The Official World Encyclopedia of
SPORTS AND GAMES

The Official World Encyclopedia of
SPORTS AND GAMES

The rules, techniques of play and equipment for over 400 sports and 1,000 games

Created by the
DIAGRAM GROUP

PADDINGTON PRESS LTD

NEW YORK & LONDON

Library of Congress Cataloging in Publication Data

Diagram Group
The official world encyclopedia of sports and games.

An abridged ed. of two works: Rules of the game (1974) and
The way to play (c1975).
Includes index.
1. Games — Rules. 2. Sports — Rules. I. Title.
GV1201.D48 1979 790 79-10380
ISBN 0 448 22202 7 (U.S. and Canada only)
ISBN 0 7092 0153 2

Adaptation and make-up by Sarisberie Design,
Salisbury, England.
Printed and bound in the United States.

In the United States
PADDINGTON PRESS
Distributed by
GROSSET & DUNLAP

In the United Kingdom
PADDINGTON PRESS

In Canada
Distributed by
RANDOM HOUSE OF CANADA LTD.

In Southern Africa
Distributed by
ERNEST STANTON (PUBLISHERS) (PTY.) LTD.

In Australia and New Zealand
Distributed by
A. H. & A. W. REED

EDITORIAL AND ART STAFF

Managing editor	Ruth Midgley
Editors	David Heidenstam, Paulin Meier, Jack Wilkinson
Assistant editor	Kathryn Dunn
Contributors	Heather Amery, Donald Berwick, Naomi Berwick, Frances Bill, Lawrence Caddell, Windsor Chorlton, Jean Cooke, Peter Eldin, Joan Faller, Peter Finch, Bridget Gibbs, Damian Grint, Barbara Horne, Joanna Jellinek, Ann Kramer, Jenny Mussell, Susan Pinkus, Allyson Rodway, Theo Rowland-Entwistle, Gina Sanders, Martin Tyler, James Walker, Joan Ward, June Weatherall, Mike Winfield
Picture researchers	Diana Phillips, Enid Moore, Jonathan Moore
Art directors	Robin Crane, Ian Wood
Designers	Jo Gait, John Seabright
Artists	Jeff Alger, Trevor Bounford, Paul Buckle, Richard Hummerstone, Elly King, Susan Kinsey, Pavel Kostal, Kathleen McDougall, Graham Rosewarne, Andy Skinner
Art assistants	Graham Blake, Bob Ho, Rupert Shaw, Sylvia Tan

Foreword

The Official World Encyclopedia of Sports and Games
was created with the cooperation and approval of more than
500 international tournament authorities, official sports-
governing bodies, coaches, athletes and game experts
around the world. This two-part encyclopedia covers more
than 1,000 games and 400 sports. Clear, concise
explanations and more than 7,000 vivid illustrations make it
a perfect home reference for game players and sports fans
everywhere — regardless of age or level of expertise.

The first part is devoted to GAMES of every conceivable
variety: family and social games; tile and board games;
gambling and casino games; card games and target games;
children's games . . . in all, fifteen separate subdivisions
under which you'll find many games that will be familiar to
you, and many that will be totally new. You'll find step-by-
step instructions on how to play each game, as well as
comments on the number of players, equipment needed
(game boards, cards, dice, counters, etc.) and scoring
procedures. The Contents on the following pages will help
you to locate games by type and also suggest new games to
you. If you are looking for a specific game and are having
trouble locating it in the Contents, consult the alphabetical
Games Index on pages 540–3. Also included is a special
listing entitled "How Many Players?" (pages 538–9), which
groups the games according to the number of players each
game requires — from games that can be played with one
person up to games that can be played by groups of nine or
more.

The second part is devoted to SPORTS, with special
attention paid to official international rules and regulations
governing competition. Included are descriptions of the
major objectives of each sport, the official dimensions of the
playing areas, plus comments on equipment, players and
officials, timing and scoring, procedures of play, and
misconduct and penalties. As in the GAMES section, the
sports have been organized under broad general categories
(athletics, gymnastics, combat sports, court sports, winter
sports, etc.). The Contents lists the sports according to their
general type; if you are looking for information on a specific
sport and are having trouble locating it in the Contents,
consult the alphabetical Sports Index on p. 543. Sports that
appear in the Olympics calendar carry a five-ringed symbol
beneath their title in the text.

Authoritative, full of facts and figures, and brimming with
new ideas, **The Official World Encyclopedia of Sports
and Games** is dedicated to sparking in the reader a lasting
understanding and appreciation of a wide spectrum of
leisure-time activities. Whether you're interested in instant
fact-finding or leisurely browsing, it will provide you with a
lasting source of reference for furthering your knowledge
and enjoyment as both a player and spectator.

Contents

Games

Games cont.

Sports

GAMES

1 Race board games

Pachisi

Pachisi is thought to have originated several thousand years ago and was the forerunner of many contemporary racing board games. Several older forms of the game are still played in Asia and South America. The game described here is played in the Indian subcontinent and is for two to four players.

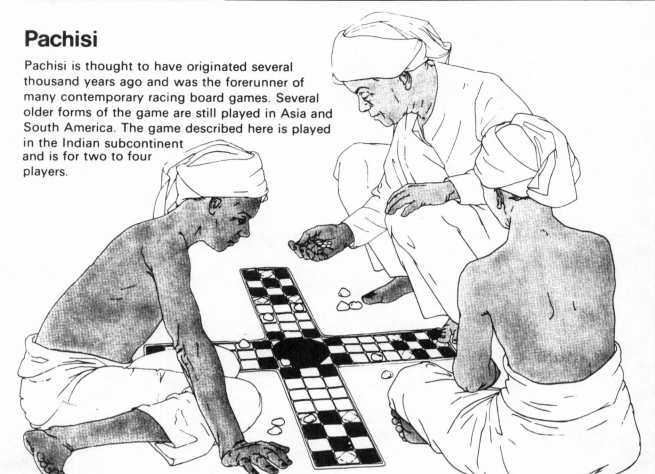

Pieces Each player has four shells, stones, or other objects that must be easily identifiable from those of his opponents.

Objective In this race game, each player tries to be the first to get all four of his pieces around the board from the starting point to the finish.

Dice Traditionally, six cowrie shells are used. They are thrown from the hand and the position they adopt indicates the number of squares a piece must be moved, as follows: two shells with their openings uppermost, two; three shells, three; four shells, four; five shells, five; six shells, six.

If only one shell falls with its opening uppermost, the player moves forward ten squares. If all the shells fall with their openings facing down, the player moves forward 25 squares. If a player throws a 6, 10, or 25 he is allowed another throw.

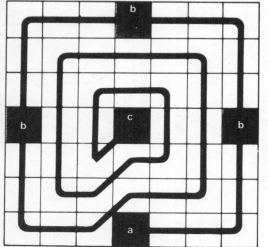

Board showing route of one player

ASHTA-KASHTE
This is a variant of pachisi and shares its objective and playing procedure. The only differences are as follows.
The board is usually divided into 49 squares.
The middle squares of each outer row are the resting squares, as well as being the starting squares (one for each player).
Pieces are moved in a spiral from their starting square to the finish at the center of the board, as shown.

a Starting square
b Resting squares
c Finish

Dice Four cowrie shells are used to indicate the number of squares to be moved, as follows:
all four shells with their openings uppermost, four squares;
three shells, three;
two shells, two;
one shell, one;
all four shells with their openings facing down, eight squares.

LUDO
Ludo is a very popular modified version of pachisi, with the same objective and basically the same rules.
The board is a square-shaped piece of cardboard, marked out as shown.
The "home base" and starting square for each player (there may be two, three, or four players), the central columns of the cross leading to the finish, and the sections of the finish itself are all colored for easy identification—usually red, green, yellow, and blue. When not traveling around the circuit, the counters are placed on a player's own "home base."
There are no resting squares, unlike in pachisi, but once a counter has reached its own colored column leading to the

Route

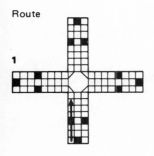

1

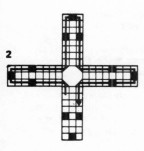

2

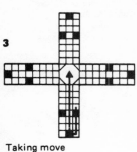

3

Taking move

Play Each player in turn throws the cowrie shells, and moves one of his pieces the number of squares indicated by the shell.

Pieces are moved in a clockwise direction around the board (see illustration).

At the start of the game each player's first piece may enter the race with any throw, but subsequent pieces (or the first piece if it has to repeat the route) may only enter the game if a 6, 10, or 25 is thrown.

A player may have one, two, three, or all of his pieces on the board at any one time.

After the players have each had one turn, they may—if they wish—miss a turn or decline to move a piece after making their throw.

Taking If a piece lands on any square other than a "resting" square already occupied by an opponent's piece, the opponent's piece is obliged to return to the start. It may only re-enter the game with a throw of 6, 10, or 25.

The player who took the opponent's piece is allowed another throw.

Once a piece has reached the central column of its own arm, leading to the finish, it cannot be taken.

Board The traditional Indian board is either woven, or made of cloth with the playing area marked out in embroidery.

The playing area is in the shape of a cross and is divided into small squares, 12 of which are distinctively colored to identify them as "resting" squares (where any number of pieces is safe from capture).

Double pieces If a piece is moved onto a square occupied by another piece belonging to the same player, both pieces may be moved together as a "double piece" on subsequent moves.

A double piece may never be overtaken by other pieces—whether the player's or an opponent's—and can only be taken if an enemy piece of equal strength lands directly on its square.

a Starting squares
b Resting squares
c Finish

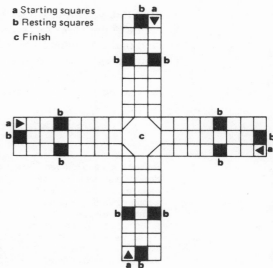

End of play The finish can only be reached by a direct throw. If, for example, a piece is seven squares away from the finish and the player throws more than a 7, he is obliged to await his next turn, or move one of his other pieces.

As soon as a piece lands on the finish, the piece is removed from the board.

The winner of the game is the first player to get all four of his pieces to the finish, and the game may be continued to determine the finishing order of the other players.

© DIAGRAM

finish, it cannot be followed or taken.

Other equipment Each player has four plastic or cardboard counters—of one of the board's four colors.

One die is used; it may be thrown from the hand or from a small plastic dice cup.

Objective Players race each other in trying to be the first to get all four of their counters to the finish.

Play Each player chooses a set of counters.

The die is thrown to determine the order of play, the person throwing the highest number starting first.

Players take it in turn to throw the die for a 6—the number needed to get a counter from its home base onto its starting square.

Whenever a player gets a 6 he

is allowed another throw, moving one counter the number of squares indicated by the die.

Counters are moved around the circuit in a clockwise direction, as in pachisi.

If a player has more than one counter on the circuit and he has a double throw (a 6 followed by another throw), he may move a different counter for each part of the throw.

Should a player throw two 6s in succession, he is allowed a third throw.

Taking If a counter lands on a square already occupied by an opponent's counter, the opponent's counter must be returned to its home base and can only re-enter the circuit on a throw of 6.

End of play The finish can only be reached by a direct throw.

For example, if a counter is four squares away from the finish and the player throws more than a 4, he must either await his next throw or move one of his other pieces.

The winner is the first player to get all four of his counters to the finish.

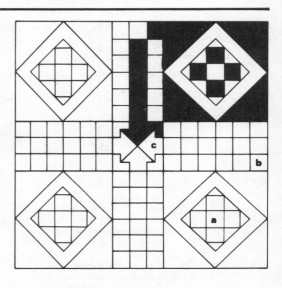

a Home base b Starting square c Finish

Game of goose

Reputedly invented in sixteenth-century Italy, the game of goose was a favorite in Europe until the end of the nineteenth century. It was the forerunner of many race board games in which the participants' progress may be either hindered or advanced by landing on certain specially marked squares.

Boards of many different designs were used, but the main feature of all of them was a spiral route divided into 63 numbered spaces—starting at the outside and finishing at the center. The boards were often illustrated by, for example, scenes from history or mythology.

In addition, certain spaces on the route were marked with symbols and printed instructions—sometimes these instructions were shown at the center of the board. One of these symbols, appearing on about every fifth space, was a goose.

By landing on a marked space, the player was instructed to either:
have another throw;
forfeit a turn;
advance a certain number of spaces; or
retreat a certain number of spaces.

Sometimes the instructions would be linked with the theme of the illustrations. For example, on a board with a military theme, the instruction might state that because of an injury received in battle, the player must forfeit a turn.

For contemporary play, the circuit may be drawn on paper or other suitable material. Geese should be drawn on about every fifth space, and other symbols or instructions may be marked at random on the circuit. (See also the section on play.)

Other equipment To mark his position on the circuit, each player needs a colored counter or other object different from his opponents'. One die is used.

The objective is to travel around the circuit as quickly as possible, the first player to land on the finish with an exact throw being the winner.

Play Throwing the die in turn, players move their counters the thrown number of spaces. If a player's counter lands on a goose space, the player may throw again.

By landing on another of the specially marked spaces, the player is instructed to either:
a) miss one or more turns;
b) advance a prescribed number of spaces; or
c) move back a prescribed number of spaces.

18th and 19th century board games

In the 18th and 19th centuries the emphasis of board games was primarily educational. Scores of games were invented, designed not only to while away long winter evenings, but also to impart useful facts or moral teachings. Many of these games are still played in one form or another today.

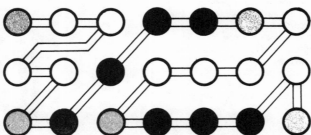

1

2

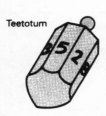

Teetotum

Boards were usually colored by hand or stencil and often had protective card or cloth cases. They were usually magnificently illustrated, and their attractiveness has made them popular collectors' items today.

Designs were extremely varied, with numbered circuits or routes in every possible arrangement.

Booklets containing useful information often accompanied the boards; sometimes descriptive passages were printed on the board itself.

Other equipment Dice or teetotums marked with numbers were used.

Players usually had a counter or "marker" made of card, although other objects such as buttons or dried peas were also used to mark the players' positions on the board.

Objective Many of the games were straightforward race games along a numbered route from start to finish.

Other games had hazards or rewards (linked to the theme of the game) that might impede or advance the players' progress.

For example, in a game about geography and travel, the "explorer" might be allowed to advance four numbers on discovering a foreign land.

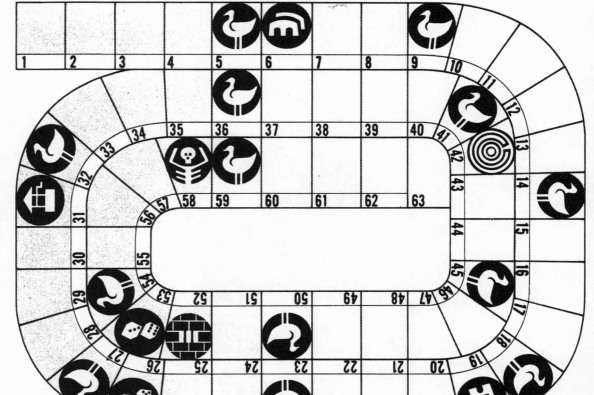

End play The finish can only be reached by an exact throw. Thus a player throwing more than the number required to reach the finish must go back the number of spaces by which he has exceeded the finish. For example, if his counter is on 62 and the player throws a 3, he must move his counter one space forward to the finish, and then back two spaces to space 61.

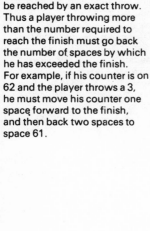

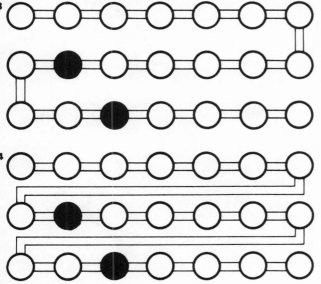

Examples of routes:
1) rambling;
2) spiral;
3) horizontal (backward and forward);
4) horizontal (left to right);
5) branching (choice of paths).

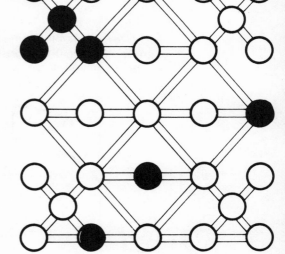

Categories

History Scenes from the past, historical personages, and famous battles were all popular subjects and were accompanied by the relevant dates and descriptive information.

Geography was the theme of many games, being an easy way of enlarging children's knowledge.

Some boards were illustrated with maps of different parts of the globe, and showed characteristic landscapes, animals, or local scenes. During the last century, "grand tours" of Europe or America were much in vogue. This resulted in another type of board design that showed familiar tourist haunts or beauty spots.

Other educational themes included natural history, astronomy, and the arts. Some of these were barely disguised educational exercises, but many were beautifully illustrated and a pleasure to play.

Moral teaching games were especially abundant in the nineteenth century. Scenes from everyday life

were often depicted, with a strong emphasis on the triumph of good over evil.

Amusement Toward the end of the nineteenth century, games designed principally for their participants' amusement became more usual. Well-loved animals or fictional characters were popular subjects, and this type of game is still common today.

Snakes and ladders

Snakes and ladders is a development of earlier games such as the game of goose, and has become a top favorite family game. Like many other race board games its outcome is entirely dependent on chance.

The board is divided into 100 squares.
Snakes and ladders—usually about ten of each—are arranged around the board. Although the positioning of the snakes and ladders may vary from board to board, the snakes' heads are always on a higher number than their tails.
The board is often decorated with scenes of children encountering hazards or having fun.

Other equipment comprises one die, and one differently colored counter for each player.
Objective Players move their counters around the board—hoping not to be "swallowed" down to a lower number by a snake but instead to be given a helping hand up a ladder to a higher number.
The first player to land on the hundredth square wins the game.

Alleyway

Alleyway is a family game popular in Eastern Europe. It is great fun to play, because although its rules are simple, winning is tantalizingly difficult!

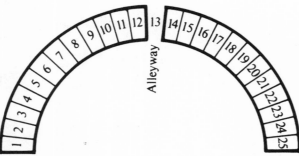

Equipment A semi-circle is drawn on a piece of paper or cardboard, and marked with 25 numbered spaces as shown. The thirteenth space or "alleyway" is left open. Each player—of whom there may be any number—has a counter of a different color. One die is used.

Play Each player throws the die and sets his counter on the space with the corresponding number. Players then take turns to throw the die and move their counters the number of spaces indicated by the die.
If at any time a player's counter lands on a space that is already occupied by an opponent's counter, the opponent's counter must be moved back a certain number of spaces, as follows.
a) If the opponent's counter was on any of the spaces from 1–12 or in the alleyway, it must go back to the beginning.
b) Once past the alleyway, however, a counter need only be moved back two spaces—and should that space also be occupied, that counter also

must move back the appropriate number of spaces.
c) If the opponent's counter is on space 14 or 15 and has to retreat two spaces (ie to the alleyway or space 12), it has to go right back to the start. If it encounters an "enemy" counter in the alleyway or on space 12, that piece, too, has to go back to the start.

End play If a player's counter lands on space 25, it has to retreat to space 14. Thus the winner is the first player whose throw gets him beyond space 25.

Play Each player in turn moves his counter along the squares in numerical order, in accordance with the number obtained by the throw of the die.

If a player's counter lands on a square bearing the foot of a ladder, the player may move his counter up the ladder to the square at its top—thus "jumping" the intermediate squares.

If a counter lands on the head of a snake, the counter must go down the snake to the square at its tail.

End play The game continues with players throwing the die in turn until one of them reaches the hundredth square with an exact throw.

If a player's throw is higher than the number needed for his counter to land on the last square, he has to count the difference in descending order.

For example, if the counter is on square 97 and the player throws a 5, he must move forward three squares to 100 and back two squares to square 98.

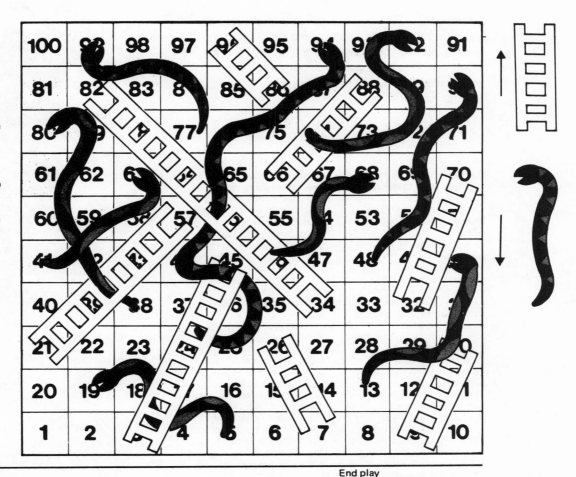

© DIAGRAM

End play

Horseshoe

Horseshoe is a game very like alleyway, its main difference being that it is played for small stakes. Any number of players may take part.

Equipment The layout is drawn onto paper or cardboard and is in the shape of a horseshoe, divided into 30 numbered spaces as shown.

Instead of using counters, players mark their progress along the horseshoe with a stake—such as a candy, coin, or nut.

The only other equipment needed is a die.

Play Each player throws the die and places his stake on the corresponding space.

Players then take turns to advance their stakes along the horseshoe in accordance with the throw of the die.

Every time a player's stake lands on an occupied space, the occupier's stake has to retreat to space 1.

End play If a player's throw is higher than the number needed for his stake to reach space 30, he must move his stake around the horseshoe past space 30 and on to space 1 or beyond. For example, if his stake is on space 28 and the player throws a 5, he must move his stake five spaces to space 3.

He must then continue round the course from that space.

Winner The first player to get an exact throw onto space 30 wins the game and all the stakes.

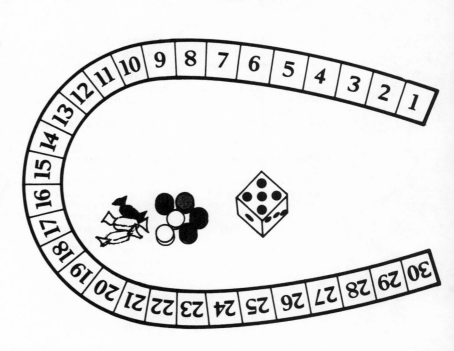

Contemporary board games

Almost every family is familiar with the fun and excitement of a race board game, in which even young children can participate. The outcome of many of the simpler games depends solely on the throw of a die—other games are more sophisticated.

Equipment Boards are usually of stout cardboard, covered with paper and edged with tape or cloth binding. They are printed in bright colors.

Luxury versions, of wood or leather, are sometimes made. The boards are usually sold in a protective cardboard or wooden box, together with printed playing instructions, counters, dice, and any other necessary equipment (such as picture cards, dice, cups, etc).

The objectives of contemporary race board games fall basically into two categories.

1) Straightforward race games—often those designed for children—are those in which players race their opponents along a prescribed route or numbered course in accordance with the throw of a die.

There may or may not be hazards to overcome, or "bonuses" that help the player reach the finish more quickly (the first person to do so being the winner).

2) In more sophisticated games, the winner is usually the first person to achieve a set objective.

As this type of game can often last for many hours, participants sometimes decide to end the game before an absolute winner has been determined. In this case, the winner is the player who is in the most advantageous position when the game is brought to an end.

Although these games require a certain amount of skill and decision making, the inexperienced player can still win by a combination of fortunate dice throws and sheer luck!

Categories As in earlier times, many contemporary race board games combine pleasure with learning. There are many historical or geographical games that differ little from the type of game played a hundred years ago.

Other games deal with current topics such as high finance, space exploration, or spying.

CHILDREN'S GAMES
Many contemporary race board games can be played by adults and children alike. There are others, however, designed specifically for young and even pre-school age children.

These games (invariably straightforward race games) are a useful way of teaching the rudiments of counting and reading, and of encouraging the child to plan or think ahead.

Familiar things like trains, household objects, and animals are popular subjects. Characters from books, films, and fairy tales are also prevalent.

Popular examples are Winnie-the-Pooh, Tom and Jerry, and Pinocchio.

MONOPOLY
Monopoly is perhaps the best-known and most popular board game of its kind. Invented in the United States in the 30s, it was patented by Parker Brothers of America in 1935. The game is now played in many countries on boards showing different cities. Monopoly is a fast-moving game of make-believe property deals and financial bargaining, in which real estate and public utilities are bought and sold; rents, mortgages, and taxes have to be paid; and fines and spells in jail are among the hazards. Between two and eight players may take part, the winner being the last person to evade bankruptcy.

Simple race board games

CLUEDO

Cluedo (a registered trademark of John Waddington Limited of Great Britain) is a mystery game in which each player attempts to solve a murder that takes place in a large house. Players move their pieces around the board from room to room. By a process of questioning and deduction, they seek to discover the murderer, the murder weapon, and the scene of the crime.

DIPLOMACY

This compelling game of strategy and political maneuvering needs foresight, shrewdness, diplomacy—and also luck—to win.
Each player takes the role of a different country and is given control of armed forces.
By waging land and sea battles and forming—and breaking—alliances with other countries, each player tries to achieve the winning objective of capturing the majority of the bases situated around the board.
Diplomacy is patented by Games Research Incorporated.

SCRABBLE

Although Scrabble was not the first "crossword puzzle" game invented, it has rapidly superseded other games of this type since its appearance in the late 1940s and has been adapted for play in many different languages. (Scrabble is patented in the United States of America by Selchow and Righter.)
Each player draws tiles printed with a letter of the alphabet and a numerical value. Players form their tiles into words on the board to build a crossword puzzle formation. They score points for the letters used and for making use of specially marked bonus squares.
Scrabble requires a good vocabulary and ingenuity in positioning the words—but there is also a degree of luck involved.

Sophisticated race board games

a Warfare
b Crime
c Big game hunting
d Space travel
e High finance
f Geography
g Word building

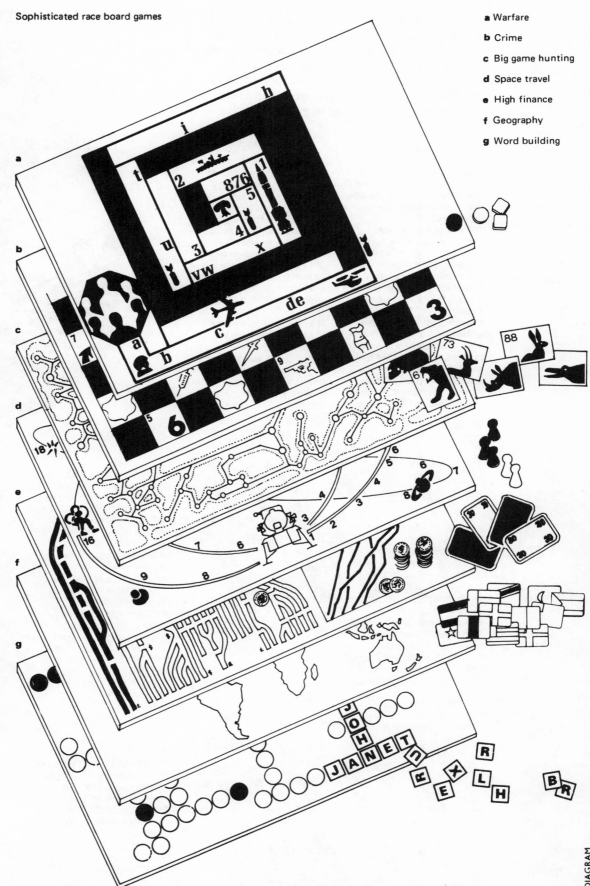

©DIAGRAM

Backgammon

Backgammon is an ancient board game developed in the Orient and now played all over the world. It is an excellent game in which the opportunities for strategic play add to the excitement of a race around the board. The fine calculation of odds involved in skilled play has a strong attraction for the player who is prepared to gamble.

Pieces Each player has 15 pieces, similar to those used in checkers. One player has dark pieces (Black) and the other light pieces (White).
The pieces are variously known as "counters," "stones," or "men." In the modern game "men" is the commonly accepted term.
Dice Each player has two dice and a dice cup in which to shake them.
Doubling cube In a game where players agree to bet on the outcome (there is no need to play for anything but fun), a doubling cube is used. This is a large die on which the faces are numbered 2:4:8:16:32:64. (Its significance is explained in the section on gambling.)

Players Only two players compete, but others may participate in the betting when matches are played for money.
Objective According to the numbers thrown on the dice, each player moves his men toward his own inner table. Once all a player's men are located in his own inner table he attempts to remove them—by a process called "bearing off."
The first player to bear off all 15 of his pieces wins the game.
Although the basic objective of the game is simple, the rules and strategies governing a player's moves are much more complex.

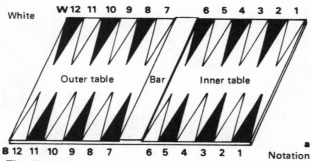

White

Outer table | Bar | Inner table

Black

a
Notation

The direction of play for each player is always from his opponent's inner table, through his opponent's outer table, through his own outer table, and into his own inner table.
Thus White always moves his men clockwise and Black moves counterclockwise.

Board Backgammon is played on a rectangular board divided into two halves by a "bar." One half of the board is called the "inner table" or "home table," and the other the "outer table."
Along each side of the board are marked 12 triangles, alternately light and dark colored (this coloring has no special significance.)
Each triangle is called a "point." For the purpose of notation, points are numbered 1–12 as shown (**a**). (No numbers actually appear on the board.)
Points 1 (the first points in the inner table) are called "ace points"; points 7 (the first points on the outer table) are called "bar points." No other points are specially designated.
The board is placed between the two players (called Black and White) so that Black has his inner table to his right.
The points on Black's side of the table are known as Black points; those on White's side as White points. In simple notation, points are indicated by their number and the initial B or W.

Start of play Players draw for color and then place their men in their prescribed starting positions (**b**).
White places two men on B1; five men on W6; three men on W8; and five men on B12.
Black places two men on W1; five men on B6; three men on B8; and five men on W12.

b
Start of play

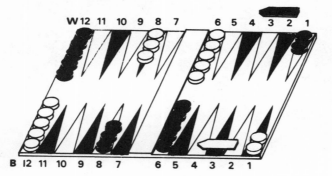

Having placed their men on their starting positions, each player throws a single die to determine the order of play. The player throwing the higher number has first move. If both players throw the same number they must throw again.

For his first move the opening player moves according to the numbers on both his own and his opponent's dice.

Thereafter, play alternates and each player moves according to the numbers on both his own dice.

Play A player throws both his dice to determine how many points he can move.

For a valid throw the dice must be:

thrown from the cup;

thrown in the player's own half of the board;

thrown so that one face of each die rests wholly on the board;

thrown only when an opponent has completed his turn.

The player then moves according to the numbers thrown on the dice.

Moving men A player attempts to move the number of points shown on each of his die. He may not merely add them together and move the combined total.

The position of the men on the board may affect a player's choice of moves or may even prevent him from moving at all. Provided that none of his men is off the board, a player may move to any point that is:

a) clear of any other men;

b) occupied by one or more of his own men; or

c) occupied by only one of his opponent's men.

When there is only one man on a point, this man is called a "blot."

A player who moves a man to a point on which he already has one man is said to "make" that point, as his opponent cannot then land on it.

(Also see sections on play after a mixed throw and play after a double.)

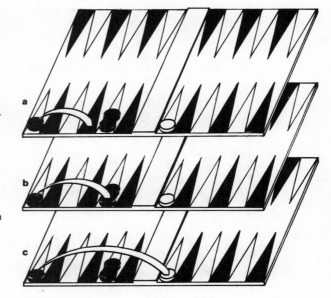

Moving men

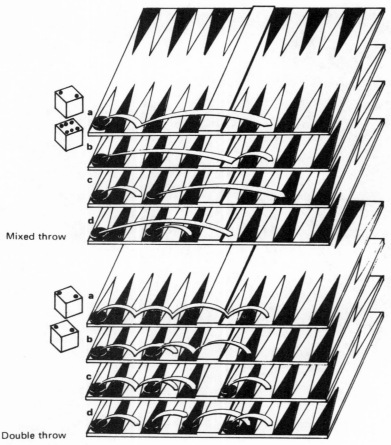

Mixed throw

Double throw

Play after a mixed throw

If the numbers on the two dice are different, the player may make one of four possible moves. For example, a player throwing a 2 and a 6 may move:

a) one man two points, then the same man six points further;

b) one man six points, then the same man two points further;

c) one man two points, and another man six points;

d) one man six points, and another man two points.

At first glance alternatives a) and b) appear to be the same. This is not in fact the case, since the order in which the numbers are taken can affect whether or not a man may be moved (see the section on moving men).

If he can use only the number shown on one of his dice, the other number is disregarded. If he has a choice of two numbers, he must use the higher one.

Play after a double

If a player throws a double, then the number shown on both dice is played four times (or as many times as possible up to four).

Thus if a player throws two 2s he may move:

a) one man four times two points;

b) one man twice two points and another man twice two points;

c) one man twice two points and another two men two points each;

d) four men two points each.

As before, the number shown on the dice is the limit of a move. A player moving one man four times two points must land on open points at the end of each two point move.

Hitting a man

If a player moves a man onto a point on which his opponent has only one man (**a**) he is said to "hit" that man.

The hit man is removed from play and placed on the bar (**b**). A player who has any hit men on the bar must re-enter them before he can move any of his men on the board.

Re-entering men

To re-enter a hit man, a player must throw the number of an open point on his opponent's home table. He may then use the number on his second die to re-enter another man or, if all his men are on the board, to move any of his men the number of points shown on that die.

Bearing off men

Once a player has succeeded in moving all his men into his own inner table, he bears them off by removing them from those points corresponding to the numbers thrown.

For example, if White throws a 4 and a 2 when he has men on both W4 and W2 he may bear off a man from each of these points.

If he throws a 4 and a 2 when he has a man on W4 but not on W2, he may bear off a man from W4 and must then move another man two points down from his highest occupied point.

If he wishes, a player may always move men down the board from his highest point rather than bearing off from the points corresponding to the numbers on the dice.

If both numbers thrown are higher than the player's highest point, the player bears off from his highest point.

If a player's man is hit after he has started bearing off, that man must re-enter and be moved around again to the inner table before bearing off is resumed.

Bearing off continues until one player succeeds in bearing off all his men.

Hitting a man

Fouls and penalties In addition to the rules on throwing the dice, players must observe the following:
a) a player may not change his move after taking his hand from a moved piece;
b) if a player makes an incorrect move, his opponent may insist that the error be corrected provided that he has not made his own following move;
c) a game must be restarted if the board or pieces are found to be incorrectly set up during play.

Scoring The game is won by the player who first bears off all his men. The number of units scored depends on the progress of the loser:
a) if the loser has borne off at least one man and has no men left in the winner's inner table, the winner scores one unit;
b) if the loser has not borne off any men, the winner has made a "gammon" and scores two units;
c) if the loser has not borne off any men and also has a man on the bar or in the winner's inner table, the winner has made a "backgammon" and scores three units.

Gambling Backgammon is often played for an agreed base stake for each game. This stake may be doubled and redoubled during play (in addition to the double payment for a gammon and treble for a backgammon). A doubling cube is often used to show the number of times that the stake has been doubled. (At the start of play it should be placed with the number 64 face uppermost.) Unless players previously agree otherwise, stakes are automatically doubled if the dice match at the first throw of a game. In this case both players then throw again. The number of automatic doubles is usually limited by agreement to one or two per game. There is no limit to the number of voluntary doubles.

Either player has the right to offer the first voluntary double —after which the right alternates between players. A player who wishes to double the stake must offer to do so before throwing the dice when it is his turn to play. His opponent then has the choice of accepting the doubled stake or of forfeiting the game and the stake.

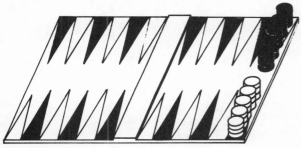
Start of play

PLAKATO
This form of backgammon is widely played in Greek cafes. It is the same as the basic game described here except that:
a) each player positions all his men on his opponent's number 1 point for the start of play;
b) a blot is not hit but is blocked and cannot be moved as long as an opposing man is on the same point;
c) a player must move all his men all 24 points instead of bearing them off when they reach his inner table.

GIOUL
This popular Middle Eastern form of backgammon is played in the same way as the basic game except that:
a) each player positions all his men on his opponent's number 1 point for the start;
b) a blot is not hit but is blocked and cannot be moved while an opposing man is on the same point;
c) when a player throws a double, he attempts to move for the double thrown and then for each subsequent double in turn up to double 6 (for example if he throws double 4 he goes on to move for double 5 and double 6);
d) if a player is unable to use any of his moves from a double, all these moves may be taken by his opponent.

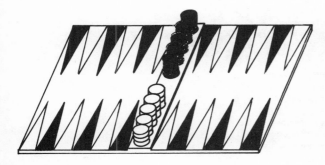
Start of play

DUTCH BACKGAMMON
This is the same as the basic game except that:
a) all the men are placed on the bar for the start of play and players must enter all 15 before moving any man around the board;
b) a player may not hit a blot until he has advanced at least one of his own men to his own inner table.

ACEY DEUCEY
This is an elaboration of Dutch backgammon and is popular in the US Navy. It differs from the basic game in the following ways:
a) men are entered from the bar as in Dutch backgammon;
b) if a player throws a 1 and a 2 (ace-deuce), he moves his men for this throw and then moves his men as if he had thrown any doublet that he chooses;
c) the stake is usually automatically doubled when an ace-deuce is thrown;
d) some players give each man an agreed unit value and the winner collects as many units as the opponent has left on the board.

2 Strategic board games

Nine men's morris

Nine men's morris, also called mill, morelles, or merels, is one of the oldest games played in Europe and was particularly popular during the Middle Ages. It is a game of strategy for two people in which each player attempts to capture or block his opponent's pieces.

Board The game is played on a specially marked-out board, with three squares one inside the other and with points in the centers of the squares' sides connected by ruled lines. Bought boards are now usually made of wood. In the past, boards have been carved out of stone or, often, cut out of turf.
A perfectly satisfactory board can be quickly drawn on a piece of paper.

Pieces At the start of a game each player has nine "men" (counters, stones, or other appropriate pieces) distinguishable in color from those of his opponent.

Objective By the placing and maneuvering of men on the board, each player attempts to capture all but two of his opponent's pieces or to make it impossible for his opponent to move any piece at his turn.

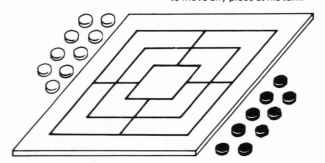

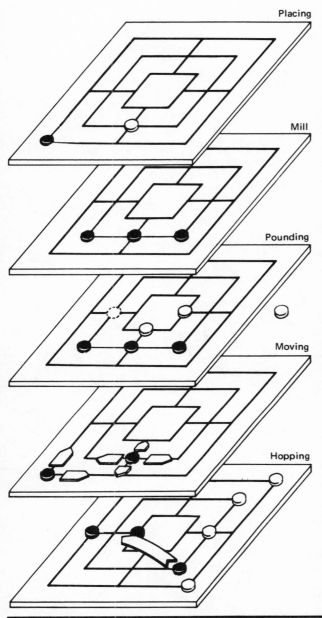

Placing

Mill

Pounding

Moving

Hopping

Play There are usually three stages of play:
1) placing the men on the board;
2) moving the pieces around;
3) "hopping" them.
(The third stage is sometimes disallowed, as it gives one player a distinct advantage over his opponent.)

Placing the pieces The players decide which of them is to start.
Each one, in turn, then places one man of his own color on the board at any point of intersection not already occupied by another piece. Players aim to get three of their own men into a straight line along one of the lines of the board, so forming a "mill."

Pounding Once a player has formed a mill he is entitled to "pound" his opponent by removing one enemy piece from the board.
A player may not, however, remove an opponent's man that is part of a mill, unless there is no other man available. Once removed from the board, a piece is dead for the rest of the game.
Players continue their turns (nine turns each) until each of their men has been placed onto the board.

Moving the pieces Still taking alternate turns, players now move their men to try to form new mills and so pound their opponent.
A move consists of moving a man from his existing position on the board to any adjoining vacant point of intersection. (According to some rules players may take pieces by passing over an enemy piece to a vacant spot beyond it, as in checkers.)

Players may form new mills by opening existing mills. This is achieved by moving a man one place from his position in a mill, and then returning him at the next move to his original position. Mills may be broken and re-made any number of times, and each new mill formation entitles the player to pound his opponent.
Play continues until one of the players is reduced by successive poundings to having only two men on the board; or until one player's pieces have been so blocked by his opponent's men that he is unable to make any move. Should a player's only remaining pieces form a mill and it is his turn to move, he must do so even if this results in his losing a piece and the game at his opponent's next move.

Hopping is an optional stage of play, and begins when either player has only three men remaining.
The player is now no longer restricted to moving his men along a line to an adjacent point of intersection, but may "hop" to any vacant spot on the board.
This freedom of movement gives him a certain advantage over his opponent, and so restores his chance of winning.

Result A player is defeated when either:
he is reduced to having only two pieces; or
his pieces are blocked by enemy men in such a way as to prevent further moves.
(If hopping has been allowed the game ends when one player has only two pieces remaining.)

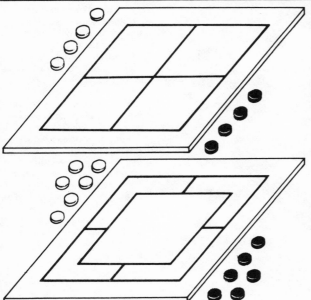

THREE MEN'S MORRIS
Three men's morris is a game for two players, each player having four counters of his own color.
The board is marked out as shown.
Players take turns to put one man on a point of intersection, in an attempt to form a mill. The first player to achieve this is the winner.

SIX MEN'S MORRIS
This game is played in much the same way as nine men's morris.
Players each have six counters and take it in turns to place them, one at a time, on the board (which is marked out as shown).
The objective is to form a mill along one of the sides of either of the squares. If a

player succeeds in doing this, he may pound his opponent.
As in nine men's morris, once all the men have been played onto the board, the game continues with players moving their men to form new mills. When one player only has two men left, he loses the game.

Ringo

Ringo is a game of strategy for two people. Invented in Germany, it is played on a circular board and has certain similarities with fox and geese. One player (the "attacker") attempts to capture the central area of the board known as the "fortress," while the other player (the "defender") tries to ward off the attack.

The playing area may be drawn on a sheet of paper. It comprises a large circle divided into eight segments of equal size. One of the segments is distinctively colored and is called the "neutral zone."

The central circle or fortress is also distinctively colored. Six concentric rings spread out beyond it, and the resulting sections are alternately light and dark colored (ie each segment has three light and three dark colored sections).

Pieces Each player has counters (or other suitable objects) distinguishable from his opponent's. The defender has four pieces and the attacker seven.

For the start of play, the defender's pieces are arranged around the fortress (but not in the neutral zone), and the attacker's pieces on the outermost ring.

Start of play

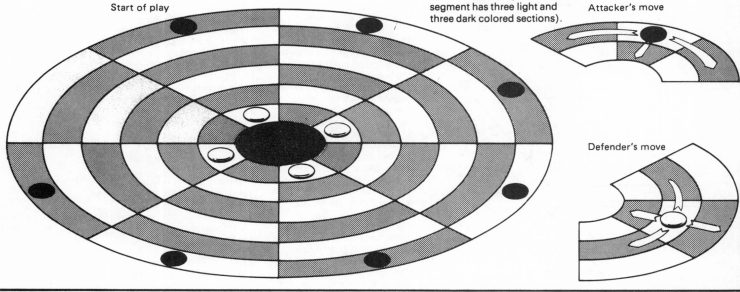

Attacker's move

Defender's move

Queen's guard

Queen's guard is an interesting old board game for two players. It can be played with counters on an improvised board. Players attempt to position their pieces in the winning pattern.

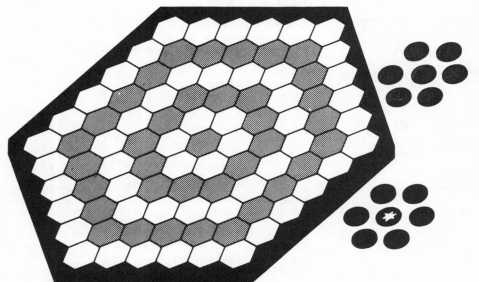

The board is in the shape of a hexagon, with 91 small hexagons in alternating dark and light bands.

Pieces There are two sets of pieces. Each set is a distinctive color and consists of one "queen" and six "guards."

Objective The game is won when one player succeeds in positioning his "queen" on the center hexagon and his six guards in the hexagons immediately surrounding it.

Start of play There are two methods of starting play:
a) the pieces are positioned as shown;
b) each player positions his pieces in turn, one at a time, anywhere he likes on the board.

Objective Each player tries to capture or immobilize as many enemy pieces as possible in order to achieve his objective. The attacker's objective is to capture the fortress by getting two of his pieces into it; the defender's objective is to prevent him from doing so.

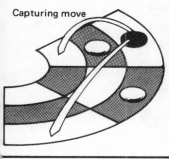

Capturing move

Play The players decide which of them is to attack and which to defend.
The attacker has the first move, and thereafter players take alternate turns.
The attacker may only move his pieces forward (ie toward the center) or sideways.
The defender—although having fewer pieces—has the advantage of being able to move them in any direction except diagonally. He may not actually enter the fortress, although he is allowed to jump over it when capturing.
When moving sideways (ie into another segment) pieces must remain on the same ring as the one on which they were standing.
Both players may move their pieces into the neutral zone—although the attacker may only have as many pieces in the neutral zone as the defender has on the board. For example, if the defender has only two pieces left on the board, the attacker may only have two pieces within the neutral zone.

Capturing Both players may capture enemy pieces, although there is no compulsion to do so.
A piece is captured by jumping over it from a touching section onto a vacant section beyond it. The captured piece is then removed from the board.
As in ordinary moves, the attacker is restricted to capturing in a forward or sideways direction, while the defender may also capture in a backward direction.
When making a sideways capture, the taking piece and the piece being captured must both be on the same ring.
A player may capture only one piece in a move.
All pieces are safe from capture when within the neutral zone. However, it is permissible for a piece to use the neutral zone as its "take-off" or "landing" area in a capturing move. Although the defender may not actually enter the fortress, he may jump over it in order to capture an enemy piece within it, provided the section directly opposite is vacant (see illustration).

End play The attacker may enter the fortress from any segment (including the neutral zone).
Should a defending piece be positioned on the innermost ring, an attacking piece may jump over it into the fortress (thereby capturing the defending piece).
If the attacker gets one of his pieces into the fortress, it is still prone to capture by a defending piece. Should the attacker succeed in getting two of his pieces into the fortress, however, he wins the game.
The defender wins the game if he either captures all but one of the attacker's pieces, or immobilizes the attacker's pieces so that he is unable to get two pieces into the fortress.

Capture of an attacker in the fortress

Moves Each player moves one piece in a turn.
A piece may only be moved into a vacant hexagon.
A player who touches one of his pieces must move that piece or forfeit his turn.
Except when a piece is trapped between opposing pieces, it may be moved one hexagon sideways or toward the center of the board (**a**).
If a "guard" is trapped between two opposing pieces (**b**), its owner must in his next turn move it to any hexagon in the outside band.
If a "queen" is trapped between two opposing pieces (**c**), its owner must in his next turn move it to any vacant square that his opponent requires.
If more than one piece is trapped, the player must move them back one in each turn. "Guards" may be moved back in any order, but a "queen" must always be moved before a "guard."
Only a "queen" may be placed in the center hexagon. A player forfeits the game if, when the center hexagon is empty, he positions all his six guards in the band immediately surrounding it.

Start of play

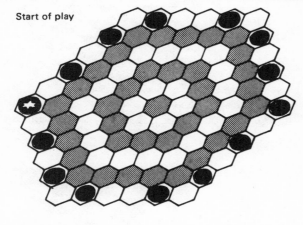

Moves

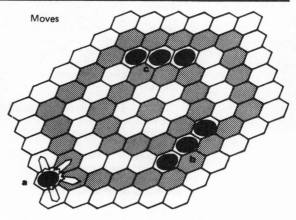

Forfeited game

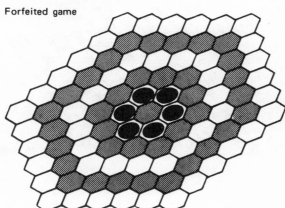

Won game

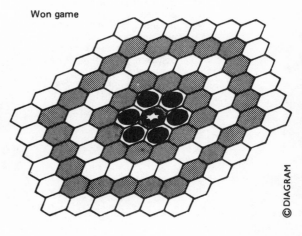

Checkers (Draughts)

Checkers, or draughts as it is called in the United Kingdom, is a board game for two players. It was played in southern Europe in medieval times and appears to have been derived from much older games played in the Middle East. Each player attempts to "take" (capture and remove) his opponent's pieces or to confine them so that they cannot be moved.

Board The game is played on a board made of wood, plastic, or cardboard and $14\frac{1}{2}$–16in square.
It is divided into 64 squares, eight along each side. The squares are alternately a light and a dark color (usually black and white, or sometimes black and red or red and white). Play is confined to squares of only one color—usually the darker color.

Pieces Each player has a set of 12 pieces—wooden or plastic disks $1\frac{1}{4}$–$1\frac{1}{2}$in in diameter and about $\frac{3}{8}$in thick. One set is usually white, and the other red or black.

Objective A player aims to "take" all his opponent's pieces or to position his own pieces so that his opponent is unable to make any move.

Start of play The players sit facing each other, and the board is positioned so that the players have a playing square at the left of their first row.
Lots are drawn to decide who will have the darker pieces for the first game. Each player has the darker pieces for alternate games.
For the start of play each player positions his pieces on the playing squares in the three rows of the board nearest him.
The player with the darker pieces always makes the first move in a game.

Moving A player may make only one move at a turn.
As play is confined to squares of only one color, all moves are diagonal.
Individual pieces or "men" may only be moved forward (**a**); double pieces or "kings" may be moved either forward or backward (**b**).
A piece may only be moved into a square that is vacant.

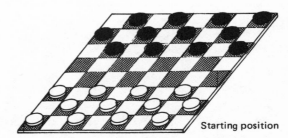

Starting position

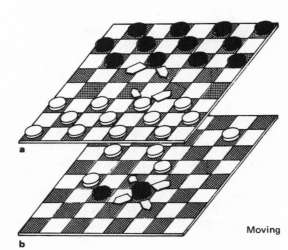

a

b

Moving

Touch and move Except when he has given notice of his intention to arrange pieces properly in their squares, a player whose turn it is must when possible make his move with the first piece that he touches.
If he first touches an unplayable piece, he is cautioned for a first offense and forfeits the game for a second offense.

Time limit for moves If a player fails to make a move within five minutes, an appointed timekeeper shall call "time." The player must then move within one minute, or forfeit the game through improper delay.
(At master level in some tournaments, players must make a prescribed number of moves within set time limits.)

A non-taking move Except when "taking" an opponent's piece, a player may only move a piece into a touching playing square.

A taking move One of the game's objectives is to "take" (capture and remove) the opposing pieces.

A piece may be taken if it is in a playing square touching the taker's square when there is a vacant square directly beyond it (**1**).

Several pieces can be taken in one move provided that each one has a vacant square beyond it (**2**).

Whenever possible, a player must make a taking move rather than a non-taking move (even if this means that his own piece will in turn be taken).

If a player has a choice of taking moves he may take a smaller instead of a larger number of pieces (**3a**), but if he begins the move enabling him to take the larger number he must continue until he has taken all the pieces possible (**3b**).

Failure to take If a player fails to take a piece when he is able (**4a**), modern tournament play rules state that his opponent should point this out and so force him to take back the wrongly moved piece and make the taking move instead (**4b**).

This ruling has replaced the old "huff or blow" rule, by which a player who failed to make a possible taking move forfeited the piece moved in error.

Crowning When a man reaches the farthest row on the board (known as the "king row" or "crownhead"), it becomes a "king" and is "crowned" by having another piece of its own color placed on it (**5**).

A player's turn always ends when a man is crowned.

A tied game occurs when neither player can remove all his opponent's pieces or prevent him from making a move (**6**).

If one player appears to be in a stronger position, he may be required to force a win within 40 of his own moves or else place himself at a decided advantage over his opponent. If he fails, the game is counted as tied.

1

2

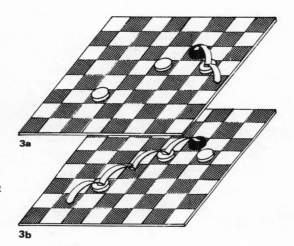

3a

3b

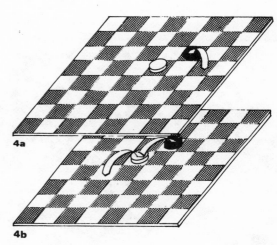

4a

4b

5

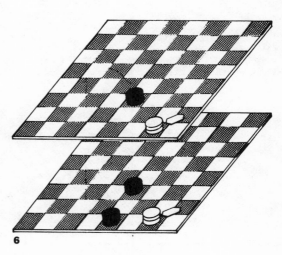

6

TOURNAMENT CHECKERS

To reduce the number of tied and repeated games at expert level, a system of restricted openings is applied at major championships and tournaments in the United States and elsewhere.

The first three moves of each game are determined by cards bearing the various openings and subsequent moves. The cards are shuffled and cut, and the top card is turned face up. Opposing players then play two games with the prescribed opening, each player making the first move in one of the games.

LOSING or GIVEAWAY CHECKERS

is played under the same rules as standard British or American checkers. The tactics, however, are very different, as the objective is to be the first player to lose all his pieces.

©DIAGRAM

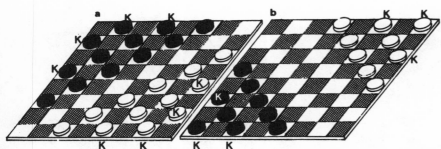

DIAGONAL CHECKERS is

an interesting variant of the standard game.
It can be played with 12 pieces per player, in which case starting position (**a**) is used, or with nine pieces each if starting position (**b**) is used.

Men are crowned when they have crossed the board to reach the opponent's corner squares (marked K in the diagrams).
Otherwise, rules are the same as for standard checkers.

ITALIAN CHECKERS is

played in the same way as standard British or American checkers except that:
a) the board is positioned with a non-playing square at the left of each player's first row;
b) a player must make a taking move whenever possible—or forfeit the game;
c) a man cannot take a king;

d) if a player has a choice of captures he must take the greater number of pieces;
e) if a player with a king to move has a choice of capturing equal numbers of pieces, he must take the most valuable pieces (ie kings rather than men).

SPANISH CHECKERS is

played in the same way as Italian checkers, except that kings are moved differently. A player may use his king to take a piece anywhere on a diagonal, provided that there are no pieces between and there is an empty square beyond it. (This is sometimes called the "long move.")
The jump need not end in the

square immediately behind the taken piece, but may continue any distance along the diagonal if there are no intervening pieces (**a**).
The king must make all its jumps before any taken pieces are removed, and these pieces may not be jumped a second time in the same move (**b**)

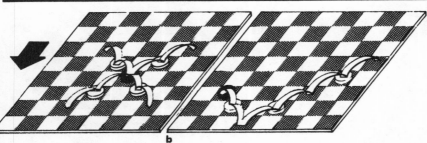

GERMAN CHECKERS is

played in the same way as Spanish checkers except that:
a) men can make taking moves either forward or backward;
b) a man is only crowned if its move ends on the far row—if it is in a position to make further jumps away from that line it must always take them.

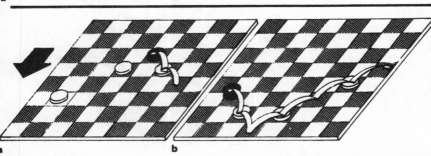

RUSSIAN CHECKERS is

played like German checkers except that:
a) a player with a choice of captures need not take the larger number of pieces;
b) a man is made into a king as soon as it reaches the far row and then jumps as a king for the rest of the move.

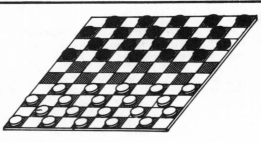

CONTINENTAL or POLISH CHECKERS is

played on a board with 100 squares, 10 along each side. Each player has 20 pieces—positioned on the first four rows for the start of play.
The game is played under the same rules as German checkers.

CANADIAN CHECKERS is another variant of German checkers.
It is played on a board with 144 squares, 12 by 12.
Each player has 30 pieces—positioned on the first five rows for the start of play.

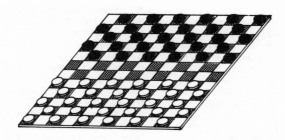

TURKISH CHECKERS may be played on a standard checker board, but the traditional Turkish board has squares all the same color.
Each player has 16 pieces—positioned on each player's second and third rows for the start of play (**a**).
Men move as in British or American checkers, but directly forward or sideways and not diagonally (**b**).
Kings move any number of squares directly forward, sideways, or backward.
Multiple captures by kings are made as shown (**c**)—as for Spanish checkers except that moves are not diagonal and pieces are removed as soon as they are jumped (instead of staying on the board to prevent further jumps).

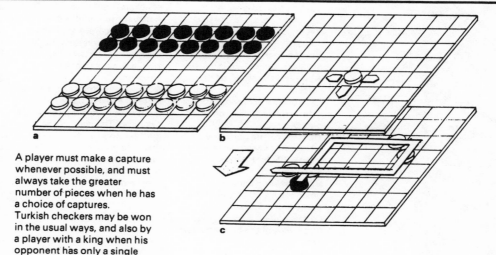

A player must make a capture whenever possible, and must always take the greater number of pieces when he has a choice of captures.
Turkish checkers may be won in the usual ways, and also by a player with a king when his opponent has only a single man remaining on the board.

© DIAGRAM

CHECKERS GO-MOKU is an adaptation of the Japanese game described on page 56.
Play is on all the squares of a standard checker board, and the two players have 12 checkers each.
The board is empty at the start of a game, and the players take it in turns to place one checker on any square. After all the checkers have been placed, a player uses his turn to move one checker into any vacant, adjoining square.
If, at any stage of the game, a player succeeds in placing five checkers in a row (horizontally, vertically, or diagonally), he is entitled to remove any one of his opponent's checkers from the board.

The game is won when a player has removed all his opponent's checkers.

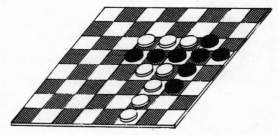

CHECKERS FOX AND GEESE Two versions of fox and geese are often played on a standard checker board and are particularly popular with children. (Other versions on other boards are described on page 30 .)
In both checkers versions, one player has one dark checker (the "fox") and his opponent has several white checkers (the "geese").
Play is only on the black squares of the board. A player moves only one checker at a turn.
The fox wins the game if it can break through the line of geese. The geese win if they can trap the fox so that it cannot move.

Four geese version
At the start of play, the player with the geese positions them on the four playing squares of his first row; the player with the fox positions it wherever he chooses (**a**).
The geese move diagonally forward like the men in British or American checkers.
The fox moves diagonally forward or backward one square at a time; it is not permitted to jump over the geese, so there is no taking in this version.

Twelve geese version (sometimes played with a "wolf" and "goats"). At the start of play the geese are positioned on the first three rows, as for British or American checkers; the fox is positioned on one of the corner playing squares on the opposite side of the board.
The geese move like the men and the fox like a king in British or American checkers. (Jumping and taking geese is permitted in this version.)

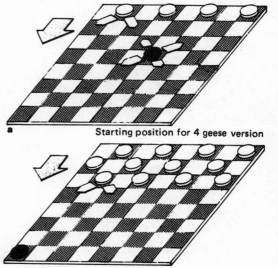

Starting position for 4 geese version

Starting position for 12 geese version

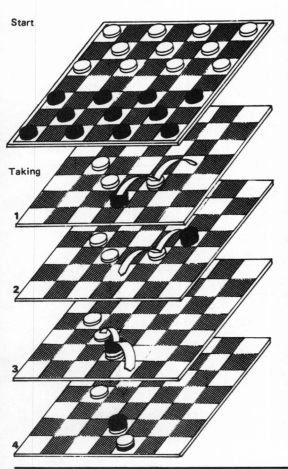

Start

Taking

1

2

3

4

LASCA

This is an interesting game in the checkers family. It is characterized by its unusual method of taking, and by the consequent building up of "columns" of pieces.

The board has 49 squares, seven along each side. The squares are alternately light and dark, and play is only on the light squares.

(A standard checker board can be used if the squares along two sides are covered, leaving a light square at each corner.)

Pieces Each player has a set of 11 pieces; one set is usually white and the other red or black.

Each piece is marked on one side—with a sticker, paint, pen, or pencil.

Objective The game is won when one player makes it impossible for his opponent to make any move.

Start of play Each player positions his pieces, with their unmarked sides face up, on the white squares in the three rows of the board nearest him.

Turns alternate, and each player makes only one move in a turn.

A **"soldier"** is a piece with the unmarked side face up. All pieces are soldiers at the start of play.

A soldier moves diagonally forward like a man in British or American checkers.

An **"officer"** is a piece with the marked side face up.

A soldier becomes an officer after it has crossed to the farthest row of the board (like "crowning" in standard checkers).

A player's turn ends whenever a soldier becomes an officer. An officer moves diagonally backward or forward like a king in American or British checkers.

A **"column"** may be a single piece or a pile of pieces.

A **"guide"** is the top piece of a column. The color of the guide shows to which player that column belongs, and its rank (soldier or officer) determines how the column may be moved.

Taking In Lasca, unlike other checkers games, a piece is not removed from the board when it is taken. Instead, it is added to the bottom of the column that takes it.

If a column contains several pieces, only the guide is taken when another column jumps over it.

In the example illustrated:
1) the red column takes the white guide from the white column;
2) the red column (led by an officer) takes the other white piece and red's turn ends;
3) the other white column (led by a soldier) takes the red guide and white's turn ends (**4**).

If a taken guide was an officer it retains this rank in the other column.

As in British and American checkers, a player must take a piece whenever possible, but if he has a choice of captures, he need not take the larger number of pieces.

REVERSI

This game of strategy was invented in the late nineteenth century and has recently been revived.

Board Bought boards have 64 playing circles with interconnecting lines. Reversi can also be played on the 64 squares of a standard checkers board.

Taking move

Multiple take

Pieces 64 pieces are needed. Each piece must have two easily distinguishable faces. Pieces can be improvised by: a) sticking or drawing symbols (eg stars and circles) on the two faces of 64 checkers; or b) sticking counters of two different colors (eg red and white) together to make a set of double-faced counters. Before play starts the players decide which of them will play with which face of the pieces up.

Objective Play ends when there is a piece on every square; the winner is the player who has the most pieces with his face up at the end of the game.

Turns alternate. In his turn each player attempts to place one piece on the board with his color or symbol face up.

First four pieces Each player's first two plays must be in the center four squares of the board. Of the possible starting patterns, (**a**) is generally preferred by expert players.

Starting patterns

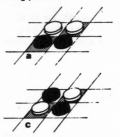

Taking After the first four pieces are placed, each player attempts to make one move in each turn.

Only taking moves are permitted, and if a player is unable to make a taking move he loses his turn. (Both players are, however, limited to a maximum of 32 plays.)

A taking move is made by positioning a piece so that: a) it is in a square next to a square containing an opposition piece; and b) it traps at least one opposition piece in a line in any direction between itself and another of the taker's pieces.

(In the example shown, reds could be positioned in the squares marked R and whites in those marked W).

When a piece is taken it is turned over to show the other player's symbol or color. A piece may be turned over many times during a game as it passes from one player to the other. Pieces are never removed from the board when they are taken.

Multiple takes By positioning a single piece a player may simultaneously take several pieces in more than one line (eg if a red were placed in the square marked T in the situation illustrated). Note that pieces may not be taken if a line is completed only when a piece is turned over.

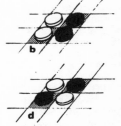

SALTA

This game was invented in about 1900 and takes its name name from *salta*, a Latin word meaning "jump."

Board The game is played on a continental checker board, 10 squares by 10.

Pieces There are two sets of 15 pieces. Each set is of a different color, eg red and white, and has pieces numbered 1 through 15. Sets can easily be made by drawing or sticking numbers on checkers pieces, though original sets have stars on pieces 1 through 5, moons on pieces 6 through 10, and suns on pieces 11 through 15.

Objective The game is won by the first player to move all his pieces onto the corresponding squares originally occupied by his opponent's pieces (eg white 4 onto the square that was occupied by red 4).

Start of play Players position their pieces as shown, with pieces 1 through 5 on the black squares of the first row, 6 through 10 on the second row, and 11 through 15 on the third row.

Starting position

Moves A player may make only one move in a turn. The following moves are permitted:
a) one square diagonally forward or backward, or
b) a jumping move diagonally forward or backward over one piece of either color that has a vacant square beyond it. Multiple jumps are not permitted in this game, and no jumped piece is removed from the board.

If a player can make a jumping move rather than an ordinary move he must do so—hence the strategic importance of forcing a player to jump his pieces back toward his own starting line.

120-move rule Some players like to play to the 120-move rule.

By this rule, play automatically ends after 120 moves. Each of the players then calculates how many moves he would need to achieve his objective. The winner is the player who is nearest his objective when play ends.

CONQUEST

Conquest is an interesting game that can be played with checkers pieces on an improvised board.

Board The game is played on a checkered board with 81 squares (nine squares by nine).

The central nine squares, called the "fortress," are enclosed within a red line.

Pieces There are two sets of pieces, one for each player. Each set is of a different color and comprises eight ordinary pieces and one specially marked king.

Objective Players attempt to capture the central fortress according to one of the four possible plans of occupation (see illustration).

The plan for a particular game must always be agreed before play starts.

Start of play Players position their pieces as illustrated: in diagonally opposite corners of the board and with the kings surrounded by the ordinary pieces.

Turns alternate, and each player makes only one move at a turn.

Moving The only permitted move for any piece is one square diagonally forward or backward (so that each piece stays on squares of the same color throughout the game) (**a**).

Exiling If a player traps an opponent's piece between two of his own pieces in a diagonal line (so that all three pieces are on the same color square) (**b**), the player may "exile" the trapped piece to any other square of the same color.

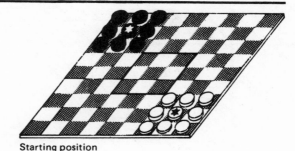

Starting position

Plans of occupation

a   b

Halma

Halma, which takes its name from a Greek word for a jump, was invented in England toward the end of the last century. It is a checkers type of game for two, three, or four persons. There are also halma solitaire problems to provide an interesting diversion for one player.

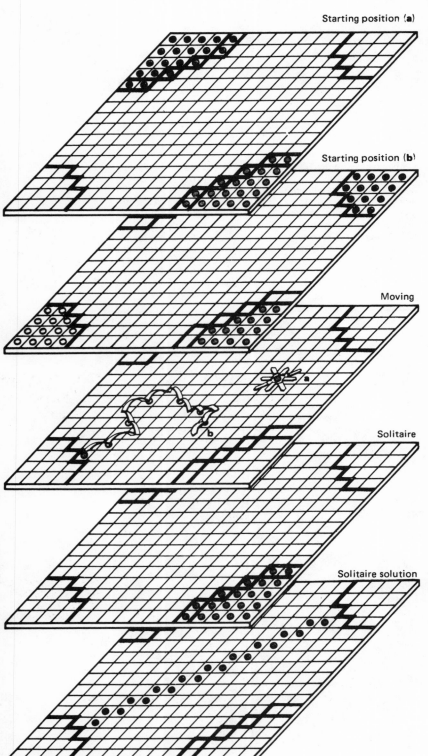

Starting position (a)

Starting position (b)

Moving

Solitaire

Solitaire solution

Board Halma is played on a board with 256 small squares, 16 along each side.
Heavy lines mark off "yards" in the board's corners. Each corner has a yard with 13 squares, and two diagonally opposite corners have an additional heavy line marking off a yard with 19 squares.
Pieces There are four sets of pieces—each of a different color. Two sets have 19 pieces and the other two only 13. The pieces may be:
a) small checkers or counters;
b) wooden or plastic cones;
c) wooden or plastic men resembling small chess pawns.
Forms of play The game may be played:
a) by two players;
b) by three or four players, each playing separately;
c) by four players, each with a partner.
Partnership halma can be played in two ways:
a) pairs are formed by players with pieces in adjacent yards;
b) pairs are formed by players with pieces in yards that are diagonally opposite.
(The second form provides more scope for partners to help each other.)
Objective Each player attempts to move his pieces from his own yard into the yard diagonally opposite. The game is won by the first player or pair to achieve this objective.
Start of play Starting positions vary with the forms of play:
a) when there are two players, each one takes a set of 19 pieces and positions them in the yards with 19 squares;
b) when there are three or four players, each one takes a set of 13 pieces and positions them in the yards with 13 squares.
Turns pass clockwise around the table if there are more than two players. A player may move only one piece in a turn.

Moving Pieces may be moved in any direction—straight or diagonally, forward or backward, to one side or the other.
Two types of move are permitted:
a) a "step"—by which a player moves a piece into an adjoining square;
b) a "hop"—by which a player moves a piece over a piece in an adjoining square into a vacant square directly behind it.
A player may hop over his own or another player's pieces, and all hopped pieces are left on the board.
A player may make several hops in one move, but may not combine steps and hops in a move.
There is no compulsion to make any hop.
HALMA SOLITAIRE
An interesting halma solitaire problem requires the player to place 19 pieces in one of the yards and then in 19 moves position them in a symmetrical figure across the board's diagonal.
This problem can be solved in several hundred ways, and the interest therefore derives from the variety of solutions. A fairly skillful player should be able to find 50 different solutions without too much difficulty.

Chinese checkers

Chinese checkers is a modern game derived from halma. It can be played by two to six persons, playing individually or with partners.

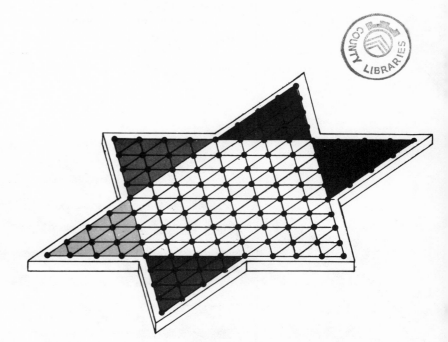

The board is made of metal, plastic, wood, or heavy card. The playing area is a six-pointed star, with holes or indentations to hold the pieces. Each of the star's points is a different color.

The pieces There are six sets of 15 pieces. Each set is the same color as one of the star's points.

The most common types of pieces are:
a) plastic pegs;
b) marbles.

Objective Players attempt to move their pieces into the opposite point. The game is won by the first player or pair to do so.

Start of play For a game between two players, each positions 15 pieces of appropriate colors in opposite points of the star (**a**).

When there are more than two players, each one positions 10 pieces in a point (**b**).

Partners usually take opposite points.

Turns Each player moves one piece in turn.

Moves may be made along any of the lines, ie in six directions.

Moves may be "steps" or "hops." A player may hop over his own or another player's pieces and may make several hops in one move. Steps and hops may not be combined in a single move. There is no compulsion to make a hop. All hopped pieces are left on the board.

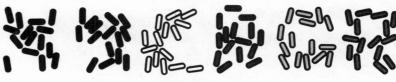

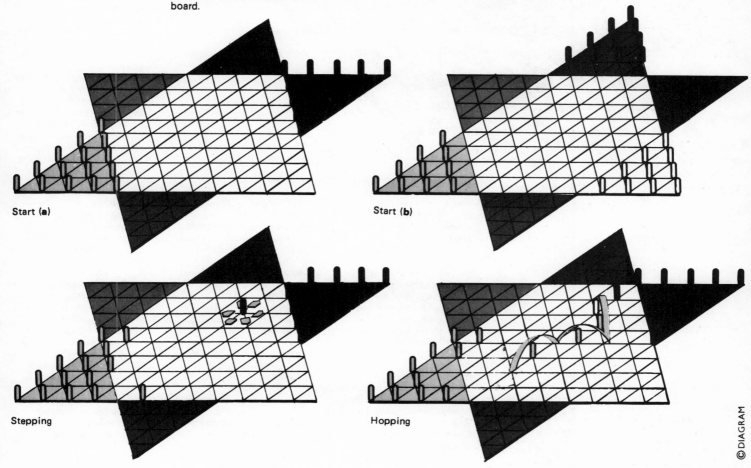

Start (**a**)

Start (**b**)

Stepping

Hopping

Brax

Brax was invented in England in the late nineteenth century and can be played by two, three, or four players. Pieces are moved along colored lines on the board, and players attempt to capture all opposing pieces.

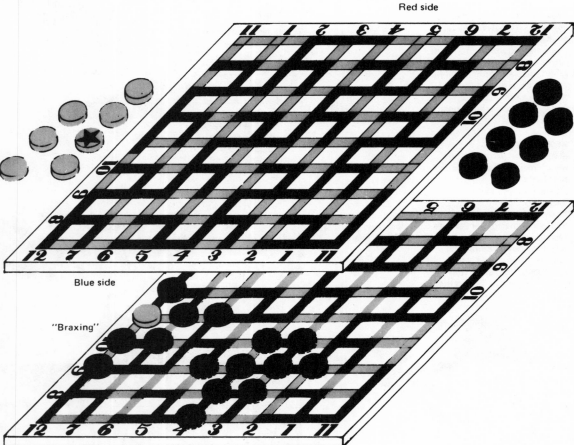

Red side

Blue side

"Braxing"

Moving

The board has short red and blue lines making the pattern illustrated. The lines form 64 squares (eight by eight), but all play is on the lines and on the points where the lines meet. There is no play within the squares.
There are numbered starting points along the board's edges.
The pieces are all identical in shape—seven red and seven blue. Each piece has one face plain and the other marked with a star.
Forms of play The basic game is for two players, but there are adaptations for three and four players.
The objective is to remove all enemy pieces from the board by capture.
Start of play Positions of pieces vary with the number of players.

Moving A player may move only one piece in a turn. Pieces are moved along the lines so that they come to rest at a point where two lines meet.
A piece may be moved in any direction, but may not be moved onto a point occupied by a piece belonging to the same side or over a point occupied by any piece of either side.
The distance a piece can be moved depends on the color of the line(s) on which it is moved:
a) a piece moving on a line of the opposing color may move only one space, ie from one point to the point immediately adjacent to it;
b) a piece moving on a line of its own color may move either one or two spaces as

the player wishes.
A piece moving two spaces may change direction in the course of that move (**c**), providing that it remains on a line of its own color and does not return to the point from which it started.
Capture A piece is captured when an opposing piece is moved to its point. A captured piece is immediately removed from the board.
"Braxing" A piece is said to "threaten" an opposing piece when it could capture it in one move —ie when it is one space away, or two spaces if it can reach the opposing piece along a line of its own color.
A player who threatens an opposing piece may call "brax" and so force his opponent to move that piece

immediately. The call must be made immediately after the threatening player has moved one of his own pieces.
If more than one piece is threatened when a player has called "brax," then the opposing player has the choice of which threatened piece to move. The threatening player may not then call "brax" again until after he has moved one of his own pieces.
When "brax" has been called, a threatened piece may move in any direction available to it. It may capture the piece threatening it, if that piece is within reach.
When one player has only one piece and the other player only two pieces left on the board, both players lose the right to brax.

BRAX FOR TWO PLAYERS

Pieces The game for two players is played with all 14 pieces, seven for each player. The pieces may be used with either face up.

Start of play Each player starts with his pieces on the points numbered 1 to 7 on his side of the board.

Play The players decide who will make the first move and then take alternate turns.

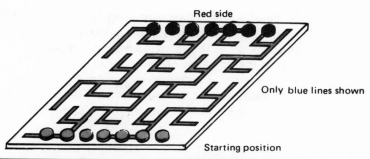

Red side

Only blue lines shown

Starting position

BRAX FOR FOUR PLAYERS

In the game for four players, two players act as allies against the other two. No consultation is allowed between allies.

Pieces Six red and six blue pieces are used. In each pair, one player uses three pieces with the star face up and his ally uses three pieces of the same color with the plain face up.

Start Each pair begins with the three plain pieces on points 1,2, and 3, and the three star pieces on points 8,9, and 10.

Play The players decide which pair will have the first move.

Turns are then in the order:
a) first pair, player with the plain pieces;
b) second pair, player with the plain pieces;
c) first pair, player with the star pieces;
d) second pair, player with the star pieces.

Retiring If a player's three pieces are all captured, he retires from the game and the remaining players continue to play in their regular order.

Braxing A player may brax only those opposing pieces that can move immediately after his move, and he can be braxed only by a piece that moves immediately before his move.

BRAX FOR THREE PLAYERS

In the game for three players, two players act as allies against the third. No consultation is allowed between allies.

Pieces The single player has five pieces of one color. The allies use six pieces of the other color: one player uses three pieces with the plain face up and his ally uses three with the star face up.

Start The single player starts with his pieces on points 1,2,3,4, and 5.
The alliance player with the plain pieces positions them on points 1,2, and 3, and the player with the stars positions them on points 8,9, and 10.

Play The single player always plays first, followed by the alliance player with the plain pieces and then the alliance player with the starred pieces. At his turn the single player moves two pieces. He may not, however, move the same piece twice in one turn (and so may make only one move when he has only a single piece left on the board).

Retiring If an ally's three pieces are all captured, he retires from the game.

Braxing Because the single player has two moves, he may be braxed by both players. If one of his pieces is braxed he must move that piece before moving any other piece. If two of his pieces are braxed he must move both pieces in his turn, but in any order.

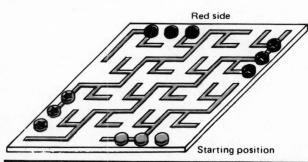

Red side

Starting position

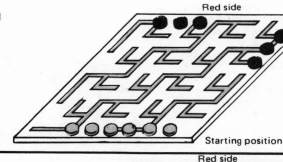

Red side

Starting position

BRAX FOX AND GEESE

This variant of brax makes an interesting game for two players.

Pieces One player uses one piece of one color (the "braxer"), and the other player uses five pieces of the other color (the "enemy").

Start of play The braxer is placed on point 4 on one side of the board.
The enemy pieces are placed on points 11,1,4,7, and 12 on the other side of the board.

Objective The player with the enemy pieces attempts to move any one of them across the board onto any one of points 11,1,4,7, or 12.
The player with the braxer wins the game if he captures all the enemy pieces before any one of them reaches one of the winning points.

Sequence of play The braxer moves first, and moves again every time an enemy piece has moved.
The enemy pieces always move in the sequence: 11,1,4,7, and 12 (the numbers being taken from the pieces' starting points).
For convenience, the enemy pieces can all begin the game with the same face up and each one can be reversed each time it is moved.

Moves The braxer moves in the usual way.
The enemy can only move forward in a straight line, and must always move as far as the colors of the lines allow, ie two spaces when on their own lines, and one space on lines of the opposing color.

Capture When an enemy piece is captured, the remaining enemy pieces continue to move in their original sequence. The braxer continues to have one turn for every move by an enemy piece.

Braxing Although the enemy pieces can only move in a straight line forward, they threaten all points within their reach in any direction—as in the standard game. The braxer cannot move to, and must move from, any point that they threaten.
When the braxer braxes an enemy piece, the braxed piece must retreat in a straight line as far as the color of the line allows. This does not count as an enemy turn and is followed by a normal move before the braxer's next turn.

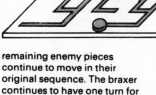

Red side

Starting position

©DIAGRAM

Chess

Originating in the East over a thousand years ago, chess has developed into one of the most popular of all games. Although it is a highly complex and sophisticated game, chess can also be enjoyed at a simpler level by inexperienced players. It is a game of strategy for two people, with each piece—from the king to the pawn—representing units in an army.

The board is a large square divided into eight rows of eight squares each.
The squares are alternately dark and light colored (usually black and white).
The board is placed between facing players so that each has a white square at the near righthand corner.
The rows of squares running vertically between facing players are called "files"; those running at right angles to the files are called "ranks." Rows of squares of the same color that touch only at their corners are called "diagonals."

Pieces At the start of a game 32 pieces are positioned on the board. 16 of these pieces are dark in color, 16 light. They are called black and white respectively and make up the two sides.
A player's side is made up of six different kinds of pieces. These are—in descending order of importance: king, queen, rook (castle), bishop, knight, pawn.
Each player has one king and one queen; two rooks, bishops, and knights; and eight pawns.

File

Rank

Diagonal

Objective The objective of each player is to capture his opponent's king.
Unlike the other pieces, the king cannot be removed from the board; it is held to be captured when it has been "checkmated" (see section on check and checkmating).
The player forcing checkmate wins the game—even if the pieces he has left on the board are outnumbered by the opponent's pieces.
A player, seeing the imminent checkmate of his king or recognizing a losing situation, will often resign. The player forcing the resignation wins the game.

Moves Each kind of piece can move a certain distance in one or more directions.
Moves are limited by conditions on the board at the time of play.
A piece may move to any square within its range, provided that:
a) the square is unoccupied by a piece of its own color;
b) if the square is occupied by an opponent's piece, that piece is first "captured" and removed from the board;
c) it does not, with the exception of the knight's move, cross a square that is occupied by a piece of either color.

Start of play

Individual pieces and moves
The king is the most important piece on the board, and its capture by checkmate ends the game. It is represented diagrammatically by a crown.
The king can move one square in any direction, provided that this square is not one where he can be taken.
Opposing kings can never stand on touching squares.
Castling The only time that a king may move more than one square is in the "castling" move involving the rook.
A player can make a castling move only once in a game.
The move is made to produce a defensive position around the king and to allow a rook to come into play. It comprises:

King

1) moving the king two squares to left or right from its original position and toward one of the rooks; then
2) transferring that rook to the square over which the king has just passed.
Castling is permitted only if:
a) neither the king nor the rook involved has moved from its original position;
b) no piece of either color is between the king and the rook involved in the castling move;
c) the square that the king must cross is not under attack by an opponent's piece.
All other pieces have a different attacking value, directly related to the number of squares to which they can move.

King's move

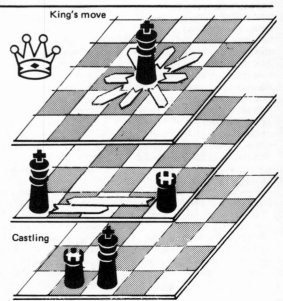

Castling

The queen, represented diagrammatically by a coronet, is the most powerful attacking piece. It can move to any square on the rank, file, or either of the two diagonals on which it is placed.

The rook, sometimes called the castle, is represented diagrammatically by a tower. It can move to any square on the rank or file on which it is placed.

In addition, either one of the rooks in each side may be involved with the king in the castling move.

The bishop, represented diagrammatically by a miter, can move to any square on the diagonal on which it is placed. In each side, therefore, each of the two bishops is restricted to moving on the diagonal of the same color as that on which it was originally placed.

The knight is represented diagrammatically by a horse's head. In a single move it travels two squares in any direction along a rank or file, then one square at right angles to that rank or file.

Thus whenever a knight moves from a black square it must land on a white square—and vice versa.

In moving, a knight may cross a square occupied by any other piece; it is the only piece allowed to do this.

The pawn, represented diagrammatically by a small ball on a collared stem, has the most restricted movements of any piece: it can only move forward.

In its opening move (**a**) a pawn may be moved forward either one or two squares on the file that it occupies. Thereafter, a pawn can only move forward one square at a time, except when capturing. Unlike other pieces, a pawn does not capture in the same way that it moves. Instead of capturing in a forward direction, it does so diagonally —taking a piece that occupies either of the two squares diagonally next to it (**b**).

In addition, a pawn may capture an opposing pawn "*en passant*" (in passing) (**c**).

If the opposing pawn moves forward two squares in its opening move, the square that it crosses is open to attack as though the pawn had only advanced one square.

Thus the capturing pawn may make its usual taking move (ie one square diagonally forward) onto the square just crossed by the opposing pawn —the opposing pawn is then considered "captured" and is removed from the board. (The *en passant* capture must be made immediately the opposing pawn has moved forward two squares.)

Pawn promotion Whenever a pawn reaches the end of the file on which it is moving (ie it reaches the far side of the board) it must—in the same move—be exchanged for a queen, rook, bishop, or knight.

The choice of piece is made by the player promoting the pawn, and is made without taking into account the number and kind of pieces on the board.

Theoretically, therefore, a player could have up to nine queens on the board.

The effect of the promoted piece on play is immediate.

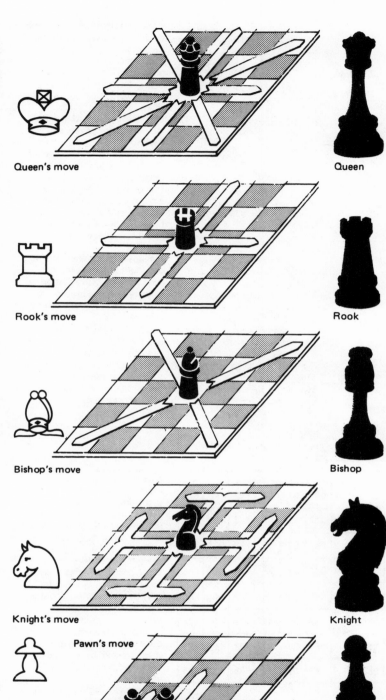

Queen's move

Queen

Rook's move

Rook

Bishop's move

Bishop

Knight's move

Knight

Pawn's move

Pawn

Capture "en passant"

Pawn capture

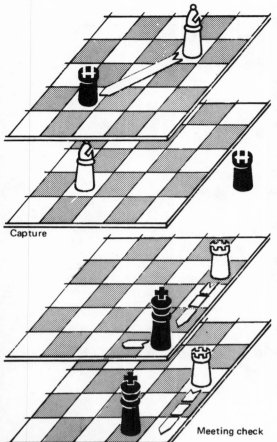

Capture

Meeting check

Starting procedure Players draw for sides, and position their pieces on the board. The player drawing white makes the first move, and thereafter the players move alternately.

Play The position of the pieces at the start of play is such that each player can move only a knight or a pawn. After the first move by each player, more pieces can come into play.

In moving their pieces, players are governed not only by the movements laid down for each piece but also by rules that affect how pieces can be handled.

If a player touches a piece that can legitimately be moved, then he must move that piece —unless he has previously warned his opponent that he is adjusting the piece on its square. The usual warning used is "*J'adoube*" (I adjust). Similarly, if a player touches an enemy piece that can be taken, the touched piece must be captured unless the player has given a prior warning.

A move is completed when:
a) a player's hand has left a piece after it has been moved to a vacant square;
b) a player, having captured a piece and placed his attacking piece on the captured square, removes his hand from the piece;
c) in castling, a player's hand has left the rook (once the king has been moved, the castling move must always be completed);
d) in pawn promotion, a player's hand has left the piece that replaces the pawn.

Phases of play Chess players commonly divide a game into three phases: opening game, middle game, and end game.

These phases are not clear-cut divisions—they simply reflect the strategies and tactics employed.
1) In the opening game, both players position their pieces into what each considers to be an advantageous situation. Castling moves are usually made during this phase.
2) In the middle game, players attempt to capture enemy pieces, thereby reducing the opponent's attacking material.

However, as the main objective is to checkmate the opponent's king, moves or captures should not be made unless they weaken the opponent's defense of his king. The player should also beware of making moves that jeopardize his own position.
3) In the end game, players attempt to checkmate the opponent's king.
If, during this phase, a player has little attacking material, he will attempt—where possible —to promote a pawn to a more powerful piece.

Check and checkmate
Whenever a king is attacked by an opposing piece, the king is said to be "in check."
The check must be met on the following move by either:
a) moving the king one square in any direction onto a square that is not attacked;
b) capturing the piece that is checking the king; or
c) interposing a piece between the king and the attacking piece (if the king is checked by an opponent's knight, it is not possible to intercept the check in this way).
A piece that intercepts a check can—in the same move —give check to the opposing king.

Black

QR1	QKt1	QB1	Q1	K1	KB1	KKt1	KR1
QR2	QKt2	QB2	Q2	K2	KB2	KKt2	KR2
QR3	QKt3	QB3	Q3	K3	KB3	KKt3	KR3
QR4	QKt4	QB4	Q4	K4	KB4	KKt4	KR4
QR5	QKt5	QB5	Q5	K5	KB5	KKt5	KR5
QR6	QKt6	QB6	Q6	K6	KB6	KKt6	KR6
QR7	QKt7	QB7	Q7	K7	KB7	KKt7	KR7
QR8	QKt8	QB8	Q8	K8	KB8	KKt8	KR8

QR8	QKt8	QB8	Q8	K8	KB8	KKt8	KR8
QR7	QKt7	QB7	Q7	K7	KB7	KKt7	KR7
QR6	QKt6	QB6	Q6	K6	KB6	KKt6	KR6
QR5	QKt5	QB5	Q5	K5	KB5	KKt5	KR5
QR4	QKt4	QB4	Q4	K4	KB4	KKt4	KR4
QR3	QKt3	QB3	Q3	K3	KB3	KKt3	KR3
QR2	QKt2	QB2	Q2	K2	KB2	KKt2	KR2
QR1	QKt1	QB1	Q1	K1	KB1	KKt1	KR1

White

Chess notation is the method by which moves in a game are recorded.
Two of the systems officially recognized are: the descriptive system and the algebraic system.

Descriptive system
Each piece is represented by its initial letter, but the knight may be represented by either Kt or N.
With the exceptions of the pawns and the king and queen, pieces are further distinguished by the side of the board on which they stand:
pieces to the right of the king take the prefix K;
pieces to the left of the queen take the prefix Q.
Thus the rook to the left of the queen is a queen's rook and is represented as QR.

Each file is represented by the initials of the pieces that occupy the squares at either end.
The eight files (from left to right for white, and inversely for black) are represented as follows:
QR, QKt, QB, Q, K, KB, KKt, KR.

KKt – KR3

Each rank is numbered from 1 to 8; both players count from their own ends of the board. Consequently each square has two names: one name as seen from white's side, and one from black's.
For example, QKt3 (white) equals QKt6 (black).
A move is described by the initial letter of the piece moved and the square to which it moved.
For example, the king's knight move to the third square of the king's rook file is represented by KKt–KR3.
If two pieces of the same kind can move to the same square, both the square from which the piece moved and the square it arrived at are given.

For example, KKt (KB4)–KR3 means that the knight on the fourth square of the king's bishop file made the move, although another knight on the board could have reached the same square in the same move.

Other explanatory abbreviations are:
a) O-O or Castles K denotes a castling move involving the KR.
b) O-O-O or Castles Q denotes a castling move involving the QR.
c) x denotes captures.
d) ch or + denotes check.
e) ! denotes well played.
f) ? denotes a bad move.

If the check cannot be met then the king is deemed "in checkmate" or simply "mate." When a checking or checkmating move is made, it is customary for the player making such a move to declare "Check" or "Checkmate" as appropriate.

Winning A player wins if he:
a) checkmates his opponent's king; or
b) forces his opponent to resign.

Checkmate may be made, or a player may resign, at any time during the course of the game.

Drawn game Many games of chess do not end in a victory for either player. A game is deemed drawn in any of the following cases.
a) When the player whose turn it is to move can make no legal move (a situation known as "stalemate").
b) When neither player has sufficient pieces to force checkmate.
c) When a player can check the opponent's king indefinitely but cannot checkmate it (a situation called "perpetual check").
d) When no capture or pawn move has been made by either side during 50 successive moves of each player.
e) When the same position recurs three times, always when it is the same player's turn to move. The right to claim a draw then belongs either to the player who is in a position to play a move leading to such repetition (provided that he declares his intention of making this move); or to the player who must reply to a move by which the repeated position is made.
f) When both players agree to call the game drawn.

Illegal positioning If an illegal move is made during the course of a game, the pieces are set up as they were immediately before the illegal move. If this is impossible, the game is annulled.

If pieces are accidentally displaced and cannot be correctly repositioned or if the initial position of the pieces was incorrect, the game is also annulled.

If the chessboard is found to have been incorrectly placed, the pieces on the board are transferred to a correctly placed board in the same positioning as when the error was discovered and play then continues.

Competition chess is strictly controlled. It differs from the informal game in the following ways.
a) Each player must write down every move made.
b) Each player must make a certain number of moves in a given time (time is kept by a special control clock).
c) If a game is adjourned, the player whose turn it is must write down his move and place it in a sealed envelope, together with his and his opponent's scoresheets. The sealed move is made on the resumption of play.
d) It is forbidden to distract or worry an opponent; ask or receive advice from a third party; use any written or printed notes; or to analyze the game on another chessboard.
e) A designated person must direct the competition. The competition director must ensure that the rules of play are strictly observed—he may impose penalties on any player who infringes these rules.
(These notes on competition chess are an outline only. The official international governing body—the Fédération Internationale des Echecs (FIDE)—lays down the full

Examples of checkmate

rules and interprets any problems arising in the game. Its decision is binding on all affiliated federations.)

Bf1–d3

Ktf3–h2

a8	b8	c8	d8	e8	f8	g8	h8	Black
a7	b7	c7	d7	e7	f7	g7	h7	
a6	b6	c6	d6	e6	f6	g6	h6	
a5	b5	c5	d5	e5	f5	g5	h5	
a4	b4	c4	d4	e4	f4	g4	h4	
a3	b3	c3	d3	e3	f3	g3	h3	
a2	b2	c2	d2	e2	f2	g2	h2	
a1	b1	c1	d1	e1	f1	g1	h1	White

Algebraic system
Each piece, with the exception of the pawns, is represented by its initial letter (and the knight by Kt or N). The pawns are not specially indicated.
The eight files (reading from left to right for white) are represented by the letters from a to h.
The eight ranks (counting from white's first rank) are numbered from 1 to 8. Initially, the white pieces stand on ranks 1 and 2, and the black pieces on ranks 7 and 8. Thus each square is represented by the combination of a letter and a number.

A move is described by the initial letter of the piece moved and the square from which it moved, plus the square at which it arrived.
For example, a bishop moving from square f1 to square d3 is represented by Bf1–d3 or in a shortened form by Bd3.
If two pieces of the same kind can move to the same square, both the square from which the piece moved and the square it arrived at are given. For example, two knights stand on the squares f3 and g4; if the knight on f3 makes the move to h2, the move is written Ktf3–h2 or in the shortened form by Ktf–h2.

The other abbreviations used in the algebraic system are the same as those for the descriptive system, with the following additions:
a) : or x denotes captures;
b) ‡ denotes checkmate.

Shogi

Shogi is the Japanese member of the chess family. It is widely popular there and supports professional players. There have been many forms of shogi since its introduction in about the eighth century. A feature peculiar to shogi since the sixteenth century is that captured pieces become members of the capturing side and can be returned to any position on the board.

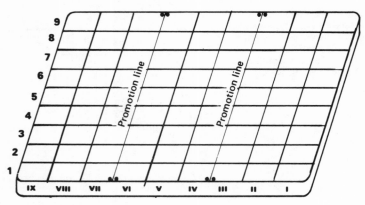

The board is nine squares by nine, giving 81 squares in all. The "squares" are in fact slightly oblong, and the board is placed between the two players so that they are facing each other down its longer length.

Black dots mark the two "promotion lines."

The notation used for referring to squares on the shogi board is shown.

The pieces Each player begins with 20 pieces. Using Western chess names as far as possible and with Western notation in brackets, these pieces are:

a king (K);
a rook (R);
a bishop (B);
two gold generals (G);
two silver generals (S);
two knights (Kt);
two lances (L);
nine pawns (P).

Shogi pieces are all the same shape: they are distinguished only by size and by the Japanese characters written on them.

Shogi pieces are also all the same color—although we have color-coded them for easy recognition in our diagrams. The two players' pieces are distinguished on the board by being pointed toward the opposing player.

The objective is to
"checkmate" the enemy king.
A king is checkmated when,
in the next enemy turn, it
could be captured either on
its present square or on any
square to which it could move.

Pieces and their moves
Pieces are only permitted to
move on the board in certain
ways. Each piece has a
different move:
a) the king can move one
square in any direction;
b) the gold general can move
one square in any direction
except diagonally backward;
c) the silver general can move
one square directly forward or
one square in any diagonal
direction;
d) the pawn can only move
one square directly forward
(unlike the pawn in chess, the
pawn in shogi makes the
same move when capturing);
e) the knight can move, in a
single turn, one square
directly forward and then one
square diagonally forward
(the square directly forward
may be vacant or occupied,
but if it is occupied by an
enemy piece that piece is not
captured);

f) the rook can move an
unlimited number of squares
in any direction except
diagonally;
g) the bishop can move an
unlimited number of squares
in any diagonal direction;
h) the lance can move an
unlimited number of squares
but only directly forward.
Pieces that can move an
unlimited number of squares
(the rook, bishop, and lance)
must halt:
if they reach a piece belonging
to their own side (in which
case they can go no farther
than the last vacant square
before they reach that piece);
or
if they reach an enemy piece
(in which case the enemy
piece is captured).

Value of pieces Players
trying out a game of shogi will
probably be helped by a rough
guide to the value of the
pieces.
As a game ends when a king
is checkmated, the king is
obviously the most important
piece.
The rook is the most powerful
piece on the board and its
importance increases as the
game progresses.
The bishop is almost as
powerful as the rook and is
most useful in the game
opening.
The gold and silver generals
are the intermediate pieces,
with the gold slightly more
useful especially in defense.
The knight and lance are
minor pieces, roughly equal
in value and of real use only in
attack.
Pawns are of very little
importance and, unlike in
chess, a one pawn advantage
is very seldom significant.

Pawn		d
Lance		h
Knight		e
Silver general		c
Gold general		b
Bishop		g
Rook		f
King		a

Moves

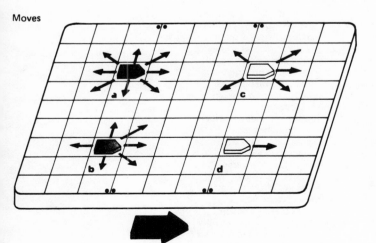

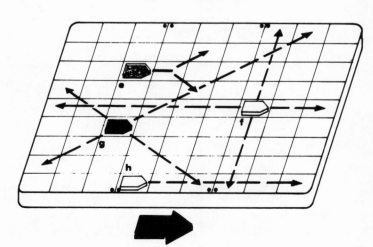

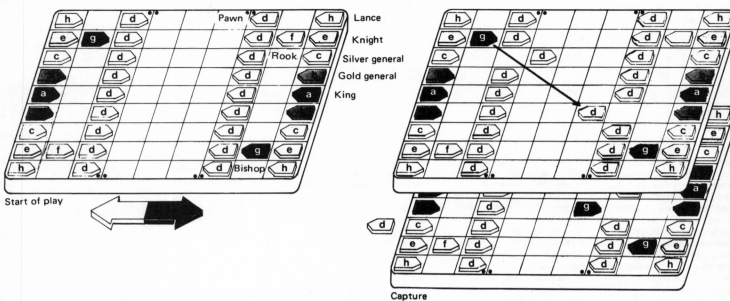

Start of play

Capture

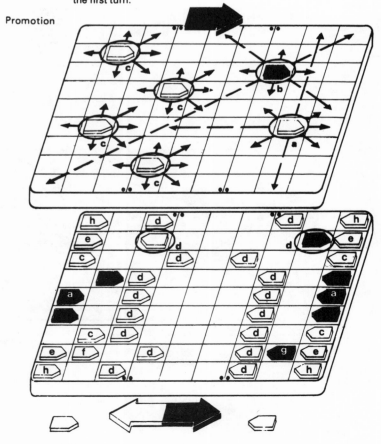

Promotion

Start of play The pieces are placed on the board as shown. When a game is being described, the players may conveniently be referred to as "black" and "white," even though their pieces are not distinguished by color. Pointers at the side of the board indicate each player's direction of play.
Players usually draw lots, and the player drawing black has the first turn.

Play The two players make alternate moves. In a move a player may either:
a) move one of his pieces on the board to a vacant square;
b) capture an enemy piece; or
c) replace a previously captured piece on the board.

Capture A player captures an enemy piece by moving one of his own pieces to the square occupied by that piece.
When a player captures a piece it becomes part of his own side, and in any future turn can be returned to the board on any vacant square.
(In the capture illustrated it is black's turn to play.
He moves by capturing the white pawn with his bishop.)

Promotion When a piece crosses the far "promotion line," its powers of movement may be changed if its player wishes.
Promoted pieces move as follows:
a) a rook keeps its original move and adds the power to move one square at a time in any diagonal direction;
b) a bishop keeps its original move and adds the power to move one square at a time in any non-diagonal direction;
c) a silver general, a lance, a knight, and a pawn are all promoted to gold generals.
A gold general does not acquire any new powers when it is promoted.
In play, promotion is shown by turning the piece over to expose a different Japanese character underneath.
In diagrams of a game, promotion is shown by drawing a circle around the original piece (**d**).
Once a piece has been promoted, it retains its new powers even if it retreats so that it is no longer beyond the far promotion line.
A piece receives its promotion in the turn in which it crosses the promotion line, or in any subsequent turn, according to

the player's wishes. Its new powers become available to it in the next turn after promotion.
A lance or pawn that reaches the last rank must be promoted; so must a knight that reaches the last two ranks. (Since these pieces cannot be moved backward, promotion is essential if they are to be moved again.)
A promoted piece loses its promotion when captured. For example, if black captures a promoted white pawn, it joins his side as a pawn not as a gold general. (He can, of course, play in such a way that it is again promoted.)

Attacking the king A king is "in check" when it is exposed to capture—ie when it is on a square onto which the opposing player could move one of his pieces in his next turn.

If a player's king is in check he must immediately escape check:

a) by moving the king to a square that is not being attacked;

b) by taking the attacking piece with the king; or

c) by taking the attacking piece with another piece. Whatever he does, however, his turn must not end with his still being in check from any enemy piece.

It is "checkmate" when a player's king is exposed to capture and there is no move that he can make that does not leave it so exposed.

Use of captured pieces A captured piece is removed from the board and becomes the property of the player who made the capture.

In any turn, instead of moving a piece already on the board, a player may place a piece that he has captured on the board on any vacant square. This is called a "drop." The piece is placed so that it points in the same direction as the player's other pieces.

A dropped piece, placed on the board beyond the far promotion line, does not receive promotion as soon as it is placed on the board but must first make a move on the board. Therefore a player must not place a pawn or a lance on the last rank, or a knight on one of the last two ranks, since these pieces would not be able to move again.

There are two restrictions on pawn drops:

a player must not place a pawn on the same file as one of his own unpromoted pawns;

a player cannot checkmate the enemy king by placing a pawn on the square directly in front of the king.

(It is because of the power of the drop as a maneuver that the king in shogi almost always stays in one corner of the board surrounded by a heavy guard.)

Examples of checkmate

a) Basic checkmate: the gold general moves to 9viii and so mates the king. (If the gold general moved to 8viii the king would have been in check but the gold general, unprotected by the bishop, would have been taken in the king's next move.)

b) Checkmate by promoting: the knight moves to 6viii, is promoted, and so mates the king.

c) Checkmate by not promoting: white chooses not to promote his silver general, moves it to 2ix, keeps it unpromoted, and so mates the king. (If the silver general had been promoted to gold general it would have been unable to attack along the reverse diagonal.)

d) Checkmate by promoting and then retreating: the promoted rook returns from beyond the promotion line to 2iv and so mates the king. (The rook needs the additional power given by promotion in order to mate.)

e) Checkmate by forced exchange: white's silver general moves to 9ii, giving check and forcing black's silver general to take it; black's silver general is in turn taken by white's gold general, which, covered by white's lance, then mates black's king.

Checkmate by drop

a) Black takes white's gold general with his bishop, promotes it, and so gives check. White's king must take black's bishop to escape check.

b) Each player now has a captured piece in hand alongside the board: black has the gold general and white the bishop. Black drops the gold general onto 8ii—and so mates white's king.

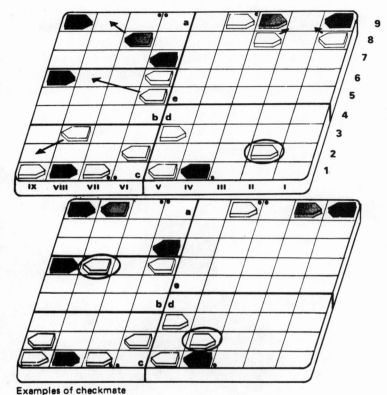

Examples of checkmate

Checkmate by drop

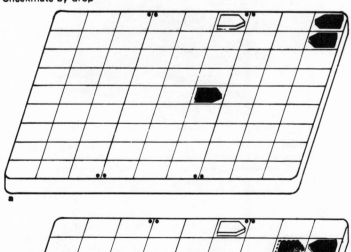

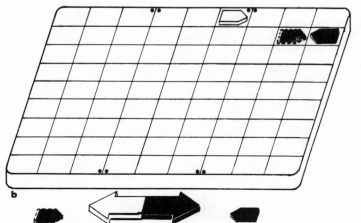

Go (Wei-ch'i)

Go is thought to be one of the oldest games in existence. It originated in China over 3000 years ago (its Chinese name is wei-ch'i) and was later adopted by Japan and other oriental countries. It is considered one of the greatest games of strategic skill. Two players compete to secure as much of the playing area as possible.

Pieces There are two sets of stones: a set of 181 black stones and a set of 180 white stones (361 in all). Each player has one set.

The stones are disk shaped, about $\frac{7}{8}$ in in diameter, and $\frac{1}{8}$–$\frac{1}{2}$ in thick.

The stones may be kept in a lacquered box (go-tsubo) or other container.

Board The traditional Japanese go table (go-ban) is made of wood and is stained yellow. It is about $17\frac{1}{2}$ in long, 16in wide, and 4–5in thick, and has four legs roughly 3in high.

The playing area (about $16\frac{1}{2}$ in by 15in) is marked out in black lacquer in a grid pattern of 19 parallel lines and 19 lines at right angles to these, forming a total of 361 intersections or points.

The intersections of the fourth, tenth, and sixteenth lines in each direction are marked by dots and are known as handicap points.

The two players kneel opposite each other, at the shorter sides of the table.

Objective By the positioning of his stones on the board, each player aims to surround more unoccupied territory and enemy stones than his opponent.

Order of play Players take alternate turns. The opening move is usually made by the player with the black stones. (Players take it in turn to play black unless there is a known disparity of playing skill—see handicapping section.)

A turn consists of placing a stone on an unoccupied point. Except in the "ko situation," a stone may be placed on any vacant point.

Once in position the stone is not moved again during the game unless it is captured, in which case it is removed from the board.

Handicapping The player taking the first turn is at an advantage.

Black (the opening turn) normally alternates between players. If there is a known disparity of playing skill or if one player wins three consecutive games, the weaker player may be allowed to keep the black stones.

If further handicapping is necessary, the weaker player may place two or more of his stones on the dotted handicap points before the game starts (see the table below), and the opening move then goes to the player with the white stones. Should the stronger player continue to win, the number of handicap stones may be increased.

Table showing positions for handicap stones

Handicap	Positions
2 stones	D4, Q16
3 stones	D4, Q4, Q16
4 stones	D4, D16, Q4, Q16
5 stones	D4, D16, K10, Q4, Q16
6 stones	D4, D10, D16, Q4, Q10, Q16
7 stones	D4, D10, D16, K10, Q4, Q10, Q16
8 stones	D4, D10, D16, K4, K16, Q4, Q10, Q16
9 stones	D4, D10, D16, K4, K10, K16, Q4, Q10, Q16

Playing procedure At the beginning of the game the board is empty except for any handicap stones.

Stones must be placed on the points (line intersections) and not on the squares formed by the lines.

Each player places his stones to form connected groups or chains in such a way as to surround as many vacant points and opponent's stones as possible.

Should all the points adjacent to one or more stones be occupied by stones of the other color, the former stone or group of stones is captured and removed from the board. (Adjacent points are those that are linked directly to a point by a line, and not diagonally.)

It is possible to win a game without capturing any stones, since the objective is territorial gain.

Explanation of diagrams

1) Playing area and standard go notation.

2) Capture of single stones.

3) Capture of groups of stones: a white stone played onto the dotted position would capture the black group attacked.

4a) and **5a**) Black cannot play onto the point marked with a cross, as the stone would be immediately captured (the arrowed point is vacant—white is not completely surrounded).

4b) and **5b**) Black can play onto the dotted point because the play puts the white stones out of contact with any empty point. The white stones are captured and removed. All black stones remain.

6a) and **6b**) A *ko* situation. In (a) a black stone placed on the crossed point captures the white stone; in (b) a white stone replaced on the captured point would recapture the black stone.

6c) A *seki* situation. Neither player can place his stone on the point marked with the cross without losing his formation.

Ko situations A *ko* (threat) situation is one that can be repeated indefinitely.

In *ko* situations the second player may not recapture until he has made at least one move elsewhere on the board. (Forcing play at other parts of the board is therefore important.)

A single *ko* situation may involve many stones. If there are three *ko* situations on a board at any one time, the game is declared drawn.

Seki situations A *seki* (deadlock) situation exists on any part of the board where opposing groups are so placed that neither player can occupy an uncontrolled point without losing his own pieces.

Seki situations are left untouched until the end of the game, and all free points in them are disregarded in scoring.

Dame points are vacant points between territories that cannot be played to with benefit by either side.

Dame points are left untouched until the end of the game, and then disregarded in scoring.

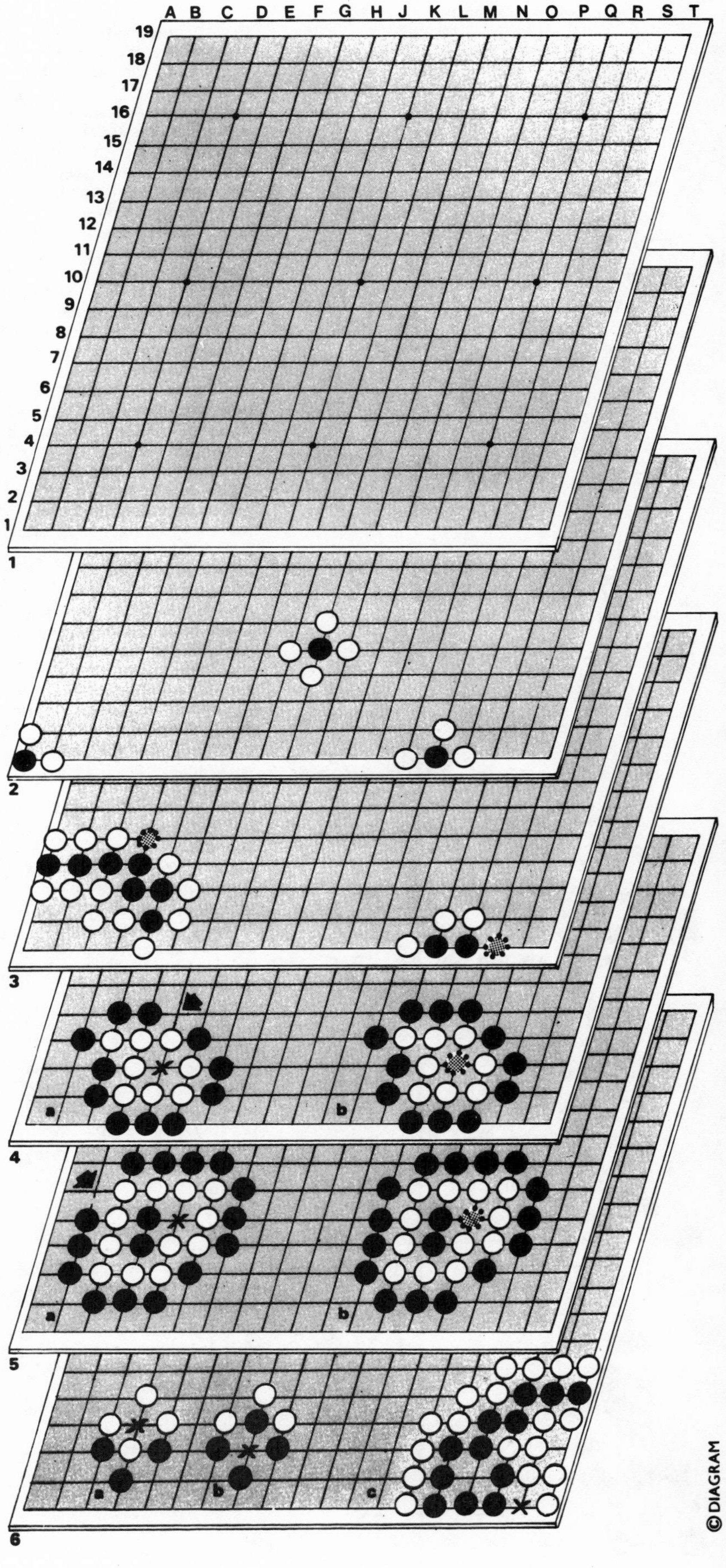

© DIAGRAM

Simplified 9 x 9 board

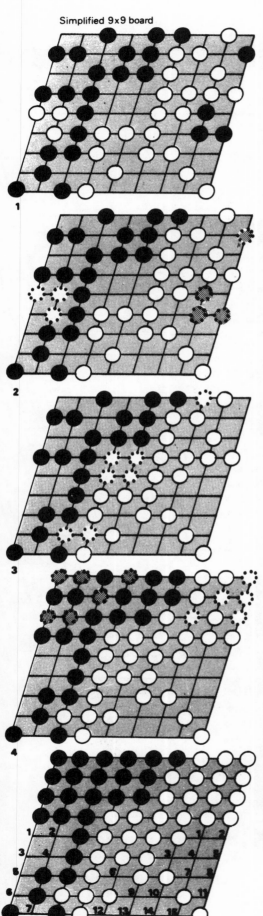

Prohibitions No move may be made that causes repetition of a position formed earlier in the game.

A stone must not remain on the board if it is entirely surrounded by enemy stones. A stone must not be played onto a point that is completely surrounded by stones of another color, unless the move causes the immediate capture of enemy stones.

End of play The game ends when both players agree that there are no further advantages to be gained by either side.

If only one player considers the game to be over, his opponent may continue to make moves until he too is satisfied that no points or stones remain to be secured.

(The first player may continue play, if he wishes, until both players agree that the game is over. But he may not resume play once he has actually missed a turn.)

Scoring An imaginary board, nine lines by nine lines, has been used to illustrate the basic scoring process. (It should be thought of as a simplified complete board, not as a section of a board.)

1) At the end of play all stones left in enemy territory are ruled captured.

2) These captured stones are removed from the board and added to each player's collection of captured enemy stones.

3) Any vacant points in neutral and *seki* situations have stones placed on them to discount them in the scoring. Either player may use his unused stones for this purpose.

4) In order to facilitate counting, black places all the white stones he has captured on vacant points in white's territory and white places all the captured black stones on vacant points in black's territory.

5) The number of vacant points left in each territory is counted.

Result The winner is the player with the larger number of vacant points left in his territory. He scores the difference between his own and his opponent's count. The game is tied if both players have an equal number of points.

GO-MOKU

This is a straightforward game played on a go board. It originated in Japan and is sometimes called go-bang or spoil five.

Players It is a game for two players.

Board A go board is used.

Pieces Each player has a set of 100 stones: one set black and the other white.

Objective Players aim to position five stones so that they form a straight line (horizontally, vertically, or diagonally).

Play The board is empty at the start of the game, and black has the opening move.

The players take it in turns to place a stone on any point (line intersection).

Once a stone has been placed it may not be moved again until the end of the game.

If all the stones are used up before either player has succeeded in forming a "five," the game may either be declared drawn, or the players may take it in turns to move one stone one point in a horizontal or vertical direction until a "five" is formed.

HASAMI SHOGI

Hasami shogi is an interesting Japanese game that can be played on a go board.

Players It is a game for two players.

The board is nine squares by nine. A quarter of a go board is generally used—but note that play is on the squares not the points.

Pieces Each player has a set of 18 stones: one set black and the other white.

The objective is to capture all the opposing stones.

Start of play Each player places his stones on his two home rows.

Play Players take alternate turns. A player may move only one stone in a turn.

Moves All moves must be forward, backward, or to the side. No moves may be diagonal. A stone may:
a) move into an adjacent square;
b) jump over a stone, of either set, into a vacant square beyond it.

Jumped stones are not removed from the board. Double jumps are not permitted.

Capture A stone is captured if an opponent's move traps it between two opposing stones. A stone is not captured if it is flanked diagonally by opposing stones.

A stone is not captured if it moves into a vacant square between two enemy stones. A stone is captured if an enemy move traps it in a corner of the board.

Hasami shogi: starting position

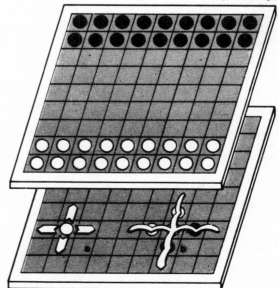

Hex

Hex is a game for two players invented by a Dane, Piet Hein. Hex sets are available in some places, but the game can also be played with improvised equipment. Each player tries to form an unbroken line of pieces between his two sides of the board.

The board has a diamond-shaped playing area made up of adjoining hexagons. Two opposite sides of the board belong to black; the other two to white.

The pieces are all identical in shape, and are in two sets of equal number, one colored black and one white. The highest number of pieces that a player can require for a game is 61; usually he will need far fewer.

Objective The game is won by the first player to place his pieces so that they form a line joining his two sides of the board.
The line does not have to be straight, but it must be unbroken. Corner hexagons belong to both players, and either player may use them as hexagons touching his sides of the board.

Play Each player takes one set of pieces.
The first player places one of his pieces on the board, on any hexagon he chooses.
Turns then alternate, with each player placing one of his pieces on any unoccupied hexagon.
Pieces may not be moved once they have been placed on the board.

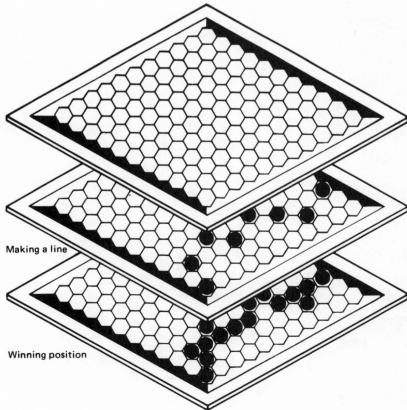

Making a line

Winning position

Solitaire board games

Solitaire board games are an excellent diversion for one person. Board solitaire originated in France, where it is said to have been invented by an imprisoned nobleman. It was introduced into England in the late 1700s and has since spread to other parts of the world.

The objective of some solitaire games is to clear the board of all the pieces; in other games the player tries to position the pieces in a specific pattern.

Equipment Solitaire is played with a special board and a set of pegs or marbles made of ivory, bone, wood, or plastic. The traditional French board is octagonal and has 37 holes to accommodate the same number of pegs.
Traditional English boards are circular and have 33 hollows to hold 33 marbles. A channel running around the edge of the board holds pieces eliminated from the game.
Some solitaire games require all the pieces—others only a certain number of them. The pieces are positioned before the start of play.
(The boards illustrated have been numbered, so that the solutions to the different games can be given.)

English board

French board

Play Pieces are moved in the same manner in all solitaire games.
Each peg or marble is "jumped" over an adjoining piece to an empty hole beyond—the piece that has been jumped over is then removed from the board. Pieces may only be moved horizontally or vertically.

Result A game is considered won only if its objective has been exactly met. For example, the standard game is a success only if the board has been completely cleared of all but one of the pieces.
Although some games can be won by more than one method, a player will usually have to make numerous attempts until he has worked out a winning solution.

Moving

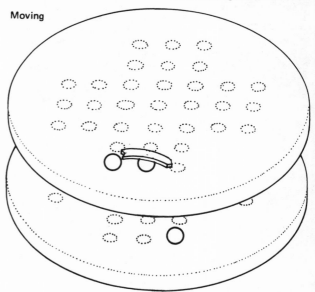

STANDARD SOLITAIRE
The objective of the basic solitaire game is the same whichever type of board is used.
The player tries to clear the board so that at the end of the game only one piece is left—either in the central hole or in some other hole predetermined by the player.
Play starts from the center of the board, after the middle piece has been removed.

It is vital that no pieces are left isolated from the others during play, as they cannot then be cleared.
If the player wishes, the board can be cleared from some other chosen starting point—leaving the center hole filled and removing a piece from elsewhere on the board in order to make a starting space.

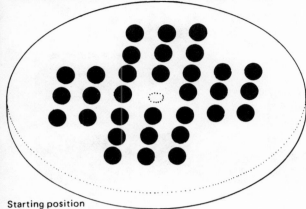

Starting position

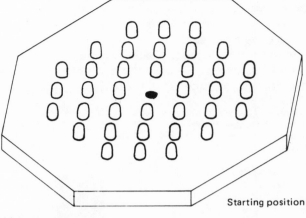

Starting position

SOLITAIRE VARIANTS
There are numerous variations of board solitaire, particularly for play on a French board. A player may wish to devise a variant of his own—which will require patience, persistence, and plenty of time. Every move of every attempt to make a certain pattern must be noted until an exact solution has been found. The following are a selection of existing solitaire games.

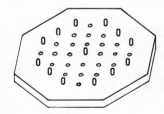

The world: solution

PATTERN FORMING GAMES
Many pattern forming games are designed for play on a French board.
Those illustrated all begin with all 37 pieces in position. The central piece is then removed, and the player tries to end the game by forming the patterns shown.

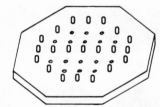

The apostles: solution

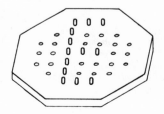

The letter E: solution

THE CROSS
The cross is played using only nine pieces, positioned as shown.
The object is to remove eight of the nine pieces from the board, leaving only one at the center.
(The cross can be played on either the French or the English board.)

The cross: English start

THE CORSAIR
At the start of the game all the 37 holes of a French board are filled. Any one peg at an angle of the board is then removed (ie 1, 3, 15, 29, 37, 35, 23, or 9).
The objective is to remove all the pieces except one—which should end up in the hole diametrically opposite the starting hole.
For example, if the game were begun at hole 37 the last peg should be in hole 1.

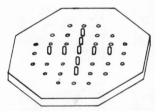

The cross: French start

THE OCTAGON
Octagon is a game for play on a French board.
All the holes except those at the angles of the board are filled (ie not 1, 3, 15, 29, 37, 35, 23, and 9).
The player tries to end the game so that only one piece—at the center of the board—remains.

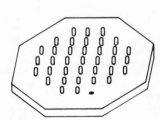

The corsair: start

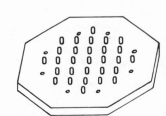

The octagon: start

Solutions

Standard solitaire (English)	The octagon
5—17	27—37
12—10	31—33
3—11	37—27
18—6	20—33
1—3	19—32
3—11	33—31
30—18	30—32
27—25	36—26
24—26	17—30
13—27	26—24
27—25	30—17
22—24	34—21
31—23	21—19
16—28	18—20
33—31	16—18
31—23	8—21
4—16	21—19
7—9	7—20
10—8	11—25
21—7	20—18
7—9	25—11
24—10	11—13
10—8	2—12
8—22	13—11
22—24	10—12
24—26	4—6
19—17	6—19
16—18	
11—25	**The world**
26—24	32—19
29—17	30—32
	17—30
	28—26
The cross (French)	25—27
12—2	14—28
26—12	34—21
17—19	32—34
19—6	4—17
21—19	6—4
2—12	18—5
12—26	13—11
32—19	5—18
(English)	27—13
10—2	7—20
24—10	
15—17	**The letter E**
17—5	32—19
19—17	34—32
2—10	20—33
10—24	29—27
29—17	33—20
	36—26
The corsair	30—32
35—37	26—36
26—36	18—31
25—35	20—18
23—25	7—20
34—32	15—13
20—33	20—7
37—27	22—20
7—20	6—19
20—33	4—6
18—31	18—5
35—25	23—25
5—18	16—17
18—31	9—11
29—27	2—12
22—20	8—6
15—13	12—2
16—18	
9—11	**The apostles**
20—7	32—19
7—5	28—26
4—6	37—27
18—5	35—37
1—11	25—35
33—20	27—25
20—18	24—26
18—5	11—25
5—7	25—27
36—26	16—18
30—32	19—17
32—19	6—19
19—6	4—6
2—12	17—4
8—6	2—12
12—2	8—6
3—1	2—7
	6—8
	22—20
	15—13
	12—14
	27—13
	13—15

© DIAGRAM

3 Tile games

Dominoes

Games with dominoes are played in many countries all over the world. They are now particularly popular in Latin America. It is thought that dominoes may have been brought from China to Europe in the fourteenth century. Certainly domino games were played in Italy in the eighteenth century. In most Western games players add matching dominoes to a pattern or "layout" formed in the center of the table.

Suits Dominoes belong to different suits according to the number of spots on each of their halves.
There is a suit for each number, a blank suit, and a doubles suit. "Mixed number" dominoes belong to two number suits or to a number suit and the blank suit.
Doubles belong to one number suit and to the doubles suit.

General features of play
Western domino games are characterized by the principle of matching and joining dominoes end to end.
In some games, players add dominoes to either end of a line of dominoes.
More common, are games in which players may build on four ends of a pattern or "layout." In one game, Sebastopol, the layout has up to eight ends.
Doubles in most games are placed across the line of dominoes, and in some rules (eg tiddle-a-wink) a player who, for example, plays a double 6 may immediately play another domino with a 6 at one end.
In some games, players use only the dominoes picked up at the start of play, and must miss a turn (called "renouncing," "passing," or "knocking") whenever they are unable to add a matching domino to the pattern.
In other games, players must draw a domino from the boneyard whenever they are unable to play a matching domino.

General rules
No domino may be withdrawn after it has been added to the layout.
If the wrong domino is accidentally placed face up by a player during his turn, it must be played if it matches an end of the layout.
A player is liable to lose the game if:
a) he fails to play within two minutes;
b) he renounces when he is able to play;
c) he plays a domino that does not match (except that the domino is accepted if the error is not noticed before the next domino is played);
d) he makes a false claim that he has played all his dominoes.

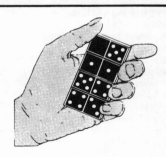

The dominoes are rectangular tiles made of wood, ivory, bone, stone, or plastic, They are sometimes called "bones," "stones," or "pieces." Typical dimensions are 1 in by 1 $\frac{7}{8}$ in by $\frac{3}{8}$ in.
Each domino's face is divided by a central line and each half is either blank or marked with indented spots (sometimes called "pips").
Dominoes with the same number of spots on either side of the central line are called "doubles" or "doublets."
A domino is said to be "heavier" than another if it has more spots, or "lighter" if it has less spots. So a double 6 is heavier than a 6:5.
The standard Western domino set has 28 tiles (with double 6 the heaviest domino). Larger sets have 55 dominoes (double 9 the heaviest) or 91 dominoes (double 12 the heaviest).
Players Some domino games are for two players only; others for two or more players playing singly or as partners. Partnerships may be decided:
a) by mutual agreement;
b) by draw—in which case each player draws one domino and the two players with the heaviest dominoes form one pair.
Partners sit opposite each other at the table.
Playing area Dominoes can be played on a table or any other flat surface.

Drawing a hand All the dominoes are placed face downward in the center of the table and are then moved around by all the players. (These dominoes in the center of the table are called the "boneyard.")
Each player then selects the number of dominoes required for the particular game to be played—usually seven or five. Except in the few games in which players do not look at their own dominoes—eg Blind Hughie—players keep their dominoes:
a) standing on edge on the table;
b) on a rack;
c) concealed in their hand.

Turns There are several ways of deciding which player is to have the first turn.
a) The player who draws the heaviest domino in a preliminary draw.
b) One player draws a domino and his opponent guesses whether its spots add up to an odd or an even number.
c) Each player draws his dominoes for the game and the first turn goes to the player with the heaviest double or, if there are no doubles, to the player with the heaviest domino.
In most countries, turns then pass clockwise around the table; in Latin America, the direction of play is counterclockwise.

End of play Games end:
a) when one player has played all his dominoes—after which he calls "domino!" or makes some other recognized signal;
b) when no player can add a matching domino in games with no drawing from the boneyard;
c) in drawing games when no player can add a matching domino and only two dominoes remain in the boneyard.

Result Most domino games are played to a set number of points.
In some games, the player who first plays all his dominoes claims one point for each spot on his opponents' unplayed dominoes.
If all play is blocked, the player with fewest spots on his unplayed dominoes claims the difference between the number of spots on his own and his opponents' unplayed dominoes. The hand is replayed if opponents' dominoes have an equal number of spots.
In other games—eg Bergen—players score points for adding a domino that makes the two ends of the layout match.

BLOCK DOMINOES

The basic block dominoes game is usually played by two, three, or four players using a standard set of 28 dominoes. (More players can play with larger sets.)

Two players usually play with seven dominoes each, and three or four players with five dominoes each.

The first player begins by laying any of his dominoes in the center of the table.

Turns then pass around the table—with players adding matching dominoes to either end of the line or missing a turn if none of their dominoes matches.

Spots are counted and points scored after one player has played all his dominoes or the game is blocked so that no one can play.

The winner of one hand plays first in the next hand.

A game is usually played to 100 or 200 points.

PARTNERSHIP BLOCK DOMINOES

The partnership form of block dominoes is played by four players with a standard set of 28 dominoes.

Play is the same as for basic block dominoes except that:
a) players sitting opposite each other form a pair;
b) each player draws seven dominoes at the start of the game;
c) the player with the double 6 starts the first hand by laying it on the table;
d) subsequent hands are started by the winner of the previous hand and this player may play any of his dominoes to start;
e) pairs score jointly—as soon as one player has played all his dominoes, he and his partner score the sum of the spots on each of their opponents' unplayed dominoes.
f) in blocked games, the pair with the lowest total of spots on their unplayed dominoes score the difference between their own and their opponents' total of spots on their unplayed dominoes.

LATIN AMERICAN MATCH DOMINOES

This Latin American form of dominoes is played in the same way as partnership block dominoes except that:
a) the player with the double 6 always starts;
b) each hand won counts as one game;
c) a match ends when one pair has won 10 hands;
d) a match win is scored only if the other pair failed to win five hands—otherwise the match is tied.

TIDDLE-A-WINK

This is a form of block dominoes particularly suited to larger groups of people. It is often played with sets of 55 or 91 dominoes.

At the start of each hand the dominoes are shared out equally between the players; any remaining dominoes are left face downward on the table.

Play proceeds as for the basic block game except that:
a) the player with the highest double always starts;
b) any player who plays a double may add another domino if he is able;
c) a player who has played all his dominoes calls "tiddle-a-wink."

(Another version of the game is played by six to nine players with three dominoes each from a set of 28 dominoes. In this version, dominoes are added to only one side of the starting double and bets are made as in domino pool.)

DOMINO POOL

The rules of standard block dominoes apply to domino pool except that, before each hand, players place equal bets in a pool or pot.

The winner of the hand takes all; or if players tie they share the pool between them.

BLIND HUGHIE

Blind Hughie is a block dominoes game of chance.

If four or five players are playing with 28 dominoes, each draws five dominoes without looking at them; two or three players each draw seven dominoes. Each player lays his dominoes in a line face downward in front of him.

The first player starts play by taking the domino at the left of his line and laying it face up in the center of the table.

Turns then pass around the table. At his turn each player takes the domino at the left of his line:
a) if it matches an end of the layout, he plays it;
b) if it doesn't match, he lays it face downward at the right of his line.

Play continues until one player finishes his dominoes or until the game is obviously blocked.

Doubles

DRAW DOMINOES

Draw dominoes is characterized by the drawing of dominoes from the boneyard after the start of play. Players usually start with seven or five dominoes each.

Play is as for basic block dominoes except that:

a) a player who is unable or unwilling to add a domino to the layout must draw dominoes from the boneyard until he draws one that he is able or willing to play, or until only two dominoes remain in the boneyard;
b) when only two dominoes remain in the boneyard, a player who cannot play a domino must end or miss a turn;
c) a player who draws or looks at an extra domino, or who turns a domino up so that other players see it, must keep that domino.

DOUBLES

This game, also called Maltese Cross, is played in the same way as basic draw dominoes except that:
a) the player with the heaviest double leads;
b) play is on four ends from the starting double;
c) a player may add a mixed number domino only if the double of the number he is matching has already been played (eg in the hand illustrated, a player could add 2:3 to the double 2 but could not play the same domino as 3:2 on the 5:3).

FORTRESS, SEBASTOPOL, CYPRUS

These are names for two closely related games.
a) The first game, usually called fortress but sometimes called Sebastopol, is a block dominoes game for four people with 28 dominoes. Each player draws seven dominoes and the player with the double 6 starts. Play is on four ends from the double 6, and a domino must be added to each of these ends before play proceeds as for standard block dominoes.
b) The second game, more usually called Sebastopol but sometimes called Cyprus, is a draw dominoes game played with a set of 55 dominoes. Four or five players start with nine dominoes each; more players start with seven or five. Double 9 always starts and if no player has this domino, players should draw one domino in turn until someone draws it. Play is on eight ends from the double 9, and all ends must be opened before a second domino may be added to any end. Players draw one domino from the boneyard whenever they are unable to add a domino to the layout.

Fortress

Sebastopol

ALL FIVES

This game, also called muggins and fives up, is a form of draw dominoes that is particularly popular in the United States. It is an interesting game characterized by its scoring system based on multiples of five.

Using a 28-domino set, two, three, or four players start with five dominoes each.

The first player may lead with any domino—and scores if its ends add up to five (a) or 10. The next player scores if the ends of the layout still add up to five or a multiple of five after he has played, (b). If he is unable to score, he may play another domino (eg the 1:3, which would make the ends of the layout add up to seven), or may draw one domino from the boneyard.

The first double of the game

(c) opens up a third end (in this case there would be no score since 6 + 6 + 4 = 16). The next domino (d) opens up the fourth and final end of the layout (and in this case it scores since 6 + 6 + 4 + 4 = 20). Play continues on four ends of the layout until one player finishes all his dominoes or until the game is blocked.

Scoring In one version of the game, a player scores one point for each spot whenever the layout's ends total five or a multiple of five. The winner of a hand also scores points for the spots on his opponents' remaining dominoes. Game is usually 150 or 200 points. More usual, however, is the scoring system in which players score one point when the ends total five, two points for 10, three for 15, and so on.

The winner of the hand scores a fifth of the face value of his opponents' remaining dominoes. In this version, the game is won by the first player to score exactly 61 points. If a player fails to claim his points after playing a domino, the first opponent to call "muggins" (or sometimes "fives") claims those points for himself.

The game is sometimes played by partners—in which case the dominoes left in the losing partner's hand are ignored for scoring purposes.

ALL THREES

All threes, or threes up, is played in the same way as all fives but scoring is based on multiples of three.

FIVES AND THREES

This is played in the same way as all fives, but scoring is based on multiples of both five and three.

A player scores one point for each spot whenever the ends of the layout total five or a multiple of five, or three or a multiple of three.

If a number is a multiple of both five and three, the player scores two points for each spot. The winner also scores for each spot on an opponent's remaining dominoes.

All fives

a   b   c   d

MATADOR

In this unusual draw game, dominoes are played when they make a specified total with a domino on an end of the layout. There are also wild dominoes called "matadors" that can be played at any turn. There are versions of the game for different sizes of domino sets.

When a 28-domino set is used, added dominoes must make a total of seven and the matadors are the 6:1, 5:2, 4:3 (ie those with ends totaling seven), and the 0:0.

For a 55 set the required total is 10 and the matadors are the 9:1, 8:2, 7:3, 6:4, 5:5, and 0:0. (In the game illustrated, play opened with the double 9. This was followed by the 7:3, a matador, and then by three dominoes making totals of 10.)

For a 92 set the total is 13 and the matadors are the 12:1, 11:2, 10:3, 9:4, 8:5, 7:6, and 0:0.

Players usually start with seven or five dominoes each, depending on the number of players and the size of set. The players with the heaviest double starts. In this game doubles are not placed crossways and the layout has

only two ends.

If a player is unable or unwilling to add a domino, he must draw one domino from the boneyard. When only two dominoes remain in the boneyard, he must play a domino if he is able.

A hand is won by the player who finishes his dominoes or who holds dominoes with the fewest spots if the game is blocked. Points are scored for the spots on an opponent's remaining dominoes, and game is an agreed number of points.

BERGEN

Bergen is a draw dominoes game in which players score points when there are matching dominoes at the ends of the layout.

Using a set of 28 dominoes, two or three players start with six dominoes each and four players with five dominoes each.

The player with the highest double starts. Subsequent play is on two ends only, and a player who is unable or unwilling to add a domino to the layout must draw one domino from the boneyard.

A player scores two points whenever two ends of the layout match (a "double

heading")—as, for example, the 6:2 and the 3:2 in the illustration (ie before the addition of the double 2).

A player scores three points for a "triple heading"—ie when there is a double at one end and a matching domino at the other, as after the addition of the double 2 in the example illustrated.

A player scores two points for winning a hand. If no player finishes his dominoes and the game is blocked, the hand is won by the player holding no doubles, the player with fewest doubles, or the player with fewest spots on his dominoes.

Game is usually 10 or 15 points.

Bergen

Matador

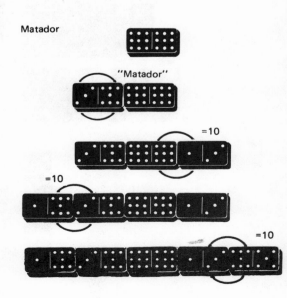

FORTY-TWO

Forty-two, or domino rounce, is an adaptation of a card game for play with dominoes. The object is to score points by winning tricks.

The game is usually played by four players with a set of 28 dominoes. Play is usually with partners. Each player draws seven dominoes at the start of a hand.

Bidding is the first stage of play, and tricks are valued as follows:
a) one point for each trick taken;
b) five additional points for a trick containing the 5:0, 4:1, or 3:2 (ie the dominoes with a total of five spots each);
c) 10 additional points for a trick containing the 5:5 or 6:4 (ie 10 spots each).
The total tricks value is 42 points (and hence the name of the game).

The player holding the 1:0 domino makes the first bid, and the other players bid in turn. Players may make only one bid and no bid may be for less than 30 points or be lower than a preceding bid. A player may pass if he does not wish to bid.

Taking tricks The player or pair with the highest bid then attempts to take tricks worth the value of their bid (or more).

There are eight suits—blanks, the numbers 1 through 6, and doubles. Except when a trump is led, the highest number on a domino determines the suit. The highest bidder plays the first domino and this establishes the trump suit for the hand. If he leads a "mixed number" domino he calls out which number is the trump suit. The other players then play one domino in turn. Except when a trump or a double is played, a trick goes to the player who played the heaviest domino of the correct suit. A double is the strongest domino of its suit, and can be taken only by a trump. As in

card games a higher number in the trump suit takes a lower one.

The player who takes a trick always leads for the next trick. (In the examples illustrated: a) double 3 takes the trick—and scores five extra points because the 3:2 is taken; b) if 2s are trumps, the 2:1 takes the trick—and scores 10 extra points because the 6:4 is taken.)

Scoring If the bidder and his partner take tricks worth as many or more points than the bid, they score the full value of their tricks plus the number of points bid.

If the bidder and his partner fail in their objective, their opponents score the number of points bid plus the value of the tricks that they have taken.

Value of tricks with 2s as trumps	
28 points a	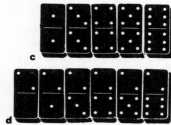
14 points b	

BINGO

This is another game in which dominoes are used like playing cards and players score points for taking tricks.

It is a game for two players with a set of 28 dominoes. Players make a preliminary draw to determine who will lead for the first trick.

At the start of play, each player draws seven dominoes from the boneyard. The leader then establishes trumps for the hand by turning over a domino in the boneyard. This domino is left exposed and its highest number becomes the trump suit for the hand.

The leader for the first trick then plays one domino and his opponent follows him. There is no need for a player to follow suit, except when the game is "closed" or the boneyard is empty.

Taking a trick The double blank, called "bingo," takes any other domino;
If two trumps are played, the higher trump takes the trick;
If one trump is played, the trump takes the trick;
If no trumps are played, the heaviest domino wins the trick;
If no trumps are played and both dominoes have the same total of spots, the leader's domino takes the trick.

As long as any dominoes remain in the boneyard, each player draws a domino after each trick. The winner of a trick always draws first and then leads for the next trick. When only two dominoes remain in the boneyard, the winner of the preceding trick may take the trump domino or the domino that is face down, and the losing player takes the remaining domino.

Value of tricks There is no score just for taking a trick. The value of a trick depends on the dominoes it contains. Only the following dominoes have any points value (with 2s as trumps in the examples illustrated):
a) the double of trumps is worth 28 points;
b) except when blanks are trumps, "bingo" is worth 14 points;
c) other doubles are worth their total number of spots;
d) trumps other than the double are worth their total number of spots;
e) the 6:4 is worth 10 points;
f) the 3:0 is worth 10 points.

10 points e

10 points f

Value of doubles A player can also claim points for having more than one double in his hand at any time when it is his turn to lead.

To claim these points he should play one double and expose the others.
For two doubles in his hand he calls "double" and claims 20 points;
for three doubles he calls "triples" and claims 40 points;
for four doubles he calls "double doublet" and claims 50 points;
for five doubles he calls "king" and claims 60 points;
for six doubles he calls "emperor" and claims 70 points;
for all seven doubles he calls "invincible" and claims 210 points;
if "bingo" is among his doubles he claims an extra 10 points.

A player is not entitled to these points if he fails to claim them when laying down a double; nor do they count if he fails to take the trick.

Closing If a player with the lead believes that he can bring his score from tricks and doubles to at least 70 points without drawing any further dominoes, he can "close" the game by turning over the trump domino.

After the game is closed neither player may draw any further dominoes and rules for following suit come into force.

Following suit After the game is closed or the boneyard is empty, a player is obliged when possible to follow suit. If a trump is led, he must play another trump.

If a domino that is not a trump is led, he must try and follow its higher number or, failing that, its lowest number. If he can follow neither of these, he may play a trump. Only if he has none of these is he permitted to discard.

Scoring A game is won by the first player to score seven sets or game points.

Sets are scored as follows:
a) one set for every 70 points from tricks or doubles;
b) one set for being the first player to reach 70 points if the other player has at least 30 points;
c) two sets for reaching 70 points after the other player has won a trick but has not scored 30 points;
d) three sets for reaching 70 points before the other player wins a trick;
e) one set for taking the double of trumps with "bingo."

DOMINO CRIBBAGE

This game is an adaptation of playing card cribbage.

The basic domino game is for two players, using a standard set of 28 dominoes.

As in the card game, the score is usually kept on a cribbage board.

Objective The game is won by the first player to score 61 points. Scoring takes place during play and also at the end of a hand.

Play Each player draws six dominoes at the start of play. He then discards two of them, face downward, to form the crib (an extra hand scored by the dealer after the other hands have been scored).

The leader then turns over a domino in the boneyard. This domino is the "starter." It is not used during play but is scored with all hands after play.

Turns alternate. The leader's opponent begins by placing any domino from his hand face upward on the table in front of himself and calling out its total number of spots.

The leader then turns over one of his dominoes and calls out the sum total of spots on both dominoes played so far.

Play proceeds in this way, with each player calling the sum total of spots played, until the "go" rule comes into play.

If, at his turn, a player is unable to play a domino that will bring the count to 31 or below, he must call "go."

The other player must then play as many tiles as he can until he reaches 31 or is unable to play.

Once a count of 31 has been reached, or if no one can play, a new count from 0 is begun. (Pairs etc cannot be carried over into the next count.)

After both players have played all their dominoes, the leader's opponent scores the points in his hand.

The leader then scores the points in his hand and then the points in the crib.

The lead then passes to the other player and another hand is started.

Scoring during play

For turning up a double for starter, one point.

For reaching a count of exactly 15, two points.

For a "pair" (playing a domino with the same total spot count as the last played domino), two points.

For a "triplet" (a third domino with the same total spot count), six points.

For a fourth domino with the same spot count, 12 points.

For a run of three or more dominoes, not necessarily in order (eg dominoes totaling 6,4,5,3), one point for each tile of the run.

For reaching exactly 31, two points.

For being nearest to 31, one point.

For the last tile of the hand, one point.

For reaching 15 with the last tile, three points.

Scoring after play

For a combination totaling 15, two points.

For a double run of three (a three-tile run with a pair to one of them), eight points.

For a double run of four (a run of four with one pair), 10 points.

For a triple run (a triplet with two other dominoes in sequence), 15 points.

For a quadruple run (two pairs and a domino in sequence with both), 16 points.

Scoring during play

Pair, 2 points

15, 2 points

Run, 3 points

31, 2 points

Scoring after play (the "show")

Runs, 6 points

Pair, 2 points

15, 2 points

"Starter"
Total, 10 points

PICTURE DOMINOES

Dominoes with pictures are very popular with young children and can be easily bought or made.

A typical set contains 28 brightly colored dominoes with combinations of seven different pictures. They are usually made of wood or heavy card.

All the dominoes are shared out among the players, who should keep the pictures hidden from the other players. One player starts by placing one domino face upward on the table. Players then take turns at adding a matching domino. If a player doesn't have a matching domino he misses his turn.

The winner is the first player to add all his dominoes to the row on the table.

Mah jongg

Mah jongg is a tile game of Chinese origin that reached the West in the 1920s. Its name means "the sparrows." Each of four (or three) players plays for himself. Players collect sets of tiles with the object of completing their hands in a prescribed manner. Scores are settled after each hand, and the winner is the player with the most points when play ends.

Players Mah jongg is best played by four players, but can be played by three. Each player plays for himself.
Deciding the winds Each player is designated the name of a wind—east, south, west, and north.
Winds for the first hand are decided after the players are seated, when each player takes a turn to throw two dice. The player with the highest total throw becomes east. The other players' winds are determined by their position at the table relative to east: west sits opposite east, south sits to east's right and north to east's left (not like a compass). If the player who is east wind does not win the first hand, the winds pass counterclockwise around the table. Thus east becomes north, south becomes east, west becomes south, and north becomes west.
If the player who is east wind wins a hand, the players retain the same winds for the next hand.

The tiles Mah jongg tiles are made of bone, ivory, bamboo, wood, or plastic.
Tile designs vary. Sets sold in the West usually have Arabic numerals in one corner of the suit tiles, and letters denoting the four winds.
A standard set has 144 tiles—136 playing tiles and eight flower or season tiles.
Suit tiles There are three different suits: circles (or dots), bamboos (or bams), and characters (or craks). Each suit comprises tiles numbered 1 through 9, and there are four of each type of tile.
The 1 bamboo usually shows a symbolic bird. All other tiles have symbols for the suits.

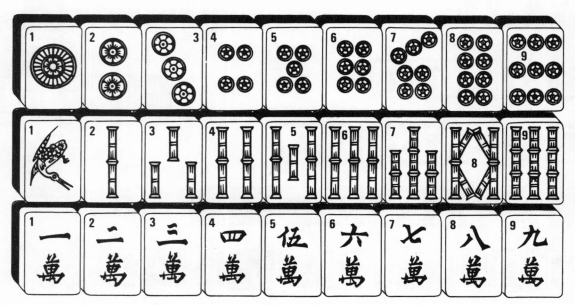

Duration A complete game consists of four rounds, but the game is in no way spoiled if players choose to stop at the end of any hand.
Each round bears the name of a wind: the first is east, the second south, the third west, and the fourth north.
As well as indicating the stage of the game, the "wind of the round" has an effect on scoring.
A round consists of however many hands are taken before the fourth player has lost a hand as east wind.

Building the wall All the tiles are placed face down on the table, and are thoroughly shuffled by the players.
Then, without looking at the tiles' faces, each player builds a wall that is 18 tiles long and two tiles high (with the long sides of the tiles touching and the faces down).
Each player then pushes his wall toward the center of the table until the four walls meet to form a hollow square representing a city wall.

Breaching the wall takes place once the wall is built. There are two stages.

a) East throws two dice to determine which side of the wall is to be breached. If he throws two 1s, he must throw again. Otherwise, he takes the total thrown and, starting with the length of his own wall as one, counts out the total counterclockwise around the table. The breach is to be made in the side of the wall where his count ends.

b) The player whose wall is to be breached now throws the two dice and adds his total to the total previously thrown by east. The new total is used to determine exactly where the breach will be made.
The player counts clockwise along the top of his tiles, beginning at the right-hand corner. If the total is more than 18 he continues along the next wall.
When the count ends, the player takes the two tiles from that stack and places them as shown. These moved tiles are called "loose tiles."

Drawing the hands After the wall is breached east takes the two stacks (four tiles) from the opposite side of the breach to the loose tiles.
South then takes the next two stacks, west the next two, and north the next two. The draw continues in this way until each player has 12 tiles.
East, south, west, and north then take one more tile in turn, and finally east takes one extra tile from the top of the next stack.
At the end of the initial draw east has 14 tiles and the other players have 13 tiles each.

Flower and season tiles drawn in the initial hand or later in the game must be placed face up in front of the player and replaced by a loose tile. Replacement at the start of the game must be in rotation, with east playing first.
For scoring purposes, each wind has its own season and flower. This is usually shown by numbers on Western mah jongg sets—with east 1, south 2, west 3, and north 4.

Breaching

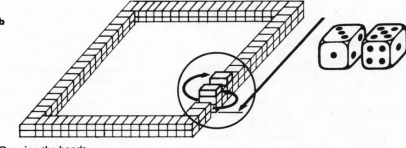

a

b

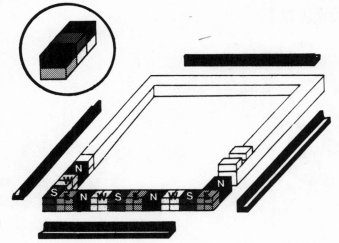

Drawing the hands

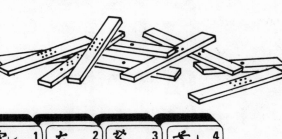

Dragon tiles There are three different dragons: white, red, and green (left to right in the illustration). As with the suit tiles, there are four of each type of tile.
Wind tiles East, south, west, and north winds are represented. Again there are four of each type of tile.
Flower and season tiles These are eight individually marked tiles.
Racks Each player is provided with a rack to hold his tiles. The player who is east wind takes the different colored rack.

Other equipment includes:
a) two dice;
b) scoring counters (small sticks) or a scoring pad;
c) optional wind indicators—either rotating indicators or separate disks.

© DIAGRAM

Objective Each player aims to complete his hand and go "mah jongg" (sometimes called going "woo").

Starting play East starts play by discarding any one of his 14 tiles.

Discarding tiles When a player discards a tile he must always call out its name, eg red dragon, east wind, 6 bams. Discarded tiles are placed in the center of the table—usually face up in Western countries but face down in China and elsewhere in the East.

Playing order Play passes counterclockwise around the table except when a player interrupts the order to claim a discarded tile.
If more than one player claims a discarded tile, the order of precedence is:
1) a player claiming the tile to go mah jongg;
2) a player claiming the tile to make a *pung* or *kong*;
3) a player claiming the tile to make a *chow*.
If the playing order is interrupted for a claim, intervening players lose their right to any turn they may have missed. Thus if player 1 discards a tile and player 4 claims it, players 2 and 3 lose their turns and player 1 has the next turn unless player 4's discard is claimed by another player.

Playing a turn If no player claims the tile that was last discarded, the player to the right of the last player to discard now takes a tile from the wall.
The new tile is taken from the end of the wall without the loose tiles. The player may conceal the tile's face from his opponents.
If he wishes to keep the new tile, he does so and discards another tile from his rack. Otherwise he discards the new tile.

Claiming tiles Only the tile that was last discarded may be claimed. It may be claimed to complete a *chow*, *pung*, or *kong*, or to go mah jongg. Claims may be made even after the next player has taken a new tile from the wall—in which case the tile drawn from the wall must be replaced. Claims are not permitted if the next player has already made his discard.

Claiming a chow Only the player sitting to the right of the player who discarded is permitted to claim for a *chow*. The claiming player must already hold in his rack the other two tiles needed for the *chow*.
To claim the discard the player must call "chow," pick up the tile, and then "expose" the complete *chow* by laying it face up in front of him.
The player then ends his turn by discarding a tile from his rack.

Claiming a pung Any player may claim the last discarded tile for a *pung* provided that:
a) he holds in his rack two tiles identical with the tile he is claiming;
b) he has played an intervening turn if he failed to *pung* that same tile on an earlier discard.
To claim the discard he must call "pung," pick up the tile, and "expose" the *pung*.
He then ends his turn by discarding a tile from his rack.

Concealed chows or pungs A player who has a *chow* or *pung* in his original hand, or who completes a *chow* or *pung* with a tile drawn from the wall, may keep these tiles "concealed" on his rack.
This gives him greater maneuverability, conceals the state of his hand from his opponents, and doubles the value of a *pung*.

Claiming a kong Any player may claim the last discarded tile for a *kong* if he holds in his rack three tiles identical with the tile he is claiming.
To claim the discard he must call "kong," pick up the tile, and "expose" the complete *kong*.
The player then draws a loose tile before discarding in the usual way.
(A loose tile is always drawn after a *kong* because a complete hand has one extra tile for each *kong* it contains.)

Concealed kong

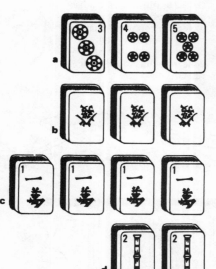

Mah jongg A complete hand usually consists of four *chows*, *pungs*, or *kongs*, plus an identical pair.
A chow is a run of three tiles of the same suit, eg 3,4,5 dots (**a**), or 7,8,9 craks. Mixed winds or mixed dragons do not count as *chows*.
A pung is a set of three identical tiles, eg three green dragons (**b**), three 8 bams, or three south winds.

A kong is a set of four identical tiles (**c**).
A pair may be any two identical tiles (**d**).

Special mah jongg hands that do not follow the conventional pattern are accepted by some players as alternative ways of going mah jongg.
These special hands normally score the maximum permitted for any one hand.
Most commonly accepted of these special hands are:
a) "hand of the thirteen odd majors" and
b) "calling nine tiles hand."

Converting an exposed pung into a kong A player may convert an exposed *pung* into a *kong* if he draws the fourth similar piece from the wall. (This is the only time that an exposed set of tiles may be interfered with.)
Players are not permitted to claim discards to convert exposed *pungs* into *kongs*.
After a player has converted an exposed *pung* into a *kong*, he ends his turn by drawing a loose tile and then discarding in the usual way.

A concealed kong A kong is "concealed" if:
a) all four tiles are in a player's original hand; or
b) a player with a "concealed" *pung* in his hand draws the fourth similar tile from the wall.
A player with a concealed *kong* may lay it on the table at any time when it is his turn to play.
A concealed *kong* laid on the table is worth double points and is distinguished from an exposed *kong* by turning over the end two tiles.
If another player goes mah jongg while a player has a concealed *kong* on his rack, he scores only for a concealed *pung*.
Only after a player has laid a concealed *kong* on the table may he draw the loose tile needed to bring his hand up to the number of tiles required to go mah jongg.

Drawing loose tiles Loose tiles are used to make a player's hand up to the correct number of tiles—after a flower or season tile has been drawn or after a *kong*.
The tile farthest from the breach is used first and then the other loose tile. After both loose tiles have been used they are replaced by the two tiles at that end of the wall—the top tile going farthest from the breach.

Wrong number of tiles A player with the wrong number of tiles in his hand (on his rack and laid out on the table) cannot go mah jongg.
Excluding extra tiles in *kongs*, each player should always have 14 tiles after drawing or 13 tiles after discarding.
A player with the wrong number of tiles must draw and discard tiles normally until another player goes mah jongg.
If the player in error had too many tiles, he pays the other players their scores without deducting any score for his own hand.
If he had too few tiles, he deducts the score for his own hand before making payment.

Wrong tile drawn If the wall is breached in the wrong place or if tiles are drawn in the wrong order, the tiles should be reshuffled and the wall rebuilt.

Incorrect combinations If a player exposes an incorrect combination of tiles as a *chow*, *pung*, or *kong*, he must rectify the error before the next player discards or his hand is declared "dead."
A player with a dead hand must pay the other players their scores with no allowance for his own hand.

Last 14 tiles A hand is declared "dead" if no player goes mah jongg before play reaches the last 14 tiles in the wall (including the loose tiles).
There is no scoring and a new hand is played with the same player as east wind.

Calling A player is "calling" (or "fishing") when he requires only one tile to complete his hand.
If two players are calling and both claim the same tile, precedence goes to the player whose turn would have come first.

A standing hand East wind may declare a "standing hand" if he is calling after making his first discard.
Any player may declare a standing hand if he is calling after drawing and discarding for the first time in a hand.
A player who has declared a standing hand must not change any of the 13 tiles then in his hand. At each turn, he draws a tile from the wall in the usual way and then discards it if it is not the tile required to go mah jongg.
A player who completes a standing hand receives a bonus of 100 points.

Snatching a kong A player who is calling may complete his hand by "snatching a *kong*"—ie claiming a tile drawn from the wall by another player who uses it to convert an exposed *pung* into a *kong*.

Going mah jongg As soon as a player completes his hand, he stops play by calling "mah jongg."
All players then expose their hands for scoring, turning over the middle tile of any *pungs* that were concealed in their hands.

Incorrect mah jongg If a player who has called "mah jongg" completely exposes his hand and then finds he has made an error, he must pay double the points limit to each of the other players.
If his hand is only partially exposed when the error is discovered, he may cancel his call and put the tiles back on his rack.

Hand of the thirteen odd majors comprises a 1 and a 9 of each suit, one of each dragon, one of each wind, and a pair to any of these tiles.

Calling nine tiles hand is made up of tiles from the same suit—three 1s, three 9s, one each of tiles 2 through 8, and any one other tile of the same suit.

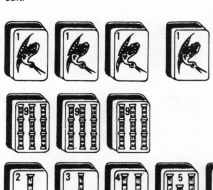

Settling the scores After calculating the value of their individual hands, the players settle with each other in the following way.

If east wind goes mah jongg, he receives double the total value of his score from each of the other players.

If another player goes mah jongg, he receives double the value of his score from east wind, and the value of his score from each of the other players.

Each loser also settles with each of the other losers.

When two losers settle (except when one of them is east wind), the player with the lower score pays the difference between his score and the other player's score.

When east wind is a loser, he pays or receives double the difference when settling with another loser.

Scoring Point values vary in different scoring systems, but the system given here shows the typical characteristics. With the exception of certain limit hands (described separately), the points value of each player's hand is calculated from the tables.

Using table A:
points are scored by all players for *pungs* and *kongs* and for each flower and season tile (no points are scored for *chows*);
the player going mah jongg also scores for some pairs.

Scoring a sample hand

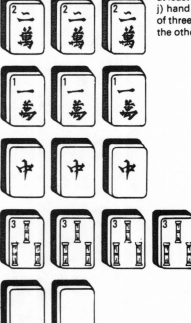

Using table B:
the player going mah jongg adds any bonus points.
Using table C:
players double their points as indicated, and again there are additional doubles for the player going mah jongg.
Limit hands Most scoring systems have specified "limit hands," designed to prevent the scoring of an excessive number of points with a single hand.

Limit hands score a fixed number of points—usually 500—regardless of their actual face value. East wind pays or receives double the limit.

Most limit hands may be obtained only by the player going mah jongg. Typical examples are:
a) hand of all winds and dragons;
b) hand of all 1s and 9s;
c) hand of concealed *pungs* and *kongs*;
d) hand of the thirteen odd majors;
e) calling nine tiles hand;
f) an original hand (east wind's hand when play begins);
g) hand completed with east's first discard;
h) east wind's thirteenth consecutive mah jongg.
Other hands score the limit whether or not completed. If the player with these hands fails to go mah jongg, he scores the limit from the other losers.
Examples are:
i) hand with *pungs* or *kongs* of at least three dragons;
j) hand with *pungs* or *kongs* of three winds and a pair of the other wind.

Table A — Tile values

All players	Exposed	Concealed
Any *chow*	0	0
Pung of tiles 2 through 8 of any suit	2	4
Pung of 1 or 9 of any suit	4	8
Pung of winds or dragons	4	8
Kong of tiles 2 through 8 of any suit	8	16
Kong of 1 or 9 of any suit	16	32
Kong of winds or dragons	16	32
Any season or flower	4	
Player going mah jongg		
Pair of any dragon	2	
Pair of player's own wind	2	
Pair of wind of the round	2	

Table B — Bonus scores

Player going mah jongg	
For going mah jongg	20
Winning tile drawn from the wall	2
Winning with only possible tile (ie with all other similar tiles exposed)	2
Winning with the last piece from the wall	10
Winning with a loose tile	10
For having no *chows*	10
For having no scoring value (except flowers or seasons)	10
Completing a standing hand	100

Table C — Doubling

All players	Number of times doubled
Pung or *kong* of any dragon	1
Pung or *kong* of player's own wind	1
Pung or *kong* of the wind of the round	1
Player's own season or flower	1
Four seasons or four flowers	3
Player going mah jongg	
Hand with no *chows*	1
Hand with no scoring tiles except flowers and seasons	1
Hand all one suit except for winds and/or dragons	1
Hand all 1s and 9s except for winds and/or dragons	1
Snatching a *kong* to go mah jongg	1
Hand all one suit	3
Hand all winds and dragons	3
Original hand (east wind's 14 tiles when play begins)	3

Scoring a sample hand

Tile values (see table A and diagram)	*Running total*
Total value of tiles in hand 20 points	20
Bonus scores (see table B)	
For going mahjongg 20 points	40
For having no *chows* 10 points	50
Doubling (see table C)	
Pung of dragons (double once)	100
Hand with no *chows* (double once)	200

Sap tim pun (Ten and a half)

Sap tim pun, or ten and a half, is a gambling game popular among the Chinese in Malaysia. This version is played with mah jongg tiles, but there are obvious similarities to the ten and a half card game known in the Netherlands as "saton pong" (page 172).

Tiles The game is played with one standard set of 144 mah jongg tiles.
The tiles have the following point values:
a) suit tiles count their numerical face value;
b) dragons, flowers, seasons, and winds are each worth $\frac{1}{2}$ point (except that special rules apply if an east wind tile is picked up in the first draw).

Objective Each player tries to get a hand with a point count that is higher than that of the banker—though not in excess of $10\frac{1}{2}$.

Building the walls The tiles are turned face down on the table, shuffled, and then built into four walls. Each wall is 18 tiles long and two tiles high, with the long sides of the tiles touching.

Turns pass clockwise around the players, as in standard mah jongg and Chinese domino games.

First draw and betting
1) the banker for the round declares the maximum stake.
2) Each player in turn draws one tile from the wall, with the player to the banker's right drawing first and the banker drawing last. Each player looks at his tile and then lays it face down in front of him.
3) Players other than the banker place a stake beside their tile and then turn the tile face up.
4) If the banker has drawn an east wind tile, he now turns it over and takes all the stakes on the table. He then discards the east wind tile and replaces it with another tile from the wall.
5) If any other player has drawn an east wind tile, and provided that the banker has not also drawn an east wind, the player receives his stake from the banker, replaces the east wind tile with another tile from the wall, and places a new stake beside it.

Drawing additional tiles
Each player in turn has the opportunity of drawing an additional one or two tiles (to make a maximum of three tiles in his hand).
A player must draw a further tile if his hand with one or two tiles is worth less than 6 points; he has the choice of drawing or standing if his hand is worth 6 points or more. The drawn tiles are kept concealed unless the player's hand totals more than $10\frac{1}{2}$ points—in which case he throws in his tiles and passes his stake to the banker.

Banker's hand When all the other players have drawn or stood, the banker turns over his first tile and then draws or stands according to the same rules as other players.

Settlement
a) If the banker's hand exceeds $10\frac{1}{2}$ points, he pays the stake of all players still in the game.
b) If his hand totals exactly $10\frac{1}{2}$, he receives all stakes laid.
c) If his hand is less than $10\frac{1}{2}$, he receives the stakes of all players with fewer points and pays all players with more points.

Rotating bank After each round the bank passes one player to the right.

Mah jongg (American)

This modern form of mah jongg, developed and organized by the US National Mah Jongg League, enjoys considerable popularity in North America. It is challenging and rewarding, while also easier to learn and score.

Tiles The modern American game is played with 152 tiles: the 144 tiles of the standard set (but with eight flower and no season tiles), plus eight big jokers (wild tiles with special rules governing their use).

Cards are sometimes used in place of tiles.

Players The basic game is for four players, but is easily adapted for two or three players.

Deciding the winds For the first hand, winds are decided as in the standard game. Thereafter, winds pass counterclockwise around the table after each hand—regardless of whether east wins or loses the hand.

Building the wall is as for the standard game except that each side of the wall has an extra two tiles.

Breaching the wall is as for the standard game, except that there are no loose tiles.

Picking the hands is as for the standard game.

Passing tiles At the start of the American game, players exchange tiles in a series of passes. Tiles are always passed face down. (Big jokers may not be passed.)

The first Charleston is compulsory and comprises three passes:
1) at the first pass each player gives three tiles to the player to his right;
2) at the second pass he gives three tiles to the player opposite;
3) at the third pass he gives three tiles to the player to his left.
(If a player does not have three unwanted tiles for his third pass, he may make a "blind pass" ie take one, two, or three tiles from the pass he is given and, without looking at them, use them in his own pass.)

The second Charleston takes place only if all four players agree. It comprises the following passes:
1) three tiles to the player to the left;
2) three to the player opposite;
3) three to the player to his right.
(A blind pass is permitted at the third pass.)

An optional pass is permitted, if all players agree, after the second Charleston (or after the first if there is no second Charleston).
At an optional pass, one, two, or three tiles are exchanged with the player sitting opposite.

Objective As in the standard game, the players aim to collect a complete mah jongg hand of 14 tiles.

Start of play East starts play by discarding any one of his 14 tiles (except when he has a complete mah jongg hand after the passes).

Discarding tiles When a player discards a tile he must call out its name and place it face up in the center of the table.
A player is not permitted to exchange a discard once he has laid it on the table and named it.

Claiming a discard Any player may claim another player's discard:
a) to complete an "exposure" (a group of like tiles making part of an exposed mah jongg);
b) to go mah jongg (to complete a hand that is either exposed or concealed).

A player claims a discard by calling "take." He may not claim until the discard has been named. Nor may he claim after the player to the discarder's right has drawn a tile from the wall and made his discard.
If several players claim a discard, the tile goes to the player nearest in turn to the discarder (except that a player who wants a tile to go mah jongg has precedence).
A successful claimant picks up the claimed tile and lays his complete exposure (or mah jongg) face up in front of him. After completing an exposure, the claimant discards any one tile from his hand.
The player to the discarder's right has the next turn (unless the new discard is claimed by another player).

Playing a turn Except when a discard is claimed, turns pass counterclockwise around the table.

At his turn a player:

1) picks the end tile from the wall (tiles being picked in a clockwise direction);

2) looks at the picked tile and either immediately discards it or keeps the picked tile and discards any other tile concealed in his hand.

A player is not permitted to "look ahead," ie to pick a tile from the wall before the player to his left has discarded.

Flower tiles In the American game, flower tiles are used in exactly the same way as suit tiles (whereas in the standard game, special rules apply).

Big Jokers Special rules apply to big jokers.

One or more big jokers may be used in place of any tile or tiles in any exposure or when going mah jongg.

If a player holds or picks a tile for which a big joker has been substituted in an exposure, he may, at his turn, exchange this tile for the big joker.

Big jokers may be discarded at any time during play and called the name of the previous discard.

If a big joker has once been exposed in a hand, this hand cannot be counted as a jokerless hand even if the big jokers are later replaced.

Miscalled tiles If a tile is miscalled, a claimant who wants the discard for an exposure must wait until the discarder calls the tile correctly. (In this case there is no penalty for the player who miscalled.)

However, if a player needs only one tile to complete his hand and another player discards a tile and mistakenly gives his discard the name of the tile for which the other player is waiting, the waiting player may claim this tile for mah jongg and the player who made the error must pay four times the value of the claimant's hand.

Wrong number of tiles If players have the wrong number of tiles before the Charleston, the wall must be rebuilt and a new start made. At any other stage in the game, a player's hand is declared "dead" if he has the wrong number of tiles in his hand or in an exposure. A player with a dead hand may not discard or pick, cannot go mah jongg, and pays the winner the same as the other losing players. If two players have dead hands, the other two players may continue playing. If three players' hands are declared dead, the game should be replayed.

Going mah jongg As soon as a player completes his hand, he stops all play by calling "mah jongg" and exposing all his tiles.

Mah jongg in error A player should never throw in or expose his hand before the "winner's" hand is verified. If a player calls mah jongg in error but realizes his mistake before his hand is exposed, or before any other player disturbs his hand, the game continues without penalty. If a player calls mah jongg in error and exposes his hand, provided that no other player also exposes his hand, the caller's hand is dead and the other players continue. If a player calls mah jongg in error and one other player throws in his hand, both these players' hands are dead and, when the hand ends, each pays the winner the same as the other loser. If a player calls mah jongg in error and two other players throw in their hands, whether or not the caller exposes his hand the hand ends, and the caller pays double the value of his miscalled hand to the player whose hand is intact.

Redeeming big jokers If a player who calls mah jongg in error has been playing an exposed hand, any other player may exchange a like tile in his hand for a big joker correctly exposed by the miscaller before his error. Players may not redeem big jokers when a concealed hand is incorrectly exposed for mah jongg.

Scoring The method of scoring used for the modern American game is extremely straightforward.

Every hand has a set scoring value (called its "limit"), which is listed with the requirements for the hand. According to difficulty, a hand is worth 20, 25, 30, or 35 points.

When a player goes mah jongg after picking his fourteenth tile from the wall, all other players pay him twice the points value of his hand. When a player goes mah jongg after claiming a discarded tile, the player who made the discard pays him twice his hand's value and the other players pay him the value of the hand.

© DIAGRAM

Typical mah jongg hands

National Mah Jongg League Each year the League sends its members a card showing approximately 50 mah jongg hands for the year's play.

Hands are made up of the following groups of tiles:

a) quints (five flowers or four like tiles and a big joker);

b) *kongs* (four like tiles);

c) *pungs* (three like tiles);

d) pairs (two like tiles).

In every case, all 14 tiles needed for a mah jongg are specified.

Some hands are valid only if they are "concealed." A concealed hand must be built up on the rack from picked tiles, except that the fourteenth tile may be a claimed discard. Other hands, classified as "exposed," may be built up

from picked tiles or from claimed discards.

Specified hands are valid only when jokerless.

The illustrations and table show typical hands from the League's 1974 card.

Further details available from: National Mah Jongg League, Inc, 250 West 57th St, New York, NY 10019, USA

x Exposed
c Concealed

x 20	1	1	9	9	7	7	7	4	4	4
c 25	1	1	2	2	3	3	4	4	5	5	5
c 20	F	F	F	F	1	3	3	1	1	3	3
x 25	9	9	9	9	9	9	9	9	9	2	7

4 Children's target games

Marbles

Games with marbles have been popular for thousands of years and are played in countries all over the world. The names and rules of marbles games vary tremendously from place to place, but the basic objective of any marbles game is to test how accurately a player can aim his marbles.

Marbles are small, hard balls made from stone, wood, baked clay, plastic, glass, or steel. They are usually about ½in in diameter.
A marble actually being used by a player is sometimes called a "taw."

Shooting In some games players throw or drop their marbles. Usually, however, marbles must be rolled along the ground.
Maximum accuracy and distance can be obtained by shooting the marble as illustrated—a method sometimes called "knuckling down."
The knuckle of the forefinger is placed on the ground, the marble is balanced on the forefinger, the thumb is put behind the forefinger—and then released to shoot the marble.

Shooting

Claiming marbles is a feature of many marbles games.
In some games a player may keep an opponent's marble if his own marble hits it.
Other games are played for points—with the difference in players' scores at the end of the game being settled by the payment of an agreed number of marbles for an agreed number of points.

CAPTURE
This is a simple marbles game for two players.
Player A shoots his marble and then player B attempts to hit it with his marble.
If player B hits A's marble, he may keep it.
If player B's marble misses A's marble, B's marble stays where it is and A attempts to hit it with a shot from where his marble lay after his first shot. If A hits B's marble he keeps it, otherwise turns alternate until one player takes the other's marble.

Spanning

SPANNERS
Spanners, or hit and span, is a variation of capture.
As in capture, a player who hits his opponent's marble may keep it. But in this game, a player may choose to

attempt a "span" if his marble is near enough to his opponent's. He does so by placing his thumb on his own marble and a finger on his opponent's marble, and then flicking them together.
In one version of the game a successful span entitles him to take his opponent's marble as if he had hit it with his shot, but an unsuccessful span means that he loses his own marble.
In another version a player gains one point for a successful span—after which both players pick up their marbles and the player who did not win the point shoots first in the next play. (An unsuccessful span is ignored in this version.)

SPANGY
Spangy is a game for five players.
A square is marked on the floor, and each player places one marble in the square to make the pattern illustrated.
Each player then plays in turn, always shooting his taw from the same point about 10yd from the square.
A player may claim any marble that he knocks out of the square, and if his taw stops within a "span" of any other marble he may also claim that marble if he makes a successful span (see spanners).
Each player picks up his taw at the end of his turn.

Spangy

RING TAW

Ring taw is a game for any small number of players. Two circles are drawn on the ground—an inner circle about 1ft in diameter and an outer circle about 7ft in diameter.

At the start of the game each player puts one or two marbles in the inner circle.

Each player then shoots in turn from any point outside the outer circle.

If a player knocks one or more marbles from the inner circle, he wins them and is entitled to another shot. This shot is taken from where his "taw" (the marble he last shot with) came to rest.

If a player fails to knock any marble from the inner circle, his turn ends and he must leave his taw where it stopped. Succeeding players may shoot at any marble within either of the circles—taws as well as the marbles originally placed in the inner circle.

Whenever a taw is hit its owner must pay one marble to the player who hit it.

After his first turn, each player shoots his taw from where it came to rest at the end of his previous turn.

The game ends when all marbles have been cleared from the inner circle.

INCREASE POUND

In this variation of ring taw the inner circle is known as the "pound" and the outer ring as the "bar."

Play is exactly the same as for ring taw except that: there is no extra shot for hitting a marble out of the pound;

a player whose taw stops in the pound must lift his taw and pay a marble into the pound;

a player whose taw is struck by the taw of another player must pay that player one marble plus all the marbles that he has won up to this stage of the game.

FORTIFICATIONS

This is another variation of ring taw, for which players draw four circles one inside the other.

At the start of the game each player places three marbles in the innermost circle or "fort" (**a**); two marbles in the next ring out (**b**); and one in the next (**c**). The outermost ring is left empty.

Each player plays in turn. With his first shot, made from any point outside the outer circle, each player attempts to knock a target marble from

ring (**c**). If he succeeds, he keeps the target marble and leaves his taw in the target marble's place. If he fails, he pays one marble into ring (**c**) and drops out of the game.

If a player's taw hits an opponent's taw at any stage of the game, the opponent's taw remains in its new position until its owner uses it for his next turn. When requested, a taw may be temporarily lifted to allow a player a clear shot at a target marble.

For all turns after the first, each player still in the game plays his taw from where it lies or from any point on the outside circle. As in his first turn, he claims any target marble that he hits and, unless he is entitled to an extra shot, leaves his taw in the target marble's place.

As long as any target marbles remain in ring (**c**), players must attack that ring and are allowed only one shot in a turn. A miss at this stage of the game, however, does not compel players to drop out. Once ring (**c**) is cleared of target marbles, players must attack ring (**b**). Play then proceeds exactly as for ring (**c**), except that a player who hits one target marble in ring

(**b**) is allowed a second shot. Once ring (**b**) is cleared of target marbles, players may attack ring (**a**). This time the only difference in procedure is that a player is entitled to a third shot if his first two shots both claim a target marble.

Ring taw

Fortifications

Bounce eye

BOUNCE EYE

In this game for two or more players, each player places one or more marbles in a central cluster in a circle about 1 ft in diameter.

The first player then stands over the ring and drops a marble onto the cluster. He may claim any marbles that roll out of the circle, but if no marbles roll out of the circle must add one marble to the cluster.

Players then drop a marble in turn until all the marbles in the central cluster have been claimed.

WALL MARBLES

In this variation of capture several players shoot or throw their marbles against a wall. The first player sends a marble against the wall and leaves it where it stops.

Each of the other players then follows in turn, and:

a) leaves his marble where it stops if it fails to hit another marble as it rebounds from the wall; or

b) claims all the marbles on the ground if his rebounding marble hits any other.

If no player has hit another marble when all the players have had a turn, play continues in the same way but with each player delivering his marble from where it stopped in the first round.

Wall marbles

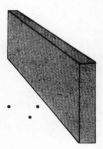

DIE SHOT

In die shot, or die marble, players shoot their marbles at a target comprising a die balanced on a marble that has been filed down to make it more stable.

Each player becomes "die-keeper" for one round, while the other players make one shot in each turn.

Before making a shot, each player must pay the die-keeper one marble.

If a player knocks the die off the marble, the die-keeper must pay him the number of marbles shown on the uppermost face of the die.

Die shot

HUNDREDS

This game for two players is usually played outdoors but can easily be adapted to indoor play. Outdoors, players shoot marbles into a shallow hole; indoors, a drawn circle can be used.

At the start of the game each player shoots one marble toward the ring.

If both players' marbles stop in the ring, both players shoot again.

When only one player's marble stops in the ring, he scores 10 points and then continues shooting and scoring until he misses or scores 100 points.

If he misses, his opponent shoots and scores until he misses.

The game is won by the first player to reach 100 points.

Hundreds

THREE HOLES

This game can also be played indoors with drawn rings instead of holes.

Three rings, about 3in in diameter and 5ft apart, are marked on the floor.

The game is won by the player who "kills" (puts out) all his opponents or is first to shoot a marble into each ring in the correct order.

Each player plays in turn, and gains an extra shot if his marble stops in the correct ring or hits another player's marble. At the end of his turn a player must leave his marble where it lies.

Only after a player has scored the first ring may he "kill" another player by hitting his marble. Before he scores the first ring, however, he may move another player's marble by hitting it.

When a player is "killed" he must pay his hitter the marble that was hit plus any marbles won in the game.

Three holes

ARCHBOARD

In archboard, or bridge board, players attempt to shoot their marbles through arches cut out of a narrow piece of card or board.

Each player is keeper of the arches for one round of the game, while the other players shoot one marble in each turn.

Before making a shot, each player pays the keeper one marble.

When his marble passes completely through an arch a player receives from the banker the number of marbles shown above that arch. (Usually numbers are higher toward the outside of the bridge.)

If a player's marble misses the bridge completely, he must pay another marble to the keeper.

PICKING PLUMS

Picking plums is a game for any small number of players.

Each player places one or two marbles in a row—with room for two marbles to pass through the gaps.

Each player then shoots in turn and may keep any "plums" knocked from the line.

A player is entitled to an extra shot whenever he picks a plum; all shots are made from the original position and not from where the marble lies after the previous shot.

DOBBLERS

This game is played in the same way as picking plums except that:

a player's taw stays where it lies at the end of a turn; subsequent turns are played from where the taw lies; a player whose taw is hit by another player's taw must add one marble to the row.

ONE STEP

One step is another game in which the target is a row of marbles made up by the players.

It is played in the same way as dobblers except that:

a player's first shot is made by taking one step and then throwing his taw from an upright position; subsequent shots are made from an upright position but with no step forward; a successful shot entitles a player to an extra shot from where his taw lies.

Archboard

Picking plums

One step

Conkers

Conkers is a popular game with British children. Two players each have a "conker" threaded on a knotted string. Players take alternate hits at their opponent's conker and the game is won when one player destroys the other's conker.

The conkers The game is usually played with nuts from the horsechestnut tree, but is sometimes played with hazelnuts (often called "cobnuts").

When preparing their conkers, players make a hole through the center with a sharp instrument such as a meat skewer, or a compass or a pair of geometry dividers. Many players then harden their conkers by soaking them in vinegar or salt and water and/or baking them for about half an hour. Excellent conkers are obtained by storing them in the dark for a year.

When the conker is ready, a strong piece of string or a bootlace is threaded through the hole and knotted at one end. The string should be long enough for about 9in to hang down after it is wrapped once or twice around the hand.

The game Players take alternate hits at their opponent's conker.

The player whose conker is to be hit first, holds his conker as shown (**a**)—with the string wrapped around his hand. He must adjust the height of his hand to suit his opponent, and must then keep his conker perfectly still for the hit.

The striker takes his conker in one hand and holds the opposite end of his string in the other hand (**b**). For the strike, he first draws the conker back and then releases it in a fast swinging motion in the direction of his opponent's conker (**c**).

If the striker misses his opponent's conker he is allowed a maximum of two further attempts to make a hit. If the players' strings tangle, the first player to call "strings" can claim an extra shot. Play continues until one of the conkers is destroyed—ie until no part of it remains on the string.

Scoring Conkers are usually described according to the number of victories won with them—eg a "oner," "fiver," "seventy-fiver."

A conker adds one to its title each time it destroys a conker that has never won a game. A conker that defeats a conker with previous wins claims one for defeating it plus all the defeated conker's wins—so a "fiver" that defeats another "fiver" becomes an "elevener."

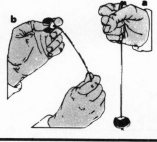
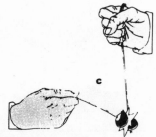

CONQUERORS

This is a similar game to conkers and seems to have been very popular in the eighteenth and nineteenth centuries.

Two players press empty snail shells tip to tip until one of them breaks.

Scoring is the same as for conkers.

SOLDIERS

This game is now usually played with lollipop, or ice cream, sticks.

One player holds his stick with both hands, one at each end. The other holds his stick in one hand and gives his opponent's stick a sharp blow. Turns at striking alternate as in conkers, and the game continues until one of the sticks breaks. Scoring is as for conkers.

The game used to be played with stalks from the ribwort plantain—the winner being the first player to knock the head off his opponent's stalk.

Coin throwing games

Money has been changing hands in games of chance and skill since time immemorial. In another, much smaller group of games it is the coins themselves that play the principal role.

BROTHER JONATHAN
This coin throwing game originated in North America in the eighteenth century.
It is a game for two or more players, playing for themselves or in teams.
The board may be marked on the ground, or drawn on a large sheet of paper laid on the floor. It is a rectangle divided into sections, with a scoring value marked in each one. Note that the larger sections bear the lower scores whereas the smaller sections contain higher numbers.

Play Each player takes it in turn to pitch a coin from a previously designated spot onto the board.
If a coin touches any of the dividing lines it does not count towards the player's score.
The winner may be decided in one of two ways:
a) the first player or team to score an agreed total; or
b) the player or team with the highest score after an agreed number of throws.

WALL JONATHAN
This game is played in the same way as Brother Jonathan except that players must throw their coins against a wall in such a way that they rebound onto the board.

CRACK LOO
In this game, players score points by throwing coins onto numbered cracks on a wood floor (or onto lines drawn on a large sheet of paper).
Otherwise play is the same as for Brother Jonathan.

COVER IT
Cover it is a game for two or more players.
The first player throws a coin against a wall and leaves it where it comes to rest on the ground.
Then each player in turn throws a coin against the wall. If his coin is touching another coin when it comes to rest, he picks up both coins. If it is not touching another coin, he leaves his coin on the ground. (This game is also played with playing cards or other small cards.)

HITTING THE MUMMY
This is a variation of cover it in which the first coin thrown is designated the "mummy" and players aim only to cover this one coin.
A player whose coin is not touching the mummy after being thrown against the wall, must leave his coin where it lies.
A player whose coin is touching the mummy, is entitled to pick up all coins on the ground except the mummy. If he mistakenly picks up the mummy, he must pay one coin to each of the other players.

PENNIES ON THE PLATE
A metal plate or lid is placed on the ground.
At his turn a player throws an agreed number of coins at the plate. The coins must be thrown one at a time from an agreed distance of several feet. The player who gets the most coins to stay on the plate wins the game. (It is usually quite easy to hit the plate, but much more difficult to ensure that a coin falls in such a way that it does not immediately bounce or roll off it.)

TOSSING A COIN

Tossing a coin is a widely known method of deciding the order of play for many different games between two players or teams.

The coin is tossed by a player or non-player, who:

a) flicks the coin into the air by releasing his thumb from between his clenched fingers;

b) catches the coin in his other hand;

c) quickly turns this hand over to lay the coin on the back of his tossing hand.

If a non-player makes the toss, he asks one of the players to "call." If a player makes the toss, his opponent should call. A player calls either "heads" or "tails" in an attempt to forecast which side of the coin will be face up after the toss. He should make his call while the coin is in the air.

A player who "wins the toss" (ie makes a correct forecast) generally has the right to choose the order of play for the game.

HEADS OR TAILS

Heads or tails is an adaptation of tossing a coin to make a game for any number of players.

Each player tosses a coin in turn, and all players, including the thrower, guess whether it will fall with the head or tail up.

The winner is either:

a) the first player to make an agreed number of correct guesses; or

b) the player with the most correct guesses after an agreed number of throws.

Tossing

CATCH

The skills of juggling and coordination play an important part in the game of catch.

For the first round, each player:

a) balances one coin on his elbow;

b) drops his hand and tries to catch his coin as it falls.

For the second round, players balance and attempt to catch two coins together, and the number of coins is then increased by one for each further round.

Any player who fails to catch the required number of coins for a round is eliminated from any further rounds, and the winner is the last player left in the game.

SPINNING A COIN

This game is played in the same way as heads or tails, except that the coins are spun instead of tossed.

(Probably the easiest method of spinning a coin is to hold it on its edge on a smooth, hard surface and then spin it between the thumb of one hand and the forefinger of the other, as shown.)

Spinning

Catching

HOLE IN ONE

For this game players need a coin and a plastic tumbler or similar receptacle.

The tumbler is placed on its side on the floor and the players take it in turn to try rolling a coin into it.

The winner is the player who gets the coin into the tumbler most times, out of an agreed number of shots.

ROLL A GOAL

This game is played in the same way as hole in one, except that players attempt to roll a coin between two "goalposts" made from folded paper, books, or other objects.

COIN ARCHBOARD

This is a coin version of marbles archboard (p 126). Players attempt to roll coins through arches in a board and, when successful, score the number of points indicated above the arch.

PENNY ROLL

This game is popular at fairgrounds in many parts of the world. It can easily be played at home with improvised equipment. Players roll coins down a metal and wood chute onto a board divided into numbered squares.

If a player's coin stops completely within a square, he receives a sum of money in accordance with that square's number.

Fivestones and Jacks

Fivestones and jacks are two almost identical games derived from knucklebones, a primitive form of dice played with the knucklebones of sheep. Knucklebones probably originated in Asia Minor, and later became popular in ancient Greece and Rome. Today, fivestones and jacks are played in many countries. In both these games, players in a crouching position throw small objects in the air and catch them in various ways in a usually increasingly difficult series of throws.

FIVESTONES
The game of fivestones (sometimes called chuckstones or jacks) is played with five small rounded stones or with five small plastic cubes of different colors.
The objective is to complete a series of throws in an agreed sequence, each throw to be successfully completed before the next is attempted.
Players The game can be enjoyed by a player on his own —or two or more players may attempt to be first to complete an agreed sequence of throws.

Turns If there are two or more players, the usual practice is to play in turn.
First turn may be decided by a preliminary throw, by the toss of a coin, or by agreement. A player's turn ends when he fails to accomplish any part of a particular throw, and his next turn begins with another attempt at the failed throw.
Throws There are many hundreds of variations of the game, but those given here are among the most widely known.

Basic throw

Basic throw For the basic throw, sometimes called the "jockey," the player must:
a) put the five stones in the open palm of one hand;
b) toss the stones up in the air;
c) while the stones are in the air, turn his hand over and catch the stones on the back of his hand;
d) toss the stones from the back of his hand;
e) turn his hand over and catch the stones in the palm of his hand.

Ones The player attempts the basic throw. If he catches all the stones, he goes on to twos. If he fails to catch any stones his turn ends.
If he catches one or more stones, he must:
leave any stones on the ground where they lie;
transfer to his other hand all but one of the stones he has caught;
throw the single stone in the air;
pick up one stone from the ground with his throwing hand;
catch the thrown stone with the same hand.
The player must repeat the procedure for picking up individual stones until all have been retrieved.

Twos The player scatters the the stones on the ground, taking care that they do not land too far apart.
He then selects one stone, throws it up in the air, and must pick up two other stones from the ground with his throwing hand before catching the thrown stone with that same hand.
When he has done this, he transfers the two stones to his other hand, tosses up the third stone, and must pick up the remaining two stones from the ground.

Threes is like twos, except that the player must pick up one stone followed by three, or three stones followed by one.
Fours In fours, all four stones are picked up at one time.

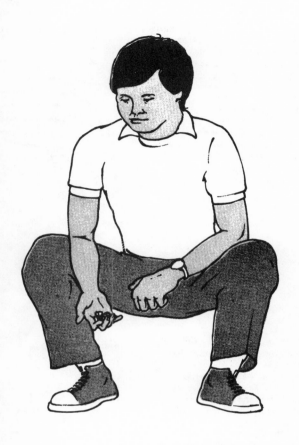

Pecks The player attempts the basic throw. If he succeeds in catching all five stones, he goes on to bushels. If he fails to catch any stones his turn ends.

If he catches one or more stones, he must:

keep the caught stones in his throwing hand;

push one stone out between his forefinger and thumb and then:

toss the pushed out stone into the air (**a**);

pick up one stone from the ground with his throwing hand (**b**);

catch the thrown stone with his throwing hand (**c**);

repeat this procedure until all stones are picked up.

Bushels If the player succeeds with a basic throw, he goes on to claws. If he fails to catch any stones his turn ends.

If he catches one or more stones, he must:

throw all the caught stones in the air;

pick up one stone from the ground with his throwing hand;

catch the thrown stones;

repeat this until all stones on the ground are picked up.

Claws The fivestones are tossed from the palm onto the back of the hand—as in the basic throw.

If all five are caught, the player attempts to complete the basic throw and if successful may go on to ones under the arch.

If none is caught on the back of the hand, the player's turn ends.

If one or more are caught on the back of the hand, the player:

leaves the caught stones on the back of his hand;

picks up the stones on the ground between the outstretched fingers of his throwing hand, with only one stone between any two fingers or between finger and thumb;

tosses the stones from the back of his hand and catches them in his palm;

maneuvers the stones from between his fingers into his palm.

Pecks

Under the arch

Ones under the arch The player first scatters the stones on the ground and makes an arch near them with the thumb and forefinger of his non-throwing hand.

He then selects one stone and throws it up in the air (**a**). While the stone is in the air, he knocks the other stones through the arch (**b**), and then catches the thrown stone (**c**). When all four stones have been knocked through the arch, the player throws the fifth stone in the air and before catching it must pick up the other four stones.

Twos under the arch is similar to ones under the arch, except that the stones must be knocked through the arch in two pairs.

Threes under the arch is similar except that the stones are knocked through as a three and a one or a one and a three.

Fours under the arch requires all four stones to be knocked through together.

Horse in the stable The stones are scattered on the ground and the non-throwing hand is placed near them, with the fingers and thumb spread out, the fingertips touching the ground, and the palm raised. The gaps between the fingers and thumb are the "stables."

One stone is then thrown into the air (**a**), and before catching it the player must knock a stone into or toward one of the stables (**b**). No more than one stone may be knocked into any one stable.

The player continues throwing, knocking, and catching in this way until all four stables are filled.

He then moves his non-throwing hand away from the four stones, tosses the throwing stone and before catching it must pick up the four stones from the ground.

Horse in the stable

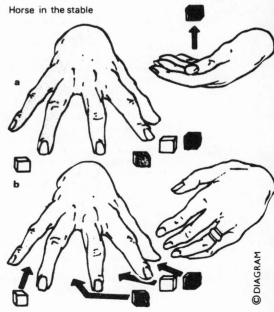

©DIAGRAM

Toad in the hole The stones are first scattered on the ground. A "hole" is then made by laying the thumb of the non-throwing hand straight along the ground and curling the fingers around so that the tip of the forefinger touches the tip of the thumb.

One stone is then thrown into the air, and before catching it the player must pick up one of the other stones, a "toad," and drop it into the hole.

This is repeated until four toads are in the hole. The player then moves his non-throwing hand, tosses up the single stone and before catching it must pick up all four toads.

Over the line The non-throwing hand is placed with the palm on the ground, and four stones are scattered on the ground to its outer side. The player then throws the fifth stone in the air, and before catching it must transfer one of the other stones to the other side of his non-throwing hand. This is repeated until all four stones on the ground have been transferred. (It is advisable to place the transferred stones as close together as possible.)

The player then throws up the fifth stone and before catching it must pick up the other four stones in his throwing hand.

Over the jump is similar to over the line, except that the non-throwing hand is placed on edge to make a jump or wall —so making the transference of stones more difficult.

Threading the needle is also similar, but the stones have to be dropped one at a time through a circle formed by the thumb and forefinger of the non-throwing hand held about 8in above the ground.

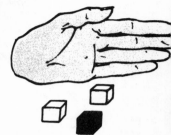

Over the jump

Snake in the grass The player sets out four stones in a straight line, with a gap of several inches from one stone to the next.

He then throws the fifth stone in the air, and before catching it, must pick up one of the end stones, use it to trace part of the pattern illustrated, and lay the picked up stone down at the point of the pattern reached.

A player is allowed any number of throws to complete his tracing, but his turn ends if he drops the throwing stone, fails to touch the stone he is using for tracing, or touches any other stone.

Building a tower can only be played with fivestones that are cubes.

The player first scatters four of his stones. He then throws the other stone and before catching it moves one of the stones on the ground away from the others.

At his second throw he places a second stone on top of the first, at his third throw he places a third stone on top of the other two, and at his fourth throw he completes the tower.

Demolishing a tower is the obvious sequel to building a tower. At each throw, the player must remove a single stone from the tower.

Snake in the grass

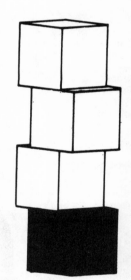

Building a tower

Backward ones After first scattering four stones on the ground, the player throws the fifth stone in the air and catches it on the back of his throwing hand.

He then tosses the fifth stone into the air from the back of his hand and before catching it in the normal way must pick up one stone from the ground. The player then throws the two held stones in the same manner and picks up a third stone. The three held stones are used for the next throw, and four stones for the throw to pick up the fifth stone.

Backward twos is similar to backward ones, except that the player must pick up two stones at his first throw and then the remaining two.

Backward threes is similar except that three and then one or one and then three stones must be picked up.

Backward fours requires the player to pick up all four stones at one time.

JACKS

Jacks or jackstones are small, six-legged, metal objects. They are usually bought in sets of five or six.

As well as the jacks, a player needs a small rubber ball. This is thrown in the air and then must be caught after agreed moves have been made with the jacks.

Most fivestone games can be adapted for play with jacks.

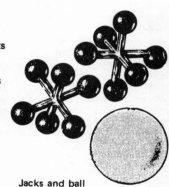

Jacks and ball

Spellicans

Spellicans and jackstraws are two similar games that test a player's skill at removing straws or small sticks from a pile, one at a time and without disturbing any of its neighbors. They are games for any number of players.

SPELLICANS

This game, sometimes called spillikins, originated in China and is played with a set of about 30 thin strips of ivory, wood, or plastic.

These strips, called spellicans, have carved heads representing animals, people, etc. There is also a carved hook for moving the strips.

Start of play The order of play is determined by the throw of a die or some other means.

The last person in the playing order then takes all the spellicans in one hand and drops them on to the table or floor. He must not interfere with any spellican after it has left his hand.

Play At his turn, each player takes the carved hook and attempts to remove a spellican from the pile without disturbing any of the others. Once a player has started moving a particular spellican he is not permitted to transfer his attack to a different spellican.

If he successfully removes a spellican from the pile, he keeps it and tries to remove another spellican from the pile. A player's turn continues until he disturbs a spellican other than the one that he is attacking.

Play continues in this way until all the spellicans have been taken.

Scoring Each spellican has a points value, and a game is won by the player with the highest score.

Spellicans that are generally fairly easy to move have a low value, and more elaborate and difficult to move spellicans have a correspondingly higher value.

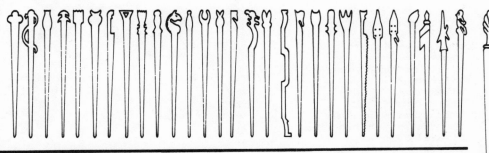

JACKSTRAWS

This variant of spellicans is also variously known as jerkstraws, juggling sticks, pick-up sticks, and pick-a-stick.

It is played with about 50 wood or plastic sticks or straws. These are about 6in long, rounded, and with pointed ends, and colored according to their points value.

Play The rules are the same as for spellicans except that players remove the sticks with their fingers or, in some versions of the game, may use a stick of a specified color after they have drawn one from the pile.

MAGNETIC JACKSTRAWS

This is a modern form of jackstraws in which the straws are made of metal and must be removed from the pile by means of a small horseshoe magnet.

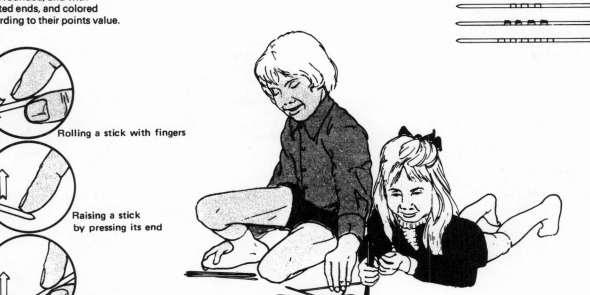

Rolling a stick with fingers

Raising a stick by pressing its end

Using one stick to move another

Tiddlywinks

Tiddlywinks is a game for any small number of players. In the standard game, each player attempts to put small disks or "winks" into a cup by shooting them with a larger disk called a "shooter." Various tiddlywinks games based on sports such as tennis and golf can be bought or easily improvised.

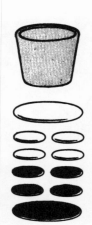

Playing area The game is played on the floor or on a table.
Any shape of table may be used but a square or round one is best for more than two players. The table should be covered with a thick cloth or piece of felt.

Equipment For the standard tiddlywinks game players need "winks," "shooters," and a target cup.
Winks and shooters must be slightly pliable and are usually made of bone or plastic. Winks are usually about $\frac{5}{8}$ in and shooters about 1 in in diameter. Each player's winks and shooter should be a different color.
Cups are made of plastic, wood, or glass and are usually $1\frac{1}{2}$ in across and 1–2 in high.

Players The standard game is usually played by two, three, or four players with four winks each.

Start of play The cup is placed in the center of the table, and each player places his winks in a line in front of him.

Turns Order of play is often decided by a preliminary shot —the first shot of the game going to the player who gets his wink nearest the cup.
Play is then usually clockwise around the table.
Each player shoots one wink in a turn plus one extra shot each time he gets a wink into the cup.

Scoring Tiddlywinks may be scored in two ways:
a) players count the number of games they win;
b) players score one point for each wink in the cup when each game ends.

Objective The game is won by the first player to get all his tiddlywinks in the cup.

Out of play Any wink that is partly covered by another is out of play. A player whose wink is covered by an opponent's wink must either wait until the opponent moves his wink or attempt to remove the opponent's wink by hitting it with one of his own winks. Any wink that stops against the side of the cup is out of play until it is knocked level on to the table by another wink. A wink that is shot off the table does not go out of play. It must be replaced on the table at the point where it went off.

Partners Tiddlywinks can be played by partners in the same way as the standard singles game except that:
players pair up with the player sitting opposite;
partners play alternately and may play either their own or their partner's winks.

Shooting A player shoots a wink by stroking and pressing the edge of his shooter against the edge of the wink and so making the wink jump into the air.
A wink is shot from where it lies after the player's previous turn.

FORFEIT GAME

An interesting variation of the standard game is played by drawing six concentric circles around the cup.

Play is the same as for the standard game except that any wink that lands in one of the circles is forfeited and immediately removed from the table.

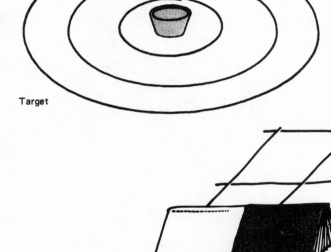

Forfeit

TARGET GAMES

Variations on the standard tiddlywinks game can be played by using numbered targets.

Typical layouts are:
a) a target with concentric circles each worth a set number of points;
b) a raised target with numbered scoring areas.

Target tiddlywinks games are played in the same way as the standard game except that: players score a set number of points for landing their winks on different parts of the target (a wink touching two scoring areas always scores the lower number);

a wink may not be shot again once it has landed on any part of the target, but may be knocked by another wink.

Target

TIDDLYWINKS TENNIS

The lines of a tennis court should be marked on the floor or the tiddlywinks cloth. (Dimensions for the court should be varied to suit the skill of the players and the height of the net.)

An improvised net can be made with folded paper or card, or with a row of books. Players shoot a wink back and forth over the net—gaining points whenever their opponent fails to get the wink over the net or shoots it so that it goes outside the limits of the court.

Rules for service can be modified to suit the skill of the players—eg extra shots allowed to get the wink over the net or no restrictions on where in the opponent's court the wink must land.

A match is scored in games and sets as in ordinary tennis.

©DIAGRAM

Tennis

TIDDLYWINKS GOLF

Tiddlywinks golf sets, with tiddlywinks, greens, obstacles, and holes, are produced by various toy manufacturers. The game can also be played on an easily improvised course. Nine "holes" should be positioned at intervals around the course. Holes can be egg cups, napkin rings, or just circles drawn on the tiddlywinks cloth.

The course is then made more interesting by the addition of obstacles—such as rumpled or corrugated paper under the cloth to make rough ground, upturned books to make bunkers, and box or jar lids for water obstacles.

The game can be scored by "stroke" or by "hole" as in real golf. In the first, each player counts the number of shots he takes to complete the course. In the second, players score one for each hole won and a half for each hole tied.

Golf

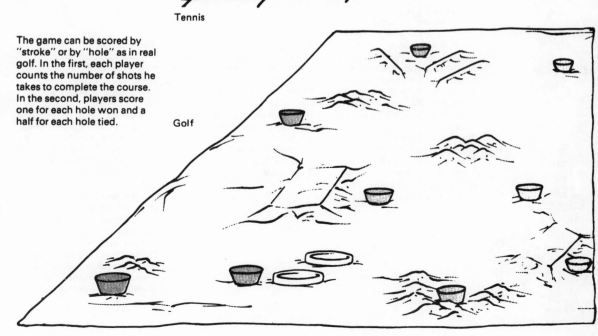

Ball games

Although ball games are usually associated with outdoor play, there are many enjoyable games that can be played indoors. A table tennis ball is recommended for minimum damage !

Cup and ball

Containers

CUP AND BALL

Cup and ball is a game for one person that was first played several hundred years ago. It was especially popular among children in the late nineteenth century and can still be bought today.

The cup and ball are made of wood and joined by a length of string. Sometimes the cup is replaced by a wooden spike and the ball has a hole bored through its center.

The player holds the cup around its base and stretches out his arm so that the ball hangs toward the ground. He then swings his arm and tries to catch the ball in the cup—with a little practice this can be done almost every time.

The version with a spike is more difficult to accomplish, as the ball has to be impaled on the spike.

JAM JARS

This is a game needing only a few table tennis balls and some jam jars for equipment. Five or six jam jars are placed close together on the floor or on a table.

Players stand a few feet away and take it in turns to throw a set number of table tennis balls (usually two or three) in an attempt to get them into the jars.

As table tennis balls are extremely bouncy, this task is more difficult than it might at first seem !

The player who manages to get the most balls into the jam jars after each round of play is the winner. (Any number of rounds may be played.)

IN THE BOWL

In the bowl is a game very like jam jars.

A deep bowl or bucket is placed on the floor.

Each player in turn tries to throw a table tennis ball so that it lands (and remains !) in the bowl.

If the player is successful he may throw again.

At the end of a set time, the player with the most successful throws wins the game.

CONTAINERS

This game is played in the same way as in the bowl, except that players try to get a ball into one of several containers—each with a points value depending on its size.

The player with most points wins the game.

Blow football

Holey board game

BLOW FOOTBALL

Blow football is a game played at a table by two players or by two teams of two or three. Each person blows through a drinking straw at a table tennis ball, and tries to get the ball into the opposing goal.

The player or team that scores the most goals after a given time wins the game.

Equipment Blow football is best played at a long table, although it can also be played on the floor.

A goal must be marked at each end of the table—using pencils or other suitable objects.

It is a good idea to make a wall around the edges of the table to help keep the ball in play. (Strips of wood or cardboard can be used.)

Each player is given a drinking straw, and the only other equipment needed is a table tennis ball.

Play The table tennis ball is placed in the middle of the table. At a given signal, the players start to blow through their straws in an attempt to get the ball into the opponents' goal—while at the same time defending their own goal from attack.

Whenever a goal is scored (ie the ball passes between the "goalposts"), the ball is repositioned at the center of the table and the game is restarted.

If the ball is blown off the table, the opposing side places the ball on the table at the spot where it came off and then takes a "free" blow before the other side may continue blowing.

HOLEY BOARD GAME

This is a target game in which players score points by throwing a table tennis ball through a "holey board."

The holey board can be made quite easily out of stiff cardboard. A random number of holes is cut out, each one a different size. (The smallest hole should be just big enough for a table tennis ball to pass through it.) A scoring value is written above each hole—the bigger the hole, the lower the value.

The board is propped up between two chairs—books can be used to keep it in position. Players stand as far away from the board as possible and take turns to throw the ball.

Each time a player gets the ball through a hole, he scores the number of points written above the hole. (The smaller the hole, the more difficult it is to get the ball through it!)

The player with the highest score after a set number of throws is the winner.

Once players have become quite skilled, they can try throwing the ball so that it bounces on the floor before going through a hole.

THROUGH THE TUNNEL

Through the tunnel is very like the archboard game (see the section on marble games). Playing procedure is exactly the same, but table tennis balls are used instead of marbles, and the arches through which they are rolled are correspondingly bigger.

© DIAGRAM

5 General card games

Basic rules

The origin of playing cards is a mystery. Chinese playing cards, it seems, grew out of a marriage between divinatory arrows and paper money. Such cards may have reached Europe via the Crusades or the China trade. Alternatively Western playing cards may have had a separate European origin— seeming to have appeared quite suddenly, around 1370, in almost their present form.

THE CARDS
The deck The standard international deck of playing cards consists of 52 cards, divided into four suits of 13 cards each. Many decks also contain two jokers, sometimes used as wild cards.
The suits are named hearts, diamonds, spades, and clubs, and each card of the suit bears the appropriate symbol, as shown. Hearts and diamonds bear red symbols, spades and clubs black symbols.

The cards in any one suit are all of different denominations: nine are numbered from 2 to 10; three are "court" or "face" cards (jack, queen, king); the remaining card is the "ace," which is the "1" but is often the most powerful card of the suit.
The denomination of numbered cards is shown by both numbers and by the appropriate number of suit symbols.
The ace is shown by an "A" and a single large suit symbol. Court cards are shown by stylized drawings and by initial letters, which vary according to the country of origin of the deck. In English language countries these letters are "J" (for jack), "Q" (for queen), and "K" (for king).

The rank of cards is usually either:
2 (low), 3, 4, 5, 6, 7, 8, 9, 10, j, q, k, a (high); or
a (low), 2, 3, 4, 5, 6, 7, 8, 9, 10, j, q, k (high).
In either list, a card beats any card listed before it.
These rankings are referred to in the text as "cards rank normally, ace high," and "cards rank normally, ace low."
A meld is a scoring combination of cards in certain games.
It is usually either:
three or more cards of the same denomination; or
three or more cards in consecutive order of rank and of the same suit.

Trumps In games in which tricks are taken, it is often ruled that certain cards are made trump cards (trumps).
If so, any trump card ranks above any other card.
Usually, all the cards of one suit are chosen as trump cards (trump suit).
But in some games only some cards of one suit are the trump cards; or in other games there are other trump cards in addition to the trump suit.
Within a trump suit, cards rank in the standard order for the game being played.
Choice of trump suit The method depends on the game being played.
Some games use a permanent trump suit, chosen by agreement or convention at the beginning of the game.
But usually a suit has the role of trump suit for only one deal at a time. In this case, the trump suit for a deal is decided in one of the following ways, depending on the game being played:
a) by competitive bidding among the players;
b) by chance, ie turning a certain card face up—the suit revealed becomes trumps;
c) by set order of rotation among the suits.

PREPARING AND DEALING
Choice of partners for partnership play is usually by an initial draw. Each of the four players draws one card from the deck: the two players with the two highest ranking cards form one partnership and the other two players form the second.
Choice of first dealer
a) By high cut. Any agreed player acts as temporary dealer and shuffles the cards. Any other agreed player cuts them.
Each player then cuts the deck, beginning with the player to the temporary dealer's left, going clockwise, and ending with the temporary dealer.
Each cut consists of lifting a section of cards from the top of the face-down deck. The card cut by the player is that at the bottom of this section.
The section is held so all players can see this card.
After each cut, the two sections of cards are restacked in their original order, before passing to the next player.
The player cutting the highest denomination card becomes the first dealer. Cards rank normally; ace ranks high or

Shuffling

low according to the game played. Players who cut equal highest cut again until a decision is reached between them.
b) By deal of cards. Any agreed player acts as temporary dealer and shuffles the cards. Any other agreed player cuts them.
The temporary dealer then deals one card face up to each player, including himself, beginning with the player to his left and going clockwise, until the first card of a specified denomination is dealt (eg the first ace). The player receiving this card becomes the first dealer.
Shuffle and cut are often required before every deal.
The dealer shuffles. Any other player also has the right to shuffle, but the dealer has the right to shuffle last.
The procedure of shuffling is not governed by rules— providing that an adequate shuffle is given to the cards in some way. One simple and satisfactory procedure is illustrated.
The player to the dealer's right is offered the cards to cut. If he declines the player to his right is offered the cut, and so on.

If no player wishes to cut, the dealer must cut.
A cut consists of lifting a section of cards from the top of the deck, placing it on the table, and placing the other section on top of it.
Cards remain face down and unexposed throughout.
There must be at least five cards in each section.
The deal Unless otherwise stated, the dealer gives one card at a time to each player, beginning with the player to his left and going clockwise. This rotation is repeated until each player has the required number of cards. The deal must be from the top of a face-down deck.
Deal in packets is a deal in which each player receives more than one card at once. It is required for certain games. On the deal, the dealer gives each player a specified number of cards (eg three cards), before going on to the next player.
Otherwise the deal follows normal procedure.
Sometimes the number of cards specified changes during the deal. For example, in solo whist:
when the dealer goes around the circle of players for the

first, second, and third times, he gives each player three cards each time;
when he goes around the fourth (last) time, he gives each player one card, as in a normal deal.
A widow is a batch of cards dealt separately from the players' hands. Its role varies from game to game.
The stock is, in certain games, the part of the deck which remains undealt after the deal is complete but which becomes available to players in the course of play.

ROTATION OF PLAY
Unless otherwise stated, play begins with the player to the dealer's left, and continues with the other players in clockwise rotation.

Complete deck of cards

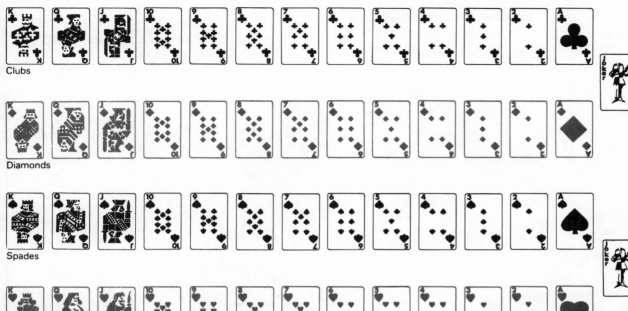

Clubs

Diamonds

Spades

Hearts

TRICKS
A trick signifies, in certain games, one round of cards during play—one card being contributed by each active hand.

It also means the cards themselves when gathered together.

On each trick one player plays first ("has the lead"), and the other players follow in clockwise rotation.

Each player's action consists of taking one card from his hand and placing it face up in the center of the table.

The lead is held, in most games:

on the first trick after a deal— by the player to the dealer's left;

on the remaining tricks of a deal—by the player who won the previous trick.

Choice of cards The lead may play any card he wishes. The other players must "follow suit" if possible, ie each must play a card of the same suit as the lead card if he has one. If a player cannot follow suit, he may play any other card that he has.

A trick is won by the highest ranking card of the suit led— providing that no trump is played.

If one or more trump cards are played, it is won by the highest ranking trump card. A player may usually only play a trump card if he cannot follow suit.

The player playing the winning card takes the trick: he gathers the cards together, and places them face down on the table, usually near his (or his partner's) position.

Revoking A player who has failed to follow suit when he in fact had a card of the required suit, is said to have "revoked."

Penalties for this vary from game to game.

NOTES ON BETTING
Betting chips When these are required, any counters, matchsticks, or other agreed objects may be used.

An ante is compulsory in certain games. It is a small contribution to the betting pool before a deal.

It is usually required either of all players or of the dealer only.

Odds The recognized forms in which payment odds are stated are:

either "x to y" (eg 30 to 1, 15 to 2)—which signifies that the player's stake is returned in addition to the win payment; or "x for y" (eg 30 for 1, 15 for 2)—which signifies that the player's stake is returned as part of the win payment.

For example, a player staking 1 chip at 30 to 1 receives 30 chips and his 1 chip stake back. At 30 for 1 he receives 29 chips and his 1 chip stake back.

"30 to 1" can also be written "30–1."

IRREGULARITIES
Rules on irregularities in play vary from one game to another. But the following rules are general.

A misdeal should be declared:

if, during a deal, a card is found face up in the deck;

or if the rules of shuffling, cutting, or dealing are broken.

Imperfect deck If the deck is found to have cards missing, or added, or duplicated, the hand being played is immediately abandoned. However, any scores made so far on that hand are valid.

Lead

Trick

Trumps

Trumping a trick

Whist

Whist evolved in the eighteenth century from an earlier game called triumph. It has since given rise to a whole family of games, including the popular contract bridge and solo whist. The rules are comparatively simple, but a great deal of skill is needed to play really well.

Players Whist is a game for four players, two playing against two as partners. Partnerships are decided by draw (see p 80).

Players sit around a table, with partners facing each other. By convention, players are referred to by the points of the compass, with North and South playing against East and West.

Cards A standard deck of 52 playing cards is used. Cards rank normally, with ace high. The suits are not ranked, except that one suit is designated the trump suit for each hand. A card of the trump suit beats any card from any other suit.

Objective Players aim to win tricks. A trick consists of four cards, one played by each player.

Choice of first dealer is by high cut, with ace ranking low (see p 80).

Shuffle and cut Any player has the right to shuffle, but the dealer has the right to shuffle last. The player to the right of the dealer cuts the cards and passes them to the dealer.

Rank

Deal Beginning with the player to his left and going clockwise, the dealer deals out all but one of the cards, face down and one at a time. The remaining card is placed face up on the table and its suit indicates the trump suit. The dealer adds it to his hand when it is his turn to play.

Misdeal It is a misdeal if:
a) more or fewer than 13 cards are dealt to any player; or
b) any card other than the last one is exposed.
It is not a misdeal if a player is dealt two or more successive cards and the dealer rectifies the error at once.
If there has been a misdeal, players may agree to accept the deal after the error has been rectified.
Any player, however, has the right to demand a new deal until the first trick is completed. After that the deal must stand. If there is to be a redeal, players throw in their cards and the deal passes one player to the left.

Play The player to the dealer's left leads by placing any one of his cards face up in the center of the table.
Each of the other players in turn plays a card to the center of the table.
If a player has a card of the same suit as the card led, he must play this card. This is called "following suit," and failure to do so is penalized (see the section on revoking). If he does not have a card of the suit led he may play any other card.
The trick is won:
a) by the player of the highest trump card, or
b) if no trump cards have been played, by the player of the highest card of the suit led.
The winner of one trick leads to the next. Play continues in this way until all 13 tricks of a hand have been played.
The deal passes to the next player in a clockwise direction. The cards are reshuffled and cut for the new deal.

Revoking is failing to follow suit when able to do so.
A player is not penalized if he corrects his error before the trick is turned over, and the partner of a player who fails to follow suit may caution him by asking if he does not have any cards of the suit led.
Once the trick has been turned over but before play to the next trick has begun, the opposing partnership may challenge and claim a revoke. Points penalties for revoking vary with the different scoring systems for the game.
A partnership cannot win the game in any hand in which it revokes. If both partnerships revoke in the same hand, all cards are thrown in and a new deal is made.
Calling If a player exposes a card, other than when playing it to a trick, he must leave it face up on the table until one of his opponents "calls" on him to play it to a trick where it will not cause a revoke.
Scoring There are a number of ways of scoring, but the following systems are most common.

In America a seven-point game is usual, with two ways of scoring game points.
1) The first six tricks played are discounted. Thereafter, each trick taken scores one game point.
2) Revoking also provides game points, as the pair that failed to follow suit transfers two of its game points to the other pair.
The first pair to get seven game points scores the difference between seven and the losers' score.
English whist uses a five-point game including the scoring of honors. Games are grouped into rubbers.
There are three ways of scoring game points.
1) Discounting the first six tricks played, one game point is scored for each trick taken.
2) The honors are a,k,q, and j of trumps. A partnership scores four game points if it is dealt all four honors, and three game points if dealt any three. However, if both pairs reach five game points in the same deal, the trick points from that deal take precedence over the honors points. At least one trick must be taken in the last deal before declaring game. After game, the losers' honors

score, if any, is no longer counted in their game points total.

3) There are three alternative rulings concerning the penalties for revoking:
a) the revoking pair loses three game points;
b) the revoking pair transfers three game points to its opponents; or
c) the opponents gain three points.

After each game, additional points are scored by the winners as follows:
a) three points if the opponents had no game points;
b) two points if the opponents had one or two game points; and
c) one point if the opponents had three or four game points.
A rubber is the best of three games.

If the first two games are won by the same pair, a third game is not played.
The winners of two out of three games score two extra points for the rubber. All points are then totaled, and the partnership with the highest score wins.

TERMS USED IN WHIST
Finessing consists of playing the third-best card of a suit when also holding the best—trusting that the opponents do not hold the second best.

Forcing is playing a suit in which another player is void.

Long trumps are the remaining trump or trumps left in a hand after all other trumps in the deck have been played.

Loose card is a card of no value.

Quarte is any four cards of the same suit in sequence.

Quarte major is a sequence of a,k,q,j in the same suit.

Quinte is any five cards of the same suit in sequence.

See-saw occurs when each member of a partnership is trumping a suit, and each plays these suits to the other for that purpose.

Slam is winning every trick.

Tenace consists of holding the cards immediately above and below the opposing side's best in suit, for example ace and queen when the opponents hold the king.

SOLO WHIST
Temporary partnerships are formed in solo whist, but each player scores for himself. Basically play is as for whist, but the game has its own bidding and scoring systems.

Players Solo whist is a game for four players. At the start of each hand each player is on his own.

Cards A standard deck of 52 playing cards is used. Cards rank normally with ace high.

Objective Each player tries to contract and fulfill a bid.

Choice of first dealer is by high cut, with ace low. (See p 80.)

Shuffle and cut are normal (see p 80).

Deal The dealer deals out all the cards, beginning with the player to his left and going clockwise. The cards are dealt three at a time, with a final round of single cards. All but the last card are dealt face down; the last card, dealt to the dealer, is dealt face up and indicates trumps for some bids. Rules for misdeals are the same as for whist.

Bidding Each player in turn, beginning with the player to the dealer's left, may make a bid or pass without making a bid. In certain circumstances players may have a second chance to bid.

The bids are ranked in the following order, with each outbidding the one before.
a) Proposal and acceptance, or "prop and cop," involves a temporary partnership of two players. A call of "I propose" or "Prop" indicates that the player will try to win eight tricks in partnership with any of the others. Play is with the trump suit indicated at the deal. In his turn, a subsequent bidder may call "Accept" or "Cop" to become the partner.
b) "Solo" is a bid to take five tricks playing alone against the other three. Play is with the trump suit indicated at the deal.
c) "Misère" or "nullo" indicates that the player will try to lose every trick, playing with no trump suit.
d) "Abondance" is a bid to take nine tricks, playing with a trump suit nominated by the bidder. He does not announce the trump suit until all remaining players have passed.
e) "Royal abondance" or "abondance in trumps," is a bid to take nine tricks, playing with the trump suit indicated at the deal.

f) "Misère ouverte" or "spread" indicates that a player will try to lose every trick, playing with no trumps and turning his remaining cards face up on the table after the first trick has been taken.
g) "Abondance declarée" is a bid to take 13 tricks, playing with no trump suit.

Second bids may be made in the following cases:
a) by the player to the left of the dealer to accept a proposal;
b) by any player who has been overbid and wishes to make a higher bid;
c) by a proposer who has not been accepted and wishes to amend his proposal to a higher bid.

No bid hands If all players pass, the cards are thrown in and the deal passes to the left.

Play The player to the dealer's left leads first, unless the bid is abondance declarée in which case the bidder leads. The rules for making tricks and trumping are the same as for whist.
It is not always necessary to play a hand right out.
For example after a bid of misère the hand ends as soon as the bidder takes a trick.

Revoke A revoke (see p 81) loses or wins three tricks depending on the bid and on which player made the error. A hand is always played out after a revoke, and a bidder who revokes must pay for the three tricks even if he makes his bid without them.

Scoring Chips are usually used for scoring: red ones worth five points each and white ones worth one point. Alternatively a written record may be kept.
Scores are as follows. For a successful proposal and acceptance bid, one partner receives five points from one opponent, and the other partner the same from the other opponent. For an unsuccessful bid, partners pay instead of receive the points. For all other bids, the bidder receives points from each of the other players if successful, or pays each of them if unsuccessful. The number of points varies with the bids:
solo, 10 points;
misère, 15 points;
abondance, 20 points;
royal abondance, 20 points;
misère ouverte, 30 points;
abondance declarée, 40 points.

In addition, for bids other than misère, misère ouverte, or abondance declarée, one extra point changes hands at each payment for each overtrick (trick in excess of the bid) or undertrick (trick fewer than the bid).

THREE-HANDED SOLO
The game can be adapted for three-handed play as follows.
Cards There are two alternative changes:
1) A 40-card deck is used— obtained by stripping the 2s, 3s, and 4s from a standard deck. 39 cards are dealt out and the 40th indicates the trump suit.
2) A 39-card deck is used— obtained by stripping out the whole of one suit. The trump suit is indicated by the last card dealt.
Bids There is no proposal and acceptance bid. Misère overbids abondance and misère ouverte overbids abondance declarée.
Scoring Misère is worth 20 points and abondance 15 points. Misère ouverte is worth 40 points and abondance declarée 30 points.

Rank of cards in three-handed solo

BOSTON

This game developed from whist and is itself an ancestor of the now more popular solo whist. It was very popular at the time of the American Revolution.

Players The game is for four players, each playing for himself.

Cards Two standard decks are used: one in play and the other for determining the "preference" and "color" suits. (If the preference and color suits are determined before the deal the game can be played with only one deck.) Cards rank normally, with ace high.

Chips A large number of chips are required for scoring purposes. (To make settlement simpler, players sometimes use chips of different values.)

Objective Each player tries to contract and fulfill a bid.

Choice of first dealer is by high cut, with ace low.

Pool Before each hand, each player pays 10 chips into a pool.

If the pool exceeds 250 chips, the excess is put aside for the next pool.

Deal The dealer deals out all the playing deck, beginning with the player to his left and going clockwise. The cards are dealt three at a time, with a final round of single cards.

If there is a misdeal, the dealer must pay 10 chips into the pool. The deal then passes one player to the left.

Determining preference and color suits After the deal, the second deck is cut by the player sitting opposite the dealer.

The top card of the bottom section is turned face up and denotes the preference suit. The other suit of the same color is called the color suit.

Bidding Each player in turn, beginning with the player to the dealer's left, may make a bid or pass.

The bids are ranked in the following order, with each outbidding the one before:
a) "Boston," ie a bid to win five tricks with one of the plain suits as trumps;
b) six tricks;
c) seven tricks;
d) "little misery," ie a bid to lose 12 tricks, playing with no trumps and after each player has discarded one card face down;
e) eight tricks;
f) nine tricks;
g) "grand misery," ie a bid to lose every trick, playing with no trumps;
h) 10 tricks;
i) 11 tricks;
j) "little spread," ie a bid to lose 12 tricks, playing with no trumps and the hand exposed;
k) 12 tricks;
l) "grand spread," ie a bid to lose every trick, playing with no trumps and the hand exposed;
m) "grand slam," ie a bid to win all 13 tricks.

Trumps There are no trumps for misery and spread bids. For other bids the player chooses his own trump suit, usually stating what it is only when his bid has been accepted.

However, if two or more players wish to make a bid for the same number of tricks, the bids are ranked as follows according to the proposed trump suit: preference suit (high), color suit, plain suits (low).

No bid hands If all players pass, each one throws in his cards and pays 10 chips into the pool. The deal then passes one player to the left.

Play The player to the left of the dealer leads to the first trick. Play is as for whist. A player who revokes loses the hand and must pay 40 chips into the pool.

Settlement If a player fulfills his bid he receives chips from each of the other players and, if his bid was for seven tricks or higher, he also receives the chips in the pool.

If a player fails to fulfill his bid he pays chips to each of the other players and must also double the chips in the pool.

For misery and spread bids the bidder pays or receives chips as follows:
20 for little misery;
40 for grand misery;
80 for little spread;
160 for grand spread.

If a player fulfills any other bid he is paid according to table A.

If a player fails to fulfill any other bid he pays according to the number of tricks by which he fails—as given in table B. A player is said to be "put in for" the number of tricks by which he fails.

OH HELL

Also known as blackout, this game has many features in common with whist. It is a game for three or more players, each playing for himself.

Cards A standard deck of 52 cards is used. Aces rank high.

Objective Each player tries to win the exact number of tricks he has bid.

Deal Each game involves a series of deals. Players cut for the first deal (highest card deals) and thereafter the deal passes in a clockwise direction around the table.

In the first deal, each player is dealt one card; in subsequent deals, the number of cards dealt to each player is increased each time by one card.

When the size of the hand can no longer be increased by one card per player, the game is finished.

Thus with four players, the cards will be dealt 13 times, and with five players ten times. At the end of each deal, the dealer turns the top card of the stock face up to denote trumps.

If in the final deal there is no spare card to turn face up, the hand is played without trumps.

Bidding Starting with the dealer, each player in turn bids the number of tricks he expects to win, or "nullo" if he expects to lose every trick.

In the first deal, possible bids are one or nullo; the number of possible bids increases with the size of each hand.

Play is opened by the player to the dealer's left. He leads with any card, and the other players must follow suit; if unable to do so they may trump or discard.

The winner of a trick leads to the next.

Scoring Every player who fulfills his bid exactly scores one point for each trick of his bid and a ten point bonus.

There is no standard score for making nullo; sometimes ten points are awarded, sometimes five, or five points plus the number of tricks in the deal.

If a player wins more or fewer tricks than the number he bid, he neither scores nor pays a penalty.

Optional scoring A successful bid of small slam—winning all but one of the tricks in the hand—with a hand of more than five cards earns a 25 point bonus.

Similarly, a successful bid of grand slam—winning all the tricks in the hand—earns a 50-point bonus.

Table A

Tricks bid	5	6	7	8	9	10	11	12	13
Payment	10	15	20	25	35	45	65	105	170

Table B

Tricks bid	Numbers put in for													Tricks bid
	1	2	3	4	5	6	7	8	9	10	11	12	13	
	Payment													
5	10	20	30	40	50									5
6	15	25	35	45	55	65								6
7	20	30	40	50	60	70	80							7
8	25	35	45	55	70	85	100	115						8
9	35	45	55	65	80	95	110	125	140					9
10	45	55	70	80	95	110	125	140	155	170				10
11	70	80	95	110	125	140	155	170	185	200	220			11
12	120	130	145	160	180	200	220	240	260	280	300	320		12
13	180	200	220	240	260	280	300	320	340	360	390	420	450	13

The winner is the player with the highest cumulative score after all the deals have been played.

VINT

Another member of the whist family, vint is a game for four players playing in partnerships of two.

Cards A standard deck of cards is used. The cards rank in ascending order from 2 through ace. The suits rank spades (lowest), clubs, diamonds, hearts, and no trumps (highest).

Objective Each partnership aims to make and fulfill a bid by taking tricks.

Deal The entire deck is dealt out, one face-down card at a time to each player. The deal passes clockwise around the table with each round of play.

Bidding Starting with the dealer, each player in turn bids or passes.

Each bid indicates the intention to take six tricks plus the number called, in the suit named or with no trumps. Thus the lowest bid is one spade (ie taking seven tricks with spades as trumps); and the highest is seven no trumps (ie taking thirteen tricks).

A bid is overcalled by a bid of more tricks in the same suit, or the same number of tricks in a higher ranking suit or no trumps.

When a player is overcalled he may call higher when his turn comes round again, even if the only other bidder is his partner.

Play is opened by the player to the left of the highest bidder, and proceeds in a clockwise direction around the table.

Each player must follow suit if able to do so; if he cannot, he either plays a trump or discards.

The winner of a trick leads to the next trick.

Scoring Each partnership records its score on a scorepad or piece of paper divided into two sections by a horizontal line (as in bridge, p 92).

Game points are entered below the line. Each partnership scores for each trick taken—whether or not the bid is fulfilled.

However, the number of tricks bid determines the value of each trick, ranging from ten points per trick for a bid of one, 20 points per trick for a bid of two, and so on up to 70 points per trick for a bid of seven.

The first partnership to score 500 game points wins the game—even if it reaches this score partway through a hand, and regardless of whether or not it won the bidding.

Bonus points are entered above the line. They are scored as follows:
a) winning a game, 1000 points;
b) winning a rubber (two out of three games), 2000 points;
c) "little slam" (12 tricks) made but not bid, 1000 points;
d) little slam bid and made, 6000 points;
e) "grand slam" (13 tricks) made but not bid, 2000 points;
f) grand slam bid and made, 12,000 points.

Honor points are scored above the line and comprise the a, k, q, j, and 10 of trumps and the other aces. In a trump suit, the ace is counted twice, both as an honor and an ace. When playing no trumps, only the four aces are honors.

The partnership holding the most honors scores ten times the trick value for each honor held in trumps, or 25 times the trick value for each honor (ace) held when playing no trumps.

For example, if the final bid is three trumps, each trick is worth 30 points and therefore each honor is worth 300 points (10 × 3 = 300).

If one partnership has a majority of aces and the other a majority of honors, those two majorities are compared, and the partnership that has the bigger majority scores for the difference.

For example, if side A has two honors and one ace, but side B has one honor and three aces, the two honors are deducted from the three aces and side B scores for one honor, worth ten times the trick value.

But if side A has three honors and one ace, and side B has one honor and three aces, neither side scores, as the three honors and the three aces cancel each other out.

If both sides hold two aces: at no trumps, neither side scores; at trumps, the side that wins most tricks scores for its honors.

Coronet Any player holding three aces or a sequence of three cards in a plain suit—known as a "coronet"—scores 500 points, entered above the line.

If a player holds the fourth ace, he scores a further 500 points; and each extra card in a sequence also scores a further 500 points.

If the sequence is in the trump suit, or in any suit when no trumps has been declared, coronet is worth double.

Unfulfilled bids If a partnership fails to make its bid, it is penalized for each undertrick by 100 times the value of each trick (entered above the line); but it also scores game points below the line for the number of tricks it took.

For example, if the bidding partnership made a bid of five no trumps (ie 11 tricks) and took only eight tricks (ie it failed by three tricks), scoring would be as follows:
a) $3 \times 50 \times 100 = 15,000$ penalty points;
b) $8 \times 50 = 400$ game points;
c) the opponents score game points in the usual way for the number of tricks they took: $5 \times 50 = 250$ game points.

PREFERENCE

This is a fairly straightforward game usually played for small stakes. Three players take part, each playing for himself.

Cards A standard deck with all the 2s,3s,4s,5s, and 6s removed is used.

The cards are ranked as follows: ace (high), k, q, j, 10, 9, 8, 7 (low).

The suits, in descending order, rank: hearts (known as "preference"), diamonds, clubs, spades.

Objective Each player tries to be the highest bidder and fulfill the contract.

Preliminaries Before the start of play, each player puts an equal agreed number of chips into the pool.

Players must also decide:
a) how much a successful bidder should receive from the pool, depending on the rank of the trump suit; and
b) the payment to be made into the pool by an unsuccessful bidder.

Deal Any player may deal the first hand; thereafter the deal passes clockwise around the table.

The dealer gives ten face-down cards to each player, and also deals two cards face down in the center of the table as the "widow," as follows.

He first deals a packet of three cards to each player, then he deals the widow, then another packet of four cards to each player, and finally a packet of three cards to each player.

Bidding Each player in turn, beginning with the player to the dealer's left, either bids a suit or passes.

By bidding a suit, the player indicates that he intends to win at least six tricks of the possible ten, with the named suit as trumps.

Each player is permitted one bid only, and each bid must be in a higher ranking suit than the previous bid.

If all three players pass in the first round of bidding, there is a second round in which each player can either pass or put chips into the pool. The player putting most chips into the pool then wins the right to name the trump suit; he may also discard any two of his cards and take the widow into his hand.

If a player bids in the first round, the widow is not used.

Play The player to the left of the successful bidder leads to the first trick.

Every other player must follow suit if he can; if he cannot he may play a trump or discard any card.

The highest card in the suit led or the highest trump played takes the trick.

The winner of a trick leads to the next trick, and the game continues until all ten tricks have been taken.

Settlement If the bidder fulfills his bid (takes at least six of the ten tricks) he wins the agreed number of chips from the pool, depending on the rank of the trump suit.

If the bidder fails in his contract, he pays the agreed number of chips into the pool.

Rank of cards in preference

Euchre

Euchre is a derivative of écarté and dates back at least to the 1800s. For a time it was the national game of the United States. It is a game for two to six players depending on the version played; perhaps the most popular form is four-handed euchre.

Tricks bid	♠	♣	♦	♥	No trumps
6	40	60	80	100	120
7	140	160	180	200	220
8	240	260	280	300	320
9	340	360	380	400	420
10	440	460	480	500	520

Rank

Rank of trumps

FOUR-HANDED EUCHRE

Four people play in partnerships of two. Each player sits opposite his partner.

Deck A 32-card deck is used: a standard deck with the 6s, 5s, 4s, 3s, and 2s removed.
Ace ranks high, and 7 low.

Trumps The jack of trumps, called the "right bower," ranks as the highest trump. The other jack of the same color, called the "left bower," ranks second.
For example, if diamonds are trumps, the jack of hearts is the left bower.
Thus the trump suit ranks: rb (high), lb, a, k, q, 10, 9, 8, 7 (low).

Objective Each partnership tries to win the most tricks.

Deal Players draw for first deal, lowest card dealing. Each player is dealt five face-down cards, in packets of three and two.
The dealer then turns the next card face up to indicate trumps.
The deal passes clockwise around the table.

Nominating trumps Each player, beginning with the player to the dealer's left, has the option of accepting the suit of the face-up card as trumps, or refusing it in the hope of nominating a different suit.
To accept, the dealer's opponents say "I order it up;" the dealer's partner says "I assist;" and the dealer says nothing but indicates his acceptance by discarding one card, and adding the face-up card to his hand.
To refuse, the non-dealers say "I pass," and the dealer puts the face-up card under the stock.
Once one player has accepted, play begins.
If all four players refuse, there is a second round in which each player in turn has the right to nominate the trump suit or pass. Once a player has nominated a suit, play begins. If all the players pass, the hands are thrown in and the

cards are dealt by the next dealer.

Play The player who nominated trumps is called the "maker." Before play begins, he may decide to play the hand without his partner, in which case he says "I play alone."
His partner then lays his hand face down on the table. Although he does not play the hand, he still shares in any stakes.
Rules of play are the same as in whist.

Scoring If the maker and his partner win all five tricks, this constitutes a "march," and scores two points. If the maker is playing alone, he scores four points for a march.
If the maker and his partner win four or three tricks, they score one point; if they win fewer than three tricks they are said to be "euchred," and their opponents score two points.

Game is generally five points, but some players prefer to set a target of seven or ten.
Players may use counters to keep the score, but it is customary to use a 3 and a 4 from the unused cards as markers, one card being face up, the other face down, as illustrated:
the 3 exposed with the other card across it signifies one point; 4 exposed with the other card across it is two points; 3 on top of the other card is three points; and 4 on top is four points.

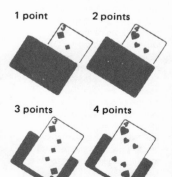

1 point   2 points

3 points   4 points

RAILROAD EUCHRE

In this variation of four-handed euchre, the joker is used as an additional trump, ranking above right bower.

TWO-HANDED EUCHRE

The deck is reduced to 24 cards by discarding the 8s and 7s. Rules are the same as for four-handed euchre, except that there is no need for a declaration to play alone.

THREE-HANDED EUCHRE

In three-handed euchre (also called cutthroat euchre) the maker plays on his own, with the other two players in partnership against him.
The maker scores three points for march; otherwise scoring is the same as in the four-handed game.

CALL-ACE EUCHRE

This is a version for four, five, or six players, each playing for himself.
The rules are the same as for four-handed euchre, with the following differences.

Calling The maker has the right to decide whether to play on his own or with a partner. To choose a partner he says "I call on the ace of . . ." and nominates a suit.
If a player holds the ace named, he plays as the maker's partner, but does not declare his partnership until he plays the ace.
As the ace may in fact not have been dealt, the maker may find he is playing alone!

Scoring A lone maker wins points as follows:
a) march, as many points as there are players;
b) four or three tricks, one point. A partnership wins points as follows:
a) march, two points for each player if there are three or four players, and three points for each player if there are five or six;
b) four or three tricks, each partner scores one point.
If the maker, with or without partner, is euchred, the other players score two points each.

FIVE HUNDRED

Five hundred is a variant of euchre for three players. It has certain similarities to bridge and whist.

Deck As for euchre, plus a joker (giving 33 cards in all).
In the trump suit cards rank, in descending order, as follows: joker, right bower (jack of the trump suit), left bower (other jack of the same color), a, k, q, 10, 9, 8, 7.
In no-trump hands, there are no right and left bowers. The holder of the joker may then nominate it to represent any suit he pleases;
the joker automatically ranks as the highest card of that suit and takes any trick to which it is led or played.

Objective Each player aims to make a contract by bidding and to win enough tricks to fulfill it.

Deal Players cut for deal (king ranks high, ace low, and joker lowest); lowest card deals.
Ten face-down cards are dealt to each player, in packets of either three, two, three, two; or three, three, three, one.
The remaining packet of three cards constitutes the "widow," and is placed face upward on the table.
The deal passes clockwise around the table.

Bidding Each player in turn makes a bid, starting with the player to the dealer's left.
Each player specifies the number of tricks he intends to take and his choice of trumps.
The lowest number of tricks that can be bid is six, and the highest ten.
For bidding the calls are ranked: no-trumps (highest), hearts, diamonds, clubs, spades (lowest).
Any player who passes cannot make a further bid in that round of play.

Widow The player who wins the contract adds the three widow cards to his hand and discards face down any three cards of his choice.

Play Rules of play are the same as in whist.

If a player leads the joker in a no-trump hand, he cannot nominate it to a suit in which he has either declared himself void or that he has failed to follow when able.

The winner of a trick leads to the next trick.

Scoring The players opposing the contract play as partners, but each always scores ten points for each trick he makes. The bidder scores points according to the table, provided he has made his contract.

If he fails to score sufficient tricks, he loses the value of the contract.

Bonuses There are no bonuses for overtricks (ie tricks over the number bid).

However, a player who has made a contract of less than eight clubs but has scored "grand slam" (all ten tricks), receives a total of 250 points.

(There is an optional system for when grand slam is scored after a bid of eight clubs or better. In this system, the successful player scores a bonus equal to the contract. For example, a bid of eight diamonds that results in a grand slam is worth 280 points plus a bonus of 280.)

Players losing contracts may well find their scores going into minus figures.

Game is 500 points. If two players reach this total in the same deal, the player who reached 500 first wins.

TWO-HANDED FIVE HUNDRED

This is played in the same way as the three-handed game, except that a third hand, known as a "dead hand," is dealt. It remains face down throughout the game, and adds a degree of uncertainty to the bidding and play.

FOUR-HANDED FIVE HUNDRED

This game is also played like the three-handed game, but facing players act as partners. The deck is increased to 43 cards by adding the 6s, 5s, and two 4s—one of each color.

ECARTE

Ecarté is a card game for two players that first became popular in France in the early 1800s. Its name is the French word for "discarded."

Deck A 32-card deck is used: a standard 52-card deck with the 6s,5s,4s,3s, and 2s removed.

Cards rank: k (high), q, j, a, 10, 9,8,7.

Objective Each player tries to take tricks and to score points.

Deal Players cut for deal, highest card dealing first (the cards rank as in play). The dealer gives each player five face-down cards, in packets of either two then three, or three then two. Whichever system is used must be kept throughout the game.

The deal passes clockwise around the table.

Trumps The eleventh card is placed face up beside the stock and indicates trumps.

Exchanging cards The non-dealer may propose an exchange of cards. To do this he says "Cards".

If the dealer accepts, the non-dealer exchanges as many cards as he wishes for cards drawn from the stock. The dealer may then do likewise.

The non-dealer may repeat the proposal, and players go on exchanging cards until the stock is exhausted. But if the dealer refuses at any time, by saying "Play," there is no more exchanging.

If the non-dealer does not wish to exchange at any time, he says "I play."

The dealer cannot propose an exchange.

Play The non-dealer leads first. Players must follow suit if they can, and may trump if they cannot.

A player must always take a trick if he can. The winner of a trick leads to the next trick.

Scoring is as follows:

a) "point" or "the trick" (three tricks won), scores one point;

b) "the vole" (all five tricks won), scores two points;

c) king turned up to indicate trumps, scores one point for the dealer; and

d) king of trumps held in the hand, scores one point if it is, declared before the holder plays his first card.

Game is five points.

Penalties If a player has refused to exchange and fails to make at least three tricks (point), his opponent scores an extra point if he makes point.

There is no penalty if the opponent scores vole.

Five hundred

Deal

Player 2

Player 1   Player 3

Widow

Ecarté

Deal

Player 1   Player 2

Trumps

Stock

NAPOLEON

Also called nap, this game is in some ways similar to euchre. Any number of players from two to seven may take part. There are no partnerships.

Deck A standard 52-card deck is used; ace ranks high.

Objective Each player aims to contract a bid and take tricks to fulfill it.

Deal Players cut for deal, highest card dealing first. Each player is dealt five face-down cards, one at a time. The stock is then placed face down on the table. The deal passes in clockwise rotation.

Bidding Beginning with the player to the dealer's left, each player can either pass or bid two, three, four, or "Napoleon" —indicating the number of tricks he intends to win. (Napoleon signifies five tricks.)

Each bid must be higher than the previous bid, and the player with the highest bid becomes the bidder.

There is only one round of bidding.

Trumps The bidder leads to the first trick, and the suit of his opening card denotes trumps.

Play is the same as in whist.

Scoring Napoleon is played for stakes, the usual ones being:

two units for a bid of two; three units for three; four units for four; and ten for Napoleon.

If the bidder wins his contract, each of the other players pays him the stake. If he fails to win his contract, he pays each of the other players the stake. If he fails on a bid of Napoleon, he pays only half the stake.

Optional bids The following optional bids are sometimes used.

a) "Wellington" is a declaration to win all five tricks at double stakes. It cannot be called unless Napoleon has already been called.

b) "Blücher" overcalls Wellington, and is for five tricks at triple stakes.

c) "Misère" or "misery" is a declaration to lose every trick. In the bidding it ranks between three and four, and carries the same stakes as three. There are no trumps in this bid.

PURCHASE NAP

The rules of purchase nap are the same as for Napoleon, except that each player may exchange any number of cards for fresh ones from the stock, on payment of one unit for each card.

The payments are put in a kitty, won by the first player to make a bid of Napoleon.

SEVEN-CARD NAP

In seven-card nap, each player receives seven cards. Play is the same as for Napoleon, but bids of Wellington and Blücher are not permitted.

The order of bids with their stakes are as follows:

three bids, a stake of three; four, stake of four; nap and misère (optional), stake of 10; six, stake of 18; and seven, stake of 24.

Players losing nap, misère, six, or seven pay half stakes.

THREE-CARD LOO

Loo, or lanterloo as it is sometimes called, was once one of the most widely played card games in Europe. It has several variations but is always played for stakes.

Players Three or more people can play, but the best number is about six.

Deck A standard 52-card deck is used. Ace ranks high.

Objective Each player tries to win at least one trick.

Deal Players cut for deal, lowest card dealing.

Each player is dealt three face-down cards, one at a time.

An extra hand known as a "miss" is also dealt, as either the first or the last hand of each deal.

The top card of the remaining cards is turned face up and denotes trumps.

The deal passes clockwise around the table.

Pool In an optional opening deal called a "single," no miss is dealt, and only the dealer puts three counters into a pool. In subsequent deals, or if no single has been played, a miss is dealt and each player contributes three counters to the pool.

The choice Beginning with the player to the dealer's left, each player in turn chooses one of the following:

a) to play with the cards he holds;

b) to throw in his own cards and play with the miss; or

c) to pass.

To indicate their choice, players say "I play," "I take the miss," or "I pass," as appropriate.

If a player passes, he throws in his cards and takes no further part in that deal. If every player passes, the dealer takes the pool.

If only one player decides to play but has not taken the miss, the dealer must play him, using the cards in the miss. If the dealer loses, he does not pay, nor is he paid if he wins.

If only one player decides to play and has taken the miss, the dealer may either play him with standard scoring, or just let him take the pool.

Play The first player to choose to play leads to the first trick, with his highest trump if he has one.

Each player who did not pass plays a card to each trick.

If possible, he must:

a) follow suit; and

b) play a higher card of the leading suit than any already played to that trick.

If a player cannot follow suit, he should trump the trick with a higher trump than any already played to that trick; if he cannot do this, he may discard.

The winner of a trick must lead with a trump if possible.

Scoring The winner of each trick takes one third of the pool.

Looing A player who has not won a trick is said to be "looed."

In limited loo, a looed player pays an agreed amount (usually three counters) into the pool.

In unlimited loo, he pays as many counters as there were in the pool at the beginning of the hand.

Penalties A player is also looed if he breaches the rules, including:

a) playing out of turn;

b) looking at the miss without taking it;

c) failing to take a trick when possible; and

d) failing to lead the ace of trumps when holding it.

Variations

a) The trump card is not turned up until a player cannot follow suit.

b) If a player is dealt three trumps, he collects the pool. The hands are thrown in, and the cards are shuffled and dealt for the next round.

FIVE-CARD LOO

This variant is played in the same way as three-card loo, except for the following changes.

Deal Each player receives five cards.

Pool Contributions to the pool are five instead of three counters.

Miss is never dealt.

Exchanges Each player may exchange up to five cards for the same number of cards drawn from the stock. A player who exchanges must then play his hand.

Pam The jack of clubs, called "pam," ranks as the highest trump regardless of suit. If a player leads the ace of trumps and says "Pam be civil," the pam cannot be played to that trick.

Flushes are five cards of the same suit, or four of the same suit plus pam. The holder of a flush exposes it before play and wins the pool. Each of the other players is then looed unless he also holds a flush or flush with pam.

If there is more than one flush, a trump flush wins over one in a plain suit, and if there is a clash between plain suit flushes, the highest card wins. If two or more plain suit flushes are equal, the pool is divided.

Blaze This is an optional winning hand, entirely made up of court cards. The same rules of precedence apply as with flushes, and a blaze outranks a flush.

IRISH LOO

This is played like three-card loo, with the following differences.

a) Miss is not dealt.

b) Exchanging is carried out in the same way as in the five-card game.

c) "Club law:" if clubs are trumps every player must enter the game.

SPOIL FIVE

Spoil five is similar to loo but has an unusual and complex ranking system. It is especially popular in the Republic of Ireland.

Players Two or more people can play, but the game is best played with five or six. Each person plays for himself.

Deck A standard deck of playing cards is used. The cards are ranked, in descending order, as follows.

Spades and clubs
Plain suits (ie non-trump): k,q,j,a,2,3,4,5,6,7,8,9,10.
Trump suits: 5,j,a of hearts, ace of spades or clubs, k,q,2,3, 4,6,7,8,9,10.

Diamonds
Plain suit: k,q,j,10,9,8,7,6,5,4, 3,2,a.
Trump suit: 5,j,a of hearts, a of diamonds, k,q,10,9,8,7,6,4,3, 2.

Hearts
Plain suit: k,q,j,10,9,8,7,6,5,4, 3,2.
Trump suit: 5,j,a,k,q,10,9,8,7, 6,4,3,2.

Note that the ace of hearts is always the third-best trump, regardless of suit; the 5 of the trump suit is highest; and the jack of the trump suit second-highest.

Objective Each player tries to win three tricks and to prevent anyone else from doing so.

Deal Players draw for deal, using standard ranking with ace high and 2 low. Lowest card deals.
Five face-down cards are dealt to each player in packets of two then three, or vice versa. The next card is turned face up to indicate trumps. The deal passes clockwise around the table.

Pool Each player puts an agreed number of counters into the pool. It is won by a player taking three tricks in one hand.

Exchanging If the face-up card denoting the trump suit is an ace, the dealer may exchange it for a card in his hand before the first card is led. This is called "robbing." If a player has been dealt the ace of trumps he may, if he wishes, exchange any card in his hand for the face-up card. If he does not exchange a card, he must announce that he has the ace at his first turn of play —otherwise the ace becomes the lowest-ranking trump for that round, even if it is an ace of hearts.

Play The player to the left of the dealer leads to the first trick and the winner of each trick leads to the next.
Rules of play are the same as for whist, with the following differences.
If a card of a plain suit is led, a player may either trump or follow suit. He may discard another plain suit card only if he can neither follow suit nor trump.
If a card of the trump suit is led, a player must follow suit if he can. He need not play any of the top three trumps if the leading card was a lower trump—holding back a card in this way is called "reneging."

Jinxing A player who wins three tricks may take the pool and the hand ends.
Alternatively, he may call "Jinx," implying that he will try to win the remaining two tricks. Play continues, and if he wins the extra two tricks he takes the pool, plus a sum from each player equal to his original contribution to the pot. If he does not make both tricks he loses the pool and the hand counts as a "spoil."

Spoil is when nobody wins three tricks, or a winner fails to win all five after jinxing. The cards are dealt for a new hand but only the new dealer contributes to the pot. Only when the pot is won do all the players contribute to a new pot.

FORTY-FIVE

In this variant of spoil five only an even number of players can take part, divided into two equal and opposing sides. There is no pool.

Scoring The winning partnership scores as follows:
a) three tricks, 5 points; and
b) five tricks, 10 points; or
alternatively:
a) three tricks, 5 points;
b) four tricks, 15 points;
c) five tricks, 25 points.
Game is 45 points, and the first side to reach it wins.

AUCTION FORTY-FIVE

Auction forty-five is very popular in parts of Canada. Its basic rules are the same as for spoil five, with the following variations.

Players Four or six people play in partnerships of two or three respectively. Each player sits between two players of the opposing side.

Bidding The player to the left of the dealer bids first, followed by each player in turn to his left.
The bids, indicating the number of points each side is contracted to make, are 5,10, 15,20,25, and 30. Each bid must outbid the previous bid. The dealer has the option of "holding" ie outbidding the previous bid without increasing it.
Each of the other players who bid may then bid again; but the dealer has the option of holding a second time.

Trumps are nominated by the highest bidder.

Discards Each player may exchange as many cards as he likes for cards drawn from the top of the stock.

Play The player to the left of the highest bidder leads first.

Scoring Each trick counts five points, and the highest trump in play scores five extra points to whichever side takes it.
If a side fulfills its contract it scores the number of points bid plus the points scored with its tricks.
If it fails, it loses the number of points bid.
The side that did not make the contract scores all the points it makes in play.
Game is 120 points.

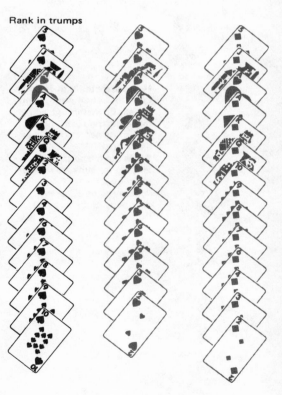

Spoil five
Rank in plain suits
Spades and clubs — Hearts — Diamonds

Rank in trumps

Contract bridge

For very many people, contract bridge is the most fascinating of card games: it is played in houses, clubs, and tournaments throughout the world. Its origins can be traced back some 400 years to the development of whist in England, but it was only in 1896 that the game of bridge itself evolved. In 1925 contract bridge was developed, and within a few years it was by far the most popular form of the game.

GENERAL
Cards A standard deck of 52 cards is used. By convention a second deck, with contrasting backs, is also used, so that while one player deals another can shuffle the alternate deck in readiness for the next deal.
The cards rank: ace (high) through 2 (low). The 2 is commonly called a "deuce," and the 3 a "trey."

Players As in whist, there are four players, each pair forming a partnership. Partners sit opposite each other. One partnership is usually called North-South, the other East-West.
Objective Each partnership aims to win a "rubber," by winning the most points in the best of three games.
A game is won by scoring 100 points, earned by taking tricks that have been contracted for.

Honors

Rank of suits

Rank of cards

Honors are the high-ranking cards in the trump suit, from the ace down through and including the 10. In "no trump" games, the four aces are honors.
Suits For the purpose of bidding the suits are ranked as follows:
spades (highest), hearts, diamonds, clubs (lowest).

The draw At the beginning of a bridge game, one deck is spread out face down on the table, and each player draws one card from the deck.
The two players who draw the highest cards form one partnership; the other two players form the second. The player with the highest card becomes first dealer and chooses his seating position; his partner sits opposite him. If cards of the same denomination appear on the draw, they are ranked according to suit, as for bidding.
Shuffle and cut The player to the left of the dealer shuffles the deck; the player to the dealer's right cuts the deck.
As the cards are being dealt, the alternate deck is shuffled by the dealer's partner.
The deal begins with the player to the dealer's left. The cards are dealt in a clockwise direction, one at a time and face down, until each player including the dealer has 13 cards.

BIDDING
The auction begins once players have had a chance to study their cards. It opens with the dealer and continues in clockwise rotation. Each player, according to his hand, makes a "call," that may be a bid, pass, double, or redouble. If a player passes, he may still make another call at a later stage in the bidding. But when a bid, double, or redouble is followed by three passes in succession, the auction ends. If there are four passes at the opening of bidding, one from each player, the cards are "thrown in" to the center of the table and shuffled. A new hand is then dealt by the next dealer.
A pass indicates that a player does not choose to make any other call at that time in the bidding.

A bid is a statement of a number and a trumps suit, eg "three clubs," or "five no trumps." It offers an undertaking that if that suit is trumps (or if there are "no trumps") the bidding player's partnership will take a certain number of tricks.
Bidding refers to the number of "odd" (ie additional) tricks that a bidder undertakes to make over six tricks.
A bid of "one club," for instance, means that a player thinks that his partnership can make seven tricks in all, if clubs are trumps.
A bid of "four no trumps" offers the undertaking to make ten tricks in all, if no suit is trumps.
Continuing the bidding As the auction continues, each successive bid must be higher than any preceding bid— either by calling a greater number of tricks or by naming a higher ranking suit.
For instance, a bid of "two spades" is higher than two hearts, diamonds, or clubs. A no trump call ranks above all suits. So, for example, a bid of "two no trumps" is higher than two spades. The next player to bid would have to bid at least "three clubs."

The contract The highest bid of the auction becomes the "contract." The players in the partnership making that bid must, in play, make as many tricks as they have contracted for, or more. Their opponents have only to prevent them from doing this—it does not matter what they themselves have bid.

The first six tricks taken by the contracted bidders are commonly referred to as "making the book."

Slam The maximum number of tricks in any played hand is 13. This gives a maximum bid of "seven," when one side believes it can take all the tricks: the book (of six), plus seven odd tricks.

If a side succeeds in bidding and winning 13 tricks, this is known as a "grand slam." A "small slam" occurs if a side bids and wins a total of 12 tricks.

Doubling If a player says "Double" after any of his opponents' bids, it means that he believes he could prevent them making their bid, if it became the contract.

A bid that has been doubled need not become the contract: it can be overbid in the usual way, by either partnership. If, however, it does become the contract and succeeds, the contracting players' score is doubled. Should the bidders "go down" (ie not make their contract) the side that doubled gets twice the score that it would otherwise have had.

Redoubling If a bid has been doubled, either player of the bidding partnership may say "Redouble." This confirms his confidence in the bid, and —as in doubling—the scoring is affected whether or not the contract is made (see the section on scoring).

A bid that has been redoubled can be overbid in the usual way.

The declarer The player in the contracting side who first made a bid in the trump suit of the contract (spades, hearts, diamonds, clubs, or no trumps), is referred to as the "declarer." He plays both hands of the contracting partnership's game.

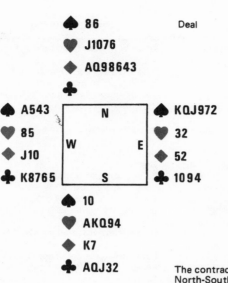

Deal

♠ 86
♥ J1076
♦ AQ98643
♣

♠ A543   ♠ KQJ972
♥ 85   ♥ 32
♦ J10   ♦ 52
♣ K8765   ♣ 1094

N
W   E
S

♠ 10
♥ AKQ94
♦ K7
♣ AQJ32

The contract is four hearts North-South have made the contract and South is declarer

S	W	N	E
1♣	double	1♦	1♠
2♥	2♠	3♦	double
3♥	pass	pass	3♠
4♥	pass	pass	pass

PLAY

A trick consists of four cards, one played from each player's hand, in clockwise rotation. The player who must play first is called the "lead."

The lead The opening lead is held by the player to the dealer's left. He plays the first card after the bidding ends. After this, the winner of each trick makes the next lead.

A player may lead any card, and the other three players must follow suit if possible. If a player cannot follow suit, he may play any other card in his hand.

Winning the trick If none of the four cards is a trump, the trick is won by the highest card played in the suit led.

If one or more of the four cards is a trump, the trick is won by the highest trump.

No trump When a "no trump" bid becomes the contract, all suits have equal rank and the highest card in the suit led always wins the trick.

Dummy As soon as the opening lead has been made, declarer's partner lays down his cards face up on the table, sorted out by suit, with trumps to his right.

The exposed cards, and declarer's partner himself, are referred to as "dummy" for that hand.

Only declarer can choose the cards to play for the dummy hand. The dummy partner may not participate in that hand, other than to physically play a specified card at declarer's request.

Plays from dummy must be in correct order of rotation, ie following a card played by the player to declarer's left. Declarer must play a card in dummy that he touches (except when rearranging the cards or touching a card next to the one to be played).

Gathering won tricks is done by either player of the side winning the trick.

The four cards are gathered together and placed face down on the table.

All declarer's and dummy's tricks are placed in front of declarer; all the opponents' tricks are placed in front of one opponent.

The arrangement of gathered tricks must show clearly how many tricks have been won and in which order. Common procedure is to bunch the first six of declarer's tricks into one group, so that it is clear how many odd tricks have been made.

A trick may be inspected by the declarer or by either opponent, until a player of the inspecting side has led or played to the following trick.

Laying out dummy's hand

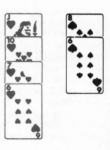
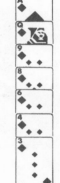

SCORING

It is important to master the scoring in contract bridge as it strongly affects the game's strategy.

Both sides should keep score in case of disagreement.

A scoring pad has a central vertical line dividing "we" (one partnership) from "they" (its opponents).

A horizontal line is initially drawn across the scoring pad, and a partnership can score points either "below the line" or "above the line."

Trick points are entered below the line. Only declarer's side can score trick points on a hand, and only if the contract is made. Only the odd tricks contracted for can be scored below the line.

Trick points show each side's progress toward winning the current game.

Premium points are scored above the line, and may be scored by both sides in any hand. They are won for:
overtricks;
successful doubling or redoubling;
bidding and making a slam;
having a certain number of honors cards in one hand in the deal; or
winning the final game of a rubber.

Undertricks If declarer's side fails to make the contract, the number of tricks it has failed by are known as "undertricks."

These are credited to the opponents' premium points and scored above the line.

Vulnerable A partnership is "vulnerable" if it has won its first game toward the rubber. (It is therefore possible for both partnerships to be vulnerable.)

Winning a game The first side to reach a score of 100 or more, either in one or in several hands, wins the game. A horizontal line is then drawn below the trick scores of both sides.

Trick scores for the next game are entered below this line, both sides beginning again from zero.

Winning the rubber When one side has won two games, the rubber ends.

This side earns 700 premium points if its opponents have won no game, and 500 premium points if its opponents have won one game.

All trick and premium points are then totaled, and the side with the higher total wins the rubber.

The back score indicates an individual player's standing. It is used in any competition in which partners rotate.

After a rubber, the difference between the two sides' final scores is calculated by subtracting the lower from the higher.

This difference is rounded to the nearest 100 (50 and above become 100), and divided by 100. For example, 753 becomes 800, giving 8. Each player of the winning partnership is then given a score of plus 8 and each opponent a score of minus 8. In subsequent rubbers, with different partnerships, the same procedure is followed. The player with the highest plus score at the end is the overall winner.

Contract bridge scoring table

Trick score: scored by declarer below the line

	♣	♦	♥	♠	NT
First trick over six bid and made	20	20	30	30	40
Subsequent tricks bid and made	20	20	30	30	30
Doubling doubles trick score					
Redoubling doubles doubled score					

Premium score: scored by declarer above the line

	Not vulnerable	Vulnerable
Small slam	500	750
Grand slam	1000	1500
Each overtrick undoubled	Trick value	Trick value
Each overtrick doubled	100	200
Each overtrick redoubled	200	400
Making a doubled or redoubled contract	50	50

Rubber, game, and partscore: scored above the line

	Points
For winning rubber, if opponents have won no game	700
For winning rubber, if opponents have won one game	500
For having won one game in an unfinished rubber	300
For having the only partscore in an unfinished rubber	50

Honors: scored by either side above the line

	Points
Four trump honors in one hand	100
Five trump honors in one hand	150
Four aces in one hand, no trump contract	150

Undertricks: scored by opponents above the line

	Undoubled	Doubled	Redoubled
First trick, not vulnerable	50	100	200
Subsequent tricks	50	200	400
First trick, vulnerable	100	200	400
Subsequent tricks	100	300	600

Explanation of scoring diagrams

a) "We" score 70 trick points.

b) "We" score 30 trick points and 150 premium points. "We" win the first game and are now vulnerable.

c) "We" go under by two tricks. "They" score 200 undertrick points.

d) "They" score 60 trick points and 150 premium points.

WE	THEY
70	

WE	THEY
150	
70	
30	

WE	THEY
150	200
70	
30	

WE	THEY
	150
150	200
70	
30	
	60

DUPLICATE CONTRACT BRIDGE

Duplicate contract bridge is very popular among advanced bridge players. It is the only form played in international tournaments. All groups of players are presented, in turn, with the same deal of cards. In this way, the game relies more on skill than on luck of the deal.

Equipment:
1) one table for each deal to be played in the tournament;
2) the same number of duplicate boards or trays;
3) one deck of cards for each board.

Players Competing units may be individuals, pairs, or teams of four or six, depending on the nature of the tournament.

In individual events, partnerships change during the tournament; in team events, partnerships change at half-time; and in pairs matches, the same partnerships are preserved throughout.

A duplicate board is used at each table. Each board has four pockets, an arrow or label indicating North's side, and markers indicating the dealer and the vulnerability or otherwise of partnerships.

Before the tournament the boards are arranged so that a quarter have North-South vulnerable, a quarter East-West vulnerable, a quarter both pairs vulnerable, and a quarter neither pair vulnerable. Within each category, the position of dealer is distributed equally between the pairs.

Basic procedure Each board maintains the same deal of cards throughout the tournament.

The boards and players move from table to table in a specified way.

The tournament ends, according to the system used, either:
when all North-South players have met all East-West players; or
when all players have played with and against all other players.

Deal For the first hand at each board, the designated dealer shuffles and deals the cards in the usual way.

Thereafter, following each hand, this original deal is preserved. Each player's cards are placed in the appropriate board pocket, in readiness for the next set of players.

The auction for any hand takes place in the usual way, commencing with the player indicated as dealer.

If all players pass, there is no redeal.

Play on any hand proceeds as in contract bridge, except that after each trick is completed the cards are not gathered together.

Each player takes back his card, and turns it face down on the table in front of him. He points the card lengthwise toward the partners who won the trick; this allows players to keep track of the number of tricks won by each side.

Scoring a hand No points are given for winning a rubber. If a side bids and makes a contract that gives it a game (100 trick points), it gets 500 premium points if vulnerable, 300 if not.

Additional premium points for making a grand slam are 1500 if vulnerable, 1000 if not; and for a small slam 750 if vulnerable, 500 if not.

If a side bids and makes a contract less than game, it gets 50 premium points.

A score made on one board cannot be carried forward to affect scoring on the next.

Unless cumulative tournament scoring is used, no premium points are given for holding honors in one hand.

Scoring the tournament
a) Match point procedure is always used if the competing units are individuals. It can also be used for pairs.

The comparison is between scores made at the same board, ie success in playing the same deal.

Each score is given two points for each lower score made in the same position on that board, and one point for each exactly equal score.

Each individual in an individual event receives points for the score made by his partnership. The individual or pair with the highest number of match points wins the competition.

b) International match point (imp) scoring is usually used for teams. Each partnership's surplus (or deficit) of points over its opponents is calculated for each hand, and added together at the end to give a team total. This is then converted into match points on the basis of an established scale.

c) Cumulative (total point) scoring is still sometimes used for team competitions.

AUCTION BRIDGE

A forerunner of contract bridge, auction bridge evolved from the game of whist.

Except for the scoring—which greatly affects the strategy of the game—its rules are as for contract bridge.

Major differences The two major differences in scoring are as follows:
1) In auction bridge there is no concept of vulnerability. If one partnership has won a game there is no extra penalty (as in contract bridge) for failure to make a contract.
2) All odd tricks, whether contracted for or not, are scored "below the line." They contribute to winning the game, provided that declarer has succeeded in making the minimum number of tricks named in the contract.

Trick points

	♣	♦	♥	♠	NT
Undoubled	6	7	8	9	10
Doubled	12	14	16	18	20
Redoubled	24	28	32	36	40

Game The first side to score 30 points below the line wins a game. A horizontal line is drawn across the scoring pad, as in contract bridge, to indicate that a game has been completed.

Rubber The first side to win two games out of three wins the rubber and is awarded an additional 250 points.

Honors If either side has three or more honors in the trump suit (or aces at no trumps) then—whether or not that side is declarer—the following scores are given above the line:

three honors or aces, 30 points;
four honours or aces, divided 40 points;
five honors, divided, 50 points;
four honors, one hand, 80 points;
five honors, divided four to one, 90 points;
four aces, one hand 100 points;
five honors, one hand, 100 points.

Bonuses 50 points are given above the line if a doubled contract is bid for and made.
In addition, declarer's side gets 50 points for each trick in excess of the contract.
If declarer succeeds in making a redoubled contract, both the bonuses mentioned above are raised to 100 points each.

Undertricks If declarer's side fails to make its contract, the opponents are given the following points (above the line) for each undertrick:
undoubled contract, 50;
doubled contract, 100;
redoubled contract, 200.

Slams If either side makes a small slam (12 tricks), it receives 50 points above the line—regardless of the bidded contract.
If a grand slam (13 tricks) is won, 100 points are awarded.

Hearts

Penalty cards

Hearts is one of the avoidance games—meaning that it is based on the principle of not taking penalty cards rather than of winning tricks. It evolved in the nineteenth century, since when many interesting variants have appeared.

HEARTS: BASIC GAME

Players Three to seven people can play. There are no partnerships.

Cards A standard deck of 52 playing cards is used.
2s are discarded as follows:
one 2 with three players;
none with four players;
two with five players;
three with seven players.
If possible, the 2 of hearts is not discarded.
The cards rank normally, with ace high. There are no trumps.

Choice of first dealer is by low cut (see p 80).

Deal The dealer deals out all the cards one at a time and face down, beginning with the player to his left and going clockwise.

Play The player to the dealer's left leads to the first trick. Thereafter the winner of one trick leads to the next.
Each player after the lead must follow suit if he can. If he cannot, he may play any card he likes.
A hand ends when all the hearts suit has appeared in play.

Revoking If a player fails to follow suit when he is able to, he may correct his mistake without penalty if he does so before the trick is picked up. Otherwise he scores 13 penalty points and the hand ends. No other players can score penalty points on that hand.

Scoring Each player scores one penalty point for each card of the hearts suit contained in tricks taken by him.

Continuing play After each hand, the deal passes one player to the left.

The winner is the player with the fewest penalty points after an agreed number of hands.
Alternatively, the winner is the player with the fewest penalty points when one player reaches a set number of points (eg 50 points).

SPOT HEARTS

Also called chip hearts, this game is played in the same way as basic hearts except that each heart card counts as many penalty points as its face value. The king counts 13, the queen 12, and the jack 11. (Almost any hearts variant can be scored in this way.)

13 points   12 points   11 points

BLACK LADY HEARTS

In this popular version the queen of spades is an extra penalty card, scoring 13 penalty points. Each heart card counts one penalty point. Sometimes it is ruled that a player must take the first possible opportunity to discard the queen of spades.

13 points

GREEK HEARTS

In this variant the penalties are the same as for black lady hearts, but play and scoring differ in the following ways.

Exchanging Before play begins, each player, after looking at his cards, passes three cards of his choice face down to the player to his right. No player may look at the cards he is receiving until after he has passed on his own cards.

Scoring Each heart is scored as in spot hearts, and the queen of hearts counts 50 penalty points. Except that if one player takes all the penalty cards he does not score at all for this hand and instead all the other players score 150 penalty points each.

50 points

DOMINO HEARTS

The penalty values are as in the basic hearts game, but play varies as follows.

Deal Six cards are dealt to each player, and the remainder are placed face down to form the stock.

Play If a player cannot follow suit he draws cards one at a time from the top of the stock until he can follow suit. Drawn cards of other suits remain in his hand to be played later. When the stock is exhausted players may discard as in the basic hearts game.
Each player drops out when he has played all his cards. The last player left in scores one penalty point for each heart card left in his hand as well as for those in his tricks.
If a player wins a trick with his last card, the lead passes to the next player to the left.
The winner is the player with the lowest score when one player reaches 31 points.

JOKER HEARTS

In this hearts game, the 2 of hearts is discarded and a joker used.
The joker ranks between the 10 and jack of hearts, and wins any trick in which it is played, regardless of the suit led, unless a higher heart also appears in that trick—in which case the higher heart takes the trick.
A high heart played when the joker is not played is a discard as usual, unless hearts were led.
The joker counts five penalty points.

5 points

HEARTSETTE

In this variant of hearts a widow hand is dealt face down in the center of the table.
The 2 of spades is not used if there are three or four players.
The size of the widow depends on the number of players:
with three or four players, three cards;
with five players, two cards;
with six players, four cards.
All other cards are dealt out to the players.
Play and penalties are as in the basic hearts game except that the winner of the first trick adds the widow to it and scores penalty points for any penalty cards it contains.

TWO-HANDED HEARTS

This is an adaptation of the basic game for two players.
It is played like basic hearts except that 13 cards are dealt to each player and the remainder are placed face down to form a stock.
After each trick the winner takes the top card from the stock and the loser takes the next card.
The game continues until all the cards have been played.

BLACK MARIA

This very popular version is also known as Slippery Anne. Play is as for basic hearts except as follows.

Penalty cards As well as hearts (one point for each card), there are three penalty cards:
the ace of spades, seven points;
the king of spades, 10 points;
the queen of spades (Black Maria), 13 points.

Exchanging occurs before play as in Greek hearts.

Each hand ends when all the penalty cards have been played.

7 points   10 points   13 points

Grand

Grand is a combination of whist, euchre, and hearts (see pages 82, 86, and 94 respectively). Each hand is played like one of these three or a fourth option, depending on the choice of the bidder.

KNAVES
In this game the principles of avoidance games and normal trick-taking games are combined.
Players Knaves is a game for three players.
Cards A standard deck of 52 cards is used.
Objective Each player tries to win tricks without taking any jacks.
Deal and play are as for whist.
Tactics Each player plays for himself, but if one player is winning the other two often act as a temporary partnership to try and reduce his lead.
Scoring At the end of each hand, each player scores one point for each trick he has taken.
If he has taken any jacks, he then subtracts points as follows:
jack of hearts, four points;
jack of diamonds, three;
jack of clubs, two;
jack of spades, one.
A player may have a minus score.
The winner is the first to reach 20 plus points.

POLIGNAC
This is another game in which players try to avoid taking tricks with jacks in them.
Players Four to six can play.
Cards For four players a standard deck without the 2s,3s,4s,5s, and 6s is used. For five or six players the two black 7s are also removed.
Deal and play are as in whist except that there are no trumps.
Scoring At the end of each hand, each player scores penalty points for each jack he has taken, as follows:
one point each for the jacks of hearts, diamonds, and clubs;
two points for the jack of spades (polignac).
"General" A player may decide to try and take all the tricks in a hand. This is known as general, and the player must announce his intention before the lead to the first trick.
If he succeeds, all the other players score five penalty points.
If he fails, he scores five penalty points and the jacks score penalty points in the usual way against the players who take them.
The winner is the player with the fewest points after an agreed number of hands.

Players Four people play, in partnerships of two.
Deck A standard deck of playing cards is used. The rank of the cards depends on the type of game being played.
Objective Each partnership aims to make a contract and fulfill it.
Deal Players cut for the deal (ace ranks low), and highest card deals. Cards are dealt in a clockwise direction, one at a time and face down, until each player has 13 cards.
Bidding Each player in turn, starting with the player to the left of the dealer, has one chance to either bid or pass. The bids are five and multiples of five, and indicate the number of points the bidder expects to score in that hand if he is the highest bidder.
At the end of bidding the highest bidder names which game (whist, grand, euchre, or hearts) will be played for that round.
If the first three players pass, the dealer must make a bid.
General play Unlike whist, euchre, and hearts, the bidder always leads to the first trick.

Whist
If whist is chosen, the bidder names the trump suit. Play is the same as in whist.
Scoring Each trick more than six counts five points. For example, on a bid of 25 the bidding partnership needs to take 11 tricks to score.
If the bidding partnership makes a grand slam (winning all 13 tricks), it scores for all 13 tricks, making 65 points. No points are scored for honors.
Setbacks If the bidding partnership fails to make its bid, the entire amount of its bid is deducted from its previous score.
In addition, the opposing partnership wins five points for each trick that it takes above six tricks.

Grand
If grand is chosen, play is the same as in whist, except that there are no trumps.

Scoring Each trick more than six scores nine points. A grand slam also scores 40 points for the first six tricks, making a total of 103 points. If either partnership makes a grand slam, it wins the game—regardless of its score.
Setbacks are scored in the same way as in the whist option, except that each trick counts nine points.
The opponents also win nine points for each trick they take over six tricks.

Euchre
Euchre can only be chosen on a bid of 25 or less. The bidder names the trump suit. Each player then discards eight cards face down—he may not keep any trumps lower than 8. Play is the same as in euchre with the following differences.
If the bidder calls less than 20 he cannot play alone. If he bid 20, he may choose whether or not to play alone. If he bid 25, he must play alone.
If playing alone, the bidder may exchange any one of his cards for the best card in his partner's hand. The bidder's partner puts his cards face down on the table.
Scoring Points are scored by either partnership as follows:
a) three tricks, 5 points;
b) four tricks, 10 points;
c) five tricks if made in partnership, 20 points;
d) five tricks if made by lone hand, 25 points.
Setbacks If the bidding partnership fails to make its bid, the amount bid plus 20 points is subtracted from its score.
If a lone hand fails to make his bid, he loses twice the amount bid.

Hearts
Hearts can only be selected on a bid of 50 or less.
Play is the same as in hearts.
Scoring If the bidding partnership does not take any tricks containing hearts, it wins 50 points.

Setbacks If the partners do take tricks containing hearts, the amount bid plus one point for each heart taken is subtracted from their score. The opponents are set back one point for each heart they take.
Heart bid option If the first bidder passes when the dealer's partnership has a score of less than 70, it is generally regarded as an indication that he is prepared to play hearts.
If the dealer's side has 70 or more points, the first bidder may determine that hearts are played by leading a heart and saying "Hearts."

Game is 100 points, but the game may finish at the end of a time limit or after a set number of rounds.
Final result The scores at the end of play are used to calculate the final result.
1) The difference between 100 and the lowest score at the end of play stands as a separate score for the side with the highest score at the end of play.
2) The difference between the number of times each side has been setback is multiplied by ten. This stands as a separate score for the side with the fewer setbacks.
3) The result of this final scoring indicates the winner.
For example, if at the end of play side A has a score of 80 with seven setbacks and side B has a score of 60 with five setbacks, then the final result is calculated as follows:
1) 100 − 60 = 40 (awarded to side A);
2) (7 − 5) × 10 = 20 (awarded to side B);
3) therefore side A wins with a total of 40 against side B's total of 20.

Seven up

Seven up is a card game for two or three players that originated in England in the seventeenth century. Other names by which it is known are all fours, high-low-jack, and old sledge.

 4 points   3 points   2 points   1 point   10 points

BASIC SEVEN UP

Deck A standard deck of cards is used. Ace ranks high.

Objective Each player tries to score seven points and so win the game.

Deal Players cut for the deal, highest card dealing. Each player is dealt six face-down cards in packets of three.
The next card is turned face up and denotes trumps, and if it is a jack the dealer scores one point.
The deal passes clockwise around the table.

Trumps If the player to the dealer's left is happy to play with the trump suit shown, he says "Stand" and play begins. Should he prefer to play another trump suit he says "I beg," and the dealer can choose whether or not to change trumps.
If the dealer chooses to keep the same trump suit he says "Take one" to the player, who scores one point. Play then commences.
If the dealer agrees to change the trump suit, he sets aside the face-up card, deals a further three cards to each player, and turns the next card face up to denote trumps. If this card shows a different suit from the first face-up card, play begins with this suit as trumps—and if it is a jack, the dealer scores one point.
Should the face-up card be the same suit again, however, another three cards are dealt to each player and a third card is turned face up. This procedure is repeated until a new trump suit is determined, and the dealer scores one point for each jack that is turned up, provided it is not of the same suit initially rejected.
If the deck is exhausted before a new trump suit is turned up, the entire deck is shuffled and redealt.

Discarding If the trump suit has been changed, each player discards face down a sufficient number of cards to reduce his hand to six.

Play is the same as in whist.

Scoring At the end of each round the tricks are turned face up for scoring. Points are scored as follows:
a) "high," one point for the player dealt the highest trump;
b) "low," one point for the player dealt the lowest trump;
c) "jack," one point for the player who takes the jack of trumps in a trick;
d) "game," one point for the player who takes the highest total value of cards in tricks. The cards are valued as follows:
four for each ace;
three for each king;
two for each queen;
one for each jack;
ten for each 10.

Game The first player to make seven points wins the game. If more than one player reaches seven points in the same hand, the points are counted in the following order so as to determine the winner: high, low, jack, game.

FOUR-HANDED SEVEN UP

In this version four people play in partnerships of two. Each player sits opposite his partner.
Play is the same as in the basic game, except that the two players to the right of the dealer do not look at their cards until after trumps have been determined.

ALL FIVES

With the exception of the scoring, all fives is just like seven up.
One point is scored for "game," but not for high, low, or jack. Instead, points are scored for taking certain trump cards in tricks, as follows:
four for the ace;
three for the king;
two for the queen;
one for the jack;
ten for the 10; and
five for the 5.
Game is 61 points.

CALIFORNIA JACK

This variant of seven up is sometimes called draw seven or California loo. It is played by two people and differs from seven up in the following ways.

Trumps The first card turned face up denotes trumps. After each trick, first the winner and then the loser of that trick take a card from the top of the stock. The next card of the stock is then turned face up and denotes trumps for the next trick.
When the stock is exhausted, each player's remaining cards are played out using the last trump suit, the winner of each trick leading to the next.

Scoring One point is scored for taking each of the following in tricks: the highest trump, the lowest trump, and the jack of trumps.
The first player to make 10 points wins.

AUCTION PITCH

This is the most popular variation of seven up in the United States, and is also called set back. It is a game for two to seven players.

Deal Players cut for the deal, highest card dealing. Each player is dealt six face-down cards in packets of three.

Bidding Each player in turn, starting with the player to the dealer's left, makes one bid of one, two, three, or four; or passes.
Each bid must be higher than the previous bid—but the dealer may hold the previous bid if it is under four.
Each bid indicates the number of points the bidder intends to make.
A bid of four is called "shoot the moon," "slam," or "smudge."
The highest bidder, or the dealer if he held a previous bid, is called the "pitcher."

Play The pitcher leads to the first trick and his card denotes trumps for the deal.
In a trump suit players must follow suit or, if they cannot, discard one card. In a plain (non-trumps) suit, players may either follow suit or play a trump card—if they can do neither, they discard.
The winner of a trick leads to the next.

Scoring Points are scored for high, low, jack, and game as in seven up; each player except the pitcher scores for these as before.
The pitcher only scores if his score is equal to or greater than his bid. If he fails to make his contract, he is set back by the number of points he bid. This means his bid is subtracted from his previous score. If this leaves him with a minus number, he is said to be "in the hole."

Game is usually seven points, but players can decide to play for 10,11, or 21 points.
If the pitcher ties with another player, the pitcher is the winner.
For ties between other players, points are counted in the order: high, low, jack, and game.

AUCTION PITCH WITH JOKER

A joker is added to the deck for this version of auction pitch. It ranks as the lowest card of the trump suit in play.
If the pitcher leads the joker to the first trick, the trump suit is spades.
The player who takes the joker in a trick scores one point.
"Low" is scored by the player who is dealt the lowest trump card above the joker.
Game is 10 points. If there is a tie, the order for counting points is: high, low, jack, joker, and game.

All fives

 5 points

Auction pitch with joker

 1 point

Casino

Casino can be traced back to the fifteenth-century gambling games of France. In the United States, its era of greatest popularity was eclipsed by the gin rummy boom of the 1930s. Although appearing comparatively simple, casino is in fact a game of considerable mathematical skill.

Capturing

Groups

Court cards

Pairs

BASIC CASINO

Players The game can be played by two, three, or four players.

A deck of standard playing cards is used.

Court cards have no numerical value; aces count 1; and other cards count their face value.

Objective Each player tries to "capture" certain cards during play and to score the most points.

Deal Players cut for the deal and the lowest card deals. If there are two players, two cards are dealt face down to the non-dealer, then two cards face up to the center of the table, then two cards to the dealer. This procedure is repeated, so that each player has four cards and there are four face-up cards in the center of the table.

If there are three or four players, the dealer deals two cards to each player including himself, two face-up cards to the center of the table, two more cards to each of the players, and then two more cards to the center.

Each time the players have played the cards in their hands, they are each dealt a further four cards in packets of two—no more cards are dealt to the center.

Players take it in turns to deal the whole deck.

Play Beginning with the player to the left of the dealer, players take it in turns to play one card. Each player may "capture," "build," or "trail" with each card.

Capturing Cards are captured in the following ways.

a) Pairs: if a face-up card has the same numerical value as a player's card, the player may capture the face-up card. He does this by placing his card face down on the face-up card, and then moving the pair toward him.

For example, a 7 of spades may capture a 7 of diamonds.

If two or more face-up cards match a single card in the player's hand, he may capture them all at the same time.

b) Groups: if the combined value of two or more face-up cards is equal to the numerical value of a player's card, the player may capture all the face-up cards involved.

He puts the face-up cards in a pile in front of him and places his own card face down on top of them.

For example, a 9 could capture a 2,3, and 4 from the center. If one of a player's cards has the same numerical value as both a single face-up card and a group of face-up cards, he may capture all the cards involved at the same time.

For example, a 9 of spades could capture both a 9 of diamonds and a group of cards (eg a 2, 3, and 4) totaling 9.

c) Court cards: if a player holds a court card, he may either capture one matching face-up court card, or alternatively three matching face-up court cards if he holds the fourth.

This means that if, for example, he holds a queen and there are two face-up queens, he can only capture one of them in a turn (but had there been three face-up queens, he could have captured all of them in a turn).

Building may be done in either one of two ways: single or multiple.

Single build: a player may build a card face up onto a central face-up card provided:

a) the combined numerical value of the cards does not exceed ten; and

b) he holds another card that is of equal value to the build he is making, so that in his next turn he would be able to take that build.

For example, if a player holds a 4 and a 7, he may build the 4 onto a face-up 3 (ie 4 + 3 = 7) and say "Building 7."

A build may be increased by either player with a card from his hand, provided that the total of all the cards in the build still does not exceed ten, and that he holds a card equal in value to the build he is making.

For example, if the opponent

holds an ace and an 8, he may build the ace onto an existing build of 7, saying "Building 8."

Multiple build A single build can be changed to a multiple build by duplicating the single-build value with other cards.

For example, a player may add an ace from his hand to a build of 7 in order to make a build of 8 (ie 3 + 4 + 1 = 8), and add to that build another build of 8 (eg 2 + 6) and say "Building 8s."

Once a multiple build has been established, its stated value cannot be altered.

A multiple build is captured by a card equal in value to its stated value (8 in the example above).

Next turn If a player makes or adds to a build, unless his opponent plays to the build immediately, he must in his next turn either:

a) capture it himself (placing the captured build face down in front of him);

b) make a new build; or

c) add to a build.

Trailing If in his turn a player cannot build or capture, he simply places one card from his hand face up on the table.

End of a round When all the cards have been dealt out, the last player to capture cards takes all the remaining face-up cards for scoring.

Scoring Points are scored for capturing certain cards as follows:

a) one point for the 2 of spades ("little casino");

b) two points for the 10 of diamonds ("big casino");

c) one point for each ace;

d) one point for seven or more spades;

e) three points for 27 or more cards.

In addition, one point is scored for capturing all the center face-up cards in any single turn during the course of play; this is known as "making a sweep."

Game Players may either: count each deal as a separate game (the player with most points being the winner); or end the game as soon as one player (the winner) has made a set number of points (usually 21).

ROYAL CASINO

This differs from casino in that the court cards are given numerical values and can be included in builds and captured in tricks like other cards.

A jack numbers 11, a queen 12, and a king 13. Aces may count either one or 14 as the player chooses.

DRAW CASINO

In draw casino only the first 12 cards are dealt. Thereafter, each player draws a card from the stock every time he plays a card.

Otherwise, play is the same as in casino.

SPADE CASINO

Spade casino is played like the basic game, but has additional scoring as follows:

a) jack of spades, two points;

b) 2 of spades, two points as before; and

c) the other spades, one point each.

Game is 61 points.

Pope Joan

Pope Joan is a card game for three or more players
that was invented by combining two earlier games,
commit and matrimony. Contestants try to play
their cards in such a way as to win as many
counters as possible.

Cards A standard deck of 52
cards is used, but with the 8
of diamonds removed.
The cards are referred to in the
usual way, except for the 9 of
diamonds which is called
Pope Joan. Aces count low.
Counters At the start of a
game, each player should have
an equal number of counters.

Betting layout A board or
other betting layout is required
for the game.
Layouts are usually circular or
square (**a**), and are divided into
sections labeled ace, jack,
intrigue, queen, matrimony,
king, Pope Joan, and game.
Some traditional Pope Joan
boards comprise a circular tray
revolving on a central stand.
A layout can easily be drawn
on a sheet of plain paper or
material. Each section should
be large enough to hold at
least 20 counters.
Objective Each player aims
to win as many counters as
possible by playing certain
cards. Counters are also won
by the first contestant to use all
his cards.

Bet and deal Players decide
upon a dealer.
Each player, including the
dealer, then places counters in
the different sections of the
betting layout. This may be
done in one of two ways,
either:
a) each player, including the
dealer, puts out the same
agreed number of counters,
dividing them equally between
the different sections; or
b) each player, including the
dealer, puts four counters in
the pope section, two in
matrimony, two in intrigue,
and one in each of the other
sections (**b**).
The dealer then deals one
hand to each player including
himself, and one extra hand.
He deals by giving one card to
each player in a clockwise
direction, beginning with the
player to his left.
The card for the extra hand is
dealt just before he deals to
himself.
All cards are dealt face down.
The deal continues in this way
until all the cards but one have
been dealt; this card is placed
face upward or top of the
extra hand.

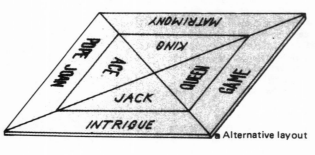

a Alternative layout

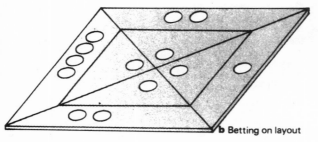

b Betting on layout

The exposed card If the card dealt face upward is Pope Joan (the 9 of diamonds), the dealer wins all the counters in the pope and game sections (**c**). (In an alternative version of play the dealer wins all the counters on the layout.)
The round ends and the player to the dealer's left becomes the new dealer.
If any other card is dealt, its

suit determines trumps for that hand.
If the card dealt face upward is an ace or a face card, the dealer wins the counters on the section with the same name.
Play Each player examines his own hand, but no player may look at the extra hand.
The player to the dealer's left begins. He plays any one card

from his hand face up onto the middle of the playing area and says its name, eg "3 of hearts."
The player with the 4 of hearts then plays it, followed by the player with the 5, the 6, and so on.
This continues until no player can add to the sequence because either:
a) the sequence has been

completed by reaching the king;
b) the next card needed is the 8 of diamonds; or
c) the next card needed is hidden in the extra hand or has already been played.
At this point the cards already played in the sequence are turned face down, and whoever played the last card begins a new sequence by playing any card of his choice.
Claiming counters Anyone who plays the ace, jack, queen, or king of trumps receives all the counters in the section marked with the same name (**d**).
If a player plays the jack and queen of trumps in sequence, he wins all the counters in the intrigue section, as well as those on jack and queen (**e**).
If anyone plays the queen and king of trumps in sequence, he receives all the counters in the matrimony section, as well as those on queen and king (**f**).
A player putting out Pope Joan wins all the counters on that section (**g**).
It should be noted that these cards only win counters when played in the correct way, ie by starting or adding to a sequence. They win nothing if they are still unplayed at the end of a round.
Ending the round The round continues until any one player has played all his cards, when he may take all the counters in the game section. All the other players have to give him one counter for every card still in their hand, with the exception of anyone holding the unplayed Pope Joan, who is exempted from playing for the cards left in his hand.
Unclaimed counters Any counters that are not won in a round remain on the betting layout until won in subsequent rounds.
New counters are added as usual to all sections at the beginning of each round.
Any counters left at the end of a game are distributed by redealing the cards, face up, without an extra hand. The players who receive the ace, jack, and queen of diamonds and the Pope Joan take any remaining counters in those divisions. Any counters in the matrimony section are divided between the holders of the king and queen, and those in the intrigue section between the holders of the queen and jack.

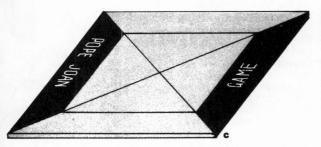

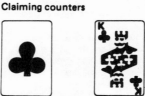

Exposed card

Claiming counters

Trump suit

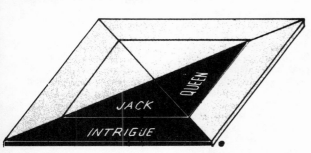

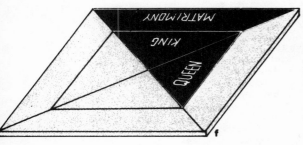

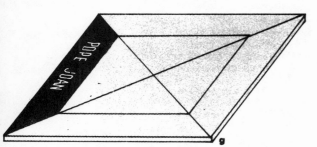

Michigan

Michigan is a popular and fast-moving game usually played for low stakes. It is easy to learn but can also be a challenging game for the experienced player. Other names by which Michigan is known are boodle, Newmarket, Chicago, and Saratoga.

Boodle cards

Players Any number from three to eight can play.
Cards In addition to one standard deck of playing cards, an ace, king, queen and jack—each in a different suit—from a second deck of cards are used. These four cards are called "boodle" cards and are placed face up in the center of the table.
Cards rank normally, with ace high.
Chips Each player is given a supply of betting chips or counters.
Objective Each player tries to play certain cards, thereby collecting chips, and to be the first to get rid of all his cards.
Ante Before each hand is dealt, every player must ante by putting one chip on each of the four boodle cards.
Deal Players cut for the deal, highest card dealing.
The dealer gives one face-down card at a time to each player and to an extra hand (widow) to the dealer's left. Each player must have the same number of cards. Any card or cards left over at the end of the deal are placed face down on the table.
Auction Before the start of play the dealer has the right to exchange his hand for the widow. If he does so, he discards his hand face down. If the dealer chooses not to take the widow, the other players may bid for it. The highest bidder pays the dealer in chips, discards his hand face down, and takes the widow.
If no player wants the widow, it is left face down without being seen by any player.
Play begins with the player to the dealer's left. He places his lowest card in any suit face up in front of him.
The player with the next card higher in that suit (ie either the same or another player) plays it face up. This continues with cards played in sequence until either the ace is reached or nobody has the next card in the sequence.

Usually, players announce the rank and suit of cards as they play them.
Each player forms a pile of face-up cards in front of him. Once a card is covered, it cannot be inspected.
Stopped play At the end of a sequence play is said to be "stopped." The last person to have played a card starts a new sequence with his lowest card in any other suit. If he cannot do this, the next player to his left able to lead with another suit does so.
If none of the other players can lead another suit, the first player may lead with his lowest card in the same suit as the previous sequence.
Boodle winnings Whenever a player lays down a card that matches one of the four boodle cards, he wins all the chips on that card.
If no player claims the chips on a boodle card during a hand, the chips remain on the card and carry over to the next deal. Before each hand, each player antes one chip on each boodle card.
Play ends as soon as one player has got rid of all his cards. Every other player must then pay him one chip for each card still in his hand.
Penalty If a player fails to play a card in a sequence when able to, he must pay one chip to each of the other players.
If by failing to play a card he prevented another player from winning boodle chips, he must make up the loss to the dispossessed player with his own chips. The chips on the boodle card remain and are carried over to the next deal.
The winner of a game is either:
a) the first person to win an agreed number of chips; or
b) the player with the most chips at the end of a set number of deals or a time limit.

Calabrasella

Calabrasella is an interesting and fast-moving card game for three players. Its characteristic features are a stripped deck, unusual ranking of cards, and the absence of a trump suit.

Cards A standard deck of playing cards with the 8s, 9s, and 10s removed is used.
The cards rank: 3 (high), 2,a, k,q,j,7,6,5,4 (low).
Players: three
Objective Each player tries to take certain tricks.
Deal Players cut for the deal and lowest card deals.
The dealer gives each player 12 face-down cards in packets of four.
The four remaining cards are placed face down in a pile in the center of the table as the widow (extra hand).
Bidding Starting with the player to the left of the dealer, each player in turn may choose either to play or pass.
The first player to choose to play is opposed by the other two players in partnership for that round.
If none of the three players wishes to play, the hand is thrown in and the cards are redealt.
Widow The player who decided to play may discard, face down, up to four of his cards and replace them with cards from the widow, turned face up. The discarded cards, if any, and any remaining widow cards are then placed face down in a pile. These four cards will go to the winner of the last trick.
Play The player to the left of the dealer leads to the first trick with any card he likes. In turn, each of the other players must follow suit if possible, or discard if not.
The winner of each trick leads to the next.
Scoring Players score for taking certain cards in tricks as follows:
a) aces, three points each;
b) 3s,2s,ks,qs, and js, one point each.
The player who takes the last trick scores an extra three points, and also scores for the four spare (widow or discard) cards.
Thus the maximum possible score is 35 points.
Each side totals its score, and the difference between them is the final score for that hand.

Rank

Payoff If the single player wins, each of the opponents pays him the final score in counters or points.
If he loses, he pays each opponent the final score.
If one side scored the maximum of 35 points, the payoff is 70 points or counters.
Game is 100 points. Alternatively, play can continue until one player has lost all his counters.

Bezique

Bezique is a card game that originated in France, and is based on games played over 350 years ago. It became particularly popular in the mid-nineteenth century. The standard game is for two players, but there are variants for three or more players. The popular American game of pinochle is derived from bezique.

STANDARD (TWO-HANDED) BEZIQUE

The deck comprises a double piquet deck, or two standard 52-card decks from which the 2s, 3s, 4s, 5s, and 6s have been removed—making a total of 64 cards in play.

The cards rank: a (high), 10, k, q, j, 9, 8, 7.

The objective of the game is to make winning melds or declarations, and to take tricks containing certain scoring cards known as *brisques*.

Deal Players cut for deal. The dealer gives eight cards to each player, dealing three, two, and three cards at a time. The next (the seventeenth) card is placed face up on the table and indicates the trump suit for that hand. If this card is a 7, the dealer scores 10 points.

The remaining cards are turned face down in a pile, forming the "stock."

Play is in two stages.

The first stage lasts as long as there are cards in the stock. The non-dealer leads first; thereafter the winner of each trick leads to the next one. After each trick the winner may make any declaration, and then both players draw cards from the stock to replenish their hands, the winner of the trick drawing first.

The winner of the last trick takes the last stock card, and the loser takes the exposed trump card.

During this stage the players are not obliged to follow suit.

A trick is taken by the higher card of the suit led or by a trump card.

If cards of equal value are played, the card that led takes the trick.

The second stage begins when the stock is exhausted. The players must follow suit for these last eight tricks, except they may trump if they cannot follow suit. A player must win a trick if he is able to. The winner of the last trick scores 10 points.

Rank

© DIAGRAM

Standard bezique

Trumps

20 points
a

40 points
b

40 points
c

40 points
d

60 points
e

80 points
f

100 points
g

250 points
h

500 points
i

Three-handed bezique

1500 points

Declarations may be made after winning a trick.

The cards of each meld must be laid face up in front of the player, but they may be played to tricks as if they were still in the hand.

The possible declarations are as follows:

a) common marriage: king and queen of the same suit, except trumps, 20 points;

b) royal marriage: king and queen of the trump suit, 40 points;

c) bezique: queen of spades and jack of diamonds, 40 points (when spades or diamonds are trumps, some players prefer to make "bezique" the queen of clubs and jack of hearts);

d) any four jacks, 40 points;

e) any four queens, 60 points;

f) any four kings, 80 points;

g) any four aces, 100 points;

h) sequence: a,10,k,q,j of the trump suit only, 250 points;

i) double bezique: both queens of spades and both jacks of diamonds, 500 points; exchanging the 7 of trumps for the face-up card, 10 points (the holder of the other 7 of trumps scores 10 points when he plays it, which does not count as a declaration).

A player may make only one declaration after winning a trick. But if his exposed cards show a second possible declaration, he can announce that he will declare it when he next takes a trick.

No card may form part of a second similar declaration. For example, a queen of spades in "four queens" cannot form part of a second

declaration of "four queens," but she can form part of a "bezique," "double bezique," "royal marriage," or "sequence."

The cards used to form a "bezique" can be used again to form part of a "double bezique," but neither card can be used with a fresh partner for a second "bezique."

Brisques are every ace and every 10 taken in tricks, and they count 10 points each. The *brisques* are counted up by each player examining his tricks at the end of the game.

Game is either 1000 or 2000 points up.

Penalties If a player draws out of turn, his opponent scores 10 points.

If a player holds more than eight cards, his opponent scores 100 points, provided he himself has the right number of cards.

A player who plays to the next trick without having drawn a card during the first stage forfeits 10 points to his opponent.

A player who revokes (fails to follow suit although able to) during the last eight tricks, or fails to take a trick if he is able to do so forfeits all eight tricks to his opponent.

Scoring is most easily done using special bezique markers; but it can also be done with pencil and paper, counters, or with a cribbage board (each hole on the board counting as 10).

THREE-HANDED BEZIQUE

Three-handed bezique is the same as ordinary bezique, except that 96 cards are used. Each player plays for himself. Triple bezique scores 1500 points.

RUBICON BEZIQUE

Rubicon bezique is a popular variation of bezique for two players. It is similar to standard bezique, with the following differences.

The deck consists of 128 cards, or four piquet decks.

The deal consists of nine cards to each player, dealt either singly or in threes.

Trumps are established by the first sequence or marriage declared by either player. No stock cards are turned up, and the 7 of trumps has no value.

Play is the same as for standard bezique, except that the last trick counts 50 points.

Declarations are as in standard bezique, with the following additions.

a) *Carte blanche*: worth 50 points, and scored if either player is dealt a hand not containing a court card. The hand must be displayed.

If, after drawing a further card, the player's hand still does not contain a court card, *carte blanche* may be scored again, and this continues until a court card is drawn.

Once a player has held a court card, *carte blanche* cannot be scored.

b) Ordinary sequence/back

door: a sequence not of the trump suit, 150 points;

c) triple bezique: three queens of spades and three jacks of diamonds, 1500 points;

d) quadruple bezique: four queens of spades and four jacks of diamonds, 4500 points.

Cards may be reused to form the same combinations. For example, if "four queens" are declared and one queen is played, a fifth queen may be laid down to form "four queens" again. Two marriages of the same suit may be rearranged to form two more marriages.

Brisques are only counted if there is a tied score, or to save a player from being "rubiconed," ie failing to reach 1000 points.

If one player chooses to count *brisques*, the other player's *brisques* are also scored.

Game is a single deal. The player with the higher score wins 500 points plus the difference between his and the loser's score.

If the loser is rubiconed, the winner gets 1000 points, plus the sum of his and the loser's scores, plus 320 points for all *brisques*. (This applies even if the winner himself has scored fewer than 1000 points.)

If the loser fails to score 100 points, the winner scores an extra 100 points.

Any fractions of 100 points may be ignored in scoring, except if the players' scores are very close.

Rubicon bezique

Trumps

50 points
a

150 points
b

1500 points
c

4500 points
d

Six-deck bezique

Trumps	400 points	600 points	800 points	900 points	1000 points		Carte blanche 250 points
	a	**b**	**c**	**d**	**e**		

SIX-DECK (CHINESE) BEZIQUE

Six-deck bezique, also known as Chinese bezique, is a variant of rubicon bezique. The rules are the same as for rubicon bezique, with the following changes.

The deck comprises 192 cards, or six piquet decks shuffled together.

The deal consists of 12 cards to each player, dealt singly or in threes.

Trumps are indicated by the first declared marriage or sequence.

Brisques do not count at all.

Declarations can be made as in rubicon bezique, reusing cards in similar scoring combinations.

In Chinese bezique, *carte blanche* is worth 250 points, as is winning the last trick. Declarations in addition to those in rubicon bezique are, in the trump suit only:

a) four jacks, 400 points;
b) four queens, 600 points;
c) four kings, 800 points;
d) four 10s, 900 points;
e) four aces, 1000 points.

Bezique varies according to which suit is trumps, as follows:

hearts, queen of hearts and jack of clubs;
diamonds, queen of diamonds and jack of spades;
clubs, queen of clubs and jack of hearts;

spades, queen of spades and jack of diamonds.

Game is a single deal. Scores are calculated as for rubicon bezique, except that:
the winner gets a game bonus of 1000 points instead of 500; and
the rubicon point is 3000 instead of 1000.

© DIAGRAM

EIGHT-DECK BEZIQUE

Eight-deck bezique is played like six-deck bezique, with the following variations.

The deck consists of 256 cards, or eight piquet decks.

The deal is 15 cards to each player.

Declarations are the same, with the following changes and additions:
bezique, 50 points;
quintuple bezique, 9000 points.

In the trump suit only:
a) five jacks, 800 points;
b) five queens, 1200 points;
c) five kings, 1600 points;
d) five 10s, 1800 points;
e) five aces, 2000 points.

A player is rubiconed if he fails to score 5000 points.

Eight-deck bezique

Trumps	800 points	1200 points	1600 points	1800 points	2000 points	50 points	Quintuple bezique 9000 points
	a	**b**	**c**	**d**	**e**		

FOUR-HANDED BEZIQUE

Four-handed bezique is similar to rubicon bezique, but the game is played with 192 cards. The players play in partnership, two against two.

The deal is nine cards to each player; the player on the dealer's left leads to the first trick.

Declarations may be made by any player after winning a trick; alternatively he may allow his partner to make the declaration.

A player may use both his own cards and any of his partner's declared cards to make a declaration.

Scoring is as in rubicon bezique, with the following variations and additions:

a) *double carte blanche*: both players in a partnership being dealt a hand without a court card, 500 points;
b) any four jacks, 400 points;
c) any four queens, 600 points;
d) any four kings, 800 points;
e) any four 10s, 900 points;
f) any four aces, 1000 points;
g) quintuple bezique, 13,500 points;
h) sextuple bezique, 40,500 points.

Double carte blanche 500 points
a

Four-handed bezique

Trumps	400 points	600 points	800 points	900 points	1000 points	13,500 points	40,500 points
	b	**c**	**d**	**e**	**f**	**g**	**h**

Piquet

Piquet is a card game for two players that allows great opportunities for skill. It has been known, under various names, since the middle of the fifteenth century. The present French name and terminology were adopted in English during the reign of Charles I of England, as a compliment to his French wife, Henrietta Maria.

Rank of cards

Players The game is for two.
Objective Each player aims to score points, both with certain combinations of cards in his hand and by playing for tricks.
Cards A deck of 32 playing cards is used, commonly called a piquet deck. This is a standard 52 card deck from which all the 2s, 3s, 4s, 5s, and 6s have been removed. Usually two decks are used alternately, one being shuffled in readiness for the next hand while the other is being dealt into play.
The cards rank normally, from 7 low to ace high.
Choice of first dealer is by low cut (see p 80). The first dealer also has choice of seats.
Shuffle is normal. (See p 80).
Cut is by the non-dealer. There need be only two cards in each section. Otherwise the cut is normal (see p 80).
The deal is in packets of two cards, face down. The dealer gives two cards to his opponents, then two to himself, until each has 12 cards.
The remaining eight cards form the stock, which is placed face down in the center of the table. The stock is divided so that the upper five cards rest at an angle to the lower three.
Discards The dealer has the chance to discard first. Under American rules, he need not discard; under English rules, he must discard at least one card. In either case, the most cards he can discard is five. If he is discarding, he places the discards face down beside him, and draws an equal number from the stock. (Players must draw cards in the order in which they are stacked in the stock.)
Even if the dealer does not draw, or does not draw all five, he may look at the cards that he could have drawn, and then replace them without showing them to his opponent.
Then the non-dealer discards at least one card and at most as many cards as remain in the stock.
He places his discards face

down beside him and draws an equal number of stock cards, beginning with any left by the dealer.
The non-dealer may look at any cards in the stock that remain undrawn. But in this case the dealer may turn these cards face up for himself to see also.
(Sometimes it is ruled that the dealer may do this only after leading to the first trick.)
A player may inspect his own discards during play.
Scoring Points are scored in two ways. Some points are scored by "declaration," which occurs immediately after discarding and before play. Other points are scored during play.
Declarations Each player declares certain combinations of cards held in his hand, and scores points if his declaration ranks higher than his opponent's.
A player does not have to declare a potentially winning combination if he prefers not to—but he cannot then score points for it. This is called "sinking."
A player may include any card in more than one combination.
Scoring combinations
Point The player with the most cards of one suit scores one point for each card he holds in that suit.
If both players have long suits of the same length, the better point is the one with the higher face value. (Face value is calculated by counting the ace as 11, court cards as 10 each, and other cards as their numerical face value.) If the players still tie, neither scores.
A player can only score for one point—even if he has more than one suit longer than his opponent's longest.
Sequences The player with the most cards in rank order in one suit scores as follows:
tierce (three cards), three points;
quart (four cards), four points;
quint (five cards), 15 points;
sextet or sixième (six cards), 16 points;
septet or septième (seven

cards), 17 points;
octet or huitième (eight cards), 18 points.
The holder of the highest sequence can also score for any other sequences he holds.
If players tie for longest sequence, the sequence with the higher top card wins. If both sequences have the same top card, neither scores for any sequences.
Meld The player with the highest ranking meld, of three or four cards of a kind, scores as follows:
trio or "three" (three cards of the same denomination), three points;
quatorze or "fourteen" (four cards of the same denomination), 14 points.
But only aces, kings, queens, jacks, or 10s may be declared for melds (and sometimes it is ruled that 10s only count if a quatorze is held).
If both players have sets of equal length, the one with the higher ranking cards wins. The winner also scores for any other melds he holds.
Announcing the declarations is by a formal dialogue, designed to reveal no more information than necessary.
The non-dealer makes the first declaration in each category of combination, and takes them in the order point, sequence, meld.
Declaring a point Non-dealer says: "A point of ——," stating whatever number of cards he holds in his longest suit.
Dealer replies:
"Good," if he concedes the point;
"Not good," if he holds a longer suit—stating its length;
"How many?" if he holds a suit of equal length.
If the reply is "How many?" the non-dealer must then declare the face value of his point. The dealer then replies "Good," "Not good" (stating the face value of his point), or "Equal" (in which case no one scores).
Whoever has won the point then states the length of his point again (adding the face value if that also had to be declared), and announces his score.
Declaring a sequence Non-dealer says: "A sequence of ——" (or "A tierce," etc), stating the number of cards in his longest sequence.
The procedure then follows as in declaring a point—except that when the dealer holds a

sequence of equal length his reply is "How high?" The non-dealer then declares the top card of his sequence, and the dealer states "Good," "Not good," or "Equal."
Declaring a meld Non-dealer says "A three (or fourteen) of ——," naming the denomination. (Alternatively he can use the words "trio" or "quatorze".) The dealer cannot hold a meld of the same length and denomination, and so his only possible replies are "Good" or "Not good."
A sample declaration
Non-dealer: "A point of five."
Dealer: "Good."
Non-dealer: "A point of five. I score five." Then he names his best sequence: "A sequence of four (or "A quart")."
Dealer: "How high?"
Non-dealer: "Queen."
Dealer: "Not good. Ace. Also a tierce. Seven. I score seven."
Non-dealer (naming his best meld): "Three kings" (or "A trio of kings").
Dealer: "Not good. Fourteen queens (or "quatorze of queens"). I score 14. I start with 21."
Non-dealer (playing the lead to the first trick and automatically adding one point to his score—see below): "I start with six."
English style declaration
In this, the dealer only names his combinations after the non-dealer has led to the first trick. For example:
Non-dealer: "A point of five."
Dealer: "Good."
Non-dealer: "A point of five. I score five. A quart."
Dealer: "How high?"
Non-dealer: "Queen."
Dealer: "Not good."
Non-dealer: "A trio of kings."
Dealer: "Not good."
Non-dealer (playing first card): "I start with six."
Dealer: "A quart to the ace. Also a tierce. Seven. And a quatorze of queens: 14. I start with 21."
Showing combinations
Sometimes it is ruled that all winning combinations must be shown before they score. More usually, winning combinations are shown only at the opponent's request. A combination that is shown is replaced in the holder's hand as soon as the opponent has seen it.
Play The non-dealer leads to the first trick. Each player must follow suit to a lead if he can. If not he may discard any card. The winner of a trick leads to the next.

Scoring during play A player scores for tricks; also players may score additional points in various ways.

Scoring for tricks Each player scores as follows:
a) one point for leading to a trick;
b) one point for taking a trick that his opponent led to;
c) one point for taking the last trick; and
d) 10 points for taking the majority of the tricks (seven or more).
Each time a player scores he announces his total score so far.

Variation Sometimes it is played that:
a) a player scores for leading to a trick only if the card led is higher than a 9;
b) a player scores for winning a trick only if the winning card is higher than a 9.

Additional scoring Points may also be scored in the following ways.
a) Carte blanche is a hand devoid of court cards, and scores 10 points. It must be claimed by a player immediately before he discards after the deal. (Under English rules, it must be claimed before either player discards.)
b) Pique is scored by the non-dealer if he scores 30 points before the dealer scores anything. It scores 30 bonus points.
c) Repique is scored by either player if he scores 30 points on declaration, ie before the lead to the first trick. It is worth 60 bonus points.
d) Capot is scored by either player if he captures all 12 tricks in play. It is worth 40 bonus points, but the 10 standard points for taking a majority of tricks are not scored.

A game is known as a partie. It consists usually of six deals, though some players prefer to have a partie of four deals, with scores for the first and fourth deals counting double. The turn to deal alternates between the two players.

Scoring the partie
a) The scores for the individual deals are added together to give a total for each player. The procedure then depends on whether these totals exceed the "rubicon" of 100 points.
b) If both players have 100 or more points, the player with the higher total wins by the difference between the two totals plus 100 points bonus for the partie.
For example, if the dealer has totaled 120 and the non-

dealer 108, the dealer wins and scores 112 points (120−108+100).
c) If either or both players have less than 100 points, the player with the lower total is said to be "rubiconed." The player with the higher total wins by the sum of the totals plus 100 points bonus.
For example:
if the scores are 125 and 92, the player with 125 wins and scores 317 (125+92+100);
if the scores are 98 and 92, the player with 98 wins and scores 290 (98+92+100).

Piquet au cent has different final scoring. Deals continue until one player totals 100 points or more. At the end of that deal, the player with the higher total scores the difference between his own and his opponent's totals—or double that difference if his opponent's total was below 50.

AUCTION PIQUET
This variation puts more emphasis on the play of the hands.

Bidding takes place before the discard. The non-dealer bids or passes first.
If both pass, the cards are dealt again by the same player. Once a bid has been made, bidding continues until one player passes.
The minimum bid is seven. A bid may be either "plus" (winning the stated number of tricks) or "minus" (losing that number). Plus and minus bids rank equally: to continue the bidding a player must bid a greater number of tricks.
The final bid is the "contract" as in contract bridge.

Other rules are as for basic piquet, with the following exceptions.

Discards Players need not discard at all.

Declarations may be made in any order.

Sinking is not allowed on minus contracts.

Pique is scored after 29 points in plus contracts and 21 points in minus ones.

Repique is scored after 30 points in plus contracts and 21 points in minus ones.

Scoring for tricks Each player scores one point for each trick that he takes (whoever led to that trick). Players do not score for leading to a trick or for taking the last trick.

Scoring the contract If the contracted player exceeds his contract, he scores 10 points for every trick won (on plus contracts) or lost (on minus contracts) in excess of his contract.
If he fails to make his contract, every trick by which he fell short scores 10 points for his opponent.

Doubling and redoubling are allowed, as in bridge, but affect only the scores for overtricks or undertricks.

Scoring the partie Rubicon is 150 points, and bonus for the partie is also 150 points.

IMPERIAL
This game is a form of piquet, but there is a trump suit and the cards rank differently.
Players: two.
Cards A 32-card piquet deck is used—a standard deck with the 2s,3s,4s,5s, and 6s removed.
Cards rank k (high), q,j,a,10, 9,8,7 (low).
"Honors" are the k,q,j,a, and 7 of trumps.
Chips are used for scoring: 12 white chips and eight red. One red chip is worth six white.
At the beginning of the game all chips are placed together in a central pool.
Shuffle and cut is as in piquet.
The deal is as in piquet, but in packets of three.
When both players have 12 cards each, the 25th card is placed face up in the center of the table. The suit of this card becomes trumps for the hand. The undealt part of the deck is placed to one side, out of use for the remainder of the hand. There is no discarding or drawing in play.
Scoring procedure
1) Whenever a player scores, he takes the appropriate chip from the pool.
2) Whenever a player has collected six white chips, he immediately exchanges them for one red chip from the pool.
3) Whenever a player gains a red chip in any way, his opponent must put back into the pool any white chips that he holds. (His red chips are safe.)
Scoring before play occurs in the following order:
1) the dealer scores one white chip if the turned up (25th) card is an honor card;
2) either player scores one red chip if he has been dealt carte blanche, ie a hand containing no king, queen, or jack;
3) players declare and score as

in piquet for each combination that they hold;
4) players declare and score for any sequence or meld using the turned up card.
Declaring is as in piquet, except that:
a) players must show any winning combinations;
b) when players declare equally good combinations, the non-dealer wins.
Point is called exactly as in piquet. The player with the better point scores one white chip.

Imperial

Rank of cards

Sequences may be of three or four cards but may contain only kings, queens, jacks, and aces. A four-card sequence beats a three-card sequence. Three-card sequences rank according to the top card. The winner scores one red chip.
Melds Only fours of kings, queens, jacks, aces, and 7s are counted—ranking in that order, with king high. Threes do not count. The winner scores one red chip.
Combinations using the turned up card
1) Players declare any sequence that includes the turned up card. The higher ranking sequence wins one red chip.
2) A player declares if he has a meld of four using the turned up card. If so, he wins one red chip.

Honors

Play is as for piquet, except that the second player to each trick must take it if he can. (This includes trumping if he cannot follow suit.)
Cards are not collected in tricks. Each player puts the cards he has played face up in front of him, and is free to examine them at any time.
Scoring during play
1) A player taking the jack of trumps by leading the king or queen wins one red chip.
2) A player taking the ace also wins one red chip.
3) A player takes one white chip for each trump honor contained in tricks that he wins.
Scoring after play If one player takes more tricks in a hand than his opponent, he wins one white chip for every trick in excess of his opponent's total.
Thus if a player wins all 12 tricks—referred to as "capot" —he wins two red chips.
The winner is the first player to win five red chips. Hands continue until one player does this, with the deal alternating between players.
If a player gains five red chips in the middle of a hand, the hand is abandoned at once.

Chips

Pinochle

Rank of cards

PINOCHLE

This game is derived from bezique and is widely played in North America. Its name is also spelled pinocle and sometimes penuchle.

Players The basic game is for two players.

Cards A 48-card deck is used: made from two standard decks excluding all the 2s, 3s, 4s, 5s, 6s, 7s, and 8s. Cards rank a (high), 10, k, q, j, 9 (low).

Objective Each player aims to take tricks containing certain cards, and to make melds.

Choice of first dealer is by high cut. Thereafter the deal alternates.

Shuffle and cut are normal (see p 80), except that the non-dealer must cut.

Deal The dealer gives 12 cards to each player in packets of three or four.

The thirteenth card is then turned face up on the table, and its suit becomes trumps for that hand.

The rest of the deck, the "stock," is then placed face down on the table, half covering the trump card.

First stage of play This lasts as long as there are any cards in the stock.

The non-dealer leads to the first trick. Thereafter the winner of one trick leads to the next.

In this stage, players may play any card to a trick. This includes playing a trump when holding a card of a plain suit led. Each trick is won by the highest trump, or, if no trumps appear, by the highest card of the suit led. If two cards of the same denomination and suit appear, the one played first wins.

The winner of a trick places it face down in front of him. After each trick, the winner may make one meld (see the section on melding). Then, whether or not a meld has been made, the winner draws the top card from the stock and the loser draws the next card. The winner then leads to the next trick.

Drawing after tricks continues until all the stock and the exposed trump card have been drawn. (It is often ruled that the player who draws the last face-down card must also expose it.)

Melding After each trick in the first stage, the winner of the trick may claim one meld.

A meld is claimed by placing the cards involved face up on the table, and stating the score. A player can only score for one meld in a turn — even if the cards he exposes for that meld

have also given him another scoring combination.

Each card melded can also be used later to form another meld of a different class (see the section on melds) or one of a higher score in the same class. However, each new meld formed in this way requires a new turn and the addition of at least one card from the player's hand.

Any card that a player uses in a meld may still be played to a later trick, but once a card has been played to a trick it cannot then be used in further melds.

Melds There are three classes of meld. Points are scored as follows when the melds are put on the table.

Class A:
"sequence" (or "flush") — a, 10, k, q, j of trumps — 150 points;
"royal marriage" — k and q of trumps — 40 points;
"marriage" — k and q of any plain suit — 20 points.

Class B:
"pinochle" — q of spades and j of diamonds — 40 points;

Class C:
four aces, 100 points;
four kings, 80 points;
four queens, 60 points;
four jacks, 40 points.
(Note that all "fours" must contain one card of each suit.)

The second stage of play, or "play out," begins with each player taking back into his hand any cards that he has melded. The players then play for the remaining 12 tricks to use up the cards in their hands. The winner of the last trick in the first stage leads to the first trick in the second.

In this stage a player must follow suit if he can, and may only trump if he cannot.

If a trump is led, the following player must play a higher trump if he can.

(Usually it is made a general rule for this stage that a following player must win any trick he can.)

Tricks are won as in the first stage, and the winner of one trick leads to the next. No melds are made in this stage.

The "dix" is the name given to the 9 of trumps.

If the card turned up to decide trumps is a 9, the dealer scores 10 points immediately. If a player holds a dix during the first stage of play, he can declare it and win 10 points by placing it face up on the table after winning a trick. (Most players rule that a meld can also be made in the same turn.)

If the first dix to appear is one declared by a player, it is not

left face up in front of him but is exchanged for the exposed trump card at the bottom of the stock pile. The player takes that trump card into his hand and puts the dix in its place.

Scoring of tricks Points for cards taken in tricks are scored at the end of each hand. Cards are scored as follows:
a) each ace, 11 points;
b) each 10, 10 points;
c) each king, four points;
d) each queen, three points;
e) each jack, two points.
The winner of the last trick in the second stage scores a further 10 points.

Points for tricks are rounded to multiples of 10 (only 7, 8, or 9 being rounded up) before being added to the player's total score.

Game is usually 1000 points. If both players reach 1000 or more after the same hand, play continues until one player reaches 1250. If the same happens again, play continues to 1500, etc.

AUCTION PINOCHLE

In this version, players bid on how many points they expect to score. Chips are collected by successful players.

Players Three people play. Usually the game is played at tables of four, with the dealer taking no active part.

Cards The deck and rank of cards are as in basic pinochle.

Deal 15 cards are dealt to each player in five packets of three. After each player has been dealt one packet, a widow of three cards is dealt face down.

Bidding Each player in turn, starting with the player to the dealer's left, may make a bid as to the number of points he expects to score.

Bidding must start at an agreed minimum (usually 300) and must rise 10 points at a time. A player must bid or pass. If he passes, he may not bid again in that hand. Bidding ends when two players have passed. The other player is then the "bidder," and his highest bid is his contract.

The other two players together try to prevent him making his contract.

Melding The bidder takes up the widow cards, shows them to the other players, and then adds them to his hand.

He then names the trump suit and lays down his melds. No other player is allowed to make melds at any time.

Melds and their scores are as in basic pinochle, except that the dix counts as a Class A meld scoring 10 points, and is

scored only if the bidder places it on the table with his other melds.

Starting play The bidder begins by discarding three cards face down from those still in his hand. He then picks up his meld cards and leads to the first trick.

He may change his mind about his melds, discards, or trumps at any time before he actually leads to the first trick. But if he discards a meld card that he has scored for, he forfeits the game unless he corrects the mistake before leading to the first trick.

Tricks are won as in basic pinochle. Each player must follow suit if he can; and, if trumps are led, must try to win the trick if he can.

If a player cannot follow suit he must trump rather than discard. This still applies after a trick has been trumped, but he need not trump higher if he does not wish to.

The winner of each trick leads to the next.

Scoring of tricks may be as in basic pinochle.
Alternatives are:
a) 10 points for each ace or 10, and 5 points for each king or queen; or
b) 10 points for each ace, 10, or king.

Whatever the points system, the bidder scores for any scoring cards contained in the three cards he discards, and there is a bonus of 10 points to the bidder if he wins the last trick.

Game Each hand is a complete game. If the bidder makes or exceeds his contract, he wins chips from each player. Typical amounts are:
a) 300-340 bid, three chips;
b) 350-390 bid, five chips;
c) 400-440 bid, 10 chips;
d) 450-490 bid, 15 chips;
e) 500-540 bid, 20 chips;
f) 550-590 bid, 25 chips;
g) 600 or more, 30 chips.
These amounts are doubled if spades are trumps.

A kitty usually features in auction pinochle. The following are typical rules.
1) Each player must put three chips into the kitty before play begins.
2) If all players pass on a deal, all pay three chips into the kitty.
3) If a bidder makes, or fails on, a contract of 350 or more, he collects from, or pays to, the kitty, as well as each other player. Amounts are the same as for settlements between players.

Kalabriasz

Rank of trumps

Trumps

KALABRIASZ

This excellent game is also known as klaberjass, clab, and clobber. It is essentially the same as the French game, belote.

Players The basic game is for two players.

Cards Play is with a standard deck of cards from which the 2s, 3s, 4s, 5s, and 6s have been removed.

The cards rank as follows:
a) in the trump suit, j (high), 9, a, 10, k, q, 8, 7 (low);
b) in plain suits, a (high), 10, k, q, j, 9, 8, 7 (low).

Objective Players aim to meld sequences and to take certain scoring cards in tricks.

Choice of dealer for the first hand is by high cut, with ace low.

First deal The dealer gives each player six cards face down in packets of three. He then places the next card face up in the center of the table, and places the rest of the deck — the stock — face down in a pile beside it.

Determining trumps Players make bids to determine the trump suit.

1) The non-dealer opens with a bid of "Accept," "Schmeiss," or "Pass."

If he bids to accept, the suit of the central face-up card becomes trumps for the hand. A bid of schmeiss is a proposal for a new deal. The dealer then has the opportunity of agreeing to a new deal or of accepting the suit of the central face-up card as the trump suit.

If the non-dealer says "Pass," the dealer has a turn at bidding.

2) The dealer may now either: accept the suit of the central face-up card as trumps; bid Schmeiss, in which case the non-dealer must agree to the new deal or accept the suit of the face-up card as trumps; or pass, in which case there is a second round of bidding.

3) If both players pass in the first round of bidding, the non-dealer may then either: nominate any trump suit that he wishes, in which case play will be with this suit as trumps; or pass, in which case the dealer may nominate a trump suit or pass.

If both players pass in the second round of bidding, the cards are thrown in and a new first deal made.

The player who actually determines the trump suit is called the "maker."

Second deal Once the trump suit has been established, each player is dealt a further three cards, one at a time and face down.

The dealer then takes the bottom card of the stock and places it face up on top of the stock.

If the suit of the central face-up card was accepted as trumps, a player holding the 7 of that suit may exchange it for the central face-up card if he wishes. The 7 of trumps is known as the "dix."

Declaring sequences usually takes place before play begins, but may be after the non-dealer has led to the first trick. By their declarations players establish which of them holds the highest sequence.

Sequences All cards in a sequence must be consecutive and of the same suit. There are two kinds of sequence:
a) a sequence of three cards, worth 20 points; and
b) a sequence of four or more cards, worth 50 points.

For sequences cards rank in the order a (high), k, q, j, 10, 9, 8, 7 (low).

Sequences of equal value are ranked according to their highest card. Note that a sequence of four cards beats a longer sequence provided that the four-card sequence is headed by the highest card.

If sequences are of equal value and are headed by cards of the same rank, a sequence in the trump suit is higher.

If equal sequences headed by cards of the same rank are both in plain suits, some versions of the game rule that the non-dealer's sequence is higher while others rule that the sequences are equal and neither player may score.

Declaration procedure The non-dealer begins by announcing "Sequence of 50" if he has a sequence of four or more cards, or "Sequence of 20" if he has a three-card sequence.

The dealer then replies "Good" if he cannot beat it, "Not good" if he can beat it, or "how high?" if he has a sequence with the same points value.

If the dealer replies "How high?" the non-dealer states the rank of the card that heads his sequence, and then the non-dealer replies "Good" if he cannot beat it, or "Not good" if he can.

Scoring of sequences Only the player with the highest sequence scores any points at this stage of the game.

He scores for his highest sequence after first showing it to his opponent.

He also scores for any other sequences that he is prepared to show.

Play Non-dealer leads to the first trick.

Players must follow suit if they are able, and if they cannot follow suit must play a trump if they have one. If a trump is led the opposing player must take the trick if he can.

The winner of a trick places it face down in front of him and leads to the next trick.

Bella is an additional meld comprising the king and queen of trumps.

It is worth 20 points to any player who holds it, and is scored automatically when the holder plays the second of the two cards.

Scoring during play Players score points as follows for cards taken in tricks:
a) "jasz" (jack of trumps), 20 points;
b) "menel" (9 of trumps), 14 points;
c) each ace, 11 points;
d) each 10, 10 points;
e) each king, four points;
f) each queen, three points;
g) each jack but jasz, two points.

The player who takes the last trick scores a further 10 points.

The final score for each hand is calculated as follows.
a) If the player who determined the trump suit (the maker) has a points total higher than his opponent, each player scores his own total.
b) if the opposing player has a higher total, he scores both his own points total and that of the maker. This is called "going bate."
c) If the players have an equal number of points, the maker scores no points and his opponent scores his own points total. The maker's opponent is said to have gone "half bate."

Game is usually 500 points. If both players reach the agreed game total in the same hand, the one who has most points is the winner

THREE-HANDED KALABRIASZ

In the three-handed game turns pass clockwise around the table. The maker must score more than both his opponents together, or go bate. Players score their own sequences and points won in play, but opponents share the maker's points if he goes bate.

PARTNERSHIP KALABRIASZ

This differs from the basic game as follows.

All but the last card are dealt out so that the dealer has seven cards and the other players eight each.

The last card becomes the central face-up card. Before play, the player with the dix exchanges it for the face-up card, and the dealer takes the dix to complete his hand.

After one player has established the highest sequence, his partner may also score for any sequences.

Partners keep their tricks together and score as a side.

Rank of plain suits

Scoring cards

a **b** **c** **d** **e** **f** **g** Trumps

© DIAGRAM

Skat

Skat developed in Germany in the early 1800s and its rules were codified at a congress in 1896. It has since flourished on both sides of the Atlantic, being one of the most skillful of all card games. The simplified variant described here — Rauber Skat — is gradually replacing the original game.

Rank of cards with trumps

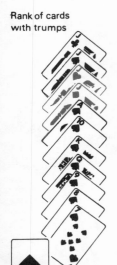

Trump suit

Plain suits

Rank in no trumps

Players Three to five people can play, but only three play on any one deal.
With four players, the dealer sits out. With five, the dealer and the third player to his left sit out: the first, second, and fourth play.
The first player to the dealer's left is called "forehand," the next "middlehand," and the last player with cards "endhand."

Cards Skat is played with a standard deck from which all the 2s, 3s, 4s, 5s, and 6s have been removed.
Rank of cards Most contracts require trumps.
The highest trumps are always the four jacks, which rank in the order clubs (high), spades, hearts, diamonds (low).
In addition there may also be a trump suit. If so, the rest of that suit rank below the lowest jack, in the order a (high), 10, k, q, 9, 8, 7 (low).
When play is with trumps, cards in plain suits also rank a (high), 10, k, q, 9, 8, 7 (low). When there are no trumps, all suits rank a (high), k, q, j, 10, 9, 8, 7 (low).
Objective Each player tries to win the right to choose the game that will be played, and then successfully to complete that game.
Choice of first dealer is by high cut (see p 80). Thereafter the deal passes one player to the left after each game.

Deal A packet of three cards is dealt to each active player. Then a "skat" of two face-down cards is set aside. A packet of four is next dealt to each active player, and finally a further packet of three.
This gives three hands of ten cards each, and two cards in the skat.
Bidding The player who makes the highest bid wins the right to name the game. He then tries to fulfill his bid and the other two players try to prevent him.
A bid states only the number of game points that the player believes he can make if he wins the right to choose the game.
The lowest permitted bid is 18; the highest practicable bid is about 100.
Bidding follows the deal. Middlehand bids first, or passes.
If middlehand bids, forehand must reply. He must state either "Pass" or "Hold." "Hold" means that he makes the same bid as middleman. By bidding hold, he retains the right to name the game, because a player cannot lose this to a player to his left unless that player has bid higher.

This continues with forehand holding bids and middlehand raising bids until either player passes.
Then endhand must either raise the bid or pass; and if he bids, the survivor of the first pair replies by passing or holding. This continues as between the first pair, until one bidder gives in.
If both middlehand and endhand pass without bidding, forehand may make a bid or may pass. Once a player has passed, he may not make a bid. The player who survives in the bidding will now be referred to as the "bidder."

The skat The bidder begins by deciding whether or not to pick up the two cards that form the skat.
If he picks up the skat, he must then discard any two cards from his hand. These discards will eventually count toward his final score.
If he does not pick up, this is referred to as "handplay." The skat is then set aside for the duration of play. At the end of the hand, the fate of the skat depends on the game that has been played.
If the bidder chooses to pick up the skat, this limits his choice of game for the hand (since for certain games it is ruled that the skat may not be picked up).

The games The bidder then chooses which game will be played in that hand. His choice is between "suits," "grand," "simple null," "open null," and "reject."

(A bidder who has picked up the skat is not permitted to choose simple null, open null, or reject.) To fulfill his bid, he must not only successfully complete the game he chooses (for example, by making sufficient trick points if that is required), but must also score sufficient "game" points to equal or exceed his bid.

Suits The bidder names a suit. All the cards in that suit become trumps, together with the jacks.

The bidder's aim is to make at least 61 trick points by taking tricks containing scoring cards.

Grand Only the four jacks are trumps. The bidder's aim is as in suits.

Simple null There are no trumps. The bidder aims to lose every trick.

Open null As in simple null, but the bidder must play with all his cards exposed. He lays them face up on the table before the opening lead.

Reject This game may only be chosen by forehand, and he may choose it only if middlehand and endhand have both passed without a bid. He does not make a numerical bid, but simply states "Reject." Only the four jacks are trumps. Each player tries to take fewer trick points than any other player.

Open If the bidder has opted for handplay, and names suits or grand, he may increase the value of his game by declaring "Open."

The player must then play with all his cards exposed, laying them face up on the table before the opening lead.

Schneider and schwarz If the bidder has named suits or grand, he may before the opening lead, declare:
a) schneider, ie he aims to win at least 91 trick points; or
b) schwarz, ie he aims to take every trick.

He need not declare either — in which case his goal remains 61 trick points.

Play Forehand leads to the first trick. Thereafter the winner of one trick leads to the next.

Other players must follow suit if possible. If unable to follow suit they may trump (if there are trumps in the game) or they may discard.

The highest trump played, or the highest card of the suit led if no trumps appear, wins the trick.

Scoring of trick points Cards taken in tricks score as follows:
a) each ace, 11 points;
b) each 10, 10 points;
c) each king, four points;
d) each queen, three points;
e) each jack, two trick points.

Scoring the skat After the last trick has been taken, the skat is allocated as follows:
a) at suits or grand, to the bidder (if he took the skat before play, he is given the cards he discarded);
b) at reject, to the winner of the last trick;
c) at null, to no one — the skat is discarded.

Whoever receives the skat (or discards) counts trick points for any scoring cards it contains.

Making the game Except at reject (see separate section), the bidder makes the game if he achieves that game's object (ie 61 trick points, 91 trick points, all tricks, or no tricks).

He must, however, then consider if he has made the number of game points that he bid.

Making the bid Except at reject, a bid is made if the bidder's game score equals or exceeds the number of game points stated in his bid. Game points are scored as follows.
a) At null games, the game value is fixed: 23 game points for making simple null, and 24 for making open null. Provided that the player's bid was not higher than this, he makes his bid.
b) At suits or grand, the game value has to be calculated — by multiplying a base game value by a number of multipliers. The player does not know how many multipliers he will qualify for until after play ends. The player makes his bid if the total game value (base x all multipliers) equals or exceeds his bid.

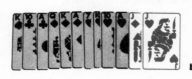

Base values for the games are:
a) diamonds, nine game points;
b) hearts, 10 game points;
c) spades, 11 game points;
d) clubs, 12 game points;
e) grand, 20 game points.

The multipliers are as follows:
a) automatic multiplier for having made game, one;
b) for holding "matadors" (see separate section), the multiplier varies but is at least one;
c) for choosing handplay, one;
d) for making schneider or schwarz (see separate section), the multiplier varies but is at least one.

The player adds all his multipliers together. The total will be between two and 14. He then multiplies the base value for his game by this total.

Matadors The jack of clubs and all other trumps in unbroken sequence in the bidder's hand (including the skat, whether or not it is used in play) are called matadors. When the bidder holds the jack of clubs, his hand is said to be "with" a number of matadors. When he does not hold the jack of clubs, his hand is said to be "without" a number of matadors.

The multiplier is the number of matadors that the bidder is with or without (it does not matter which).

Two examples are shown.
a) Spades are trumps, the player is with three matadors (the missing jack of diamonds breaks the sequence before the ace of spades). The multiplier is three.
b) Hearts are trumps, the player is without two matadors (the top two trumps are missing). The multiplier is two.

Trumps

Holding matadors

Multipliers for schneider and schwarz The bidder may only count one of the following multipliers:
a) schneider made but not predicted, one;
b) schwarz made but not predicted, two;
c) schneider predicted and made, three;
d) schneider predicted and schwarz made, four;
e) schwarz predicted and made, five.

Scoring is as follows. (Except see the separate section for reject.) Only the bidder scores.

If he has made his bid, he scores the total of his game points (which may be higher than his bid).

If he has not made his bid:
a) at suits or grand, he loses the amount of his bid at handplay — or twice that amount if he took the skat;
b) at null, he loses the absolute game value.

Reject There is no bidder and no bid. Normally the player who makes the fewest trick points scores 10. But:
a) if he takes no tricks, he scores 20;
b) if two players tie for fewest trick points, the one who did not take the last trick receives the score of 10;
c) if one player takes all tricks, he loses 30 and the others score nothing;
d) if all players tie with 40 trick points, forehand alone scores 10 for naming the game.

Winning The scores are recorded on a piece of paper and totaled at the end of a session.

The winner is the player with the highest score.

Often, an average score is worked out — players above the average then collect money accordingly, while players whose score is below average must make the payments.

Rummy

One of the most popular games in the United States, rummy is a straightforward card game for two to six players. Among its many variations, gin rummy—which can be traced back to the gambling casinos and saloons of nineteenth-century America—is the best liked and the most played.

Melds

BASIC RUMMY

Cards A standard deck of 52 cards is used.
In play, the cards rank normally with ace low.
For scoring, the jack, queen, and king are each worth 10 points; all other cards are worth their face value.

Players Two to six may play. There are no partnerships.

Objective Each player attempts to be the first to go out through having "melded" all his cards.
Cards are melded in either groups or sequences.

A group is three or four cards of the same rank (eg 4 of hearts, 4 of spades, and 4 of clubs).

A sequence is three or more cards of the same suit falling in numerical order (eg 9,10, and jack of diamonds).

Starting the game The player with the lowest cut or draw shuffles the cards, with the player to his right cutting the deck.
The cards are dealt in a clockwise direction. The number of cards dealt varies according to the number of players:
two players, 10 cards each;
three to four players, seven cards each;
five to six players, six cards each.
After the deal, the remaining cards are turned face down to form the stock. The top card from the stock is turned face up beside it to start the discard pile (this card is called the upcard).

Play Players take their turns in a clockwise direction, beginning with the player to the dealer's left.
The player starts his turn by drawing the top card from either the stock or the discard pile. He may then meld a group or a sequence face up on the table.
He may also "lay off" (add) as many cards as possible to any matched sets already melded on the table, whether the original melds were his own or an opponent's.
He ends his turn by rejecting one card from his hand and placing it face up on the discard pile. If he began his turn by drawing a card from the discard pile, he is not permitted to end the turn by discarding that same card.
If the stock is used up before any player goes out, the discard pile is turned face down (unshuffled) to form a new stock.

Going out A player goes out—and wins the hand—if he succeeds in getting rid of all his cards, with or without a final discard.

Going rummy A player "goes rummy" if he goes out by melding all his cards in one turn without having previously melded or laid off any cards.

Scoring If a player goes out, the numerical value of all the cards then left in his opponents' hands is totaled to give the winner's score for the round. This score is doubled if the player went rummy.

Continuing play The deal passes to the next player to the left if there are more than two players. If there are two players, the winner of one round deals the next.

Game The first player to reach a previously agreed total wins the game.

GIN RUMMY

Cards Two standard decks of 52 cards are used. While one player deals, the other shuffles the second deck ready for the next deal.
The cards rank normally, with ace low. They are valued as for basic rummy.

Players Basic gin rummy is for two players. It can be adapted for any larger even number by dividing players into two equal sides, and holding separate but simultaneous games between pairs of players.

Objective As in rummy each player tries to meld his cards in groups or sequences.
Unlike basic rummy, however, it is possible for a player to win a hand without melding all his cards.

Choice of first dealer The player cutting the higher card has the choice of seat, deck of cards, and whether he wants first deal.

Shuffle and cut are normal (see p 80).

Deal The dealer deals 10 face-down cards to each player, beginning with his opponent and dealing one card at a time.
The twenty-first card is then turned face up and becomes the first card on the discard pile (the upcard).
The remaining cards are placed face down on the table alongside the upcard to form the stock.

Start of play The non-dealer decides whether or not he wants the upcard.
If he decides not to take it, the dealer has the option of taking it. If the dealer does not want it, then the non-dealer must draw the top stock card. Whichever player takes a card must then discard one.

Turn of play In subsequent turns a player takes the top card from either the discard pile or the stock, and then discards.
Players do not lay melds on the table until one player ends the hand by "going gin" or "knocking."

Going gin A player goes gin if he can meld all 10 of his cards in matched sets. He declares this when it is his turn, and lays all his cards face up on the table.
His opponent may then lay down his own melds, but he may not lay off any cards onto the winner's melds.

Knocking is an alternative way of going out. It may be done if the unmatched cards—deadwood—in a player's hand add up to 10 points or less. A player can knock only when it is his turn. He draws a card in the usual way, knocks on the table, and discards one card face down. He then lays out all his remaining cards face up on the table, grouping them into melds and unmatched cards.
His opponent must then, without drawing, lay out his cards on the table. Cards should be grouped into melds and unmatched cards, but the player also has the opportunity of laying off cards onto the knocker's melds.
Each player's deadwood cards are then totaled, and the totals compared.

Scoring a hand
1) If a player goes gin he gets a 25 point bonus in addition to the value of his opponent's deadwood.
2) If a player knocks and his deadwood count is less than his opponent's, the knocker wins the hand and his score is the difference between the two counts.
3) If a player knocks and his opponent's deadwood count is lower than or the same as his own, the opponent has "undercut" the knocker and wins the hand. For this he scores a 25 point bonus as well as any difference between the deadwood counts.

"No game" The last two cards in the stock may not be drawn. If the player who draws the fiftieth card is unable to go gin or knock, the hand is a tie and no points are scored. The same dealer deals for the next hand.

Box (or line) A running total is kept of each player's score. When a player wins a hand, a horizontal line called a box (or line) is drawn under his score.

Game score The first player to score 100 or more points ends the game and has 100 points added to his score.
If his opponent has failed to win a hand, the winner then doubles his score (including the 100 point bonus).
Finally, for every hand a player has won—as shown by the boxes in his running score —he receives an additional 25 point bonus.

CANASTA

Canasta is a partnership game of the rummy family. Originating in Uruguay, it reached the United States in 1949. Here, in the early 1950s, it became one of the biggest fads in the history of card playing.

Cards Two standard decks of 52 cards and four jokers are used, shuffled together. The cards are not ranked. There are 12 wild cards: the four jokers and all eight deuces (2s).
Wild cards can be given any denomination that the holder wishes.

Players In the standard game there are four players divided into two partnerships.

The objective is to be the first side to score 5000 points over a series of hands. Points are mainly scored by making melds.

A meld is a set of at least three cards of the same denomination. They can be all natural cards, or a mixture of natural and wild cards. But whatever the size of the meld, there must be at least two natural cards and not more than three wild cards. Melds score according to the cards they contain (see table A).

Cutting for partners Each player cuts a card from the deck, and the two who cut the highest cards play against the other two.
For this purpose, cards rank normally (ace high) and suits rank spades (high), hearts, diamonds, clubs (low). Players cutting a joker or exactly equal cards cut again. The player cutting highest becomes first dealer and has choice of seats.

Shuffle and cut are normal (see p 80).

The deal begins with the player to the dealer's left. The cards are dealt one at a time and face down in a clockwise direction until each player including the dealer has 11 cards.
The remaining cards are then placed face down on the table as the stock. The top card of the stock is turned face up alongside to start the discard pile.

Play starts with the player to the dealer's left.
In a normal turn a player first takes the top card of the stock. He then makes any melds that he can, or adds to those that he or his partner have already laid out on the table.

Finally he discards by placing one card from his hand face up on the discard pile.

The initial meld of a partnership after each deal must total at least a certain number of points—how many depends on their score so far (see table B).
Once either partner has made this first meld, both partners can make new melds of any value and can add to melds that they have already laid out on the table.
A player may add to either his own or his partner's melds.

A canasta is a meld of seven cards.
A natural canasta consists of seven cards of the same rank and has a bonus value of 500 points on top of the card score.
A mixed canasta has natural cards and one to three wild cards, and has a bonus value of 300 points.
Once a canasta is completed, the cards are gathered into a pile. A natural canasta has a red card placed on top for identification, and a mixed canasta a black card.
Further cards may be added to a canasta. But a mixed canasta may not receive a fourth wild card and a natural canasta loses its value if a wild card is added.

Taking the discard pile In place of taking the top card from the stock, a player may in his turn take the upcard from the discard pile—but only if he has in his hand at least two natural cards of the same denomination.
He must lay the appropriate hand cards face up on the table and meld the upcard with them.
He then also takes all the remainder of the discard pile, and immediately uses as many cards as possible by adding to existing melds or laying out new ones. Any cards that he cannot use become part of his hand.
The player ends his turn by discarding one card to start a new discard pile.
Provided it is not "frozen," a player may also take the discard pile:
a) if he can meld the upcard with one card of the same denomination and one wild card; or
b) if the upcard matches an existing meld of his partnership.

Frozen discard pile The discard pile is frozen as follows.
1) It is frozen for a partnership that has not made its initial meld.
2) It is frozen for a player if a black 3 is the upcard. In this case it is no longer frozen after the player has drawn from the stock and discarded.
3) It is frozen for all players if the discard pile contains a red 3 or a wild card. In this case further discards are placed crosswise on top of the freezing card. The discard pile remains frozen until one player unfreezes it by melding the upcard or wild card with two natural cards from his hand.

Red 3s are bonus cards counting 100 points each. They cannot be melded.
If a player draws a red 3 from the stock, he must lay it face up on the table and draw another card from the stock.
If he is dealt a red 3 he must lay it face up on the table and draw a card from the stock in addition to his regular draw.
If a red 3 is taken as part of the discard pile, it must be laid face up on the table without any extra card being drawn from the stock.
If a partnership holds all four red 3s, these cards count 200 points each (800 points in all). All red 3 points count against a partnership if it has not made an initial meld when play ends.

Black 3s may only be melded when a player is going out. They can never be melded with wild cards. Their main use is as "stop cards" to freeze the discard pile.

Going out occurs when a player is able to meld all his cards, providing that when he has gone out his side has made at least one canasta. A player can go out without discarding if he wishes.

Concealed going out occurs when a player melds all his cards when he has not previously melded any cards. Note that he must meld a canasta unless his partner has already melded one.

Permission is usually asked to go out, in the form of "May I go out partner?" A yes or no answer is required and is binding.
This procedure is generally used as a warning to a partner to meld as many cards as possible, so that the requesting player can go out in his next turn.

Table A

Card	Points for each card in meld
Joker	50
Deuce (2)	20
Ace	20
8, 9, 10, j, q, k	10
4, 5, 6, 7	5
Black 3	5
Red 3	see text

Table B

Accumulated score of partnership	Value required for initial meld
Minus	15
0-1495	50
1500-2995	90
3000 or more	120

Table C

	Points
Natural canasta	500
Mixed canasta	300
Going out	100
Concealed going out	100 extra
Red 3s	see text

Wild cards

Melds

Natural

Mixed

A canasta

Scoring Each partnership receives the total of all bonus points earned in the hand (see table C), plus the total point value of all melded cards, less the value of any cards remaining in the hands of either player in the partnership at the end of play.
(Note that the low bonuses for going out make the completion of high-scoring melds more significant than being first to go out.)
If one partnership has failed to meld at all, the value of any red 3s it has laid down count against it.
It is possible for a partnership to make a minus score on a hand.

Hands continue until one side has made a total of 5000 points and wins the game. For each successive hand the deal passes clockwise.

Variant rules The following variations on the standard rules are widely accepted.
1) Even if the discard pile is not frozen, a player may not take the upcard to add it to a completed canasta of his own side.
2) When taking the upcard from the discard pile to make a new meld, a player must always have a natural pair to match it (ie not a matching card and a wild card).

© DIAGRAM

Cribbage

Cribbage is reputed to have been invented by Sir John Suckling, an English poet and courtier who lived in the early 1600s. Six-card cribbage for two players is the most popular form of the game today, but there are also five- and seven-card forms as well as adaptations for three and four players.

Pair, 2 points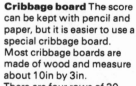

Pair royal, 6 points

Double pair royal, 12 points

Sequence, 4 points

Flush, 4 points

Fifteen, 2 points

Specimen hand worth 24 points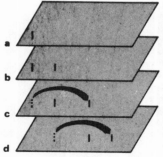

The "start"

Four fifteens, 8 points

Four sequences, 12 points

Pair, 2 points

Pair, 2 points

Cards All forms of cribbage are played with a single standard deck of 52 cards.

Card values Court cards count 10 each, and all other cards count their face value.

Cribbage board The score can be kept with pencil and paper, but it is easier to use a special cribbage board. Most cribbage boards are made of wood and measure about 10in by 3in.

There are four rows of 30 holes, two rows for each player, and additional game holes at one or both ends of the board.

Each player has two pegs, usually red or black for one player and white for the other. When there are four game holes, the players usually put their pegs in them for the start of play.

A player marks his score by moving his pegs first along his outer row and then back along his inner row of holes.

Both pegs are used to score in the following way:

a) a player marks his first score by moving one peg that number of holes from the start;

b) his second score is marked by placing his second peg that number of holes beyond his first peg;

c) his third score is marked by placing his first peg that number of holes beyond his second peg;

d) scoring continues in this way until a player's forward peg has passed all the scoring holes to end in one of the game holes.

SIX-CARD CRIBBAGE

Players The basic game is for two players.

Objective The game is won by the first player to score 121 points, ie to go "twice around the board."

The deal Players cut for deal. The player with the lower cut (with ace low) deals first, and then the deal alternates between players.

The deal is six cards, one at a time, to each player. The remaining cards are placed face down to one side.

The crib is an extra hand scored by the dealer.

It is formed by each of the players discarding two cards and placing them, face down, to the dealer's right. Each player is thus left with a hand of four cards.

The cut After the discards the non-dealer cuts the deck, and the dealer turns up the top card of the remaining stack.

This card is placed face up on the stack for the rest of the game. It is known as the "start" or "starter."

If the start is a jack, the dealer scores "two for his heels."

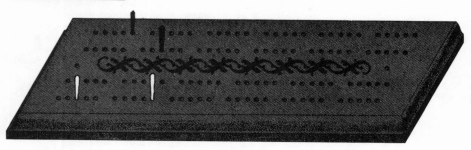

Scoring Points are scored both during the playing of a hand and when the hands are shown after play. Combinations of cards score as follows.

a) A pair, two cards of the same rank, scores two points.

b) A pair royal, three cards of the same rank, scores six points (two points for each of the possible pairs to be made).

c) A double pair royal, four cards of the same rank, scores 12 points.

d) A sequence or run is a series of cards in face order (ace low) and scores one point for each card. The cards do not have to be of the same suit.

e) A flush is four or five cards of the same suit and scores one point for each card. If a flush is also a run, points are scored for both features.

f) Fifteen is any combination of cards with a face value totaling that number. It scores two points.

Play begins with the non-dealer. He places a card face upward in front of him and calls out its face value as he does so. Court cards are called as 10.

The dealer then places one of his cards face upward in front of himself and calls out its value.

Whenever a pair, pair royal, double pair royal, sequence, or fifteen (but not a flush) is formed during play, the player putting down the card that forms it scores the appropriate points.

If the non-dealer lays down a 5 and the dealer follows it with another 5, the dealer would say "ten for a pair" and score two points. If a third 5 is played, the non-dealer would say "fifteen for eight," the eight points being made up of a fifteen and a pair royal.

A sequence of cards scores regardless of the order in which it is played. Thus if cards are played in the order ace, 2, 5, 4, 3, the player putting out the 3 can count a run of five cards. Should the second player be able to add a 6 he can score a run of six cards, and so on.

When the count during play reaches 31, the cards are turned face down and the player whose card brought the total to 31 scores two points. If a player at his turn is unable to play a card that is within the limit of 31, he says "go." His opponent then plays any of his cards that are low enough to be within the limit. If they make 31 he scores two points; if less than 31 he scores one point and also says "go." Play then resumes with the remaining cards in hand, and proceeds until all the cards are played or another 31 limit is reached.

The player who plays the last card of a hand scores "one for last."

The show After all the cards have been played, each player picks up his own cards from in front of him.

The non-dealer shows and scores his hand first, which gives him an advantage if he is very near reaching 121.

The start is taken into the reckoning as part of each hand.

A card may be ranked for scoring in any number of different combinations. Thus two 10s and two 5s would give a score of eight points for fifteens plus four points for pairs—giving a total of 12 points. The combination 4,4,5,5,6,6 scores eight points for fifteens, four points for pairs, and 12 points for sequences—giving a total of 24 points (see illustration).

If a player holds a jack of the same suit as the start, he scores "one for his nob."

A flush of four cards in hand scores four points. If the start is of the same suit the player scores five points, but a flush of four cards including the start scores nothing.

After the non-dealer has declared his score, the dealer shows and scores his own hand. After which, he shows and also scores for the crib. The crib is scored in the same way as the hands, except that the only flush allowed is a five-card one.

Muggins If a player overlooks a score, whether in his hand or in play, his opponent may call "muggins" and claim the overlooked score for himself. (Some players prefer not to employ this rule.)

Lurch If a player reaches 121 before his opponent is halfway around the board, he scores a lurch and counts two games instead of one.

Errors If an error in dealing is noticed during the deal, there should be a redeal.

If an error in dealing is found after play has started, the non-dealer scores two points and the error is rectified either by a redeal or by drawing additional cards from the stock.

If after "go" is called a player fails to play his additional cards, he may not subsequently play those cards and his opponent scores two points. Errors in counting during play are not penalized.

FIVE-CARD CRIBBAGE
This is an earlier form of the game than six-card cribbage. Except as specified, the rules are the same as for the six-card game.

Objective Game is 61 points.

The deal is five cards to each player.

The crib consists of two cards from each player.

Play Non-dealer pegs three points before play begins, to compensate for not having the crib.

Hands are not played out after 31 is reached or "go" is called. Hands are shown and scored; then there is a new deal.

SEVEN-CARD CRIBBAGE
This version is played in the same way as six-card cribbage, except that: game is 181 points; the deal is seven cards to each player (of which two go to the crib).

THREE-HANDED CRIBBAGE
The game is adapted for three-handed play in the following ways.

Game is 61 points.

The deal is five cards to each player and one to the crib. Each player then gives one card to the crib.

Play begins with the player to the left of the dealer, and passes to the left.

The player who leads also has the first show.

FOUR-HANDED CRIBBAGE
This is a partnership form of the game.

Partners sit opposite each other, and play begins with the player to the dealer's left.

Game is 121 points.

The deal is usually five cards to each player (of which one goes to the crib).

Tarot card games

The exact origins of tarot cards are not known, but it is probable that they have been used since medieval times both as a means of foretelling the future and for playing card games. Many different tarot games are played today, often using a mixed deck of tarot and standard playing cards.

Trump cards

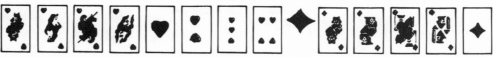

AUSTRIAN TAROCK

This is a popular 54-card tarot game played in many parts of Europe. It is played with a mixed deck of numbered tarot cards and standard playing cards.

Players It is a game for three people (**a**), but can be adapted for four players.

The player to the left of the dealer is called forehand, the next middlehand, and the dealer himself, endhand. (If four players take part (**b**), the dealer does not receive cards, but he may share in the payments for that hand. The third player is then called endhand.)

Forehand

a

(Dealer) Endhand
Middlehand

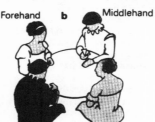

Forehand b Middlehand

Dealer Endhand

The deck comprises:
a) 32 cards divided equally into four suits—hearts, diamonds, spades, and clubs. Four of the eight cards in each suit are court cards: king, queen, knight, and jack. Cards in the red suits rank: k (high),q,kt,j,a,2,3,4 (low). Cards in the black suits rank: k (high),q,kt,j,10,9,8,7 (low).
b) 22 trump cards numbered XXII (high) through I (low). Number XXII is called the joker or "skus;" number XXI "mond;" and number I "pagat."
The trump cards are sometimes illustrated as well as bearing a number.

The objective is to make a winning bid and to score points in melds and tricks.
Deal The dealer gives eight face-down cards at a time to each player, including himself. He then deals a face-down "widow" (see p 80) of six cards to the center of the table, before dealing a further batch of eight cards to each player.
(Should any player not have received a trump card, he must immediately show his cards, and a redeal takes place after the cards have been thoroughly shuffled.)

Suit cards

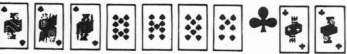

Bidding is in a clockwise direction, beginning with forehand. Players may either bid or pass. If all the players pass, the deal moves one player to the left without a score.

There are two permissable bids: a threesome (worth 50 points) and a solo (worth 100 points). The solo bid overcalls the threesome, so that if forehand opens with a solo bid, there can be no further bidding.

Threesome When the winning bid is threesome, the bidder takes up the top three cards of the widow. If these are not to his liking, he puts them face up on the table and takes the remaining three cards of the widow.

He may either incorporate these three cards into his hand (in which case the game counts double); or he may reject them face up and take up the exposed first three cards of the widow (in which case the game counts triple).

Whichever cards he chooses, he then discards any three cards, except kings, from his hand. His discards are put face down on the table but if they include a trump this must be declared.

At the end of play, the discards belong to the winning bidder and the rejected cards of the widow to his two opponents (see the section on trick scores).

After choosing his widow cards, the bidder must choose to play either:

a) game—in which case he must try to win 36 or more points in play; or

b) consolation—in which case he must try to win 35 or fewer points.

Solo When solo is the winning bid, the widow remains unexposed. At the end of play it goes to the bidder's opponents, who, in both solo and threesome, play in partnership against him.

Melds are declared after the bidding and the discarding, if any.
Possible melds are:
a) joker, mond, and pagat;
b) four kings.
Each meld scores 50 in threesome and 100 in solo. (see scoring).

Melds

5 points

5 points

5 points

5 points

4 points

3 points

3 points

Play After the bidding, forehand leads with any card he likes. The other players must either follow suit or, if this is impossible, trump. If a player can neither follow suit nor trump he may play any card he likes.

The highest trump, or the highest card of the suit led if there are no trumps, takes the trick. The winner of each trick leads to the next trick.

Points in play depend on the combination of "point" cards and "nulls" in each trick. Point cards and their point values are as follows:
a) joker (XXII), mond (XXI), pagat (I), and kings, five points each;
b) queens, four points each; and
c) knights and jacks, three points each.
Nulls are the other 35 cards and have no point values.
Each trick counts points as follows:
a) one point for three nulls;
b) the value of the point card for one point card and two nulls;
c) the sum of the point cards minus one, for two point cards and one null; and

d) the sum of the point cards minus two, for three point cards.

The bidder also scores for his discards, if any, and the opponents for the widow. The bidder fulfills his bid if either:

he chose solo or game and makes 36 or more trick points; or he chose consolation and makes 35 or fewer trick points.

Scoring At solo or game a successful bidder scores double the number of trick points he made over 35, plus 50 for threesome and 100 for solo.

If he played consolation, his score would be double the difference between 35 and his actual trick points, plus 50 for threesome.

For example, if he took 24 trick points, his score would be $(35 - 24) \times 2 + 50 = 72$.

If the bidder fails to make his bid, each of his opponents scores the value of the bid plus twice the number of points the opponent has scored over 35.

Each player then scores for any melds he has made.

Pagat Any player who wins the last trick with the pagat receives a bonus of 50 in threesome, and 100 in solo.

Before play opens the bidder may declare "Ultimo," signifying his intention of taking the last trick with the pagat.

If he does so and succeeds, he gains a bonus of twice the value of the game.

If he fails, he loses that same amount. If he has to play the pagat earlier in the game and loses it, he may score 5 points for it if he takes the last trick. He does not score if he played the pagat unnecessarily.

If the bidder declares ultimo, an opponent may declare "Contra-ultimo," signifying that he intends to win the bidder's pagat.

If he does so and succeeds, each opponent wins a bonus of 200 in threesome, and 400 in solo.

If he fails, the same bonus goes to the bidder.

Trick scores

1 point

5 points

7 points

9 points

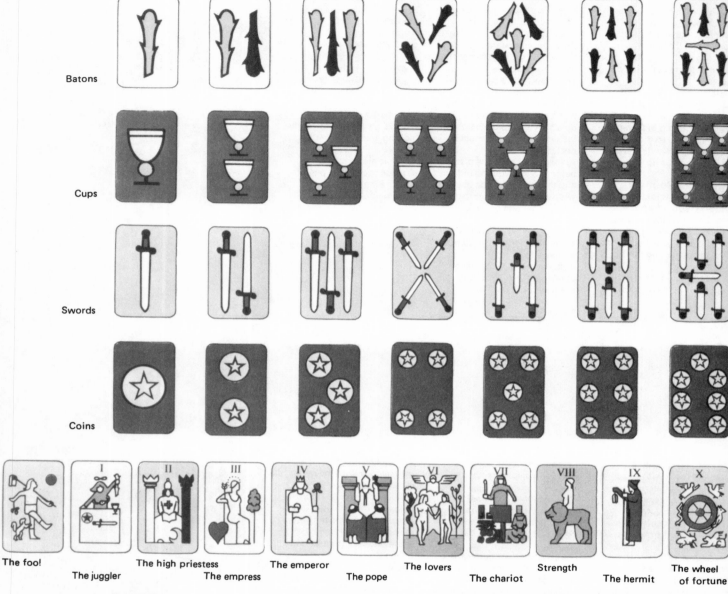

Batons

Cups

Swords

Coins

The foo! | The juggler | The high priestess | The empress | The emperor | The pope | The lovers | The chariot | Strength | The hermit | The wheel of fortune

TAROCCO

Tarocco is a tarot game played with the traditional 78-card tarot deck that is also used for fortune telling.

Players The game is for three players. Play is in a counterclockwise direction: the player to the dealer's right is called forehand, the second player middlehand, and the dealer endhand.

The deck comprises:
a) 22 cards that function as a trump suit;
b) 56 cards in four suits of 14 cards each: batons, cups, swords, and coins.

The trump cards rank from XXI (high) to I (low). (The fool, when ranked, ranks below the I.)

The suit cards rank k(high), q,kt(knight),j,10,etc.

The trump cards are:
the fool (the only one of the 22 cards that is not numbered), the juggler (I), the high priestess (II), the empress (III), the emperor (IV), the pope (V), the lovers (VI), the chariot (VII), strength (VIII), the hermit (IX), the wheel of fortune (X), justice (XI), the hanging man (XII), death (XIII), temperance (XIV), the devil (XV), the tower (XVI), the star (XVII), the moon (XVIII), the sun (XIX), the day of judgment (XX), and the world (XXI).

The world, the juggler, and the fool are called "honor" cards.

The objective is to score the maximum number of points by taking certain cards in tricks.

Deal Players draw cards for the right to deal; lowest card deals first. The deal passes one player to the right for each new hand.

Each player is dealt 24 cards, one at a time and face down. The remaining six cards are added to the dealer's hand.

Buying cards takes place as soon as the deck has been dealt.

It is an optional procedure and has many variations, but usually a player wanting a particular card may announce this and buy it from the player who holds it (assuming he is willing to part with it) by "paying" ten points ie ten points are deducted from the buyer's score and added to the seller's score.

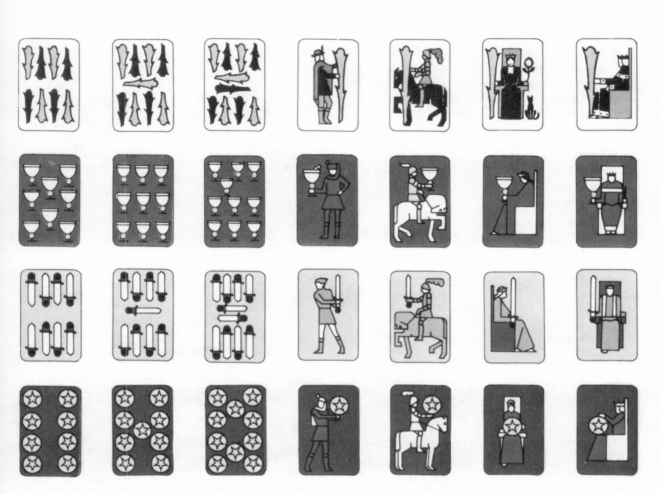

XI	XII	XIII	XIV	XV	XVI	XVII	XVIII	XIX	XX	XXI
Justice	The hanging man	Death	Temperance	The devil	The tower	The star	The moon	The sun	The day of judgment	The world

Play The dealer discards face down any six cards except honors and kings.
He then leads to the first trick by putting out face up any card of his choice. Play then proceeds in a counterclockwise direction.
If the lead is in batons, cups, swords, or coins the players must play a card of the same suit but of any value. If he cannot follow suit, he must play a trump card; if this is not possible he may play a card of any suit.
If the lead is a trump card, a player must follow with another trump card—usually a rule is applied that it should also be of a higher value; if this is not possible he may play a card of any suit.
The winner of a trick leads to the next trick.

The fool A player holding the fool may, during any trick except the last, show it instead of playing a card. The trick is then contested between his two opponents only, and the fool is placed with any tricks the player may have taken.
In the last trick, the fool counts as the lowest ranking trump card and is played normally.
The juggler If a player wins the last trick with a juggler, he scores ten points. If he plays the juggler to the last trick and loses, he forfeits ten points.

Scoring in tricks If accompanied by a low-value card (ace through 10) certain cards score as follows:
a) the world (XXI), the juggler (I), the fool, five points each;
b) kings, five points each;
c) queens, four points each;
d) knights, two points each.
The dealer also scores as above for his discards.

Bonus points A player with 15 trumps in his hand must declare them before play begins, and earns a bonus of ten points.
A player who wins all tricks receives a bonus of 20 points.
The winner is the player with the highest score at the end of three hands.
Each loser pays the difference between his and the winner's score, according to a points or money scale agreed on by the players before the game.

6 Dice games

Casting objects to see how they will fall has universally fascinated man. Modern-looking dice from 1500BC have been found in the tombs of Egypt; and in ancient India one prince wagered his kingdom and his wife at dice, and lost. Nero played happily for the equivalent of $15,000 a throw; and once, King Henry VIII of England staked—and lost—the bells of old St Paul's church.

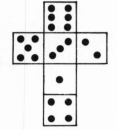

A standard modern die is a regular cube, with the six sides numbered with dots from 1 through 6. Any two opposing sides add up to 7.

The evolution of dice
Casting must have begun with common objects such as stones and shells. The Indian game of pachisi is still played with six cowrie shells, scored by which way up they fall.
Later the anklebones of sheep were used as four-sided dice. These led to the cubic dice of the ancient Etruscans.
In Asia divination sticks led to the "long dice" still used in some Eastern games. These have from two to six sides and are rolled rather than tumbled. Another Eastern type is the "teetotum" or spinning die.
Unusual dice of ancient and medieval times include many-sided dice, and dice marked on small carved figures of animals or men.

If you don't have dice:
a) dot a sugar cube with ink;
b) scratch lines on a pencil's six sides, and roll it;
c) make a "spinning die" from a pencil and card;
d) divide a sheet of paper into six numbered areas, and throw any object to see where it falls.

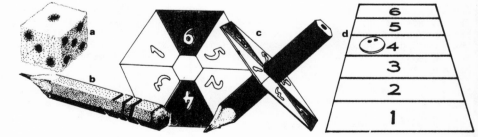

A mis-spotted die

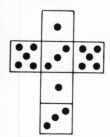

Odds With one true die, each face has an equal chance of landing face up. With two dice thrown together, some scores are more likely than others because there are more ways in which they can be made.
Cheating includes weighted, distorted, and mis-spotted dice; tampered edges; false throws; and sleight of hand.

Ways of throwing different numbers, with two dice

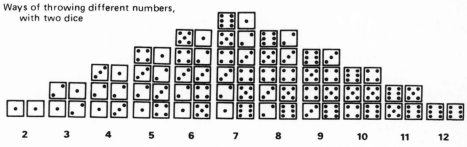

2   3   4   5   6   7   8   9   10   11   12

118

Family dice games

These are family games—ways of passing a happy hour, some games for the young and some for both young and old.

Shut the box

FIFTY

This game, for two or more players, is one of the simplest dice games. It requires two dice, and the winner is the first player to score 50 points. Each player in turn rolls the two dice, but scores only when identical numbers are thrown (two 1s, two 2s, and so on). All these doubles, except two 6s and two 3s, score five points. A double 6 scores 25 points; and a double 3 wipes out the player's total score and he has to start again.

ROUND THE CLOCK

This is a game for three or four players, using two dice.
Objective Players try to throw 1 through 12 in correct sequence. The winner is the first player to complete the full sequence.
Play Each player throws in turn, rolling the dice once only.
From 1 through 6, he can score on either of the two dice, or on both of them. For example, if he threw a 1 and a 3, but wanted only a 1, this die alone would count, and at his next throw he would try for a 2. But if he wanted a 4, he would count both dice (1+3= 4).
A player can also count both dice as separate scores, if he can use both of them. For example, if he needs 1 and throws a 1 and a 2, he can count both 1 and 2.
From 7 through 12, however, the combined spot values of both dice will obviously be needed.

SHUT THE BOX

This game, for two or more players, has long been popular in northern France.
Equipment:
1) two dice;
2) a board or sheet of paper with nine boxes numbered 1 to 9;
3) nine counters used to cover the numbers during the course of the game—in some parts of the world, specially made trays with sliding covers for the numbers are available.
Objective Players aim to cover as many of the numbers as possible, in accordance with the throws of the dice. High-numbered boxes should be covered first, since it is the player with the lowest score who wins.
Play begins after a preliminary round has decided the first shooter (usually the player with the highest score). Each player in turn throws the two dice. He then adds the spot values of the two dice and decides which box numbers he will cover.
For example, a throw totaling 10 would allow him to cover 5 and 5, 6 and 4, 7 and 3, 8 and 2, or 9 and 1.
Once the player has covered his chosen numbers, he throws again and makes a further choice. But he cannot make use of numbers he has already covered—he must use up his entire score with uncovered numbers.
When a player has covered the three highest numbers (7, 8, and 9), he is allowed to throw with only one die whenever he wishes. He continues throwing until he can no longer find combinations in his latest throw to match the numbers still uncovered. His turn is now complete and the uncovered numbers remaining are totaled and constitute his score.
All numbers on the board are once more exposed. The next player takes the dice and has his turn, and so on.

HEARTS

Hearts, or hearts due, is a game for two or more players.
Equipment Six dice are used. Special dice marked with the letters H,E,A,R,T,S instead of numbers are sometimes used, but the game is now more commonly played with ordinary dice.
The objective is simply to score more than your opponents over an agreed series of rounds, or a single round, or to be the first to reach an agreed total.
Play begins after a preliminary round has decided the first shooter (usually the player with the highest score).
Each player in turn rolls the six dice once and calculates his score according to the following ratings:
1 (H)=5 points;
1,2 (HE)= 10 points;
1,2,3 (HEA)= 15 points;
1,2,3,4 (HEAR)= 20 points;
1,2,3,4,5 (HEART)= 25 points;
1,2,3,4,5,6 (HEARTS)= 35 points.
If a double (two dice of the same spot value) or a treble appears in the throw, only one of the letters or numbers counts. But if three 1s (or Hs) appear, the player's whole score is wiped out and he has to start again.

BEETLE

This is a lively game for two or more players—more than six tend to slow down the game.
Equipment:
1) one die, either an ordinary one or a special "beetle die" marked B (body), H (head), L (legs), E (eyes), F (feelers), and T (tail);
2) a simple drawing of a beetle as a guide, showing its various parts and (when an ordinary die is used) their corresponding numbers;
3) a pencil and a piece of paper for each player.
Objective Each player, by throwing the die, tries to complete his drawing of the beetle. The first to do so scores 13 points and is the winner. The 13 points represent one for each part of the beetle (body, head, tail, two feelers, two eyes, and six legs).
Play Each player throws the die once only in each round. Each player must begin by throwing a B (or a 1); this permits him to draw the body. When this has been drawn, he can throw for other parts of the beetle which can be joined to the body.
An H or a 2 must be thrown to link the head to the body before the feelers (F or 5) and eyes (E or 4) can be added. Each eye or feeler requires its own throw.
A throw of L or 3 permits the player to add three legs to one side of the body. A further throw of L or 3 is necessary for the other three legs. Sometimes it is agreed that a player may continue to throw in his turn for as long as he throws parts of the body he can use.
Continuing play When a series of games is played, each player counts one point for every part of the beetle he has been able to draw and cumulative scores are carried forward from round to round. The winner is the player with the highest score at the end of the series, or the first to reach a previously agreed total score.

Beetle

© DIAGRAM

Drop dead

Running total   0

0

0

3

7

7

DROP DEAD

This is an exciting game for any number of players.

Equipment:
1) five dice;
2) a sheet of paper on which to record players' scores.

Objective Players aim to make the highest total score.

Play Each player in turn rolls the five dice several times. His score for each throw is the total of the numbers in that throw. However, any throw containing a 2 or a 5 scores nothing. Any dice showing those numbers must be removed from succeeding throws by that player.

For example, if a player threw 2,4,6,3,4 on his first throw, the die showing 2 would count zero, and on his second throw he would roll only four dice. Eventually he may be reduced to only one die. When this shows a 2 or a 5, he is said to have "dropped dead" and is out of the game.

It is possible, of course, for a sudden demise to result from the very first throw, eg 5,5,5,2,2; and equally possible to survive profitably for a long time with only one die!

The game can also be played with each player having several throws, exactly as above, but throwing only one die in a turn and passing it to the player to his left after each throw.

This makes the game more exciting, but after each player's throw a careful note must be made of his score so far and how many dice (if any) he has left.

CHICAGO

Chicago, also called rotation, is a game for any number of players. Two dice are used. The game is based on the 11 possible combinations of the two dice—2,3,4,5,6,7,8,9,10, 11 and 12—and so consists of 11 rounds.

The objective is to score each of these combinations in turn. The player with the highest score is the winner.

Play Each player in turn rolls the dice once in each round. During the first round, he will try to make a total of 2, during the second, a total of 3, and so on up to 12.

Each time he is successful, that number of points is added to his score.

For example, if he is shooting for 5 and throws a total of 5, he gains five points. If he fails to make the desired number, he scores nothing on that throw.

GOING TO BOSTON

Also known as Newmarket or Yankee grab, this game is ideal for three or four players, although more can play.

Equipment: three dice.

Play Each player in turn rolls the three dice together. After the first roll, he leaves the die showing the highest number on the table, then rolls the other two again. Of these, the die with the highest number is also left on the table and the remaining die is rolled again. This completes the player's throw and the total of his three dice is his score.

When all players have thrown, the player with the highest score wins the round. Ties are settled by further rolling.

A game usually consists of an agreed number of rounds: the player who wins the most games is the winner.

Alternatively, each player can contribute counters to a pool that is won at the end of each game.

MULTIPLICATION

This game is played like going to Boston, but with one important difference.

When each player has completed his turn, his score is the sum of the spot values of the first two dice rolled, multiplied by that of the third. For example, if his first throw is 5, his second throw 4, and his final throw 6, his score will be 54: $(5+4) \times 6$.

PIG

This simple game, for any number of players, requires only one die. The winner is the first player to reach a previously agreed high score (usually 100).

Order of play is determined by a preliminary round. Each player throws the die once and the player with the lowest score becomes first shooter. The next-lowest scoring player shoots second, and so on. The order of play is important because the first and last shooters have natural advantages (see below).

Play begins with the first shooter. Like the other players, he may roll the die as many times as he wishes. He totals his score throw by throw until he elects to end his turn.

He passes the die to the next player, memorizing his score so far.

But if he throws a 1, he loses the entire score he has made on that turn, and the die passes to the next player. Play passes from player to player until someone reaches the agreed total.

Given a little luck, the first shooter is the player most likely to win. But his advantage can be counteracted by allowing other players to continue until they have had the same number of turns. The player with the highest score is then the winner.

The last shooter still has the advantage of knowing the scores made by all his opponents. Provided he does not roll a 1, he can continue throwing until he has beaten all those scores.

The fairest way of playing the game is to organize it as a series, with each player in turn becoming first shooter.

Player 1   Player 2   Player 3

Pig   Out   Out   Stops, scores 24

CENTENNIAL

Also known as martinetti or Ohio, this is a game for two to eight players.

Equipment:
1) three dice;
2) a long board or piece of paper marked with a row of boxes numbered 1 to 12;
3) a distinctive counter or other object for each player.

Objective Each player tries to be the first to move his counter, in accordance with throws of the dice, from 1 to 12 and back again.

Play begins after a preliminary round has determined the first "shooter" (thrower)—usually the player rolling the highest score.

Each player in turn throws the three dice once. His throw must contain a 1 before he can put his counter in the box so numbered. After his throw, the dice are passed to the next player and so on.

Once a player has thrown a 1, he must try for 2. He can make 2 by throwing either a 2 or two 1s.

He continues to move his counter in this way from box to box.

Some throws may enable him to move through more than one box on a single throw. For example, a throw of 1,2,3 would not only take him through the first three boxes, but on through the fourth $(1+3=4)$, to the fifth $(2+3=5)$ and finally the sixth $(1+2+3=6)$.

Other players' throws must be watched constantly. If a player throws a number he needs but overlooks and does not use, that number may be claimed by any other player. He must do this as soon as the dice are passed, however, and must be able to use it at once.

EVEREST

This game is like centennial but has a different layout and scoring system.

Equipment Each player has a sheet of paper showing two columns, each divided into 12 boxes. In one column the boxes are numbered from 1 to 12 in ascending order. In the other they are numbered from 1 to 12 in descending order.

Objective Each player tries to be the first to score all 24 numbers. The numbers do not have to be scored consecutively as in centennial, but as desired and in either column.

Scoring Each die in a throw can be counted only once.

Centennial

Everest

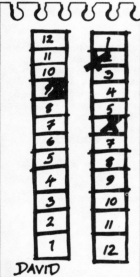

DAVID

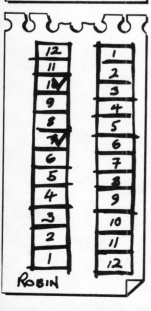

ROBIN

BASEBALL

As a dice game for two players, baseball can be played in several different ways. Of the three described below, the most popular is probably the two-dice game.

Equipment:
1) one, two, or three dice, according to the type of game being played;
2) the one-die and two-dice games require at least three counters for each player to represent his men;
3) a sheet of paper with a simple diagram of a baseball diamond drawn on it;
4) another piece of paper for recording scores.

The objective is to score the highest total number of runs in the nine innings per player that constitute the game.

If the two players have equal scores after the usual nine innings, an extra-inning game is played.

(Note that in baseball, each player's turn at bat is called a "half-inning.")

One-die baseball
The players throw the die to decide who shall "bat" first (ie shoot the die first).

Each player in turn then throws a half-inning. A half-inning is ended when a player has thrown three "outs" (see below).

Value of the throws At the start of the game, or whenever all bases are empty, a throw of 1,2 or 3 permits the player to put a man (counter) on whichever of those three bases he has thrown. A player may have only one man on a base at a time.

If he throws 1, 2, or 3 again, this permits him to move the man around the diamond by the number of bases thrown, and to place another man on the base that bears the number thrown.

For example, if he has a man on 1, and throws a 2, the man advances to base 3 (1+2) and a new man is entered on base 2.

Each time a man reaches the home (fourth) base or "home plate," a run is scored.

A single throw may give a score of more than one run if it results in more than one man reaching home base. (The rule against more than one man on a base does not apply to the fourth base.)

For example, if a player with men on bases 2 and 3 throws a 2, both men advance to home base and two runs are scored. At the same time a new man is entered on base 2.

A throw of 4 counts as a home run and advances all men on the bases to home base. The score is thus the home run plus one run for each man brought home.

Outs Throws of 5 or 6 are "outs."

A throw of 5 is as though there had been a hit and a throw-in, so that men on the bases may also be out, as follows.

a) If the shooter has only one man on the bases, he is out;
b) if he has men on all bases, the man on base 1 is out;
c) if he has men on bases 1 and 2, the man on base 2 is out;
d) if he has men on bases 1 and 3, the man on base 1 is out;
e) if he has men on bases 2 and 3, both are safe.

Men on the bases who are not out remain where they are.

A throw of 6 is also an out, but it is as if the batter were out without striking the ball; men on bases are safe, and remain where they are.

Note that three outs end a half-inning. The other player then throws his half-inning to complete the inning.

Two-dice baseball is similar to the one-die game, but the dice scores count as follows.

Any 12 or 2 is a home run.

Any 4 or 10 is a "one," any 11 a "two," any 3 a "three." With these, all men already on bases advance the appropriate number of bases, and a new man is entered on the appropriate base.

Any 6 or 9 is an out, and the men on bases do not move.

Any 8 is an out, except for double 4s (4+4), which is a "walk." On a walk, a new man is entered on first base and other basemen advance only if they are forced on by him.

Any 5 is an out, but any basemen advance one base each ("sacrifice").

Any 7 is an out, and if there are any basemen one of them is also out. When there is more than one baseman, it is the one nearest home base; the others do not move.

Three-dice baseball is the simplest and perhaps least satisfying version of baseball dice.

Each player throws the dice in turn, scoring one run for every 1 that is rolled.

When he fails to throw a 1, a player's half-inning is ended and his opponent takes over. The game consists of the usual nine innings, with extra innings to decide any tie.

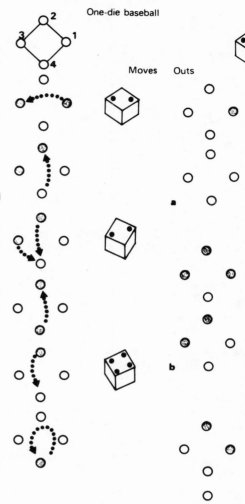

One-die baseball

Moves   Outs

a

b

c

d

BASKETBALL

As a dice game, basketball is usually played by two players, but more can take part, each player representing a team. As in the real game, the winner is the team (ie player) making the highest score in the game or series of games.

Equipment Basketball may be played with only two dice or with as many as 10. Many players use eight dice as there are then enough to ensure a rapid game and realistic scores.

Play A game consists of four quarters. In each quarter each player in turn rolls the eight dice once, their total being his score for that quarter.

If the game is played with only two dice, each player rolls the dice four times to determine his score for that quarter.

The player with the highest score for the four quarters wins the game.

If the game, or agreed series of games, ends in a tie, this is resolved by playing extra quarters until the outright winner is established.

Cheerio combinations

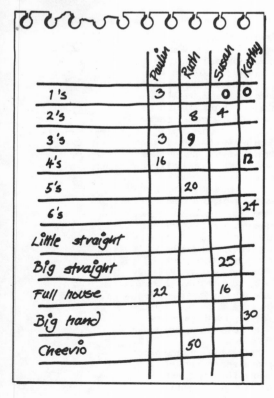

Ones

Twos

Threes

Fours

Fives

Sixes

Little straight

Big straight

Full house

Big hand

Cheerio

Cheerio score sheet

	Pauline	Ruth	Susan	Kathy
1's	3		0	0
2's		8	4	
3's	3	9		
4's	16			12
5's		20		
6's				24
Little straight				
Big straight			25	
Full house	22		16	
Big hand				30
Cheevio		50		

CHEERIO

This game can be played by any number of players up to a maximum of 12. The greater the number of players, the slower the pace of the game.

Equipment:
1) five dice;
2) a dice cup;
3) a sheet of paper showing the various combinations and a scoring column for each player.

Objective Each player tries to score the maximum possible for each of the 11 scoring combinations (see below). The player with the highest total score wins the game.

Games are often played as a series, the player who wins the most games in the series being the overall winner. Alternatively, the scores in each game can be carried forward to the next game until a player has reached a previously agreed cumulative total. If two or more players exceed the total, the player with the highest score wins. Ties are settled by an extra game.

The combinations are given here in ascending order, but that order need not be followed in play. Each player may choose the combinations for which he is rolling (see the section on rolling).

Ones Scores one point for each die showing one spot. Maximum possible: five.

Twos Scores two points for each two-spot die. Possible scores: 2,4,6,8,10.

Threes Scores three points for each three-spot die. Possible scores: 3,6,9,12,15.

Fours Scores four points for each four-spot die. Possible scores: 4,8,12,16,20.

Fives Scores five points for each five-spot die. Possible scores: 5,10,15,20,25.

Sixes Scores six points for each six-spot die. Possible scores: 6,12,18,24,30.

Little straight A show of 1,2,3,4,5 scores 20 points.

Big straight A show of 2,3,4,5,6 scores 25 points.

Full house Three of a kind plus two of a kind scores according to the numbers shown on the dice.
For example, a "full house" comprising 1,1,1,2,2 would score seven points; 2,2,2,1,1 would score eight points, and so on to a maximum of 28 points (6,6,6,5,5).

Big hand The total spot value of the dice. Maximum score: 30 points (6,6,6,6,6).

Cheerio Five of a kind in any value, 1 through 6. Always scores 50 points.

Rolling Each player in turn rolls all five dice. Having rolled the dice once, he may pick up all or any of them and roll once more in an attempt to improve his score.

He does not have to declare his combination until he has finished rolling. This gives him considerable freedom of choice. For example, if he has rolled 6,6,2,3,3 he might call sixes (score 12). But if he wanted to keep sixes for a later turn, when he might roll more than two of them, he could call twos (score 2), or threes (score 6), or even ones (zero) depending on the combinations he has still to roll.

All combinations, except big hand, may rate zero. However, once a player has scored a combination, he cannot score it again in that game.
For example, 6,6,6,5,5, a full house normally scoring 28 points, could not rate this score if the player had rolled a full house in a previous turn and counted it as such. It could only be counted as sixes (score 18) or fives (score 10). If the player had also previously rolled sixes and fives, it would rank zero and be recorded against some other combination.

GENERAL

General is a major gambling game in Puerto Rico. It has many similarities with cheerio and can be played as a family game.

Five dice are used. The combinations and the players' names are recorded on a sheet of paper. The combinations are as follows:

The numbers 1 through 6 score their spot values.

Straight Either 1,2,3,4,5 or 2,3,4,5,6, scores 25 points if made on the first throw, but only 20 points if made on the second or third throw (see the section on rolling). Only one straight is scored.

Full house Scores 35 points on first throw, but only 30 points on the second or third throw.

Four of a kind Scores 45 points on first throw, but only 40 points on the second or third throw.

Five of a kind If made on the first throw, it ranks as the "big general" and immediately wins the game. Made on the second or third throw, it is a "small general" and scores 60 points.

Aces wild "Aces" (1s) may be counted as 2 or as 6, if one or both of these are needed to complete a straight—but not as any other number or for any other purpose.

Order of play is determined by a preliminary round in which each player rolls the dice once. The player with the lowest spot score shoots first, the player with the next lowest score second, and so on.

Players Any number may play, either singly or in partnership. Partnerships are usually determined by the scores made in the preliminary round, the two highest scorers being paired, the two lowest, and so on.

Rolling A game normally consists of 10 turns ("frames") per player, but of course a game ends immediately if any player rolls a big general.

Each player may roll the dice once, twice, or three times during each frame.
If, on his first throw, he fails to make an obvious scoring combination like a straight or a full house, he may pick up all or any of the dice for his second roll. But the value of any combination he now rolls is diminished, and a big general now becomes a small general.
After his second roll he may again, if he wishes, pick up all or any of the dice for a third roll.

After the third roll, he must state which combination he has scored. His score is determined according to the combinations he still needs, exactly as in cheerio and subject to the same rules.
If the game runs its full course of ten frames, the player with the highest score wins.

Payment When general is played as a gambling game, the winner receives from each of the other players the difference between his own and that player's point score. The monetary value per point is settled before the game.

DOUBLE CAMEROON

This game is similar to general but has important differences. It is played with ten dice.
After a player has rolled them for the third time in each turn, he divides them into two groups of five, and then allots the score of each group to one of the ten combinations in the game. So in the course of a game, each player has five turns.

The combinations are:

Numbers 1 through 6 Score their spot values.

Full house Scores its spot value.

Little cameroon (1,2,3,4,5) scores 21 points.

Big cameroon (2,3,4,5,6) scores 30 points.

Five of a kind Scores 50 points.

(Unlike in "general," a score does not decrease if the combination is made on a second or third throw.)

Private betting games

These are the games for playing on a bar counter, or at a friend's over beer and cheese. They can be played for high stakes or for low, or just for counters or matchsticks for fun.

POKER DICE

This game, for two or more players, is often played in bars to decide such simple questions as who shall pay for the next round of drinks. As a gambling game, it is played for a "pot" (pool) to which each player contributes at the start of each round.

Equipment Five dice are used, and these are normally special poker dice marked with a,k,q,j,10,9 (instead of the numbers 1 through 6). The game may also be played with standard dice, with 1 ranking highest, then 6,5,4,3, 2; or alternatively as in Indian dice.

Objective Players aim to make the best possible poker "hand" in not more than two rolls of the dice (or three rolls of the dice in the old form of the game).

Rank of hands is as follows: five of a kind (highest rank); four of a kind; straight (an unbroken sequence, either a,k,q,j,10 or k,q,j,10,9); full house (three of a kind and one pair); three of a kind; two pairs; one pair; no pair (the lowest rank—five unmatched values not in sequence).

Hands of the same rank need not tie. They compare as follows.

1) Five of a kind: five aces rank higher than five kings, and so on.

2) Four of a kind: as for five of a kind.

3) Full house: the threes decide, with a,a,a,j,j ranking higher than k,k,k,q,q, and so on.

4) Straight: a,k,q,j,10 beats k,q,j,10,9.

5) Three of a kind: three aces rank higher than three kings, and so on.

6) Two pairs: the highest pair wins.

7) One pair: the higher pair wins.

8) No pair: the highest die wins.

The odd dice in any combination are used by some schools as tiebreakers. For example, a,a,q,q,j (two pairs) would rank above a,a,q,q,9.

It is more common, however, for the odd dice to be disregarded, and if two or more players make equal-ranking hands they must roll again.

Order of play is decided by a preliminary round in which each player throws a single die.

The highest scorer throws first in the first round. The second highest scorer sits to his left, and so on. Play goes clockwise and each round is commenced by a different player in turn.

Play Each player rolls in turn. He may accept the hand produced by his first throw; or, if he wishes, he may pick up one or more of the dice and roll them again in an attempt to improve his hand. Some schools limit to three the number of dice he may pick up. The outcome of his second throw completes his hand and the dice are passed to the next player.

The highest hand in the round wins. Alternatively, the lowest hand pays for the drinks! If there are only two players, the best two out of three rounds, or the best three out of five, win.

Aces wild Poker dice may be played with aces "wild," ie they may rank normally or count as any other value the player wishes. For example, a throw of q,q,q,q,a could rank as five queens; a throw of a,a,a,a,j could rank as five jacks; or a throw of k,q,j,a,9 could rank as a straight.

INDIAN DICE

Indian dice, a favorite bar game in the United States, is very similar to poker dice. It is played with five ordinary dice, with 6 ranking highest and 1s ("aces") wild. Any number of players may take part.

Objective Players aim to make the highest poker hand. The hands rank as in poker dice except that straights do not count.

Play begins after a preliminary round to decide the order of play. The highest scorer becomes first shooter, the second highest scorer sits to his left, and so on.

The player who shoots first may have up to three throws to establish his hand. He may "stand" on his first throw, or pick up all or any of the dice for a second throw. He may then stand on that throw or pick up the dice again for a third and final throw.

No subsequent player in the round or "leg" may make more throws than the first player.

A game usually consists of two legs, with the winners of each leg playing off if stakes are involved, or the lowest scoring players playing off if no stakes have been placed.

If there are only two players, the victor is the one who wins two out of three legs.

Indian dice

Poker die faces

Five of a kind

Four of a kind

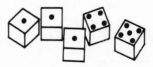
Full house

Three of a kind

Two pairs

Pair

No pair

124

Thirty six

Player 1

30 points

Player 2

33 points

31 points

Player 3

LIAR DICE

The essence of this game, for three or more players, is deception!

Equipment The game may be played with five ordinary dice, 1s (aces) ranking high, but is much more absorbing when poker dice are used. Each player also needs three betting chips (or counters).

Rank of hands is as in poker dice.

Hands of the same rank are also compared as in poker dice, but in liar dice the odd dice are always used as tiebreakers if necessary.

Order of play is established by a preliminary round in which each player throws a single die. The highest scorer becomes first shooter. The second highest scorer sits to his left, and so on.

Play Each player puts three betting chips in front of him. The first shooter then throws all the dice, keeping them covered so that the other player cannot see what he has thrown.

He declares his throw in detail, eg "full house, queens on nines" (q,q,q,9,9). This call may be true or false and it is for the player to his left to accept or challenge the call. The declaring player may call below the actual value of his throw if he wishes.

1) If the player to his left thinks the caller is lying and challenges him, all the dice are exposed.

If the caller has in fact lied, he must pay one chip into the pot; but if the value of the throw is equal to or higher than the call, it is the challenger who pays into the pot.

In either case, it now becomes the challenger's turn to throw.

2) If the player to the left of the caller accepts the call, he takes over the dice (still unexposed). He may now throw all or any of them (or none of them), but he must say truthfully how many he does throw.

Keeping the dice covered, he then makes his call, which must be higher than the call he accepted—but it need not be a higher rank of hand; it can be a higher hand of the same rank. His call may be accepted or challenged by the player to his left, and so play continues round the table.

When a player has lost all three of his chips, he is out of the game. Play continues until all but one of the players has been knocked out. The sole survivor is the winner and he collects the pot.

Start of play rotates one player to the left after each game.

Liar dice

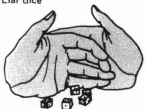

THIRTY-SIX

This is a game for any number of players, using only one die.

Order of play is determined by a preliminary round in which each player throws a single die. The lowest scorer becomes first shooter, the next-lowest second shooter, and so on.

Each player puts an agreed stake in the pot.

Objective Players aim to score a total of 36 points. Any player scoring more than 36, however, is eliminated from the game.

The winner is the player with the score nearest 36 points and he takes the pot.

Play Each player in turn rolls the dice once, totaling his score round by round. As he nears 36 he may choose to stand on his score, especially if it is 33 or more.

In the event of a tie, the pot is divided.

ACES

This is a game for any number of players. It is usually played for a pot and the winner is the player throwing the last ace (1) with the last die.

Equipment Each player requires five dice and a throwing cup.

Order of play is determined by a preliminary round in which each player tries to throw the highest poker hand. Numbers rank: 1 (high), 6,5,4, 3,2, (low).

The player with the highest ranking hand becomes first shooter. The other players then sit in clockwise order in accordance with the hands they have thrown.

Ties are resolved by further throws.

Play The first shooter throws his dice and transfers to the center of the table any 1s that come up. Any 2s in his throw are passed to the player to his left, and any 5s to the player to his right.

He continues throwing until he fails to make any of these numbers on a throw, or until he has disposed of all his dice. Although he may have no dice left, he is still in the game, since he may later receive dice from the players to his left and right.

Play continues in a clockwise direction around the table until all the dice except one have been transferred to the center.

The winner (or loser) is the player who throws the last ace with that die.

PAR

Par can be played with any number of players, but is best played with six or seven.

Equipment:
1) five dice;
2) chips (or counters) representing the betting unit.

Objective Each player tries to achieve a total score of 24 or more by throwing the dice.

Order of play is established by a preliminary round in which the highest scoring player becomes the first shooter. The second highest scorer throws next, and so on.

Play The first shooter rolls all five dice. He may "stand" on that throw if it makes 24 or more, but may throw four of the dice again if he desires. He may continue throwing to try to improve his total (or he may stand), but each time he throws, he must leave one more die on the table.

If he makes 24, he neither gains nor loses.

If he fails to make 24, he pays each other player the difference between his score and 24.

If he makes more than 24, the difference between his score and 24 becomes his "point." For example, if he has thrown 26, he has a point of 2. He then throws all five dice again (but once only), and for every 2 that appears he collects two chips from each of the other players. (If 6 was his point, he would collect six chips for every 6 that appeared.)

SHIP, CAPTAIN, MATE, AND CREW

This game may be played by any number of people. Five dice are used.

Objective Players try to throw 6 (the ship), 5 (the captain), and 4 (the mate) in that order and within three throws.

Order of play is established by a preliminary round, in which each player throws a single die. The highest scorer becomes first shooter.

Play then moves in a clockwise direction around the table.

Play The players each put an agreed stake into the pot. Each player in turn is allowed not more than three throws of the dice.

If he makes a 6 and a 5 on his first throw, he can set those dice aside. In his second throw he then rolls the other three dice hoping to make a 4. If, however, he makes a 6 and a 4 on his first throw, only the 6 can be set aside, and the remaining four dice must be rolled again for a 5 and a 4.

If the player makes 6, 5, and 4 in his three throws, the remaining two dice (the crew) are totaled as his score. But if he makes 6, 5, and 4 in his first or second throw, he may, if he wishes, use the remaining throws to try to improve the total of the crew dice.

The pot goes to the player with the highest score in the round. A tie nullifies all scores and a further round has to be played.

Start of play rotates one player to the left after each game.

TWENTY-ONE

This game is based on the blackjack card game. Any number of players may take part.

Equipment: one die, and a supply of chips or counters for each player.

Objective Players try to score 21 without "going bust" (ie throwing more than 21).

Play Each player puts one chip into the pool or kitty. Then each player in turn rolls the dice as many times as he likes in an attempt to make a total of 21 or a number near it. If, for example, a player's first four throws are 4,6,2,6 (totaling 18), it would probably be safer to "stick" on this number than risk a fifth throw that might take his total over 21.

If his total does exceed 21, he "goes bust" and is eliminated from that round.

Players often agree on a minimum number, eg 16, at which sticking is permissible. When all the players have thrown, the player with 21, or the number nearest to it, takes the pool, and a new round commences.

If two or more players have the same score, the pool may either be shared or decided by a play-off.

Start of play rotates one player to the left with each round.

BUCK DICE

This is a game for any number of players, using three dice.

Preliminaries Order of play is established by a round in which each player throws a single die. The highest scorer becomes first shooter. The lowest scorer then throws one die to determine a point number for the first game.

Objective Players aim to score a "buck" or "game" (exactly 15 points). On achieving this score the player withdraws from the game, which continues until one player is left: the loser.

Play Each player in turn takes the three dice, and each goes on throwing for as long as he throws the point number on one or more of the dice. As soon as he makes a throw that does not contain the point number, he passes the dice to the player to his left. Each player keeps count, aloud, of the number of times he has thrown the point number. Each occasion counts one point.

If, when he is nearing 15 points, a player makes a throw that carries his score beyond 15, the throw does not count and he must roll again.

Some throws rate special values. Three point numbers in one throw ("big buck" or "general") count 15 points. A player making this throw withdraws immediately from the game irrespective of any score he has made previously. Three of a kind that are not point numbers count as a "little buck" and score five points.

Variation Some players follow the rule that when a player has scored 13 points, he rolls with only two dice; and when 14 is reached, with only one die.

Continuing play Start of play rotates one player to the left after each game. The right to determine the point number also rotates in this way, so that it is always with the player to the starter's right.

Hooligan score card

Point number	K	J	P	T
1	2	4	1	
2			6	4
3	12	9	3	9
4	12			16
5		10	25	15
6	6	24	18	24
H	20	20		

HOOLIGAN

Hooligan is played with five dice and a throwing cup. Any number of players may take part.

Hooligan is a point-scoring game; the winner is the player making the highest total score.

Preliminaries Aside from a preliminary round to determine the order of play, a scoresheet must be prepared. This sheet should have a column divided into seven sections marked 1,2,3,4,5,6, and H (hooligan), against which the score of each player can be recorded.

The game consists of seven rounds, each player throwing in turn. A turn ("frame") consists of three throws. After his first throw, each player declares which of the numbers on the scoresheet (including H) he is shooting for (ie his point number). He must shoot for H on his final throw, if he has not previously done so.

"Hooligan" is a straight, either 1,2,3,4,5 or 2,3,4,5,6, and counts 20 points.

If he wishes, a player need not declare a point number after his first throw. In this case he picks up all five dice, shoots again, and then declares his point number; but this counts as his second throw, so he has only one throw left in this frame.

If he declares his point number after his first throw, he puts aside all dice bearing that number, then throws a second time with the remaining dice. Once more, any dice bearing the point number are put aside. He then makes his third and final throw with the remaining dice.

His score is determined by multiplying the point numbers he has made by the point number itself.

For example, if he were throwing for 4s and made three of them, his score would be 12.

If a player throws the maximum of five point numbers in his first or second throw, he counts this score and plays the remaining throw(s) of the frame with five dice, setting aside any dice bearing the point number after the first throw if two throws are involved.

The point numbers made on these throws are added to the five made on the first throw. A player has only one turn to shoot for each point number. He must choose a different point number for each frame. Sometimes games of hooligan are operated by a banker. Players play against the bank, and must pay to enter the game.

The odds and rules of such games vary from place to place.

Two-hand bidou betting sequence

A Bets

B Raises

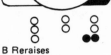
A Reraises

B Reraises

A Calls

HELP YOUR NEIGHBOR

Help your neighbor, for two to six players, is usually played for fun using counters.

Equipment:
1) three dice and a dice cup;
2) betting chips or counters for each player.

Objective Each player tries to be the first to get rid of all his counters. The winner takes the pot formed during the course of play.

Order of play is determined by a preliminary round in which each player throws a single die. This throw also decides which number(s) each player takes. The highest scoring player in the preliminary round becomes first shooter and takes the number 1. The second-highest scorer becomes the second shooter and, taking the number 2, sits to the left of 1, and so on.

If there are only two players, the higher scoring player takes numbers 1, 2, and 3, and the other the remainder.

With three players, the numbers are paired off: 1 and 2, 3 and 4, 5 and 6.

With four players, numbers 5 and 6 are "dead;" with five players, 6 is dead.

Play begins with each player placing ten counters in front of him, and then proceeds in a clockwise direction from the first shooter.

Each player in turn throws all three dice once. Any player whose number comes up in that throw has to put one counter into the pot for each of his numbers thrown.

For example, if the first shooter throws 4,6,6, the player who has number 4 puts one counter into the pot; and the player with number 6 puts two counters into the pot.

When the pot has been taken by the winning player (the first to lose all his ten counters), the next game is started by the player to the left of the first shooter in the previous game, and he now takes the number 1.

BIDOU

Bidou is a game with the same betting principles as poker—but whereas in poker the player wants to win chips or counters, in bidou his objective is to get rid of them.

Players Any number can take part, but the procedure is different when only two players are involved.

Equipment Each player needs three dice and a throwing cup. The game also requires a supply of chips or counters.

Objective Players aim to get rid of their chips. The last player still holding chips is the loser. If desired, he pays each other player a previously agreed amount, or meets group expenses.

Bidou combinations The ranking of all possible dice throws is shown in the table.

BIDOU COMBINATIONS

Highest listed first
1) 2,1,1 (bidou)*
2) 2,2,1 (bidé)
3) 4,2,1 ("421")
4) 6,6,6
5) 5,5,5
6) 4,4,4
7) 3,3,3
8) 2,2,2
9) 1,1,1*
10) 3,3,6
11) 3,3,5
12) 3,3,4
13) 3,3,2
14) 3,3,1
15) 1,1,6
16) 1,1,5
17) 1,1,4
18) 1,1,3
19) 3,2,1
20) 4,3,2
21) 5,4,3
22) 6,5,4
23–56) The remaining 34 possible combinations are ranked according to their spot total, eg 6,3,2 (=11) beats 4,3,1 (=8). (The maximum is 6,6,5=17.) But all are beaten by any of the combinations listed separately above.
* 1,1,1 beats 2,1,1, but is beaten by all other combinations listed above it.

TWO-HAND BIDOU

Two-hand bidou is played in games made up of three separate rounds. The loser is the player losing at least two of the rounds.

Starting a round Only nine betting chips are used. They are placed on the table between the two players. Each player then throws a die once. The player making the higher score becomes "captain" (first shooter) for the first hand.

Play: first round The captain takes his turn first, then his opponent.
In his turn each player may throw the dice up to three times to achieve the best possible score.
In each throw he must throw all the dice, keeping them concealed beneath his dice cup. He must declare the number of throws he makes. When both players have thrown, betting on that hand begins.

Opening the betting If both players have made the same number of throws, or if the captain has made fewer throws than his opponent, then the captain bets or passes first. If the captain has made more throws than his opponent, the latter becomes captain and makes the first bet, or passes.

Betting limits The maximum bet or raise is one chip.

Betting procedure Players use the center chips for betting until these run out. As each player states his bet, he moves the appropriate number of chips away from the center pile and slightly toward him. When all the center chips have been used up, players may use any chips they have received during the round, moving them slightly toward the center as they use them.

Betting A player need not have a strong hand to make a bet; he may choose to bluff his opponent.
Betting is as in poker. If both players pass, the hand ends.

Once one player has bet, the other must call (ie bet an equal amount), raise (ie bet a greater amount), or drop out. If one player raises, the other must call, reraise, or drop out. The betting continues until one player has called or dropped out.

Outcome If one player calls the other, both show their dice. All chips bet are then taken by the loser. The winner becomes the next captain. If one player drops out, he must take one penalty chip (from the center if possible). All other chips bet are returned to their positions before the hand began.
The player who has not dropped out is the next captain.
If both players pass, neither takes any chips, and the captaincy changes for the next hand.

Play: second round Play is exactly as in the first round, except that on any throw a player may put aside any dice whose score he wishes to keep, and throw only the remainder. The dice put aside must remain hidden from the opponent.
Having put aside dice on one throw, a player may still throw all the dice on his third throw of that turn.

Play: third round Play reverts to the rules for the first round.

"Open throw" occurs when one player has eight chips, leaving one chip with his opponent or in the center. The player with one or no chips is then entitled to not more than three throws of the dice to make the highest possible exposed combination. (Whether he must rethrow all the dice or may select, depends on the rules for the round they are playing.)
His opponent then throws in similar fashion and if he loses the throws he takes the single chip and so loses the game. If the single-chip player loses, he takes one chip from his opponent and normal play is resumed.

Multihand bidou betting sequence

A Bets

B Drops out C Raises

D Drops out E Stays in

A Calls

The showdown

MULTIHAND BIDOU
When three or more players take part no chips are placed in the center of the table. Instead, each player begins with six chips.

Captaincy A preliminary round decides who is first captain, as in two-hand bidou. Play begins with the captain and proceeds in a clockwise direction. The winner of each round becomes captain of the next.
If all players pass, the player to the left of the captain of that round becomes captain of the next.

Play is as in two-hand bidou. All players must keep their dice hidden from the others until betting has closed.

Opening the betting If all players have made the same number of throws, the same player remains captain. Otherwise, the player making the fewest throws and nearest the original captain's left becomes captain.

Betting limits The maximum bet is three chips, the maximum raise two chips.

Betting procedure Each player uses his own store of chips, and places his bets to the center of the table to form a common pot.

Betting situations
1) On a showdown between two or more players, the loser collects all chips still in the pot.
2) Players dropping out without betting receive no penalty.
3) For players dropping out after betting at least once, the following rules apply:
the first in a round to do so must take from the pot whichever amount he has put in on that hand, plus the same amount for each player still betting, plus one penalty chip;
each player dropping out thereafter on that round must take one penalty chip.
If the players remaining have bet unequal amounts, whichever number of chips is left in the pot is called or raised by the next player in turn.

4) If all players drop out after a player has raised, any chips left in the pot after penalties have been taken are returned to the raising player.
5) A player who bets his last chips has the right to stay in for the showdown, even if other players take the betting further.
If he loses, he receives back his bet and the equivalent amount from each showdown player. Other chips still in the pot are returned to the players who bet them.
6) If, in the same circumstances, there is a tie, the player who bet the last of his chips takes back his bet, and the other players take back all their chips except one each. The remaining chips are removed from the game. If there is a tie in any other circumstance, each showdown player takes back one chip, and any other chips in the pot are removed from the game.
7) If only one player bets on a round and all the others pass, he can discard one chip even if it is his last.
8) If only two players are left with chips, these two continue until one has lost. Should the two players have more than nine chips between them, each discards one chip whenever he bets and is not called, until the players have a total of nine chips between them. The two then fight out the game as in two-hand bidou.
9) Any player who passes after betting has begun automatically drops out of that round.

Poor fish is a variation that requires all players to expose their last throws, if all have passed.
The player with the highest throw is the "poor fish" and receives one chip from each of the other players.

MONTEVIDEO
Like bidou, this game requires three dice, a throwing cup, and chips or counters for each player.

However, the objective is not to lose chips but to win them on the basis of the winner ultimately taking all. Three or more players can take part.

Ante At the start of play each player has six chips. In each round he antes one chip into the pot before throwing the dice.

Betting After the dice have been thrown, betting proceeds as in poker.

Play resembles poker, but bidou combinations are used. At showdown, the highest combination wins the pot. If the game reaches a stage where only two players have any chips, it is speeded up by increasing, round by round, the number of chips each must ante into the pot, to a maximum of six. If there are many players, the same process should be made for the last three players.
Any player may, if he wishes, open the betting by "betting the pot," ie stay in without putting up chips. When this happens, any other player—even if he has already passed—may call the pot. The bet may, of course, be raised in the usual way.

CROWN AND ANCHOR
This is a fast game in which any number of players play against a banker.

Equipment Three special dice are used, each marked with a crown, anchor, heart, spade, diamond, and club. These symbols also appear on the layout, which is marked on a cloth or board set in front of the banker.

Play Each player puts a wager on one or more of the symbols on the layout. The banker then throws the three dice from a cup and pays out on the result of the throw.
The usual odds are evens on singles, 2 to 1 on pairs, and 3 to 1 on three of a kind. The advantage always lies with the banker.

ENGLISH HAZARD
This is a centuries old game played with two dice and a throwing cup. Any number may play.

Play begins when a first shooter, called the "caster," puts his stake in a circle marked on the center of the table. Any other player wishing to wager also puts his stake in the center, and the caster accepts his challenge by knocking the table with the throwing cup.
When all betting has finished, the caster throws the dice to establish a "main point," a total of either 5,6,7,8, or 9. If he throws any other total it is "no main" and he must continue throwing until a main point comes up.
Having established a main point, he throws the dice again to establish a "chance point" (a total of either 4,5,6,7,8,9, or 10—but not the same number as the main point number). When he throws to establish the chance point, the caster immediately loses the bet if he throws an "out." An out is any throw of 2 or 3(called a "crab"); or a throw of 12 if the main point is 5,6,8, or 9.
The caster wins, however, if he throws a "nick." He makes a nick if he throws an 11 when the main point is a 7, or if he throws a 12 when the main point is a 6 or an 8. If he throws the main point itself, this also counts as a nick and he wins immediately.
If he establishes a chance point, he then continues throwing. If he throws the chance point again, he wins the bet. But if he throws the main point again, he loses.

Crown and anchor layout

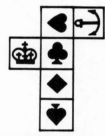

Crown and anchor die

Professional banking games

These games are found, in some countries, in fairgrounds, cheap casinos, and small gambling parlors. Many of the games flourished in frontier America, but some date back to the European society gaming houses of the eighteenth century.

Barbooth
Losing throws

Winning throws

BARBOOTH

Barbooth, also called barbudi or even-up craps, is often played for high stakes in some parts of the United States.
Equipment: two miniature dice and a dice cup.
Players Any number of players that can be accommodated at an average poker table may play.
House officials include a "cutter," who is responsible for collecting the house percentage of each winning bet. A banker is usually in attendance to take side bets, charging 5 per cent for his services and paying half this percentage to the house.
Play Only two players at a time throw the dice. The first player to throw is the "shooter." The player to his right (the "fader") throws the dice alternately with him. The shooter does not declare any wager. The fader bets whatever he likes (up to the house limit) that he will beat the shooter. If the fader loses, his stake is collected by the shooter. If the fader wins, his stake is returned with an equal amount from the shooter. The other players make side bets on the result of the contest between the shooter and the fader.
Shooter and fader throw alternately until a decision is reached.
Scoring The only meaningful throws are winning throws (3,3; 5,5; 6,5; or 6,6) and losing throws (1,1; 1,2; 2,2; or 4,4).
Continuing play When a shooter loses with a throw of 1,1; 2,2; or 4,4; and when a fader wins with 3,3; 5,5; or 6,6, the dice are taken by the fader, who now becomes the shooter. The player to his right becomes the new fader. But when the shooter loses with 1,2 or the fader wins with 6,5 the dice remain with the shooter.

TWENTY-SIX

This game, especially popular in the American Midwest in the 1950s, is still played today.
Equipment The game is played with ten dice and a throwing cup. Operators usually provide a scoresheet that also states the rules and payoffs.
Play The player chooses any number from 1 through 6 as his point number and then throws the ten dice 13 times. His score is the number of times his point number appears.
Payoffs vary. The average operator pays 8 to 1 for scores of 33 or over; 4 to 1 for 26 through 32; 4 to 1 for 11 or less; and 2 to 1 for an exact 13. No other scores count, and the game always works strongly in favor of the operator.

GRAND HAZARD

Equipment The game is played with three dice, which the operator either throws from a cup or tumbles through a hazard chute. A layout showing the payoff system is provided.
Play Players bet on the total number thrown. They may bet on individual numbers, on "high" (totals of 11 through 17), "low" (totals of four through 10), "odd" (an odd total), "even" (an even total), and "raffles" (three of a kind).
The payoffs on individual numbers are shown on the layout. Even money (1 to 1) is paid on high, low, odd, and even bets; but if the dice show three of a kind on these bets, the bank wins.
Individual raffles are paid at 180 to 1; any raffle (unspecified) at 30 to 1.
The bank's advantage is even higher if the player's stake is included in the payoff count; for example 16 is paid "30 for 1," not "30 to 1."

CHUCK-A-LUCK

Chuck-a-luck, closely related to grand hazard, has had many other names during its long history, including sweat cloth, chuckerluck, chuck luck and, more recently, bird cage.
Equipment:
1) three dice;
2) a chuck cage;
3) a simple layout showing the numbers from 1 through 6.
Play Each player places his bet on one of the six numbers. When all bets have been placed, the operator tumbles the dice in the chuck cage until they come to rest face up or drop down a chute onto the table.
Payoff If a player's number appears on one die, the operator pays him evens; if on two dice, 2 to 1; if on three dice, 3 to 1.

THREE DICE

Equipment: three dice and a throwing cup.

Play is against a banker and begins with all players putting their bets in front of them. The banker covers these bets (ie puts in an equal amount), and then throws first.

If the banker throws three of a kind, any pair plus a 6, or 4,5,6, he wins and collects all wagers. He loses to all players if he throws 1,2,3, or any pair plus a 1.

All other combinations are valueless except a pair plus a 2,3,4, or 5. On such a throw, the number on the odd die becomes the shooter's point number that others then try to beat.

If the banker makes a valueless first throw, he must throw again.

If the banker makes a point-number throw, each player in turn throws to decide whether he or the banker wins.

If the player fails to make a clear-cut winning or losing throw and throws a point number, it is the higher point number—player's or banker's—that wins.

A tie is a no decision.

If a player fails to make a pair, 4,5,6, or 1,2,3, his throw is valueless and he must continue throwing until such a combination appears.

UNDER AND OVER 7

This is a deceptively simple game in which the odds are heavily loaded in the operator's favor.

Equipment:
1) two dice;
2) a throwing cup;
3) a simple layout showing three spaces: "under 7," "over 7," and "7."

Play The player bets on any one of the three spaces and then throws the two dice. If he has bet on "under 7" and throws a total under seven, the operator pays evens. The same odds apply to successful "over 7" bets. If the player bets on the "7" space and wins, the operator pays five times his stake.

HIGH DICE

This is a fast and simple game, also known as two-dice klondike or beat the bank. It is played with two dice and a throwing cup.

The banker and the player each throw once, the banker throwing first. The score is the numerical total of the two dice, and the player must throw a higher total than the banker to win.

Ties count as wins for the banker.

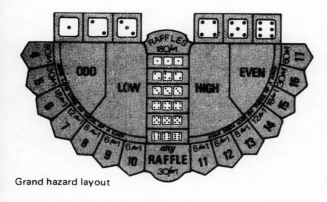

Grand hazard layout

COUNTER KLONDIKE

Equipment Five dice; they are rolled down a stepped chute.

Play The banker rolls first. Each player in turn then rolls, trying to beat the banker's score in a single throw. Ties count as wins for the banker.

Scoring The numbers on the dice rank: 1 (high),6,5,4,3,2 (low). Winning combinations in ascending order of value are: a pair, two pairs, three of a kind, full house (three of a kind and a pair), four of a kind, and five of a kind. The odd die in a combination does not count. For example, four 3s and a 1 rank equally with four 3s and any other number. Straights, and no pairs, do not count as scoring combinations.

CASINO KLONDIKE

Equipment:
1) two sets of five dice;
2) two throwing cups;
3) a layout with spaces marked "win," "lose," "beat two aces," and "klondike."

Objective Players aim to beat the banker. A player betting on the "win" space has to beat the banker's throw. If he bets on the "lose" space, he must throw less than the banker. To win on "beat two aces," he must throw not less than two pairs.

Play The banker throws first and his throw remains displayed on the "klondike" space throughout the round. Play then goes clockwise round the table, the players using the second set of dice. The banker pays or collects after each player's throw, paying evens to all winners. All ties count as wins for the banker.

Klondike layout

Craps

Craps developed in the early nineteenth century, when American negroes adapted the old English game of hazard. Today, the money wagered at craps in the United States alone makes it the biggest gambling game in history. Its attractions are its speed of action and large element of participation; yet its essence is that of a mathematical game of numbers and odds.

FORMS OF THE GAME
Three forms of craps exist today.
1) Private craps: between two or more people, making bets among themselves.
2) Open (or money) craps: typical of illegal sawdust casinos and big money games. One person banks the game, and certain bets can only be made against the bank.
3) Bank (casino) craps: played on a specially constructed table, and requiring all bets to be made against the house.

GENERAL RULES
Basic equipment is:
1) two matched dice;
2) a playing surface, preferably edged by a wall or backboard;
3) betting chips or cash.
Players: any number over two; one player can play against the house at bank craps.
General procedure
a) Any player by common agreement may shoot the dice first; thereafter the dice are passed around in a clockwise direction.
b) A new player may join a game at any stage and sit anywhere in the circle of players—provided that the house (or the players in a private game) raise no objection at the time. He takes his turn in the normal way when the dice reach him.
c) A player may leave a game at any time, regardless of his gains or losses.

Throw of the dice The shooter shakes the dice in his closed hand and throws them onto the playing area. If there is a backboard, it is usually ruled that the dice must rebound from it before they come to rest. This helps defeat controlled throws.
The two numbers face uppermost when the dice come to rest, added together, give the result of the throw.
Basic play The first throw in a shooter's turn is called a "come-out" throw as is the first throw after each time the dice win or lose.
On a come-out throw:
a) if the shooter throws a 7 or 11 he has thrown a "natural"; the dice "pass" (ie win) immediately. The shooter may keep the dice for another come-out throw.
b) If the shooter throws a 2, 3, or 12, he has thrown a "craps": the dice "miss out" or "crap out" (ie lose) immediately. The shooter may keep the dice for another come-out throw.
c) If the shooter throws a 4, 5, 6, 8, 9, or 10, he has thrown a "point": for the dice to win he must "make the point," ie throw the same number again before he

throws a 7—no other numbers matter.
If the shooter throws the same number again before he throws a 7, the dice pass (win). The shooter may keep the dice for another come-out throw.
If he throws a 7 before he throws the number again, the dice miss out or "seven out" (lose). The shooter must give the dice to the next player in turn.
A sample turn of play
1) First come-out throw: 3 (craps).
2) Second: 11 (natural).
3) Third: 6 (point). Player then throws: (11),(4),(9),(3),6 (makes point).
4) Fourth: 12 (craps).
5) Fifth: 10 (point). Player then throws: (2),(8),(11),7 (sevens out). Player loses dice.

Giving up the dice If the shooter sevens out, he must give up the dice.
He may also, if he wishes, pass the dice if:
a) he has not thrown the dice in his turn; or
b) he has just thrown a "decision:" ie a natural, a craps, or a pass on a point.
Change of dice If more than one pair of dice is being used, any player may call for the dice in use to be changed at any time. This is called a "box-up." The change is made immediately before the next come-out throw.

PRIVATE CRAPS

Private craps games can be played anywhere. Players arrange the bets among themselves, and it is important that they know the correct odds for different bets—in many games hustlers offer short odds that the inexperienced accept. Cheating, with false dice or controlled throws, is also common.

Center bet On each come-out throw, the shooter places the amount he wishes to bet in the center of the playing area. He announces the amount, saying "I'll shoot . . ."

Any of the other players then "fade" (accept) whatever part of the total they wish, by placing that amount in the center alongside the shooter's bet.

Unless agreed at the beginning of the game, there is no set order or amounts in which players fade the center bets. Players simply place money in the center until all the shooter's bet has been faded, or until no one wishes to place any further amount.

(However, it is sometimes agreed that any player who faded the entire center bet on the preceding come-out, and lost, can claim the right to fade the entire present bet.)

If the center bet is not entirely faded by the players, the shooter may either:
a) withdraw the part not faded; or
b) call off all bets, by saying "No bet."

Players may not fade more than the shooter's center bet; but if the players show eagerness to bet more, the shooter can decide to increase the amount of his bet.

Throw of dice and basic play: see the general rules.

Settlement of center bet If the dice miss out (lose), the players who faded the center bet each receive back their money together with the equivalent amount of the center bet.

If the dice pass (win), all the money in the center is collected by the shooter.

The center bet is therefore an even money (1 to 1) bet. Since the probability of the dice passing is in fact 970 occasions in 1980, the shooter has a 1.414% disadvantage on the center bet.

Continuing play The dice are retained or passed as described in the general procedure. For the new come-out throw, the shooter puts up a new center bet for any amount he wishes.

Other bets are known as side bets. Like the center bet, they must be arranged before the dice are thrown, not while they are rolling.

Note that the shooter himself may make any of the side bets he wishes, in addition to the center bet.

Right and wrong bettors
All these bets require agreement between two players.

One is the "wrong" bettor: he "lays" odds that the dice will not pass or will not make the number(s) bet on.

The other is the "right" bettor: he "takes" odds that the dice will pass or will make the number(s) bet on.

The bet and odds may be proposed by either the right or the wrong bettor; in practice, however, more experienced players tend to be "wrong" bettors and propose odds that the less experienced player will "take."

Flat bet This is a normal bet on whether a shooter's come-out throw will pass, and is made as a side bet between two players (of which one may be the shooter). Flat bets occur especially if one player has faded the entire bet.

Point bet If the shooter throws a point on his come-out throw, players may bet on whether he will "make the point." (The center and flat bets still remain to be settled in the same way.)

Come bet This is a bet on whether the dice will pass— but treating the next throw of the dice, after the bet, as the bet's come-out throw—when in fact the shooter is throwing for a point.

That is: on the shooter's come-out throw he has thrown a point (eg a 6). He continues throwing the dice to see if he makes the point or sevens out.

Before one of these throws, two players agree on a "come bet:" one player lays odds that the dice will not come, the other takes odds that they will. The first throw of the dice after the bet is the "come-out" throw for the come bet. If the shooter rolls a 7, he sevens out on his point—but for the come bet the dice "come," because a 7 on a come-out throw is a natural.

Similarly, 11 is a natural for the come bet, and 2, 3, or 12 is craps—the dice "don't come." (But all these leave the center bet undecided, because they are neither the point number nor a 7.)

If the shooter rolls a point number on the come-out throw for the come bet, this number becomes the point for the come bet. The outcome then depends, in the usual way, on whether the point or a 7 appears first.

If the shooter makes the point on his center bet without making the come bet point, the players making the come bet can agree to withdraw the bet or to continue the number sequence into the shooter's next turn.

Hardway bet (or gag bet)
This is a bet on whether the shooter will throw a certain number "the hard way"—ie as the sum of a double. Hardway bets can be placed on 4 (2+2), 6 (3+3), 8 (4+4), or 10 (5+5).

The right bettor loses if a 7 is thrown, or if the number bet on is thrown any other way before being thrown as a double.

Off-number bet Two players agree to bet on any number they choose. The right bettor wins if the shooter throws the number before he throws a 7. Bettors may call off this bet before a "decision" is reached.

Proposition bet refers to any other kind of side bet agreed upon—limited only by players' imaginations!

Such bets are always offered at odds designed to give the proposing player an advantage. There are two main categories:
a) bets on whether the specified number(s) will appear within a certain number of rolls after the bet: "one-roll bets," "two-roll bets," "three-roll bets;" or
b) bets on whether the specified number(s) will appear before other specified number(s) or before a 7.
In each case, the specified number(s) bet on may be:
a) a certain number to be thrown in any way;
b) a certain number to be thrown in a specified way;
c) any one of a group of numbers (eg a group of specified numbers, odd numbers, numbers below 7, etc).

True odds Table 1 (see p132) gives the true odds for various bets on or between single numbers, and provides the information from which the true odds for any bet between groups of numbers can be calculated. (A player should particularly avoid accepting 1 to 1 odds on 6 to 5 bets.) Table 2 (see p132) gives the true odds for hardway bets.

Irregularities at private craps: certain throws are void and the shooter must throw the dice again.

1) If the playing area has been specified at the start of the game, the throw is void if either die rolls out of the area.

2) If either die comes to rest under any object on the playing area or tilted on an obstruction, so that it is not clear which of its faces is uppermost, any agreed neutral player or bystander is nominated to decide the question. If he cannot decide, the throw is void.

3) When there is a backboard and neither die hits it, the roll is void. If only one die hits the board the roll counts, but the shooter must be reprimanded. If it occurs again, the other players may designate a player to complete the shooter's turn for him. They may also bar the shooter from shooting for the rest of the game.

4) If either die hits any object or person after hitting the backboard, the roll is counted.

5) A player may not knock either or both dice aside on the roll and call "No dice." If he does this once, the throw counts as it finally shows; if he repeats it, he may be barred from shooting for the rest of the game.

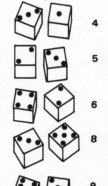

Throws

7

11

Natural throws

2

3

12

Crap throws

4

5

6

8

9

10

Point throws

Table 1: True odds for bets on or between single numbers

Number	Number of ways	Single roll	Before a 7	Comparative odds
12	1 (a)	35-1 (b)	6-1 (c)	12 (d)
11	2	17-1	3-1	2-1 11
10	3	11-1	2-1	3-1 3-2 10
9	4	8-1	3-2	4-1 2-1 4-3 9
8	5	31-5	6-5	5-1 5-2 5-3 5-4 8
7	6	5-1	—	6-1 3-1 2-1 3-2 6-5 7
6	5	31-5	6-5	5-1 5-2 5-3 5-4 1-1 5-6 6
5	4	8-1	3-2	4-1 2-1 4-3 1-1 4-5 2-3 4-5 5
4	3	11-1	2-1	3-1 3-2 2-1 1-1 3-4 3-5 1-2 3-5 3-4 4
3	2	17-1	3-1	2-1 1-1 2-3 1-2 2-5 1-3 2-5 1-2 2-3 3
2	1	35-1	6-1	1-1 1-2 1-3 1-4 1-5 1-6 1-5 1-4 1-3 1-2 2

Table 2: Hardway bets

Bet	Ways of making	Other ways of making	Ways of making a 7	Total ways of losing	Odds against hardway bet
4 (2+2)	1	2 +	6 =	8	8-1
6 (3+3)	1	4 +	6 =	10	10-1
8 (4+4)	1	4 +	6 =	10	10-1
10 (5+5)	1	2 +	6 =	8	8-1

Notes on odds table
a) Number of different combinations of two die faces that will give the number. Total of all possible combinations is 36.
b) Odds against making a number on a single roll— calculated by comparing the number of ways of making the number (x) with the number of ways of making another number (36-x).
c) Odds against throwing the number before throwing a 7: for point and off-number bets.
d) Odds against making the higher number before the lower number (eg 12 before 4: 3–1). Reverse the odds to give odds against making the lower number before the higher (eg 4 before 12: 1–3).

BANK CRAPS
This is the form of the game found in most legal casinos throughout the world. About four-fifths of the turnover of casinos in the United States comes from play at craps. A special table with betting layout is used, and all bets must be placed against the house. The odds paid give the house a mathematical advantage on any bet.
The table is about the size of a pool or billiard table. A wood rail about 10in high runs around the outside edge and forms the backboard. For most of its length the backboard is lined with sponge rubber, embossed so that the dice rebound in a random way. The backboard is faced with a 9in-high mirror over a 6ft length opposite the "stickman" (see the section on croupiers). This enables him to see both sides of the the dice when they have come to rest, and so prevent mis-spotted dice being slipped into play.
Grooves in the top edge of the rail hold players' reserves of chips.

Other equipment: bank craps also requires betting chips; one or more pairs of matched dice; and a "stick" for passing and retrieving the dice.
Players Any number of players from one upward may take part. The role of banker is taken by the house.
Croupiers The "stickman" is the croupier in charge of the dice. He calls out the number thrown, collects the dice, and —when bets have been settled—passes them to the next shooter. His name refers to the curved stick he uses to reach for and pass the dice. Opposite him are two "boxmen," who supervise every aspect of the game. At the table ends (or sometimes in other positions, depending on the layout) stand the two housemen who collect and pay out bets.

Basic rules: see the section on general rules.
Throw of the dice It is often required that the dice rebound from the backboard before coming to rest. With a double-sided layout, there may instead be an elastic cord strung across the center of the table, over which the dice must pass before hitting the table surface. Alternatively, it may be required that the dice travel past the point where the stickman is standing.
Basic play, turn of play, passing the dice, and change of dice: see the general rules for craps.
Betting In bank craps, all bets are placed against the bank; there are no side bets. The shooter must bet that the dice will or will not pass. Any other bets are at the player's discretion.
Note that some of the odds quoted below for place, hardway, and one-roll bets are altered by law in some countries to give the player less disadvantage.

Pass line bet ("Pass," "line," "win," or "do"): placed on the long narrow area marked "pass line," "pass," "line," "win," or "do," and known as the "front line." The bettor wins if the dice pass (ie throw a natural or make a point). The bet is paid at 1 to 1, giving the house a 1.4% advantage.
Don't pass line bet ("Don't," or "lose"): placed on the long narrow area marked "don't pass," "don't," or "lose," followed by the word "bar" and dice symbols, and known as the "back line." The bettor wins if the dice miss out (ie crap out or seven out)—except for a standoff on the barred result shown by the dice symbols (ie when the bettor's stake is returned). The bet is placed at 1 to 1. If 2 (1+1) or 12 (6+6) is the barred missout throw, the house advantage is 1.4%. If 3 (1+2) is the barred throw, the house advantage is 4.4%.
Come bet: placed on the space marked "come." The bettor wins if the dice pass, taking the first throw after the bet as a come-out. The bet is paid at 1 to 1, giving the house a 1.4% advantage.

The layout is printed on green baize stretched across the table surface. There are several designs.
A "double-sided" layout is one with identical patterns at each end and with a smaller central area for proposition bets. The practical differences between layouts are small, except for some of the odds offered.

Betting layout

To calculate the odds between any groups of numbers: add all ways of making the numbers in one group, and compare with the total of all ways of making the numbers in the other group.

True odds for other one-roll bets:
a) against any specified pair (eg 3+3): 35–1;
b) against any specified combination of two different numbers (eg 6+5): 17–1;
c) against any craps (2, 3, or 12): 8–1.

OPEN (OR MONEY) CRAPS

Open craps is played in many parts of the United States. At its highest levels, it brings together the leaders of business and the underworld in games in which bets may be placed in units of $10,000. Winnings of $500,000 in a session are not uncommon.

Betting This form of craps gained its name because originally all bets could be placed, at option, either with the bank or with other players ("open" bets). Today it is much more restricted. Players may bet among themselves on point numbers. All other bets are placed against the bank—including any point number bets not taken up by other players.

Bets are almost always in cash.

The layout if there is one, is usually without any space for proposition bets (see bank craps). Any propositions the bank accepts are memorized. If there is no layout, bets are placed in the same relative positions as if a layout were being used.

The bank The man who is banking the game is called the "book." The percentage he takes is called "vigorish."

Settlement The following bets are paid at bank craps odds:
1) pass/don't pass bets, and come/don't come bets;
2) one-roll bets;
3) hardway bets.
On bets on points or single (place) numbers, the bank pays players at the correct odds, but makes a house charge on the amount wagered.
In some games the bank charges a "wrong bettor" only when he loses. In other games, the charge is made on all point and box numbers.

Don't come bet: placed on the space marked "don't come."
The bettor wins if the dice do not pass, taking the first throw after the bet as a "come-out" —but making one result a standoff, as with the don't pass line bet. The bet is paid at 1 to 1. House advantages are as for the don't pass line bet.

Place bet: is a bet on a single number, either 4, 5, 6, 8, 9, or 10. A right bettor places his bet on the square marked with the number, and wins if the number bet on is thrown before a 7 is thrown.
A wrong bettor places his bet on the space behind the numbered square, and wins if a 7 is thrown before the number is thrown.
Right bets on 4 and 10 are usually paid at 9 to 5 (house advantage 6.6%), on 5 and 9 at 7 to 5 (4.0%), and on 6 and 8 at 7 to 6 (1.5%).
Wrong bets on 4 and 10 are usually paid at 11 to 5 (house advantage 3.0%); on 5 and 9 at 8 to 5 (2.5%); and on 6 and 8 at 5 to 4 (1.8%).
In the United Kingdom, right bets on 4 and 10 are paid at $9\frac{1}{2}$ to 5, and wrong bets at $10\frac{1}{2}$ to 5.

Field bet: placed on the space marked "field." The bettor wins if any one of the following numbers is thrown on the next roll: 2, 3, 4, 9, 10, 11, 12. The bet is paid at 1 to 1, giving the house a 5.5% advantage.
Variants:
a) sometimes 5 is a winning number in place of 4;
b) sometimes higher payments are made on 2 and 12; eg 2 to

1 on both, 3 to 2 on both, or 3 to 1 on 2 only, or (in the United Kingdom) 3 to 1 on 12 and 2 to 1 on 2. These variants reduce the house advantage.

Big six bet: placed on the space marked "big six." The bettor wins if a 6 appears before a 7. It is exactly the same as a place bet on the six, but paid at worse odds, 1 to 1, giving the house a 9.1% advantage—a sucker bet!

Big eight bet: placed on the space marked "big eight." As for "big six," except that the result bet on is 8.
Both "big six" and "big eight" are banned in some countries, for example in the United Kingdom.

Hardway bets: placed on the space marked with the appropriate double dice symbol. The bettor wins if the number bet on is made with a double before it is made any other way and before a 7 is thrown. Bets on 4 and 10 are paid at 7 to 1, giving the house an 11.1% advantage. Bets on 6 and 8 are paid at 9 to 1, giving the house a 9.1% advantage.
Payments in the United Kingdom are $7\frac{1}{2}$ to 1 and $9\frac{1}{2}$ to 1 respectively.

One-roll or come-out bets
Layouts usually provide for the following one-roll bets. They are placed on the space marked with the appropriate double dice symbol.
a) 12 (6+6): paid at 30 to 1 (house advantage 13.9%) or at 30 for 1 (ie 29 to 1, house advantage 16.6%). Payment is 33 to 1 in the United Kingdom.
b) 2 (1+1): as for 12.
c) 11 (5+6): paid at 15 to 1 (house advantage 13.9%) or

at 15 for 1 (ie 14 to 1, house advantage 16.7%). Payment is 15 to 1 in the United Kingdom.
d) 3 (1+2): as for 11.
e) 7: paid at 4 to 1 (5 for 1); house advantage 16.6%.
f) any craps (2, 3, or 12): paid at 7 to 1 (ie 8 for 1); house advantage 11.1%. Payment is $7\frac{1}{2}$ to 1 in the United Kingdom.
Note that where payment is quoted as "x for 1" it means that the original betting unit is counted in the winning payment.

Withdrawing bets Come and don't come bets cannot be withdrawn once the dice have rolled.
Pass line and don't pass line bets cannot be withdrawn after a come-out roll.
If the dice make a point, any undecided bet (hardway or place bet) must be declared by the bettor to be "on" or "off," ie it can be withdrawn.

Free odds bets—"do" bets If a player has placed a pass bet, and the shooter comes out on a point number; or
if a player has placed a come bet, and the shooter throws a "new" number, ie a point number for the come bet; then the player may make a further identical bet, up to the amount of his original bet, and —if the dice make the point number—the house will pay off this second bet at the true odds.
This is known as "taking the (free) odds." Accepting it reduces the house advantage on the two bets combined to 0.8%.

Free odds bets—"don't" bets If a player has placed a "don't pass" bet or a "don't come" bet, and the shooter comes out on a point or new number, then the player may make a further identical bet up to a limit that would give him winnings not higher than his original bet. If the dice do not make the point number, the house will pay off this second bet at the true odds.
Accepting the "free odds" on "don't" bets reduces the house advantage on the two bets combined to 0.8%.
Free odds bets may be withdrawn before the bet is decided. Note that (since casinos will only settle in rounded amounts) a player accepting the "free odds" needs to calculate whether the size of bet will allow such payment, at the odds effected. Otherwise, on payment, rounding down may give him worse odds on the two bets than on his original bet.

Betting limits The maximum limit varies in different casinos. The limit on proposition bets (eg one-roll and hardway bets) is usually one-third of the house's pass bet limit. The betting limit on free bets is usually half the normal maximum limit.

7 Solitaire (Patience) card games

Solitaire and patience are general names for any card game for one player. The exact origin of such games is obscure, but they have probably existed for centuries and several hundred different games exist today. Although the outcome of many of the games depends mainly on the luck of the shuffle, others involve real skill and judgment.

GENERAL PROCEDURE

Cards Solitaire games can be played with a standard 52-card deck, or with two decks shuffled together.

Some games are played with a "stripped" deck, from which certain cards have been discarded prior to play.

Special solitaire cards, smaller than ordinary playing cards, may be used; these are especially useful when playing in a confined space.

Certain games allow for the inclusion of a joker.

Ace, unless otherwise specified, ranks low.

Objective The object of many solitaire games is to build up sequences of cards in their suits onto base cards known as "foundations."

A second group of solitaires involves the pairing up of certain cards.

Other solitaires have a quite different objective, such as rebuilding the deck into a single pile, or discarding all the cards in the deck.

If a solitaire game is successful, ie the game's objective is exactly achieved, it is said to "come out" or to "go through."

If a game is "blocked," however, this means that the cards are such that the game cannot possibly be won.

Layout At the start of most solitaire games, cards are laid out in a prescribed formation that varies from game to game. This formation or "tableau," together with any other cards dealt out at the beginning of play, forms the "layout."

Foundation cards are the first cards of certain piles onto which sequences of cards are built (the objective of many solitaire games).

In some games they form part of the layout and are set out at the beginning of the game. More often, they are not included in the layout, but are put out as they come into play.

They are usually cards of a specified rank—often aces. With rare exceptions (such as in King Albert) a card cannot be removed once it has been placed on a foundation.

Spaces (sometimes called vacancies) are gaps in the layout into which cards may legitimately be played, or places from which cards have been removed and which may or may not be reoccupied, depending on the rules of the game.

Reserve In some games the layout includes one or more cards that may be brought into play as appropriate. This "reserve" of cards may not, however, be built onto—unlike the cards in the tableau.

The stock comprises those cards that remain after the layout has been dealt.

The stock is invariably kept face down, and may be brought into play in different ways according to the rules for particular games.

Waste pile or heap Cards from the stock that cannot immediately be played onto the layout are sometimes placed face up in one or more waste piles, to be brought back into the game as appropriate.

The discard pile is made up of any cards that have been set aside during the course of play and that are not brought back into the game.

The objective of some solitaire games is to discard all or most of the deck.

Available cards Any card that can, in accordance with the rules, be played onto the tableau, foundations, or spaces is termed "available." Sometimes the removal of a card "releases" the card next to it, for example when the top card of a waste pile is removed and makes the next card in the pile available for play.

Exposed cards A card is usually only available for play if it is fully exposed, ie if no other card covers it either wholly or partially.

Building

a   b   c   d   e   f

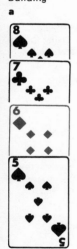

Building is the term used for placing a card onto the tableau, foundations, or a space in its correct sequence. This may be done numerically, by suit, or by color.

a) Cards may be "built down" numerically (eg a 7 is built onto an 8, a 6 onto the 7, etc).

b) Cards may be "built up" numerically (eg a 3 is built onto a 2, a 4 onto the 3, etc).

c) Sometimes the numerical sequence may be continuous or "round the corner" (eg 3, 2,a,k,q), or in twos (eg 7,9,j,k, 2,4, etc).

d) A card may only be built onto another card of the same suit (eg all hearts). Or, in other games, a card may only be built onto a card of a suit other than its own.

e) A card may only be built onto a card of the same color (eg all red cards).

f) A card may only be built onto a card of the other color (eg red, black, red, black).

Solitaire (one - deck games)

KLONDIKE

Klondike probably owes its great popularity to its combination of judgment, luck, attractive layout, and fast-moving tempo—all ingredients of a good solitaire game.
(In the United Kingdom this game is sometimes called Canfield. The game known as Canfield in the United States

is described on p 151 .)

Layout Deal a row of seven cards, with only the first card face up. Add another row of six cards, with the first card face up on the second card of the first row, and the others face down. Deal five more rows in the same way, each row having one card fewer than the row beneath it and with only its first card face up.

Objective The four aces are the foundation cards, and they are set out above the tableau as they become available. The object is to build up the four suits on their respective aces in correct ascending order.

Play The hand is played one card at a time and once only. Cards that are not immediately playable are put face up in a waste heap, the top card of which is always available. Cards are built up in their correct suits on the foundations, or added to the columns of the tableau in descending, alternate-color order (regardless of suit). The top (fully exposed) card of each tableau column is always available for play onto a foundation or another column.
By removing an exposed card,

the face-down card beneath it is turned up and becomes available.
Sequences in the tableau may be transferred from one column to another, but only as a complete unit.
Spaces created in the tableau can only be filled by kings. These may be taken (together with any cards built onto them) either from the stock or from anywhere in the tableau.

Klondike

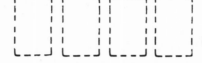

Foundations

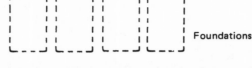

Tableau

King Albert

Reserve

Foundations

Tableau

KING ALBERT

Layout Forty-five cards are dealt face up in rows from left to right, to form a tableau of nine columns.
The first column has one card, the second column two, and so on—the last column comprising nine cards.
The cards in each column should overlap so that all are visible.
The remaining seven cards, known as the "Belgian reserve," may either be held in the hand or fanned out next to the tableau.
The objective is to free the four aces (the foundations), which are placed above the tableau as they come into play. Cards are built onto them in ascending suit sequence, from ace through king.

Play All cards in the reserve are available, as are the exposed cards of the tableau. Only one card may be moved at a time, either onto a foundation pile or in descending, alternate-color sequence on the columns of the tableau.
If an entire column becomes vacant, the space may be filled by any available card.
If the player wishes, he may transfer cards from the foundations to the tableau, provided that they fit into the correct numerical and color sequence.

Eight away

Foundations

Tableau

EIGHT AWAY (EIGHT OFF)

Layout Deal 48 cards face up in eight columns of six cards each. The cards in each column should overlap so that all are visible.
Deal the remaining four cards face up in a row below the tableau to form the start of the reserve.
Objective The player's aim is to free the aces (which are moved as they become available to form a row above the tableau), and to build on them suit sequences, ace through king.

Play The exposed cards in the tableau (those at the bottoms of the eight columns) and all the reserve cards are available for play:
They can be moved to the foundations, built in descending suit sequence on other exposed cards, or moved to the reserve—which, however, must never contain more than eight cards.
Only one card may be moved at a time. Any space that occurs in the tableau can be filled only by an available king.

Reserve

FLOWER GARDEN
Layout Deal 36 cards into six fans or "beds" of six cards each. These are collectively called the "garden" (ie the tableau).
The remaining 16 cards or the "bouquet" may be held in the hand or spread out on the table.

The objective is to free the aces, which are set out below the garden as they become available, and to build onto them suit sequences in ascending order, ace through king.

Play The exposed cards of each bed and all the bouquet cards are available for play. They may be played onto a foundation, or added to a bed in downward numerical sequence, regardless of suit. A sequence may be transferred from one bed to another, provided that the correct numerical order is preserved. If a space is created by the

removal of an entire bed, it may be filled by any available card, or by a sequence from another bed.

Flower garden

Tableau

LA BELLE LUCIE
Layout The deck is dealt out into 17 fans of three cards each and one single card.
Objective The aces are the foundation cards, and they are set out in a row above the tableau as they come into play. Cards are built onto the foundations in ascending suit sequence, from ace through king.

Play The end card of each fan and the single card are available for play. One card at a time may be moved onto a foundation, or built onto another fan in downward suit sequence.
Cards may always safely be built onto the foundations, but any building down on the fans should be carefully considered, as any cards to the

left of the built-down cards will consequently be immobilized.
Any spaces caused by the removal of a fan are left unfilled.
Redealing Two redeals are permitted.
When no further play is possible, all cards other than those on the foundation piles are gathered up, thoroughly

shuffled, and redealt into fans of three cards (any one or two remaining cards forming a separate fan).
After the second redeal, the player may pick out and play one card from any fan of his choice.

La belle Lucie

BRISTOL
Layout Deal 24 cards, face up, in eight fans each of three cards. Any kings that turn up in the deal are placed at the bottom of their respective fans. Next to this tableau, deal three more cards face up in a row to form the start of the waste heaps or reserve.

Objective The foundation cards are the aces, which are set out in a row above the tableau as they occur in play. The aim is to build four ascending sequences, ace through king, regardless of suit or color.

Play The top cards of the fans and the three waste heaps are available for play, but only one card may be moved at a time—either to a foundation or in descending sequence, regardless of suit or color, onto the exposed card of another fan.
The stock is dealt three cards at a time, one card to each of the three waste heaps.

Spaces in the waste heaps are filled only in the deal. Spaces in the tableau (caused by the removal of an entire fan) remain unfilled. Only one deal is permitted.

Bristol

Waste heaps

BELEAGUERED CASTLE

Beleaguered castle is also known by the names of sham battle and laying siege.

Layout Set out the four aces in a column as foundation cards and deal out the rest of the deck face up to form wings of six overlapping cards to the left and right of each ace.

The objective is to build up each suit in ascending numerical order, from ace through king, on its correct foundation card.

Play Only the fully exposed cards at the ends of the rows in each wing are available for play (one card only being moved at a time).

Playing onto the tableau In beleaguered castle it is essential to plan several moves in advance, rather than to play cards onto the tableau as soon as they become available. Otherwise, key cards can quickly become inaccessible and block further play. Spaces—created by the removal of an entire row—are also important to the progress of the game, and may be filled by transferring any exposed card.

Playing onto the foundations Eligible cards can, of course, be placed on the appropriate foundation card as soon as they come into play.

As far as possible, the build-up onto the four foundations should be fairly even.

Beleaguered castle

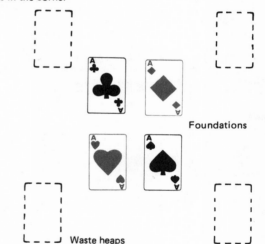

PUSS IN THE CORNER

Layout Puss in the corner has one of the most straightforward layouts of the single-deck solitaires.

The four aces are put face up in a square, and during the course of play four waste heaps are established at its corners.

The object of the game is to build up ascending sequences, ace through king, according to color but irrespective of suit.

Play Cards are played from the stock one at a time, either onto the aces (the foundation cards) or— if ineligible—onto one of the four waste heaps. The top cards of the waste heaps are always available for play.

The player can choose onto which of the four waste heaps he wishes to put a card.

It is wise to reserve one heap for court cards, and if possible low-value cards should not be buried under higher-ranking ones.

Redeal When the stock is exhausted, the cards in the waste heaps are collected in any order and redealt once without shuffling.

Puss in the corner

Foundations

Waste heaps

CALCULATION

Calculation is an aptly named game, for it involves a considerable amount of thinking ahead. (It is sometimes called broken intervals.)

Layout Set out in a row any ace, 2, 3, and 4 as the foundation cards.

The objective is to build up the rest of the deck on these base cards regardless of suit or color, but strictly in accordance with the following order:

On the ace: 2, 3, 4, 5, 6, 7, 8, 9, 10, j, q, k.
On the 2: 4, 6, 8, 10, q, a, 3, 5, 7, 9, j, k.
On the 3: 6, 9, q, 2, 5, 8, j, a, 4, 7, 10, k.
On the 4: 8, q, 3, 7, j, 2, 6, 10, a, 5, 9, k.

Play Cards are turned up one at a time and either built onto the appropriate base card or placed on one of four waste heaps immediately beside these.

Only the top card on each waste heap is available and cards cannot be moved from one waste heap to another. Any space in the waste heaps is filled with the top card of the stock.

Much of the skill of the game lies in playing the cards to the various waste heaps in such a way that they are later readily available for transfer to the foundations.

For example, it is best to keep kings in one waste heap or, if they come out early, at the bottom of waste heaps. Cards of the same rank should be dispersed between the waste heaps rather than concentrated in any single heap.

Whenever possible, cards should be played to the waste heaps in the reverse order to their build-up on the foundations.

Calculation

Foundations

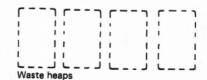

Waste heaps

BISLEY

Layout Set out the four aces at the beginning of the top row of the tableau. Deal nine cards to the right of the aces; then deal the rest of the deck to complete a layout of four rows of 13 cards each. In the course of play, as they become available, the four kings are put out in a row above their aces (king of hearts above ace of hearts, etc).

Objective The aces and kings are foundation cards, and the aim is to complete entire suits, by building up in suit sequence on the aces and building down in suit sequence on the kings. When the two sequences meet they are put together (it does not matter at which point they meet).

Play The bottom card of each column of the tableau is available for play, either onto a foundation or onto the bottom card of another column.

Building onto the bottom cards of the columns is in ascending or descending suit sequence as the player wishes, and he may at any time reverse the order.

Spaces created in the tableau are not filled.

It is evidently important to free the kings as soon as possible, and to use every opportunity of building onto the foundations.

Bisley

 Foundations

         Tableau

FRIDAY THE THIRTEENTH

Layout Set out in a row from left to right any jack, queen, king, and ace—regardless of suit. Leave enough space to the right of them for a further nine cards to be added to the row.

The objective is to establish a total of 13 foundation cards —the jack, queen, king, and ace and then any 2 through 10 as they come up in play—onto which the remaining cards (the stock) are built up four to a pile in ascending numerical order, regardless of suit or color.

Play Work through the stock, turning one card at a time face upward and building it onto one of the foundations (eg a queen onto the jack), or putting it out as the next foundation card. The foundations must be set out in their correct order, for example a 3 cannot be laid out before the 2 has been established.

If a card cannot be played immediately, it is put face up on a waste heap.

Where there is a choice, it is usually better to establish a new base card rather than to build onto an existing pile. For example, if the first card turned up were a 2, it would be wiser to use it as the next base card rather than building it onto the ace.

The waste heap Any exposed card on the waste heap is available for play. When the stock is exhausted, the waste heap is turned over and may be replayed once without shuffling.

Friday the thirteenth

Foundations

SCORPION

The unwary player may be caught out by the scorpion's "sting" at the tail end of the game—since delay in exposing the hidden cards may prevent the solitaire going through!

Layout Deal three rows of seven cards each—the first four cards in each row face down and the remainder face up.

Below these deal four more rows of seven cards each, all face up. This makes a total of 49 cards in the tableau, and the three cards left over are put face down as the reserve.

Objective The four kings are the foundations onto which the cards are built in descending suit sequence (king through ace).

The kings are not removed to separate foundation piles, but are built onto within the tableau.

Play Cards are built on the exposed cards of the layout (ie the bottom card of each column) in correct descending order and suit.

If, as in the example illustrated, the 6 of hearts is exposed, the 5 of hearts may be moved onto it. It may be taken from anywhere within the layout, but all the cards laid on top of it must also be moved.

Nothing may be built onto an ace.

Face-down cards As each face-down card is reached (by the removal of the card or cards on top of it) it is turned face up.

The sooner the hidden cards are uncovered, the better the player's chances of getting the solitaire through. It is therefore advisable to plan moves that will clear the face-down cards as rapidly as possible.

Spaces and reserve If an entire column is cleared away the space may be filled by a king (together with any cards laid on top of it).

A space need not be filled as soon as it occurs.

When no further moves are possible, the three reserve cards are turned up and added to the layout, one to the foot of each of the three left-hand columns.

Not all spaces need to be filled before using the reserve cards. It often helps to see the reserve before filling a space, and this may be done provided that all other moves have been exhausted.

Scorpion

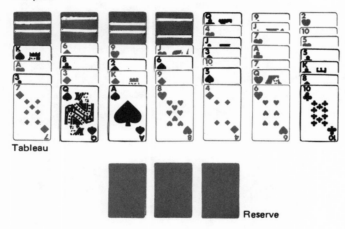

Tableau

Reserve

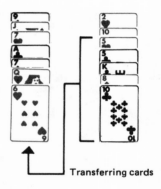

Transferring cards

FLORENTINE

Layout Deal five cards face up to form a cross. Deal a sixth card face up at the top left-hand corner. The rank of this card denotes the foundations; the other three cards of that rank being placed at the other corners as they come into play.

The objective is to build up ascending suit sequences on the four foundation cards. Aces follow kings.

Play Cards from the stock are dealt one at a time. They can be played on the foundations if eligible, or packed in downward sequences regardless of suit on the four outer cards of the cross. The center card of the cross is at all times kept clear.

If one of the outer cards is transferred to a foundation card or packed on another outer card, the vacancy thus created is filled by a card from the waste heap, or by the center card of the cross (which is then replaced by a card from the waste heap).

The waste heap can be turned over and replayed once without shuffling.

Florentine

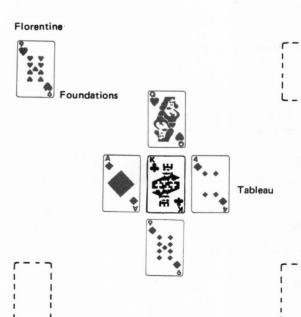

Foundations

Tableau

Canfield

Foundations

Reserve pile

Tableau

Play

Reserve

Waste heap

CANFIELD

Named for the nineteenth-century American gambler and art collector Richard A. Canfield, this game is one of the most popular single-deck games. It is known in the United Kingdom as "demon."

Layout Deal out a reserve pile of 13 cards face down, then turn the pile over to expose one card. Deal four more face-up cards to the right of the reserve to form the tableau. Above the first card of the tableau place the next card face up; this is the first of the four foundation cards and its rank determines the other three cards (which are laid out as they come into play).

Should one of the tableau cards have the same rank as the foundation, move it up into position and deal another card into the space left in the tableau.

The object of the game is to build up the four suits on the foundation cards.

The cards rank continuously, ie if the foundation cards are kings, the next cards in the sequences must be aces.

Play The stock is turned over three cards at a time, only the exposed card of each three being in play (although cards below it can be played as they become available).

If there are only one or two cards at the end of the stock, they are dealt singly.

Cards are built up by suit on the foundations, and in descending alternate-color sequence in any suit on the columns of the tableau. Provided the correct color and numerical sequences are maintained, an entire column of the tableau can be transferred to another column.

Spaces in the tableau are filled immediately from the reserve. If the reserve is exhausted, the player may fill the space from the top of the waste heap, but he need not do so immediately.

Redeal The stock may be redealt, without shuffling, as many times as necessary until the game either blocks or is won.

PYRAMID

In its opening stages this pairing solitaire game appears deceptively easy, and the player may think he is well on the way to winning. He will need a lot of lucky card combinations, however, for the solitaire to go through!

Layout Twenty-eight cards are dealt face up in seven rows to form a pyramid.

Each card is overlapped by two other cards in the row below, except for the cards in the bottom row, which are fully exposed.

Only the fully exposed cards are available for play (ie at the start of the game the seven cards in the bottom row). When two cards are discarded during the course of play, the card they were overlapping becomes exposed and available for play.

The objective is to pair off the entire deck.

Play Any two available cards that together total 13 (regardless of color or suit) are paired off and placed in a waste heap.

The kings are worth 13 and may be discarded singly. Queens are worth 12, jacks 11, and aces one.

For example, a 10 can be paired with a 3, a jack with a 2, or a 4 with a 9.

Cards in the stock are turned up one by one onto a waste heap, of which the top card is always available.

A pair may be made up of: two tableau cards; one tableau card and one card from the stock; or two stock cards (the top card from the waste pile plus the next stock card turned up).

Redeal When the stock has been dealt once and no further pairing is possible, the waste pile may be redealt without shuffling.

Some players permit two redeals; others prefer not to allow any redeal.

MONTE CARLO

Monte Carlo, also called weddings or double and quits, is a straightforward pairing game.

Layout Twenty cards are dealt out into four rows of five cards each. (Some players may prefer to deal out 25 cards in five rows of five cards each.)

Objective At the end of a successful game the player will have dealt out the entire deck and paired up all the cards, leaving an empty layout.

Play Any two cards of the same rank that touch each other top or bottom, side to side, or corner to corner, are discarded.

The spaces thus made are filled by closing up the remaining cards of the layout from right to left, moving up cards from row to row as necessary, but preserving their order as originally laid out.

Extra cards are added from the stock to complete the layout, and the process is repeated until further pairing is impossible, or until the solitaire goes through.

Pyramid

Tableau

Waste heap

CLOCK

Although the chances of winning this solitaire are slight, it is fun to play and very fast-moving.

Clock gets its name from its layout, which is in the form of a clock dial. Other names by which it is known are sun dial, travelers, hidden cards, or four of a kind.

Layout The deck is dealt face down into 13 piles of four cards each. The cards may be dealt singly or in fours.

The piles are arranged to represent a clock dial, one pile corresponding to each hour. The thirteenth pile is placed in the center.

Objective By rearranging the cards, the player hopes to end up with thirteen piles of like-numbered cards in their correct "time" position: the four aces at one o'clock, the four 2s at two o'clock, and so on around the dial.

The jacks represent 11 o'clock, and the queens twelve o'clock. The four kings make up the thirteenth, central pile.

Play The player takes the card at the top of the central pile and places it face up at the bottom of the pile of the same number or "time."

For example, if the card is a 7, it is put face up underneath the seven o'clock pile.

The player then takes the top card of the seven o'clock pile and puts it under its matching pile.

In this way the player works his way from pile to pile, always removing the top card of the pile under which he has just put its matching card.

If the player turns up a card that happens to be on its correct pile (eg a 3 is turned up from the three o'clock pile), it is still placed at the bottom of the pile in the usual way, and the next face-down card is taken from the top of the pile.

Clock

The outcome depends on the order in which the kings are turned up. If the fourth king is turned up before all the other cards are face up, then the game is blocked.

This means in effect that the game can only be won if the last card to be turned up is the fourth king. As the chance of this happening is very small, the king may be exchanged for any one face-down card in the layout. Only one exchange is allowed, and if the fourth king is again turned up before the other cards are in their correct piles, then the game is lost.

Maze

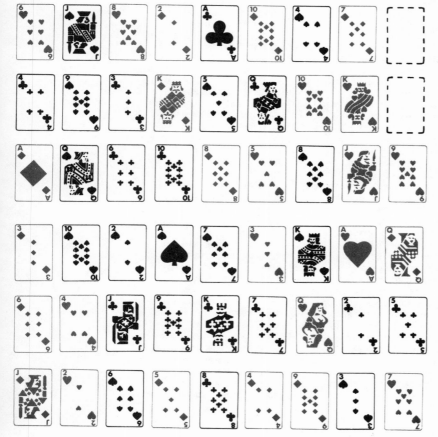

MAZE

Although maze is not one of the better known solitaire games, it is particularly satisfying and requires time and ingenuity to succeed.

Layout The entire deck is dealt face up into two rows of eight cards and four rows of nine cards.

The four kings are then discarded, leaving a total of six spaces.

Objective By rearranging the cards one at a time, the player aims to get the four suits into their correct ascending sequence, ace through queen —one suit following the next. (The order of the suits is immaterial.)

The cards must run from left to right and from the end of one row to the beginning of the next. During play the top row is counted as following on from the bottom row.

In the final sequence, the first card must be an ace and the last card a queen.

For example, in a successful game the order might be: ace of hearts through queen of hearts, ace of spades through queen of spades, ace of clubs through queen of clubs, ace of diamonds through queen of diamonds.

Play A card may be moved into any one of the six spaces provided it is in the same suit as the card to the left or the right side of the space and that it is either:

lower than the card to the right of the space, or

higher than the card to the left of the space.

(For example, a 2 of diamonds may be moved into a space that either has an ace of diamonds to its left or a 3 of diamonds to its right.)

Whenever there is a space to the right of a queen, it may be filled with any of the four aces (even if there is no matching 2 on the right of the space).

LEAPFROG

Layout Deal out 20 cards face up into four rows of five cards each.

The objective is to deal out all the remaining cards onto the table, and to end with as many spaces as possible in the layout.

Play Moves in leapfrog are very like the "taking" moves in a game of checkers.

A card in the layout may be "leapfrogged" over an adjoining card (either horizontally, vertically, or diagonally), provided that the card onto which it lands is of the same suit or rank.

A card so played now becomes the top and identifying card of a pile, and in any subsequent leapfrogging the whole pile is moved.

A move is not limited to a single leapfrog: a succession of leapfrogs is sometimes possible.

Any card leapfrogged by another card is removed to a waste heap.

Empty spaces are filled by cards dealt from the hand whenever the player wishes. (It is better to fill the gaps as soon as they occur, in order to provide a wider choice of moves.)

ACCORDION

Accordion, also called Tower of Babel, idle year, or Methuselah, is one of the most difficult single-deck games to get out. It is unusual in that there is no formal layout at the start of the game: the cards are merely dealt in a single row.

Objective The player aims to rebuild the deck into a single pile.

Play The cards are dealt out face up in a row, as many at a time as space allows.

Any card may be moved onto the card immediately to the left, or onto the third card to the left, provided it is of the same suit or has the same rank.

A pile of two or more cards, identified by its top card, can be similarly moved.

If a card matches both its neighbor and the card three to the left, the player may choose either move, taking into account the various possibilities.

POKER SOLITAIRE

Poker solitaire is a very challenging single-deck game that needs a mixture of luck, judgment, and practice to score well. It is a useful game for familiarizing the beginner with the scoring combinations used in regular poker.

Layout The tableau for poker solitaire comprises five rows of five face-up cards each.

Play The cards are dealt out one by one from a thoroughly shuffled deck. Each card may be placed anywhere within the limits of the tableau.

Once in position a card may not be moved; its placing on the tableau is therefore of great importance.

Objective Each row and each column of the tableau is the equivalent of a poker hand (ie there is a total of 10 hands). The player tries to place the cards of each "hand" to give the highest possible scoring poker combinations.

Scoring The American and British scoring systems are as follows:

Ace can rank either high or low, but may not form part of a "round the corner" sequence (ie king, ace, 2 is not allowed).

A score of about 150 (American) or 50 (British) is considered good, and a score of about 200 (American) or 60 (British) excellent.

Alternative rules

1) In order to improve his chance of a good score, the player may include a joker in the deal.
He can either:
substitute the joker for one of the 25 cards before dealing them; or
play all 25 cards in the usual way, exchanging the joker for any one card of his choice before totaling the score.
2) Another simplification of the game involves dealing out all 25 cards at the start of play in random order, and then rearranging them at will to form the best possible hands.
3) If the player wishes to make the game more taxing, he may only place a card onto the tableau if it touches a previously played card either horizontally, vertically, or diagonally (rather than placing it anywhere within the confines of the tableau).

Poker solitaire, with American scores

One pair 2 points	Flush 20 points	One pair 2 points	Flush 20 points	Straight 15 points	
					Full house 25 points
					Three of a kind 10 points
					Straight 15 points
					Four of a kind 50 points
					No score

Scoring table

Combination	American	British	Definition
Royal flush	100	30	A, k, q, j, 10 of one suit
Straight flush	75	30	Sequence of five cards in one suit
Four of a kind	50	16	Four cards of the same rank with one odd card
Full house	25	10	Three cards of one rank and two of another
Flush	20	5	Any five cards of the same suit
Straight	15	12	Five cards in sequence regardless of suit
Three of a kind	10	6	Three cards of the same rank with two odd cards
Two pairs	5	3	Two pairs with one odd card
One pair	2	1	One pair with three odd cards

Solitaire (two-deck games)

NAPOLEON AT ST HELENA

Although Napoleon was recorded as having played solitaire while in exile on St Helena, it is most unlikely that he invented or even played the many solitaires attributed to him today. The game described here is among the most interesting of this group. Its other names are forty thieves and big forty.

Layout Deal out forty cards into four overlapping rows of ten cards each. The bottom card in each column is available for play.

The objective is to build up suit sequences through to the kings on the eight aces, which are set out in a row above the tableau as they come into play.

Play The stock is turned over one card at a time and is either played onto the foundations, or built onto the tableau in downward suit sequence. If unplayable, cards are placed on a waste heap, of which the top card is always available. Available tableau cards may similarly be played one at a time onto the foundations or onto another column of the tableau.

Spaces If an entire column of the tableau is cleared away, the resulting space may be filled by any one available card from elsewhere in the tableau or from the top of the waste heap.

The player should choose this card carefully, as it may give him the opportunity of releasing useful cards.

Napoleon at St Helena

Foundations

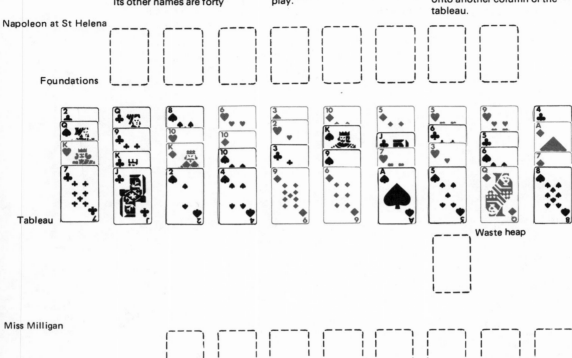

Tableau

Waste heap

MISS MILLIGAN

Objective With the eight aces as the foundations, the player aims to build up the cards into ascending suit sequences.

Play Deal out eight cards face up in a row. If any of these is an ace, set it out above the row as a foundation. Also move any cards that can be built up on the ace in correct suit sequence, or arranged in descending alternate-color sequence on other cards in the row.

Now deal out another row of eight cards, overlapping cards already in position or filling in any spaces as appropriate. Once again, study the layout to see which cards may be built onto the foundations or transferred to other columns. (Several cards may be transferred together, provided they are in correct sequence.) If at this stage a space occurs, it may only be filled by a king (plus any cards built onto it). Continue in this way until the entire stock has been dealt—always completing all possible moves before dealing out the next batch of cards.

Weaving When no cards remain in the stock, the player may lift up any one available card or build from the tableau, and set it aside as a reserve. Each of these reserve cards is available, and the player tries to rebuild them onto the tableau or foundations. If he fails in rebuilding the reserve, the game is lost. If he succeeds, however, he may repeat the "weaving" process until the solitaire goes through or is blocked.

Miss Milligan

Foundations

a) First row of eight cards is dealt

b) Player moves cards where appropriate

CRAZY QUILT

Crazy quilt is an unusual and interesting solitaire that gets its name from its layout of interwoven cards. It is also known as Indian carpet or Japanese rug.

Layout Take an ace and a king of each suit and set them out face up in a row. These are the eight foundations.

Above them, deal out a reserve or "quilt" of eight rows of eight face-up cards each, laying the cards vertically and horizontally in turn.

Any card in the quilt that has one or both of its narrow sides free is available for play. For example, at the start of play the four projecting cards at each side of the quilt are available.

Objective The aim is to build ascending suit sequences on the aces, and descending suit sequences on the kings.

Play Study the reserve to see if any available cards can be built onto the foundations. The removal of a reserve card releases one or more other reserve cards for play.

Spaces in the reserve remain unfilled.

Then turn up the stock one card at a time, putting the card in a waste heap if it cannot be played to a foundation. (The top card of the waste heap is always available.)

In order to release a useful card in the quilt, an available card may be played from the quilt to the top of the waste heap in either ascending or descending suit sequence.

The stock may be redealt once.

Crazy quilt

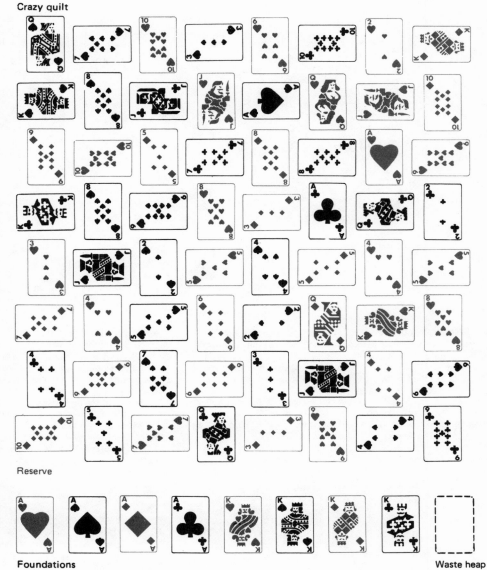

Reserve

Foundations   Waste heap

FROG (TOAD IN THE HOLE)

Layout Deal a reserve pile of 13 cards face up. If any of these cards are aces, set them out to the right of the reserve as foundations.

If no aces are turned up, take one ace of any suit from the stock to begin the foundation row.

The other aces are added to the row as they turn up in play, to complete the foundation of all eight aces.

The objective is to build on the aces ascending sequences from ace to king, regardless of suit or color.

Play Cards are turned up from the stock one at a time and played either onto the foundations or onto any one of five waste heaps.

The waste heaps are set out below the foundations, and cards may be added to them in any order the player chooses.

The top card of the reserve and the top cards of the waste heaps are available at all times for playing onto the foundations.

If a space occurs in the waste heaps it is filled from the stock; if the reserve is exhausted it is not replaced.

It is sound strategy to keep one waste heap for high-value cards such as kings and queens, and—if at all possible—to add cards to the waste heaps in descending numerical order so as to avoid burying low-ranking cards.

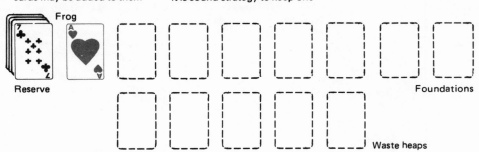

Reserve   Foundations

Waste heaps

Royal cotillion

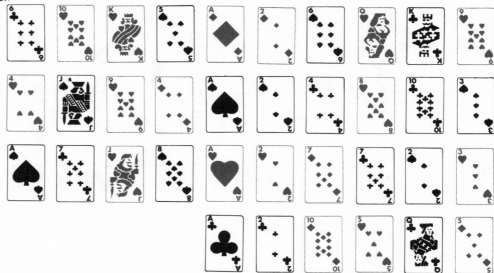

ROYAL COTILLION

Layout Set out face up in two columns an ace and a 2 of each suit.

To the left of the ace column, deal 12 cards face up in three rows of four cards each.

To the right of the 2 column, deal 16 cards face up in four rows of four cards each.

(Some players prefer to establish the two central columns by putting out the aces and 2s as they come into play.)

The objective is to build suit sequences in the following order:

on the aces, 3, 5, 7, 9, j, k, 2, 4, 6, 8, 10, q;

on the 2s, 4, 6, 8, 10, q, a, 3, 5, 7, 9, j, k.

Play Only the bottom card of each column in the left wing of cards is available for play onto a foundation card, and the space made by such a move is not filled.

All the cards in the right wing are available, however, and spaces that occur must be filled immediately, with the top card of either the waste heap or the stock.

The stock is played one card at a time. Any card that cannot be built on a foundation or is not required for filling a space, is put on the waste heap, of which the top card is always available.

There is no redeal.

Spider

SPIDER

There are numerous versions of spider; the one described here is reputed to have been the favorite solitaire of President Franklin D. Roosevelt.

Layout Deal out a tableau of four overlapping rows, each row having ten cards. Deal the first three rows face down and the fourth row face up.

Objective Cards are built onto the eight kings in descending suit sequence. Instead of setting out the kings in separate piles as they come into play, they are built onto within the tableau. Only when a sequence is complete (ie king through ace in any one suit) is it discarded from the tableau.

If the solitaire comes out, all eight completed sequences will have been discarded.

Play The face-up cards in the bottom row are all available, and may be built on any other available card in descending numerical sequence, irrespective of suit or color. When a card is moved to another column, the player must also transfer all the cards built onto it.

Nothing may be built onto an ace, which ranks low and can only follow a two.

When a face-down card is reached, it is turned face up and becomes available for play.

A space in the tableau may be filled by any available card or build.

Stock When there are no more moves to be made in the tableau and all the spaces have been filled, ten cards are dealt face up from the stock—one to the bottom of each column. Play continues in the same way, a fresh batch of ten cards being dealt from the stock each time all possible moves in the tableau have been completed.

(The last deal will be of only four cards, one to be dealt to the bottom of the first four columns.)

WINDMILL (PROPELLER)

Layout Place any king face up at the center of the playing area. Then deal out a reserve (called the "sails") of eight face-up cards: two above the king, two below it, and two to either side.

The objective is to build:
a) a descending sequence of 52 cards on the central king, regardless of suit or color and with kings following aces;
b) ascending sequences, ace through king and regardless of suit and color, on the first four aces that come up in play.

Play Cards are turned up from the stock one at a time and if unplayable are put on a waste heap. The stock is only dealt once.

The first four aces to appear are put as foundation cards in the four angles of the sails. Cards are played to the foundations from either the stock, the sails, or from the top of the waste heap (which is always available for play). The top card of any ace foundation may be transferred to the central king foundation (building on the central pile is of prime importance if the game is to go through).

Spaces A space in the layout must be filled by the top card of either the stock or the waste heap, but it need not be filled as soon as it occurs.

This means that a space can be "saved" for a useful card— and by using his judgment in the way he fills spaces, the player can greatly increase his chances of winning.

Alternative rule Some players prefer the central foundation card to be an ace and the other four foundations to be kings.

Should he choose this alternative, the player must build an ascending sequence on the central ace and descending sequences on the four kings.

Windmill

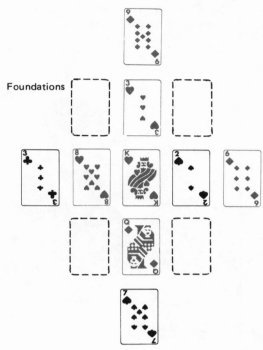

Foundations

BRAID (PLAIT)

Braid or plait is a straight-forward solitaire that gets its name from its particularly attractive layout.

Layout Twenty cards are dealt face up in the form of a braid: the cards are laid out diagonally, and alternately pointing to right and left— each card partially covering the card beneath it (as illustrated).

Columns of six face-up cards are dealt to either side of the braid; the braid and the columns together form the reserve.

The next (33rd) card is placed to the right of the reserve. It determines the rank of the other seven foundations, which are set out as they become available to make two rows of four cards.

Objective The player tries to build ascending "round the corner" suit sequences on the eight foundations (ace following king and preceding 2).

Play The bottom (fully exposed) card of the braid and all the cards in the two columns are available for play onto the foundations.

The stock is dealt one card at a time, and if the card is unplayable it is placed on a waste heap.

Any number of redeals is permitted, until the game either becomes blocked or goes through.

A space in the columns must be filled as soon as it occurs. If the top or bottom card of a column has been removed, the vacancy may be filled by the available card of the braid, or from the top of the waste heap (which is always available). If the vacancy is anywhere else in the column, it may only be filled from the stock.

Braid

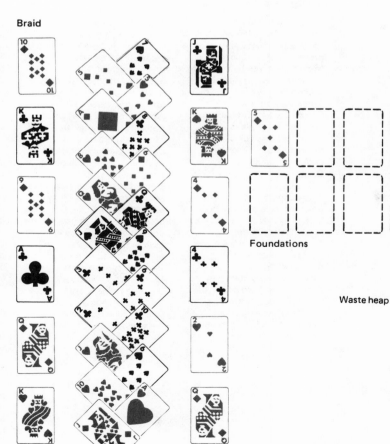

Foundations

Waste heap

Reserve

©DIAGRAM

Double solitaires

Although solitaire card games are really just for one person they can be played by two or more players in competition—either racing each other or comparing scores. In addition, there are "double solitaires" intended specifically for two players. Two of these are Russian bank and spite and malice.

RUSSIAN BANK

This popular game, also known as crapette, requires a great deal of concentration. Moves are made according to a strict procedure that, if broken, may result in the player forfeiting his turn.

Cards Two standard decks are used. Each player should have his own deck with a distinctive back in order to avoid confusion.
Cards rank: k(high),q,j,10,9,8, 7,6,5,4,3,2,a.

The objective A player's objective is to build all or as many as possible of the cards in his deck onto the foundations, the tableau, or his opponent's reserve or discard piles.

Preliminaries Each player draws a card from one of the decks: the player drawing the lower card will play first. Players then shuffle and cut their opponent's deck.

Layout To establish his reserve, each player counts out 12 cards from his deck and places them face down in a pile to his right.
Both players then deal out a column of four face-up cards above their reserve; these eight cards form the tableau and are for common use.
The remaining cards in each deck are placed face down in a pile in front of each player and form his stock.

Foundations The eight aces are the foundations. They are laid out between the two columns of the tableau as they come into play. Cards are built onto the foundations in ascending suit sequence. Building cards onto the foundations is also called building to the "center." Once a card has been built onto a foundation, it may not be removed.

Play The player who drew the lower card plays first; thereafter players take alternate turns.
Cards must be moved according to a set procedure, as follows.
1) Both players must start their opening turns by playing any available tableau cards to the center. They must then turn up the top card of their reserve and—if possible—play that to the center. If it cannot be played to the center, it may be played elsewhere on the layout.
2) In subsequent turns, players may turn over the top card of their reserve prior to making a play.
3) Building onto the foundations always takes precedence over building elsewhere on the layout. Also, if there is a choice of cards for building onto the center, cards from the reserve must always be used before cards from the tableau or stock.
4) If no more cards can be built onto the foundations, the player may build onto the tableau in descending alternate-color sequence. He may use the top card from another tableau pile, the reserve, or the stock—there is

no order of precedence. (Players should take every opportunity of rearranging tableau cards, so as to free blocked cards for play to the center.)
Cards in the tableau piles should be built in overlapping rows, so that all the cards are visible.
5) A space in the tableau may be filled by the top card of another tableau pile, the reserve, or, once the reserve is exhausted, from the stock. (Spaces need not be filled as soon as they occur.)
6) If no cards can be built to the center and the top reserve card cannot be built onto the tableau, the player may turn up the top card in his stock. If this card can be played directly to the center or the tableau, the next card in the stock may be turned up, and so on until an unplayable stock card is turned up. As soon as this happens, the player must move the unplayable card face up onto a waste pile to his left. His turn then ends.
7) Cards in the waste pile cannot be played. If the player's stock is exhausted, he may, however, take the waste pile and turn it face down and unshuffled to form a new stock.

SPITE AND MALICE

Cards Two standard decks and four jokers are used. The decks should be distinctively backed. Ace ranks low; jokers are wild.

The objective A player aims to get rid of all the cards on his payoff pile.

Preliminaries One of the decks is shuffled—without its jokers—and divided into two separate "payoff" piles of 26 cards, one for each player. The top card of each pile is turned face up and the player with the highest card will play first.
If by chance the two cards have the same value, the procedure is repeated.
The player with the lower card shuffles the second deck, including the four jokers. He then gives himself and his opponent five cards, dealing them one at a time and face down.
The remaining cards form the stock and are placed face down in a pile in the middle of the table.

Play The player who had the higher card has the opening turn; thereafter play is alternate.

1) Aces must be played to the center of the table as soon as they become available; they are the base cards of "center stacks" (equivalent to foundation piles).

Available 2s must be built on the aces whenever possible. Cards are built on the center stacks in ascending sequence regardless of suit; a card from the payoff pile, the hand, or a side stack (see paragraph 3) may be used.

Whenever a center stack has been built up through to the king, it is shuffled together with the stock at the next break in play.

2) The top card of the payoff pile may be played only to the center stacks. Whenever this happens, the player may turn up the next card in the payoff pile, and so on, until an unplayable card is turned up.

3) Each player may build up to four "side stacks" using only cards from his hand. A side stack may be started with a card of any value, and is built on regardless of suit either in descending sequence or with a card of the same value (eg a 7 on a 7). Only one build onto a side stack may be made in any one turn.

4) Jokers may take the place of any card except an ace.

End of turn A player may make any number of legal plays to the center stacks, but his turn ends as soon as he plays a card from his hand to a side stack.

A player may also finish his turn by saying "End" if he cannot, or wishes not to, make further moves.

Stock At the start of their second and subsequent turns, players take as many cards from the stock as they need to replenish their hand (ie anything up to five cards).

Result The winner is the first player to have exhausted his payoff pile. Should neither player be able to make any further moves but still have cards left in his payoff pile, the game is considered drawn.

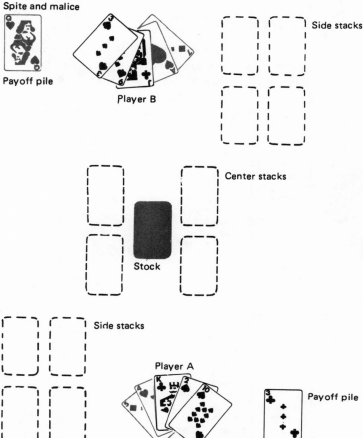

Spite and malice

Payoff pile

Player B

Side stacks

Center stacks

Stock

Side stacks

Player A

Payoff pile

Loading Once all available cards have been played to the center, the player has the option of "loading" cards onto his opponent's reserve or waste piles in up or down suit sequence.

The player may use cards from the tableau, or from his own reserve and stock.

Should the opponent's top reserve card be face down, the player may ask him at any time to turn it face up.

If an opponent has used up his reserve or waste pile (ie toward the end of the game) a player cannot off-load cards onto the resultant spaces.

Stops If a player thinks that his opponent has made an error in procedure, he may call "Stop," and play must immediately be halted.

If the error is proved, the wrongly moved card is returned to its former position and the offending player forfeits the rest of that turn. Should an error not be noticed until after further moves have been made, the offender is allowed to continue without penalty.

Result The game is won by the first person who succeeds in discarding his entire deck, ie all the cards in his reserve, stock, and waste pile.

He scores 30 points for winning, plus two points for each card left in his opponent's reserve and one point for each card left in his opponent's stock and waste pile.

If neither player succeeds in winning outright, the game is considered a draw.

Alternatively, players can evaluate their remaining cards (using the system described above); the player with fewest points then scores the difference between his points total and that of his opponent.

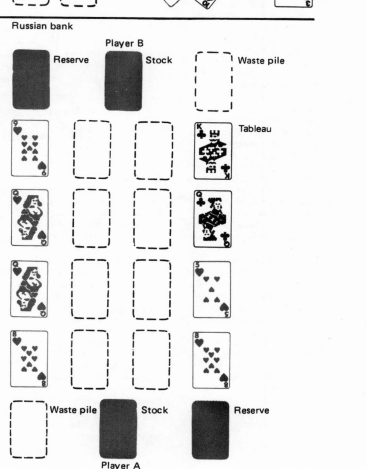

Russian bank

Player B

Reserve

Stock

Waste pile

Tableau

Waste pile

Stock

Reserve

Player A

Shove ha'penny

Shove ha'penny is an old English game sometimes played in public houses. Two players or pairs attempt to position ha'pennies or metal disks on a marked board. A game is won by the first side to "shove" three ha'pennies into each of the board's nine "beds."

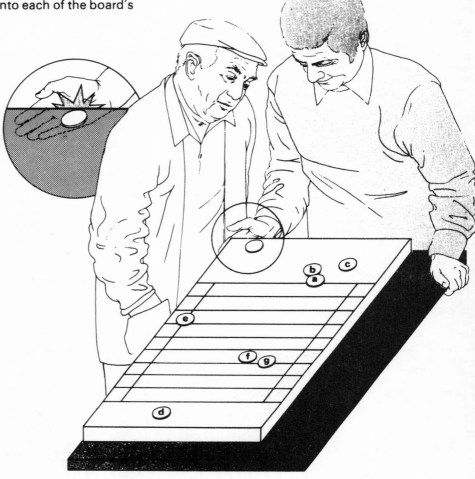

The board Shove ha'penny is usually played on a special board, but can be played on a tabletop marked with chalk or pencil.

A strip of wood under the board keeps it steady when placed over the edge of a table or other level surface.

Boards are 2ft by 1ft 2½in and are made of hardwood or slate. Wood boards have the grain running lengthways and the lines marked by shallow grooves.

Ten lines running across the board at 1¼in intervals mark out the nine "beds," and two lines at right angles to them mark the edges of the scoring area.

The squares along the edges of the board are used for recording the players' scores. Some boards have three holes in each square to hold small scoring pegs.

Ha'pennies The game was played in Britain long before decimalization of the currency in 1972. The old ha'penny was 1 in in diameter.

Players use very highly polished old ha'pennies, or metal disks of the same diameter.

Each player has five ha'pennies or disks.

Players Shove ha'penny is a game for two players or pairs.

Turns Choice of playing order may be decided by the toss of a coin, or by a preliminary shove for the nine bed (using only one ha'penny except in case of a tie).

Each player shoves five ha'pennies in a turn.

"Shoving" The ha'penny is placed partly over the edge of the board and is then shoved as illustrated. A sharp, light tap is most effective.

Shoving one ha'penny into another ("cannoning" or "caroming") is an important feature of the game.

Objective The game is won by the first side to shove three scoring ha'pennies into each of the board's nine beds.

Short shoves

a) A ha'penny that comes to rest on the nearest line of the first bed must be left in position, but may later be cannoned into the beds by another ha'penny.

b) A ha'penny that fails to reach the nearest line of the first bed after hitting a ha'penny on that line must also be left in position.

c) A ha'penny that fails to reach the nearest line of the first bed without hitting a ha'penny on that line may be retaken.

Dead ha'pennies must be immediately removed from the board and may not be retaken. A ha'penny is dead if:

d) it goes wholly beyond the far line of the ninth bed;

e) it stops wholly or partly beyond the side lines in the area used for keeping the score.

Ha'penny on another If a ha'penny stops wholly or partly on top of another, both are left on the board.

If a ha'penny is on top of another at the end of a turn, neither ha'penny can be scored.

Scoring A player's turn is scored only after he has shoved all his five ha'pennies —hence the importance of cannoning.

A ha'penny is scored if it lies completely within one of the beds for which the player needs a score (**f**).

There is no score for a ha'penny on a line (**g**), however slight the overlap.

Scores may be made in any order, but good players usually fill the far beds first.

If a player scores more than three times in any bed, the extra scores may be claimed by the opposition. Except that the score that wins the game must actually be from a shove by the winner.

Penalties A player loses all five shoves for the turn if he: touches a played ha'penny before all are played; or removes his ha'pennies before recording his score.

A player who plays out of turn is allowed no score for that turn and must miss his next turn.

Shovelboard

Table shovelboard is the ancestor of shove ha'penny and of the shovelboard, or shuffleboard, game played on ships' decks and outdoor courts. Players attempt to score points by propelling coins or disks into marked scoring areas. The game can easily be adapted for modern play.

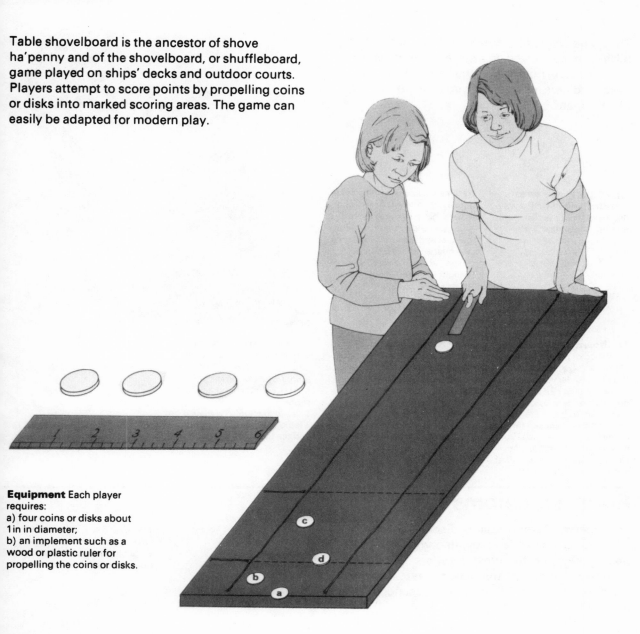

Equipment Each player requires:
a) four coins or disks about 1in in diameter;
b) an implement such as a wood or plastic ruler for propelling the coins or disks.

Table In medieval times shovelboard was played on very long, narrow tables— perhaps 30ft long and 2ft wide. The higher scoring area extended 4in from the end of the table and the lower scoring area 4ft in front of that.
It is, however, possible to play a form of shovelboard on almost any rectangular or square table—by marking off an out of play area and scaling down the dimensions of the scoring areas.

Players Shovelboard is a game for two players or two teams of equal number.
Turns In team games, each player normally plays a round against an opponent from the other team.
The two opponents in a round propel one coin alternately.
Playing a coin Players use their rulers to give the coin one push toward the scoring area. All coins, except those more than half over the out of play lines, are left on the table until the end of the round. This makes hitting one coin into another an important feature of the game.

Scoring Players score:
a) three points for any coin partly over the far edge of the table;
b) two points for any coin completely in the far scoring area;
c) one point for any coin completely in the near scoring area;
d) one point for any coin on the line between the near and far scoring areas.

Result In singles games, the winner is the first person to score an agreed number of points—for example 11.
Team games can be decided in several ways:
the team winning most rounds;
the team with most points after an agreed number of rounds;
the first team to score an agreed number of points.

Bagatelle

The name "bagatelle" is sometimes applied to a billiards game played on a baize-covered table. Better known, however, is the bagatelle game described here, which is played on a wood or plastic board.

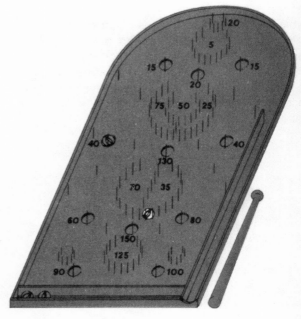

Objective Players try to strike the balls in such a way that they score the maximum number of points.

Other equipment Bagatelle is played with small steel or plastic balls. When not in play, they are ranged behind a special partition running along the near end of the board. A stick about the size and weight of a drum stick is used to strike the balls.

The board is made of varnished or painted wood or of plastic.
It is rectangular in shape (approximately 2ft by 1ft) and one of its ends is curved to form a semicircle.
The board has a raised rim—rather like a tray—and slopes very slightly, so that the far (curved) end is higher than the end nearest the player.

A number of small nails are set into the board as shown. (The arrangement of the nails may vary from board to board.) Some of the nails form semicircles (called "cups"); other nails are free standing. There are also a number of shallow depressions or "holes," just big enough to hold a ball and with nails next to them.

The cups and holes are marked with a scoring value, usually ranging from five to 150 points. The free-standing nails act as deflectors and have no score.
The board should be placed on a table or other suitable surface for play.

Burmese caroms

This ancient Burmese game displays most of the techniques and skills associated with billiard games played in the West. It differs significantly in the smaller size of the playing area, the use of disks instead of balls, and in the absence of a cue as a striker.

Players This is a game for two players or for two pairs. Opposing players face each other across the board.

Starting position

Table Burmese caroms is played on a miniature table measuring 2ft square. The playing surface is composed of a highly polished tropical hardwood, such as teak.
To reduce friction to a minimum, the surface is lightly coated with French chalk (reapplied after each game).
At each corner of the table there is a netted pocket. The width of each pocket should not exceed $1\frac{1}{2}$ times the diameter of the striker disk.
A circle 6in in diameter, with a center spot, is marked on the middle of the board.
Two rectangles, each $21\frac{1}{3}$in by $18\frac{2}{3}$in, are marked out on the board, so that their short edges are equidistant from the four sides of the table. This arrangement forms four

narrow rectangles or "boxes," from which each player makes his strokes.
Equipment There are 19 object disks: nine black, nine white, and one red or "queen" disk. These disks measure 1in across and $\frac{3}{16}$in in depth. They are made of polished hardwood and are designed to fit into the center circle.
There is also one striker disk made of bone or ivory, measuring $1\frac{1}{3}$in across and $\frac{3}{16}$in in depth.

Play The participants—of whom there may be any number—each play in turn. In his turn, the player takes a ball and places it at the head of the "guidance channel" that runs part-way along the right-hand side of the board. Holding the striking stick with one or both hands, the player then strikes the ball so that it runs along the channel and into the main area of the board. (In the follow-through, the tip of the stick may not extend beyond the end of the channel.)

If the player strikes the ball with insufficient force—so that it rolls back to the start instead of into the main area of the board—he may strike the ball again.

If, however, the ball is hit so forcefully that it shoots off the board, the player may not take the ball again and his score for that ball is zero.

The number of balls each player may strike in a turn may be determined by the players before the start of the game. The players may also choose whether to remove each ball from the board as soon as it has been played, or to leave all the balls in position until the end of a round.

Scoring A player's score must be noted after each turn. A ball cannot be judged until it has come to an absolute standstill. If it comes to a halt inside a cup or hole, it scores the corresponding number of points.

There is no score if the ball: enters a cup or hole but then rolls out again; becomes lodged against the nails outside a cup or hole; comes to a halt in any non-scoring area of the board, including the near end of the board.

If balls are left in position until the end of a round, points may also be scored by a player managing to dislodge an opponent's ball that has already scored.

For example, if the opponent's ball scored 50 points, the player may add 50 points to his own score—whether or not his ball comes to halt in a scoring area.

End play The players may decide to continue a game until:
a) a set time limit has been reached (in which case the winner is the player with the highest score at that point);
b) one player's score has reached a predetermined number of points; or
c) each player has had a predetermined number of turns—the player with the highest score then being the winner.

Alternative boards come in many different shapes and sizes, sometimes small enough to fit in the hand.

On many of these boards, the balls are fed automatically to the front of a spring-loaded trigger. By pulling and then releasing the trigger, the balls are propelled around the board.

Some of the boards are illustrated with a particular theme.

Bagatelle has also been adapted for play in fairgrounds and amusement arcades on special machines popularly known as "pinball" machines.

Objective Each player (or pair) attempts to pocket the disks of the color allotted to him by knocking them with the striker disk.

All players also attempt to pocket the queen disk—which carries bonus points.

Starting procedure The queen disk is placed on the center spot, with the other disks arranged around it as shown.

Order of play is determined by lot. The player drawing black plays first, and his objective is to pocket the black disks; his opponent's objective is to pocket the white disks.

Play Black places the striker disk anywhere within his box and, by flicking it with his middle finger, attempts to knock one or more black disks into any pocket.

A player must flick the striker disk across the front line of his box at each stroke—although if the striker crosses the front line and then spins off a side of the table in such a way as to hit a disk behind the striker's original position, the stroke is valid. (The striker disk may rebound from a side before hitting a disk.)

A player may hit one of his opponent's disks, using it to pocket one of his own disks. A player's turn ends when he either:
a) fails to flick the striker across the front line of his box;
b) fails to pocket one of his disks;
c) pockets one of his opponent's disks; or
d) pockets the striker—whether or not he succeeds in pocketing one or more of his own disks. (See also the section on fouls and penalties.)

When the turn passes to a player, the striker disk must be placed in that player's box. All shots must be played from the correct box.

Pocketing the queen disk may be done in either one of two ways (to be agreed on by the players before the start of the game).
1) The queen disk may be pocketed at any time provided that the successful player pockets one of his own disks with his next stroke.
Failure to do so results in the queen being returned to the center, together with any other of the player's disks pocketed with that stroke.

2) In the more difficult alternative, the queen disk may only be pocketed after a player has successfully pocketed all his own disks.

Fouls and penalties In addition to losing his turn, a player may also incur penalties or penalty points.
a) If a player pockets one of his opponent's disks, it remains in the pocket.
b) If a player pockets the striker disk as well as one or more of his own disks, his opponent replaces the disk or disks anywhere within the center circle.
c) If a player pockets the striker disk only, his opponent takes any one of the player's disks from a pocket and places it anywhere within the center circle. If the offending player has no disks pocketed, he has one point deducted from his score.

Scoring No scoring is carried out until one player has pocketed all his own disks, thereby winning the game. The first player to do so scores the value of his opponent's disks still on the board, plus the value of the queen if it was pocketed by him. No points can be claimed for pocketing the queen disk if it was pocketed by the loser.

Each black and each white disk is worth one point, and the queen is worth five points. Any penalty points are deducted from the players' scores.

Scores are totaled until one player has 30 points—this may take several games.

In match play the first player to score 30 points wins the set, and the winner of two out of three sets wins the match.

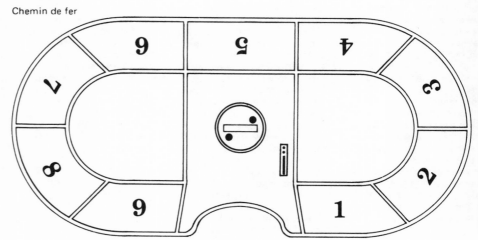

9 Casino and gambling house card games

Baccarat and Chemin de fer

Games of the baccarat and chemin de fer family originated in the baccarat that became popular in French casinos in the 1830s. In the present century they have traveled from Europe to the United States, from the United States back to Europe, and from both points to casinos throughout the world. This process has resulted in wide variations in playing rules, and what is called "baccarat" in one casino may more nearly resemble the "chemin de fer" of another. Three basic forms of play are described here.

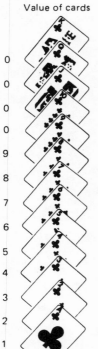

Value of cards

0
0
0
0
9
8
7
6
5
4
3
2
1

Players: at least two, but usually seven or more. Often persons without seats may also bet.

Croupier The casino provides a croupier, who assists players in making and settling bets, advises on rules and odds, and takes the casino's cut.
The croupier also plays the "bank" hand when the game is banked by the casino.
The casino makes an hourly charge for the croupier and his assistants, and for supervising the game.

The objective is to bet on a winning hand, ie on a hand with a higher point value than the other hand(s).

Hands are of two or three cards.
Cards score as follows:
a) face (court) cards and 10s, zero;
b) aces, one point;
c) any other card, its numerical value.
When scoring a hand tens are ignored—eg five plus seven counts as two not 12. Hence the highest possible score for a hand is nine.

The basic sequence of play is:
1) placing of bets;
2) dealing of hands;
3) receipt of another card on request;
4) comparison of hands and settlement of bets.

Equipment Several standard decks of playing cards are used.
Other equipment is:
a) a heavy table, padded and covered with green baize, and marked with a layout for nine or 12 players;
b) a card-holding box or "shoe," from which the cards are dealt one at a time;
c) a discard box, positioned beneath a slot in the table;
d) wooden palettes for distributing cards and payments to the players.

CHEMIN DE FER
The distinctive features of the "chemin de fer" game are that:
the role of banker rotates rapidly among the players;
only a bank hand and one non-bank hand are dealt;
bets can only be placed against the bank.
Cards Six or eight standard decks of cards are used.

The shuffle
1) The croupier places the decks face down on the table.
2) Players and croupier take groups of cards and shuffle them, and then shuffle the groups of cards into each other.
3) The croupier gathers the cards, gives them a final shuffle in large groups, gathers them all into a single

Chemin de fer

deck, and cuts the deck several times.

4) The croupier asks one of the players to make a final cut. (Often the croupier makes the actual cut, after the player has inserted an indicator (a blank or advertising) card at the point where the cut should be made.)

5) Often the croupier then inserts a second indicator card into the deck, around eight or ten cards from the bottom, to give warning of the end of the shuffled cards.

6) The croupier places the deck face down in the shoe.

7) The croupier deals three or four cards from the shoe, shows them, and discards them.

First choice of banker is either:
a) by lot;
b) by auction, with the players bidding the amounts they are prepared to put forward as the "bank";
c) by acceptance, the bank being offered first to the first player to the croupier's left or right (according to house rules), and then on around the table, clockwise or counterclockwise, until a player accepts the bank.
The croupier passes the shoe to the first banker.

Amount of the bank On the first play of a turn as banker, the bank is:
a) what the player bid for it if the bank was gained by auction;
b) any figure the banker wishes to put at risk if he gained the bank by lot or acceptance.
On all subsequent plays of a turn as banker, the bank is the amount stated on the first play plus subsequent winnings.

Betting takes place before any cards are dealt.
Players can only place bets against the bank—ie they bet that the bank will lose.
The total of bets on a single play is limited to the amount of the bank—the banker is never liable for payment of bets in excess of this.
The player to the banker's right (or left, according to house rules) has first bet.
Any amount of the bank he does not bet against ("fade"), may be bet against by the next player in turn.
Betting passes around the table until the entire bank is covered by several bets, someone has called "banco," or everyone has bet who wishes to.
Bystanders may bet if there is part of the bank left to cover or if one of them calls "banco."
If the bank is not completely covered, the amount not faded is safe for the hand and is kept by the banker whether he wins or loses.

"Banco" A player or bystander who wishes to bet against the entire bank makes this known by calling "banco." A call of "banco" makes all other bets void.
When two or more wish to banco, a player who bancoed on the preceding hand has precedence over all others.
Otherwise, a seated player has precedence over a bystander and the order of priority among players belongs to the player who is earliest in the betting order.

Play is as follows.

1) The banker deals two hands of two cards each. The cards are dealt singly and face down, alternately to the table and to the banker himself. The "table" hand represents all players betting against the bank. It is played by whoever made the highest bet against the bank. If there are two equal bets, the player nearer the banker in the betting order has priority.

2) The player and banker examine their hands without showing them.

3) If the player's hand totals eight or nine, it is a "natural," and is immediately declared and turned face up. If it is an eight hand, the player calls "la petite;" if a nine he calls "la grande."

4) If the player's hand is a natural, the banker shows his own cards. If only the player's hand is a natural, all bets against the bank win. If both hands are naturals, a nine beats an eight. If both hands are naturals of the same number, it is a "stand-off" and all bets are returned.

5) If the player's hand does not contain a natural, he says "pass." The banker then examines his own hand, and if it contains a natural he declares it immediately and wins all bets.

6) If both hands have been examined, and neither contains a natural, the player may "draw" (request another card, face up) or "stay" (not request another card). His decision must be based on the rules of mathematical advisability (see table), except that in some games a player who has bancoed is allowed to ignore these rules.

7) Whether the banker then draws another card or stays depends on the card that he has just given to the player (see table), except that in some games the banker is allowed the option when holding a five hand and having given a four. If a player has bancoed and is allowed to use his judgment, the banker may also ignore the rules for drawing or staying.

8) The hands are shown. If there has been any error, the banker must reconstruct the play as it should have been.

Player

Player holding	Action
0, 1, 2, 3, or 4	draw
5	optional
6 or 7	stay
8 or 9	face

Banker

After giving	Banker stays on	Banker draws on
0 or 1	4, 5, 6, or 7	3, 2, 1, or 0
9	4, 5, 6, 7, (or 3)	2, 1, 0, (or 3) ·
8	3, 4, 5, 6, or 7	2, 1, or 0
7 or 6	7	6, 5, 4, 3, 2, 1, or 0
5 or 4	6 or 7	5, 4, 3, 2, 1, or 0
3 or 2	5, 6, or 7	4, 3, 2, 1, or 0
Player has stood	6 or 7	5, 4, 3, 2, 1, or 0

Natural 8s   Natural 9s

Winning The hand totaling nine or nearest nine wins.
a) If the totals are the same, all bets are returned.
b) If the banker has won, he collects all bets less any casino levy. In most countries the casino levies a percentage (usually 5%) on bankers' winnings. Sometimes the winnings on a player's first hand as banker are exempt from the levy. (In countries where a percentage levy is illegal, all casino profits come from the hourly rate charged by the casino.)
c) If the banker has lost, each player collects the amount of the bank that he had covered.

Keeping the bank If the banker has won a hand, he may keep the bank for the next hand.
In this case, the new bank comprises the original bank plus the winnings after any levy.
A player who keeps the bank is not permitted to remove any of his winnings between hands.
If the original bank plus winnings exceeds the house limit on bets, the excess is not at stake.

Passing the bank If the banker has won a hand but chooses not to keep the bank, he may take his winnings and pass the bank.
In this case:
a) the bank is offered to the players in turn until one of them accepts it, after which the new banker decides the amount of his bank; or
b) the house croupier holds an informal auction, and the bank passes to a player who will put up a bank equal to the one that has just been passed.

Losing the bank If the banker loses a hand, the bank is offered to the players in turn—as when the banker chooses to pass the bank. (An auction is not held.)
Reshuffling The cards are not reshuffled until at least ⅚ of the deck has been used— and usually not until the last few cards are reached.

BACCARAT BANQUE

Also known as *baccarat à deux tables* (double table baccarat), baccarat banque is the oldest European form of the game.

The distinctive features of baccarat banque are that: the role of banker rotates more slowly among the players or may be held permanently by the casino or concessionaires; one bank hand and two non-bank hands are dealt; bets can be placed only against the bank.

Except when specifically described here, the rules are the same as for chemin de fer.

Cards Three standard decks are used.

Banker Sometimes the role of banker is held permanently by the casino—or by concessionaires who pay the casino a percentage of their takings.

Otherwise the procedure is as follows.

a) The bank is auctioned to the highest bidder, who pays 2½% of his bid to the casino.

b) The banker does not lose the bank if he loses a hand, but holds it until he loses the whole bank or passes.

BACCARAT-CHEMIN DE FER (LAS VEGAS)

The distinct Las Vegas form of the game may be called baccarat, chemin de fer, or baccarat-chemin de fer.

The distinctive features of the Las Vegas game are that: the role of banker is usually held permanently by the casino, although it may rotate slowly among the players; one non-bank hand is dealt; bets can be placed either with or against the bank.

Cards Six or eight standard decks are used.

Banker When the role of banker rotates among the players, the rules for the bank are the same as for baccarat banque.

More usually the casino keeps the bank, and the procedure is as follows.

a) The limit on bets on a hand is not the size of the bank but the house betting limit. (The house betting limit will, however, sometimes be raised when a player requests this.)

b) There is no banco bet and no need for rules of precedence in betting.

c) A single player can play.

d) The casino takes a cut (usually 5%) from winning bets that have bet the bank to win.

c) The banker cannot withdraw any money from the bank unless he passes—but any part of the bank not bet against on a hand is not at risk.

d) When a bank is lost or passed, the bank is again auctioned. As before, the casino takes a 2½% cut from the winning bidder.

Betting and play differs from chemin de fer in the following ways.

a) The banker deals three hands—one to his right, one to his left, and one to himself.

b) Bets against the bank may be placed on either the right or the left hand, or on both hands. Betting on both hands is called betting "*à cheval*" (on horseback).

c) Priority for betting on the right table hand begins with the player sitting to the banker's right; for the left table hand, with the player to the banker's left. Calling "banco" is usually allowed, but not always.

d) Each hand is played by a player on the appropriate side of the table. The player playing the right hand always plays first. On the first deal, the hands are played by the players nearest the dealer on his right and left sides. Thereafter, a player continues playing one of the table hands until he loses a hand. After a player has lost a hand, the right to play that side's hand passes to the next player in rotation.

e) Table players are bound by the same staying and drawing rules as in chemin de fer. The banker may stay or draw on any hand, and will obviously concentrate on beating the hand on which most money has been bet.

f) Players betting *à cheval* lose only if the bank wins both hands, and win only if the bank loses both hands. Otherwise their bets are returned.

Baccarat banque layout

Baccarat – Chemin de fer layout

Betting Players may bet with or against the bank.

A player betting the bank to win places his bet on the appropriate numbered section at the table center.

A player betting the bank to lose places his bet on the numbered section in front of him.

A player may also back the bank to have a natural eight or nine, and if successful, he is paid the odds of nine to one.

Play is as in chemin de fer, except that all player's and banker's options are removed to become draw plays. Thus:

a) a player must draw if holding a hand totaling five;

b) the banker must draw if holding a three hand when he has given a nine, or a five hand after giving a four.

©DIAGRAM

Faro

Faro or farobank is a very old banking card game. It was known as pharaon in the French court of Louis XIV. In the 1700s it was the most popular gambling house game in England. The following century it became equally popular in the United States, where it was often called "bucking the tiger."

Casekeeper

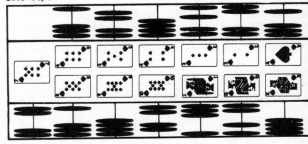

Equipment

a) A table covered with green baize, bearing the faro layout. The complete spades suit is usually used for the layout.
b) A dealing box from which one card can be slid at a time.
c) A casekeeper. This is a frame like an abacus used to show which cards in the deck have been played.
d) A standard deck of cards.
e) Betting chips.
f) Faro "coppers"—round or hexagonal chips of either red or black—used for betting a denomination to lose.
g) Bet markers—small flat oblongs of ivory or plastic—used to make bets over the limit of a bettor's funds.

Players Up to ten can play. House officials are a dealer, a lookout who supervises betting, and a casekeeper official.
The house always banks.

Objective Players try to predict whether the next card to appear, of the denomination bet on, will be a winning or a losing card.
Cards appear in play two at a time. The first in each pair is always the losing card, the second the winning card.

Shuffle, cut, and bet The dealer shuffles the cards, cuts them, and puts them in the dealing box face up. The exposed top card is called the "soda." It is ignored for betting.
Bets are now placed.

First turn The dealer puts the soda card face up to one side to start the discard pile or "soda stack."
He then takes the next exposed card from the box and places it face up to the right of the box. This card is the losing card. The card now exposed in the box is the winning card.

Between turns Any bets on the two exposed denominations are settled. Other bets may be changed and new bets made. The casekeeper is altered to show the cards that have already appeared.

Continuing play Play continues through the deck. In each turn:
1) the dealer removes the last winning card from the box and places it face up on the discard pile;
2) a new losing card is taken from the box as in the first turn;
3) the new winning card is exposed at the top of the box.

The casekeeper has pictures of the 13 denominations, with four large wood buttons on a spindle opposite each picture. At the beginning of the deal all the buttons are positioned at the inner ends of the spindles. As a card is taken from the box, one of the buttons on the relevant spindle is moved along toward the outer edge of the frame.
How far it is moved depends on whether it represents a winning or a losing card:
a) for a losing card it is moved until it touches the outer frame or an earlier button on the same spindle;
b) for a winning card a gap of about $\frac{1}{2}$ in is left between the button and the frame or between this and an earlier button.
When the fourth card of a denomination appears, whether it is a winning or a losing card, all four buttons are pushed together against the outer frame to show that betting on this denomination is at an end.

The last turn Three cards are left in the box for the last turn. The casekeeper shows which cards they are. The last card in the box is called the "hoc" or "hock" card.
For the last turn players may normally:
a) bet on any one of the cards to win or lose as usual;
b) "call the turn"—ie try to predict the precise order of all three cards (eg, queen first to lose, 6 second to win, ace last).
The turn is played in the usual way, except that when the winning card has been removed from the box the losing card is half slid out to confirm the denomination of the hoc card.
A player's bet is returned if the card that he bet to win or lose appears as the hoc card.

Continuing the game After the last turn all cards are gathered and shuffled for the next deal.

Betting There are three kinds of bet apart from bets on the last turn:
a) bets on a single denomination;
b) bets on a set of denominations;
c) bets that take action in every turn.

Bets on a single denomination are settled when a card of that denomination appears. To make the same bet again a player places a new stake on the layout.

Bets on a set of denominations are bets on groups of different numbers that appear close together on the layout (see placing of bets). They are settled as soon as any one of the denominations bet on appears. To make the same bet again, a player places a new stake on the layout.

Bets that take action in every turn remain on the layout until removed by the player. There are two such bets: a "high card" bet and an "even or odd card" bet.
a) In a high card bet the player bets that the higher denomination card of each pair will win in each turn, or, if he has "coppered" the bet, that the higher card will lose. (For this bet ace ranks low.)
b) In an even or odd card bet the player bets that either the even card or the odd card will win in each turn. (For this bet ace, jack, and king count as odd, and queen as even.)
With these two bets the player wins or loses on every turn. Each time he loses he gives the dealer a number of chips equal to his stake. Each time he wins he receives an equal number. The actual stake remains on the table until the player stops making the bet.

Placing of bets

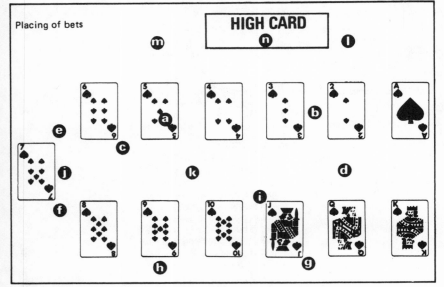

Explanation of placing of bets diagram:

a) bets a single denomination (5);
b) bets two denominations horizontally adjacent (2+3);
c) bets two denominations diagonally adjacent (6+9);
d) bets two denominations vertically adjacent (2+q);
e) bets 6+7;
f) bets 7+8;
g) bets two denominations horizontally adjacent and separated by one other denomination (j+k);
h) bets three denominations horizontally adjacent (8,9,10);
i) bets three denominations in a right angle (3,10,j);
j) bets 6,7,8;
k) bets adjacent denominations in a square (4,5,9,10);
l) bets the even denomination card in each turn (the chip position is between the 2 and the table edge);
m) bets the odd denomination card in each turn (the chip position is between the 5 and the table edge);
n) bets the higher denomination card in each turn.

Bets to win using one or several chips All bets may be made with one chip or several chips.
If several chips are used, they are stacked vertically except for bet (c). For that bet they are tilted or "heeled," by moving the bottom chip in to rest on the corner of one card and tilting the remainder toward the other card.

Bets to lose using one or several chips In general these bets are placed as for bets to win but are "coppered" —ie a faro copper is placed on top of the betting chip(s). The only exception is where bet (c) is made with a single chip. In this case the copper is placed in the usual position not far from the tip of one of the cards, with the chip on top of it tilting toward the other card.

Betting one card to win and one to lose This bet can be placed on any two adjacent denominations or on bet (g).
a) If made with a single chip, a copper is placed on the edge or corner of the lose card and the chip is tilted toward the win card.
b) If made with several chips, one chip is placed on the edge or corner of the lose card and the remaining chips are tilted on it in the direction of the win card.

This bet is settled as soon as one of the denominations appears as a winning or losing card.

Last turn bet: "calling the turn" The stake is placed on the card bet to lose and angled toward the card bet to win.
a) When made with a single chip, a copper is placed on the card bet to lose on the edge nearest the card bet to win. The single chip is placed on it, tilted toward the card bet to win. Another copper is placed on top of the single chip.
b) When made with several chips, one chip is placed on the card bet to lose on the edge nearest the card bet to win. The remaining chips are tilted on the bottom chip so that they point toward the card bet to win.
When the third card lies between the winning and losing cards, the bet is tilted toward the outside of the layout. This shows that it avoids the middle card, ie the middle card is bet to be the hoc card.

Last turn bet: "cat hop" The stake is placed as for calling the turn.

Bet markers are used when a player wants to place on the layout at one time more bets than he has funds for.
For each marker placed on the layout the player must have staked an equal value in chips elsewhere on the layout.
If one of the player's bets loses, the dealer takes payment in chips. The player must then withdraw his marker bet unless the value of his chips on the layout still exceeds the value of the markers he has used.
If one of the player's bets wins, the player wins an equivalent amount in chips.

A "split" occurs in a turn when a single bet has covered both winning and losing cards.
a) A split on a single denomination occurs when two cards of the same denomination appear in a turn. The house takes half of any bets on that denomination; the other half is returned to the bettor.
b) A split on a set of denominations occurs when two cards of a group bet on by a player appear in a single turn. The bet is returned to the bettor.
c) A split on bets that take action in every turn occurs when both cards in a turn are of the same denomination or are both odd or both even.

The bet remains on the table and the bettor neither makes nor receives any payment.

Betting on "cases" When only one card of a denomination is left in the box, this is called "cases"—eg, "cases on the queen."
Most houses forbid a player to bet on cases until after he has bet on a denomination that could be split.

"Cat hop" bet On the last turn the casekeeper may show that the three cards left are not all of different denominations. "Calling the turn" is then replaced by the "cat hop" bet. It may be made on denominations or on colors.
a) If two of the three cards are of the same denomination, a player may make a cat hop on denominations, predicting the order of denominations as usual—eg, 10,6,10. (A player may still bet one denomination to win or lose as usual.)
b) If all three cards are of the same denomination, a player may make a cat hop on color, predicting the order of suit colors—eg, red, black, red. Cat hop bets are placed in front of the dealer according to whatever temporary regulations he states.

Settlement A player who calls the turn successfully is paid at 4 to 1. A player who makes a successful cat hop bet is paid at 2 to 1. All other bets are paid at even money (1 to 1).

STUSS

Stuss is also known as Jewish faro. It is a simplified form of faro, with a larger percentage in the house's favor.

Equipment:
a) a table;
b) a dealing box similar to the faro box, but with a recess ("pocket") at the bottom of the box, deep enough for the thickness of four cards. This prevents the last four cards of the deck appearing in play.
c) a standard 52-card deck;
d) betting chips of various colors.

Players and officials are as for faro, except that there is no casekeeper or casekeeper controller.

The objective is for a player to bet on a denomination that subsequently appears as a winning card before it appears as a losing card.
Cards appear in play two at a time. The first in each pair is always the losing card, the second is the winning card.

Shuffle, cut, and bet The house dealer shuffles the cards, cuts the deck, and puts it face-down in the box.
Bets are then placed.

Betting A player may place as many bets as he wishes, but each bet is on one denomination only.
A bet is always for a denomination to win—ie that the next card of that denomination to appear will be the second (winning) card in a turn.

A turn
1) The dealer removes the top card from the box and places it face up to the right.
2) Any bets on the denomination of this (losing) card are collected by the house.
3) The dealer removes the next card from the box and places it face up to the left.
4) Any bets on the denomination of this card are won by the bettors. Their bet is returned together with an equal payment by the house.

Between turns Other bets may be changed and new bets placed.

Continuing play Play continues in this way through the deck. The two cards in play in each turn are added to those played previously, to form a winning and a losing pile.
Eventually no more cards can be dealt. There will then have been 24 two-card turns, and four cards still remain in the pocket of the box.

Pocket cards The dealer opens the box and shows the four remaining cards. If any bets had been placed on their denominations, they are all won by the house.

Splits If two cards of the same denomination appear on a turn (a "split"), any bets on that denomination are won by the house.

Second bets are bets on a denomination of which one card has already been dealt; usually they are bet on in the normal way. Some casinos, however, do not allow second bets. In this case, the last four cards are not "pocketed" but appear for play and for betting in the normal way.

Variants
1) In a very simple form of stuss, the cards are dealt from the hand.
2) Stuss is sometimes played as a private banking game; the role of banker is taken by the player willing to put up the largest bank.

Ziginette

Ziginette is the Italians' favorite way of seeing money change hands at cards. The rules given here are those played in gaming houses in the United States.

Cards used

Table card matched

Equipment:
1) one standard 52-card deck from which all the 8s, 9s, and 10s have been removed, leaving 40 cards;
2) a metal card box that allows only one card to be removed at a time.

Players Two or more people can play. One person is banker.

There are also two house officials. One, the "cutter," collects and pays bets for the banker and takes the house's percentage cut. (The house never banks the game.)

The other, the "lookout," keeps a watch on proceedings and transfers dead cards to the discard pile.

The objective is for a player to bet on a table card that is not matched by the time the banker's card has been matched. A card is "matched" when another card of the same denomination becomes visible at the top of the card box.

Choice of first banker is by deal—the first ace to appear (see p 80). The cutter carries out the deal after he has shuffled the cards and had them cut by any player.

Shuffle and cut See p 80. Any player other than the banker cuts the cards. The banker places the deck face up in the card box.

Deal The banker deals two cards from the box face up onto the table. The next card in the box is now visible: this is the banker's card.

If all three cards are of different denominations, players may now bet; if they are not, special rules govern further procedure (see the section on "playette").

Opening bet Any player other than the banker may place a bet on one or both of the table cards.

Betting limits The banker decides the minimum and maximum allowable bets and can alter them at will between stages of play.

Opening play The banker takes the banker's card from the box and places it so that one end rests beneath the card

box but most of it is visible. It stays in this position for the rest of the deal.

This exposes the next card in the box. If the card now exposed matches any card on the table (including the banker's card), any bets involved are settled. But if it does not match any card on the table, there is no further action in this turn, unless any player wishes to place a further bet.

Settlement of bets If at any time a card exposed in the box matches the banker's card, the banker loses all unsettled bets, ie he pays all outstanding bets by players on all table cards. Settlement is at even money—a winning player gets back his stake plus an equal amount from the bank. Play on this deal then ceases and the bank and deck pass one player to the right.

If a card exposed in the box matches a table card on which bets have been placed, these bets are won by the banker and he continues to operate the bank.

The house cutter pays out the banker's losses and collects his winnings for him. He takes a 10% house cut from each bet won by the bank.

Next turn of play If the banker's card has not been matched, then any settlement of bets and placing of new bets ends the turn of play. The exposed card is then taken from the card box.

1) If the exposed card has matched a table card, then the exposed card and the table card it matched are now dead (even if the table card had no bets placed on it).

The cutter takes both cards and places them to one side out of play. They are dead for the remainder of the deal, as are the other two cards of the same denomination still in the card box. When cards appear in the box that are the same denomination as cards already matched, they are removed and added to the discard pile. The discard pile is kept fanned out so that the denominations

of dead cards can be seen.
2) If the exposed card has not matched a table card, then it is placed face up on the table alongside the other table cards. It is now available for players to bet on in the usual way at the end of a turn of play, provided it is not immediately matched by the new exposed card in the box. If it is immediately matched, both it and the matching card are transferred to the discard pile in the usual way and the other cards of the same denomination are also dead.

Continuation of play Play continues in this way until the banker's card is matched.
At each turn of play:
1) The top card is removed from the card box.
2) If, on the previous turn, it had matched a table card, it is placed on the discard pile together with the card it matched.
If it was the same denomination as a card already matched, it is added to the discard pile.
If it had matched neither a table card nor a dead card, it is added to the table cards.
3) If the card now exposed in the box matches a table card, any bets involved are settled. If it matches the banker's card the banker collects all bets and the deal ends.
4) If the banker's card has not been matched, players can bet on any card now on the table. This includes any card just added to the table, providing that this card has not been immediately matched by the new card exposed in the box.

Playette This is the term used when two cards of the same denomination appear in the opening deal. It is usually ruled "no deal." The cards are removed from the box and reshuffled. Sometimes the rule is that the duplicate cards are "doubled up."

Doubling up—opening deal If two table cards match, they are placed together, and the top card from the box is dealt to fill the empty table position.

If a table card and the box card match, the box card is added to the table card's position. In either case, the next card in the box becomes the banker's card.

Doubling up—settlement of bets When any two cards have been doubled up then, with all denominations, no bets are settled until three cards of the denomination have appeared. For example, the bank does not win the bet on the 6s until a further 6 has been exposed;
the bank does not win the bet on the queen of hearts until two further queens have been exposed;
the bank does not lose until two further 10s have been exposed.

Tripling If all three cards of the opening deal are of the same denomination, then (providing "doubling up" is allowed) they are all placed together on one of the table hand positions.
No decision is reached on any bet, or on the bank, until four cards of a denomination have been exposed.

Change of banker A banker may pass the bank at any time that there are no unsettled bets on the table.
When the banker's card is matched he must pass the bank.
All cards are collected, shuffled, and cut before the new game begins.

Skinball

Skinball is a very fast action game played in the South and Midwest United States. It is very similar to ziginette and seems originally to have been a black American version of that game. It is also called skin or skinning.

Equipment:
a) one standard deck of 52 cards;

b) a card box that allows only one card to be removed at a time.

Players The game is played by three or more people. One person is banker.

There is also a house official who keeps a watch on proceedings, transfers dead cards to the discard pile, collects and pays bets for the banker, and takes the house's percentage cut. (The house never banks the game.)

The objective is for a player not to have his card matched before the banker's card has been matched. Also, if the player has made side bets, he aims not to have his card matched before the card of any player that he has bet against has been matched. A card is "matched" when another card of the same denomination is dealt from the card box.

Choice of first banker is by deal—the first ace to appear (see p 80).

Shuffle and cut See p 80. After the cut, the banker places the deck face down in the card box.

Betting limits are decided by the banker and can be altered by him at will.

Opening play The banker slides the top card from the card box and deals it face up to the first player to his right. The player may accept the card or may refuse it for any reason. If a player refuses a card he is out of the game until the next turn of play. The card that has been refused is offered to the next player to his right.

As soon as a player accepts this first card, the banker deals a second face-up card from the box to himself: this is the banker's card.

Opening bet The player who has accepted the card states his bet. This may be for any amount within the betting limits.

Even if the bet is within the limits, however, the banker need not accept it. He may reduce it to any amount he chooses. If the banker does this, the player must accept the decision; he cannot withdraw.

Whichever bet the banker accepts, he places the corresponding amount of money in the center of the player's card.

The player then makes his bet by literally "covering" the banker's money with his own.

Next card in play The banker deals a third card from the box. If this card's denomination matches either the banker's or the player's card, then the bet involved is settled.

If the card matches the banker's card, the amount on the player's card is won by the player.

If the card matches the player's card, the amount on his card is won by the banker.

If the third card does not match either of the earlier cards, it is dealt to the next player in turn. He may accept or refuse it. If he refuses it, it is offered to the next player in turn. Once the card is accepted, a bet is placed against the banker in the usual way.

Bets between players
When more than one player has accepted a card, bets may be made between them.

A player bets that the other player's card will be matched before his own.

Either of the two players may suggest the bet; the other player must be in agreement for the bet to take place. Money involved in bets between players is stacked to one side.

Matched cards Each time a card is matched, the houseman takes both cards and puts them in a discard pile. The other two cards of the same denomination still in the deck are not allowed to enter play. When one appears it is put directly into the discard pile and a further card is dealt.

Continuation of play As long as the banker's card is not matched, the deal and betting continue as above until each player has been offered a card. The banker then continues to deal further cards (one at a time and face up) to the table. Any card that appears that does not match either a player's card, a discarded card, or the banker's card is called a "fresh" card.

If there is a player without a card—either because he refused an earlier card or because his card has been matched—he is offered the first fresh card to appear. If there is more than one player without a card, the fresh card is offered first to the player without a card who is nearest the banker's right. If he refuses it, it is offered to the next player to his right without a card.

Any fresh cards that appear when every player is holding a card are placed face up in the center of the table. A player may accept any one of them as soon as the card he holds has been matched.

Each time a player accepts a card, he makes a bet against the banker in the usual way. A player with a card will often have side bets against every other player, but he must bet against the banker first.

Banker's card matched
Whenever the banker's card is matched, all the players betting against him at the time win the amounts on their cards. If there are no unsettled side bets, the bank passes to the next player to the right. All cards are collected and shuffled for the next deal.

If there are unsettled side bets, the banker chooses either:
a) to continue to deal for the betting players only—he does not enter into any further bets himself and does not give out any fresh cards; or
b) to take the first fresh card dealt from the deck as his new banker's card.

Any player's cards that are matched while the banker has no card become dead without the players losing their bets. After the banker has a new card, players without cards may take fresh cards as they appear, and place new bets. Although players with outstanding side bets may make new bets against the banker, they are not obliged to do so.

When the bank is exhausted, the bank must pass.

House percentage The house takes either:
a) 25% of the last winning bet of each deal; or
b) 2% from each bet won by a player against the banker, plus 2% of the banker's winnings, if any, at the end of his deal.

Trente et quarante

Trente et quarante is one of the most popular games in French and Italian casinos, although it is rarely found elsewhere. It originated in seventeenth-century Europe and is also known as rouge et noir.

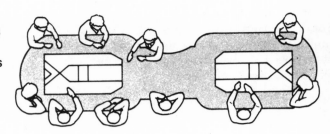

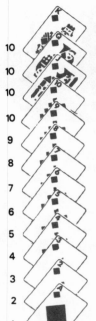

Card values

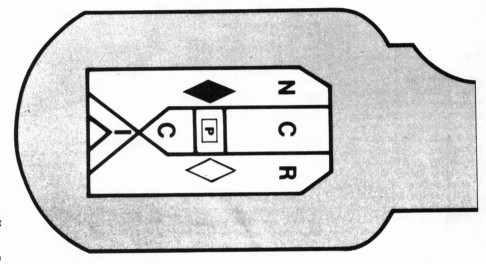

Equipment:
a) regulation table with trente et quarante double layout;
b) six standard 52-card decks shuffled together to form a single deck of 312 cards;
c) an indicator card for cutting the deck.

Players Any number of people can play up to the limit that the table will accommodate.
Five croupiers operate the game: four control the bank and one acts as dealer ("tailleur"). A supervisor sits on a stand overlooking the table.

Value of cards Face cards count 10. All other cards count their face value, with aces counting one.

The objective is to bet which of two rows of cards will give a total points count nearer 31.

Shuffle and cut At the start of a round of play the dealing croupier spreads all six decks on the table. (If it is not the first round of play, the cards must first be taken from the discard receiver and sorted until they are all face down.) All croupiers and players each take a group of cards and shuffle them.
The croupier then gathers all the cards and gives them a further shuffle. He offers one player the whole deck to cut. The player inserts the indicator card at the point at which he wants the cards cut. The dealer cuts the deck at this point and the indicator card and all cards above it go to the bottom of the deck.

Play The players place their bets (see the section on betting).
The dealing croupier then takes about 50 cards from the top of the deck and deals one card face up onto the table. He then deals further cards face up, placing them alternately to the right and left of this first card. After each card he announces the total number of points now contained in the row. When the total equals or passes 31 points he stops dealing. This first row is called the "black" row whatever the suit color of the cards it contains.
The dealing croupier in exactly the same way then deals a second row below the first. This is the "red" row. He again stops dealing when the total equals or passes 31 points.
The row with the points total nearer to 31 is the winning row. (In the example illustrated, the black row totals 33 and the red row 37. Black therefore wins.)
The winning total will always be in the range 31 to 39 inclusive—ie between 30 and 40. It is from this that the game takes its name.

Betting All bets are placed against the bank. Before the play players bet in one or both of the following ways, placing their bets on the layout.
a) Players bet which row will win, either black (N for "noir" on the layout) or red (R for "rouge").
b) Players bet whether the suit color of the very first card dealt will or will not match the color of the winning row. If they want to bet that it will match they bet on C for "couleur" on the layout. If they want to bet that it will not match they bet on I for "inverse." (In the example illustrated bets on C win since the first card was the black 3 of spades and the total for the black row was nearer 31.)

Settlement of bets After the deal the dealing croupier announces the result. Traditionally he calls the results for red and color only, ie "Rouge gagne" (red wins) or "Rouge perd" (red loses), and "Couleur gagne" (color wins) or "Couleur perd" (color loses).
The croupiers collect all losing bets. All winning bets are paid off at even money (1 to 1).
If both rows tie at more than 31 (a "refait"), all bets are returned.
If both rows tie at 31 ("refait de trente et un") the bank takes half of all bets and returns the remainder; or, rather than lose half of his bet, a player may decide to leave his bet in "prison" (P on the layout) for the next deal. If his original bet is successful in this next deal, his bet is returned but earns no money. If it is unsuccessful he now loses all his bet. (Sometimes with a bet in prison the player may choose whether to maintain his original bet or transfer it to its opposite.)

Insurance bet Before a hand is dealt, a player can indicate that he wishes to insure against a tie at 31. The charge for this is 5% of his wager.

Black 33

Red 37

Card craps

This game was created to bypass laws banning dice craps. It is necessary to understand the game of dice craps (see page 130) before attempting card craps.

Equipment:
a) a special deck of 48 cards. It is made up of six denominations only—ace, 2, 3, 4, 5, and 6. In each denomination there are eight cards, two in each suit. For example there are eight 6s made up of two hearts, two spades, two diamonds, and two clubs;
b) betting chips.

Players Any number can play from two upward. One person is dealer and is known as the "shooter."

Choice of first shooter is by any agreed method.

Shuffle See p 80.

Cut Any player may cut; but the player to the dealer's left has the right to cut last. If he does not wish to do so, the right to cut last passes clockwise.

Play The shooter deals two cards from the top of the deck face up onto the table. This constitutes a "throw." The value of the two cards added together gives the score for the throw in just the same way as the two dice in dice craps.

Play follows the basic rules for craps. The first two cards on a come-out give either a natural (7 or 11), a craps (2,3, or 12), or a point (4,5,6, 8,9, or 10) that must be repeated before a 7 is thrown. After every come-out throw the two cards are shuffled back into the deck by the shooter and the deck is cut by him. This happens even if no decision has been reached (ie if a point has been thrown). If the shooter then still has to make a point, he deals further throws but does not shuffle these back into the deck. This continues until he makes the point or sevens out. The entire deck is then shuffled together and cut. If, on a point, the whole deck is used without a decision, the deck is reshuffled and cut by the shooter; he then continues, trying for the same point.

Change of shooter If the shooter sevens out he must give up the cards. He may also give up the cards if:
a) he has not made any throw in his turn; or
b) he has just thrown a decision.
The cards pass to the next player to the left.

Change of deck When two decks are available, any player may request a change of deck at any time. The change is made immediately before the next come-out throw.

Betting and odds See rules for private craps, p 175–176.

Double hardway Players may arrange bets on the "hardway" as usual. A "double hardway" is not a bet but a double payment made when the shooter throws a point number (4,6,8, or 10) with two cards that are pairs of the same suit, eg 8 with two 4s of hearts.

The payment is made by wrong bettors to those who have taken a normal "right bet" on the shooter making the point. This serves to equalize the right and wrong bettors' chances on even number points. Otherwise point number payment is as in private craps (see table on p176).

Open card craps is played as in open dice craps, with the "book" accepting bets and making a 5% (or 3%) charge.

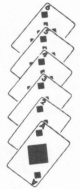

Cards used

Payment by wrong bettor when cards make point

Point number	Point made normally	Point made "double hardway"
4	2-1	4-1
5	3-2	-
6	6-5	12-5
8	6-5	12-5
9	3-2	-
10	2-1	4-1

Monte bank

Monte bank is the major banking card game of illegal gambling clubs in America. It is also called monte or Spanish monte.

Cards used

Cards A 40-card deck is used —a standard deck with the 10s, 9s and 8s removed.

Players From two to as many as can get around the gaming table. One of the players is banker.

There is also a non-playing house official called a "cutter." He assists the banker and collects a 25% cut from certain bets. When the bank passes, the amount collected by the cutter is divided equally between the house and the retiring banker.

The objective for a player is to bet on the layout card or cards that will first be matched in play.

Normally a card is "matched" when another card of the same denomination appears at the top of the deck.

Top layout

Pair in top layout

Triple in top layout

a   b   a   b   c

Bottom layout

Choice of first banker/ dealer is by low cut (see p 80).

Bank The banker places in front of him, in cash, the total amount he wishes to put at risk. The banker does not have to pay out an amount greater than this on any one hand. If the result of a hand presents a banker with losses exceeding the bank total, he pays off the highest bet first, then the next highest, until the bank is exhausted. Other bets are then void and are returned to the players.

Betting limits The minimum bet is governed by house rules. The maximum bet is the amount of the bank. A player betting the maximum on a hand does not prevent other players betting because his bet may lose.

Shuffle and cut The dealer shuffles. Any other player may claim the right to shuffle before the cut but the dealer shuffles last.

The dealer then places the cards in front of the player to his right. Any other player may claim the right to cut but the player to the dealer's right must cut last.

Dealing the layout Holding the deck face down, the banker deals two cards from the bottom. He places them face up on the table, slightly apart. These form the "top layout." He then deals two cards from the top of the deck and places them face up on the table just below the first two cards and slightly apart. These form the "bottom layout."

Pairs and triples If the two cards of the bottom layout are of the same denomination, the deal is void. The cards are collected and reshuffled.

The same applies if two cards, one in each layout, are of the same denomination.

If the two cards of the top layout are of the same denomination (**a**), the dealer places them one on top of the other and deals another card alongside (**b**).

If this card is also of the same denomination, it is placed with the others and a further card is dealt (**c**).

If this card is the fourth of the the same denomination, the deal is void.

The cards are collected and reshuffled.

Betting involves predicting which of two cards or two groups of cards on the layout will be matched earliest. Players back a certain card or cards to be matched before another specified card or cards. Normally a card is "matched" when another card of the same denomination appears at the top of the undealt portion of the deck.
Bets are placed in cash on the layout. The position of a bet shows the card(s) bet and the card(s) bet against. There are four types of bet:
1) circle bet;
2) crisscross bet;
3) doubler bet;
4) Monte carlo bet.
Circle bet The player bets that a specified card will be matched before any of the other three cards on the layout. A successful circle bet is paid at 3 to 1.
Crisscross bet The player bets that the specified card will be matched before another one specified card on the layout.
A successful crisscross bet is paid at evens (1 to 1).
Doubler bet The player bets that one of the cards (unspecified) in the top layout will be matched before either one of the cards in the bottom layout, or vice versa. Alternatively, he bets that one of the cards (unspecified) to the dealer's right will be matched before either one of the cards to the dealer's left, or vice versa. A successful doubler bet is paid at evens (1 to 1).
Monte carlo bet This is a combination of the other three types of bet.

Sample betting
a) bets 7 of spades;
b) bets ace of diamonds;
c) bets 7 of spades against 3 of clubs;
d) bets king of hearts against ace of diamonds;
e) bets 3 of clubs against king of hearts;
f) bets ace of diamonds against 7 of spades;
g) bets left layout;
h) bets bottom layout.
Sample play with pairs
Cards turned up:
1) jack of clubs, no action;
2) ace of hearts, bet (d) loses (crisscross bet not involving pair); all other bets undecided;
3) 7 of hearts, bet (a) wins, paid 3—1; bets (c) and (g) win, paid evens; bets (b), (f), and (h) lose; bet (e) undecided;
4) 6 of clubs, no action;
5) king of diamonds, bet (e) loses.

Matching with pairs and triples in the layout When cards of the same denomination have been dealt to the top layout, they are placed together (see the section on pairs and triples). A pair or triple is matched as usual when a further card of the same denomination appears from the undealt part of the deck.
But other cards on the layout are not necessarily matched when a card of their own denomination appears. To give all cards an equal chance, the color of the cards appearing at the top of the deck is taken into consideration.
Matching with pairs in the layout When a denomination in the top layout has been paired, then another card on the layout is matched only by a card which is of its own denomination and of a different color.
Matching with triples in the layout When a denomination on the layout has been tripled, another card on the layout is matched only by a card which is of its own denomination and of the same color.

Crisscross bets An unmatched pair or triple will be involved in some way in all bets on a layout, with the exception of those crisscross bets in which neither of the two cards bet is the pair (or triple).
Such crisscross bets are settled as soon as one of the two cards involved is matched in the normal way, ie by the appearance of any other card of its denomination.
For other purposes the card is not considered matched.
Play After bets have been placed the cutter says "That's all."
The dealer then turns the deck face up, showing the bottom card only.
If the card matches any of the cards on the layout, all bets involved are settled and the matched card is removed from the layout.
If the card does not match any card on the layout, or if there are still other bets unsettled, the dealer removes the bottom card and places it to one side, exposing the next face-up card. This continues until all bets have been won or lost, each exposed card being added to the discard pile.
The deal is complete as soon as the last bet on the layout has been settled. (This will happen before all cards on the layout have been matched.) The dealer then gathers all cards and shuffles them for the next deal.

House cut and banker's cut When a player wins because the card he has backed is matched by the very first card exposed, the house takes a 25% cut from the player's winnings.
When the bank passes, the total collected is divided equally between the house and the retiring banker. House cuts are collected by the cutter.
Change of banker A banker may hold the bank for as long as he wishes, or he may be limited to a set number of deals agreed by players beforehand. However, a banker may pass the bank at any time that there are no unsettled bets on the table. He indicates that he is passing the bank by saying "Aces."
If the bank becomes exhausted, the role of banker passes immediately.
The role of banker always passes to the next player to the left.
Variant Sometimes the dealer adds unmatched cards from the deck to the layout. Players may place further bets on them as in ziginette (see p 160).

Sample betting

Matching with pairs
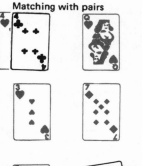
Does not match   Match

Matching with triples

Do not match   Matches

Sample play

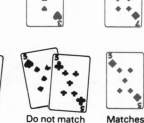

Blackjack

Blackjack is the world's most widespread banking card game. It is also known as BJ, twenty-one, vingt-et-un, pontoon, and vanjohn. There are two main forms: that with a "changing bank"—the usual private game; and that with a "permanent bank"—the casino game. The two forms of the game have many features in common.

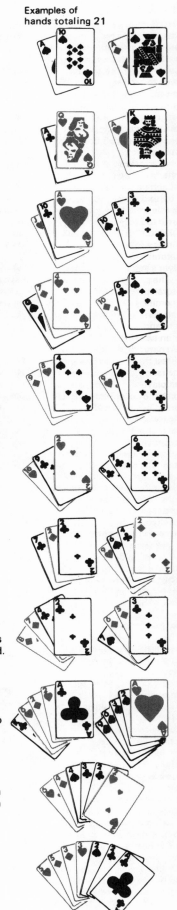

Examples of hands totaling 21

Card values

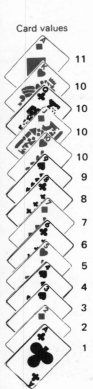

11
10
10
10
10
9
8
7
6
5
4
3
2
1

GENERAL FEATURES

Players Games are played by a banker/dealer and from one to six or seven or more other players (private games can have as many as 14 other players).

Value of cards Standard playing cards are used.
a) An ace counts as 1 or 11, at the option of the holder.
b) A "face" or "court" card counts as 10.
c) All other cards count their numerical face value.
A joker, if used, is only an indicator card and does not enter play.

Objective Each player tries to get a higher point count in his hand than the dealer—but the value of his hand must not exceed 21. A hand whose point count exceeds 21 is immediately lost.
A two-card hand with a value of exactly 21 (a face card, or 10, and an ace) is called a "natural" or a "blackjack."

Betting With the exception of the dealer, each player bets at the beginning of each hand. Only bets against the dealer are allowed.
At the end of each hand, the dealer pays those with point counts higher than his own. Onlookers may be allowed to bet on any player's hand, but not on the dealer's hand.

Basic sequence of play
1) Betting, and deal of two cards to each player.
2) Receipt of further cards on request by each player in turn —with the dealer last.
3) Settlement of bets.

BLACKJACK WITH A CHANGING BANK

Cards A standard deck of 52 cards (or sometimes two decks shuffled together), plus a joker that does not enter play.

Choice of first banker/ dealer is by deal: usually the first ace, but in some versions the first black jack, decides (see p 80 for procedure.)

Change of banker/dealer There are two alternative systems.

1) Each player has five deals as banker/dealer, after which the role passes to the next player to the left.

2) The deal passes whenever there is a hand in which a "natural" is dealt—ie when a player's first two cards total 21. The player with the natural has the option of becoming the new banker/ dealer on the completion of that hand.

When two or more players hold naturals, the player nearest the dealer's left has the first option.

If all players with naturals refuse the option, the present banker/dealer continues— unless he also refuses, in which case the role is offered around the table clockwise, beginning with the player to the immediate left of the present banker/dealer. If all refuse, a new banker/dealer is chosen in the same way as the original one.

Auctioning the bank Private games are occasionally run so that the banker/dealer is always decided by auction. In all private games, however, a player who no longer wants to be banker/dealer may, between hands, put the bank and deal up for auction. However, if there are no bids he loses the bank and deal to the first player to his left (or, if that player refuses, the bank and deal are offered clockwise around the table until accepted or until a new dealer has to be chosen in the original way).

Shuffle and cut

1) The dealer shuffles the cards. (Any player has the right to shuffle at any time but the dealer has the right to shuffle last)

2) Any other player cuts the cards. If several players want to cut, each of them must be allowed to do so.

3) The deck is placed, face down, on an upturned joker, which acts as an indicator card. (If no joker is available, the dealer "burns" a card—ie he takes the top card from the deck, shows it to all players and places it face up at the bottom of the deck.

An ace may not be burned, and if an ace is turned up the deck must be reshuffled and cut again.)

Betting limits The dealer decides the minimum and maximum allowable bets, and can alter them at will between hands.

Bet and deal for the two forms of the private game

The betting and dealing stage of the private game takes two main forms.

a) As in the casino blackjack game, the players place their bets before they have seen any of their own cards.

b) As in the pontoon game of the British Commonwealth, the players bet after looking at their own first card.

There is no standard way of distinguishing between these: American rules for private blackjack games may quote the pontoon form, while a few Americans use "pontoon" to mean standard blackjack. We have used the name "blackjack" for form (a), and "pontoon" for form (b).

Bet and deal: "blackjack"

1) Before any cards are dealt, each player but the dealer puts his bet in front of him in full view.

2) The dealer deals one card to each player but himself, face down, beginning with the player to his immediate left and going clockwise. He then deals one card to himself, face up.

3) A second card is then dealt to each player, including the dealer, face down.

4) If the dealer's face-up card is an ace or a card worth 10 points, the dealer looks at his face-down ("hole") card to see if he has a natural.

If he has, he immediately announces this and turns his cards face up. The other players then show their own cards. The dealer collects the bets of all players not having naturals; players with naturals usually have their bets returned, but in some versions of the game they also pay the dealer.

5) If the dealer's face-up card is not an ace or a 10 point, or if he finds that he does not have a natural, then the player to the dealer's left commences play.

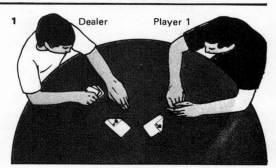
Dealer   Player 1

Bet and deal: "pontoon"

1) The dealer deals one card face down to each player, including himself, beginning with the player to his immediate left and going clockwise.

Each player, including the dealer, looks at his own card.

2) Each player, except the dealer, puts his bet in front of him in full view.

The dealer may call for all bets to be doubled. Any player refusing to double drops out of the hand and loses his original bet.

If the dealer has doubled, any other player may then redouble his own individual bet.

3) The dealer deals a second card, face up, to each player including himself.

4) The dealer then considers if he has a natural, as in the "blackjack" game. If he has a natural, he collects from each player twice the amount of that player's current bet—except that from any other player with a natural he collects only that player's bet.

5) If the dealer's face-up card is not an ace or a 10 point; or if he finds that he does not have a natural, then the player to the dealer's left commences play.

Dealer   Player 1

©DIAGRAM

First player's hand The player to the dealer's left looks at his hand and commences play.

a) If he has 21 points, he shows his cards, claims a natural, and is paid by the dealer unless the dealer also has a natural.

b) If his card total is less than 21 points, he has the option of taking further cards.

If he feels that the points count he already holds is closer to 21 than the dealer is likely to achieve, then he can say "I stand," and he receives no further cards.

If he decides to attempt a total closer to 21, he can say "I draw" or "hit me," and receives another card face up. He can repeat this until he is satisfied with his hand, when he says "I stay." However, if his point count goes over 21, he must announce this immediately by saying "bust." If a player goes "bust," he turns his cards face up, the dealer collects his bet, and the player's cards are placed face up at the bottom of the deck. He is then out of the game until the next hand.

Subsequent player's hands Once a player has said "I stand," "I stay," or "I bust," play passes to the player to his left. This continues until all players have had the chance of drawing further cards.

Dealer's hand The dealer plays last.

If all players have bust, he simply discards his cards and begins the next hand. Otherwise he turns his hidden card face up, and decides to stay or to "draw" (giving himself further cards, face up) until he is satisfied or he exceeds 21 (busts).

Once the dealer's hand is completed, all hands still in the game are shown.

Doubling down is a procedure allowed in the "permanent bank" game and often incorporated in the "blackjack" form of the "changing bank" game.

In his turn a player may, after looking at his first two cards, decide to "double down"—ie with his original two cards face up, he doubles his original bet and receives one further card only, face down. He may not look at this card until the dealer turns it up after all other players and the dealer have completed their turns of play. (Sometimes doubling down is allowed only when the first two cards total 10 or 11.)

Buying is a procedure sometimes played in the "pontoon" form of the "changing bank" game.

At his turn, a player may "buy" a card: instead of receiving a further card face up, he adds to his original bet and receives a further card face down.

The amount of the additional bet must be at least the minimum, but not greater than the original bet.

Buying can be repeated for further cards if the player wishes; or he may "twist"— ie draw further cards face up in the normal way. However, once a player has twisted he is not allowed to buy.

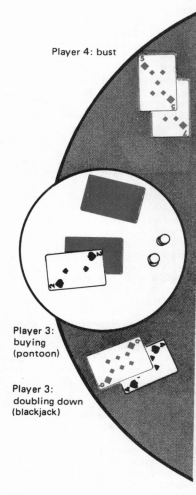

Player 4: bust

Player 3: buying (pontoon)

Player 3: doubling down (blackjack)

Irregularities

a) If a player is missed on the first round of dealing, he must ask for a card from the top of the deck before the second round of dealing begins, or must stay out for that deal.

b) If a player receives two cards on the first round of dealing, he has the choice of: discarding either one; or playing both hands with his original bet on each.

c) If a player in the "pontoon" game receives his first card face up, he can either:
bet, and receive the next card face down; or
drop out of that hand.

d) If a player receives two cards on the second round of dealing, he discards either one.

e) If a card appears face up in the deck, a player has the choice of accepting or refusing it.

f) If a player receives a card that he did not ask for, he may either keep or discard it.

g) If a player has stood on a total of over 21, he pays the dealer twice his original bet even if the dealer has bust. (All discards are placed face up at the bottom of the deck. They may not be claimed by the next player in turn.)

Settlement If the dealer goes bust, he pays all players who have not bust.

If he does not bust, he collects the bets of all players with a lower total, and pays out to all players with a higher total who have not bust. Where a player and the dealer have the same total, rules vary. Sometimes the player's bet is returned, but often (more commonly in the "pontoon" game) the dealer collects. All winning bets are paid off by the dealer at even money, except that a player who has beaten the bank with a natural is paid off at two to one.

Continuing play As each bet is settled, the player's cards are given to the dealer and placed face up at the bottom of the deck.

Play of further hands then continues from the same deck, without a shuffle, until the face-up cards are reached. All face-up cards are then shuffled by the dealer, cut by another player, and a joker or burnt card is used as an indicator as before.

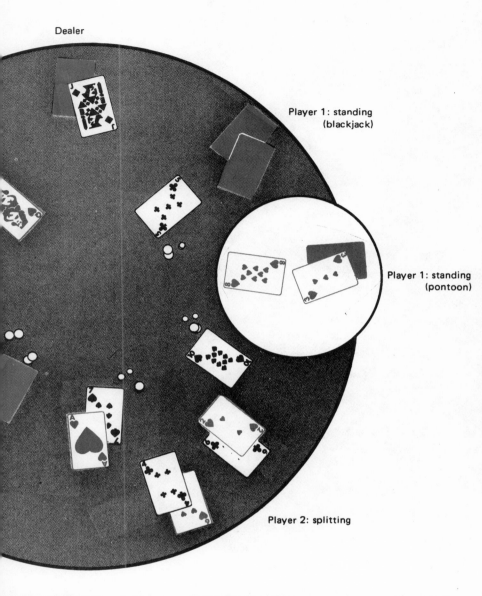

Dealer

Player 1: standing (blackjack)

Player 1: standing (pontoon)

Player 2: splitting

Splitting pairs is a procedure allowed in the "permanent bank" game, and often incorporated in both the "blackjack" and "pontoon" forms of the "changing bank" game.

If a player's first two cards are a pair (eg two 6s or two kings), they may be "split" if the player wishes—ie they may be treated as the basis of two separate hands.

In his turn of play, the player with the pair turns it face up—one card to his right and one to his left. He places his original bet by one of the cards and an equal amount by the other. The dealer then deals one card, face up, to the card to the player's right—after which the player plays this hand off in the normal way. When he has finished (stood, stayed, or bust), he receives another face-up card, dealt to the card to his left, and then plays off this hand.

If, on splitting and receiving a new card other than an ace, a player forms a further pair, he may split the pair again if he again puts out an amount equal to his original bet. Any further pairs may also be split. If aces are split, one card may be drawn to each split ace. A 21 point count made in two cards after splitting does not count as a natural—it is paid off at even money and the bank does not change hands.

Bonus payments In the "pontoon" game, a player other than the dealer can win his bet with certain special hands. These hands are declared and paid off as soon as they have been achieved.

a) A hand with five or more cards totaling 21 or under: for a five-card hand, a player receives double his bet; for a six-card hand, a player receives four times his bet; for a seven-card hand, eight times his bet, and so on. The win stands even if the dealer achieves a total nearer to 21.

b) Triple 7s: for a 21 made with three 7s, a player receives three times his bet.

c) 8,7,6: for a 21 made with an 8,7, and 6, a player receives double his bet.

None of these is a special hand if held by the dealer. They are then judged only according to their points count: a banker's five-card hand is beaten by a player's hand with a higher point count, and a player's win on a natural stands against a banker's triple 7s or 8,7,6.

a

b

c

© DIAGRAM

BLACKJACK WITH A PERMANENT BANK
Equipment:
 a) a regulation blackjack table, with six or seven betting spaces on the layout;
 b) a rack containing betting chips;
 c) a card-dealing box ("shoe");
 d) a discard receiver;
 e) one, two, or four standard 52-card decks, shuffled together;
 f) two blank or advertising cards to be used as indicator cards—one to cut the deck and one to mark the end of the shuffled cards.

Participants:
1) a permanent house dealer/banker;
2) one to six or seven active players.
There is also a casino observer/supervisor, who controls play and whose decision is final.

Shuffle and cut
1) Only the dealer shuffles. He may reshuffle at any time.
2) After he has shuffled, he offers the deck to a player to cut. (Casino regulations may require an "indicator card" cut, in which the dealer holds the deck and the player inserts a blank or advertising card to indicate the point where he wants the deck cut. The dealer then cuts the deck, with the indicator card going to the bottom.)

3) In many casinos, the dealer then inserts a second indicator card about 40 cards from the bottom of the deck to prevent the last cards of any shuffle coming into play.
4) If a shoe is being used, the dealer places the deck in it, face down.
5) The dealer then deals a few (usually three) cards from the top of the deck and places them to one side, out of play.

Betting limits The casino sets the minimum and maximum bet limits. (A casino will often agree to raise the maximum at a player's request.)

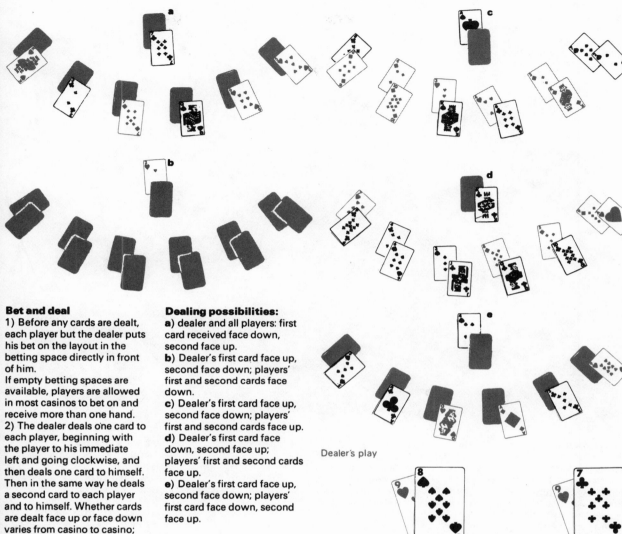

Bet and deal

1) Before any cards are dealt, each player but the dealer puts his bet on the layout in the betting space directly in front of him.

If empty betting spaces are available, players are allowed in most casinos to bet on and receive more than one hand.

2) The dealer deals one card to each player, beginning with the player to his immediate left and going clockwise, and then deals one card to himself. Then in the same way he deals a second card to each player and to himself. Whether cards are dealt face up or face down varies from casino to casino; possibilities are illustrated here.

3) If the dealer's face-up card is a 10 point or an ace, he looks at his face-down card to see if he has a natural, exactly as in the "changing bank" game. If he has a natural, he immediately collects the bets of all players who do not have naturals; players with naturals always have their bets returned.

(In some casinos, to prevent cheating by the collaboration of a player and a crooked dealer, the dealer is not allowed to look at, or sometimes even to deal, his own face-down card until all other players' hands are completed.)

4) If the dealer's face-up card is not a 10 point or an ace; or if he finds that he does not have a natural; or if he may not look at his face-down card: then the player to the dealer's left commences play.

Dealing possibilities:

a) dealer and all players: first card received face down, second face up.
b) Dealer's first card face up, second face down; players' first and second cards face down.
c) Dealer's first card face up, second face down; players' first and second cards face up.
d) Dealer's first card face down, second face up; players' first and second cards face up.
e) Dealer's first card face up, second face down; players' first card face down, second face up.

Dealer's play

a Stay on 17   **b** Draw on 16

Insurance bet If the dealer's face-up card is an ace, players are in many casinos allowed to place an insurance bet against being beaten by a dealer's natural.

Before the dealer looks at his face-down card, a player wishing for insurance puts out an amount equal to half his present bet. If the dealer has a natural, the player receives two to one on his insurance bet; otherwise the insurance bet is lost.

Play If a player is playing more than one hand, he must play out the hand farthest to his right before looking at his next hand or hands.

Play is as for the private game, with splitting and double downing but no buying allowed.

Dealer's play In the "permanent bank" game, the dealer has no decisions to make:

a) if his count is, or reaches, 17 or more—he must stay;
b) if the count is 16 or less he must draw;
c) when he holds an ace he must accept a count of the ace as 11 and not draw if this gives him 17 or more without busting.

(As the dealer has no option in his play, it does not matter if he sees the players' hands. For this reason players' hands are dealt face up in some casinos.)

Settlement is as for the "changing bank" game, except that:

a) when a player and the dealer have the same total, the player's bet is always returned;
b) naturals are paid at odds of three to two, not two to one;
c) there are no bonus payments.

Irregularities are treated in the same way as in the "changing bank" game.

VARIANTS OF BLACKJACK

There are a number of games whose basic differences from blackjack are the card values and the points count that the players are attempting to reach.

Card values

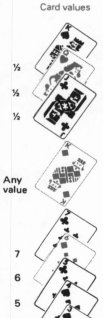

½
½
½

Any value

7
6
5
4
3
2
1

SEVEN AND A HALF

This is an Italian-American variant of blackjack. The rules are as for blackjack with the following exceptions.

Cards The 8s,9s, and 10s are removed from a standard deck to give a deck of 40 cards. No indicator card is used.

Objective Players aim to get a total points count of 7½: non-court cards count their numerical face value, with aces counting 1 point; the king of diamonds can be given the value of any card the holder chooses; other court cards each count ½ point.

Play The player receiving the king of diamonds in a preliminary deal becomes the dealer for the first hand.
The dealer decides and alters betting limits at will. A player not wishing to bet on a round can say "Deal me out."
The deal is one card face down, after which a player stands or draws one or more cards face up.
7½ in two cards is announced and settled immediately.
Unless the dealer also has 7½ in two cards, it is paid double and wins the bank (If two or more players have 7½ in two cards, the bank goes to the player nearest the banker's left).
Bust—8 or more with any number of cards—is also settled immediately.
The dealer then plays, and pays surviving players with a higher total. He returns the bet of any player with the same total as himself.
The dealer shuffles the deck after every round.

Card values

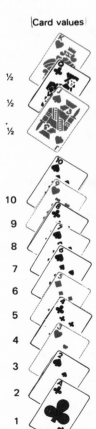

½
½
½

10
9
8
7
6
5
4
3
2
1

TEN AND A HALF

Ten and a half or "*saton pong*" is the Dutch equivalent of seven and a half. The rules are as for seven and a half, with the following exceptions.
It is played with a standard 52-card deck.
Players aim for a total points count of 10½. A count of 10½ is always announced immediately. 10½ in two cards is paid double.
The dealer places discards at the bottom of the deck, face up. The deal changes by passing to the left when the whole deck has been used—though the current dealer is allowed to reshuffle used cards to complete a half finished hand.

MACAO

Macao or "three naturals" is a variant of blackjack that was popular in the 1920s and 1930s.
It is played with a standard 52-card deck.
Players aim for a total points count of 9 in one or more cards.

Card values are:
zero for court cards and 10s; the numerical face value of all other cards (with aces counting 1).
The deal is one card, face down.
A player with a 9,8, or 7 in one card announces it immediately. The dealer then shows his own card, and pays if the player's card is higher.

For a 9 in one card a winning player is paid three times his bet, for an 8 twice, and for a 7 one for one.
Players and dealer without a 7,8, or 9 in one card, then draw one or more cards toward a total of 9.
The dealer then collects and pays out on remaining bets.
A player who ties with the dealer has his bet returned.

Card values

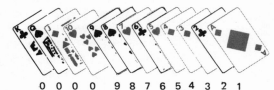

0 0 0 0 9 8 7 6 5 4 3 2 1

FIFTEEN

Fifteen, also called quince, cans, or ace low, is a blackjack variant for two players with one acting as dealer.
Players aim for a points count of 15. Court cards count 10; other cards their numerical face value (with ace as 1).
Dealer and non-dealer place equal amounts in a pool before the deal.

The deal is one card face down. The non-dealer stands, or draws one or more cards face up. He does not announce if he busts—he says only "I stay." The dealer then stands or draws.

Both players then show their face-down cards. The player nearer 15 without busting wins. If both players tie or bust, bets are left in the pool for the next deal.
The loser of one hand deals for the next.

Card values

10 10 10   10 9 8 7 6 5 4 3 2 1

FARMER

This is an interesting variant of blackjack for two to eight players.
One player, the "farmer," is the equivalent of the banker/dealer in other games of the blackjack family, but in this game players also make an ante bet into a central pool or "farm."
The money in the farm is won only when a player has a points count of exactly 16; other settlements are made between player and farmer after each round.
Cards 45 cards are used: a standard 52-card deck with all the 8s and three of the 6s removed (the 6 of hearts is retained in the deck).
Objective Players aim for a total points count of 16: court cards count 10 points; other cards their face value (with aces counting 1).
Choice of first farmer is as for the banker/dealer in blackjack, except that the deciding card is the 6 of hearts.
Ante bet Each player puts one unit into the farm.
Shuffle The farmer shuffles. Any other player has the right to shuffle, but the farmer has the right to shuffle last.
Cut The player to the farmer's right is offered the cut. If he does not wish to cut, any other player may do so. If no other player wishes to cut, the farmer must cut.
Deal The farmer deals one card face down to each player, including himself, beginning with the player to his left and going clockwise.

Play The player to the farmer's left begins. He looks at his card and then receives one further card from the farmer.
If his total now exceeds 16, he does not announce this but says "I stay" and receives no further cards. He does not show his hand.
If his card total is less than 16, he can either stay or receive further cards as he wishes. When he is satisfied with his hand or when his total exceeds 16, he says "I stay," receives no further cards, and keeps his hand concealed.
Play then passes to the player to the first player's left, and play continues as described until all other players, including the farmer, have received at least one further card and had the chance to draw others.
Settlement At the end of the round, all hands are shown and settlement is as follows.
a) Each player who has a count of over 16 points must pay one unit to the farmer who dealt the hand. (The farmer does not have to pay anyone if his hand exceeds 16 points.)
b) A player holding 16 points wins the farm (the central pool) and becomes the next farmer. If more than one player holds a total of 16, the order of precedence when deciding the new farmer is:
the player with the 6 of hearts;
the player with fewest cards;
the current farmer if he has 16 points;
the player nearest the farmer's left.

c) If no-one holds a total of 16, the farm is not won. The player with the total nearest 16 then receives one unit from each player with a lower total (but not from players who have bust).
If two or more players have equal totals, they divide the units won from the other players. The same farmer then deals the next hand, and all players put a further ante into the farm.

Farmer

Player 3: loses

Player 1: bust, pays one unit

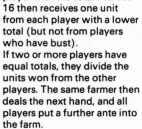

Player 2: wins the farm

10
10
10
6
10
9
7
5
4
3
2
1

Card values

Poker

Poker is played all over the world. It has been called the national card game of the United States of America, where it developed its present form. Poker ranks with blackjack among card games. Although the betting element is central to both games, they also allow for great skill; it is this that sets them apart from most pure gambling games.

GENERAL RULES
Equipment
1) One standard deck of 52 cards (see also the section on arrangements p179).
2) One or two jokers as "wild" cards if desired (see also the section on wild cards p176).
3) Betting chips or cash.

Players: two to eight or more. Certain forms of poker can be played by up to 14 people. No alliances are allowed; a player may play only for himself.

Basic terms The usage of some poker terms is not standard. In the following text a "hand" means the cards, or the particular combination of cards, held by a player.
A single game, from one shuffle to the next, is here called a "play" (rather than a "hand").
Objective Each player tries to maximize his winnings.
On each play all bets are put into a common pool (the "pot").
One player wins the pool on a play if:
a) he holds a higher ranking hand than anyone still betting at the end (the "showdown"); or
b) all other players drop out of the betting before the showdown in the belief that they cannot win (see also the section on bluffing p177).

Rank of cards Cards rank in the normal order (see p80). Ace ranks high, except in the 5,4,3,2,ace sequence; in a "high-low" game it may rank either high or low (see p183). Sometimes low-ranking cards (2s, 3s, and even 4s and 5s) are removed from the deck to speed up the game.
The suits are not ranked.

Poker hands In standard poker all hands must, for scoring (showdown) purposes, contain five cards, although fewer than or more than this may be held at different stages of the game.
The following hands are universally recognized. Each hand loses to the one listed before it, and defeats the one listed after it. This order derives from the mathematical probabilities involved.

1) Straight flush Five cards in sequence of the same suit. (A, k, q, j, 10 of the same suit is known as a "royal flush.")
2) Four of a kind or "fours" Four cards of the same denomination, and one unmatched card.
3) Full house Three cards of one denomination, and two cards of another denomination.
4) Flush Five cards of the same suit, but not in sequence.
5) Straight Five cards in sequence, but not of the same suit.
6) Three of a kind or "threes" Three cards of the same denomination, and two unmatched cards.
7) Two pairs Two cards of one denomination, two cards of another denomination, and one unmatched card.

Straight flush · Four of a kind · Full house · Flush · Straight · Three of a kind · Two pairs · Pair

8) One pair Two cards of the same denomination, and three unmatched cards.
9) High card Five unmatched cards.
Other hands are sometimes accepted locally (eg a "blaze" denotes any five court cards). Their inclusion and their ranking should be agreed before the game begins.

High card

Hands of the same rank
When poker hands are of the same rank, the winning hand is decided by the rank of the cards involved.
The following rules apply where no wild cards are used.
1) Straight flush: the highest ranking card in a sequence decides the best hand. Thus a royal flush is the highest when there are no wild cards. Note that the ace in a 5, 4, 3, 2, ace sequence ranks low, so this hand would be beaten by 6, 5, 4, 3, 2. The same rule applies to straights.
2) Four of a kind: the hand with the highest ranking matched cards wins.
3) Full house: the hand with the highest ranking "three of a kind" wins.
4) Flush: the hand with the highest ranking card wins. If the highest cards are the same denomination, the next highest are compared. This continues down to the lowest, until a difference is found.
5) Straight: as for straight flush.
6) Three of a kind: as for four of a kind.
7) Two pairs: the hand with the highest ranking pair wins. If the higher pairs in two hands are the same, the lower pairs

are compared. If both pairs in two hands are the same, the hand with the best-ranking unmatched card wins.
8) One pair: the hand with the highest ranking pair wins. If the pairs in two hands are the same, the highest unmatched cards are compared. If these are the same, the next highest are compared. This continues down to the lowest, until a difference is found.
9) High card: as for flush.

Hands tie if they contain exactly the same denominations: the suits are irrelevant. Hands that tie as highest in a showdown divide the pool between them. If the pool is not exactly divisible, the amount left over goes to the player who was "called" (ie the player who first made the highest bet).

176

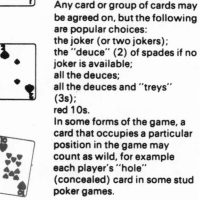

Wild cards Sometimes players agree at the beginning of a game to designate certain cards "wild." A wild card is one that may represent a card of any denomination.
Any card or group of cards may be agreed on, but the following are popular choices:
the joker (or two jokers);
the "deuce" (2) of spades if no joker is available;
all the deuces;
all the deuces and "treys" (3s);
red 10s.
In some forms of the game, a card that occupies a particular position in the game may count as wild, for example each player's "hole" (concealed) card in some stud poker games.

Wild cards

Two alternative rules govern the use of a wild card. The holder may either:
a) use it to represent any card (denomination and suit) he does not hold; or
b) use it to represent any card even if he holds that card.
In either case, a wild card ranks the same as the card it represents.

If a joker is used as a wild card, it may be used either like any other wild card, or alternatively as a "bug." The bug may be used to represent only an ace or any card the player needs to complete a straight or a flush. Again, the use of the joker as the bug may or may not be limited to cards that the player does not hold.

Hands with wild cards
Wild cards rank exactly the same as the cards they stand for, so when comparing hands of the same rank, ties are possible between same-denomination fours, full houses, and threes. With fours and threes, the rank of the other cards in the hands decides the winner where possible.
If hands with wild cards are of identical rank, the hand with no or fewer wild cards wins. If there are the same number of wild cards, the hands tie.

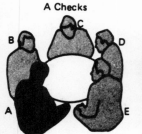 A Checks  B Opens for 1  C Drops out  D Stays in  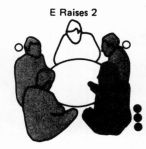 E Raises 2

Example of a betting interval

Betting intervals In a single play there will be at least one betting interval, and normally two or more.
These always follow receipt of cards by players, but the precise number and when they occur depend on the form of poker being played.
In each betting interval, a certain player will have the right to bet or not to bet first. (How he is chosen depends on the form of the game.)
Thereafter players bet or do not bet in clockwise rotation.

Principles of betting All bets on a play are placed together near the center of the table to form a pool. One player bets first ("opens the betting"). Thereafter, each player in turn must either "drop out," "stay in," or "raise."
In his turn, a player announces what he is doing before he places any chips in the pool.
For a first bet or a raise, he also announces the amount of the bet or raise.
A bet is not considered made until the better has removed his hand from the chips bet: until then it can be withdrawn.

a) Drop out (or "fold"): the player discards his hand and gives up his chance of winning the pool on this play.
A player may drop out at any time, even if he has previously bet on this play in an earlier interval or in this interval; but any chips he has already bet remain in the pool and go to the pool winner.
A player who has dropped out is no longer "active," and may not take further action in this play.
b) Stay in (or "call" or "see"): the player puts in just enough chips to make the total he has bet so far in this play exactly equal to the total bet by the player with the highest total bet.
c) Raise (or "up" or "go better"): the player puts in enough chips to stay in, plus an additional number. The additional amount is that by which he "raises the last bet." Every other player in the game must then either stay in (by bringing his total bet up to the raised amount), drop out, or raise again ("reraise").

Checking is allowed in many games of poker. A player who checks at the beginning of a betting interval stays in the game for the moment without making a bet. If all active players check, the betting interval ends. But if one player bets, the interval continues as usual: all other players (including those who have checked) must now stay in, drop out, or raise. To stay in, a player who has checked must equal the highest bet made so far.
If all players check on the first betting interval, the play is void and ends. The next player in turn deals the next round (see the section on pattern of play, p178).

A betting interval ends when either:
a) all players have checked;
b) only one player is still active (and therefore wins), all the others having dropped out; or
c) the bets of active players are equalized. This happens when all players still active have put equal amounts in the pool, and the turn has come round again to the last person to raise (or, if no one raised, to the person who opened the betting): he may not then raise again. As long as the bets are unequal any player may raise, but as soon as the bets are equal, no one may raise.

Where wild cards are used for any card (even one held by the player) two new hands are possible.

1) Five of a kind Five cards of the same denomination. This ranks as highest hand, above a straight flush.

2) Double ace high flush Flush including two aces. This ranks above flush and below full house.

Sometimes, a wild card may be used only to make five of a kind—but not to make double ace high flush. This must be decided before the start of play.

Five of a kind

Double ace high flush

Prohibitions A player may not:
a) attempt to make a private agreement with any other player (eg divide the pool without a showdown);
b) waive his turn as dealer, unless physically unable to deal;
c) look at the discards (either before or after showdown), at undealt cards, at another player's hand, or at a hole card (in stud poker);
d) take chips or money from the pool during play, except as correct change for a verbally stated bet;
e) leave the table taking his cards with him (he should ask another player, preferably a non-active one, to play his hand for him—if he fails to do so and misses his turn, his hand is dead).

Bluffing is allowed (ie trying to mislead other players by actions, statements, gestures, or manner). Bluffing may include:
making announcements out of turn about one's hand or plan of play that are not true or are not subsequently kept to; playing so as to make one's hand seem weaker than it is. Sarcasm, heckling, and derision are allowed—genuine help is not!

A Stays in

B Raises 1

D Drops out

E Stays in

A Stays in

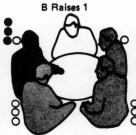
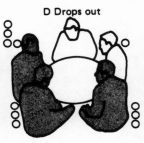
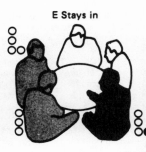

Example of a betting interval

Player	bet	action	total bet
A	0	checks	0
B	1	opens for 1	1
C	0	drops out	(0)
D	1	stays in	1
E	3	raises 2	3
A	3	stays in	3
B	1	raises 1	4
D	0	drops out	(1)
E	1	stays in	4
A	1	stays in	4

The betting interval ends. The only three players still active have bet equal amounts; B may not raise the betting again.

Passing may mean either: to drop out; or to check (where checking is allowed).
In games where checking is allowed, a player who says "Pass" is assumed to be checking, if checking is available to him. (A player shows that he is dropping out by discarding his hand.) Games in which no checking is allowed are referred to as "pass and out" (or "pass out" or "bet or drop").

Sandbagging is poker slang for either:
a) checking to disguise a good hand—this is sometimes considered unethical, but is better accepted as a regular part of bluffing; or
b) constant raising and reraising by two players, forcing a third along with them if he wishes to stay in the play. Raising to force out other players is an essential part of poker, but beyond a certain point it can spoil the game's character. Two optional rulings can keep it in check: limiting raises, and freezing raises.

A limit on raises is often agreed beforehand. Possible limits are:
a) three (or sometimes two) by one player in one betting interval;
b) a total of three by all players in one betting interval.

Freezing the raise is becoming accepted procedure. If there have been two or more raises (whether by one or several players) in a single betting interval, any player who has not raised in that interval may "freeze the raise." In addition to betting sufficient to stay in, he bets a previously agreed amount, usually two to five times the normal maximum bet (see the section on betting limits). Other active players must then drop out or stay in by equaling his bet.
The action only freezes the raise for that betting interval.

Side bets are sometimes made between players. For example, in a "high card bet" in stud poker, players bet on who will have the highest first upcard.

Bonuses It is sometimes agreed before play that, on showdown, a player holding a royal flush, straight flush, or four will receive a payment from each player, whether active or not. The amount agreed is usually three to five times the maximum bet.

Prohibitions A player may not:
a) bet for another player;
b) borrow money or chips from another player during a play;
c) take back a bet once it has been placed in the pool and the better's hand removed. An inadequate bet must be added to, otherwise it is lost and the player's cards are dead.

Betting limits The system to be used must be decided upon before play. The betting limits are also the raise limits.

Note that a player forced to bet, for example, the maximum amount to stay in, may still in that turn raise by the maximum (or by any lesser amount).

1) Specified limits: fixed Minimum and maximum amounts are specified before play starts. Sometimes it is agreed that either:

a) any amount between the limits is acceptable as a bet or raise;

b) only specified amounts between the limits are acceptable as a bet or raise; or

c) no amount between the limits is acceptable as a bet or raise.

2) Specified limits: varying The minimum and maximum limits change during a play; for example, limits for the final betting interval are always twice the earlier limits.

3) Last bet limit The opening bet is governed by agreed limits. Thereafter, the maximum bet or raise is the amount put in the pool by the previous bettor's action. Players must decide either:

a) that each betting interval recommence at the original limits; or

b) that continuous growth be allowed over a single play.

4) Pot limit The opening bet is governed by agreed limits. Thereafter, the maximum bet or raise is the total amount in the pool at the time. To calculate this, a player wishing to raise may include in the pool total the amount needed for him to stay in.

Agreement on an absolute maximum (eg 50 chips) is still necessary.

5) Table stakes Before the session, each player puts any amount of money he wishes onto the table, or buys chips to that amount. (A minimum is agreed beforehand, and sometimes a maximum too.) Any amount a player wins is added to his table amount. He may also, from his own pocket, increase his table amount— but not during a play, and only by at least the agreed minimum.

During a play, a player may not:

borrow from, or owe money to, the pool;

decrease his table amount or withdraw chips from it;

sell chips back to the banker until he withdraws from the game.

The maximum betting limit for a player is his table amount at the time (the minimum is the amount agreed beforehand).

If a player's table amount is used up in a play, he has the right to remain in for the main pool showdown. Any amounts bet by other players, above the amount he has bet, are put into a side pool.

In the example shown: of three active players, player B has only 30 units left on the table. Player A bets 40 units: 30 go into the main pool; 10 start a side pool.

Player B bets his 30 units, if he wants to stay in the main pool. Player C bets 50 units: 30 go into the main pool, the rest into the side pool.

Betting between A and C then continues until their side pool bets have been equalized.

B makes no further bets, and there are no further payments into the main pool, on this or any further betting intervals in this play.

At the showdown, B wins the main pool if he has the best hand. The side pool can only be won by A or C.

6) No limit A player can bet or raise any amount. He may borrow during a play, if he can, but he may not put IOUs in the pool. To stay in, he must equal the highest bet.

In the old no limit games, a player had 24 hours to raise money for a bet.

No limit games have now virtually disappeared.

Table stakes:
a player's table amount is used up.

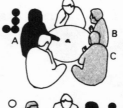

Freeze-out This can be played with any limits system except table stakes.

Before the session, each player puts an equal number of chips on the table in front of him. Winnings are added to this amount, but no player may add new chips, lend chips, or remove chips from the game. As soon as a player has lost all his chips, he drops out. The session continues until one player has won all the chips.

Jackpot This ruling can be played with any limits system. It applies if all other players drop out in a play, after one player has opened the betting. In the next play and before the deal, the others must each "ante" (put) into the pool an amount equal to the single bet made in the previous play. The new maximum limit (for this play only) is the total amount now in the pool before play starts (providing that this is higher than the normal maximum).

The minimum is as usual.

Whangdoodle This ruling can be played with any limits system. After the appearance of any very good hand (eg full house or better), the usual or opening limits are doubled for the next play.

Sometimes the special limits hold for the next round of play, ie one deal by each player.

PATTERN OF PLAY

Rotation of play is clockwise. No player acts until the active player nearest to his right has acted.

Choice of first dealer is by deal: the first jack to appear (see p 80).

Shuffle and cut See p 80.

The deal is clockwise to active players only, beginning with the active player nearest the dealer's left.

Play varies from one form of poker to another.

Showdown After the final betting interval, players still active expose their hands (in draw poker) or hole card(s) (in stud poker), beginning with the player being called, and in a clockwise direction. Each player announces the rank of hand he is claiming. In any discrepancy the cards "speak for themselves"—this includes giving the hand a higher rating than claimed, except if there are wild cards (when the player's announcement cannot be improved on).

The hand of highest rank wins. Tied hands divide the pool equally.

Change of dealer After each play, the deal passes one player to the left of the previous dealer.

Play rotates clockwise

Deal passes to left

ARRANGEMENTS

Banker Poker is not a banking game. Bets are made as contributions to a pool. The "banker" simply supervises the supply of betting chips. He records how many have been issued to each player, including himself, and keeps the payments and the unissued stock to one side.

Players must not make exchanges or transactions among themselves. A player needing more chips must purchase them from the banker's stock; a player with surplus chips may sell them back into stock.

The banker is either the host; or any player chosen by lot (eg high cut) or agreement.

The kitty is a fund for buying new cards or refreshments, set up by agreement before the game starts.

Usually, one betting unit is contributed to it from any pot in which there has been more than one raise or, alternatively, where the winner holds a hand of a specified rank or better. The banker arranges all this. Any chips in the kitty at the end of the game are divided equally among those still playing. (A player who leaves before the end loses the right to any part of the kitty.)

Betting chips are almost always used rather than cash. Usually different colors represent different values, for example: white, one unit; red, five units; blue, 10 units; and, sometimes, yellow, 25 units. A game with seven or more players needs about 200 chips. The best value distribution depends on the maximum betting limit.

At the start of play, each player buys chips to the same total value, for example 50 units.

A player's stock of chips must always be kept in full view of other players, and not taken from the table except for cashing in.

Two decks of cards with contrasting backs are usually used in club play. At the end of one play, one deck is collected and shuffled by the player who dealt last, while the other is dealt into play by the new dealer.

New deck(s) of cards may be called for by any player at any time.

Seating at the start of a session is random, unless a player demands a reseating after the first dealer has been chosen but before play begins.

On reseating, the first dealer has first choice of seat. He then shuffles the deck, has it cut by the player to his right, and deals one card face up to each player in rotation, beginning with the player to his left.

The player with the lowest ranking card sits to the dealer's left, the player with the next lowest card to that player's left, and so on. Of two cards of the same denomination, that dealt first ranks higher.

The dealer then gathers the cards and has them shuffled and cut for play.

After play starts, or after a reseating, no one may demand a reseating for at least an hour, provided no one joins or leaves the game.

If a player joins the game after it starts and someone questions the seat he takes, the dealer, between plays, deals a card to each existing player, and the new player takes his seat to the left of the player with the lowest card. This is done separately for each player joining.

If a player replaces another player, he must take the seat vacated, provided no one objects.

Two players may exchange seats just before any play, provided no one objects.

Time limit The time at which the game will end should be agreed before play starts, and be strictly observed.

Any players who then wish to continue can do so, but should set a new time limit.

Time limit for a decision by a player during play (eg how many cards to draw, how to bet) is five minutes. This is important in a high-limit game. If a player fails to act within this time, his hand is dead.

Rules to be agreed before the start of a game (and best written down) are:
a) the form of game to be played;
b) wild cards and their use;
c) any special hands and rulings;
d) the value of chips;
e) betting limits and checking;
f) limits on raises and/or payment for freezing a raise;
g) bonus payments and payments to the kitty.

Club and casino poker The management supplies table, chips, cards, dealer and/or inspector. It takes a cut—usually as a direct charge on the winner of each pool, but sometimes rents tables at an hourly rate and supervises the game to prevent cheating.

Irregularities Because poker can be played for very high stakes, innumerable rules govern irregularities of play, both accidental and deliberate. It is impossible to treat all these here. The reader who wishes to play poker for high stakes should consult an advanced book on the subject.

FORMS OF POKER

There are two main forms of poker.

1) Closed poker, usually played in the form of draw poker. Players receive their cards face down. After a betting interval, they discard the cards they do not want, and receive replacements from the deck.

A second betting interval is followed by a showdown if more than one player is still active.

2) Open poker, known as stud poker. Players receive some cards face down, some face up. Betting intervals interrupt the deal. After the deal, players cannot receive replacements, but (in versions where more than five cards per player are dealt) each chooses only five cards to form his final hand.

A final betting interval is followed by a showdown if more than one player is still active.

The form of poker chosen may be decided by the host or by club rules; but if a decision has to be made, two factors should be taken into account.

1) Number of players. The best games for a particular number of players are as follows.

Four or under, stud poker; five to eight, any form of poker; nine or ten, five card stud; more than ten, any variant with fewer than five cards per player—or split into two tables.

2) Relative experience. If some players are considerably more experienced than others, it is best to choose one of the less common variants in which the element of skill is lower.

Dealer's choice If it is agreed to play "dealer's choice," the dealer chooses the game to be played: a standard form, a known variant, or any new and easily explained variant he can devise.

He designates any wild cards. He may not, however, alter the betting limits, add cards to or remove them from the deck, or alter basic poker rules.

His choice of game holds by agreement, either:
a) for his deal only; or
b) for a complete round of dealing. The next dealer in turn then chooses for the next complete round.

Sometimes, a play or round of dealer's choice is played whenever a very good hand appears (eg full house or better).

STUD POKER

Stud poker is a faster game than draw poker and allows for greater skill. As there is no exchange of cards, the average rank of winning hands is lower than in draw poker.

STANDARD GAME: FIVE-CARD STUD

Players Up to ten may play.

Ante Usually, a small compulsory bet is made by all players; alternatively no ante is made.

Opening deal One card is dealt face down to each player (the "hole" card), then one card face up. Each player examines his hand.

First betting interval The player with the highest ranking face-up card must open or drop. A wild card is considered higher than an ace. If two players hold equal-ranking cards, the player nearer the dealer's left opens. After the opener, each player drops, stays in, bets, raises, or reraises in the normal way until betting is equalized.

Continuing play Further rounds of dealing one card face up to each player alternate with betting intervals, until the end of the fourth interval (when each player has one face-down and four face-up cards).

On these deals, the dealer leaves the deck resting on the table and takes cards one at a time from the top.

On the betting intervals, the player with the right to open is the one with the highest ranking completed hand in exposed cards—the dealer announces the player and also announces exposed pairs or better hands, possible flushes and straights, and the last deal. The showdown follows the fourth betting interval; all active players expose their hole cards.

Additional rules

1) If all the players check, the betting interval ends and the play continues.

2) If a player drops out, he turns all his cards face down and does not reveal his hole card.

3) If on any betting interval only one active player is left, he wins and the play ends. He need not show his hole card.

4) A "four flush" is often ruled a ranking hand in stud poker, ie four cards of the same suit plus one other. At showdown (and in deciding the start of a betting interval) it beats a pair but loses to two pairs.

Deal

 Player 2

Player 1 Player 3

 Dealer

End of betting

Player 3, dropped out

DRAW POKER

The basic pattern of the game is as follows:

1) Ante: a small compulsory bet is made by all players.

2) Deal: five face-down cards are dealt to each player in the normal way. Players count their cards, then look at them.

3) First betting interval: the player to the dealer's left has the right to bet first; if he does not bet, the other players may bet in turn.

4) Draw: each active player in turn may discard one or more cards and receive from the dealer the same number, face down, from the undealt part of the deck. A player need not draw—he may "stand pat."

5) Second betting interval: the player who made the first bet in the first interval has the right to bet first. If he has dropped out, the first active player to his left may bet.

6) Showdown takes place if more than one active player is left at the end of the second betting interval.

STANDARD GAME

Players Up to ten may play. No more than six should play in high-betting games, since with more players it may be necessary to use discards to complete the draw.

Ante Either:

a) each player puts an equal agreed amount into the pool; or

b) only the dealer antes ("dealer's edge").

The ante amount is usually the same as the minimum bet.

First betting interval There are two forms:

1) "Jacks or better." A player may not open the betting unless he holds a pair of jacks or any better hand. (Before betting is opened, players may check.)

After betting has opened, a player may bet on any hand, and must bet or drop out. At the end of the play, the opener must show the cards he opened on.

2) "Pass and out" (or "pass out" or "bet or drop"). A player may open the betting on any hand. Each player must bet or drop out; no one may check.

In either case, the player to the dealer's left is the first to "speak."

Once the betting has opened, it proceeds in the normal way. If no one opens, all players ante again, and the next dealer deals for the next play.

The draw occurs if more than one player is still active after the first betting interval. The dealer offers the draw to each player in turn in normal rotation, beginning with the player to his left and ending with himself.

Each player in his turn either:

a) states the number of cards he requires and places that number from his hand face down on the table in full view —the dealer then gives him the same number from the undealt part of the deck; or

b) says "I stand pat," or knocks on the table, to indicate that he wishes to keep the hand that he has.

In his turn, the dealer also either states the number of cards he has drawn (exchanged), or indicates that he is "standing pat."

Normally it is ruled that a player may draw one, two, or three cards at his discretion. With four or fewer players, four and five card draws are sometimes allowed.

A player may use the draw to bluff in any way he wishes about the value of his hand. The dealer must answer truthfully how many cards he himself drew. No other question need be answered

VARIATIONS OF STUD POKER

Six-card stud This is like five-card stud, except that after the fourth betting interval each player receives a sixth card face down. This is followed by a fifth (final) betting interval.
At the showdown, each active player chooses five cards from his six to form his final hand.
Seven-card stud (or seven-toed Pete or down the river) This game is for two to eight players.
The opening deal is of three cards: two hole cards, then one face up. Betting intervals and rounds of dealing face-up cards then alternate as usual, until each player has seven cards (including the two hole cards).
After a final betting interval, each active player chooses five cards from his seven to form his showdown hand.

Seven-card stud: low hole card wild As above, but each player's lower ranking hole card is wild—as, for him, is any other card of that denomination. Sometimes players are allowed to choose either one of their hole cards (and its denomination) as wild.
Mexican stud is like five-card stud, except that all cards are dealt face down.
After the second and each subsequent dealing round, each player turns up any one of his face-down cards, leaving one chosen card as hole card. Sometimes a player's final hole card is ruled wild, together with any other cards of that denomination that he holds.
Other five-card stud variants
1) Last card down: the last card is dealt face down, giving two hole cards.
2) Last card optionally down: a player may turn up his hole card before the last dealing round and receive his fifth card face down.
Low-hand stud The lowest hand wins the pool. The lowest exposed hand begins each betting interval. Other rules are as for the form of stud being played.

truthfully by anyone.
The bottom card of the deck is not used. If further cards are required, the bottom card and the cards discarded so far are shuffled together and cut to allow the draw to continue. The usual rules apply, but the player who is due to draw next cuts last.
No other shuffling or cutting on the draw is allowed.
Sometimes, in "jacks or better," the opening bettor discards one of his "openers" (ie one of the cards that gave him the right to open). If he does so, he must state this, and the discarded opener is kept to one side to be inspected at the end of the play. It is not used if the discards are reshuffled.
Second betting interval
This follows the usual rules. All players may check, even if "pass and out" was enforced for the first interval. If all the players check, the interval ends. If all players except one drop out, that player wins without showing his hand (except for showing his openers in "jacks or better," if he opened the betting).
Showdown Each active player in turn must place all his five cards face up on the table, to be seen by all players

(active or otherwise). At the same time he announces the value of his hand—he must do this even if he sees he is beaten.
If all players checked in the second betting interval, the opener shows his hand first; but if bets were placed in the second betting interval, the player who was called shows first.
In either case, other active players then follow in normal rotation.
Dropping out In draw poker a player indicates that he is dropping out by placing his cards face down on the table when his turn in the betting interval arrives.
As long as a player wishes to remain in the game he must keep his cards in his hands, above table height, unless he is forced to put down the cards temporarily for some reason, in which case he must state this.

Seven-card stud Deal
 Player 2
Player 1 Player 3
 Dealer
End of betting

Player 1, dropped out

Deal
Player 2
Player 1 Player 3
Dealer
Showdown
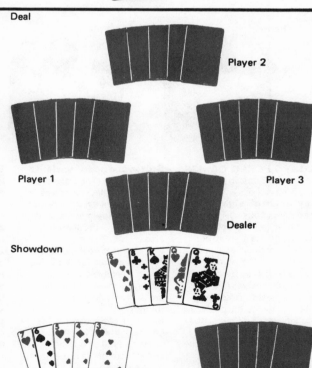
Player 3, dropped out
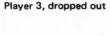 ©DIAGRAM

VARIATIONS OF DRAW POKER
"Jacks or better" variations

1) Progressive openers: if no one opens on a play, two queens or better are required to open on the next play. If again no one opens, two kings or better are required on the next play; then two aces or better; then back down to two kings or better, two queens or better, and two jacks or better.

Each time, players must ante again; and sometimes the limits are doubled. Once a player opens, the next play reverts to jacks or better (and limits go back to normal).

2) "Jacks or bobtail" to open. This is like "jacks or better" but a player may also open on a "bobtail" (four cards of the same suit plus one other card) or a "bobtail straight" (four cards in sequence plus one other card—but the sequence may not be a,k,q,j or 4,3,2,a). These hands have no showdown value.

Blind opening (or "blind tiger" or "blind and straddle"). In this variation, players bet "blind," ie before receiving their hands.

Before the deal:
1) the dealer antes only one chip;
2) the player to his left bets one chip blind ("edge");
3) the next player raises him, betting two chips blind ("straddle").

After the deal, the next player after the blind raiser has the first voluntary bet. He may call (two chips), drop out, or raise (three chips). The betting interval then proceeds as normal. The maximum raise before the draw is one chip. (Note that the dealer's ante does not count toward staying in, but the two players' blind bets do.)

In the second betting interval, the bet and raise limit is two chips. Betting begins with the first blind bettor or the (still active) player nearest his left. Players may check until a bet is made.

Sometimes, in the predeal betting, up to three voluntary blind bets—each doubling the last bet—are allowed after the blind raise. These bets count toward staying in the game in the first interval.

Shotgun Play is as in the standard game, except for an additional (first) betting interval during the deal, after each player has received three cards.

Any hand can open. There is no checking.

Spit in the ocean There are many versions of this; some are given in the section on closed poker games.

1) Basic game: each player receives four cards. The next card is dealt to the center of the table. The game proceeds as usual, but at showdown each active player must count this table card as the fifth card in his hand.

2) Pig in the poke: as above, but the face-up card and all the others of the same denomination are wild (or sometimes only cards of the same denomination as the face-up card, but not the face-up card itself).

Stormy weather Each player receives four cards. Three face-down cards are dealt to the table, one each after the second, third, and fourth dealing rounds.

There is then a betting interval. A player may open on any hand. There is no checking. In the draw, each player may change up to four cards.

After the draw, the dealer turns up the table cards one at a time, with a betting interval as each one is turned up.

At the showdown, a player uses any one of the table cards as his fifth card. None of the table cards is wild.

Sequence of play

Draw poker
Deal

Betting

The draw

Betting

Showdown

CLOSED POKER GAMES
These are variants in which there is no draw.

Showdown straight poker (or cold hand poker) There is one betting interval before the deal. The deal is normal, but the cards are dealt face up and the best hand dealt wins.

Double barrel shotgun
Each player receives five face-down cards. Beginning with the player to the dealer's left, all the players then expose any one of their cards.

Betting intervals then alternate with further rounds of exposing one card each. On the fifth and final round of exposure, the best hand wins.

Spit in the ocean variants
1) Criss-cross (or X marks the spot): each player receives four cards. Five cards are then dealt face-down to the center of the table in the shape of a cross.

Players examine their hands. The dealer then turns up any one of the table cards except the one at the center of the cross. A betting interval follows.

Exposure of the cards in the cross alternates with betting intervals until all but the central card of the cross have been exposed.

After the fourth betting interval the center card is exposed; showdown follows immediately.

The center card of the cross is wild, as are all other cards of the same denomination.

Each player mentally selects his final five-card hand from any cards in his hand and the table cards. (Sometimes, he is only allowed to choose table cards from any three that form a straight line in the cross.)

2) Cincinnati: five cards are dealt to each player, and the next five cards are dealt face down to the center of the table.

The game is the same as criss-cross, but without the cross pattern. None of the table cards is wild; a player may use any of the table cards in his final hand.

3) Lame brain Pete: this is played like Cincinnati, but the lowest-ranking table card is wild, as are all the other cards of that denomination.

Three-card poker Each player receives three face-down cards, and there is a betting interval after each round of cards is dealt. Showdown follows immediately after the third interval.

The rank of hands (with the highest given first):
threes; three-card straight flush; three-card flush; three-card straight; pair; high card.

Two-card poker (usually played with wild cards) comprises: a deal of two face-down cards to each player; a single betting interval; and a showdown.

Pairs and high cards are the only hands.

Spit in the ocean

Deal

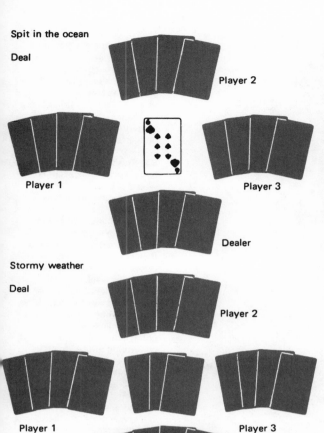

Player 2

Player 1

Player 3

Dealer

Stormy weather

Deal

Player 2

Player 1

Player 3

Dealer

Stud poker
Deal

Lowball is often played during "jacks or better" sessions. When no one has openers for "jacks or better," lowball is played for that play only.

In lowball the lowest hand wins. Rules are as for the standard game, with the following exceptions.

1) Ante: the dealer and the player to his left (sometimes also the second player to his left) ante.

2) First betting interval: the player to the left of the last player to ante must open or drop out. No checking is allowed. The limit is the ante amount. Antes count toward staying in.

3) Draw: before the draw the dealer "burns" (exposes and then discards) the top deck card.

4) Second betting interval: this begins with the active player nearest the dealer's left. Checking is allowed, but a player who checks cannot later raise on that play. Limits are agreed beforehand.

5) Showdown is won by the lowest hand.

Ace always counts low, and straights and flushes do not count. Therefore a,2,3,4,5 (known as a "bicycle") counts as five low cards and is the lowest hand—regardless of suits.

The joker can be used for any card not in the player's hand.

Low ball: lowest hand

Betting

Further dealing

Betting

Showdown

HIGH-LOW POKER

Almost any standard game or variant, draw or stud, can also be played as a high-low game. Especially popular is seven-card high-low stud. At showdown, the highest and lowest hands split the pool. Usually a player must declare, just before showdown, whether he is competing for highest hand, lowest hand, or both.

It is possible to declare for both in any game where a player has more than five cards from which to select his final hand, for he is then allowed to select two different hands.

Rank of cards is as usual. If a player is competing for the lowest hand, ace ranks low; if for the highest hand, high or low, as he wishes; if for both,

both high and low, if he wishes.

Rank of hands is as usual. Hence the lowest possible hand, without wild cards, is 6,4,3,2,a, in different suits (5,4,3,2,a would be a straight).

The usual rules for comparing hands apply—highest card first, then next highest, until a difference is found. Thus, 9,7,6,5,4 ranks lower than 9,8,4,3,2.

Wild cards A wild card can only be given one denomination and suit at showdown.

If declaring for lowest hand, a wild card ranks the same as a low ace, without pairing any ace in the hand. Thus, 4,3,2,a, wild card becomes the lowest possible hand.

Declaring follows the last betting interval. There are two methods.

a) Beginning with the player to the dealer's left, each active player in turn declares himself as competing for highest hand or lowest or both.

b) Each player takes one of his chips in his hand, without revealing its color. He takes a white one if declaring low, a red one if declaring high, or a blue one if declaring both. When all the players have decided, they show their chips.

The highest hand and lowest hand divide the pool equally (if an exact division is impossible, the highest hand receives any odd chips).

A player can only win the part of the pool for which he has declared. If more than one

player has declared the same way, the player with the best hand wins that part of the pool. If all the players have declared the same way, the player with the best hand wins the whole pool.

If a player has declared for both high and low, he must at least tie each way at showdown, or his hand is dead and he receives nothing.

High-low: lowest hand

THREE - CARD BRAG

This is the basic form of the game.

Players: from three to 12.

The objective on each deal is to win the pool by holding the best ranking hand on a showdown or by having all the other players drop out of the betting.

Betting limits are agreed beforehand. Typical limits would be:

1) maximum one unit bet or raise;

2) one to five or one to ten units bet or raise.

Ante Sometimes rules specify that, before each deal, each player must contribute one unit to the pool.

Deal The dealer deals one card face down to each player, including himself, beginning with the player to his left and going clockwise, and continuing until each player has three cards.

Play Players look at their hands and bet accordingly, beginning with the player to the dealer's left and going clockwise. Bets are placed in a central pool. Players may bet on any hand—bluffing is unrestricted.

There is only one betting interval. A player cannot "pass" and stay in the game—he must bet or drop out. If all the players but one drop out the remaining player wins the pool.

Otherwise betting continues until there is a showdown, when the player with the best hand wins. A showdown is not allowed until all players but two have dropped out. Dealt cards are replaced at the bottom of the deck, face down. The cards are reshuffled for the next hand only if a pryle has just appeared on showdown.

GENERAL RULES

Brag was one of the ancestors of poker and still remains very popular in Britain. There are many forms and variants but basically the game is a form of three-card poker with no "draw."

Equipment:

a) one standard deck of 52 cards;

b) betting chips or cash.

Rank of hands A "hand" at brag contains only three cards. Originally only threes and pairs scored but today, through poker influences, all the following are generally recognized (with the highest listed first).

a) "Pryle": three cards of the same denomination.

b) "On a bike" run: three cards in sequence from the same suit.

c) Run: three cards in sequence.

d) Flush: three cards of the same suit.

e) Pair: two cards of the same denomination and one unmatched card.

f) "High card": three unmatched cards.

Rank of cards The cards rank in normal order, with ace high, except:

a) ace can rank low to make a 3,2,ace run or on a bike run—which then counts as the highest hand of that rank, beating a,k,q.

b) for pryles only, a specified denomination varying with the game played (eg three 3s) is ranked above three aces.

Wild cards Today brag is usually played with no wild cards, or sometimes with 2s (deuces) wild.

However, the traditional wild cards for the game, listed in order of rank, are:

ace of diamonds;

jack of clubs;

9 of diamonds.

Hands of the same rank are valued according to the denomination of cards used—as in poker. For two special cases, see "rank of cards." Otherwise:

1) for pryles, on a bike runs, flushes, and high cards, the hand with the highest denomination card wins;

2) for pairs, the hand with the higher denomination pair wins or, if these match, the hand with the higher ranking odd card wins.

Rank of hands with wild cards A hand using wild cards is valued in the usual way (with the wild card valued according to the card it represents). However, a hand using wild cards loses to a hand that uses none.

Note that a pair using a wild card loses to the same pair in natural cards even if the wild card hand has the higher odd card.

Arrangements:

1) choice of first dealer is by low cut (see p 80).

2) shuffle and cut are normal (see p 80).

Pryle · On a bike run · Run

Betting principles There are several alternatives:
a) "round the table";
b) "bet or raise";
c) poker betting.

Round the table betting
Each time it is his turn to bet a player must bet one unit or drop out.

This continues even when there are only two players left, but then either player may in any of his turns pay a double amount to "see." Both players then show their cards without further betting.

Bet or raise In this system limits are agreed beforehand and affect only the opening bet and raises.

In the betting interval betting is as for the round the table system, but in any turn a player may choose to bet more than one unit.

All active players must then bet exactly the same amount each time their turn comes around—or must drop out or raise again.

Raises are therefore not like the raises in poker. Instead of players just having to "call," they set a new minimum contribution to the pool per turn.

Each player must contribute at least that full amount in subsequent turns—regardless of his previous contributions to the pool—or must drop out. Each time the bet is raised only the increase is limited. The total bet of a player in a turn can therefore exceed the "limits."

As in the round the table system this can continue when only two players remain—until one of them pays double the amount at that time to see.

Poker betting is sometimes used (see poker, p176). In this system the interval ends when bets are equalized.

However, unless modified, poker rules can leave more than two active players at showdown. This can be accepted, or the following rules may be observed:
a) when there are three or more active players, a player may not call if this equalizes all players' bets (he must raise or drop out);
b) if a player drops out and so equalizes the bets between the remaining three or more active players, the last player to raise must raise again.

"Blind" betting It is sometimes ruled that a player may bet without looking at his cards.

In this case, any player who has looked at his cards must in each turn pay double the blind bettor if he is to stay in.

When only two active players are left an "open" bettor cannot double his stake to see a blind bettor. To remain in the game he must continue to bet until the blind bettor doubles his bet to see him.

When the last two active players are both blind bettors either of them can pay double to see the other.

Covering the kitty If a player runs out of money during a betting interval he places his hand face down on the pool.

Subsequent bets by other players are then placed in a side pool.

Showdown is then between three players: between the last two active players for the side pool and between these two and the player who covered the kitty for the main pool.

SEVEN-CARD BRAG
This version is for two to seven players.

Before each deal, players contribute equal amounts to a pool.

Each player then receives seven cards, looks at them, discards one face down, and visibly splits the remainder into two unexposed three-card brag hands.

When all are ready, each player in turn exposes one hand, beginning with the player to the dealer's left.

Then each player in turn exposes his other hand, beginning with the player whose first hand was highest.

A player has complete discretion on how he splits his cards between the two hands, but he must expose the best hand first.

The rank of cards is as in three-card brag, except that the highest pryle is three 7s, followed by three aces. (Three 3s rank normally—below three 4s and above three 2s.)

If the same player has the highest hand both times, he wins the pool.

Alternatively, a player whose original seven cards contain four cards of the same denomination wins the pool if he declares this at once without discarding.

Otherwise the pool is not won, but players still contribute again before the next deal.

A deal is usually one card at a time, face down. It may, however, be three cards to each player, followed by another three, and then by a single card.

In the latter case, dealt cards are usually not shuffled between hands but replaced face down at the bottom of the deck with no shuffle or cut.

NINE-CARD BRAG
This is similar to seven-card brag. A maximum of five can play, as nine cards are dealt to each player. The deal is usually in ones, but sometimes in threes.

Players divide their cards into three brag hands, exposing the highest hand first.

Any player with the highest hand in all three exposures wins the pool (or, under some rules, the pool is won by a player with two out of three highest hands).

Alternatively, as in seven-card brag, the pool is won immediately by a player with four cards of a kind.

The rank of hands is as in three-card brag, except that the highest pryle is three 9s, followed by three aces. (Three 3s rank normally—below three 4s and above three 2s.)

If no one wins the pool, players still contribute again before the next deal.

Sometimes a pool may not be won for many hours—by which time it can be very large.

STOP THE BUS
This British students' game is a variant of three-card brag.
All players start with an equal number of betting chips. An additional three-card hand—the dummy—is dealt face up onto the table.

In play, each player in turn may exchange one card in his hand for one from the dummy. The discarded cards go into the dummy face up.

This continues until one player does not wish to alter his hand.

All players then show their cards, and the lowest hand pays a previously agreed amount into the pool (eg five units).

Further hands are played until only one player has any chips remaining. He then wins the whole pool.

Flush

Pair

High card

Wild cards

11 Private gambling card games

The following private betting games are "banking games," in which one person takes on the wagers of all other players. He also has a different role to other players in play. But unlike in casino banking games, no one person is banker continuously. Instead, to equalize players' chances, the role of banker moves around—often after every hand

CARD PUT-AND-TAKE
Equipment:
1) one standard deck of cards;
2) betting chips.
Players: from two to eight.
Objective On the "take" deal each player aims to hold, and on the "put" deal not to hold, cards of the same rank as those turned up by the banker.
Choice of first banker/ dealer is by high cut (see p 80).
Shuffle and cut are standard (see p 80).
Deal The banker deals five face-up cards to each player but himself, dealing them one at a time in a clockwise direction.
Betting limits Payments are one to 16 chips. One chip's value is agreed beforehand.
Play
1) Players look at their cards.
2) The put deal is made. The banker deals five face-up cards one at a time onto the table.
After each card is dealt, any player holding a card of the same rank must pay chips into a pool. The payment doubles with each card: one chip for the first card turned up; two for the second; four for the third; eight for the fourth; and 16 for the fifth. A player with two or more cards of the same rank as the banker's card must pay for each one.
The banker makes no payments.
3) The banker takes the five cards from the table and places them face up at the bottom of the deck.
4) The take deal is made, for which the banker deals five more cards as before. This time each player takes chips from the pool for each of his cards of the same rank. The number of chips taken increases exactly as in the put deal.
5) Any chips left in the pool after the five cards have been played go to the banker. Any chips still owing are paid by the banker from his own chips.
Change of banker/dealer After each hand the bank and deal pass to the player to the banker's left.

VARIANTS
Ante payment Sometimes each player but the banker puts one chip into the pool before each hand.
Easy go has an additional payment and claim. Players pay—and take—one additional chip for each card that, besides being of the same rank as the card played by the banker, is also of the same color.
Red and black has an additional payment and claim for any player with three or more cards of the same suit as the card played by the banker. Players pay—and take—one chip for the first card the banker turns up; two for the second; three for the third; four for the fourth; and five for the fifth, in addition to the regular payments.
Up and down the river has a different payment and claim system. Each player pays—and takes—according to the rank of the matching cards, not according to whether it is the first, second, third, fourth, or fifth card turned up. Payment for an ace is one chip; for a jack, 11 chips; for a queen, 12 chips; and for a king, 13. Payments on other cards match their face value.

Put-and-take

Player 2

−16+21

Player 1

−14+0

Player 3

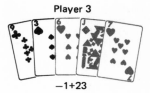

−1+23

Put deal

1   2   4   8   16

Take deal

RED AND BLACK

Equipment:
1) two standard decks of 52 playing cards;
2) betting chips.

Players: two or more.

Objective Each player tries to forecast correctly whether he will hold more red or more black cards in his hand.

Choice of first banker is by high cut (see p 80).

Shuffle and cut are standard (see p 80)—with the two decks shuffled together to form a single deck.

Betting limits are agreed beforehand.

Betting Each player bets on red or black. He bets any amount within the limits. A player bets on black by placing his bet in front of him to his left; he bets on red by placing it in front of him to his right.
(Alternatively each player may be given two colored tokens: one red and one black. He places one of these beside his bet.)

Play The banker deals five cards, one at a time, face up, to the player to his left.
He deals them directly in front of the player, so that it is clear whether the player's bet lies to the right or left.
If the first four cards consist of two red and two black cards, the player may double his bet before he receives his fifth card.
After the first player's bet is settled, the banker deals to the next player to the left. He continues dealing until all players but himself have received a hand.

Settlement of bets A player wins from the banker if he is dealt three or more cards of the color bet on. If he has three of that color, he wins the amount of his bet. If he has four, he doubles his bet. If he has five, he wins four times his bet.
A player loses to the banker if he is dealt three or more cards of the color not bet on. If he has three, he loses his bet. If he has four, he pays the banker twice his bet (his original bet and a further payment equal to it). If he has five cards, he pays four times his bet (his original bet plus a payment equal to three times his bet).

Change of banker After the banker has dealt a hand to all the other players, the bank and deal pass one player to the left.

HORSE RACE

Equipment:
1) one standard deck of 52 cards;
2) betting chips.

Players The game is for three or more players.

Objective Players try to "win the race" by betting on the first suit to appear eight times in a deal.

Choice of first banker is by high cut (see p 80).

The "horses" The banker takes the four aces from the deck and lines them up in any order.

Shuffle and cut are standard (see p 80).

The "course" After the shuffle and cut, the banker deals seven face-up cards in a line at right angles to the horses. If five or more of the cards dealt are of the same suit, the banker takes them all up, reshuffles, and deals the course again.

Betting limits are decided by the banker for each race.

Betting The banker declares the odds on each horse (suit), taking into account the cards that have appeared to form the course. If one suit has appeared predominantly in the course, there will be fewer cards of that suit to appear in the race.
The table gives an example of the odds that a banker might offer. He will choose odds that give him some degree of advantage; it is up to each player whether or not to place a bet at those odds.
The players then state their bets, placing their stakes in front of them. The banker makes a note of how much each player bets on each horse and what the odds are.

The "race" The banker deals the top card from the deck face up onto the table. The horse (ace) of the same suit as the dealt card is then moved up the course one space. The banker then deals another card face up on top of the first, and again moves the horse of the corresponding suit one space. This continues until one horse has passed the end of the course. This horse is the winner.

Settlement of bets The banker collects all bets placed on the losing horses. He pays at the quoted odds each bet on the winning horse.

Change of banker After each hand, the bank and deal pass one player to the left.

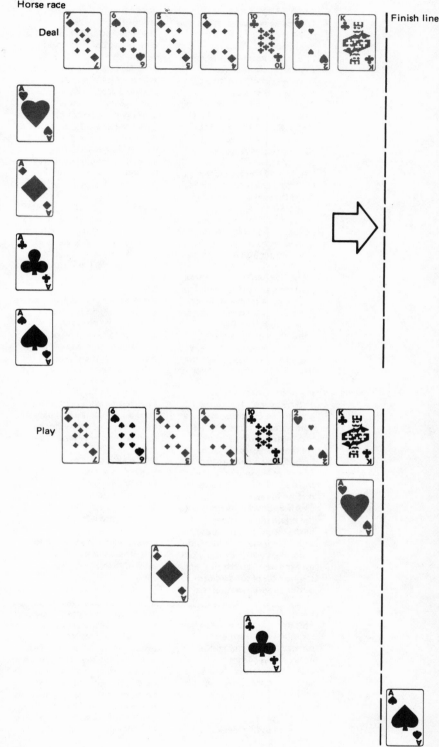

Horse race

Deal

Finish line

Play

Betting odds

Number of cards of suit in course	Odds offered on suit
0	Evens
1	2-1
2	3-1
3	5-1
4	10-1
5 or more	Layout redealt

SLIPPERY SAM

This game is related to red dog (p 247).

Equipment:
1) one standard deck of cards;
2) betting chips or cash.

Players: ideally six to eight but two or more can play.

Rank of cards is normal (ace high). Suits are not ranked.

Objective Players aim to hold a card in the same suit but of a higher rank than the banker's card.

Choice of first banker is by high cut (see p 80).

Shuffle and cut are normal (see p 80).

Bank The banker places in the center of the table the amount he wishes to put at risk. This is any amount above an agreed minimum.

Deal The banker deals three cards to each player, dealing them one at a time and face down. He then deals one card face up to himself.

Play Players bet without looking at their hands. Play begins with the player to the banker's left. He may agree or refuse to bet against the exposed banker's card.

1) If he agrees, he bets any amount he chooses, above an agreed minimum, up to the total amount in the bank. He then looks at his cards. If he holds a card in the same suit but of higher rank than the banker's card, he wins; if not, he loses.

2) Alternatively, he refuses to bet against the exposed banker's card. In this case he says "Deal me another card." For this privilege he must pay into the bank an amount equal to one fifth of the bank (or, under alternative rules, he pays a previously agreed amount).

The exposed banker's card is then discarded and another card dealt from the top of the deck face up onto the table. This becomes the new banker's card. The player either bets against this card in the usual way, or pays again for a new banker's card to be dealt. A player may reject the banker's card up to three times on a single hand, paying the same amount each time. After the third rejection, the player may either bet in the usual way against the banker's card now exposed, or he may pass his turn without betting.

3) If the player has bet and won, he shows his winning card only. His bet is returned plus an equal amount from the bank.

If he has bet and lost, he shows all his hand and his bet is added to the bank.

Whether he has won or lost, his hand is then added face down to a discard pile.

4) Bet and play then pass one player to the left, and continue in the same way. Each player's turn begins with the banker's card on which the last player bet or passed: a new banker's card is dealt only when paid for.

When all players except the banker have had a turn, the banker collects whatever amount is now in the bank. Bank and deal then pass one player to the left.

If the bank is emptied ("bust") before each player has had a turn, the bank and deal pass immediately.

Deal

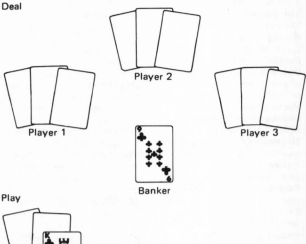

Banker

Play

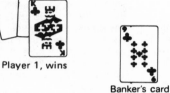

Player 1, wins

Banker's card

Player 2, loses

Banker's new card

Player 3, wins

LANSQUENET

This game is said to have been popular with German mercenaries in the 1600s. Its name derives from *Landsknecht*, the German word for mercenary. It is closely related to ziginette and skinball.

Equipment:
1) one standard deck of cards;
2) betting chips.

Players: two or more.

Objective Players aim to bet on a card that has not been "matched" by the time the banker's card is matched. A card is matched when a card of the same denomination is dealt from the deck.

Choice of first banker is by deal: first ace to appear. (See p 80.)

Shuffle and cut are normal (see p 80).

Dealing the layout Provided that none of the cards dealt for the layout matches, the procedure is as follows. The banker deals the top two cards from the deck (the "hand" cards) face up onto the table. He then deals one card face up to himself (the "banker's card"), followed by another one face up (the "players' card").

Matching cards in the layout The following procedure must be observed if matching cards are turned up while dealing the layout.

1) If the card dealt for the second hand card matches the first, it is placed on top of it. A further card is then dealt as the second hand card. If necessary this process is repeated until the hand cards do not match.

2) If the card dealt as the banker's card matches one of the hand cards, it is placed on top of that card and a new banker's card dealt. This process is repeated if necessary until the banker's card is of a different denomination from those of the hand cards.

3) If the card dealt as the players' card matches one of the hand cards, the procedure is as for the banker's card. If the players' card is the same denomination as the banker's card, the deal is void and a new deal made.

Betting limits are decided by each banker for the duration of his hand.

Betting Each player places his bet alongside the players' card. If all chips are of the same color, the bets may be placed at different corners of the card to distinguish them.

First turn The banker deals one card from the top of the deck face up onto the table. If the dealt card does not match any card on the layout, it is placed face up next to the players' card. It is now a further players' card, on which players may place bets. If the dealt card matches one of the hand cards, it is placed on top of the matched card. This denomination is now out of play. The hand cards have no effect, except to remove two denominations from the betting.

If the dealt card matches the players' card, the banker wins the players' bets. There is then no further betting on the matched denominations for the rest of the deal.

POLISH RED DOG

This game is also known as stitch and Polish pachuk.

Equipment:
1) one standard deck of 52 cards;
2) betting chips (or cash).

Players The game is for two to ten players.

Rank of cards is normal, with ace high. The suits are not ranked.

Objective Players aim to hold a card in the same suit but of a higher rank than the banker's card.

Choice of first banker is by deal: first ace to appear. (See p80.)

Shuffle and cut are normal (see p80).

Bank The banker places in the center of the table the amount he wishes to put at risk. A minimum is usually agreed before the game.

Deal The banker deals three face-down cards to each player but himself, dealing one card at a time.

Play Players bet without looking at their cards. Play begins with the player to the banker's left. He places his bet in front of him: this may be any amount up to half the total of the bank.

The banker then "burns" the top card of the deck, ie he turns it face up, shows it to all players, and places it face up at the bottom of the deck. He then turns up the next card and this becomes the banker's card.

The first player then turns his own cards face up. If he holds a higher ranking card of the same suit as the banker's card, he wins; if not, he loses.

If he has won, he receives back his bet and twice that amount from the bank.

If he has lost, his bet is added to the bank.

His cards are then placed face up at the bottom of the deck. Bet and play then pass one player to the left. After the player has bet, the banker burns one card before exposing a new banker's card.

Change of banker If the bank is emptied at any time, the bank and deal immediately pass one player to the left and a new round is begun.

If the bank is not emptied at the end of a round, the same banker continues to deal.

If, at the end of any round, the bank has increased to three or more times the size it was when the present banker began, then the banker declares a "stitch" round. He deals one more round, and, at the end of this, collects anything left in the bank. Bank and deal then pass one player to the left.

A player must continue to act as banker until the bank is emptied or a stitch round has been completed.

Deal

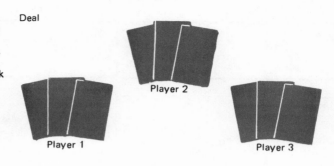

Player 2

Player 1

Player 3

Play

Player 1, wins

Banker's card

Player 2, loses

Player 3, wins

The matched and matching cards are dead, but are left on the layout, on top of each other, as a reminder that this denomination is out of play. Any further cards of that denomination are placed on top of the matched cards. If the dealt card matches the banker's card, the banker pays all bets at even money, ie each winning player receives his stake plus an equal amount from the bank. Play on this deal then ceases and the bank and deal pass one player to the left.

Continuing play If the banker's card is not matched immediately, play continues in the same way until it has been matched—when the banker pays all outstanding bets.

A card is dealt in each turn—

and either matches a card on the layout or becomes a new players' card.

Each time one of the players' cards is matched, the banker collects the bets on that card. Between turns, players may place new bets on the players' cards. But a bet that has once been placed may not be removed or transferred to another card.

Explanation of play diagram
a) The 8 was dealt first, and became a players' card.
b) The king was dealt, matching a hand card and having no effect on play.
c) The 6 was dealt. It matches the banker's card—so players win all bets and the deal ends.

Betting

Players' card

Hand cards

Banker's card

Play

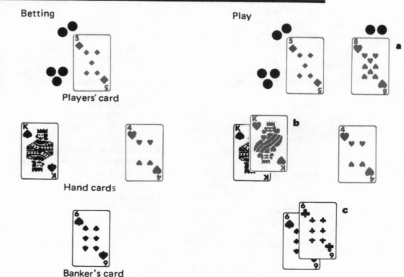

Hoggenheimer

33rd card

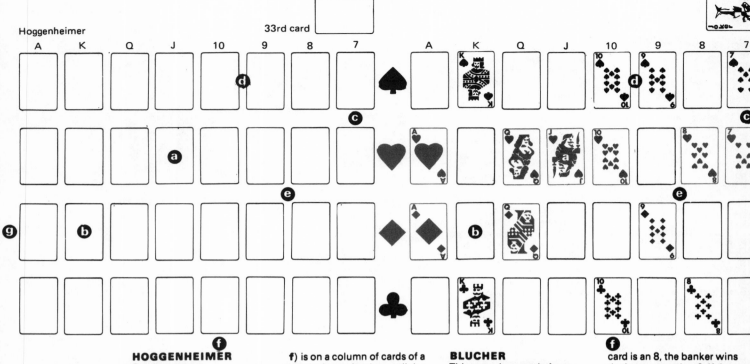

HOGGENHEIMER
Equipment:
1) one standard deck of 52 cards from which the 2s, 3s, 4s, 5s, and 6s have been removed.
2) one joker (or any one of the discarded cards if a joker is not available);
3) betting chips.
Players The game is for two or more players.
Objective Players try to bet on a card (or cards) exposed before the joker is exposed.
Choice of first banker is by high cut (see p 80).
Shuffle and cut are normal. (See p 80).
Dealing the layout The banker deals four rows of eight cards face down, and the 33rd card face down to one side. He takes care that no card's face is seen during the deal.
Betting limits are agreed beforehand.
Betting Each player but the banker places as many bets as he wishes.
The card bet on is shown by the position of the bet on the layout. The top row represents spades, the next hearts, the next diamonds, and the bottom row clubs. The column furthest to the right represents 7s, the next 8s, and so on; the column furthest to the left represents aces.
Examples of betting are shown in the illustration:
a) is a bet on the jack of hearts;
b) on the king of diamonds;
c) is on two adjacent cards— the 7s of spades and hearts;
d) is on two adjacent cards— the 9 and 10 of spades;
e) is on four cards in a square —the 8s and 9s of hearts and diamonds;

f) is on a column of cards of a single denomination—all the 10s;
g) is on a row of cards of the same suit—a bet on all the diamonds.
Play The banker turns the 33rd card face up.
If it is a joker the deal ends and the banker collects all bets.
If it is any other card the banker places it face up in its correct position on the layout. Any bet on that position is replaced on top of the card. The face-down card that was in that position is removed, turned face up, and placed in its correct position in the layout.
Play continues in this way until the joker appears.
Settlement A player's bet wins if all the cards bet on are turned up before the joker. The banker collects all other bets.
In the example illustrated: bets **(a)**,**(c)**, and **(d)** win; bets **(b)**,**(e)**,**(f)**, and **(g)** lose.
Bets on single cards are paid 1 to 1.
Bets on two cards are paid 2 to 1.
Bets on four cards in a square or column are paid 4 to 1.
Bets on eight cards in a row are paid 8 to 1.
Continuing play The bank and deal pass one player to the left. This rotation overcomes any bias in the settlement odds. All cards are collected for the next hand.

BLUCHER
This game is named after a German general who fought against Napoleon. Modified rules are given here.
Equipment:
1) one standard deck of cards;
2) betting chips;
3) a betting layout with areas representing each denomination of card (it can be made up of cards from another deck, or may be drawn on paper).
Players: three or more.
Objective Players aim to bet on a denomination on the layout that is not matched during the hand.
A denomination is matched when the dealer, having called that denomination, turns up a card of that rank.
Choice of first banker is by high cut (see p 80).
Shuffle and cut are normal (see p 80).
Betting limits are agreed beforehand.
Betting Each player but the banker places as many bets on the layout as he wishes. Each bet must be placed on only one denomination.
Play The banker turns up cards one at a time from the top of the deck to form a face-up pile on the table. As he turns the first card up he says "Ace." He says "Deuce" for the second, and so on. For the eleventh, he says "Jack," for the twelfth, "Queen," and for the thirteenth, "King."
For each card, if the denomination of the exposed card matches the rank called, the bank collects any bets placed on that denomination on the layout.
For example, if the eighth

card is an 8, the banker wins the bets on section 8; if the twelfth card is a queen, he wins the bets on the queen's section.
Each time the banker wins a bet on the layout, he is paid an additional equal amount by the player who made that bet. When the banker has counted to king he begins again from ace, still turning up a card from the deck for each rank he calls. The players may not add to, remove, or change their bets. The banker collects bets as before, if rank and card match.
Play continues in this way until the banker has counted from ace to king four times. All the deck has then been dealt.
Doubling This occurs if at any time the banker counts from ace to king without any of the 13 cards matching the rank called. The banker must then, with his own chips, double all players' bets that are then on the layout. However, the bets stay on the layout and are still at risk. This doubling only takes place once in a single deal. If the banker counts from ace to king again without any cards matching, he does not add again to the players' bets. If the banker wins a player's bet that has been doubled, he wins all the doubled bet plus an equal amount from the player.
Final settlement Any bets still on the layout at the end of the game are returned to the players who placed them.
Continuing play Bank and deal pass one player to the left. All the cards are collected for the next deal, and new bets are placed.

CHINESE FAN-TAN

This simple game works on the same principle as the Chinese bean game of fan-tan (p214). It was once an American gambling house game but disappeared because it gives no advantage to the banker.

Equipment:
1) one standard deck of cards;
2) one joker to be used for the betting layout;
3) betting chips—preferably a different color for each player.

Players The game is for two or more players.

Objective Players aim to guess how nearly the number of cards in a section cut from the deck will be divisible by four.

Choice of first banker is by high cut (see p80).

Betting limits are agreed beforehand.

Bank Because each player may make more than one bet, the betting limits do not limit a bank's losses. A banker therefore places to one side, before his first hand as banker, any of his fund of chips he is not prepared to put at risk. The remainder constitutes the bank. Any winnings gained during a player's turn as banker must remain at risk in the bank until the role of banker passes to the next player.

The betting layout consists of the joker, turned face up in the center of the table. The card is placed so that one of its short sides is facing the banker.

Each of the joker's corners is allocated a number. As the banker looks at the card, the bottom left hand corner is 1, the top left hand corner 2, the top right hand corner 3, and the bottom right hand corner 4.

Bets at the corners of the joker are on one number only.

Bets along the side of the joker are on the numbers of the two adjacent corners.

In the example illustrated, bet (a) is on 3, bet (b) on 3 and 4, and bet (c) on 4 and 1.

A player may place as many bets as he likes, provided each bet is within the betting limits.

For each bet, he puts down the number of chips he wishes to put at risk.

More than one player may make the same bet. The banker does not bet.

Shuffle The player to the banker's left shuffles the deck thoroughly and gives it to the banker.

Play The banker cuts a section of at least one third of the cards from the deck, and then counts them out face down onto the table in groups of four. If the section divides exactly into groups of four, 4 is the winning number.

If a number of cards is left over after counting out in fours, the number left over is the winning number.

In the example illustrated, the section comprised 19 cards—four groups of cards and three over.

Settlement of bets The banker first collects losing bets and then pays winning ones. Bets on single numbers are paid at 3 to 1—bet (a) in the example illustrated. Bets on two numbers are paid at evens—bet (b). (Bet (c) loses.) The banker first pays any winnings due to the player to his left and then those due to the other players in turn.

If the bank is emptied before all winnings have been paid, the winning bets that remain unpaid are simply returned to the bettors.

Change of banker Unless the bank has been emptied, bank and deal remain with one player for a set number of hands agreed beforehand. After this the banker receives all the chips then in the bank, and bank and deal pass one player to the left.

The bank and deal pass immediately if a bank is emptied.

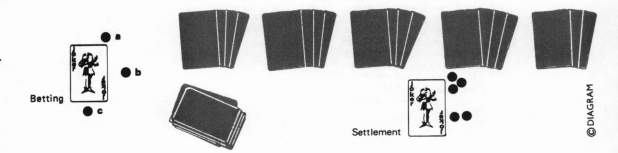

Betting

Settlement

© DIAGRAM

Private monte bank

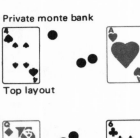

Top layout

Bottom layout

"Gate"
Gate matches
bottom layout

Rank of cards

MONTE BANK (PRIVATE)

This is a simple version of the gambling club game (p164). Cards are matched by suit not by denomination.

Equipment:
1) one standard deck of 52 cards with all 10s, 9s, and 8s removed to leave a 40-card deck;
2) betting chips.

Players The game is for two or more players.

Objective Players bet that one of two cards on a "layout" (pair of cards) will be matched.
A card is matched when the next card exposed from the deck is of the same suit.

Choice of first banker/dealer is by low cut (see p 80).

Shuffle and cut are normal (see p 80).

Dealing the layouts
Holding the deck face down, the banker deals two cards from the bottom. He places them face up on the table, slightly apart. These form the "top layout."
He then deals two cards from the top of the deck and places them face up on the table, slightly below the first two cards. These form the "bottom layout."
The deal is valid whatever suits appear—even if all four cards are of the same suit.

Betting Each player but the banker may bet on the top or the bottom layout or on both. A bet on a particular layout is shown by placing the chips between that pair of cards.

Betting limits are agreed beforehand.

Play The banker turns the deck face up, exposing the bottom card. This card is known as the "gate."
If the gate card's suit matches one (or both) of the cards in a layout, the players win any bets on that layout.
If the gate card matches cards in both layouts, the players win their bets on both layouts.
If no layout card is matched all bets are lost.

Settlement The banker collects all losing bets. Winning bets are paid at 1 to 1, even if both cards in a layout were matched.

Continuing play The banker collects together the layout cards, and places them to one side to form a discard pile.
He then turns the deck face down, takes the next gate card from the bottom of the deck and puts it on the discard pile.
He then deals the layout cards for the next hand. There is no shuffle or cut.

Change of banker Bank and deal remain with one player for a previously agreed number of hands (up to a maximum of six). At least 10 cards of the deck should remain unplayed to prevent players calculating which suits remain.
The bank and deal then pass one player to the left. All cards are collected, and the deck shuffled and cut as before.
If the bank and deal is emptied at any time bank and deal pass immediately.

BANKER AND BROKER

This simple game has very fast betting action. Also known as Dutch bank and blind hookey, it is played in a number of slightly different ways.

Equipment:
1) one standard deck of cards;
2) betting chips (or cash).

Players: two or more.

Rank of cards is normal (ace high). Suits are not ranked.

Objective Players try to bet on a card of higher denomination than that bet on by the banker.

Choice of first banker is by high cut (see p 80).

Shuffle and cut are normal (see p 80).

Betting limits are as agreed.

Basic form of play
1) The banker cuts a number of sections from the deck: one for himself and one for each of the other players.
2) The other players lay bets on their sections by placing chips (or cash) beside them.
3) The banker turns all the sections face up to show the bottom cards.
4) The banker collects the bets on sections showing a lower denomination card than his own. He pays 1 to 1 on sections showing a card of higher denomination.

Points of variation

1) Discarding the bottom card: either the banker removes and discards the bottom card from the deck before cutting; or, he leaves an unused bottom section after cutting.
2) Timing of bets: bets are placed either before or after the sections are cut.
3) Number of sections cut: either the banker cuts one section for each player and one for himself (up to a limit of seven), and each player may only bet on the section cut for him;
or, the banker cuts three sections, two for the players and one for himself, and each player bets at will on either or both of the players' sections;
or, the banker cuts as many sections as he likes, varying the number from deal to deal if he wishes, and the players bet as they please but leave one section for the banker.
4) When the banker's denomination is the same as that bet on by a player: either the bank wins or the player's bet is returned.
5) Change of banker: either the bank passes one player to the left after each deal or set number of deals;
or, players cut for the bank after each deal or set number of deals;
or, the bank is passed when a player bets on an ace.
If two players (or player and banker) both have an ace, or if two players have bet on the same ace, the deck is cut and the bank goes to the player with the higher card.

Banker and broker

Deal

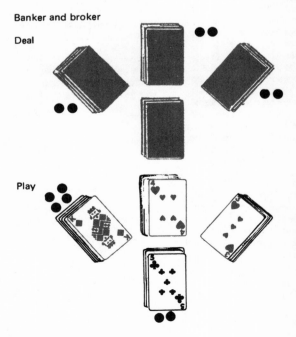

Play

A HUSTLER'S GAME: ACE-DEUCE-JACK

The odds in this game are so heavily loaded that it is found only as a hustler's game.

Equipment:
1) one standard deck of cards;
2) cash for betting.

Players Two or more can play. One player is banker.

WITH THE HUSTLER AS BANKER

Objective Players bet that none of the three cards exposed in play will be an ace, deuce (2), or jack.

Betting limits are agreed beforehand.

Shuffle and cut The banker shuffles. Any player has the right to shuffle but the banker has the right to shuffle last. Any player other than the banker then cuts the deck.

Preparation
1) The banker takes three cards face down from the bottom of the deck, making sure that no one sees their denominations. These three cards are ruled "dead," and are put to one side.
2) The banker then cuts two groups of cards from the deck, taking care that no one sees the bottom card of each cut. He places each group face down alongside the deck, so that there are now three groups of cards on the table.

Bet and play Each player but the banker may place a bet. The banker then turns the three sections face up, exposing the bottom card of each section.

Settlement If any one of the three cards is an ace, deuce, or jack, the banker takes all bets. If none of the cards is one of these denominations, the banker pays 1 to 1 on all bets.

Continuing play All cards in the deck are collected, shuffled, and then cut for the next turn of play.

WITH THE SUCKER AS BANKER

Sometimes the sucker wants to be banker. The hustler then suggests the following version, in which players bet on which denomination will appear. "You bank, and we'll do the guessing too," says the hustler. "You can't help but win."

On a big hustle, with a planned victim, the hustler may set up this version from the beginning.

Objective Players bet that one of the three cards exposed in play will be one of three specified denominations.

Betting limits are agreed beforehand.

Shuffle, cut, and preparation are as for the version with the hustler as banker.

Betting Each player but the banker may place a bet. Sometimes the betting denominations are as in the first version, ie ace, deuce, jack.

But usually the three denominations change for each hand, and are chosen by the players as they place their bets.

This "guessing" process gives the banker the impression that the odds are with him.

Play The banker turns the three sections face up, exposing the bottom card of each section.

Settlement If none of the three cards is one of the three denominations bet on, the banker takes all bets.

But if any one or more of the denominations appear, the banker pays 1 to 1 on all bets. (Note that he pays only 1 to 1 even if two or three denominations appear.)

Continuing play is as in the first version.

The hustle There are high odds that the three exposed cards will include one of any three specified denominations. This will occur on average nearly 60 times in 100 plays—which is enough to ruin anyone betting against these odds.

The hustler simply has to ensure that the sucker is on the wrong side of the appropriate version of the game.

Ace-deuce-jack

Dead cards

Deal

Show

© DIAGRAM

Pool games

In the private gambling games that follow, there is
no banker. Instead, all players' bets take the form of
contributions to a central pool. In many games the
entire pool is then won by a single player—usually
at the end of every hand—but in other games the
pool acts as a reservoir of chips, from which
payments are made to players according to their
success.

INJUN
This fast, amusing game is very
simple to play. But it can see a
lot of money change hands
very rapidly, and offers
opportunities for skillful
judgment to anyone familiar
with mathematical odds.
Equipment:
a) a standard deck of 52
cards;
b) betting chips or cash.
Players: from two to about
15.
Rank of cards The cards
rank in normal order, with ace
high. The suits are not ranked.
The objective is to bet on
holding a higher ranking card
than any other player.

Choice of first dealer is by
deal: first ace to appear (see
p 80).
Shuffle and cut are normal
(see p 80).
Ante Before each deal, each
player, including the dealer,
puts an equal amount into the
center of the table to form a
pool. This amount is known as
the "ante."
Deal The dealer deals one
card face down to each player
including himself, beginning
with the player to his left and
going clockwise.
Play Players are not allowed
to look at their own cards.
Each picks up his own card
and puts it against his
forehead.
He holds it there, face
outward, so that all the other
players in the game can see
the card.
Players should watch carefully
at this stage of play to check
that no player glimpses his
own card.

Betting begins with the
player to the dealer's left, and
goes clockwise.
Each player bets according to
his judgment of whether his
own card, which he cannot
see, is likely to be higher in
rank than all the other players'
cards—which he can see.
A player must bet to stay in
the game. If he drops out at
any time, he places his card
face down on the table in
front of him.
All bets are placed in the pool.
Betting principles There are
two alternatives:
a) poker betting;
b) brag betting.

Poker betting In this
alternative each player in turn
bets, calls, raises, or drops out
until the bets are equalized.
When this happens, betting
ends and there is a showdown
between all active players.
Brag betting In this
alternative, betting is as in the
"round the table" system in
brag. Each player in each of
his turns contributes one unit
to the pool, or drops out.
No one can raise and betting
continues until all but two
players have dropped out.
These last two active players
then continue to put bets of
one unit each into the pool,
until:
a) one of them drops out
leaving the other player the
winner; or
b) one of them pays two units
to "see the other" and there is
a showdown between these
two players.

Showdown On showdown
all active players look at their
own cards.
The player with the highest
card wins the play and takes
the pool.
Ties for highest card divide the
pool.
"Covering the kitty" If a
player runs out of money
during betting he places his
card face down on the pool—
allowing all other players to
remind themselves of its rank
before he does so.
Subsequent bets of other
players are then placed in a
side pool.
Showdown is then between
three players: between the
last two active players for
the side pool, and between
these two and the player who
covered the kitty for the main
pool.
Continuing play After the
pool has been won the deal
passes one player to the left
and all players ante for the next
play.

RED DOG

This fast betting game, also known as high card pool, is very popular among American news reporters. It needs little skill and is usually played for low stakes.

Equipment:
1) one standard deck of cards;
2) betting chips (or cash).
Players: from two to ten.
Rank of cards is normal (ace high). Suits are not ranked.
Objective Players aim to hold a card in the same suit but of higher rank than a card dealt from the deck.
Choice of first dealer is by deal: first ace to appear. (See p 80.)
Shuffle and cut are normal (see p 80).

Ante Before each deal, each player, including the dealer, puts an equal amount into the pool. This amount is known as the "ante."
Deal The dealer deals five face-down cards to each player including himself, beginning with the player to his left and going clockwise. (Four cards each are dealt if players prefer or if more than eight are playing.)

Betting All players look at their cards. Play begins with the player to the dealer's left. He must bet if he wants to stay in the game. To bet he places his stake in front of him, near the pool.
The minimum bet is equal to the ante. The maximum bet is equal to the total in the pool at the time. The dealer must keep note of all bets.
If a player does not wish to stay in the game, he must pay a forfeit equal to the minimum bet but may then place his hand face down on the table without showing it.

Red dog

Deal

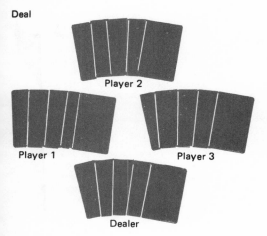

Player 2

Player 1

Player 3

Dealer

Play

Play The dealer deals the top card from the deck face up onto the table in front of the bettor. If the player holds a card of higher rank in the same suit, he wins; if not, he loses. If he has won, he shows the winning card only (**a**); he receives back his bet and an equal amount from the pool. If he has lost, he shows all his hand (**b**), and his bet is added to the pool.
In either case, his hand is then placed face down in front of him.
Bet and play then pass one player to the left.
When all players including the dealer have had a turn of play, the deal passes to the next player to the left. Any money in the pool remains, but all players ante again before the next round is dealt.
Empty pool If the pool is emptied during a round, all players ante again to allow the round to continue. They must still ante again before the next round begins.

Division of the pool
Sometimes the pool becomes too large for the level of betting. It is best if a limit for the pool is agreed beforehand. If the pool passes that limit, it is divided among the players at the end of that round.
Irregularities
1) If a player receives no hand, or too many cards in his hand, he may not take part in the round. The dealer is not penalized.
2) If a player receives too few cards in his hand, he may bet if he wishes, or he may discard his hand without showing it and without betting or paying a forfeit. The dealer is not penalized.
3) If the top card of the deck is accidentally exposed, it is discarded.
4) Once a player has stated his bet, he cannot alter it. A bet paid into the pool in error cannot be returned. A bet received from the pool in error cannot be taken back once the top card for the next player has been dealt.

VARIANTS OF RED DOG
Burning card version The dealer "burns" a card from the top of the deck before each card that he exposes to settle a bet. That is, at each bettor's turn, the dealer discards the topmost card after turning it face up and showing it to all the players. The next card is then turned up to decide whether the bettor has won or lost.

Banking version Red dog can also be played as a banking game. The current dealer acts as banker. He does not deal himself a hand. Before the hand, the dealer places in front of him the money or chips he wishes to put at risk. This can be any amount he wishes. The players do not ante.
Each player in turn, excluding the banker, bets any amount he wishes up to the total then in the bank.
Any amount left in the bank at the end of the hand is returned to the banker. The bank and deal then pass one player to the left.
If the bank is emptied before all the players have had a turn, the hand ends and the bank and deal pass at once.

196

Deal

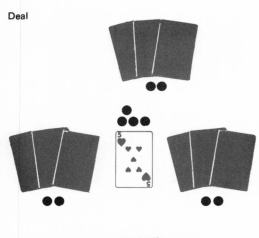

Play

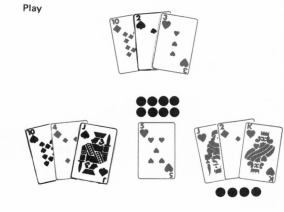

SIX-SPOT RED DOG
Equipment:
1) one standard deck of 52 cards;
2) betting chips (or cash).
Players The game is for two to 15 players.
Rank of cards is normal (ace high).
Objective Players aim to hold a card in the same suit but of higher rank than the pool card.
Choice of first dealer is by deal: first ace to appear. (See p80.)
Shuffle and cut are normal (see p80).
Ante Before each deal, each player including the dealer puts an agreed equal amount into the pool.
Deal The dealer deals three face-down cards to each player including himself, beginning with the player to his left and going clockwise. The dealer then deals one card from the top of the deck face up to the center of the table.
If it is a 6 or lower (6,5,4,3 or 2) it becomes the pool card. If it is a 7 or higher, it is discarded and the next card from the top of the deck is dealt face up onto the table. This procedure is repeated until a 6 or lower card is dealt to become the pool card. If there is no such card left in the deck, the hand is redealt.

Betting All players including the dealer bet immediately without looking at their cards. The minimum bet is one chip (or a previously agreed amount of money). The maximum bet is the amount then in the pool. More than one player may bet the maximum.
Play Players then turn their hands face up. If a player has a card of the same suit but ranking higher than the pool card, he has won. If not, he has lost.
Settlement of bets is supervised by the dealer. He first adds to the pool the bets of all the players who have lost. Then he pays out to those players who have won, beginning with the player to his left and going clockwise. Winning bets are returned together with an equal amount from the pool.
If the pool is emptied before all winning players have been paid, the remaining players receive back only their bets. If anything remains in the pool after all bets have been settled, this amount is carried over to the next round.
The deal then passes one player to the left, and all players ante again to begin the next round.

VARIANT: BANKING VERSION
Six-spot red dog can also be played as a banking game. The dealer acts as banker. He does not deal himself a hand or bet.
Bank Before the hand, the banker places in front of him the money or chips he wishes to put at risk. This can be any amount he wishes. The players do not ante.
Deal The banker deals to the players as usual but excludes himself. He then deals one card at a time to the table in the usual way, until a 6 or lower card is dealt. This is now referred to as the banker's card.
Betting begins with the player to the banker's left. He may bet ("cover") any amount up to the total of the bank. Subsequent players may only bet against any amount of the bank that has not yet been "covered." The total of bets against the bank cannot therefore exceed the amount in the bank.
If all the bank has been covered before all players have bet, the remaining players are not allowed to bet on that hand.
Any part of the bank that is not covered when all players have bet is not at risk in that hand.
Play and settlement of bets takes place in the usual way. When all bets have been settled, any amount left in the bank is returned to the banker. The bank and deal then pass one player to the left.

THIRTY-FIVE
Thirty-five is a modern version of the Italian game of trentacinque.
Equipment:
1) one standard deck of 52 cards;
2) betting chips (or cash).
Players The game is for two to five players.
Rank of cards Court cards count 10 points; others count their pip value.
Objective Each player aims to hold a total of 35 points or more in one suit.
Choice of first dealer is by high cut (see p80).
Shuffle and deal are normal (see p80).
Ante Before each hand, each player including the dealer places an agreed equal amount in the center of the table to form the pool.
Deal
1) The dealer deals one card face down to each player including himself and then one card face down to the center of the table. He continues in this way until each hand, including the hand on the table, contains four cards. He then deals no further cards to the center of the table, but continues dealing to each player,

THIRTY-ONE (SCHNAUTZ)
Equipment:
1) one standard deck of cards;
2) betting chips (or cash).
Players: from three to 15.
Value of cards Aces count 11, court cards 10, and all other cards their pip value.
Rank of cards is normal, ace high. Thus although court cards all count 10, king beats queen and queen beats jack.
Objective Players aim to obtain the highest points count from three cards of the same suit or rank.
Choice of first dealer is by low cut (see p80).
Shuffle and cut are normal (see p80).
Ante Before each hand, each player including the dealer puts an agreed equal amount into a pool.
Deal The dealer deals one card face down to each player including himself, beginning with the player to his left and going clockwise; and then one card to the center of the table. This continues until all players and the table hand (the "widow") each have three cards.

including himself, until each has a further five cards. Thus the hand at the center of the table contains four cards and the other hands nine cards each.

2) The remaining cards of the deck are placed to one side and do not enter subsequent play.

3) The players then examine their cards. A player who holds cards in any one suit to the value of 35 or over announces this and takes the pool. If two or more players have 35 or more, the pool is divided between them.

4) If no player claims the pool, bidding begins.

Bidding for the "buy"
Betting takes the form of bidding for the table hand—the "buy."

Bidding begins with the player to the dealer's left. His opening bid may be any amount up to the total in the pool. (If he does not wish to bid, he throws in his cards.) Thereafter, each player may raise the bid or throw in his cards until only one player is left prepared to bid. He then takes the table hand and adds it to the nine cards he already holds.

Settlement involves only the pool and the player who has taken the table hand. If the player now holds cards to the value of 35 or over in any one suit, he declares this, shows his cards, and takes an amount from the pool equal to his bid. If his bid exceeded the amount of the pool, he takes all the pool but has no further claim. If the player does not hold cards in one suit to the value of 35 or more, he pays into the pool an amount equal to his bid.

Division of the pool
Sometimes the pool becomes too large for the level of betting. It is best if a limit for the pool is agreed beforehand. If the pool passes that limit, it is divided among the players.

Change of dealer The deal passes one player to the left after each hand.

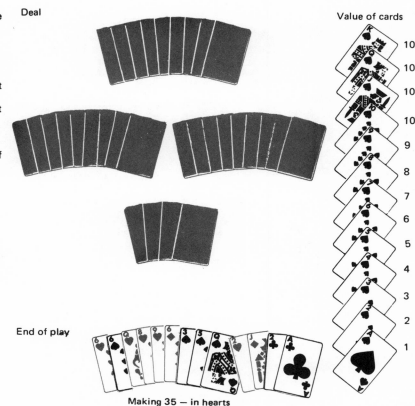

Deal

End of play

Making 35 — in hearts

Value of cards

10
10
10
10
9
8
7
6
5
4
3
2
1

Play Each player examines his cards and announces immediately if he holds:

a) three cards of one suit—with a points total of 31 ("31 points");

b) any three cards of the same rank ("three cards");

c) three cards of one suit—with a points total that he feels is high enough to win ("x points").

If a player announces immediately, all players show their hands and the highest point count wins.

If no player announces immediately, the player to the dealer's left must exchange one of his cards with any face-up card on the table. (Sometimes it is agreed that two or even three cards may be exchanged in one turn.) He is not allowed to pass.

The next player then does the same. Cards that have been put out by a player may subsequently be picked up. Play continues around the table in this way until one player has 31 points or is satisfied with his cards.

If a player has 31 points he must announce it immediately, and all exchanging ends. All players then show their hands. If a player is satisfied with his

hand he knocks on the table instead of exchanging a card in his next turn. In this case, hands are not shown until each of the other players in turn has had the option of exchanging one more card. The pool is won by the player who shows the best hand. The deal then passes to the next player to the left.

Scoring of hands A hand with three cards of the same rank scores $30\frac{1}{2}$; all others score their points count. Illustrated examples are:

a) 31 point hand comprising ace, queen, 10;

b) $30\frac{1}{2}$ point hand comprising three 6s;

c) 30 point hand comprising king, jack, 10;

d) 29 point hand comprising king, queen, 9;

e) 28 point hand comprising ace, king, 7.

Where two or more players have hands scoring the same number of points, the hand containing the higher ranking card wins. For example: ace, king, queen beats ace, queen, jack; and three 6s beats three 5s. (Note that a score of 25 or 26 points often wins.)

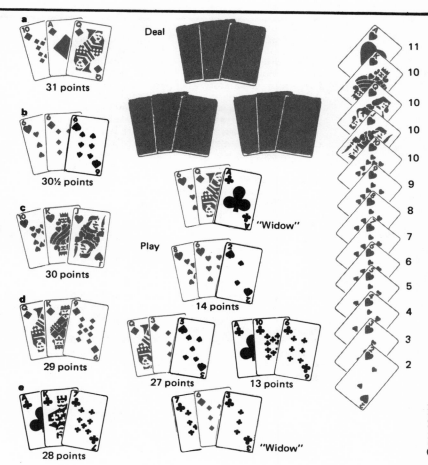

a 31 points

b $30\frac{1}{2}$ points

c 30 points

d 29 points

e 28 points

Deal

"Widow"

Play

14 points

27 points

13 points

"Widow"

Value of cards

11
10
10
10
10
9
8
7
6
5
4
3
2

©DIAGRAM

Deal

Play

Player wins

Player loses

Consecutive cards: no bet

YABLON

This game is also called in between and ace-deuce.

Equipment:
1) one standard deck of cards;
2) betting chips (or cash).

Players: from two to eight.

Rank of cards is normal, ace high. Suits have no significance.

Objective Each player hopes to draw a card ranking between his first two cards.

Choice of first dealer is by deal: first ace to appear. (See p 80.)

Shuffle and cut are normal (see p 80).

Ante Before each deal each player including the dealer puts an equal agreed amount into the pool.

Deal The dealer deals two face-down cards one at a time to each player including himself.

Play begins with the player to the dealer's left.
1) He examines his cards and decides whether to bet.
2) If he does not wish to bet he says "No bet," and returns his cards to the dealer to be placed on a discard pile. Play then passes to the left.
If the first player does wish to bet, he places his bet in front of him near the pool. The minimum bet is the same amount as a player's ante; the maximum is the total amount then in the pool.
3) The dealer deals him the top card from the deck, face up. This is called the player's draw card.
4) The player turns his two original cards face up.
5) If his draw card ranks between his original two cards, the player wins. For example, if he has a 5 and a 9 he must draw a 6, 7, or 8 to win; if he has a 2 and an ace he can draw any card except a 2 or an ace to win. Note that if a player holds two identical cards (eg two 6s) or two consecutive cards (eg 10 and jack), he cannot win and will not bet.
6) If the player has won, he retains his bet and takes from the pool an amount equal to his bet. If he has lost, his bet goes into the pool.
7) Each player including the dealer has a turn of play, with turns passing to the left.

Continuing play After each player has had a turn, the deal passes to the player to the dealer's left. He collects all the cards, shuffles them, and has them cut for the next hand.

Any money left in the pool remains for the next hand, but players also ante again.

Division of pool If the pool passes a limit agreed beforehand it is immediately divided among the players.

YABLON VARIANT

Yablon can also be played as a banking game. The dealer acts as banker and does not deal himself a hand.

Before the hand, the dealer places in front of him the money or chips he wishes to put at risk. This can be any amount he wishes. The players do not ante.

Each player in turn bets any amount he wishes, up to the amount then in the bank. The dealer does not have a turn. Any amount left in the bank at the end of the hand is returned to the banker. The bank and deal then pass one player to the left.

If the bank is emptied before all the players have had a turn, the hand ends and the bank and deal pass at once.

BANGO

Equipment:
1) two standard decks of cards, with different backs;
2) betting chips.

Players The game is for three to ten players.

Objective Each player aims to be the first player to turn all his face-up cards face down.

Choice of first dealer is by deal: first ace to appear. (See p 80.)

Shuffle and cut The dealer and the player to his left each shuffle one deck of cards. Each deck is then offered separately to the player to the dealer's right to be cut in the usual way (see p 80).

Ante Before each deal, each player including the dealer puts an equal agreed amount into the pool.

Deal From one deck, the dealer deals five cards to each player including himself, dealing them face up and one at a time. The rest of this deck is then put to one side out of play.

Play The players arrange their cards face up in front of them. The dealer then takes the second deck of cards and deals the top card face up onto the table, stating its rank and suit

as he does so.
If any player including the dealer has the identical card from the first deck face up in front of him, he now turns that card face down.
The dealer then takes the next card from the top of the second deck and deals it face up onto the table, stating its rank and suit as he does so.
Play continues in this way until one player has turned all his cards face down. He announces this by calling "Bango."

Checking The dealer checks the hand of the player who called against the cards that have been dealt from the second deck, and if no mistake has been made that player wins the pool.

Change of dealer The deal passes one player to the left after each hand.

BANGO VARIANT

In this game players take into account only the rank of the cards turned up by the dealer. The dealer calls the rank and players turn face down all cards of that rank in their hands.

Deal

End of play

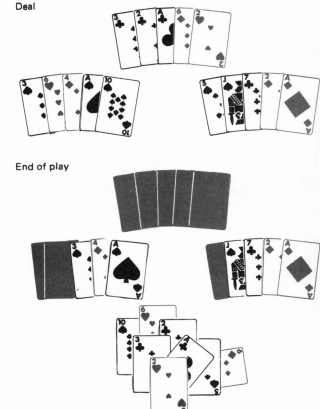

KENTUCKY DERBY

Also called pasteboard derby, this game has a varied race and simple betting.

Equipment:
1) one standard deck of cards;
2) betting chips (or cash).

Players: three or more.

Objective Players try to bet on the winning "horse."

Choice of first dealer is by high cut (see p 80).

Shuffle and cut The four aces are removed from the deck. The rest of the deck is shuffled and cut in the normal way (see p 80).

The "course" After the shuffle and cut, the dealer forms the course by dealing seven face-down cards in a line.

The "horses" The four aces are the horses—they can be given the names of favorites. They are lined up just below the first course card, in the order: hearts, diamonds, spades, clubs.

To make judging easier, the two red aces are put to one side of the course and the two black aces to the other.

The player to the dealer's left lines up the aces and moves them during the race.

Ante Before the game, each player including the dealer puts an equal agreed amount into the pool.

Betting Each player decides which horse he will back. A player may only bet on one horse; more than one player may bet on the same horse. A horse still runs even if no one bets on it.

It is best to write down the selections if there are several players. This is done by the player to the dealer's right. He also has charge of the pool and pays out the winnings at the end.

Starting the race The dealer deals the top card from the deck face up onto the table just behind the ace of hearts.

The player to the dealer's left moves the ace of hearts the appropriate number of spaces up the course, if any (see moves table).

The dealer then deals a card behind the ace of diamonds, and so on.

Running the race How far a horse moves depends on the card dealt. The dealer deals one card to each ace in turn, in the order: hearts, diamonds, spades, clubs, and then starts again.

Further cards dealt to each ace are placed face up on top of the cards first dealt, forming four discard piles.

Finishing the race A horse finishes when it passes the last course card.

But the winner is only decided when all horses have had an equal number of turns. The winner is then the ace that has gone furthest over the finishing line.

If the second place horse is to be decided too, and only the winning horse has crossed the finishing line, then the winner's discard pile is turned face down, and play continues with the remaining aces.

Splitting "dead heats"
Sometimes two aces have gone an equal distance over the finishing line on the same turn.

Each is then dealt a further card from the deck. This continues until, with an equal number of cards dealt, one horse has gone further past the post than the other.

Settlement: winning horse only With fewer than six players, races are run for first place only.

The pool is won by the player or players betting on the winning horse.

If there are two or more successful bettors, the pool is split equally between them. If the pool does not divide equally, any chips over stay in the pool for the next race.

Settlement: winner and second place With six or more players, races may be run for first and second places. Bettors on the second place horse receive back their ante from the pool.

The remainder of the pool is won (and divided if necessary) by the player(s) who bet on the winning horse.

Preparing for the next race
The deal passes to the player to the dealer's left. He collects all the cards (except the aces) and reshuffles them.

The player to the new dealer's left controls the horses, and the player to his right the bets.

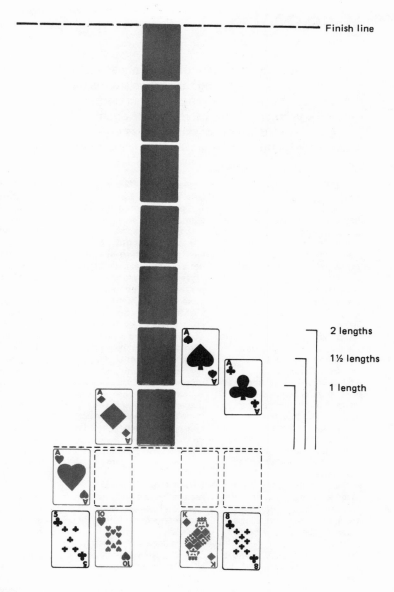

Finish line

2 lengths

1½ lengths

1 length

The moves

	Card played	Distance moved
Ace moves forward	king	2 lengths
	queen	1½ lengths
	jack	1 length
	7, 8, 9, or 10 same color as ace	1 length
	3, 4, 5, or 6 same color as ace	½ length

Any card dealt of same suit as ace adds ½ length

Ace moves back	2 of same color as ace	½ length back
	2 not of same color as ace	1 length back

2 dealt while ace still on starting line   No move

12 Word and picture games

Word games

Play with words is a popular form of amusement, newly devised games taking their place alongside old favorites. Word games range from straight-forward spelling games to more complex games requiring verbal dexterity or skilful guesswork. Most of the games can be played by any number of people.

STANDARD SPELLING BEE

One person is chosen as leader, and the other players sit facing him.
The leader is either given a previously prepared list of words or he makes one up himself. It is a good idea to have a dictionary to hand in case of disputes.
Play The leader reads out the first word on his list and the first player tries to spell it. He is allowed ten seconds in which to make an attempt at the correct spelling.
If he succeeds, he scores one point and the next word is read out for the next player.
If he makes a mistake, the leader reads out the correct spelling. The player does not score for that word, and the next word is read out for the next player. (Alternatively, the player is eliminated from the game for an incorrect answer.)
Play continues around the group of players until all the words on the list have been spelled.
The winner is the player with the most points at the end of the game.

GREEDY SPELLING BEE

In this version of standard spelling bee, if a player spells a word correctly he is given another word to spell. Only when he makes a mistake does the next player take a turn—and he starts with the incorrectly spelled word.
One point is scored for each correct spelling, and the player with the highest score at the end of the game wins.

BACKWARD SPELLING BEE

In this more difficult version of the standard game, players must spell their words backward.
Scoring is the same as in standard spelling bee.

RIGHT OR WRONG SPELLING BEE

The players should form two teams of equal size, and get in line opposite each other.
The leader calls out a word to each player in turn, alternating between teams. Each time a player spells a word, the player standing opposite him must call out "Right" or "Wrong." If he calls a correctly spelled word wrong or a misspelled word right, he is eliminated from the game and must leave the line. (Players may move around once their numbers have been depleted, so that there is a caller for each player in the other team.)
If the caller makes a correct call, he gets the next word to spell.
The last team to retain any players wins the game.

GRAB ON BEHIND

Also called last and first or alpha and omega, this is another good game for a lot of players.
Players decide on a specific category, such as flowers, cities, or insects.
The first player calls out a word in the chosen category. The next player then follows with another word in the category—but it must begin with the last letter of the previous word. Play continues in this way around the group. For example, if the category were flowers the words might be: mimosa, anemone, edelweiss, sweet pea, and so on.
Players have only five seconds in which to think of a word and may not repeat a word that has already been called.
Anyone failing to think of a word or calling an incorrect word drops out of that round. The last player to stay in wins.

GHOSTS

Ghosts needs concentration and a good vocabulary to win. The players sit round in a circle and take it in turns to contribute a letter to an unstated word. They try to keep the word going for as long as possible—any player who completes a word loses one of his three "lives."
For example, the first player thinks of any word (about) and calls out its first letter (A). The second player thinks of a word with more than three letters starting with the letter called (agree) and calls out its second letter (G). The third player thinks of a word that begins with AG (agate) and calls out its third letter (A). The next player, thinking of "again," calls out "I."
The fifth player, unable to think of anything other than "again" is forced to add N and thus complete a word. He may also try to bluff his way out of the situation by calling out a letter of an imaginary word, in the hope that none of the others will notice—if they do notice, they may challenge him.
Challenging If a player hesitates for too long or the other players suspect that he has no particular word in mind they may challenge him. The challenged player must state his word, and if he cannot do so he loses a "life."
If his explanation is satisfactory, however, the challenger loses a life.
Scoring Whenever a player completes a word he loses a life and becomes "a third of a ghost." Losing a second life makes him "two-thirds of a ghost," and if he loses a third life he becomes a whole ghost and must drop out of the game.
The player who survives until the end is the winner. (For a longer game, the number of lives may be increased to four or five.)

I-SPY

I-spy is an excellent game for children learning to spell. It is also fun for older children, who can try and outwit each other by "spying" (seeing) inconspicuous objects.
Objective Each player tries to be the first to guess which visible object one of them has spied.
Play Two or more people can play, and one of them is chosen to start.
He says "I spy, with my little eye, something beginning with . . ." and gives the first letter of an object that he has secretly chosen, that must be visible to all the players. (They may have to turn their heads in order to see the object, but they should not need to move about.)
For example, if he chose a vase, he would give the letter V or, if he chose a two-word object, the first letter of each word (eg PF for picture frame).
If the player chooses an object, such as a chair, of which there may be more than one in the room, the other players must guess the particular chair he has in mind.
The game ends as soon as someone has spotted the object that was chosen—he may then spy the next object.
Variation I-spy may be played by very young children if colors rather than first letters are given.
For example, a player may say "I spy, with my little eye, something red" and the others then look for the red object that he has in mind.

1234 Buzz

200

INITIAL LETTERS

The players sit in a circle. One of them puts a question—it may be as farfetched as he likes—to the others. Each of them in turn must reply with a two-word answer, beginning with the initials of his or her name. Players have only five seconds in which to think of an answer.

For example, if the question were "What is your favorite food?" Bruce Robertson could reply "Boiled rice," and Robert Chapman might say "Roquefort cheese."

When all the players have answered, the second player asks a question.

Any player who fails to answer after five seconds or who gives a wrong answer drops out of the game; the winner is the last person to stay in.

INITIAL ANSWERS

This is a good game for a large group of people. The players sit in a circle and one of them starts by thinking of any letter of the alphabet (eg S). He must then think of a three-letter word beginning with that letter and give a definition of his word, for example "S plus two letters is a father's child."

The second person in the circle has to try and guess the word ("son"), and he then thinks of a word of four letters also beginning with S. He might choose "soup" and define it as "S plus three letters makes a tasty start to a meal" for the person sitting next to him to guess.

This next person, after guessing the word correctly, must think of a five-letter word—perhaps "snail"—defining it as "S plus four letters carries a house on its back."

The game continues in this way, with each person having to think of a word beginning with the chosen letter, and each word having one letter more than the previous word. Any player who fails to think of an appropriate word, or who fails to guess a word must drop out.

The last person left in the game is the winner.

A different letter of the alphabet should be chosen for the next round.

TRAVELER'S ALPHABET

In this game, the first player says "I am going on a journey to Amsterdam," or any other town or country beginning with A.

The next person then asks "What will you do there?" The verb, adjective, and noun used in the answer must all begin with A; for example, "I shall acquire attractive antiques."

The second player must then give a place name and an answer using the letter B, the third player uses the letter C, and so on around the players. Any player who cannot respond is eliminated from the game.

If the players wish to make the game more taxing, they may have to give an answer that is linked to the place they have chosen. For example, a player might say "I am going to Greece to guzzle gorgeous grapes."

If a player gives an inappropriate answer he may be challenged by another player. If that player cannot think of a more fitting sentence, the first player may stay in the game. Should the challenger's sentence be suitably linked, the first player is eliminated.

BUZZ

This game should be played as briskly as possible for maximum enjoyment.

The players sit in a circle. One player calls out "One," the next player "Two," the next "Three," and so on.

As soon as the number five, or any multiple thereof, is reached, the players must say "Buzz." If the number contains a five but is not a multiple of five, only part of it is replaced by buzz. (For example, 52 would be "buzz two.")

If a player forgets to say buzz or hesitates too long, he drops out; the last player to stay in the game is the winner.

FIZZ

This is played exactly like buzz, except that players say "Fizz" for sevens or multiples of seven.

BUZZ-FIZZ

Buzz-fizz combines the two games, so that 57, for example, becomes buzz-fizz.

I LOVE MY LOVE

In I love my love, players have to think of an adjective beginning with each letter of the alphabet to complete a given statement.

The first player starts by saying "I love my love because she is . . ." using any adjective beginning with A. The next person repeats the phrase, but his adjective must begin with B, the next person's with C, and so on through the alphabet.

Alternatively, each player must say a different refrain, as well as using an adjective with a different letter. The refrains may be:
"Her name is . . . ;
She lives in . . . ;
And I shall give her . . ."
Players may write down the refrains decided upon if they wish, but there must be no hesitation over the answers. Any player who hesitates or gives an incorrect answer drops out of the game, and the winner is the last person left in.

A WAS AN APPLE PIE

This is a similar game to I love my love, but players must think of a verb instead of an adjective.

The first player says: "A was an apple pie, A ate it," and other players might add "B baked it," "C chose it," "D dropped it," and so on.

TABOO

In taboo—sometimes called never say it—players try to avoid saying a particular letter of the alphabet.

One player is the questioner and chooses which letter is to be "taboo."

He then asks each of the players in turn any question he likes. The respondent must answer with a sensible phrase or sentence that does not contain the forbidden letter— if he does use the taboo letter, he is out.

The last player to stay in the game wins and becomes the next questioner.

I—spy

© DIAGRAM

6 Fizz 8 9 Buzz 11 12 13 Fizz Buzz 16 1 Fizz 18 19 Buzz Fizz 22 23 24

JOIN THE CLUB

This game needs players who have not played it before. Only when they guess a secret solution, known only to the leader, are they allowed to "join the club."

The leader says: "Mrs Pettigrew doesn't like tea, what does she like?"

The other players suggest different things and the leader tells them whether they are right or wrong—if they are wrong they must drop out. Play continues until all the players have dropped out, or until one of them guesses the solution; "tea" is really the letter T, so that any answer given should not contain it. For example, answers like "chocolate," "tomatoes," or "tequila" would eliminate a player.

If a player guesses the solution, the leader says "Join the club!"

Other questions the leader could ask are:

"Our cook doesn't like peas, what does he prefer?"; or "The G-man never takes his ease, what does he take?"

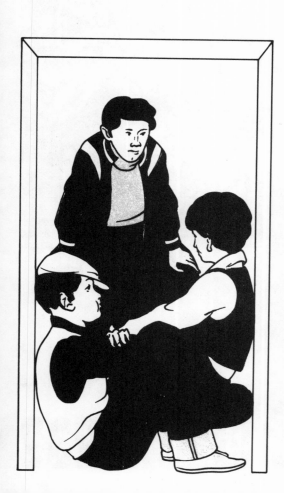

COFFEEPOT

Coffeepot is a word substitution game that is easily learned and a lot of fun.

The objective is for one player to guess an activity chosen by the other players. He does so by asking questions in which he substitutes the word "coffeepot" for the unknown word.

Play One player leaves the room while the others choose a verb or participle describing an activity—for instance "laugh" and "eat" or "laughing" and "eating." The player then returns to the room and puts a question to each of the players in turn, saying something like "Do you often coffeepot?" The players must answer truthfully, with either a straight "Yes" or "No," or with answers like "Only sometimes" or "When it rains."

As the guesser does not know what the activity is, some of the questions will be hilarious —which is where the fun of the game lies.

If he manages to guess the word, the player whose answer enabled him to do so becomes the next guesser. If he cannot guess the word within a reasonable time, he must take another turn at guessing.

TEAKETTLE (TEAPOT)

As in coffeepot, one of the players leaves the room while the others think of a word for him to guess.

The choice of word might be quite tricky, as it must be one with several meanings. Examples are: rain, reign, rein; or way, weigh, whey.

The player comes back into the room and listens to the others as they make conversation; he may join in if he likes. Sentences must have "teakettle" in place of the chosen word, so that a player might say: "It always seems to teakettle(rain) when I take my baby for a walk."

As soon as he guesses the word, another player takes a turn at guessing a new word.

A variation of teakettle is for the first player to select the word, and the other players to guess what it is as he makes up different sentences. The first person to guess the word correctly may then take a turn at choosing a word.

ASSOCIATIONS

Associations needs quick thinking, as the slightest hesitation eliminates a player from the game!

One person starts by saying any word (preferably a noun). As quickly as possible, the player next to him says the first word that the first player's word brought to mind, and so on around the group, beginning again with the first player.

If a player hesitates before saying a word, he drops out— if he manages to stay in the game longer than all the other players, he wins.

ASSOCIATION CHAIN

This game can be played as a continuation of the last game. As soon as the chain has been formed, the last player to have called out a word starts to repeat the chain backward. If he makes a mistake, he drops out, and the player before him continues to unravel the chain. This goes on until either the first word is reached, or only one player is left.

The more obvious or striking the associations, the easier it is to unravel the chain.

NUMBER ASSOCIATIONS

Number associations needs a person to call out any number between 1 and 12.

As soon as he has said a number, the players call out an appropriate association. For example, if the number called is seven, a player could call "Deadly sins."

The first player to call out a correct association scores one point. Other players may challenge a reply if they feel it is inappropriate. If the leader agrees with the challenge, that player loses one point from his score.

An association may not be repeated.

At the end of the game, the winner is the person with the highest number of points.

I WENT ON A TRIP

Each player tries to remember and repeat a growing list of items.

One of the players chooses any article he likes—for example an umbrella—and says "I went on a trip and took my umbrella."

The next player repeats that sentence and adds a second item after "umbrella." In this way the players gradually build up a list of articles. Each time his turn comes, a player repeats the list and adds another item. Whenever a player cannot repeat the list correctly, the list is closed and the next player in the group begins a new list.

CITY OF BOSTON

City of Boston is very similar to I went on a trip, but the additions are made at the beginning of the sentence. Thus the first player might say "I shall sell you a nosegay of violets when you come to the City of Boston," and each of the other players repeats that sentence, adding an item he will "sell" to the list.

ONE MINUTE PLEASE

One minute please calls for quick wits and imagination as players try to speak for one minute on a given topic.

One player is chosen as timekeeper, and also picks a topic for each player to talk about.

When it is his turn to speak, the player is told his topic. This may be anything from a serious topic such as "The current political situation" to something frivolous like "Why women wear hats."

The player may choose to treat the subject in any manner he pleases and what he says may be utter nonsense, provided he does not deviate from the topic, hesitate unduly, or repeat himself.

Other players may challenge the speaker if they feel he has broken a ruling. If the timekeeper agrees, then that player must drop out and the next player is given his topic. The winner is the player who manages to speak for an entire minute. If two or more players achieve this, the others decide which of the speeches was the best, or alternatively further rounds may be played.

WHAT IS MY THOUGHT LIKE?

This is a game for those with a lively imagination and the ability to bluff.
Any number of players may take part. One of them thinks of a thing or a person and asks the other players "What is my thought like?"
Each of them then makes a totally random guess (as no clues have been given) as to the object thought of.
Once all the players have made their guesses, they are told the object and are given a moment or two in which to think of a way of justifying the relationship between the object and their own guesses.
For example, if the object were a tiger and the first player had suggested a fire engine, he might legitimately explain "A fire engine is like a tiger because they both roar down the road!"
As some of the explanations may be rather farfetched they may be discussed among the other players. Any player whose explanation is disallowed must pay a forfeit. If all the players give satisfactory answers, the questioner must pay a forfeit.
A different questioner is chosen for each subsequent round.

WHO AM I?

This is a fairly simple game, in which one player does all the guessing.
He leaves the room while the other players think of any well-known personality—real of fictional, dead or alive.
The guesser returns to the room and asks "Who am I?"
The other players each reply with a clue to the character's identity.
If the character is Napoleon, for example, answers given might be:
"You are rather short and stout;"
"You are a great strategist at war;"
"You underestimated the Russian winter."
When each of the players has given a reply, the guesser may make three guesses as to the identity of the person.
If he fails to guess correctly, he is told the answer.
Another player is always chosen for the next round.

PROVERBS

In this guessing game, one player has to discover a proverb hidden in the other players' answers to his questions. (It is sometimes called hidden proverbs, or guessing proverbs.)
While he is out of the room the other players select a proverb. He returns to the room and asks each player in turn a question—it may be about anything at all, such as "What did you have for breakfast today?"
Each answer must contain one word from the proverb in the correct order. As soon as all the words have been used up, the players begin again with the first word of the proverb. The questioner may make as many guesses at the proverb as he wishes within a time limit of, say, ten minutes. If he cannot guess the proverb, he is told the answer and another player takes over as guesser in the next round.

BOTTICELLI

This is another game featuring famous people, and requires a good general knowledge.
One person chooses a personality, and tells the other players the initial of his surname. For example, he might say "M" for Groucho Marx.
Taking turns, each player must think of a character whose name begins with that letter, and give a description of him without naming the person he has in mind. If he thought of Mickey Mouse, he would ask "Are you a Walt Disney cartoon character?"
If the first player recognizes the description, he answers "No, I am not Mickey Mouse," and another player may make a guess.
If the first player does not recognize the description, however, the player who gave it may then ask a direct question that will give him and the other players a lead, such as "Are you in the entertainment business?" The first player must give a truthful "Yes" or "No" reply.
The first person to guess the personality wins the round and may choose the next character.
If nobody succeeds in guessing the personality after a reasonable length of time, the first player tells them the answer and may choose again for the new round.

ANIMAL, VEGETABLE, OR MINERAL

Sometimes called twenty questions, this game is one of the oldest and most familiar word guessing games. It may be made as simple or as difficult as the players wish, and can provide plenty of scope for intellectual dexterity as the players try to guess an object thought of by one of the others.
Players The game needs two or more players, or two teams. It is often helpful to have a non-playing person to act as referee.
Play One of the players thinks of an object. It may be general (eg "a ship"), specific (eg "the Lusitania"), or a feature (eg "the bridge of the Lusitania").
Sometimes the player then tells the others the composition of his chosen object (ie animal, vegetable, or mineral)—in an alternative version the players must guess it themselves.
The three categories may be defined as follows:
1) animal: all forms of animal life or anything of animal origin, eg a centipede, a tortoiseshell comb;
2) vegetable: all forms of vegetable life or anything of vegetable origin, eg flax, a wooden mallet;
3) mineral: anything inorganic or of inorganic origin, eg soda water, a mirror.
Objects are often a combination of categories, for example a can of beer or a leather shoe (The referee may be consulted if the player is unsure as to the category of an object.)
The player usually indicates the number of words in the object—excluding the definite or indefinite article. The other players then ask anything up to 20 questions to try to guess the object. They should ask questions of a general nature rather than make random guesses, until they feel confident that they are near to knowing the object. As each question is put to the player, he must reply either "Yes," "No," or "I don't know" as appropriate. In one version of the game, he may be allowed to qualify his answer if necessary by saying, for example, "Yes, in certain conditions."
The referee may intervene if he feels the player has given a wrong or misleading answer; he may also be consulted for guidance on a particular point.

End The first player to guess the object correctly may choose an object for a new round of play.
If no one has guessed the object by the time 20 questions have been asked (usually the referee keeps a count) the players are told what it was, and the same person may choose an object for the next round, or—if two teams are playing—a person in the other team may choose.

MAN AND OBJECT

In man and object, a player thinks of a person and something identified with him.
The person may be someone known personally to all the players, or a famous personality or fictional character. Examples might be an eskimo and his igloo, or Dante and the Inferno.
Playing procedure is the same as for animal, vegetable, or mineral—except that the players may be allowed to ask more than 20 questions.

Associations

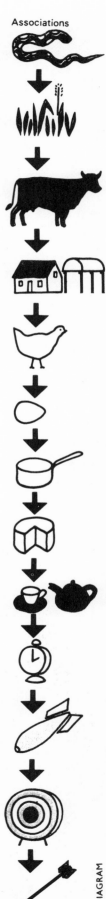

©DIAGRAM

Acting word games

In charades, "the game," dumb crambo, and in the manner of the word, one team mimes a word for the other team to guess. All these games are old favorites requiring only a lively imagination and a little acting ability. Amusement derives not only from the players' acting attempts but also from the often bizarre guesses made by the other team.

Players Acting guessing games can be played by any number of players divided into two teams.

One team chooses a word or phrase according to the rules of the particular game and then the other team attempts to guess it.

The teams change roles whenever a correct guess is made.

Costumes and other props are not necessary for these games but they can add to the players' enjoyment.

CHARADES
Charades is probably the best known and most popular of all acting and guessing games.
The objective is for one team to guess a word with several syllables that is acted out in mime by the other team.
Play The acting team leaves the room and decides on a suitable word. Usually words of three syllables are chosen, but players may choose words of only two syllables or of four or more.
This word is then presented to the other team in mimed scenes representing the different syllables, and then in a final scene representing the whole word.
Usually there is one scene for each syllable, although players may choose to represent two syllables in a single scene. (For example, the word "decorate" could be broken down as "deck-or-rate" or as "decor-ate.")
A member of the acting team must announce the number of scenes before miming begins. The actors usually leave the room between scenes and the guessing team is then free to discuss its ideas.
It is advisable for players to agree on a time limit for guessing words after the final scene.
An example of the sort of word that might be chosen is "nightingale," which was used in a charade scene in the book Vanity Fair by the nineteenth-century English novelist, William Thackeray.
Nightingale breaks down into three syllables and could be represented by:
a) a "night" scene with people going to bed or sleeping;
b) an "inn" scene with people drinking and making merry;
c) a "gale" scene with people being blown down a street;
d) a "nightingale" scene with people flapping their arms and imitating bird song.

CATEGORY CHARADES
This game is played in the same way as standard charades except that teams must choose words that belong to a previously agreed category and there is no miming of the full word.
Ideas for categories are:
a) towns (eg "came-bridge," "prince-ton");
b) people's names (eg "rob-in," "car-row-line");
c) animals (eg "lie-on," "buff-a-low");
d) flowers (eg "snow-drop," "butter-cup").

PROVERB CHARADES
Proverb charades is played in the same way as standard charades except that teams choose a proverb or well-known quotation, which they then act out word by word or in groups of several words. A good proverb for this game would be "a bird in the hand is worth two in the bush."

SPOKEN CHARADES
This game is played in the same way as standard charades except that the actors speak. Instead of miming scenes representing the syllables and then the full word, players must mention them while acting in the different scenes. This game is easier to play than most charades games, and for this reason is particularly popular with younger children.

THE GAME

This is a fascinating variation of charades. It is called "the game" because its early enthusiasts claimed that it was truly the game of all games. The players are divided into two teams, and each team nominates a different person to be its actor for each round.

Objective Using conventional gestures and free mime, the actor must convey to his teammates a well-known phrase chosen by the opposing team. The teams compete on a time basis.

Categories Phrases for this game must belong to one of a number of categories previously decided by both teams. Typical categories are the title of a book, play, television series, song, or painting, or a quotation, slogan, or proverb.

Play One team chooses a phrase and whispers it to the actor from the other team. The actor then begins miming, and a person appointed as timekeeper makes a note of the time. The actor should use conventional gestures where possible.

His teammates are allowed to speak, and make guesses as the acting proceeds. The actor, however, is only allowed to reply to their guesses with gestures.

If a correct guess is made, the timekeeper records the time and the teams change roles. (It is advisable to have a time limit, after which the teams must change roles even though the phrase has not been guessed.)

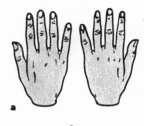
a

b

c

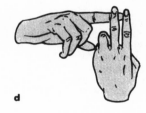
d

e

Gestures Players may improvise in their miming, but "the game" is characterized by the use of previously agreed gestures.

Firstly the actor indicates the category of the phrase. For example he can mime holding a book (**a**) for a book title. To indicate the number of words in the phrase the actor then holds up that number of fingers (**b**).

If the actor is going to mime the entire phrase he forms a circle, either with his thumb and forefinger (**c**) or with his arms.

If he wishes to mime only part of the phrase, he indicates a word by tapping the appropriate finger (**d**). He then counts his fingers to show how many letters there are in this word (**e**). If he wishes to use only part of a mimed word, he must make chopping actions to divide the word into syllables.

When his team makes a correct guess, the actor nods his head. If a guess is along the right lines, he beckons; if totally wrong, he makes a brushing away gesture.

Scoring The game is always scored on the basis of the time taken to guess the phrases. There are, however, two different scoring systems:
a) a round is won by the team that guesses its phrase most quickly and a game is won by the team that wins the most rounds;
b) times for the different rounds are added together and the game is won by the team with the shortest total guessing time.

THE GAME (SIMULTANEOUS)

Some players prefer to have both teams acting the same phrase simultaneously.

In this case it is necessary to appoint a referee, who thinks of a phrase, writes it on two slips of paper, and hands the slips to an actor from each of the teams.

Acting takes place in different rooms—so that players cannot hear the guesses of the opposing team.

A round is won by the team that is first to guess the phrase correctly. A game is won by the team that wins the most rounds.

THE GAME (RELAY)

This is played in the same way as the simultaneous version except that it is organized like a relay race.

The teams must be of equal size and each team member has a turn at being the actor. As soon as a team guesses a phrase, its next actor goes to the referee, tells him the last phrase, and is given a new one. A game is won when a team guesses its last actor's phrase.

DUMB CRAMBO

Dumb crambo is a very old game of the charades family. It was particularly popular in the nineteenth century.

Objective After receiving a rhyming clue, a team attempts to guess and mime a word, usually a verb, chosen by the opposing team.

Play The first team chooses a word, for example "feel," and then tells the second team a word rhyming with it, for example "steal."

It is obviously best for this game to choose a word that has several words rhyming with it. For example, other words that rhyme with "feel" are "heal," "keel," "reel," "deal," and "peel."

The second team then attempts to guess the chosen word and must mime its guesses. A maximum of three guesses is allowed.

If a guess is incorrect, members of the other team hiss or boo; if a guess is correct, they clap their hands.

A team scores one point each time it guesses a word.

Teams change roles after a word is guessed or after three incorrect guesses.

The game is won by the team with most points when play ends.

IN THE MANNER OF THE WORD

This is an amusing acting guessing game in which players attempt to guess adverbs.

Play One player chooses an adverb, such as rapidly, quietly, or amusingly.

The other players, in turn, then ask him to carry out some action "in the manner of the word." For example, a player might say: "eat in the manner of the word," "walk in the manner of the word," or "laugh in the manner of the word."

The player who chooses the adverb must do as the other players ask, and the other players may make guesses as soon as acting begins.

The first player to guess an adverb correctly scores one point. If no one guesses the word after each of the players has asked for an action, the player who chose the adverb receives one point.

The game is won by the player with most points after each of the players has had a turn at choosing an adverb.

Pencil and paper games

Pencil and paper games need only the simplest equipment, yet they can provide great scope for the imagination, increase a player's general knowledge, and—above all—be a highly enjoyable way of passing time. Pencil and paper games fall basically into two categories: word games and games in which pictures or symbols are drawn.

DOG
COG
COT
CAT

KEYWORD

Keyword, sometimes called hidden words, can be played by any number of people. The players choose a "keyword" containing at least seven letters. Each player then tries to make as many words as possible from the letters in the keyword. The letters may be used in any order, but a letter may be used in any one word only as many times as it appears in the keyword.
Generally, proper nouns (capitalized words) or words with fewer than four letters are not allowed; nor are abbreviations or plurals.
The game may be played just for interest, with players working together; or it may be made into a contest, with individuals competing to find most words in an agreed length of time.

JUMBLED WORDS (ANAGRAMS)

Any number of players may take part. One of them prepares a list of words belonging to a particular category (eg flowers, cities, poets) and jumbles up the letters in each word.
Each of the other players is given a list of the jumbled words and their category, and tries to rearrange the letters back into the original words.
For example, "peilmidhun" should be "delphinium" and "wodronsp" should be "snowdrop."
The first player to rearrange all the words correctly, or the player with most correct words after a given time, wins the game.
More experienced players may like to make up anagrams of their own by rearranging the letters in a word to make one or more other words, eg "angered" is an anagram of "derange."

ACROSTICS

Acrostics is another word-building game. A word of at least three letters is chosen. Each player writes the word in a column down the left-hand side of a sheet of paper; he then writes the same word, but with the letters reversed, down the right-hand side of the page.
The player fills in the space between the two columns with the same number of words as there are letters in the keyword—and starting and ending each word with the letter at either side.
For example, if the keyword is "stem," a player's words might read: scream, trundle, earliest, manageress.
The winner may be either the first person to fill in all the words, or the player with the longest or most original words.

TRANSFORMATION

Two words with the same number of letters are chosen. Each player writes down the two words. He tries to change the first word into the second word by altering only one letter at a time, and each time forming a new word.
For example, "dog" could be changed to "cat" in four words as follows: dog, cog, cot, cat. It is easiest to begin with three or four letter words until the players are quite practiced—when five or even six letter words may be tried.
The winner is the player who completes the changes using the fewest number of words.

FILL INS

A list of 30 to 40 words is prepared and kept hidden from the players.
Each player is then given the first and last letters and the number of letters missing from each word on the list.
The winner is the first player to fill in all the blanks correctly.
Alternatively, the players may be allowed an agreed length of time and then the winner is the player with the most correct words.

CATEGORIES

Perhaps one of the best-known pencil and paper games, categories can be played at either a simple or a sophisticated level.
Preparation Each player (there may be any number) is given a pencil and a piece of paper.
The players decide on between six and a dozen different categories; these may be easy ones for children (eg girls' or boys' names, animals, colors) or more difficult for adults (eg politicians, rivers, chemicals). Each player lists the categories on his piece of paper.
One of the players chooses any letter of the alphabet—preferably an "easy" letter such as "a" or "d" if children are playing. Experienced

players can make the game more challenging by choosing more difficult letters such as "j" or "k."
Players may decide to play to an agreed time limit of say 15 minutes.
Play The players try to find a word beginning with the chosen letter for each of the categories (eg if the chosen letter is "p" all the words must begin with that letter). They write down their words next to the appropriate category.
The more unusual or original the word, the better—thus even if simple categories have been chosen, there is still plenty of scope for ingenuity.
Scoring Writing must stop as soon as the time limit is up, or as soon as one player has finished.

Each player in turn then reads out his list of words. If he has found a word not thought of by any of the other players, he scores two points for that word. If, however, one or more of the other players has also chosen the same word, each of them scores only one point. If the player could not find a word at all, or if his choice of word did not correctly fit the category, he gets no points. (Any disagreement about the relevance of a word to a category must be solved by a vote among the other players.)
The winner is the player with the highest score for his list of words.
Subsequent rounds Any number of rounds may be played, using either the same or different categories; the chosen letter, however, must

be different for each round. Players may take it in turns to choose a letter at the start of a round.
Players make a note of their scores at the end of each round. The winner is the player with the highest points total at the end of the final round.

GUGGENHEIM

Guggenheim is a slightly more complicated version of categories. Instead of choosing only one letter for each round of play, the players choose a keyword of about four or five letters.
The letters of the keyword are written spaced out to the right of the list of categories, and players try to find words for each of the categories beginning with the letter heading each column.

CROSSWORDS

This intriguing game can be adapted for play by any number of people.

If up to five people are playing, each of them draws a square divided into five squares by five on a sheet of paper.

If more people take part, or if players wish to lengthen the game, the number of squares can be increased to, say, seven by seven.

Each of the players in turn calls out any letter of the alphabet. As each letter is called, all players write it into any square of their choice, with the objective of forming words of two or more letters reading either across or down. Generally, abbreviations or proper nouns (names, etc) may not be used.

Once a letter has been written down, it cannot be moved to another square.

Players continue to call out letters until all the individual squares have been filled.

The number of points scored is equal to the number of letters in each word (one-letter words do not count). Thus a three-letter word scores three points. If a word fills an entire row or column, one bonus point is scored in addition to the score for that word.

No ending of a word can form the beginning of another word in the same row or column. For example, if a row contains the letters "i, f, e, n, d" the player may score four points for the word "fend" but cannot in addition score two points for the word "if." Each player adds together each of his horizontal and vertical totals; the winning player is the one with the highest score.

SYNONYMS

A list of 10 to 20 words is prepared, and a copy given to each player.

The objective is to find a synonym (word with the same meaning) for each word on the list. If a player can think of more than one synonym for any word he should write down the shortest one.

After an agreed length of time, the players' lists are checked.

The winner is the player who finds a synonym for the most words, or, if two or more players have an equal number of synonyms, the player with the lowest total of letters in his synonyms.

GEOGRAPHY RACE

This is an ideal game for a large group of players, and a good way of brushing up one's knowledge of geography! The players are formed into two teams, and one person acts as umpire. If possible, the teams should sit in parallel rows. The first person in each team is given a piece of paper and something to write with.

The object of the game is for each person in a team to write down the name of a town or city that lies in a specified direction of the last town on the list.

Play The umpire chooses the name of any well-known town or city and specifies in which compass direction the other towns must lie.

For example, he might say "Towns to the east of Berlin." He gives a start signal, and the first person in each team must write down a town that lies to the east of Berlin.

The player then hands the pencil and paper to the next person in his team, who writes down a town to the east of the town chosen by the first player.

Play continues in this way until the last member in the team has written down a town.

Scoring As soon as one team has finished, the umpire checks both teams' answers. The team that finished first scores a bonus of five points. In addition, each correct answer scores one point, and one point is deducted for each incorrect answer.

The team with the highest number of points after one or more rounds wins.

TELEGRAMS

Players are given a list of 15 letters, and must use each of them—in the order given—as the initial letter of a word in a 15-word telegram.
(Alternatively, the players are given a word of about 10–15 letters, eg blackberries, so that the first word must begin with "b," the second with "l," and so on.)

The telegram may include one or two place names and may—if the player wishes—have the name of the "sender" as the last word.

Stops (or periods) may be used for punctuation.

The winner is the first player to complete his telegram, or, if a time limit has been set, the player whose telegram is judged to be the best at the end of the time set.

Acrostics

S C R E A M
T R U N D L E
E A R L I E S T
M A N A G E R E S S

Categories

Categories	Letters	P.	S.
Composer		Paderewski	Strauss
City		Port o' Spain	Sydney
Mountain		Pilatus	Stromboli
Girl's Name		Phyllis	Sarah

Guggenheim

Categories	G	A	M	E
Composer	Grieg	Albinoni	Mozart	Elgar
City	Georgetown	Amsterdam	Mombassa	Essen
Mountain	Grossglockner	Anapurna	Matterhorn	Etna
Girl's name	Gertrude	Abigail	Michelle	Elinor

Telegrams

BLACKBERRIES

BRING LAMP AND CHISEL STOP KNOW BEST ENTRY ROUTE STOP REST IS EASY STOP
SID

Crosswords

F	A	K	E	D	6
U	N	N	H	U	0
R	A	I	N	C	4
R	N	F	K	T	0
Y	I	E	L	D	6
6	4	6	0	4	TOTAL 30

F	E	R	N	D	4
U	K	I	F	U	2
N	E	A	R	N	4
N	I	L	D	K	3
Y	A	C	H	T	6
6	3	0	0	4	

TOTAL 32

Consequences

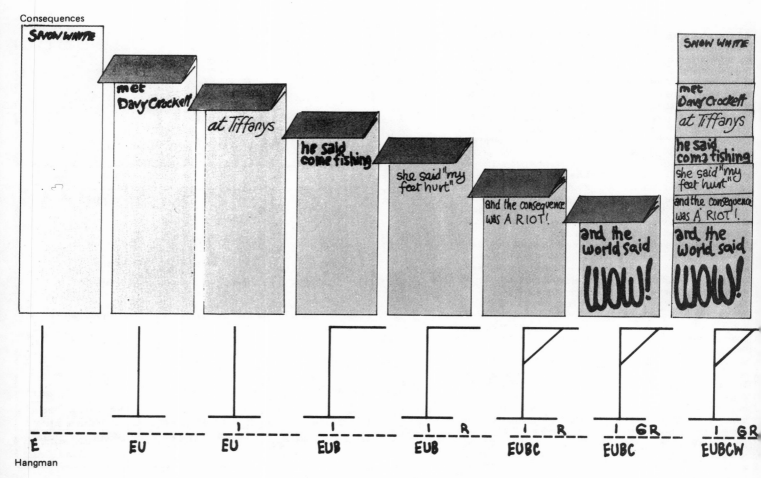

Hangman

CONSEQUENCES

Consequences is a favorite among children and is a game purely to be enjoyed—there are no winners or losers. Any number of players can take part, and each of them is provided with a sheet of paper and a pencil.

The objective is to write as many stories as there are participants, with each person contributing to each of the stories.

Play One person is chosen as "caller" (this does not exclude him from taking part). He calls out the first part of the story. Each person writes down an appropriate name, phrase, or sentence, making it as humorous as possible. He then folds over the top of the piece of paper to hide what he has written, and passes the paper to the player to his left.

Squiggles 1

The caller then says the next part of the story, and the players write something on the paper they have just received from their neighbors.

This procedure is repeated until the story is complete. Any theme may be used, but the one decribed here is perhaps the best known.

a) "A girl . . ." (players write the name of someone known to them, or alternatively a famous personality or fictional character);

2) "met a boy . . ." (again, the players may choose any name of their choice);

3) "at . . . beside . . . in . . ." (the players may choose any location);

4) "he said . . .";

5) "she said . . .";

6) "the consequence was . . .";

7) "and the world said . . ."

When the story is complete, each player passes the piece of paper on which he wrote the last sentence to the person to his left. The pieces of paper are unfolded and the stories read out one by one—they may not be fictional masterpieces but are sure to provide a lot of fun !

PICTURE CONSEQUENCES

This game follows the same principle as standard consequences, but instead of writing words the players draw parts of the human figure dressed in funny clothing— starting with the head and finishing with the feet. When the pieces of paper are folded over, a part of the last drawing is left showing, so as to give a lead to the next player. For example, after drawing the head, the paper should be folded so that the edge of the neck is showing. Parts of animals or birds can also be drawn in addition to (or instead of) humans. After drawing the feet, players may write down the name of the person whom they want the figure to represent !

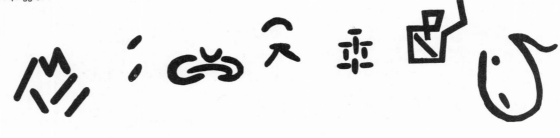

Picture consequences

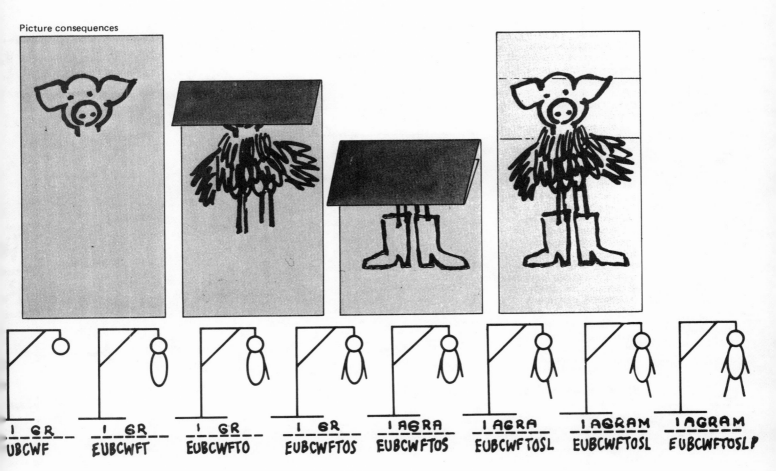

PICTURES

Pictures is best played by two teams of at least three players each. In addition, there must be an organizer who belongs to neither team.

The organizer makes a list of half a dozen or so book titles, proverbs, or other subjects (they need not be in the same category).

The organizer whispers the first title on the list to one player from each team. This player returns to his team (the teams should preferably be in separate rooms) and must draw a picture representing the title. He may add to his drawing or make further drawings—until one of his teammates has correctly guessed the answer. (No verbal clues may be given, however!)

As soon as one player has guessed the title, he may go to the organizer for the next title on the list.

The winning team is the first one to guess all the titles on the organizer's list.

HANGMAN

Hangman is a popular game for two or more players. One person thinks of a word of about five or six letters. He writes down the same number of dashes as there are letters in his word.

The other players may then start guessing the letters in the word, calling one letter at a time. If the guess is a successful one, the letter is written by the first player above the appropriate dash—if it appears more than once in a word it must be entered as often as it occurs.

If the guess is an incorrect one, however, the first player may start to draw a hanged man—one line of the drawing representing each wrong letter.

The other players must try to guess the secret word before the first player can complete the drawing of the hanged man.

If one of the players guesses the word (this should become easier as the game progresses) he may take a turn at choosing a word. If the hanged man is completed before the word is guessed, the same player may choose another word.

To make the game more difficult, longer words may be chosen, or even a group of words making a proverb or title of a book or film—the player gives the others a clue as to the category.

SQUIGGLES

This is a game for two people, each of whom should have a piece of paper, and a pencil different in color from the other player's.

Each player scribbles very quickly on his piece of paper—the more abstract the squiggle, the better.

Players then exchange papers and set themselves a time limit of, for example, two minutes, in which they must use every bit of the squiggle to make a picture. Ingenuity is more important than artistic ability—a third person could be asked to judge which of the players has used his squiggle more inventively.

Squiggles 2

Tick-tack-toe

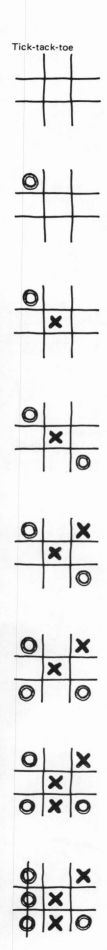

TICK-TACK-TOE

A favorite for generations, tick-tack-toe (or noughts and crosses) is a game for two people that may be over in a matter of seconds!

Two vertical lines are drawn with two horizontal lines crossing them, forming nine spaces.

Players decide which of them is to draw noughts (circles) and which of them crosses. Taking alternate turns, the players make their mark in any vacant space until one of them manages to get three of his marks in a row (either horizontally, vertically, or diagonally). He then draws a line through his winning row and the game comes to an end. If neither player succeeds in forming a row, the game is considered drawn.

As the player who draws first has a better chance of winning, players usually swop their starting order after each game.

THREE-DIMENSIONAL TICK-TACK-TOE

Based on the standard game, the three-dimensional version offers a lengthier and more challenging alternative. Three-dimensional tick-tack-toe can be bought as a game, but can equally well be played with pencil and paper.

The cube may be represented diagrammatically by 64 squares—as shown. For actual play, each "layer" of the cube is drawn out individually.

Playing procedure is similar to standard tick-tack-toe, but the winner is the first player to get four of his marks in a row (see illustrations).

Three-dimensional tick-tack-toe

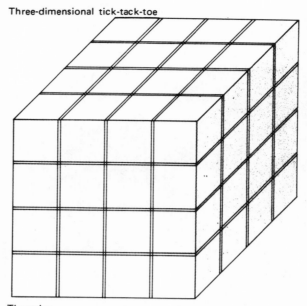

The cube

Playing layout

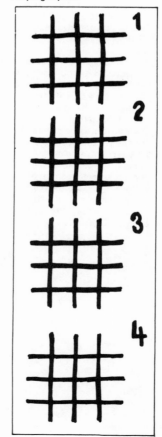

Nine winning rows

Boxes

Crystals

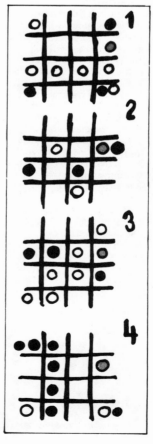

BOXES

This is a simple but amusing game for two players. Any number of dots is drawn on a piece of paper—the dots are drawn in rows to form a square. Ten rows by ten is a good number.

Players take alternate turns. In each turn they may draw a horizontal or vertical line to join up any two dots that are next to each other.

The objective is to complete (with a fourth line) as many squares or "boxes" as possible. Whenever a player completes a box he initials it and may draw another line. He may continue his turn until he draws a line that does not complete a box.

As soon as there are no more dots to be joined—all the boxes having been filled—the game ends. The player with the highest number of initialed boxes is the winner.

Another way of playing is to try to form the lowest number of boxes—the players join up as many lines as they can before being forced to complete a box. The winner is the player with the fewest initialed boxes.

Sprouts

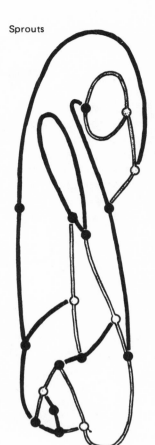

SPROUTS

Sprouts has certain similarities with boxes, but needs rather more ingenuity to win!

Two players take part. About six or so dots are drawn—well spaced out—on a sheet of paper (more may be drawn for a longer game).

Taking alternate turns, each player draws a line joining any two dots or joining a dot to itself. He then draws a dot anywhere along the line he has just made, and his turn ends.

When drawing a line, the following rules must be observed:

1) no line may cross itself or cross a line that has already been drawn;
2) no line may be drawn through a dot;
3) a dot may only have three lines leaving it.

The last person able to draw a legitimate line is the winner.

Disallowed sprouts

CRYSTALS

In this sophisticated pattern visualizing game, each player tries to form symmetrical shapes known as "crystals."

Equipment All that is needed is a sheet of squared (graph) paper and as many differently colored crayons as there are players.

The number of squares used for each game depends on the number of players: if two take part (the best number) about 20 rows of 20 squares each would form a suitable area.

Objective Each player attempts to "grow" crystals on the paper with the aim of filling more squares than his opponent.

A player does not score points for the number of crystals he grows, but for the number of squares his crystals cover.

A crystal is made up of "atoms," each of which occupies a single square. In growing crystals, players must observe certain rules of symmetry that determine whether or not a crystal is legitimate.

The symmetry of a crystal can be determined by visualizing four axes through its center: horizontal, vertical, and two diagonal axes. Once the axes

have been "drawn," it should theoretically be possible to fold the crystal along each of the four axes to produce corresponding "mirror" halves that, when folded, exactly overlay each other (ie are the same shape and size).

In addition to the rules of symmetry, players must observe the following:

a) a legitimate crystal may be formed from four or more atoms drawn by one player only;

b) the atoms forming a crystal must be joined along their sides—they may not be connected only by their corners;

c) a crystal may not contain any empty atoms (ie holes).

Play Players decide on their playing order and each one in turn shades in any one square of his choice—each player using a crayon of a different color.

In their first few turns, players rarely try to grow a crystal. Instead, they place single atoms around the playing area in order to establish potential crystal sites. As play progresses, players will see which atoms are best placed for growing crystals and add to them as appropriate.

When a player thinks he has grown a crystal, he declares it, and rings the area that it covers.

A player with a winning advantage will try to retain the lead by either blocking his opponents' attempts at growing crystals, or by growing long narrow crystals that—although not high scoring—restrict the playing area.

Play ends when no blank squares are left, or when the players agree that no more crystals can be formed.

Scoring Players work out which of the crystals are legitimate, and count the number of squares each crystal covers.

Any crystal that does not demonstrate symmetry around each of the four axes is not legitimate and does not score. The number of squares in the legitimate crystals that each player has grown are added, and the player with most squares wins the game.

Disallowed

Allowed

©DIAGRAM

There are numerous theories as to why gambling should always have held so much fascination. Perhaps the only certainty is that man will never run short of things on which to make a wager, be it on the roll of a die or the outcome of a political election. Some forms of betting involve a degree of skill or judgment, but the games described here are games of pure chance—ranging from simple guessing games played for fun to highly organized games on which vast sums of money are gambled each year.

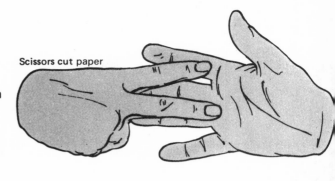

Scissors cut paper

Paper wraps stone

Stone blunts scissors

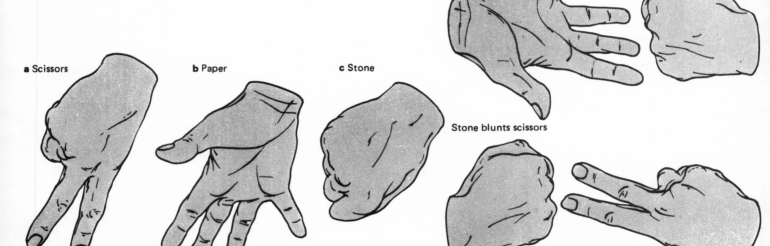

a Scissors   **b** Paper   **c** Stone

SCISSORS, PAPER, STONE

This ancient game, also known as hic, haec, hoc and by many other names, is played all over the world.

It is a game for two players. Three objects (scissors, a piece of paper, and a stone) are indicated by different positions of the hand:

a) two fingers making a V shape represent scissors;
b) an open hand represents a piece of paper; and
c) a clenched fist represents a stone.

Each player hides one hand behind his back and adopts one of the three positions. One of the players calls "One, two, three" (or "Hic, haec, hoc") and as the third word is called the players show their hands.

The rule of the game decides the winner: scissors can cut paper, paper may be wrapped around a stone, and a stone can blunt the scissors. Thus if one player chooses scissors and the other player paper, the player who chooses scissors wins the round. If both players decide on the same object, the round is a draw.

Players usually play a predetermined number of rounds.

SPOOF

This is an intriguing game of bluff for at least two players, in which each person tries to guess the total number of objects the players are concealing in their hands. Each player requires three small objects, such as coins or matches. He hides any number of them (or none if he wishes) in his outstretched fist.

One by one, in a clockwise direction, the players call out the number of objects they think are contained in the players' hands—but no two players may say the same number.

When all the players have guessed, they open their fists and the objects are counted. The player who guessed correctly, or whose guess was nearest the correct number, wins the round.

Obviously, much depends on the ability to determine whether a player is bluffing when he calls a number. For example, guessing high might indicate that the caller has a full hand of three objects (especially if he happens to be the first caller in a round). Similarly, guessing low could mean a low number of objects —or an attempt to deceive the other players as to the contents of a hand.

Spoof: two players

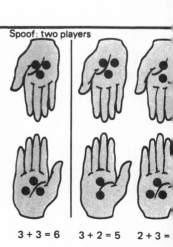

3 + 3 = 6   3 + 2 = 5   2 + 3 =

6   **5**

213

Mora

MORA

Mora, also known as fingers, is another finger guessing game for two players.

The object of the game is to guess the number of fingers that will be "thrown" (displayed).

The players stand facing each other, each with a closed fist against his chest. At a given signal they throw a chosen number of fingers (or extend their clenched fist to indicate zero) and simultaneously call out the total number of fingers that they think will be thrown by both players (thumbs count as fingers). A call of "Mora!" indicates that the player is betting on ten fingers.

If neither player guesses correctly, the round is considered void. If one player guesses correctly he wins that round; if both players guess the right number, the round is a draw.

A mora session usually comprises 10 or 15 rounds.

SHOOT

Shoot is rather like mora, except that the two players must guess not the number of fingers thrown, but whether it will be an odd or an even total. The players may throw the fingers on one or both hands (ie each player may throw any number from zero through ten).

As they show their hands, the players call out "Odds!" or "Evens!" The fingers are counted (zero is considered an even number) and the winner is determined as in mora.

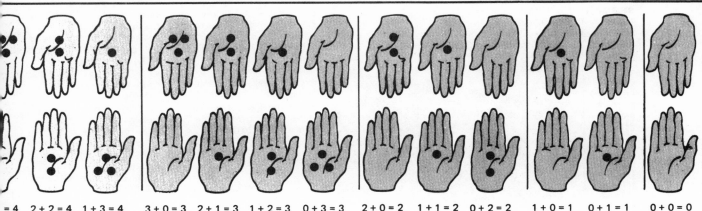

= 4   2 + 2 = 4   1 + 3 = 4   3 + 0 = 3   2 + 1 = 3   1 + 2 = 3   0 + 3 = 3   2 + 0 = 2   1 + 1 = 2   0 + 2 = 2   1 + 0 = 1   0 + 1 = 1   0 + 0 = 0

4   **3**   **2**   **1**   **0**

©DIAGRAM

FAN-TAN

Fan-tan is a gambling game that originated in China several centuries ago. It is still very popular in Asia and in Chinese communities throughout the world.

Fan-tan is played on a board or table with the corners numbered 1, 2, 3, and 4 (**a**). The players bet on the numbers, placing their stakes on the appropriate corner of the playing area.

When the bets have been made, the banker takes a random handful of beans or other small objects and places them in the middle of the playing area (**b**).

Using a small stick as a rake, he then counts off the beans in groups of four (**c**).

The groups are disregarded until the last batch—the one that determines the winner. If it contains four beans, the players who bet on 4 win; if it contains three beans (**d**) those who backed 3 win, and so on. The banker takes a percentage of all the stakes, usually 25 per cent.

DOLLAR POKER

No relation to card poker, dollar poker is a betting game played with one-dollar bills. Its other names are money poker and liar poker.

Objective The game is based on the eight digits contained in the serial number on the bill (its two letters are ignored). Players bid the total number of any one digit that appears on all the dollar bills held by the players. The player with the highest successful bid is the winner, and collects one dollar from each player. If he fails to justify his bid, he loses and pays each player one dollar.

Deal The best number of players is about five or six, and one of them is chosen as dealer.

Each player gives the dealer five or more one-dollar bills. The dealer shuffles the bills with their serial numbers face down, and deals them out one at a time and in a clockwise direction to all the players including himself, beginning with the player to his left.

Each player selects any one bill from those he has just been dealt, and the other bills are put to one side for later games.

Play Bidding is started by the player to the dealer's left and then passes from player to player in a clockwise direction. Each player has the option of bidding or passing (ie missing his turn). If he passes, he may reenter the bidding whenever it is his turn to play.

The player who bids first may bid (call out) any digit and amount he chooses; but thereafter each bid must be successively higher, either in the amount of that digit or in the same amount of a higher-ranking digit. Rank is 0 (high), 9, 8, 7, 6, 5, 4, 3, 2,1 (low).

For example, if the opening bid is two 4s, the next bid must be either two 5s (or two of any higher ranking digit), or three 1s, 2s, 3s, or 4s.

If only one player bids and all the other players pass, he is the winner if he justifies his bid at the "showdown," or the loser if he fails to do so.

Showdown When bidding stops, the last bidder (inevitably the player who made the highest bid) must try to justify his bid. He declares the quantity of the bid number on his own bill, and then each player in turn does likewise.

If the sum total of the bid number is equal to or exceeds the amount called, the bidder is paid one dollar by each player. If it is less, he loses and must pay one dollar to each of the other players.

For example, if the bidder called ten 7s and his dollar bill has three 7s, he calls "Three," and each of the other players calls out the number of 7s on his bill. If the final total of 7s equals ten or more, the bidder wins—but if it is less than ten he loses.

Any player is entitled to see the serial numbers of all the bills in play at the showdown in order to verify the outcome of the game, but it is more usual to assume that the players have been honest in their declarations.

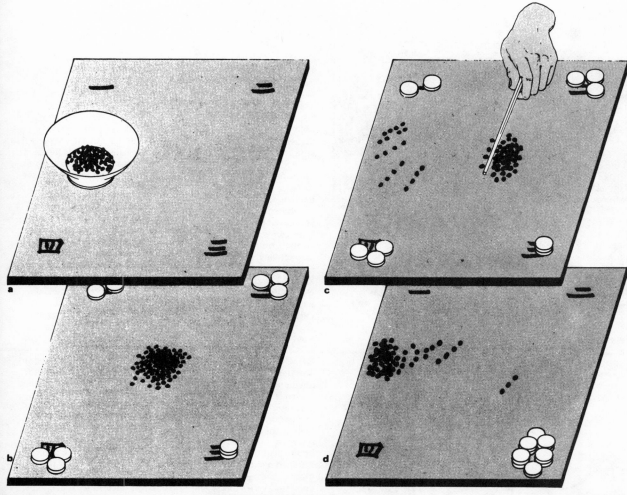

Subsequent rounds Each player selects another dollar bill from his stock for the next round of play.
The first bid is made by the player to the left of the previous round's winner. If, however, the last bidder in that round lost, it is he who must make the first bid.
Play continues as before.

PUT AND TAKE TOP

Around 1940 this was a big gambling craze in the United States of America but "loaded tops" and rampant cheating meant it soon died out.
However, it now seems to be coming back into fashion.
An eight-sided top is used, with sides marked as shown.
Any number can play and each player contributes an agreed amount to a pot. Players then take it in turns to spin the top. If the top falls with a put side uppermost, the spinner puts the amount indicated (1, 3, 4, or all) into the pot. For put all, the spinner doubles the amount in the pot. If the top falls with a take side uppermost, the spinner takes the amount indicated. For take all, he takes all the money in the pot.

PUT 1
TAKE 1
PUT 3
TAKE 3
PUT 4
TAKE 4
PUT ALL
TAKE ALL

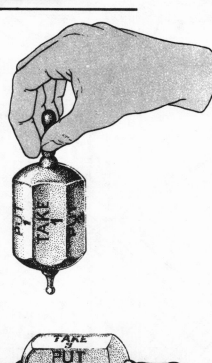

LOTTO

This family game—the forerunner of games like bingo—originated in Italy. Other names by which it is known are housey housey, tombola, and bolito.

Equipment Lotto is played with special rectangular cards divided into either three or five horizontal and nine vertical rows.

Each horizontal row has five numbered and four blank squares in random arrangement. The vertical rows contain, from left to right respectively, numbers selected from 1 to 10, 11 to 20, 21 to 30, and so on up to 90. No number is duplicated on any other card, and no two cards are alike.

Complementary to the cards is a set of 90 small card counters, numbered from 1 to 90.

Play As many players may take part as there are cards. Each player is given one card —or more than one if there are any left over.

One player (who may take part in the game if he wishes) is the caller. He puts the card counters into a sack or other container and mixes them well. The caller takes out one counter at a time, calls its number, and gives it to whichever player has the card on which the number appears. That player places the counter on the appropriate square.

End As soon as one player has covered all the numbers on his card in this way, he calls out "Lotto!" His card and counters are checked, and if they are correct he wins the game.

BINGO

This descendant of lotto has developed into a commercial bonanza. Millions of people play regularly at bingo halls and parlors all over the world, lured by big cash prizes in return for only a modest financial outlay. Many bingo sessions are organized to raise money for charities or community projects.

Equipment resembles lotto equipment but is much more sophisticated.

Bingo cards The typical North American bingo card is divided into five rows of five squares each and has the letters B, I, N, G, O printed at the top of the card, one letter relating to each column. Numbers selected from 1 to 75 fill all the squares except the one at the center, which is specially marked and called the "free-play" square. In the United Kingdom two types of bingo are played. "Prize" bingo—usually played at fairgrounds or at non-commercial sessions—is played for prizes other than cash, using the type of card described above (but without a free-play square).

The more usual "cash" bingo (for cash prizes) is played with cards of three rows of ten squares each. Each row has five numbered and five blank squares, arranged at random. The numbers are selected from 1 to 99. There is no free-play square.

At commercial bingo sessions cards are sometimes pasted on a piece of cardboard called a lapboard—this forms a convenient table and ensures that players do not take their cards home at the end of the session.

Cardboard or plastic markers may be used to cover the numbers, and sometimes cards have slides that can be finger-tipped across the numbers.

Bingo balls Like the cards, bingo balls in North America are both numbered and lettered. B-balls are for numbers 1 to 15, I-balls 16 to 30, N-balls 31 to 45, G-balls 46 to 60, and O-balls 61 to 75. Sometimes a colored "wild" ball with neither letter nor number is added, giving some special advantage to the player when it is drawn. For example, it might allow him to cover any number on his card, or perhaps the final number needed to complete a line. In the United Kingdom, the bingo balls usually bear only numbers, from 1 to 99.

Machines to mix and select the numbers may be either wire mesh cages, or glass or plastic "blower" machines. Many are partly or fully automatic.

The balls are released from the machines one at a time. Many establishments have a master board connected to a lighted signal board; this displays the numbers as they are placed on the master board and can also be used to check previously called numbers.

card no	253	BLUE		NO 5505
B	**I**	**N**	**G**	**O**
		32	47	63
			50	66
		FREE PLAY	52	67
	25	41	55	70
14	27	43	58	71
nos 1 to 15	nos 16 to 30	nos 31 to 45	nos 46 to 60	nos 61 to 75

PICTURE LOTTO

This is a variation of standard lotto, using pictures instead of numbers. It is an excellent test of recognition for young children.

The cards used in picture lotto are usually divided into six or eight squares, each showing a different symbol or picture, eg flowers, animals, or household objects.

Each picture has a matching card. At the start of the game the caller gathers these small cards together, mixes them thoroughly, and picks out one at a time for the players to see. The player who claims the small card takes it and covers the appropriate picture on the large card with it. As in lotto, the first player to cover all the pictures on his card wins the game.

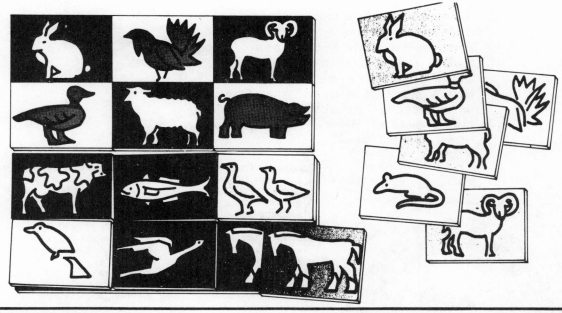

Play At the start of each round of calling, the players buy one or more cards. Often they hope to increase their chances of success by buying as many as ten or more cards. As each ball emerges from the selector machine, the caller announces its number (and letter) and places it on the master board.

Any player whose card shows the drawn number covers the appropriate square. (The same number may appear on more than one card, although no two cards are exactly alike.) The first player to complete a line of numbers—vertically, horizontally, or diagonally—calls "Bingo!" His card is then read back aloud to the caller by a floor attendant, and if it tallies with the master board, he gets a prize.

But the single line rarely brings in the big money! Most players have their sights set on the jackpot. This is won by the first player to achieve a "blackout" or "coverall" (ie covering all the numbers on his card). Some bingo halls place a limit on the amount of the jackpot; others let it accumulate from week to week until it is won.

Other winning variations include:
covering the eight numbers around the central free play square;
covering the numbers at the four corners of the card;
covering specific lines, or lines that intersect to form a stated letter of the alphabet.

When a game has been won, any player may keep or exchange his card(s) for a further game, or buy additional cards, but the selection of numbers starts afresh.

Drawing the lucky number

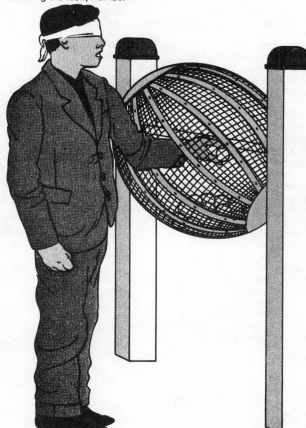

LOTTERIES

Organized lotteries as we know them today probably began in the fifteenth century. Then as now, they provided an attractive and easy means of raising money—be it for the benefit of the community or for less philanthropic reasons. Nowadays, many countries have lotteries that are organized or supervised by the state. Tickets or bonds are sold to the public and a small percentage of the income raised from their sale is used in prize money. The winning tickets are drawn by lot.

After the deduction of the running costs, the profit goes to the government—as revenue, for charity, or for other purposes.

The manner in which money is raised and given out in prizes may vary; occasionally the lottery may also be linked to an event such as a horse race. But in all lotteries, no skill or judgment is involved and the winners are determined solely by chance.

Many people—including those who would never consider themselves gamblers—are happy to spend a small amount on what may turn out to be a ticket to fortune!

Roulette

Spinning wheels have fascinated gamblers ever since ancient Greeks wagered on the turn of a battleshield spun on the point of a sword. Today roulette is one of the great casino games—being simple to play and yet offering the hope of dazzling success. The impersonality of the turning wheel lures players who believe that magical numerologies or "scientific systems" can help them "break the bank."

American wheel

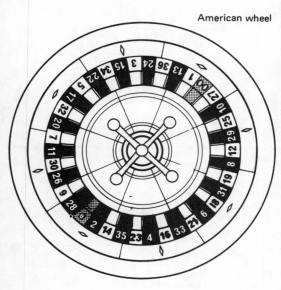

French wheel

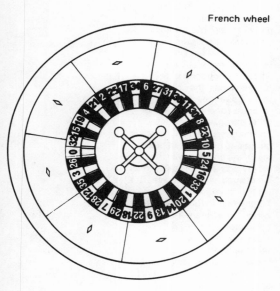

Equipment for roulette is:
a) a table, marked with the betting layout;
b) a roulette wheel;
c) a roulette ball;
d) a rake for the croupier;
e) betting chips.

The table is usually mahogany. A standard table has the betting layout at one end and the wheel at the other. A "double ended" table has a wheel at the center and layouts at each end.

The "wheel bowl" is a wood bowl-shaped recess in the table. It forms a stationary surrounding to the wheel. High on its side is a groove known as the "back track." Below the back track is the gently sloping "bottom track" —lined off into eight equal arcs, each with a diamond-shaped metal obstacle. At the bowl's center, hidden by the wheel, is the steel spindle on which the wheel spins.

The wheel (or "wheel head") is a solid wood disk. At its center is the "spinner"—a metal ornament used to spin the wheel.

The wheel's perimeter is divided by paint lines into 37 or 38 numbered sections of equal size.

The French wheel has sections numbered 1 through 36, plus one 0 section. There are never more than two odd or two even numbers consecutively. The American wheel has sections 1 through 36, plus 0 and 00 sections. Any number always has a consecutive number directly opposite it. On both types of wheel the sections are numbered in gold. They are colored alternately red and black, except that 0 and 00 sections are green. Directly next to each numbered section is a pocket painted the same color as the section. Pockets are divided by metal partitions known as separators.

The roulette ball is about $\frac{1}{2}$in–$\frac{3}{4}$in in diameter and made of ivory or plastic.

The betting layout is painted on green baize. Gold lines divide it into a large number of sections, each bearing a number, symbol, or label.

Players place chips in different positions on the layout according to the bets they wish to make.

Sections numbered 1 through 36 are colored black or red to match the corresponding section of the wheel.

French and American layouts differ in shape and labeling, but the only difference that affects the game is the 00 section on American layouts. (The addition of this section increases the casino's mathematical advantage.)

Players The number of players varies from one to as many as can get around the roulette table.

0		
1	2	3
4	5	6
7	8	9
10	11	12
13	14	15
16	17	18
19	20	21
22	23	24
25	26	27
28	29	30
31	32	33
34	35	36

PASSE   PAIR   MANQUE   IMPAIR

◆   ◇

12ᴾ 12ᴹ 12ᴰ   12ᴰ 12ᴹ 12ᴾ

French layout

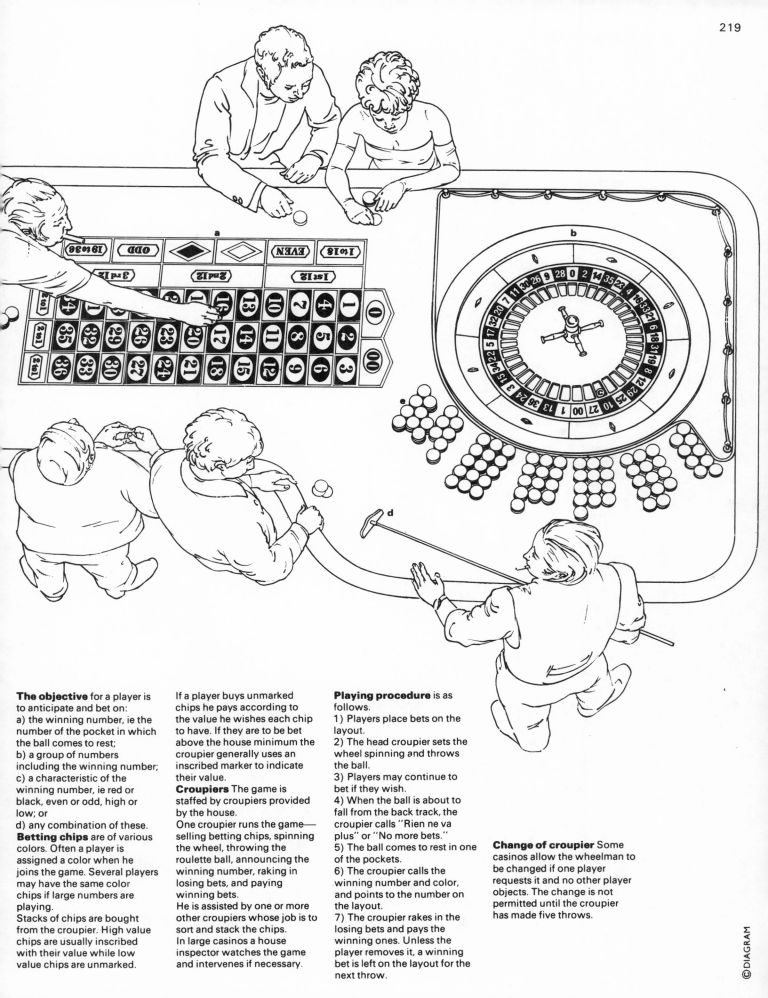

The objective for a player is to anticipate and bet on:
a) the winning number, ie the number of the pocket in which the ball comes to rest;
b) a group of numbers including the winning number;
c) a characteristic of the winning number, ie red or black, even or odd, high or low; or
d) any combination of these.
Betting chips are of various colors. Often a player is assigned a color when he joins the game. Several players may have the same color chips if large numbers are playing.
Stacks of chips are bought from the croupier. High value chips are usually inscribed with their value while low value chips are unmarked.

If a player buys unmarked chips he pays according to the value he wishes each chip to have. If they are to be bet above the house minimum the croupier generally uses an inscribed marker to indicate their value.
Croupiers The game is staffed by croupiers provided by the house.
One croupier runs the game—selling betting chips, spinning the wheel, throwing the roulette ball, announcing the winning number, raking in losing bets, and paying winning bets.
He is assisted by one or more other croupiers whose job is to sort and stack the chips.
In large casinos a house inspector watches the game and intervenes if necessary.

Playing procedure is as follows.
1) Players place bets on the layout.
2) The head croupier sets the wheel spinning and throws the ball.
3) Players may continue to bet if they wish.
4) When the ball is about to fall from the back track, the croupier calls "Rien ne va plus" or "No more bets."
5) The ball comes to rest in one of the pockets.
6) The croupier calls the winning number and color, and points to the number on the layout.
7) The croupier rakes in the losing bets and pays the winning ones. Unless the player removes it, a winning bet is left on the layout for the next throw.

Change of croupier Some casinos allow the wheelman to be changed if one player requests it and no other player objects. The change is not permitted until the croupier has made five throws.

©DIAGRAM

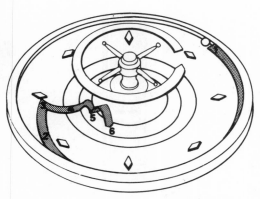

Throwing the ball

Throw of the ball
The croupier first takes the ball from the pocket in which it last came to rest.

If the wheel's spin has slowed, or if the casino requires the wheel's direction of spin to change for every throw, he then turns the wheel's spinner with whichever hand is most visible to the players. (If the direction of spin does not change, the spin is usually counterclockwise.)

Using the same hand, the croupier next throws the ball at speed into the wheel bowl so that it travels in the opposite direction to the wheel.

The path of the ball is as follows:
1) It travels at speed high against the bowl's side, in the groove known as the back track.

2) As its speed slows, it drops to the gently sloping bottom track.

3) On the bottom track the diamond-shaped obstacles can make it ricochet unpredictably.

4) It passes onto the outer wheel perimeter, where the contrary motion slows it abruptly and then carries it around with the wheel.

5) The ball may hover over two or three neighboring numbers, be hit by one of the separators, or go into a pocket and bounce out again.

6) Eventually it settles into one of the pockets.

Betting
There are three types of bet:
a) single numbers;
b) groups of numbers;
c) all numbers of a specified characteristic (red or black, odd number or even, high number or low).

Bets on a group of numbers are paid if any one of the numbers comes up.

Bets on a characteristic are paid if any number with that characteristic comes up.

Betting on American layout

Betting on French layout

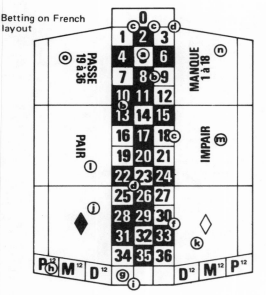

Bets available

Coverage	American term	French term	Payment	Numbers bet
1	Straight bet	En plein	35-1	Any one number (a)
2	Split bet	A cheval	17-1	Any two adjacent numbers (b)
3	Street bet	Transversale plein	11-1	Three numbers in a row; or 0, 1, 2; or 0, 2, 3; 00, 2, 3 (c)
4	Square/quarter	En carré	8-1	Four numbers in a square; or 0, 1, 2, 3 (d)
5 (US)	Line bet		6-1	0, 00, 1, 2, 3 (e)
6	Line bet	Transversale simple	5-1	Six numbers in two adjacent rows (f)
12	Column bet	Colonne	2-1	All 12 numbers in a vertical row (g)
12	Dozens bet	Douzaine	2-1	All 12 numbers in block 1-12, or 13-24, or 25-36 (h)
24	Two column bet	Colonne à cheval	2-1 on	All 24 numbers in adjacent vertical rows (i)
18	Black bet	Noir	1-1	All black numbers (j)
18	Red bet	Rouge	1-1	All red numbers (k)
18	Even number	Pair	1-1	All even numbers (l)
18	Odd number	Impair	1-1	All odd numbers (m)
18	Low number	Manque	1-1	All numbers 1 to 18 (n)
18	High number	Passe	1-1	All numbers 19 to 36 (o)

Placing bets on the layout
a) Single number bet: on any number, not touching any lines.

b) Two number bet: on the horizontal or vertical line separating any two numbers.

c) Three number bet: on the outside vertical line of the layout alongside any line of numbers. Or (on the French layout) to bet the 0, 1, 2 or 0, 2, 3: on the intersection of the three numbers.

d) Four number bet: on the intersection where any four numbers meet. Or (on the French layout) to bet 0, 1, 2, 3: on the outside vertical line of numbers against the line separating the two lines of numbers.

e) Five number line bet (American): on the outside vertical line of the layout against the lines separating 00 and 3.

f) Six number line bet: on the outside vertical line of the layout against the line separating any two lines of numbers.

g) Vertical 12 number bet: on any one of the three spaces at the base of the number columns.

h) Black 12 number bet: on the appropriate space on the layout. American: first, second, or third dozen. French: P¹², M¹², D¹²—either one of the pairs of these.

i) Vertical 24 number bet: on the line between any two of the three spaces at the base of the number columns.

j) Black number bet: on the space containing the black diamond.

k) Red number bet: on the space containing the red diamond.

l) Even number bet: on the space marked "even" (American) or "pair" (French).

m) Odd number bet: on the space marked "odd" (American) or "impair" (French).

n) Low number bet: on the space marked "1-18" (American) or "manque" (French).

o) High number bet: on the space marked "19-36" (American) or "passe" (French).

Boule

Boule is a simple version of roulette played in European casinos. It first appeared in the eighteenth century and remains popular because of its simplicity and low minimum stake.

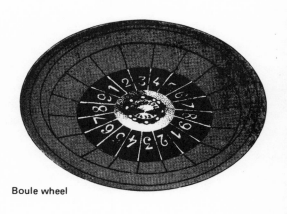

Boule wheel

Zero and double zero The 0 and 00 may be bet as single numbers in the usual way.
They may also be included in a two or three number bet with adjacent numbers, ie 1, 2, and 3. (On the American layout 0 cannot be bet with 3 or 00 with 1.)
They may also be included in a four number bet (French) or the five number bet (American).
They are not, however, covered by any other bet—either on a group of numbers or on characteristics of numbers. 0 and 00 are therefore known as house numbers.
If there is a bet on a group of numbers and the 0 (or 00) comes up, the bet is lost.
If there is a bet on a characteristic and the 0 (or 00) comes up, the bet is lost (American rules), put "in prison" (some European casinos), or half lost (other European casinos).
Bet in prison A bet in prison must be left on the layout, and its fate is decided by the next throw of the ball.
If the characteristic bet (eg red) comes up next, the bet is returned to the player but with no winnings. If the opposite characteristic (eg black) comes up, the bet is lost.
If the 0 comes up again, rules vary (since these are European casinos there is no 00):
a) in some casinos the player loses half the bet and the other half is returned;
b) elsewhere the player loses half the bet, while the other half remains in prison to have its fate decided by the next throw of the ball in exactly the same way (the bet in prison is halved for each further 0 that appears consecutively).
Betting limits House regulations lay down the minimum and maximum bets allowed.
The house advantage derives from the difference between the true odds and the odds offered.
The house advantage where there is both 0 and 00 is 5.26% on all bets—except for the five number line bet, which has a 7.8% house advantage.
When there is only a single 0, the general house advantage is 2.7%. If 1–1 bets are put in prison when the 0 appears (or half the stake is returned), the house advantage on even money bets is only 1.35%.

Equipment consists of a table, bowl, ball, betting layout, and betting chips or cash.
The table has at one end an area of polished wood centering on the bowl. At the other end there is an area of green baize printed with one or two layouts.
The bowl is a wood recess in the table; it contains no wheel or moving part.
Since the bowl is set slightly below the table's surface it is edged by a low rim. A groove cut into this rim runs right around the bowl's circumference.
The surface of the bowl itself slopes gently down toward a slightly raised hub at its center. This surface is divided into 18 segments, numbered consecutively in a clockwise direction from 1 to 9 twice.
At the point of each segment, just before the raised hub, are one or more holes to catch the ball. The holes are marked with the number of the segments to which they belong.
The holes are colored alternately black and red, except that the two 5s are any contrasting color (usually yellow).
Holes of segments with the same number are always the same color.
The ball is made of rubber. Ball sizes vary.
The betting layout is an oblong area divided into sections and printed in gold on the green baize.
One section is printed with one or more red diamonds and another with one or more black diamonds. All other sections are labeled in gold.
Players place bets on different positions on the layout according to the bets they wish to make.
Players The number of players may be from one to as many as can get around the table.

Croupiers The game is staffed by one or more croupiers provided by the house. If there are two croupiers, one controls the play of the ball and the other supervises the betting.
The objective for a player is to anticipate and bet on:
a) the winning number, ie the number of the hole in which the ball comes to rest; or
b) a characteristic of the winning number, ie red or black, even or odd, high or low.
Playing procedure is as follows.
1) Players place bets on the layout.
2) The croupier calls "Rien ne va plus," after which no more bets may be placed.
3) The croupier throws the ball into the bowl so that it travels at speed around the groove in the bowl's rim.
4) The ball slows, descends toward the bowl's hub, and comes to rest in one of the holes.
5) The croupier calls the winning number and color.
6) The croupier rakes in losing bets and pays winning ones.
Betting There are two types of bet:
a) single numbers;
b) all numbers of a specified characteristic (red or black, even or odd, high number or low).
Bets Players may make the following bets.
a) Single number bet: bets the number shown on the section of the layout on which the bet is placed.
b) Black numbers bet: bets all black numbers.
c) Red numbers bet: bets all red numbers.
d) Odd numbers bet: bets all odd numbers except the 5.
e) Even numbers bet: bets all even numbers.
f) Low numbers bet: bets all numbers below 5.
g) High numbers bet: bets all numbers above 5.

Betting on boule layout

(f) MANQUE	1234	
1	(d) IMPAIRS 1379	2
3	5	4
6		7
8	PAIRS 2468 (e)	9
PASSE	6789 (g)	

(b) ◆ (a) ◇ (c)

The five Players may bet on the 5 as a single number, but it is not covered by any bet on a characteristic.
Betting limits are usually low.
Settlement A successful single number bet is paid at 7 to 1. All other bets are paid at 1 to 1.

©DIAGRAM

14 Children's party games

Musical games

These are all active games in which players move around to music. When the music stops, the players must immediately stand still or change what they are doing. All the games require someone to organize the music.

MUSICAL CHAIRS
Play Chairs are placed around the room in a large circle. There should be one chair fewer than the number of players.
The players stand in the circle and, when the music starts, all dance around.
When the music stops, each player tries to sit on a seat.
The player left without a seat is eliminated.
One chair is then removed from the circle and the music is restarted.
The last person to stay in the game is the winner.

MUSICAL BUMPS
This is like musical chairs, except that it is played without the chairs.
When the music stops, players sit down on the floor. The last person to sit down is out.

OWNERSHIP MUSICAL CHAIRS
In this version of musical chairs there is one chair per person.
Before the music starts each player sits on a chair and marks it as his own.
When the music starts, the players dance around the circle in the same direction.
When the music stops, the players continue moving around the circle. As each player comes to his own chair he sits down. The last player to sit on his chair is out and remains seated.
The organizer may vary the game by calling directions to the players as they move around—eg walk backward, or turn to the right.
The last person to stay in the game is the winner.

MUSICAL BLACKOUT
This is played like musical chairs except that when the music stops, the lights are switched off for five seconds. When the lights are switched on again, any player who has not found a chair is eliminated.

MUSICAL HOTCH POTCH
In this game, players race for objects instead of chairs.
Play A pile of objects, numbering one fewer than the number of players, is placed in the center of the room.
When the music starts, players hop or dance around the pile.
When the music stops, each player dives for an article from the pile.
The larger the objects, the less likely are the players to bump their heads!
The player left without an object is out.
One object is removed from the pile and the game continues.

Musical hotch potch

MUSICAL MAGIC CARPET
The organizer chooses a part of the floor as a "magic patch" but keeps its position a secret.
Play When the music starts the players dance in pairs.
When the music stops, they stop dancing.
The pair nearest the magic patch wins a prize, and the game continues until all the prizes are won.
Alternatively, the game can be played for points. The pair nearest the magic patch scores a point, and the game is won by the pair with most points after an agreed time.

HIGH STEPPERS
Preparation Pairs of chairs with their fronts touching are placed around the room to form a circle of hurdles.
Play The players space themselves around the room in pairs.
When the music starts, they march around the room and must climb over the hurdles as they come to them.
When the music stops, any pair touching a hurdle is eliminated.
The music starts again and the game continues.
The winning pair is the last one left in the game.

High steppers

Musical chairs

MUSICAL STATUES

Players dance around the room to music.

When the music stops, the players immediately stop dancing and stand as still as statues.

Any player seen moving after the music stops is eliminated. The music is started again fairly quickly and the game continues.

Eliminated players can help to spot moving statues.

The last player to remain as a dancer is the winner.

Statues

MUSICAL RINGS

This is a game for a large room and many players.

Play Players space themselves around the room. When the music starts, they dance around.

When the music stops, the organizer announces a number and players quickly arrange themselves into groups of this size.

Any spare players unable to form a group of the right size are out.

The game ends when only two players remain. These players are the winners.

MUSICAL ISLANDS

This is another game for a large room.

Preparation Small mats, newspapers, pieces of cardboard, etc are scattered over the floor to form "islands."

Play When the music starts, players walk around in a circle.

When the music stops, players must stand on an island. More than one player may stand on one island. Anyone unable to get onto an island or falling off into the "water" is eliminated. The music starts again and the game continues.

Islands are gradually removed during the game.

The last player left in the game is the winner.

Musical islands

GODS AND GODDESSES

This is a game requiring fairly slow and gentle music.

Play Each player is given a book. When the music starts, the players walk around the room balancing the books on their heads.

When the music stops, each player goes down on one knee. If a player's book falls off, he is eliminated.

The music starts again and the game continues.

The last player left in the game is the winner.

Gods and goddesses

Blindfold games

In these games the blindfolded player's movements are a source of much amusement. It is a good idea if an adult ties on the blindfold and checks that it is tied neither too tight nor so that the blind man can peep out.

Blind man's buff

BLIND MAN'S BUFF
Objective A blindfolded player tries to catch and identify another player.
Play A "blind man" is chosen and blindfolded. He is turned around three times in the center of the room and then left on his own.
The other players dance around, taunting him and dodging out of his way to avoid capture.
When the blind man catches someone, he has two or three guesses at the name of his prisoner.
If he guesses correctly, the prisoner becomes the new blind man.
If wrong, he continues to be the blind man and tries to catch another player.

TEN STEP BUFF
Objective As in blind man's buff, a blindfolded player tries to catch and identify another player.
Play The blind man stands in the center of the room.
The other players scatter around him and stand still.
The blind man takes ten paces and stretches out his hands.
If he touches a player, that player becomes the blind man. If not, he takes another ten paces and tries again.

SQUEAK-PIGGY-SQUEAK
Objective A blindfolded player attempts to identify another player by getting him to squeak.
Play One player is blindfolded, given a cushion, and turned around three times in the center of the room.
The others sit down around the room.
The blind man must then place his cushion on another player's lap and sit on it.
He then calls "squeak-piggy-squeak" and the person he is sitting on squeaks like a pig.
If the blind man recognizes the person, he changes places with him.
Once the new person is blindfolded, the players all change seats before he tries to sit on a player's lap.

BLIND MAN'S STICK
Objective A blind man tries to identify a player from the noises he makes.
Play One player is blindfolded and given a stick. The others form a circle and slowly move around him.
If the blind man touches a player with his stick, the player must grasp the stick. The blind man then asks the player to imitate a noise—for example a creaking door.
If the blind man guesses the player's name, that player becomes the new blind man.
If he guesses incorrectly, the blind man must touch another player.

BLIND POSTMAN
Objective A blindfolded player tries to sit in a vacant seat while two players are changing places.
Preparation One person is chosen to be postmaster. All the others choose a town, and the postmaster makes a list of their choices.
Play One player is blindfolded and becomes the first postman. All the other players sit in a circle. The postman stands in the center of the circle, and is turned around several times by the postmaster.
The postmaster then announces that a letter has been sent between two of the towns on his list, for example from Cambridge to Birmingham.
The two players whose towns are called then try to change places before the postman sits in one of their empty seats.
If the postman gets a seat, the player without a seat becomes the new postman.
More than one letter may be sent at a time.
Mode of travel The postmaster can also say how the letter traveled—and so indicate how the players should move. For example, if the letter went:
a) by air, they hop;
b) by sea, they walk backward;
c) by train, they crawl; and
d) by Pony Express, they bunny hop.

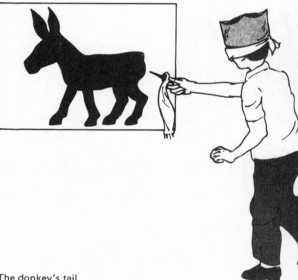

The donkey's tail

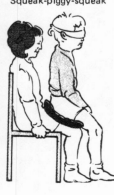

Squeak-piggy-squeak

Jailer

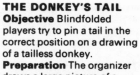

THE DONKEY'S TAIL
Objective Blindfolded players try to pin a tail in the correct position on a drawing of a tailless donkey.

Preparation The organizer draws a large picture of a donkey without a tail and fastens it onto a pinboard propped upright.
He also makes a donkey's tail out of cardboard or wool and sticks a large pin through the body end.

Play Each player in turn is blindfolded and turned around so that he is in front of and facing the donkey.
He is then given the tail and attempts to pin it on the correct part of the donkey.
The organizer marks the position of each player's attempt.
The player who pins nearest the correct place is the winner.

DRAW THE ELEPHANT'S TAIL
This is similar to the donkey's tail but instead of pinning on a tail players draw one.
Each blindfolded player is given a crayon and draws a tail on a picture of an elephant (or any other animal).

BLIND MAN'S SORT OUT
Objective Blindfolded players race to sort a collection of objects into categories.

Preparation The organizer collects a selection of buttons, screws, nails, beans, beads, etc.

Play The game is usually organized as an elimination contest—with two players competing at a time.
The objects are divided into two similar piles. The first two players are then blindfolded and each placed in front of a pile of objects.
When the organizer calls "Go!" each of the blindfolded players starts sorting his objects into groups of buttons, screws, etc.
The first player to finish sorting his objects into categories goes forward into the next round of the contest.
All the other players then compete in pairs, and the winners all go into the next round.
Further rounds are held until only two players remain for the final. The winner of the final wins the game.

A BLIND JUDGMENT
Play One player is blindfolded and placed on a "seat of judgment."
Another player then stands quietly in front of him, and the player in the judgment seat gives a brief description of whoever he thinks might be standing in front of him.
If the other players think that the "blind judgment" was reasonably accurate, the player in front of the

blindfolded player becomes the new blind man.
If his judgment was inaccurate, the original blindman must pass judgment on another player.

MURALS
Preparation The organizer cuts out large pieces of paper for drawing on.

Play Each player in turn is blindfolded, given a crayon, and asked to draw a picture on a piece of paper pinned on the wall.
The subject for the picture is chosen by the other players— good examples are a house, a person, or some kind of animal.
The artist feels the edges of the paper and has one minute in which to draw the chosen subject.
When everyone has had a turn, the drawings can be judged by an adult or by all the players together.

Murals

THIEVES
Objective A blindfolded player tries to catch players stealing from him.

Play One player is blindfolded and given a rolled newspaper to hold in his hand.
The blindfolded player sits in the middle of a circle made by other players, and a pile of treasure—necklaces, brooches, bracelets, etc—is placed in front of him.
Players in the circle quietly take it in turns to steal a piece of treasure.
If the blindman hears a thief, he strikes at him with the newspaper and calls "thief, thief."
If he touches a thief, the thief must return empty-handed to his place to await his next turn.
The thief who collects most treasure wins the game.

JAILER
This is similar to thieves except that the blindfolded man is guarding a bunch of keys.
The organizer names a player, who then has to take the keys from the jailer and carry them around the outside of the circle and back to his place.
The jailer listens for the thief and if he hears him points at him.
If the jailer locates the thief the thief takes over as jailer.

BLIND MAN'S TREASURE HUNT

Objective Each player chooses a parcel by touch and tries to identify the contents before opening it.

Preparation Objects of different shape and feel are wrapped up—one parcel per player. The parcels are piled on a table.

Play Each player in turn is blindfolded and led to the table to choose a parcel. He then takes off his blindfold and waits until all the players have chosen a parcel.

Each player then guesses what is in his parcel before opening it.

Presents This game is an excellent way to give out small presents at a party.

SWEET TOOTH

Objective Each player tries to identify foods that he has eaten while blindfolded.

Play Each player sits down and is then provided with a plate of goodies such as chocolate, fudge, nuts, liquorice, and pieces of orange.

When all the players have eaten or tasted all their goodies, any leftovers are taken away and the blindfolds are removed.

The children then write down what they think they have eaten.

If the players are too young to write, they can whisper their answers to an adult.

MURDER IN THE DARK

Although players are not blindfolded for this game, a "detective" attempts to identify an unseen "murderer." The opening stages of play take place in the dark.

Preparation One small piece of paper per player is folded and placed in a hat. One is marked with a cross, another with a D, and all the others are blank.

Play Each player draws a piece of paper from the hat. The player who gets the paper with the cross is the murderer and the one with the D the detective.

The detective first leaves the room and the lights are switched off.

The other players then dance slowly around the room in the dark. The murderer catches a victim and puts his hands on the victim's shoulders. The victim must scream and fall to the ground.

The lights are then switched on and the detective is called in.

The detective tries to identify the murderer by questioning everybody except the victim. All the players except the murderer must answer his questions truthfully.

After the questioning the detective accuses his prime suspect of the murder, saying "I charge you (name of suspect) with the murder of (name of victim)."

If the accusation is correct, the murderer must admit his guilt.

Hunting and observation games

Hunting games have always been popular and there is a great variety of games of this type. In some, players hunt for hidden objects. In others, they hunt for another player who may or may not himself be hidden. Observation is obviously a vital part of hunting, but there are also games of pure observation and memory.

HUNT THE THIMBLE

This very popular game is usually played with a thimble, but any other small object will do just as well.

Play All the players but one leave the room while this player hides the thimble somewhere in the room or on his person.

He then calls the other players back into the room to look for it.

The game is won by the first player to find the thimble and take it to the player who hid it. The finder then has a turn at hiding the thimble.

SIT DOWN HUNT THE THIMBLE

This is played in the same way as the last game except that when a player sees where the thimble is hidden he sits down on the floor.

The last person to see the thimble and sit down must pay a forfeit.

The player who sat down first has the next turn at hiding the thimble.

SINGING HUNT THE THIMBLE

This is played like hunt the thimble except that only one player leaves the room while one of the others hides it.

On his return, the players who stayed in the room try to guide him to the thimble by singing. They sing more loudly as he moves closer to the thimble and more quietly as he moves away.

HOT AND COLD THIMBLE

As in singing hunt the thimble, only one player leaves the room while the thimble is hidden.

The other players help him find the thimble by telling him how "hot" he is in different parts of the room.

If he is in the wrong part of the room he is "very cold" or "cold." As he approaches the thimble he is "getting warmer"—until he becomes "warm," "hot," and finally "very hot" just before he touches the thimble.

Hunt the ring

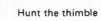

Hunt the thimble

BLINDFOLD OBSTACLE WALK

Preparation Everyone lays out obstacles—a pile of books, a glass of water, cushions, etc—from one end of the room to the other.
Play Several of the players volunteer to walk the course. They then leave the room to be blindfolded.
Meanwhile the others quickly and quietly remove all the obstacles.

Each of the blindfolded volunteers is then brought in one at a time.
The blindfolded player then attempts to walk across the room without hitting the obstacles. To add to the fun all the onlookers utter appropriate gasps and shudders.
When he has completed the "course" the blindfold is removed.

NELSON'S EYE

This game plays on a blindfolded person's heightened imagination.
Play Several volunteers who do not already know the game are asked to leave the room. They are blindfolded and brought back into the room one at a time.
One of the other players begins by asking the blind man to feel "Nelson's good leg"—and the blind man's hands are guided so that he can feel someone's leg.
He is then asked to feel Nelson's bad leg—and his hands are guided to a chair leg.
Next the blind man must feel Nelson's good arm—and feels someone's arm. Then he must feel Nelson's bad arm, which can be a stuffed stocking.

This is followed by Nelson's good eye, which can be a marble.
Finally he is asked to feel Nelson's bad eye—and is presented with a squashy pickled onion or a soft flour and water mixture.
The blind man usually becomes rather squeamish at this point—much to the amusement of the other players!

Nelson's eye

HUNT THE SLIPPER

In this game one player tries to find which of the others is holding the slipper. A little acting greatly adds to the fun of this game.
Play All the players but one sit with their feet touching in a circle on the floor. These players are the cobblers.
The other player has a small slipper (or shoe) which he says is in need of repair. He then gives the slipper to the cobblers and asks them to mend it.
He walks away and returns several times to see if it is ready. Each time the cobblers pretend that it is not quite finished. Finally, however, they admit that they have lost it.
The hunt The cobblers now pass the slipper from one to another under their knees.
The customer tries to touch a cobbler while he is holding the slipper. When he succeeds, the slipper is "found" and the customer and the cobbler holding the slipper change places.

HUNT THE RING

This is another game in which one player tries to find which of the others is holding an object.
Preparation A curtain ring is threaded onto a long piece of string. The two ends of the string are then tied together with a knot that is small enough to allow the ring to pass easily over it.
Play One player stands in the middle of the room and the others form a circle around him.
The players in the circle each hold the string with both hands—and one of them also holds the ring so that the player in the middle cannot see it.
When the player in the middle says "Go!" the others pass the string through their hands—passing the ring from hand to hand at the same time.
The player in the center tries to locate the ring by touching any hand he thinks conceals it.
A player must open his hand if it is touched. If it concealed the ring, he must change places with the player in the center. If his hand is empty, the original player stays in the middle.

UP JENKINS!

This game is similar to hunt the ring but is played with any small object instead of a ring on a string.
Play One player sits on the floor in the middle of a circle formed by the other players sitting around him.
The players in the circle sit with their hands behind their backs and one of them holds the small object.
When the player in the middle says "Go!" the players in the circle all pass, or pretend to pass, the ring around the circle behind their backs.
When the player in the middle says "Up Jenkins!" the players in the circle, including the one with the object, must all raise their clenched fists.
When the player in the middle says "Down Jenkins!" the players in the circle must put their hands palms down on the ground—and the player with the object must, of course, do his best to keep the object concealed at this stage of the game.
The player in the middle then tries to identify which of the players is hiding the object.

Jigsaw hunt

Easter egg hunt

© DIAGRAM

Finding the thimble

BEAN HUNT
Preparation The organizer hides a large quantity of beans around the room. A small container such as a paper cup is needed for each player.
Play Each player collects as many beans as he can within a given time limit. The player who finds most beans is the winner.

BUTTERFLY HUNT
This game is played in the same way as bean hunt except that players look for paper butterflies hidden by the organizer. The winner is the player who finds most butterflies after an agreed time limit.

HIDDEN OBJECTS
In this game players look for objects hidden all around the house.
Preparation The organizer hides about 20 objects in different rooms. It should be possible to see the objects without moving anything. A list of the objects is prepared for each of the players.
Play Each player is given a list and tries to locate the objects, noting down wherever he finds one.
The game is won by the first player to locate all the objects and take his list to the organizer.

JIGSAW HUNT
Preparation One "jigsaw" is needed for each player. The organizer makes the jigsaws by cutting picture postcards into four irregular pieces.
Three pieces from each jigsaw are hidden in the room.
Play Each player is given one of the jigsaw pieces that was not hidden.
The first player to find the three pieces missing from his jigsaw wins the game.

PRESENT HUNT
Each player is given a piece of paper with a written clue to guide him to his present.

COLOR HUNT
This game is played in the same way as present hunt except that each player is given a small piece of wrapping paper and then hunts for and keeps the present wrapped in the same sort of paper.

EASTER EGG HUNT
Each player hunts for a chocolate Easter egg wrapped in a particular color of paper. Alternatively, a tag with the name of one of the players may be attached to each hidden egg.

DETECTIVE TREASURE HUNT
This game requires more preparation and ingenuity than most hunting games.
Preparation The organizer thinks up a series of clues such that the solution of each clue will lead players to the hiding place of the next one. The solution of the last clue may lead to:
a) a prize for the first player or pair to find it;
b) a pile of presents, one for each player; or
c) the party table.
Play Sometimes players take part on their own. Alternatively they may play in pairs.
The organizer gives each player or pair the first clue. As the other clues are discovered, they should be left in their places for the other players to find.

CARD HUNT
In this game players form two teams and look for playing cards hidden around the room.
Preparation Two decks of playing cards are needed. The cards from one deck are hidden around the room within reach of the players. The other deck is divided into two piles—one of red cards and one of black cards.
Play Each member of one team is given a black card and each member of the other team is given a red one.
Each player searches for the hidden card that matches the card he has been given.
When a player finds the card he is looking for he takes it to the organizer who gives him another card of the same color.
Play continues in this way until one of the teams has found all its cards.

STOREKEEPERS
This is another team hunting game. It is best if there are about four teams each with three or more members. Each team represents a different store.
Preparation The organizer takes a number of plain cards and writes the names of a commodity on each one. These commodities should be items sold in the stores that will be represented. There should be an equal number of cards for each store. These cards are hidden around the room.
Play The players form teams and each team is given the name of a store—for example the bakery or the grocery store.
The players are told how many commodities are missing from the stores.
Each team chooses a "storekeeper," who stands in the middle of the room. The other players then look for the cards and when they find a card for their own store take it to their storekeeper.
The game is won by the team that first finds all its hidden commodities.

CUT-OUT PAIRS
This is a good game for introducing players to each other at the start of a party.
Preparation All sorts of pictures are cut out of magazines, comics, etc. Each picture is pasted onto cardboard and cut into two oddly shaped pieces. (Picture postcards may be used to save time.) There should be one picture for each pair of players.
Play Each player is given one piece of a picture. He then tries to find the player with the other half of the same picture.
When two players have a complete picture they write a suitable caption for it.
Pictures and captions are displayed and the writers of the funniest caption may win a prize.

MOTHERS AND BABIES
This is another pairing game along the lines of cut-out pairs. For this game players are given a card showing a mother or a baby animal—for example a cow or a calf, a frog or a tadpole. Players then have to find the player with the card showing the other member of their family.

HIDE AND SEEK
Children enjoy organizing this game themselves.
Play Players choose somewhere to be "home"— for example a chair or a door. They also choose someone to be the first "seeker." The seeker then shuts his eyes and counts to 40 while all the other players hide.
When he reaches 40, he shouts "Ready!" and goes and looks for the other players.
When he finds a player, that player must try and reach home before the seeker can touch him.
The first player to reach home untouched becomes the next seeker.

SARDINES
This is a type of hide and seek usually played in the dark. The more rooms the children can play in the more exciting the game becomes.
Play One player is chosen as the first sardine. He then leaves the room and finds a place to hide—preferably somewhere big enough for most of the others to squeeze in too.
When the first sardine has had time to hide, the other players split up and look for him.
When a player finds the hiding place he creeps in and hides with the first sardine.
The last sardine to find the others usually becomes the first sardine for the next game.

KIM'S GAME
Sometimes called memory test or the memory game, this is an excellent test of the players' powers of observation.
Preparation The organizer puts about 20 small objects on a tray. He then covers them with a cloth until play begins.
Play The organizer uncovers the objects and allows the players about 3 minutes in which to memorize them. The players are not allowed to make any notes.
At the end of the time limit the organizer covers the tray with the cloth and gives each player a pencil and paper.
The players are then asked to write down as many of the objects as they can.
The winner is the player who remembers most objects.

MISMATCHES

This is a team observation game, in which one team tries to spot all the "mismatches" made by the other.

Play Players divide into two teams. One team leaves the room while the other makes its mismatches by altering things in the room.

For example the team making the mismatches might change the position of objects—such as turning a vase upside down —or might change something about a person—such as putting a cardigan on inside out.

At the end of a time limit the other team returns and tries to spot the mismatches.

At the end of another time limit, any mismatches that have not been noticed score one point to the team that made them.

The teams then change roles, and the winning team is the team that scores most points.

RUMORS

This is a competitive form of the popular old game of Chinese whispers.

Objective Each player tries to pass on a message that has been whispered to him.

Play Players divide into two equal teams and each team sits down in a circle. Players take it in turns to be team leader. The organizer decides on a message and whispers it to the two leaders.

Each leader then whispers the message to the player to his right. This player then whispers the message as he heard it to the player to his right, and so on around the circle. Whisperers are not allowed to give the message more than once.

The last player of each team tells the leader the message as he heard it. The leader then tells the message as it began. The team that kept the message most intact wins the game.

WRONG!

In this game players try to spot deliberate errors in a story that is read to them.

Preparation The organizer writes a short story in which there are numerous errors of fact—for example he might say that he went to the antique shop and bought a new clock.

Play The organizer reads out the story.

If a player spots a mistake he shouts "Wrong!" The first player to call out a mistake scores one point. A player who shouts when there has been no mistake loses one point.

The player with most points at the end of the story wins the game.

HAPPY TRAVELERS

Each player tries to be the first to sort the pages of a newspaper into the correct order.

Preparation For each player the pages of a newspaper are put together in the wrong order—some pages may be upside down or back to front —and then folded.

Play Players sit facing each other in two rows. They should sit very close together like passengers on a crowded train.

Each player is given one of the newspapers.

At the word "Go!" each player tries to rearrange the pages of his newspaper into the correct order.

The first player to succeed wins the game.

PRINTERS' ERRORS

In this game players try to set out jumbled lines of a printed article into their correct order.

Preparation A jumbled article is needed for each player. The organizer makes as many copies of the article as he needs and then jumbles each one by cutting it into pieces after each line.

Play Each player is given his jumbled article. When the organizer gives the signal players start to sort out their articles.

The winner is the first player to put his article into the correct order.

Hide and seek

Trickery games

In these games players try to trick others into carrying out some action for which they will be penalized. As these games are usually played, a player must drop out if he makes a mistake. Alternatively, players may be allowed to stay in the game if they carry out a forfeit.

Simon says

SIMON SAYS
Simon says is an old party game that remains a great favorite. It is sometimes called O'Grady says.
Play One player is the leader and the others spread around the room in front of him.
The leader orders the others to do various actions—such as touching their toes or raising their arms.
Whether or not they must obey his orders depends on how the orders are given.
If the leader begins the order with the words "Simon says," the players must obey.
If he does not begin with these words, they must not do the action.
If a player makes a mistake he is out of the game.
The leader encourages mistakes by:
a) giving rapid orders;
b) developing a rhythm with a repeated pattern of movements and then breaking it;
c) doing the actions himself for the others to follow.
The last person left in the game is the winner and becomes the next leader.

DO THIS, DO THAT!
This is played like Simon says except for the way in which the leader gives his orders.
If the leader says "Do this!" the players should mimic his action.
If he says "Do that!" they should remain still.

IN THE DITCH
This game is simpler than Simon says but calls for a lot of energy.
Play A line is marked along the floor with cushions or two parallel strands of yarn.
One player is the leader and the others space themselves out down one side of the line. One side is called "the bank" and the other side "the ditch."
The leader orders the players to jump from side to side by calling out "In the ditch!" or "On the bank!" He can try to trick the players by calling the orders very quickly and repeating an order instead of alternating them.
A player must drop out if he makes a mistake. The winner is the last person left in the game.

Parcel games

Everyone loves to unwrap a parcel and find a present inside. Pass the parcel is an old party favorite and is enjoyed by children of all ages. There are also a number of entertaining variations on the parcel-opening theme.

Pass the parcel

PASS THE PARCEL
Preparation A small present is wrapped in layer after layer of paper. Each layer should be secured with thread, glue, or a rubber band.
Music is needed for this game—and a non-player to start and stop it.
Play Players sit in a circle and one of them holds the parcel. When the music starts, players pass the parcel around the circle to the right.
When the music stops whoever is holding the parcel unwraps one layer of wrapping. The music is then restarted and the parcel passed on again.
The game continues in this way until someone takes off the final wrapping and so wins the present.

MY LITTLE BIRD

This game is played in countries all over the world. Other names for it include flying high and birds fly.

Play One player is the leader and the others stand in a row in front of him. Alternatively everyone sits around a table.

The leader starts by saying "My little bird is lively, is lively," and then goes on to name something followed by the word "fly"—for example he might say "eggs fly."

If whatever he names can fly—for example cockatoos—the players raise their arms and wave them about.

If it cannot fly—as with eggs—the players should remain still.

A player who makes a mistake is out. The last player left in the game wins.

YES-NO BEANS

In yes-no beans players must guard against being tricked while at the same time trying to trick others.

Play Each player starts with five beans or any other unit of exchange.

The players circulate round the room, asking each other questions and replying to any questions that another player asks them. Players must not use the words yes or no in any of their replies.

Whenever a player succeeds in tricking another into saying yes or no, he gives that player one of his beans.

The first player to get rid of all his beans wins the game.

LAUGHING HANDKERCHIEF

This game is often a riot of infectious laughter. It will be won only by a player who can start and stop laughing at will.

Play One player is the leader and stands in the center of a circle formed by the others. The leader has a handkerchief which he drops as a signal for the other players to laugh. They must start laughing as soon as he lets go of the handkerchief and must stop when it touches the floor.

A player is out if he does not laugh the whole of the time that the handkerchief is falling or if he continues laughing after it has landed.

The last player left in the game wins and becomes the next leader.

In the ditch

FORFEITS PARCEL

This game is the same as pass the parcel except that a forfeit is written on each layer of wrapping.

A player who is holding the parcel when the music stops must carry out the next forfeit before taking off the next layer of wrapping.

MYSTERY PARCEL

Preparation A parcel is prepared as for pass the parcel but with a message written on each layer of wrapping. Typical messages are "Give to the player with the whitest teeth!" and "Pass to the person to your left!"

Music is needed.

Play The parcel is passed around to music as in pass the parcel.

When the music stops, the player holding the parcel reads out the message and hands the parcel to the player who fits the description in the message. This player then unwraps the next layer of paper before the music is restarted.

HOT PARCEL

Preparation A present is given a single strong wrapper.

Music is needed.

Play is as for pass the parcel except that when the music stops the person holding the parcel drops out of the game. The last player left in the game unwraps the parcel and wins the present.

LUCKY CHOCOLATE GAME

Preparation A chocolate bar is wrapped in several layers of paper. Each layer should be secured with thread.

The parcel and a knife and fork are then put on a breadboard on a table.

A chair with a hat, scarf, and gloves on it is then placed at the table.

One die is also needed.

Play The players sit in a circle on the floor and take it in turns to throw the die.

If a player throws a 6, he puts on the hat, scarf, and gloves, sits on the chair, and uses the knife and fork to remove the wrappings.

If another player throws a 6 he changes places with the player at the table.

When the chocolate is unwrapped, players at the table use the knife and fork to eat the chocolate.

The game continues until all the chocolate has been eaten.

Lucky chocolate game

Contests

In these games players perform various feats of skill. Some of the games are a test of physical strength or ability, others need ingenuity in order to outwit opponents. It is a good idea in case of dispute for someone to act as referee.

Card and bucket contest

Balloon flights

Limbo

Apple on a string

BALLOON FLIGHTS
Objective Each player tries to flick a balloon the farthest distance.
Play Players form a straight line. Each person balances a balloon on the palm of one hand. Balloons should all be a different color, or marked with the players' initials.
The referee counts "One, two, three, go," and each player then flicks his balloon with the first finger and thumb of his other hand.
The player whose balloon makes the longest flight is the winner.

STATIC ELECTRICITY
Objective Each player tries to have the most balloons clinging to a wall at the end of a time limit.
Preparation Plenty of balloons are inflated and their necks tied.
Play The balloons are placed in a pile in the center of the room and each player is allocated an area of wall.
On the word "Go," each player takes a balloon, rubs it on his clothing to create static electricity, and then tries to make it cling to the wall.
If he succeeds, he takes another balloon and does the same, and so on with as many balloons as possible.
If a balloon falls off the wall any player may use it again.
End At the end of a time limit, the player with the most balloons still clinging to the wall wins.

CARD AND BUCKET CONTEST
Objective Players try to flick all their cards into a bucket or other large container.
Play Each player is given ten playing cards—preferably old ones—and writes down which ones they are.
The players then form a large circle around a bucket. At a call of "Go!" each player tries to flick his cards into the bucket.
When all the players have flicked all their cards, the cards in the bucket are identified.
The winner is the player who gets most cards into the bucket. Several rounds may be played.

APPLE PARING
Objective Each player tries to peel the longest unbroken paring from an apple.
Play Each player is given an apple, a knife, and a plate. All the apples and all the knives should be of similar quality.
The players then peel their apples.
The winner is the one to produce the longest and narrowest paring.

CANDY WRAPPER

This game is similar to apple paring, but instead of fruit the children get a candy to eat.
Objective Each player aims to tear a candy wrapper into a long, thin, spiral strip.
Play Each player is given a candy, which he unwraps. While eating the candy, he tears its wrapping paper, starting at the outer edge and tearing round and round towards the center.
The player with the longest unbroken strip of paper wins.

HOPPIT

Objective Each player tries to hop the farthest while making progressively larger hops.
Play Using strands of yarn, two straight lines are marked on the floor. The lines are about 1ft apart at one end of the room and fan out to about 6ft apart at the other.
Players take turns at hopping back and forth across the two lines. They start at the narrow end and move down the room.
The player who gets the farthest down the lines before failing to hop right across the two lines, is the winner.

SINGING HIGH JUMP

This is a test of vocal range—each player aims to sing the most widely spaced low and high notes.
Play The referee stands by a "take-off" line ready to score each player's attempt.
In turn, each player runs up to the take-off line, stops, and sings two notes: the first as low as possible, the second as high as possible.
The player who makes the highest musical "jump" is the winner.

APPLE ON A STRING

An old favorite for Halloween, players try, without using their hands, to eat apples suspended from strings.
Play A piece of string is hung across the room, well above head height.
One apple (or currant bun) per person is suspended from it, also on a string.
The players try to eat their apples or buns without using their hands.
The first player to eat the apple down to its core, or to completely eat the bun, is the winner.

LIMBO

Originally a West Indian acrobatic dance, this is a test of suppleness and sustained contortion.
Play Two people gently hold a long stick horizontally and at chest height.
Each player in turn bends backward and edges himself under the stick.
He must neither touch the floor with his hands nor touch the stick.
If a player, after two attempts, fails to pass under the stick he is eliminated.
After each round the stick is lowered a little.
The last person to stay in the game is the winner.

GRANDMOTHER'S FOOTSTEPS

Objective Each player tries to be the first one to creep up behind the "grandmother" without her seeing him move.
Play One person is chosen as the grandmother and stands with his face against a wall and eyes shut.
The other players line up across the opposite wall. When everyone is ready, the players start to creep up behind the grandmother—but whenever she looks round they must "freeze" into statues.
The grandmother may look round as often as she likes. If she sees anyone moving, she points to him and he has to go back to the start. The grandmother turns round to face the wall, and the players move forward again.
End The first player to touch the grandmother's wall wins and takes the next turn at being grandmother.

TWO-MINUTE WALK

Objective Each player tries to walk from one end of the room to the other in exactly two minutes.
Play Players line up along one wall.
On the word "Go," they set off across the room. Without using a watch or a clock, each player tries to reach the other side of the room in exactly two minutes.
The organizer times the players' walks.
End When all the players have finished, the player whose time was nearest two minutes wins.

STORK FIGHTING CONTEST

Play Two players tie their left ankles together with a scarf, and hop on their right feet. Each player then tries to make his opponent's left foot touch the ground—without putting down his own left foot.
If a player's left foot touches the ground, or if his hands touch the ground, his opponent scores a point.
The winner is the player with the most points at the end of a time limit.

COCK FIGHTING CONTEST

Objective Each player tries to tip over his opponent.
Play Two players crouch on the floor facing each other. Each brings his knees together under his chin and clasps his legs with his arms.
A walking stick is then passed under his knees and over his arms.
The two players then try to tip each other over.
The first player to succeed is the winner.

TRIANGULAR TUG-OF-WAR

This is a game for three players.
Play A circle is made from a rope about 3yd long.
Three players space themselves around the rope and hold it taut, forming a triangle.
A handkerchief is placed at each corner of the triangle, out of reach of the player. On the word "Go!" each player tries to pick up the handkerchief nearest him without letting go of the rope.
The first player to pick up his handkerchief is the winner.

ARM WRESTLING

Objective Each player tries to prove he has the strongest arm muscles!
Play Two players sit facing each other at either side of a table.
Resting their right elbows on the table and with crooked arms, they clasp each other's right hands. (Both players may use their left arms if they prefer.)
On the signal to begin each player tries to force his opponent's right hand back until it touches the table. Elbows must be kept firmly on the table.
The winner is the first to succeed.

Stork fighting

© DIAGRAM

Cock fighting

Triangular tug-of-war

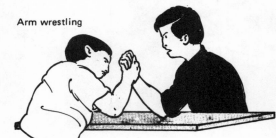
Arm wrestling

Goal scoring games

Although goal scoring games are often based on energetic outdoor sports, they can safely be played in the home if a balloon, soft ball, or large rag is used. Playing with balloons is particularly enjoyable as they are difficult to control and unlikely to cause damage.

AVENUE GOALS
Players try to score goals by patting a ball or balloon so that it goes beyond their opponents' end of the avenue.
Players The players form two lines about 5ft apart, and sit facing each other on the floor. Counting from one end, the odd-numbered players in one line belong to the same team as the even-numbered players in the other line.
Each team is allotted one end of the avenue as its goal.
Play The organizer puts the ball into the center of the avenue.
Each team tries to score by patting the ball by hand down the avenue into its opponent's goal. Players are not allowed to hold or throw the ball.
The ball is put back into the center of the avenue after each goal.
The winning team is the one with most goals at the end of a time limit.

OVERHEAD GOALS
Players try to score goals by patting a balloon over their opponents' heads.
Players The players form two teams in rows about 4ft apart, and sit facing each other on the floor.
Play The organizer tosses the ball into the center.
Each team tries to score goals by knocking the balloon over the heads of the opposing team and onto the ground behind them.
The winning team is the one with most goals at the end of a time limit.

Avenue goals

Scoring races

In all these games players are in some way singled out from their teams to take a turn at competing for points. In each case, the competition takes the form of a race between members of opposing teams.

NUMBER PARADE
Objective Each team tries to be the first to parade a number called by the organizer.
Preparation Single digits from zero to nine are drawn on separate pieces of card. The digits should be several inches high.
There may be either one or two cards for each player but there should be the same set of digits for each team.
In addition, a list of numbers using the digits available to each team is drawn up.
Play The teams form lines and each player is given either one or two of the cards.
The organizer calls out a number—for example he might call "469."
Immediately the players in each team with the digits 4,6, and 9 rush to the front and line up holding their digits so that they read "469."
The first team to parade the number correctly scores a point.
Players return to their teams and another number is called.
To make the game more interesting the organizer can set easy sums for the players to solve and parade.

WORD PARADE
This is played like number parade except that letters are written on the cards and words are called out to be spelled and paraded by the players.

BALLOON VOLLEYBALL
In balloon volleyball players hit a balloon over a piece of string held taut by two players standing on chairs.

Players The players divide into two teams, one on either side of the string. Players within a team take turns at serving (hitting the balloon into play at the start of play or after a break).

Play Players hit the balloon back and forth over the string with the aim of making a shot that their opponents will not be able to return.

A team scores a point whenever it hits the balloon over the string onto the floor on its opponent's side.

If the ball goes under the string, the opposing team serves it.

The winning team is the one with most points at the end of a time limit.

BLOW VOLLEYBALL
This is played in exactly the same way as balloon volleyball except that the balloon is blown rather than hit, and the string held lower.

ASTRIDE BALL
This is a goal scoring game without teams.

Players One player stands in the center of a circle formed by the other players standing with their legs apart.

Play The center player has a ball to be rolled along the ground. If he rolls it between the legs of a player in the circle, he "scores a goal" and changes places with that player.

The players in the circle should keep their hands on their knees except when trying to prevent a goal.

HOCKEY RAG TIME
In this game team members take turns at trying to shoot a goal.

Players The players form two rows about 6ft apart and sit down facing each other on the floor. Each team member is given a number, starting with one.

A rag and two walking sticks are laid on the floor between the two rows of players. A chair is placed at each end of the avenue as a goal. Each team is allotted one of the goals.

Play The organizer calls out a number.

Each player with that number picks up a walking stick and uses it to maneuver the rag into his opponent's goal.

The successful player scores a point for his side.

The rag and walking sticks are replaced and the organizer calls another number.

The winning team is the one with most goals at the end of a time limit.

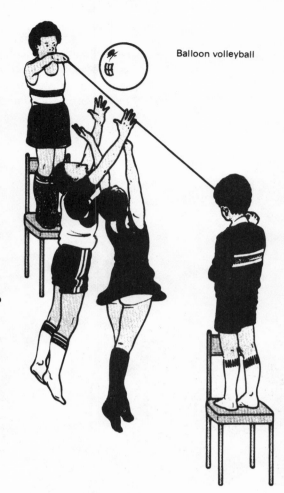

Balloon volleyball

MYSTERY NUMBERS
Objective Each team's players try to be fastest at solving clues and running around their teams.

Preparation It is a good idea to prepare a list of clues indicating particular numbers. If there are seven players in a team, clues for numbers one through seven will be needed. For example for number six the clues might be: half a dozen, a hexagon, an insect's legs, June, the sides of a cube.

Play Players line up behind their leaders and sit down. In each team players are numbered off starting with the leader as number one.

The organizer calls out a clue. As soon as a player recognizes that it refers to his number, he jumps up, runs around his team, and sits down in his place again.

The first player back scores a point for his team.

When all the players are seated again, the organizer calls out another clue.

End The team with the most points at the end of a time limit wins the game.

SIMPLE NUMBERS
This is played in the same way as mystery numbers except that the numbers are not hidden in clues. The organizer simply calls out each number.

LADDERS
Ladders can be played like either mystery numbers or simple numbers.

The difference is that the teams sit in two rows facing each other. It is recommended that players take off their shoes for this game. Each player sits with his legs outstretched and his feet touching those of the opposing player with the same number as himself. When a player's number is called or indicated he runs up between the lines over the other players' legs, back down behind his team, and then up between the lines to return to his place.

MY MOTHER'S CAKE
This is played in the same way as ladders except that players are given the name of an ingredient instead of a number.

The organizer then tells a story about how the cake was made and while telling it he mentions all the various ingredients. When a player hears the name of his ingredient he must race around as in ladders.

Mystery numbers

© DIAGRAM

Passing races

These are all games in which teams of players race to pass objects to each other in different ways. In each game, the contestants need to strike a balance between speed and skill.

Nose in the matchbox

Switchback

Passing the orange

PICK AND CUP

Objective Each team tries to be the first to pass assorted objects down its line of players.

Preparation Identical piles of various objects—eg fruit, beans, buttons, pebbles, etc—are collected together, one pile for each team.

Play Players divide into teams and sit down beside their leaders.

One pile of objects is placed beside each leader.

On the word "Go!" each leader picks up an object and drops it into the cupped hands of the player next to him.

The third player in the line picks the object out of the cupped hands and places it into the fourth player's cupped hands.

This continues down the line to the last player, who puts the object on the floor.

The leader can then pick up the next object and pass it down the line as before.

End The first team to transfer all the objects down the line wins.

NOSE IN THE MATCHBOX

Play Players divide into teams and line up beside their leaders.

A matchbox lid is given to each leader.

On the word "Go!" he lodges it on his nose and passes it onto the next player's nose without using his hands.

In this way the matchbox lid is passed down the line.

If a player touches the lid with his hands or drops it, it is returned to the leader to start again.

End The first team to successfully pass the matchbox lid down the line wins.

DOUBLE PASS

Objective Players in each team try to pass objects behind them and in front of them in two directions.

Preparation Two identical piles of objects are collected, one for each team.

Alternatively, a deck of cards may be divided between the teams.

Play Players divide into teams and sit in a line to the left of their leaders.

One pile of objects, or cards, is placed beside the leader.

On the word "Go!" he starts passing the objects, one after the other, down the line. Only right hands are used until the object reaches the end of the line. Then the left hands are used to return the objects behind the players' backs.

As objects arrive back at the beginning again, the leader makes a pile of the returned objects.

End The first team to return all the objects wins.

SWITCHBACK

Objective Each team tries to be quickest at passing through a hoop.

Play Players divide into teams and line up behind their leaders. A hoop is given to each leader.

On the word "Go!" the leader puts the hoop over his head, drops it to the ground, and steps out of it.

The next player steps into the hoop, lifts it over his head, and hands it to the next player.

The hoop is passed down the line in this way, players putting the hoop over their heads and stepping into it alternately.

When the last player has passed through the hoop, he runs with it to the front of the line and passes it back as before.

This continues with each player taking a turn at the head of the line.

End The first team with its leader at the front again wins.

BALLOON PASS

Objective Each team tries to be quickest at passing a balloon overhead.

Play Players divide into teams and form lines behind their leaders.

Each leader is given a balloon. On the word "Go!" he passes it over his head to the player behind him. This player in turn passes the balloon back over his head.

In this way the balloon is passed down the entire line. When the last player gets the balloon, he runs to the front of his line and passes the balloon back in the same way as before.

Thus each player takes a turn at the head of the line.

The winning team is the first one to have its leader at the front of the line again.

TUNNEL BALL

This is played like balloon pass except that players stand with their legs apart and pass the balloon back between their legs.

STRAWS AND BEANS

Objective Each team tries to be quickest at using straws to pass beans from player to player.

Play Players divide into teams and sit in a line beside their leaders.

A saucer with six beans on it is placed next to each leader, and an empty saucer is placed at the other end of each team.

Every player is given a drinking straw.

On the word "Go!" the leader picks up a bean and transfers if from his hand to the next player's cupped hand by sucking the bean onto the end of his straw and holding his breath.

In this manner all the beans are passed down the line and placed in the empty saucer. If a bean is dropped, it is returned to the beginning again.

End The first team to successfully transfer all its beans wins.

SUGAR AND SPOONS

This is played like straws and beans, except that players hold teaspoons in their mouths and tip sugarlumps from spoon to spoon.

PASSING THE ORANGE

Objective Seated players try to pass an orange down the line using their feet, or (in an alternative version) by using their chins!

Play Players divide into teams and sit in a line on the floor beside their leaders.

Each leader is given an orange and, with his legs together, cradles it on his feet.

On the word "Go!" he passes the orange onto the feet of the next player.

(Alternatively, the leader tucks the orange under his chin. The next player takes the orange from him, also using his chin—neither player may use his hands.)

Using either one of these ways, the orange is passed from player to player.

If the orange drops onto the floor, or if a player uses his hands, the orange is returned to the leader to start again.

End The first team to successfully pass the orange down the line wins.

PALMS

Objective Each team tries to be quickest at passing coins with flat hands.

Play Players divide into teams and form rows to the left of their leaders.

Each leader is given six large coins that he holds in his left hand.

On the word "Go!" he places one coin on the flat palm of his right hand and slaps it onto the flat palm of the next player's right hand.

In this manner each coin is passed down the row.

If a coin is dropped, it is returned to the leader to start again.

End The first team to successfully pass all six coins from one end to the other wins.

Tunnel ball

Balloon pass

Straws and beans

Sugar and spoons

Passing the orange

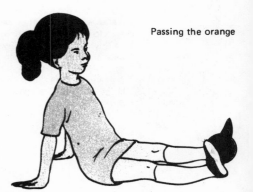

©DIAGRAM

Strange races

Individuals, pairs of players, and sometimes larger teams compete in these races. They can all be run in heats leading to a final if there is not enough room or equipment for everyone to compete at once.

Newspaper walk

Rabbit race

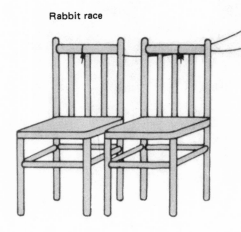

NEWSPAPER WALK
Each player tries to be the first to walk the length of the room on two sheets of newspaper.
Play Players stand in a line at one end of the room.
Each player is given two sheets of newspaper to stand on, one sheet under each foot.
At the word "Go!" he starts to move across the room on his newspaper.
If he touches the floor with any part of his body he must go back to the beginning again.

TORTOISE RACE
Each player tries to be the last to finish.
Play Players line up along one side of the room.
At the word "Go!" they each start to move across the room as slowly as possible. They must head straight for the opposite wall.
A player is disqualified if he stops moving or changes direction.

FISHERMEN
Each player tries to be the first to wind in his "fish."
Preparation Each player requires a fishing line and fish —made by tying a teaspoon to a length of strong thread wrapped around a spool.
Play Players stand in a line at one end of the room.
Each player is given a spoon and spool. He places the spoon on the floor and then unwinds the thread in a straight line to the other end of the room.
At the word "Go!" each player starts to wind in his spoon by turning the spool round and round in his hands.
He is not permitted to hold the thread in one hand and wind it around the spool.

RABBIT RACE
Each player tries to be the first to jerk his "rabbit" along his piece of string.
Preparation One rabbit shape for each player is cut out of heavy card. A small hole is made in its center and a piece of string about 6ft long threaded through the hole and tied to a chair.
Play Each player holds the free end of one of the pieces of string and moves the rabbit to that end.
At the word "Go!" each player, without touching his rabbit, must jerk it along the string to the chair.

BOTTLE FISHING
Each player tries to be the first to ring his bottle.
Preparation Several bottles of the same size and shape are needed, together with an equal number of rings large enough to slip over the necks of the bottles. Each ring should be tied to a length of string.
Play Players sit or stand in a line, with a bottle in front of each of them. Each player then tries to "catch" his bottle, by getting his ring over his bottle's neck.

BACK TO BACK RACE
Pairs of players try to be the first to run the course.
Play Players form pairs and line up at one end of the room. Each pair of players stands back to back with their arms linked.
At the word "Go!" the linked players race to the other end of the room. Pairs who become unlinked must go back to the beginning and start again.

PIGGY BACK RACE
This is another race in which pairs of players try to be the first to run a course.
Play Players form pairs and line up at one end of the room. One player from each pair gets on the other's back to be carried.
At the word "Go!" the pairs race to the other end of the room, where they must change places so that the carrier becomes the carried. They must then race back to the original end of the room. If a player touches the floor while he is being carried, that pair must start again.

Bottle fishing

THREE-LEGGED RACE
Pairs of players try to be the first to run from one end of the room to the other.
Play Players form pairs and line up at one end of the room. A scarf is needed for each pair so that the right leg of one of the players in the pair can be tied to the left leg of his partner.
At the word "Go!" pairs race to the other end of the room.

PATCHES
Players race to sew patches on their partners' clothes.
Preparation A square of material, a needle, and thread are needed for each pair of players.
Play Each player finds a partner and one of them is given a square of material, a needle, and a length of thread.
At the word "Go!" a player from each pair quickly sews his patch on his partner's clothes. (Big stitches are allowed!)
The first player to finish wins the heat.
The other player in each pair then has a turn at sewing.

NECKLACE RACE
Each pair tries to be the first to thread all its beads.
Preparation 12 beads on a saucer, a needle, and a length of thread are needed for each pair of players.
Play Players line up in pairs along one side of the room. Each saucer of beads is placed opposite a pair of players at the other end of the room. One player in each pair is given a needle and length of thread.
At the word "Go!" each player with needle and thread must thread his needle and tie a large firm knot at one end of his thread.
At the same time his partner runs to the saucer, picks up two beads, and returns with them.
When the first player in each pair has threaded his needle he takes the two beads from his partner and threads them while his partner goes back to the saucer for two more beads.
Play continues in this way until all 12 beads have been threaded. If any beads are dropped they must be picked up and threaded normally.
When a player has threaded all 12 beads, he removes the needle and ties the bead necklace around his partner's neck.
The game is won by the first pair to finish its necklace.

YARN TANGLES
Teams of four players try to be first to untangle balls of yarn wrapped around chairs.
Preparation A chair and four different colored balls of yarn are needed for each team.
Play Players form into teams of four. Each team is given four balls of yarn and a chair. Teams are then allowed about one minute in which to tangle their yarn around their chairs. They are not allowed to lift up their chairs or to make deliberate knots in the yarn.
At the end of the time limit the organizer calls "Stop!" and teams must move around to a different chair.
At the word "Go!" teams start to disentangle the yarn from their new chair. Each player winds one of the balls of yarn. Players are not allowed to pick up the chair or deliberately break the yarn.
The game is won by the first team to untangle the yarn into four separate balls.

DUMB ARTISTS
Each pair tries to be the first in which one player recognizes an animal drawn by the other. Players are not allowed to speak to each other during this game.
Play Players form pairs, and partners stand opposite each other at different ends of the room.
The players at one end are each given a pencil and a card with the name of an animal written on it.
At the word "Go!" each of these players runs to his partner and, with the animal's name face down, tries to draw the animal.
When his partner thinks that he recognizes the drawing, he takes the pencil and writes down the animal's name.
If his answer is correct, his partner nods his head and both players run to the other end of the room.
If his answer is incorrect, his partner shakes his head, takes the pencil back, and continues drawing.
The game is won by the first pair to reach the other end of the room after the animal has been guessed.

CROCODILE RACE
This is an amusing race for teams of players.
Play Players divide into teams and line up behind their leaders at one end of the room. Players then squat on their heels, each with his hands on the shoulders or waist of the player in front of him.
At the word "Go!" the "crocodiles" move forward by little jumps or bounces.
If a player loses contact with the player in front of him, his team must stop and reassemble. For reassembling, the hind end of the crocodile must stay where it is while the front end moves back to join it.
The first team to reach the other end of the room intact wins the race.

Back to back race

Three-legged race

Piggy back race

Relay races

In relay races players in each team take it in turns to perform the same action one after the other. Two or more teams can take part in any of the races described here. Relay races are particularly enjoyable for large numbers of players.

Flying fish

Burst the bag

FLYING FISH
Objective In this game (also known as kippers in the United Kingdom) teams race each other at fanning "fish" across the room.
Preparation A "fish" about 10in long is made for each player out of fairly thick paper—the plumper the fish, the better it will "fly."
Each team is given a folded newspaper or magazine.
Play Players line up behind their leaders at one end of the room. A plate is placed on the floor at the other end of the room opposite each team.
At the word "Go!" each leader places his fish on the floor and fans it with the newspaper, down the room and onto the plate.
As soon as he has done this, he races back to his team and hands the newspaper to the next player in line.
Each player in turn fans his fish across the room and onto the plate, and the first team to finish wins the game.

BURST THE BAG
Objective Teams race each other to be the first to blow up and burst paper bags.
Play Players line up behind their leaders.
Paper bags, one for each player, are placed on chairs opposite each team leader.
At the word "Go!" each leader runs to the chair, takes a paper bag, blows it up, and bursts it with his hands.
As soon as he has done this, he runs back to his team and touches the next player. As soon as this player is touched, he takes his turn at bursting a bag.
Play continues in this way until each player has burst a bag—the first team to finish being the winners.

FRUIT COLORS
Objective Each team tries to be the first to color in pictures of fruit.
Preparation For each team, outlines of fruit (one per player) are drawn on a large sheet of paper. The drawings should be the same for each team.
The sheets of paper are attached to a wall or laid out on a table.
Play Teams line up behind their leaders at the opposite end of the room to the drawings.
Each leader is given a box of crayons.
At the word "Go!" he runs to his team's sheet of paper and colors in one of the pieces of fruit.
He then goes back to his team, hands the box of crayons to the next player and stands at the back of his team.
As soon as the second player gets the crayons, he goes and colors in another fruit and so on down the line of players.
If a crayon is dropped on the floor, the player with the box must pick it up.
End The first team to color in all its fruit wins.

SURPRISE SENTENCES
Objective Each team tries to write a sentence, with each player in the team writing one word of it.
Preparation For each team, a large sheet of paper is attached to a wall or to a board propped upright.
Play Each team lines up opposite its sheet of paper and the leader is given a pencil.
At the word "Go!" he runs up to his paper and writes any word he likes.
He then runs back to his team, hands the pencil to the next player, and goes to the end of his team.
As soon as the next player gets the pencil, he goes to the paper and adds a second word either in front of, or behind the leader's word.
Play continues in this way with each player adding one word. The words should be chosen and put together so that they can be part of a grammatically correct sentence.
Each player, except the last, must avoid completing the sentence. The last player should be able to complete the sentence by adding just one word, and he also puts in the punctuation.
Players may not confer and choose a sentence before writing their words.
End The first team to construct a sentence with one word from each player wins the game.

EMPTYING SOCKS

Objective Each team tries to be the first to remove a variety of objects in their correct order from a long sock.

Preparation Identical groups of small objects are put into long socks, one sock for each team. There should be only one item of each kind in each group. The objects might be buttons, beans, coins of different sizes, hairpins, pebbles, etc.

Play Teams line up opposite their leaders. Each leader is given a sock to hold.
The organizer announces the first object to be found.
Immediately the first player in each team runs to his leader and puts his hand in the sock. He feels for the object and picks it out of the sock.
If he makes a mistake, he returns the object that he took and tries again.
If he is right, he gives the object to the organizer and is told the next object to be retrieved.
He returns to his team, tells the next player what to search for and stands at the back of his team.
As soon as the next player knows what to find, he takes his turn at feeling for an object in the sock.
Play continues in this way until each object has been retrieved, and the first team to finish wins.

EGG CUPS

Objective Each player tries to blow a table tennis ball from one egg cup to another without dropping it.

Play Players divide into teams and line up beside their leaders.
Two egg cups and a table tennis ball are given to each leader.
At the word "Go!" the leader blows the table tennis ball from one egg cup to the other. He may hold the egg cups so that they touch, but he may not merely tip the ball from one cup to the other.
As soon as the leader has finished, he hands the cups and the table tennis ball to the next player; and so on down the line, until each player has blown the ball from one egg cup to the other.
If the ball is dropped, handled, or tipped instead of blown, it is returned to the leader who must start again.

End The first team whose players have all correctly blown the table tennis ball from one cup to the other wins.

HAT AND SCARF

Objective Players of each team try to be the quickest at dressing up and running around the team.

Preparation A hat, a scarf, a coat, and a pair of gloves are collected for each team.

Play Teams line up behind their leaders and a set of clothes is placed on a chair in front of each team.
At the word "Go!" each leader runs to the chair, puts on the clothes, and runs around his team.
He then takes off the clothes and gives them to the next player to dress up in.
Play continues in this way down the line. When the last player has run around his team, he places the clothes on the chair.

End The first team with its set of clothes back on the chair wins the game.

BALLOON HOP

Objective Teams try to be the first to find and inflate all the balloons belonging to them.

Preparation Balloons of as many different colors as there are teams should be bought, and each player in each team will need a balloon.

Play Players line up behind their leaders. Each team is allotted a color.
The balloons are placed in a pile at the other end of the room.
At the word "Go!" each leader hops across the room, finds a balloon of his team's color and hops back with it to his team.
When he returns, the next player hops across to find a balloon; and so on, until each player has a balloon.
When players return to their teams, they inflate the balloons and fasten the necks.
If a player has a lot of difficulty tying his balloon, another player in his team may help him.

End The first team with all its balloons blown up and tied wins.

HURRY WAITER!

Objective This game also needs a table tennis ball for each team, and the players try to balance it on a plate as they weave in and out of a line of their teammates.

Play Players divide into teams and stand in a line behind their leaders.
Each leader is given a table tennis ball on a plate.
At the word "Go!" he weaves in and out between the players in his team as quickly as he can without dropping the table tennis ball.
When he reaches the end of the line, he runs straight to the head of the line again and hands the plate and ball to the next player, saying "Here is your breakfast Sir (or Madam)" as he does so.
This procedure is repeated, with each player beginning at the head of the line and returning to his place as soon as he has handed the "breakfast" to the next player in turn.
If a player drops the ball, he must go back to the head of the line and start again.
The first team to finish wins the game.

Hat and scarf

15 Children's card games

All the card games in this chapter are fast-moving and easy to learn. Some old favorites like snap and happy families are primarily games for children. Others—like racing demons, cheat, and memory—are enjoyed by adults and children alike.

SNAP

Amusing and noisy, snap is among the most familiar of all children's card games.

Players Two or more can play.

Cards Special snap cards can be bought but the game is just as much fun with standard playing cards.

It is best to use old cards in case of damage, and it does not matter if any of the cards is missing.

If there are more than three players it is a good idea to use two decks of cards.

Objective Players aim to win all the cards.

Deal One player deals out all the cards in a clockwise direction—one at a time and face down. It does not matter if some players have one card more than the others.

Each player puts his cards into a neat pile face down in front of him.

Players are not allowed to look at their cards.

Play The player to the dealer's left turns over the top card of his pile and places it face up to start a face-up pile of cards next to his face-down pile. The next player to his left turns the same, and so on around the players until any player sees

that the cards on the top of any two face-up piles have the same value (eg two 10s).

Snap The first player to shout "snap" when there are matching cards on the top of two face-up piles, collects both these piles of cards and puts them at the bottom of his own face-down pile.

Players now continue turning cards over as before, beginning with the player to the left of the last player who turned over a card.

Snap pool If two players shout "snap" together, the matching face-up piles are put face up in a pool in the center. Players then continue to turn over cards, and the pool is won by the first player to shout "snap pool" when the top card of any player's face-up pile matches the top card of the pool.

No more cards When a player runs out of face-down cards he simply turns over his face-up cards when it is next his turn to play.

Penalty There are different rules for when a player calls "snap" in error:
a) the player gives one card from his face-down pile to each of the other players;
b) the player's own face-up

pile is put into a central pool to be won like an ordinary snap pool.

End The game ends when only one player has any cards.

EASY SNAP

This version is particularly suitable for very young children. Instead of having individual face-up piles, each player plays his cards onto a central face-up pile. Players shout "snap" when the top two cards are of the same value.

SPEED SNAP

In this faster version of snap, players still turn their cards up one at a time but all players do so together.

MENAGERIE

This hilarious and noisy game is similar to snap. It is sometimes called "animals."

Players It can be played by two players but is better with three or more.

Cards One or two decks of standard playing cards are used.

Objective Players aim to win all the cards.

Choosing the animals Players first choose the name of an animal with a long and tongue-twisting name. After checking that everyone has chosen a different animal, each player is given a small piece of paper on which he must write his animal's name. (An older person can help anyone who hasn't learned to write.)

All the pieces of paper are folded and then shaken together in a bag or hat.

Each player then takes one piece of paper—and the name on that paper is his animal for the game.

Players should then learn the animal names of all the persons playing.

Deal The cards are dealt as for snap.

Play is the same as for snap, except that animal names are used instead of calling "snap." Whenever the top card on any two player's face-up piles are the same (eg two 7s), each of these two players must call out the other player's animal name three times.

The first player to do so, wins the other player's face-up pile and adds these cards to the bottom of his own face-down pile.

Penalty If a player wrongly calls out a name, he must give all his face-up cards to the player whose animal name he called.

Snap!

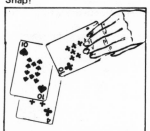

ANIMAL NOISES
This game is played in the same way as menagerie, except that:
a) players choose animals that make distinctive noises (eg dog, cat, or duck);
b) players imitate their opponents' animal noises instead of repeating their animal names.

SLAPJACK
This is an exciting game that needs no skill. It can be enjoyed by the very young as the only requirement is that players can recognize a jack.
Players Two or more can play.
Cards Standard playing cards are used. If there are more than three players it is a good idea to mix two decks together. It does not matter if a few cards are missing.
Objective Players aim to win all the cards.
Deal One player deals out all the cards in a clockwise direction—one at a time and face down. It does not matter if some players have one card more than others.
Each player puts his cards into a neat pile face down in front of him.
Players are not allowed to look at their cards.
Play The player to the dealer's left turns over the top card of his pile and places it face up in the center.
Turns then pass around to the left, with each player placing his card on top of the previous player's card.

Slapping a jack When a jack is turned up, each player tries to be the first to put his hand on the card—ie to "slap the jack."
The successful player wins the central pile of cards and shuffles them with his own cards to form his new face-down pile.
The player to the winner's left starts the next round, placing a card face up in the center.
If more than one player puts his hand on the jack, the winner is the player whose hand is underneath.
If possible it is a good idea to appoint a referee to settle arguments.
If a player loses all his cards he can stay in the game if he is first to slap the next jack.
If he fails to slap the next jack he must retire from the game.

Penalty If a player slaps a card that is not a jack, he must give his top card to the player whose card he slapped in error.
End The winner of the game is either:
a) the first person to collect all the cards; or
b) the player with the most cards at the end of a time limit set at the start of the game.

Slapping a jack

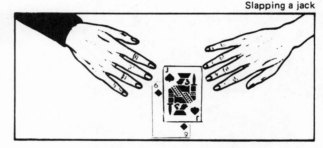

WAR
An easy game, war is a good way of introducing young children to card playing.
Players This game is for two people.
Cards A complete deck of standard playing cards is used.
Objective Each player aims to win all the cards.
Deal One player deals all the cards.
Each player puts his cards into a neat pile face down in front of him.
Players are not allowed to look at their cards.
Play Both players turn over the top card of their piles, and place them face up, side by side, in the center.
The player who has played the higher card, regardless of suit, wins both cards and places them face down at the bottom of his pile.
Aces are the highest cards, followed by kings, queens, jacks, and so on down from the 10s to the 2s.
The "war" If the two cards turned up have the same value, the war is on.
Each player puts one card face down on top of his first card in the center. He then puts another card face up on top of this.

The two new face-up cards are compared, and the highest card wins all six cards in the center.
If the face-up cards match again, the war continues.
Each player puts out another face-down card with a face-up card on top.
Play continues in this way until someone plays a card higher than the other.
End The winner of the game is either:
a) the first player to win all the cards; or
b) the player with the most cards at the end of a time limit set at the start of the game.

WAR FOR THREE PLAYERS
This version of war is for three players.
Deal The cards are dealt out as in war for two, except that the last card is not dealt out. (In this way, all three players begin with the same number of cards.)
Play is the same as in war for two, except that:
a) when two cards of the same value are turned up, all three players engage in war;
b) when three cards of the same value are turned up, the players engage in double war.
In double war each player puts out two cards face down and then one card face up. If the cards still match, the three players then continue with single war.

PERSIAN PASHA
Persian pasha, also called pisha pasha, is a similar game to war.
Players It is a game for two players.
Cards A complete deck of standard playing cards is used.
Objective Each player aims to win all the cards.
Deal Cards are dealt as for war.
Play Each player turns over his top card and places it on a face-up pile next to his face-down pile.
Players continue turning over cards until their top face-up cards are of the same suit.
The player with the higher card then takes all the other player's face-up pile and puts these cards at the bottom of his face-down pile.

Rank of cards

War

MEMORY

This card game for any number of players is also called pelmanism or concentration. It is easy to play and is an excellent test of memory and observation.

Cards One or two standard decks of playing cards are used, depending on the number of players.

The cards should be clean and reasonably new, so that when they are lying face down they cannot be identified by creases, marks, or torn corners!

The playing area must be flat and as large as possible—the floor or a big table is best.

The deal One player shuffles the cards and lays them face down on the table—in all directions and so that no card is touching another.

Objective Each player tries to collect as many cards as possible by turning up pairs with the same rank (number or picture).

First player The player to the left of the dealer starts the game. He turns over two cards at random and allows the other players to see them.

If the rank of the two cards is the same, for example two aces or two kings, he takes them and may turn over two more cards. He continues in this way until he turns over two cards that do not match. If the cards that are turned over do not match, the player must put them face down in their original positions. His turn then ends.

Second player The person to the first player's left now turns over any two cards.

If the first card matches one that has already been turned over he must try to remember where that card is. If he is successful he takes the pair. He continues his turn until he fails to turn over a matching pair.

Successive players Play continues with the players taking their turns in a clockwise direction, until all the cards have been collected.

The winner is the player with most cards at the end of the game.

OTHER CARD-MATCHING GAMES

Memory and other card-matching games may be played with special cards. These can be smaller than standard playing cards and any number of pairs may be used, depending on the number of players.

The cards are printed with colored pictures, patterns, or symbols, and are particularly popular with young children. Rules for these games are like those for memory, with players trying to get matching pairs of, for example, pineapples, eskimoes, or boats.

To make play simpler for very young children, the cards may be laid out at the start of the game in rows, and fewer pairs may be used.

BEGGAR MY NEIGHBOR

Beggar my neighbor is an easy and exciting game. No skill is required as the outcome is wholly decided by the luck of the deal.

Players There may be two to six players.

Cards Any deck of standard playing cards may be used, and it need not be complete. For more than three players it is a good idea to mix two decks together.

The objective is to win all the cards. But, as the game may go on for a very long time, the winner may be the player who has the most cards at the end of an agreed length of time.

Deal One player deals out all the cards in a clockwise direction—one at a time and face down. It does not matter

if some players have one card more than the others.

Each player puts his cards into a neat pile face down in front of him.

Players are not allowed to look at their cards.

Play The player to the dealer's left turns up the top card in his pile and places it in the center of the playing area.

Each player in turn, in a clockwise direction, then places the top card from his pile face up on the central pile. This continues until one player turns up an ace or a court card (a jack, queen, or king).

Payment of cards The player next to him then has to "pay" him by placing a certain number of cards on the central pile:

four cards for an ace;

three cards for a king;

two cards for a queen;

one card for a jack.

If, however, one of the payment cards is an ace or a court card, the payer stops turning over his cards and the player next to him has to pay the correct number of cards. This goes on until a player paying out cards turns over the correct number of cards with no aces or court cards.

When this happens, the last player to have turned over an ace or a court card may take the central pile and place it face down at the bottom of his own pile.

The payer then starts a new round by playing his next card face up in the center of the playing area.

As soon as a player has no more cards, he is out.

DONKEY

Donkey is a fast and noisy card game in which players are penalized with letters from the game's name.

Players Three or more can play.

Cards Special cards can be bought but donkey is usually played with sets of cards taken from an old deck of standard playing cards.

Each set consists of four cards with the same picture or number. The number of sets used is the same as the number of people playing. For example if there are five players, the aces, kings, queens, jacks, and 10s might be used.

Spoons, buttons, or some other unbreakable objects should be placed in the center of the table at the start of each round. There must be one object fewer than the number of players.

The objective is to collect a set of four cards and at the same time to avoid being the "donkey" (ie the first player to lose six rounds of the game). A player is penalized with one letter from the word donkey each time that he fails to pick up an object at the end of a round.

Play Keeping his cards hidden from the other players, each player chooses one card that he does not want and places it face down on the table. All the players then pass their unwanted card to the player to their left.

Each player than looks at his new card and again chooses a card to pass to his neighbor.

He may pass the new card if he wishes.

The game continues in this way, as quickly as possible, until one player has a set of four cards of the same value. When a player has a set of cards, for example four 10s, he should quietly put them face up on the table and pick up an object from the table.

As soon as any player does this, the other players must reach for an object whether they have a set of four cards or not.

The player who fails to pick up an object loses the round and is penalized with a letter.

Donkey The first player to be penalized with all the letters of the word donkey loses the game and must "hee-haw" three times.

PIG

Pig is a similar game to donkey. The number of players and the cards used are the same as for donkey, but in pig there is no need for any unbreakable objects.

The objective is to collect a set of four cards of the same value while also avoiding becoming the "prize pig."

Play is the same as for donkey, except that when a player has a set of cards he puts his finger to his nose. The last player to do so is pig for the round.

Prize pig The game is lost when one player becomes prize pig after losing ten rounds. As a forfeit, the prize pig must say "oink-oink" three times.

PIT

Pit is a very lively trading game played with special cards. It is trademarked and copyrighted by Parker Brothers of Salem, Mass.

Players attempt to collect sets of cards representing commodities traded on the American Corn Exchange: wheat, barley, corn, rye, oats, flax, and hay.

The game is made more exciting by the inclusion of bonus and penalty cards: a bull and a bear.

Cards are exchanged by any two players wishing to trade the same number of cards, and as all players are trying to trade at once the game often develops into a happy free for all.

MY SHIP SAILS

An easy game for beginners, my ship sails is also great fun when played at speed by those familiar with it.

Players Four to seven people may play.

Cards A standard deck of playing cards is used.

Objective Each player aims to be the first to collect seven cards of the same suit, for example seven spades.

Deal Each player cuts the cards and the one with the highest card (ace high) is the dealer.

He deals out the cards in a clockwise direction, one at a time and face down, until each player has seven cards. The remaining cards are not used.

Play Each player sorts his cards into suits in his hand and decides which suit he will try to collect. This will probably be the suit for which he has most cards at the start of a round, but he may change his mind during the course of play.

Exchange of cards Each player takes one card that he does not want and puts it face down on the table. When all the players are ready, they pass these cards to the next person to the right.

The players pick up their new cards, decide on another card to discard, and then pass it in the same way.

End Players continue to exchange cards until one person collects seven cards of the same suit. He then calls "my ship sails," and wins the game. If two players call together, the first to start calling is the winner.

My ship sails!

HAPPY FAMILIES

Happy families is a peaceful game much loved by children.

Players Three or more can play.

Cards Special cards are normally used, each illustrated with one of four members of a family.

Usually there are 10–13 families—often shown as different animals. Each family has a father, mother, son, and daughter. For example one family might be Mr Lion, Mrs Lion, Master Lion, and Miss Lion—each represented on a separate card.

(The game may also be played with standard playing cards—see "authors.")

Objective Each player tries to collect as many complete families as possible.

Deal One of the players deals out all the cards. If more than one round is played, the players can take it in turns to deal.

It does not matter if some players have one card more than others.

Play Each player looks at his cards and sorts them into families.

It is important that players keep their cards hidden from each other. (With young children it is a good idea if they can lay out their cards out of view of the other players.)

When all the players are ready, the person to the dealer's left asks any player, by name, for a particular card (eg Master Lion). He must already possess at least one member of the same family (eg Mrs Lion). If the person asked has the card, he gives it to the first player, who may again ask anybody for a card of any family as long as he already has one card belonging to that family.

He continues to do this until he fails to obtain a card.

If the person asked does not have the card requested, it is his turn to ask for cards.

When a player collects all four cards of the same family, he puts them into a pile face down in front of him.

End Play continues until all the families have been completed.

The person who collects most families is the winner.

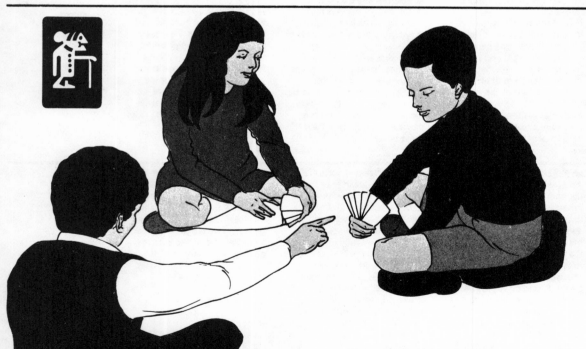

OLD MAID

Old maid is a simple card game that is a great favorite with young children. It can be played with special cards, or with standard playing cards.

Players Old maid is a game for three or more players.

Cards Special decks of old maid cards consist of a single card with a picture of the "old maid" and pairs of cards showing other colorful characters.

If standard playing cards are used, one of the queens is is removed to leave the deck with an odd queen—the "old maid."

A pair of butchers

AUTHORS

This game is essentially the same as happy families. In some countries it is possible to buy special cards showing famous authors and the names of four of their works.

The name authors is, however, probably more commonly used for the variation of happy families played with standard playing cards.

To use standard playing cards, the ranks of the cards become the family names or "author," while the suits become the members of the families or the "books." For example, a player with the 8s of spades, clubs, and diamonds would ask for the 8 of hearts to complete his "family of 8s."

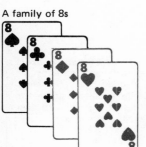

A family of 8s

Authors

FISH

This game is similar to happy families but the element of luck in winning is greater.

Unlike happy families it can be played by only two people—although it is better with more.

Cards Fish is usually played with standard playing cards but young players may prefer to use happy families cards.

Deal All the cards are dealt out as for happy families but a spare hand is also dealt—ie if there are four players, five hands are dealt.

The spare hand is placed face down in the center of the table and called the "fish pile."

Play This is the same as in happy families except that when a player is asked for a card he does not have, he says "fish."

Then the player who asked him takes the top card from the fish pile.

Play continues with the player who said "fish" asking for cards.

End The winner is the first player to have no cards other than his completed families. If two players finish at the same time, the one with the most completed families is the winner.

Fish

Deal One player deals all the cards face down, one at a time, to all players. It does not matter if some players have one card more than the others.

Objective Each player aims to get rid of all his cards by discarding pairs of equal value. The player who is left with the old maid card when play ends is the loser. There are no winners in this game.

Play Each player looks at his cards, making sure that none of the other players can see them.

If he has any pairs—two matching character cards or two playing cards with the same value, eg two 9s or two kings—he lays them face down on the table.

A player with three cards of the same value may only put down two of them and must keep the third, but a player with four cards of the same value may put down all four as two pairs.

The player to the dealer's left fans out his cards, keeping their faces toward him, and offers them to the player to his left.

The player who is offered the cards must take any one of them. He then looks to see

whether the new card pairs up with any of the cards already in his hand. If it does, he lays the pair face down on the table. If not, he adds the new card to the cards in his hand. He then fans out his cards and offers them to the player to his left.

Play continues in this way until all cards but the "old maid" have been played. The player holding the "old maid" is the loser, and all the other players call him "old maid" before a new game is started.

Variation To make the game last longer, cards may be considered as pairs only if their color matches as well as their number, for example two red 7s or two black aces.

LE VIEUX GARCON

This French game is similar to old maid.

It is played with a standard deck of playing cards, with the jacks of hearts, diamonds, and clubs removed.

The game is lost by the player left with the jack of spades—called "le vieux garçon" or "old boy."

BLACK PETER

This game is very popular in Germany. It is usually played with special cards, but standard playing cards can be substituted as for other games of this type.

Special decks of cards consist of a single "Black Peter" card, often showing a fierce black cat wearing boots and a hat, and pairs of other cards showing different animal characters.

It is played in the same way as old maid, and the loser is the player left with the "Black Peter" card.

A pair of 9s

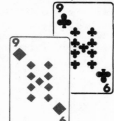

A pair of red 7s

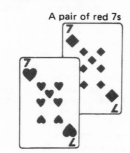

Animal pairs

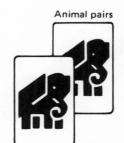

Stealing bundles

STEALING BUNDLES

As soon as a player can spot that two cards have the same rank (face value), he is old enough to play stealing bundles. Other names for this game are old man's bundle and stealing the old man's bundle.

Players Two or four people can play.

Cards A standard deck of playing cards is used.

Objective Each player tries to collect as many cards as possible.

Deal One person is chosen as dealer. He deals the cards in a clockwise direction, one at a time and face down, until each player has four cards.

The dealer then places four cards face up in a row in the center.

Play The player to the left of the dealer begins.

If he has a card of the same rank as one of the cards in the center, he captures that card. He places the captured card and his matching card face up in a pile in front of him. This is the beginning of his "bundle."

If two or three center cards have the same rank as one of the player's cards he may capture them all in the same turn.

If none of the player's cards matches a center card, he must place one of his own cards face up in the center. This is called "trailing."

Each player then plays one card in turn. In place of or in addition to capturing cards from the center, he may steal another player's bundle if his card matches the top card of that bundle.

Every time a player captures cards he places them in his bundle with the matching card face up.

If none of his cards matches any face-up card he must "trail" one of his cards.

Extra deals When all the players have played each of the four cards in their hands, the dealer deals out four more cards to each player. No cards are dealt to the center. Play then continues as before.

End The game ends when all the cards have been dealt and played.

The winner is the player with most cards in his bundle when play ends.

I DOUBT IT

Also known as cheat, this game is great fun for those who like taking risks and calling people's bluffs.

Players A minimum of three people are needed to play, but the more the better.

Cards One or two decks of playing cards are used.

Objective Each player aims to be the first to get rid of all his cards.

Deal One player deals out all the cards. Some players may have one extra card.

Play Players look at their cards. The player to the left of the dealer places one to four cards of the "same" rank (eg all 7s) face down in a pile in the center. He calls their rank as he does so. (In fact, the cards need not be what he claims—see cheating.)

Subsequent players must then play—or claim that they are playing—one to four cards of the rank one higher than those played by the preceding player.

Cheating There are at least two ways of cheating.

a) Instead of putting down cards of the correct rank, a player can put down any other cards, as long as he pretends that they are all the same, and of the next highest value to those just played.

If a player does not have cards of the required value, he has no alternative but to do this. It is important that a player should avoid giving the others reason to doubt him.

b) A player may put down more cards than he states. Again, he should avoid

drawing people's attention to this.

Calling a player's bluff If a player suspects another of cheating, he can challenge him by calling "I doubt it" or "Cheat" before the suspect's cards are covered by those of the next player.

The challenged player must then turn over his cards for inspection.

If the player who called "I doubt it" is correct, the person who cheated picks up all the cards in the central pile and adds them to his hand.

If the player did not cheat, the challenger must pick up the central pile of cards.

The player who picks up the cards from the center starts the next round.

End The winner is the first person to succeed in playing his last card—ie either:
a) he withstands a challenge from another player; or
b) his cards are covered by the next player's before anyone has challenged him.

UP AND DOWN CHEAT

The only difference between this game and ordinary I doubt it or cheat is in the rank of the cards that can be played. Instead of only claiming to play cards in ascending rank, a player may also claim that he is playing cards that are either of the same rank or one rank lower than the last player's cards.

Go boom

GO BOOM
Go boom is a straightforward game for two or more players, which can be played by quite young children.
Cards A standard deck of playing cards is used.
Objective Each player aims to be the first to get rid of all his cards.
Deal The players cut for deal; the one with the highest card (ace ranks high) deals out the cards in a clockwise direction, one at a time and face down, until each player has seven cards. Spare cards are placed face down in a neat pile in the center.
Play Each player looks at his cards and sorts them in his hand. Turns pass clockwise around the players, starting with the player to the dealer's left.
The first player chooses a card from his hand and places it face up in the center. Each of the other players in turn, making a central face-up pile, plays a card that is either:
a) of the same suit, or
b) of the same rank (number or picture) as the card put down by the person before him.
If a player cannot follow suit or rank, he takes cards one at a time from the top of the central face-down pile until he has a card that he can play onto the central face-up pile.
If all the cards have been taken, the player says "pass" and play moves on to the next player.
When each player has played a card or "passed," the cards are compared for the highest card (ace ranks high) and the player of the highest card starts the next round.
If two or more players tie for the highest card, the first one to play his card starts the next round.
End The winner is the first player to get rid of all his cards and shout "boom."

SCORING GO BOOM
This is a variation of go boom that is made more interesting by the introduction of a scoring system.
It is played in the same way as basic go boom, except that several rounds are played and points are scored for going boom.
When a player goes boom, he scores points for all the unplayed cards still in the other players' hands. Points are scored as follows:
a) 10 points for each king, queen, or jack;
b) one point for each ace;
c) the numerical face value of all other cards.
A game is won by the first player to score an agreed number of points (usually 250).

CRAZY EIGHTS
Crazy eights is the same basic game as go boom except that the 8s are wild.
A player may play any 8 after any card, and then decides what suit should follow.
As in scoring go boom, the first player to play all his cards scores points for the unplayed cards still in the other players' hands.
Points are scored as follows:
a) 50 points for an 8;
b) 10 points for each king, queen, or jack;
c) one point for each ace;
d) the numerical face value of all other cards.
If the face-down pile of cards is exhausted before any player plays all his cards, the game is blocked and the player with the lowest count in his remaining cards scores the difference in count between his own hand and the other players' hands.

SNIP-SNAP-SNOREM
A game with funny words to say, snip-snap-snorem is noisy, fast-moving, and fun to play.
Players It is a game for three or more players.
Cards A standard deck of playing cards is used.
Objective Each player aims to be the first to get rid of all his cards.
Deal Each player cuts the cards and the one with the highest card (ace high) is the dealer.
He deals out all the cards in a clockwise direction, one at a time, and face down.
It does not matter if some players have one card more than the others.
Play Each player looks at his cards without letting any other player see them, and sorts them in his hand.
Turns pass clockwise around the players, starting with the player to the dealer's left.
The first player places any one of his cards face up in the center (a).
If the next player has a card of the same rank (eg another queen if the first player played a queen), he places this face up in the center of the table and shouts "snip" as he plays it (b).
If he has another card of the same rank he keeps it until his next turn.
If he does not have a card of the same rank, he says "pass" and play moves on around the players.

The next player with a card of the same rank (c) shouts "snap" when he plays it, and the player of the fourth card (d) shouts "snorem!"
The player of the fourth card starts the next round.
End The winner is the first player to play all his cards.
Variation If a player has more than one card of the same rank, he must play them all in the same turn, saying the appropriate words.

JIG
This is played exactly like snip-snap-snorem except that instead of playing four cards of the same rank, a sequence of four cards is played.
For example, if the first player puts down a 5, this is followed by a 6, then a 7, and finally an 8.
The cards can be from different suits.
Players call out "jiggety, joggety, jig" when playing the cards.

Crazy eights

 a
Snip
 b
Snap
 c
Snorem!  d

250

Play or pay

PLAY OR PAY
This easy game, sometimes called round the corner, is fun for players learning about the rank and sequence of playing cards.
Players Three or more can play.
Cards A standard deck of playing cards is used.
Counters Each player starts with 20 counters. (Beans or matchsticks could be used.)
Objective Each player aims to be first to get rid of all his cards.
Deal One player is chosen as dealer. He deals out all the cards in a clockwise direction, one at a time and face down. It does not matter if some players have one card more than others.
Play The player to the left of the dealer chooses any one of his cards and places it face up in the center.
The next player to his left then looks at his cards to see if he has the next card "in sequence."
A card is in sequence if it belongs to the same suit as the last card that was played and follows the order a, 2, 3, 4, 5, 6, 7, 8, 9, 10, j, q, k. If the last card was a king, the next card in sequence for this game is the ace of the same suit. This

is called a "round the corner" sequence.)
If the player has the next card in sequence he plays it face up onto the card in the center. If he does not have this card, he must pay one counter into the center.
Play continues with each player in turn either playing the next card in sequence or paying a counter.
When all the cards of a suit have been played, the player who put down the last card has an extra turn and may play any card that he chooses.
End The first player to get rid of all his cards is the winner of the round and takes all the counters from the center. Each loser must also pay him one counter for every card left in his hand.
The winner of the game is the player with most counters after an agreed number of rounds.

SEQUENCE
This game is easily learned but calls for a little skill in choosing which card to play when starting a sequence.
Players Two or more can play sequence but it is best with four or five players.
Cards A standard deck of playing cards is used.
Objective Each player aims to be first to get rid of all his cards.
Deal One player is chosen as dealer. He deals out all the cards in a clockwise direction, one at a time and face down. It does not matter if some players have one card more than others.
Play The player to the left of the dealer starts by putting his lowest card of any suit face up in the center. (2s count as the lowest cards and aces as the highest.)
The player with the next card in sequence then plays it face up onto the card in the center. A card is in sequence if it is of the same suit as the last card that was played and follows the order 2, 3, 4, 5, 6, 7, 8, 9, 10, j, q, k, a.
Play continues in this way until the ace is played and the sequence ends.
A player who ends a sequence starts another by playing any card from his hand.
When part of a suit has already been played, a sequence ends with the highest card yet to play. The following sequence is then started by the player who played this highest card.
End The first player to get rid of all his cards is the winner.
Scoring If more than one round is to be played, players may each start with 10 counters or beans.
At the end of every round each loser pays the winner one bean for every card still in his hand. The winner is the player with most counters or beans after an agreed number of rounds.

CARD DOMINOES
This game of luck and skill is also called sevens, parliament, and fan tan. A player can increase his chances of winning by carefully choosing the order in which he plays his cards.
Players The game is for two or more players.
Cards One complete deck of standard playing cards is used.
Objective Each player aims to be first to play his cards onto a central pattern of cards in sequence.
Deal One player deals all the cards in a clockwise direction, one at a time and face down.
Play Each player looks at his cards and sorts them in his hand according to suit and sequence.
The player with the 7 of diamonds starts the game by putting it face up in the center. The player to his left must then try to put down either the 6 or 8 of diamonds or another 7. If he plays the 6 or 8 of diamonds he puts it respectively below or above the 7. If he plays another 7 he puts it next to the 7 of diamonds.
If, however, he does not hold any of these cards he "passes" and the play then goes to the next player to the left.
Play continues in this way, with each player in turn adding a card to one of the sequences, putting down a 7, or passing. The sequences are built up from 7 through 8, 9, 10, jack, and queen to king, and down from 6 to ace.
End The game is won by the first player to put down all his cards, but play usually continues until every card has been played and there are four complete suit sequences.

Card dominoes

ROLLING STONE

This popular game is highly unpredictable in its outcome. Just as a player is on the verge of winning he can get a new handful of cards to play. It is also known as enflay or schwellen.

Players Four, five, or six people can play.

Cards A standard deck of playing cards is used, but with cards removed so that there are eight cards per player.

The following cards should be removed before play:
a) for four players, the 2s, 3s, 4s, 5s, and 6s;
b) for five players, the 2s, 3s, and 4s;
c) for six players, the 2s.

Objective Each player aims to be the first to get rid of all his cards.

Deal Each player cuts the cards and the one with the highest card (ace high) is the dealer. He deals out all the cards in a clockwise direction, one at a time and face down.

Play Each player looks at his cards and sorts them into suits in his hand.

The player to the dealer's left starts play by choosing a card from his hand and placing it, face up, in the center.

The other players, in turn, then try to play one card of the same suit.

If all the players are able to "follow suit," these cards (called a "trick") are put to one side and are out of play for the rest of the game. The player who played the highest card (with ace high) then starts the next trick by playing another card into the center.

If any player is unable to follow suit, he must pick up the cards already played for that trick and add them to his own hand. He then plays the first card of the next trick, but must not use any of the cards that he has just picked up.

End The winner is the first person to play all his cards.

A trick, five players

LINGER LONGER

Linger longer is an ideal introduction to the principles of trump play that form the basis of many more complicated card games.

Players Three or more people can play. Four to six is best.

Cards A standard deck of playing cards is used.

Objective Each player tries to be the last person with cards in his hand. Players obtain new cards by winning tricks.

A trick comprises one card from each player played into the center.

Except when a trump has been played a trick is won by the highest card belonging to the suit that was led—ie to the same suit as the first card played in that trick.

A trump is a card belonging to the trump suit. The trump suit is determined before each game is played. A trump card beats any card belonging to the suit led.

Deal One player deals out the cards in a clockwise direction, face down and one at a time, until each player has the same number of cards as there are players. For example if there are five players, each one of them receives five cards.

The remaining cards are placed in the center in a face-down pile called the stock.

The last card dealt to the dealer is shown to all the players. The suit of this card is the trump suit for the game.

Play The player to the left of the dealer plays any card he likes face up into the center. Each player in turn then plays one card into the center. (These cards together form a trick.) If possible, players must play a card of the same suit as the first card—this is called "following suit." If a player is unable to follow suit, he may play a trump card or any other card.

A trick is won by the player who played the highest trump card or, if no trump was played, by the player who played the highest card of the suit led. Ace ranks high for this game.

A player who wins a trick places these cards face down in front of him. He then draws the top card from the stock and adds it to the cards in his hand (no other player draws). This player plays the first card of the next trick.

Players continue playing tricks in this way as long as they have any cards in their hand—ignoring the cards in any tricks that they have won. A player with no cards in his hand must drop out of the game.

End The last player left in the game wins.

KNOCKOUT WHIST

Knockout whist is another easy game with trumps. The players are eliminated until only one remains.

Objective Each player aims to win all the tricks of a hand.

Players Two to seven people can play this game.

Cards A standard deck of playing cards is used.

Deal One player deals out the cards face down, one at a time, and in a clockwise direction until each player has seven cards.

The remaining cards are put face down in a pile in the center.

Each time the cards are dealt, the number dealt to each player is decreased by one.

Play The top card of the center pile is turned over and this determines the trump suit for the first hand.

The player to the dealer's left then starts the first trick by playing any card he chooses. Each player in turn then plays a card, following suit if he can.

The trick is won as in linger longer and the winner starts the next trick.

When all seven tricks have been played anyone who has not won a trick drops out of the game.

The dealer collects all the cards, shuffles them, and deals six cards to each remaining player.

The winner of the most tricks in the first round chooses the trump suit and plays the first card in the second hand.

Play continues in this way—with players without tricks dropping out at the end of each hand.

End The first player to win all the tricks in a single hand is the overall winner.

If play continues to the seventh hand, each player will have only one card and there will be only one trick to win.

A trick, four players

Trumping a trick

Trumps

252

Racing demon

SPIT
Spit is an excellent game that calls for alertness and speed.
Players Two persons can play.
Cards A complete deck of standard cards is used.
Deal All the cards are dealt out equally between the two players.

Before play starts, each player lays out a row of cards in front of him, as follows:
1) starting from the left, he places three cards face down followed by a fourth card face up;
2) he places a second face-down card on each of the first two face-down cards and a face-up card on the third;
3) he places a face-down card on the first pile and a face-up card on the second;
4) he places a face-up card on the first pile.
Each player then places the rest of his cards face down in a pile to the left of his row.
Objective Each player aims to be the first to get rid of all his cards.
Start of play When both players are ready, either one of them calls "Spit!"
Immediately both players take the top card from their piles of spare cards and place them face up, side by side, in the center.

Playing into the center
Each player then quickly plays as many cards as possible from his row of face-up cards onto either of the face-up cards in the center of the table. A card may be played into the center if it has a numerical value either one higher or one lower than a central face-up card. (For example, a 9 or a jack can be played onto a 10. Either a king or a 2 can be played onto an ace.)
If playing a face-up card into the center exposes a face-down card in a player's row, this card should be turned face up.
Players continue to play cards onto the central piles in this manner until neither player can put out any more of his cards.

Play to center

Play on face-up cards

RACING DEMON
Racing demon is a fast and noisy game.
Players Any number can play.
Cards One complete deck of standard playing cards is needed for each player. Old decks with different backs are recommended.
Playing area This game requires a lot of space.
Deal Each player shuffles and deals his own deck.
After shuffling, each player first deals out 13 cards, face down, in a pile in front of him. This pile is then turned over so that only the top card is visible.
He then deals four cards face up, in a row alongside his pile of 13 cards.
His spare cards should be held face down in one hand.
Objective Each player aims:
a) to get rid of his pile of 13 cards;
b) to play as many cards as possible into the center.
Start of play One of the players is chosen to be the starter. When all the players have dealt out their cards, he starts play by shouting "Go!"

Play All the players play at the same time: there is no waiting to play in turn. Players may either play cards into the center or onto their own face-up cards.
Playing into the center If a player has an ace among his face-up cards, he should place it face up in the center. Once an ace has been played into the center, anyone with a face-up 2 of the same suit can play this onto the ace. A face-up 3 of the same suit can then be added by any player, and so on through to the 10, jack, queen, and king.
Playing on face-up cards
As well as building up the piles in the center, a player can build piles of cards on the four cards alongside his original pile of 13.
Cards added to these piles must be in descending order and alternatively black and red (for example a black 6 can be added to a red 7 and then a red 5 added to the black 6).
Cards added to these piles may be:
a) the top card from the player's original pile of 13;
b) a card, or a correct sequence of cards, from one of the player's other face-up piles.

Any space left by the removal of one of the four face-up piles should be filled with the top card from the player's original pile of 13.
Spare cards If a player is unable either to play a face-up card into the center or to move any of his face-up cards, he turns to the cards that were spare after he first dealt out his cards.
These spare cards are turned over, three at a time, onto a separate pile, until one of them can be played into the center or onto a face-up pile.
When all the spare cards have been turned over, the player picks up the pile, turns it face down, and continues play.
End As soon as any player uses up all his cards from his original pile of 13, he shouts "Out!" and play ends.
Scoring The cards in the center are sorted into their separate decks.
A player's final score is the difference between the number of his cards in the center and the number of cards left in his original face-up piles.
The winner is the player with the highest score.

Spit If neither player can play any card from his row of face-up cards, one of the players shouts "Spit!"

Both players then take the top card from their piles of spare cards and place them face up on their central piles.

If possible, players then resume playing cards into the center from their face-up piles.

If players still cannot add any cards from their face-up rows, the other player calls "Spit!" and both players again play the top card of their spare piles. They continue in this way until either player can play a card from his row.

If a player wishes to call "Spit!" and the players' spare piles have been used up, each player takes his own central pile and turns it face down to form a new spare pile. The player then calls "Spit!" and play continues as before.

End of a round When a player has played all the cards from his face-up row into the center, he shouts "Out!" and wins the round. He then picks up his spare pile.

The other player then collects both central face-up piles, picks up the cards left in his row, and adds all these cards to the bottom of his spare pile.

Starting a new round
Players lay out their cards as for the first round.

New rounds are played in the same way as the first round, except that if one player does not have enough cards for a spare pile he does without and both players play onto a single central pile.

End of game A game is won by the first player to get rid of all his cards.

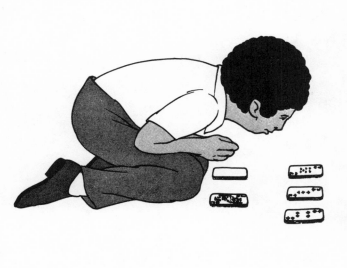

GIVE AWAY
Give away is a simple game that requires players to stay alert. The faster it is played the better.

Objective Each player aims to be first to get rid of all his cards.

Players Two or more can play this game.

Cards A standard deck of playing cards is used.

Deal One player deals out all the cards in a clockwise direction—face down and one at a time. It does not matter if some players have one card more than others. Players do not look at their cards but put them in a neat face-down pile in front of them.

Play The player to the left of the dealer turns over the top card of his face-down pile.

If it is not an ace, he places it face up by his face-down pile and ends his turn.

If it is an ace, he puts it face up in the center of the table and turns over another card. His turn continues until he turns over a card that he is unable to play to the center—a card may be played to the center if it is an ace or if it can be built in rank order (a, 2, 3, 4, 5, 6, 7, 8, 9, 10, j, q, k) onto a center card of the same suit. When he turns over a card that cannot be played to the center he places it face up by his face-down pile and ends his turn. Each player then plays in turn. As well as playing to the center a player may play a card onto another player's

face-up pile—provided that it is one higher or lower in rank than the top card of that pile. When a player plays his last face-down card onto his face-up pile, he waits until his next turn before turning over his face-up pile to start again. If he plays his last face-down card into the center or onto another player's pile, he turns over his face-up pile immediately and continues his turn.

End The first player to get rid of all his cards wins the game.

Give away

Play to center

Play on face-up cards

Spit

©DIAGRAM

SPORTS

Athletics is a sport comprising a wide range of events and demanding a variety of different skills from its participants. There are two broad categories of athletics events – track and field. Track programs are made up of sprint, middle distance, relay, hurdle, and walking events. Field programs include throwing events, and jumping for distance and height.

Maximum inclinations For running and jumping events the maximum inclinations are 1:100 in the lateral direction and 1:1000 in the running direction.
For throwing events the maximum inclinations for the runways are 1:100 in the lateral direction and 1:1000 in the running direction;

throwing fields have a maximum inclination of 1:1000.
Direction of running All races are run with the competitors' left hands toward the inside of the track.
Lanes All lanes are of uniform width.
Finish All races should end at the same point.

General rules for field events Competitors compete in the order drawn by lot. Unless competing in a simultaneous track event, a competitor missing his turn in a field event is not permitted to take the trial so missed.
A competitor who unreasonably delays a trial is liable to have that trial disallowed and recorded as a fault.
After a second delay in a competition, he shall be debarred from further trials though credited with any performance made up to that time.

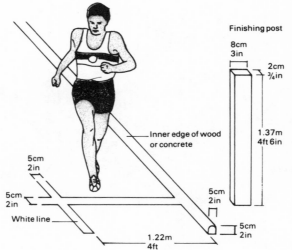

Finishing post

8cm 3in · 2cm ¾in · 1.37m 4ft 6in · Inner edge of wood or concrete · 5cm 2in · White line · 5cm 2in · 5cm 2in · 5cm 2in · 1.22m 4ft

Olympic athletics events

Men / Women

Track races Sprints 100m 200m 400m

Middle distance 800m 1500m

Long distance 5000m 10,000m

Relays 4 x 100m 4 x 400m
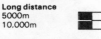

Hurdles 100m 110m 400m

Steeplechase 3000m

Road races Marathon

Walks 20km

Throwing events Javelin Shot put Discus Hammer

Jumping events High jump Pole vault Long jump Triple jump

Combined events Decathlon Pentathlon
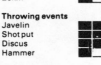

STANDARD 400M TRACK

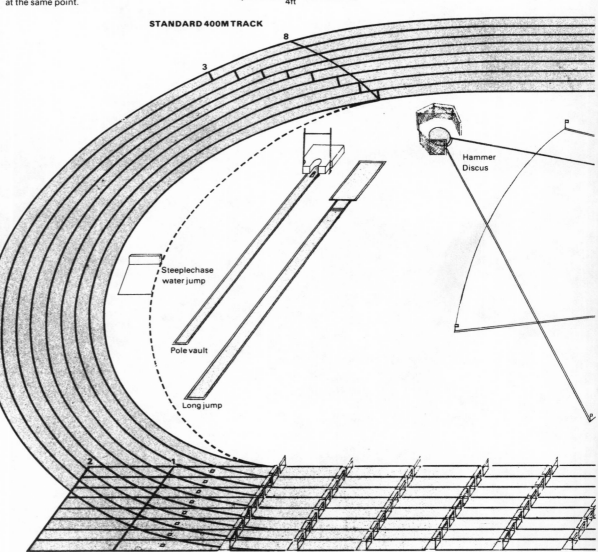

Hammer Discus · Steeplechase water jump · Pole vault · Long jump

The referee may award a substitute trial to any competitor hampered in the course of a trial.
Fingers must not be taped together, but tape is allowed on a cut or wound.
Rosin or a similar substance is allowed on the hands.

Dress Clothing (**a**) must be clean, non-transparent even when wet, and designed and worn so as not to cause offense.

Numbers Competitors must wear numbers (**b**) corresponding to the numbers given in the program. In the high jump and pole vault, competitors may wear one number on either their back or their front; competitors in all other events must wear numbers on both their back and front.

Footwear Competitors may compete in bare feet, or with shoes on one or both feet. Styles of footwear (**c**) vary for different events, but all must conform to certain general specifications: a maximum of six sole and two heel spikes is permitted; spikes must not project more than 25mm (1in) or exceed 4mm (0.16in) in diameter; grooves and ridges are permitted on sole and heel; soles must not exceed 13mm ($\frac{1}{2}$in) in thickness; heel thickness must not exceed sole thickness by more than 13mm ($\frac{1}{2}$in) for walking events or 6mm ($\frac{1}{4}$in) for all other events.

Starts
1 100m and 100m hurdles
2 110m hurdles
3 200m
4 400m
5 800m
6 1500m
7 3000m steeplechase
8 5000m
9 10,000m

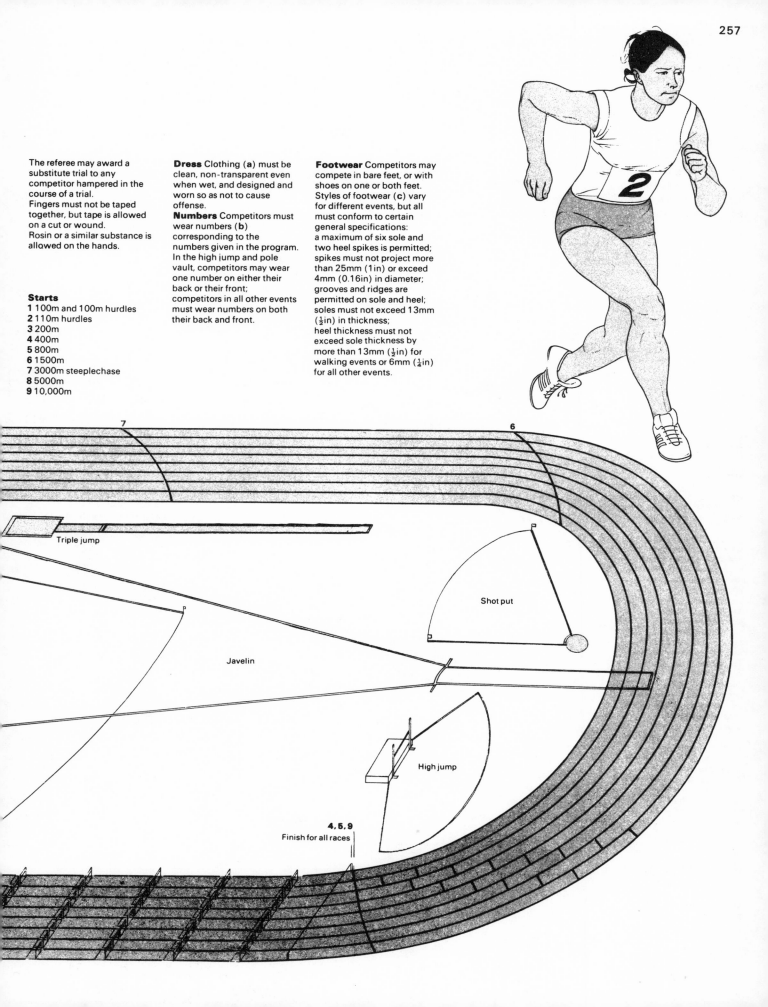

Triple jump

Javelin

Shot put

High jump

4, 5, 9
Finish for all races

Track events

Running events

The Olympic Games include individual track events run over distances ranging from 100m to 10,000m. There are men's and women's events over 100m, 200m, 400m, 800m, and 1500m, and men's events over 5000m and 10,000m.

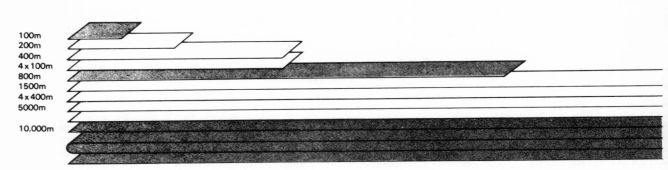

100m
200m
400m
4 × 100m
800m
1500m
4 × 400m
5000m

10,000m

Distances are measured from the edge of the starting line farthest from the finish to the edge of the finish line nearest the start.

Heats Preliminary rounds (heats) are held when there are too many competitors for a satisfactory single-round competition.
Only in circumstances approved by the referee may a competitor take part in a heat other than that in which his name appears in the program.

The start Races run around bends have curved or staggered starts so that all competitors have to run the same distance.
The starter, in his own language, gives the commands "on your marks" and "set" in races up to and including the 800m, and "on your marks" in all longer Olympic races.
The pistol is then fired when the competitors are all steady in position.

False starts It is a false start if a competitor:
fails after a reasonable time to comply with the command "set";
starts before the pistol is fired.
Competitors are recalled by a pistol shot after a false start. The competitor(s) responsible must be warned. Competitors are disqualified after causing two false starts, or three in the decathlon or pentathlon.

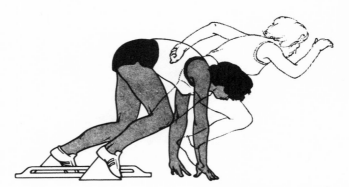

Lanes All the individual races shorter than 800m are run completely in lanes.
Also run in lanes are the first two bends of the 800m and the first three turns of the 4 × 400m relay.
Lanes are decided by lot.
Any competitor who deliberately leaves his lane shall be disqualified; if the offense was not deliberate, disqualification is at the referee's discretion.
Marks may be placed on or beside the track only for relay races.

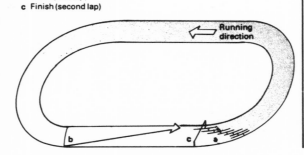

800m
a Staggered start
b End of section run in lanes (first lap)
c Finish (second lap)

Running direction

Relay events

Events There are four Olympic relay events: men's and women's 4 × 100m, and men's and women's 4 × 400m.
Procedure Each of the four team members runs one stage of the race.
A baton is carried in the hand, and transferred in the take-over zone from one runner to the next. If dropped, the baton must be picked up by the competitor who dropped it.
Composition of teams may be changed after a heat only in the case of injury or illness certified by the official medical officer.

A team may change its running order.
No competitor may run more than one stage in a race.
The relay baton is a smooth, hollow tube made of rigid material in one piece. It must weigh not less than 50g (1¾oz).

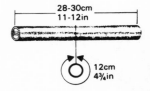

28-30cm
11-12in

12cm
4¾in

Shoes with a maximum of six spikes in the sole are worn for track running events.

Pistol Races are started by the report of a pistol, or similar apparatus, fired upward into the air.

Starting blocks may be used in individual races up to and including 800m, and by the first runner in relay races in which the stages are not greater than 800m.

They must be constructed entirely of rigid materials. They may be adjustable, but must be without springs or any other device whereby the athlete might obtain artificial assistance.

Athletes in the "set" position must have both feet touching the track.

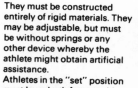

Leaving the track Any competitor who voluntarily leaves the track or course may not then continue running in a race.

Obstruction A competitor who jostles, runs across, or otherwise obstructs another competitor is liable to disqualification.

After a disqualification the referee may order the race to be re-run, or, in the case of a heat, permit any affected competitor to compete in the next round.

Assistance Permission must be obtained to inform track competitors of intermediate times.

Track competitors will be disqualified for receiving any other assistance from persons within the arena.

The finish Competitors are placed in the order in which any part of their torso (as distinguished from their head, neck, arms, legs, hands, or feet) reaches the vertical plane of the edge of the finish line nearest to the start. (Competitor(a)is the winner in the finish illustrated at right.)

Timing Electrical timekeeping equipment is used for the Olympic Games and some other major meetings; otherwise timing is by timekeepers using stopwatches.

Times are taken from the flash of the pistol to the moment when the competitor's torso reaches the finish.

Individual and relay races up to and including the 1500m are timed to one-tenth of a second.

Longer races are timed to one-fifth of a second, but recorded as multiples of two-tenths of a second.

Ties In a tie for first place in a final, the referee decides whether it is practicable for those tying to run again. If a tie in a heat affects qualification for the next round, the tying competitors run again only if it is impracticable for both to qualify.

All other tied results stand.

© DIAGRAM

a Staggered start
b First take-over zone
c Second take-over zone
d Third take-over zone
e Finish

Lanes 4 × 100m relay races are run entirely in lanes. 4 × 400m relay races are run in lanes as far as the exit from the first bend of the second lap.

Take-overs The baton must be handed over within the marked take-over zone Runners about to take over must not start running more than 10m before the take-over zone.

In the stages of the 4 × 400m not run in lanes, competitors must return to their own lanes for the take-over unless they can use the inside position

without causing an obstruction.

After handing over the baton, competitors should remain in their lanes or zones until the course is clear.

Teams will be disqualified for deliberately causing an obstruction or for pushing or giving any other assistance at a take-over.

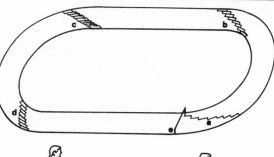

10m
11yd

Take-over zone   20m
22yd

Track events

Steeplechase

The Olympic steeplechase is a men's event run over 3000m. It comprises 28 hurdle jumps and seven water jumps. Competitors may jump, vault, or stand on the hurdles. The hurdles numbered (3) and (4) are positioned after the competitors have passed by on the first lap. Competitors run outside the water jump on the first lap.

Steeplechase hurdles have a base on either side and must weigh 80–100kg (176½–220½lb). They are positioned across the three inside lanes.

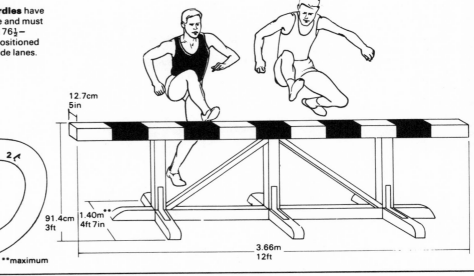

12.7cm
5in

91.4cm
3ft

1.40m**
4ft 7in

3.66m
12ft

Start

Running direction

3

2

Water jump

Finish

4

1

**maximum

Hurdle events

Olympic hurdling events are held over 110m and 400m for men, and over 100m for women. In addition, the decathlon includes a 110m hurdles and the pentathlon a 100m hurdles race.

All hurdling events are run in lanes, and there are 10 hurdles in each lane.

100m women's hurdles

110m men's hurdles

a b b b b b b b b b c

a b b b b b b b b b c

a b b b

Hurdles are made of metal with the top bar of wood. They are designed so that a force of 3.6–4kg (8lb–8lb 13oz) applied to the center of the top edge of the crossbar is required to overturn them.
The height of the hurdles varies with the length of the race.

Disqualification A hurdler will be disqualified if he:
trails his foot or leg alongside any hurdle;
jumps any hurdle not in his own lane;
deliberately knocks down any hurdle with his hand or foot.

400m

Start and finish

Running direction

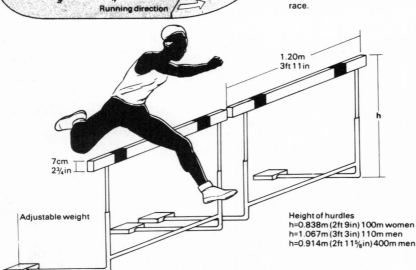

1.20m
3ft 11in

h

7cm
2¾in

Adjustable weight

70cm
2ft 3½in

Height of hurdles
h=0.838m (2ft 9in) 100m women
h=1.067m (3ft 3in) 110m men
h=0.914m (2ft 11⅝in) 400m men

Marathon

The marathon is 42.195km (26mi 385yd) long. The start and finish are usually in the arena, but the rest of the race is run on made-up roads.
Distances, in kilometers and miles, are displayed to the competitors along the route.
Competitors must leave the race if ordered to do so by the medical staff.

Refreshments Approved refreshments may be taken at official refreshment stations, sited at about 11km (7mi) and then at every 5km (3mi). No other refreshments are allowed. Additional sponging points, supplying water only, are provided midway between the refreshment stations.

The water jump is the fourth jump in each lap. The water jump hurdle stands the same height as the other hurdles, but is sunk into the ground.
Disqualification A steeplechaser will be disqualified if he:
steps to either side of a jump;
fails to go over or through the water;
trails his foot or leg alongside any hurdle.

12.7cm
5in

91.4cm
3ft

70cm
2ft 3½in

3.66m
12ft

3.66m
12ft

Concrete

Matting

100m women's hurdles: a=13m, b=8.5m, c=10.5m
110m men's hurdles: a=13.72m, b=9.14m, c=14.02m
400m men's hurdles: a=45m, b=35m, c=40m

400m men's hurdles

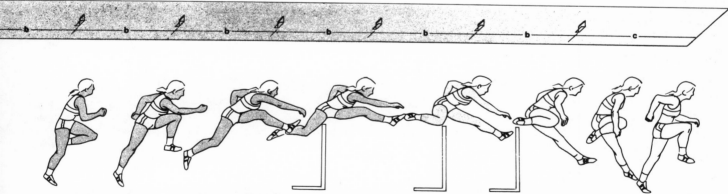

Walking events

The walking events most frequently included in international competitions are the 20km and 50km road walks.

Action Walkers must maintain unbroken contact with the ground. Thus the rear foot (**r**) must not leave the ground before the advancing foot (**a**) has made contact. The leg must be momentarily straightened while a foot is on the ground.

Refreshments Approved refreshments may be taken at official refreshment stations in walking races exceeding 20km.
Stations are sited at 10km and then every 5km.
No other refreshments are allowed.
Additional sponging points, supplying water only, may be provided at points after 20km.

Disqualification A competitor is entitled to one caution, signaled with a white flag, before being disqualified, signaled with a red flag.
Action is taken against a competitor after the independent recommendation of three judges, or two judges if one is the chief judge.
In track races a disqualified competitor must immediately leave the track. In road races he must immediately remove his number.
If immediate notification is impracticable, competitors may be disqualified immediately after a race ends.

Walking shoes Soles may be up to 13mm (½in) thick. Heels must not exceed the sole thickness by more than 13mm (½in).

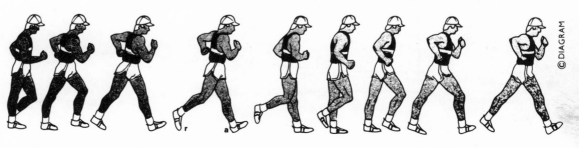

© DIAGRAM

Field events

Javelin

The javelin is thrown from behind an arc and must land within the marked sector. If there are fewer than eight competitors, each one generally has six trials; otherwise competitors generally have three trials, and then the best eight competitors have a further three. The winner is the competitor with the best distance in his six trials. A tie for first place is decided by the competitors' second-best throws.

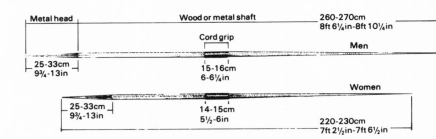

Shoes Sole and heel spikes are recommended. A maximum of six sole and two heel spikes is permitted.
The javelin must be without mobile parts. The cord grip is around the center of gravity and its circumference must not exceed that of the shaft by more than 25mm (1in). The minimum weight for men is 800g (1lb 12.218oz) and

for women 600g (1lb 5.163oz).
Landing The javelin must land tip first, but it need not stick in the ground. It must land within the inner edge of the sector lines.
Broken javelin If the javelin breaks in the air, a trial is not counted, provided the throw was made in accordance with the rules.

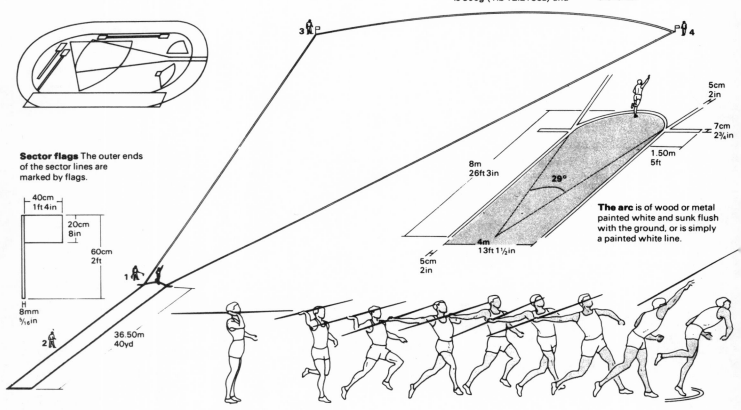

Sector flags The outer ends of the sector lines are marked by flags.

40cm 1ft 4in
20cm 8in
60cm 2ft
H 8mm 5/16in

36.50m 40yd

8m 26ft 3in
29°
4m 13ft 1½in
5cm 2in
5cm 2in
7cm 2¾in
1.50m 5ft

The arc is of wood or metal painted white and sunk flush with the ground, or is simply a painted white line.

Practice throws Before any throwing event practice throws in the arena are permitted only from or near the circles or scratch line. Implements must always be returned by hand either in practice or during the competition.
Throwing action
The javelin must be held at the grip. It must be thrown

over the shoulder or the upper part of the throwing arm. It must be neither slung nor hurled. The competitor is not permitted to turn his back to the arc after preparing to throw and before discharging the javelin.
A throw is a foul if the competitor touches with any part of his body the arc or scratch lines or the ground

beyond them.
The parallel lines may be crossed during run-up, but the competitor must be between them when the javelin is released.
The competitor must not leave the delivery area until the javelin has landed, when he must leave from behind the arc and scratch lines.

Judging A white flag indicates a fair throw and a red flag a foul.
Judge (1) watches whether the competitor touches or crosses the arc or scratch line. Judge (2) watches the approach and the way the javelin is held. Judges (3) and (4) watch the landing of the javelin.

Measurement A throw is measured from the nearest mark made by the head of the javelin (a) to the inner edge of the circumference of the arc (b). Measurement is along a line from the mark and through the center of the radius of the arc (c). Distances are recorded to the nearest even unit of 2cm (1in) below the distance thrown.

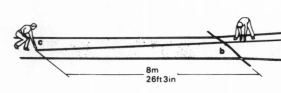

8m 26ft 3in

Shot put

The shot is put from a circle and must land within the marked sector. If there are fewer than eight competitors, each one generally has six trials; otherwise competitors generally have three trials, and then the best eight competitors have a further three. The winner is the competitor with the best distance in his six trials. A tie for first place is decided by the competitors' second-best throws.

The shot is made of solid iron, brass, or any metal not softer than brass, or a shell of such metal filled with lead or other material. It must be spherical in shape and smooth-surfaced. The minimum weight for men is 7.257kg (16lb) and for women 4kg (8lb 13oz).

Shoes are without spikes since a concrete surface is recommended for within the circle.

The circle is bounded by a painted white line or by a white-painted band of iron, steel, or wood. Concrete is recommended for the surface within the circle. There is a raised stopboard for this event.

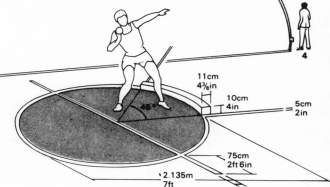

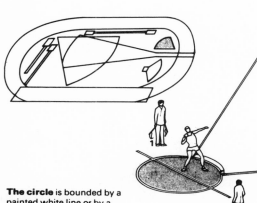

Judging A white flag indicates a fair throw and a red flag a foul. Judge (**1**) watches the position of the arm and judge (**2**) watches for infringements by the foot or any other part of the body. Judges (**3**) and (**4**) check the landing and help measure the put.

Putting action The competitor must begin his put from a stationary position. Only one hand may be used and throughout the putting action this hand must not be dropped below its starting position. The shot must not be brought in front of the line of the shoulders. A put is invalid if the competitor, after commencing

his action, touches with any part of his body the top of the stopboard (**s**) or the ring bounding the circle, or the ground outside (**g**). He is permitted to touch the inside of the stopboard or ring. The competitor must not leave the circle until the shot has touched the ground, when he must, standing, leave from behind the dividing line.

Interrupting a trial Provided there has been no infringement, a competitor is permitted one interruption for each trial. When interrupting a trial, the competitor may lay down his shot. He must then restart from a stationary position. **Landing** The shot must land within the inner edge of the sector lines.

Measurement takes place immediately after each trial. Puts are measured from the nearest mark made by the shot to the inner edge of the ring bounding the circle. Measurement is along a line from the mark and through the center of the circle. Distances are recorded to the nearest 1cm ($\frac{1}{2}$in) below the distance put.

Field events

Discus

The discus is thrown from a circle and must land within the marked sector. If there are fewer than eight competitors, each one generally has six trials; otherwise competitors generally have three trials, and then the best eight competitors have a further three. The winner is the competitor with the best distance in his six trials. A tie for first place is decided by the competitors' second-best throws.

219-221mm 8⅝-8¾in

Men

44-46mm 1¾-1⅞in

50-57mm 2-2¼in

Women

37-39mm 1½-1⅝in

180-182mm 7⅛-7¼in

The discus A smooth metal rim is permanently attached to the body of the discus, which is made of wood or other suitable material. A weight is secured in the center. Minimum discus weights are 2kg (4lb 6.547oz) for men, and 1kg (2lb 3.247oz) for women.
Holding the discus The most usual method is

illustrated. Fingers must not be taped together.
Shoes without spikes are worn for discus and hammer events.

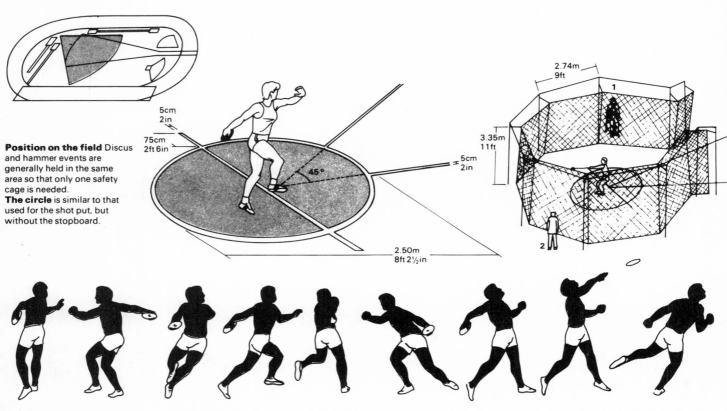

Position on the field Discus and hammer events are generally held in the same area so that only one safety cage is needed.
The circle is similar to that used for the shot put, but without the stopboard.

5cm 2in

75cm 2ft 6in

45°

5cm 2in

2.50m 8ft 2½in

2.74m 9ft

3.35m 11ft

5cm 2in

Throwing action The competitor must begin his throw from a stationary position. He may hold the discus as he wishes and use any throwing technique. His throw is a foul if, after commencing his action, he touches with any part of his body either the top of the ring bounding the circle or the ground beyond it. This rule

remains in force while the discus is in flight.
At the end of the throw the competitor must, from a standing position, leave the circle from behind the dividing line.
Interrupting a trial Provided there has been no infringement, a competitor is permitted one interruption for each trial. When

interrupting a trial, the competitor may lay down his discus. He must then recommence his action from a stationary position.
Landing The discus must land within the inner edge of the sector lines.

Judging Five judges are needed. Judges (**1**) and (**2**) watch on their own side for infringements within the circle. (Their positions are reversed for left-handed throwers.) Three judges are needed in the field since the landing area is unpredictable.

Measurement A throw is measured from the nearest mark made by the discus (**a**) to the inner edge of the ring bounding the circle (**b**). Measurement is along a line from the mark and through the center of the circle (**c**). Distances are recorded to the nearest 2cm (1in) below the distance thrown.

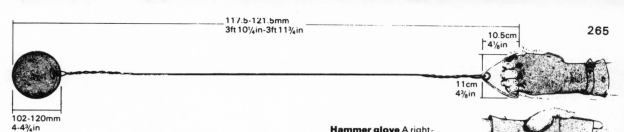

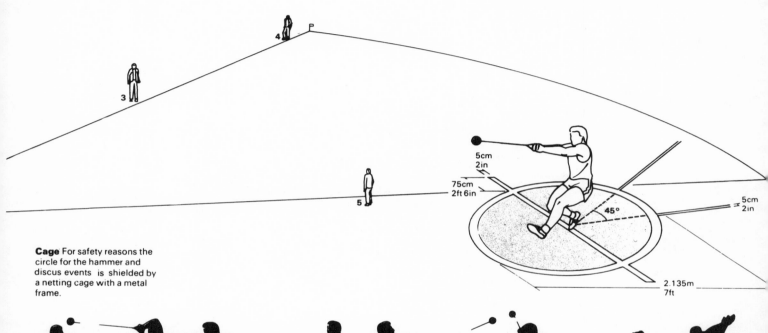

Hammer

The hammer is thrown from a circle and must land within the marked sector. As in other throwing events, some competitors may be eliminated after three trials. The winner is the competitor with the best distance after six trials. A tie for first place is decided by the competitors' second-best trials.

Hammer glove A right-handed competitor should wear a glove on his left hand.

The hammer The spherical head is of any metal not softer than brass, or has a shell of such metal filled with lead or other material. The head is attached by a swivel to the handle, which is a single length of steel wire with a diameter of 3mm ($\frac{1}{8}$in).

The grip may be a single or a double loop but must not have hinging joints. Neither the handle nor the grip must stretch appreciably during throwing. The minimum weight for a complete hammer is 7.257kg (16lb).

Cage For safety reasons the circle for the hammer and discus events is shielded by a netting cage with a metal frame.

Judging Hammer throwing is judged by five judges. Positions and responsibilities are as for discus throwing.
Throwing action The competitor must begin his throw from a stationary position, when he is permitted to rest the head of the hammer on the ground inside or outside the circle. The head of the hammer may also touch the ground during preliminary turns or swings (**a**).
A throw is a foul if, after commencing his action, the competitor touches with any part of his body either the top of the ring bounding the circle or the ground beyond it (**b**).

The competitor must not leave the circle until the hammer has landed, when he must, from a standing position, leave from behind the dividing line.
Landing The hammer must land within the inner edge of the sector lines.
Broken hammer A trial is not counted if the hammer breaks during throwing or flight, provided the throw was made in accordance with the rules. Nor is it counted a foul if the broken hammer caused the competitor to lose his balance and infringe the rules.

Interrupting a trial As in other throwing events, a competitor is permitted one interruption for each trial. He must not, however, interrupt a trial during which the hammer head has touched the ground during the preliminary swings or turns.
Measurement A throw is measured from the nearest mark made by the head of the hammer to the inner edge of the ring bounding the circle. Measurement is along a line from the mark and through the center of the circle. Distances are recorded to the nearest 2cm (1in) below the distance thrown.

©DIAGRAM

Field events

High jump

The high jump is made over a crossbar between
rigid uprights. The crossbar is raised after each
round, and competitors remain in the competition
until eliminated by three consecutive failures.

Judging Two or three judges
ensure that the apparatus and
landing area are in order and
that all jumps are correctly
made.

Shoes Heel spikes and
plastic heel cups are
recommended when jumping
for height.

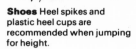

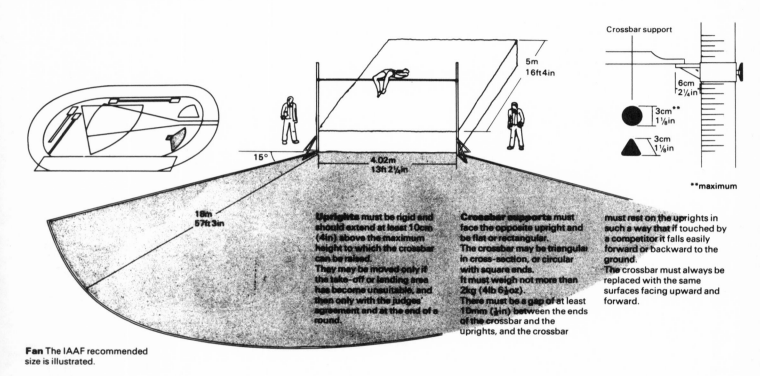

5m
16ft 4in

15°

4.02m
13ft 2¼in

18m
57ft 3in

Crossbar support

6cm
2¼in

3cm**
1⅛in

3cm
1⅛in

**maximum

Fan The IAAF recommended
size is illustrated.

Uprights must be rigid and
should extend at least 10cm
(4in) above the maximum
height to which the crossbar
can be raised.
They may be moved only if
the take-off or landing area
has become unsuitable, and
then only with the judges'
agreement and at the end of a
round.

Crossbar supports must
face the opposite upright and
be flat or rectangular.
The crossbar may be triangular
in cross-section, or circular
with square ends.
It must weigh not more than
2kg (4lb 6½oz).
There must be a gap of at least
10mm (⅜in) between the ends
of the crossbar and the
uprights, and the crossbar

must rest on the uprights in
such a way that if touched by
a competitor it falls easily
forward or backward to the
ground.
The crossbar must always be
replaced with the same
surfaces facing upward and
forward.

Run-up The length of run-up
is unlimited.
Marks may be placed for
run-up and take-off, but may
not be placed in the landing
area.
A handkerchief, or similar
marker, may be placed on the
bar for sighting purposes.
Competitors may not use
weights or grips.

Procedure Starting heights
for each round are announced
by the judges before the
event begins.
Competitors may start
jumping when they wish, and
choose whether to attempt
any subsequent height.
Elimination occurs after three
consecutive failures,
regardless of the height at
which they occur.

Failures A jump is counted
a failure if the competitor:
takes off from two feet (1);
touches the ground or landing
area beyond the plane of the
uprights without first clearing
the bar (whether or not he
makes a jump);
knocks the bar off the
supports (2) (even if he has
landed before the bar falls).

Measurements are made
perpendicularly from the
ground to the lowest part of
the upper side of the bar.
New heights are measured
before jumping begins, and
heights are remeasured after
jumping if a record is to be
established.

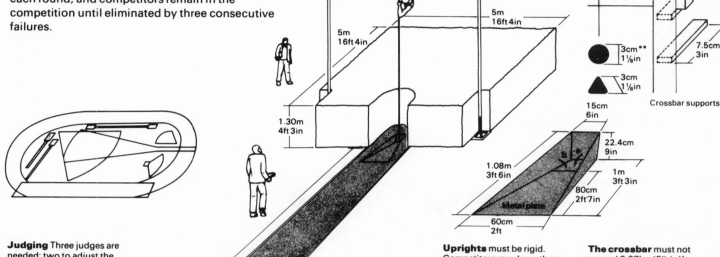

Typical vaulting pole

Handgrip — 4.90m / 16ft — Base

Binding

30cm / 1ft

Pole vault

Competitors use a flexible pole to vault a crossbar between two uprights. The crossbar is raised after each round, and competitors remain in the competition until eliminated by three consecutive failures.

3.66-4.32m / 12-14ft 2in

5m / 16ft 4in

5m / 16ft 4in

1.30m / 4ft 3in

Pole A competitor may use his own pole, provided it is approved by the judges. A pole may be of any material(s), but must be smooth-surfaced. It may be of any length or diameter (typical dimensions are shown). Bindings, except at the foot of the pole, must not exceed two layers of adhesive tape of uniform thickness.

3cm** / 1⅛in

3cm / 1⅛in

7.5cm / 3in

Crossbar supports

15cm / 6in

22.4cm / 9in

1.08m / 3ft 6in

80cm / 2ft 7in

1m / 3ft 3in

Metal plate

60cm / 2ft

Judging Three judges are needed: two to adjust the apparatus and record the vaults, and a third to watch the run-up and liaise with competitors.

45m / 147ft 6in

1.22m / 4ft

Uprights must be rigid. Competitors may have them moved in either direction, but never more than 60cm (2ft) from the continuation of the inside edge of the top of the stopboard.
The box is sunk level with the ground. It is made of metal or of wood with the bottom lined with metal. Angle (**a**) should be 105° and angle (**b**) about 120°.

The crossbar must not exceed 2.27kg (5lb). If touched by a competitor or his pole, it should fall easily toward the landing area.
Crossbar supports are smooth pegs with a uniform diameter not exceeding 13mm (½in).

2

1

© DIAGRAM

Run-up The length of the run-up is unlimited. Marks may only be placed alongside the runway.
Procedure Starting heights for each round are announced by the judges before the event begins. Competitors may start vaulting when they wish, and choose whether or not to attempt any subsequent height.

Elimination occurs after three consecutive failures, regardless of the height at which they occur.
Failures A failure is counted if a competitor:
1) before taking off touches with his body or pole the ground (including the landing area) beyond the vertical plane of the stopboard;

2) knocks the bar off the supports with his body or pole;
3) leaves the ground to make a vault but fails to clear the bar;
4) after leaving the ground places his lower hand above the upper one or moves his upper hand higher up the pole.
5) A failure is also counted if anyone touches the pole

when it is falling toward the crossbar or uprights and is likely to displace them.
(It is not counted a failure if a competitor's pole breaks.)
Measurements are made perpendicularly from the ground to the lowest part of the upper side of the bar. Heights are measured before each round, and after a vault

if a record is to be established. When special measuring apparatus is available, heights are also measured after the uprights have been moved.

Field events

Long jump

Competitors leap from a take-off board into a sand landing area. If there are fewer than eight competitors, each one generally has six trials; otherwise competitors generally have three trials, and then the best eight competitors have a further three. The competitor with the longest jump in his six trials is the winner. A tie for first place is decided by the competitors' second-best jumps.

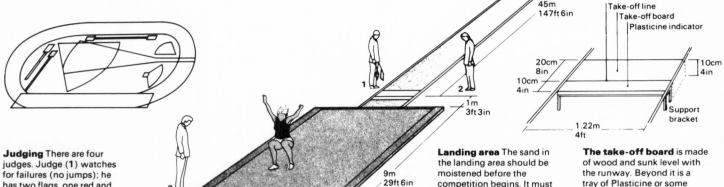

1.22m
4ft

45m
147ft 6in

Take-off line
Take-off board
Plasticine indicator

20cm
8in
10cm
4in

10cm
4in

1m
3ft 3in

1.22m
4ft

Support
bracket

9m
29ft 6in

2.75m
9ft

Judging There are four judges. Judge (**1**) watches for failures (no jumps); he has two flags, one red and one white. Judges (**2**) and (**3**) measure the jump after judge (**3**) has marked it. Judge (**4**) calls up competitors and clears the runway.

Landing area The sand in the landing area should be moistened before the competition begins. It must be raked level with the take-off board before every jump.

The take-off board is made of wood and sunk level with the runway. Beyond it is a tray of Plasticine or some other similar soft substance for recording foot faults.

Run-up The length of the run-up is unlimited. Marks may not be placed on the runway, but may be placed alongside it. Marks may not be placed beyond the take-off line.
Take-off A failure is counted if a competitor touches with any part of his body the ground beyond the take-off line or take-off line

extended. This rule applies whether he makes his jump or merely runs up without jumping. Long jumpers may not use weights or grips.
Landing It is a failure if a competitor, when landing, touches the ground outside the landing area nearer to the take-off than the nearest break in the landing area.
Measurement A jump is measured from the nearest break in the landing area made by any part of the competitor's body (**m**). Measurement is up to the take-off line and at right angles to it.
Distances are recorded to the nearest 1cm ($\frac{1}{4}$in) below the distance jumped.

Take-off | Plasticine
board | indicator

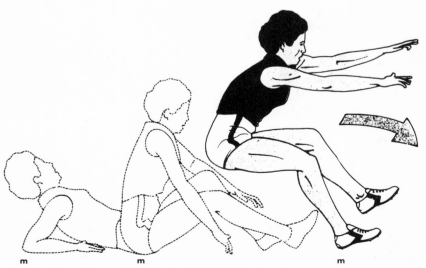

m   m   m

Shoes Heel spikes are recommended for use on grass. Plastic heel cups may be used to protect the heel bones.

Triple jump

The triple jump comprises a hop, step, and jump sequence. As in other field events, some competitors may be eliminated after three trials. The winner is the competitor with the best distance after six trials. A tie for first place is decided by the competitors' second-best trials.

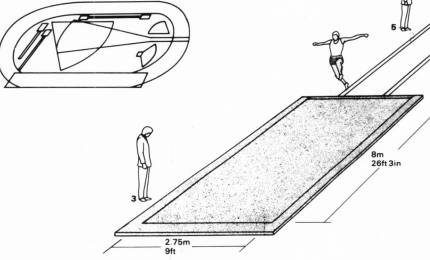

1.22m
4ft

45m
147ft 6in

13m
42ft

8m
26ft 3in

2.75m
9ft

Judging There are five judges: four as for the long jump and a fifth between the take-off board and landing area to watch the competitors' feet.

Jumping action Long jump rules apply for the run-up, initial take-off, landing, and measuring of triple jumps. Additional rules involve the hop, step, and jump action. For the hop, the competitor must land on the foot from which he first took off (l). For the step, he must land on the other foot (r). It is counted as a failure if the competitor touches the ground with his "sleeping leg" at any point during the triple jump action.

Jumping area The landing area and take-off board are the same as for the long jump, but for the triple jump in international competitions there must be 13m between them.

Hop   l   Step   r   Jump

Decathlon and pentathlon

Two Olympic athletics competitions are made up of a number of events. The decathlon is a men's competition of 10 events and the pentathlon a women's competition of five events. Competitors score points for their performance in each event.

Order of events Events are held in the set order listed. A competitor is considered to have withdrawn from the competition if he fails to take part in any event.
The order of competing is drawn before each event.

Rules IAAF (International Amateur Athletic Federation) rules generally apply for each event. Exceptions are that competitors are allowed only three trials in each field event and that three false starts in a track event result in elimination without points from that particular event.

Scoring According to IAAF tables. Points are awarded not for placings, but for achieving set times, heights, and distances. In a tie, the competitor with most points in the majority of events wins. If the tie remains, the person with most points in any one event wins.

Decathlon
First day
A 100m
B Long jump
C Shot put
D High jump
E 400m

Second day
F 110m hurdles
G Discus
H Pole vault
I Javelin
J 1500m

Pentathlon
First day
A 100m hurdles
B Shot put
C High jump

First or second day
D Long jump
E 200m

A B C D E F G H I J

A B C D E

©DIAGRAM

Special Olympic Games

The Special Olympic Games are held to encourage mentally retarded children and adults to train and compete as athletes. Such physical activity improves coordination, strengthens muscles, and helps mental developments such as adjustment to surroundings, sportsmanship, recognition of numbers and distances, a concept of time, and discipline. Competitors are divided into categories based on their age and ability. They compete in a series of local and regional contests to reach the finals. The first international Special Olympics were held in the United States in 1968. Other competitions have since taken place in Canada and France. Medals are awarded and the "Olympic" opening and closing ceremonies enacted.

Competitions National Special Olympics held every four years; state Games held annually in late spring and early summer; local and area Games held annually in early spring.

Competitors Individuals are eligible if they have been assigned to training programs designed to meet the needs of the mentally handicapped. Normally they have a maximum IQ of 80. Competitors must be at least eight years old and are not eligible if they take part in regular school athletic competitions.

Training programs Participants are involved in training programs throughout the year. These have a broad range and are not confined to specific Special Olympic sports.

Events Competitions include: track events, field events, gymnastics, bowling, volleyball, basketball, floor hockey, swimming, diving, ice skating.

Special procedures Some of the conventional rules of sports included in the Special Olympics are modified to meet the needs of the competitors.

Objective The main objective of these Games is not to produce world champions and record breakers, but to provide opportunities for the mentally retarded to participate in sports.

Basketball

Floor hockey

Track events

Field events — long jump

Olympics of the Paralysed

The Olympics of the Paralysed, also known as the Stoke Mandeville Games after their birthplace, are an international competition for paralyzed athletes. They were started in 1948 to encourage men and women with spinal cord lesions from injury or disease to train for and participate in as wide a range of sports as possible. In 1952 the Stoke Mandeville Games became an annual international event and at the Games of 1972, held at Heidelberg in Germany, 1000 paralyzed athletes from 45 countries competed for the prizes.

Fencing

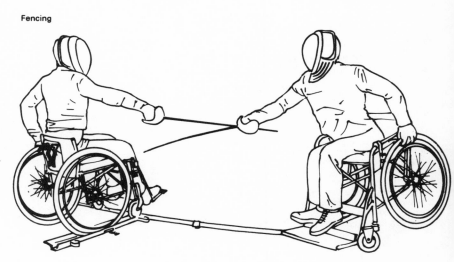

Competitions Olympics of the Paralysed are held annually at Stoke Mandeville, and every four years either immediately before or after the Olympic Games and, where possible, in the country of the Olympics.
Other meetings are the British Paraplegic Commonwealth Games and the annual National Stoke Mandeville Games for the Paralysed.
Competitors Those confined to wheelchairs because of complete or partial paralysis due to spinal cord affliction.
Equipment Standard equipment is used and standard dress worn.

Field events — discus

Bowling

Events All the normal rules of each sport are applied, except where wheelchairs or disability make certain amendments necessary. Events include: archery, swimming, basketball, bowls, snooker (men only), table tennis (singles and doubles), dartchery (a combination of darts and archery), and:
Field events Club throw, shot put, javelin, precision javelin, and discus.
Pentathlon Archery, field, track, and swimming.
Track events 60m dash, 100m dash, 4 × 60m relay.

Swimming (For which all starts are made in the water.) Breaststroke 25m, 50m, and 100m; freestyle 25m, 50m, and 100m; butterfly 25m, 50m, and 100m; individual medley 3 × 25m and 3 × 50m; freestyle relay 4 × 50m.
Benchpress weightlifting (Men only – from a prone position.) Light, light feather, feather, middle, light heavy, and heavy.
Fencing Individual and team events for men in saber, épée, and foil. Women's individual and team events in foil, and novice foil for men and women.

Archery

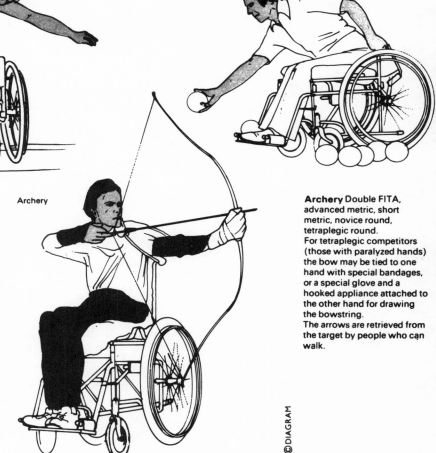

Archery Double FITA, advanced metric, short metric, novice round, tetraplegic round.
For tetraplegic competitors (those with paralyzed hands) the bow may be tied to one hand with special bandages, or a special glove and a hooked appliance attached to the other hand for drawing the bowstring.
The arrows are retrieved from the target by people who can walk.

©DIAGRAM

Cross-country running

Cross-country races are governed more by local conditions than detailed rules. But, generally, cross-country running is a winter sport in which individuals and teams compete over courses through the countryside. The first runner to complete the course is the winner; team performances are determined by the aggregate placings of individual team members.

Course For major events the course should be confined to open country, fields, heathland, and grassland. A limited amount of plowed land is allowed. Woodland sections must be clearly marked. Roads should be avoided. There should be no high obstacles, deep ditches, dangerous ascents or descents, thick undergrowth, or any other excessively difficult obstacle. Artificial obstacles should only be used when absolutely necessary. The competitors should be allowed an unrestricted run for the first 1500m (mile).
Markings The course should be clearly marked, with red flags on the left, and white flags on the right. Flags should be visible from 125m (140yd).
Distances Senior men's distances should be at least 8km (5 miles); international races should be at least 12km (about 7½ miles); national championships at least 14½km (about 9 miles). Women's senior events should be between 2km and 5km (1¼–3⅛ miles).

In international events a team must have at least six and no more than nine runners, plus five reserves.
Assistance Competitors may not receive assistance or refreshment during a race.
Start Races are started with a pistol shot. A 5-minute warning may be given if there is a large number of competitors.
Team scoring After the race the placings of the scoring members of each team are added together. The team with the lowest aggregate is the winner.
If there is a tie, the team whose last scoring runner finished before the other team's last scoring runner is awarded the higher place.
Officials for major events should include: a referee, a judge, a timekeeper, a starter, funnel judges and funnel controllers, result recorders, and assistants.

Competitors Runners may compete individually or in teams; a race may include both competitions.
Teams Except in national championships and international events, a team is allowed to enter and run twice the number of runners entitled to score. Reserves equal to the number of scoring runners may be allowed.

Dress Competitors wear starting numbers on their chests and backs. Running shoes with studs, not spikes, are usually worn.

Fell running

Fell running is similar to cross-country running, but involves much steeper and frequently longer courses. It is a sport confined to the highland areas of Britain. Competitors race between prominent geographical features.

Courses are planned over a number of prominent points that the competitors have to ascend.
Courses may be circular or consist of a run to and back from a specified point.
The courses are not marked and competitors are permitted to choose their own routes.

Distances vary considerably and may be in excess of 20 miles.

Dress Competitors may wear track suits (or similar clothing); a cagoule (cape); and fell-running shoes with spikes in the heels and soles.
Equipment Maps and compasses are allowed for navigation, especially in cloudy and misty conditions.

Start Runners begin together in a massed start.
Result The first runner to complete the course is the winner.

Orienteering

Orienteering is a sport in which individuals or teams compete on foot across rough country. Competitors reach the finish by way of a number of control points discovered through the use of a map, a compass, and their own initiative.

Orienteering map

Orienteering compass

Control marker

30cm
11¾in

30cm
11¾in

A

©DIAGRAM

Map A map of the course is given to competitors before the race.
For major competitions, the map scale is 1:20,000 or 1:25,000.
Overprinted on the map, or printed on sheets given to the competitors, are the location of the controls (numbered in the correct order), the out-of-bounds areas, and any special information relevant to the course.
Each contestant must have a mapholder in which to secure his map, and a red pen with which to plot the course.
Course Orienteering courses vary considerably according to the nature of the competition. But they are invariably heavily wooded areas with restricted visibility to prevent competitors from following one another.
In first-class competitions the course must be topographically neutral with a certain amount of relief, but not too great a height difference.
Lengths of courses vary with the different classes. The usual length for senior élite competitions is about 8 miles, and for the youngest classes about 1–2 miles.
Details of the course are kept secret before a competition so that no competitor is able to survey the area beforehand.
Each course must have a start area able to cope with large numbers of competitors, who are started at intervals, and a finish area with facilities for calculating the time taken by each competitor.
Officials Orienteering needs a large number of officials, the most vital of whom is the course setter. He is totally responsible for the positioning of the controls and for the general outline of the competitive area.
Officials and timekeepers must be present at the start and finish of the event. There is usually an official at each control point in major events.

Control points The number of control points varies with the length of the course and the type of competition.
Score orienteering competitions have roughly twice as many control points as point orienteering competitions.
A control marker consists of a three-sided prism, each side of which is a 30cm square divided diagonally with the upper half white and the lower half orange or red.
Each control is numbered. Refreshments are offered at some controls.
Control card Each competitor is issued with a control card, which he stamps when he reaches a control point.

Compulsory tracks or paths are marked by white and orange/red tape or flags.
Dress The choice of clothing is entirely free; tracksuits and athletics clothing are the most usual.
Studded athletics shoes are the most suitable footwear for the rough terrain.
A peaked cap will protect the eyes from brambles and overhanging branches.
For championship events starting numbers are worn on the chest.
The start Competitors assemble in a pre-race area close to the actual starting line.
Individuals start the race at intervals of 1 to 3 minutes, depending on the rules of the competition.

Compass An orienteering compass should have:
1 transparent base plate
2 rotating compass housing
3 orienteering lines
4 direction marker
5 magnifying lens
6 distance marker
7 safety cord

Duration varies with the type of competition. Some events end only when the course is completed. Others have a time limit.
Scoring In point orienteering (a straight race around a circuit of control points), relay orienteering (in which the circuit is completed by a team of participants), and line orienteering (where the complete route is marked out), the competitor or team with the fastest time wins. Team scores are obtained by adding together the times of the team members.
Score orienteering is performed to a strict time limit (usually 1–1½ hours). In that time contestants visit as many controls as possible. Each control has a points tariff, varying from 5 to 50

points. Controls are deployed in such a way that competitors have to decide whether to visit many low-scoring controls or a few high-scoring ones. The competitor or team with the highest aggregate tariff score is the winner, but penalty points are deducted for every minute by which a competitor exceeds the time limit. There are no bonuses for finishing early.
Misconduct Competitors are disqualified if they miss a control (except in score orienteering) or if they stamp their control card incorrectly. The orienteerer must conduct himself in a sporting manner, and must not try to gain information from spectators or other competitors about the nature of the course.

Modern pentathlon

The modern pentathlon is an Olympic event comprised of riding, fencing, shooting, swimming, and cross-country running contests. Individual and team classifications are based on points awarded for competitors' performances in each of the five disciplines. Teams have three members.

Classification The points scored for each discipline are added together to give the final classification.
Only competitors who start in all five disciplines will be considered.
A competitor who withdraws or is disqualified from one of the five disciplines may remain in the competition, but will receive 0 points for that discipline.
The team classification is obtained by adding together the points obtained by the team members, excluding any points obtained by team members fencing against opponents who are not members of a team.

Ties In the event of a tie, the competitor or team with the highest number of wins in the different disciplines wins the event.
If there is still a tie, the disciplines are valued in the order: cross-country running, swimming, shooting, fencing, riding.

Participants Nations may enter four competitors, but only three actually take part in the competition.

Rules Modern pentathlon events are governed by the rules of the UIPMB (Union Internationale du Pentathlon Moderne et Biathlon) and of the international governing bodies of the five disciplines involved.

Order The event takes place on five days:
1) riding
2) fencing
3) shooting
4) swimming
5) cross-country running

Draw A draw to determine the order of participation in each event takes place one day before the start of the riding.

Doping control Doping tests are carried out on every day but the first. The penalty for doping is elimination.

Substitution A competitor can be replaced if he withdraws due to injury from the riding competition.
If the injury occurs after he has mounted but before he passes the starting line, the replacement must start at the time drawn for the injured competitor.
If the injured competitor had passed the starting line, a replacement may be entered provided:
the doctor in charge issues a statement that the injured competitor is unable to take part in the remaining disciplines;
the replacement starts in the fencing with 0 points for riding.
Substitution is not permitted at any later stage in the event.

RIDING

Horses One horse is provided for every two competitors, plus one reserve horse for every 10 competitors. All horses are carefully selected to ensure equality between them.

Riders must weigh at least 75kg.

The course is 800m long, with 15 obstacles including a double and a triple combination.
Obstacles may not exceed prescribed dimensions:
a straight fence may not exceed 120cm in height;
a water jump may not exceed 300cm in width;
a spread fence may not exceed 110cm in height and 130cm in width.
The course is inspected by a jury two days before the competition. This is the last opportunity for changes to be made to the plan of the course or to any obstacle. Competitors may view the course on the day before the competition.

Scoring Competitors can receive a maximum of 1100 points – for a clear round in the time allowed (2 minutes). Penalty points are deducted as follows:
for each commenced second above the time allowed, 2 points;
for a knockdown or a horse's foot in the water, 32 points;
for a fall of the horse, rider, or both, 64 points;
for a first refusal, 24 points;
for a second refusal, 48 points;
for a third and subsequent refusal(s), 72 points.
If a refusal causes an obstacle to be knocked down the penalty depends on where the disobedience occurred:
for a first disobedience on the course, 36 points if at a single obstacle or part A of a combined obstacle, 40 points at part B, 44 points at part C;
for a second disobedience, 60 points at a single or part A of a combined obstacle, 64 at part B, 68 at part C.
for a third disobedience, 84 points at a single or part A of a combined obstacle, 88 at part B, 92 at part C.

FENCING

Area Fencing pistes with all-copper mats, measuring 17m by 1.80m, and 10cm thick.

Equipment Epées approved and inspected by the FIE (Fédération Internationale d'Escrime).
Electrical touch recorders are used.

Dress must conform to international fencing regulations. Numbers must be worn on the opposite thigh to the weapon arm.

Bouts All fencers meet each other, aiming for one touch; coup doubles are not counted.
Each competitor must compete in at least 20 bouts; a second round will be held if there are less than 21 competitors.
One bout lasts 3 minutes, and competitors are informed when there is only 1 minute left.
If there is no decisive touch, the bout counts as a loss for both competitors (double defeat).
If a competitor is disqualified in the fencing, all his bouts are disregarded.

Scoring Winning 70% of the bouts yields a total of 1000 points.
Points are gained or lost for each victory above or below this percentage; these points are calculated by dividing 1100 by the number of bouts. A deciding bout may be held to determine the fencing winner, but the number of points scored is not affected.

SHOOTING

Pistols The caliber must be 5.6mm (0.22). The maximum size is 300mm by 150mm by 50mm, with a 5% tolerance in one direction. The maximum weight is 1.26kg.

Ammunition Bullets must be made of lead or a similar soft, homogeneous substance.

Targets Silhouette targets approved by the UIT (Union Internationale de Tir) must be used. There must be a backing target 1m behind each target so that doubtful shots can be judged more easily.

Shooting distance is 25m.

Procedure Four series of five shots are fired by each competitor. (A practice series of five shots may be taken before the first series.) Competitors must not raise their shooting arm more than 45° from the vertical line before firing.
All commands are given in French.

Scoring 194 out of a possible 200 target points gives a score of 1000 points. 22 competition points are gained or lost for each target point over or less than 194.

SWIMMING

The pool must conform to the standard approved by FINA (Fédération Internationale Natation Amateur).

Race 300m freestyle. Competitors are divided into heats according to the starting list and the number of lanes.
The starting signal is a pistol shot.
Only injured competitors may start in the water.

Scoring Swimming the distance in 3 minutes 54 seconds gives a competitor 1000 points. Every 0.5 of a second faster or slower than this time gains or loses 4 points.

CROSS-COUNTRY RUNNING

The course is 4km long, with a total climb of 60–100m. It is marked with white tape and with signposts marked by pairs of flags, red on the left and white on the right.

Viewing On the morning of the cross-country competition, competitors view the course and are given a contour map.

Dress Competitors must wear their team colors. On their backs they must wear their own number; and on their chests their starting number for the cross-country.

Procedure Competitors start at 1-minute intervals. A competitor who starts prematurely must start again; he will be timed from his official starting time. Late starters are timed from their official starting times.

Scoring Completing the course in 14 minutes 15 seconds gives a competitor 1000 points. Every second faster or slower than this time gains or loses 3 points.

17 Gymnastics

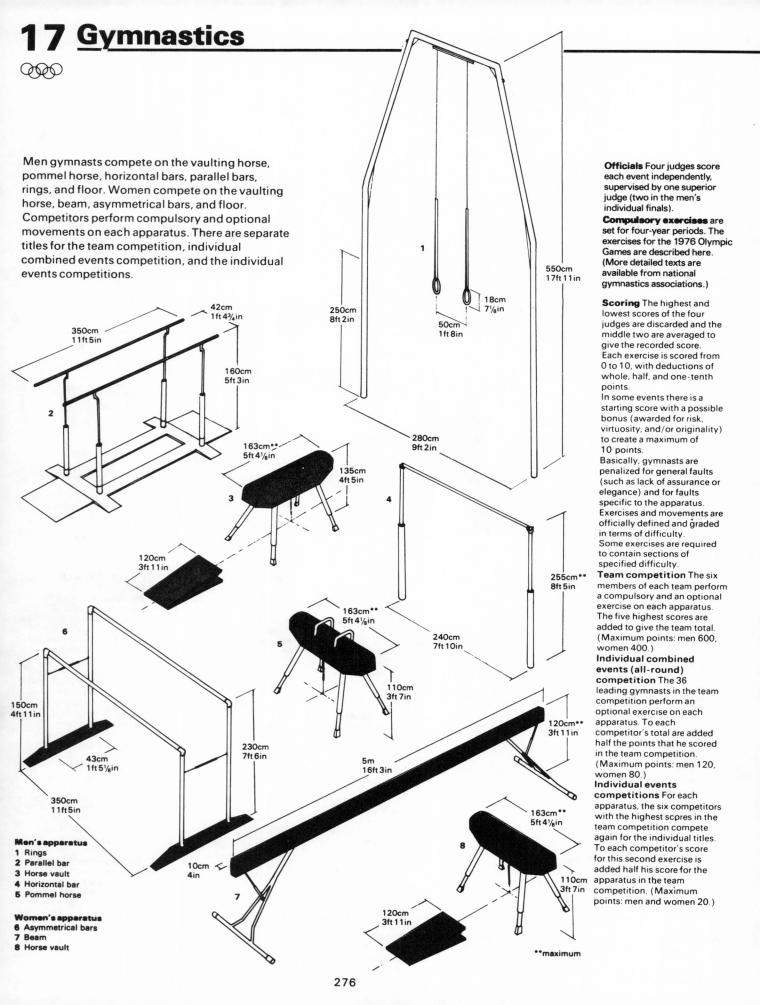

Men gymnasts compete on the vaulting horse, pommel horse, horizontal bars, parallel bars, rings, and floor. Women compete on the vaulting horse, beam, asymmetrical bars, and floor. Competitors perform compulsory and optional movements on each apparatus. There are separate titles for the team competition, individual combined events competition, and the individual events competitions.

Officials Four judges score each event independently, supervised by one superior judge (two in the men's individual finals).

Compulsory exercises are set for four-year periods. The exercises for the 1976 Olympic Games are described here. (More detailed texts are available from national gymnastics associations.)

Scoring The highest and lowest scores of the four judges are discarded and the middle two are averaged to give the recorded score. Each exercise is scored from 0 to 10, with deductions of whole, half, and one-tenth points.
In some events there is a starting score with a possible bonus (awarded for risk, virtuosity, and/or originality) to create a maximum of 10 points.
Basically, gymnasts are penalized for general faults (such as lack of assurance or elegance) and for faults specific to the apparatus. Exercises and movements are officially defined and graded in terms of difficulty.
Some exercises are required to contain sections of specified difficulty.

Team competition The six members of each team perform a compulsory and an optional exercise on each apparatus. The five highest scores are added to give the team total. (Maximum points: men 600, women 400.)

Individual combined events (all-round) competition The 36 leading gymnasts in the team competition perform an optional exercise on each apparatus. To each competitor's total are added half the points that he scored in the team competition. (Maximum points: men 120, women 80.)

Individual events competitions For each apparatus, the six competitors with the highest scores in the team competition compete again for the individual titles. To each competitor's score for this second exercise is added half his score for the apparatus in the team competition. (Maximum points: men and women 20.)

Men's apparatus
1 Rings
2 Parallel bar
3 Horse vault
4 Horizontal bar
5 Pommel horse

Women's apparatus
6 Asymmetrical bars
7 Beam
8 Horse vault

**maximum

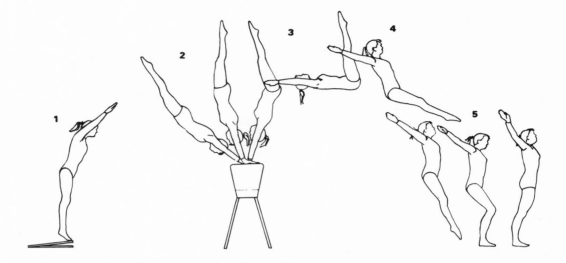

WOMEN'S HORSE VAULT

All vaults must be performed with the hands placed on the horse.

In both compulsory and optional exercises the gymnast may make two vaults; the better one is recorded.

In the optionals the two vaults may be different.

A gymnast is allowed one supplementary run for the two vaults without penalty, provided she does not touch the horse.

Generally, there are three types of vault:
handstands;
horizontal vaults;
vaults with turns.

Out of a team's 12 vaults, only four may be the same.

Each vault is divided into sections and sub-sections:

First flight
a) take-off (position, arms, legs, trajectory, lift of the body);
b) arriving on the horse (position of hands, arms, shoulders, hips, legs).

Second flight
a) repulsion;
b) balance (compared to first flight);

c) stretch and extension of body;
d) descent (balance on floor);
e) general direction of the vault;
f) general balance.

Landing One step is allowed without penalty, provided it is in the direction of the descent and is not caused by loss of balance.

Compulsory vault (1976)
Yamashita vault:
1 jump, body and arms outstretched;
2 inverted support sideways;
3 turn forward through a piked flexed position;
4 straighten body after leaving the horse;
5 landing with back to the horse.

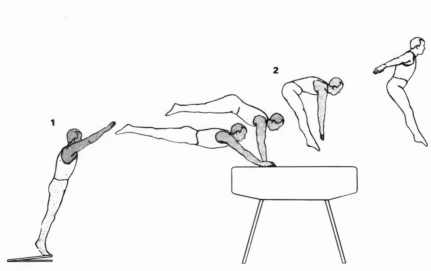

MEN'S HORSE VAULT

Approach The maximum length for the approach is 20m (66ft). The gymnast may select the length of the springboard. The approach is not scored.

Preflight is the time from take-off until the hands leave the horse.

The horse is divided into three zones; the support (hands placed on the horse) must be in one of the end zones.

All jumps must be executed with the support of one or both hands.

The angle of the body is the important factor. When the support is at the near end the body should be at least horizontal before the hands leave the horse.

Second flight lasts from when the hands leave the horse until landing. It must produce the effect of the jump by the power, amplitude, and flight of the movement in height and length.

For jumps from both ends the body must rise above the horse so that the buttocks are approximately $\frac{4}{5}$ of the horse's height above it.

The body should reach a horizontal position before the gymnast lands in a standing position. The landing distance beyond the horse should be $1\frac{1}{4}$ times the length of the horse for vaults at the far end, and the length of the horse for vaults from the near end. The direction of the flight must follow the line of the length of the horse.

Compulsory vault (1976)
1 stoop vault with hands on the near end of the horse;
2 second flight as described.

WOMEN'S FLOOR EXERCISES

The gymnasts incorporate their own optional exercises into a series of compulsory exercises. Sequences must suit the level of difficulty of the various exercises, and also the build and temperament of the gymnast. They must be varied and original, and display her grace, suppleness, and energy.

The gymnast must display:
a) sureness of acrobatics;
b) sureness of turns;
c) sureness of balance;
d) amplitude of movements;
e) general posture of body;
f) coordination;
g) lightness;
h) suppleness;
i) relaxation.
The gymnast's feet must not go off the edge of the mat.

The musical accompaniment must personalize the gymnast, and contribute to the exercise. Only one instrument is allowed. The music must not be too loud, and must finish in a logical fashion with the end of the exercise.

Compulsory exercises
1 step right foot forward;
2 step left foot forward;
3 step right foot oblique forward; full turn to right;
4 leap, left leg to rear;
5 leap and cabriole;
6 lunge right;
7 two steps; full turn on half-bent right leg;
8 step onto ball of left foot;
9 ¼ turn left;
10 ¼ turn left; hurdle jump;
11 round off; two flic-flacs; step out; ½ turn right; front handspring; step out;
12 chasse forward;
13 step and develop;
14 rise on ball of right foot;
15 one step to left;
16 cross legs, ¾ turn left;
17 step backward, arms up;
18 step back; cat leap backward onto left foot;
19 step back, ¼ turn left; legs split in air;
20 step across, ⅜ turn left;
21 swing right leg sideward;

MEN'S FLOOR EXERCISES

Optional exercises must form a harmonious and rhythmic whole, with alternating gymnastic movements, displaying balance, hold, strength, jumps, kips, handsprings, and saltos. The display must express the gymnast's personality.
All elementary movements of trunk and limbs must be technically correct.
Points are deducted for excessively long runs, depending on the difficulty and risk of the subsequent movements.
All available floor space should be used in all directions.

Compulsory exercises
1 jump turn followed by
2 handspring to front somersault (tucked);
3 two headsprings;
4 cartwheel to arabesque;
5 turn; arab spring; side somersault;
6 leg circles to handstand; roll forward;
7 cartwheel; handspring; fall to prone;
8 lift to handspring;
9 straddle down; back roll through handstand; turn; cabriole jump turn;
10 run; arab spring; two flic-flacs; back somersault (tucked).

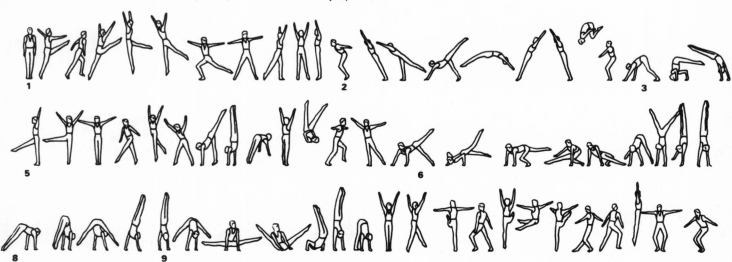

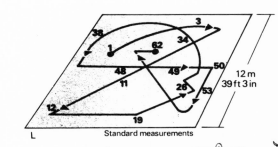

Standard measurements

12 m
39 ft 3 in

22 cartwheel right;
23 step to side; ¼ turn left;
24 ½ circle of left leg;
25 weight onto left leg;
26 cartwheel to handstand; ½ turn to left; onto knees;
27 straighten body; ½ turn right on left knee;
28 ¼ turn left and stomach roll to front lying position;
29 roll over left to back lying position;

30 lift left leg high;
31 raise body to sit;
32 ⅛ turn onto left knee;
33 stand on right foot;
34 running steps; stag leap;
35 chasse (left, right);
36 step left; fish hop;
37 three running steps;
38 dive handspring; step out;
39 step left, ½ turn right;
40 lunge on right leg;
41 hop and ¼ turn to left;

42 side lunge right; ¼ turn right on right leg;
43 step left forward, ½ circle of right leg;
44 step right forward; ½ circle of left leg;
45 step left, arms downward;
46 step right; ½ turn left;
47 step back; hop forward;
48 step back; ¼ turn left;
49 chasse sideward; step left with ¼ turn left;

50 swing leg forward; hopping ½ turn left; split jump;
51 land on slightly bent right leg;
52 ¼ turn to left on right foot;
53 step and tinsica forward;
54 two steps forward;
55 step right forward; ⅜ turn to right on right foot;
56 quick steps forward;
57 hurdle step; dive cartwheel with ¼ turn back; two mounter

flip flops into lunge;
58 cross step left;
59 swing right leg sideward, rising onto ball of left foot;
60 ⅛ turn left; chasse forward;
61 weight on right leg, left leg backward;
62 stretch legs, swinging right arm, following with head.

Standard measurements

12 m
39 ft 3 in

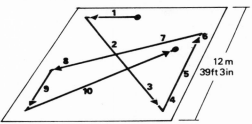

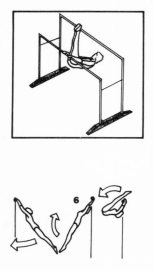

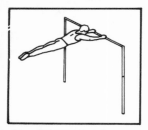

WOMEN'S ASYMMETRICAL BARS

The most important features of the exercises are:
a) swinging movements;
b) the passage of the hands between the bars;
c) changing hand grasps on each bar;
d) suspension;
e) difficult elements.
The exercises should be continuous; two stops are allowed, if necessary, for balance or concentration. Dismounts must be from a handgrasp. It is forbidden to dismount by somersault from the lower bar.
Only two gymnasts from the same team may use identical mounts or dismounts.
If a gymnast falls she may resume within 30 seconds.

Compulsory exercises
1 run a short distance; leap to place hands on low bar; straddle over low bar to momentary stretched hang on high bar;
2 kip to front support on high bar;
3 roll forward; swing backward to a front lying position with hand on low bar;
4 cast legs backward; straddle over low bar; half turn (stretched) on high bar;
5 release grip and jump in suspension; grasp low bar with closed legs; forward glide kip on low bar, immediately releasing hands to grasp on high bar; into hang backward on high bar; lift legs into lying hang backward on low bar;
6 kip to support on high bar;
7 forward roll to support forward;
8 high cast out to swing;
9 swing forward and turn backward on low bar; Hecht jump over low bar to sidestand rearways.

MEN'S HORIZONTAL BAR

Optional exercises must consist exclusively of swinging parts without stops, including:
a) forward and backward giant swings;
b) changes of grip;
c) other variations, such as free hip-circles and twists.
The minimum requirements for a maximum score include at least one combination leaving the grips simultaneously and regrasping the bar with both hands simultaneously.

Compulsory exercises
1 jump to hang with reverse grip; shoot-up toward handstand;
2 on backward swing uprise and place feet between hands on the bar; straighten body to handstand;
3 giant swing forward, with changing of left hand to regular grip; do half turn left, swinging through hang in mixed grip;
4 on the upward swing, vault over the bar with quarter turn; regrasp in hang, swinging forward in regular grips;
5 squat legs between hands; extend body and swing forward in extended hang; uprise to support rearways;
6 circle backward; disengage legs and swing forward with half turn left; swing forward with mixed grips, changing to both hands in reverse grip at end of this swing;
7 kip to handstand and immediately make half turn left forward to handstand;
8 one giant swing backward;
9 on second giant swing backward do half turn to giant swing forward (direct change);
10 one giant swing forward; fall-over to Hechtstraddle dismount.

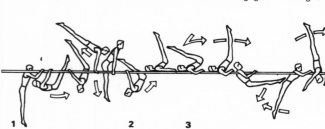

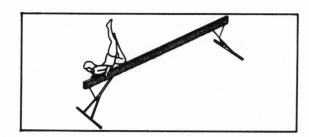

WOMEN'S BEAM

This is essentially an exercise of balance and must include:
a) balancing elements;
b) turns (large and small);
c) jumps and leaps;
d) running steps;
e) steps.

Elements of difficulty must be logically distributed.

The whole length of the beam must be used.

There should not be too many lying and sitting positions.

The rhythm must be varied, generally dynamic, and uninterrupted.

Three stops are allowed.

The exercise should last 80 — 105 seconds. The time begins when the gymnast's feet leave the floor and ends when her feet touch the floor. If she falls, she may resume within 10 seconds.

Only two gymnasts from the same team may use identical mounts or dismounts.

Compulsory exercises

1 run 2—3 steps; leap to riding seat with ½ turn;
2 rise to squat stand;
3 ballet stand with ½ turn;
4 three steps forward;
5 hop on left foot;
6 ballet position;
7 step forward; ½ turn;

one-arm cartwheel; ¼ turn; lunge;
8 step forward; ½ turn;
9 sink to low squat;
10 stand on slightly bent leg;
11 step left; jump to squat;
12 ½ turn to left while raising to stretched stand;
13 step forward; leap changing legs to rear; leap;
14 hop; swing leg into step;
15 ¼ turn left; ½ turn left; straddled stand;
16 lunge to side; ¼ turn right; stand, one leg raised behind;
17 step, swinging other leg forward; momentary lunge;
18 ballet stand; swing left leg to full turn right;
19 step forward; ½ turn left;
20 step forward; leap; run; ½ turn left to ballet stand;
21 cross legs; ballet stand left; raise right leg in front;
22 bend left leg halfway;
23 2 steps forward; stag leap;
24 step and ½ bend left leg;
25 ballet stand; ½ turn right;
26 step forward; handstand; lower right leg to beam;
27 weight onto left leg; ¼ turn to left into side stand;
28 ¼ turn right;
29 2—3 steps forward; layout somersault forward with ½ turn to stand forward.

MEN'S PARALLEL BARS

The optional exercises must contain:
a) swinging and hold elements;
b) a certain measure of strength.

Swinging and flight movements should predominate.

In the team competition the exercise should contain a more difficult part, executed under or over the bars, simultaneously

releasing and recatching both grips.

In the combined and individual events the release must be both under and over the bars.

Compulsory exercises

1 from a stand between the bars, felge to cross support;
2 swing forward and cast to upper arm hang; swing backward to
3 forward roll; swing

backward to
4 Stutzkehre backward to cross support; swing backward to
5 pirouette forward through handstand and immediately
6 lower to upper arm hang; swing forward to backward roll through handstand;
7 Stutzkehre forward to forward swing in upper arm hang (30° at least);

8 front uprise to cross support and
9 swing backward; straddle forward to "L" support (hold);
10 press bent body, straight arms, legs together, to handstand (hold);
11 salto backward to outer cross stand, without support of the hand.

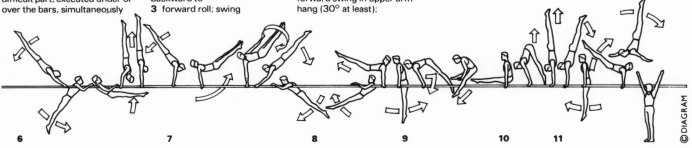

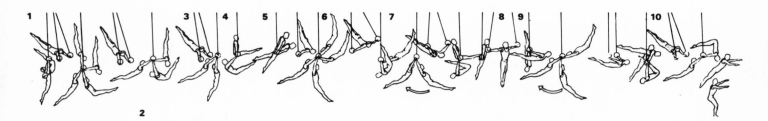

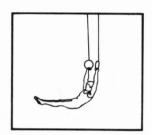

MEN'S STATIONARY RINGS

Optional exercises contain movements alternating between swing, strength, and hold parts, without swinging the rings. There must be:
a) at least two handstands (one executed with strength, the other with swing from a hang, inverted hang, or support);
b) an additional strength part of a difficulty that conforms to the total difficulty of the exercise.

Compulsory exercises

1 from hang, raise legs forward to kip position; dislocate backward;
2 felge to handstand (hold);
3 fall backward through hang; giant dislocate backward through hang;
4 front uprise with straight arms to "L" position (hold);
5 straight body, bent arm press to handstand (hold);
6 fall over forward through hang; high inlocate, straight body;
7 swing downward and inlocate to straight body inverted hang; immediately bend body to kip position and kip to support;
8 lower to cross (hold);
9 turn forward to straight body inverted hang; swing downward and backward to back uprise; fall backward to kip position;
10 dislocate backward; salto backward with bending and straightening body to stand.

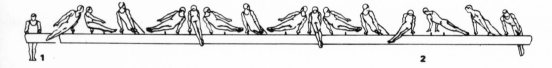

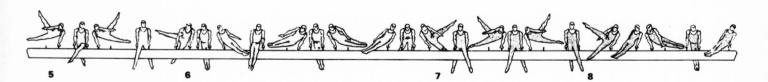

MEN'S POMMEL HORSE

Optional exercises must be composed of clean swings, without stops, including:
a) undercuts of one leg;
b) circles of one and both legs;
c) forward and reverse scissors, at least one of which must be executed twice in sucession.
Double leg circles must be predominant, and all parts of the horse must be used.

Compulsory exercises

1 from side stand kehre in; circle both legs 2½ times;
2 double front vault (Double Swiss);
3 double leg circle and kehre out;
4 travel sideways into saddle;
5 undercut and scissors backward;
6 circle right leg backward to two clockwise circles;
7 circle left leg forward; two front scissors;
8 circle right leg forward to one circle both legs;
9 travel out and kehre in; two circles;
10 double front vault dismount.

Trampolining

There are trampolining competitions for individuals, teams of five, and synchronized pairs. Each type of competition includes compulsory and voluntary routines of 10 movements each. Marks are awarded for execution and difficulty, and deductions are made for form breaks, loss of rhythm, loss of height, and lack of synchronization.

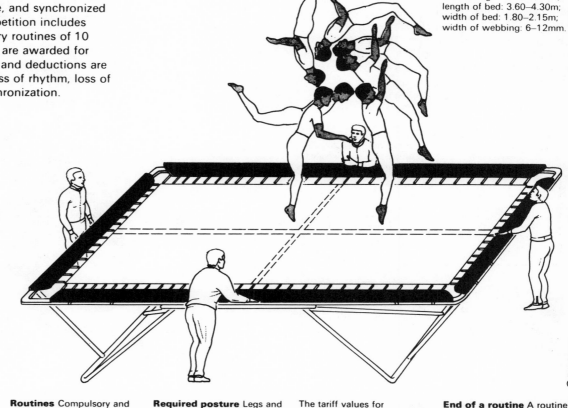

Frame height: 0.95–1.05m; length of bed: 3.60–4.30m; width of bed: 1.80–2.15m; width of webbing: 6–12mm.

© DIAGRAM

Trampolines The beds must be woven and the frames covered with safety pads. Trampoline mats must cover the floor around the trampolines.
For synchronized competitions, the trampolines must be parallel and 2m apart.
Hall Must be at least 7m high.
Dress Sports shirts and long gymnastic trousers for men. Leotards for women: Trampoline shoes. Spotters must wear training suits.
Officials One referee; four judges for execution, two for difficulty, and two for synchronized jumping; chief recorders; assistants; arbitration jury comprising a member of the organizing committee, the president of the technical committee, the referee, and two judges.
Spotters are compulsory at each side and end of the trampoline to ensure the safety of competitors. They are forbidden to speak to competitors; 0.3 of a mark is deducted each time this rule is disregarded.
Individual competitions
The ten best competitors in a preliminary round go forward to a final round. The preliminary round comprises one compulsory and one voluntary routine. The final comprises one voluntary routine.
Team competitions Teams have five members, all of whom perform one compulsory and two voluntary routines.
Team scores are obtained by adding a team's four best scores for each routine.
Synchronized competitions Pairs of competitors jump the same routine simultaneously. Each competitor may start in only one pair.
Competitions consist of one compulsory and one voluntary routine; the compulsory routine is the same as for individual competitions.

Routines Compulsory and voluntary routines each consist of 10 movements. Second attempts at routines are permitted only if the jury decides that a competitor was obviously disturbed (by faulty equipment, spectators, etc.).
Competition cards
Competitors enter details of their voluntary routines on their competition cards and must give them to the referee two hours before the competition. Entries are then checked by the judges of difficulty. Competitors may still change the order of their routines.
Warming up Two hours' training on the competition apparatus is allowed before the competition starts. Competitors are also allowed one practice routine before each round for which they have qualified.
Start The referee signals after the competitor is on the trampoline. Competitors may make as many preliminary jumps as they wish. Scoring starts with the first actual part of the routine.

Required posture Legs and hips must be straight, piked, or tucked. Knees and toes must be kept together. Arm positions are free except in the tucked position, when hands must grasp below the knees. In the tucked and piked positions the upper body and thigh must be at an angle of at least 90", except in a twisting somersault.
Repetition If a jump is repeated in the voluntary routine, there is no score for the degree of difficulty of the repeat.
Multiple somersaults with twists in the first, middle, and last phase have the same degree of difficulty; they are regarded as different jumps (not repeats). Tucked, piked, or straight positions are considered different jumps.
Degree of difficulty
Marked in tenths of a point from 0.1. All jumps without rotation have no degree of difficulty. Other jumps are rated on the principle:
90° somersault, 0.1;
360° somersault, 0.4;
180° twist, 0.1;
360° twist, 0.2 points.

The tariff values for somersaulting and twisting are added together for twisting somersaults.
Piked and straight somersaults without twists are awarded an extra tenth of a point for difficulty.
Interruption A routine is interrupted if:
a competitor does not perform the compulsory routine in the written sequence;
the elasticity of the bed after landing is not used for the immediate continuation of the next movement and a break is caused;
any part of the competitor's body touches the frame or the suspension system during the routine;
the competitor is physically helped by a spotter;
the competitor leaves the trampoline during the routine due to insecurity;
the sequence of jumps in a synchronized competition is changed.
After an interruption the referee tells the judges what the highest deduction mark should be. The routine is only judged to the point of interruption.

End of a routine A routine ends with a foot landing after the tenth movement. The competitor may then make one more jump in a stretched position.
If he fails to land on his feet after the tenth movement, he is judged to have made an additional movement, for which 1 point is deducted. The competitor must stand upright for at least 3 seconds after landing, or 1 point is lost for insecurity.
Result The winner is the competitor or team with the highest total of points. Competitors with equal marks in individual and synchronized competitions are given the same placing, except that a jump-off (a third voluntary routine) is held for first place. In team competitions all places are shared in a tie.
Scoring Of the execution judges' marks, the highest and lowest are disregarded and the other two averaged. The recorder then makes deductions for mistakes in synchronization and doubles the result. The final score is obtained by adding the marks for difficulty and making deductions for interruptions.

Weightlifting

Competitors attempt to lift a weighted bar by two different methods: the snatch and the jerk (or clean and jerk). In each type of lift, each competitor makes a maximum of three attempts to lift the bar. There are individual and team classifications for the snatch and the jerk, and for the total weight of the competitor's best performances in the two types of lift.

Dress Lifters must wear either a full-length costume with athletic support, or a short-sleeved shirt, trunks, and support. The shirt must be collarless.
A belt, if worn, must not exceed 10cm in width.

Categories Lifters are grouped into nine categories; the maximum body weight for each category is given in the table.

Lifter's weight limits	Kg
Flyweight	52
Bantamweight	56
Featherweight	60
Lightweight	67.5
Middleweight	75
Light heavyweight	82.5
Middle heavyweight	90
Heavyweight	110
Super heavyweight	over 110

Boots must be of normal shape and not widened; heels must not exceed 4cm in width.
Bandages are allowed on the wrists and knees. They must not exceed 8cm in width. Wrist bandages may be up to 1m long, and knee bandages up to 2m long.
Alternatively, leather wrist straps and elastic knee caps may be worn.
Bandages are not permitted around the hands or body.
Adhesive bandages (no more than two layers) may be worn on the thumbs. If there is a hand injury, an official doctor may apply adhesive bandages.
Competitors In major championships nine competitors and two reserves are allowed from each country.
Competitors are spread over the weight categories, with a maximum of two in any one category.
A competitor may compete only in one weight division.
There are two classes of lifters – seniors, and juniors aged under 20.

Platform All lifts must take place on a wooden platform, 4m square. The lift must be completed on the platform; if the lifter steps off it during a lift, it is a "no lift."
Weighing-in occurs 1¼ hours before any category of competition. Weighing-in is conducted by the referees and lasts 1 hour.
Lifting order The weight categories are competed in sequence, from the lightest weights up to the heaviest. The order of the competitors is drawn at the weigh-in. This draw is used to decide precedence if several lifters wish to make their first attempt on a lift at the same weight.
A lifter making his first attempt at a weight precedes any competitor who is making his second or third attempt. Similarly, a lifter's second attempt precedes another's third.

Duration After being called, a competitor is allowed 2 minutes' delay before he makes his attempt. He is then allowed a further 1 minute before the attempt is discounted.
The lifter is not called until the barbell is loaded.
The timing is stopped when the lifter has raised the barbell above his knees.
Officials in international competitions consist of referees, a jury, and a timekeeper.
Referees There are three referees whose task is to ensure that the equipment and the lifts are correct. The chief referee must be positioned not less than 6m from the center of the platform. He signals the end of each lift by ordering the lifter to replace the barbell.
The jury, composed of category 1 referees from the participating countries, ensures that the technical rules are applied. It can correct refereeing mistakes.
The timekeeper ensures that lifters make their attempts within the time allowed.

Judging The three referees decide whether a lift has been performed correctly.
They announce their decision (usually by lights) after the lifter has replaced the barbell on the platform.
If the majority approve the lift (white lights) it is a "good lift"; otherwise (red lights) it is a "no lift."
Scoring The snatch and the jerk (or clean and jerk) are won by the competitors lifting the heaviest weights in these lifts.
There is also a combined winner – the competitor lifting the heaviest combined weight in the snatch and the jerk.
If a tie occurs, the lighter competitor is ranked first. If the tied lifters weigh the same, both before and after the competition, they are classified as equal.
A lifter who does not achieve a lift in either the snatch or the jerk is eliminated from that competition, the combined total competition, and the team classification. He is, however, allowed to continue in the competition for the other type of lift (snatch or jerk), or for a record.

In a team match where the result is decided by the team total instead of the individual totals in each category, a lifter who fails to achieve a lift is permitted to attempt the following lift.
In major international championships countries are classified by the awarding of points to the leading 10 competitors.
If countries tie for a place, the one with most first places is classified first. If they have the same number of first places they are classified by the number of second places, and so on.

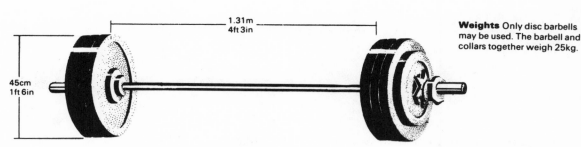

1.31m
4ft 3in

45cm
1ft 6in

Weights Only disc barbells may be used. The barbell and collars together weigh 25kg.

The grip

The grip Hooking is permitted; the competitor covers the last joint of the thumb with the fingers of the same hand at the moment of gripping the bar.

The discs are marked with their weights. They are loaded on the barbell with the largest inside and the smallest outside. They are locked onto the bar with a collar. The discs weigh: 25kg (red); 20kg (blue); 15kg; 10kg; 5kg; 2½kg; 1¼kg.

The snatch

The jerk

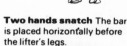
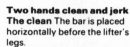

©DIAGRAM

Lifting In a competition, weights must be lifted using one of two methods: the snatch and the jerk (or clean and jerk).
A lifter is allowed three attempts in each type of lift.
If he succeeds at a weight in one attempt, he progresses to a heavier weight for his next lift; but if he fails at a weight in one attempt, he repeats it at the next.
A lifter states in advance the weights that he intends to attempt, assuming he succeeds at each attempt; but these selections can be changed during the competition.
During competition for a particular lift the bar is made progressively heavier, and lifters take their turns when it reaches the weights they wish to attempt. Once it has been lifted by any competitor at a particular weight it cannot then be made lighter. In general, the bar's weight is increased by 5kg at a time, but a lifter can request an increase of 2½kg over the last weight if he is making his final attempt.

Two hands snatch The bar is placed horizontally before the lifter's legs.
The lifter grips the bar, palms down, and pulls it in a single movement from the ground to the full extent of both arms vertically above his head, while splitting or bending the legs.
The bar must pass along the body with a continuous movement.
After the weight is fully extended above his head, the lifter is allowed unlimited time to adjust his position (the "recovery").
He must then become motionless, with his arms and legs extended and his feet on the same line.
The referee signals for the bar to be replaced.
Prohibitions The lifter must not:
pause during the lift;
turn his wrists over until the bar has passed the top of his head;
extend his arms unevenly or incompletely; or
finish with a press-out.

Two hands clean and jerk
The clean The bar is placed horizontally before the lifter's legs.
The lifter grips it palms down, and brings it in a single movement to the shoulders, while splitting or bending the legs.
He may then rest the bar on his collar bones, his chest, or on his fully bent arms.
The lifter must not:
clean in the squat position;
touch his knees or thighs with his elbows or upper arms;
let the bar touch his trunk before it reaches his shoulders;
place the bar on his chest before the elbows are turned over.
The recovery The lifter is allowed unlimited time before the jerk to return his feet to the same line and straighten his legs.
He may also:
lower the bar onto his shoulders if it is causing inconvenience;
withdraw his thumbs or unhook from the bar;
change the width of his grip.
These adjustments may not be part of the clean or the jerk.

The jerk The legs are bent and then the arms and legs are extended.
The lifter may make another recovery before becoming motionless. Then the referee signals for the bar to be replaced.
Any apparent jerking movement must be completed.
Any apparent effort from the shoulders, if the lift is not completed, will constitute a "no lift"; this includes lowering the body or bending the knees.

No lift In either the snatch or the jerk the lift is invalid and a "no lift" is declared:
a) for pulling from the "hang";
b) if the bar reaches the knees in an unfinished attempt;
c) if the bar touches and stops against the thighs (but it is permissible for it to touch the legs below the knees or move along the thighs without stopping);
d) if oil or grease is used on the thighs to help the bar to slide;
e) if any part of the body other than the feet touches the floor;
f) if the lifter replaces the bar before the referee's signal to do so;
g) if, after the referee's signal, the lifter drops the barbell or fails to hold it with both hands until it is replaced (he must lower it on to the platform);
h) if the lifter leaves the platform during any part of the lift;
i) if the arms are bent or extended during the recovery, when the lifter adjusts his position before the final motionless position;
j) if the arms are extended unevenly above the head.

Boxing

Boxing is an ancient sport but in its modern form, as basically defined by the Marquess of Queensberry in the 1860s, two fighters contest a bout of limited duration using only their gloved hands to hit each other in certain areas of the upper body. Bouts are won by a count-out, by forcing an opponent to retire, or on points.

The ring Most contests are held in a three-roped ring, though amateur bouts may be held in a two-roped ring. The floor must be canvas over an undercover of felt or rubber.
The maximum ring dimensions are 20ft square; minimum dimensions are 12ft square for amateurs and 14ft square for professionals. There must be at least 1ft 6in floor space beyond the ropes.

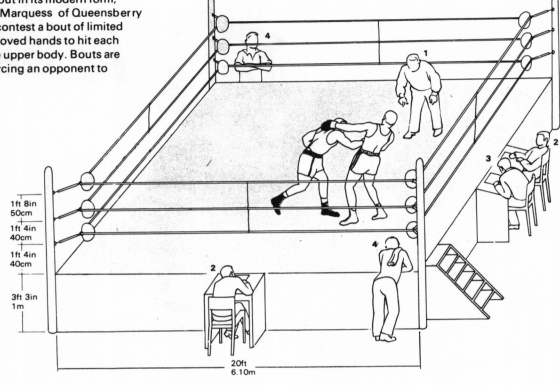

1ft 8in 50cm
1ft 4in 40cm
1ft 4in 40cm
3ft 3in 1m
20ft 6.10m

Weigh in Amateur boxers must weigh in on the day of the contest, stripped or in boxing gear.
Professionals must weigh in at 11.00am for afternoon tournaments or at 1.00pm for evening tournaments.
(Licenses are issued only after very strict medical examination.)

Officials In both amateur and professional contests there are:
1 a referee, who is responsible for controlling the bout;
2 judges, who score the contest;
3 a timekeeper;
4 an official second for each boxer (up to four seconds are allowed in professional contests).

Referees In Great Britain professional bouts are scored only by the referee; elsewhere the referee acts as one of three judges.
The referee is always responsible for:
looking after the boxers in the ring;
administering cautions when necessary;
controling the corners;
giving the count;
stopping the contest when necessary.
Seconds must leave the ring when ordered by the referee. They must not coach during a round. They are permitted certain medical equipment for treating cuts and injuries.

| Weight limits Kg | | | | |
Event	ABA	BBBC	EBU	WBC
Light flyweight	48.081	—	—	—
Flyweight	50.802	50.802	50.802	50.802
Bantamweight	53.978	53.524	53.524	53.524
Featherweight	57.153	57.153	57.153	57.153
Junior lightweight	—	—	58.967	58.967
Lightweight	60.328	61.235	61.235	61.235
Light welterweight	63.503	—	63.503	63.503
Welterweight	63.956	66.678	66.678	66.678
Light middleweight	70.760	—	70.760	70.760
Middleweight	74.842	72.574	72.574	72.574
Light heavyweight	80.739	79.378	79.378	79.378
Heavyweight	over 80.739	any weight	any weight	any weight

ABA (Amateur Boxing Association)
BBBC (British Boxing Board of Control)
EBU (European Boxing Union)
WBC (World Boxing Council)

Scoring Bouts can be won:
on points;
by a count-out (for a count of 10 seconds);
on a stoppage by the referee;
by the opposition being unable to continue;
on a disqualification.
Points decisions Each round in a contest is worth a fixed number of points to the winner.
In amateur boxing the winner of a round generally receives 20 points, and the outscored boxer receives less points in proportion to the number of scoring blows he has struck to the target area.
There are no draws in amateur boxing. If the scores are equal at the end of a bout, the winner is the boxer who did more attacking. If the bout remains undecided, the boxer with the better style wins. If the tie still persists, the boxer with the better defense is the winner.
Similar principles apply in professional boxing. The maximum number of points for a round is 10 in most countries.
Points are awarded for attack, defense, showing initiative, and for style. If scores are equal at the end, the bout is declared a draw.
(To score, all blows must be delivered with the knuckle part of the closed glove and must land on the target area.)

Gloves 8oz gloves are used by amateurs and professionals. 6oz gloves are used at professional welterweight and below. 10oz gloves are used by heavyweights in some countries.

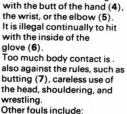

Fouls Punching on certain areas outside the target is illegal – eg below the belt (**1**), the back of the neck (**2**), and in the kidneys (**3**).
Pivot or backhanded blows are also fouls, as is hitting with the butt of the hand (**4**), the wrist, or the elbow (**5**). It is illegal continually to hit with the inside of the glove (**6**).
Too much body contact is also against the rules, such as butting (**7**), careless use of the head, shouldering, and wrestling.
Other fouls include: persistently ducking below the waistline (**8**);
failing to step back from a clinch when ordered to "break";
hitting on the break; deliberately punching an opponent on the floor or when he is falling (**9**);
holding onto the ropes with one or both hands for defense or attack; not trying to win. The referee may rule as a foul any act that he considers to be outside the rules.
Fouls are punished by a warning – with consequent loss of points.
Persistent misconduct leads to disqualification.

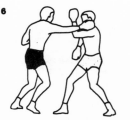

Equipment for amateur and professional boxers:
1 gumshield
2 gloves
3 tape
4 protector
5 boots

Tape On each hand amateurs are allowed up to 8ft 4in of 1¾in soft dry bandage or 6ft 6in of 1¾in Velpeau dry bandage.
Professionals are allowed, on each hand, up to 18ft of 2in soft bandage, or 9ft (below middleweight) or 11ft of 1in zinc oxide tape.
Tape must not be put over the knuckles.

Dress Amateurs wear shorts and undershirts; professionals wear only shorts. Boots are worn.

Duration In competitive **amateur** boxing:
contestants in the open (senior) category box three 3-minute rounds;
intermediate class contestants usually box two 2-minute rounds and one 3-minute round;
novices box three 2-minute rounds.
Professional title contests are over 15 3-minute rounds;
title eliminator contests are over 10 or 12 3-minute rounds;
other contests are over six 2-minute rounds, or six, eight, or 10 3-minute rounds, depending on the experience of the contestants.
(There is a 1-minute break between rounds in all contests.)

The bout The referee first calls the boxers together to ensure that the rules are understood. The boxers then shake hands.
(In professional contests the handshake is repeated at the start of the final round; amateurs must shake hands after the result has been announced.)
During the bout boxers must obey all the referee's instructions.
At a knock-down, the standing boxer is ordered to a neutral corner, and the referee takes up the count. If the fallen boxer rises, the count is over (though in amateur and some professional contests there is a mandatory count of eight). The boxers then continue.

In professional boxing the count must continue if a knock-down occurs at the end of a round.
The referee has the power to end the contest if he judges that one boxer is unfit to continue.
The referee raises the winner's hand when the contest is over.

©DIAGRAM

Wrestling

Wrestling is an ancient sport with two modern Olympic forms: freestyle and Greco-Roman. (Contestants may not use their legs in Greco-Roman wrestling.) Contestants take part in a series of elimination rounds until only three wrestlers remain for the final. Classification is by a system of penalty points.

The mat for international contests is 12m square, with a circular contest area 9m in diameter. There is a center circle 1m in diameter. The two diagonal corners of the mat are marked in red and blue. If the mat is on a platform, it must be no more than 1.1m high.

Dress Tight-fitting, one-piece, red or blue costume; jock strap or support belt; handkerchief. Light knee-guards are permitted; bandages only when prescribed by a doctor. Shoes must not have heels, nailed soles, rings, buckles, etc. Covering the skin with oils or grease is forbidden. Wrestlers must be clean-shaven unless their beards are several months old. Fingernails must be cut short.

Officials
1 referee
2 mat chairman
3 judge
4 timekeeper

Mat chairman is the chief official and his decision is final. Only he communicates with the judge and referee. He indicates decisions by raising a wrestler's color.

Referee wears white, with a red armband on one arm and a blue armband on the other. His duties are to:
start, interrupt, and end bouts;
warn or caution wrestlers;
indicate points scored and placing in danger;
inspect wrestlers at the start of each round;
stop a bout by making a T sign to the timekeeper if wrestlers rest under some pretense.
He must not make untimely interventions or obstruct the view of officials or the public if a fall is likely.

Judge raises his baton with the appropriate color to declare anything missed by the referee, and gives a score sheet to the mat chairman when a bout ends.

Duration Three rounds of 3 minutes actual wrestling time, unless a victory is obtained before the time limit.
The timekeeper announces the time every minute. At the end of a round the timekeeper rings the bell and the referee then blows his whistle; no action is valid between the bell and whistle.

In the intervals a wrestler may be instructed and attended by his trainer and masseur until 5 seconds before the bell.
If a wrestler is forced to halt for any reason beyond his control, the referee suspends the bout; the bout ceases if interruptions exceed 5 minutes.

Start of bout Wrestlers shake hands in the center of the mat, are inspected, and return to their corners until the referee's whistle. Each round starts in the standing position (**1**).

Wrestling on the ground Wrestling may continue if a wrestler is brought to the ground. The wrestler underneath may counter his opponent and get up. If he goes off the mat he must resume in the kneeling position (**2**), with hands and knees at least 20cm apart. He may change his position only when the referee has blown his whistle after the uppermost wrestler has made first contact by placing both hands on the other's shoulder blades.

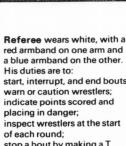

1
Standing position

The uppermost wrestler must not resume by jumping on his opponent.
A wrestler who has brought his opponent to the ground must be active; if both wrestlers are passive they must resume in a standing position.

2
Kneeling position

Placing in danger A wrestler is placed in danger (of a fall) when he goes beyond 90°, with his back turned to the mat, and resists with the upper part of his body.
Examples occur when a wrestler:
forms a bridge (**3**) to avoid a fall;

3
The bridge

rests on his elbows to keep his shoulders off the mat;
is lying on one shoulder with the other shoulder 90° beyond the vertical line;
is turned with his chest or stomach to the mat to create a placing in danger position after his upper body has passed through 90°.

4
The fall

The referee counts seconds up to five as long as placing in danger continues.
The fall (**4**) Both shoulders must be in contact with the mat for a count of three. A fall is signaled by the referee striking the mat with his hand and blowing his whistle.

Weight limits	kg
Light flyweight	48
Flyweight	52
Bantamweight	57
Featherweight	62
Lightweight	68
Welterweight	74
Middleweight	82
Light heavyweight	90
Heavyweight	100
Heavyweight plus	over 100

Wrestling on the edge of the mat If the wrestler who is underneath is within the limits of the mat (even if one competitor has both legs, and the other one or both legs, off the mat), the bout continues for as long as the wrestling takes place within the confines of the mat.

If either wrestler executes a hold outside of the limits and so puts himself and his opponent off the mat, the bout must be interrupted and resumed standing in the center of the mat.

If the head and shoulders of the wrestler underneath go off the mat, the bout must be stopped.

If, as a result of an attack, the head of the wrestler who is underneath touches the floor off the mat, the bout must be interrupted and resumed on the ground.

Scoring a bout A contestant may win a bout by a fall or on points. If points are equal or there is less than one point difference, the bout is declared a draw.

One point is scored for: bringing an opponent to the mat and holding him down in control; moving from the underneath to the uppermost position in control; applying a correct hold without causing an opponent to touch the mat with his head or shoulder; a caution.

Two points are scored: for applying a correct hold and placing an opponent in danger for less than 5 seconds; if an opponent is in an instantaneous, accidental, or rolling fall; if an opponent rolls from side to side to form a bridge using the elbows and shoulders.

Three points are scored for: keeping an opponent in danger for 5 seconds; a series of rolling falls or bridges lasting for 5 seconds continuously.

The final is contested by the last three contestants. If any finalists have not met in previous rounds, they must take part in a final bout. If they have met in previous rounds, the penalty points for such bouts are carried forward and they do not meet again.

The result The competition is won by the finalist with the least penalty points.

If two finalists have equal penalty points, the winner is the contestant who defeated the other.

If three finalists have equal penalty points, in both the final and during earlier bouts, they are rated by the number of falls, wins on points, and draws. If the tie is still unbroken, the winner is the wrestler with least cautions in the final.

If none of these tie-breaking procedures produces a result, the competition is declared drawn.

Fouls The laws forbid:
1 stepping on an opponent's feet;
2 touching an opponent's face between his eyebrows and mouth;
3 gripping the throat;
4 forcing an elbow or knee into an opponent's stomach or abdomen;
5 gripping the mat edge;
6 tripping and sideways striking with the feet or legs; pulling an opponent's hair, flesh, ears, private parts, or costume; twisting his fingers or toes; brawling, kicking, throttling, and pushing; applying holds liable to endanger life, fracture limbs, or torture into submission; bending an opponent's arm more than 90°; head holds using both hands; head locks; scissor grips by the legs to an opponent's head or body; speaking to a wrestler during a bout; forcing an opponent's arm behind his back; closing his arm and forearm with pressure; lifting an opponent from a bridge to throw him onto the the mat (a bridge must be pressed down, but not collapsed by pushing in the direction of the head).

A wrestler applying a hold from behind, in the standing position, with his opponent's head turned down, may only throw the opponent to the side and must ensure that part of his own body, other than his feet, touches the mat before his opponent's body.

A double head-hold (double Nelson) is permitted, but must be applied from the side and the legs must not be used against an opponent's body.

Greco-Roman wrestling also forbids:
seizing an opponent's legs; gripping an opponent with the legs; using the legs to push, lift, or exert pressure when they are touching an opponent's body.

Passive obstruction is: continually obstructing an opponent's holds; continually lying flat on the mat; willfully running off the mat; holding both an opponent's hands.

Cautions are given for: passive obstruction (after a warning); lack of discipline; infringements and fouls; failing to heed the referee after two warnings; arguing with the judge or mat chairman; making no action or points in the first 3 minutes.

When the referee cautions a contestant, he raises one arm and holds the offender's wrist with his other hand.

After two cautions, the mat chairman co-opts another official to assist him.

A competitor loses the bout if he receives three cautions (for which there must be a majority decision of three, including the mat chairman).

Disqualification A contestant may be disqualified from an entire competition only for a serious offense, not for receiving three or more cautions.

©DIAGRAM

Penalty points The result of a bout is converted into penalty points using the official table.

Elimination Contestants are eliminated after receiving six penalty points.

Elimination rounds continue until only three wrestlers remain with less than six penalty points.

Penalty points	Result of bout
0	Win by a fall
0	Win by 12 or more points
½	Win by 8-11 points
1	Win by less than 8 points
3	Lose by a fall
4	Lose by 12 or more points
3½	Lose by 8-11 points

Penalty points	Result of bout
3	Lose by less than 8 points
4	Lose by passivity
0	Win by passivity, winner uncautioned
1	Win by passivity, winner 1 caution
2	Win by passivity, winner 2 cautions
4	Disqualified, declared loser, or retired through injury

Judo

Originally a method of self-defense developed in the Orient, judo has become so popular in recent years that it was made an Olympic sport in 1964. Its rules are based on an essential combination of strength and balance, and contests are won by displaying superior holding and throwing techniques.

Weight limits	Kg
Lightweight	63
Light middleweight	70
Middleweight	80
Light heavyweight	93
Heavyweight	over 93
Open	any weight

The mat In international competitions the contest area (*shiaijo*) is a 9m-square green mat around which there is a 1m-wide red danger area. This is surrounded by a safety area of green matting to prevent injuries. The entire competition area measures 16 × 16m.

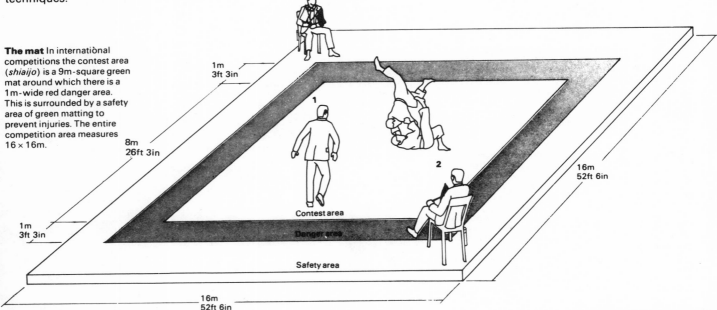

1m
3ft 3in

8m
26ft 3in

1m
3ft 3in

16m
52ft 6in

16m
52ft 6in

Contest area

Danger area

Safety area

Officials The contest is governed by:
1 Referee , who generally remains within the contest area and conducts the bout;
2 Two Judges , who assist the referee from their positions at opposite corners of the safety area.

At the end of an undecided contest the referee places the competitors in the starting position and calls "*hantei*". The judges then raise a white or red flag to indicate the winner or both flags for a draw. The referee adds his decision and the result is given according to the majority.

Out of bounds The contest must be fought within the limits of the contest area.

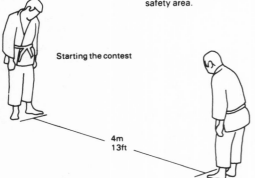

Starting the contest

4m
13ft

Scoring an *ippon*

1

2

3

Start Contestants face each other, at a distance of 4m, make a standing bow, and begin when the referee calls "*hajime*". Movements must begin in a standing position within the contest area.
Duration Minimum of 3 minutes and maximum of 20, arranged in advance. The contest may be temporarily halted, on the call of "*matte*".

if the contestants are about to leave the contest area;
after a foul;
if there is illness or injury;
to adjust the costume;
to disentangle unproductive holds.
At the end of the contest competitors return to their starting places, face each other, and make a standing bow after the decision.

Scoring Contestants are judged on throwing technique (*nagewaza*) and holding technique (*katamewaza*). Violations are also a determining factor. By achieving an *ippon* (one point) a competitor wins outright. *Ippon* is awarded for:
1 a throw of considerable force;

2 lifting the opponent from the mat to shoulder height;
3 making an effective stranglehold or lock; maintaining a hold for 30 seconds.
If the contestant just fails to make an *ippon*, he may be awarded a *waza-ari*. Two *waza-ari* equal one ippon. If a contestant scores only one *waza-ari* but has a serious

violation committed against him by his opponent, then he also wins outright.
The judges may award a draw and a bout may be lost by default. In the event of injury, illness, or accident the referee and judges decide on the result.

3-5cm
1⅛-2in

5—8cm
2—3⅛in

Dress The costume (*judogi*) must be white or off-white. The jacket (**1**) must cover the hips and is generally slit about 18cm up each side. It has continuous strengthened lapels about 4cm wide and reinforced stitching at the armpits and below the waistline. Sleeves must be loose and cover more than half the forearm.

Trousers (**2**) must be loose and cover over half the lower leg.
The belt (**3**) fastens the jacket at the waist and is long enough to go twice round the body. It is tied with a large square knot and its ends are about 15cm long.
A white or red sash distinguishes contestants.

Groundwork Contestants may apply ground techniques (*ne-waza*): if the attacker moves directly into *ne-waza* after throwing his opponent; when one contestant falls; when *ne-waza* follows a successful stranglehold or lock in the standing position;

after any skilful technique that does not qualify as a throw; or in any other situation in which a contestant falls to the ground.

Fouls It is forbidden to:
1 sweep an attacking opponent's supporting leg from the inside (although it is permissible to hook his instep);
2 attempt to throw an opponent by entwining a leg around his leg (*kawazu-gake*);
3 fall back deliberately when an opponent is clinging to the back and when either contestant controls the other's movements;
4 adopt an excessively defensive attitude either physically or by not attacking;
5 pull the opponent down in order to start groundwork;
6 take hold of the opponent's foot or leg in order to change to *ne-waza*, unless exceptional skill is shown;
7 put a hand, arm, foot, or leg directly on the opponent's face or to take his *judogi* in the mouth;
maintain, while lying on the back, a leg hold around the opponent's neck when he manages to stand, or to position the knees to lift him up;
apply joint locks (*kansetsu-waza*) except at the elbow joint;
endanger the opponent's spine or neck;
lift an opponent who is lying on his back off the mat in order to drive him back onto the mat;
break back fingers;
intentionally go outside or force the opponent to go outside the contest area;
continuously hold the opponent's costume on the same side with both hands, or the belt or bottom of the jacket with one hand;
seize the inside of the sleeve or bottom of the trousers;
continuously stand with fingers interlocked with the opponent's;
deliberately disarray the costume;
wind the belt around the opponent;
disregard the referee;
make derogatory remarks or gestures;
do anything contrary to the spirit of judo.

1

2

3

4

5

6

7

Penalties The referee has the power to award four penalties of increasing gravity: *shido*, *chui*, *keikoku*, and *hansoko-make* (disqualification). For *keikoku* and *hansoko-make* the referee must consult his judges and obtain a majority decision before imposing the punishments. Each of the first three penalties counts against the offender in the judges' assessment at the end of the contest.

©DIAGRAM

Karate

Karate is a practical, empty-handed fighting technique, a formal method of physical and mental training, and a competitive combat sport. Contests of sport karate are held as sparring matches, in which some karate techniques are not permitted and only a few used very often. To avoid injuries all punches, blows, strikes, and kicks are controlled and pulled back before contact.

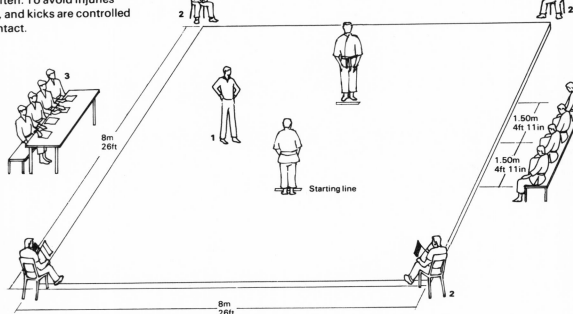

8m
26ft

1.50m
4ft 11in

1.50m
4ft 11in

8m
26ft

Starting line

Match area A flat, 8m-square surface without obstacles.
Officials
1 a referee, in the fight area;
2 four judges, one seated at each corner of the match area;
3 arbitrator, seated to one side of the match area.
Also: timekeeper(s), record-keeper(s), and administrator(s).
The referee conducts the match, awards points, announces fouls, and issues warnings and disciplinary action.
In the event of a draw he casts the deciding vote.
He may extend the duration of a match when necessary. He receives advice from the judges. If only one judge signals, the referee may ignore him; if two or more judges signal, then he must suspend the match and consult them.
Only he may suspend or terminate a match.
The judges Each judge carries one red flag, one white flag, and a whistle, with which to signal:
a point scored;
a foul or imminent foul;
a contestant out of the area.
The judges also indicate any disagreement with the referee's decision, and may overrule him if they are unanimous.
They continuously evaluate the performance of the contestants, and vote when awarding a victory by majority decision.
The arbitrator judges protests and directs the timekeeper and record-keeper.
Procedure The referee takes up his position. The contestants stand facing each other with their toes to the starting line and bow to one another.
On the referee's call of "shobu ippon hajime," the match begins.
Halting the match If the referee sees an ippon scored, he signals "soremade" and the contestants return to the starting lines. The referee

Target area

Scoring an ippon

returns to his position, raises his left or right hand to indicate the winner, and calls out the scoring technique used.
The contestants bow to each other and the match ends.
If the referee sees a waza-ari scored, he calls "yame," and the contestants return to the starting lines. The referee returns to his position and announces "waza-ari," pointing to the scorer and calling out the scoring technique used.
On the referee's call of "hajime" the match recommences (unless one contestant has accumulated two waza-ari).
Temporary halts The referee may call "yame" and temporarily halt the match if: it develops into infighting

with no effective technique;
there is deadlock;
one or both contestants is out of the match area;
he wishes a contestant to adjust his dress;
he sees a contestant about to commit a foul;
there is injury or illness;
a rule is broken;
a judge signals.
If necessary, the referee may consult with the judges and return the contestants to the starting lines before recommencing.
If the halt is longer than 10 seconds, it is not counted in the match time.
No score If the match ends with no ippon scored, the referee calls "soremade." He and the contestants then return to their positions.
The referee gives the

judges time to make a decision, and then calls "hantei" and blows his whistle. The judges then vote by signaling with their flags. If necessary the referee gives the casting vote.
Team matches may be organized in one of two ways:
a) individual contestants are paired off for fights and the winning team is the one with the most individual winners;
b) a winning individual continues to meet new opponents from the other team until he is defeated.
In both cases ties are broken by the greater number of ippons, then by the greater number of waza-ari and wins by decision.
Fouls and disqualifications count as ippons.

If the tie still remains, then an extra match is held.
Extra matches, if held, are between one chosen representative from each team.
An extra match lasts 2 minutes and is repeated until a winner is established.
After two repeats, each contestant is replaced by another team member.
If after a number of extra matches the result is still inconclusive, the panel of judges may decide the match by conference.

Dress Contestants must wear a white *karate-gi*, with a colored belt (*obi*) indicating the formal grade they have reached.

For identification during the fight, one contestant has a white string fastened to his belt and the other contestant a red string.

No badges or metallic objects may be worn.

Protective or safety devices may only be used if permitted by the judges.

Duration A match normally lasts 2 minutes, but this may be extended to 3 or 5 minutes. Stoppages for injury or inquiry are not included in the match time.

The timekeeper signals with a gong or buzzer at the end of the match and 30 seconds before the end.

Winning To win a match it is necessary:
a) to be the first contestant to score one *ippon* (full point) or two *waza-ari* (half points), or
b) for the other contestant to be disqualified, or
c) to be awarded the match by decision of the referee and judges.

No score

Scoring is by using recognized competition karate techniques, in good form, on the permitted scoring area on the opponent's body. Actual physical contact is strictly limited and is not required for scoring. Light contact is permitted on the body. Only very light contact is permitted on the face and head.

Points can be awarded for controlled techniques having a focus within 2in of the target surface.

Excessive physical contact always results in disqualification.

Ippon (one point) is awarded for a blow that is struck with: good form, good attitude, strong vigor, *zanshin* (constant alertness of mind), proper timing, and correct

distancing. Blows may be *tsuki* (thrusts), *uchi* (snaps), *ate* (hits), or *keri* (kicks).

Waza-ari (half point) is awarded for a blow that is less correct but still effective – if, for example:
the opponent is moving away from the blow;
the blow is slightly off target;
the blow is delivered from an unstable position.

Other *ippons* A full point is still given for less powerful blows if:
the attack was delivered just at the moment when the opponent began to move toward the attacker;
the attack was delivered just at the moment when the opponent was thrown off balance by the attacker;
a combination of effective blows was applied;

a combination of *tsuki* and *keri* or of *tsuki* and *nage* (throw) techniques was used;
the opponent had lost his fighting spirit and turned his back on the attacker;
the attack was delivered on defenseless parts of the opponent.

Not *ippons* An ippon is not awarded if an attacker fails to deliver a blow the moment he has seized or thrown his opponent.

If two opponents score simultaneously, neither point is counted.

Scoring techniques delivered simultaneously with the end of time signal are counted, as are techniques delivered if an attacker is inside the match area but his opponent outside it.

Victory by decision
Hanteigachi (superiority) may be awarded to a contestant who has scored a half point, or by considering:
the number of escapes outside the match area;
any warnings due to fouls;
the comparative vigor and fighting spirit shown by the contestants;
the comparative ability and skill of the contestants;
the number of attacking moves;
the comparative excellence of the strategy used.

Protests A contestant's team officer may protest against a decision by appealing to the arbitrator, who then consults the referee and judges.

Injuries If a contestant is badly hurt it is usually because a foul has been committed against him by his opponent. The opponent is disqualified and the injured contestant wins the match, even if he cannot continue.

If a contestant refuses to continue, or requests permission to quit after a minor injury not serious enough to disable him, he is the loser.

Similarly, he loses the contest if he cannot continue or requests permission to quit for reasons other than injury.

If an injury is not the responsibility of either contestant, or if both competitors are injured simultaneously and both are responsible, the one who quits is the loser.

If an injury is unintentional – for example, running onto a controlled blow – the decision rests with the judges.

If injuries are not attributable to either contestant, the match is a draw.

Penalties A foul may result in: private warning by the referee in a quiet voice (*chui*);
public warning by the referee in a loud voice (*hansoku-chui*);
disqualification, announced by the referee (*hansoku*).

Disqualification may be due to repeated fouls after warning. It may also be imposed if the contestant:
fails to obey the referee;
becomes over-excited to the extent of being considered a danger to his opponent;
breaks rules with malicious intent; or
breaks match rules in some other way.

© DIAGRAM

Fouls The following are fouls:
1) direct attacks to the body other than the arms and legs;
2) dangerous techniques, such as blows to the eyes or testicles;
3) dangerous throws;
4) persistent attacks directly on the shin;
5) direct attacks to the hips, knee joints, or insteps;
6) unnecessary grabbing, clinching, or body crashing;
7) excessive moving out of the match area, or moves wasting time;
8) ignoring contest rules;
9) unsportsmanlike behavior.

Kendo

One of the traditional Japanese martial arts, kendo is presented as a modern competitive sport. Two contestants, wearing protective armor, fight with bamboo swords. Footwork is vital – kendoka use short, fast, gliding steps, and sometimes a jump for counter attacks.

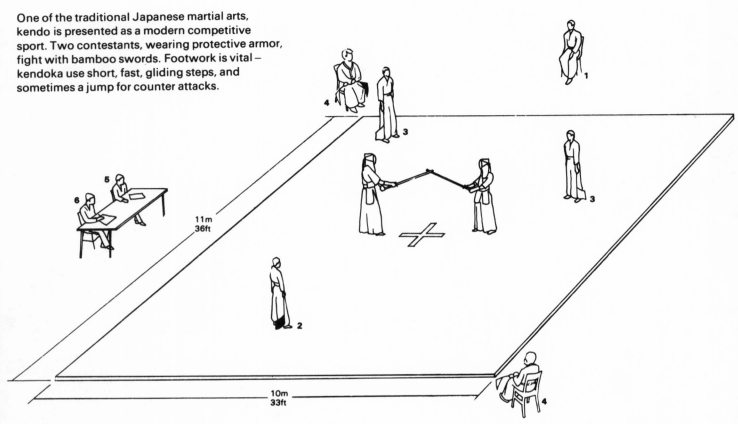

Effective cut or thrust

No effective blow

Cannot judge

Interrupt the match

Separate contestants

Area A smooth, wooden-floored rectangular area, usually 10m by 11m. The center is marked with a cross or circle, the boundary with lines 5–10cm wide. Two starting lines are also marked. Around the boundary is a clear surround space at least 1.5m wide.

Duration 3 or 5 minutes. Extra time if needed for a result: 3 minutes. Interruptions are not included in time.

Officials
Judge in chief (**1**) (or a judge in charge, as his representative), sitting outside the area.
One chief (**2**) and two assistant judges (**3**) inside the area, two of them "forward" and one "rear". Using red and white flags, these judges control conduct, point out and rule on valid techniques and infringements, and, where necessary, decide the victor.
Two line judges (**4**).
Timekeeper and assistants (**5**).
Scorekeeper and assistants (**6**).

Signals used by judges in the area:
effective cut or thrust, flag raised diagonally upward in the direction of the scorer;
no effective blow, both flags waved downward in front of the body;
cannot judge, both flags held crossed downward in front of the body, red flag out;
interrupt the match, both flags raised;
separate contestants when hilt-to-hilt, both flags extended forward, parallel, shoulder high.
(If the other judges are not in agreement, the judge in chief decides.)

Announcements *Men ari* (or *koto, do,* or *tsuki ari*): successful scoring technique at the area named;
Yame: interruption;
Nikomme: re-start after one point is scored;
Shobu: re-start after one point each;
Encho hajime: re-start for extra time;
Shobu ari: end of match, a victory;
Hikiwake: a draw.
Contestants are separated:
a) if a contestant falls or drops his *shinai,* and his opponent does not immediately strike an effective blow (re-start at the starting lines);
b) if contestants are in a prolonged hilt-to-hilt with no apparent intention of striking a blow (re-start at the same point).

Procedure Contestants bow, cross *shinai,* and take up starting positions (both standing or both squatting). The match begins on the chief judge's call of *Hajime* and continues until his final call of *Yame.*

Dress
1 *Keikogi* (shirt)
2 *Hakama* (ankle-length "divided skirt")
3 *Hachimaki* (toweling headcloth)
Protective equipment
4 *Men* (mask)
5 *Kote* (gauntlets)
6 *Do* (breastplate)
7 *Tare* (apron)
Shinai Made of equal sections of bamboo, held together by leather and strings at the tip, halfway point, and hilt.

If one *shinai* is used: it must be under 118cm in length and weigh 468gm.

If two *shinai* are used: the longer has a maximum length of 110cm and must weigh 375gm, and the shorter has a maximum length of 60cm and a minimum weight of 265gm.

©DIAGRAM

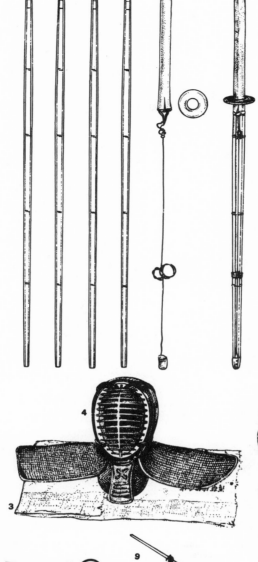

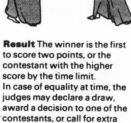

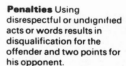

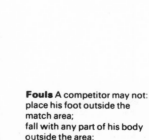

Scoring techniques
Cuts (made with the forward third of the *shinai*); thrusts (with the tip of the *shinai*).
Scoring areas
For cuts:
8 left and right temples;
9 left and right breastplate;
10 left and right wrist (left wrist permitted only when the left hand is at shoulder height or higher).
11 For thrusts: the throat.
Effective techniques One point is awarded for a blow delivered with full spirit and correct form. The vote of one judge is sufficient if the others are undecided.
Techniques are still effective if delivered as the opponent drops his *shinai*, steps or falls out of bounds, or as time is called.

Result The winner is the first to score two points, or the contestant with the higher score by the time limit.
In case of equality at time, the judges may declare a draw, award a decision to one of the contestants, or call for extra time. If there is extra time, the winner is the first contestant to score.
Team matches may be to one of two systems: pairing or elimination (see karate for details).

Fouls A competitor may not: place his foot outside the match area;
fall with any part of his body outside the area;
use his *shinai* as a prop to prevent his body from going outside the area;
trip his opponent;
illegally shove or thrust with his *shinai*;
strike or thrust at his opponent's unprotected parts;
grasp his opponent with the hands;
use his *shinai* hilt to break his opponent's grasp of his *shinai* hilt;
grasp his opponent's *shinai* above the hilt after dropping his own *shinai*;
use disrespectful or undignified acts or words.

Penalties Using disrespectful or undignified acts or words results in disqualification for the offender and two points for his opponent.
Other fouls result in a warning, and one point to the opponent after the third foul in a match.
Injuries The match ends if a contestant is injured so that he cannot continue.
If his opponent caused the injury, the injured man wins with one point;
otherwise, the injured man forfeits the match and his opponent is awarded two points.
If a contestant requests an end or halt without sufficient reason, he forfeits the match and his opponent is awarded two points.

Aikido

Aikido is a competitive fighting sport, based on an ancient Japanese system of self-defense. Force is not met with counter-force but with avoiding action, enabling the defender to take advantage of the attacker's temporary loss of balance to score with a successful aikido technique.

Area At least 9m square, preferably with a surrounding safety area.

Types of competition
Kata is a formal event. *Ninin dori, tanto randori,* and *randori kyoghi* are three types of fighting event.

Dress As for judo. For identification, one contestant wears a red belt (or string or tape at the belt), the other white. Metal badges, jewelry, etc are prohibited.

Officials For *kata* and *ninin dori,* one senior judge and two or four assistant judges. For *tanto randori* and *randori kyoghi,* one referee in the competition area and two judges at opposite corners. For all competitions, a scorer and a timekeeper.

9m
29ft 6in

9m
29ft 6in

1 Senior judge
2 Assistant judges
3 Scorer
4 Timekeeper

Terms used in aikido are:
hajime, begin;
soremade, finish (of round or fight);
yame matte, stop (the competitors return to their initial positions and timing is interrupted);
ippon, one point;
tanto ippon, one point for knife strike;

waza-ari, half point;
waza-ari awazette ippon, second half point, making one full point;
hantei, call for score or judgment;
hikkiwake, draw;
chui, warning.

Referee's signals (for *tanto randori* and *randori kyoghi*) are:
ippon, arm raised above the head;
waza-ari, arm raised to shoulder height;
no score, right hand waved from side to side, above the head or in front of the body;

hajime, rapid lowering of the arm from outstretched position in front of the body or above the head;
hantei, right arm raised centrally above the head.
Judges' signals Made with a red or white bat (or flag) to indicate each contestant. Competitor outside the area: bat pointed to area edge and waved from side to side.

Competitor stayed in the area: bat raised, hand pointed to the area edge.
Scoring technique: bat raised.
Did not see: both flags waved in front of legs.
Vote on judgment: red or white bat raised for a win, both for a draw.

KATA
Two participants work together in a set routine of defense and attack.
Procedure One participant is *tori* (thrower) and the other *uke* (attacker). They stand 4m apart, facing *joseki* (the chief guest), and bow. They then turn and face each other. They begin on the call of "*hajime.*" When they have finished, the senior judge calls "*hantei.*" All judges then display their score for the joint performance. These scores are totaled by the recorder. The participants then turn to *joseki,* bow, and leave the area.

Assessment Performances should be polished, well placed, smooth, continuous, purposeful, and coordinated. Participants must show good understanding of their *kata* and between each other.
Scoring Each judge can give up to 10 points. Scores may be given to one decimal place.

NININ DORI
Three participants work together in a spontaneous mock fight. Each is *tori* (defender) for 1 minute.
Procedure The three participants stand at the area edge, face *joseki,* and bow. The first *tori* takes up position in the area center with *joseki* on his right. The two *ukes* face *tori,* about 2m from him. Each 1-minute round begins on the call "*hajime*" and ends with "*soremade.*" The *uke* on *tori*'s right always begins the attack. On "*soremade,*" participants return to starting positions. After rounds one and two, the new *tori* changes places with the previous one. After round three, the participants retire to the area edge, hear the score for their joint performance, and bow

TANTO RANDORI

Free fighting between two contestants, over two rounds of 1 minute each. The defender (unarmed) in the first round becomes the attacker (armed with a rubber-composition "knife") in the second.

Procedure The two contestants and referee stand at the area edge, facing *joseki*, and bow. The two contestants then face each other at the center, 4m apart. The first attacker is to the referee's right. On the command "*rei,*" they bow to each other. Before each round, the current attacker collects the "knife" and red belt from the referee. Each round begins on "*hajime*" and ends on "*soremade.*" A round may be interrupted by "*matte*" or "*yame.*" After the second round, the referee calls "*hantei,*" and the recorder announces each contestant's total score. The referee indicates the winner. Both contestants bow to each other, bow to *joseki*, and leave the area.

Interruptions The referee will call "*yame*" and interrupt the fight and timing:
if a contestant goes out of the area;
if a contestant breaks the rules;
for accident, injury, or illness;
for adjustments to clothing;
for any other reason he considers necessary.
The contestants return to their starting positions and the fight resumes on "*hajime*."

Scoring as attacker The target area is the chest (from shoulder line to the line of the sternum).

A scoring attack must:
start from the hip line;
be a thrusting movement;
start at least one pace away from the defender;
strike with the knife tip first;
have the attacking arm fully extended at the moment of striking.
An unimpeded attack scores one point.

An attack does not score:
if it is deflected by the defender and then hits the target area;
if it is deflected by the defender who then hits the "knife" because he starts an aikido technique.

Scoring as defender The defender can score with any skilful aikido technique in which the attacker is thrown, made to submit, or made harmless.
A perfect technique scores one point;
an 80% correct technique scores a half point.
A score is awarded:
if the attacker drops the "knife" due to a correct defense technique; or
if the attacker is thrown out of the area and the defender has been in the area throughout.

After a score the referee calls "*matte.*" Both contestants return to their starting positions. The referee announces "*ippon*" (one point) or "*waza-ari*" (half point), indicating the scorer. On "*hajime,*" the fighting resumes. A technique delivered simultaneously with the end of time scores.

Winning The winner is the contestant with the higher number of total points. If both scores are equal, the contestant scoring highest as defender wins. If these scores are also equal, the winner is the contestant judged to have the better bearing and technique.

Fouls Unsportsmanlike, dangerous, forbidden, over-forceful, or non-aikido behavior or techniques; grasping the clothing, grappling, or preventing action in any other way; disobeying the referee, or stopping and adjusting clothing without his permission; repeatedly stepping outside the area.

Penalties Fouls make contestants liable to warning, the loss of one point, or disqualification.

to *joseki*. Rounds may be interrupted by the judge's call "*yame.*"

Rules *Uke's* attack:
may be from any direction;
must begin when *uke* is one step away from *tori*;
must be positive and realistic;
must not include kicks.
Competitors must stay in the area.
The senior judge's decision is final.

Assessment For good posture and technique, variations in attack and defense, speed of performance, use of area, tactics, stamina, and *tori's* reactions and awareness under stress.

Scoring As for *kata*.

RANDORI KYOGHI

Aikido free-fighting between two unarmed contestants, for one round.

Procedure As for *tanto randori*, except for one round only and with no "knife". A full round lasts 2 minutes or more, but the fight ends if one contestant scores two full points.

Scoring As for the defender in *tanto randori*. Contestants must maintain basic aikido posture and attack with *shomenate* action.

After scoring As for *tanto randori*.

Winning The winner is the first contestant to reach two full points;
otherwise the contestant with the higher number of total points at the end;
otherwise, the contestant judged to have the better bearing and technique.

Interruptions, fouls As for *tanto randori*.

© DIAGRAM

Fencing

Modern fencing has its roots in the historical traditions of swordsmanship. Two opponents contest an assault or bout using one of three weapons: foil, épée, or saber.

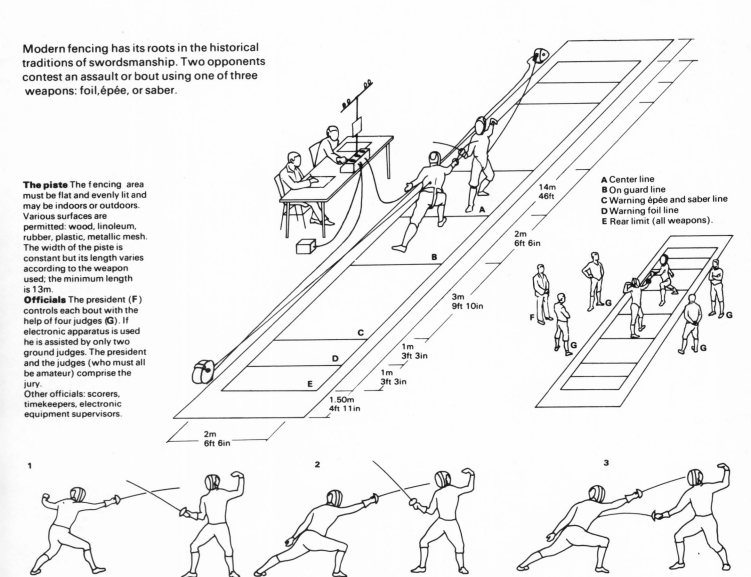

The piste The fencing area must be flat and evenly lit and may be indoors or outdoors. Various surfaces are permitted: wood, linoleum, rubber, plastic, metallic mesh. The width of the piste is constant but its length varies according to the weapon used; the minimum length is 13m.

Officials The president (**F**) controls each bout with the help of four judges (**G**). If electronic apparatus is used he is assisted by only two ground judges. The president and the judges (who must all be amateur) comprise the jury.
Other officials: scorers, timekeepers, electronic equipment supervisors.

14m
46ft

2m
6ft 6in

3m
9ft 10in

1m
3ft 3in

1m
3ft 3in

1.50m
4ft 11in

2m
6ft 6in

A Center line
B On guard line
C Warning épée and saber line
D Warning foil line
E Rear limit (all weapons).

Duration of bouts In men's fencing the winner is the first competitor to score five hits; in ladies' foil, the first to score four hits.
The time limit is 6 minutes for men and 5 minutes for women. Timing is halted at each stoppage during the bout.
If the fencers are equal when time expires in foil and saber, a deciding bout is fought. The competitor ahead when time is up wins the bout.
A tie in épée counts as a defeat for both competitors.
Playing procedure The first fencer called stands with his open side toward the president. The contestants stand facing each other 2m from the center of the piste.

The president orders "on guard," asks the competitors if they are ready, then calls "play."
The bout only stops when the president calls "halt," which he may do:
at dangerous play;
if a competitor is disarmed;
if a player leaves the piste, etc.
After a valid hit, the contest resumes with both fencers behind the on guard lines. If a hit is invalid, play continues at the spot where fencing was halted.
Hits made before "play" or after "halt" is called, are annulled.
In non-electric foil and saber, fencers change ends after one competitor has scored half the possible number of hits.

Attack and defense For a hit to be valid in foil and saber the fencers' movements must follow the correct phrase. Basically, when attacked a fencer must parry before he can make a riposte (counter-attack). The attacker is the fencer who first threatens the target with his sword arm outstretched (**1**); he remains on the attack until the opponent has parried the attack (**2**).
In the case of a composed attack (several movements made to mislead the opponent), the defending fencer may make a stop hit at his opponent (**3**), provided that hit reaches the target before the final movement of the attack has started.

In simple terms: the phrase must follow the sequence of attack, parry, riposte, counter-riposte. Variations depend on the speed of movement and the line and complexity of the attack.
In épée there is no fencing phrase and no priority of movement.
In all weapons the *flèche*, or running attack, is allowed.

Scoring To score a hit the fencer has to strike his opponent's target area with the sword point. In saber, a cut with the edge or the top third of the back edge also counts.
The fencer must be on the piste for his hit to count. Hits that land off the target in foil and saber become valid if the fencer who is hit has taken up an extreme position to avoid being hit on target.
A hit off-target brings the phrase to an end.
Electronic scoring equipment may be used in foil and épée. Fencers use electronic apparatus that indicates hits on the target area by a system of lights.

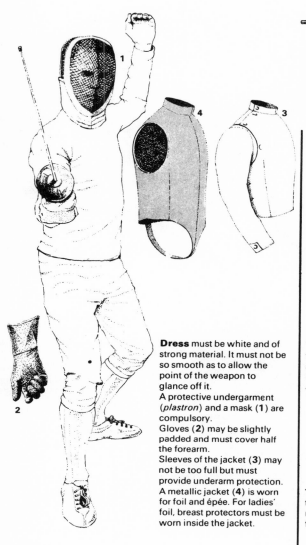

All weapons have a flexible steel blade with a button at the end, a hilt by which to hold the weapon, and a guard. A martingale is obligatory for foil and épée when no electric equipment is used.

In foil and épée (thrust weapons) hits can only be made with the point. The saber can be cut and thrust, scoring with all of the front edge and the top third of the back edge.

The foil must weigh less than 500g. The flexibility of the blade should measure 5.5–9.5cm if a 200g weight is hung from the button and the

blade held firm 70cm from the end. In an electric foil, a hit must register only if the pressure on the point exceeds 500g.

target area

The épée must weigh less than 770g. The blade must be as straight as possible. Flexibility should measure 4.5–7cm (measurement as

for foil). In an electric épée, a hit must register only if the pressure on the point is more than 750g.

The saber must weigh less than 500g. The blade must not be too rigid nor too flexible. Any curve must be

continuous, of less than 4cm, and not in the direction of the cutting edge.

Dress must be white and of strong material. It must not be so smooth as to allow the point of the weapon to glance off it.
A protective undergarment (*plastron*) and a mask (**1**) are compulsory.
Gloves (**2**) may be slightly padded and must cover half the forearm.
Sleeves of the jacket (**3**) may not be too full but must provide underarm protection.
A metallic jacket (**4**) is worn for foil and épée. For ladies' foil, breast protectors must be worn inside the jacket.

In foil, the jury must still analyze the materiality (validity) of the hit before awarding it.
In épée the light is the only judge; if both fencers make a hit within 1/25 of a second of each other a double hit is recorded.
There can be no double hit in foil or saber. If both fencers make a hit at the same time it is either simultaneous action, in which case both hits are annulled, or it is the result of one fencer breaking the convention of the phrase. The president must then decide on the offender and award the hit to his opponent.

Judging hits The president awards hits and punishes fouls. His judges aid him in spotting hits. As soon as a judge sees a hit he raises his hand to inform the president, who reconstructs the phrase. He consults the judges and/or the electronic equipment to decide on the materiality of each hit. If both the materiality and the fencing phrase are satisfactory, the hit is awarded.
Before the beginning of an assault the president must check the electronic equipment to ensure that no false scoring is registered.

Fouls and penalties
Fighting at close quarters is only allowed if the fencers can wield their weapons correctly. Bodily contact (*corps à corps*) (**1**) in foil and saber is punished first by a warning, then by a penalty of one hit. In épée, bodily contact is permitted as long as there is no excessive violence. Ducking and turning are allowed and the unarmed hand may touch the piste, but if the fencers pass each other the president must halt the bout and reposition the contestants. A hit in the act of passing is valid; one made after passing is not.
For crossing the piste limits laterally: the fencer loses ground; 1m at foil and 2m at épée and saber.

Any hit he makes off the piste is invalid.
For going over the side lines to avoid being hit, he is penalized one hit if he has already been warned. The same penalty is imposed for crossing the rear limits after a warning.
For causing prolonged interruptions the penalty is a warning followed by one hit.
Dishonest or incorrect fencing, intentional brutality, or vindictive actions are punished by the president. Refusal to obey the orders of the president and other officials is penalized by a warning at the first offense, a penalty hit at the second, and then by exclusion from the competition.

The weapon must be held in one hand; changing hands is only allowed when permitted by the president.
The weapon may not be thrown; the hand must not leave the hilt.
The use of the free hand for defensive or attacking purposes (**2**) is prohibited. Any hit made using the unarmed hand is annulled. Persistent infringement is punished by conceding a hit.

Horseshoe pitching

In horseshoe pitching, competitors pitch specially manufactured "horseshoes" at stakes from alternate ends of a court. Although there are two basic methods of scoring, the object in both is to pitch the shoes as near the stake as possible. A game may last for 50 pitches from each player or pair, or until a player or pair scores 50 points.

Horseshoes are specially made for pitching. The ends of a shoe have rolled-down edges called "heel calks" and the closed end has a "toe calk." The maximum weight is 2½lb.

Officials A tournament committee organizes the contest.
A referee decides disputes about scores.
Each court has an official scorer.
Contests There are various types of contest.
Two players usually play the best of 11 games.
In tournaments contestants play one game against each of the other players.
Qualifying rounds may be held to divide competitors into classes. Each player may have to pitch 50 or 100 shoes alone. The winners of each class may play each other.

Court The target area is of moist clay, prepared so that the shoes will not bounce or roll.
Pitching platforms are flush with the ground on outside courts. For indoor courts, they may be up to 6in above the ground. The ceiling must be at least 12ft high.
Women and players under 17 years of age pitch a distance of 30ft.

Singles Each player has two shoes and uses the same pitcher's box. Players pitch both shoes in turn at the opposite stake to complete an inning. They then walk to that stake, tally the score, and pitch back toward the first stake.
Doubles Partners separate, one at each stake. Shoes are pitched from one box by two players, then pitched back by the other two. No movement between the boxes is necessary. The partners' scores are added together.
Start Players toss a coin; the winner decides who pitches first. If there is more than one game, the choice of starting alternates thereafter.

Pitching The pitcher must stand on one of the pitching platforms. His feet must stay behind the foul line until the shoe has left his hand.
His opponent must remain on the opposite side of the stake, either in the rear quarter of the other pitching platform or behind the pitching box, with the toes of one foot touching that platform.
He must not talk, move, or in any other way distract the pitcher. Such an offense incurs a loss of score in that inning.
No player may walk to the opposite stake, or be informed of the position of the shoes before an inning is complete.
Once thrown, shoes may not be moved or touched until the scores have been decided. Such an offense incurs a loss of score in that inning.

Scoring Shoes must be within 6in of the stake to score.
A shoe that first strikes the ground outside the target area cannot be scored, nor can any shoe thrown from an invalid position. Such shoes may be removed from the pitching box on the request of the opponent.
A shoe landing in the area and breaking is not scored; it is removed and another pitch taken.
A "ringer" is a shoe that encircles the stake so that a straight edge could touch the two prongs without touching the stake.
Three-handed games If two players score a ringer in an inning and the third does not, then his shoes are disregarded.

Cancellation scoring Each ringer scores three points. Each shoe closer than an opponent's scores one point. Innings continue until one player reaches 50 points.
Only the difference between the scores in each inning counts. If the result of an inning is equal, then no score is recorded.
The scorer in one inning pitches first in the next inning. If no points are scored, the order of pitching alternates.

Count-all scoring Each ringer scores three points and one point is scored for every shoe within 6in of the stake, regardless of the position of an opponent's shoes.
A game consists of 25 innings, 50 shoes being pitched by each player.
Ties are broken by pitching an extra inning. The order of pitching alternates.

Darts

A traditional English "pub" game, darts now has enthusiasts in many different countries. Players throw darts at a circular target divided into different scoring areas. Games are played by individuals, pairs, or teams. In the standard game, players aim to reduce a starting score exactly to zero. Other games provide a great variety of objectives designed to test the players' skill.

Standard dartboard Most dartboards are made of cork, bristle, or elm, with the divisions and sector numbers marked by wires.
The standard tournament board is 18in in diameter and has twenty sectors, an outer "doubles" ring, an inner "trebles" ring, and an inner and outer "bull" in the center. Adjacent sectors are differentiated by color.
Darts Each player has a set of three darts.
Designs vary, but most darts are about 6in long. All darts have:
a sharp point, usually made of steel;
a barrel, with finger grips, made of metal (usually brass), of plastic weighted with metal, or of wood;
a tail, "flighted" with feathers, plastic, or paper.

Yorkshire

Narrow five

Target

Irish black

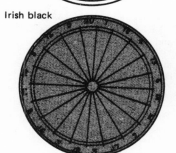

Unusual dartboards
Examples of unusual dartboards are:
a) the Yorkshire board, with a single bull, diamonds between the numbers 14 and 9 and 4 and 13, and no trebles ring;
b) the Irish black, again with a single bull and no trebles ring;

c) the narrow five board from London's East End, with three 20s, three 15s, three 10s, and three 5s; and
d) the target board, with circles increasing in value toward the center.

Games using different boards Any game played on the standard tournament board can be played on the Yorkshire board or the Irish black—the only difference being that there are no trebles and no outer bull.
The narrow five board—now very rare—is used for a game in which players seek to be first to reach a set target score. The target board—a very early type—is used for a game in which players throw three darts in a turn and aim to be the first to throw 1000 points.

STANDARD TOURNAMENT GAME

Players Games are played by individuals, pairs, or teams of any fixed number of players.

Starting Each player, or one member of each pair or team, must get a dart in the doubles ring to begin scoring.
The starting double is scored, as are darts thrown after but not before it in the same turn.

Turns In singles games, each opponent throws in turn. In pairs and team games, the different sides throw in turn, with members of each side playing in the order established at the start of the game.
The first turn goes to the player, pair, or team that wins the toss of a coin or gets a dart nearest the bull in a preliminary throw.

Scored throws A throw is invalid if the player is not behind the toe-line when throwing.
Only those darts sticking in the board at the end of a player's turn are scored. Thus darts are not scored if they rebound, stick in another dart, fall from the board, or are knocked out before the player ends his turn. Re-throws are not permitted. (Also note starting and finishing procedures.)

Scoring Scored throws are deducted from a starting total —usually 301, 501, or 1001. Darts in the inner bull score 50, and in the outer bull 25. Darts in a sector score according to the sector number—unless they are within the outer (doubles) ring, when they score double the sector number, or the inner (trebles) ring, when they score three times the sector number.

Finishing The game ends with a double bringing the score exactly to zero.
If the scores in a player's turn take him past zero, or to one, he goes back to the score before that turn and forfeits any darts remaining in that turn.

The scoreboard is a slate or blackboard, usually positioned to one side of the dartboard. Each side's score is recorded in chalk.

"Chalking" Traditionally in English pubs, a person who wishes to play on the dartboard when other players are using it, must offer to "chalk" (keep the score) for these players. Chalking entitles him to play the winner of the game then in progress.

Playing area The dartboard is hung on a wall, with the center 5ft 8in from the ground. Toe lines may be marked on a mat or on the floor, at distances of 8ft, 8ft 6in, and 9ft from the dartboard.

8ft
8ft 6in
9ft

©DIAGRAM

AROUND THE CLOCK

This is a singles game for any number of players. Each player throws three darts in a turn.
After a starting double, each player must throw one dart into each of the sectors, in order, from 1 to 20. Darts in the doubles or trebles rings of the correct sector are usually allowed.
The winner is the first player to finish.
As a variation, players may be awarded an extra turn for scoring with the last dart of a turn.

SHANGHAI

Shanghai is another "around the clock" game for any number of players with three darts each.
In his first turn, each player throws all his darts at sector number 1. Singles, doubles, and trebles all score their value.
In his second turn, each player throws all his darts at sector number 2 (even if he made no score in his first turn).
Play proceeds in this manner right "around the clock," and the winner is usually the player with the highest total score.
In a popular variation of this game, a player may win by going "Shanghai," ie by scoring in one turn a single, double, and treble of the required number.

SCRAM

Scram is a game for two players throwing three darts in each turn.
The player with the first turn is the "stopper," and any sector he hits with a dart is closed to his opponent.
The second player is known as the "scorer," and he aims to score as many points as possible before all the sectors are closed.
When all the sectors are closed, the two players change roles.
The winner is the player who scores most when playing scorer.

CLOSING

This is a game for two players, each with three darts.
Each player aims to make as high a score as possible while seeking to prevent his opponent from making a high score.
As soon as one of the players has scored three times from any one sector, that sector is "closed" and no further score may be made from it by either player.
Doubles and trebles score their value, and count as two and three scores respectively.
The winner is the player with the highest score when the last sector is closed.

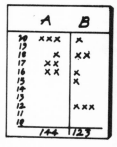

Closing

KILLER

Killer is probably best with four to eight players, but can be played by either more or less.

In his first turn, each player throws one dart with the hand that he normally does not use for playing darts. This throw decides a player's own sector for the rest of the game. Unless a very large number of people are playing, it is usual for a

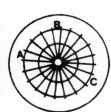

First turn

Second turn   A

Third turn

player to throw again if a sector has already been given to another player.

In every other turn, each player throws three darts with his usual hand.

The game has several versions, but in all cases the winner is the player left in the game when all other players have lost all their "lives."

First version In one version of the game, all players begin with no lives and a player's first objective is to acquire three lives by throwing three darts into his own sector (two lives for a double and three for a treble).

Once a player has three lives he becomes a "killer" and starts throwing darts at other players' sectors (in the

example illustrated, players B and C become killers after their second turns and player A after the first throw of his third turn).

If a killer throws a dart into the sector of a player with three or two lives, that player loses one life (or two for a double or three for a treble).

If a killer throws a dart into the sector of a player with one or no lives, that player is out (player B after C's third turn in the example illustrated).

A killer who loses a life loses his right to kill until he makes up his lost life by throwing another dart into his own sector.

Second version All players start with an agreed number of lives—usually three or five. To start killing, a player has to throw a double of his own number. Kills are made by throwing doubles and trebles of other players' numbers— one kill for a double and two kills for a treble. Lost lives cannot be won back again.

A	✗	
B	✗ ✗ ✗	
C	✗ ✗ ✗	

A	✗ ✗ ✗	
B̶	✗ ✗ ✗	
C	✗ ✗ ✗	

HALVE IT

Halve it is a game for any number of players, each throwing three darts in a turn.

Before play begins, players select a series of objectives and chalk them up on the scoreboard. A typical series would be: 20, 19, 18, any double, 17, 16, 15, any treble, 14, 13, 12, double, treble, 11, 10, bull.

In his first turn, each player aims for 20 and scores for each dart in that sector (doubles and trebles count their value). Players then take turns to make their way through the list of objectives, scoring for each dart in the correct sector or halving their total score (rounding down) whenever none of their darts scores.

There are no minus scores, and

a player whose score is reduced to zero stays at zero until he throws a dart that scores.

	A	B
20	–	20
19	19	37
18	37	75
Double	18	105
17	9	122
16	4	61
15	19	30
Treble	9	70
14	4	45
13	30	71
12	15	95

FIVES

Fives can be played by two players or sides using a standard dartboard.

The winner is the first player to reach an agreed number of points, usually 50.

Each player throws three darts in a turn. He scores only if the sum of his three darts can be divided by five—in which case he scores the result of this division.

A player who throws a dart out of the scoring area when he has a total divisible by five, scores no points for that turn.

DARTS FOOTBALL

This is a game for two players, each throwing three darts in a turn.

A dart in the inner bull "gains control of the ball." This player can then start scoring

"goals"—one for each double. He continues scoring until his opponent "takes the ball away" by scoring an inner bull. The first player to score ten goals wins the game.

DARTS CRICKET

Darts cricket is a game for two teams of equal size.

The team that wins the toss of a coin decides whether to "bat" or to "bowl."

Turns alternate between teams, and each player throws one dart in a turn.

When "batting," a team aims to score as many "runs" as possible; when "bowling," to "take wickets" by scoring inner bulls.

The teams change roles after five wickets are taken.

The team with the highest batting score wins the game.

DARTS BASEBALL

This is a darts game for two players, each representing a baseball team.

There are nine innings, and each player has a turn at "bat" in each inning. A player's turn consists of three throws.

In the first inning players throw darts at sector 1, in the second inning at sector 2, through to sector 9 in the ninth inning. Extra innings are played if there is a tie.

A single "run" is scored by getting a dart into the correct sector for the inning (with two runs for a double and three for a treble). Getting a bull at any stage of the game is a "grand slam home run" and scores four runs.

DARTS SHOVE HA'PENNY

This game for two players or pairs is based on the rules of an old English board game (p 151).

Each player throws three darts in a turn, and the objective is to score three times in each of the sectors numbered 1 through 9.

The scores may be made in any order, and doubles count as two scores and trebles as three.

If a player scores more than three times in any one sector, the extra scores are given to the opposition. The score that wins the game, however, must always be actually thrown by the winner.

The game is won by the first side to finish.

Target archery

In target archery competitors shoot a specified number of rounds. Each round consists of a certain number of arrows shot from prescribed distances. Each arrow that hits the target scores according to its distance from the center.

Men

90m line
99yd

Women

70m line
77yd

60m line
66yd

90m
99yd

*minimum

50m line
55yd

15°

130cm
4ft 3in

30m line
33yd

Permanent
shooting line

5m*
16ft 3in

Waiting line

5m*
16ft 3in

The field All competitors compete on one field. Men and women are separated by a clear lane at least 5m wide. Buttresses are numbered and pegged securely to the ground. There are one to three (usually two) targets in each lane. Lanes must be clearly marked. The points on the shooting line directly opposite each buttress must be marked and numbered accordingly. Archers shoot from a sequence of distances. Men shoot at: 90m, 70m, 50m, and 30m. Women shoot at: 70m, 60m, 50m, and 30m. In club shooting, the target line is usually permanent and the shooting line is moved up at each distance.

Officials These may include: an organizing committee; a director of shooting (or field captain) and his deputy; a scores committee; scorers (one per target): a technical commission of at least five members.

Competitors Archers compete as individuals and as teams. National teams comprise three archers.

Scoring generally occurs after every end (three arrows). Archers call their own scores, with other archers in the group verifying. Scores are determined by the position of the arrow shaft on the target face. An arrow touching two colors or a dividing line scores the higher value. An arrow passing through the target (**1**), an arrow rebounding from the target (**2**), or an arrow rebounding from another arrow, will only score if their marks on the target face or arrow can be identified. An arrow embedded in another arrow scores the same as that arrow. An arrow deflected from another arrow scores as it lies in the target. Arrows that hit the wrong target or hit their target after rebounding from the ground do not score. No archer may touch the arrows or the target face until the scores have been verified. After arrows have been drawn from the target, all holes are marked.

The target Targets are made of straw ropes stitched together. Target faces are made of paper, cloth, or other suitable material. There are two standard circular FITA (Fédération Internationale de Tir à l'Arc) target faces of 122cm and 80cm diameters. They are divided into ten concentric scoring zones of equal width: 6·1cm on the 122cm target face, and 4cm on the 80cm target face. The targets are also divided into five concentric color zones. The 80cm target face is used at 50m and at 30m. Competitors are drawn for targets. There is a maximum of four (preferably three) archers to each target.

3 FITA international 122cm target face:
a white (outer) 1 point
b white (inner) 2 points
c black (outer) 3 points
d black (inner) 4 points
e blue (outer) 5 points
f blue (inner) 6 points
g red (outer) 7 points
h red (inner) 8 points
i gold (outer) 9 points
j gold (inner) 10 points

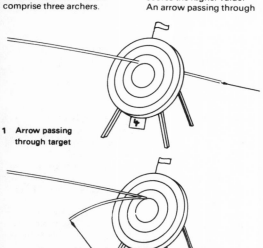

1 Arrow passing
through target

2 Arrow rebounding

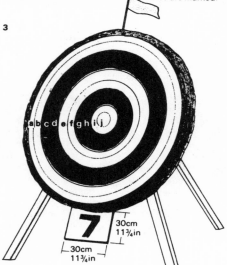

3

abcdefghij

7

30cm
11¾in

30cm
11¾in

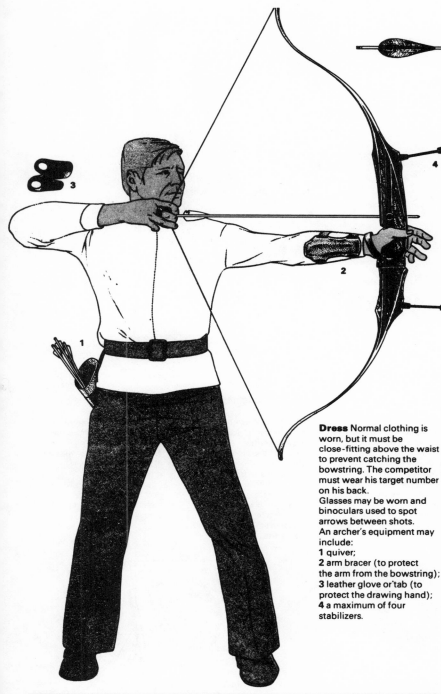

©DIAGRAM

Arrows are generally of tubular aluminum alloy. Length, weight, and stiffness vary to suit the archer and the bow.
The ideal length is from the base of the thumb to the archer's chin, in the sideways shooting stance. The weight is usually less than 28g. The stiffness of the spine of the arrow determines (for a given bow) whether it will drift to left or right. The arrow is not held on the string but the string, at the nocking point, fits into the nock of the arrow. The "serving" at this point is made thick enough for the arrow to hang on to the string. Arrows must be marked to identify the archer.

Dress Normal clothing is worn, but it must be close-fitting above the waist to prevent catching the bowstring. The competitor must wear his target number on his back.
Glasses may be worn and binoculars used to spot arrows between shots.
An archer's equipment may include:
1 quiver;
2 arm bracer (to protect the arm from the bowstring);
3 leather glove or tab (to protect the drawing hand);
4 a maximum of four stabilizers.

The bow Any form of bow is allowed except the crossbow. Generally, most advanced archers use steel or composite bows made of fiberglass, wood laminations, and plastic.
There is no specified length for a bow. Longer bows are steadier in the hand; shorter bows shoot a faster arrow, less affected by wind.
All bows may be fitted with foresights, bowsights, or bowmarks for range and to compensate for lateral drift. Alternately, a "point of aim" mark may be placed on the range. One lip or nose mark is allowed on the string.

Certain attachments, including lenses, prisms, rearsights, mechanical releases, and excessively long stabilizers are forbidden.
The draw-weight is the weight of pull at full draw (when the bowstring is pulled back). This is usually between 35–45lb for men, and 24–28lb for women.

Tournaments A single FITA round may be shot over one or two days, and consists of 144 arrows, 36 arrows at each distance. Distances shot are:
Men: 90m, 70m, 50m, 30m.
Women: 70m, 60m, 50m, 30m.
The longest distance is shot first. If shot over two days, the two longest distances are shot on the first day.
A complete tournament is either one or two FITA rounds (two at world championships).
Starting Under the control of the field captain, each competitor begins each day with six sighting arrows, which are not scored.
The shooting then divides into ends of three arrows from each archer.

Shooting Except for the disabled, shooting is from an unsupported standing position, with a foot each side of the shooting line. Archers shoot in turn, usually one archer per target. The target group member who shoots first changes with each end. During an end an archer shoots three arrows consecutively, then returns behind the waiting line while other members of the group shoot.
Each archer has a maximum of 2½ minutes for his three arrows, from the moment he steps up to the shooting line.

A warning signal is given after two minutes. Twenty seconds is allowed between archers. Arrows shot outside the allotted time are forfeited. All time signaling is by colored lights or plates, or by whistle blast.
While on the shooting line archers may not receive any information.
An arrow is not regarded as being shot, and may be returned, if the archer can touch it with his bow without moving his feet from their position at the shooting line.

Result Competitions are won by the archer with the highest total score after the prescribed rounds have been completed.
A few competitions under local rules are decided by the most hits or the most golds.
Ties If the score total is tied, the winner is the archer with the greatest number of scoring hits. If a tie persists, the winner is the archer with most golds, and then the most hits scoring nine points. If a tie still persists the archers are declared equal.

Ties in team competitions are decided for the tying team with the archer who has the highest individual score; then, if the tie persists, for the tying team with the archer who has the second highest individual score. If the tie persists, the tying teams are declared equal.

Field archery

There are two major types of field archery: freestyle and barebow (or instinctive). Freestyle allows the equipment used in target archery, but barebow forbids any artificial forms of aiming. Both styles use targets of four different sizes located around a course. Under international rules competitors shoot two rounds: the hunters' round and the field round.

The range The targets are set out in sequence over natural terrain in two courses, one course for each round. Each course is of one or two units, of 14 targets each. Direction of shooting and shooting distances vary. Shooting distances are marked by posts. In the field round, 11 targets each have one distance post, and three have four posts. In the hunters' round, all have four posts.
Where there are four posts, competitors shoot from all four posts—beginning with the farthest post and gradually approaching the target.
In the hunters' round at championship level, competitors are not informed of the measured distances of the posts from the targets.
Dress is as for target archery. Competitors may not use fieldglasses or other visual aids; any aids for calculating distances; any memoranda for improving scores.
The bow There are two classes of bow: freestyle and instinctive.
Freestyle includes any bow that may be used for target archery.
Instinctive prohibits any attachments that would aid the aim.
Draw weights tend to be heavier than for target archery
Arrows are similar to those used in target archery, but may have larger fletches.
Officials are similar to those in target archery. One competitor in each group is target captain, and two are scorers.
Duration A tournament consists of two rounds—a field round and a hunters' round shot on separate days. Each round is of 28 targets (two units, or two circuits of the same unit) and requires 112 arrow shots from each archer.
Shooting Competitors shoot from marker posts driven into the ground. The shooting stance is with both feet

behind the post.
Competitors move around the course in groups of three to five (preferably four).
The field captain assigns the post from which each group will start its round, so that all groups start shooting at the same time, each from a different post.
Within each group the shooting order rotates; members may shoot singly or in pairs— as indicated at each post.
Each archer shoots four arrows at each target. Where there is one distance post, he shoots all four arrows from that post. Where there are four distance posts, he shoots one arrow from each post. An arrow is not considered to have been shot if the archer can touch it with his bow without moving his feet from behind the shooting line.
Scoring Arrows passing through or rebounding off a target can be scored (except in US national field archery competitions). Otherwise the rules are as for target archery.
The accumulated total scores decide the result of competitions. Ties are decided by most targets hit, then by most scoring arrows. If a tie persists, there is a shoot-off.
The scores are recorded after all the archers in the group have shot their arrows; except on the 30cm face, where scores may be taken after two archers have shot; or on the 15cm face after each archer has shot.
The maximum possible score for a target is 20 points, and for a round 560 points.

Targets There are four standard circular target faces: 60cm, 45cm, 30cm, and 15cm in diameter.
In both the field round and the hunters' round, all the faces are divided into an outer ring, an inner ring, and a center circular spot.
The inner ring is half the diameter of the outer ring; the center spot is $\frac{1}{4}$ the

diameter of the outer ring.
In the field round, the outer ring and center spot are black and the inner ring is white.
In the hunters' round, both the inner ring and the outer ring are black, with a thin dividing line, and the center spot is white.
Except in FITA championship events, the targets may be

drawn on animal figures, but the center spot must always be clearly visible.
Target faces must always be at least 15cm from the ground.
The outer ring scores three points; the inner ring, including the center spot, scores five points.

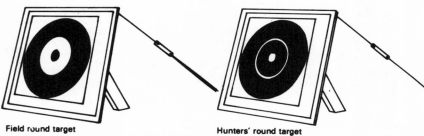

Field round target

Hunters' round target

The field round: consists of two units each of 56 arrows. Each unit comprises:

Number of arrows from each distance	Distance	Number of targets	Number of posts for each target	Diameter of target faces	Total arrows
4	15m, 20m, 25m, 30m	4	1	30cm	16
4	35m, 40m, 45m	3	1	45cm	12
4	50m, 55m, 60m	3	1	60cm	12
4	35m	1	1	45cm	4
1	6m, 8m, 10m, 12m	1	4	15cm	4
1	30m, 35m, 40m, 45m	1	4	45cm	4
1	45m, 50m, 55m, 60m	1	4	60cm	4
					Total 56

Shots are mixed to give maximum variety.

The hunters' round: consists of two units each of 56 arrows. Each unit has a total distance of 1480m. Competitors shoot one arrow from each of four different distance posts for each target. These are:

Number of arrows from each distance	Distance	Number of targets	Total distance for arrows	Diameter of target faces	Total arrows
4	5-15m	2	80m	15cm	8
4	10-30m	4	320m	30cm	16
4	20-40m	5	600m	45cm	20
4	30-50m	3	480m	60cm	12
			Total 1480m		Total 56

Beyond these general rules, distances do not have to be notified to competitors..

Crossbow archery

Bolts may be of any material and may be any length over 12in. They must not cause unreasonable damage to the target boss. All bolts must be clearly marked for identification purposes.

Crossbow archery shares many of the rules of longbow archery, although the two weapons are not used in the same competitions. Competitors shoot at similar targets from several distances to complete a round. Each part of the target is worth a specific number of points. The winner is the competitor with the highest score after a specified number of rounds.

Shooting Crossbowmen shoot at a target in pairs. They must stand to shoot. For target shooting an offhand position must be used; any position may be adopted for field shooting.

Officials A crossbow field captain exercises duties corresponding to those of a field captain in target archery.

Duration A competition lasts for a specified number of rounds.
A double championship round consists of:
5 dozen bolts at 60yd;
5 dozen bolts at 50yd;
5 dozen bolts at 40yd.

Penalties A competitor may be disqualified if he handles his weapon carelessly or endangers others.

Targets are made of woven or firmly compressed straw and are 24in in diameter. The center circle has a white center 2.4in in diameter, surrounded by a black band 1.2in wide. The four concentric bands are all 2.4in wide.
The bands score 1, 3, 5, and 7 points, from the outside inwards. The black circle and the center circle score 9 points.

Crossbows may be made of any material, but usually the stock is made of walnut or some other good quality hardwood, the bow of laminated fiberglass and maple, and the string of dacron.
Crossbows must be drawn by hand; no mechanical aids are permitted.
Telescopic or magnifying sights are forbidden. Binoculars or a spotting telescope may be used for target shots.

Rifle shooting

Rifle shooting is divided into three basic categories: smallbore, bigbore, and air rifle. These are determined by the type of rifle used, and there are further subdivisions in competition shooting based on the type of shooting position used (prone, kneeling, and standing). The competitor who records the highest score with his total of shots wins the competition.

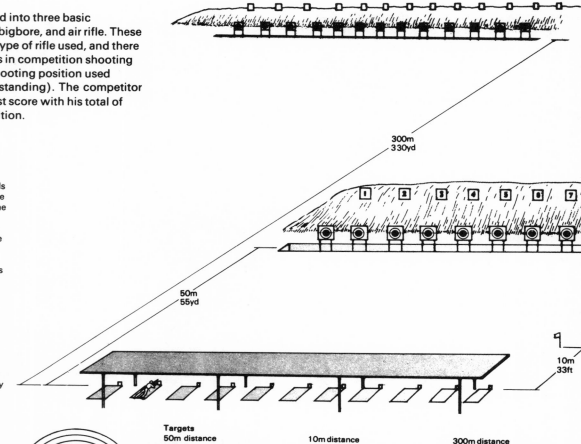

300m
330yd

50m
55yd

10m
33ft

Range Competitors shoot in line, shoulder to shoulder, and there must be enough space behind them for officials and spectators. The targets are numbered to correspond to the firing points.
Sighting (or practice) targets are clearly marked and may be removed during the competitive shooting.
Outdoor targets are fixed so as to remain stationary even in high winds; wind flags are placed 10m in front of the competitors.
Behind the targets there must be bullet catchers, and an earth wall or adequate dead ground.
Distances are measured from the target face to the firing line, where the competitor may place his forward foot or elbow.
Clocks are used to inform competitors of remaining shooting time.
10m range: indoor or outdoor. The target height is 1.5m above the level of the shooting station and may be adjusted to the competitor's height. The background must be light-colored and non-reflecting. Horizontal deviation from an angle of 90° may not exceed 25cm. The competitor usually changes the targets himself.
50m range: indoor, semi-indoor, or outdoor. The optimum target height above the level of the shooting station is 50cm. Horizontal deviation from an angle of 90° may not exceed 1m.
300m range: the line of targets can be lowered into a covered pit and the range may be surrounded by walls for security. The optimum target height above the level of the shooting station is 3m. Horizontal deviation from an angle of 90° may not exceed 6m.
Teams Shooting teams include a team leader.
If a competitor drops out after his first sighting and competitive shots, he may not be replaced.

Targets
50m distance
smallbore rifle events:
diameter 162.4mm
"bull" diameter 112.4mm

Officials include:
a jury, in general control;
a chief range officer and his deputies for each event, who supervise shooting;
register keepers, who record shooting;
target and pit officers, who supervise the targets.
Target procedure (50m and 300m events). After firing, the competitor observes the target with a telescope. The register keeper signals to the pit marker, who lowers the target and records the value of the shot. He then raises the target or a new target and signals the score.

Targets are made of non-reflective material that registers shots without excessive tearing or distortion. The size of the target varies with the distance.
Targets are divided into nine concentric circles scoring between 1 and 10 points, the innermost circle scoring 10.
Shots breaking the boundary between two scoring zones score the higher value.

Targets
10m distance
air rifle events:
diameter 46mm
"bull" diameter 31mm

Shooting ranges are available for training before the competition.
Target and shooting order are decided by lot; an elimination series may be held to reduce the number of competitors per target.
Conditions must be as consistent as possible, with special allowances for left-handed competitors.
All events are shot in series of 10 shots, which are not interrupted except for emergencies. If a competition lasts more than a day, all competitors must fire an equal number of shots and use the same positions each day.

Targets
300m distance
big and smallbore rifle events:
diameter 1000mm
"bull" diameter 600mm

Warming up shots are only allowed in smallbore competitions, to warm the rifle before the start of the event.
Sighting shots may be fired before the competition and between each series of shots, and they are included in the shooting time. A new sighting target may be raised at the competitor's request.
In smallbore free and bigbore free competitions, 15 minutes is allowed to change positions.
Shots fired after the time limit has expired are registered as misses, unless the competitor has been allowed extra time.

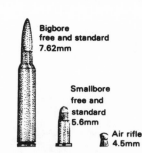

**Bigbore
free and standard
7.62mm**

**Smallbore
free and
standard
5.6mm**

**Air rifle
4.5mm**

Ammunition
Air rifles: maximum caliber
5.6mm; steel projectiles are
forbidden.
Smallbore: lead or similar
soft material.
Bigbore: tracer, armor
piercing and incendiary
ammunition are forbidden.

Rifles
Smallbore free
Maximum weight: 8kg
Maximum caliber: 5.6mm for
rimfire (0.22)
The right-hand grip must not
rest on the sling or the left arm.
Maximum length of the hook
of the butt end is 15.3cm. The
stock or butt end must not give
special support against the
body. The butt plate has a
maximum adjustment of 3cm.
Smallbore standard
Maximum weight: 5kg
Maximum caliber: 5.6mm
Thumb holes, spirit levels,
hand stops, and thumb, palm,
or heel rests are forbidden.
Bigbore, free and standard
Maximum caliber: 8mm
Minimum trigger weight
(bigbore standard): 1500g
Other specifications as for
smallbore.
Air rifle
Any compressed air or CO_2
rifle, of conventional
appearance and 4.5mm
caliber.
Dimensions and prohibited
features as for smallbore
standard.
Sights No lens, lens systems,
or telescopic sights are
permitted. Correcting glasses,
if needed, may be worn by the
shooter.

Air rifle

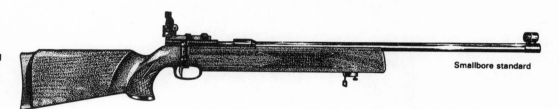

Smallbore standard

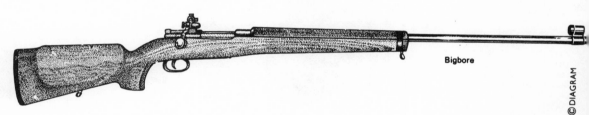

Bigbore

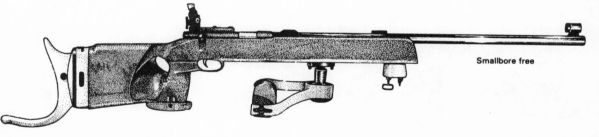

Smallbore free

© DIAGRAM

Course events
Smallbore free: English match 50m
60 shots prone, and 15
sighting shots; or two series
each of 30 shots and 10
sighting shots. Duration: full
match 120 minutes; half match
80 minutes.
Smallbore free: three position 50m
120 shots: 40 prone, 40
standing, 40 kneeling; and 10
sighting shots for each
position. (The 40 shots prone
may be combined with the
first 40 shots of an English
match.) Duration: prone, 90
minutes; standing, 120
minutes; kneeling, 105
minutes.

Smallbore standard 50m
60 shots: 20 prone, 20
standing, 20 kneeling; and 6
sighting shots for each
position. Duration: 150
minutes.
Air rifle 10m
40 shots standing, and 10
sighting shots. Duration: 90
minutes.
Bigbore free 300m
120 shots: 40 prone, 40
standing, 40 kneeling; and 10
sighting shots for each
position. Duration: prone, 90
minutes; standing, 120
minutes; kneeling, 105
minutes.

Bigbore standard 300m
60 shots: 20 prone, 20
standing, 20 kneeling; and
6 sighting shots for each
position. Duration: 150
minutes.
Unless each competitor has
his own target, the maximum
time allowance for a four-man
team is:
smallbore free (three
positions), 21 target hours;
smallbore standard, 10 target
hours;
bigbore standard, 10 target
hours.
Misses If a competitor fails to
hit a target (the shot is
outside the scoring ring), the
shot may be repeated with a
deduction of 2 points.
If he fires a sighting shot on to
another competitor's sighting

target, there is no penalty but
he is not allowed another
shot.
If he fires a sighting shot on to
another competitor's
competition target, 2 points
are deducted and no other
shot is permitted.
If he fires a competition shot
on to any target of another
competitor or on to his own
sighting target, he is
penalized 2 points. If the shot
can be identified or if the shots
are of equal value, the
respective scores are recorded.
If the shots cannot be
identified, both competitors
may either repeat the shot or
accept the shot with the
lower value. If the shot is
repeated, it may not score
more than either of the two
original shots.

Excess shots If a competitor
fires too many sighting shots,
he is penalized 2 points for
each shot.
If he fires too many
competition shots, he is
penalized 2 points for every
excess shot after the first two,
which do not incur a penalty.
He must then fire
correspondingly fewer shots
at the next target.
If there are also too many hits
on his competition target
(disregarding any from
another competitor), his best
hits are nullified up to the
number of surplus shots.

Accessories
a) Telescopes are permitted to locate shots, but may not be attached to rifles.
b) Compensators and muzzle brakes are prohibited.
c) Slings, with a maximum width of 40mm, may be worn only over the upper part of the left arm and must be connected to the front end of the rifle stock.
d) Palm rests must not extend more than 20cm below the barrel axis.
e) Ground cloths or pads of canvas or other thin material are provided by the organizers.
f) A cylindrical kneeling pad or roll is allowed for the kneeling position, with a length of 20cm and diameter of 12–18cm.

Dress Restrictions on material, construction, size, and thickness prevent any artificial support in the different firing positions.
Competitors may wear numbers on their backs for identification.

Kneeling position

Standing position

Prone position

Shooting stations must be level at the front and insulated against vibration. The floor is of earth or gravel, covered to prevent competitors acquiring elbowgrip when shooting in the prone position. Tables used for the prone position must be stable.
The firing point should be equipped with: loading bench, ground cloth, official mat for the prone position, official cushion for the kneeling position, a chair for the competitor, and the register keeper's equipment.

10m ranges must be at least 1m wide. Ground cloths, mats, and kneeling rolls are not required. Targets are collected by the register keeper.
50m ranges are usually 1.6m wide. Competitors are sheltered from the weather. There is a signaling system between the register keeper and marker, and a telephone system between these and the range officers.
300m ranges are normally 1.6m wide, and provide protection from the weather. There is a signaling system between the register keeper and the target pits.

Shooting positions There are three recognized shooting positions:
Prone The rifle is supported by both hands, one shoulder, and a sling. It may touch the competitor's cheek.
Standing Both feet must be on the ground. The left (or right) arm and elbow may be supported on the chest or hip, but slings are prohibited. The rifle is held with both hands, a shoulder and the adjacent chest, and the cheek.

Kneeling The toe of the right foot, the right knee, and the left foot touch the ground. The rifle must be held as in the prone position. The left elbow may rest on the left knee. A sling may be used, also a cushion under the right instep. The reverse positions apply for left-handed competitors.

Extra time If a competitor has to stop shooting for more than three minutes, he may ask for extra shooting time. If he has to stop for more than five minutes, he is also entitled to two extra shots.
If a competitor has to change or repair his rifle, he may be allowed extra shooting time and two sighting shots.
Penalties Infringements may be penalized by:
a warning;
a deduction of two points;
disqualification.
In team competitions a disqualification automatically disqualifies the whole team.

Pistol shooting

Rapid fire pistol shooting is sometimes referred to as silhouette shooting, because of the shape of the targets. Competitors fire a total of 60 shots at five targets from a distance of 25m. These shots are fired in groups of five, each at different targets that turn simultaneously from a side-on to a face-on position and are exposed for a few seconds.

Range A line of targets with revolving silhouettes is placed 25m away from, and parallel to, the firing line.

Targets The silhouettes are placed 75cm apart in groups of five. They appear and disappear simultaneously and are presented face-on for a specified time of 8, 6, or 4 seconds. They turn through 90° at a maximum speed of 0.4 seconds (0.2 seconds in the Olympics and world championships).
Each target is 160cm high and 45cm wide. It is black with a white edge of about 1mm width, and is divided into 10 zones, each with a different scoring value of between 1 and 10. The center of the 10-point zone is always between 80cm and 160cm above the level of the firing platform.

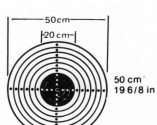

Standard 20yd pistol target

Target revolver

Target pistol

Rapid fire pistol

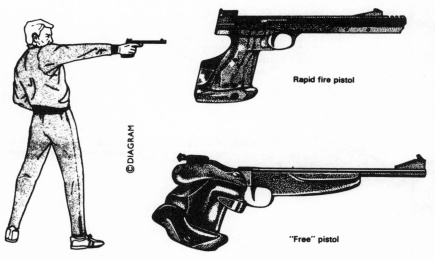

"Free" pistol

Rapid fire target

Ammunition Bullets must be made from lead or a similar soft and even substance.

5.6mm

Weapons Any type of 5.6mm (0.22 caliber) automatic pistol or revolver may be used provided:
it is officially approved;
the butt is not prolonged to create extra support;
the central line of the barrel passes above the upper part of the hand in the normal firing position;
the height of the barrel, including all accessories, does not exceed 40mm;
its weight, including all accessories, does not exceed 1260g;
the weapon fits into a rectangular box with interior measurements of 30cm by 15cm by 5cm.
The use of optical lenses is forbidden.
No support may be given to the weapon above the hand.

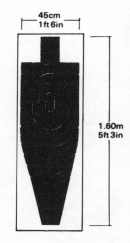

© DIAGRAM

Shooting position The competitor must stand without any kind of support. The weapon must be held in one hand only, so that the wrist may move freely. Leather bracelets and other forms of protection around the wrist are forbidden.

Shooting There are 60 shots divided into two courses of 30. Each course consists of six series of five shots, and in each series one shot is fired at each of the silhouettes from the moment they appear face-on until they disappear. A competitor has the opportunity to use a telescope to observe his shots. Before each course, competitors may fire five sighting shots, one at each silhouette.

Duration of each course:
2 series each of 8 seconds;
2 series each of 6 seconds;
2 series each of 4 seconds.

Scoring Each silhouette is divided into 10 sections, scoring between 1 and 10 points. A shot that strikes the demarcation line between two zones will score the higher value. The competitor with the highest total of points wins.

Misfires If the shot does not leave the weapon, the competitor must place the weapon on the table. The referee then decides whether the failure was caused by a misfire or other malfunction. The competitor may be allowed to fire another series of five shots. Should the substitute series score less than the original shots, the latter are counted.
Such a procedure is only allowed twice in a course of 30 shots.
If the referee decides that the failure was not due to a misfire or malfunction, the shots that were fired in that interrupted series are cancelled.

Free pistol

In free pistol shooting over 50m competitors are allowed 60 shots, divided into six series, which must be completed within two and a half hours. The competitor with the highest score wins.

Range Competitors shoot over a distance of 50m.

Targets Each target is a white square. The scoring rings within it are valued from 1 to 10 from the outside inwards. The inner ring is 5cm in diameter. The diameter of each of the other rings is 5cm wider than the one inside it, making the outside ring 50cm in diameter.

Shooting The pistol must be held in one hand, and the shooting arm must be unsupported and free from the body.
The 60 shots are divided into six series, and 15 sighting shots are allowed. The target is changed after each series. The competition lasts 2½ hours.

Pistol The pistol bore must have a caliber of 5.6mm. The grip of the pistol must not be extended to give extra support to the arm. Optical sights are prohibited.

Clay pigeon shooting

Olympic trench shooting

Clay pigeon shooting includes three types of competition: Olympic trench, down-the-line, and skeet. In all types, competitors with shotguns aim at saucer-shaped clay targets released from traps around the range. The targets' paths resemble the flight of game birds at take-off. The positions of shooting stations and traps vary with the type of competition. The rules of Olympic trench follow.

Shooting range Five shooting stations and fifteen traps. Each shooting station is a marked square, with a table or bench on which to place cartridges, etc. The traps are in five groups, three opposite each station.

a 1-5 firing points spaced 10ft 6in (3.20m) apart
b Distance to trap 49ft 3in (15m)
c Trap (group of three)

Gun Any shotgun, 12 gauge bore or smaller, including automatic models. Compensators, etc that may disturb other shooters are not allowed.

 Side by side

Single barrel

Over and under

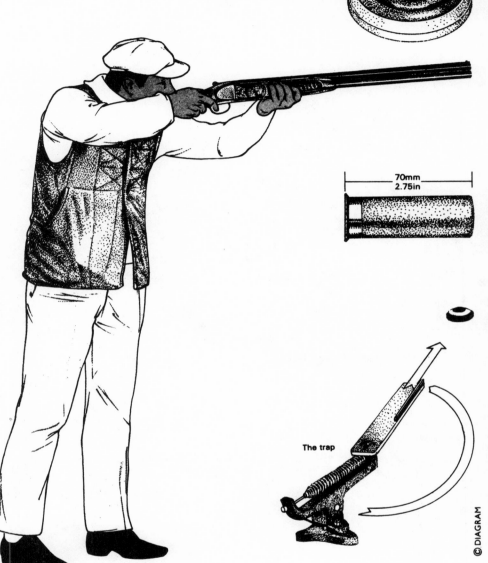

Targets Height 25–27mm; weight 100–110g.
The color chosen for a competition must be identical throughout (black, white, or yellow) and clearly visible. A low barrier is often built in the distance to help judges see that targets have left the trap properly.

110mm
4.29in

70mm
2.75in

Ammunition Maximum loaded cartridge length 70mm. Maximum diameter of shot 2½mm (No 6 European or No 7 US).
Maximum load of shot 32g. Black powder, incendiary, and tracer cartridges are prohibited.

Traps The three traps in a group are fixed to fire in different directions. At the best angle of elevation targets must travel 70–80m if measured over level ground. Traps are adjusted each day and then sealed.
The center trap of each group is indicated by a line or mark on the roof, visible from the corresponding shooting station.
Pits and screens protect the trap loaders.
Traps are released, electrically or mechanically, by a puller operating where he can clearly see and hear all shooters.
Selector systems conceal from which trap of a group the next target will be released, so that the flight path of a station's next target is unknown to all.

The trap

© DIAGRAM

Officials A referee decides hits, misses, and repeat targets. Two assistant referees assist in the scoring. In international competitions, a jury of five controls the competition,and three scorers record misses and misfires, and control the scoreboard.
The traps are loaded by trappers and fired by a puller.
Shooting is usually in squads of six. The firing order within each squad is decided by ballot each day.
Five competitors stand at the shooting stations; the sixth stands ready to take over number 1 station. Each station receives a target; then the shooters move to the next station on the right, and the number 5 shooter crosses

behind to stand ready for number 1.
Shooting continues for a round of 25 "birds" (targets) per competitor (ie five birds at each station), though a shorter round can be used for smaller competitions.
Shooting may be interrupted by the referee, eg for bad weather or to repair traps.
The shooter stands with both feet entirely within the shooting box. He loads two cartridges, and calls when ready to shoot. The target is thrown immediately. If he misses with the first cartridge, he may shoot at the same target with his second.
Misfires If a gun or ammunition fails, the target is repeated, provided that the shooter:
did not cause the failure;

does not open his gun or touch the safety catch before the referee's inspection;
does not fire his second shot if his first misfired.
Only three misfires per shooter are allowed in a round.
If a first shot has missed, and a second misfired, then on the repeated target the shooter must also miss with his first shot, or the target is lost.
A shooter may change a faulty gun if no delay is caused and if it cannot be repaired quickly.
Scoring
A dead target (hit) is one properly thrown and shot at, and visibly broken or reduced to dust. Competitors may not pick up a target to see if it has been hit.

A lost target (miss) occurs when the target has not visibly broken in the air (even if dust rises).
No bird If the target's timing is wrong (thrown before the shooter's call or not immediately after) and the shooter has not fired at it, a new target is allowed.
If it is irregular in some other way, a new target is allowed whether the shooter has fired or not.
The referee may also allow another target:
if the shooter is materially disturbed;
if another competitor has shot at the same target.
The shot is not scored if a competitor shoots out of turn or before calling.

Ties The three leading places are decided by further 25-bird rounds. Shooting continues until scores differ.
Penalties Competitors breaking rules of conduct or equipment may be warned, fined a number of targets, or disqualified.
World championships Teams consist of four shooters from each country. The individual contest comprises 200 targets, of which the first 150 also decide the best national team.

Clay pigeon shooting

Skeet shooting

Shooting range There are eight shooting stations with two traphouses—the "high house" on the left and the "low house" on the right.
From the high house the target emerges at 3·05m above the ground.
From the low house it emerges at 1m.
Targets must pass through a central area and travel 65—70m in still air (except in the UK, where they must travel a minimum of 50·5m).
A timer mechanism releases the target from 0 to 3 seconds after the shooter's call. (Under UK rules the targets are released immediately.)
Targets are the same as for trench shooting.
The traps throw targets at angles that are set within certain limits.

a 1-8 shooting stations
b high house
c low house
d 120ft 9in (36.82m)
e 63ft (19.21m)
f 18ft (5.49m)
g shooting boundary marker 66ft (20.13m) from target crossing point

Firing position

Ready position

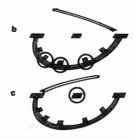

Guns are the same as for trench shooting.
Ammunition The maximum cartridge length is 70mm.
The shot must be spherical, of lead or lead alloy, and 2mm in diameter.
The maximum load of shot is 32g.
Only one type of cartridge may be used by a competitor in a single round.
Black powder, tracer, or incendiary cartridges are forbidden.
Cartridges must be of normal loading, with no internal changes to give special dispersion.
Officials are as for trench shooting.

Shooting Usually squads of five shoot in turn from each station.
At stations 1, 2, 6, and 7 (**a**) a shooter receives, on separate calls:
a single target from the high house;
a single target from the low house;
two targets simultaneously, one from each house (doubles).
At station 3,4, and 5 (**b**) and 8(**c**) a shooter receives, on separate calls:
a single target from the high house;
a single target from the low house;
This totals 24 targets. Also each competitor is allowed one extra shot to complete a 25-bird round.

The extra shot is either a repeat of the first target he misses; or, if there are no misses, it is another low house target at station 8.
After a missed double, only an extra single is given.
The shooter must stand with both feet completely within the shooting box.
At stations 1 and 8 the shooter may raise the gun to his shoulder for a practice aim.
On each call, under international rules, the gun must be held in the "ready" position until the target(s) appears. (Under UK rules there is no defined position.)
Doubles targets must appear simultaneously, whether immediately on the call or up to three seconds after. The shooter aims first at the target from the nearest house.

Only one cartridge may be fired at any target, and only while the target is within shooting bounds. From stations 1 to 7 the target must be within the shooting boundary markers; at station 8 it must be fired at before it crosses the center line.
Scoring The system is the same as for Olympic trench. Repeat targets are allowed in various circumstances, but only two repeats are allowed for misfires in any round. One repeat is also allowed if the shooter's shooting or gun position was wrong, providing he has not already been warned in the same round.

No bird is allowed for doubles targets if:
both barrels go off simultaneously, providing the first target was hit;
both targets are broken with the same shot (only allowed three times);
the shooter aims for the first and accidentally hits the second (in this case the first is lost, and in the repeat only the second target can score).

Down-the-line shooting

Shooting range Five stations, each 18in square, all using a single variable-direction trap.
The trap shoots targets at unpredictable heights and angles, within adjustable limits.
Single-rise shooting Only one target is thrown; the trap is set for it to fall in a defined area.
Double-rise shooting Two targets are thrown simultaneously; the trap is set for them to fall in two separate defined areas.
Targets are the same as for trench shooting.

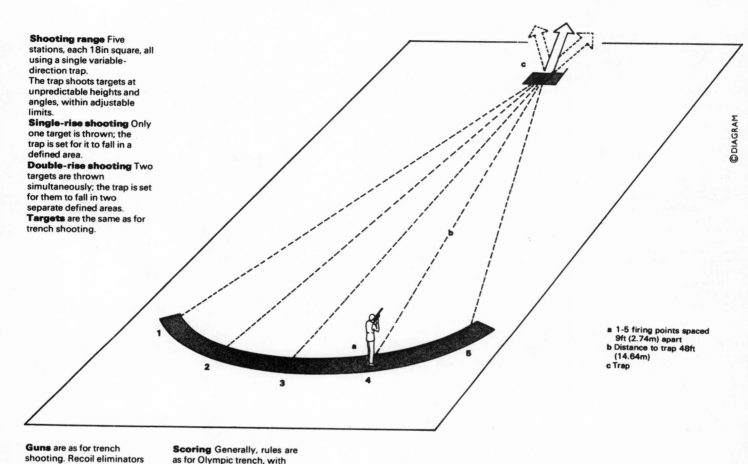

a 1-5 firing points spaced 9ft (2.74m) apart
b Distance to trap 48ft (14.64m)
c Trap

©DIAGRAM

Guns are as for trench shooting. Recoil eliminators are not allowed.
Ammunition is as for trench shooting.
Officials include a referee (whose decision is final), a scorer, a puller, and trappers. There is no jury.
Shooting is normally in squads of five, one at each station. Targets are released at the shooter's call of "pull." Each station receives a target in turn until each competitor has completed an "innings." This is usually five targets per station in a 25-bird "stage." Each shooter then moves to the station at his right. Number 5 moves to number 1.

Scoring Generally, rules are as for Olympic trench, with the following exceptions:
Single-rise shooting "Kills" (hits) are also marked according to which shot hits the target.
Three points are awarded for a first shot kill, two points for a second shot.
Simultaneous shooting of both barrels is not scored— another target is thrown.
Double-rise shooting The shooter may only shoot once at each target.
No birds Additional no birds are declared and two further targets allowed in double-rise shooting if:
only one target is thrown;
a target breaks when thrown;
both targets are broken by one shot;
both barrels discharge simultaneously;
one barrel misfires and the competitor does not fire the other;
the targets are not thrown simultaneously;
the flight of one target is irregular.

1

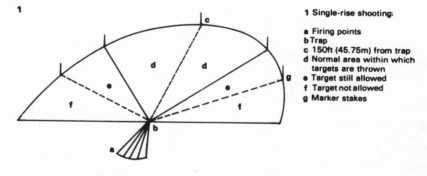

1 Single-rise shooting:

a Firing points
b Trap
c 150ft (45.75m) from trap
d Normal area within which targets are thrown
e Target still allowed
f Target not allowed
g Marker stakes

2

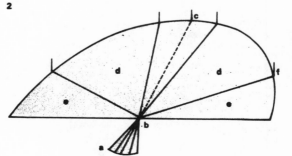

2 Double-rise shooting:

a Firing points
b Trap
c 150ft (45.75) from trap
d One target to fall in each area
e Target not allowed
f Marker stakes

English billiards

English billiards is played on a special table by two players or pairs. Three balls are used – white, spot white, and red. Players use a cue to propel their cue ball across the table to score points by pocketing balls (hazards) or by hitting both other balls (cannons).

The table is a slate bed, covered with green baize. The dimensions given are those of the standard size table. Scaled down tables are sometimes used.
1 cushion (width 2in)
2 top pocket (width 3½in)
3 center pocket (width 4in)
4 bottom pocket (width 3½in)
5 the spot
6 center spot
7 pyramid spot
8 balk line
9 balk line spot
10 the "D"
11 the balk
12 long butt cue (9ft), half butt cue (7ft), and rest (8ft)
13 half butt rest (5ft)
Lighting Billiard tables must be well lit, and special lighting equipment is normally used.

6ft 1½in
1.86m

12ft
3.66m

2ft 5in
73.7cm

2ft 10½in
87.7cm

Starting position

Balls The white and spot white are the cue balls, one used by each player (or pair of players). The red ball is never touched with a cue; it is only hit by knocking other balls against it.
Officials In tournaments a referee controls the game and is the sole judge of fair play. He may be assisted by the marker, who keeps the score.
Duration Play lasts an agreed length of time, or until one player or side reaches an agreed number of points. A game is known as a frame.

Stringing Players "string" for choice of balls and order of play, ie each plays a cue ball up the table from the "D", and the choice goes to the player whose ball stops nearer to the bottom cushion. Playing order is kept throughout the game.
Start The red ball is placed on the spot, and the striker places his cue ball at any point in the "D" and plays the first shot.
When his turn is ended, the second player brings his cue ball into play.
When bringing a cue ball into play, no shot may be made directly at any ball within the balk area. If both balls are in this area, the cue ball must strike a cushion outside the balk before it can touch either ball.

Making a shot The striker uses the tip of his cue to hit his cue ball in the direction of another ball. Chalk is applied to the cue to improve contact. The cue ball must be struck and not pushed; and at the moment of striking, the player must have a foot on the floor. Balls must not be forced off the table.
Rests Players may use a rest to support the cue for a shot.
Distraction The non-striker must not do anything to distract the striker.
Making a break The shots comprising a player's turn are called a break.
Each time a player scores from a shot he is entitled to another shot. Only when he fails to score does he forfeit his turn. All points scored up to that time are scored for the break.

Balls touching If the striker's ball comes to rest against another ball, the red ball is replaced on the spot. The non-striker's ball, if on the table, is placed on the center spot; if off the table, it is left off, and the striker plays from the "D".
Pocketed balls If the non-striker's cue ball is pocketed during a break, it remains off the table until the break ends.
When the red ball is sunk, it is immediately replaced on the spot. When the cue ball is pocketed, the striker brings it back into play by playing from the "D".
Fouls and penalties A striker who makes any foul shot loses his turn and any score he has made in that break. In addition, he

concedes points to his opponent for the following fouls:
touching his ball more than once in a stroke, one point;
forcing a ball off the table, three points;
not playing out of balk from the "D" correctly, one point;
making a push shot, one point.
The following fouls incur no penalty points:
playing with both feet off the floor;
playing the balls before they are still;
striking the ball with anything but the cue;
playing the wrong ball;
playing out of turn;
playing from outside the "D" when required to play from within it.

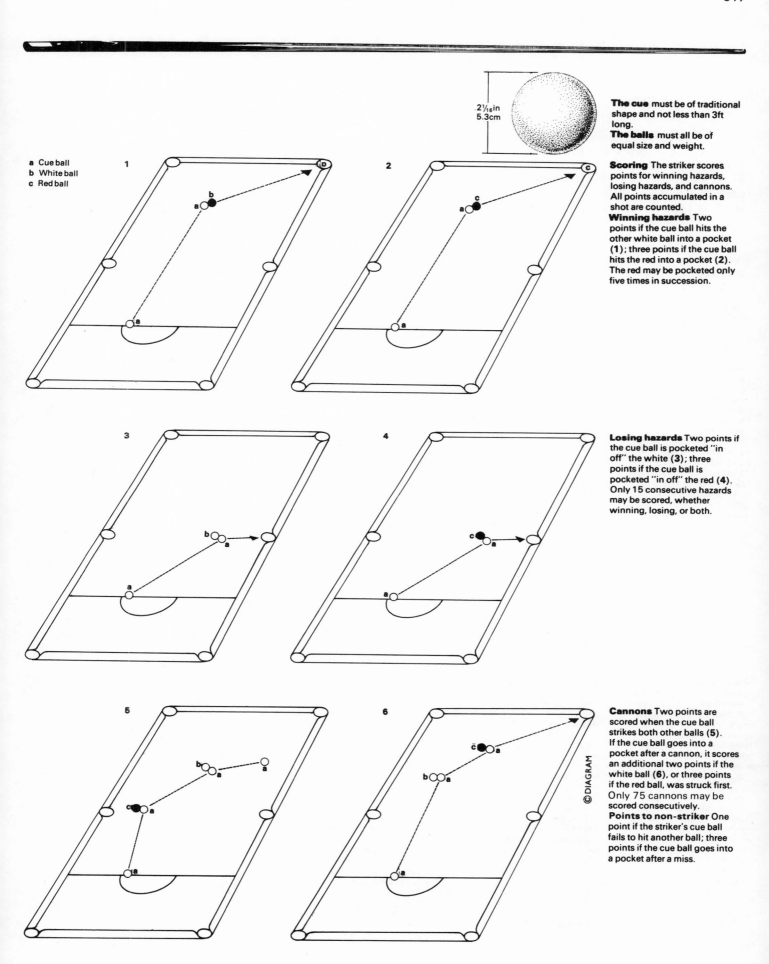

**2¹⁄₁₆in
5.3cm**

a Cue ball
b White ball
c Red ball

The cue must be of traditional shape and not less than 3ft long.
The balls must all be of equal size and weight.

Scoring The striker scores points for winning hazards, losing hazards, and cannons. All points accumulated in a shot are counted.
Winning hazards Two points if the cue ball hits the other white ball into a pocket (**1**); three points if the cue ball hits the red into a pocket (**2**). The red may be pocketed only five times in succession.

Losing hazards Two points if the cue ball is pocketed "in off" the white (**3**); three points if the cue ball is pocketed "in off" the red (**4**). Only 15 consecutive hazards may be scored, whether winning, losing, or both.

Cannons Two points are scored when the cue ball strikes both other balls (**5**). If the cue ball goes into a pocket after a cannon, it scores an additional two points if the white ball (**6**), or three points if the red ball, was struck first. Only 75 cannons may be scored consecutively.
Points to non-striker One point if the striker's cue ball fails to hit another ball; three points if the cue ball goes into a pocket after a miss.

©DIAGRAM

Carom billiards

Carom billiards is played on a billiard table with no pockets. It is played with three balls: red, white, and spot white. A carom, scoring one point, is made when the cue ball glances off one object ball on to the other. The first player to reach an agreed number of points wins the game.

The table has a slate base, covered with green baize. There are no pockets. A carom billiards table can be 5ft by 10ft, 4½ft by 9ft, or 4ft by 8ft.
1 foot cushion
2 foot string
3 foot spot
4 center string
5 center spot
6 head string
7 head spot.
8 head cushion
9 side rails
10 diamond
11 red ball (first object ball)
12 white object ball
13 cue ball
(Strings are imaginary lines through the spots and parallel to the ends of the table.)

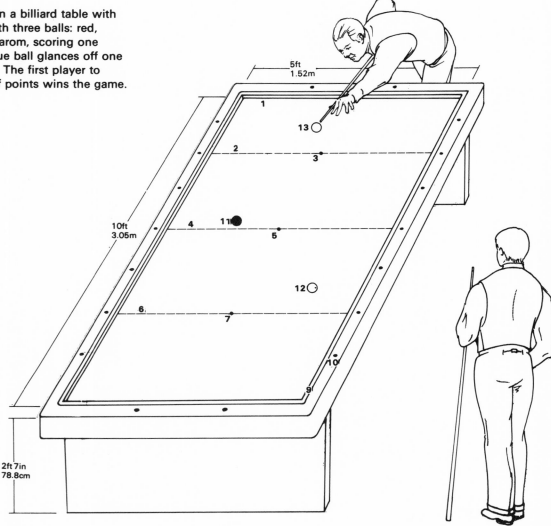

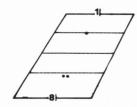

Starting position

Playing order If there are more than two players, the order may be decided by lot. If there are two players or two teams, the order is decided by lagging. In lagging, the red ball is placed on the foot spot.
Each player takes a cue ball, and plays it against the foot cushion from behind the head string. One player lags to the right, and the other to the left, of the red ball. Choice of playing order and cue ball goes to the player whose cue ball at the lag comes to rest nearest the head of the table. Cue balls may touch the side rails during lagging.
A player loses the lag if his cue ball interferes with the red ball on the foot spot, or is clearly out of line and inter-

feres with his opponent's ball. The lag is repeated if both players are in error or if the result is a tie.
Break shot The break or opening shot is made with the red ball on the foot spot and the white object ball on the head spot. The cue ball is played from the head string, within 6in (center to center) from the white object ball. The cue ball must contact the red ball first.
Rules of play In any shot but a break shot, a player's cue ball may contact either of the object balls first. A player's turn continues until he fails to score, when he also loses one point if his last shot was not a successful "safety."
Officials are a referee and a scorekeeper.

Playing out of turn If the offending player fails to score, it is a foul. The offender loses one point and ends his turn, and the incoming player must accept the balls in position.
If the offending player scores, his opponent must detect the error before a second shot is played. If the error is detected in time, the offender loses one point and ends his turn. If the error is not detected in time, all points scored count and the player's turn continues until he misses. The offending player must wait for his next turn until all the other players have had a turn, and the new playing order is then retained throughout the game.

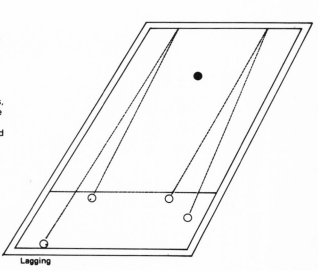

Lagging

Cue A carom billiards cue is similar in size and shape to an English billiards cue.
Balls Carom billiards is played with one red object ball, a white ball, and a white ball with two small spots. Each player or side has one of the white balls for a cue ball.

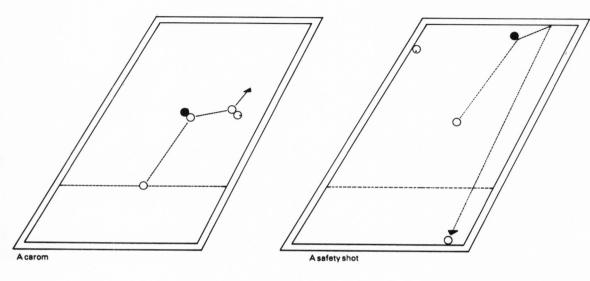

A carom

A safety shot

Scoring a carom A carom count or carom score of one point is gained when the cue ball glances from one object to the other. It may do so directly or by way of touching a cushion.
A safety shot allows a player to end his turn without penalty. The cue ball must either contact a cushion after striking an object ball, or drive an object ball to a cushion.
Safety shots are generally not permitted in consecutive innings.

© DIAGRAM

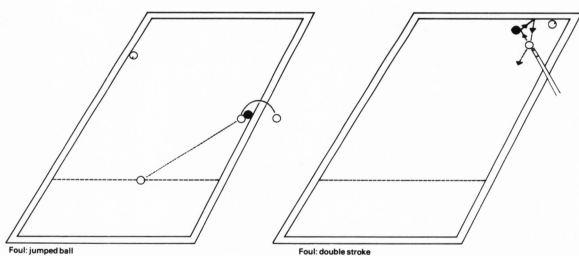

Foul: jumped ball

Foul: double stroke

Playing from safety It is a foul if a player fails to make an obvious attempt to score on his return to the table after a safety shot. There is a one point penalty and the player loses his turn. Rules on playing from safety continue to apply until the player opens a turn with a deliberate attempt to score.
Additional one point penalties are incurred for each infraction.
Kiss shots are all counted, whether they assist in a score or deprive a player of points. The cue ball may kiss from one object ball to another. An object ball already struck by the cue ball may kiss the second object ball either into or away from the path of the cue ball.

Jumped balls If his cue ball jumps off the table, the player loses one point and ends his turn. The cue ball is placed on the head spot or, if it is occupied, on the foot spot. If both are occupied, the cue ball is placed on the center spot.
If the red ball jumps off the table, it is replaced on the foot spot. If the white object ball jumps off the table, it is replaced on the head spot. Any score made before either or both object balls jump off the table is counted and the player continues shooting. If all the balls jump off the table, it is a foul.
The offending player loses one point and ends his turn. The incoming player makes a break shot.

Bounce on rail The cue ball remains in play if it bounces onto and rides the rail and then returns to the table. It is treated as a jumped ball if it remains on the rail.
Frozen balls are balls that are touching each other or a cushion.
Frozen object balls remain in play as they are.
If his cue ball is frozen, a player can shoot away from the frozen object ball or have the balls spotted for a break shot. Failure to do either is a foul (resulting in the loss of one point and the end of a turn).
If his cue ball is frozen against a cushion, it may be first played against that cushion.

Fouls All fouls cause the loss of one point and the end of the offender's turn. The following constitute a foul.
Balls in motion: making a shot when any ball is in motion.
Cueing ball: touching the cue ball during "warm up" stroking. The offender may not claim that the touch was his stroke.
Push or shove shot: making a push or shove shot, which is defined as a shot in which the cue tip remains in contact with the cue ball after the cue ball has struck an object ball.
Double stroke: making a double stroke, defined as one in which the cue tip again contacts the cue ball after the cue ball has struck an object ball.

Cue and object ball: touching an object ball with the cue.
Wrong cue ball: shooting the wrong cue ball; the incoming player must accept the balls that are in position.
Foot on floor: not having one foot touching the floor when making a shot.
It is a foul if any player causes interference. The offender loses a point and the incoming player must accept the balls in position.
A miscue is not a foul.

Pool

Pool is played on a pocket billiard table with one white cue ball and fifteen numbered object balls. It can be played by two individuals, pairs, or teams. Points are scored for pocketing designated balls in designated pockets. The first player or side to reach an agreed number of points wins the game.

The table A slate base, covered with green baize. There are six pockets. Table sizes range from 3½ft by 7ft to 5ft by 10ft; the length is always twice the width.
 1 foot cushion
 2 foot string
 3 foot spot
 4 center string
 5 center spot
 6 head string
 7 head spot
 8 head cushion
 9 long string
 10 side rails
 11 pocket
 12 cue ball
 13 object balls
(Strings are imaginary lines through the spots and parallel to the ends of the table.)
Officials are a referee and a scorekeeper.

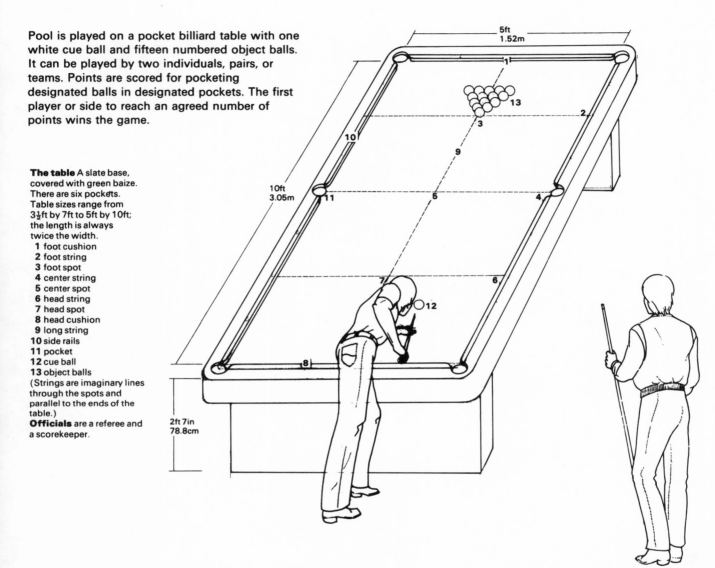

Lagging Players "lag" to decide the order of play. The choice goes to the player whose cue ball comes to rest nearest the head of the table after being stroked against the foot cushion from behind the head string.
The cue ball may touch the side rails.
The player winning the lag usually chooses to play after his opponent.
Duration A match is made up of an agreed number of "blocks." Each block is played to an agreed point requirement—usually 125 or 150 in title play.
Scoring One point is scored for pocketing a designated ball in a designated pocket.

An additional one point is scored for every other object ball pocketed in the same stroke.
Break shot Starting with his cue ball behind the head string, the opening player must either:
1 drop a called (designated) ball into a called pocket; or
2 drive the cue ball and two object balls to a cushion.
He may shoot directly at the object balls or make the cue ball touch one or more cushions before contact with the balls.
Failure to achieve either objective is a foul, and the player loses two points. At the option of his opponent, he then either ends his turn or, with the balls reframed; is compelled to break again. Two points are lost for each consecutive

failure to meet the break requirements. The 15-point penalty does not apply.
If, however, the opening player drives two balls to a cushion and scratches the cue ball into a pocket (3), he loses only one point and ends his turn. This scratch counts towards a three scratch 15-point penalty.
When the opening player legally breaks the object balls without pocketing a called ball, the incoming player accepts the balls in position.
Pocketing balls A player must always designate the ball he is aiming to pocket and the pocket in which he is aiming to score.
He must notify the referee, unless his intention is obvious. In the latter case, the

referee calls the ball and the player must make any necessary correction before striking the cue ball.
Combination, carom, and kiss shots are all legal, and the player need not state the type of shot he intends to employ.
Illegally pocketed balls are spotted on the long string.
Ball bouncing from pocket If an object ball falls into a pocket and then rebounds on to the table, it is not considered pocketed.
If the ball was the called ball, the player ends his turn.
The ball remains in play where it comes to rest on the table.
Continuous play A player may pocket 14 object balls successively. The 15th object ball is left in position on the table and

becomes the break ball. The cue ball is also left in position. The 14 pocketed balls are racked by the referee, who leaves space for one ball at the foot spot apex of the triangle. The player then continues his turn. If he chooses, he may call and pocket one of the racked object balls. Otherwise, his procedure is to pocket the break ball in a designated pocket and carom the cue ball from the break ball into the triangle of racked balls. If he is successful, his turn continues. If not, rules for misses apply.
A player may continue counting 14 balls, having them reracked, and breaking until he misses, scratches, or scores the required number of points for the game.

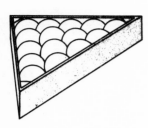

Balls Pool is played with 15 object balls numbered from 1 to 15, and a white cue ball. Balls must be of uniform weight, between 5½ and 6oz.

2¼in
5.7cm

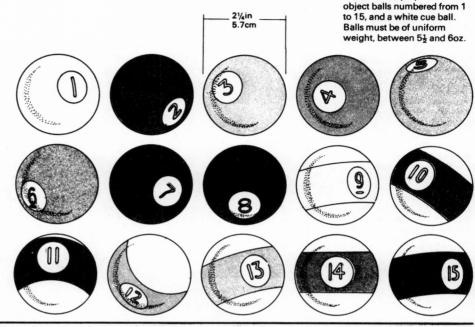

Racking It is recommended that the 15-ball is placed in the apex of the triangle on the foot spot. The 1-ball is placed in the left apex of the triangle and the 5-ball in the right epex. The highest numbered balls should be placed near the foot spot apex and the lowest numbered balls near the base of the triangle.

The break:

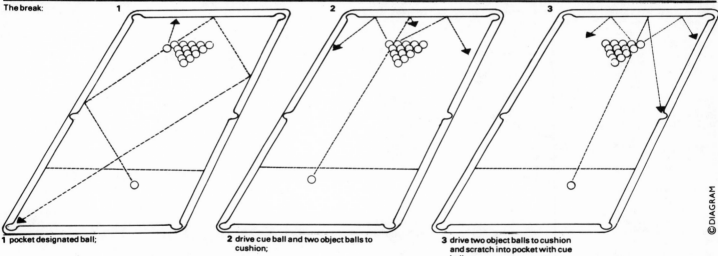

1 pocket designated ball;

2 drive cue ball and two object balls to cushion;

3 drive two object balls to cushion and scratch into pocket with cue ball.

©DIAGRAM

Interference with the rack If an unpocketed 15th ball interferes with the racking of the 14 balls, the unpocketed ball is placed on the head spot. If an unpocketed 15th ball and the cue ball both interfere with the racking of the 14 balls, the 15 object balls are racked and the player has the cue ball in hand.
If the cue ball interferes with the racking of the 14 object balls:
the cue ball is in hand if the break ball is not within the head string;
the cue ball is placed on the head spot if the break ball is within the head string;
the cue ball is placed on the center spot if the break ball or the 15th ball is resting on the head spot.
In any case of interference

with the rack, the player has the option of shooting at a ball in the rack or at the unracked break ball. If he elects to shoot into the rack, he must either drive an object ball to a cushion, cause the ball to hit a cushion after contacting an object ball, or pocket a ball. Failure is a foul, incurring a one point penalty.
Pocketing the 15th ball If a player by one stroke legally pockets the 14th and 15th balls of a frame, he scores both balls. The 15 object balls are reframed, and the player continues play from where the cue ball came to rest.

Misses A player's turn ends if he misses the shot called. A miss carries no penalty, provided the cue ball hits a cushion after hitting an object ball, or drives at least one object ball to a cushion or into a pocket. Otherwise, the player has fouled, ends his turn, and loses one point.
Scratching A player may scratch the cue ball into a pocket at the break shot or during continuous play. Scratches are also incurred during safety play on a ball frozen to a cushion, and when a player's cue ball jumps off the table.
At his first scratch, a player ends his turn, loses one point, and has one scratch marked against him on the scoreboard.

This scratch may be removed by pocketing a ball at his next turn, or by playing a legal safety.
If he scratches a second time without removing the first scratch, he ends his turn, loses one point, and has two scratches marked against him.
Three scratch 15-point penalty At his third scratch in succession, a player loses one point for the third scratch, plus 15 points for the three successive scratches. The player is then required, with the cue ball in hand, to break the balls as at the start of a game.
End of a block The first player to reach the point requirement must continue to play until all but one of the

object balls on the table are pocketed.
If he fails to clear the table, his opponent attempts to do so. Whichever player clears the table makes the opening shot in the next block. Subsequent blocks are won by the player who first scores the agreed number of points. But if the winner of the block is behind in total points for the match, play continues until one of the players has a score equal to the point requirement for one block multiplied by the number of blocks played. In the final block, play ends when a player pockets the ball that brings his total to the specified number of points for the match.

→

Safety play In attempting a safety, a player must either:
1 drive an object ball to a cushion;
2 cause the cue ball to strike a cushion after contacting an object ball; or pocket an object ball.
Failure is a foul with a one point penalty.
The player need not declare his intention to play safe.
If a player has obviously resorted to safety without declaring his intention, the referee announces "safety" after the balls stop rolling.

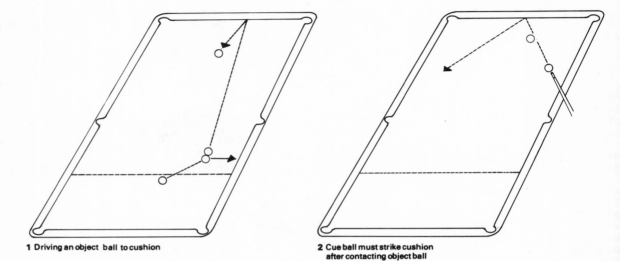

1 Driving an object ball to cushion

2 Cue ball must strike cushion after contacting object ball

Jump shots It is a jump shot if the player causes the cue ball to rise from the bed of the table.
A jump shot is legal if the player causes the cue ball to jump accidentally as the result of a legal stroke, or deliberately, by elevating the butt end of the cue ball in the center or above center.
A jump shot is a foul, with a one point penalty, if the player digs under the cue ball with the tip end of the cue.
Jumped balls If the cue ball jumps off the table, it is a foul. The player ends his turn, loses one point, and has a scratch marked against him. The incoming player has the cue ball in hand.
If the called object ball jumps the table, it is a miss and ends the player's turn. The retrieved ball is spotted.
If a player scores the called object ball and then, as a result of the stroke, causes another object ball to jump the table, he scores the ball legally pocketed. The jumped ball is spotted, and the player continues play.
A ball that comes to rest on a rail is considered a jumped ball. But a ball that returns to the table bed after riding a rail or hitting overhead lighting equipment is not considered a jumped ball and remains in play where it comes to rest.

Balls in motion A stroke is not complete until all balls on the table have come to a dead stop.
A stroke made before the balls stop moving is a foul. The offender ends his turn and loses one point. The incoming player can accept the balls in position or insist that conditions prior to the foul be restored.
Object ball within the string If a player has the cue ball in hand and the object balls are within the head string, the object ball closest to the string is spotted on the foot spot.
If two balls are equidistant from the string, the lowest numbered ball is placed on the foot spot. The player then plays the cue ball from any point within the head string, shooting at the ball on the foot spot.
Cue ball within the string It is a foul if a player, with the cue ball in hand, fails to shoot from within the head string after a warning from the referee.
The offender ends his turn and loses one point. The incoming player accepts the balls in position and can insist that all balls are positioned as before the foul.
If a head string foul is not detected until a player shoots and scores, he is credited with all balls pocketed and continues play. If he misses, it merely ends his turn.

Frozen cue ball When the cue ball is in contact with an object ball, a player may play directly at the object ball in contact with the cue ball, provided the object ball is moved and the cue ball strikes a cushion, or provided the object ball in contact with the cue ball is driven to a cushion.
Failure to comply with this rule is a foul carrying a one point penalty.
Ball frozen to a cushion A player forfeits one point if he stops the cue ball in front of an object ball frozen against a cushion, whether his cue ball contacts the object ball or not.
When playing such a shot (as a safety measure) the player must either pocket the object ball, cause the cue ball to contact a cushion after striking the object ball, or drive the object ball to another cushion.
Each player is allowed only two legal shots in safety procedure on a ball frozen to, or within a ball width of, a cushion. On the third shot he must either drive the cue ball to a different rail or drive the cue ball to any rail after contact with the object ball.
If a player fails to make this shot correctly, all 15 balls are racked and he must break as at the opening of a game.
(Three scratch 15-point penalty rules apply to scratches acquired through safety play on a ball frozen to a cushion.)

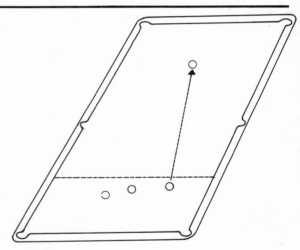

Object ball within headstring

Foot on the floor It is a foul if a player makes a stroke with both feet off the floor. The offender ends his turn and loses one point.
Interference by a player If a player accidentally disturbs a ball with any part of his body or clothing, it is a foul. He ends his turn and loses one point.
If a player touches a ball with any part of the cue but the tip, it is declared a deliberate foul. He loses 15 points and must break as at the start of a game.
Outside interference If anyone other than a player disturbs a ball, it must be replaced as near as possible to its position before the interference.

Time limit on protests If a player considers that his opponent is guilty of a foul, he may ask the referee for a ruling. He must do so before his opponent makes his next stroke.
Disqualification The referee and/or tournament manager may disqualify a player for unsportsmanlike conduct.

Eight-ball pool

Eight-ball is one of the officially recognized variants of pool. Unlike pool, the aim is not to score points but to pocket a designated set of object balls. Its appeal lies in the fact that not until the final stroke is made can a player be certain of winning.

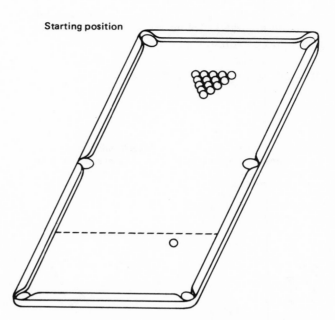

Starting position

Objective Unlike its parent game, eight-ball is not won by scoring points. The aim of each player or team is to pocket a designated group of object balls.

The numbered object balls are split into two groups: from 1 to 7 and from 9 to 15. Each player or team chooses, or is allotted, one of the groups; the 8-ball belongs to neither group.

Each player attempts to pocket the balls of his designated group. When all the balls of his group have been pocketed, a player attempts to pocket the 8-ball.

The game is won by the first player or team to pocket the 8-ball.

Starting procedure Players 'lag' to determine the order of play (see pool), and the winner of the lag usually allows his opponent to play first.

After the lag, the object balls are "racked" at the foot spot, with the 8-ball in the center of the triangle.

With the cue ball placed behind the head string, the opening player makes his stroke at the racked object balls.

If he pockets an object ball on the break, the group to which this ball belongs is his designated group.

If he pockets one or more object balls from each group, he may designate either group.

If he fails to pocket an object ball, turns alternate until someone legally pockets an object ball and so determines his group of balls.

Play The player who pocketed the first object ball continues play. His turn continues until he commits a foul, or fails legally to pocket a ball of his own group.

Except after a successful safety shot, the incoming player starts his turn by playing the cue ball from anywhere within the head string.

Table For championship games, a standard pool table is essential. Informal games can be played on any pocket billiard table.

Cues are as for pool.

Balls One white cue ball and a full set of 15 pool balls are required.

Players The game is for two players or teams.

Pocketing balls A player does not have to call which ball he is trying to pocket, or which pocket he is aiming for. If he pockets one of his opponent's balls, even with a foul stroke, that ball remains pocketed and is credited to his opponent.

A ball from a player's own group is legally pocketed only if the player's cue ball first strikes a ball from his own group. A legally pocketed ball remains pocketed; an illegally pocketed ball is replaced on its spot.

A player may legally pocket more than one of his own balls with one stroke.

If a player legally pockets an opponent's ball along with one of his own balls, both balls remain pocketed and the player's turn continues.

A player loses the game if he pockets the 8-ball before he has pocketed all the balls of his group.

Safety play A player may end his turn by playing to safety. For a successful safety shot, the cue ball must contact a ball from the player's own group and then either the cue ball or a ball from the player's group must be driven to a rail.

After a successful safety shot, the incoming player must play the cue ball from wherever it rests.

End play When a player has pocketed all the balls in his group, he must attempt to pocket the 8-ball in a designated pocket.

A player makes a foul stroke and loses the game if, when attempting to pocket the 8-ball he:

a) fails to drive the 8-ball or the cue ball to a cushion if the 8-ball is not pocketed;
b) pockets the 8-ball in a pocket not designated before the stroke;
c) pockets the cue ball;
d) fails to hit the 8-ball if the cue ball was bounced off the cushion;
e) hits a ball from his opponent's group before the cue ball strikes the 8-ball.

Fouls and penalties General rules of conduct are the same as for other pool games. Similarly, the rules applying to balls bouncing from pockets, jump shots, jump balls, balls in motion, etc are substantially the same as for pool.

However, as the eight-ball game is not a game in which points are scored, the usual penalty for a foul stroke is for the player to end his turn and for any advantage derived from the foul stroke to be canceled.

Groups of object balls

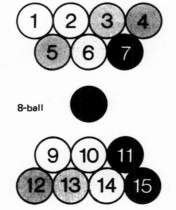

8-ball

Snooker

The game of snooker is played on a pocket billiard table. Fifteen red balls, six colored, and one white cue ball are used. Points are scored by pocketing balls and by forcing an opponent to give away points through "snookers." It may be played by two persons, pairs, or teams.

Triangle A triangular rack is used to position the red balls for the start of play.
Cues and rests are the same as for English billiards.
Balls Snooker is played with:
a) one white cue ball;
b) 15 red balls;
c) yellow ball;
d) green ball;
e) brown ball;
f) blue ball;
g) pink ball;
h) black ball.
The 22 balls must all be of equal size and weight. English balls are $2\frac{1}{16}$ in in diameter, American $2\frac{1}{8}$ in.

Table Snooker may be played on any pocket billiard table.

Starting position

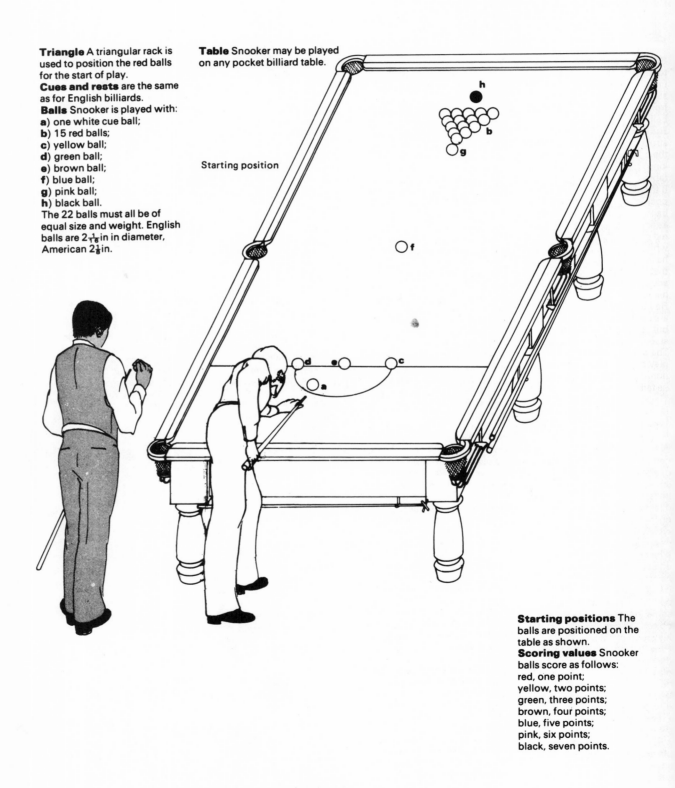

Starting positions The balls are positioned on the table as shown.
Scoring values Snooker balls score as follows:
red, one point;
yellow, two points;
green, three points;
brown, four points;
blue, five points;
pink, six points;
black, seven points.

Scoreboard

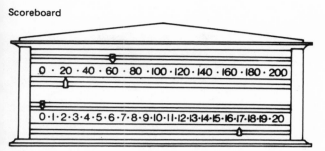

Scoreboard The score is recorded on a board showing units, tens, and hundreds.

Starting play A coin is tossed to decide who will play first. The game begins with the starter playing the cue ball from within the "D" at any red ball.

Rules of play The initial stroke of each turn must strike the cue ball against a red, so long as any red remains on the table.

If the striker succeeds in pocketing a red, he scores that ball and continues his break by attempting to pocket any non-red ball: he must nominate which ball he is aiming for and he must hit the cue ball against that ball. If he pockets it, he adds the value of that ball to his score.

Red balls that are pocketed are not replaced on the table; but colored balls are, at this stage, immediately respotted. The player's break continues, playing alternately a red and a nominated colored ball, until he fails to score on any stroke. The sum of points in his break is then added to his total score for the game to that stage, and it is his opponent's turn to attempt a break.

The opponent plays from wherever the cue ball has come to rest. If the cue ball is pocketed at any time, the break ends, and it is next played from the "D."

Play continues in this way until there are no red balls left on the table. The player pocketing the last red may attempt to pocket any colored ball. If he succeeds, that colored ball is respotted. Thereafter the colored balls must be struck by the cue ball and pocketed only in strict ascending order of value; and once pocketed, they are not put back on the table. A break ends when a player fails to pocket the colored ball of lowest value left on the table.

"On" ball The ball that is next to be struck is referred to as "on."

Duration The player with the highest score when all the balls are cleared from the table is the winner.

When only the last ball (the black) is left on the table, the first score or penalty ends the game—unless this makes the scores equal, in which case the black is respotted and the players draw lots for the choice of playing at the black from the "D." The next score or penalty ends the game.

Pairs and teams play as for singles, with turns alternating between the sides, ie a player of one side is followed, at the end of his break, by an opponent. Order of play within a side must remain the same throughout a game.

Respotting balls Red balls are not respotted, even if illegally pocketed. But any colored ball pocketed while there is a red on the table, or illegally pocketed at any stage, is immediately respotted (ie even during a break).

If the appropriate spot is covered, the ball is replaced on the first available spot in descending order of value, beginning with the black spot. If all spots are covered, any ball except the black or pink is replaced as near as possible to its own spot, on the top cushion side (ie away from the "D"), and without touching any other ball.

Where there are various equally close positions, preference goes to the one that is also nearest the top cushion.

The pink or black is replaced as close as possible to its spot, on the side toward the "D" and on the centerline of the table.

Balls touching If the cue ball comes to rest against another ball, it must be played away from that ball without moving it, or it counts as a push shot.

If it is touching an "on" ball, the striker incurs no penalty for missing the "on" ball or for striking another ball.

Balls touching

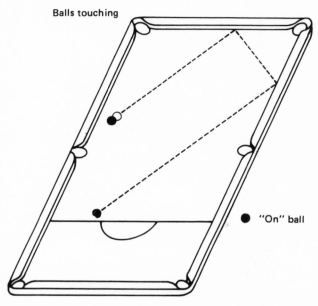

"On" ball

A "snooker" A player is snookered when a ball he must not play obstructs a straight line between the cue ball and the ball that is "on."

He must attempt his shot, and will be penalized for missing the "on" ball or for first hitting any other ball.

If he is snookered by an opponent's foul stroke, he may play any ball that he nominates. If he pockets it, it is treated as a red, unless all the reds are off the table, in which case it is treated as the "on" ball from which he is snookered.

A snooker

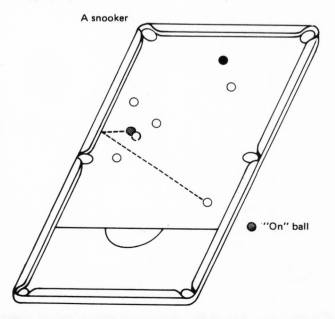

"On" ball

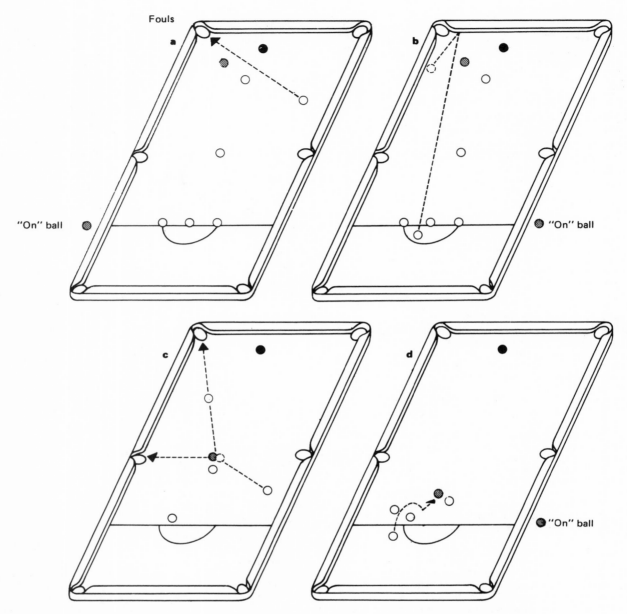

Fouls

a

"On" ball

b

"On" ball

c

d

"On" ball

Fouls and penalties After any foul shot, the striker loses his turn and any score that he may have made on that break. His opponent receives the appropriate penalty score, and has the option of playing the balls where they have come to rest or of asking the other player to do so.

The minimum penalty score is four points. The following apply only if they give a higher penalty.

1) For pocketing the cue ball (**a**), missing all the object balls (**b**), or first hitting a ball that is not "on," the penalty is the value of the "on" ball.

2) For striking simultaneously, or pocketing with one shot (**c**), two balls (other than two reds, or the "on" ball and a nominated ball), the penalty is

the higher value of the two balls struck.

3) For a push stroke, jump shot (**d**), or playing out of turn, the penalty is the value of the "on" ball, or of the ball struck or pocketed, whichever is greater.

4) For forcing a ball off the table, or moving a ball when the cue ball is touching it, the penalty is the value of the "on" ball, or of the ball off the table or moved, whichever is greater.

5) For pocketing the wrong ball, the penalty is the value of the "on" ball, or of the ball pocketed, whichever is greater.

6) For playing with other than the cue ball, or playing at two reds with successive shots, the penalty is seven points.

7) For playing with both feet off the floor, or playing improperly from the "D," the penalty is the value of the "on" ball, or of the ball struck, or of the ball pocketed or improperly spotted, whichever is greatest.

8) For playing the balls before they have come to rest, or before they have been spotted, or when they have been wrongly spotted, the penalty is the value of the ball struck, or pocketed, or of the ball wrongly spotted, whichever is greatest.

9) For playing the ball with anything but the cue, the penalty is the value of the "on" ball, or of the ball touched, whichever is greater.

Skittles

Skittles is a game for an even number of players from two to 24. As a team game it is usually played five a side. The participants roll or throw a ball or a thick, flat disc at nine skittles at the end of an alley and score a point for each one knocked down.

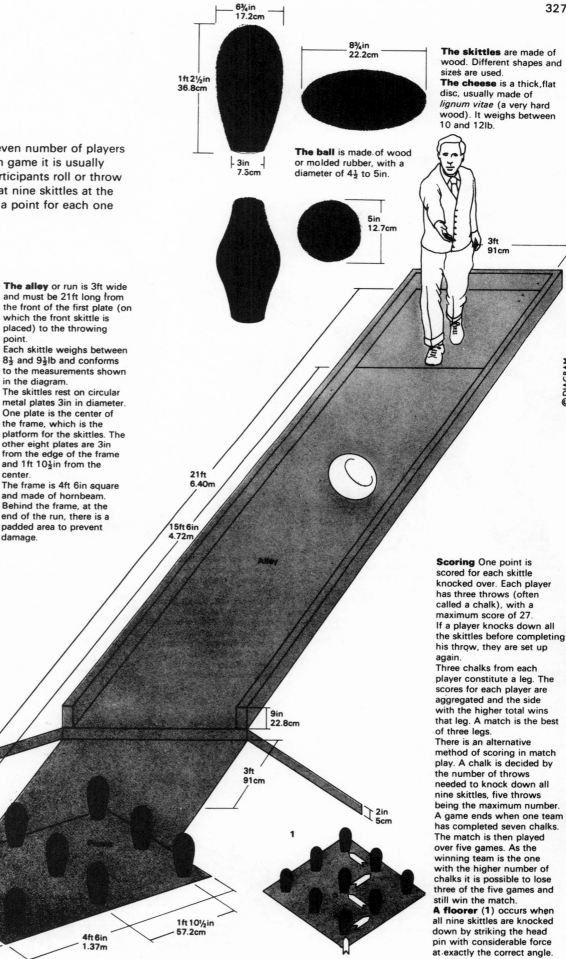

6¾in 17.2cm

8¾in 22.2cm

1ft 2½in 36.8cm

3in 7.5cm

The skittles are made of wood. Different shapes and sizes are used.
The cheese is a thick, flat disc, usually made of *lignum vitae* (a very hard wood). It weighs between 10 and 12lb.

The ball is made of wood or molded rubber, with a diameter of 4½ to 5in.

5in 12.7cm

3ft 91cm

© DIAGRAM

Rules of play The player must stand with the heel of one foot at least 21ft from the frame. He is allowed one step forward before releasing the cheese or ball.
Once it leaves his hand he may take a further pace toward the frame, but he must not cross a line 15½ft from the frame until the cheese or ball has become stationary.
He must stay within the limits of the run until the cheese or ball and the skittles are motionless.
If the cheese or ball hits the side of the alley before hitting the skittles, it is a foul throw. After hitting the skittles the cheese or ball may hit the side, providing it does not bounce back and hit the skittles again.
Skittles that have been displaced must be repositioned.
Players throw in an agreed order—either from alternate sides or one team at a time—until each participant has completed a chalk.
Officials Competitive matches are played under the complete control of a referee. During a game each team provides a setter-up, who stands near the skittles, though not in direct line with the throws. He sets up the pins at the end of a chalk as well as removing the cheeses or balls after foul throws.

The alley or run is 3ft wide and must be 21ft long from the front of the first plate (on which the front skittle is placed) to the throwing point.
Each skittle weighs between 8½ and 9½lb and conforms to the measurements shown in the diagram.
The skittles rest on circular metal plates 3in in diameter. One plate is the center of the frame, which is the platform for the skittles. The other eight plates are 3in from the edge of the frame and 1ft 10½in from the center.
The frame is 4ft 6in square and made of hornbeam. Behind the frame, at the end of the run, there is a padded area to prevent damage.

21ft 6.40m

15ft 6in 4.72m

Alley

9in 22.8cm

3ft 91cm

2in 5cm

4ft 6in 1.37m

4ft 6in 1.37m

1ft 10½in 57.2cm

1

Scoring One point is scored for each skittle knocked over. Each player has three throws (often called a chalk), with a maximum score of 27.
If a player knocks down all the skittles before completing his throw, they are set up again.
Three chalks from each player constitute a leg. The scores for each player are aggregated and the side with the higher total wins that leg. A match is the best of three legs.
There is an alternative method of scoring in match play. A chalk is decided by the number of throws needed to knock down all nine skittles, five throws being the maximum number. A game ends when one team has completed seven chalks. The match is then played over five games. As the winning team is the one with the higher number of chalks it is possible to lose three of the five games and still win the match.
A floorer (1) occurs when all nine skittles are knocked down by striking the head pin with considerable force at exactly the correct angle.

Tenpin bowling

Tenpin bowling may be played by two or four players, or by teams of up to five a side. A rubber composition or plastic ball is propelled along a lane with the aim of knocking down ten wooden pins that are positioned in a triangle at the end of the lane.

Footwear Bowling shoes have soft soles so as not to scar the approach surface. Ideally, shoes for a right-handed bowler should have leather on the left shoe sole, and rubber tipped with leather on the right sole. Heels are made of hard rubber.

The four-step delivery

The bowling lane conforms to the measurements shown below.
Gutters run on either side to catch badly aimed balls.
The lane's surface is wood, most often pine or maple.
At least 15ft must be allowed before the foul line in order to give bowlers sufficient approach space.
Most bowling lanes have automatic machinery to replace the pins and return the ball.

Dress Clothes should be lightweight and allow full freedom of movement.

Rules of play Players take their turn to bowl. A turn is completed when the contestant has bowled a frame.

Fouls The ball must be delivered underarm, so that it runs along the surface of the lane.
The bowler usually employs a four-step delivery.
He must not touch or cross the foul line, even after having sent the ball down the lane.
If he does, the foul judge or automatic foul-detecting device will signal an illegal ball. Any pins knocked down by that ball do not score.
If the first ball in a frame is a foul, all the pins must be reset. Should they then all be knocked down by a legal second ball, a spare and not a strike is scored.
If the foul ball is the second in a frame, only those pins knocked down with the first ball are counted.

Officials For major competitions a foul judge is appointed, unless the lane is equipped with an automatic foul-detecting device.

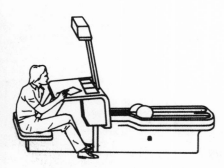

a ball rack/scoring table
b approach area (min. 15ft)
c foul line
d lane (width 3ft 6in)
e guide marks (7ft from the foul line)

The pins The ten pins are made of maple wood, and are often plastic coated. Their weight varies from 3lb 2oz–3lb 10oz. They stand on spots marked within a 3ft triangle, and are numbered from one to ten.

8½in
21.6cm

1ft 3in
.38.1cm

The grip Balls have finger holes for gripping. Most bowlers use a three-finger grip.

The ball weighs not more than 16lb. Lighter balls are used by ladies and juniors. The ball measures 8½in in diameter, and is made of a hard rubber composition or of plastic.

© DIAGRAM

Ready for first ball ☒ Strike   First ball   ☐ Spare   Second ball

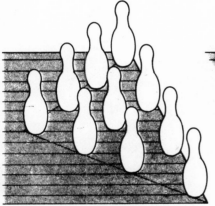

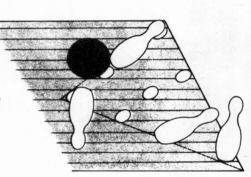

Duration A game of tenpin bowling consists of ten frames.
Every player bowls twice in each frame, unless he knocks down all ten pins with his first ball (a strike).
In competitions, matches are decided by the totals of several games.

Scoring The winning player or team has the highest score at the end of ten frames.
One point is scored for every pin knocked over, and a bonus is given for a strike or a spare.

A strike is scored when a player knocks down all ten pins with his first ball of a frame.
A strike scores ten points, plus the score from the next two balls bowled.
If a player scores a strike in his final frame, he is allowed an extra two balls to complete his bonus.

If a strike is achieved in every frame and with both bonus balls, the maximum score of 300 is achieved.
A spare is scored when a player knocks down all ten pins with both balls in a frame. (This includes knocking down all ten pins with the second ball of a frame.)

A spare scores ten points, plus the score from the next ball bowled.
If a player scores a spare in his final frame, he is allowed one extra ball to complete his bonus.

f guide marks (12–16ft from the foul line)
g gutter
h ball return
i visual pinfall guide
j pins

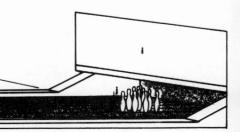

60ft
18.30m

Canadian fivepin

Canadian fivepin bowling is played by two players or by two teams of equal numbers. Each player in turn propels a ball at five pins, and points are scored to the value of the pins knocked down.

Officials Competitive matches are controlled by a judge of play. He ensures that the contest is conducted within the rules, and settles any disputes.
Official scorers are appointed for competitions.
Duration One game of Canadian fivepin bowling consists of ten frames.
Each player bowls three balls consecutively in each frame, unless he scores a strike or a spare.
Dress should be lightweight and loose fitting to allow full freedom of movement.
Special bowling shoes are worn to provide comfort and the necessary slide.

Fouls A foul is committed if a ball is fairly delivered but any part of the bowler's body or clothing touches any part of the lane, the foul line, or any part of the alley extending beyond the foul line.
If a player knows he has fouled but realizes that his error has not been noticed, he should step onto the foul line so that his transgression may be recorded.
Fouls may be called by:
the foul-line judge;
a foul-detecting device;
a member of one of the opposing teams,
an official scorer.

The bowling alley conforms to the dimensions shown.
a foul line
b lane (width 3ft 6in)
c guidemarks (13–16ft from the foul line)
d gutter
e ball return
f pins

Fouls

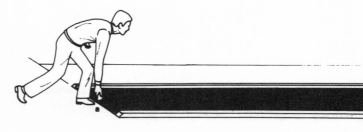

Dead ball No foul is scored when a bowler plays in the wrong lane or out of turn. This is called a dead ball, and the player then takes his proper turn in the correct lane.
Penalties When a player delivers a ball and commits a foul, all the pins knocked down are counted but a penalty of 15 points is deducted from the final score. As many as three fouls may be scored in one game.
At the end of the game, a player cannot score less than zero, even if the total number of foul points is greater than the number of legitimate points scored.

The pins are made of wood, with a strip of rubber around the middle to deaden the force of the ball. They are smaller than those used in tenpin bowling, and measure 12½in in length.

The grip The ball is held between the thumb and fingers. The fingers are spread out and a space is left between the ball and the palm of the hand.

The ball is made of hard rubber composition. It is 5in in diameter, and has no finger holes.

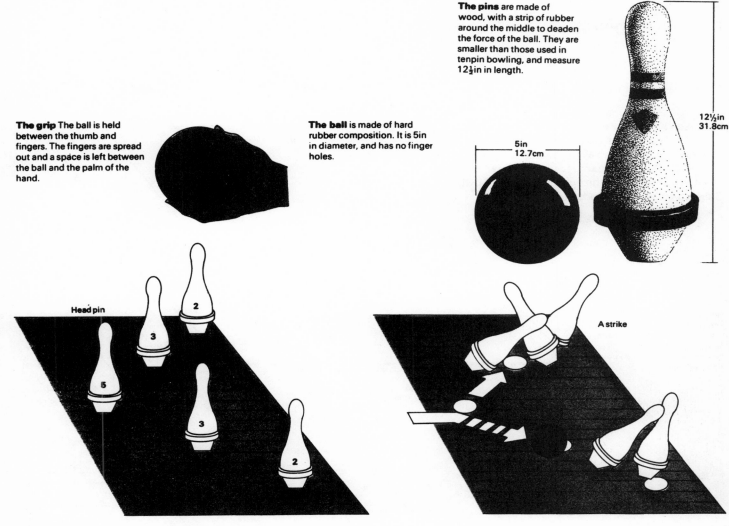

5in
12.7cm

12½in
31.8cm

Head pin

2

3

5

3

2

A strike

Scoring Pins have different values. The head pin is worth five points, the two pins immediately behind it are worth three each, and the remaining two skittles are each worth two points. A pin counts as being knocked down when it is felled by a fair ball before it leaves the lane surface. Pins do not count as being knocked down if they are felled by a ball that has rebounded off any foreign object in the lane, or the gutter.

A strike is scored if a player knocks down all the pins with his first delivery in a frame. The frame is then complete, and the player scores 15 points for that frame plus the score from the first two balls of the next frame(s).
If a player scores a strike in his tenth frame, he is allowed an extra two balls to complete his bonus.
A spare is scored if a player has knocked down all the pins after his first two deliveries in a frame. He scores 15 points for that frame plus the score from the first ball in the next frame. If a spare is scored in the tenth frame, a bonus of one ball is awarded.

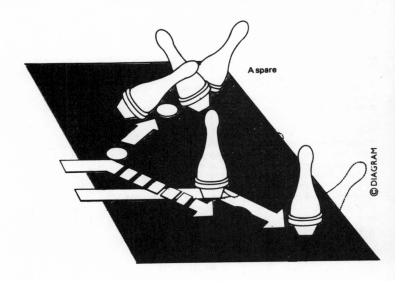

A spare

© DIAGRAM

60ft
18.30m

Flat green bowls

Flat green bowls is played by two players or by
two sides of up to four players. Points are scored
after each "end" (when all the bowls have been
delivered). One point is scored for each bowl
nearer to the jack than the opposition's best bowl.
Games are decided by ends or by points.

The green is a level grass
playing area. Square greens
must have sides 33–44yd
long (minimum of 40yd for
international competitions).
Rectangular greens are
sometimes permitted, with the
same minimum and maximum
lengths.
The green is bounded by a
ditch and bank.

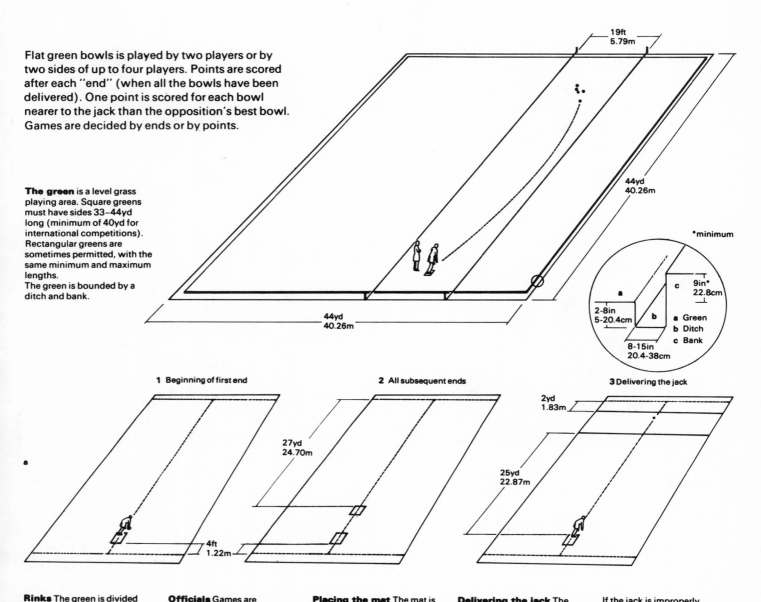

Rinks The green is divided
into rinks, 14–19ft wide and
numbered consecutively.
Rink boundaries are marked
by green threads attached to
pegs at the rink corners. The
center of each rink is marked
on the bank at each end by a
peg or similar object.
White markers on the side
banks indicate a distance of
27yd from each end ditch.
Competitions There are
various types of competition,
such as league or knock-out,
and competitors may play
individually or in teams.
Competitions may be played
on one rink or on several
rinks.
Teams may be divided into
smaller units of one (singles),
two (pairs), three (triples), or
four (fours), each competing
on a different rink.

Officials Games are
controlled by an umpire. The
score is kept by a marker.
Start Teams draw for rinks.
For each rink the winner of the
toss decides who bowls first.
A trial end is allowed.
Duration Games are divided
into ends, played alternately
in opposite directions.
Games are played for a
specified period of time, a
specified number of ends, or
until a specified number of
points has been scored by one
side.
Play may be interrupted (eg
because of the weather) by
the umpire or by the mutual
consent of the players.
Play resumes with the same
score, but uncompleted ends
are ignored.
Players may not leave the rink
for more than 10 minutes.

Placing the mat The mat is
positioned at the start of each
end and must not be removed
until the end is finished.
At the beginning of the first
end, it is placed lengthwise on
the center of the rink, with its
back edge 4ft from the rear
ditch (1). In all subsequent
ends, the back edge of the
mat shall be not less than 4ft
from the rear ditch, and the
front edge not less than 27yd
from the front ditch, and in the
center line of the rink of
play (2).

Delivering the jack The
player to bowl first begins by
delivering the jack.
For a delivery to be valid the
jack must travel at least 25yd
from the mat.
After delivery, the jack is
centered in the rink; if the
jack stops less than 2yd from
the ditch it is centered 2yd
from the ditch.
If the jack is improperly
delivered, an opponent may
move the mat in the line of
play and deliver the jack, but
not the first bowl.

If the jack is improperly
delivered for a second time,
the back edge of the mat
must be placed 4ft from the
rear ditch and no further
movement of the mat is
permitted until completion of
the end.
Whoever delivers the valid
jack, the players deliver their
bowls in the order previously
arranged.

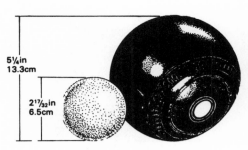

5¼in
13.3cm

2¹⁷⁄₃₂in
6.5cm

The bowls are made of wood, rubber, or composition, and may be black or brown. Each set must carry a distinguishing mark. Wooden bowls have a maximum diameter of 5¾in and a maximum weight of 3½lb. They may not be weighted.

Rubber or composition bowls must be 4½–5⅛in in diameter, and weigh 3–3½lb. All bowls are biased to move along a curved path. The degree of bias is prescribed, and bowls must be officially tested. The biased side is marked.

The jack must be white, weigh 8–10oz, and have a diameter of 2¹⁵⁄₃₂–2¹⁷⁄₃₂ in.

Dress Players and officials wear footwear with smooth rubber soles and no heels.

The mat is made of rubber and is black with a 2in-wide white border.

2in
5cm

1ft 2in
35.5cm

2ft
61cm

© DIAGRAM

Correct

Singles Two players each have four bowls, which they deliver alternately.
The score is taken after each end (after all eight bowls have been delivered toward the jack).
Once an end is completed, the players bowl back along the rink for the next end.
The winner of one end bowls first in the next end; if the end is tied or void, the same player bowls first in the next end.
The first player to score 21 points wins the game.

Correct

Pairs Two opposing players alternate until they have bowled two, three, or four bowls each, as previously decided.
Then their teammates alternate until they have bowled the same number.
A game lasts for 21 ends. The pair with the higher score wins.
Triples The opposing players play in pairs, bowling alternately.
Each player delivers two or usually three bowls.
A game usually lasts 18 ends, the trio with the highest score wins.

Incorrect

Fours is the main form of bowls.
Each of the four teammates has special duties.
The first player (lead) places the mat, and delivers and centers the jack.
The second player (second) keeps the scorecard, compares it with his opposite number after each end, and gives it to his skip at close of play.
The third player (third) may measure all disputed shots.
The fourth player (skip) has charge of the team. He directs his players and may settle disputes with the opposing skip.
Each player has two bowls, which he delivers as in triples.
A game lasts for 21 ends. The team with the highest score wins.

Incorrect

Scoring One point is won for each bowl nearer the jack than the opponents' best bowl.
If the nearest bowl from each side is equidistant, the end is drawn and is not scored.
The last player may always choose not to play his last bowl in an end.
Either side may claim a maximum of 30 seconds after the last bowl has stopped moving to allow all the bowls to settle.
Result Games are won when a side wins an agreed number of points or ends, or by the side with most points after an agreed time.

Foot faults At the moment of releasing the bowl or jack, one foot must be completely on or above the mat.
If a player foot faults, he is warned by the umpire. If he continues to foot fault, the umpire may have the bowl stopped and declare it dead.
If an invalid bowl disturbs the jack or a valid bowl, the opponent may choose to leave the jacks or bowls in position, reset them, or have the end replayed.
Wrong bowl If a bowl is played out of turn the opposing skip may stop it while it is running and have it replayed in its proper sequence.
If a wrong bowl displaces a jack or bowl, the positions may be accepted or the end replayed.
A wrong bowl shall be replaced, where it stops, with the player's own bowl.
If a bowl is delivered out of order and the live bowls and jack have not been disturbed, the opponent bowls two successive bowls.
A player who omits to deliver a bowl may not play that bowl later in the end.

A dead bowl is one that:
stops within 15yd of the mat;
stops completely outside the rink boundaries;
is driven beyond the rink boundaries by another bowl;
finishes in the ditch without having touched the jack on the green;
rebounds from the far bank without having first touched the jack on the green.
All other bowls are live, including "line bowls" on a boundary.
The skips (or, in singles, both players) agree when a ball is dead.
Dead bowls are immediately removed from the rink and placed on the bank.

Bowls

15yd
13.72m

Dead bowls

Live bowls

Dead jack A jack becomes dead if a bowl drives it:
over the bank;
completely over the side boundary;
into a hole or irregularity in the bank;
so that it rebounds within 22yd of the mat.
The end is then void and must be replayed in the same direction.
(A jack remains in play if it rebounds from the far bank onto the rink.)
Damaged jack If a jack is damaged the end is declared dead and a new jack substituted.

Jacks

22yd
20.13m

a live jacks
b dead jacks

Movement of jack in ditch

Live and dead jack

A toucher is a bowl that touches the jack during its course.
It is not a bowl that first rebounds from the far bank or touches the jack as a result of a subsequent bowl.
If the jack is lying in the far ditch, subsequent bowls cannot become touchers.
Touchers are immediately marked with a chalk these marks are removed after each end.
Jack in ditch A jack in the ditch is still live, but may not be moved again except by a previous toucher or by a non-toucher that hits it without leaving the green. If these return the jack to the green it comes back into normal play.

A jack's position in the ditch may be marked by an object about 2in across, placed above the jack on the top of the bank. (Touchers in the ditch may be similarly marked.)
Displacing bowls and jacks A bowl or jack on the green that is displaced by a non-toucher rebounding from the bank should be restored to its original position by a player of the opposing side.
Players may not disturb a jack, live bowls, or a jack or bowl in motion until the end is completed and scored (except when a bowl is moved for measuring).
If a player disturbs the jack or a bowl, the opposing captain may:
have the bowl or jack restored to its original position;
accept the new position;

declare it dead (if it is a bowl);
have the end replayed in the same direction.
Boundary jack A jack driven onto the side boundary remains live.
Players may play toward it from either side, even though the bowl passes outside the boundary.
A bowl coming to rest within the rink remains live even if it missed the boundary jack (1).
A bowl coming to rest outside the rink is dead even if it touched the boundary jack (2).

Boundary jack

Offenses It is forbidden to:
play on the same green, on the same day, prior to the competition;
place any object, bowl, or jack on the green for assistance, except for marking a live jack or toucher in the ditch;
distract opponents while they are bowling;
stand less than 1yd behind

the end of the mat or in front of the jack when someone is bowling, except for a skip or third man directing play (the player is not allowed to remain in front of the jack after the bowl is delivered);
change bowls during a game except after an objection or if they have been damaged;
play a bowl out of turn;
play the wrong bowl.

Crown green bowls

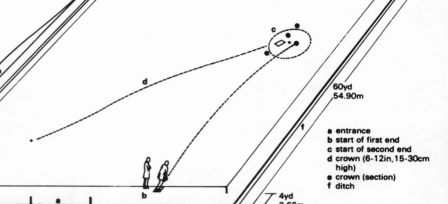

The bowls Each player has two bowls. There are no restrictions on size, weight, or bias.
The jack is biased and must weigh 20–23oz.
The footer is a round mat 7–10in in diameter.

3¾—3⅞in
19.5—19.8cm

Crown green bowls is played on a grass surface that rises to a crown in the center. Games are played between two players, who each have two bowls. The green is not divided into rinks, and ends start from near where the jack was last positioned. A player scores one point for each bowl nearer the jack than his opponent's best bowl, and a game usually lasts until one player scores 21 points.

60yd
54.90m

a entrance
b start of first end
c start of second end
d crown (6-12in,15-30cm high)
e crown (section)
f ditch

4yd
3.66m

60yd
54.90m

The green A grass area, 30–60yd square.
The surface rises gently to a central crown 6–12in higher than the edges.
The green is marked at the center, the entrance, and 4yd from the boundaries.
Start The players toss to decide who bowls first. The winner of the toss, or of the previous end, is the leader.
For the first end the leader places the footer within 3yd of the green entrance and 1yd from the edge of the green.
For subsequent ends he places it within 1yd of the last position of the jack.
The last player in an end carries the footer to the jack.
The leader delivers the jack, attempting to "set a mark."
A mark is set when the jack:
stops at least 21yd from the footer;
does not stop within 3yd of the center;
does not stop within 4yd of the same boundary as the footer;
has not gone off the green.
If the leader fails to set a mark, the players alternate until a suitable mark is set.
The player delivering the jack must allow the opponent to see which bias the jack is

given and watch the course of the jack from near the footer.
Duration A game lasts until one player wins the game by reaching a predetermined number of points (usually 21).
If the game is interrupted, the position of the jack is marked for the resumption.
Scoring The player whose bowl is nearest the jack wins the end.
Each bowl nearer than an opponent's best bowl scores one point; the maximum score for an end is two points.
If a player moves the jack or bowls before the score is agreed, the opponent can claim one point for each of his bowls in play.
No measuring is allowed before an end is finished; bowls and jacks may be disturbed only by the referee.

Delivery A player bowling with his right (left) hand must keep the toe of his right (left) foot in contact with the footer until the bowl or jack has left his hand.
A player must use the same hand throughout the game, for both bowls and jacks.
For a first fault the bowl is stopped and rebowled; after later faults the bowl is dead.
A player may not move or use the footer until his opponent's bowl has stopped moving. If the footer is moved before an end is finished it must be replaced.
A bowl delivered out of turn must be returned and replayed properly.
A bowl or jack that may interfere with another game should be stopped and replayed.

Setting a mark

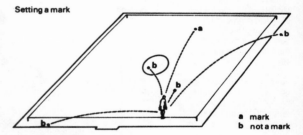

a mark
b not a mark

A leader may set another mark if he is unable to deliver his first bowl because another game is measuring up.
Offenses It is forbidden to:
change bowls or jacks during a game (except when damaged);
commit ungentlemanly and unfair acts;
approach within 3yd of an own bowl before it stops;

follow a bowl without allowing an opponent an uninterrupted view of its course;
obstruct the view of the jack;
stand within the radius of the bowls at the jack end;
impede a moving bowl;
disturb a bowl that it is still.

Officials A referee controls the game. Scorers record and confirm the scores.

Moving the jack The jack becomes void if it is struck off the green, and the player who set that mark makes the first attempt to set a new one.
Play resumes from the original footer position if two or more bowls are still to play
Otherwise play resumes from a new position 1yd from the edge of the green where the jack went out of play.
An end is void if:
a jack at rest is displaced by an outside cause (including a jack or bowl from another game) and the players cannot agree where to replace it;
a jack in motion makes contact with any person, or with a bowl or jack from another game.

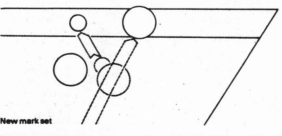

New mark set

Displacing bowls A player who impedes or displaces a still or moving bowl forfeits both bowls in that end.
If a still bowl is displaced by other causes, it must be replaced as near as possible in its original position.

If a moving bowl is impeded by other causes, it must be played again. (If it is the leader's first bowl he may choose to set a new mark.)

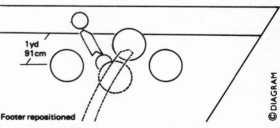

1yd
91cm

Footer repositioned

Dead bowls A bowl is immediately out of play if:
it travels less than 3yd from the footer;
it is played or struck off the green;
it falls from a player's hand and leaves the footer;

it is placed instead of bowled;
it is played while the jack or preceding bowl is still in motion;
a player delivers an opponent's bowl by mistake (the bowl is returned to the opponent).

©DIAGRAM

Boules (boccie)

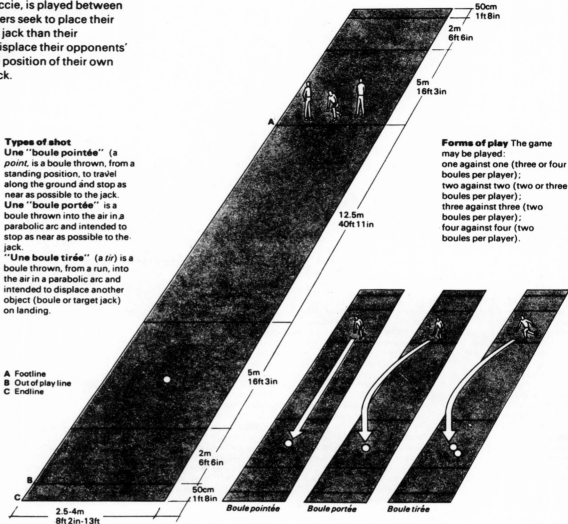

Boule portée

The game of boules, or boccie, is played between two players or teams. Players seek to place their boules nearer to the target jack than their opponents' boules, or to displace their opponents' boules and so improve the position of their own boules in relation to the jack.

The pitch Any type of surface may be used.
The lines are traced with a *baguette*; they must be clearly visible and may be retraced if necessary. (Lines must have been challenged before a shot if any allowance is to be made.)
The standard pitch length is 27.5m; it may be reduced to a minimum of 24.5m.
For international matches, the minimum pitch width is 3m, and there must be end banks at least 20mm high.
Umpire The umpire's decision is final. If he is temporarily absent, any person may settle a question provided both teams first agree to accept his decision.
Scoring When both teams have played all their boules, one team scores one point for each of its boules that is nearer to the jack than the nearest of the opposition's boules.
Delays If a team delays a start or resumption of play, the opposing team receives one point for each 5 minutes, or part of 5 minutes, after the first 10 minutes.
The opponents win when they have 6 points (just from time points or from previous play).
If both teams are late, both are penalized.
Throwing the target jack At the beginning of the game, the right of first throw of the jack is decided by lot; thereafter it belongs to the team that last scored.
The jack is thrown from behind the footline . A throw is valid when the jack comes to rest in the 5m rectangle at the far end ; the jack's whole circumference must be within the lines.
If the first throw fails, the same team has the right to try again, provided there was no foul.
After two attempts, the opposing team may place the jack in the 5m rectangle (at least 50cm from any line.
If they place it wrongly, they can be asked to move it, but the request must be made before the first boule is thrown.

Types of shot
Une "boule pointée" (a *point,* is a boule thrown, from a standing position, to travel along the ground and stop as near as possible to the jack.
Une "boule portée" is a boule thrown into the air in a parabolic arc and intended to stop as near as possible to the jack.
"Une boule tirée" (a *tir*) is a boule thrown, from a run, into the air in a parabolic arc and intended to displace another object (boule or target jack) on landing.

A Footline
B Out of play line
C Endline

50cm
1ft 8in

2m
6ft 6in

5m
16ft 3in

12.5m
40ft 11in

5m
16ft 3in

2m
6ft 6in

50cm
1ft 8in

2.5-4m
8ft 2in-13ft

Boule pointée   *Boule portée*   *Boule tirée*

Forms of play The game may be played:
one against one (three or four boules per player);
two against two (two or three boules per player);
three against three (two boules per player);
four against four (two boules per player).

Position of players When the jack is thrown, all other players must stand behind the same footline as the thrower.
If a teammate is out of position, the throw is annulled, and the team loses the right to a second throw — a member of the opposing team then places the jack.
If an opposing player is out of position, the umpire may grant an extra throw.
(The penalties are the same if a player stops or deviates a thrown jack.)
Throwing the boule The team that threw the jack throws the first boule (though it need not be the same person who throws). The first opponent then throws.

It is then the turn of the team not winning the point — except that if a thrown boule goes out of play or is annulled, the next throw goes to the other team.
If two opposing boules are at an equal distance from the jack, the team that threw last throws again.
If the tie remains, the other team throws, and so on.
When one team has delivered all its boules, the other team continues until all its boules are delivered.
The players then measure to decide the score, and then change ends.
If two opposing boules tie for nearest, the end is void and is replayed in the other direction with the same team delivering the jack.

Throwing position Both feet must be behind the footline, except for a *tir* when one foot may be put on the line.
The advantage rule is followed after any foul.
Other players must be beyond the footline of the far 5m rectangle. If the pitch allows it they must stand outside the lateral lines but as near alongside them as possible. At the moment of the throw, other players must stand motionless and not stare at the thrower.
Teammates of the thrower must not point at lines or objects on or off the pitch.
For fouls by opponents, the umpire imposes penalties; for fouls by teammates, the advantage rule applies.

Interfering with the pitch The throwing team may remove obstacles from the pitch, retrace boundary lines, and smooth or level the surface. They may not create mounds, channels, obstacles, or signs.
After the jack is thrown the pitch may only be touched to mark positions, to efface landing, measuring, and positioning marks, and to mark and efface radius marks for *tirs*. (The umpire may allow the pitch to be leveled if normal play becomes impossible.)
No-one must touch the pitch when a boule is moving.

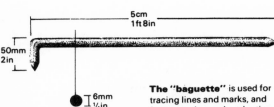

5cm
1ft 8in

50mm
2in

6mm
¼in

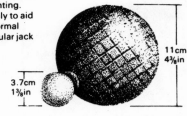

11cm
4⅜in

3.7cm
1⅜in

Boules must be made of metal or synthetic material. They must not be nailed, or weighted with lead. They must be 8.8–11cm in diameter and weigh 0.7–1.3kg. Any boule disallowed by the umpire must be replaced.

The jack must be made of wood, and without hobnails, ridges, or lead weighting. It may be colored only to aid visibility under abnormal conditions. An irregular jack must be replaced.

The **"baguette"** is used for tracing lines and marks, and for measuring and evaluating distances. Both teams' *baguettes* must be identical.

"Points"

A regular **"point"** is when a boule *pointée* or *portée*:
a) does not go out of play;
b) does not run on more than 1m after displacing a boule or jack on the pitch;
c) does not displace such an object by more than 1m;
d) approaches within at least 2m of the front edge of the far 5m rectangle.
(Displacement may be indirect.)

An irregular "point" A *point* is irregular when:
it does not fulfill the conditions to be regular;
a foul has been whistled.
After an irregular *point*, the opponents follow the advantage rule (unless the only irregularity is that the boule *pointée* has run on more than 1m, in which case the

boule *pointée* stays where it is and all other positions may be retained or replaced.
Sideline **"point"** A *point* landing near a sideline is regular if over half the landing mark is within the line; otherwise all objects are replaced by an opponent and the boule is annulled.

"Tirs"

Designating a target Before making a *tir*, the player must designate one target object (either the jack or an opponent's boule) within the 5m rectangle. If he fails to do this clearly, it is assumed that he has designated the opposition boule nearest to the jack.
Tracing arcs Before a *tir* is made, the opposing team traces arcs with a *baguette*:

a) 50cm in front of the designated target;
b) 50cm in front of any objects within 50cm of the designated target—providing such an arc is also within 50cm of that target. Arcs are normally 15–20cm long, but an arc in front of a designated target may be extended.
Any object that prevents tracing may be temporarily moved.
An arc must be challenged before the *tir* if it is to be ruled invalid.
The umpire will decide in favor of the thrower in cases of doubt caused by unclear or missing lines.
A regular **"tir"** must fulfill three conditions:
a) the landing point (where

it first strikes the ground) must be within 50cm of the designated target;
b) the landing point must be within 50cm of the first object to be struck;
c) the object first struck must be within 50cm of the designated target.
(Measurement is to the object's farthest circumference.)
In these cases, a *tir* is regular even if the object first struck is a boule of the thrower's team or if the object is struck before the boule *tirée* touches the ground.
An irregular "tir" A *tir* is irregular when:
it does not fulfill the conditions to be regular;
there has been a foul.
After an irregular *tir*, the

opponents follow the advantage rule. If the boule *tirée* is still in play, it may be accepted or rejected.
(In disputed cases all marks must be left for the umpire to see. Landing points are judged according to whether or not the outside edge of the relevant arc is broken.)
Special cases
a) If a *tir* is regular and an object is displaced indirectly, the position is accepted even if in front of the landing mark.
b) A *tir* is regular if it touches an object before landing near a lateral line; if it touches the ground before or as it strikes the object, it is regular if the landing mark is within the line (otherwise the boule *tirée* is annulled and all objects are replaced by the opposition).
c) A *tir* is annulled if it comes to rest on the pitch without touching any object.

The *tir* — tracing arcs using a *baguette*

15-20cm
6-8in

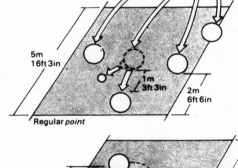

5m
16ft 3in

1m
3ft 3in

2m
6ft 6in

Regular *point*

50cm
1ft 8in

50cm
1ft 8in

5m
16ft 3in

Tracing arcs

50cm
1ft 8in

50cm
1ft 8in

5m
16ft 3in

Regular *tir*

©DIAGRAM

Marking objects The position of the jack and all boules must be marked before each throw, using lines at 90° drawn with the *baguette*. The jack's position is marked by the team that threw or placed it—or if it has been displaced, it is marked by the scoring team.
Measuring is by the team that thinks it has scored; the opponents may verify. A boule may be temporarily lifted during measuring. If a measurer disturbs any object:
the opponents score, unless the measuring team is still winning the point after disadvantaging itself;
a moved boule stays in its new position, but a moved jack is replaced.

If objects are disturbed by the umpire, points are considered equal and equidistance rules apply, except that a team scores if it is disadvantaged but still winning the point.
Foul when boule is thrown
After a foul by the opposing team, the throwing team may:
a) accept the throw; or
b) reposition the objects and retake the throw.
After a foul by the throwing team, the advantage rule applies.
The advantage rule The opposing team may:
a) accept the position of all objects; or
b) have all objects repositioned.

In either case the fouling boule may be left in place, or annulled and removed from the pitch.
The inversion rule is applied in cases where:
a) a fouling boule is wholly or partially occupying the former position of another object;
b) under the advantage rule, the opposing team asks for the displaced boules to be repositioned and the fouling boule left in position.
Under this rule the positions of the fouling boule and the displaced boule are simply exchanged.
If the fouling boule partially occupies the former positions of two objects, the team applying the advantage rule chooses which object will be moved.

Misuse of boules
a) The first time a player accidentally plays another's boule, the opposing team puts the correct boule in the position of the boule played in error; the advantage rule applies on subsequent occasions.
b) Deliberately exchanging boules is forbidden, except with the umpire's agreement when a boule is damaged. Both boules are annulled if a player deliberately plays the wrong boule.
c) The opposition wins if a player deliberately delivers too many boules.

d) If the jack is in the 7m rectangle and a player holding a boule enters the rectangle, the carried boule is annulled.
e) Unplayed boules left out of position after a warning will be annulled. Unplayed boules should be in the rack provided or along the side of the pitch allocated to each team.

Playing while boules are moving is a foul and the advantage rule applies.
If the last-played boule touches a moving boule of the same team, the opponents may annul both boules.
If it touches an opponent's boule, the opponents may accept the new position or replay the boule and in either case may accept or annul the last-played boule.

Objects stopped or displaced
a) If during a regular throw, the opponents may reposition or accept the new position of all objects. In either case the thrown boule may be annulled or accepted, or, if the thrown boule was impeded by the opposition, the throwing team may retake the throw.

b) If during an irregular throw, the procedure is as for a regular throw, except that if both teams have fouled, all objects must be repositioned and the thrown boule annulled.
c) A boule impeded by a non-player, animal, or other agency is replayed if within the 7m rectangle; otherwise it is left in position.

Boule out of play A boule is out of play if it crosses a side-line or "out of play" line. Out of play or annulled boules must be placed in the rack or at the far end of the pitch.

Jack out of play The jack is out of play if it crosses any boundary of the 7m rectangle.

a) If during an end, the jack is replayed in the same direction except that if only one team has still to play it scores as many points as it has boules left to play.
b) If at the last boule, the end is replayed in the other direction with the jack thrown by the team that last threw it.

Out of play—special cases
a) An object is annulled if after a regular or an accepted irregular *point* it touches an object that is out of play.
b) If a *boule pointée* joins a group of objects that are touching and therefore annulled, the *point* becomes irregular and the opponents can either accept the boule *pointée* (in which case the touching objects are annulled)

or have the touching objects put back in position and the boule *pointée* annulled.
c) A boule is annulled if it stays on the pitch only because it meets a boule that is out of play or annulled.
d) If an object that was not moving is displaced by an out of play boule returning to the pitch, the object is put back in position. If a moving object is similarly displaced, it is annulled.
(Players may always prevent out of play boules from returning to the pitch.)
e) A boule remains in play if it meets an obstacle overhanging the pitch; a jack goes out of play.
f) If a boule on or near a sideline touches an object on an adjacent pitch, that boule is annulled. Objects are

repositioned if they are displaced after the boule contacted the boule on the adjacent pitch. The advantage rule applies to boules displaced before the boule on the adjacent pitch was contacted.
(Boules should not be thrown until all boules on an adjacent pitch are motionless. Throwers may ask for a boule on an adjacent pitch to be temporarily lifted. All players may attempt to prevent a boule from touching an object on an adjacent pitch.)

Object from another pitch modifying the game.
a) If disturbance occurs during a *point*, any affected object that was previously motionless is repositioned but the boule *pointée* is retaken only if its effect was altered.
b) If disturbance occurs during a *tir*, the umpire may decide that the *tir* was regular or otherwise all objects are repositioned and the *tir* is retaken.

Disturbance by a player
a) If a boule is accidentally disturbed by a teammate of the thrower, the opposition follows the advantage rule.
b) If disturbance is by an opponent, the thrower may accept the situation or have all objects replaced and then retake his boule.

Chance disturbance (by a non-player, animal, or other agency):
a) If a disturbed object modifies the path of a boule *pointée* (by striking against it or being removed from its path), the object is repositioned and the *point* retaken.
b) If at a *tir* the designated object, or any object within 50cm of it, is disturbed, all objects are repositioned and the *tir* is retaken.
c) In case of a disturbance with no apparent cause, a *tir* is treated as regular and a *point* as under case a) of this rule.

Broken jack The umpire decides whether or not a jack is broken. A broken jack is annulled and must be replaced within a time limit fixed by the umpire. Time penalties will be imposed for delays.

Buried jack
a) If the jack is more than half buried after a regular *tir*, the advantage rule applies (ie the opposition can accept the *tir* and have the jack annulled or reject the *tir* and have all objects unburied).
b) If the jack is less than half buried after a regular *tir* or is at all buried after a *point*, it can be unburied by either team at any time unless this would involve permanently moving any boule.

Broken boules The umpire decides whether or not a boule is broken.
A broken boule may be replaced, along with a player's other boules, within a brief time allowed by the umpire. If a broken boule cannot be replaced, the player must continue with one boule fewer.
All effects (even if caused by a splinter) are counted if a boule is broken during a regular throw; the advantage rule applies if the throw was irregular.

Buried boules
a) After a regular *point* any boule that is more than half-buried is unburied and remains in play; any boule that is less than half-buried is left in position.
b) If after a regular *tir* the boule *tirée* is more than half-buried it is unburied and left in position; any other boule that is more than half-buried is annulled. A boule that is less than half-buried is left in position.
c) After an unaccepted irregular *point* or *tir*, any buried boule is unburied and left in its original position.

Repositioning objects
a) An object irregularly displaced by a *tir* or *point* is repositioned by the opposition.
b) An object moved accidentally is repositioned by the opposition.
c) A boule moved by chance or with no apparent cause is repositioned by the team it belongs to; a jack is repositioned by the team currently winning the end.
d) If an object is moved deliberately, the offender is excluded from the game and steps are taken to see that the other team does not suffer.

e) When the advantage rule is being applied, the opposition can no longer accept the new situation once they have moved any object nor reject it once they have effected any mark.
f) Unmarked or badly marked objects may not be repositioned by the team that marked them.

Major fouls are:
a) unsporting conduct;
b) irregularly composed teams;
c) infringing competition substitution rules (in case of illness or other serious cause, two substitutes per team are permitted in fours and one in pairs and triples);
d) not making the most of opportunities;
e) deliberately prolonging a match;
f) deliberately stopping or moving an object against the rules;

g) stopping an object that is on the line but not yet out of play;
h) positioning an obstacle to affect a throw;
i) failure to observe a decision by the umpire;
j) agreeing with another player to ignore any rule;
k) fraud;
l) protesting to an opponent instead of the umpire.

Penalties, imposed at the umpire's discretion, are:
a) warning;
b) temporary or permanent exclusion of players or teams;
c) loss of the game;
d) the awarding of points to the opposing team or the reduction of the offending team's points.
Increasingly severe penalties are awarded for deliberate or persistent fouling.
A team with one or more players excluded may continue with its other players. Serious indiscipline is penalized by the total elimination of a team; only in this case can penalties affect results already obtained.

Curling

Stones are round, not more than 36 in in circumference or less than 11.45cm high. They must not weigh more than 44 lb including the handle and bolt. They are concave on the top and underneath. A bolt through a center hole screws into a goose-neck handle, which is used to deliver the stone.

Two teams of four players deliver round stones across a measured length of ice to a marked target area, or "house." One point is scored for each stone inside the house and closer to its center, or tee," than any opponent's stone.

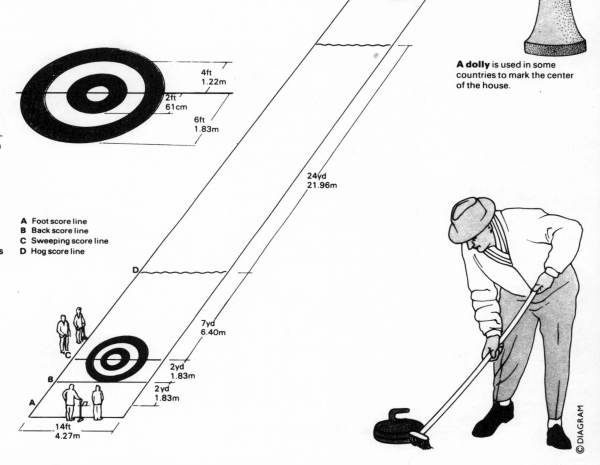

A dolly is used in some countries to mark the center of the house.

Playing area An area of ice 46yd long, with two target circles or houses 38yd apart. The houses are usually marked by blue outer and red inner circles.
Behind the circles are hacks or crampits – rubber- or metal-covered footholds from which players deliver their stones.
Officials Umpires supervise the measuring at the end of each head, settle disputes, and have the final decision.
Dress is usually informal and gloves are a matter of choice. Rubber-soled shoes or boots are usually worn. A more easily sliding sole is sometimes worn on one foot. Spikes on footwear, which would damage the ice, are not allowed.

A Foot score line
B Back score line
C Sweeping score line
D Hog score line

4ft 1.22m
2ft 61cm
6ft 1.83m
24yd 21.96m
7yd 6.40m
2yd 1.83m
2yd 1.83m
14ft 4.27m

Competitions There are many national and international competitions, played under the jurisdiction of the International Curling Federation and the Royal Caledonian Curling Club.
Competitors Two teams, called rinks, compete against each other for the highest score. Each rink has four members: lead, number 2, number 3, and the captain, or skip.
Matches Each match consists of a number of heads (also called ends), usually 10 or 12, sometimes more, or is played to a time limit.
In the case of a tie, another head is played to break it.
Procedure The two skips agree by lot, or sometimes by other means, which team shall deliver the first stone.
Each member has two stones, which are played alternately against his opponent.
A team's order of play is decided by the skip and remains the same throughout the match. At the end of each head, the winning rink starts in the next head.
A head is considered started when the first player is on the hack and the skip is in position.

Each player must deliver his stone from the hack and no part of his body or equipment may cross the hog score during delivery.
After a stone is delivered the player's side may sweep the ice from the nearest hog score to the sweeping score.
Opposing skips may sweep behind the sweeping score (behind the tee). Sweeping is directed by the skips and must always be to the side.
No sweepings must be left in the path of a moving stone.
No stone may be substituted for another after a match has started.
If a stone breaks, play continues to the end of that head with the largest fragment. Another stone is used for the rest of the match.

Any stone that finishes on its side or upside down is removed from the ice.
If, during delivery, the handle comes out of a stone, the shot may be replayed.
Any stone that does not pass the hog score is removed, unless it has struck another stone in position.
Penalties
1) Any rink not having four players is disqualified. In the case of illness or accident during a match, the lead plays four stones.
2) If a stone is played from the wrong hack, the stone is removed from the ice.
3) If a player delivers out of turn, his stone is stopped and returned to him.
4) If a player touches a moving stone of his own team, it is removed from the ice. If a

stone is touched by a member of the opposing team, it is placed in a position decided upon by the player's skip.
Scoring When all stones have been played, the head is completed and the score taken. The scoring side gains one point for each stone inside the house and closer to its center, or tee, than any stone of the opposing team. Measurements are taken from the tee to the nearest part of the stones.

Brooms Brushes are usually used in Scotland and elsewhere in Europe. In the United States and Canada whisk brooms are made of corn straw, nylon, flagged polypropylene, or horsehair. On instruction from his skip, each player uses his broom to sweep frost and moisture from in front of the running stone. This helps to keep the stone straight and make it run farther. The skip also uses his broom to direct his team.

© DIAGRAM

Croquet

Croquet is a game for two or four players. The object is to score points by hitting balls with a mallet through a course of hoops and against a center peg. The game is won by the side that finishes the course first with both balls or scores most points in an agreed time.

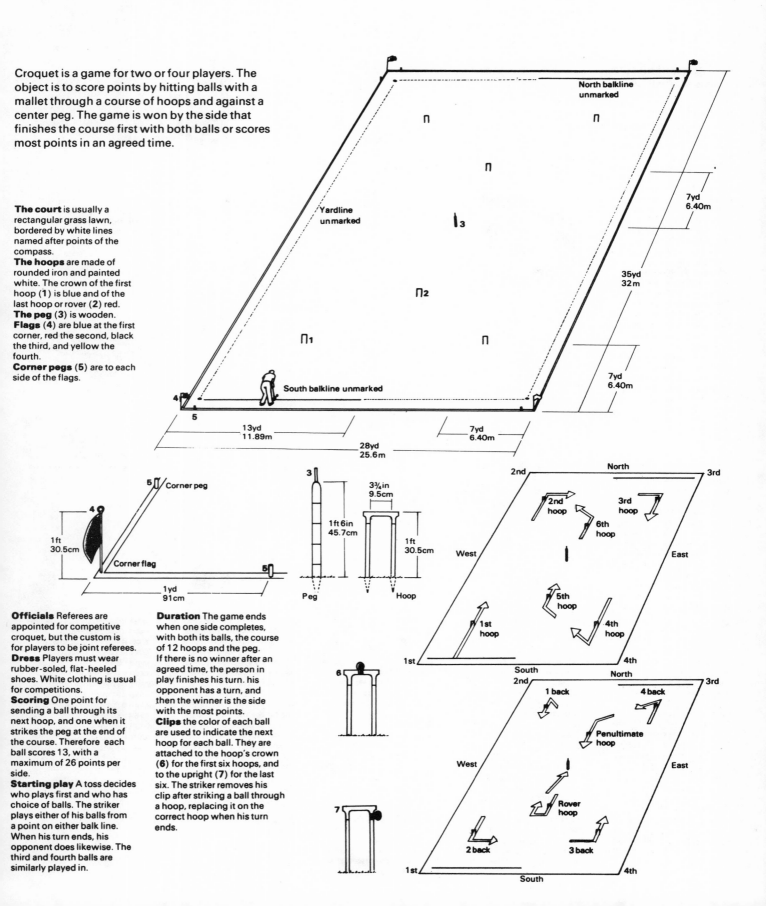

North balkline unmarked

Yardline unmarked

7yd 6.40m

35yd 32m

7yd 6.40m

South balkline unmarked

13yd 11.89m

7yd 6.40m

28yd 25.6m

5 Corner peg

4

1ft 30.5cm

Corner flag

5

1yd 91cm

3

1ft 6in 45.7cm

3¾in 9.5cm

1ft 30.5cm

Peg   Hoop

2nd   North   3rd

2nd hoop   3rd hoop

6th hoop

West   East

5th hoop

4th hoop

1st hoop

1st   South   4th

2nd   North   3rd

1 back   4 back

Penultimate hoop

West   East

Rover hoop

2 back   3 back

1st   South   4th

6

7

The court is usually a rectangular grass lawn, bordered by white lines named after points of the compass.
The hoops are made of rounded iron and painted white. The crown of the first hoop (**1**) is blue and of the last hoop or rover (**2**) red.
The peg (**3**) is wooden.
Flags (**4**) are blue at the first corner, red the second, black the third, and yellow the fourth.
Corner pegs (**5**) are to each side of the flags.

Officials Referees are appointed for competitive croquet, but the custom is for players to be joint referees.
Dress Players must wear rubber-soled, flat-heeled shoes. White clothing is usual for competitions.
Scoring One point for sending a ball through its next hoop, and one when it strikes the peg at the end of the course. Therefore each ball scores 13, with a maximum of 26 points per side.
Starting play A toss decides who plays first and who has choice of balls. The striker plays either of his balls from a point on either balk line. When his turn ends, his opponent does likewise. The third and fourth balls are similarly played in.

Duration The game ends when one side completes, with both its balls, the course of 12 hoops and the peg. If there is no winner after an agreed time, the person in play finishes his turn. his opponent has a turn, and then the winner is the side with the most points.
Clips the color of each ball are used to indicate the next hoop for each ball. They are attached to the hoop's crown (**6**) for the first six hoops, and to the upright (**7**) for the last six. The striker removes his clip after striking a ball through a hoop, replacing it on the correct hoop when his turn ends.

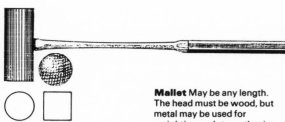

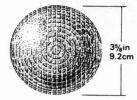

Mallet May be any length. The head must be wood, but metal may be used for weighting and strengthening.

The faces, any shape, must be identical and parallel. Only a damaged mallet may be changed during a turn.

Balls must be of even weight, 15¾–16½oz. One player or pair takes the blue and the black, the other the red and the yellow.

3⅝in 9.2cm

Turns alternate throughout the game. Either, but only one, of the side's balls may be used in a turn. Initially a turn is only one stroke, but extra strokes are gained:
a) by sending a ball through its next hoop – one ordinary shot (a continuation stroke);
b) by making a roquet.
Making a roquet (when the striker's ball hits another) is always followed by a croquet shot and then (unless either ball has been sent out of play) by a continuation stroke. Each ball may be roqueted only once in a turn unless the striker's ball scores a point by going through a hoop.
If the striker's ball hits two balls in one shot, the roqueted ball is the one hit first.
The croquet shot The striker places his ball alongside the roqueted ball. He then hits his ball and so moves the croqueted ball.
It is a foul if the croqueted ball does not at least shake, in which case the balls are replaced and the turn ends.

Making a roquet

Croquet shot

Scoring a hoop point

© DIAGRAM

1

2

3

4

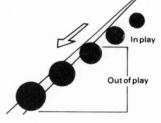

In play

Out of play

Foul strokes The striker must not:
touch the head of the mallet with his hand (**1**);
kick or hit the mallet onto the the ball (**2**);
rest either the mallet or a hand or arm used in the shot against his leg or foot;
rest the mallet shaft or his hand or arms on the ground;
strike the ball with any part of the mallet but its face;
push or pull his ball when it is touching another, without first striking it distinctly;
hit the ball twice in one shot;
move a stationary ball by hitting a hoop or peg with the mallet;
strike the ball into a hoop upright (**3**) or the peg when it rests directly against it;

touch any other ball with his mallet or any ball including his own with any part of his person;
fail to move the croqueted ball in a croquet shot.
The penalty after a stroke fault (provided it is claimed before the next stroke) is the end of the striker's turn and no point scored.
A ball in hand is a ball that has to be moved:
when any part of it is over the inside edge of the border (**4**);
when it is in the yardline area (the striker's ball is in hand only at the end of his turn; others may be in hand after each stroke).
Balls in hand are to be placed, before the next stroke, on the yardline at the point where the ball crossed the border.

If two or more balls have to be replaced, the striker decides the order.
Obstacles The striker may move his ball or another if a fixed obstacle outside the court is likely to interfere with his shot.
Any loose impediments (eg leaves) may be moved, and the striker's ball or any ball from which he is taking croquet may be moved from a worn corner spot.
Allowance may be made for damage (eg holes made by a mallet) and any ball may be wiped at any time by the striker.
No player may make guiding marks either on or off the court.

If part of a hoop or of the peg is in a straight line between his ball and all the others, or if part of the peg or hoop will interfere with the mallet in a roquet shot, the player may play his ball from any point on either balk line, provided his opponent was responsible for the ball being so positioned.
Doubles The rules are generally as for singles, with the following major exceptions:
turns alternate, but each player takes the same ball throughout;
the striker's partner faces the same penalties as the striker if he contacts a ball incorrectly;
a player may advise his partner, set his balls for a croquet shot, and indicate the

direction his mallet should swing, but he should be well away from him when the stroke is actually made; either player may make a replay if they have received false information.
Handicaps There is an accepted handicapping system, ranging from 16 to minus 3.
In singles, one extra turn is given for each unit of difference (called a bisque) between players' handicaps. In doubles, half a turn is given for each unit of difference. When taking a half turn (half bisque), no point can be scored.

Golf

Golf consists of playing a ball with a club into a series of holes by successive strokes. Players may compete individually or in teams, playing the course together in groups of two, three, or four. The two basic forms of competition are match play and stroke play. In match play the side winning the majority of holes wins the match. In stroke play the winner is the player who finishes with the fewest strokes.

Clubs A player may use a maximum of 14 clubs. He may replace damaged clubs during a round, or add extra clubs if he started with fewer than 14, provided he does not exceed the total. The 14-club rule applies to partners sharing a set of clubs.

There are three types of clubs.
a A "wood" is one with a head that is relatively broad from front to back, and is usually made of wood, plastic, or a light metal. Woods are numbered from 1 to 7 according to shape, and are used for long shots.
b An "iron" has a head that is relatively narrow from front to back, and is usually made of steel; irons are numbered from 1 to 10 and are used for shorter shots; a 3 iron is equivalent to a 4 wood.
c A "putter" is a light metal club used for playing the ball on the putting green.
Each club except the putter has only one striking face. The face may be scored or indented, but may not be shaped or finished in such a way as to cause extra movement of the ball. The length of shaft and the angle of the face of each club vary according to the kind of shot it is designed to play. Steeply angled faces give sharply lifting shots. The grip of the club must not be shaped to fit the hands in any way.

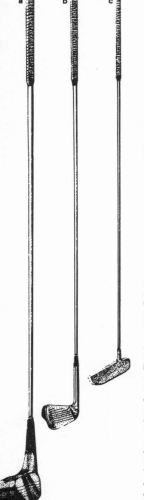

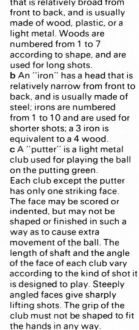

Players must not stop play because of bad weather unless they are ill or there is danger from lightning; and they must play without unnecessary delays.
Artificial devices to assist play or strokes, or to measure distance or conditions, are forbidden.
A player may ask advice from, or give advice to, only his partner or either of their caddies. He must not ask for or accept physical assistance or protection from the weather.
He may have someone to indicate the line of play to him—except on the putting green; but the line must not be marked.
Caddies Each player is allowed one caddie to carry his clubs. The caddie may mark the position of the ball.

Course A standard golf course consists of 18 holes, and has a total length of 6500–7000yd. Holes vary in length from 100–600yd. Holes contain the following features:
a) a tee, a smooth level area on which play begins;
b) the fairway, a closely-mown strip along which players aim to hit the ball;
c) the rough, unprepared areas flanking the fairway;
d) hazards, consisting of bunkers (sand traps) or areas of water;
e) the putting green, in which the hole is located.
The length and features of each course vary with local conditions and planning. The boundaries must be clearly defined.

Scoring A player who completes each hole, or in certain games the whole course, with the least number of strokes is the winner. If two players have the same score for a hole, that hole is said to be "halved".
Par is the score that in theory a perfect player would take to complete a hole. Par is calculated on the length of a hole, and is higher for women than for men. It ranges from par 3 up to par 6. One stroke under par is a "birdie;" two strokes is an "eagle;" one over par is a "bogey".
Handicaps are based on the total par score for a course. A man may receive a handicap of up to 24 strokes, and a woman up to 36 strokes.

Match play The game is played by holes.
A hole is won by the side that holes the ball in fewer strokes. (In a handicap match the lower net score wins the match.)
A hole is halved if each side holes out in the same number of strokes.
A match consists of a stipulated number of holes. It is won by the side that wins the majority of the holes, and a match can be won before the round is completed.
In three-ball matches each player plays two matches simultaneously.
In best-ball matches one player plays against the better ball of two, or the best ball of three, players.

In four-ball matches two players play their better ball against the better ball of their opponents.
Stroke play Generally, match play rules apply, but the winner is the player who completes the round or rounds in the fewest strokes. Each competitor has a marker to record his number of strokes on a score card, which the competitor and the marker must sign before it is handed in at the end of the round.
In four-ball stroke play two competitors play as partners, each playing his own ball. The lower score of the partners is the score of the hole.
Practice Competitors are not allowed practice strokes during a round, but a practice swing is allowed.

1.62in (UK)
1.68in (US)

Alger
1

The ball is made of rubber with a liquid core, and has a surface dimpled to improve accuracy and distance of flight. Maximum weight is 1·62oz. Minimum diameter is 1·68in for USA; 1·62in for UK, Canada, and international team competitions.

If the ball is damaged and unfit for play, another ball may be substituted where the original ball lay. It must be substituted in the presence of the opponent (match play) or the marker (stroke play).
A ball interfering with play may be lifted; it is replaced after the stroke has been made.

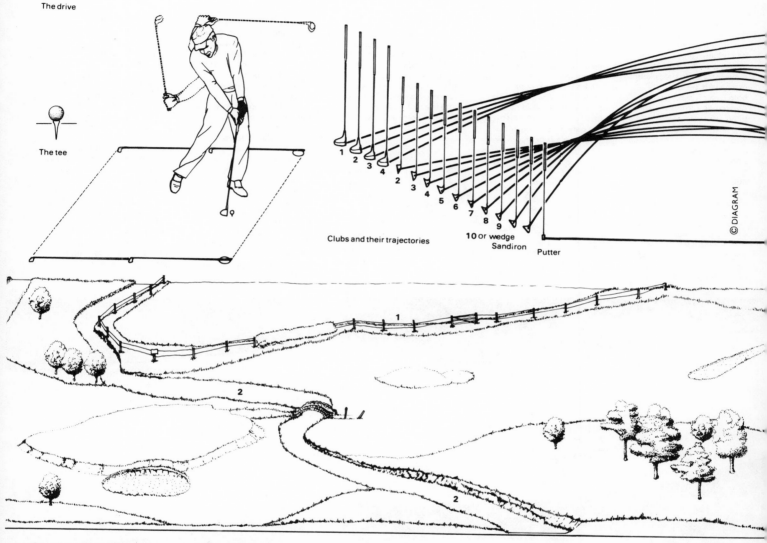

The drive

The tee

Clubs and their trajectories

1 2 3 4 2 3 4 5 6 7 8 9 **10** or wedge Sandiron Putter

© DIAGRAM

1 2 2

Starting play (1) Each player plays a ball from the first teeing ground. The ball may be played from the ground, from a heap of sand, or on a wooden or plastic tee.
A draw decides who plays first. Subsequently, the side that wins a hole decides who plays first at the next teeing ground (the "honor"). If a hole is halved the side that last had the honor retains it. Partners play the ball alternately.
Out of turn In match play if a player plays out of turn, his opponent may require him to replay the stroke, without penalty; in stroke play, the ball is deemed to be in play, without penalty.
Outside tee If the ball is not played from the teeing ground, in match play the

opponent may require it to be replayed from the teeing ground without penalty; in stroke play the player must restart from the teeing ground, but the stroke or strokes he has already made are counted. Failure to rectify the mistake is penalized by disqualification.
Off tee If the ball falls off the tee before the stroke it may be re-teed; if the stroke has been made, it is counted. No penalty is incurred in either case.
Playing the ball The ball must be played as it lies: it must not be deliberately moved or touched except when addressing it (that is, when the player has rested his club on the ground preparatory to making the stroke).
A player must not try to improve his shot by moving,

bending, or breaking anything that is fixed or growing. Nor may he remove or press down sand, loose soil, or cut turf. But he may make such adjustments in order to take his stance or swing the club, tee a ball, or repair damage to the green. The player can move loose impediments without penalty unless the impediments or the ball lie in or touch a hazard.
The stroke The ball must be struck with the head of the club—it must not be pushed, scraped, or spooned. A player must not strike the ball twice: if he does the stroke is counted and a penalty stroke is incurred.
The player must not play a moving ball unless it is in water, or moves after the stroke begins.

Order The ball furthest from the hole is played first.
If a player plays out of turn in match play, his opponent may require him to replay the stroke; in stroke play the game continues.
Water hazards (2) are water courses (even when containing no water), or any other areas of water. They include sea, lakes, ponds, rivers, ditches.
A lateral water hazard is one that runs approximately parallel to the line of play so that any ball played over it will not lie between the player and the hole.
A player may search in water for his ball, and no penalty is incurred by moving it.
If a ball lies in or is lost in a water hazard, the player may drop a ball (with a

penalty of one stroke) either as near as possible to the point from which the ball was played, or so that the hazard lies between the ball and the hole.
At a lateral water hazard the player also has the choice of dropping the ball outside the hazard, within two clubs' lengths of either edge of the hazard and opposite the point at which the ball last crossed the edge of the hazard. The ball must not stop nearer to the hazard than that point. Again, a penalty of one stroke is incurred.
A player may make a stroke at a ball moving in water, but he must not delay the stroke until the ball is in a better position.

Interference covers any deliberate or accidental act that interferes with the ball while in play.

Wrong ball If a player plays the wrong ball, except in a hazard, he loses the hole (match play) or incurs two penalty strokes (stroke play).

In a hazard, strokes at the wrong ball are not penalized or counted, provided the player then plays the correct ball. If the wrong ball belongs to another player, it must be replaced.

Moving ball If a moving ball is accidentally stopped or deflected by any outside agency (a) it must be played from where it lies, and the original stroke may not be replayed. It is defined as a "rub of the green."

If the ball lodges in anything that is moving, the player must drop a ball (or place it, if on a putting green) as near as possible to the place where the ball became lodged. If a ball is stopped or deflected by its owner, his partner, or either of their caddies (b) or equipment, the player loses the hole (match play) or incurs two

penalty strokes (stroke play). If a ball is stopped or deflected by an opponent, his caddie, or their equipment (c), the opponent's side loses the hole in match play; in stroke play it is reckoned a rub of the green and the ball is played from where it comes to rest.

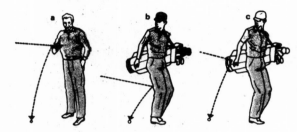

Ball at rest If a ball at rest is moved by any outside agency except the wind, the player must replace it before making his stroke; if he or his caddie moves the ball, there is a one-stroke penalty. If a player moves the ball after addressing it, he incurs one penalty stroke (but there is no penalty if he knocks it accidentally off the tee). If the ball is moved by an opponent, his caddie, or his equipment, the opponent incurs one penalty stroke in match play; in stroke play the ball must be replaced, but there is no penalty. If a player's ball moves an opponent's ball there is no penalty; the opponent may play the ball as it lies or replace it in its original position.

Ball on green The rules differ for match play and stroke play.
a) In match play, if an opponent's ball might interfere with the putt, the opponent must lift it. If the ball when played stops where the opponent's ball was, a second stroke must be played before the removed ball is replaced.

If a player's ball knocks an opponent's ball into the hole, the opponent is deemed to have holed out with his last stroke. If the opponent's ball is knocked clear of the hole, he may replace it.

A player may concede that his opponent would hole out with his next stroke; he may then move the ball before playing his own stroke.

A bunker (3), also called a sand trap, is an area of bare ground, often a depression, covered with a deep layer of sand.

Long grass and bushes (4) may be moved only to enable a player to find and identify a ball that is lying among them. He is not necessarily entitled to see the ball when actually playing the stroke.

Other obstructions A movable obstruction may be removed; if the ball is moved by so doing, it must be replaced without penalty. If the ball is in or near an immovable obstruction, including casual water (any temporary accumulation of water), ground under repair, or a hole made by a burrowing animal, the player may play the ball as it lies or take relief—that is, drop or place the ball in a new position not nearer the hole.

Dropping the ball is done when the ball has to be repositioned anywhere except on the green, and must be done by the player himself. He must face the hole, stand erect, and drop the ball behind him over his shoulder (d). Any other method of dropping the ball incurs one penalty stroke.
If the ball touches the player before it reaches the ground (e), it is redropped without penalty. If it rests against the player after it touches the ground he may play it without penalty even if it moves when he moves.
A ball must be dropped as near as possible to where it lay, but not nearer the hole. In a hazard (f) the ball must be dropped within the hazard.

If a dropped ball rolls into a hazard, out of bounds, or more than two clubs' lengths from where it struck the ground, or stops nearer the hole than the original position, it may be redropped without penalty.
If it rolls into a similar position it may be placed where it was dropped, without penalty.

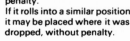

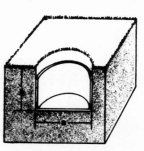

a) 4¼ in (10.8cm)
b) 4 in (10.2cm)*
*minimum

The hole should be 4½ in in diameter , and at least 4in deep. Any lining must be sunk at least 1in below the surface of the putting green.

b) In stroke play, if a competitor's ball might interfere with his opponent's stroke, the opponent may ask for it to be removed.
If a player thinks his ball could assist a competitor, he may remove it or play first, without penalty.
If a player's ball strikes another on the green, he incurs a two-stroke penalty. He must play his ball as it lies, and the competitor's ball must be replaced.
Lifting A ball to be lifted may be lifted only by the owner, his partner, their caddies, or another person authorized by the owner.
In stroke play, if the ball is lifted (except as provided for in the rules) before holing out, the owner must replace it and incur a two-stroke

penalty or be disqualified. He must replace it before he makes a stroke from the next teeing ground or leaves the final green.
Placing The owner, his partner, or either caddie may replace a ball.
If a ball fails to remain where it is placed, it can be placed in the nearest spot—not nearer the hole—where it will rest. If the original lie of the ball has been altered, it must be placed in the nearest possible lie similar to the original, not nearer the hole and not more than two clubs' lengths from the original lie.

Lost or unplayable If a ball is lost or out of bounds —that is, outside the confines of the course—the player may play his next stroke as near as possible at the spot from which he originally played the ball (adding a penalty stroke to his score), except if it is in a water hazard. If the ball was played from the teeing ground, it may be played from anywhere in that area.
If the ball is unplayable the player may play again from the original spot, or drop the ball within two clubs' lengths of where it lay, but not nearer the hole. He incurs a penalty stroke.
He is the sole judge whether a ball is unplayable.
He may stand out of bounds to play a ball on the course.

Provisional ball To save time when a ball is out of bounds or lost (except in a water hazard), a player may play another ball from as near as possible to where the original ball was played. This is a provisional ball. He must play the provisional ball before a search begins. Once the provisional ball has passed beyond the point where the original ball is likely to be, that ball is deemed lost.
If the original ball is found and is not out of bounds, it comes back into play and the provisional ball is abandoned. A player has five minutes to find his ball.
Penalties for infringements are loss of hole in match play, and two strokes in stroke play.

The flagstick

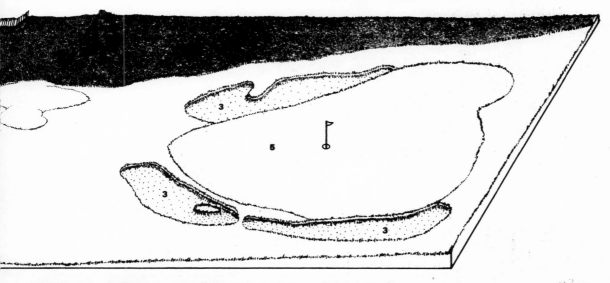

© DIAGRAM

The putting green (5) is the area around the hole specially prepared for putting. A ball on the wrong putting green must be lifted and dropped off the edge before being played.
The flagstick is centered in the hole to show its position. A player may have it held up or removed before he plays his stroke. It must not be touched while the ball is in motion.
If the ball rests against the flagstick while it is in the hole, the flagstick may be removed. If the ball falls into the hole, the player is deemed to have holed out with his last stroke. A flagstick is said to be attended when it is being held. The ball must not strike the flagstick, or any person

attending it: penalty in match play is loss of the hole, and in stroke play, two strokes.
The putt The line of the putt must not be prepared, except for the removal of loose impediments, such as stones. The player may not press anything down with his club, though he may ground the club in front of the ball when addressing it.
If the line of the putt is obstructed by something that cannot be moved, such as casual water or an animal hole, the player may lift the ball and place it in a position to avoid the obstruction— but not closer to the hole. The player may repair any damage to the green caused by the ball's impact, and he may also clean the ball.

The line of the putt may be indicated by a partner or a caddie, but must not be marked or touched. The player must not test the surface by rolling a ball. When a ball is in motion after a stroke on the putting green no other ball may be played or touched. If the ball is stopped or deflected by any outside agency, the stroke is cancelled; the ball is replaced and played again. If the ball hangs over the edge of the hole for more than a few seconds, it is deemed to be at rest.

Foul putt

Correct putt

Court handball

Court handball is a ball game played by two players (singles) or two pairs (doubles) on a walled court. The ball is struck with a gloved hand in such a way that it is difficult for the opponent to return it. The court may have one, three, or four walls. The four-wall game is the most popular.

The court for the four-wall game must conform to the measurements shown in the diagram.
The lines on the floor must be red or white and 1½in wide.
Officials Each match is controlled by a referee who is, where possible, assisted by a scorer. Larger tournaments are under the overall control of a chairman.
The referee is responsible for:
checking the equipment;
briefly checking that the players are aware of the court regulations;
all decisions during the match;
ruling a player out of the match for unsporting conduct, leaving the court without permission, or reporting late for the start.

Duration The first player or pair to win two games wins the match.
Each player or pair is allowed three 30-second time-outs in each game. A 2-minute interval is permitted between the first and second games, and a 10-minute interval between the second and third.

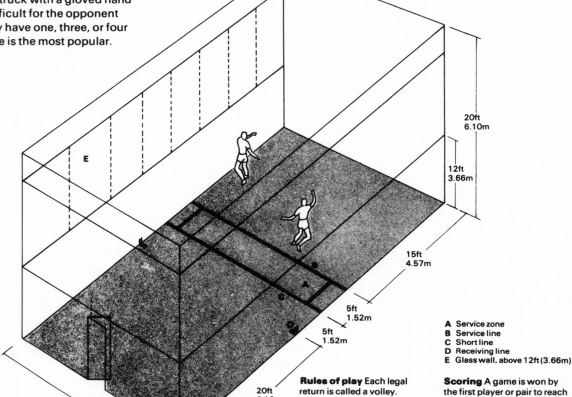

A Service zone
B Service line
C Short line
D Receiving line
E Glass wall, above 12ft (3.66m)

Rules of play Each legal return is called a volley.
The ball may be struck with any part of the hand, but only by one hand. No other part of the body may be used.
Each player is allowed only one touch of the ball, but if a player aims to hit the ball and misses he may play it again or, in doubles, his partner may play it.

Scoring A game is won by the first player or pair to reach 21 points. Points are awarded only if the side that is serving wins the rally. If the non-serving side wins a rally the serve passes to that side.

Obstructions or hinders
There are two types of obstruction:
dead ball hinders, after which the point is replayed;
avoidable hinders, after which the offender is punished by losing a point or the serve.
Dead ball hinders occur when:
the ball passes through an opponent's legs and there is no fair chance of seeing or returning the ball (1);
there is any unintentional hindrance that unsights an opponent;
a returned ball, without first bouncing, hits an opponent before striking the front wall;
any body contact with an opponent interferes with the seeing or striking of the ball.

1

2

Avoidable hinders take place when:
a deliberate block is made to prevent a player from reaching the ball (2);
a player does not move out of the way to allow an opponent his shot;
deliberate pushing takes place;
a player moves into the path of the ball.

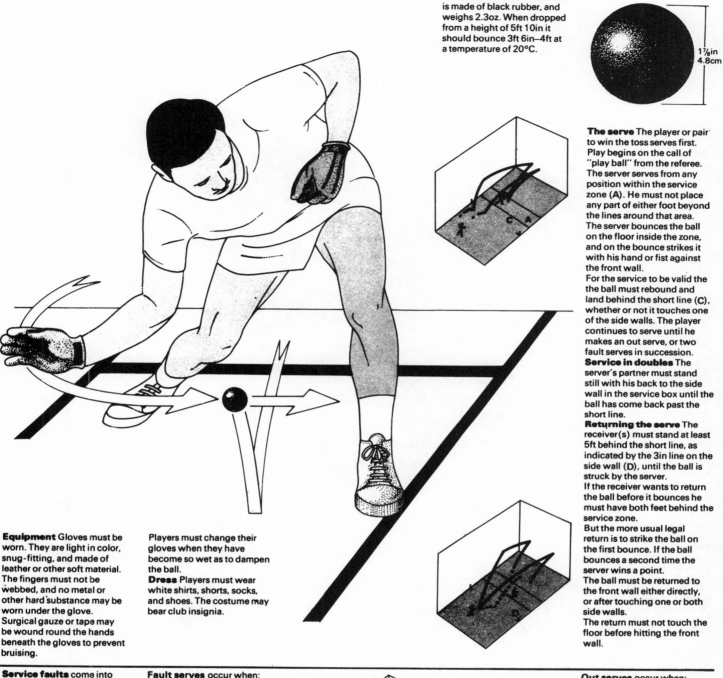

The ball A standard handball is made of black rubber, and weighs 2.3oz. When dropped from a height of 5ft 10in it should bounce 3ft 6in—4ft at a temperature of 20°C.

1⅞in
4.8cm

The serve The player or pair to win the toss serves first. Play begins on the call of "play ball" from the referee. The server serves from any position within the service zone (A). He must not place any part of either foot beyond the lines around that area. The server bounces the ball on the floor inside the zone, and on the bounce strikes it with his hand or fist against the front wall.

For the service to be valid the the ball must rebound and land behind the short line (C), whether or not it touches one of the side walls. The player continues to serve until he makes an out serve, or two fault serves in succession.

Service in doubles The server's partner must stand still with his back to the side wall in the service box until the ball has come back past the short line.

Returning the serve The receiver(s) must stand at least 5ft behind the short line, as indicated by the 3in line on the side wall (D), until the ball is struck by the server.

If the receiver wants to return the ball before it bounces he must have both feet behind the service zone.

But the more usual legal return is to strike the ball on the first bounce. If the ball bounces a second time the server wins a point.

The ball must be returned to the front wall either directly, or after touching one or both side walls.

The return must not touch the floor before hitting the front wall.

Equipment Gloves must be worn. They are light in color, snug-fitting, and made of leather or other soft material. The fingers must not be webbed, and no metal or other hard substance may be worn under the glove. Surgical gauze or tape may be wound round the hands beneath the gloves to prevent bruising.

Players must change their gloves when they have become so wet as to dampen the ball.

Dress Players must wear white shirts, shorts, socks, and shoes. The costume may bear club insignia.

Service faults come into three categories:
1) dead-ball serves, after which the player takes another serve without penalty;
2) fault serves, two of which result in the service passing to the opponent; and
3) out serves, after which the serve passes straight to the opponent.

Dead-ball serves occur when:
in doubles, the ball hits the server's partner on rebounding from the wall while he is in the serving zone and before the ball touches the ground;
the server, or his partner, obscures the receiver's view of the ball.

Fault serves occur when:
the server (S) or his partner (P) steps out of the service zone before the ball has passed the short line;
the ball hits the floor in front of the short line (1);
the ball hits a side wall before crossing the short line (2), or hits the ceiling;
the ball hits the back wall without first bouncing;
the ball hits the crotch (where the front wall joins the floor) (3). A crotch serve into the back wall is allowed.

© DIAGRAM

Out serves occur when:
the server (S) bounces the ball more than three times before serving;
the server aims his hand to serve the ball and misses;
the ball strikes a side wall (1), the ceiling, or the floor (2) before hitting the front wall;
the ball rebounds and touches the server, or his partner (P) while he is out of the service box;
in doubles, the pair serves out of order.

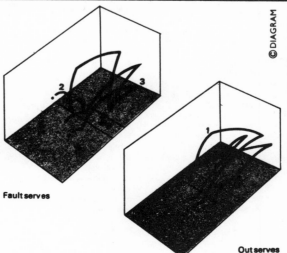

Fault serves

Out serves

Rugby fives

Rugby fives is a ball game played on a four-walled court by two players (singles) or four players (doubles). The ball is struck with a gloved hand with the object of making it difficult for an opponent to return the ball as it rebounds off the front wall of the court. Points are scored only by the player or pair receiving the serve.

The ball is hard and white, with an inner core of cork and string and an outer skin of leather. Its circumference is 5¾in, and its weight 1½oz.
Equipment Padded gloves are worn on both hands. Players usually dress in white shirts, shorts, socks, and rubber-soled shoes.

The court must conform to the measurements shown in the diagram. The walls of the court should be black and the floor red. The floor has no markings and is made of stone. A wooden board runs across the front wall 2ft 6in from the floor.
Officials The match may be controlled by an umpire, whose decision is final on all incidents.

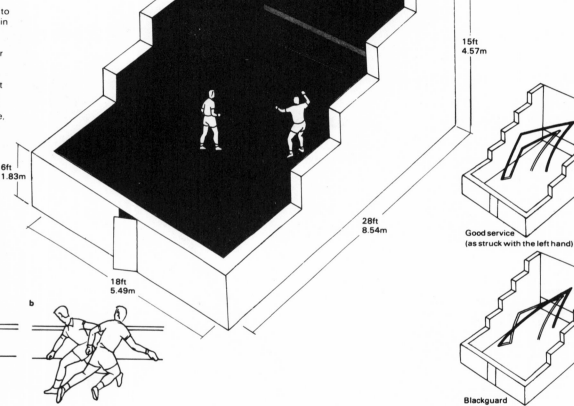

15ft
4.57m

6ft
1.83m

28ft
8.54m

18ft
5.49m

Good service
(as struck with the left hand)

Blackguard

Lets

a

b

Duration The first player to score 15 points is the winner unless the score has reached 14 all. In that event the first to reach 16 is the winner. In a match consisting of more than one game, a three-minute interval is allowed between games.
Scoring Unlike squash or court handball, only the receiver of service can score points. When the receiver wins a rally, he gains a point. If the server wins a rally, he then becomes the receiver.
Starting play Before play begins a preliminary rally is held. The winner becomes the receiver, while the loser serves.
Serving Play starts with the server, or the receiver if requested, throwing the ball

so that it first hits the front wall and then a side wall of his choice (according to whether he is right-handed or left-handed) before falling into court.
After the ball has bounced the server then hits the ball against the same side wall and on to the front wall above the board.
A blackguard is a service that reaches the front wall without hitting the side wall. The receiver may elect to return a blackguard provided that he states that he is going to do so before he hits the ball. He may not, however, return a blackguard if he needs only one point to win. If three successive blackguards are served, all untaken by the receiver, then the receiver wins a point.

Returning service The ball may be allowed to bounce off any of the four walls before being returned, as long as it touches the floor only once. The ball may then be struck to hit any number of other walls before hitting the front wall.
Rules of play After the service and its return, the players strike the ball alternately on to the front wall, either directly or after it has hit the side walls. The ball may bounce once before it is struck.
Rallies are won by a player when:
a) his adversary misses the ball, allows it to bounce twice, hits it below the board line, strikes it into the roof, sends it out of court, or

directs it on to the floor before it strikes the front wall;
b) his opponent hits him with the ball when his return would not have gone "up" (ie above the board line);
c) his opponent allows the ball to strike his person before it has bounced;
d) his opponent hits the ball with any part of his body other than the hand or forearm.
Lets The point is replayed when:
a) a player is hit by a return that would have gone "up;"
b) a player is impeded in his attempt to return the ball;
c) the striker is hit by the ball after it has bounced;
d) the server, about to serve, changes his mind and fails to hit the ball, or calls "no" after striking it.

Doubles The basic rules of singles play all apply. The pair that wins the preliminary rally has the option to receive or to serve. The receiver remains "in" until his side loses a rally. Then the first of the opposing pair receives until they lose a rally, after which the second opponent receives until his side loses another rally. The right to receive then passes to the other side. The serving side must change servers every time the opponents score.
Only the receiver may return service, unless he or his partner chooses to return a blackguard. If either side plays in the wrong order it must be pointed out before the next rally, otherwise that rally stands.

Jai alai (pelota)

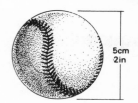

The pelota has a hard rubber core, covered with a layer of linen thread and two layers of goatskin. The diameter is 2in and the weight $4\frac{1}{2}$oz.

5cm
2in

Jai-alai (pelota) is a fast ball game played in a three-walled court (*fronton*) by two players, or by several teams of players. Players attempt to hit a ball (*pelota*) with a wicker basket (*cesta*) against the front wall (*frontis*) so that their opponents will be unable to return it and will therefore lose a point. The game originated in northern Spain. The rules given here are for the game now played in the United States.

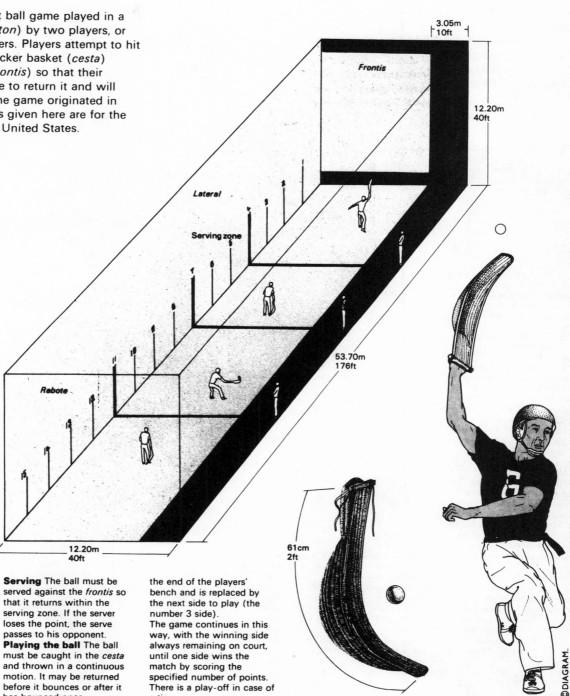

3.05m
10ft

Frontis

12.20m
40ft

Lateral

Serving zone

53.70m
176ft

Rebote

12.20m
40ft

61cm
2ft

©DIAGRAM.

The court has three walls. The front wall is called the *frontis*, the back wall the *rebote*, the side wall the *lateral*.
The *frontis* is made of granite blocks; the *rebote*, *lateral*, and floor are made of gunite, a pressurized cement.
The fourth side of the court has a clear screen through which spectators watch the game.
The court is divided into 15 numbered areas. The serving zone is the space between areas 4 and 7.
Officials There are three judges, standing opposite lines 4, 7, and 11. Officials wear *tuxedos*, and carry rackets to protect themselves from the ball.
Players The game can be played as singles, doubles, or triples.
The *quiniela* (betting) version of the game is played as singles or doubles involving a maximum of eight one- or two-man teams.
Scoring A match is played for a number of points, ranging from 6 (singles) to 40. Only the server scores. He gains a point if his opponent:
a) returns the ball after it has bounced more than once;
b) misses the ball;
c) does not return the ball on to the *frontis*;
d) plays the ball on to the floor next to the screen;
e) fails to catch the ball and throw it in a continuous motion.

Serving The ball must be served against the *frontis* so that it returns within the serving zone. If the server loses the point, the serve passes to his opponent.
Playing the ball The ball must be caught in the *cesta* and thrown in a continuous motion. It may be returned before it bounces or after it has bounced once.
The ball must be returned to the *frontis* and be played within the green areas on the walls.
Quiniela The first two players or teams begin play, with the number 1 side serving.
Play continues until one of the sides loses a point. The losing side then returns to

the end of the players' bench and is replaced by the next side to play (the number 3 side).
The game continues in this way, with the winning side always remaining on court, until one side wins the match by scoring the specified number of points. There is a play-off in case of a tie.
Seven-points system In games where eight teams or players are playing for seven points, one point is scored for each win in the first round (ie until all eight players or teams have played once) and two points for each win in subsequent games.

The cesta is a wicker basket made to a player's specifications. It has a chestnut frame, covered with woven reed.
Front court players usually have smaller *cestas* than rear court players.
The player's hand is inserted into a leather glove which is sewn to the outside of the

cesta. A long tape is wrapped around the glove to keep it on the hand.
Dress Players wear white trousers; a colored sash or belt; a white or colored shirt bearing a number; white rubber-soled shoes; and a helmet.

Squash

Squash is a racket game played in an enclosed court. The object of the game is to keep the ball in play while making it difficult for the opponent to do so. The rules and court dimensions vary from country to country; the basic rules given here are those of the ISRF (International Squash Rackets Federation).

SINGLES

The court The dimensions of an international court are shown on the large diagram. The small illustration shows an American court.

The telltale (also termed the board or tin) is a strip of resonant material running along the foot of the front wall. It is outside the playing area and makes a distinctive sound when hit.

The walls should be white or off-white and completely smooth. The door of the court should have a flush handle that will not deflect the ball. Court markings must not exceed 5cm in width and are painted red.

The floor is usually made of hardwood planks laid parallel to the side walls.

Officials The game is controlled by a marker and a referee, who sit in the center of the gallery. The marker calls the play and the score. The referee is in overall charge, and decides all appeals.

Dress Men wear white shirts and shorts; women wear white dresses, or white blouses and skirts. All players wear white socks and shoes. The soles of the shoes must not be black, in order to avoid marking the court.

Duration Players are allowed 5 minutes for a knock-up before play begins. A match is the best of five games. Play is continuous except for a 1-minute interval between games and a 2-minute interval if the score reaches 2-all.

Scoring The international singles game is played to 9 points. At 8-all the receiving player may call "no-set" (in which case the game ends at 9 points) or "set 2" (in which case the game ends at 10 points).

In North America the game is played to 15 points. At 13-all the receiving player may call: "no set" (game 15); "set 3" (game 16); or "set 5" (game 18).

Winning points Under international rules, only the server can score points. (Under American rules both server and receiver can score.) A player wins a point if his opponent fails to make a good return.

A return is good if, before the ball bounces twice on the floor, it is returned by the striker onto the front wall above the telltale and below the out-of-court line. The ball must reach this area without touching the floor, and it must not touch any part of the striker's clothing or be hit twice.

If a good return has been made in the direction of the front wall but is deflected by an opponent or his racket (a), the striker is awarded the point.

If the ball would not have reached the front wall (b), the striker loses the point.

If the server fails to keep the ball in play the service passes to his opponent.

If the server wins a point he keeps the service.

If the ball is deflected when it would have hit a side wall and then the front wall, a let is played.

Out of court line

Service line

15ft
4.57m

6ft
1.83m
19in
48cm

Telltale board

Short line

Side wall line

Service box

7ft
2.15m

Half court line

32ft
9.75m

10ft 6in
3.20m

5ft 3in
1.60m

14ft
4.30m

21ft
6.40m

5ft 3in
1.60m

International singles court

American singles court

17in
43cm

16ft
4.88m

6ft 6in
1.98m

18ft
5.49m

12ft
3.66m

9ft 3in
2.82m

4ft 6in
1.37m

32ft
9.75m

18ft 6in
5.64m

Deflection

a   b

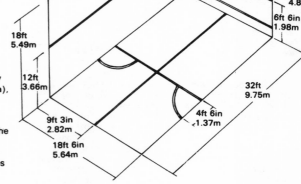

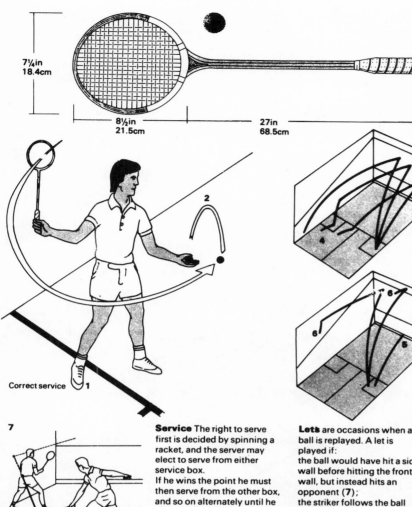

7¼in
18.4cm

8½in
21.5cm

27in
68.5cm

Correct service 1

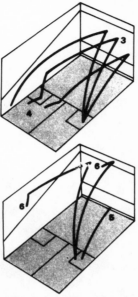

The racket must have a wooden-framed head, though the shaft may be of wood, cane, metal, or fiberglass. Any suitable material may be used as a grip.

The ball is made of rubber or a composition of rubber and butyl, and must have a matt finish. ISRF specifications are:
weight 23.3–24.6g;
diameter 39.5–41.5mm.

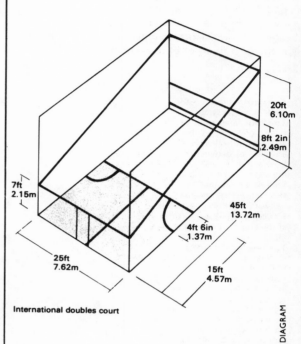

International doubles court

20ft
6.10m

8ft 2in
2.49m

7ft
2.15m

45ft
13.72m

4ft 6in
1.37m

25ft
7.62m

15ft
4.57m

© DIAGRAM

Service The right to serve first is decided by spinning a racket, and the server may elect to serve from either service box.
If he wins the point he must then serve from the other box, and so on alternately until he loses the service. When the service returns to him he again has the choice of box for his first service.
The service may be forehand, backhand, or overarm, but the server must:
have at least one foot in the service box (1);
throw the ball into the air (2);
serve the ball above the service line (3);
serve the ball in such a way that, unless volleyed, it will return from the front wall to land behind the short line in the opposite back quarter of the court (4).

Faults An incorrect service is a fault. If a player serves a fault he may serve a second time. In singles the receiver may elect to play a fault, and by doing so makes the service good. The receiver may take the service on the volley.

Loss of service The server loses the service if:
the ball is served onto or below the telltale (5);
the ball is served out of court (6);
the ball is served against any part of the court before it hits the front wall;
he misses the ball, strikes it more than once, or serves two consecutive faults;
he touches the ball in any way before it hits the floor twice or his opponent hits it.

Lets are occasions when a ball is replayed. A let is played if:
the ball would have hit a side wall before hitting the front wall, but instead hits an opponent (7);
the striker follows the ball around, thus turning before making his stroke, and the ball hits his opponent on its way to the front wall (8);
the position of the player about to strike the ball makes it impossible for his opponent to avoid being hit or, if the striker refrains from making the stroke, avoid hitting the other player (9);
the receiver is not ready to receive service and does not try to play the ball;
the ball strikes any object lying on the floor or is damaged in any way.
It is generally the player's responsibility to claim a let by calling "let please."
If a player misses a stroke completely, he may play another shot provided he can retrieve the ball before it bounces twice.

Obstruction With play taking place in such a confined space, a player must make every effort to give his opponent freedom of movement and full view of the ball.
If the referee considers that a player is making insufficient efforts to avoid obstructing his opponent, he may award that volley to the opponent.

DOUBLES
The doubles game is played on a larger court than the singles game; the dimensions of an international court are shown above.
Rules are the same as for singles, with the following exceptions.

Scoring The game is played to 15 points, with set calls as for North American singles. If the non-serving side wins a rally, a point is added to its score.

Service The two players on the serving side serve one after the other to the receiving side. The first server serves until his side concedes a point and is then relieved by his partner. This order is maintained throughout the match.
When a further point is lost, the serve passes to the first player of the opposing pair. When he loses a point, the fourth player takes his turn to serve.

At the beginning of each new game, however, the serving side loses the right to serve after the loss of only one point. The side winning a game has the choice of serving or receiving at the beginning of the next game.
At the start of each game one player of each pair is designated to receive service in the left-hand court, the other in the right-hand court. The receiver may not return faulty serves.

Obstruction A hinder or balk may be called when the striker is being hindered unnecessarily by his opponents, and a point is awarded against the offending side, even if the striker was not actually prevented from hitting the ball.
It is not a balk simply to impede an opponent's view of the ball.

7

8

9

Paddleball

Paddleball is played by two, three, or four players on a court with one, three, or four walls. A small ball is played against the walls with a paddle (bat). The serving side may win points by serving an ace or winning a volley. The first side to score 21 points wins the game. A match is the best two out of three games.

The court is marked out with lines 1½in wide.

The four-wall court has three high walls, a ceiling, and a lower back wall. A line midway between the front and back walls is called the short line (**A**), and in front of it is another line, the service line (**B**). The space between these lines is the service zone (**C**). Each end of the service zone is marked off to form a service box (**D**)

The one-wall court has a 4ft wire fence along the top of the wall. The sidelines are extended beyond the end line at the back of the court to help in judging long balls and serve-outs. The markings are different from those of the four-wall court: the service line is behind the short line. There should be a playing space of at least 6ft around the court.

The three-wall court is similar to the one-wall court, except that the side walls extend as far as the short line.

Officials A referee controls each match, assisted by a scorer.

The referee stands in the center and above the back wall in four-wall courts; on the side near the end of a side wall in three-wall courts; and on the side and toward the front of the court on an elevated platform in one-wall courts.

The scorer keeps a record of play, announces the score after each exchange, and helps the referee generally.

Players A match may be played between two players (singles), by three players (cut-throat), or by four players (doubles).

Dress Players must wear white shirts, shorts, socks, and shoes. Warm-up suits must also be white if worn in a match. A glove may be worn on the hand holding the paddle. Knee and elbow pads of a soft material may be worn.

Duration Matches last for the best of three games. A two-minute interval is allowed between the first two games. A 10-minute interval is allowed after the second game, during which the players are allowed to leave the court.

Time-outs Play is continuous during games except for time-outs. Two time-outs per player or side are allowed in a game. They must not exceed 30 seconds. They may be requested by serving or receiving players. Play may be suspended for 15 minutes for an injured player, but he forfeits the game if he is then unable to continue or is forced to stop again.

Scoring Only the serving player or side scores points. Points are scored when the opposition:
is unable legally to return a serve or volley;
deliberately hinders the serving player or side.
A point is lost if the ball goes out of court, even if it rebounds off the front wall or goes out of play from the first bounce after hitting the front wall.

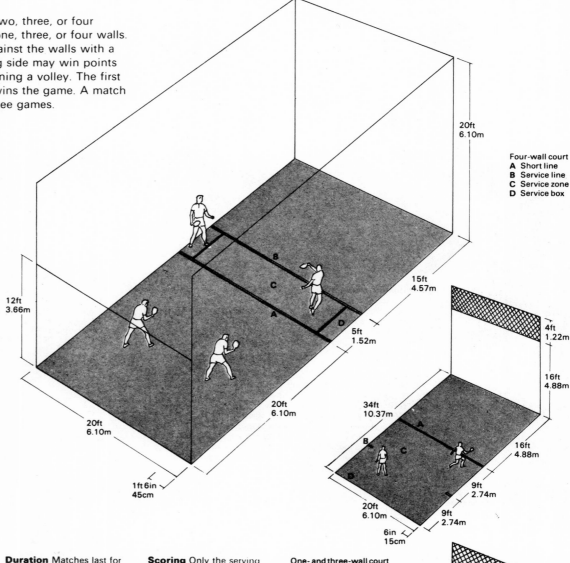

Four-wall court
A Short line
B Service line
C Service zone
D Service box

20ft
6.10m

12ft
3.66m

15ft
4.57m

5ft
1.52m

20ft
6.10m

1ft 6in
45cm

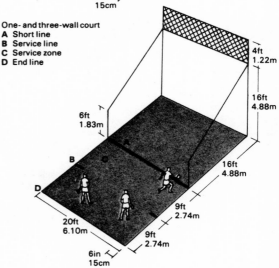

One- and three-wall court
A Short line
B Service line
C Service zone
D End line

4ft
1.22m

16ft
4.88m

34ft
10.37m

16ft
4.88m

9ft
2.74m

20ft
6.10m

9ft
2.74m

6in
15cm

6ft
1.83m

4ft
1.22m

16ft
4.88m

16ft
4.88m

9ft
2.74m

20ft
6.10m

9ft
2.74m

6in
15cm

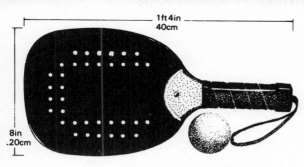

1ft 4in 40cm

8in 20cm

The paddle is made of wood and may be oval or square. Stringed rackets are not allowed. A leather thong is attached to the handle and must be worn around the wrist during play. The paddle is approximately 8in wide by 1ft 4in long, and weighs about 1lb.

The ball is black. When dropped from a height of 6ft it should rebound approximately 3ft 6in.

1⅞ in 4·8cm

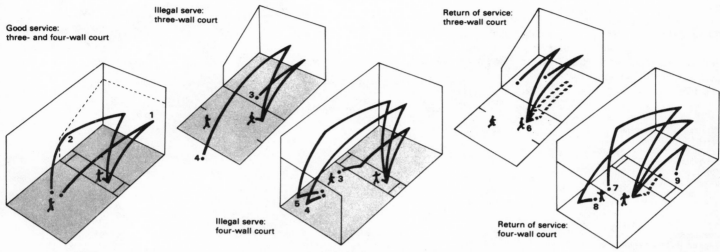

Good service: three- and four-wall court

Illegal serve: three-wall court

Illegal serve: four-wall court

Return of service: three-wall court

Return of service: four-wall court

Playing the ball When returning an opponent's service or shot a player may hold the paddle with one or both hands, but may not switch it from hand to hand. The safety thong must always be around his wrist.
He may not hit the ball with his arms, hands, or any part of the body.
The ball may be touched once only; it may be played onto any of the walls.
Service is decided by tossing a coin. The server in the first game also serves first in the third game. Before each service the server calls the score, giving his own score first. He must not serve until his opponent is ready.
The player may serve from anywhere in the service zone. He may step on a line bounding it, but no part of either foot may be beyond either line of the service zone. The server must remain in the service zone until the ball has crossed the short line.
Method The player drops the ball on the floor within the service zone and strikes it with the paddle on the first bounce so that it hits the front wall (**1**).
The ball must rebound directly behind the short line. In four-wall and three-wall games the ball may touch a side wall first (**2**). In one-wall and three-wall games the ball must rebound within or on the sidelines or the back line.

Illegal serves A serve is illegal if:
the ball hits the floor before crossing the short line (**3**) – a short serve;
the ball rebounds from the front wall to the back wall or over the end line before hitting the floor (**4**) – a long serve;
the ball rebounds to the ceiling before hitting the floor – a ceiling serve;
the ball rebounds from the front wall and hits two or more walls before hitting the floor (**5**);
the ball goes out of court;
the server leaves the service zone before the ball has crossed the short line – a foot fault.

Loss of service A player loses service if:
a) he makes two consecutive illegal serves;
b) he bounces the ball more than twice before striking it when serving;
c) he drops the ball and hits it in the air;
d) he strikes at the ball and misses the serve;
e) he touches his clothes or body with the ball when serving;
f) the serve simultaneously hits the front wall and the ceiling, the floor, or a side wall;
g) the ball hits a side wall before the front wall;
h) the ball goes out of court.
A serve-out is a single action that causes a loss of service.

Return of service The receiver must remain:
in four-wall, at least 5ft behind the short line until the ball is struck by the receiver;
in one-wall and three-wall, behind the service line until the ball passes the short line.
A legally served ball may be returned to the front wall before it bounces (volleying) or after one bounce (**6**).
The ball may touch the side walls (**7**), back wall (**8**), or ceiling, but a return touching the floor and the front wall simultaneously is a bad return (**9**).
When the receiver volleys the ball no part of his body may cross the short line until the return is made.

Obstruction Players must not prevent their opponents from seeing and playing the ball. They must not deliberately hinder an opponent's movements, or make physical contact. The point is replayed if obstruction is accidental. If the obstruction is deliberate the player loses either a point or the serve.

© DIAGRAM

DOUBLES
The doubles game generally conforms to the rules of singles, with some additions.
Service After the first serve-out the service passes to the other side. But thereafter in that game both players of a side are allowed to lose their service before the service passes to the opposition.
Partners' positions
a) In four-wall the server's partner must stand in the service box with his back toward the wall and both feet on the floor until the ball has crossed the short line.
If he is not in his proper position it is a foot fault.
If he is in a legal position and the ball either hits him before it touches the floor or passes behind him, the serve is replayed.
If he is out of the box and is hit by the ball it is a serve-out.
b) In one-wall and three-wall the server's partner must stand outside the sideline between the short line and the back line until the ball has crossed the short line.
If the player is not in this position during a serve it is a foot fault.
If he enters the playing area (ie between the sidelines) before the served ball passes him it is a fault.

Badminton

Badminton is a racket game played by two players (singles) or four players (doubles). A shuttle, generally made of cork and feathers, is hit over a high net that divides a marked court. The object of the game is to hit the shuttle to the floor on the opponents' side of the net. The game derives from the ancient "battledore and shuttlecock."

The court The game may be played out of doors, but it is best played indoors in a draft-free environment.
The floor of the court should have a non-slip surface, and is usually made of wood.
Markings should be in white, yellow, or some other easily distinguishable color. The lines should be 1½in wide. They are included within the overall dimensions of the court.

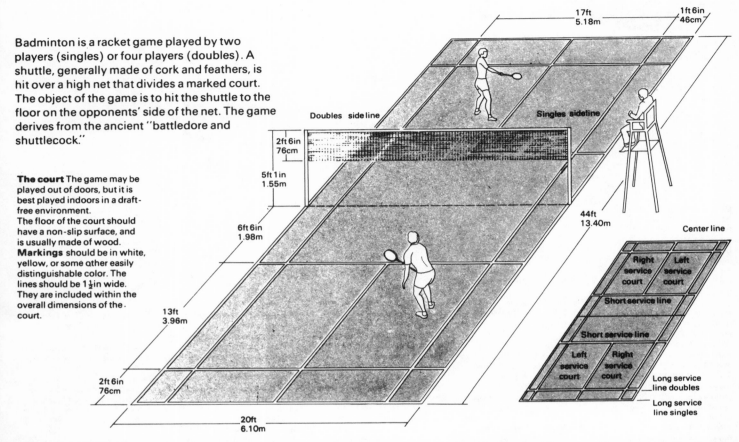

Doubles side line

Singles sideline

Center line

Right service court

Left service court

Short service line

Short service line

Left service court

Right service court

Long service line doubles

Long service line singles

17ft 5.18m

1ft 6in 46cm

2ft 6in 76cm

5ft 1in 1.55m

6ft 6in 1.98m

44ft 13.40m

13ft 3.96m

2ft 6in 76cm

20ft 6.10m

Walls The space between the court and its enclosing walls should not be less than 3ft from court to side walls, and 5ft from court to end walls.
Ventilation Any ventilation system must not move the air.
The net is made of cord with a mesh size of ⅝–¾in. It is tightly stretched so that its upper edge is flush with the top of the posts.

The posts are fixed into the surface of the court on the outside boundary lines, and should be rigid enough to support the net under tension. If the net is fixed by supports outside the court area, a thin post or strip of material should be fixed to the boundary line and rise vertically to the upper edge of the net.

Officials The umpire (1) is the sole judge of the scoring. He may appoint service judges and linesmen.
If a tournament has an overall referee, players may appeal to him only on points of law.
Dress is white and usually consists of a shirt, shorts, socks, and rubber-soled shoes.

Duration Play should be continuous, though some national organizations allow a rest between the second and third games of a match.

Changing ends The players change ends after every game, and during the third game when the leading player's score reaches 8 points in a game of 15 points; 6 in a game of 11 points; and 11 in a game of 21 points.

Scoring Only the serving side can win a point.
In doubles and men's singles, a game consists of either 15 or 21 points.
In women's singles, a game is 11 points.
A match generally consists of the best of three games.
Setting If both players or sides reach the same score during the last stages of a game, play may be extended by "setting" a new deciding score.
If, for example, the score reaches 13-all in a 15-point game, the first player to reach 13 may choose to "set the game to 5", raising the deciding score to 18 points.
If the option to "set" is not taken up at 13-all, it may be taken at 14-all and set to 3.

In a 21-point game, "setting" may take place at 19-all (set to 5) and 20-all (set to 3).
In an 11-point game "setting" may take place at 9-all (set to 3) and 10-all (set to 2).
A player wishing to "set" the game must do so before the next service is taken.
When the game is "set" the score reverts to 0–0 (love-all) and proceeds to 2, 3, or 5 as decided. The final score is recorded as the total number of points scored in the game.

Correct service stroke

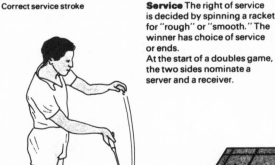

Service The right of service is decided by spinning a racket for "rough" or "smooth." The winner has choice of service or ends.
At the start of a doubles game, the two sides nominate a server and a receiver.

Singles The serving court is always decided by the server's score – if it is even, the right-hand court is used; if it is odd, the left-hand court. If the game is "set" the relevant score is the total number of points gained by the server. The shuttle is served into the service court diagonally opposed to the server.

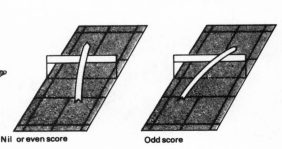

Nil or even score

Odd score

The racket is light and made of wood or steel. The weight is usually 4–5oz.

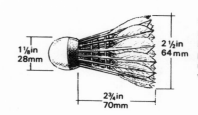

The shuttle is generally made of 14–16 feathers fixed in a cork base, but nylon and plastic are allowed by some national associations. The weight is 4.73–5.50g.

1⅛in 28mm

2½in 64mm

2¾in 70mm

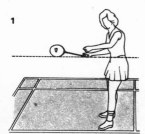

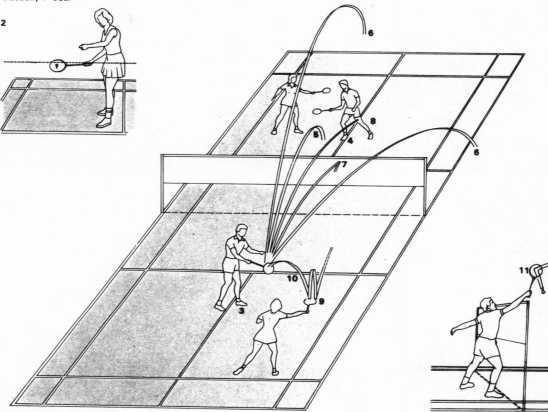

Faults are infringements that end a rally. If the server commits a fault, the service passes to his opponent. If the non-server commits a fault, the server wins a point.

Service faults It is a fault if, in service:

the shuttle is hit above waist level (**1**);

the head of the racket is not completely below the level of the hand holding the racket (**2**);

the server's feet are not in the correct service court;

both the server's feet are not in contact with the floor (**3**);

a feinting movement is made;

the receiver is not standing within the correct service court (**4**);

the receiver moves before the shuttle is struck;

the shuttle lands outside the correct service court (**5**).

General faults It is also a fault if:

the shuttle drops outside the court (**6**);

the shuttle fails to go over the net (**7**);

a player is struck by the shuttle (**8**);

a player hits the shuttle twice during a shot (**9**);

a player and his partner hit the shuttle with successive shots (**10**);

the shuttle is struck before it crosses the net (**11**);

a player touches the net while the shuttle is in play;

a player obstructs his opponent;

there is any other transgression of the laws.

Lets A let allows a rally and resulting score to be disregarded. The server restarts the game by serving again from the same service court. Lets are given by the umpire without appeals made by the players.

Singles Lets in singles are played when the server serves from the wrong court, or his opponent receives service while standing in the wrong court, but only if the offending player wins the rally. If he loses, the score stands. The score also stands if the mistake is not realized before delivery of the next service. A let is also played if the server and receiver commit faults at the same moment, or if the shuttle is caught in the net after passing over it.

Doubles Similar let rules apply in doubles games. A let is awarded if a player wins a point after serving out of turn or from the wrong court.

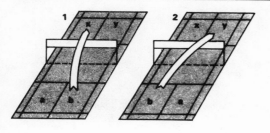

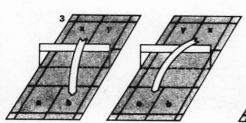

Doubles In doubles the principles of serving are more complicated:

1) If the server (**b**) wins the first point,

2) he then serves into his opponent's left service court from his own left service court; the opponent (**y**) who did not receive on the first point now becomes the receiver.

3) When the serve is lost, it passes to the opponent who was in the right service court at the start of the rally (**x**). After the service has thus changed ends at the beginning of each game, the receiving side (**a,b**) must win two rallies to retrieve it. The first opponent to serve (**x**) does so from alternate courts until he loses a rally.

4) Then his partner (**y**) takes over, serving from the court he occupied at the beginning of the losing rally. He serves from alternate courts until he loses a rally.

5) The service then passes across the net, and both of that pair (**b,a**) serve.

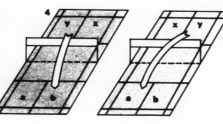

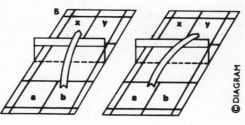

© DIAGRAM

Lawn tennis

Lawn tennis is a racket game in which individuals (singles) or pairs (doubles) compete against each other. The game is played on a court divided by a net. The object of the game is to propel the ball over the net in such a way that it bounces in court and beats any attempt by an opponent to return it.

Court The surface may be grass, a variety of asphalt, wood, porous concrete, or other composition. It is marked out with white lines as shown in the diagram. The lines are included within the limits of the court.

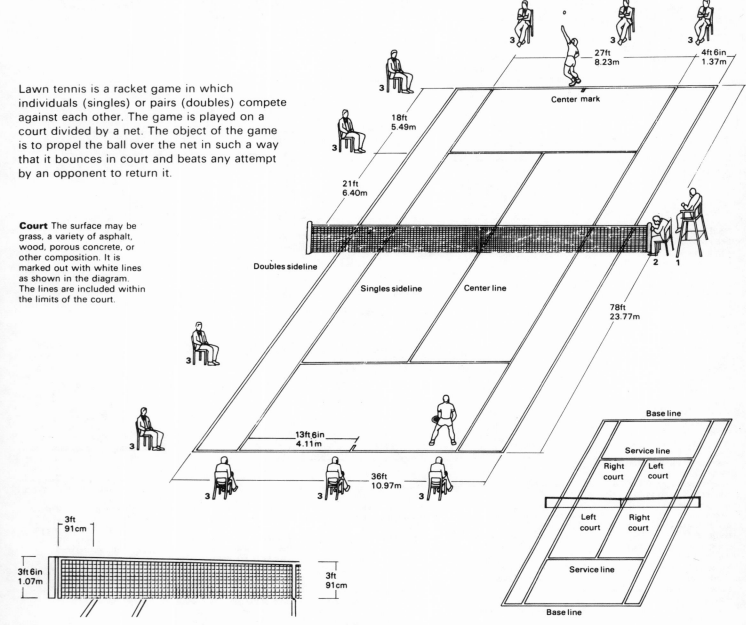

The net is suspended between two posts from a cable covered by white tape. At its center it is kept taut by a vertical strap which is firmly fixed to the ground. The height of the net may be adjusted by a handle attached to one of the posts.

Players Normally men play against men and women against women, except in mixed doubles, where opposing pairs each consist of a man and a woman.

Dress By tradition the shirts and shorts of the men and the skirts, blouses, and dresses of the ladies are white, though certain professional tournaments allow colored clothing. White socks and rubber-soled shoes are worn.

Duration A match lasts a maximum of five sets for men and three for women. A men's match ends when one side has won three sets, and a women's match when one side has won two sets. Play is continuous, though in certain circumstances and some countries players are allowed a rest of up to 10 minutes after the third set for men and the second for women. This break may be 45 minutes in equatorial countries.
Play is never delayed to enable a player to recover his strength or receive advice.
The umpire may suspend play indefinitely if factors such as crowd disturbance are affecting play.

Officials consist of an umpire (**1**) assisted by a net-cord judge (**2**), linesmen (**3**), and foot-fault judge
Start of play The choice of service and sides (ends) is decided by spinning a racket in the air and calling "rough" or "smooth"—the two different faces of the racket.

Scoring A match is scored in games and sets.
In each game a player begins with no score ("love"). His first point scores 15, his second 30, his third 40, and his fourth wins the game unless there is a "deuce," which is called at the score of 40-all. After deuce, the next point won is scored as an advantage to the player who won it, and if he wins the following point he wins the game. Should his opponent redress the balance the score returns to deuce, and so on until the end of the game.
The first player to win six games wins the set, unless each player has won five games, when play continues until one player is two games ahead.

Tie-break To prevent long sets, some tournaments use a tie-break system which comes into operation at a specified equal score (6-all or 8-all).
There are several systems in use. In the United States, the favored version is for the first player or partnership to score 5 out of the next 9 points to be the winner. In the "7 out of 12" version the first player to score 7 points with a 2-point lead is the winner. If the score reaches 6-all the game continues until one player leads by 2 points.
In some tournaments, the tie-break is not used in a final set, which must be played out in the ordinary way.

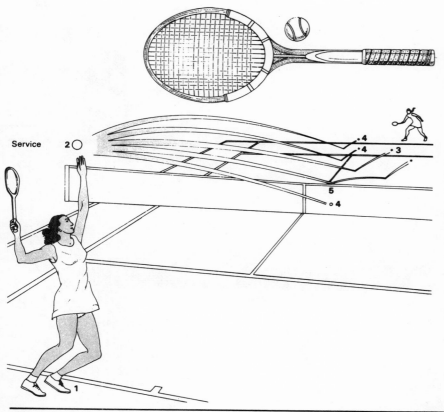

Rackets have wood or steel frames. A man's racket generally weighs 13½-14oz (382.7g-396.9g) and a woman's 13-13½oz (368.5g-382.7g).
Tennis balls must be white or yellow. They should weigh 2-2$\frac{1}{16}$oz (56.7g-58.5g).

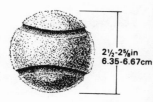

2½-2⅝in
6.35-6.67cm

Service

Service The server starts play by sending the ball over the net into the service court. He serves from alternate sides, first from behind his right court, and then his left court.
He must serve with both feet behind the base line and within imaginary continuations of the center mark and side line (1).
To serve, the ball must be thrown into the air and struck with the racket before it hits the ground (2).
Throughout delivery of service the server must not change his position by walking or running, nor touch with either foot any area other than that behind the base line within the imaginary extensions of the center mark and the side line.

For the service to be good the ball must cross the net without bouncing and pitch into the service court diagonally opposite (3) The lines bounding that court are part of its area.
If the server or the service infringes any rule (4) a fault is recorded. A second service is then permitted; if that is a fault the server loses a point.
It is not a fault if the ball touches the net but still falls into the appropriate court (5). This constitutes a "let," and the serve is taken again. A let is also called if the ball is served before the receiver is prepared. The receiver must allow the ball to bounce before he returns it.
In the next game the service passes to the receiver.

Losing a point

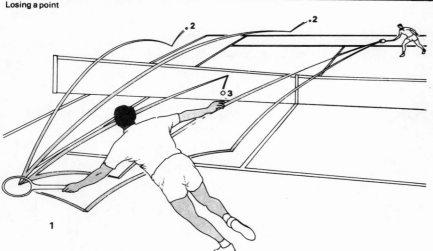

Changing ends Players change ends at the end of the first and third games and any subsequent alternate game in each set.
A change of ends at the end of a set occurs only if the total number of games in that set is an odd number. If the number is even the change takes place after the first game of the new set.
Losing a point A point is lost when the player:
fails to return the ball over the net before it touches the ground twice on his side of the net (1);
returns the ball so that it first hits the ground outside his opponent's court, or strikes any object outside that court (2);
hits the ball into the net (3);

hits the ball twice;
hits the net with his person or racket;
plays the ball before it has crossed to his side of the net;
is hit by the ball anywhere other than on his racket;
deliberately hinders an opponent (a let is played if any hindrance is accidental).
A return is good if it bounces within the court after crossing the net.
The ball may touch the net or cross outside the post as long as it lands in the correct court.
A player's racket may pass over the net after hitting the ball as long as the player did not strike the ball before it crossed the net.

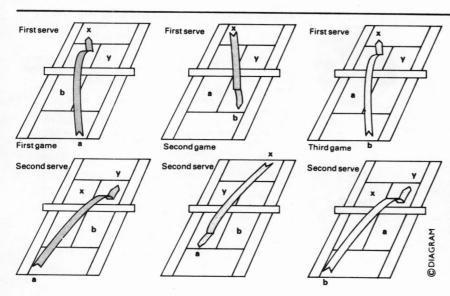

First serve   First serve   First serve
First game   Second game   Third game

Second serve   Second serve   Second serve

The doubles game is played within a wider playing area. Except for the order of service, the same rules apply as for singles.
Service The pair about to serve in the first game (a, b) decides which player shall serve for that game (a).
The opposing pair (x, y) decides similarly for the second game (x).
The player in the first pair who did not serve in the first game (b) serves in the third game, while the fourth player (y) serves in the fourth game. The same order is kept throughout each set.
Receiving The pair about to receive in the first game (x, y) decides which player shall receive the first

service (x). That player then receives all the first services in the odd games of that set. Similarly, the pair due to receive in the second game (a, b) makes a choice, and the chosen player (b) receives the first service in the even games of that set.
In each game partners receive the service alternately. During a rally each pair plays the ball alternately, either partner of each pair being allowed to return the ball.

©DIAGRAM

Table tennis

Table tennis is a game for two players (singles) or four (doubles) and is normally played indoors. Rackets, sometimes called "bats," are used to hit a small, light ball backward and forward across a table divided by a low net. The object is to win points by making shots that an opponent is unable to return.

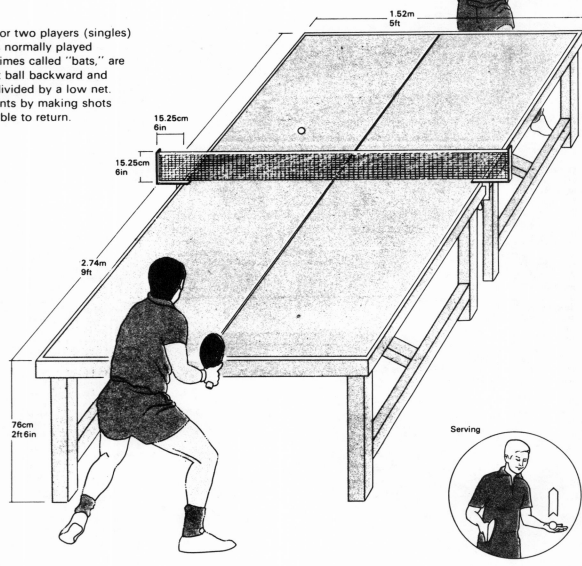

1.52m
5ft

15.25cm
6in

15.25cm
6in

2.74m
9ft

76cm
2ft 6in

The table may be of any substance but must give a uniform bounce of not less than 22cm or more than 25cm when a standard ball is dropped from 30.5cm above its surface.
The playing surface should be dark-colored, preferably green, and matt, with white marking lines.
A white line 2cm wide, marks the edges of the table. The sides of the table-top are not considered part of the playing surface.
For doubles, the playing surface is divided into halves by a 3mm white line.
The net, 1.83m long, is suspended across the center of the table by a cord attached to a post at either end.
The playing area should extend at least 1.5m on either side of the table, and at least 2.5m at the ends. The maximum height is 3.5m.
Dress Players should not wear white clothing, though white edging to playing shirts is permitted. Match uniform generally consists of a dark shirt, shorts or skirt, and flat-soled shoes.
Officials A referee controls play. He may suspend a player for misconduct.

The racket may be any size, weight or shape. The blade should be of wood, continuous, of even thickness, flat and rigid. (The use of other materials may be allowed by national associations for an experimental period.)
Each side of the blade must be of a uniform, dark color, but the two sides need not be of the same color.
That part of the blade nearest the handle and gripped by the fingers may be covered with any material.
The blade may be covered with:
a) plain, pimpled rubber, with pimples outward, of a total thickness not exceeding 2mm;

b) a sandwich of cellular rubber surfaced with plain, pimpled rubber, with pimples inward or outward, of a total thickness not exceeding 4mm.
(A side not used for hitting is exempted from covering rules.)

a) 2mm
0.08in
b) 4mm
0.16in

A game is won by the player or pair first scoring 21 points, unless both shall have scored 20 points, when the winner shall be the first to score two points more than the opposition.
A match consists of one game, the best of three, or the best of five games.
Play must be continuous throughout except that either player or pair may claim up to five minutes rest between the third and fourth games of a match, and not more than one minute between any other successive games of a match.

Choice of ends and the right to serve or receive is decided by tossing a coin. If the winner of the toss decides to serve or receive first, the loser has the choice of ends, and vice versa.
The winner of the toss may require the loser to choose first.
In doubles, each pair decides which of them is to serve and receive first in the first game.

Serving

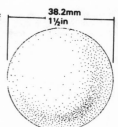

The ball should be made of celluloid or a similar plastic, white or yellow, with a matt surface. Its weight must be between 2.40g and 2.53g (0.085oz-0.09oz).

38.2mm / 1½in

A good service

A good return

Volleying is not allowed

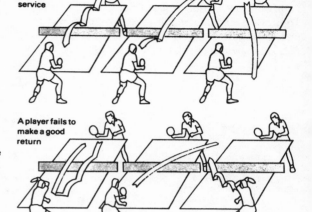

A player fails to make a good service

A player fails to make a good return

Order of play The period when the ball is in play is termed a "rally."
The player who first strikes the ball in a rally is termed the "server"; the second is the "receiver."
"Struck" means hit with the racket or the racket hand below the wrist.
A stroke made with the hand alone, after dropping the racket, is not good; nor is a stroke made by the racket alone after it is dropped or thrown.
In singles the server must first make a good service, the receiver must make a good return, and then server and receiver make good returns alternately.
In doubles the server must make a good service, the receiver a good return, the

server's partner a good return, the receiver's partner a good return, and so on in this sequence.
Serving The ball is placed on the palm of the free hand, which must be stationary, above the level of the playing surface, and not cupped. The fingers must be kept together, with the thumb free.
The ball is then thrown by hand only, without imparting spin, near vertically upward, so that it is at all times visible to the umpire and so that it visibly leaves the palm. On descent, the ball is struck to touch the server's court first and then, passing directly over or around the net, to touch the receiver's court. (Around the net is defined as under or around the

projection of the net and its supports outside the side line.)
The ball must be struck at the first attempt. At the moment of striking, the racket must be behind the end of the table or an imaginary continuation of it.
In doubles the ball must touch the right-hand half of the court on the serving side and then the diagonally opposite court or line.
Returning service The ball must be struck to pass directly over or around the net to touch the opponent's court. If the ball, in passing over or around the net, touches the net or its supports, it is considered to have passed directly.
The ball must not be allowed to bounce twice before

return, nor must it be struck by a player more than once consecutively.
Volleying—striking the ball in play before it has touched the playing surface on that player's side of the table—is not allowed, and loses a point.
The ball is considered out of play once it has touched any object other than the

net, supports, playing surface, racket, or racket hand below the wrist. A stroke made with the hand alone, the racket having been dropped, also puts the ball out of play.
Change of ends The players or pairs change ends after each game until the end of the match. They also change ends in the last game when the first player or pair scores 10 points.
Wrong ends If the players are playing from the wrong end they must change ends as soon as the error is discovered, unless a game has been completed since the error, in which case the error is ignored. In any circumstances, all points scored since the error are counted.

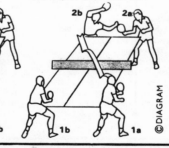

©DIAGRAM

Points are scored by a player when his opponent: fails to make a good service; fails to make a good return; strikes the ball out of sequence in a doubles game (except by mistake); touches the playing surface with his free hand when the ball is in play.
A player also scores when: anything his opponent wears or carries comes into contact with the ball before it has passed over the end line or side lines while not having touched the playing surface; his opponent (or his racket or something he wears or carries) touches the net or its supports or moves the playing surface while the ball is in play.
Under the expedite system, a receiver also scores after

13 good returns.
A let is a rally from which no point is scored. It occurs when:
a) the ball touches the net or its supports in service, provided the service is otherwise good or has been volleyed by the receiver;
b) a service is delivered when the receiver or his partner is not ready, provided no attempt has been made to return the ball;
c) a player fails to make a good service or return through an accident beyond his control, such as a movement by a spectator or a sudden noise;
d) the ball is broken in play;
e) a rally is interrupted to correct a mistake in playing order or ends;

f) a rally is interrupted to apply the expedite system.
Change of service With certain exceptions, the service in singles and doubles passes from one player to another after every five points scored.
The service sequence in doubles is: the player to serve first of one pair (1a) serves to the player who serves first of the second pair (2a); 2a then serves to 1a's partner, 1b; 1b serves to the fourth player, 2b; and 2b serves to 1a.
From the score of 20-all, or under the expedite system, the serving sequence is unchanged, but each player serves once only in succession until the game ends.

The player or pair who served first in a game receives first in the next game.
In each game of doubles the initial order of receiving is opposite to that of the previous game.
In the last game of a doubles match the receiving pair changes its order of receiving when the first pair scores 10.
Any error in serving or receiving must be corrected as soon as it is noticed; all points scored after the error count.

The expedite system is introduced if a game is unfinished 15 minutes after the start. It then applies to the rest of that game and to all remaining games of the match.
The umpire interrupts play after 15 minutes by calling "let." If the interruption occurs between rallies the game is restarted by a service from the player who is next due to serve.
The return strokes of the receiving player or pair are counted out loud, from 1 to 13, by an official other than the umpire. After 13 good returns the point goes to the receiving player or pair.

Volleyball

Volleyball is a team game played by six players on each side. The object is to send a ball over a net and within the boundaries of a court so that the opposing team are unable to return it or prevent it from hitting the ground. Any part of the body above the waist may be used to propel the ball.

The court includes the boundary lines, and the ball must clear them completely to be ruled out of court. The attack lines extend indefinitely beyond the side lines.
The net is 1m deep and 9.50m long, made of 10cm-square mesh. Along the top is a double thickness of white canvas with a flexible cable stretched through it. Vertical tapes run down each side of the net, and vertical aerials project above its top.
Temperature Competitive volleyball should not be played when the temperature is below 10°C.

Service area
3m 9ft 9in
3m 9ft 9in
Back line
80cm 2ft 8in
1m 3ft 3in
1.43m 4ft 8in
Center line
3m 9ft 9in
Attack line
18m 59ft
6m 19ft 6in
15cm 6in
Players' rotation
9m 29ft 6in

Dress Players wear jerseys and shorts in team colors, with numbers on the back and front of their jerseys. Numbered track suits may be worn in cold weather. Shoes must be light and pliable and without heels; players may obtain permission to play barefoot. Headgear or articles that may cause injury must not be worn.

Officials The game is controlled by:
the referee (1); aided by the umpire (2);
the official scorer (3); and two linesmen (4).
Team officials Team coaches, managers, and captains are responsible for team discipline; they may ask for a time-out or a substitution. At a time-out or substitution

the coach must not enter the court, though he may speak to his players.
Captains are the only players allowed to speak to officials. Any dispute over the interpretation of rules is to be settled on the spot by the referee and the disputing captain.
There is no appeal during the match against any decision.

Positioning At the moment of service the players must take up the positions shown. But once the ball is served they may move anywhere on their own side of the net. Any positional error incurs a fault, and the offenders lose all points scored while at error (the opponents retain all theirs).

Correct positions must be resumed when a positional error is spotted.
On the change of service, members of the team that is to serve rotate one position clockwise before serving. The order of rotation must remain constant in each set; it may be changed for a new set if the scorer is informed.

Duration In international competitions a match is the best of five sets.
Intervals are allowed between sets: 2 minutes for the first three intervals and up to 5 minutes between the fourth and fifth sets.
Up to 3 minutes are allowed for injury stoppages.
If bad weather etc interrupts a game, it may be resumed from where it was halted if on the same court and within 4 hours; otherwise the interrupted set must be replayed.
Ends Before play starts, the captains toss a coin for choice of ends or the right to serve first.

Teams change ends after each set unless the next set is the decider; then there is a fresh toss of a coin to decide ends or service. In a deciding set the teams change ends after one side has reached eight points.
Scoring If a team fails to return the ball correctly over the net, a fault is recorded against it. If the penalized team is serving, it loses service. If the penalized team is not serving, the serving team scores a point. Only serving teams score points. A set is won when one team reaches 15 points with a two-point lead. If the game is tied at 14/14 it continues until one team has a two-point lead.

The serve After the referee's whistle the player in the rear right-hand corner puts the ball into play.
The server stands within the service area and hits the ball with his hand (open or closed) or any part of his arm to send it over the net into his opponents' court. He must release the ball from his other hand before striking it.

After hitting the ball he may land on the serving line or within the court. The serving team must not distract opponents during the service. A fault is conceded if the ball touches the net, the net aerial or its imaginary extensions, or a player of the serving team; or if it lands outside the opponents' court.

A player continues to serve until his team commits a fault and a side-out is called. Then the serve passes to the other team. A new set is begun by the team not serving at the end of the preceding set, but the ball must be served by the correct player.

Underarm serve

Tennis serve

Hook serve

The ball is made of supple leather casing with a bladder, or of rubber or a similar synthetic product. It must be all one color. The circumference must be 65–67cm and the weight 260–280g.

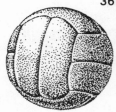

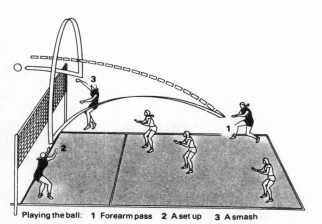

Playing the ball: 1 Forearm pass 2 A set up 3 A smash

Playing the ball Each team may touch the ball up to three times before sending it over the net (1, 2, 3).
Contact is allowed with any part of the body above the waist as long as the hits are clean and the ball is not held, scooped, or carried in any way.
4 If two or more teammates play the ball at the same moment, it counts as two touches (except in blocking). The ball may be played while the player is in contact with a teammate as long as he is not using him as a prop.
5 If two players go for the same ball but only one touches it, only one touch is counted.
6 When two opponents simultaneously commit a foul, a double fault results and the point is replayed.
A hit (except a service) is good if the ball touches the net between the side-markers and drops in court. The ball is out of play if it touches the ground or any object outside the court.

Blocking A blocking act is an attempt to stop, with any part of the body above the waist, the ball coming over the net.
One or more front-line players may block, provided they indicate their intention to do so by raising a hand above the top of the net.
Any blocking player is entitled to a second play at the ball (this counts as the second of his team's touches). If the ball touches more than one blocking teammate, this counts as only one touch even if the contacts are not simultaneous.
Blockers may reach over the net, but they must not attempt to touch the ball unless their opponents are attacking – sending the ball over the net. If two opponents simultaneously touch the ball above the net, the player whose team does not receive the ball as it falls is deemed to have made the last touch. The normal rules of play apply as soon as the ball drops. It is a double fault if the ball is held.
Back-line players may only send a ball from the attack area (or its extended limits) into the opponents' court when it is below net height.

Blocking

From behind the attack line, they may use any permissible manner to hit the ball into the opponents' court.
Substitution Each team may make six substitutions in each set, but only when the ball is dead and on the request of the captain or coach.
Substitutes must report to the scorer before joining the play. While not playing, substitutes must sit with the coaches on the side of the court opposite the referee; they may warm up outside the playing area provided they return to their correct place.
A time-out is charged for any delay in substitution; if the team has already taken its time-outs, it must forfeit the serve or a point.
Anyone playing at the start of a set may be replaced only

once. The original player may go back during the same set, but he must return to his previous rotational position.
A substitute who leaves the game may not return in the same set.
A substitute may be replaced only by the player whose position he originally took. If after six substitutions have been made an injury occurs, the injured player may be replaced.
If after six substitutions, one player is sent off, the team forfeits that set but retains the points it has scored.
Play must resume immediately after a substitution.
During a substitution no one is allowed to advise the players on court.

Fouls A team loses the service or a point if:
1 a player "spikes" the ball above the opponents' court;
2 a player crosses the vertical plane of the net and touches the court or an opponent;
a player interferes with an opponent's play;
the ball touches the ground;
a team plays the ball more than three times in succession;
the ball touches a player below the waist;
a player touches the ball twice consecutively;
a team is out of position at the service;
the ball is held or pushed;
a player touches the net or vertical aerials (unless the ball knocks the net against him);
a player crosses the center line when play is in progress;

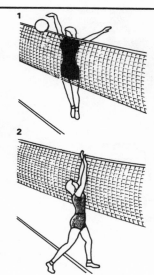

a back-line player in the attack area returns the ball from above net height;
the ball does not pass over the net between the vertical rods (or their assumed extension);
the ball touches the ground outside the court;
the ball is returned with the use of a teammate as a support;
a player receives a personal warning;
a coach or a substitute, having been warned, continues to instruct;
a player reaches under the net and touches the ball or an opponent while the ball is on the opponents' side;
the game is persistently delayed;
a substitute joins the play illegally;

a team requests a third time out after a warning;
a team extends a second time-out beyond 30 seconds;
a team delays a substitution after taking two time-outs;
players leave the court without the referee's permission;
a player intimidates an opponent;
a block is illegal;
a serve is illegal.
Disqualification Persistent misconduct by players, substitutes, or coaches will lead to disqualification for the rest of the set or match.

Time-outs Two 30-second time-outs may be requested in each set, but only when the ball is dead. They may be taken consecutively, or a time-out may be followed by a substitution, or a substitution by a time-out.
The captain or coach must make it clear whether he wants a time-out or a substitution.
No player may leave the court during a time-out, and only the coach may give advice. If a team requests a third time-out the referee gives a warning, and then punishes with a fault any further requests in the same set.

© DIAGRAM

Basketball

Basketball is a fast, exciting game played by two teams of five players, who may pass, throw, roll, bat, or dribble the ball. The object of the game is to score points by throwing the ball into the opposing team's basket.

1 referee
2 umpire
3 scorer
4 timekeeper
5 30-second operator

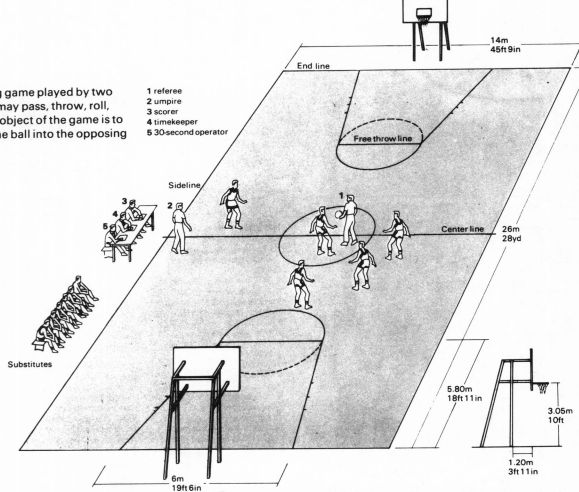

The court must have a hard surface (not grass). Its width may vary by 1m and its length by 2m but the proportions must be kept. The ceiling must be at least 7m high. Lighting must be uniform and not hinder players from throwing for a goal.

Backboards are made of hardwood or a single piece of equally rigid transparent material, with lines and edges to contrast with the background – usually black on white, or white on transparent. The supports are bright in color to be easily visible, and at least 40cm clear of the end lines.

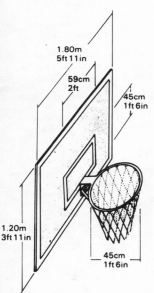

Baskets consist of white cord nets to hold the ball briefly as it drops through. They are suspended from orange metal rings attached rigidly at right angles to the backboards.

Teams consist of five players and five (in some cases seven) substitutes. Players may leave the court only with official permission except at the end of each half.

Dress Players wear shirts and shorts with basketball boots or sneakers. Shirts carry numbers front and back in contrasting color. Only numbers from 4 to 15 are used.

Coaches inform the scorer of the names and numbers of the players and the captain, and any changes of numbers. The captain may act as coach; if disqualified or injured, he is replaced as coach by the substitute captain. There may also be an assistant coach.

Technical equipment consists of:
a) stopwatches, including game watch and time-out watch;
b) device for administering the 30-second rule, visible to players and spectators;
c) official scoresheet;
d) scoreboard;
e) markers, numbered 1–4 in black, 5 in red, to show the number of fouls per player.

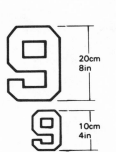

Officials are the referee and umpire, assisted by the scorer, timekeeper, and 30-second operator. They wear grey trousers and shirts. The referee and the umpire divide the court between them, exchanging places after each foul involving a free throw penalty and after each jump ball decision. They use whistles and hand signals to make and explain decisions.

Starting Visitors choose ends; on a neutral court the teams toss up. The teams change ends at half time. Each team must begin with five players on court. The game starts with a jump ball.

Scoring A goal is scored when a live ball enters a basket from above and stays in or passes through. Goals from the field count two points, from free throws one point.

Duration A game consists of two halves of 20 minutes each, with an interval of 10 or 15 minutes. If the score is tied, play continues for as many extra 5-minute periods as necessary. Teams toss for baskets for the first period, then change ends for the others.

Forfeited game A game is forfeited if a team:
does not have five players ready 15 minutes after starting time;
is not on court within 1 minute of the referee's signal;
does not have at least two players on court.
If the team to which the game is forfeited is ahead, the score stands; otherwise the score is recorded as 2–0 in its favor.

The ball is spherical and has a leather, rubber, or synthetic case, with a rubber bladder. Its circumference is 75–78cm. It should weigh 600–650g. When inflated, it should bounce between 1.20m and 1.40m on a solid wooden floor if dropped from a height of about 1.80m.

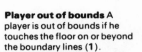

Jump ball starts each game. The referee throws the ball up in the center circle, and the opposing forwards leap up and try to tap it away. The jumpers must stand in the half of the circle nearest their own baskets, with one foot touching the center line. The ball is thrown up at right angles to the sideline so that it drops between them. Each player is allowed two taps before the ball touches the ground, a basket, a backboard, or another player. The jumpers must remain in position until the ball is tapped. Other players must be outside the circle, and must not interfere with the jumpers. Any violation of the jump ball rules is penalized if the opponents do not gain an advantage from it. The toss is repeated if it is a bad one or if both teams violate the rules. A jump ball also occurs if neither team has control when the ball becomes dead. It takes place in the nearest circle. If the ball lodges on the basket supports, the jump ball takes place from the nearest free throw line.

Play The ball may be passed, thrown, batted, tapped, rolled, or dribbled, but it may not be carried or kicked deliberately. It goes into play when an official administers a jump ball or free throw, or a player is about to throw in.

Live ball! The ball becomes alive when a player taps it in a jump ball, when it is thrown in, or during a free throw.

Control A player has control if holding or dribbling a live ball. A team is in control if one of its members has control or the ball is being passed between them. Team control ends with a goal, a dead ball, or loss of possession to the opponents.

Dead ball occurs when:
a goal is made;
a violation occurs;
a foul occurs;
on a throw for a technical foul by the coach or his substitute;
at the first of two free throws it is obvious the ball will not go into the basket;
a held ball occurs;
the ball lodges in the basket supports;
the whistle blows or time expires, unless an attempt at a goal is being made.
The ball does not become dead if a foul occurs during an attempt at a goal, or if the penalty for a jump ball violation is ignored.

Player out of bounds A player is out of bounds if he touches the floor on or beyond the boundary lines (**1**).

Ball out of bounds The ball is out of play when it touches any person or object on or beyond the boundary lines, including the rear of the backboard or its supports. Possession is awarded to the team that did not touch the ball last; a player forced out by slight contact may also be awarded the ball.

Return to play The player nominated to return the ball stands outside the court at the point where the ball went out. He may throw, roll, or bounce the ball into court (**2**). No other player may step out of bounds during the throw in. If the ball goes out across the sideline but between the center line and the end line, an official must hand the ball to the player who is to throw in.
It is forbidden to:
carry the ball into court;
touch the ball in court before another player has done so;
take more than 5 seconds to throw in.
The officials may regard repeatedly putting any part of the body over the line before the ball, or playing an opponent's throw in, as technical fouls.

Held ball occurs when two opposing players are both firmly holding the ball (**3**), or when a closely guarded player takes more than 5 seconds to shoot, pass, roll, bat, or dribble.
Officials should not call a held ball too hastily. A player lying on the floor in possession of

the ball must have a chance to play it, unless he is in danger of injury.
After a held ball, play resumes with a jump ball at the nearest circle.

Dribble occurs when a player throws, bats, rolls, or bounces the ball and then touches it again before another player does so (**4**). The ball must touch the floor, except at the start of the dribble when the player may toss the ball into the air and touch it once more before it touches the floor.
The dribble is completed when the player touches the ball with both hands at once, or lets it rest in one or both hands.
The player may take any number of steps between bounces or when the ball is not in contact with his hand.
A second, consecutive dribble is forbidden unless the ball has touched the basket, the backboard, or another player, or has been batted out of his control by an opponent.

Moving with the ball A player may pivot on one foot – which he must keep stationary on the floor – while stepping once or more than once in any direction with the other foot (**5**). A moving player may stop or dispose of the ball using a two-count rhythm (**6**). The first count (one) occurs as or after he takes the ball when one or

both feet touch the ground. The count of two comes the next time one or both feet touch the ground.
If a player makes a legal stop he may then use only the rear foot as pivot unless both feet are together.
A player who receives the ball while standing still or comes to a legal stop while holding the ball may lift his pivot foot

to jump, but must pass or shoot before one or both feet touch the floor again. If he is going to dribble he must release the ball before lifting his pivot foot.

©DIAGRAM

Interference No player is allowed to touch a basket or its backboard while the ball is in or on the basket.
In attack a player in the restricted area must not touch the ball in its downward flight above the level of the ring, whether during a try for a goal or a pass, until the ball has touched the ring (**1**). No point can be scored. The opponents throw in from the sideline near the place where the violation occurred.
In defense a player must not touch a falling ball above ring level during an opponent's throw for a goal until the ball touches the ring or will obviously miss (**2**). This applies only to a throw for a goal. If such a violation occurs the ball becomes dead. The thrower gets one point if it occurs during a free throw, two if it occurs during a try for a goal. The game is restarted as if a goal had been scored and no violation had taken place.

Throwing for a goal begins with the throwing motion and lasts until the player regains his balance after the ball leaves his hands. On a jump ball neither player has possession, so even if one taps it into the basket he is not deemed to be in the act of throwing for a goal.

Restart after goal After a field goal play restarts by a throw in from, or a pass behind, the end line.
The team against whom the goal is awarded takes the throw in. Once a member of the team has the ball, play must restart within 5 seconds.

The referee or umpire handles the ball only to save time. The scoring team must not handle the ball, or a technical foul is awarded against it.
Allowance is made for accidental handling.

Time-out The game watch stops when an official signals a violation, a foul, a held ball, unusual delay in getting a dead ball into play, the end of a 30-second period, suspension of play for an injury, or any other official suspension of play.
Charged time-out Each team is allowed two charged time-outs per half, each of 1 minute. They may not be saved up for a subsequent half. One charged time-out is allowed for each extra period of play. The request for a time-out is made by the coach to the scorer, who stops the game watch when the ball is dead.

Time-out for injury The officials may order a time-out for injury; it is not charged if the injured player is replaced within 1 minute, or is ready to resume in that time. The officials must wait for the team in possession to complete its play before signaling time-out unless an immediate stop is needed to protect the injured player.
Time-in is the resumption of play after a time-out. Play is resumed by a throw in by a member of the team that had control of the ball; by a jump ball if neither team had control; or by a free throw. The game watch is restarted when the ball is legally tapped in a jump ball, or when the ball touches a player on court after a throw in or an unsuccessful free throw.

Substitutes must report to the scorer and be ready to play at once. The scorer signals the substitute's entry when the ball is dead; the substitute waits for the official's signal before entering the court. He gives the official his name or number and that of the player to be replaced (except at the beginning of the second half). A time-out is charged if more than 20 seconds is taken to replace any number of players.
After a violation the offending team may field substitutes only if their opponents do so. After a successful free throw only the thrower may be replaced, and the request must be made before the ball comes into play for the last free throw. A player involved

in a jump ball may not be replaced.
Three-second rule No player may remain more than 3 seconds in the restricted area between his opponents' end line and free throw line (the lines included) while his team has possession (including throw ins).
This rule does not apply when the ball is being thrown at the goal, is rebounding from the backboard, or is dead. An allowance may be made for a player who dribbles in to throw for a goal.
Thirty-second rule A team must try for a goal within 30 seconds of gaining possession. A new 30-second period begins if the ball goes out of play; the opponents gain the ball if it was purposely sent out. A period

continues if the ball touches an opponent but the team keeps control.
Ten-second rule A team that has possession of the ball in its back court must move it into the front court within 10 seconds. It may not return the ball to the back court.
This rule applies at all times except:
at jump balls in the center;
after technical fouls by the coach or a substitute;
when the team chooses a throw in after a foul.

© DIAGRAM

A free throw is taken after a technical foul, or a personal foul on a player in the act of shooting. After a personal foul the fouled player takes the throw. If he is about to leave the field to allow a substitute to come on, he must take the free throw first, unless he leaves because of injury. If the ball is sent into the wrong basket the throw is taken again. After a technical foul any player may attempt the free throw.

Free throw positions Two opponents must stand in the two places nearest the basket (**1**), with other players in alternate positions outside the free throw lane. The thrower stands immediately behind the free throw line (**2**). Other players can stand where they like as long as they do not interfere with the thrower or the officials, and stay outside the free throw lane until the ball hits the basket, ring, or backboard, or will obviously miss. The ball must be thrown within 5 seconds once it is passed to the thrower.

Free throw violations Generally, after a violation by the thrower's team, or if the ball misses the ring, the opponents are awarded a throw in – unless the throw is given for a technical foul by the coach or a substitute. A violation by opponents is penalized by another free throw. If both teams interfere with the ball before it reaches the basket, a jump ball occurs on the free throw line. After a technical foul by the coach or a substitute players do not line up. The ball remains in play if the last free throw for a personal foul is missed, unless it goes out of bounds; in that case the opposition takes a throw in from the sideline. If the ball misses the ring and falls on the court, it must be thrown in by the opposition from the sideline opposite the free throw line.

Fouls and violations A violation is an infraction of the rules, penalized by loss of the ball. A foul is an infraction involving personal contact with an opponent or unsportsmanlike conduct, which is recorded against the offender and may be penalized by a free throw at the basket.

After a violation the ball becomes dead, and if a goal is scored it is not counted. After a foul the official indicates to the scorer the number of the offender, who at once faces the scorer and raises his hand (failure to do so is a technical foul).

If a player not shooting is fouled, his team is awarded a throw in near the place of the foul.

If a shooting player is fouled the goal counts if scored, and an end-line throw in follows. If the goal is missed the thrower has two free throws – unless a jump ball is awarded for a double foul.

Personal fouls Blocking an opponent who is not in possession (**1**), holding, personal contact when guarding from the rear, pushing, charging, tripping, and otherwise impeding an opponent by personal contact are forbidden. Hand-to-hand contact is allowed if it is an attempt to play the ball, but is illegal if the opponent is shooting.

2 A player who obstructs an opponent and makes little effort to play the ball is not fouled if the opponent, moving normally, pushes or charges him.

3 A dribbler must not try to dribble between two opponents, or between an opponent and the boundary line, if personal contact is probable. But once his head and shoulders are past, subsequent contact is the opponent's responsibility.

4 A dribbler must not be crowded out from a straight path, but he must stop the dribble or change path if the opponent is in a legal defensive position in that path. There is no penalty for accidental contact.

Intentional foul is a serious deliberate personal foul. Persistent offenders are disqualified.

Technical fouls

By a player It is a technical foul for a player to:
disregard or be disrespectful to an official;
use unsportsmanlike tactics, such as offensive language, baiting an opponent, or delaying the game.
Unintentional technical infractions not affecting the game and administrative infractions are not technical fouls unless repeated after a warning.
Any play that continues before a foul is discovered is valid, but a penalty is given on discovery.
The penalty is two free throws for the opposing team.

By a coach or substitute It is a technical foul for a coach or substitute to:
enter the court to attend an injured man without official permission;
leave his place to follow the action from the boundary line without permission;
disrespectfully address officials, assistants, or opponents.
The coach may address his team in a charged time-out if he does not enter the court and the players do not leave it (unless permission is granted). Substitutes may listen if outside the court. As with players, unintentional technical infractions are not fouls. The penalty for a foul by a coach is one free throw; by a substitute, two free throws.
For persistent or flagrant infractions a coach may be banished from the vicinity of the court, and replaced by the captain or assistant coach.

In an interval Play resumes with a jump ball after two free throws have been taken.

Double fouls When two players foul at the same time a personal foul is charged against each. Play resumes with a jump ball between them.

Multiple fouls When two or more teammates foul against the same opponent at approximately the same time, a personal foul is recorded against each player. The offended player takes two free throws.
If the offended player was shooting, a goal counts if scored, there are no free throws, the fouls are recorded, and the ball is put into play from the end line.

Double and multiple fouls When a double foul and another foul occur at the same time, the double foul is dealt with first, and the other foul is penalized as if no double foul had occurred.

Dead ball fouls Further fouls when the ball is dead are treated as if they occurred when the initial foul caused the ball to become dead. Thus any number of fouls can be called at the same time against both teams.
If the team in possession scores a field goal all fouls are recorded, and any free throws or throw in penalties not yet taken are canceled.

Other fouls include:
a) fouls committed at approximately the same time or when the ball is dead – each offense is penalized;
b) simultaneous fouls by both teams involving similar penalties result in no free throws – play is restarted with a jump ball at the nearest circle, or the center if in doubt. Penalties awarded against only one team stand, but no team may receive more than possession of the ball and two free throws.

Disqualification follows five fouls, personal or technical. The player must automatically leave the game. A player may be disqualified immediately after a flagrant breach of the rules.

Netball

Netball is a seven-a-side team game usually played by women. As in basketball, points are scored by sending the ball through a ring at the opponents' end of the court. Players may pass the ball by throwing it but they must not run with it. Unlike basketball, players are restricted to certain areas of the court.

The court should have a hard surface. Each goalpost is supported by a socket in the ground, or by a metal base that should not protrude into the court.

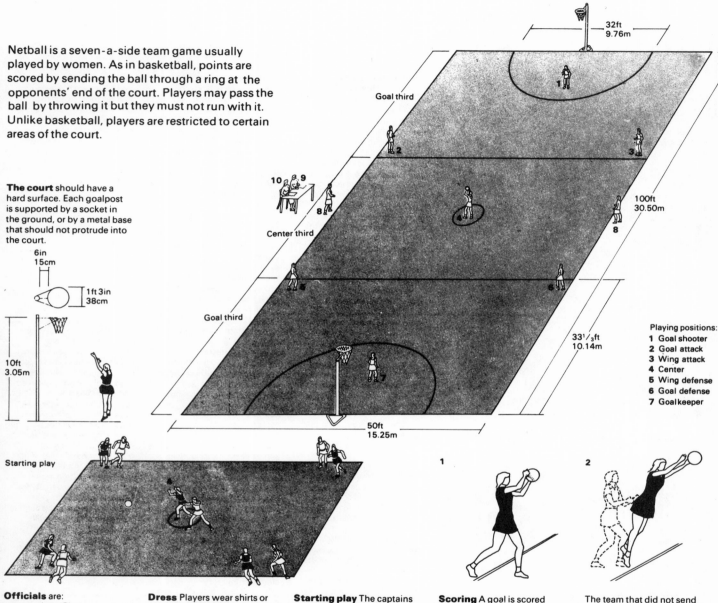

32ft
9.76m

Goal third

Center third

Goal third

100ft
30.50m

33¹⁄₃ft
10.14m

50ft
15.25m

6in
15cm

1ft 3in
38cm

10ft
3.05m

Playing positions:
1 Goal shooter
2 Goal attack
3 Wing attack
4 Center
5 Wing defense
6 Goal defense
7 Goalkeeper

Starting play

1

2

Officials are:
two umpires (**8**);
official scorer (**9**);
timekeeper (**10**).
In women's international matches, all officials must be women.
Umpires must check the court and all equipment before play starts. Each umpire controls half of the court and gives decisions on infringements in that half, though she must be prepared to assist the other if asked. Umpires keep outside the court. Each umpire has a whistle to stop and start play.

Dress Players wear shirts or blouses, skirts or shorts, socks, and shoes that must not be spiked.
Duration A game is divided into four quarters of 15 minutes each. Between the first and second and the third and fourth quarters there is a 3-minute interval. Half-time is 10 minutes. Injury time is added to each quarter in which injury occurs.

Starting play The captains toss for choice of ends or for the first center pass. The players then take up the positions shown.
The center (**4**) who is to make the first center pass takes the ball in the center circle and must pass it within 3 seconds of the starting whistle.
The opposing center may not come within 3ft of the center circle, and the other players must be within their own areas, until the whistle is blown. The first pass must go to a player in the center third of the court.

Scoring A goal is scored when the ball is sent through the ring by a goal shooter, goal attack, or a defender's attempt to intercept a shot at goal. (A penalty shot may not be intercepted.)
The shooting player must be inside the shooting circle for the goal to count.
Out of play The lines are part of the court and the ball is out of play only if it touches the ground or any object outside them.
The ball is also out if it is held by a player standing outside the court (**1**).
Players standing outside the lines cannot jump to play the ball from out of the court (**2**). The ball is returned to play by a throw in from immediately behind where it crossed the line.

The team that did not send the ball out of play takes the throw.
The thrower must be alongside her own playing area, and must not enter that area until she has released the ball. The throw must be made within 3 seconds.
If the ball is sent out of play by two opponents at the same moment, play is restarted by the umpire throwing up the ball in the court between the two players opposite where the ball went out.

Ball A size 5 soccer ball is used. It can be made of leather or rubber, and must weigh 14–16oz.

Playing areas Each player must remain within the areas illustrated (right). Players may change positions only during an interval or after an injury stoppage.

Offside A player is offside if she goes over the boundaries of her area. She may catch the ball over the line, but her feet must remain within the area.

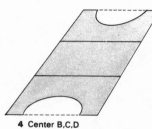

Playing areas

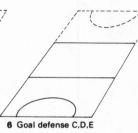

1 Goal shooter A,B

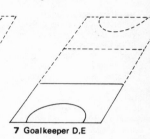

2 Goal attack A,B,C

3 Wing attack B,C

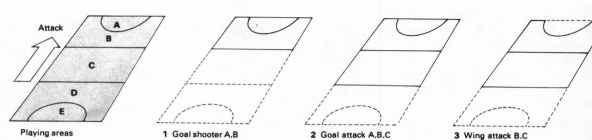

4 Center B,C,D

5 Wing defense C,D

6 Goal defense C,D,E

7 Goalkeeper D,E

Playing the ball

1

2

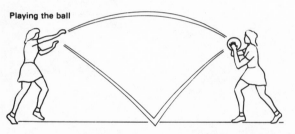

Correct passing   Incorrect passing

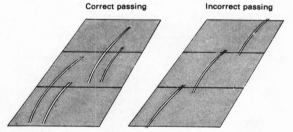

3

4

3ft 91cm

5

Playing the ball Players may catch the ball in one or two hands, or deflect it to another player.
Having taken possession, they may throw it or bounce it to another player. No player may hold the ball longer than 3 seconds.
Players may not roll the ball, run with it, throw it in the air and catch it again, bounce it, or drop it and pick it up. They may not deliberately kick it, grab it from an opponent, punch it, or play the ball while they are on the ground. Players must not use the goalpost as a means of support, nor pull at it to keep a shot out of the ring.

Passing A pass must cover a distance that allows a third player to move between the thrower and the receiver. A pass may not be thrown over a whole third of the court unless it is touched by a player in that third.
Moving with the ball A player may not step with the first foot grounded after catching the ball, but may move the other foot in any direction any number of times (**1**). Pivoting on a foot (**2**) does not count as a step. Hopping is not allowed.

Fouls No player, with or without the ball, may come into physical contact with an opponent (**3**) or try to knock the ball from a player's hands. Any player coming closer than 3ft to the player with the ball is guilty of obstruction (**4**), though any attempt at interception may be made from outside this distance. Any intimidating movement is treated as obstruction.
Penalties An offense against the contact and obstruction rules is penalized by:
a) awarding the opponents a penalty pass if the offense is outside the circle;

b) the option of a penalty pass or a penalty shot if the offense is inside the circle. In either case the offender must stand beside the thrower and take no part in the play until the ball has left the thrower's hands.
A penalty shot may not be intercepted.
Any other offense results in the award of a free pass from where the infringement took place.
A throw up (**5**) is used to restart play when two opponents commit the same foul simultaneously, or when the umpire is undecided about a ruling.

Substitutes Up to 5 minutes stoppage is allowed to treat an injured player. Substitutes for injured or ill players are allowed, but once called into play they cannot be replaced by the original players.

©DIAGRAM

Korfball

Korfball is played by two teams, each with six men and six women. The teams are positioned within three zones on the pitch. Goals are scored by throwing the ball into the opponents' basket. It is essentially a passing game that forbids physical contact, but allows tight marking.

The pitch A grass pitch is marked by white tapes; other types of pitch are marked with yellow tapes, or with ropes. Flags about 1.5m high may be positioned at the corners but not at the ends of the center lines.
Spectators are not allowed within 2m of the pitch.
Baskets should be all one color, preferably yellow. The posts are cylindrical, made of wood or metal, and fitted into the ground or a base. Posts must not protrude above the baskets.

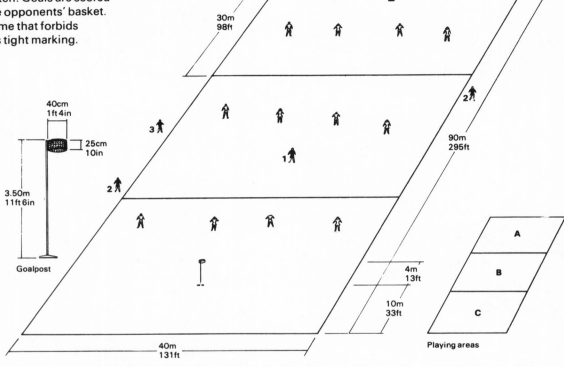

40cm 1ft 4in
25cm 10in
3.50m 11ft 6in
Goalpost

30m 98ft
90m 295ft
40m 131ft
4m 13ft
10m 33ft
Playing areas

A
B
C

Officials
The referee (1) controls the game. He decides the suitability of the pitch and weather; starts, stops, and restarts play; enforces the rules; settles disputes.

The linesmen (2) judge when the ball is out of play and draw attention to fouls and other infringements. The referee may change his decisions on their advice.
The timekeeper (3) warns the referee before the end of each half. A linesman may act as timekeeper.

Teams A team consists of six men and six women; two men and two women are positioned in each zone.
Captains Each team has a captain, who wears a distinctive band on the upper part of his left arm.
The captain may approach the referee and is responsible for the conduct of his team.

Substitutes may play only with the referee's permission. Except in case of injury, the opposing captain's permission is also required.
Dress Teams must wear distinctive uniforms. Dangerous footwear is forbidden, including shoes with strengthened toe caps, heavy heels, or metal studs, spikes, or protruding nails.

Leather studs must be no longer than 4mm.
Playing areas Every time two goals are scored players move to another zone. Those from A move to B, those from B to C, and those from C to A. When teams change ends at half time, A becomes C and C becomes A and the players in those zones change over.

Fouls Players may not:
a) touch the ball with the leg or foot;
b) hit the ball with the fist;
c) take possession of the ball when on the ground;
d) run with the ball;
e) avoid passing;
f) dribble;
g) hand the ball to a player;
h) waste time – for example by delaying a pass or free throw, kicking or throwing the ball away, or by playing the ball into the rear zones except for attacking purposes;
i) knock, take, or run the ball out of an opponent's hand;
j) push, cling to, or hold off an opponent, whether deliberately or not and even if the opponent does not have possession;
k) excessively hinder an opponent in possession;

l) hinder a member of the opposite sex or a player who is already hindered;
m) play the ball or hinder an opponent outside the proper zone;
n) throw the ball over the center zone without it touching a player on the ground;
o) shoot from a defended position;
p) shoot after cutting past an attacker or from the center zone, a free throw, or a throw up;
q) shoot when not playing against a personal opponent;
r) influence a shot by moving the post, or take hold of the post when jumping, running, or moving away;
s) violate a free throw or penalty.

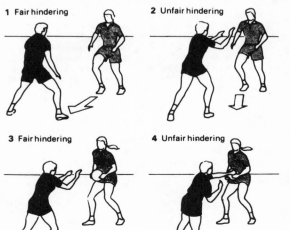

1 Fair hindering
2 Unfair hindering
3 Fair hindering
4 Unfair hindering

Interference (hindering)
Players must not impede the free movement of opponents by physical contact or other forms of obstruction, whether deliberately or not.
A defender may stand in the path of an attacker, but must not extend the arms or legs to prevent him or her from running past nor cause an unavoidable collision.
A player may attempt to influence the direction of a throw or attempt to block the ball provided he does not hinder a member of the opposite sex or someone who is already being hindered.
A player may not hinder an opponent when standing outside his or her own zone.

The ball Either a number 5 soccer ball or a special korfball is used. Its circumference must be 68–71cm and its weight 425–475g.

Starting play The home team throws off and chooses the end at which it will shoot. (Captains toss if there is no home team.) Both teams position their players in the different zones.
Duration Two periods of 45 minutes, with an interval of 10–15 minutes. Extra time is played for stoppages. The teams change ends at half time.

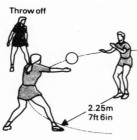

Throw off

2.25m
7ft 6in

Throw up

Throw off The ball is thrown off from the middle of the center zone to start the game and at the beginning of the second half. After each goal the team that did not score throws off.
Throw up The referee restarts play by throwing the ball up between two opponents if:
a) two opponents seize the ball simultaneously;
b) the ball touches a spectator or an object within the field of play – unless there is no doubt which side would have won possession;
c) neither side is entitled to the ball after an interruption. The referee selects two opponents from the same zone. They must be of the same sex and of similar height.

A free throw is awarded to the other team after an offense or if the ball is sent out of play.
The throw is usually taken where the incident occurred or where the ball went out of play.
It must be taken within a few seconds of the referee's whistle, and must be retaken if thrown before the whistle. All other players must stay at least 2.25m from the thrower until he makes a throwing action (whether he throws the ball or not). A violation is penalized by a free throw to the opposition; persistent violations by the award of a penalty.
A goal may not be scored directly from a free throw.

Scoring A goal is scored when the ball passes completely and legally through the opposing team's basket.
A goal is not scored:
if the attackers have committed an offense;
if the ball is thrown through the bottom of the basket and then falls back through it;
if the referee has blown his whistle, except when the offense was committed by a defender and the ball had left the attacker's hand and was out of the defender's reach before the whistle was blown.

Playing the ball Players may use their hands to catch and pass the ball. They must not play the ball with their legs or feet, or with a fist – even if the ball hits the wrist or the back of the hand.
They must not play the ball when lying on the ground, unless they fall when in possession.
No player may play the ball outside his or her zone unless he or she plays the ball in the air after jumping from that zone.

1

2

Moving with the ball
Players are not allowed to run with the ball. A player who has stopped with the ball may pivot on one foot.
If taking a long throw from a standing position (**1**), it is permissible to place one foot forward and lift the other foot before the ball has left the hands.
A player may jump and land without releasing the ball providing he or she lands in the same position.
A player who seizes the ball when running (**2**) may stop with the ball or may pass it while running provided the seizing and throwing are combined into one flowing movement.

The referee must use his discretion in such cases, considering the player's speed, the condition of the pitch, and the need for continuous play, especially in the center zone.
Passing Players must attempt to pass the ball whenever possible. They must not:
a) deliberately change position without passing;
b) throw the ball with the intention of replaying it;
c) hand the ball to another player (a pass is made only if the ball passes freely through the air or along the ground);
d) dribble the ball, ie tap the ball along the ground and run alongside it.

(If two opponents compete for a ball, one of them may touch the ball several times before seizing it; this is not a dribble and the player may shoot after playing the ball in this way.)
Out of play The ball is out of play if it:
touches a boundary line;
touches the ground, a person other than a player, or an object outside the playing area.
If the ball is out of play, a free throw is awarded against the team that last played the ball.

1 Defended position

2 Defended position

3 Shot from center zone

4 Cutting

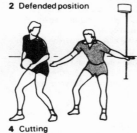

© DIAGRAM

Throwing for goal Shots at goal are forbidden when the shooting position is defended. It is defended when a defender satisfies the following conditions:
a) the defender is nearer the post than the attacker (**1**);
b) the defender is so near the attacker that he or she can touch the attacker without having to bend forward (**2**);
c) the defender faces the attacker and attempts to block the shot (whether the attempt succeeds or not)
A shot at goal may not be made from the center zone (**3**)
Cutting (**4**) occurs when an attacker runs so close past another attacker that a defender cannot follow the first attacker without the risk of colliding with the second attacker.

Cutting is not an offense in itself, but it is an offense if the first attacker goes on to throw for goal.
A penalty is automatically awarded for any offense that deprives a team of a chance to score – for example by pushing, or preventing a pass to, a player with a chance to score.
A penalty may also be awarded for an offense that illegally hinders the attackers.
A player may score directly from a penalty.
A penalty is taken from the penalty spot 4m in front of the opponents' post. It must be taken by an attacker.
The player taking the penalty must not touch the ground between the penalty spot and the post until the ball has

been thrown, nor throw the ball until the referee has blown his whistle. If he does either, the penalty must be retaken.
Other players must remain at least 3.50m from the thrower until the ball is thrown and must not interfere with the throw.
If an attacker approaches too near the thrower, the defenders are awarded a free throw.
After any violation by a defender, the penalty will be retaken if the throw fails to score.
Extra time may be added to each half for a penalty to be taken.

Team handball

Team handball is one of the world's fastest team games. It is played by two sides of seven players and five substitutes. The object is to score most goals, and attackers pass or dribble the ball with their hands until a shooting opportunity is created. When a team loses possession it immediately forms a defensive formation around its goal area.

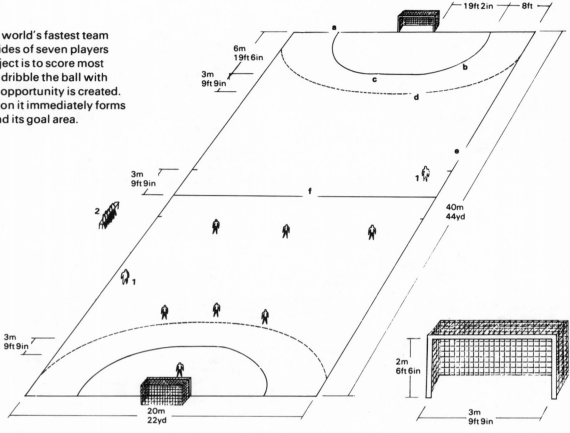

The playing area must be 38–44m long and 18–22m wide. Markings are:
a goal line
b goal area line
c penalty line
d free throw line
e touch line
f center line

Officials Each game is supervised by two referees (**1**), who are in control of the game. One referee is stationed behind the defense (the goal line referee), the other behind the attack (the court referee). The referees change position as play swings from one end of the playing area to the other; they do not change ends at half time.
There is also a scorer and a timekeeper.

Teams Each team has up to 12 players (including two goalkeepers), of whom seven (including one goalkeeper) may be in play at any time. Goalkeepers may not play in any other position, though other players may become goalkeepers.
At least five players must be on the court at the start of the game, but at other times play continues if one or both teams have fewer than five players in play.

Substitutes (**2**) may enter the game at any time and as often as required. They need not notify the timekeeper provided the players to be replaced have already left the court. Substitutes must enter from the substitutes' area.

Dress The goalkeeper must be distinguishable from his teammates. Players wear the numbers 1–12 on the backs of their shirts, the first goalkeeper wearing 1 and the second goalkeeper 12. Footwear may have studs or bars of leather, rubber, or approved synthetic material. Bars must be flat and at least 12mm wide; studs must be cylindrical and at least 12mm in diameter. Spikes are forbidden.

Start The captains toss for choice of ends or throw off.

Throw offs are taken from the center, within 3 seconds of the referee's whistle. Every player must be in his own half of the court, and opponents must be at least 3m from the thrower until the ball has left his hand.
A goal cannot be scored directly from a throw off.

Duration
Men Two periods of 30 minutes with a 10-minute interval, or (in tournaments) two periods of 15 minutes without an interval.
Women Two periods of 25 minutes with a 10-minute interval, or (in tournaments) two periods of 10 minutes without an interval.
General Teams change ends after the interval, and the game is restarted with a throw off by the other team. If the first half ends prematurely and the players leave the court, play restarts after the interval with a referee's throw from the center, or, if appropriate, with a throw from the goal, and continues until the outstanding time is completed. The teams then change ends. Time may be added on to each period and for a free throw or penalty throw. To achieve a result two extra halves may be played after a 5-minute interval. For men each extra half is 5 minutes, for women 3½. Ends are changed without an interval.
If the score remains a draw, the teams may play two more halves. If they are still drawn, the match must be replayed.

Scoring A goal is scored when the whole ball crosses over the goal line between the posts and under the crossbar.
A goal is not scored if the whole of the ball has not crossed the line when an official signals to interrupt the game.
The referee may award a goal if any unauthorized person or object prevents the ball from going into the net, provided that he is convinced that a goal would otherwise have been scored.
After a goal, play restarts with a throw off from the center by the team that did not score.
A game is won by the team with most goals when play ends.

Tackling
3

Tackling In play it is permissible to:
a) use hands and arms to win possession;
b) use the flat of the hand to play the ball from another player (**3**);
c) obstruct an opponent with the body whether or not he has possession (**4**).
It is forbidden to:
a) snatch the ball with one or both hands, or violently strike it from an opponent's hands;
b) obstruct an opponent with hands, arms, or legs;
c) catch an opponent with one or both hands, or handle him roughly by hitting, pushing, running into, jumping into, or tripping him, or by throwing oneself before him;

4

The ball has an outer casing of colored leather.
For men the weight is 425–475g and the circumference 58–60cm.
For women the weight is 325–400g and the circumference 54–56cm.

Playing the ball

Moving with the ball

© DIAGRAM

Playing the ball A player may:
a) stop, catch, throw, bounce, or strike the ball in any manner and in any direction using hands, fists, arms, head, body, thighs, or knees;
b) hold the ball for 3 seconds but no longer;
c) pass the ball from one hand to the other;
d) stop the ball with one or both hands and then catch it, providing he does not move;
e) pass the ball when sitting, kneeling, or lying on the ground.
It is forbidden to:
a) touch the ball more than once unless it touches the ground, another player, or the goal, or is fumbled or passed from one hand to the other;
b) touch the ball with any part of the leg below the knee, or with the foot;
c) dive for the ball lying or rolling on the ground, except for the goalkeeper in his own area;
d) deliberately play the ball across the touchline or the goal line.

Moving with the ball A player may take only three steps while holding the ball, but he may then stop, bounce the ball once with one hand, and then take three further steps. If a running or jumping player catches the ball, his steps are not counted until after both feet have in turn or together touched the ground. He may bounce the ball repeatedly with one hand while running with it or standing. Having caught the ball, he is allowed three steps and 3 seconds to hold it before passing.
He may catch, bounce, and catch the ball again when it has touched another player or the goal. There is no limit on the steps between bouncing and recatching the ball.
A player may roll the ball along the ground with one hand. "Bouncing" only occurs if the player has control of the ball. If the player fails to control the ball when attempting to catch it he is considered not to have touched it.

d) push or force an opponent into the goal area;
e) deliberately throw the ball onto an opponent, or move it toward him as a dangerous feint.
Goal area Only the goalkeeper is allowed in the goal area.
Any ball that touches or crosses the goal area line may only be played by the goalkeeper.
Any ball that enters and leaves the goal area without being touched by the goalkeeper remains in play.
If a player deliberately plays the ball into his own goal area and the ball does not leave the goal area without being touched, his team will concede:

a) a goal, if the ball enters the net;
b) a penalty throw, if the goalkeeper prevents a goal;
c) a free throw in all other cases.
(Play continues if the ball was not deliberately played into the goal area.)
The goalkeeper (1) may defend the goal in any way, except that he may only use his legs below the knees or his feet if the ball is moving toward the goal or goal line. Within his area he is exempt from rules limiting the number of steps or the time taken to throw the ball; outside his area he shares the restrictions imposed on other players.
A goalkeeper is not penalized for accidentally leaving his area.

A goalkeeper may not play or take the ball into his area, or touch the ball outside his area while lying or rolling inside it.
Throw in If the whole of the ball passes over the touchline a throw in is awarded against the team that last touched the ball. It is taken from where the ball crossed the line.
The thrower must:
a) face the court (2);
b) have both feet touching the ground behind the touchline (3).
A goal throw is awarded if the whole of the ball crosses the goal line outside the goal, having been last touched by an attacker or by the defending goalkeeper.
It is also awarded if the ball enters the goal direct from a throw off, throw in, or goal throw.

It is thrown by the goalkeeper from within his area, though his hands when holding the ball may be outside the court (4).
The ball is in play again as soon as it crosses the goal area line (5). The goalkeeper must not play the ball again before it touches another player. He cannot score directly from a goal throw. Opponents may not enter the area between the free throw line and the goal area line (6), nor even touch the free throw line before the throw is taken.

Advantage If a team is infringing the rules the referees may allow play to continue if they consider that the offending team is gaining no advantage from the offense.
Suspension The referees will caution a player guilty of ungentlemanly conduct. If he repeats the offense he may be suspended or excluded. Suspension is for 2 or 5 minutes. A second suspension is for 5 minutes. If a player is sent off for a third time he is disqualified.
Substitutes may not be fielded for suspended or excluded players, except for the goalkeeper (but another player must then leave the court).

Throw in

Goal throw

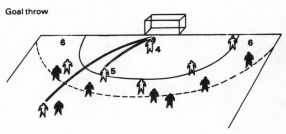

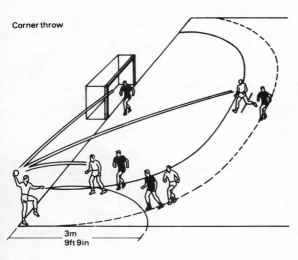

Corner throw

Corner throw If any defender except a goalkeeper is the last player to touch the ball before it crosses the goal line outside goal, a corner throw is awarded to the attackers.

It must be taken within 3 seconds of the referee's whistle, from the intersection of the touch line and goal line on the side on which the ball went out.

The thrower must keep one foot continuously on the ground until the ball has left his hand, but he may lift the other foot or move it inside or outside the court.

The hand or hands with which he holds the ball may be outside the court. The thrower must throw the ball and not just hand it to a teammate. He must not touch the ball again until it has touched another player or part of the goal.

The thrower may throw the ball in any direction and may score direct from a corner throw.

Opponents must be at least 3m away from the thrower until the ball leaves his hand.

Referee's throw A game is restarted with a referee's throw if:
a) it is halted because both teams infringe the rules simultaneously;
b) it is interrupted without any infringement;
c) a player accidentally falls on the ball and delays the game.

To take the throw the referee bounces the ball vertically where play was interrupted; but if play was interrupted between the goal area line and the free throw line, the referee's throw is taken from the nearest point outside the free throw line.

Players must be at least 3m from the referee before the ball touches the ground, and none of the attackers must be touching the free throw line or across it.

Free throw

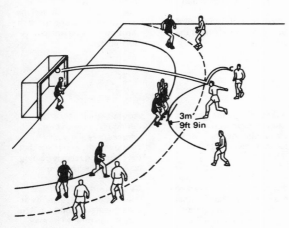

A free throw is awarded for:
a) illegally entering or leaving the court;
b) an illegal throw in;
c) illegally playing the ball;
d) deliberately putting the ball out of play;
e) illegal obstruction, tackling, or defense;
f) infringements in the goal area by court players;
g) deliberately playing the ball into one's own goal area;
h) infringements by the goalkeeper, except those which incur penalty throws;
i) ungentlemanly conduct.

A free throw may be taken immediately from the spot where the offense occurred, without the referee blowing his whistle.

If the infringement was committed by a defender between his goal area line and the free throw line, then the free throw is taken from the nearest point outside the free throw line.

If the free throw is delayed the referee will blow his whistle: the free throw must then be taken within 3 seconds, or a free throw is awarded to the other team. The attackers must not touch or cross their opponents' free throw line before the throw is taken. When a free throw is to be taken from the free throw line the defenders may stand on their goal area line.

A goal may be scored direct from a free throw.

The ball may be thrown in any direction. The defender must keep one foot continuously on the ground. He must not touch the ball again until it has touched another player or the goal. Opponents should be 3m away until the ball has left the thrower's hands.

Penalty throw

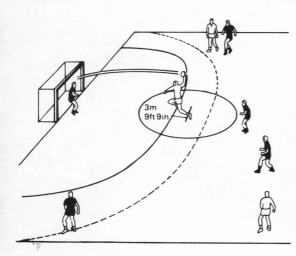

A penalty throw is awarded:
a) for serious personal offenses in a player's own half;
b) for serious personal offenses anywhere on court if they destroy a clear chance of a goal;
c) if a defender deliberately enters his own goal area for defensive purposes;
d) if a defender deliberately plays the ball into his own goal area and it touches the goalkeeper;
e) if the goalkeeper carries or throws the ball into his own goal area;
f) if a player enters the goal area to deputize for the goalkeeper without informing the referee.

The thrower may not cross the penalty throw line before the ball leaves his hand.

He must throw the ball in the direction of the goal and keep one foot continuously on the ground, though the other may be lifted or moved. Both feet must stay behind the line.

The throw must be taken within 3 seconds of the referee's whistle.

A suspended player is not allowed to take a penalty throw.

The goalkeeper must be at least 3m from the thrower, but he may move about within his area. The throw is retaken if the goalkeeper fouls.

All other players must be outside the area between the free throw line and the goal area line. Opponents must be at least 3m from the thrower until the ball leaves his hand, and they must not attempt to distract him.

If an attacker touches or crosses the free throw line before the ball is thrown: the throw is retaken if a goal is scored;
a free throw is awarded to the defense if the ball strikes the goal or goalkeeper and rebounds outside the area; play continues if the goalkeeper stops or holds the ball.

If a defender touches or crosses the free throw line before the ball is thrown: a goal is scored if valid; otherwise the throw is retaken.

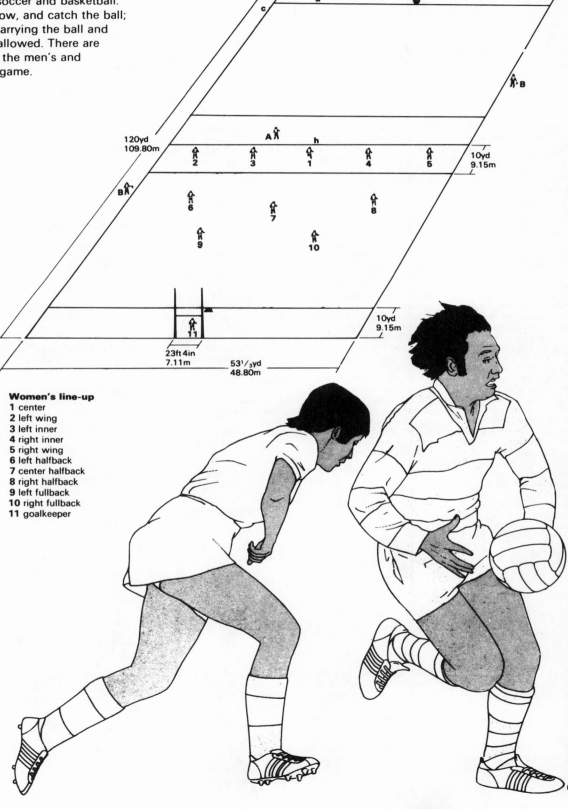

Speedball

The ball is an official soccer ball, with a circumference of 27–28in and a weight of 14–19½oz. (A basketball may be used on a small pitch.)

Speedball combines the elements of several team sports, particularly soccer and basketball. The players may kick, throw, and catch the ball; there is no offside rule. Carrying the ball and physical contact are not allowed. There are slight variations between the men's and women's versions of the game.

Pitch A full-size pitch is 120yd long by 53⅓yd wide. The various features are:
a goal;
b end line;
c sideline;
d goal line;
e restraining line;
f end zone and penalty area;
g penalty kick mark;
h middle line.
Teams There are two teams, each of 11 players.
Substitutes Each team is allowed five substitutes, who may be put into play without limitation after reporting to a linesman. They may go onto the pitch only after the ball is dead.

120yd 109.80m

10yd 9.15m

10yd 9.15m

23ft 4in 7.11m

53⅓yd 48.80m

Men's line-up
1 center
2 left end
3 left forward
4 right forward
5 right end
6 left halfback
7 fullback
8 right halfback
9 left guard
10 right guard
11 goal guard

Women's line-up
1 center
2 left wing
3 left inner
4 right inner
5 right wing
6 left halfback
7 center halfback
8 right halfback
9 left fullback
10 right fullback
11 goalkeeper

Dress Players wear uniforms of jerseys and shorts. Football boots are worn. Dangerous equipment is prohibited.
Officials A referee (**A**) who is in charge of the game. Two linesmen (**B**) on opposite sides and in different halves of the pitch, who whistle to indicate fouls, when the ball is out of play, etc. A scorer, who keeps a record of the game. A timekeeper, who, on the referee's order, excludes time when the ball is not in play.

© DIAGRAM

Duration Each game consists of four quarters lasting 10 minutes. There are intervals of two minutes after the first and third quarters, and 15 minutes after the second.
Extra periods of five minutes are played if the score is tied when the game would normally end.
Time outs Each team is allowed five time outs in a game. Each time out must not exceed two minutes. A team may not request a time out when the ball is in play unless it has possession.
A time out is not charged if requested for the purpose of substituting a player.
Starting play The team that won the toss has the choice of goal or kick off. The loser has the same choice at the start of the second half.
At the start of a half and after a score the game is started with a place kick from the center of the kicking team's restraining line. The ball must reach the opposition's restraining line unless it is touched by another player. The rest of the kicking team must be behind the ball. Their opponents must be behind

their restraining line. Artificial tees may not be used.
Ends are changed for the second and fourth quarters. In the men's game, the ball is then put into play with a punt, drop kick, or pass from the sideline at a point opposite where the ball was in play when the previous quarter ended. It is put into play by a member of the team that last had possession. In the women's game, quarters begin with a restraining line kick off by the team last in possession.
Teams also change ends for every period of extra time after the first. Each such period begins with a kick off from the kicking team's restraining line.
After a time out the ball is put in play from the sideline; the team last in possession makes a pass, drop kick, or place kick. The ball must not be put in play nearer to the opposition goal line than where it went out.

Playing the ball The method of playing the ball depends on whether it is an aerial (or fly) ball, or a ground ball.
An aerial ball is one that has been kicked into the air. It remains an aerial ball until it hits the ground.
A loose aerial ball (ie an aerial ball not in a player's possession) may not be kicked (**1**) or kneed.
It may be played with the hands or caught (**2**), but not until the kicker's foot has left the ground or the ball has left his foot or leg.
A ball that has been caught may not be dribbled by bouncing on the ground (**3**) It may be dribbled overhead (**4**). An overhead dribble is made by throwing the ball in the air and then running and catching it before it hits the ground. Players are not permitted to make a touchdown by an overhead dribble, nor make consecutive overhead dribbles.

A player who has caught an aerial ball is not permitted to run with it in his hands (**5**). If he catches the ball in the air he may put both feet on the ground. He may make one step in any direction.
A player who has caught an aerial ball may play it to his feet and make a dribble, punt, or drop kick.
A ground ball is one that is stationary, rolling, or bouncing. It may be kicked, headed, or bounced off the body.
It may not be played with the hands, but may be converted into an aerial ball with the feet.
Tackling A player may only guard an opponent who has the ball. He may attempt to play the ball, but must not hold or obstruct the opponent.
If two players are challenging for the ball they must play the ball and not the man.

A tip off is held if: two players hold the ball simultaneously; there is doubt which side put the ball out of play; there is a simultaneous foul by opponents.
The tip off takes place where the incident occurred, except that it may not be within 5yd of a boundary. The referee or linesman tosses the ball between two opponents, who stand opposite each other, between their own goal and the opponent within an imaginary 4ft circle.
The players attempt to tap the ball to a teammate. They must not tap the ball until it reaches its highest point, nor may they tap it more than twice before it hits the ground or is touched by another player.
If they fail to tap the ball before it touches the ground, the tip off is retaken.
No other player is allowed within 6ft of the tip off.
If the tip off is in the end zone and the ball is caught by an attacker there is no score although the ball remains in play.

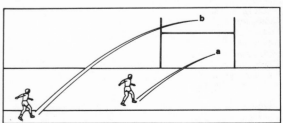

Drop kick   Field goal

Types of kick
A punt (**9**) occurs when the player drops the ball and kicks it before it touches the ground.
A drop kick (**10**) occurs when the player kicks the ball after it has bounced once.
A place kick (**11**) occurs when the player positions the ball and kicks it while it is stationary.

Scoring The methods of scoring are the same for the men's and the women's versions of the game, but the number of points scored is different.
(If a score is made after the end of a period, it is recorded provided the attackers did not give further impetus to the ball after the whistle was blown.)

Men's scoring is by:
a field goal (3 points);
a drop kick (2 points);
a touchdown (1 point);
a penalty (1 point);
an end kick (1 point).
Women's scoring is by:
a drop kick (3 points);
a touchdown (2 points);
a field goal (1 point)
a penalty (1 point).

A field goal (**a**) is scored when a ground ball is kicked or legally sent over the end lines between the goalposts and under the crossbar.

A drop kick (**b**) scores when the ball is legally caught and then kicked over the crossbar, providing the drop kick is made outside the defenders' end zone.

Converting a ground ball into an aerial ball Players may not use their hands (**6**), but they may use one foot (**7**), or both feet (**8**).

© DIAGRAM

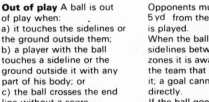

Out of play A ball is out of play when:
a) it touches the sidelines or the ground outside them;
b) a player with the ball touches a sideline or the ground outside it with any part of his body; or
c) the ball crosses the end line without a score.
A ball that rebounds off the goalposts or crossbar remains in play although a touchdown cannot be scored from it.
The ball is put in play from where it went out. It is returned by either a place kick, a drop kick, a punt, or a pass.
The player returning the ball has five seconds to play it, or it is awarded to the opposition. He must be outside the pitch when he returns the ball, and may not play it again until it has been touched by another player.

Opponents must be at least 5 yd from the ball until it is played.
When the ball goes over the sidelines between the end zones it is awarded against the team that last touched it; a goal cannot be scored directly.
If the ball goes across the sideline from a kick off the opposition kicks it into play from where it went out.
A touchback occurs when an attacker puts the ball over the sideline in the end zone or over the end line without scoring; the defense puts it in play.
A safety occurs when a defender plays the ball over the end line without scoring; the attackers put the ball in play. No score may be made until the ball has passed outside the end zone.

Personal fouls include: kicking; tripping; pushing; holding; blocking; or any unnecessary rough play against an opponent.
Technical fouls include: illegal substitution; taking more than five time outs; unsportsmanlike conduct; more than 11 players from one team appearing on the pitch simultaneously; time wasting.
Violations include: carrying the ball; touching a ground ball with hands or arms; making two successive dribbles; infringements at kick offs, free kicks and penalty kicks; infringements at tip offs; infringements when returning the ball into play; kicking or kneeing an aerial ball unless a player has first caught it.

Penalties vary according to the offense committed.
Personal fouls When a personal foul is committed by a player outside his end zone, a free kick is awarded to the opposition. It is taken either from where the offense occurred or from where the ball was when the foul occurred, whichever is nearer to the offender's goal.
When a player commits a personal foul within his own end zone, two penalty kicks are awarded to the opposition, the first without a follow-up, the second with a follow-up. The fouled player must take the kicks; the ball will be dead after the first attempt.
Technical fouls If a technical foul is committed the opposition is awarded a penalty kick without a follow-up. Any member of the team may take the kick.

Violations If a player commits a violation outside his end zone the opposition is awarded a free kick.
If he commits a violation within his end zone the opposition is awarded a penalty kick, with a follow-up if missed.
Suspension A player may be suspended from the game for unsportsmanlike conduct. A player who commits five personal fouls in a game is automatically suspended.
A free kick may be a punt, drop, or place kick. The ball may be kicked in any direction. It must travel its own circumference. The kicker may not play it again until it is touched by another player. The kicking side may stand anywhere; all opponents must be at least 10 yd away from the kicker.

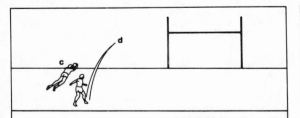

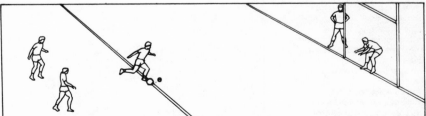

A touchdown (**c**) may be made by a player who receives a forward pass when in the opposition end zone. The receiver must be completely within the end zone and not be touching any boundary line.

An end kick (**d**) is scored by legally kicking a ground ball from within the opponents' end zone over the end line outside the goal. (Teams decide before a game whether end kicks are to be scored.)

A penalty kick (**e**) is scored when the ball is kicked into the goal from the penalty mark after a personal or a technical foul.
Only one defender is allowed in goal, and he must stand on the end line until the ball is kicked.

After some offenses the kicker's teammates are permitted to attempt to score (follow-up) if the kicker misses.
The kicker may not play the ball again until it touches another player; his teammates must be behind the ball.
The opposition (except the goalkeeper) must be outside the end zone; they may

stand on the end line outside the goal.
If there is no follow-up the ball is dead immediately the kicker misses.
If a team incurs more than one penalty kick with a follow-up for successive fouls or violations, then all but the last kick will be without a follow-up.

Gaelic football

Gaelic football is governed by some of the same rules as hurling, and is played on the same size pitch. Players may catch, fist, and kick the ball, and attempt to score points by getting the ball into the opponents' goal space. The winning team is the one that scores the greater number of points.

Pitch The minimum size of a pitch is 140yd by 84yd; the maximum size 160yd by 100yd.
Officials are :
a referee, who controls the game;
two linesmen, one at each side of the field, who change ends at half time;
four goal umpires, one outside each goalpost, who do not change ends.
Teams Each team has 15 players. Three substitutes per team are allowed, but they may only take up their positions during stoppages.
Duration Playing time is usually 60 minutes with a maximum interval of 10 minutes at half time, after which the teams change ends. Playing time for the All Ireland senior finals and semi-finals is 80 minutes.
Start The captains toss for choice of ends. Two players from each side stand in two lines at the center of the field; the other players position themselves behind the 50yd lines. The referee then throws in the ball over the heads of the players.

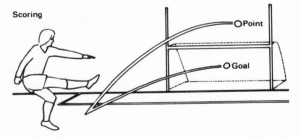

14yd line
21yd line
50yd line
21yd 19.21m
160yd 146.40m
50yd 45.75m

1 referee
2 linesmen
3 goal umpires

21ft 6.40m
8ft 2.44m
8ft 2.44m
4yd 3.66m
5yd 4.57m
15yd 13.72m
The parallelogram

100yd 91.50m

Scoring

O Point
O Goal

Scoring A goal is scored when the ball passes between the posts and under the crossbar, except when thrown or carried by a member of the attacking side.
A goal scores three points. One point is scored if the whole of the ball goes over the crossbar and between the posts, except when thrown by an attacker.

The team scoring the greater number of points wins.
The parallelogram No point is scored if an attacking player enters the parallelogram before the ball, unless the ball reenters the area before the player can leave it – provided he is not involved in the play – or unless the ball is sufficiently high to be out of reach of players in the parallelogram.

Kick out In a kick out from goal, the ball is kicked from the ground within the parallelogram.
All opponents must be outside the 21yd line; all defendants other than the kicker and goalkeeper must be outside the 14yd line.
After a score the ball is kicked out from the 21yd line; no player may stand nearer than 14yd until the ball is kicked.

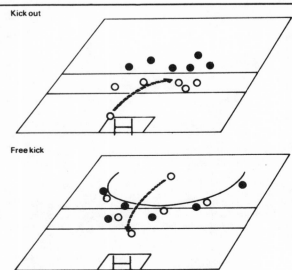

Kick out

Free kick

A free kick is awarded for all infringements, and, except for penalty kicks, is usually taken from the spot indicated by the referee.
The player taking the kick may not touch the ball again until another player has touched it, unless it rebounds off the crossbar or upright.
If a player stands nearer than 14yd, or illegally charges a free kick or a 50yd kick, the opposing team is awarded a free kick from where he stood or charged. If he charged from within the parallelogram, a penalty kick is awarded to the other team.
If a player other than the kicker kicks a placed ball, he is sent to the sideline.

A side kick is awarded to the opposition if a player plays the ball over a sideline. The ball is kicked from where it crossed the line, and is placed by a linesman. No other player may stand nearer than 14yd.
The kicker may not play the ball again until it has been touched by another player.

The ball weighs 13–15oz and has a circumference of 27–29in.

Dress Players wear shirts, shorts, and socks in their team colors, and football boots.

Fisting the ball   Passing the ball

© DIAGRAM

Playing the ball A player may:
kick the ball;
fist the ball;
pass the ball from hand to hand;
strike the ball with his hands when it is off the ground;
hop (bounce) the ball with one or both hands.
The goalkeeper, when he is within the parallelogram, may pick the ball off the ground with his hand or fist it up from the ground.
A player may not:
throw the ball;
hold the ball longer than it is necessary to pass it;
hold the ball for more than four steps, or tip the ball (bounce it on the hand).
A player other than the goalkeeper may not play a ball that is on the ground with his hands, unless he was knocked to the ground with the ball – in which case he may fist it away.

Tackling A player may charge an opponent shoulder to shoulder.
If a player who is being fairly charged deliberately turns so as to make the charge come from behind, that charge will not be termed a foul.
A goalkeeper may not be charged within the parallelogram unless he has the ball or is obstructing an opponent.

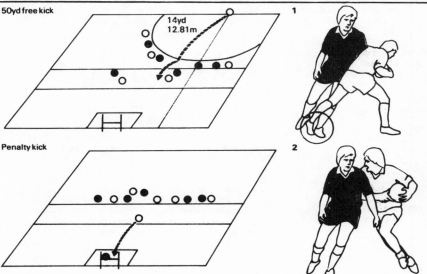

A 50yd free kick is awarded to the attacking side when a defender plays the ball over the end line. It is taken on the 50yd line opposite where the ball crossed the line.
A penalty kick If a defender commits a foul inside the parallelogram, a penalty kick is awarded to the attacking team from the center of the 14yd line.
All players other than the kicker and goalkeeper must stand outside the 21yd line.

50yd free kick

14yd
12.81m

Penalty kick

1

2

Fouls A player may not: push, kick, trip (**1**), hold, strike, or jump at an opponent; obstruct a player with his hand or arm (**2**) even if he is not actually holding him; reach from behind a player who has the ball; charge a player from behind; charge or interfere with an opponent who is not playing or moving to play the ball.
Interference If anyone other than a player prevents the ball from crossing a sideline, a sideline kick is awarded against the last player to have touched the ball.
A goal, point, or 50yd kick is awarded if the ball is similarly prevented from scoring or crossing an endline.

Australian rules football

Australian rules football is played on a large oval pitch between two teams, each of 18 players. The teams try to score goals (six points) through the center posts, or behinds (one point) through the outer posts. The ball may be kicked or punched (handballed), but it may not be thrown.

Pitch An oval grass pitch should be 110–155m wide and 135–185m long.

Officials A match is controlled by a field umpire(**1**), two goal umpires(**2**), two boundary umpires(**3**), and two timekeepers. The officials ensure that the ball is kept in play and that the game is played in accordance with the laws.

Teams consist of 20 named players, two of whom are substitutes.

Substitution A substitute may not normally enter the field until the player he is replacing has left it. If a player appears to have been so seriously injured that he cannot be removed immediately, he may be replaced before he has left the field at his captain's request and with the field umpire's permission.
A replaced player may not return to the game.

Start The captains toss for choice of ends. At the start of each quarter and after a goal the field umpire blows his whistle and bounces the ball in the center circle. (He may throw the ball in the air if the ground is unsuitable.) No player may enter the circle and, until the ball touches the ground, only four players are allowed inside the square.

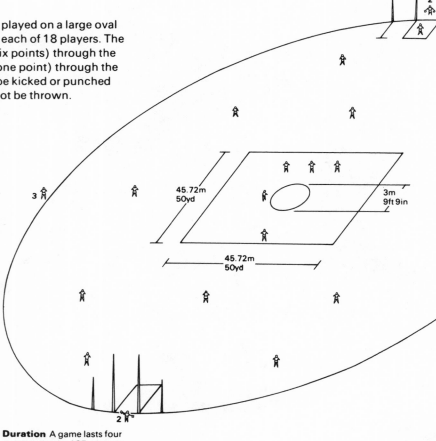

Duration A game lasts four quarters, each of 25 minutes playing time. Teams change ends after each quarter.
A maximum of 3 minutes is allowed between the first and second quarters; 15 minutes at half-time; and 5 minutes between the third and fourth quarters.
The timekeepers sound a bell at the end of each quarter. Play ceases when the field umpire blows his whistle to indicate that he has heard the bell.
Time on may be added when there has been an undue delay, for example in getting the ball when it is out of play.

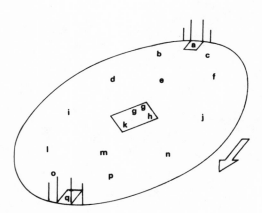

Playing positions
a full back
b right full back
c left full back
d right half back
e center half back
f left half back
g followers (two)
h rover
i right center (wing)
j left center (wing)
k center
l right half forward
m center half forward
n left half forward
o right full forward
p left full forward
q full forward

Start of play

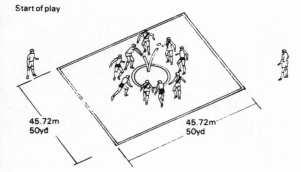

45.72m
50yd

45.72m
50yd

Bouncing the ball The field umpire bounces the ball:
a) at the start of each quarter;
b) after a goal;
c) when there is doubt over which player has taken a mark;
d) when a player kicking off from behind, kicks off from outside the kick-off lines;
e) in scrimmages;

f) when a player is unable, through accident, to kick from a mark or free kick;
g) when the ball has been bounced and has gone over the goal line, behind line, or boundary line, without having been touched by any player;
h) when a player claims a mark, the ball having been

touched, and retains possession when held by an opponent, if the field umpire is satisfied the player has not heard his call "play on";
i) when the goal umpire cannot see whether the ball crossed the goal line.

The ball is of hide with a rubber bladder inside. It is normally provided by the home team. The ball may only be changed with the consent of both captains. A standard ball weighs 454-482g and has a short circumference of 57.2cm and a long circumference of 73.6cm.

Dress Players wear jerseys, shorts, socks, and studded boots.

©DIAGRAM

Scoring The team scoring the most points wins; if the score is equal, the game is drawn.

A goal (6 points) is scored when an attacker kicks the ball over the goal line between the goalposts (the center posts) without it touching either the posts or another player.

A behind (1 point) is scored:
a) when the ball goes between the goalposts without fulfilling all the conditions for a goal to be scored;
b) when the ball touches or passes over a goalpost; or
c) passes over a behind line without touching a behind post;
d) when the ball is kicked or carried over the behind or goal line by a defender.
If a ball touches or passes over a behind post, it is out of play.
When a player is kicking at goal from a mark or free kick, the kick must be on a direct line through the mark to the center of the goal line.

Scoring after time is allowed if:
a) the ball was in transit before the first bell;
b) the player was awarded a free kick;
c) the player took a mark before the bell.
Scoring is not allowed after time if the ball was touched in transit or if it touched any player below the knee.

Scoring

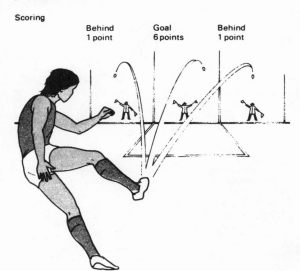

Behind
1 point

Goal
6 points

Behind
1 point

Kick off After a behind, unless a free kick has been given, the defending side kick the ball from within the kick-off lines.
No opponent is allowed within 10m of those lines. The ball must be kicked clear of the hands and feet, but does not have to be kicked over the kick-off line.

Playing the ball A player may kick the ball, but may not throw it; he may pass the ball with the hands only by handballing (punching) it. A player may hold the ball until he is held by an opponent. Players are allowed to tackle an opponent who has the ball (as permitted by the laws), or block opponents near the ball but not in possession.

Running with the ball A player may run with the ball, but he must bounce or touch it on the ground at least once every 10m.
If, when running with the ball, a player hits it over an opponent's head and catches it, he must bounce or touch it on the ground, or pass it, within 10m.

Running with the ball

10m
33ft

A mark is awarded when a player catches and holds the ball directly from the kick of another player at least 10m away (**1**). (The ball must not have been touched before the mark.)
A mark is also awarded if the ball strikes an official but is caught by another player before it touches the ground.

The player who made the mark is allowed an unhindered kick from anywhere behind where he marked. Only one opponent is allowed to stand at a mark and no other player is allowed within a 10m semicircle behind the mark. If an opponent "crosses the mark" when a player successfully kicks for goal, the goal is awarded; if no goal is

scored the player may make another kick.
A mark is allowed if it was made by a player before the ball crossed the boundary. It is also allowed on a goal line.

Holding the ball (**2**) A player is holding the ball if he retains possession when firmly held by an opponent. A player who lies on or over the ball is in possession.

Handball (**3**) A player may pass the ball with the hands only by holding the ball in one hand and hitting it with the clenched fist of the other hand.

Awarding free kicks A free kick is awarded to the nearest opponent of a player who:
a) infringes at a center bounce;
b) kicks or deliberately forces the ball out of play;
c) deliberately wastes time;
d) interferes with an opponent when the ball is out of play or is more than 5m away;

e) deliberately holds back or throws an opponent who has kicked or handballed the ball;
f) trips (**6**), kicks (or attempts to), or slings an opponent;
g) is guilty of dangerous kicking when not in possession;
h) strikes or attempts to strike an opponent with his hand, arm, or knee;

i) seizes an opponent below the knee or above the neck (including the top of the shoulder) (**7**);
j) charges an opponent;
k) pushes an opponent from behind (**8**), except when legitimately going for a mark;
l) pushes an opponent in the face (**9**);

m) pushes an opponent who is in the air for a mark;
n) handballs the ball incorrectly;
o) throws or hands the ball to another player while the ball is in play (**10**).

Taking a free kick A player may take a free kick from any point behind where it was awarded.
No other player may be within 10m and only one opponent is allowed at that distance.
The field umpire will allow play to continue if a free kick would benefit the offending side.

Holding the man (4) A player may hold an opponent who is in possession of the ball, but must allow him a reasonable chance to dispose of the ball by kicking or handballing it.
If the player in possession is forced to lose the ball (for example, by being swung off balance), play continues.

Checking (5) A player with the ball may be tackled with the hip, chest, shoulder, arms, or open hands.
A player without the ball may be pushed in the chest or side in the proper manner in accordance with the laws, providing the ball is within 5m of him.

Out of play To be out of play the ball must be completely outside the boundary line. The field umpire must be informed, and, unless a free kick has been awarded, the ball is returned to the position in the field where it went out.
If, after a mark or free kick, the player does not put the ball back into play from

outside the boundary line, the ball is returned to the field at the point where the original mark or free kick took place.
If a defender, kicking from behind the goal line or behind line, hits a post, time and another kick are allowed.

Throw in When the ball is over the boundary line, the boundary umpire may be directed by the field umpire to throw the ball over his head toward the center of the field. It must travel between 10 and 15m at a minimum height of 10m.

If an opponent deliberately delays a free kick or a mark, it may be advanced a maximum of 15m toward the offending team's goal.
If the offending team commits another offense before the free kick is taken, the kick shall be taken where the second offense occurred if that is to the disadvantage of the offending team.

If the offense was against a player who had disposed of the ball, his team may take the kick from:
a) where the ball touched the ground;
b) where the ball was caught;
c) where the ball was marked;
d) where the ball went out of play;
e) where the offense occurred.

Scoring from a free kick If an offense by an opponent occurs during a successful kick at goal, the goal will count. If a behind is scored, another kick is awarded.
If an attacker commits an offense during his team's kick for goal, no points may be scored and a free kick is

awarded to the opposition.
If a player is fouled immediately after a score and "all clear," another free kick is awarded where the offense occurred. There may then be another score before the ball is bounced in the center circle or kicked off.

Suspension The field umpire can caution offenders and report them to the controlling body, which may suspend them from further matches.

American football

In American football two teams with 11 players on the field attempt to score points by kicking goals or putting the ball behind their opponents' goal line in an approved manner. The winning team is the one that scores the greater number of points.

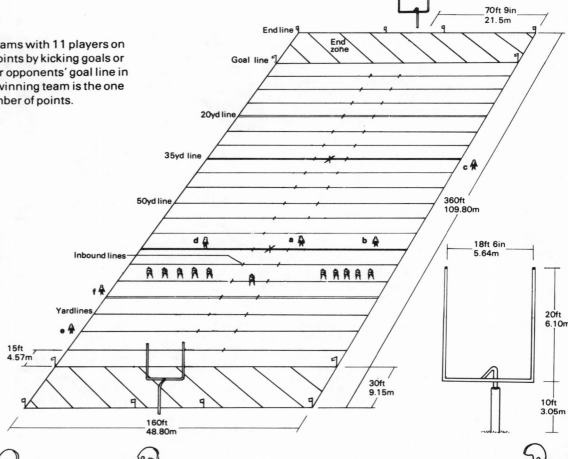

The field The area between the end lines and sidelines is the field of play.
The field is divided between the goal lines by parallel yardlines, 5yd apart. These are intersected by short inbound lines 70ft 9in from each sideline. Between the inbound lines there are marks at 1yd intervals. All measurements are made from the inside edges of the lines. Sidelines and end lines are out of bounds; goal lines are in the end zones. No benches or rigid fixtures are allowed within 5yd of the sidelines.

Kick offs

Officials have individual functions, but they are equally responsible for signaling and recording fouls. They all wear uniforms, including a white cap with a visor, and carry a whistle and a flag. The officials are:
a) the referee, who is the chief official in control of the game;
b) the umpire, with special responsibility for equipment and the scrimmage lines;
c) the linesman, who operates on one side of the field and changes sides at half time. He has special responsibility for offsides, encroaching, scrimmages, the chain crew, and covering his side zone;
d) the field judge, with special responsibility for kicks from scrimmages, forward passes across the defensive end line, and similar loose balls;

e) the back judge, who operates on the same side as the line judge, 17-20yd deep, and has to check the number of defensive players at a snap and the eligible receivers of a pass on his side of the field;
f) the line judge, who operates on the opposite side to the linesman, and has special responsibility for timing, recording team time-outs, winning the toss, the score, illegal movements behind the scrimmage line and illegal shifts.

Teams Each team fields 11 players, one of whom is the captain. No team is allowed more than 40 players in uniform.
Substitution Unlimited substitution is allowed, but substitutes are only allowed on the field when the ball is dead (not in play). Disqualified players and players requiring more than the permitted time out for injury or repairs must be substituted. Players must leave the field on their own side between the end lines.

Starting play The captains toss 30 minutes before the start for choice of kicking off receiving, or defending a goal. For the second half the captain who lost the toss has the choice.
Goals are changed at the end of the first and third periods, but possession and the relative position of the ball etc remain unchanged.
Play is started on or between the inbound lines, with a kick off (free kick) from:
a) the 35yd line, at the start of each half and after a field goal or try for extra point;
b) the 20yd line, after a safety.
Kick offs may be taken in one of the following ways:
1 a tee may be used for a place kick;
2 the ball may be drop kicked;

3 another player may hold the ball for a place kick.
A punt kick, when the ball does not touch the ground, is only permitted from the 20 following a safety.
During kick off, all players must be in bounds. The kicking team, except for the kicker and the holder of a place kick, must be behind the ball; the opposition must be at least 10yd away.
The ball must travel across the opposition line unless touched by an opponent. It should not go out of play.
After a kick off (or any other free kick), if the opposing team gains possession it may advance with the ball; if the kicking team gains possession the ball is dead and is put in play again from where it was legally recovered.

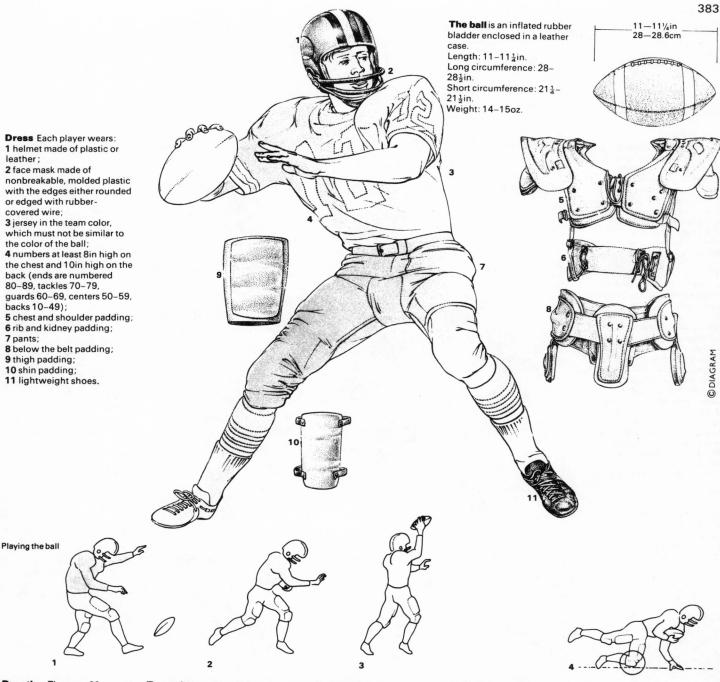

Dress Each player wears:
1 helmet made of plastic or leather;
2 face mask made of nonbreakable, molded plastic with the edges either rounded or edged with rubber-covered wire;
3 jersey in the team color, which must not be similar to the color of the ball;
4 numbers at least 8in high on the chest and 10in high on the back (ends are numbered 80–89, tackles 70–79, guards 60–69, centers 50–59, backs 10–49);
5 chest and shoulder padding;
6 rib and kidney padding;
7 pants;
8 below the belt padding;
9 thigh padding;
10 shin padding;
11 lightweight shoes.

The ball is an inflated rubber bladder enclosed in a leather case.
Length: $11–11\frac{1}{4}$in.
Long circumference: $28–28\frac{1}{2}$in.
Short circumference: $21\frac{1}{4}–21\frac{1}{2}$in.
Weight: 14–15oz.

$11–11\frac{1}{4}$in
28–28.6cm

©DIAGRAM

Playing the ball

Duration There are 60 minutes' actual playing time, divided into four quarters, of which two comprise a half. Playing time excludes stoppages and other interruptions. There is a 2-minute interval between the periods of each half; only an incoming substitute may enter the field. There is a 15-minute interval at half time.
Overtime period If the game ends in a tie a 15-minute sudden-death period is played. The kick-off is determined by the toss of a coin. The game is won by the first team to score in the extra period. If there is no score, the tie stands.

Team time-outs Each team is allowed three time-outs per half. A time-out lasts $1\frac{1}{2}$ minutes, and 3 minutes are allowed to repair equipment. A time-out is not charged to a team if a player is injured, unless:
he stays on the pitch;
he receives unauthorized assistance from the field;
the injury occurs in the last 2 minutes of a half;
a player confers with the coach on the sideline.
Otherwise, a team time-out is at the captain's request.

During the last 2 minutes' play a fourth time-out is only allowed in order to remove an injured player.
Subsequent time-outs for injuries are penalized by 5yd. The same conditions apply in the last 2 minutes of the first half if the score is equal or if the team in possession is behind.

Playing the ball Players may kick, carry, and throw the ball (**1, 2, 3**) subject to certain restrictions, such as the number of forward passes allowed.
They may not bat or punch:
a loose ball toward the opponents' goal line;
a loose ball in an end zone;
the ball when a player has possession.
A pass in flight may be batted in any direction by the defending side; but the offensive side may only bat such a ball to prevent the other team intercepting the ball.
If the player with the ball touches the ground with any part of his body except his hands or feet, the ball is dead (**4**).

A team in possession is allowed 30 seconds to put the ball into play.
A down is a period of action starting from the moment the ball is put into play and ending when the ball becomes dead (goes out of play).

Scrimmage Each team provides a line of at least seven players who stand on either side of the ball and parallel to the goal line. The line of scrimmage for each team is a line passing through the end of the ball nearest a team's own goal line. The area between the scrimmage lines is the neutral zone.

The remainder of the team, except for the player who receives the snap, must be at least 1 yd behind the scrimmage line.

The snap is a backward pass through the legs of one of the players in the line, which puts the ball into play. The snap must be one quick and continuous action. The snapper may not slide his hands along the ball before grasping it, nor move his feet or lift a hand until after the snap. Other players must be stationary until the ball is snapped. No player may enter the neutral zone or move toward his opponents' goal line at a snap.

The snap must be to a player not on the scrimmage line unless the ball touches the ground, in which case play continues as after any other backward pass.

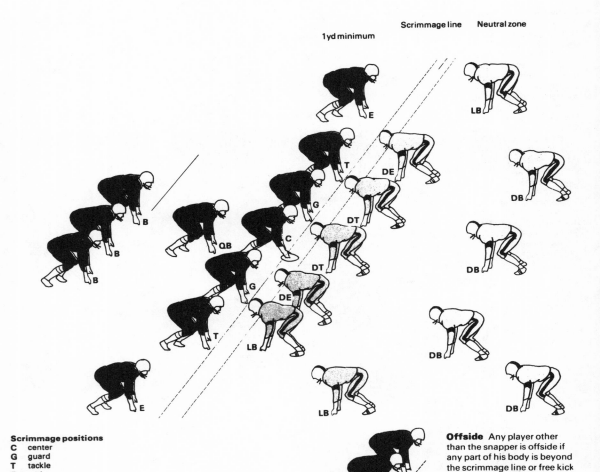

Scrimmage line   Neutral zone

1 yd minimum

Scrimmage positions
C   center
G   guard
T   tackle
E   end
QB   quarter back
B   back
DT   defense tackle
DE   defense end
LB   line backer
DB   defense back

Offside Any player other than the snapper is offside if any part of his body is beyond the scrimmage line or free kick line when the ball is put into play.

Moving with the ball When a team has possession, it is allowed four downs in which it has to advance 10 yd to the necessary line or to the goal line.

If it advances that distance while still in possession, it is allowed another four downs. If it does not advance 10 yd the ball is awarded to the opposition from the point at which it became dead.

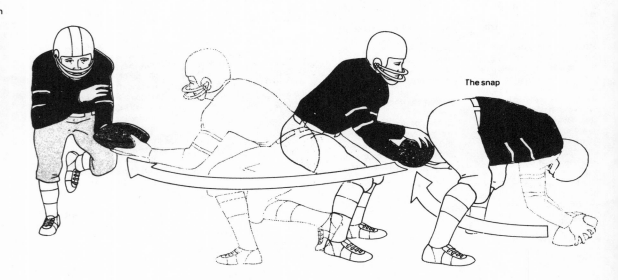

The snap

Fair catch When the ball is in flight from a kick, an opposing player may claim the right to catch the ball by raising one hand at full arm's length above his head. He is then entitled to field the ball without being impeded or tackled.
If he catches the ball it becomes dead at that spot and the captain chooses any form of free kick or a snap to put the ball in play again. The player is not allowed to advance with the ball after signaling for a fair catch.

Backward pass A runner may make a backward pass at any time. A teammate may catch the pass or recover the ball after it touches the ground in an advance. If an opponent catches the pass, he may also advance; but if he recovers it after the ball has grounded, the ball is dead and his team snaps at the point of recovery.
Fumble If a runner fumbles the ball, either team can recover and advance, whether or not the ball touches the ground. If the ball is deliberately fumbled forward, it is an illegal forward pass.
Forward pass The team in possession is allowed one forward pass during each play from a scrimmage, providing the passer (**1**) is behind his line. Any other forward pass by either team is illegal, and is a foul if made by the passing team. If an illegal pass is intercepted, play continues. All the opposing players are eligible to receive a forward pass, but only those of the passer's team who are on the ends of the scrimmage line (**2**) (except a center, guard or tackle), or are standing at least 1yd behind that line (**3**) may receive the ball.
If an opponent touches the ball, all the passing side is eligible to receive the ball. If the pass occurs behind the passer's goal line, it is a safety (when a dead ball is on or behind a team's own goal line) unless thrown from behind the line of scrimmage.
The ball at any forward pass becomes dead if it:
goes out of play;
hits the ground;
hits a goalpost or crossbar.

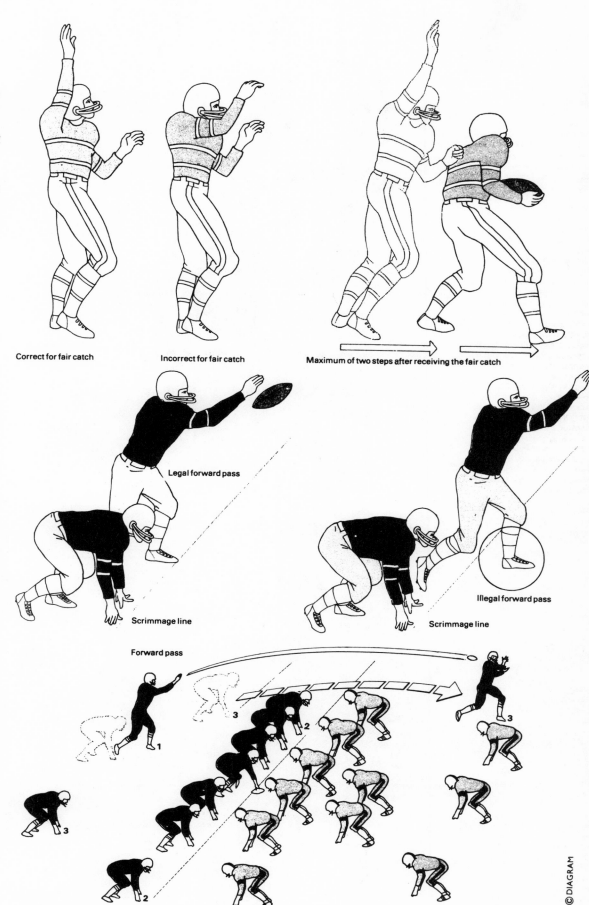

Correct for fair catch

Incorrect for fair catch

Maximum of two steps after receiving the fair catch

Legal forward pass

Scrimmage line

Illegal forward pass

Scrimmage line

Forward pass

© DIAGRAM

Scoring
Touchdown (6 points) occurs when a player carries the ball across the opponents' goal line, or recovers a loose ball on or behind the opponents' goal line.

Extra point (1 point) After a touchdown the scoring team is allowed an attempt to score an additional point from a scrimmage taken between the inbound lines and at least 2yd from the opponents' goal line. The point may be scored from a kick, another touchdown, or a safety. As soon as the opposition touches the kicked ball it is dead.

Field goal (3 points) occurs when a player kicks the whole of the ball through the opponents' goal, without it touching the ground or any of his own players, from a place kick or drop kick after a scrimmage, or from a free kick after a fair catch. After a missed field goal attempt, the ball is returned to the line of scrimmage or the 20yd line, whichever is farther from the goal line.

Safety (2 points) occurs when a team sends the ball into his own end zone and it becomes dead in its possession, or out of play behind its goal line. It is also awarded if a team in possession commits a foul behind its goal line.

The touchdown

Out of play
1 When the ball is kicked out of play, other than from a free kick, it is awarded to the opposition for a scrimmage at the inbounds spot.
2 If the ball goes out of play between the goal lines from the kick off, without being touched by an opponent, it is kicked off after a 5yd penalty against the kicking team.
3 If a player with the ball runs out of play, his team restarts play with a scrimmage at the inbounds spot.
4 If the ball is fumbled or back passed out of play between the goal lines, the side last in possession restarts play with a scrimmage at the inbounds spot.
5 If the ball is passed forward out of play, that team restarts with a scrimmage from where

the penalty for an incomplete or illegal pass is enforced.
6 If the ball is passed, kicked, or fumbled out of play behind the goal lines by the opposition, the defending team snaps from its 20yd line, between the inbounds lines.

Out of play

Direction of attack

—— Flight of ball

S Scrimmage or snap
K Kick

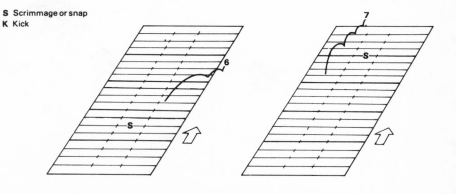

Tackling is the use of hands or arms by a defensive player in an attempt to hold the runner (the player in possession of the ball), or throw him to the ground.

Blocking is the use of the body above the knees by a defending or an attacking player in order to obstruct an opponent.

The hands must be cupped or closed and kept inside the elbows and not outside the body of either player. Arms may not be extended to push. A blocker may not push, clamp down on, hang on, or encircle an opponent. Players may block an opponent at any time, provided this does not interfere with a pass, a fair catch, a kicker, or a passer and provided it is not too rough. A wide receiver may not be cut down by a block below the knees. A wide receiver may not block an opponent below the waist if he is blocking back toward the ball (crackback block).

A defensive player may not tackle or hold any opponent except the runner, although he may use his hands or arms to remove or evade a blocking opponent.

Once a receiver is 3yd beyond the line of scrimmage, he can be hit only once by any defender.

An offensive player is allowed to assist the runner by blocking opponents, but he may not:
push or lift the runner;
cause a teammate to obstruct an opponent;
grasp or tackle an opponent with his hands or arms.
If an offensive player is trying to recover the ball after a backward pass or fumble, he may use his hands or arms only in a personal attempt to recover the ball.

The runner may ward off opponents with his hands or arms.

Fouls Players may not:
strike with their fists (**1**);
kick or knee a player (**2**);
strike the head, face, or neck of an opponent with the side, back, or heel of the wrist, or with the forearm, elbow, or clasped hands;
block an opponent and strike him below his shoulders with the forearm or elbow;
hit an opponent above the knee with a foot (**3**);
hit or trip an opponent below the knee (**4**);
tackle a player who is

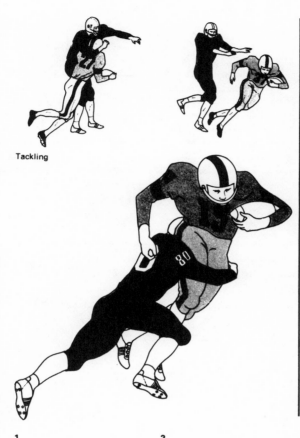

Tackling

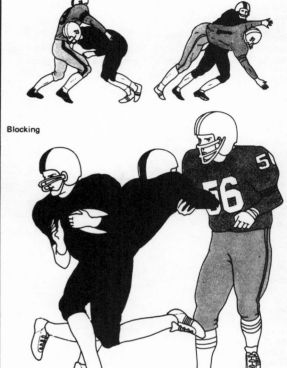

Blocking

1

2

3

4

5

6

© DIAGRAM

obviously off the field fall on a prostrate player (**5**) or on a runner after the ball is dead (piling on);
grasp an opponent's face mask.

A defensive player may not:
use his palms above an opponent's shoulders except during an initial charge at a line;
deliberately run into a kicker (**6**);
throw the runner to the ground when the ball is dead;
run into a passer after the ball has left his hand.

A runner may not advance after any part of his body (other than his hands or feet) has touched the ground (crawling).

Players must not behave in an unsportsmanlike manner.

Penalties Infringements are penalized by one or a combination of the following: loss of a down, when the team, loses that one of its downs; loss of yards, when the team concedes 5yd, 10yd, or 15yd (an offense by the attacking team may be penalized by the loss of more yards than an offense by the defending team); disqualification.

A team may be penalized by the loss of yards for offenses by its officials, who may also be disqualified.

Canadian football

Canadian football is very similar to American
football, but is played on a larger field and with 12
players in a team. Other major differences are
that: only three downs are allowed to gain 10 yd;
there are no team time-outs; there is no fair catch;
there is an extra means of scoring (a rouge); and a
greater number of distances is used to penalize
offenses and restart play.

The field The area between
the goal lines and sidelines is
the field of play. It is divided
between the goal lines by
parallel lines 5yd apart. These
lines are intersected by short
lines 24yd from the sidelines
(hash marks). The boundary
lines are outside the field of
play.

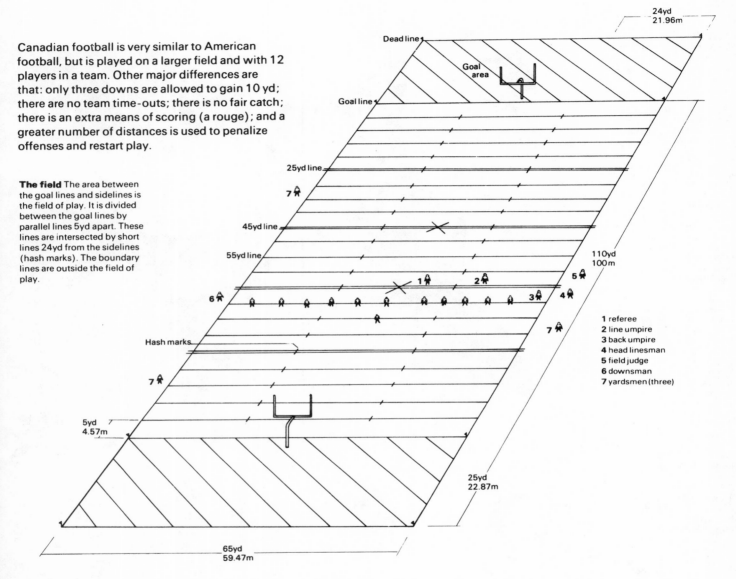

1 referee
2 line umpire
3 back umpire
4 head linesman
5 field judge
6 downsman
7 yardsmen (three)

The field officials have
individual functions, but are
equally responsible for the
conduct of the game; any of
them may stop the game for a
foul.
The referee is the chief
official in control of the game.
The line umpire has special
responsibility for scrimmage
lines.
The back umpire has special
responsibility for players of
both teams behind the
scrimmage line of the team
not in possession.
The head linesman supervises
the yardsmen, records downs,
checks substitutions, and
covers the scrimmage line and
his sideline.
The field judge has duties
identical to those of the head
linesman except for yardsmen
and downs.

The sideline officials are:
the downsman who indicates
the down, and the forward
point after each play;
two yardsmen, equipped to
assist in measurements, and
a third on the opposite
sideline;
the timekeeper, who has to
notify field officials when a
period, or half, is about to end;
the scorer, who records the
score and substitutes.
Teams Each team fields 12
players, one of whom is the
captain. Substitutes may enter
the field at any time when the
ball is dead. A replaced player
must go directly to his team
bench.

Starting play Either the
captain of the visiting team or
the one that wins the toss may
choose to kick off, receive the
kick off, or choose the goal he
wishes to defend. For the
second half the other captain
has the choice of these
alternatives.
Goals are changed at the end
of the first and third periods.
At the start of the second and
fourth periods play continues
at a point corresponding
exactly to where it was in the
other half when that period
ended.
Play is started between the
hash marks from:
the 45yd line, at the start of
each half or after a touchdown
with a kick off (the conceding
team may insist that the
scoring team kicks off from its
45yd line after a touchdown);

the 35yd line, with a kick off or
scrimmage, by a team that
concedes three points;
the 35yd line, by the
conceding team, after a safety
touch or a rouge, with a
scrimmage (except in the last
three minutes of a half, when
it must kick off following a
safety touch).

Kick offs The players of the
kicking team must be behind
the ball, except the player
holding the ball for the kick off.
Opponents must be at least
10yd away.
From a kick off the ball must
travel at least 10 yd toward
the opponents' goal line,
unless touched by an
opponent. It must hot be
kicked out of play.
After the kick off the
receiving team may interfere
with its opponents, but the
kicking team must recover the
ball before interfering with the
opposition.

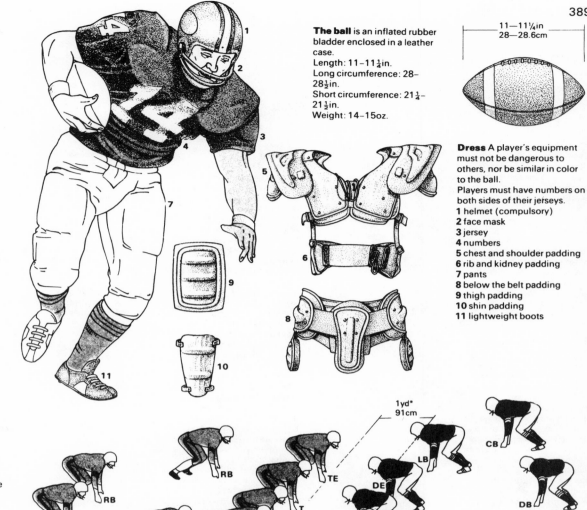

The ball is an inflated rubber bladder enclosed in a leather case.
Length: 11–11¼in.
Long circumference: 28–28½in.
Short circumference: 21¼–21½in.
Weight: 14–15oz.

11–11¼in.
28–28.6cm

Playing positions:

C	center
G	guard
T	tackle
TE	tight end
SE	split end
QB	quarter back
RB	running back
F	flanker
DT	defense tackle
DE	defense end
LB	line backer
CB	corner back
DB	defense back
S	safety
MLB	middle line backer

Dress A player's equipment must not be dangerous to others, nor be similar in color to the ball.
Players must have numbers on both sides of their jerseys.
1 helmet (compulsory)
2 face mask
3 jersey
4 numbers
5 chest and shoulder padding
6 rib and kidney padding
7 pants
8 below the belt padding
9 thigh padding
10 shin padding
11 lightweight boots

1yd*
91cm

© DIAGRAM

Duration There are 60 minutes' actual playing time, divided into four quarters. A 15-minute interval is allowed between the second and third periods.
A team is allowed to complete a play, a convert, or a penalty beyond normal time in any period.
The timekeeper stops the time when the ball is dead.

Extra time If the game must produce a winner and the score is tied at full time, extra periods of 20 minutes, divided into halves, are played. Each 20 minutes must be completed.
There are no team time-outs.

Playing the ball Players may kick, carry, strike, and throw the ball, with certain exceptions.
A player has possession if the ball is firmly held by a hand, arm, or leg, or under the body. If two opponents have possession, the ball is awarded to the player who gained it first, or, if possession was simultaneous, to the team that last touched it.
If the player with the ball touches the ground with any part of his body except for his hands or feet, the ball is dead. If a player gains possession in his own goal area and is held or kneels on the ground, the ball is dead. The team in possession is allowed 20 seconds to put the ball in play.

Moving with the ball When a team has possession it is allowed three downs to gain 10yd. If it gains the 10yd, it is allowed another three downs. If it does not gain the 10yd, the ball is awarded to the opposition from the position in which it became dead.
A down is measured by the forward point of the ball. If it is necessary to measure the distance gained, the ball is rotated so that its long axis is parallel to the sidelines. A down starts from when the ball is put into play at a scrimmage.

Scrimmage The teams are separated by the scrimmage zone, which is the area between the sidelines that extends on each side of the scrimmage line.
The scrimmage line is an imaginary line, parallel to the goal line, through the point of the ball farthest from the goal of the team in possession. The players of the team in possession must be either clearly in the line (within and behind the scrimmage line) or in the backfield (clearly behind the line players). There must be at least seven line players, five of them in a continuous line and ineligible for a pass. The two end players and all backfield players may receive a pass. The opponents must be at least 1 yd behind their side of

the scrimmage line until the ball is in play.
The snap One of the line players (the center) facing the opposition goal, snaps the ball back in one continuous action. He may not handle the ball again until it has been played by another player.
No player is allowed to move so as to draw an opponent offside deliberately. No line player may move at all after adopting his stance, until the ball is snapped. If a team is in possession within a yard of the goal line the scrimmage occurs 1yd from that goal line.

Offside A player is offside if the ball has last been touched by one of his own team behind him, except when onside, hand off, and forward pass rules apply. A player in an offside position is played onside if the ball touches an opponent or if a teammate carries the ball past him. If a player moves across the line of scrimmage before the ball is put into play, he is also offside.

Scoring

Touchdown (6 points) is made when the ball is in the possession of a player who is in his opponents' goal area, or who crosses or touches their goal line.

Convert (1 or 2 points). After a touchdown the scoring team is allowed an attempt to score extra point(s) from anywhere on or outside the opponents' 5yd line. A successful place kick counts 1 point; running, or completing a pass, into the goal area counts 2 points.

Field goal (3 points) Scored by a drop kick or a place kick (except at a kick off) when the ball goes over the crossbar without touching the ground after being kicked.

Safety touch (2 points) Scored when a team plays the ball into its own goal area and the ball becomes dead in the team's possession or touches or crosses the dead line or sideline in goal.

Rouge or single point (1 point) Scored when the ball is played into the opposition goal area and becomes dead in the opponents' possession, or it touches or crosses the boundary lines or touches the ground, player, or any object beyond those lines.
If a team, having played the ball into its own end zone, makes an offside pass in its goal area and retains possession, the opposition may claim 2 points. If a team gains possession in its area from an opponent's kick or fumble, and makes an offside pass, the opposition gains 1 point or the "option."

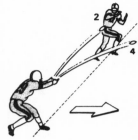

Passing

Forward pass (1) Only one forward pass is allowed in any one down. It is thrown from behind the scrimmage line toward the opponents' dead line and to any eligible receivers. The ball must not touch the ground, goalposts, crossbar, officials, or other object.

Onside (or lateral) pass (2) occurs when the ball is thrown, handed, knocked, batted, or fumbled by a player parallel to, or in the direction of, his own dead line. The place where the ball strikes the ground, a player, or an official, or is caught or goes out of play determines whether it is an onside or offside pass.

Hand off pass (3) occurs when the ball is handed, not thrown, to another player behind the scrimmage line. There are no restrictions on the number of hand off passes during a play, but the player receiving the ball must not occupy a lineman's position.

Offside pass (4) occurs when the ball is passed from in front of the scrimmage line toward the opponents' dead line, or when it is knocked with the hand or arm toward the opposition dead line. If a player is offside when a teammate fumbles or blocks the ball in an offside direction, he may recover the ball subject to a penalty. Offside passes in a team's own goal area may be penalized by:
the loss of points;
the option of taking advantage of playing from that position;
a scrimmage (on its own 10yd line if it intercepts an opponent's forward pass and then makes an offside pass from within its own goal area).

Tackling is grasping the ball carrier with hands or arms.

Interference is when a player obstructs, blocks, or charges an opponent in order to prevent his approach to the ball carrier, potential ball carrier, or the ball.

Screening is interference without direct contact.

Defensive players may only tackle the player with the ball, although they may interfere with opponents who are attempting to shield him and who are penetrating their defense for a forward pass.

Offensive players, except when the ball has been thrown forward or kicked across the scrimmage line, may interfere with any opponent in order to protect the player with the ball. After a forward pass across the scrimmage line, only the eligible receivers may interfere with opponents.

Out of play

Out of play The ball is out of play if it or the player in possession touches a sideline (in front of or beyond the goal), dead line, the ground, or any object beyond those lines.
Generally, the ball is put into play at a scrimmage between the hash marks opposite the place where it went out. When the ball is carried off the field or is thrown out by a forward pass, that team retains possession, except on the third down when no yards have been gained.
When the ball is kicked out of play the opposition is awarded possession at that point. But if a kick off is kicked out, they may instead have the kicking team repeat it from 10yd further back. If a kick off goes through the

opponents' goal area untouched, or hits the goal, the ball is dead. The opposition puts it into play at its 25yd line.
fumbled out of play or touches a player before going out, the team that last touched the ball has possession. It is scrimmaged 24yd from the sideline opposite the point at which it went out or was last touched, whichever is nearer the goal line of the team in possession.
A player who goes off the field, except as a result of bodily contact, must remain out of that play.

Fouls Players may not:
hold an opponent, other than the one with the ball, with their hands or arms;
tackle an opponent, other than the one with the ball, from the rear (clipping);
kick an opponent;
strike an opponent with the fist, heel of the hand, knee, or elbow;
charge or fall on a player with the ball when it is dead (piling);
trip an opponent;
tackle an opponent off the field;
grasp an opponent's face guard;
combine together or give assistance, by direct contact, to the rear of the ball carrier (**5**);
use the body of another player to rise up in an attempt

to play the ball (**6**);
hold hands or lock arms at a scrimmage (**7**);
touch the kicker when he is kicking from a scrimmage;
contact an opponent in any other unnecessarily rough or unfair manner;
abuse opponents, officials, or spectators.

Penalties Infringements are penalized by any one or combination of the following:
loss of a down, when the team loses that one of the permitted number of downs;
loss of yards, when the team concedes 5, 10, or 25yd (but it cannot also lose that down);
loss of the ball;
an option, when the non-offending team may choose between the penalty or the advantage of the position;
a first down, awarded

automatically to the team in possession when the other team commits certain offenses;
removal of a player, with substitution permitted.
A team will be penalized on the field for offenses by its officials, who may also be disqualified.

COMPARISON OF CANADIAN AND AMERICAN FOOTBALL

A summary of the major differences between the two North American football games.

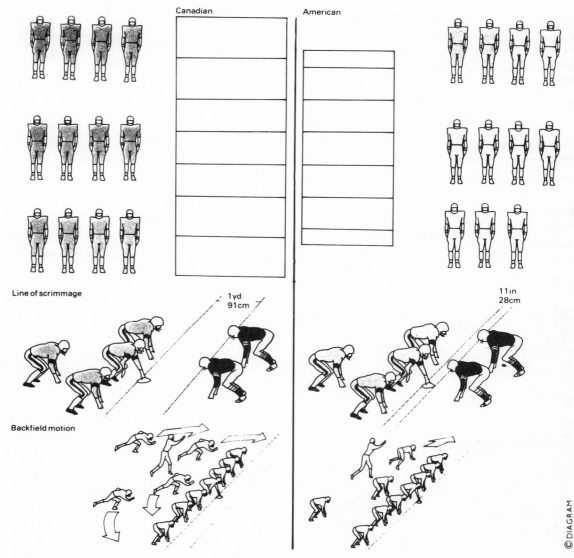

Canadian

American

Line of scrimmage

1yd
91cm

11in
28cm

Backfield motion

© DIAGRAM

Field The Canadian field is larger than the American field. Canadian goalposts are on the goal line; American goalposts on the end line.
Teams Canadian football allows 12 players on the field. American football allows 11.
Ball into play In Canadian football time is allowed for lining up and substitution, and the attackers then have 20 seconds in which to put the ball into play.
In American football the attackers have 30 seconds to put the ball into play.
End of a period In Canadian football there is a further complete play if any time remains when a play ends. In American football there is no further play if a period ends before the ball is returned to play.

Time-outs There are no team time-outs in Canadian football.
American football allows three team time-outs in each half.
Kick offs In Canadian football there is a kick off from the 45yd line at the start of each half and after a touchdown.
In American football there is a kick off from the 35yd line at the start of each half and after a score.
Punt returning In Canadian football there is no fair catch. Tacklers may not approach within 5yd of the receiver until he has touched the ball; the punter or a player "onside" to the punter, however, may legally recover the ball if he gets to it before the receiver. The punt returner concedes a rouge if

he fails to run or kick the ball out of the end zone. In American football punts may be allowed to roll dead; be received for a fair catch; or be returned with the aid of blocking by the returning team. If the receiving team touches or fumbles the ball, the kicking team may legally recover it.
There is a touch back if the punted ball crosses the goal line.
Downs Three downs are needed in Canadian football to make 10yd.
Four downs are needed in American football to make 10yd.

Scrimmage line In Canadian football the offensive line is at the forward point of the ball and the defensive line 1yd beyond it. In American football the offensive and defensive lines are at each end of the ball before it is put into play.
Backfield motion In Canadian football all backfield players may move in any direction at a snap. In American football only one attacking back may move backward or parallel to the line of scrimmage at the snap.
Scoring One point is scored for a single or rouge in Canadian football.
There is no equivalent in American football.

Penalties Canadian football has 5, 10, 15, and 25yd penalties, and penalties are the same for attackers and defenders.
In American football there are 5, 10, and 15yd penalties, and differences between offensive and defensive penalties.

Rugby union

Rugby union is an amateur game played by two teams of 15 players, who are allowed to carry, kick, and throw the ball. Players attempt to score points by placing the ball over the opponents' goal line (a try), or by kicking it over the crossbar (a goal).

The pitch must be of grass, or clay or sand provided the surface is not dangerous. The touchlines are not part of the playing area.

Officials The referee (1) is in charge of the game, although he may take the advice of the touch judges (linesmen). He uses a whistle to indicate the start and end of play, scores, and infringements. Players must not dispute his decisions and must obtain his permission to leave and reenter the pitch during play. The two touch judges (2) remain off the playing area except when standing behind the posts to judge a kick at the goal. They indicate touch and other decisions with a flag.

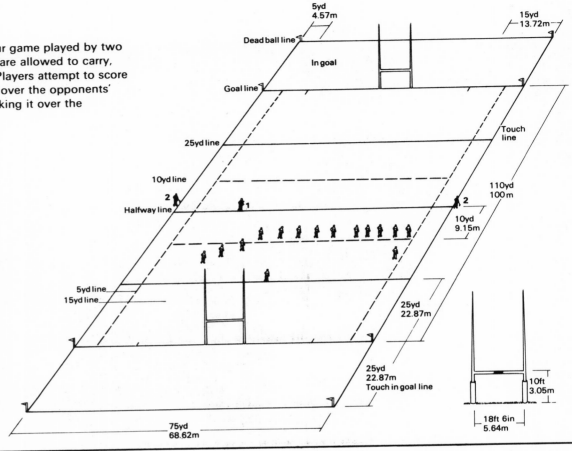

Rugby league

Rugby league is similar to the union game from which it developed, but it has its own procedures and a different style of play. The game is played by professionals, and there are 13 members in each team.

The pitch conforms to the measurements shown in the diagram. The touch lines are not part of the playing area.

Officials The referee (1) controls the game and its timing, and signals with a whistle.
Two touch judges (2) assist the referee. They stand on either side of the pitch, except when judging kicks at goal. Each has a flag to signal when the ball goes out of play.

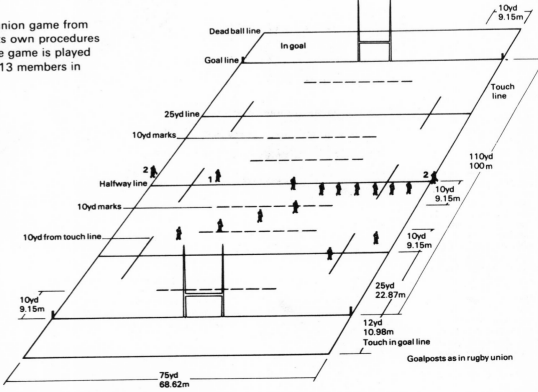

Ball A rugby ball is oval and made of leather or other approved material. It weighs $13\frac{1}{2}$–$15\frac{1}{2}$oz. A rugby league ball is slightly shorter and thinner than a rugby union ball.

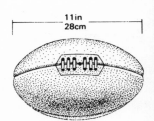

11in
28cm

RUGBY UNION
Starting play Captains toss for kick off, which is a place kick (**1**) from the center spot. A place kick is also taken by the conceding team after a goal, and a drop kick (**2**) after an unconverted try. Opponents must stand behind their 10yd line, which the ball must cross unless first touched by an opponent. If the ball goes into touch (crosses the touchline) without bouncing, opponents may accept the kick, have it retaken, or scrummage in the center.
If the ball goes into touch in goal, over the dead ball line, or after some touch downs, defenders restart with a drop out (a free drop kick) on or behind the 25yd line.

If the ball does not cross the 25yd line, the opposition may choose to form a scrum or to retake the kick. If the ball pitches directly into touch, they may also accept the kick. Opponents may not cross the 25yd line until the kick is taken.
Scoring
A try (**3**) (4 points) is scored by grounding the ball in the opponents' in goal area. The player must be touching the ball as it is grounded. A penalty try may be given if a foul prevents a try.
Conversion (2 points) A place kick or drop kick at goal follows a try. It is taken on a line through where the try was scored; except after a penalty try, when it is taken as if the try was scored between the posts.

The kicker's team must be behind him; opponents must remain behind the goal line until the kicker runs at the ball, when they may charge or jump.
A dropped goal (3 points) is scored during play when the ball is dropped from the hands and kicked over the crossbar on the half volley.

A penalty goal (3 points) is scored from a free kick awarded for an infringement. (Goals are valid if the ball strikes the crossbar or posts, or is blown back after passing correctly through the posts.)

UNION/LEAGUE
Duration There are two halves of 40 minutes each. Teams change ends at half time after a five-minute interval. The referee adds on any time lost by stoppages.
Substitutes Union only allows substitutes in internationals and certain trials, when a maximum of two injured players may be replaced. Substituted players may not rejoin the match.
League allows two substitutes for any reason, but only with the referee's permission during a stoppage or when the ball is out of play.
Playing the ball A player may run with the ball and kick it in any direction, but he may not throw or knock it toward his opponents' goal line. Any player holding the ball may be tackled.
Touch down In both league and union a defender may ground the ball in his own in goal area.
In league, defenders restart the game with a drop out from the goal line.
In union, it is restarted by a scrum 5yd from the goal line if the player carried the ball over it, or by a drop out from the 25yd line if he was behind the line. Both occur opposite the point of grounding.

Dress Players wear jerseys, shorts, socks, and boots. Headbands or scrum caps may be worn. Shin guards are optional, and league players may also wear other protective clothing, provided it is not rigid.

1 Place kick

2 Drop kick

3 Try

Goal

Headband

Scrum cap

Shin guard

© DIAGRAM

RUGBY LEAGUE
Starting play Captains toss for ends, and the losing team kicks off with a place kick from the center spot. A place kick is also taken by the conceding team after a try or a goal.
Defenders restart the game with a place kick from the center of the 25yd line after an attacker:
sends the ball into touch in goal or over the dead ball line;
infringes in the in goal area;
is tackled in goal before he grounds the ball.
The game is restarted by the defending team with a drop kick from the center of the goal line after a defender:
sends the ball over the dead ball line or into touch in goal;
breaks the laws accidentally;

touches down, is tackled, or kicks straight into touch from his own goal area. The kicker must not cross the appropriate line, kick the ball straight into touch, or send it less than 10yd. Opponents must allow the ball to travel 10yd before touching it.
Scoring
A try (3 points) is scored by grounding the ball in the opponents' in goal area, or if opposing players simultaneously ground the ball in the in goal area. It is also scored if the ball touches the ground in front of the goal line, but the player's momentum then carries him over the line.
A penalty try may be awarded if a foul prevents a try.

A conversion (2 points) must be a place kick.
A drop goal (3 points in England, 1 point elsewhere).
A penalty goal (2 points) may be drop kicked.

Rugby boots have studs of leather, rubber, aluminum, or plastic, which must be circular and securely fixed. In league, boot studs must be at least $\frac{5}{16}$ in in diameter.

RUGBY UNION

Scrummage Players are formed into a scrummage, usually by their forwards, at or near the place of the infringement and parallel to the goal lines.
There should be at least three players in each front row. The front rows interlock, leaving a clear tunnel between them. Other

Scrum positions and numbers in rugby union are usually:
1 prop forward
2 hooker
3 prop forward
4 lock forward
5 lock forward
6 flank forward
7 flank forward
8 No. 8 forward
9 scrum half back
10 stand off or outside half back
11 left wing threequarter back
12 left center threequarter back
13 right center threequarter back
14 right wing threequarter back
15 full back

forwards bind with at least one arm onto a teammate; opponents may be held with only one arm to steady the scrum. Other players remain behind the line of the rear foot of their pack.
The scrum should be steady until the ball is put in by the scrum half of the non-offending team. He stands 1yd away, midway between

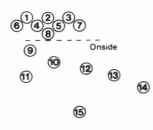

Onside

the front rows, holding the ball in both hands between his knee and ankle. He aims it to hit the ground just beyond the width of the near prop's shoulders. If the ball runs straight through the scrum, it must be put in again.
If there is any doubt, the ball is awarded to the team moving forward.
The two hookers strike for possession; they must not be lifted off their feet.
Front players must not raise a foot until the ball touches the ground. All players may try to play the ball, but they must keep one foot on the ground. No player may handle the ball.
A ruck occurs in free play when one or more players from each team close around the ball when it is on the ground

between them. Players must be on their feet, and must bind with at least one arm around a teammate.
Players may not:
return the ball into the ruck;
handle it or pick it up except to handle a try;
jump on other players;
make the ruck collapse;
stop the ball coming out (which is penalized by a penalty kick at the place of the infringement).
A maul occurs in free play when one or more players from each team close around a player who is carrying the ball. It ends:
if a player with the ball frees himself;
in a ruck if the ball becomes loose;
in a scrummage if the ball becomes unplayable.

Ruck

Maul

A mark is awarded when a stationary player with both feet on the ground catches the ball cleanly and cries "mark." He may catch it directly from a kick, knock on, or throw forward. He may then take a free kick, which may be directly at the goal or to gain an advantage; in both cases it must be taken from on or behind where the mark was made.

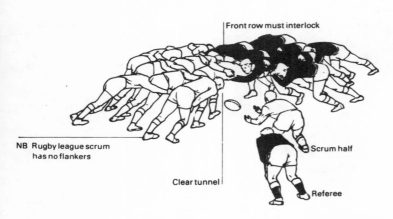

Front row must interlock

NB Rugby league scrum has no flankers

Clear tunnel

Scrum half

Referee

RUGBY LEAGUE

A scrum is formed by the forwards of each side to restart play whenever the game is not restarted by a kick off, a penalty kick, a drop out, or a play-the-ball.
It is normally formed where the infringement occurred, but it must be at least 10yd from the touchline and 5yd from the goal line. The six forwards pack into a three-two-one formation. Once the scrum is correctly established, the forwards may push to gain an advantage.
The ball is played straight into the center of the tunnel by the scrum half of the non-offending team.
The front row forwards may not raise a foot until the ball is put in, and may not strike the ball before the hookers.

Onside

No players may handle the ball. If a ball goes into touch, play is restarted by a scrum 10yd infield from that point. If a forward ball goes straight into touch, a scrum is formed where contact with the ball was made. If a penalty kick is sent straight into touch, the kicking side restarts with a place kick 10yd infield from that point.

Scrum positions and numbers in rugby league are usually:
1 full back
2 right wing threequarter
3 right center threequarter
4 left center threequarter
5 left wing threequarter
6 stand off half
7 scrum half
8 front row prop forward
9 hooker
10 front row forward
11 second row forward
12 second row forward
13 loose forward

Tackling A player is tackled when he:
is held by one or more opponents and the ball or his arm holding the ball touches the ground;
is held so that he can make no progress;
is lying on the ground and an opponent lays a hand on him.
He must not move from the place where he is tackled.

The play-the-ball

5yd
4.57m

5yd
4.57m

The play-the-ball In rugby league, a tackled player is allowed to be released immediately he indicates that he wishes to play-the-ball. He must then without delay stand up, face forward, and drop or place the ball on the the ground in front of his foremost foot. Once on the ground, the ball may be kicked or heeled in any direction, and from that contact the ball is in play. One opponent may mark the tackled player, and a player from each side may support these two players; all other team members must stand at a distance of at least 5yd behind his teammate in the play-the-ball.

The team in possession is allowed three successive play-the-balls (five in Britain and Australia), but at the fourth tackle (the sixth in those countries), providing an opponent has not touched the ball in this period, play is restarted by a scrum.

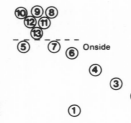

Line out If the ball or the player carrying it touches or crosses the touchline, the ball is "in touch" and in union play is restarted by a "line out."

The ball is thrown in at right angles to where it went into touch and between players of both teams who line up to receive the ball. Other players must be 10yd away from the imaginary line bisecting the two lines of players. The thrower is from the team that did not touch the ball last. After an improper throw opponents choose to throw in or scrummage.

If the ball pitches straight into touch, a line out occurs opposite to where the ball was kicked or where it went into touch, whichever is nearer the kicker's goal. This does not apply to penalty kicks or if the ball is kicked from within the player's 25yd line.

Unless jumping or peeling off from a scrummage, players must stay in the line at least 1yd from the next player in their team and 2ft from an opponent, until the ball touches the ground or another player.

Peeling off in order to catch the ball from a teammate in the line may only occur after the ball has left the thrower's hands. Players must not push, charge, bind, lift, or move within 5yd of the touchline or beyond the farthest player, until the ball has passed overhead. Any consequent scrum must be 15yd infield.

Line out

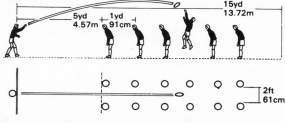

A ruck at a line out is regarded as a maul; it will not end a line out until all the feet of the players involved have moved beyond the line of touch.

Fouls Players may not: strike, hack, kick, or trip an opponent;
make a dangerous tackle or tackle with a stiff arm;
willfully charge, obstruct, or grab an opponent who does not have the ball, except in a ruck.
Obstruction and deliberate time wasting are penalized by a penalty kick or a penalty try.
It is not an offense to shoulder charge a player in possession.
A deliberate knock on or forward throw is punished by a penalty kick or, if unintentional, by a scrummage. It is not an offense if:
the ball bounces forward after hitting the ground or a player;
a fair catch is allowed;
the ball is charged down;
the ball is knocked forward in an attempt to catch a kick, but is retrieved before it hits the ground.
It is always an offense if the ball is knocked forward during an attempt to pick it up.

Offside A player is offside if he is in front of the ball when a teammate is playing it. He may be penalized if he then plays the ball or obstructs or tackles an opponent.
An offside is penalized by a penalty kick at the point of infringement, or, in free play, the option of a scrum at the place the offenders last played the ball.
A player in an offside position may be made onside if a teammate carries the ball past him, or kicks the ball past him and pursues it.
No penalty will be given if the player's position is unavoidable and he retires immediately and without interfering with an opponent. If he cannot avoid contact he is "accidentally offside" and a scrummage is formed.

Penalties The referee may caution and dismiss players and award penalty kicks and tries. A dismissed player is reported and may not rejoin the match.
A penalty kick may be taken by any player, but he must indicate if he is making a shot at goal.

Advantage If a non-offending team gains a tactical or territorial advantage from an offense by the other team, the referee does not whistle for an infringement and play continues.
Advantage cannot be played: at a kick off;
when the ball emerges from either end of a tunnel;
from an incorrect drop out;
when the free kick is void;
when the referee creates an advantage by touching the ball or the player carrying it — in which case a scrum should be awarded to the team that last played the ball.

1 Knock on

2 Knock on

5 Offside interference

6 Offside tackle

Fouls It is forbidden to: deliberately trip, strike, or obstruct a player:
attack unnecessarily an opponent's head;
drop knees-first on to a grounded opponent;
use a dangerous throw in a tackle;
deliberately break the laws;
use obscene language;
argue with the referee;
reenter the play without the referee's permission;
abuse the spirit of the game.
A knock on occurs when the ball is propelled forward from a player's hand (**1**) or his arm (**2**). An accidental knock on will not be punished if the player kicks the ball before it hits the ground. Charging down a kick does not count as a knock on.

3 Forward pass

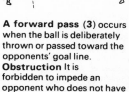

© DIAGRAM

4 Obstruction

A forward pass (**3**) occurs when the ball is deliberately thrown or passed toward the opponents' goal line.
Obstruction It is forbidden to impede an opponent who does not have the ball (**4**).
Offside Unless in his own goal area, a player is offside when the ball is played or held by a member of his own team behind him.
An offside player must make no attempt to join in the play (**5**). Nor must he encroach within 5yd of any player who is waiting for the ball (**6**); he must move 5yd from any opponent who gains possession.
He may be placed onside if:
an opponent carries the ball more than 5yd;

an opponent touches the ball without holding it;
a teammate runs in front of him with the ball or chases a kick forward;
he retires behind the point where the ball was last played by a teammate.
Penalties The referee may caution or dismiss offenders and award penalty kicks for misconduct, unless this acts to the offending team's advantage.
The penalty kick is taken from or behind where the offense occurred, by punting, drop kicking, or place kicking the ball. The kicker's team must remain onside; opponents must retire 10yd or to their goal line.

If a defender who scores a try is fouled by a defending player, a penalty is awarded at the center of the line 10yd from the goal line.
This penalty is a kick at goal only, and is taken after the attempted conversion of the try and in addition to the conversion.

Soccer

Soccer (Association football) is a ball game
played by two teams, each of 11 players. The
object of the game is to put the ball into the
opponents' goal, and the winning team is the one
that scores the greater number of goals.

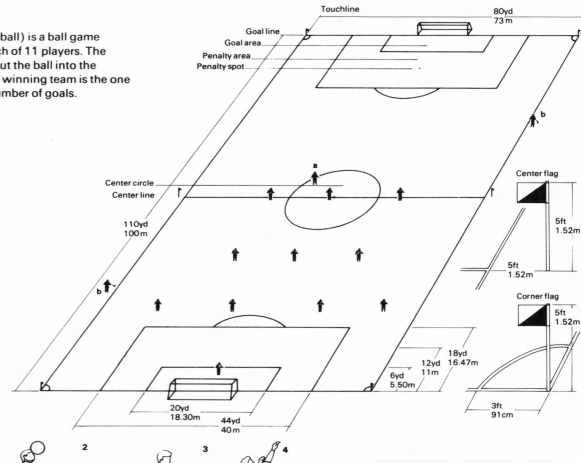

Touchline
Goal line
Goal area
Penalty area
Penalty spot
80yd
73 m

Center circle
Center line
110yd
100m

Center flag
5ft
1.52m
5ft
1.52m

Corner flag
5ft
1.52m

18yd
16.47m
12yd
11m
6yd
5.50m

20yd
18.30m
44yd
40 m

3ft
91cm

The field is rectangular and
must be 50–100yd wide and
100–130yd long.
At either end there is a goal
and a goal area enclosed in
the larger penalty area. The
posts and crossbar of the
goals must be of equal width
and of the same width as the
goal line.
The touchlines and the goal
lines are part of the playing
area.
At each corner of the field
is a flag on a post that is at
least 5ft high and must not
have a pointed top. Flags on
either side of the center line
are optional, but must be set
back at least 1yd from the
touchline.

Playing the ball

1

2

3

4

8ft
2.44m
24ft
7.32m

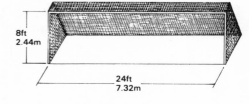

Officials A referee (**a**)
controls the game and is
assisted by two linesmen (**b**).
The referee:
acts as timekeeper and keeps
a record of the game;
enforces the laws;
stops the game at injuries,
infringements, etc, and
restarts it appropriately;
cautions or sends off
offenders;
may end the game because
of bad weather, interference
by spectators, etc.

The linesmen, one on each
touchline, indicate when the
ball is out of play, and which
side has the right to put the
ball into play again with a
throw in, corner kick, or goal
kick. They raise their flags to
indicate any infringement, and
the referee may choose
whether or not to act on this
signal.

Teams Each team has 11
players, one of whom is the
goalkeeper.
Substitutes One or two
substitutes are usually
permitted, depending on the
competition and for any
reason, but must be
named before the game.
Once substituted, a player
may not return to the game.
The referee must be informed
of any substitution.
In the event of an injury,
an outfield player may
become the goalkeeper
provided he obtains the
referee's permission and
wears a distinctive jersey.

Duration The game is
played in two halves of 45
minutes each; the teams
change ends at half time.
The half time interval may
not exceed five minutes,
except by consent of the
referee.
The referee adds on time for
moments lost through
injuries, time wasting, etc.
Time is also extended to
allow a penalty kick to be
taken at the end of either
period.

Playing the ball Except at
throw ins, the goalkeeper is
the only player allowed to
play the ball with his hands
or arms, and he may only do
so within his own penalty
area.
A player may, however, use
any other part of the body in
order to stop, control, or pass
the ball, move with it, or
score. He may use his:
1 feet
2 head
3 thigh
4 chest

The ball is made of leather or other approved material. At the start of a game it must weigh 14–16oz, and should be inflated to a pressure of 15lb per square inch.
The ball may not be changed during a game without the referee's permission.

Dress The goalkeeper (**1**) must wear different colors to distinguish him from the other players and the referee. All other players in the team (**2**) must wear uniform jerseys or shirts, shorts, and socks.
Shin pads (**3**) are an optional protection.
Boots (**4**) may be studded or have bars of leather and rubber across the soles. Studs must be of solid leather, rubber, plastic, aluminum, or similar material, but they must be rounded and not less than $\frac{1}{2}$in in diameter or more than $\frac{3}{4}$in long from the mounting. Studs that are molded as part of the sole must be of a soft material; provided that there are at least 10 studs on each sole, the minimum diameter of each stud may be $\frac{3}{8}$in.
Gloves (**5**) are frequently worn by goalkeepers.
Numbers (**6**) are usually worn on the back of the jersey.
Players may not wear anything that could injure another player, particularly faulty studs. Any player wearing dangerous equipment may be expelled from the game until it is replaced.

© DIAGRAM

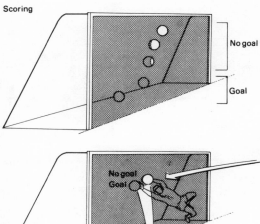

Scoring

No goal

Goal

No goal
Goal

Scoring A goal is scored when the whole of the ball has crossed the goal line under the crossbar and between the goal posts, provided that the attacking team has not infringed the laws.
Result The team scoring the greater number of goals wins. If the number of goals scored is equal the result is a draw, though in some competitions draws are resolved by:
replays;
a period of extra time (usually two halves of 15 minutes each) immediately after the 90 minutes;
a series of penalty kicks;
the toss of a coin.

Starting and restarting the game The two captains toss a coin for choice of ends or for the right to kick off. On the referee's whistle the team kicking off shall play the ball from a stationary position on the center spot into the opponents' half of the field.
At that moment every player must be in his own half and no opponent may come into the center circle until the ball is played.
Once played, the ball must travel its own circumference and the player taking the kick off must not kick it again until it has been touched by another player.

After a goal is scored play is restarted the same way by the team that has conceded the goal. The second half is begun with a kick off by the team that did not start the first half.
If during play the referee stops the game when the ball is in play and there is no reason to award a free kick to either team, the referee may restart the game by dropping the ball at the place where it was when play was stopped. A player may not play the ball until it has touched the ground.

398

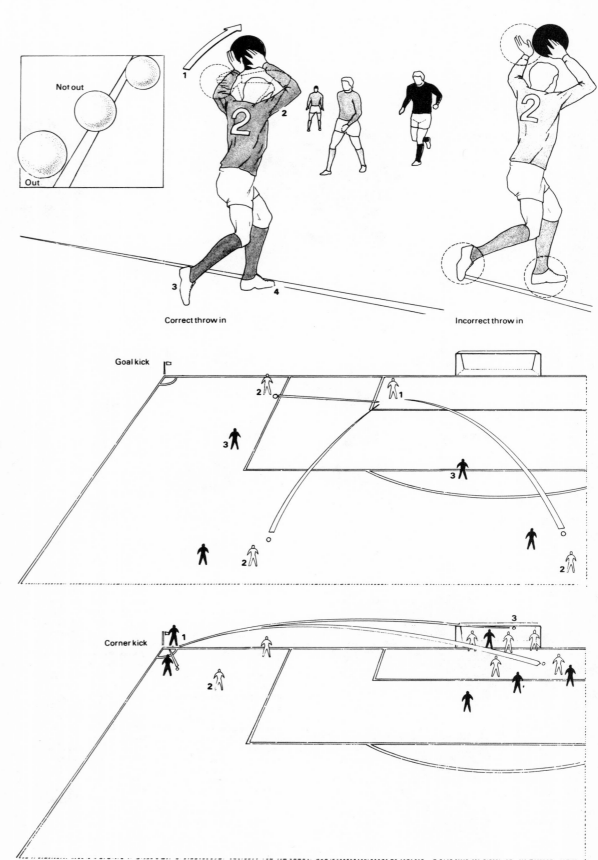

Out of play The ball is out of play when it completely crosses the boundaries of the pitch, or when the game has been stopped by the referee. Play is restarted by a throw in when the ball has crossed the touchlines, or by either a goal kick or a corner kick when it has crossed the goal line.

A throw in is taken along the touchline at the point where the ball went out of play. It is awarded against the team that last touched the ball before it went out of play.

The ball must be thrown into play with both hands, from behind and over the head (**1**). The thrower must face the play (**2**). As he releases the ball, part of each foot must be on the ground either behind (**3**) or on (**4**) the touchline. If these rules are infringed the throw in passes to the opposition.

No goal can be scored from a throw in, and the thrower may not play the ball again until it has been touched by another player.

A goal kick is awarded to the defending team when the ball crosses their goal line after having been last touched by an opponent. The kick may be taken by any player of the defending side, including the goalkeeper.

The ball is placed within the half of the goal area nearer the point where it crossed the goal line (**1**). The kick must send the ball out of the penalty area (**2**) and the kicker may not touch the ball again until it has been played by another player. All opponents must retreat outside the penalty area until the kick is taken (**3**).

No goal can be scored directly from a goal kick.

A corner kick is awarded to the attacking team if the ball crosses the goal line having been last played by one of the defending team.

It is taken from the quarter circle by the corner flag on the appropriate side of the pitch (**1**). The flag must not be moved to help the kicker. Opponents (**2**) must remain 10yd away until the kick is taken (until the ball has traveled its circumference). A goal can be scored direct from a corner kick (**3**), but the kicker must not play the ball again until it has been touched by another player.

Correct throw in

Incorrect throw in

Goal kick

Corner kick

Not out

Out

A free kick is either direct or indirect and is taken from where the offense occurred.
A direct free kick is one from which the player taking the kick can score direct (**1**).
An indirect free kick is one from which a goal cannot be scored until the ball has been touched by another player (**2**). At any free kick all opponents must be 10yd from the ball (**3**), except at an indirect free kick less than 10yd from the goal, when they must stand between the goal posts.
If the defending side is given a free kick in its own penalty area the ball must be kicked out of, and no opponents may enter, the area until the kick is taken.
The ball must be stationary at a free kick and the kicker may not replay the ball until another player touches it.

Direct free kick

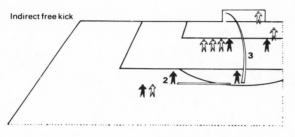

Indirect free kick

Penalty kick Any offense that incurs a direct free kick is punished by the award of a penalty kick to the opposing team when it is committed by a defending player in his own penalty area.
A penalty kick is taken from the penalty spot. All players except the goalkeeper and the player taking the kick must stand outside the penalty area, at least 10yd from the penalty spot.
The player taking the kick must propel the ball forward and he may not play it a second time until it has been touched by another player. The goalkeeper must stand on the goal line, without moving his feet, until the ball is kicked.

The kick is retaken if:
the defending team breaks the law and a goal is not scored;
the attacking team, with the exception of the kicker, infringes and a goal is scored;
there are infringements by players of both sides.
If the kicker breaks the law, for instance by kicking the ball twice, the defending side is awarded an indirect free kick.

Offside

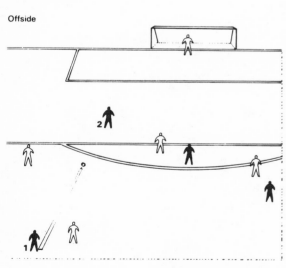

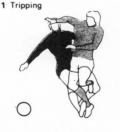 **1 Tripping**

2 Holding

 **3 Handling the ball**

4 Dangerous play

 **5 Charging without the ball**

 **6 Obstruction**

©DIAGRAM

Offside An attacking player is offside if, when the ball is played (**1**), he is nearer the opposing goal than two opponents and the ball (**2**), unless:
he is in his own half of the pitch;
an opponent was the last player to touch the ball;
he receives the ball direct from a goal kick, a corner kick, a throw in, or when the referee drops the ball.
Although a player is technically in an offside position, he is not penalized unless in the opinion of the referee he is interfering with play or with an opponent, or is seeking to gain an advantage by being in an offside position.

Fouls and misconduct
A direct free kick (penalty kick) is awarded for the following intentional fouls if they are committed by a defender in his penalty area:
1 tripping;
2 holding an opponent with a hand or arm;
3 playing the ball with a hand or arm (except for the goalkeeper in his penalty area);
kicking or attempting to kick an opponent;
jumping at an opponent;
charging in a violent or dangerous manner;
charging from behind (unless the opponent is guilty of obstruction);
striking or attempting to strike an opponent;
pushing an opponent with the hand or any part of the arm.

An indirect free kick is awarded:
4 for dangerous play;
5 for charging fairly, as with the shoulder, but when the ball is not within playing distance;
6 for intentionally obstructing an opponent while not attempting to play the ball, in order to prevent him reaching it;
for charging the goalkeeper – unless the goalkeeper is holding the ball, obstructing an opponent, or has gone outside his goal area;
when a goalkeeper takes more than four steps while holding the ball, throwing it in the air and catching it, or bouncing it, without releasing it to another player, and when he wastes time;
for offside;

when a player taking a kick off, throw in, goal kick, corner kick, free kick, or penalty kick plays the ball a second time before another player has touched it;
for dissenting from the referee's decisions;
for entering or leaving the game without the referee's permission;
after a player is sent off for an offense not specified in the laws;
for ungentlemanly conduct;
for using a teammate to gain height to head the ball.

Cautioning and sending off The referee must caution a player if he:
enters or leaves the game without the referee's permission;
continually breaks the laws;
shows dissent from any of the referee's decisions;
is guilty of ungentlemanly conduct.
The referee has the power to send a player off the field for the rest of the game if he:
commits acts of violence or serious foul play (including spitting);
uses foul or abusive language;
continues to break the laws after a caution.

Baseball

Baseball is played by two teams, each of nine players, who attempt to score more runs than their opponents. In each batting period the players attempt to make the circuit of the bases as many times as possible. However, when the fielding team has put out three opponents, the whole of the batting side is out and becomes the fielding side.

Area The playing field is composed of the infield and the outfield. The infield is the area bounded by the four bases. The outfield is the area beyond this section bounded by the extension of the two foul lines.

Home base is a five-sided slab of whitened rubber, while the other three bases are marked by white canvas bags. The pitcher's plate is a rectangular slab of whitened rubber, usually set on a raised mound of earth.

2ft
61cm

18ft
5.49m

60ft 6in
18.45m

Home base plate

1st, 2nd, 3rd base bag

1ft 5in
43cm

1ft 3in
38cm

8½in
21.5cm

8½in
21.5cm

1ft 3in
38cm

Pitcher's plate

2ft
61cm

6in
15.5cm

6ft
1.83m

4ft
1.22m

8ft
2.44m

4ft 3in
1.29m

7

8

9

Outfield   Grass line

Fielding positions
1 pitcher
2 catcher
3 first baseman
4 second baseman
5 third baseman
6 shortstop
7 left fielder
8 center fielder
9 right fielder

Umpire

4

6

Infield

5

1

3

15ft
4.57m

10ft
3.05m

Manager's box

Manager's box

20ft
6.10m

90ft
27.45m

Umpire

2

On-deck circle
for next batter

60ft
18.30m

90ft
27.45m

Grandstand or fence limit

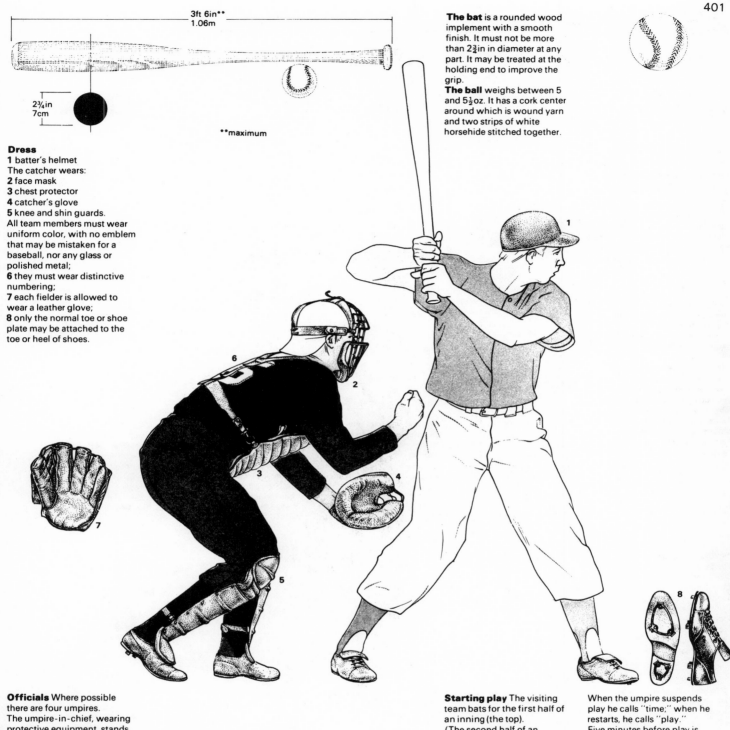

3ft 6in**
1.06m

2¾in
7cm

**maximum

The bat is a rounded wood implement with a smooth finish. It must not be more than 2¾in in diameter at any part. It may be treated at the holding end to improve the grip.
The ball weighs between 5 and 5½oz. It has a cork center around which is wound yarn and two strips of white horsehide stitched together.

Dress
1 batter's helmet
The catcher wears:
2 face mask
3 chest protector
4 catcher's glove
5 knee and shin guards.
All team members must wear uniform color, with no emblem that may be mistaken for a baseball, nor any glass or polished metal;
6 they must wear distinctive numbering;
7 each fielder is allowed to wear a leather glove;
8 only the normal toe or shoe plate may be attached to the toe or heel of shoes.

Officials Where possible there are four umpires.
The umpire-in-chief, wearing protective equipment, stands behind the catcher specifically to judge on strikes, but he is also the overall judge on all decisions.
The other umpires stand near the first, second, and third bases to judge whether a runner safely reaches the bag. For each game an official scorer is appointed to record the statistical details of the play.

Umpire-in-chief

©DIAGRAM

Starting play The visiting team bats for the first half of an inning (the top).
(The second half of an inning is termed the bottom.)
Before the players take the field, the umpire must check that the playing area is correctly marked and that the players' equipment conforms to the regulations.
The umpire must also receive from the home club a number of new baseballs for use in the game.
The manager of the home team is the sole judge if the weather conditions make play doubtful, but once the game is under way, it is the umpire who decides in bad weather if play should be stopped, restarted, etc.

When the umpire suspends play he calls "time;" when he restarts, he calls "play."
Five minutes before play is due to start, the umpire must receive each team's batting order in duplicate. He keeps one copy for himself and passes the other to the opposing manager.
The players of the home team then take their defensive positions, the batter takes up his position, and on the call of "play," the game begins.
The batting team may have two coaches in the coaches' boxes during their half-inning.

Batting Each member of the batting side takes his place in the batter's box according to the order decided by the team manager.

The batter must stand with his feet within the box. He attempts to score runs by striking the ball as it is pitched to him.

The strike zone is the area over home plate between the batter's armpits and knees (as in his normal stance).

A strike is called by the umpire when the batter does not swing at a pitch in the strike zone, or swings at any pitch and misses, or hits the ball into foul territory with fewer than two strikes against him.

A ball is a pitch delivered outside the strike zone that is not struck at by the batter. After four balls the batter may walk to first base.

Running The batter becomes a runner when he has hit the ball into fair territory, walked on four pitched balls, is hit by a pitch, or if the catcher drops a third strike.

Strike zone

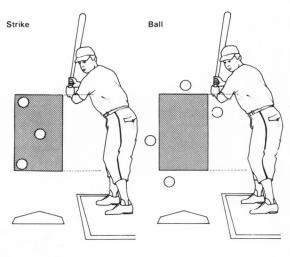

Strike   Ball

A force play is when the batter runs to first base and forces any runner on that base to move to second base; if there is a runner on second base he must move to third base.

A runner is "safe" at a base if he touches the bag before the fielder with the ball touches him or the base.

He may stay there until he is dismissed or until he is forced to move on by the arrival of another runner.

A steal is when a runner gains a base without the help of a hit, walk, or error; usually by running to it while the pitcher has the ball or if the batter fails to make contact with the pitch.

The runner is out if he fails to beat a throw to the base to which he is running.

Tagging up A runner may vacate a base on a caught fly only after the ball hits a fielder's glove. If he has left the base he must return and tag up before he may advance. If the ball is returned to the base ahead of him, he is forced out.

Force play

Steal

Duration A game lasts a specified number of innings; American professionals play nine. Each side has a turn at bat to complete an inning.

A half-inning is completed when three of the batting side are out.

With a tie score after the specified innings, extra innings are played until one team is ahead at an inning's end.

Scoring The team that scores most runs is the winner.

A run is scored when a player completes a circuit of the bases, touching each in turn.

1 If a batter hits the ball away from the fielders into the distant outfield, he may make a home run (ie get around all the bases in one turn). It is also awarded if he hits a fly ball (one that does not touch

the ground) over a boundary fence that is more than 250ft from home base and in fair territory.

(A grand slam home run is a home run hit when the bases are loaded, ie when three men are on base. It scores four runs, the maximum possible from one hit.)

2 If a fair ball bounces over the fence, the batter may go to second base. More often, he will reach first base and then continue around as following batters take their turns.

Whenever a batter hits the ball into the field of play, he must run to first base.

Substitutes may be introduced at any time when the ball is dead. A substitute takes the replaced player's position in the batting order; once substituted that player may not return to the game.

A substitute may take the place of any player on the field, providing the umpire is informed.

No player whose name is on the batting order may become a substitute runner.

Relief pitchers usually warm-up in the "bull-pen" before they come into the game.

The use of substitutes is at the manager's discretion, as are all decisions on the strategy of the game.

Fielder's misconduct If a fielder stops a batted ball by throwing his glove or cap at it when it would have gone out of the playing area, the batter is awarded a home run.

The batter may take three bases if the fielder throws any part of his equipment or uniform at any other fair batted ball and so stops it.

If runners are obstructed by fielders, they are allowed to reach at least one base beyond the last base legally touched before the obstruction occurred.

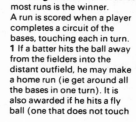

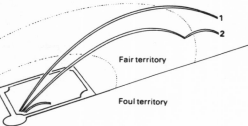

1
2

Fair territory

Foul territory

Set position

Wind-up position

Illegal pitch

Illegal pitch

Pitching The pitcher is allowed no more than eight practice pitches before he starts play or takes over from another pitcher.
He may deliver the ball only from either the set position, or the wind-up position.
At any time before he pitches, he may throw the ball to a base, providing he steps in that direction.

He may only rub the ball between his hands; any attempt to shine it on his clothing, apply saliva or any foreign substance to it, or rub it on the ground, is an offense. Any violation leads to disqualification.
The pitcher must not pitch the ball directly at the batter.
He must not delay the game

and must pitch the ball 20 seconds after receiving it.
A balk The pitcher concedes a no ball or strike (called a balk):
for an illegal pitch, when his foot is not in contact with the pitcher's plate;
if he pretends to pitch and does not do so;
if he fails to step directly toward a base when he is

throwing to that base;
if he pitches when not facing the batter;
if he delays the play;
if he makes any sort of feinting movement;
if he drops the ball while in the pitching motion;
if he pitches when the catcher is not in position.
A balk allows any runners to walk on to the next base.

A base runner may also advance one base:
when a wild pitch or a throw from the pitcher to a base goes into the stand;
when a pitch beats the catcher and lodges in the umpire's clothing.

1 Caught

2 Bunt to foul territory

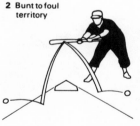

3 Tag

4 Out

4 Not out

Putting out batters and runners More than one of the batting side may be out between consecutive pitches.
A batter is out:
1 if he hits the ball and it is caught "on the fly" by a fielder, even if it is caught in "foul" territory;
2 when he attempts to bunt (tap) the ball down in front of him on a third strike and it goes into foul territory;
if he fails to make contact with three strikes (providing the catcher catches the third strike or the first base is occupied and there are less than two outs);
if he hits the ball so that it can be caught in the infield when there are less than two out and runners on first and second or on first, second, and third (infield fly rule).

Double play

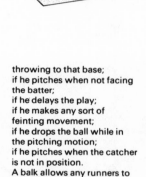

when he is touched by the ball as he tries to hit a third strike;
when a runner is hit by a batted ball;
when the umpire judges that a spectator has prevented a fielder from catching a fly ball;
if he deliberately strikes the ball twice;
if he interferes with or obstructs a fielder.

A runner is out:
3 if a fielder tags (touches) him with the ball when he is not in physical contact with a base;
if he runs more than 3 ft off a straight line to avoid being tagged;
4 if a fielder with the ball tags a base at which a force exists before the forced runner reaches the base.

A double play occurs when two outs are recorded between consecutive pitches such as a runner from first forced at second and the batter forced at first on the same ground ball.

A triple play occurs when three outs are recorded between consecutive pitches such as when a fly ball is caught and two runners are forced before they can tag up.

© DIAGRAM

404

Softball

Softball is a sport derived from baseball. The batting side attempts to score runs by making a circuit of four bases while the fielding team attempts to dismiss them. The major differences are that softball is played by men and women, the field of play is smaller, the ball is larger, the game lasts only seven innings, pitching is underhand, and players may not steal runs off their bases.

The field The pitching distance is 46ft for men, and 40ft for women.
The home plate is made of rubber or other suitable material.
The pitcher's plate is made of rubber or wood, and its top is level with the ground.
The bases are made of canvas or other suitable material, and must be securely fastened in position.
Officials Matches are controlled by:
a) the plate umpire, who judges batting, appeals, and forfeited matches; and
b) the base umpire, who takes up different positions on the playing field from where best to render base decisions.
The umpires share equal authority to:
judge illegal pitches and stealing bases;
expel players or team officials; suspend play.
Fielding positions
1 pitcher
2 catcher
3 first baseman
4 second baseman
5 third baseman
6 shortstop
7 left fielder
8 center fielder
9 right fielder
Teams A team consists of nine players, who must all be present to start or continue a game.
Pitchers and catchers must stand in their prescribed positions. Other players may be stationed anywhere on fair ground.
Substitutes All players except the pitcher may be substituted at any time.
The pitcher may only be replaced after the opposing batter has completed his turn or the side has finished its half of the innings in the field.
A player who has been substituted may not return to the game.
Starting play Teams toss to determine the batting order.

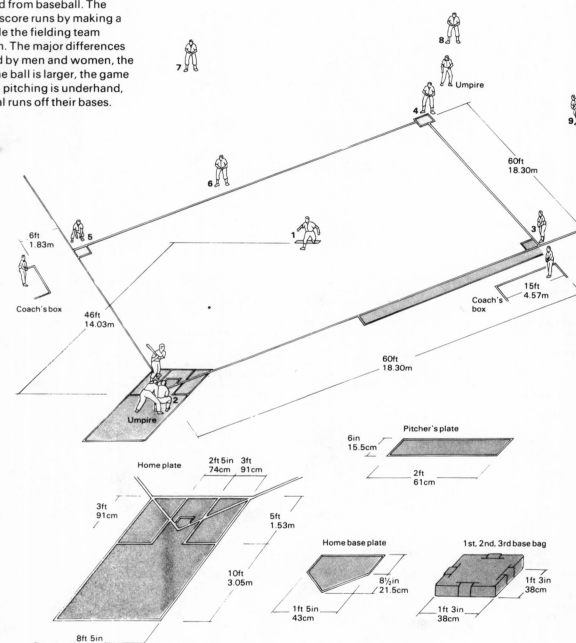

Duration A game consists of seven innings. A full seven innings need not be played if the second batting team scores more runs in six innings or before the third player is out in the last half of the seventh inning.
A tied game continues for additional innings until one side has scored more runs at the end of a completed inning, or until the side batting second scores more in their half of an inning before their third dismissal.
A game that the umpire ends prematurely is considered finished if five or more completed innings have been played.

Scoring The winning team is the one that scores the greater number of runs.
A run is scored when a player completes a circuit of the bases, touching each in turn.
A player may not score a run ahead of a preceding runner. If the batter hits a ball into the air (fly ball) over the boundary, he is entitled to a home run. If, however, that fly ball, or any other fair ball, passes out of the field less than 200ft from the home base, the batter and runners are only allowed to proceed two bases.
A forfeited game scores 7–0 in favor of the team not at fault.

2ft 10in
86.5cm

The bat is round in cross-section, and made of hard wood or metal. Wooden bats have safety grips of cork, tape, or composition material. A plastic cap may be attached to the handle.
The ball is made of kapok or of a mixture of cork and rubber. It is covered in horse or cow hide. Circumference $11\frac{7}{8}$–$12\frac{1}{8}$in; weight $6\frac{1}{4}$–7oz.

©DIAGRAM

1

2

3

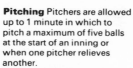

Dress Uniforms are similar to those worn for baseball. Umpires' uniforms are navy blue.

Gloves may be worn by any player, but mitts (**1**) may only be worn by the catcher and first baseman. No top lacing, webbing, or other device between the thumb and body of a glove or mitt may exceed 4in, unless worn by the catcher.

Shoes (**2**) may have metal plates with spikes a maximum of $\frac{3}{4}$in long.

Catchers and plate umpires must wear masks (**3**). Body protectors (**4**) may be worn and are compulsory for women catchers.

Batting Players bat in the order listed on the scoresheets; substitutes in the order of the players they replace.

If a player has not completed his turn when the team's half of the inning at bat is ended, he becomes the first batter in its next inning at bat.

The batter must stand within the lines of the batter's box.

A strike is a ball pitched into the strike zone at which the batter does not swing, or at which he swings and misses. A batter is allowed three strikes.

A ball is a ball pitched outside the strike zone and not struck at by the batter. After four balls the batter may walk to first base.

Running The batter becomes a runner:

when he hits the ball into fair territory;

when the catcher fails to field the third strike before it touches the ground;

when two players are out or first base is unoccupied;

after four balls;

after interference by the catcher;

when a batter does not play a pitch and it hits him while he is in the box;

when a fair ball hits the umpire in foul territory.

A runner may move to the next base while the ball is in play:

when the ball leaves the pitcher's hand on a pitch or if he drops it during his wind-up or backswing;

when the ball is overthrown;

when the ball is batted into fair territory.

He may also move to the next base without threat of dismissal:

when the batter is awarded a base;

after an illegal pitch;

when a fielder obstructs a runner;

when a fielder illegally stops the ball;

when the ball is pitched into or past the backstop;

when the ball is overthrown into foul territory and is ruled out of play.

Runners must return to their bases:

when a foul ball is legally caught;

when the ball is batted illegally;

after interference by a batter or runner;

when the batter is hit by a pitched ball, whether he swings at it or not;

when a throw by the catcher or a fair throw by a fielder hits an umpire.

Pitching Pitchers are allowed up to 1 minute in which to pitch a maximum of five balls at the start of an inning or when one pitcher relieves another.

1 The pitcher must stand:

with both feet on the pitcher's plate;

facing the batter and with his shoulders in line with the first and third bases;

holding the ball with both hands in front of his body. This position may be kept for 1–20 seconds. The catcher must be in position before the pitcher assumes the pitching position.

2 The delivery starts when the pitcher removes one hand from the ball. It must be delivered underhand, and the hand must be below the hip, and the wrist no further from the body than the elbow.

3 The pitcher may take only one step forward, in the direction of the batter and simultaneous with delivery. The release of the ball and the follow through of the hand and wrist must be in a forward direction, past the straight line of the body. Any type of wind-up is allowed, provided:

the ball is pitched immediately after the pitching motion;

one hand is not removed from the ball and returned to the ball after the swing;

there is no halt or reverse in the forward motion;

there is not more than one revolution in a "windmill" pitch;

the wind-up does not continue after stepping forward.

A no-pitch occurs if the pitcher:

pitches during a halt in play;

attempts to pitch before the batter has taken up position, or is off balance after the previous pitch;

pitches when a runner is out for leaving a base too soon.

Dismissals

A batter is out if:

the third strike is caught by the catcher;

he misses the third strike and the ball hits him;

he bunts (taps) the third strike into foul territory;

a foul ball is legally caught;

he is caught in the infield when there are fewer than two teammates out and runners on the first two or three bases (an infield fly);

a fielder deliberately drops an infield fly or line drive (an aerial ball batted sharply and directly into the playing field) with any of the bases occupied and fewer than two players dismissed;

he has three strikes when fewer than two teammates are out and the first base is occupied;

the preceding runner interferes with an attempt to field the ball – the runner is then also dismissed.

A runner is out if:

before he can reach or return to a base the fielder touching the base receives the ball;

before he can reach or return to a base he is legally touched with the ball by a fielder;

he runs more than 3ft from a direct line between the bases to avoid being touched with the ball by a fielder;

he overtakes a preceding runner;

he fails to return to touch a base after a halt in play;

he deliberately interferes with an attempt to field the ball or with a thrown ball;

he is hit by a fair ball off base before the ball has touched or passed a fielder;

he deliberately kicks the ball;

he is on third base and the batter interferes with play at the home plate when fewer than two players are out;

the coach physically assists him;

teammates gather at a base to which he is running in order to confuse the fielders;

he circuits the bases in the wrong order;

he leaves the base before the ball is pitched.

A force-out occurs when the runner loses the right to his base because the batter has become a runner and the fielder on the next base is holding the ball.

A runner is not out if, after touching the base, he overruns it and is about to return to it.

Misconduct by players or team officials is punishable by a warning for a first offense and expulsion from the game for a second offense.

Rounders

Rounders is an English game similar to baseball and softball. A batter attempts to strike a ball and run around an area marked by posts to score a "rounder." The team that scores the most rounders wins the match. It is usually played by women and children.

The pitch Four vertical posts are set at the corners of the running track. The lines of the batting and bowling squares are considered part of those squares.

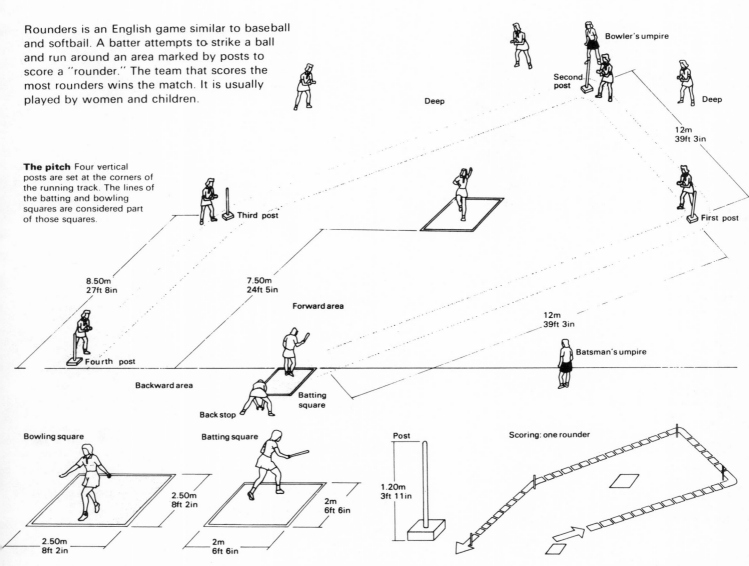

Bowler's umpire

Deep

Second post

Deep

12m
39ft 3in

Third post

First post

8.50m
27ft 8in

7.50m
24ft 5in

Forward area

12m
39ft 3in

Fourth post

Batsman's umpire

Backward area

Batting square

Back stop

Bowling square

2.50m
8ft 2in

2.50m
8ft 2in

Batting square

2m
6ft 6in

2m
6ft 6in

Post

1.20m
3ft 11in

Scoring: one rounder

Teams Each team consists of nine players. The fielding positions shown are usual but not obligatory.
Substitutes An injured batter may be substituted by another player.
With the opposing captain's consent, a reserve for an injured player may field, bat, or bowl for the rest of the match.
When acting as a runner, the substitute must stand behind and to the right of the batter, until the ball has been hit or has passed the batter.

Officials A match is controlled by the batter's umpire, who must be able to see both the batting square and the first post without turning her head; and by the bowler's umpire.
The umpires' decisions are final. They may consult each other and both record the scores. They exchange positions after both first innings have been completed.

Start of play Captains toss for choice of inning. A team must retain the same batting order throughout an inning.
Duration Each team has two innings. An inning ends when all the batters are out. A team leading by ten or more rounders may require the other team to follow on.

Scoring
One rounder is scored if a batter hits the ball into the forward area and runs around the track to touch the fourth post before another ball is bowled—unless she is dismissed or the next post is "stopped" (touched by a fielder with the ball in her hand).
A half rounder is scored if the batter:
completes the track as for a rounder but without hitting the ball;
completes the track from first post after the ball comes back into the forward area after a backward hit.

A penalty half rounder is awarded to the batting team when the bowler delivers three consecutive no-balls to the same batter, or if a batter is obstructed by a fielder.
It may be awarded in addition to a rounder if a batter scores a rounder despite either of these offenses. Two penalty half rounders are awarded if a batter scores a rounder despite both offenses.
A penalty half rounder may be awarded to the fielding team if the waiting batting side obstructs the fielders.

46cm
1ft 6⅜in

17cm
6¾in

The stick is round in cross-section and made of wood. It must be no more than 17cm around the thickest part. The maximum length is 46cm and the maximum weight 370g.
The ball weighs 70–85g. Its circumference should be approximately 19cm.

Batting
1 After a fair ball, the batter must move to the first post.
2 The batter's feet must be within the batting square until the ball leaves the bowler's hand, and her feet must remain behind the front line until she has hit the ball or it has passed her.
3 A backward hit occurs if the ball is hit directly into the backward area.
4 A batter may take a no-ball and score in the usual way as long as she is not caught out. She is deemed to have accepted the ball if she reaches first post. When only one player in a team remains to be dismissed, she may have one minute's rest between rounders and is allowed a choice of three good balls at each turn.

Running A batter must pass outside, or halt at, each of the first three posts in order to reach the fourth, preferably carrying her stick. She must touch the fourth post with her hand or stick. When waiting (even temporarily) at a post, the batter must maintain contact with it—either with her hand or bat—until the ball has left the bowler's hand. She may run on whenever the bowler is not in possession of the ball and is in the bowling square.
She must not overtake another runner, nor stay at the same post as another batter.

She may not run beyond the first post after a backward hit until the ball has been returned to the forward area, nor return to a post unless ordered to do so by an umpire. A member of the batting side may run on from a post if a no-ball is bowled that the batter does not accept.
A runner need not run after every ball bowled, unless the batter immediately behind her has to run.

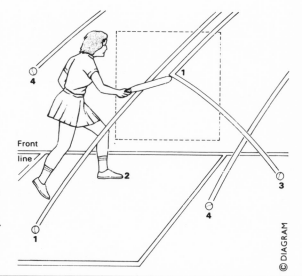

Front line

© DIAGRAM

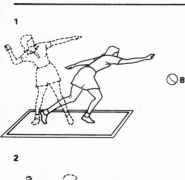

Dismissing the batters
More than one batter may be out between consecutive balls.
A batter is out if:
1 she has one or both feet over the front line of the batting square before she has hit the ball or it has passed her;
2 she runs on the inside of a post—unless she is obstructed;
3 she is run-out by a fielder who touches (with the ball or the hand holding the ball) the post to which she is running;
4 after hitting, attempting to hit, or missing a good ball, or taking a no-ball, a fielder touches her with the hand holding the ball while she is still in the batting square or running around the track; she obstructs a fielder or deliberately deflects the ball; she overtakes another batter; her substitute runner leaves her place before the batter has hit the ball or it has passed her; she leaves a post before the ball has left the bowler's hand.
Side out When there is no batter waiting to bat, all the running batters can be out simultaneously if any fielder throws the ball directly into the batting square before one of the runners reaches fourth post (5).

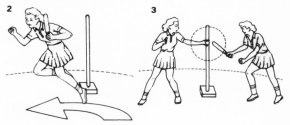
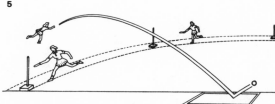
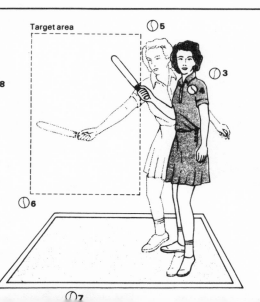

Target area

Bowling A bowler may be changed only after delivering a good ball. She may leave the bowling square in order to field the ball.
No-balls A ball is considered a no-ball if:
1 it is not bowled with a continuous and smooth underarm action;
2 the bowler fails to keep both feet within the bowling square until the ball is released;
3 it is bowled on the wrong side of the batter;
4 it is aimed at the batter's body;
5 it is bowled higher than the batter's head, or
6 lower than her knee;
7 it hits the ground before it reaches the batter;
8 it is bowled "wide" (out of reach of the batter, in the position she was in when the ball left the bowler's hand).
Obstruction is caused if:
a fielder in any way impedes the batter's stroke or her run;
a batter does not run directly on the running track, thereby impeding a player fielding the ball.
The batting side, while waiting to bat, must stand in the backward area away from the backstop (the fielder positioned behind the batter) and the fourth post fielder.

Cricket

Cricket is a ball game played by two teams of eleven players. It is played on a pitch with two wickets placed 22yd apart. Each team bats (takes its innings) in turn. The object of the batting side is to make runs, while the bowling and fielding side tries to dismiss the batsmen. The winning team is the one that scores more runs.

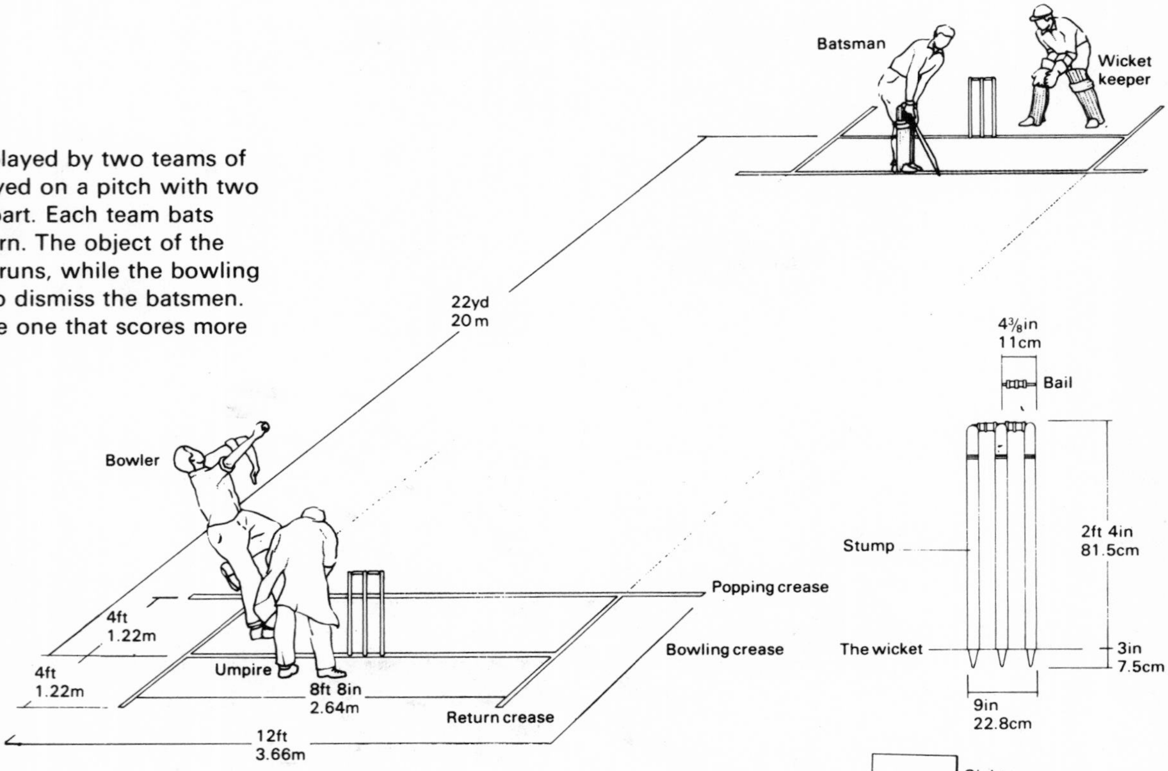

The pitch is the area between the two bowling creases and extending 5ft in width on either side of a line joining the center of the wickets. The pitch, of grass (or approved matting), is prepared before the game to be level and with the grass trimmed short. In first-class cricket, regulations govern when and how often the pitch is to be rolled, mown, watered, or covered.

The rest of the playing area is enclosed by a boundary line.

The wicket at each end of the pitch is composed of three vertical stumps on top of which are placed two horizontal bails.

The return and popping creases are unlimited in length.

Teams There are eleven players in a team.

Fielding positions (for a right-handed batsman):
1 bowler
2 wicket keeper
3 slips
4 leg slip
5 backward short leg
6 square short leg
7 forward short leg
8 silly point
9 gully
10 silly mid off
11 silly mid on
12 mid wicket
13 square leg
14 backward point
15 point
16 cover
17 short extra cover
18 extra cover
19 deep extra cover
20 mid off
21 deep mid off
22 mid on
23 deep mid on
24 short fine leg
25 deep fine leg
26 short third man
27 third man
28 long leg
29 deep square leg
30 deep mid wicket
31 long on
32 long off

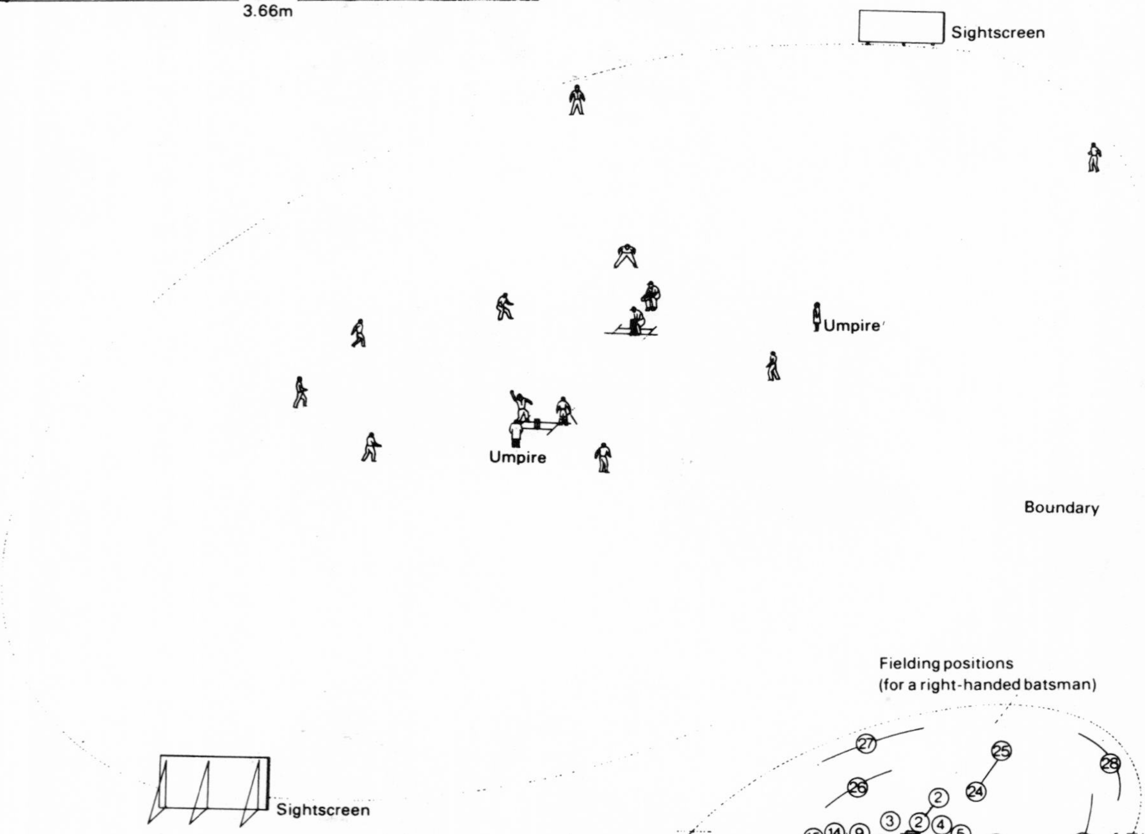

Batsman
Wicket keeper

22yd
20m

4⅜in
11cm
Bail

Stump

2ft 4in
81.5cm

The wicket

3in
7.5cm

9in
22.8cm

Bowler

4ft
1.22m

4ft
1.22m

Umpire

Popping crease

Bowling crease

8ft 8in
2.64m

Return crease

12ft
3.66m

Sightscreen

Umpire

Umpire

Boundary

Sightscreen

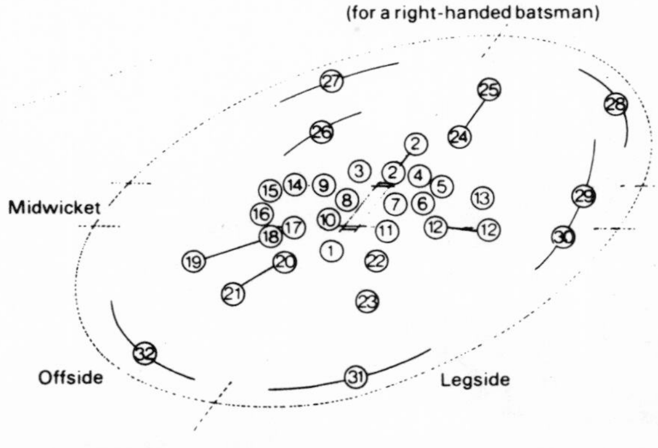

Fielding positions
(for a right-handed batsman)

Midwicket

Offside

Legside

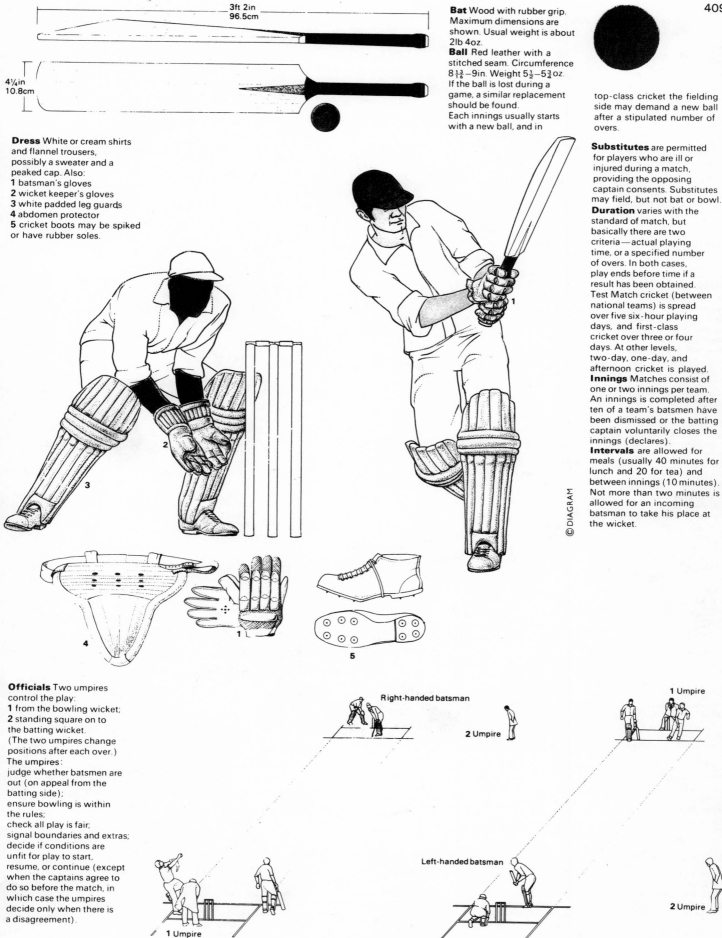

3ft 2in
96.5cm

4¼in
10.8cm

Bat Wood with rubber grip. Maximum dimensions are shown. Usual weight is about 2lb 4oz.

Ball Red leather with a stitched seam. Circumference $8\frac{13}{16}$–9in. Weight $5\frac{1}{2}$–$5\frac{3}{4}$oz. If the ball is lost during a game, a similar replacement should be found.

Each innings usually starts with a new ball, and in top-class cricket the fielding side may demand a new ball after a stipulated number of overs.

Dress White or cream shirts and flannel trousers, possibly a sweater and a peaked cap. Also:
1 batsman's gloves
2 wicket keeper's gloves
3 white padded leg guards
4 abdomen protector
5 cricket boots may be spiked or have rubber soles.

Substitutes are permitted for players who are ill or injured during a match, providing the opposing captain consents. Substitutes may field, but not bat or bowl.

Duration varies with the standard of match, but basically there are two criteria—actual playing time, or a specified number of overs. In both cases, play ends before time if a result has been obtained. Test Match cricket (between national teams) is spread over five six-hour playing days, and first-class cricket over three or four days. At other levels, two-day, one-day, and afternoon cricket is played.

Innings Matches consist of one or two innings per team. An innings is completed after ten of a team's batsmen have been dismissed or the batting captain voluntarily closes the innings (declares).

Intervals are allowed for meals (usually 40 minutes for lunch and 20 for tea) and between innings (10 minutes). Not more than two minutes is allowed for an incoming batsman to take his place at the wicket.

© DIAGRAM

2

1

3

4

1

5

Officials Two umpires control the play:
1 from the bowling wicket;
2 standing square on to the batting wicket.
(The two umpires change positions after each over.)
The umpires:
judge whether batsmen are out (on appeal from the batting side);
ensure bowling is within the rules;
check all play is fair;
signal boundaries and extras;
decide if conditions are unfit for play to start, resume, or continue (except when the captains agree to do so before the match, in which case the umpires decide only when there is a disagreement).

Right-handed batsman

2 Umpire

1 Umpire

1 Umpire   1 Umpire

Left-handed batsman

2 Umpire

Starting play Each team bats in turn. The choice of batting or fielding first goes to the captain who wins the toss of a coin.

Two members of the batting team take up their positions, one at each wicket. A member of the fielding side bowls from one end to the batsman defending the opposite wicket. The rest of the fielding side is positioned to stop runs and to help dismiss the batsmen.

The umpire calls "play" at the start of a day or an innings, and "time" at the close of play.

The follow on In a two-innings match, each side takes its innings alternately unless it is forced to "follow on" (to take its second innings immediately after its first).

A team batting second may be asked to follow on by the opposing captain if it scores:

200 less than the opposition in a five-day match;
150 less in a three-day or four-day match;
100 less in a two-day match;
75 less in a one-day match.

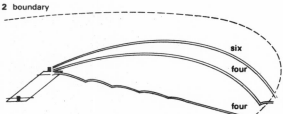

1 run

2 boundary

Scoring is in runs.

1 A run is scored when both batsmen, after a hit or at any time the ball is in play, pass each other and reach the opposite wicket. The run does not count if a batsman runs short, is run out, or is caught.

2 When the ball crosses the boundary on the full pitch, it counts six runs; if it touches the ground first it counts four.

The batsmen then resume their original positions; only the boundary score counts, not any runs between the wickets.

Extras are runs scored without hitting the ball with the bat. They may be scored from

3 a wide;
4 a bye;
5 a leg bye;
a no ball.

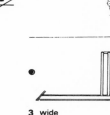

3 wide

3 wide

4 bye

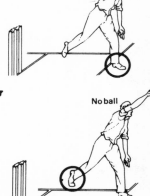

5 leg bye

Result The match is won by the team with more runs after both teams have completed the required number of innings. If any innings is incomplete, the match is a draw. If scores are equal when the innings are completed, the match is a tie.

In limited-over cricket, the match is won by the team scoring more runs in the overs allowed. Draws are possible only when the weather interferes with play.

The result of a won match is expressed as a win by the number of runs by which one team beat the other, or as a win by the number of wickets still to fall if the last side to bat exceeds the other's total of runs.

Fair ball

Bowling is in "overs" of six or eight balls (as in the agreed conditions and consistent throughout a match).

Overs are delivered from alternate wickets.

A bowler must bowl a complete over unless he is injured or suspended.

Bowlers may change ends as often as they wish, but must not bowl two successive overs in one innings.

They may bowl from either side of the wicket provided they inform the batsman.

The umpire at the bowling end shall call "over" after the sixth or eighth ball, once he sees that both sides have ceased to regard the ball as in play.

A no ball is called if the bowler:

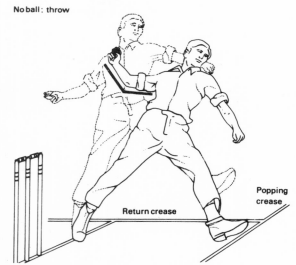

No ball: throw

Return crease

Popping crease

throws instead of bowls the ball,

in his delivery stride has no part of his front foot grounded behind the popping crease; does not ground his back foot within the return crease or its forward extension.

Either umpire may call and signal "no ball" immediately on delivery.

The receiving batsman may

hit a no ball and make runs from it, but he can only be dismissed by being run out, handling the ball, hitting the ball twice, or obstructing the field.

If the batsman fails to make any runs from a no ball, one run is added to his team's total score.

A wide is called if the bowler sends the ball so high

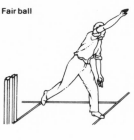

Fair ball

Fair ball

over or so wide of the wicket that it passes out of the batsman's reach.

The umpire shall signal the wide as soon as the ball passes the batsman and one run is added to the team's score.

Batsmen may be out stumped, run out, handling the ball, or obstructing the field.

A bye is a run taken when the

No ball

No ball

ball has not touched the batsman's bat or any part of his person.

A leg bye is a run taken when the ball touches but is not deliberately deflected by any part of the batsman's body except his hands.

(Runs scored when the ball comes off the batsman's gloves are added to his own score.)

Dismissing the batsman

A batsman may be out in the following ways:

Leg before wicket (lbw) If any part of his body, except the hand, prevents the ball hitting the wicket, provided that the ball has not first touched his bat or hand, and that:
1 the ball pitched on the offside of the striker's wicket, or
2 the ball pitched or would have pitched on a straight line from the bowler's to the striker's wicket.

Caught When a fielder within the playing area catches the ball before it touches the ground after it has come from the bat or the batsman's gloves.

Hit wicket If the batsman breaks the wicket with his bat or body while playing a shot or while setting off for a first run.

Run out If the batsman has his wicket broken by the opposition when he is out of his ground going for a run or for any other reason when the ball is in play.

Stumped If in receiving a ball the batsman moves out of his ground, other than to attempt a run, and the wicket keeper without another fielder's intervention breaks the wicket.

(In both run out and stumping decisions the batsman is out unless his bat or some part of his body is grounded behind the line.)

Bowled When the ball delivered by the bowler hits the wicket and dislodges a bail, even if the ball strikes the bat first.

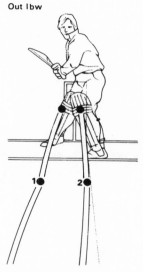 Out lbw 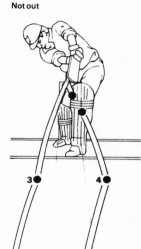 Not out

1 ball pitched on offside
2 ball pitched straight before wicket
3 player first hits ball with bat or hand
4 ball pitched outside leg stump

Handled the ball If the batsman touches the ball with his hand when it is in play unless the hand is holding the bat or unless he is requested to touch the ball by the opposition.

Hit the ball twice If the batsman strikes or stops the ball with any part of the bat or his person and then willfully hits it again unless he is protecting his wicket.

Obstructing the field If the batsman willfully obstructs any member of the opposition. (Dismissals by handled the ball, hit the ball twice, obstructing the field, and run out are not credited to the bowler.)

Retiring A batsman may retire at any time, but may only resume his innings with the consent of the opposing captain.

Fielding A fielder may stop the ball with any part of his body, but if he uses any other means (eg his cap) the batting side is awarded five runs.
Not more than two fielders may field behind the popping crease on the leg side; if they do, the umpire will call a no ball.
The wicket keeper must stay behind the stumps until the ball passes the wicket or touches the striker's bat or body, or until the batsman attempts a run.

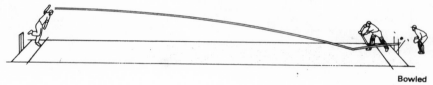  Bowled / Hit wicket
 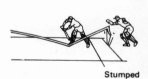 Run out / Stumped
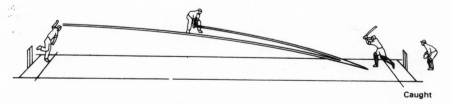 Caught

Dead ball The ball is "dead" when:
it settles in the hands of the wicket keeper or bowler;
it goes over the boundary;
it lodges in the clothing or equipment of a batsman or umpire;
a batsman is out:
a penalty is awarded for a lost ball or a fielding infringement.

The umpire may call "dead ball" at his discretion:
in the case of a serious injury;
if the striker is not ready;
if the bowler drops the ball.
The bowl is not dead if:
it strikes an umpire;
a wicket is broken (unless the batsman is out);
an unsuccessful appeal is made.

The ball is in play the moment the bowler starts his run.
Misconduct The umpires will intervene if:
players lift the ball's seam to obtain a better grip;
bowlers use wax or resin to shine the ball, though they may dry the ball with sawdust or a towel;
the fielding side attempts

to distract the receiving batsman or tries to help its own bowlers by damaging the pitch;
bowlers persistently bowl "bouncers" (short, fast deliveries);
batsmen attempt to "steal" runs during a bowler's run up.

Lacrosse

Two versions of lacrosse are played internationally: the 12-a-side game for women, and the 10-a-side men's game. The major differences, apart from team size, are in the pitch, substitution rules, and the amount of body contact and stick checking allowed. In both versions the ball is caught, thrown, and carried using sticks fitted with nets; and play is allowed behind the goals.

Pitch Women's pitches are not marked by boundary lines; approximate dimensions are shown.

Teams

Men's lacrosse The 10 players in a men's team are the goalkeeper, three defenders, three midfielder's, and three attackmen. Each team must at all times keep four players in its own half, and three in the opposing side's half.
For internationals, men's teams may have up to nine substitutes and substitution may be made at any stoppage of play (Some countries have more restrictive substitution laws.)
Each team has a playing captain, and only he may appeal to officials.
Women's lacrosse is always played with teams of 12 players and one substitute.

Men's pitch

59ft 18m
46ft 14.03m
End line
Sideline
40yd 36.60m
Wing area
Wing area
59ft 18m
110yd 100.65m
Goal area
70yd 64.05m

6ft 1.83m
18ft 5.50m
6ft 1.83m

Women's pitch
100yd 91.50m
120yd 110m
82yd 75m

Officials

Men's lacrosse:
two referees on the field (**1**);
a timekeeper (**2**);
a scorer, who records goals and fouls (**3**).
Women's lacrosse:
a center umpire, in charge of the game;
and two goal umpires, who do not change ends during the game.

Duration

Men play four "quarters," each of 15 minutes' playing time. Teams change ends after each quarter. There is a 10-minute interval at half time, and there are 2-minute intervals after the first and third quarters.
A team is allowed two time-outs per half, of up to 2 minutes each. They may be called only when the ball is dead, or when the ball is in the possession of that team and in the opponents' half.

If the score is equal at full time, the match continues for 4-minute periods, changing ends after each, until a goal is scored. Two further time-outs are allowed to a team in the first overtime period.
Women play two halves of 25 minutes.
Starting play The team captains toss for choice of ends. The match begins with a "face" for men or a "draw" for women. It restarts in the same way after intervals, goals, and some stoppages.

Playing the ball Players may pass, throw, catch, or carry the ball in their sticks (**1**); and roll or kick it (**2**).
A goalkeeper may touch the ball with his hand, but only to deflect a shot within his goal crease — he must not catch or throw it.
A player must be gripping his stick with at least one hand before he can play the ball or become involved in the game in any way.

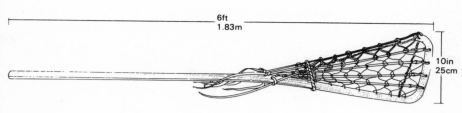

6ft
1.83m

10in
25cm

The stick is strung so that the ball should not become lodged in it, and shaped so that it cannot be used to hook an opponent or his stick. Metal may not be used in its construction.
Men's sticks must be at least 3ft long and 5–12in wide. Usual dimensions are as shown. Women's sticks may be any length.

The ball India rubber, colored white or orange. It should weight 4½–5oz and bounce 47–50in when dropped from 100in onto concrete. Its circumference is 7¾–8in.

Dress

Men players wear:
1 shirt numbered front and back
2 helmet and/or faceguard
3 shorts
4 elbow pads
5 gauntlets
6 shin guards
Goalkeepers may also wear:
7 body pad
8 tracksuit trousers and thigh pads.

Women goalkeepers wear body and leg padding. Other players sometimes wear shin pads and gloves.

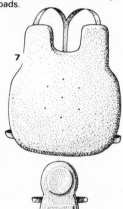

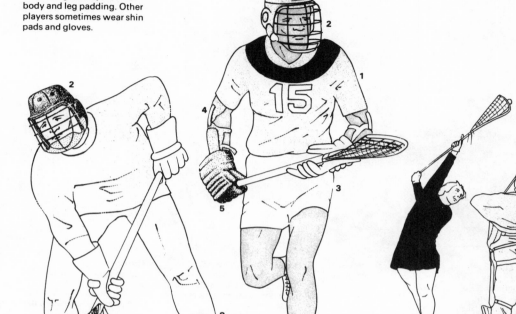

Scoring A goal is scored when the ball passes completely over the goal line. It may be conceded by a defender, but it cannot be deflected by the foot or leg of an attacker, or by a non-player. A goal cannot be scored: after an official has whistled; after the period has ended; if offside applies; if any part of the

attacker is inside the goal crease; or when the attacking team has too many players on the field.

Neutral throw In women's lacrosse, the game may be restarted with a throw:
if two players are equidistant from the ball when it goes out of bounds or play is stopped;
when the ball lodges in a stick or clothing;
when two opposing players foul simultaneously;
when the ball goes into the goal off a non-player;

when an unintentional incident has stopped play;
when the game has been stopped for any other reason.
The two players to compete for possession stand at least 1m apart, the defending player nearer her own goal. The umpire stands with her back to the center of the field, 5–10m from the players, and throws the ball with a short high

throw so that the players take it as they move in.
No throw is permitted within 10m of the goal or a boundary.

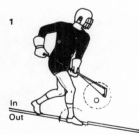

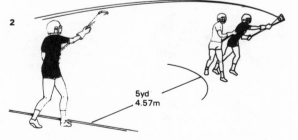

5yd
4.57m

Out of play The ball is out of play if it, or the player in possession of it, passes over a boundary line (**1**).
Possession is given against the team that last touched the ball —except for "out of play" after a shot at goal, when the ball is awarded to the player of either side nearest to the ball when it went out.

The game is restarted by a free play. All other players must be at least 5yd from the team member taking the play (**2**).

Entering the goal crease
The goal crease is the circle surrounding each goal area. No attacking player is allowed within the crease at any time. If he touches the ground within the crease with any part of his body (**3**), his side loses possession. But he may reach into the crease to catch the ball or play a loose ball (**4**).

If the goalkeeper gains possession of the ball while within the crease, his stick may not be checked by an opponent. But the goalkeeper, or any defender with the ball, may only remain within the crease for 4 seconds. No defender in possession of the ball may enter the crease.

Offside If a men's team does not have its players properly distributed in the two halves, it is offside.
If a team has four or more players off the field in the penalty box, it will not be penalized for having fewer than four players in its own half, provided it keeps three players in the opponents' half and the rest in its own.

©DIAGRAM

The face

The draw

The face (men's lacrosse)

The ball is placed on the ground between the backs of the sticks of two opposing players, who crouch with their backs to the goal they are defending.

Their sticks must be parallel to and touching the ground, and 1in apart. Their hands must be on the handles of their sticks and at least 1ft 6in apart, but not touching the stringing of the stick. The ball is rested between the backs of the sticks.

When the referee blows his whistle, the two players attempt to direct the ball with sticks or feet.

No other player may stand within 5yd.

A face may be used after a stoppage in any part of the field, except within 20yd of the goal line or a boundary line (but a face directly behind the goal, 20ft from the end line, is allowed).

A face at the center spot is used at the start of a quarter or after a goal is scored.

The draw

is used in the women's game, instead of the face.

The two center players stand each with one foot toeing the center line. They hold their sticks in the air, about hip level, wood to wood, parallel to the center line, so that each stick is between the ball and the player's goal.

No other player may be within 10m.

The umpire places the ball between the sticks and orders "ready, draw." The two players then draw their sticks up and away from each other. A player may turn her stick under the ball as the stick is swept away. A left-handed player may swing her stick behind her head instead of in front of it.

Tackling

Men players may:
charge an opponent shoulder to shoulder when competing for a ground ball (**1**);
body check an opponent who has the ball or is about to receive it (a body check is placing the body in the way of and facing an opponent);
check an opponent's stick with their own if the opponent had the ball or is about to receive it (**2**).

Fouls

A player may not:
charge an opponent in a reckless or dangerous manner (**3**);
hold or trip an opponent (**4**);
interfere with an opponent's stick, except by a legal stick check;
strike an opponent with the stick (**5**);
obstruct or impede an opponent (**6**), except by a legal body check (a player does not have to move from an opponent's path);
throw the stick;
wave or hold the stick in front of an opponent (**7**).

Women's lacrosse

allows no body contact and only limited stick checking.

1

2

3

4

5

6

7

Penalties

Men's lacrosse Time penalties are awarded for fouls. For "technical" (ie minor) fouls: the ball is either given to the other team, or the offending player is suspended for 30 seconds.

For "personal" fouls, players are suspended for 1-3 minutes.

For "expulsion" fouls (flagrant offenses against other players or officials), a player may be suspended for the rest of the game.

Women's lacrosse A "free position" is awarded for all fouls: the player who has been fouled is given the ball, and all other players must be at least 5m away. On the whistle, the player with the ball may pass, run, or shoot.

Roller hockey

3ft–3ft 9in
91—114cm

2in
5cm

The stick must be of the dimensions shown and must not weigh more than 18oz. It is made of wood and must have no metal parts. Binding is allowed. The blade must be curved, and flat on both sides.
Ball It must be of one color and contrast with the rink. Weight 5½oz. Circumference 9in.

Skates Roller skates must be bolted to the boots. There must be at least 4¾in between the axles. The wheels must be at least 1¼in in diameter. No metal or projections are allowed on the boots.

Roller hockey is played by two teams of five players on a firm and level rink surrounded by a barrier. Players are allowed to play the ball only with their sticks, although they may stop it with any part of their bodies except the hands. Teams score goals by hitting the ball into the net from within their opponents' half. The game is similar to ice hockey, but it is played on roller skates.

Dress Players wear protective padding including knee pads. Only goalkeepers may wear pads on their legs outside their clothing. Goalkeepers are allowed to wear helmets, face masks, and gloves.

Rink The surface must be firm but not slippery, and must be surrounded by a barrier 8in high.

Teams Each team has five players, including a goalkeeper. Five substitutes, including a substitute goalkeeper are allowed. There must always be at least two players on the rink.
Substitution Players can be substituted during the game; goalkeepers only during a stoppage.
Officials include a referee who controls the game, assisted by:
two goal judges;
two timekeepers;
an official to keep a record of the match.
Starting Captains toss for choice of ends. The game then starts with a strike-off at the center.
Strike-off Two opponents face each other, with their backs to their own goals. Their sticks must be before them, the blades touching the floor and 9in behind the ball. They play the ball when the referee whistles.
Duration In international matches a game consists of two periods, each of 20 minutes playing time. Otherwise, a half varies from 10–20 minutes. There is an interval of 3 minutes.
Extra time If both sides are equal at the end of the regular playing time, a 3-minute rest is allowed. Then the teams begin a play-off, with the first team to score a goal winning. If neither team has scored after 10 minutes, they are given another 3-minute rest, then change ends, and begin another 10-minute period. This system is continued until a winner is determined.

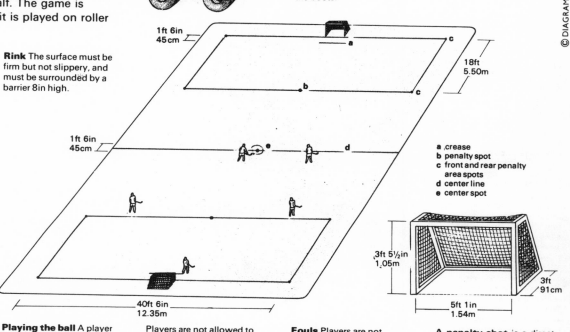

1ft 6in
45cm

18ft
5.50m

1ft 6in
45cm

a ,crease
b penalty spot
c front and rear penalty area spots
d center line
e center spot

3ft 5½in
1.05m

3ft
91cm

5ft 1in
1.54m

40ft 6in
12.35m

© DIAGRAM

Playing the ball A player may only play the ball with his stick, which may not be raised above his shoulders. He may stop the ball with his skates or any part of his body except his hands, provided it is not knocked forward to his team's advantage. He is not allowed to kick, pick up, carry, push, or drag the ball with any part of his body or his skates. When shooting, it is forbidden to hit the ball with the acute edge of the blade (chopping); the ball may be hit only with the flat part of the blade. The ball must not rise above 5ft, except when it ricochets off two sticks outside the penalty area. (Inside the penalty area a face-off is awarded from the nearest base spot.) The goalkeeper is allowed to play the ball within his penalty area with any part of his body, including his hands, even if he is on the ground. But he must not deliberately trap the ball. If the ball lodges in his clothing or in the external netting of the goal, a face-off is awarded from the nearest base spot in the penalty area.

Players are not allowed to interfere with play:
if a skate is damaged or removed from the boot;
if the wheels of a skate are not running freely;
without a stick;
when any part of the body is touching the rink;
when holding the barrier or the goal cage (the goalkeeper is allowed to hold onto his goal cage).
Scoring A goal can only be scored from within the opponents' half unless a player touches the ball before it enters his own net. The whole of the ball must cross the line between the posts.
Out of play If the ball is played out of the rink, the opposition is awarded an indirect free hit. It is taken 2½ft from where the ball crossed the barrier. A strike-off is awarded: if the ball ricochets off two sticks; if it was deliberately played to obtain a free hit; or if the referee is uncertain which team last played the ball.

Fouls Players are not allowed to:
play the ball illegally;
charge unfairly;
obstruct deliberately;
fight, trip, kick, throw, hold an opponent, use the stick against an opponent; tackle unfairly.
Penalties Violations of the rules may be penalized as follows.
An indirect frank hit (free hit) may be awarded. The ball must be stationary for the hit. Opponents must be at least 9ft away. The player taking the hit may not play the ball again until it has been touched by another player. A goal may not be scored direct from an indirect frank hit.
A direct frank hit is awarded for more serious fouls. All players, except the one taking the hit and the goalkeeper, must be 15ft behind the ball; they must not move until the ball is played. The goalkeeper must be behind the crease line, but his stick may be in front of it. A goal may be scored direct, but a direct shot is not necessary.

A penalty shot is a direct shot from the penalty spot; awarded for grave or serious infringement of rules within the penalty area. All players, except the one taking the penalty shot and the goalkeeper, must be behind the center line. The goalkeeper must be behind the crease line. No player, including the goalkeeper, may move until the ball is played. The striker may not play the ball again unless it has hit the goalkeeper or the outside of the goal.
Expulsion A player may be sent off for any period up to 5 minutes playing time, or for the rest of the game. He cannot be replaced by a substitute. For a second offense, a player must be sent off for the rest of the match.

Field hockey

Hockey is a field game played by both men and women. Each team has 11 players, who use a curved stick to hit the ball along the ground. The object of the game is to send the ball into the opponents' goal, and the team to score the greater number of goals wins.

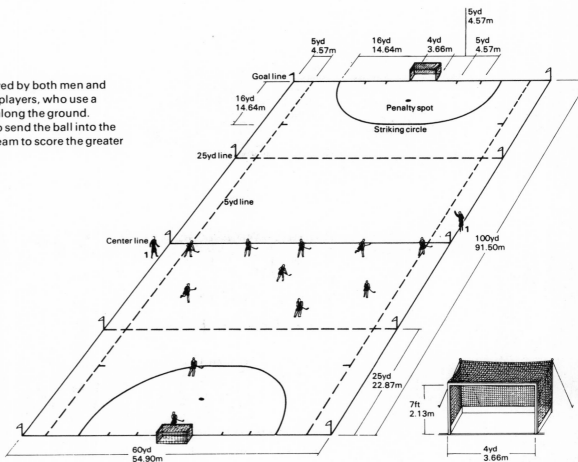

The pitch conforms to the measurements shown. Women's hockey pitches do not have penalty spots, but have a line 5yd in from each touchline, on which there is a mark 16yd from the goal line.

Officials Two umpires (**1**) and one or two timekeepers. Each umpire supervises play in his half of the pitch and controls the game with a whistle. An umpire may not penalize a team's offense if its opponents thereby gain an advantage.

Teams have a maximum of 11 players, including a captain. No substitutes are allowed in men's hockey; two are allowed for injury only in women's hockey.

Dress Shirt, shorts (or skirt), socks, and boots. No dangerous objects or boots with metal studs, spikes, or nails may be worn.

Goalkeepers wear special protective clothing:
1 faceguard
2 gloves
3 pads
4 heavy boots

Duration There are two periods of 35 minutes each. Teams change ends at half time, when there is an interval of 5—10 minutes. In the event of an injury, the game is suspended and lost time is added to the half.

Playing the ball Players may only control the ball with the flat side of their sticks, but within his own circle the goalkeeper may (except in a penalty bully) kick the ball or stop it with any part of his body.

Shinguard

Scoring A goal is scored when the whole ball has passed over the goal line between the posts and under the crossbar, provided it has been played by an attacker from within the striking circle. (It remains valid if the ball is deflected off a defender.) If the posts or bar are displaced, the umpire decides if the goal is valid.

The bully- start

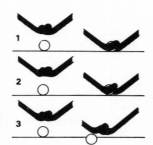

Starting play Team captains toss for choice of ends and the game starts with a ''bully'' at the center of the pitch.

The bully One player from each team stands squarely facing the sidelines, with his own goal line to his right. The ball is placed on the ground between the two players, and each then taps his stick first on the ground on his own side of the ball, then—with the face of the stick—his opponent's stick above the ball. This is done three times, after which one player must strike the ball. All other players must stand at least 5yd from the ball and between it and their own goal line. If there is any infringement, the bully is replayed.

A bully at the center line also restarts play after a goal and half time, and elsewhere on the pitch after an injury, etc. If taken from the striking area, the bully must be at least 5yd from the goal line.

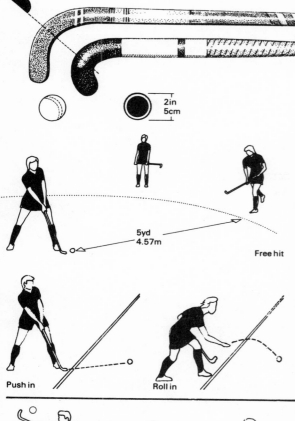

2in
5cm

The stick has a flat face on its left-hand side. The head is made of wood, and must have no metal fittings, sharp edges or splinters. It must be narrow enough to pass (including its binding) through a ring with an interior diameter of 2in. Weight: 12–28oz (men); maximum 23oz (women).

The ball is white, and made of cork and twine covered in stitched or seamless leather. It weighs 5½–5¾oz.

Free hits are awarded to the non-offending side for infringements, and are usually taken where the offense occurred.

The ball must be stationary and be hit with a legitimate stroke (men's hockey forbids the scoop stroke at free hits). Other players must be at least 5yd away. The hitter may not replay the ball (and men may not approach within playing distance of it) until another player has touched it.

In men's hockey, if an attacker fouls within 16yd of the goal line, the free hit may be taken anywhere within that distance along a line on which the offense occurred.

In women's hockey, after an offense by an attacker inside the circle, a free hit may be taken anywhere in the circle.

5yd
4.57m

Free hit

Push in

Roll in

If opposing players foul simultaneously, they take a bully at that spot.

A push-in (men) or a roll-in (women) is awarded to the opposition if a player hits the ball wholly over the sideline. A push-in is played along the ground with the stick; a roll-in is played by hand and must touch the pitch within 1yd of where it crossed the line. Other players and their sticks must be at least 5yd away, or beyond the 5yd line in women's hockey.

The person putting the ball into play may not touch it again (and men may not approach within playing distance of it) until another player has touched it.

Any violation by the player putting the ball into play is penalized by a push-in or

roll-in to the opposition. If another player violates this, it is retaken.

Behind There are three methods of restarting play if the ball crosses the goal line without scoring.

A free hit occurs from 16yd opposite where the ball crossed the line if the ball was last played by an attacker, or if a defender unintentionally hit it over the line from at least 25yd away.

A corner is awarded to the attacker if a defender plays the ball unintentionally over the line from less than 25yd away.

A penalty corner is given if a defender intentionally plays the ball over the goal line.

A corner hit is taken by an attacker on the goal line or sideline within 3yd (men) or 5yd (women) of the opponents' corner flag nearer where the ball crossed the line. Six defenders stand with their feet and sticks behind their goal line. Other defenders (men) must be beyond the center line until the corner is taken, or beyond the 25yd line (women) until the ball has been touched by another player or has gone outside the circle. Attackers must be outside the striking circle. No attacker may shoot at the goal from a corner hit unless the ball is stopped first, or touches a defender's stick or person.

1 "Sticks"

2 Tripping

3 Charging

4 Between feet

© DIAGRAM

Fouls A player must not: raise any part of his stick above the shoulder when playing or attempting to play the ball ("sticks") (1); trip (2), shove, charge (3), strike, or handle an opponent; obstruct an opponent with the body or stick; play the ball with the rounded side of the stick; interfere in the game without a stick; undercut or play the ball in a potentially dangerous way; stop the ball in the air or on the ground with any part of the body other than the hand; use the foot or leg to support the stick in order to resist an opponent; pick up, kick, throw, carry, or propel the ball except with the stick;

hit, hook, hold, or interfere with an opponent's stick. Women may not hit the ball between their feet (4); and men are not permitted to change sticks temporarily.

Penalty corners are awarded against defenders for: deliberately playing the ball over the goal line; offenses within the circle (unless a penalty stroke or penalty bully is taken); after a deliberate foul within the 25yd line; after an infringement at a corner (men's hockey). It is taken anywhere on the goal line, at least 10yd from the goalpost. In men's hockey not more than six defenders stand behind their goal line.

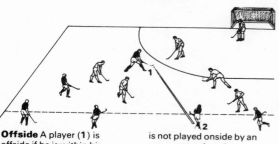

Offside A player (1) is offside if he is within his opponents' half when the ball is played by a teammate (2) further from the goal line than he is, and when there are fewer than two (three in women's hockey) opponents nearer the goal line than he is. An offside player is only penalized if he gains an advantage. In men's hockey he

is not played onside by an opponent unless that opponent deliberately touches the ball.

An offside is penalized by a free hit to the opposition at the spot where it occurred.

A penalty stroke (men's hockey) is awarded against defenders in the circle for an intentional foul, an unintentional foul that prevents a goal, or persistent and deliberate positioning infringements at penalty corners.

It is taken from the penalty spot by an attacker, who may take one step forward to hit the ball. Thereafter, he may not replay the ball or approach the goal.

The goalkeeper may not raise his stick above shoulder level, leave the goal line or move either foot until the stroke has been made. All other players must stand beyond the 25yd line.

If the goalkeeper illegally prevents a goal, it is still awarded unless the attacker

induced the offense. If the ball halts outside the circle or passes out of it, the penalty stroke is ended. If no goal is scored, or if an attacker commits an offense, the game restarts with a free hit 16yd in front of the center of the goal line.

A penalty bully (women's hockey) is awarded for the same offenses as the penalty stroke.

It is taken by the offender (or defending back if the offender is injured or suspended) and any selected opponent, 5yd in front of the center of the goal line. All other players stand beyond the 25yd line.

A goal may be scored off the attacker's stick, or the body or stick of the defender. It may be awarded for an offense (other than a mis-bully) at the bully

by a defender. If the defender hits or deflects the ball over any part of the goal line within the circle, the bully is retaken. If the ball goes outside the circle, or after an offense by the attacker, the game restarts with a bully at the center of the 25yd line.

If both players foul simultaneously, the bully is retaken; it is also retaken if another player interferes or if the ball lodges in the dress of a player, goalkeeper, or umpire. Extra time is allowed to take a penalty bully if half or full time is already completed.

Hurling

Hurling is a Gaelic field game played by two teams of 15 players. The ball may be struck with or carried on the hurley and, when off the ground, may be struck with the hand or kicked. The object is to score most points. A goal (3 points) is scored when the ball passes between the posts and under the crossbar; one point is scored when it passes between the posts and over the crossbar.

Pitch The minimum size is 140yd by 84yd; the maximum 160yd by 100yd.

Teams Each team has 15 players and may have three substitutes. Substitution is permitted only during a stoppage.

Officials The game is controlled by a referee (**1**). He is assisted by two linesmen (**2**), who change sides at half time, and four goal umpires (**3**), who stand one outside each goalpost and do not change ends at half time.

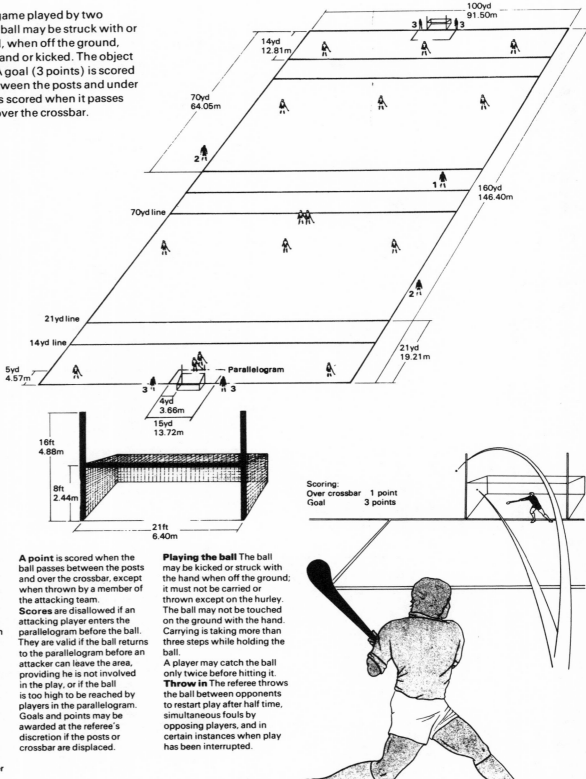

Start The captains toss for choice of ends. Two players from each side then line up at the center and the other players position themselves behind their own 70yd line. The referee then throws the ball along the ground between the players.

Duration Playing time is 60 minutes, with a maximum interval of 10 minutes at half time, after which the teams change ends.

Scoring The team scoring most points wins.

A **goal** (3 points) is scored when the entire ball passes between the posts and under the crossbar, except when thrown or carried by a member of the attacking team.

A **point** is scored when the ball passes between the posts and over the crossbar, except when thrown by a member of the attacking team.

Scores are disallowed if an attacking player enters the parallelogram before the ball. They are valid if the ball returns to the parallelogram before an attacker can leave the area, providing he is not involved in the play, or if the ball is too high to be reached by players in the parallelogram. Goals and points may be awarded at the referee's discretion if the posts or crossbar are displaced.

Playing the ball The ball may be kicked or struck with the hand when off the ground; it must not be carried or thrown except on the hurley. The ball may not be touched on the ground with the hand. Carrying is taking more than three steps while holding the ball.

A player may catch the ball only twice before hitting it.

Throw in The referee throws the ball between opponents to restart play after half time, simultaneous fouls by opposing players, and in certain instances when play has been interrupted.

The hurley is a curved stick with a broad blade. It is 4in at its widest and tapers to each end. There is no standard weight.

The ball generally has a cork center with a cover of horsehide. Circumference 9—10in. Weight $3\frac{1}{2}$—$4\frac{1}{2}$oz.

3ft
91cm

Dress Players wear:
1 shirt
2 shorts
3 socks
4 boots
5 helmet (optional)

Penalties

A free puck is awarded for infringements. It is taken where the offense occurred unless:

a) the offense was committed by a defender in the 21yd area (when it is taken from the opposite point on the 21yd line);

b) a player is fouled after delivering the ball (when it is taken where the ball lands, unless a goal is scored or the ball goes out of play, in which case the free puck is taken where the ball went out).

Except for sideline pucks, the ball must be on the ground or lifted with the hurley and struck above the ground. The ball may not be transferred from the hurley to the hand at a free puck.

The player may not play the ball again until it has been touched by another player. If it hits a non-player direct from the free puck, the free puck is retaken.

If a player stands within 21yd or illegally charges a free puck, the opposing team is awarded a free puck from where he stood or charged.

A puck-out is awarded to the defenders when an attacker hits the ball across the end line. It is taken from within the parallelogram.

The ball may be held, but must be hit on the first stroke; if missed, it may not be held again but may be raised or pucked off the ground.

The player may hit the ball more than once before another player touches it.

All opponents must be beyond the 21yd line. If the opposition encroaches into the 21yd area, the defense takes a free puck on that line opposite where the offender stood.

A 70yd free puck is awarded to the attacking team when the ball is played over the end line by a defender. It is taken on the 70yd line, opposite where the ball crossed the line.

If a player stands within 21yd or charges before it is taken, a free puck is awarded from where he charged or stood.

A side puck is awarded against a player who plays the ball over the sideline. It is taken as a free puck where the ball crossed the line.

The linesman positions the ball; the player must not move it before striking it.

All other players must be at least 14yd away; a free puck is awarded after an offense.

Tackling A player may charge an opponent shoulder to shoulder. A player is not fouled if he turns deliberately to make a fair charge come from behind.

A goalkeeper may not be charged within the parallelogram, unless he has the ball or is obstructing an opponent.

A player may strike another player's hurley only if both are striking the ball.

Fouls A player may not: push, kick, trip (**1**), hold, strike, or jump at an opponent obstruct a player with his hand or arm, even if not holding him, reach from behind a player who has the ball;

charge a player from behind (**2**), or charge or interfere with an opponent who is not playing the ball or moving to play the ball;

deliberately touch a player with the hurley;

reach for the ball with the hurley over another player;

throw the hurley.

Interference If anyone but a player prevents the ball crossing the sidelines, a side puck is awarded against the last player to hit the ball.

A goal, point, or 70yd puck is awarded if the ball is similarly prevented from scoring or from crossing an end line.

Expulsion The referee may send off any player guilty of violent or threatening conduct. A whole team may be disqualified and suspended for rough play. Players may also be cautioned.

Foul - tripping

Foul - barging in the back

©DIAGRAM

Shinty

Shinty is a Gaelic field game of Scottish origin, played by two teams of 12 men each. A caman (club) is used to hit a ball, and the object is to score goals in a match lasting 90 minutes divided into two halves.

10yd 9.15m
10yd 9.15m
2
20yd 18.30m
3
200yd 183m
3
10yd 9.15m
a
h 1
10ft 3.05m
4ft 6in 1.37m
12ft 3.66m
d
f
e
3
10yd 9.15m
2
g
c
b
100yd 91.50m

The field The minimum size of the field is 70yd by 140yd. The fronts of the goalposts are white. Only at the top may the front and back goalposts be connected by a bar, strut, or board.
The byelines and sidelines should be fenced.
Alternatively, both goals should be protected by a barrier of wood, wire, or rope a minimum distance of 15ft from either side of the goalposts. All fences, posts, etc, except corner flags, are at least 6ft from byelines and sidelines.

a side line
b byeline
c flag posts, not less than 3ft 6in high (1.06m)
d penalty spot
e 10yd area
f goal line
g barrier
h center spot

Players Each team has 12 players. An injured goalkeeper and one outfield player may be replaced by substitutes at any time.
Dress Players wear jerseys, shorts, socks, and boots without spikes or tackets (hobnails or studs). The goalkeeper must wear a jersey of a different color.
Officials The referee (1) controls the game. He is assisted by goal judges and linesmen, who do not change ends at half time and report only at the referee's request. Goal judges (2) observe goal scoring, fouls in the 10yd area, when the ball crosses the goal line and who last hit it, and whether an attacker is in the 10yd area when the ball enters it.
Linesmen (3) are responsible for one half of a sideline each. They observe when the ball crosses the sideline and who hit it.
Duration Games last 90 minutes, with an interval of at least 5 minutes at half time. Extra time is allowed for a penalty hit to be taken.
The ball must be in play when each half ends.

The start Play is begun and restarted after a goal with a throw up in the center.
After half time, play restarts with a throw up where the ball was last in play, unless it was in the 10yd area or where a set blow is necessary.
The throw up The referee blows his whistle and starts the game by throwing up the ball to a minimum height of

12ft between two opposing players standing on the center spot.
The two players must stand at least 3ft apart, with camans crossed. They shall not move away until the ball is hit in the air or touches the ground.
If the two center players are one left-handed and one right, each has choice of his side in the throw up for half the match.

No other player is allowed within 5yd of the center spot until the ball is played.
Playing the ball Players may use both sides of the caman to hit the ball.
Only the goalkeeper may use his hands to stop or control the ball.
Kicking the ball is not allowed. The ball may be passed without touching the ground.

A player within striking distance of the ball is allowed to hook an opponent's caman.
Scoring For a goal to be scored, the ball must pass wholly over the goal line between the posts and under the crossbar.

A throw up

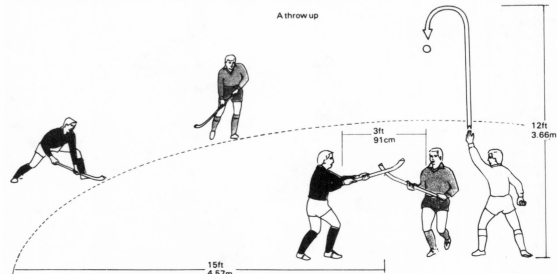

3ft 91cm

12ft 3.66m

15ft 4.57m

2½in
6.4cm

The caman (club) is wooden, without metal attachments. It should not stand higher than hip level. The "bas" (head) must pass

through a 2½in diameter ring. The "bas" is triangular, the "cas" (shaft) cylindrical. Leather or tape binding is used to give a good grip.

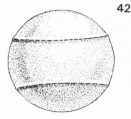

The ball is made of cork and worsted, with a leather covering.
Weight: 2½–3½oz.
Circumference: 7½–8in.

Out of play
A 10yd hit is awarded from anywhere within the 10yd area to the defending side if an attacker sends the ball across the goal line without a goal being scored.
A corner hit is awarded from the 2yd quarter circle to the attacking side if a defender hits the ball across his own goal line. A goal may be scored directly from a corner hit.
A hit in is awarded to the opposition if the ball is accidentally hit across the sideline.
The hit is taken where the ball crossed the line. The player faces the pitch with both feet on the ground. No player may be within 5yd of the striker before the ball is in the air. The ball is returned to the field by an overhead hit with the back of the caman.
If the player misses the ball completely, he may retake the hit. If he does not take the hit correctly, it is awarded to the opposition. If he hits the ball more than once, a set blow is awarded to the opposition. After the hit, the striker may not participate again until another player has hit the ball. A goal may be scored directly from a hit in.

Offside An attacker can only be offside if he is in the 10yd area when the ball enters it.
A set blow to the opponents is the penalty imposed for infringements, including offside, unless it would give an advantage to the offender. The ball is placed on the ground where the infringement occurred and is struck with the club in any direction.
No other player may be within 5yd of the striker until the blow is taken, or the referee may order a retake. If the player misses the ball completely, the blow is retaken.
After the blow, the striker may not participate again until the ball has touched the club, body, or clothing of another player. A goal may be scored directly from a set blow.

A hit in

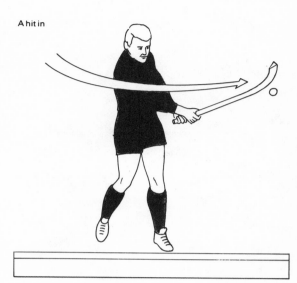

A set blow

Offside

Fouls No player shall: kick (**1**), catch (**2**), or throw the ball (though the goalkeeper inside his 10yd area may stop and slap the ball with his open hand); use his hands, arms, legs, knees, or club to hold, obstruct, push, charge, trip, hack, jump at, or throw an opponent; deliberately throw his caman at the ball, or join play without his caman, or part of it, in his hand (**3**); deliberately hinder another player while not himself playing the ball (he is penalized for obstruction) (**4**); deliberately put the ball over the sideline (a set blow is awarded to the opposition at the point of striking); cleek (hook) an opponent's caman when the player hooking is not himself within striking distance of the ball (**5**). Hooking when within striking distance of the ball is allowed (**6**).

Cautions and suspension
The referee may caution or expel a player for: rough or reckless play; misconduct; willful infringement of the rules; or ungentlemanly speech or behavior on the field.
A suspended player may not be replaced.
Penalty hit A penalty hit is awarded against a defender for an infringement in the 10yd area.
The ball is hit direct at goal from the penalty spot.
Until the hit is taken, all players except the striker and defending goalkeeper, who shall remain on his goal line, must stand behind and not closer than 5yd to the ball. The referee may order a retake if players are out of position.
If the ball fails to reach the goal line, the hit is deemed a bye and the ball is played by a defender.
If the ball strikes the goalposts or crossbar and rebounds onto the field, it shall be in play.
The striker may not hit the ball again until another player has touched it.
A goal may be scored directly from a penalty hit.

© DIAGRAM

Ice hockey

Ice hockey is played by two teams on an ice surface known as a rink. Five players and a goalkeeper from each team are allowed on the ice at any time. The object is to score points by hitting the puck with the stick into the opposing team's goal.

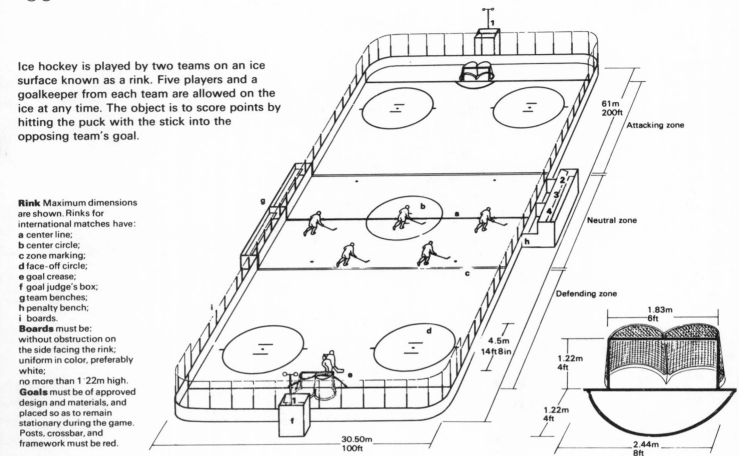

Rink Maximum dimensions are shown. Rinks for international matches have:
a center line;
b center circle;
c zone marking;
d face-off circle;
e goal crease;
f goal judge's box;
g team benches;
h penalty bench;
i boards.
Boards must be:
without obstruction on the side facing the rink;
uniform in color, preferably white;
no more than 1.22m high.
Goals must be of approved design and materials, and placed so as to remain stationary during the game. Posts, crossbar, and framework must be red.

Team benches, one for each team, able to hold 19 persons. Only players in uniform, managers, coaches, doctors, and trainers are allowed on the benches. The coach must stay within an area the length of his bench.
Penalty bench with space for eight players and extra seating for the timekeepers, scorer, and announcer.

Officials There must be: two neutral referees (international rules), or one referee and two linesmen (national rules); two goal judges(**1**); game timekeeper(**2**); penalty timekeeper(**3**); official scorer(**4**).

Players A team may have 15 players and a regular and spare goalkeeper in uniform at the start of a game. Players must wear numbers, and a list of final names and numbers must be given to the referee or scorer before the start.

A team may have only six players, including a goalkeeper, in play at any time; a bench minor penalty is imposed for an offense.

Goalkeeper A team may have only one goalkeeper on the ice at any time. Another player may be substituted for the goalkeeper, but without goalkeepers' privileges.

Starting line-up The visitors' manager or coach shall when asked:
give his starting line-up to the referee or scorer before the start of a game or period;
place a playing line-up on the ice.
A minor penalty is imposed if the starting line-up is changed.
Failure to play If a team in the dressing room fails to start play within 5 minutes of being so ordered, it shall forfeit the game and be reported to its federation.
If a team fails to appear because of accidental or unforeseen circumstances, the referee shall allow a further 15 minutes, after which the game shall be canceled and the incident reported to the authorities.

If a team withdrawn from the ice fails to return and play when the referee orders, it shall receive a bench minor penalty after one minute and forfeit the game after 2 minutes. The official responsible shall be suspended and reported to his federation.
Ends The home team has choice of ends at the start, or captains toss if there is no home team. Teams change ends after each period, and midway through the third and each overtime period.
Start The game begins with a face-off at the center of the rink.

Playing line-up
1 goalkeeper
2 right defense
3 left defense
4 center
5 right wing
6 left wing

Duration Three 20-minute periods of actual playing time, with 10 minutes' break between.
If any unusual delay occurs within 5 minutes of the end of the first or second periods, the referee may order the next intermission to be taken at once and the balance of that period to be added to the next one.
The ice is usually flooded between periods.
Result The team scoring most points wins. In general, if the score is equal after the three regular periods, the game is a tie (subject to national regulations).

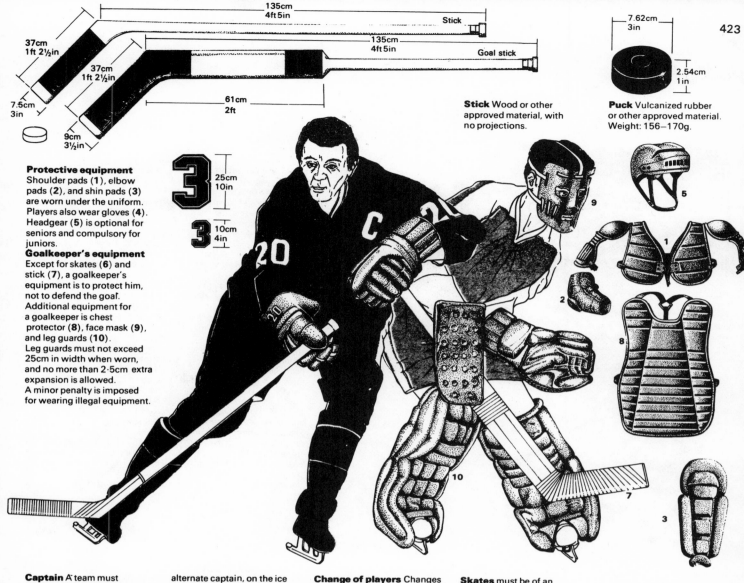

Defender

Attacker

9

Attacker

Scoring A team scores one point for each goal or assist. For a goal the puck must legally and completely cross the goal line, between the goalposts, and below the crossbar. A maximum of two assists may be awarded after certain types of goal.
A goal and assist(s) are scored when:
a) an attacker legally puts the puck into the goal with his stick;
b) the puck is deflected into the goal from the shot of an attacker off the stick, person, or skates of a teammate (provided it was not deliberately kicked, thrown, or otherwise directed into the goal).
In case a) the goal is credited to the scorer (**2**) and an assist to the player (**1**) or players who took part in the play preceding the shot.
In case b) the goal is credited to the deflecting player and the assist to the shooting player.

A goal but no assist is scored when:
a) the puck is put into the goal in any way by a defender (except as under "interference");
b) an attacker kicks the puck and it is deflected into the net by a defender other than the goalkeeper.
In case a) the goal is credited to the last attacker, and in case b) to the player who kicked the puck.
Awarded goals A goal is awarded to the attackers if, when the goalkeeper has been removed from the ice, an attacker with the puck is beyond the center line with no opponent between himself and the goal and is then interfered with by an opponent who:
illegally enters the game;
throws his stick;
fouls him from behind.
A goal is also awarded to the attackers if a goalkeeper throws his stick at the puck or an attacking player at a penalty shot.

Passing Rules govern the passing of the puck from zone to zone. In all cases the position of the puck, not the passing player's skates, determines the zone from which a pass is made. A pass is completed when the puck touches the body, stick, or skates of a teammate who is legally onside.
a) Any player may pass to a teammate in the same zone.
b) A player who was in the zone from which a pass was made may follow and play the puck in any zone, or over his opponents' goal line if the "icing" rule does not apply.
c) A defending team may make and take forward passes from their defending zone to the center line, but the pass must be completed by a player who is onside at the center line or follows the puck over that line.
d) If an attacker passes the puck back from his attacking zone, an opponent who was not in the zone where the pass was made may play the puck anywhere, provided the puck precedes him into his own attacking zone.
After all other types of pass, a face-off is held where the pass was made.

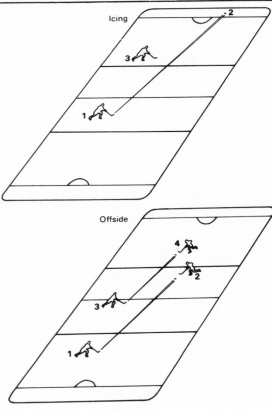

Icing

Offside

Icing the puck The puck is iced when a player (**1**) shoots the puck from behind the center line to beyond his opponents' goal line (**2**). The referee will call "icing" if the player attempted to pass the puck to a teammate who failed to touch it (**3**).
The puck is not iced:
if it enters the goal, in which case the goal counts;
if, from a face-off, it goes beyond the goal line at the other end of the ice;
if the referee considers that an opponent other than the goalkeeper was able to, but did not, play the puck before it passed his goal line;
if an opponent's person, skates, or stick touched the puck before it crossed the goal line.
If the referee wrongly calls "icing," the puck is faced in the neutral zone at the face-off spot farthest from the goal of the team last in possession of the puck.

Offside A player is offside if both his skates are completely beyond the relevant line when the puck is passed:
from the defending zone (**1**) to beyond the center line (**2**);
from the neutral zone (**3**), across the center line, and into the attacking zone (**4**).
A player who is offside may stop the puck before it crosses the line, return to his own side of that line, and then hit the puck over it.
If the referee considers that offside play was deliberate, a face-off is held at the end face-off spot in the offender's defending zone (except when the offender's team has fewer players than its opponents, in which case the face-off is from where the pass was started).

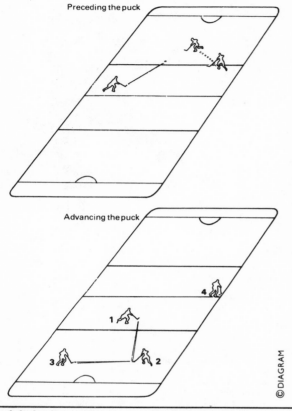

Preceding the puck

Advancing the puck

© DIAGRAM

Preceding the puck into the attacking zone is obligatory except:
when a player actually propelling the puck was first in possession of the puck with both feet in the neutral zone;
when the puck is cleanly intercepted by a defender and carried or passed into the neutral zone by the defenders;
when the player legally carries or passes the puck back from the neutral zone into his defending zone while an opponent is in the latter zone.
After an offense, a face-off is held in the neutral zone at the face-off spot nearest the offender's attacking zone

Advancing the puck A face-off is held at either end face-off spot in the defense zone if:
a player (**1**) outside his defense zone passes or carries the puck into his defense zone in order to delay the game;
a team in possession in its defense zone, unless prevented by opponents, fails to advance the puck towards the opponents' goal—player (**2**) to player (**3**).

A minor penalty is imposed if a player (**4**), other than a goalkeeper and unless checked by an opponent, deliberately holds the puck against the boards or goal.

Unplayable puck The puck is out of play if it:
a) leaves the playing surface;
b) hits an obstacle above the surface other than the boards, glass, or netting;
c) becomes lodged in the netting on the outside of a goal.
In cases a) and b), if the puck was accidentally put out of play, a face-off is held where the puck last touched a player (except when the rules state otherwise). If the puck was deliberately put out of play, a face-off is held where the offense occurred (except when the rules state otherwise).
In case c), if the puck was put out of play by a defender, a face-off is held at either end face-off spot. If an attacker was responsible, the face-off is at the nearest face-off spot in the neutral zone.

Puck out of sight If the referee is unable to see the puck in a scramble or under a fallen player, play is stopped and resumed in the same place with a face-off.

Illegal puck If during play another puck appears on the ice, play continues with the legal puck until the end of the play then in progress.

Puck striking referee Play continues if the puck strikes the referee, except when it is deflected directly into the goal (see face-off rules).

Injuries An injured player other than a goalkeeper may be replaced by a substitute without the teams leaving the ice.
An injured goalkeeper shall be replaced by the spare goalkeeper, unless both a team's goalkeepers are injured, in which case the players may leave the ice and the team has 10 minutes to prepare another goalkeeper.
An injured penalized player may go to the dressing room if a substitute sits on the penalty bench. If the injured player returns to his team bench before his penalty expires, he may take his place on the penalty bench when play next stops.
If an injured player is unable to go to his bench, play stops:
a) at once if his team had possession, though they may first shoot if in a shooting position;
b) after the opposing team loses possession if they had possession at the time of the injury, though the referee may stop play at once if an injury is serious.

Broken stick A player other than a goalkeeper may play without a stick, or with a broken stick if he drops the broken portions.
A new stick must not be thrown to him; he must collect it from his team bench.
A goalkeeper may play with a broken stick until a stop in play, or until he obtains a new stick. A goalkeeper may receive a new stick from a teammate without going to his team bench.
A minor penalty is imposed for any offense. If the goalkeeper illegally receives a stick, the minor penalty is served by a player then on the ice.

Leaving the benches A player who leaves his team bench during a disagreement on the ice shall receive a misconduct penalty.
A player who leaves the penalty bench except at the end of a period or when his penalty expires is penalized with:
a minor penalty if he does not enter a disturbance on the ice;
a minor penalty plus a misconduct penalty if he does enter such a disturbance (the penalties to be served at the end of his unexpired penalty).
If a penalty timekeeper's error causes a player to return prematurely to the ice, he shall serve only his unexpired time.
If a player is illegally on the ice (whether by his own error or not):
any goal scored by his team is disallowed;
any penalty imposed on either team is to be served.

Interference A minor penalty is imposed if a player:
interferes with or impedes the progress of an opponent not in possession of the puck;
deliberately knocks the stick from an opponent's hands, or prevents an opponent who has lost his stick from retrieving it;
by means of his stick or body interferes with or impedes the movements of the goalkeeper by actual contact, while the goalkeeper, but not the puck, is in the goal crease;
when on either bench, uses his stick or body to interfere with the puck or an opponent on the ice.
A gross misconduct penalty is imposed if a player on either bench:
throws any article on to the ice;
molests or interferes with an opponent or official.
Unless the puck is in the goal crease, a goal will be disallowed if an attacker not in possession stands or holds his stick in the goal crease or stands on the goal crease line—except when he is forced into that position by the interference of an opponent. (A face-off at the

nearest face-off spot in the neutral zone is held after a disallowed goal.)

Spectators' interference The referee will stop play if:
play is interfered with by objects thrown onto the ice;
a player is interfered with by a spectator (if that player's team has a scoring position, the referee will first allow the play to be completed).
Play will resume with a face-off where the stoppage occurred.

Delaying the game A bench minor penalty is imposed for deliberately delaying the game.
A minor penalty is imposed if a player leaves his team bench to instruct a teammate, unless he remains on the ice as a substitute.
If a player deliberately moves the goal, a minor penalty is imposed, except that a penalty shot is awarded if the minor penalty would not have expired before play ends.

FOULS

Charging into an opponent (**1**). It is a charge if a player takes more than two normal steps.

A minor penalty is imposed; a major penalty if injury is caused or if the charge is against an opponent from behind or against a goalkeeper within his crease.

High sticks (**2**) is carrying the stick above shoulder height.

A minor penalty may be imposed at the referee's discretion.

Hitting the puck with a high stick is penalized by a face-off, unless the offending side loses possession or scores against itself.

A goal scored from a high stick is disallowed, but a body deflection into goal while the stick is high is allowed.

Kneeing and elbowing (**3**) A minor penalty is imposed, or a major penalty if injury is caused.

Spearing, butt ending, or cross checking Spearing (**4**) and butt ending (**5**) are poking with the point or butt end of the stick.

In a cross check (**6**) both hands are on the stick and no part of the stick is on the ground.

A minor penalty is imposed; a major penalty if injury is caused or if the offense is against a goalkeeper in his crease.

Tripping (**7**) may be with the stick, knee, foot, arm, hand, or elbow.

A minor penalty is imposed, except when a puck carrier is tripped from behind when in the attacking zone with only the opposing goalkeeper to beat. In the latter case a penalty shot is awarded. No penalty is imposed if a player obtains possession by hook-checking.

Excessive roughness, board checking (**8**)**, and slashing** (**9**) may be penalized by a major penalty even when no injury is caused.

Board checking is causing an opponent to be thrown violently into the boards. Slashing is swinging the stick to impede or scare an opponent.

Hooking (**10**) A minor penalty is imposed on a player who impedes or seeks to impede the progress of an opponent by hooking with his stick; a major penalty if injury is caused.

Holding (**11**) A minor penalty is imposed on any player who holds an opponent with his stick or in any other way.

Clipping is falling and sliding into a puck carrier's path so that he loses possession.

A minor penalty is imposed on any player who clips an opponent; a major penalty if injury is caused. No penalty is imposed if the puck is hit from the opponent's possession before the player falls.

Kicking a player or deliberately injuring or attempting to injure any person are offenses penalized by a match penalty.

Fighting is penalized as follows:
starting a fight, match penalty;
fighting back, major penalty;
continuing to fight back, match penalty;
fighting on the playing surface or with another player off the playing surface, game misconduct penalty.

Throwing the stick is penalized as follows:
if a defender throws his stick or any article at the puck in his defending zone, a penalty shot is awarded to the attackers if they have not scored when that play is completed;
any other incident in the playing area incurs a major penalty;
any incident outside the playing area incurs a misconduct penalty.

Handling the puck A minor penalty is imposed if a player other than the goalkeeper closes his hands on the puck, or picks it up while play is in progress.

A penalty shot is awarded if a defending player other than the goalkeeper picks up the puck within the goal crease area.

A minor penalty is imposed if a goalkeeper:
holds the puck for more than 3 seconds;
throws it toward his opponents' goal (unless an opponent takes it);
deliberately drops it into his pads;
deliberately throws or bats it out of the playing area.

All players are permitted to stop or bat the puck in the air with the open hand, or to push it along the ice using the hand; but if another player of the same team plays the puck next, a face-off is held.

If a puck is knocked into the goal by the hand of an attacking player, directly off a defender, the goal is disallowed; but a puck sent into the goal by the hand of a defender is allowed as an own goal.

1 charging

2 high sticks

4 spearing

5 butt ending

6 cross checking

7 tripping

8 board checking

9 slashing

10 hooking

3 elbowing

Penalty shot

©DIAGRAM

Falling on the puck A minor penalty is imposed if any player other than a goalkeeper falls on or gathers the puck to his body in any way while standing or lying. A minor penalty is also imposed if the goalkeeper commits these offenses when the puck is behind the goal line and his body entirely outside his goal crease. A penalty shot is awarded if a defender commits these offenses when inside his goal area.

Misconduct toward officials A misconduct penalty is imposed on any player who:
uses obscene, profane, or abusive language;
persists in disputing, or shows disrespect for, the referee's rulings;
intentionally knocks the puck out of the referee's reach when he is retrieving it;
bangs his stick on the ice to show disrespect;
refuses to go at once to the penalty bench when penalized (the new penalty is imposed on his substitute);
unnecessarily enters or stays in the referee's crease while he is consulting with a game official;
persists, after a warning, in any conduct designed to incite an opponent into incurring a penalty;
molests an official.
If the referee cannot identify the culprit, a bench minor penalty is imposed on the offending team.
If a manager, coach, or trainer is guilty of any such misconduct, he is ordered to the dressing room for the rest of the game and the matter is reported.

PENALTIES
Minor penalty For a minor penalty the offender is ruled off the ice for 2 minutes' actual playing time.
No substitute is allowed.
If a team scores while the opposing team is shorthanded (has fewer players on the ice) following one or more minor (or bench minor) penalties, the first of these penalties automatically ends provided that the goal was not scored from a penalty. When the minor penalties of two teammates end at the same time, their captain designates which player will resume play first.
A bench minor penalty is imposed when an offense is by a team or when the actual offender is unknown. A bench minor penalty lasts for 2 minutes and is served by a team member designated by the manager or coach through the captain.
Major penalty For his first major penalty in a match, an offender is ruled off the ice for 5 minutes. For his second major penalty he is ruled off the ice for 15 minutes, and for his third for the rest of the match. A substitute is allowed after 5 minutes of a major penalty.
When a player receives a major and a minor penalty at the same time, the major penalty is served first.
Misconduct penalty For a misconduct penalty the player is sent off the ice for 10 minutes; a substitute is allowed immediately. After the penalty, the player may rejoin the game only at a stoppage of play.

Match penalty The offender is sent off for the rest of the game, and excluded from future games until his case has been dealt with. (See **Fouls** for details of when substitutes are permitted.)

Penalty shots The puck is placed on the center face-off spot. The captain chooses any player not serving a penalty to play the puck. Except for the opposing goalkeeper, all other players must withdraw behind the center line.
The opposing goalkeeper must remain in his goal crease until the puck crosses the blue line. He may then try to stop the puck or player in any legal way.
For the shot, the puck must be kept in motion toward the goal; a goal cannot be scored from a rebound.
If a player awarded a penalty shot is penalized in the same incident, he takes the shot before serving his penalty.
If a shot fails because an opponent distracts the player or a spectator interferes, the shot is retaken (the opponent receives a misconduct penalty).
Time for a penalty shot is not counted as playing time or overtime.
If a goal is scored, the puck is centered; if not, it is faced-off at either spot in that zone.

Game misconduct penalty For a game misconduct penalty the player is sent off for the rest of the game. A substitute is allowed at once. A second misconduct penalty by a player is automatically a game misconduct penalty.
Goalkeeper's penalties No goalkeeper can be sent to the penalty bench for a minor, major, or misconduct penalty. These penalties are served by a teammate then on the ice and chosen by the captain. For a second major penalty, a goalkeeper receives a game misconduct penalty. If given a game misconduct or match penalty, he is replaced by another player—but not by the substitute goalkeeper. The player receives the goalkeeper's full equipment and privileges.
A goalkeeper leaving his crease to enter an altercation incurs a bench minor penalty for his team.
Delayed penalties If a player is penalized while two teammates are serving penalties, he goes to the bench at once and his penalty time begins only when that of one of the other two players ends. A substitute may take his place on the ice until his penalty time begins.
In such a case, any player whose penalty expires can return to the ice only if play is stopped or the substitute is removed (except that if two teammates' penalties expire together, one may return immediately).
Calling of penalties Following a minor, major, or match penalty offense by a player of a side in possession, play is stopped at once.
If a minor penalty is signaled against a shorthanded team and a goal is scored by the other side before the whistle is blown, the goal is allowed and the delayed penalty forgotten (all other penalties continue)
All fouls before or after the referee stops play are penalized, even if they are by the same player.

11 holding

Bandy

Bandy is related to ice hockey, but there are certain basic differences between the two games. Bandy is played on a larger ice rink and there is no play behind the goals; 11 players from each team may be on the ice; they play a ball with curved sticks. The aim, as in ice hockey, is to score a greater number of goals than the opposing team.

Rink The minimum dimensions for major matches are 100m by 55m. The rink is surrounded by a movable wooden barrier. If the barrier shifts more than 1m and the ball touches a part of the rink that has moved, play is stopped and restarted by a stroke-in or a face-off.

Officials are:
a referee (or two referees for major matches) (**1**) in control of the game and responsible for timekeeping;
two goal umpires (**2**), who judge incidents on the goal line;
two line umpires (**3**) (if there is no barrier), who judge balls played over the touchline.

Teams Each team has 14 players (including two goalkeepers), of whom 11 may be on the ice at any time.

Substitutes may be used at any time, provided that the players they replace have left the rink before the substitutes enter it. Replacement must always be made at the same spot: across the touchline close to the halfway line.

Duration There are two halves of 45 minutes each, with a five-minute interval at half-time when the teams change ends.
If there is a tie, extra time of two 15-minute halves is sometimes played, and this may be repeated until one team wins.

Starting play The teams toss for stroke-off or choice of ends.
A stroke-off from the center begins each half and restarts play after a goal.
Players remain in their own half, and must be at least 5m away from the ball, until the ball is passed. The player stroking-off plays the ball into the opponents' half, and may not play the ball again until another player has touched it.
A stroke-in is awarded to the opposition if the ball is played over the touchline. The ball is placed on the ice within 1m of where it crossed the line. All opponents must be at least 5m away.

Face-off After an accidental stoppage, play restarts with a face-off at the point where the ball was when play stopped.
Two players, one from each team, face each other with their backs to their own goal line. Their sticks must be parallel and on either side of the ball, which is played in at the referee's signal. All other players must be at least 5m away.
If play stopped within the penalty area, the face-off is taken at the nearest free-stroke point.

A goal throw is awarded against an attacker who plays the ball over his opponents' goal line.
The goal umpire rolls the ball along the ice to the goalkeeper, who must be within 5m of a goalpost. All opponents must be outside the penalty area.
The goalkeeper throws the ball into play on the rink, and may only hold the ball for a maximum of 5 seconds and move with the ball for up to 5m. He may not play the ball again until another player has touched it.

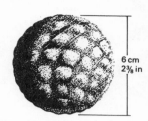

1.20m
3ft 11in

6 cm
2⅜ in

© DIAGRAM

The stick is made of wood or similar material, without metal fittings or a handstrap. Maximum length: 120cm. Maximum width: 6cm.

The ball is made of colored plastic or other approved material. When dropped on the ice from a height of 1·5m it should bounce 15—30cm. It weighs 58—62g.

Dress
Skates (**1**) must not have sharp points or projections. The captain wears an armband (**2**) on his left arm.
The goalkeeper wears a distinctive costume, with padded gloves and leg pads (**3**).
Players also wear a helmet (**4**), mouth protector (**5**), and padded gloves (**6**).

Goalkeepers A goalkeeper must not use a stick.
He may only be challenged when he has the ball or is impeding an opponent.
Within his own penalty area he may use his skates or any part of his body to play the ball. After catching the ball he may carry it in one or both hands. He may not bounce or release it on the ice and then hold it again.
He must release the ball back into play as soon as possible and may only hold it for up to 5 seconds without moving.
When he throws the ball, it must touch the ice or a player before crossing the halfway line. If he is unable to release the ball, the referee may award a free stroke to the defending team.
Outside his own penalty area he may use any part of his body other than his arms or hands to play the ball.

Playing the ball A player may:
play the ball with his stick;
kick the ball;
control the ball with his body, provided he has both skates on the ice;
jump off the ice, provided he does not endanger other players.
A player may not:
play without a stick nor play with a broken stick;
use his arms, hands, or head to control the ball;
play the ball when kneeling or lying on the ice;
play or attempt to play the ball with his stick above shoulder height;
play the ball above the illuminated area when the game is under artificial lighting.

Tackling A player may physically challenge an opponent who has the ball or is challenging for it.
He may not:
kick, trip, push, grasp, or impede an opponent or his stick;
throw his stick at the ball.
A penalty is awarded against a defender in the penalty area for dangerous or violent play against an opponent or for illegally preventing a goal.
The player taking the penalty must hit the ball forward from the penalty spot; if no goal is scored he may not play the ball again before it has been touched by another player.
The goalkeeper must stand still behind the goal line. No other players are allowed in the penalty area or behind the goal line.
Time is extended to allow a penalty to be taken.
If the attacking team commits an offense and the ball enters the goal, the penalty is retaken; if the ball missed, play continues. If the defending team commits an offense and no goal is scored, the penalty is retaken.
Expulsion A player guilty of severe or repeated infringements or misbehavior may be expelled from the rink for 5 minutes, 10 minutes, or the entire game.
An expelled player may not be replaced by a substitute.

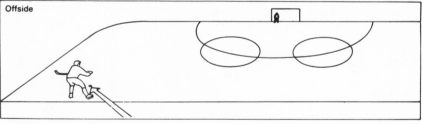

Offside

A corner stroke is awarded against a defender who plays the ball over his own goal line.
An opponent plays the ball in from within 1m of the nearest corner angle. He may not play the ball again until it has been touched by another player.
Defending players must be behind their own goal line and at least 5m from the ball. Although their sticks may touch the ice across the goal line, they may not cross the line until the ball has been played. Attacking players must be outside the penalty area.

Offside A player is offside if, when the ball is played or touched by a teammate, he is in front of the ball within his opponents' half, unless there are at least two opponents nearer their goal line than he is.
A player may stand offside as long as he does not interfere with the game and the ball is not passed to him directly or indirectly. He is not offside if the ball has last been played by an opponent.

A free stroke is awarded against offenders for most infringements outside the penalty area, but the referee must not deprive the offended side of a chance to score.
The free stroke is taken from where the offense occurred unless it took place in the penalty area, when it is taken from the nearest fixed free-stroke point.
The player who makes the stroke may not touch the ball again until it is played by another player. Opponents must be at least 5m away.

Scoring A goal is scored when the whole of the ball crosses the line between the goalposts and under the crossbar.
It cannot be scored directly from a stroke-off, corner stroke, goal stroke, goal throw, stroke-in, face-off, or direct throw by the goalkeeper.
It may be scored directly from a free stroke or penalty.
A goal is scored if the ball deflects off the referee, but not if it deflects off an umpire (in which case a goal throw or corner stroke is awarded).
The team that scores the greater number of goals wins.

429

Swimming

Swimming is both an individual and a team water sport. Participants compete in races and the first swimmer to cover a predetermined distance is the winner. Competitions are held in four major categories of swimming stroke—freestyle, breaststroke, butterfly, and backstroke.

Backstroke turning line

False start line

50m
55yd

5m
16ft 3in

21m
23yd

75cm
2ft 6in

2.50m
8ft 2in

The pool Competitions are held in pools of varying lengths, but in the Olympic Games, where swimming is the second largest sport, a 50m pool is used.
The pool is divided into eight lanes, numbered one to eight from right to left. Each swimmer must remain in his own lane.
In all events except the backstroke, swimmers begin the race by diving in from starting blocks.
Dress Men must wear swimming trunks, and ladies a one-piece costume with shoulder straps extending from front to back. All swimwear must be non-transparent. Caps are optional.

Officials Minimum international requirements are a referee, a starter, at least two placing judges, two stroke judges, two turning judges, and when electronic timing devices are not being used a minimum of two or preferably three timekeepers per lane plus additional timekeepers to take the times of the first and second in each race.
The referee (a) has overall control, ensuring that the rules are obeyed, inspecting the course, and adjudicating in any disagreements between officials or competitors.
The starter (b) controls the competitors until the race has begun. He must ensure that each swimmer is in his correct lane, and he and the referee are the sole judges of whether the start is valid.
Placing judges (c) decide the order of finishing and act as turning judges at the finishing end.
Stroke judges (d) observe whether the swimmers' stroke mechanics conform to the approved pattern for each race. They have the authority

to disqualify swimmers who infringe stroke rules.
Turning judges (e) observe all turns and relay take-overs. They may disqualify swimmers who infringe turning rules.
The chief timekeeper (f)
Lane timekeepers (g) record the time for the competitor swimming in their lane on cards to be reviewed by the chief timekeeper.
The recorder (h) keeps a complete record of the race results.
Stewards ensure that the swimmers behave in an orderly manner, and arrange the swimmers in their proper heats and lanes.
The start Except in the backstroke, the competitors shall step up to the back of the starting blocks at the referee's call. Then, on the starter's command "Take your marks," they step forward to the front of the blocks and assume a starting position. Only when they are all quite stationary will the starter give the signal for the race to begin. The starting signal may be a shot, klaxon, whistle, or the word "go."

False start The starter may call two false starts, but must then warn the competitors that if a third false start occurs, a swimmer who breaks before the signal will be disqualified. The swimmers are recalled after a false start by the lowering of a rope onto the water.
In handicap races any competitor who makes a false start is disqualified unless he makes a fresh start from the side of the pool.
In backstroke races the swimmers line up in the water, facing the edge of the pool. They may grip the end of the rail with their hands, but their feet must be on the wall under the water and not curled over the starting edge. On the starting signal, they push away from the wall.

The spearhead principle
In each event the competitor with the fastest entry time is assigned the center lane or, in pools with an even number of lanes, the lane on the right of the center.
The other swimmers are placed alternately left and right of him in descending order of speed, so that the slowest swimmers are in the two outside lanes.
If the entry times are a true indication of form, the swimmers will fan out into a spearhead formation during the race.

The spearhead

Starting position for forward strokes

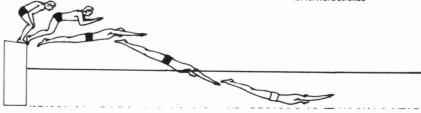

Front crawl stroke

Backstroke

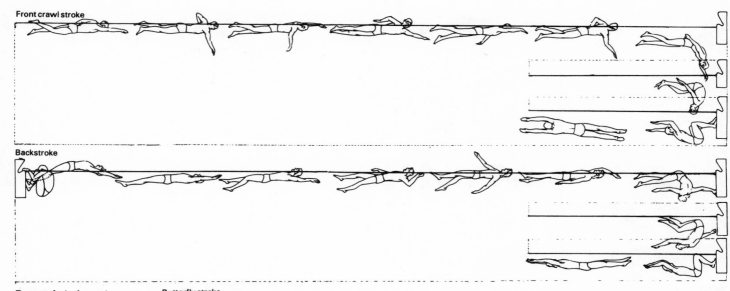

Butterfly stroke

Breaststroke

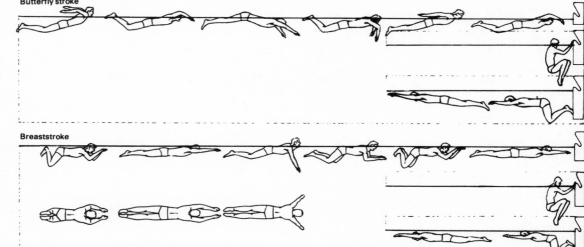

Freestyle In freestyle a swimmer may use any stroke he chooses, and rules relating to breaststroke, butterfly, and backstroke do not apply.

In turning and finishing, the swimmer must touch the end of the pool; he may do so with any part of his body. The stroke generally chosen is the front crawl.

Front crawl The main characteristics of this stroke are the following: each arm is alternately brought over and then into the water, while the legs perform a kicking action. The swimmer generally breathes on one side in the trough made by the arm pull.

Backstroke Competitors must swim on their backs throughout the race. They are permitted to use a somersault turn, but any swimmer turning beyond the vertical before he touches the end of the pool will be disqualified. A swimmer will also be disqualified for changing from his back before his head or hand touches the finishing line.

Butterfly The arms in this stroke are brought forward at the same time to enter the water at some point in front of the shoulders and are then pulled backward under the water. No alternating movement of the arms is permitted. The shoulders must at all times be parallel to the surface of the water. The feet must be moved in an up and down direction and knee movement is permitted. The feet must move simultaneously with

no outward or inward movement; they do not have to be in the same horizontal plane. There must be no alternating movement of the feet during the kick.

Breaststroke The body must at all times be parallel to the surface of the water. The hands must be pushed forward together from the breast, and then brought back on or under the surface of the water.

In the leg kick the feet must be turned outward in the backward movement; a dolphin kick is not permitted. A part of the head must always be above the general water level, except that at the start and at each turn, the swimmer may take one arm stroke and one leg kick while wholly submerged.

At the turn and on finishing the race, the touch must be made with both hands simultaneously at the same level, either at, above, or below the water level.

Medley events In individual events competitors swim an equal distance of four strokes; the sequence is butterfly, backstroke, breaststroke, and freestyle. In medley relays, each swimmer swims one stroke for the set distance; the order is backstroke, breaststroke, butterfly, and freestyle.

Disqualification A competitor is liable to disqualification for: impeding or obstructing the progress of another swimmer (including swimming out of lane);

appearing at the starting blocks after the swimmers have been called to the start;

permitting any misconduct, using abusive language, or failing to follow directions; walking on the floor of the pool;

finishing a race in a lane other than the one in which he started;

entering the water while a race is in progress;

using any equipment such as fins to aid his performance.

Olympic events (For men and women except where specified.)
100m freestyle
200m freestyle
400m freestyle
800m freestyle (women)
1500m freestyle (men)
100m breaststroke
200m breaststroke
100m butterfly
200m butterfly
100m backstroke
200m backstroke
400m individual medley
4 × 100m freestyle relay (women)
4 × 200m freestyle relay (men)
4 × 100m medley relay

© DIAGRAM

Water polo

Water polo is a team game played by two teams of up to 11 a side, only seven of whom may be in the water at the same time. The ball may be propelled one-handed, but not punched by any player other than the goalkeeper. Each team attempts to score by putting the ball into its opponents' goal.

Playing area Maximum dimensions are illustrated; minimum dimensions are 20m long by 8m wide. The minimum depth is 1m, or 1.80m in Olympic, world championship, and international competitions. All lines must be visible throughout the game; suggested colors are: goal line and half-distance line, white; 2m line, red; 4m line, yellow. There must be sufficient room for the referee to walk along the edge of the pool and for the goal judges to walk along the goal line. Goals must be painted white, and fixed firmly. Dimensions (illustrated) vary with the depth of the water.

Half-distance line

Team bench

30m
33yd

2m
6ft 6in
4m
13ft

4m line

2m line

Goal line

20m
22yd

Dress Players wear trunks. One team must wear blue caps, the other white. Goalkeepers wear red caps. All caps must be tied under the chin. If a player loses his cap, he must replace it at the next stoppage. Caps are numbered on the sides—the goalkeeper being number 1 and the other players 2–11. No dangerous articles may be worn. No player may grease or oil his body.
Officials The game is controlled by between five and seven officials.
1 A referee, who uses a whistle and two flags (one blue, one white) on a stick. He stops and starts the game, decides fouls, goals, and throws. He also applies an advantage rule by not declaring a foul if the offending team would benefit from the stoppage. He has the power to order any player out of the water.
2 Two goal judges, who each have a white flag to signal goal throws and a red flag to signal corner throws. They raise both flags for a goal. They are positioned, opposite the referee, at each end of the

pool directly level with the goal line.
3 Timekeepers, who use stopwatches to record the time when the ball is actually in play. They use a whistle to indicate the end of a period.
4 Secretaries, who record major fouls and signal with a red flag when any player is awarded a third personal fault. They also control players' periods of exclusion by signaling when an excluded player may re-enter the game
Teams A team comprises 11 players, of whom four are substitutes.
Substitution Except in case of injury or accident, a substitute may only enter the game:
during the interval after a goal;
before extra time;
after a teammate has been excluded from the rest of the game for showing disrespect, wearing oil, or committing a third personal fault.

The team captain must inform the referee of all substitutions.
No substitutes are allowed in cases of illness or brutality.
Duration Play lasts for four periods of five minutes' actual playing time. There is a two-minute interval between each period for changing ends.
Players in the water may only leave at an interval, when injured, or with the referee's permission.
For an accident or injury the referee may suspend play for up to three minutes. A player with cramp must leave the pool as quickly as possible; the game proceeds as soon as he has left the water.

If there is a tie and a definite result is required, there is a five-minute break, then two periods of three minutes play with a one-minute interval between. This pattern is continued until a decision is reached.
Start of play Players take up position on their own goal lines about 1m apart and at least 1m from either goal post (only two players are allowed between the posts).
The referee then blows his whistle and throws the ball into the center of the pool.

Restarting play
a) After a goal, players may take up any position in their own half. The team conceding the goal restarts play when the referee whistles—by one player passing the ball to a teammate, who must be behind the half-distance line when he receives the ball.
b) After a stoppage for injury etc, or after a simultaneous foul by two opponents, the referee throws the ball into the water as near as possible to where the incident occurred and giving both teams an equal chance of gaining possession.

3m
9ft 9in

90cm
3ft

More than 1.50m (4ft 11in) deep

3m
9ft 9in

2.40m
7ft 10in

Less than 1.50m (4ft 11in) deep

The ball A water polo ball must be round and fully inflated. It must be completely waterproof. Its circumference must be 68–71cm and its weight 400–450g.

Playing the ball

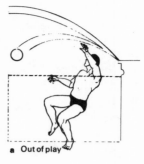
a Out of play

b Out of play

Playing the ball Apart from the goalkeeper, players are not permitted to:
touch the ball with both hands simultaneously;
strike the ball with a clenched fist;
hold the ball underwater when tackled.
They are permitted to:
dribble with the ball (**1**);
seize the ball (**2**);
lift the ball out of the water (**3**);
remain stationary with the ball (**4**);
pass or shoot the ball (**5**);
play the ball when it is in the air.
A team must concede a free throw if it fails to shoot or pass the ball within 45 seconds of gaining possession.

Goalkeepers A goalkeeper may stand, jump from the floor of the pool, walk, use both hands, and punch the ball within the 4m area. He must not cross the half-distance line or directly send the ball beyond it. He must not hold the bar, rail, or trough at the end of the pool.
Scoring A goal is scored when the ball completely crosses the goal line between the posts and under the crossbar, providing:
it has not been punched;
at least two players have touched it after a start or restart (not including a goalkeeper's attempt to stop a shot).
The ball may be dribbled into goal.

The team scoring the most goals is the winner.
Out of play The ball is out of play when:
a) it hits the side of the pool and bounces back into the water;
b) it is sent out at the side of the pool;
c) it completely crosses the goal line.
In cases a) and b), the ball is returned to play by the nearest opposing player, who takes a free throw from where the ball went out.
If an attacker sends the ball out of play over the goal line, a goal throw is awarded.
If a defender sends the ball over his own goal line, a corner throw is awarded.

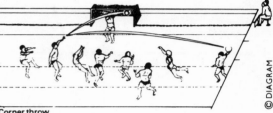
Corner throw

A corner throw is taken by the attacker nearest where the ball went out of play. It must be taken from the 2m mark on the side of the pool where the ball went out. Only the defending goalkeeper may be in the 2m area when the throw is taken.

A goal throw is taken by the defending goalkeeper. It must be taken from the goal line between the goal posts and must not go beyond the half-distance line.

Fouls

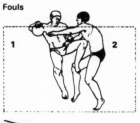

Free throw

Fouls and misconduct
Offenses are classified as ordinary fouls (penalized by a free throw to the other team) and major fouls (penalized by personal faults and periods of exclusion).

Ordinary fouls It is an ordinary foul to:
take or hold the ball under water when tackled (**1**);
swim beyond the goal line before the referee's signal to start the game;
assist a player at the start;
hold onto or push off from the goal posts or the sides of the pool, or hold onto the rails except at the start

or a restart;
stand or walk on the floor of the pool;
punch the ball;
splash water in an opponent's face;
touch a referee's throw before it reaches the water;
jump from the floor of the pool;
deliberately impede an opponent unless he has the ball;
play the ball with both hands at the same time;
push an opponent;
be within 2m of the opposing goal line unless behind the ball;
waste time (including having possession for more than 45 seconds without shooting);
take a penalty throw incorrectly. It is also an ordinary foul for the goalkeeper to throw the ball over the half-distance line.
Major fouls It is a major foul to:
kick or strike an opponent (**2**);
commit any brutal act (**3**);
illegally stop a goal inside the 4m area (**4**);
hold, sink, or pull back an opponent not holding the ball; interfere with the taking

of a free throw;
re-enter the water improperly when an excluded player or substitute;
continually commit ordinary fouls.
After a major foul, the offending player is awarded a personal fault and is ordered out of the water for one minute or until a goal is scored, whichever is the sooner.
A player is excluded from the game when he has three personal faults recorded against him.
Only if the penalized player is to be excluded from the game may a substitute take his place. He may be replaced by a substitute immediately if the foul is punished by a penalty throw, or otherwise after one minute (or a goal).
Free throw The player may:
a) throw the ball;
b) drop the ball into the water and dribble it before passing.
The throw must be made in such a way that other players can see the ball leave the thrower's hand.

At least two players must touch the ball before a goal can be scored.
Any free throw awarded for a foul in the 2m area must be taken from the 2m line opposite where the foul occurred.
Other free throws are taken from where the offense occurred.
A penalty throw is awarded for the following major fouls within the 4m area: holding, sinking, or pulling back an opponent not holding the ball;
kicking or striking an opponent;
committing any foul that prevents a probable goal.
A penalty throw is also awarded for an act of brutality anywhere in the pool.
Any player except the goalkeeper may take the penalty throw from any point along the 4m line. He must throw directly at goal.
All players except the defending goalkeeper must leave the 4m area, and no player may encroach within 2m of the thrower.
The goalkeeper must remain on his goal line.

© DIAGRAM

Diving

Competitive diving is separated into men's and women's springboard and highboard events. Competitors perform a set number of compulsory and voluntary dives, each of which is marked. A competition is won by the competitor with most marks in the final.

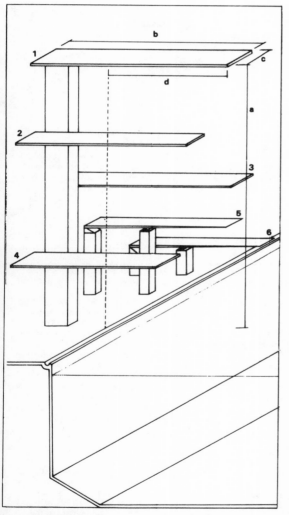

Type of board	a height	b length	c width	d to pool edge
1 Platform	10m 33ft	6m 19ft 6in	2m 6ft 6in	1.50m 4ft 11in
2 Platform	7.50m 24ft 5in	6m 19ft 6in	1.50m 4ft 11in	1.50m 4ft 11in
3 Platform	5m 16ft 3in	6m 19ft 6in	1.50m 4ft 11in	1.25m 4ft 1in
4 Platform	3m 9ft 9in	5m 16ft 3in	0.80m 2ft 8in	1.25m 4ft 1in
5 Springboard	3m 9ft 9in	5m 16ft 3in	0.50m 1ft 8in	1.25m 4ft 1in
6 Springboard	1m 3ft 3in	5m 16ft 3in	0.50m 1ft 8in	1.50m 4ft 11in

Diving apparatus
Highboard diving platforms and springboards are provided at the heights shown.
They must be rigid and covered with a layer of resilient hard wood and a surface of coconut matting or other approved non-slip material. Springboards must be made of an aluminum extrusion.
Mechanical agitation of the water's surface aids divers. Illumination must not cause glare.
Officials Competitions are judged by a judging panel consisting of the referee and judges.
The referee controls the competition and supervises the judges.
The judges (usually five or seven in major international competitions) are positioned separately on both sides of the diving board, or, if that is not possible, together on one side of the board. After each dive, each judge gives his mark when the referee signals.
Marks are recorded by two secretaries, who also record the minutes of the competition.

Preliminary contests are held when there are more than 16 competitors.
In springboard events a preliminary contest consists of 11 dives for men and 10 for women.
In highboard events 10 dives are required for men and 8 for women.
In both competitions the same dives must be performed in the final as in the preliminary contest.
The eight divers with the most points in the preliminary contest qualify for the final.
Events
Men's springboard events consist of five required dives, and six voluntary dives selected from five groups.
The required dives are: a forward dive, a backward dive, a reverse dive, an inward dive, and a forward dive with a half twist. They may be performed straight, piked, or with tuck.
Women's springboard events consist of five required dives, and five voluntary dives selected from five groups. The required dives are the same as for the men's springboard events.

Men's highboard events consist of four voluntary dives with a maximum total degree of difficulty of 7.5, and six voluntary dives without limit.
In each section, each dive must be selected from a different group.
The dives may be performed from either the intermediate or 10m platform.
Women's highboard events consist of four voluntary dives with a maximum total degree of difficulty of 7.5, and four voluntary dives without limit.
In each section, each dive must be selected from a different group.
Dives may be performed from either the intermediate or 10m platform.
Notification of dives
Before the competition each competitor must give the diving secretaries full information about each of his dives, including a written description.
A dive can be performed in three positions: straight, indicated with an (a); piked (b); and tuck (c). Difficult twist dives are indicated with a (d), and may be performed in any position.

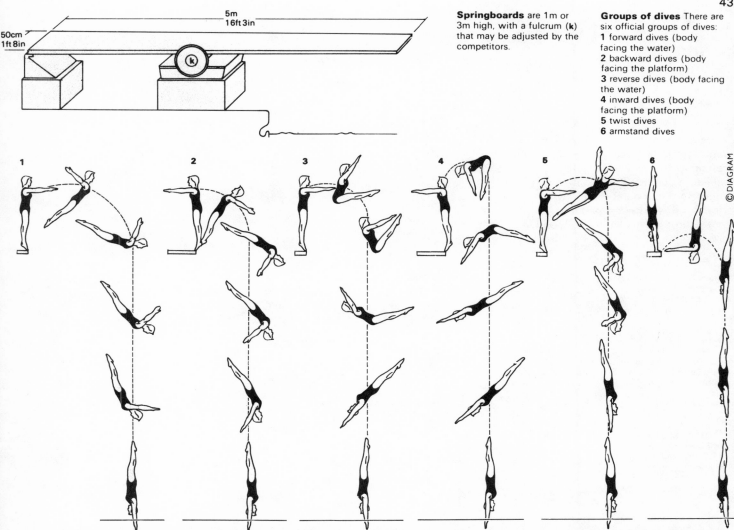

Springbroads are 1m or 3m high, with a fulcrum (**k**) that may be adjusted by the competitors.

Groups of dives There are six official groups of dives:
1 forward dives (body facing the water)
2 backward dives (body facing the platform)
3 reverse dives (body facing the water)
4 inward dives (body facing the platform)
5 twist dives
6 armstand dives

© DIAGRAM

Starting positions Divers may take off from a backward (**1**), forward (**2**), or armstand (**3**) position. Forward take-off dives may be performed either standing or running.

Standing dives The starting position for a standing dive is assumed when the diver stands on the front end of the board or platform.
The body must be straight, head erect, arms straight and to the sides or above the head. The arm swing commences when the arms leave the starting position.

Running dives The starting position for a running dive is assumed when the diver is ready to take the first step of his run.

The run must be smooth, straight, and without hesitation, and must consist of at least four steps, including the take-off from one or both feet.
The take-off must be bold, reasonably high, and confident.
In a standing dive the diver must not bounce on the board.
In an armstand dive there must be a steady balance in the straight position.

In a running dive from the springboard the take-off must be from both feet simultaneously; from fixed boards it may be from one foot.

Points may be deducted for loss of balance, restarting, touching the end of the board, diving to the side of the direct line of flight, and for lifting both feet from the board when preparing for a backward take-off.

The flight During the flight (passage through the air) the body may be straight, with pike, or with tuck. The position of the arms is the choice of the diver.
Straight (4) The body must not be bent at the knees or hips; the feet must be together and the toes pointed.
With pike (5) The body must be bent at the hips, the legs straight at the knees, and the toes pointed.
With tuck (6) The whole body must be bunched, with the knees together, the hands on the lower legs, and the toes pointed.
Flying somersault dives A straight position should be clearly held for approximately half a somersault.

Straight dives with twist The twist must not be manifestly made from the board. In pike dives with twist, the twist must follow the pike. In somersault dives with twist, the twist may be performed at any time. The twist must be within 90° of that announced, or the dive will be declared a failure.
The entry The body must always be vertical or near vertical on entering the water. The body must be straight and the toes pointed.
Head-first entries (7) The arms must be stretched above the head and in line with the body; the hands must be close together.
Feet-first entries (8) The arms must be close to the body; there must be no bending at the elbows.
Finish The dive is considered finished when the whole body is completely under the surface of the water.
Judging dives The judges consider the run, take-off, flight, and entry, but not the approach to the starting position.

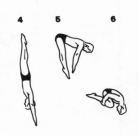

Scoring Each judge awards a mark in points and half points from 0–10 for each dive.
The secretaries cancel the judges' highest and lowest marks, total the remainder, and multiply by the degree of difficulty to give the score for the dive.
A dive other than that announced is a failed dive and scores no points.
A dive performed in a position other than that announced is deemed unsatisfactory and scores a maximum of two points.
A dive spoiled by exceptional circumstances may, with the referee's permission, be repeated.
Result An event is won by the competitor scoring most points in the final. A tie is declared if two divers have equal points.

Surfing

A surfer's basic equipment is a board, normally made to his individual specifications, with which he attempts to ride waves as they approach the shoreline. In competitions surfers may be required to ride a number of waves. Each performance is scored separately, and the points from the best waves are totaled to give a final score.

Officials The number of officials depends on the size of the competition and may include judges, a referee, a starter, and an official supervising the event.
Starting On the starter's signal the competitors enter the water and paddle out to their appropriate positions.
Duration The length of a contest depends on the number of competitors. It may be divided into heats (each of 12 to 15 minutes) and finals (of 20 minutes). Competitors are allowed to ride a certain number of waves in each heat; this number depends on the surf conditions.

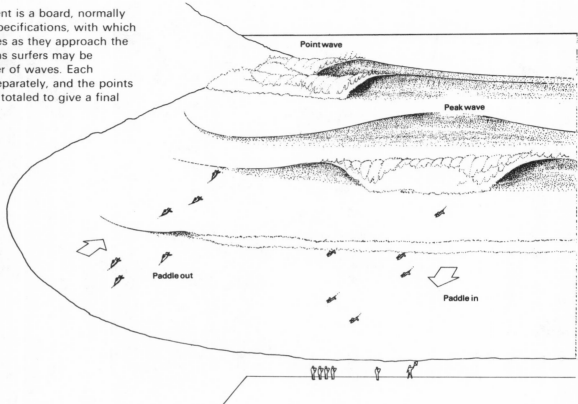

Point wave

Peak wave

Paddle out

Paddle in

Scoring Competitors are awarded points for each wave they ride. They score between 0 and 20 for:
1 making the wave;
2 beating sections;
3 tube rides;
4 turns, cut backs, and reentries;
5 nose walking;
and for style, grace, and timing.
Points may be lost for interference or other offenses.
The final total of points depends on the number of waves the surfer rides.
Waves may be judged as follows:
the best three waves out of five;
the best four waves out of six;
the best five waves out of seven;
the best three or five waves (announced prior to the competition) of an unlimited number.

Interference A competitor must not:
interfere with a rider who has wave possession (left);
interfere with the previous heat when paddling out;
surf in the contest area unless actually competing.
After a heat competitors must return at once, either kneeling or prone.

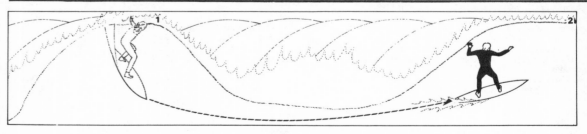

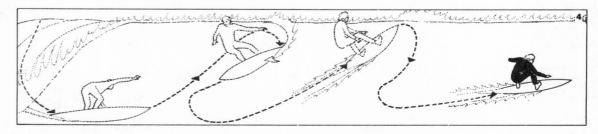

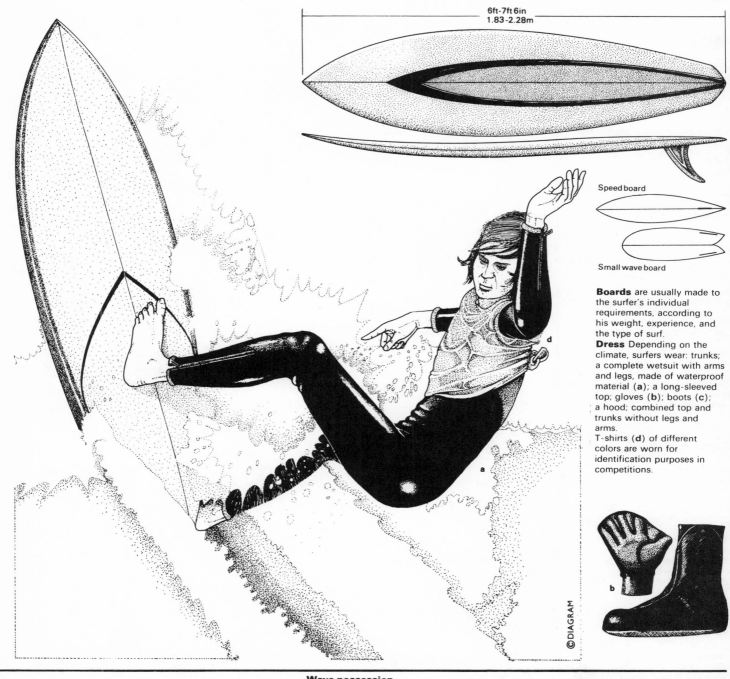

6ft-7ft 6in
1.83-2.28m

Speed board

Small wave board

Boards are usually made to the surfer's individual requirements, according to his weight, experience, and the type of surf.

Dress Depending on the climate, surfers wear: trunks; a complete wetsuit with arms and legs, made of waterproof material (**a**); a long-sleeved top; gloves (**b**); boots (**c**); a hood; combined top and trunks without legs and arms.

T-shirts (**d**) of different colors are worn for identification purposes in competitions.

©DIAGRAM

Wave possession
Whenever possible, a wave should only be ridden by one competitor.
A competitor is entitled to priority on a wave if he:
is closest to the curl (**6**);
stands up before any other competitor paddles toward that wave;
is nearest the peak on a peak wave. Should there be a contestant on either side of a peak wave (**7**) then each surfer has possession of his own side.

Penalties Offenses are penalized by loss of points or disqualification from the competition.

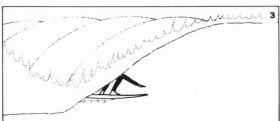
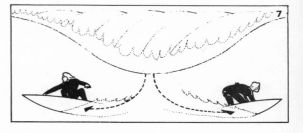
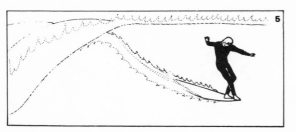

Water skiing

Water skiing as a competitive sport is divided into three distinct sections—jumping, slalom, and trick riding. The winner of a championship is the best overall performer in the three events.

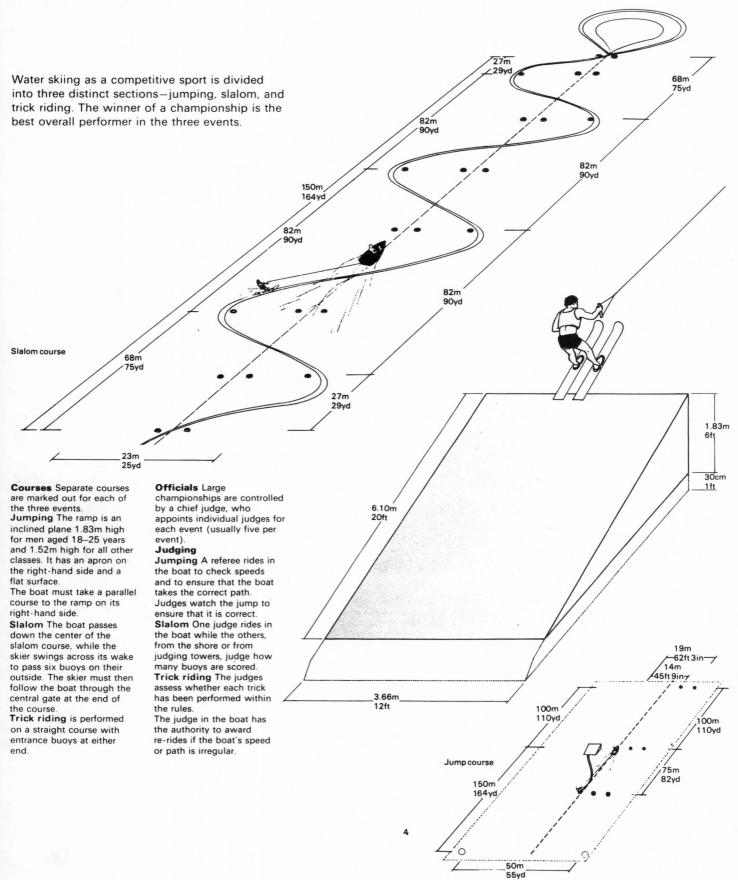

Slalom course

27m
29yd

68m
75yd

82m
90yd

82m
90yd

150m
164yd

82m
90yd

82m
90yd

68m
75yd

27m
29yd

23m
25yd

1.83m
6ft

30cm
1ft

6.10m
20ft

3.66m
12ft

Jump course

19m
62ft 3in

14m
45ft 9in

100m
110yd

100m
110yd

75m
82yd

150m
164yd

50m
55yd

4

Courses Separate courses are marked out for each of the three events.
Jumping The ramp is an inclined plane 1.83m high for men aged 18–25 years and 1.52m high for all other classes. It has an apron on the right-hand side and a flat surface.
The boat must take a parallel course to the ramp on its right-hand side.
Slalom The boat passes down the center of the slalom course, while the skier swings across its wake to pass six buoys on their outside. The skier must then follow the boat through the central gate at the end of the course.
Trick riding is performed on a straight course with entrance buoys at either end.

Officials Large championships are controlled by a chief judge, who appoints individual judges for each event (usually five per event).
Judging
Jumping A referee rides in the boat to check speeds and to ensure that the boat takes the correct path. Judges watch the jump to ensure that it is correct.
Slalom One judge rides in the boat while the others, from the shore or from judging towers, judge how many buoys are scored.
Trick riding The judges assess whether each trick has been performed within the rules.
The judge in the boat has the authority to award re-rides if the boat's speed or path is irregular.

Towing Boats must have sufficient power and conform to official dimensions.
The towing line must be fixed at the center line of the boat.
Inboard or outboard power may be used, and the boats should be fixed with adequate speedometers and two-way radios.
Drivers for the boats are selected from the appointed officials.
Tow lines must have:
12 strands with 60 yarns per strand;
a diameter of 6.3mm at 5.5kg load;
a weight per meter of 160—185g;
a minimum breaking load of 590kg.

Skis Various types of ski are used for each event, but no ski must be more than 25cm wide or 100cm long. Any type of foot binding or fixed fin may be used.
Every care must be taken to ensure that the skis are safe, with no dangerous splinters, chippings, etc.
In jumping events competitors use two skis, in slalom one, and in trick riding either one or two.

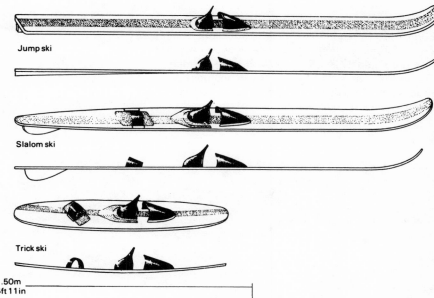

Jump ski

Slalom ski

Trick ski

23cm 9⅛in

1.50m 4ft 11in

28cm 11⅛in

Tow line

© DIAGRAM

1

2

3

4

5

Duration In major competitions there are two rounds for each event—a preliminary round and a final round for those leading after the preliminary.
Rounds
Jumping Each competitor has three jumps.
Slalom Each competitor continues to negotiate the course at increasing speeds up to specific maxima, and then with the line shortened by predetermined increments, until he misses a buoy or falls.
Trick riding Each competitor makes two passes down the course (ie travels the length of the course twice); a pass must not last more than 20 seconds.

Scoring
Jumping For a jump to score, the skier must pass over the ramp, land on the water, and then ski to the ride-out buoy that marks the end of the course.
A competitor's longest jump gives his score for the round.
Slalom To complete a successful pass the skier must follow the boat out through the finishing gate.
1 Each buoy passed scores one point. (The score counts if the skier successfully passes outside the buoy and also crosses back into the wake before passing the level of the next buoy.)
2 A competitor loses a point if he sinks a buoy. (No point is lost if he "grazes" a buoy.)

Trick riding Examples of tricks are:
3 side slide;
4 backward, toe 180°;
5 wake turn.
Each trick successfully completed inside the course has a tariff value according to its difficulty. These scores are totaled for both passes to give the score for the round.

Result In major championships the placings for each event are determined by adding together each competitor's scores for the two rounds.
Placings for the championship as a whole are determined as follows. The winners at jumping, slalom, and trick riding are each given 1000 points. The other competitors are each given a proportion of 100 depending on the proportion of their own score to that of the winner. The competitors' three scores are then aggregated to give the overall placings for the championship.

Speed
Jumping The boat for men may travel up to 57kmh; for women, up to 48kmh.
Slalom The boat must proceed at a specified speed timed by the judge in the boat.
Trick riding The skier informs the boat driver of the speed he requires.

Rowing

Rowing is divided into two basic types of
competition. Regatta events are knock-out
competitions, ending with a race between two
or more finalists. Head of the river races (which
are not used in international championships) are
processional; boats set off at intervals and the
result is decided by their times over the course.

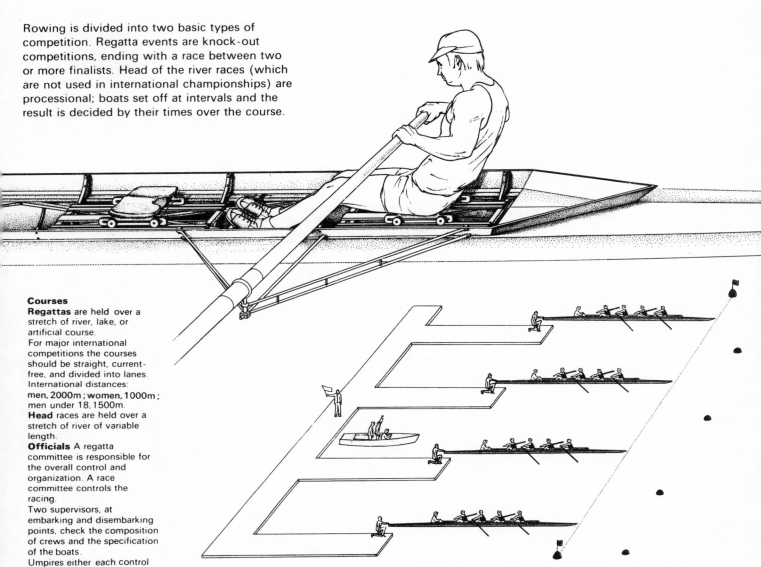

Courses

Regattas are held over a
stretch of river, lake, or
artificial course.
For major international
competitions the courses
should be straight, current-
free, and divided into lanes.
International distances:
men, 2000m; women, 1000m;
men under 18, 1500m.
Head races are held over a
stretch of river of variable
length.

Officials A regatta
committee is responsible for
the overall control and
organization. A race
committee controls the
racing.
Two supervisors, at
embarking and disembarking
points, check the composition
of crews and the specification
of the boats.
Umpires either each control
a section of the course or
follow the race in a launch.
There may also be a
separate starter and aligner.
Judges decide the results.

Competitors Within each
class of boat competitors are
divided into categories by
experience, age, or weight.
By winning certain events
oarsmen graduate from
novice status, through the
divisions of the senior class
to achieve elite status.

Dress Oarsmen and scullers
wear undershirts and shorts;
undershirts bear club or
national colors or other
insignia.

Accidents A crew must
stay at the site of any
accident in which they are
involved, unless within 100m
of the start or if the accident
was caused by an outside
agency (in which cases a
re-row may be ordered).

Substitutes are allowed
for up to half the number of
the crew, and for the
coxswain, until 30 minutes
before the first race.
(Substitutes may be allowed
later in cases of serious
illness.) No substitutes are
allowed in single sculls
events.

REGATTA RACES

The start Crews must be at
the start at least two
minutes before the race.
The aligner indicates, by
raising a white flag, when all
the crews are aligned
correctly. To aid alignment
the boats may be held by
officials in moored stake
boats.
The starter will ask, "Are
you ready?" and if there is
no objection will drop his
flag and command "go".
After a false start the boats
may be recalled (within
100m) by ringing a bell and
waving a red flag.

The race Each boat must
keep within its own lane
(if marked) or it may be
disqualified. No outside
advice is allowed.
An umpire may warn a boat
about its steering only if it is
about to impede or collide
with another boat that is
on a correct course.
If a collision occurs, or any
interference after a warning,
the umpire may disqualify the
offending crew or crews. He
may order a restart.

The finish A crew has
finished when the bows of
the boat cross the finish line.
If an oarsman or sculler falls
out, the boat can still be
placed, but not if the
coxswain falls out.
When all crews have
finished, the race umpire
raises a white flag if the race
is in order and there is no
protest; otherwise he raises
a red flag.
The judges decide the
finishing order, using
photographs if necessary.
If two or more boats finish
simultaneously, a re-row is
arranged.

HEAD RACES

There are no lanes or
stations. The overtaking crew
has the right of way. The
organizing committee must
draw up the race regulations.

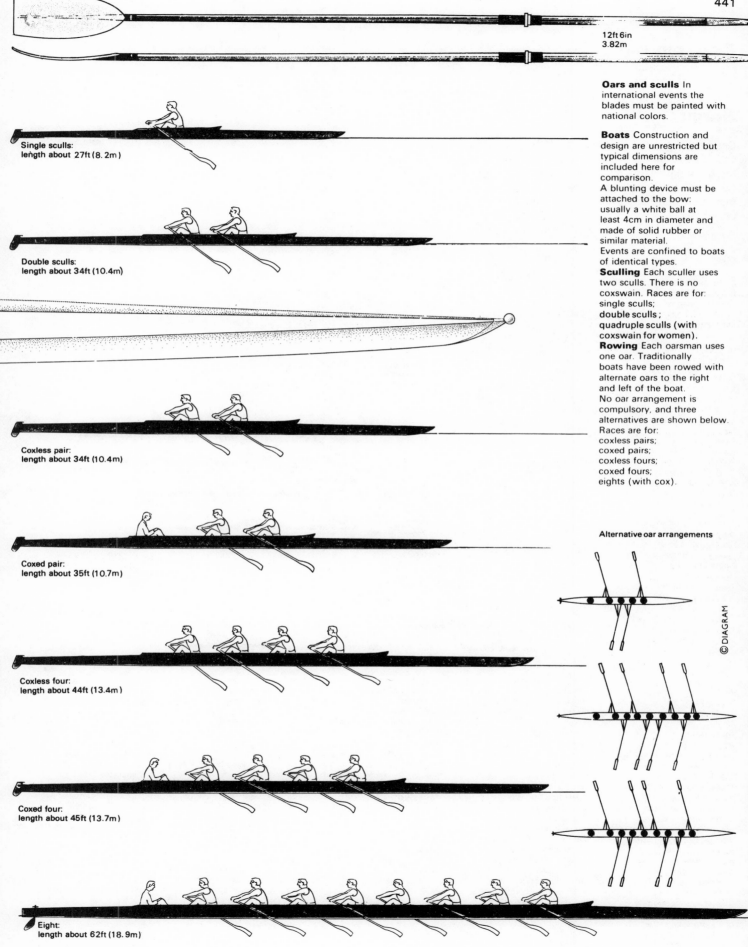

12ft 6in
3.82m

Oars and sculls In international events the blades must be painted with national colors.

Boats Construction and design are unrestricted but typical dimensions are included here for comparison.
A blunting device must be attached to the bow: usually a white ball at least 4cm in diameter and made of solid rubber or similar material.
Events are confined to boats of identical types.
Sculling Each sculler uses two sculls. There is no coxswain. Races are for: single sculls; double sculls; quadruple sculls (with coxswain for women).
Rowing Each oarsman uses one oar. Traditionally boats have been rowed with alternate oars to the right and left of the boat.
No oar arrangement is compulsory, and three alternatives are shown below.
Races are for: coxless pairs; coxed pairs; coxless fours; coxed fours; eights (with cox).

Single sculls:
length about 27ft (8.2m)

Double sculls:
length about 34ft (10.4m)

Coxless pair:
length about 34ft (10.4m)

Coxed pair:
length about 35ft (10.7m)

Alternative oar arrangements

Coxless four:
length about 44ft (13.4m)

Coxed four:
length about 45ft (13.7m)

Eight:
length about 62ft (18.9m)

©DIAGRAM

Canoeing

Sprint

Canoe sprint races are held on still water courses over 500m, 1000m, and 10,000m. International events are held for one-man, two-man, and four-man kayaks, and for one-man, two-man, and seven-man Canadian canoes.

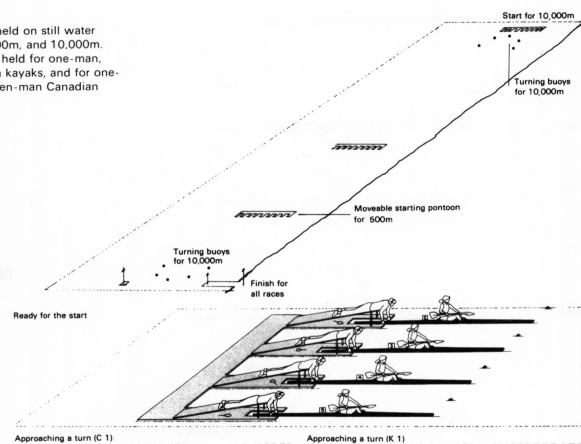

Start for 10,000m

Turning buoys for 10,000m

Moveable starting pontoon for 500m

Turning buoys for 10,000m

Finish for all races

Ready for the start

Courses should be through flat water, and be as still and windless as possible.
They are marked by buoys with flags.
Courses for 500m and 1000m races are straight, covered once only, and if possible are marked from start to finish.
Courses for 10,000m may be divided into straights (at least 1000m long) and turns (marked by red and yellow flags).
Courses with turns are raced counterclockwise.
Start and finish lines are marked by two red flags.
There must be 5m width for each boat at the start, and 45m total width at the finish.
For championships the depth over the whole course should be at least 3m if possible; otherwise there should be a uniform depth of at least 2m.
Lanes must be 9m wide for the 500m and 1000m.
For the 10,000m, the opening and intermediate straights must be at least 2000m long and the final straight at least 1000m.

Approaching a turn (C 1)

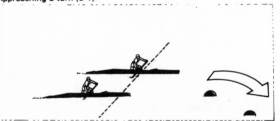

Approaching a turn (K 1)

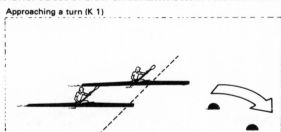

Entries for championships and Olympic events are limited to one per nation for each event.
Substitutes are permitted in all events, but a crew may not be changed after it has begun to compete in an event.
Officials Chief official; competition organizer; competition secretary; starter; aligner; course umpire(s); turning point umpire(s); finishing line judges; timekeeper(s); measurer(s); announcer; press official.
A competition committee (comprising the chief official, competition organizer, and one other) hears protests, settles disputes, and decides disqualifications.

For championships, a jury of seven, headed by the president or a leading member of the ICF (International Canoe Federation), receives any appeals against competition committee decisions.
Start Lots are drawn for starting positions.
Boats line up with their bows on the starting line. The aligner raises a white flag when all boats are level and stationary. (In championships the boats are held by officials so that their sterns touch starting pontoons.)
The starter says "ready" and after a two second pause fires a shot or says "go."
It is a false start if a competitor begins paddling after the "ready" and before the shot or "go."

A crew is disqualified for two false starts, whether it caused them or not.
If a competitor breaks his paddle within 15m of the start, there is a recall and a new start after the paddle has been replaced. (Flags indicate the 15m distance.)
Race procedure
Races up to 1000m Boats must keep to their lanes from start to finish, and approach not nearer than 5m to another craft.
Races over 1000m Boats may leave their lanes, provided they do not impede other competitors. This allows wash-hanging: positioning a canoe so that it is sitting on an opponent's bow wave.

At turns, the outside boat must give room to an inside boat if the bow of the inside boat is level with:
the front edge of the outside boat's cockpit (K1);
the forecockpit (K2, K4);
the competitor's body (C1);
the body of the foremost competitor (C2).
Otherwise, boats must follow the course as closely as possible at turning points.
Boats are not disqualified for touching when turning, except when an advantage is gained.
An overtaking craft must keep clear at all times, but the overtaken craft must not alter its course to cause difficulties for the other craft.

For the last 1000m, boats must return to their lanes and keep 5m from each other. (A sound signal warns when each boat reaches 1000m from the finish.)
The finish A canoe finishes when its bow passes between the red finishing flags.
When all the canoes have finished, the umpire shows a white flag if no rule has been infringed or a red flag if there has been an infringement.
Boats qualifying for a next round, or the first four boats in a final, are then re-measured and weighed.

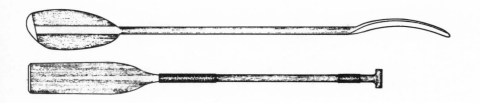

Paddles are usually made of wood and are designed for speed and lightness. The blade is spoon-shaped to give a clean entry into the water. Kayak paddles have two blades, Canadian canoe paddles have one.

Canoes Dimensions are limited according to class. Sections and longitudinal lines must be convex and uninterrupted.
Kayaks may have steering rudders.
Canadian canoes must be symmetrical upon axis of length, have no steering gear, and be open for prescribed proportions of their length.
Events Men's, women's, and junior (15–18 years) events are held for:
one-man, two-man, and four-man kayaks (K1, K2, K4);
one-man, two-man, and seven-man Canadian canoes (C1, C2, C7).
World and continental championships are held every year except Olympic years.
Championship and Olympic events are given in the table at the foot of the page.
Heats and finals For the 10,000m there are no heats, but boats may be started at intervals if necessary.
For the 500m and 1000m, heats may be held.
Heats and the final must be on the same stretch of water, and none may include more than nine canoes.
Allocation to heats and lanes is decided by lot.
The heat system should allow three canoes in each heat to proceed to the next stage, and finishing positions not times are the deciding factor.
For championships, intervals between stages must not be less than 1 hour for 500m, and 1½ hours for 1000m events.

Relays
A straight course is covered in alternating directions.
All a team's canoes must bear the same number or color.
The bows of the handover canoe must have crossed the line at the changeover point before the team's next canoe may start (the starter gives the command). Canoes must pass port-side to port-side.
An individual competitor may not paddle more than one stretch.
Membership of a crew or team may not be changed between stages, unless the chief official agrees in cases of injury. A team may alter the starting order of its boats. There should be only six teams in a final.

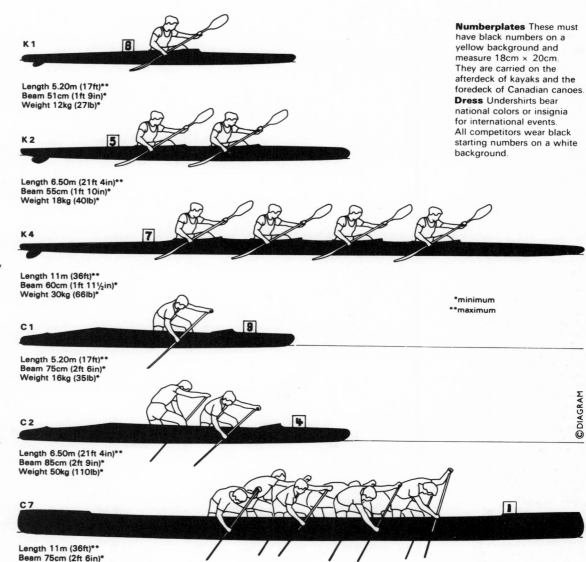

K 1
Length 5.20m (17ft)**
Beam 51cm (1ft 9in)*
Weight 12kg (27lb)*

K 2
Length 6.50m (21ft 4in)**
Beam 55cm (1ft 10in)*
Weight 18kg (40lb)*

K 4
Length 11m (36ft)**
Beam 60cm (1ft 11½in)*
Weight 30kg (66lb)*

C 1
Length 5.20m (17ft)**
Beam 75cm (2ft 6in)*
Weight 16kg (35lb)*

C 2
Length 6.50m (21ft 4in)**
Beam 85cm (2ft 9in)*
Weight 50kg (110lb)*

C 7
Length 11m (36ft)**
Beam 75cm (2ft 6in)*
Weight 20kg (44lb)*

*minimum
**maximum

©DIAGRAM

Numberplates These must have black numbers on a yellow background and measure 18cm × 20cm. They are carried on the afterdeck of kayaks and the foredeck of Canadian canoes.
Dress Undershirts bear national colors or insignia for international events. All competitors wear black starting numbers on a white background.

Disqualification
Competitors are disqualified for breaking racing rules or attempting to compete by dishonest means (including taking pace or receiving help or encouragement from boats not in the race).
Colliding with or damaging another boat (including an opponent's paddle) makes a boat liable to disqualification.
A capsize always results in elimination.
A competitor withdrawing from one event without valid reason may be disqualified from any other event in the same meeting.

Events	500m	1000m	10000m	500m relay	1000m Olympic
Men					
	K1	K1	K1	K1 × 4	K1
	K2	K2	K2		K2
		K4	K4		K4
	C1	C1	C1		C1
	C2	C2	C2		C2
	C7				
Women	500m				500m Olympic
	K1				K1
	K2				K2
	K4				

Canoe slalom

Canoe slalom is a sport testing canoe control under difficult conditions. Competitors negotiate a rapid river course with natural and artificial hazards. Gates must be negotiated in the correct order and direction. There are individual and team events for one-man kayaks and for one-man and two-man Canadian canoes.

Courses are on mountain rivers, below weirs, or on special artificial streams. The water flow must be torrent-like, and the current at least 2m per second. The stretch of water should include the following natural and artificial hazards: current, counter-current, rapids, rocks, bridge piers, and weirs.
Courses are marked by "gates" – pairs of poles strung over the river and dangling down to the water. Canoes must pass through the gates in a prescribed direction and order, giving a course up to 800m length and graded I to VI according to difficulty. (Major competitions are on grades IV or V.)
Courses must be navigable throughout (with a depth for world championships of at least 40cm).
Courses may be less difficult for women's and mixed events.
Gates Courses should have 25–30 gates, including at least four reverse gates and one team gate.
All gates are numbered in order and painted to show the direction of negotiation. The bottom of gate poles should hang as near the water as possible without being moved by the waves. The last gate should be at least 25cm before the finish line, which should be clearly marked on both sides.
Officials Chairman of the slalom; competition organizer; technical officer; chief judge; starter; raft steward; finish judge; section judges; gate judges; timekeepers; chief of the scoring office; course supervisor; boat scrutineer; first aid and rescue officer; telephone and radio service. In addition, at international competitions, a jury of three to seven international slalom experts control events, receive protests, interpret rules, and disqualify competitors.

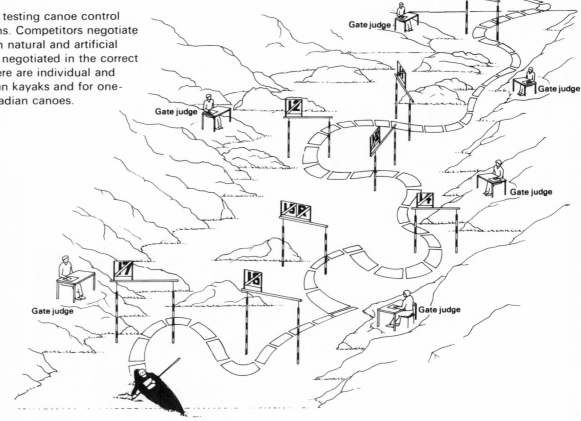

Competitors may only take part in one individual and one team event.
For world championships (held every other year), each nation may enter four boats and one reserve boat in each individual category. (Three boats per nation for the Olympic Games.)
Events Individual and team (three boats) events:
men, K1, C1, C2;
women, K1;
mixed, C2.
There is no Canadian pairs event in the Olympic Games.
Procedure After a demonstration run by a non-competitor, final acceptance of the course is agreed by the officials. Each competitor is then allowed one training run over the course.

The competition usually takes the form of two timed runs over the course by each competitor. (For team and non-international events, this may be reduced to one.) If possible, only one boat should be on the course at any time during individual events; but a shorter starting interval may be decided.
Negotiating the gates
Competitors must negotiate the gates in the correct order and direction.
Competitors must pass between the poles without either pole being touched by boat, paddle, or competitor's body
In team events, all a team's boats must negotiate the team gate within 15 seconds.

Penalties Gate judges signal penalties with red and yellow discs marked with numbers.
1 One pole touched from the inside, 10 seconds penalty.
2 Both poles touched from the inside, 20 seconds penalty.
3 Touching a gate from the outside and then correct negotiation, 20 seconds penalty.
4 Intentionally pushing a pole aside, 50 seconds.
5 Touching a gate from the outside and without correct negotiation, 50 seconds.
6 Eskimo roll while inside a gate, 50 seconds penalty.
7 Negotiation contrary to color indications, 50 seconds.

8 Gate omitted, 50 seconds.
9 Repeated attempt at a gate after competitor's body has passed the gate line, 50 seconds.
10 When gates are negotiated out of order and one gate is missed out, 50 seconds for the omission plus any penalty on the gate attempted out of order.
11 When gates are negotiated out of order and two or more gates are missed out, the penalty on the gate negotiated out of order can be nullified by going back and renegotiating one or more of the gates left out.

Paddles Kayak paddles have two blades, Canadian canoe paddles have one.

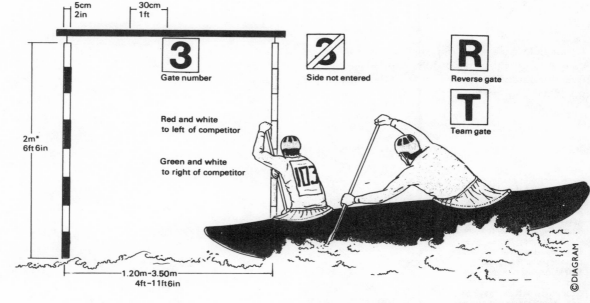

5cm
2in

30cm
1ft

3
Gate number

Side not entered

R
Reverse gate

T
Team gate

Red and white
to left of competitor

Green and white
to right of competitor

2m*
6ft 6in

1.20m–3.50m
4ft–11ft6in

©DIAGRAM

Equipment Safety helmets and lifejackets are usually required. Starting numbers are worn (by the front man only in a C2).

Capsize An Eskimo roll (a complete roll-over under water) is not considered to be a capsize.

In team races teammates may help each other roll up. If a competitor leaves his boat he is disqualified for that run (as is his whole team in a team event). Crossing the finish line upside down results in disqualification for that run.

Lost or broken paddle Only a spare carried on the boat may be used (or a teammate's spare paddle in a team event).

Clearing the course A competitor caught up by another boat must give way if the gate judge gives repeated short blasts on his whistle.

The chief judge may permit a competitor impeded by another boat to repeat his run.

Results In individual events a boat's result equals the time in seconds (from starting line to finishing line) plus any penalties.

In team events the result also includes any penalty for the team gate.

Only the best run by a boat (or team) counts for its final position, except that ties are broken in favor of the boat with the better time on its other timed run.

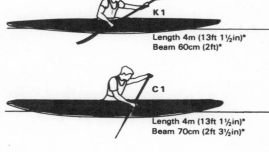

K 1
Length 4m (13ft 1½in)*
Beam 60cm (2ft)*

C 1
Length 4m (13ft 1½in)*
Beam 70cm (2ft 3½in)*

C 2
Length 4.58m (15ft)*
Beam 80cm (2ft 7in)*

*minimum

Canoes Dimensions are limited according to class. Extensions to reach minimum measurements are not permitted.

In Canadian canoes, the highest point of all cross-sections must not be higher than a line between the highest points of the stem and stern; and rounding at the stem and stern may not exceed 30cm.

Canoes must be rudderless, unsinkable, and fitted with handholds at the stem and stern (loops or toggles, or a cord running the length of the craft).

Competitors must be able to free themselves immediately from their boats.

Protests against the right of a competitor to participate, or against official decisions, must be made by team leaders.

Any appeal against the jury must be to the ICF board via the national federation.

Disqualification occurs for breaking racing rules, receiving outside assistance, or trying to win by irregular means.

If a competitor is compelled to break any rule by the action of another competitor, the jury decides what action it will take.

Wild water

Courses must be at least 3km long and be at least grade III in terms of difficulty. They should be stretches of river, with natural and artificial hazards as for slalom events. There are only occasional gates.

Competitors Team events are compulsory in world championships. Regulations are as for slalom.

Events are as for slalom. (There is no Olympic wild water event.)

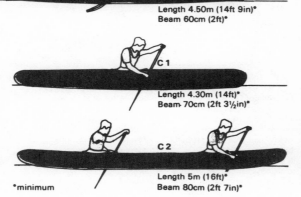

K 1
Length 4.50m (14ft 9in)*
Beam 60cm (2ft)*

C 1
Length 4.30m (14ft)*
Beam 70cm (2ft 3½in)*

C 2
Length 5m (16ft)*
Beam 80cm (2ft 7in)*

*minimum

Officials are as for slalom, except that a competition chairman replaces the chairman of slalom, course judges replace the section and gate judges, and there is no scoring office or course supervisor.

Canoes Dimensions are limited according to class. All cross-sections must be convex. Rudders are not allowed.

General safety regulations are as for slalom events.

Preliminaries The course is inspected and ratified before the race by delegates of the participating nations.

Practice runs must be held on the day before the meeting, and the water level should be as far as possible the same as for the race.

Races Each race consists of one run down the course. Starting intervals depend on the difficulty of the course and the number of competitors.

No portage (carrying of boats) is allowed.

At dangerous passages the correct channel is marked by gates.

Any competitor who is overtaken must give free passage to the overtaking craft.

Results Individual results are based on the time from start to finish. Team results are based on the time from the start of the first boat to the finish of the last.

Protests, appeals, disqualifications Rules are as for slalom.

Canoe polo

Canoe polo is played by opposing teams of five canoeists, who use their paddles to draw the ball over the water. The object is to score the most goals in the agreed time.

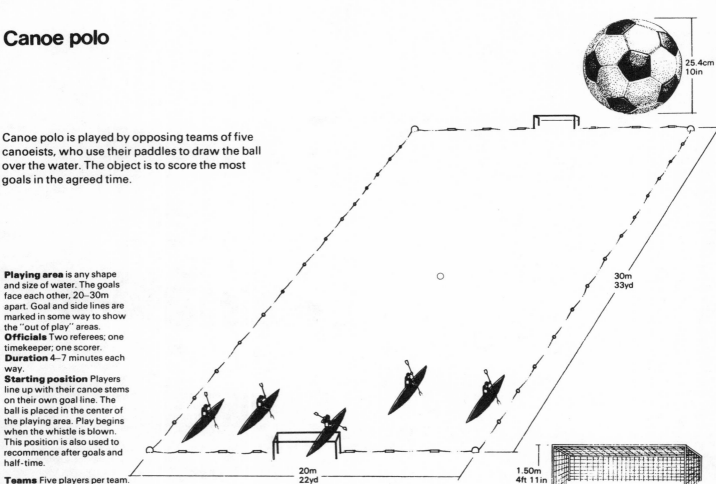

25.4cm
10in

30m
33yd

20m
22yd

1.50m
4ft 11in

4m
13ft

Playing area is any shape and size of water. The goals face each other, 20–30m apart. Goal and side lines are marked in some way to show the "out of play" areas.
Officials Two referees; one timekeeper; one scorer.
Duration 4–7 minutes each way.
Starting position Players line up with their canoe stems on their own goal line. The ball is placed in the center of the playing area. Play begins when the whistle is blown. This position is also used to recommence after goals and half-time.

Teams Five players per team. Substitution is allowed only after injury.
Dress Shirt-front insignias or other easily identifiable team marking; helmets; buoyancy aids or padded or pneumatic belts giving protection to the lower lumbar region.
Ball Size 5 plastic football.
Canoes
Length: 2–3 m
Beam: 50–60cm
End profile: all curves at least 5cm radius
Buoyancy: at least 10kg fitted.
Paddles Propulsion is by single- or double-bladed paddles or by hand. Paddles must have wooden blades without metal tips, and no part of the blade may have a radius less than 3cm.
Use of paddles The paddle may be used to stop the ball in the air or to draw it over the water. The paddle may not be used to hit the ball, either in the air or on the water. Deliberate misuse of paddles is severely penalized.

Play A player may tackle only when a man has the ball. If the ball is in play, a player must dispose of it within 3 seconds of receiving it.
Ball out of play
a) If the ball is put out over the side line, the non-offending team throws it in from the point of exit, but must not throw it in the direction of attack.

b) If the ball is put out over the goal line by an attacker, the attacking team throws from under the goal board.
c) If the ball is put out over the goal line by a defender, the attacking team throws from the corner.
d) There must be 3m between the thrower and his nearest opponent.
e) No goal can be scored from

a goal throw, corner, or penalty until after the ball has touched another object.
Player out of play If a player leaves his canoe, he is out of play until he is properly back in the canoe.
If a player leaves the playing area, he is out of play until he returns completely into it (with no part of his canoe over the boundary line).

Fouls include obstructive play, removal of an opponent's spray deck, attempts to sink or hold an opponent under water.
Penalties are imposed at the referee's discretion:
free throw to the opposing team;
player sent off for 2 minutes;
player sent off for the match;
player referred to the polo

committee of the national canoe authority.
Ties are broken by continuing play until the next goal (after a 1-minute interval and a change of ends). If no goal is scored in the time available, a tie is split by goal average, goals conceded, or the toss of a coin.

Canoe sailing

Canoe sailing is a sport more related to yacht racing than to other forms of canoeing. Sailing is under International Canoe Federation rules, and world and continental championships are held at three-year intervals.

The course An equilateral triangle marked by three buoys. Sailed in the order: start, 1, 2, 3, 1, 3, 1, 2, 3, finish. The number 1 buoy is always set to windward of the start. Each leg of the course is about 1⅛ nautical miles, giving a total distance of about 10 nautical miles.
Start and finish lines are between the buoys and the foremast of the race committee boat (which flies a blue flag when it is on station).
If the course is shortened, the race usually finishes at the number 1 buoy, giving a total distance of about 6½ nautical miles.

Officials Race committee, protest committee, measurement committee.
Protests and appeals Protests are made as in the IYRU rules. Appeals against decisions by protest or measurement committees are decided by the ICF Sailing Committee.
Wind speed Normally races are not started in winds faster than 10 meters per second.
Time limits Races are void if the first canoe fails to complete:
the first round within 1 hr 20 min;
the whole course within 4 hr;
the shortened course at an average speed of 2½ knots.
Scoring system 1st place, ¾ point; 2nd place, 2 points; 3rd place, 3 points; and so on. Retirement, maximum plus 1 point. Non-starter, maximum plus 2. Disqualification, maximum plus 3. (Maximum is the number of competitors attending the championships, after withdrawals.)
The lowest scorer wins.
If six or seven races are held, each competitor may discard his score for one race.
If less than five races are held, the championship is annulled.

Class rules All boats must be officially measured and receive certificates of conformity to class rules. These aim to make hull shapes and sail areas as uniform as possible. There are no restrictions on deck layout or sail plan.
Remeasurement is required after extensive modifications or repairs. Canoes first measured before January 1, 1971 must conform to rules in force at that time; repairs must conform to the same rules, and major reconstruction to present rules.

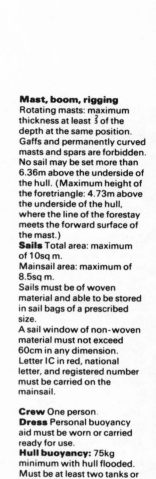

Wind

10sq m canoe
Length: 5.180m (17ft)
Beam: 1.018m (3ft 4in)
Minimum weight: 63kg (139lb)

Centerboard must not project more than 1m from the underside of the hull. It must be fixed in case of capsize and be capable of being fully raised so as not to project beyond the keel.

Sliding seat Maximum extension: 1.525m either side of the canoe.
Weight: 9–12kg, including moving parts.
Carriage must not extend beyond the sheerline.
Hull Any material or method of construction may be used. Must be to drawn design, within tolerances allowed for minor errors and ageing.

Mast, boom, rigging
Rotating masts: maximum thickness at least ⅔ of the depth at the same position. Gaffs and permanently curved masts and spars are forbidden. No sail may be set more than 6.36m above the underside of the hull. (Maximum height of the foretriangle: 4.73m above the underside of the hull, where the line of the forestay meets the forward surface of the mast.)
Sails Total area: maximum of 10sq m.
Mainsail area: maximum of 8.5sq m.
Sails must be of woven material and able to be stored in sail bags of a prescribed size.
A sail window of non-woven material must not exceed 60cm in any dimension.
Letter IC in red, national letter, and registered number must be carried on the mainsail.

Crew One person.
Dress Personal buoyancy aid must be worn or carried ready for use.
Hull buoyancy: 75kg minimum with hull flooded. Must be at least two tanks or flexible bags.

Measurements are checked with templates. The hull is completely decked and unswampable. Protective strips on the keel and centerboard are not included in measurements. Rubbing bands at the gunwales must be of certain dimensions. Stripped weight to be at least 63kg (maximum of 5kg correcting weights).

© DIAGRAM

Yacht racing

Using sail power only, competitors aim to complete a prescribed course in the shortest time. Races are organized by race committees, who issue sailing instructions on starting, sailing the course, finishing, and scoring. The rules given here are from those of the International Yacht Racing Union, and govern yacht maneuvers when racing in daylight.

The course Marks (usually buoys) must be rounded or passed in the correct order and on the required side. If necessary, because of foul weather or insufficient wind, flag signals are used to denote that the course is shortened or reversed, or that the race is canceled, postponed, or abandoned.

The start The starting line may be between two marks (usually buoys), a mark and a sighting post, or an extension from two sighting posts. The starting area may be marked by buoys.

The finish The line is marked in the same way as the starting line. There may be a time limit for finishing a race.

Racing A yacht is "racing" from her preparatory signal until she has either finished or retired, or until the race has been canceled, postponed, or abandoned. Yachts that are racing must fly a rectangular flag at the masthead.

Definitions

1 **Luffing** is altering course toward the wind until head to wind.

2 **Bearing away** is altering course away from the wind until the yacht begins to gybe.

3 **Yacht clear astern.**

4 **Overlapping yacht.**

5 **Tacking** is altering course from port to starboard tack, or vice versa, with the wind ahead. A yacht is tacking from the moment she is beyond head to wind until she has borne away to her course on the new tack.

6 **Gybing** A yacht begins to gybe when, with the wind behind, her mainsail crosses her center line. The gybe ends when the mainsail has filled on the other tack.

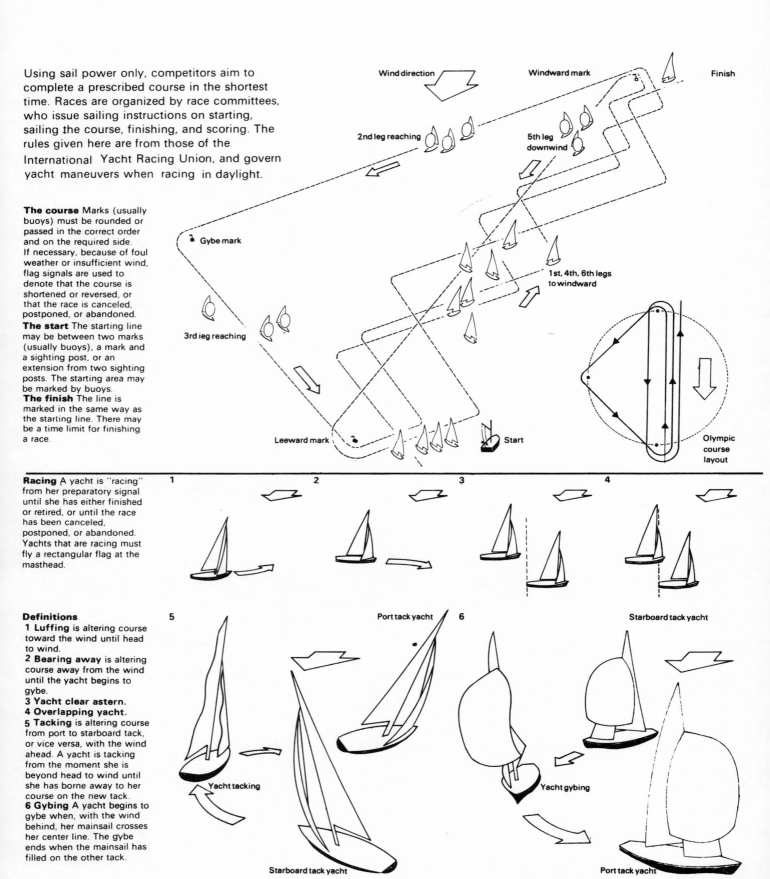

Wind direction

Windward mark

Finish

2nd leg reaching

5th leg downwind

Gybe mark

1st, 4th, 6th legs to windward

3rd leg reaching

Leeward mark

Start

Olympic course layout

1

2

3

4

5   Port tack yacht

6   Starboard tack yacht

Yacht tacking

Yacht gybing

Starboard tack yacht

Port tack yacht

Starting procedure Three flag signals are given at five-minute intervals:
1 warning signal, when the class flag is "broken out" (hoisted);
2 preparatory signal, when the "blue peter" is broken out;
3 the starting signal, when both flags are lowered.
Sound signals are given with a gun or hooter, but the flag signal is used for timing purposes.
Yachts maneuver in the starting area to be in a position to cross the line at the starting signal.
Starting prematurely Any yacht over the line at the starting signal must recross the line.
An individual premature start (**4**) is usually signaled by the class flag at half-mast and by one shot or one other sound signal; the responsibility for returning rests with the helmsman concerned.
A general recall, if several unidentified yachts are over the line, is signaled by a special flag and by two shots or two other sound signals.

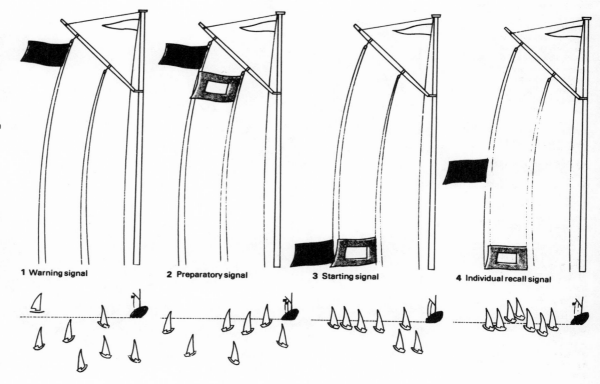

1 Warning signal   **2** Preparatory signal   **3** Starting signal   **4** Individual recall signal

Rounding a mark
1 If a yacht passes a mark on the wrong side, she must return by that side and then round or pass the mark on the correct side.
2 If a yacht touches a mark, she must either:
retire at once;
protest against another yacht for causing her offense; or
absolve herself by completing her rounding, and then re-rounding the mark without touching it.
Giving room at a mark
Provided an overlap exists at least two lengths from a mark or obstruction, an outside yacht must give room where possible to:
overlapping yachts on the same tack (**3**);
overlapping yachts on the same or opposite tacks going downwind (**4**).
This includes giving room for the inside yacht to tack or gybe if that is an integral part of the maneuver; the inside yacht must tack or gybe at the first reasonable opportunity.
(Modified rules apply before the start signal.)

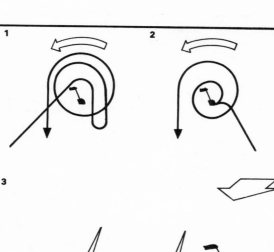

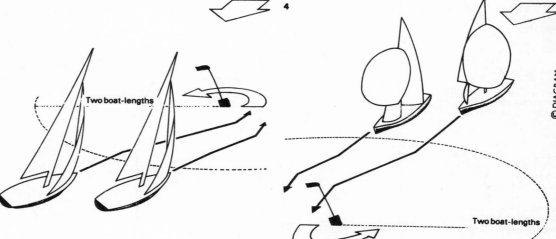

Two boat-lengths

Two boat-lengths

Yachts meeting If two yachts are on collision courses, the one that does not have the right of way must keep clear; if that yacht fails to take avoiding action the other yacht must also try to avoid collision.
A yacht with the right of way does not have complete freedom of maneuver; she must not alter course so that she prevents another yacht from keeping clear, nor obstruct a yacht that is keeping clear.
A yacht that breaks a rule should retire immediately or observe such other penalty as may be imposed in the sailing instructions. If she fails to do either, then other yachts must still observe racing rules toward her.

© DIAGRAM

Right of way Several basic rules apply:

1 When yachts are on opposite tacks, the port tack yacht keeps clear.

2 When yachts are on the same tack, the windward yacht keeps clear.

3 When yachts are on the same tack and one is overtaking, the overtaking yacht keeps clear.

4 When one yacht is changing tack, that yacht keeps clear.

5 When both yachts are changing tack, the yacht on the other's port side keeps clear.

6 When one yacht is anchored, aground, or capsized, the yacht under way keeps clear.

Exceptions

1) A yacht may hail a yacht on the same tack for room to tack to clear an obstruction.

2) If a yacht touches a mark and has to re-round it, or if a yacht is on the wrong side of the starting line at the start signal, the yacht that is sailing incorrectly must keep clear of all yachts sailing correctly.

Overtaking A yacht is "overtaking" if she establishes an overlap from clear astern and is within two lengths' distance.

1 If the overtaking yacht tries to pass to leeward, the yacht ahead must keep clear and the overtaking yacht must give her room to do so. The overtaking yacht may not luff toward the windward yacht until she has gone clear past.

2 If the overtaking yacht tries to pass to windward, the overtaking yacht must keep clear. The yacht ahead may luff the overtaking yacht and may even touch her provided that no serious damage results (the one exception to the "no collision" rule). The yacht ahead may carry the overtaking yacht to the wrong side of a sailing mark, provided that she also sails the wrong side.

A yacht may luff another only if she has the right to luff all the yachts that might be affected by her action— in which case they can all respond, even if an intervening yacht would not otherwise have had the right to luff.

3 All these rights cease as soon as the overtaking yacht's helmsman is ahead of the other yacht's mast. (Overtaking rules are modified before the start.)

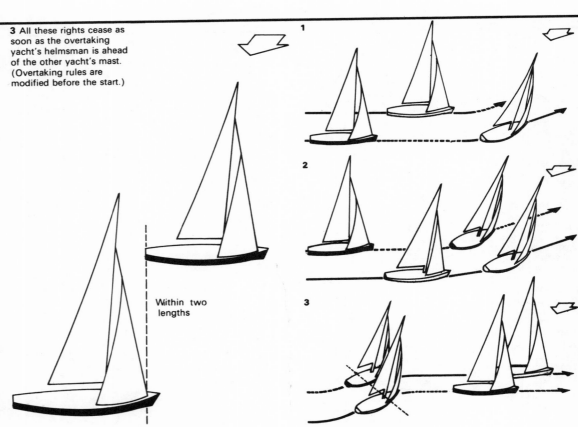

Within two lengths

Sailing the boat A yacht may be propelled only by "the natural action of wind on the sails, spars and hull, and water on the hull." Prohibited are:
"pumping" (frequent rapid trimming of the sails to fan the air like a bird's wing);
"ooching" (lunging forward and stopping abruptly);
"rocking" (persistently rolling a boat from side to side);
repeated gybing or roll-tacking in calm or near calm conditions.
Permitted when suitable wave conditions exist is "surfing" or "planing" by the frequent rapid trimming of sail and crew weight.

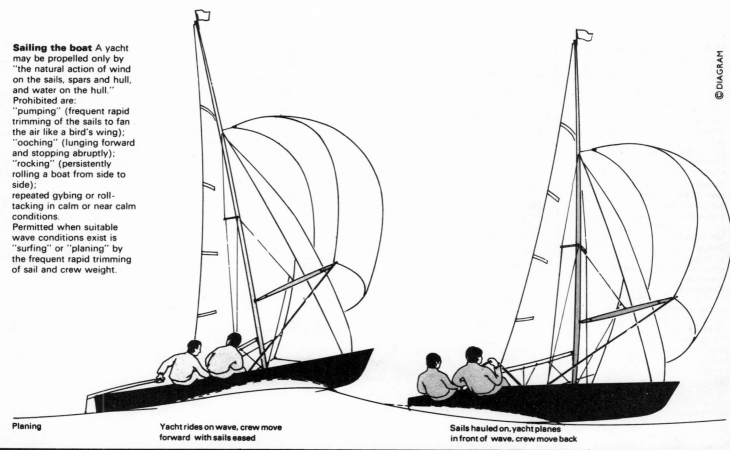

© DIAGRAM

Planing

Yacht rides on wave, crew move forward with sails eased

Sails hauled on, yacht planes in front of wave, crew move back

Infringements and protests The conditions of yacht racing do not permit referees or umpires, and competitors therefore should acknowledge their own rule infringements and enter protests about those of other yachts.
When a yacht infringes rules or instructions, or causes another yacht to do so, she must retire at once or obey sailing instructions on penalization. Causing a collision always requires retirement.
The crew member in charge of any yacht finishing must sign a declaration that all rules have been observed; and, within a time limit, enter any protests against other yachts. (Before making a protest he must usually have flown a "protest flag" during the race and hailed the offending yacht that a protest would be made.)
In national events, protests are heard by the race committee or a subcommittee; appeal is to the national authority.

In international events, protests are heard by an IYRU jury; there is no appeal. Committees and juries may also instigate hearings where no protest has been made. The outcome of a hearing may penalize a different yacht, or invoke a different rule, from those in the original protest.
If the finishing position of a yacht is "materially prejudiced" by rendering assistance, being disabled when having the right of way, or by act or omission of the race committee, the race may be canceled or abandoned, or other arrangements made.
In the Olympics, a yacht so prejudiced receives points equal to her average points (to the nearest one-tenth) for the other five races.

Penalties for acknowledged infringements
1) During the race the penalty may be two full turns through 360°, clear of other yachts, and on the same leg of the course as the infringement.
2) After the race the penalty may be to score for finishing in a place worse than the actual finishing place by 20% of the number of starters (minimum of three places lower; maximum of one place less than the number of starters).

Penalties after a hearing (ie for unacknowledged infringements):
1) for an infringement of sailing instructions the penalty may be to score for finishing in a place worse than the actual finishing place by 30% of the number of starters;
2) disqualification from the race;
3) exclusion from the series;
4) for a gross infringement the owner or helmsman or crewman in charge may be disqualified from racing for a period of time.

Olympic scoring system (Used for most major competitions):
first place, 0 points;
second place, 3 points;
third place, 5.7 points;
fourth place, 8 points;
fifth place, 10 points;
sixth place, 11.7 points;
seventh place and below, place plus 6 points.

Yachts that do not finish, or sail the course incorrectly, or retire after infringing the rules score the points for a last place finish.
Yachts disqualified, or infringing the rules and not retiring, score as for a last place finish plus 10% of the number of yachts starting.

TEAM RACING

Matches are held between two or more teams of two or more yachts each.
During races, yachts maneuver to aid teammates and hinder opponents.
Right of way rules may be waived between teammates provided there is no collision.
If there is contact between teammates, one yacht must retire immediately, or the lower scoring yacht is disqualified after the race. (Certain additional sailing rules apply for team racing.)

Scoring In team racing the first yacht to finish receives ¾ point, the second receives 2 points, the third 3 points, the fourth 4 points, and so on.

Yachts failing to start or finish (except because of an infringement) score points equal to the number of yachts entitled to start.
Yachts infringing and retiring promptly score 1 point more than the number of yachts entitled to start.
Yachts infringing and retiring tardily, or not retiring and then being disqualified, score 4 points more than the number of yachts entitled to start.

Result The team with the lowest total of points wins the race. The team winning most races wins the match when only two teams competed in each race. If more than two teams competed in each race, the match goes to the team with the lowest points score over all the races.

Ties are resolved by a sail-off if possible. Otherwise the match goes to the winner of the last race if only two teams are competing; or, if several teams are competing, to the team that beat the other tied team(s) in the most races.

In the 1976 Olympic Games there will be events for six yacht classes: Tornado, Flying Dutchman. 470, Soling, Finn, and Tempest. The 470 class has replaced the Star class, and the Tornado the Dragon class raced in previous Games. Nations may enter only one yacht in each class. There are seven races for each class, and each yacht counts her best six results for her total score.

Tornado
Catamaran
Length: 20ft (6.096m)
Beam: 10ft (3.048m)
Sail area: 235sq ft
(21.83sq m)
Minimum weight: 295lb
(133.8kg)
Construction: plywood or
fiberglass
Crew: two

Flying Dutchman
Centerboard dinghy
Length: 19ft 10in (6.04m)
Beam: 5ft 10½in (1.79m)
Sail area: 202sq ft
(18.76sq m)
Spinnaker: 144sq ft
(13.37sq m)
Minimum weight: 384lb(174kg)
Construction: mo lded
plywood or fiberglass
Crew: two (one trapeze)

470
Centerboard dinghy
Length: 15ft 4¾in (4.70m)
Waterline: 14ft 9in (4.50m)
Beam: 4ft 3in (1.27m)
Sail area: 145sq ft
(13.48sq m).
Spinnaker carried
Weight: 260lb (118kg)
Construction: fiberglass
Crew: two (one trapeze)

Soling
Keel yacht
Length: 26ft 9in (8.16m)
Waterline: 20ft (6.10m)
Beam: 6ft 3in (1.91m)
Draft: 4ft 3in (1.30m)
Sail area: 250sq ft
(23.22sq m)
Spinnaker carried
Weight: 2200lb (998kg)
Construction: fiberglass
Crew: three

Finn
Centerboard dinghy
Length: 14ft 9in (4.50m)
Beam: 4ft 11½in (1.51m)
Sail area: 107sq ft (9.94sq m)
Minimum weight: 319lb
(145kg)
Construction: molded
plywood or fiberglass
Crew: one

Tempest
Keel yacht
Length: 21ft 11¾in (6.70m)
Waterline: 19ft 3in (5.87m)
Beam: 6ft 3½in (1.92m)
Draft: 3ft 7in (1.09m)
Sail area: 247.6sq ft
(23sq m)
Spinnaker: 224sq ft
(20.80sq m)
Weight: 1299lb (589kg)
Construction: stock fiberglass
Crew: two (one trapeze)

©DIAGRAM

Yacht classes All yachts are either keel boats, dinghies, or catamarans. Keel boats and dinghies are further divided into classes. Class rules may govern the measurements, shape, weight, buoyancy, and equipment of member yachts; and every yacht must have official certificates of conformity to class rules. There are many internationally recognized classes, but all are one of three kinds.
1) In a "one design" class, all boats must be identical.
2) A "development" class allows stated variations, which may be considerable.
3) A "formula" class (for keel yachts only) does not govern individual measurements; instead a number of measurements (such as overall length, draft, sail area) are inserted into a mathematical formula and the result must not exceed a given limit.

Prohibitions A yacht must not eject or release from a container any substance (such as polymer) that might reduce the frictional resistance of the hull to the water.
Unless prescribed in a yacht's class rules or in the sailing instructions, a yacht must not use any device, such as a trapeze or plank, to project a crewman's weight outboard. Nor shall any crew member station any parts of his torso outside a yacht's lifelines, other than temporarily.

Only manual power may be used—except when class rules permit a power winch or windlass for weighing anchor after running aground or fouling an obstruction, or a power pump in an auxiliary yacht.
Only when prescribed in the class rules may a crewman wear extra clothing or equipment to increase his weight.

Required equipment for yachts is prescribed in class rules and sailing instructions. Generally included are: an anchor; racing and protest flags; specified identifying inscriptions on the sails; life-saving equipment.

1 Forward hand
2 Trapeze
3 Helmsman
4 Hiking (toe) straps
5 Rudder
6 Stays
7 Mast
8 Boom
9 Mainsail
10 Jib
11 Spinnaker
12 Spinnaker pole
13 Battens
14 Racing flag (burgee)

Port side

Stern

Bow

Starboard side

Sailing rigs

Una-rig: international A-division catamaran racing

Standing lugsail rig: junior racing/training

Sliding gunter rig: family sailing/racing

Bermudan cat rig: one-man racing

Unstayed cat rig: one-man racing

Bermudan rig sloop: two-man racing

Gaff rig sloop: two/three-man racing

Fully battened mainsail: international sloop B-division catamaran

Wing mast rig: C-division catamaran international "Little America's Cup" racing

Solid wing rig: C-division catamaran racing

Bermudan sloop high aspect ratio: inshore racing

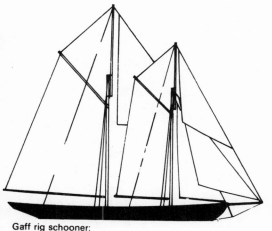

Gaff rig schooner:
non-racing type

Bermudan rig staysail
schooner:
division I ocean racing

Chinese lugsail rig schooner:
single-handed ocean racing

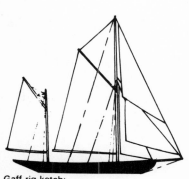

Gaff rig ketch:
non-racing type

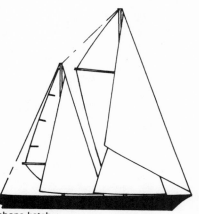

Wishbone ketch:
division II ocean racing

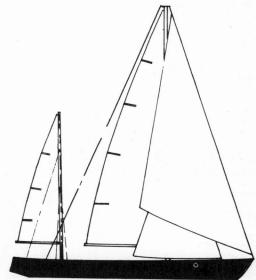

Bermudan ketch rig:
maximum size ocean racing

Gaff rig yawl:
non-racing type

Bermudan rig yawl:
division III ocean racing

Mast head sloop Bermudan
rig:
division IV ocean racing

Gaff rig cutter:
non-racing type

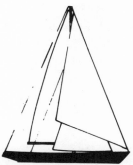

Mast head cutter Bermudan
rig:
division III ocean racing

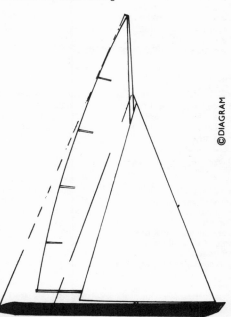

International 12-meter sloop:
"America's Cup" racing

©DIAGRAM

Offshore yacht racing

Competitors race sea-going keel yachts over offshore courses. Yachts are divided into classes, and races range from short afternoon events to great round-the-world races lasting seven or eight months.

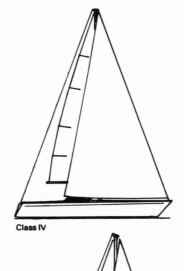

Class IV

Class V

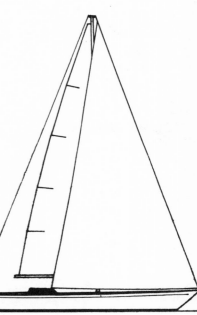

Class III

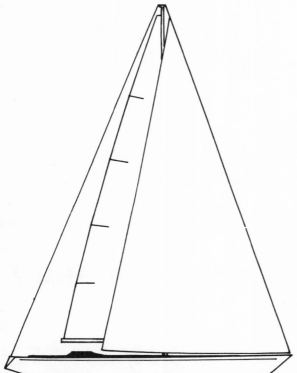

Class I

Class II

Yacht classes Yachts are divided according to their ratings into offshore classes. The five largest ones are:
I (33–70ft)
II (29–32.9ft)
III (25.5–28.9ft)
IV (23–25.4ft)
V′ (21–22.9ft)
Organization The international body for the sport is the Offshore Rating Council, and most offshore races are run under its International Offshore Rule and special safety regulations.

Race categories There are four categories, according to the course's distance from the shore.
Category 1 races are of long distance and are well offshore. Yachts must be completely self-sufficient for extended periods, capable of withstanding heavy storms, and prepared to meet serious emergencies without outside assistance.
Category 2 races are of extended duration, along or not far from the shoreline or in large unprotected bays or lakes. A high degree of self-sufficiency is required, but with the reasonable probability of outside aid in a serious emergency.
Category 3 races are across open water, most of it

relatively protected or close to the shoreline. This category includes races for small yachts.
Category 4 races are short, close to the shore in relatively warm or protected waters.
Race awards Prizes are generally awarded:
a) to a winner in each class (based on corrected times—calculated from the yachts' ratings and race times);
b) to the first boat to finish the course.

Yacht ratings Each yacht has a rating, obtained by inserting its measurements (length, beam, depth, girth, sail area, and many others) into a complex formula (the International Offshore Rule). Measurement is in two stages: hull measurements when the yacht is ashore during building or in winter; freeboard and some other measurements when afloat in full commission.
Ratings are expressed in feet or meters and are used to divide yachts into offshore racing classes.
Rating certificates are compulsory and must be renewed after alterations or a change of ownership.

Owner's responsibility The safety of a yacht and her crew is the sole responsibility of the owner. He must do his best to ensure that the yacht is thoroughly seaworthy, properly equipped, and manned by an experienced crew who are physically fit to face bad weather.
It is the sole responsibility of each yacht to decide whether or not to start or continue in a race.
Inspection A yacht may be inspected at any time. If she does not comply with official specifications her entry may be rejected, or she may be disqualified or subjected to some other penalty prescribed by the national authority or sponsoring organization.

Basic standards The hulls and equipment of offshore racing yachts must meet certain basic standards.

Hulls must be self-righting, strongly built, and fully watertight. They must be properly rigged and ballasted, and completely seaworthy.

Equipment must function properly and be readily accessible. Specifications vary according to the type of yacht and the category of course. They cover:

a) structural features, such as hatches, cockpits, and lifelines;

b) accommodation, such as bunks, galley, and the provision of drinking water;

c) navigation equipment, such as compass and spare compass, charts, piloting equipment, radio direction finder, lead line or sonar, log, and navigation lights;

d) general equipment, such as fire extinguishers, bilge pumps, anchors, first aid kits, foghorns, radar reflectors, and fuel shutoff valves;

e) safety equipment, such as life jackets, whistles, safety harnesses, life rafts life buoys, distress signals, heaving line, ship's dinghy, and white flares;

f) emergency equipment, such as spare navigation lights and power source, storm sails, emergency steering equipment, tools and spare parts, portable sail numbers, and radio receiver.

Electronic aids Permitted electronic aids are: speedometer and log; sonar; wind speed and direction indicator; radio receiver; radio direction finder (but not automatic or self-seeking); radio transmitter (for private business, emergencies, or for race reporting when included in the sailing instructions); repeating compass. The only permitted links are between radio receiver and direction finder, and between compass and compass repeaters.

Average crew of 6/8 aboard 37 ft yacht

1 Navigation lights
2 Stern lights
3 Lifelines
4 Bow rail (pulpit)
5 Stern rail (pushpit)
6 Life buoy
7 Life raft pack
8 Cockpit
9 Compass
10 Hatches
11 Winches
12 Rudder
13 Ballasted keel
14 Propeller (auxiliary engine)
15 Storm sails
16 Back stay radio aerial

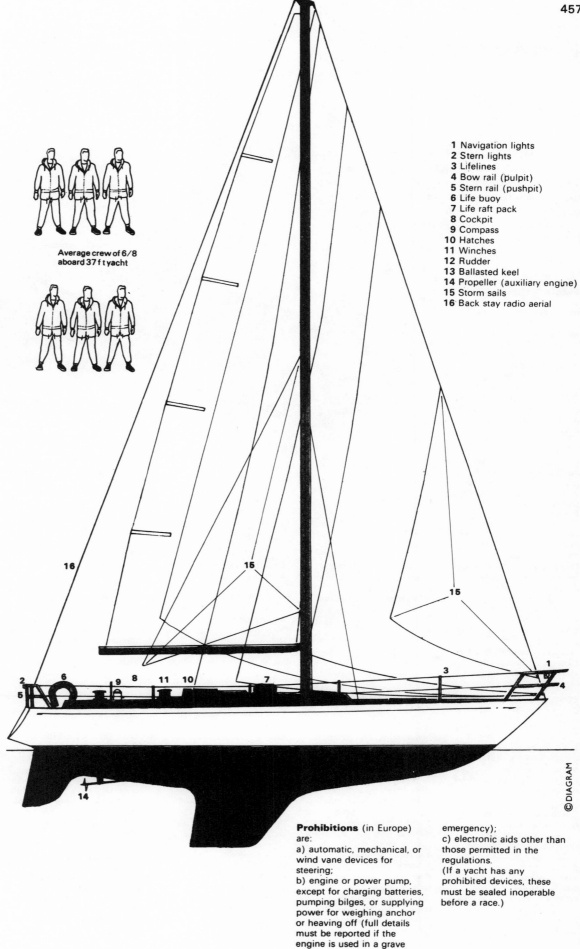

©DIAGRAM

Prohibitions (in Europe) are:

a) automatic, mechanical, or wind vane devices for steering;

b) engine or power pump, except for charging batteries, pumping bilges, or supplying power for weighing anchor or heaving off (full details must be reported if the engine is used in a grave emergency);

c) electronic aids other than those permitted in the regulations.
(If a yacht has any prohibited devices, these must be sealed inoperable before a race.)

Powerboat racing

Powerboat racing divides into sportsboat racing on inland water, and offshore racing at sea. Each division includes a variety of boat classes. Courses are marked out with buoys or racing markers. A points scoring system is used to determine the winner in races with two or more heats.

Events Competitive events are divided into:
international events open to competitors holding an international license issued by their national powerboat racing authority;
national and open invitation events open to competitors holding a national license;
club events open to members of the organizing club only, or to members of one other club in inter-club races;
basic competitive events open to members of the organizing club who hold basic licenses and taking place on a restricted course as laid down by the national powerboat racing authority.
Control
Competitors must have a valid license and third-party insurance issued by the national authority.
Organizing clubs must be affiliated to the national authority and have third-party insurance cover.
All boats entered are subject to the directions and control of the race committee, but it is the sole responsibility of each entrant to decide whether or not to start or continue in a race.

Dress
Lifejackets are compulsory for all persons on board.
Helmets are compulsory except in the cabin category of classes I and II.

Scrutineering Pre-race scrutineering shall be carried out by national officials for international and national events, and by clubs for club and basic events.

Officials In addition to the organizing race committee, independent observers are required as follows.
For national and international sportsboat races there must be one observer representing the powerboat racing authority of the country of the race.

For national offshore races there shall be three, and for international offshore races five, independent observers. The chairman of this jury of observers is appointed by the powerboat racing authority of the country of the race, the others by the organizing club.

For international events, both sportsboat and offshore, one extra observer may be appointed to the jury by each national authority taking part.
Officers of the day must not participate in any event at which they are officiating.

Courses
Sportsboat races are held on stretches of inland water. The maximum number of boats allowed in a race depends on the course's dimensions. It is recommended that boats be divided into heats according to speed.
Offshore races range from long-distance races for powerboats in classes I and II, to basic offshore races for smaller boats. Basic offshore races may not exceed 40 miles in total length and are held within an area extending not more than 2 miles offshore and not more than 8 miles from end to end.

Start Boats making a premature start are not recalled but may be penalized at the discretion of the race committee.
Finish A boat finishes when her stem crosses the finishing line.
After finishing, a driver must withdraw from the circuit without hindering other boats.
Racing flag code
Yellow flag held stationary signals caution;
Yellow flag waved means extreme danger;
Red flag signals that the race is stopped;
Black flag with a number requires the boat with that number to withdraw from the race.
Black and white checkered flag signals the end of the race.

Lap scoring and timekeeping The usual system is operated by four officials, sometimes with assistants.
A caller calls out the number of each boat as it passes the start/finish line. This is recorded by the lap scorer.
A timekeeper reads the time at which each boat crosses the line. This is noted by the recorder.
(The use of a second watch is recommended for checking the race time.)

Point scoring A point scoring system is used for races with two or more heats. The usual one is:
400 points for 1st place, 300 for 2nd, 225 for 3rd, 169 for 4th, 127 for 5th, 95 for 6th, 71 for 7th, 53 for 8th, 40 for 9th,

30 for 10th, 22 for 11th, 17 for 12th, 13 for 13th, 9 for 14th, 7 for 15th, 5 for 16th, 4 for 17th, 3 for 18th, 2 for 19th, 1 for 20th.
Publication of results
In any international, national, open invitation, or inter-club meeting with more than one heat, results are to be prominently displayed before the next heat begins.
Rescue craft must stand by for all races.
For sportsboat races, rescue craft must carry: two good swimmers, signal flags, an efficient fire extinguisher, ropes, a boathook, adequate first aid equipment. An ambulance must also be in attendance.

For hydroplane races, a rescue craft must be capable of planing at 20mph. It must be manned by at least two experienced crew and carry first aid equipment and a boarding ladder.
Hazards A boat may anchor during a race, but must weigh and recover her anchor and not slip.
A boat that grounds, or fouls a buoy, vessel or other obstruction may clear herself with her own anchors, warps, or other gear.

Powerboat classes

Sportsboat racing is divided into:
classes SJ to SZ;
classes S1 to S∞;
national stock outboard series;
junior sportsboats;
classes OF, OI, ON, and OZ.

Hydroplane racing is a subdivision of sportsboat racing. It is divided into:
classes OJ to OD;
racing inboards.

Offshore racing is divided into:
class I (28–45ft);
class II (20–28ft);
class III (over 14ft);
class IV (standard production boats over 12ft).

Eligibility All boats taking part in international or national events must conform to the appropriate class rules issued by the UIM or the national authority. All craft complying with these classes must, where required, be measured and registered with the national authority. In club and basic events, at the discretion of the organizing club, craft may be admitted which do not comply with UIM or national rules.

Sportsboat handicapping
International and national races are not run to an individual handicap system. No class may be handicapped in a series behind another class of greater capacity. A percentage disqualification clause may only be introduced to classes with three or less starters and then only in the second and subsequent heats.
For international and national events where group handicapping is used, clubs set handicap times on the fastest known boat starting in each class.
New classes may be handicapped separately or together with existing classes, depending on the entries in each race.
Classes OI and ON shall be handicapped separately from existing sportsboat classes. Mercury BP and Johnson and Evinrude GT engines in the I and N classes are handicapped separately, regardless of a boat's hull design.

Records World and national records are subject to UIM (Union Internationale Motonautique) record rules. Any person proposing to attempt a record must give at least four weeks' notice to the national authority.

1 class I offshore powerboat
2 class III offshore powerboat
3 ON class circuit powerboat
4 hydroplane
5 class IV offshore powerboat
6 cabin class powerboat

© DIAGRAM

Right of way When two boats are approaching in risk of a collision, one shall keep out of the way as follows:
1) When two boats are turning a buoy alongside each other, the boat on the outside must keep clear.
2) When two boats are crossing, the one with the other boat to her starboard must keep clear.
3) If two boats meet end on, each must alter course to starboard.
4) Every boat overtaking any other must keep clear of the overtaken boat.
5) An overtaking boat cannot set course for a turning mark until clear ahead of the overtaken boat.

A boat that is directed by these rules to keep clear shall:
slacken her speed, stop, or reverse as necessary;
avoid crossing ahead of the boat with right of way.

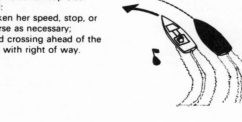
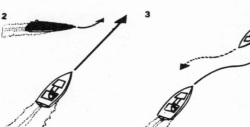

Protests A protest regarding the qualification of a boat, engine, driver, or owner, or against the validity of an entry or of the rules must be made before the start Such a protest made after the race can only be considered if the driver can prove that the relevant facts were unknown to him before the start.
Race protests can only be made by drivers who took part in the race. Such protests must be made within the time given in the program.
Protests against a result must be made within an hour of the official results being posted.
All protests must be in writing and accompanied by the appropriate fee.

Appeals Ten days after receiving the race committee's decision, the appeal, grounds for appeal, and a deposit must be sent to the race committee, who will forward it to the secretary of the national authority.

Penalties All infringements of general racing and safety rules, or any attempt by an owner or driver to gain unfair advantage over other competitors will be penalized. Clubs will be penalized if they cancel a national event without giving proper notice. Clubs will be fined for permitting infringements of licensing and insurance rules.

Speed skating

In speed skating two skaters at a time race in a counter-clockwise direction around a track. Races for both men and women are held over varying distances. Points are given in relation to the skater's time in each event, and the distance winner is the skater who achieves the fastest time. The overall winner is the skater who wins the majority of the races, or who has the lowest total of points.

Lane width
4m**
13ft

Starter

Crossing controller

Change lanes zone

70m
77yd

111.95m
122yd

b

**Lap scorer
Timekeeper
Referee**

c

d

25-26m
27-28yd

Changing lanes

**minimum

a start 500m
b finish 1000m
c start 10,000m
   finish 500m, 1500m,
   3000m, 5000m, 10,000m
d start 1500m
e start 1000m
f start 3000m, 5000m

The track An international speed skating track is a closed, two-lane circuit 333⅓m or 400m long. There must be two curved ends each of 180°, the radius of the inner curves being between 25–26m.
The width of each lane must be at least 4m, preferably 5m. The lanes are divided by snow, or by painted lines and blocks of rubber or other suitable material.
The crossing line is the whole length of the straight from the end of the curve.
Pre-start lines are marked 75cm behind the starting lines.
The start of a 1000m race on a 400m standard track is marked in the middle of the front straight (the crossing zone), and the finishing line is marked in the center of the opposite, or finishing, straight.
Every meter of the last five meters before the finishing line is marked.
Races of distances in excess of 10,000m do not have to be held on a standard track.
Officials include a referee and assistant referee; starter and assistant starter; judge; timekeepers; lap scorers; at least three track scorers; crossing controller.
Events
Men: 500m, 1500m, 5000m, 10,000m;
Women: 500m, 1000m, 1500m, 3000m.
Events take place in a specified sequence over two days.
Competitors Skaters are not allowed to compete over single distances, but they may have at least 30 minutes' rest between events.
Teams In the Olympic Games each country may enter a maximum of 12 male competitors and eight female competitors.
Men Each country may enter only four racers in both the 500m and 1500m events, and three racers in both the 5000m and 10,000m events.

Women Each country may enter a maximum of three racers in an event.
The number of racers in an event may be reduced.
Lanes are decided by either: a draw, the skater drawn first skating in the inner lane; or
performance in the preceding distance, the skater with the lower total of points skating in the inner lane.
Skaters must stand still in an upright position between the pre-start line and the starting line. Their skates may not be over the starting line.
On the command of "ready" they adopt their starting positions, and are started by a shot or a whistle.
A skater at fault in three false starts is disqualified for that distance.
Starting In some competitions the starting order for each event is decided by the racers' performances in the previous events. In the

Olympic Games there is a draw for the starting order in each event.
Competitors race in pairs in a counterclockwise direction.
Re-starts A race may be re-started:
after a false start;
if a starter is interfered with;
if a competitor or any obstacle other than a broken skate prevents a skater from finishing the race.
A skater is allowed 30 minutes' rest before a re-start. He starts the second race in the same lane as the first race. If two skaters are allowed a re-start, they draw for lanes.
Changing lanes Skaters must change lanes each time they reach the crossing straight, except in the first straight of the 1000m or 1500m race on a 400m track. It is the responsibility of the skater leaving the inner lane to avoid collision. Skaters may not change lanes or cross the lines when entering, skating on, or leaving a curve.

Overtaking A skater may only overtake if he does not impede the leading skater. When a skater has been overtaken and passed, he must remain at least 5m behind his opponent.
Any form of pacemaking— in front, alongside, or behind the other skater—is forbidden.
Finishing Skaters finish when one skate reaches the finishing line.
Penalties Skaters may be disqualified from an event, from further events, or from events already run, for: deliberate fouls; collisions caused when moving from the inner lane; three false starts; changing lanes on a curve.
Scoring Points are scored on the basis of the skaters' times:
in 500m races each second equals one point;
in 1000m races the points are half of the number of seconds;
in 1500m races the points are a third of the number of seconds;

in 3000m races the points are a sixth of the number of seconds;
in 5000m races the points are a tenth of the number of seconds;
in 10,000m races the points are a twentieth of the number of seconds.
Results The skater who achieves the best time for a distance is the winner. If more than one skater has the same time, each of them is the winner.
The overall winner is the skater who has won the majority of distances. If no skater has this majority, or if several skaters have won the same number of events, the overall winner is the skater with the lowest total of points.
In some competitions the overall winner must have competed over all the distances.

Dress The skater who starts in the inner lane wears a white armband; the skater starting in the outer lane wears a red armband.
Skates Speed skates have long, thin, straight blades, reinforced with steel tubing for lightness and strength. The shoe is made of thin leather for lightness.

Short track speed skating

There are three types of race in short track speed skating: individual races over varying distances, relay races with teams of two or four skaters, and pursuit races between two skaters.

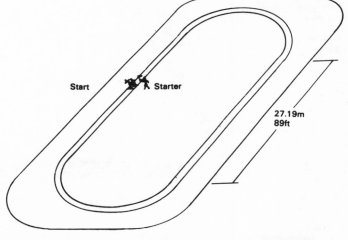

Start   Starter

27.19m
89ft

The track must be at least 4.57m wide in the straights. The distance between the apex of the semicircular end and the barrier must not be less than 3.35m.
Officials include: a referee; at least five judges; starter; timekeepers; lap scorer; recorder; two track stewards; competitors' steward.

INDIVIDUAL RACES
Events
Short-distance: 500m, 1000m, 1500m; long-distance: 3000m, 5000m.
Heat system A maximum of four skaters race together in short-distance events, and a maximum of six skaters in long-distance events.
Skaters may qualify for further rounds by either: winning a heat; being among a specified number of skaters with the fastest times; or being among the fastest runners-up.
The race winner is the first skater to finish in the final.
Elimination system A maximum of eight skaters competes. After four laps the skater in last position is eliminated. Another skater is eliminated after the next two

laps and after each successive two laps until only the winner remains.
Overtaking The leading competitor has the right of way and may only be passed on the outside, providing he keeps to the inside of the track. The responsibility for any collision or obstruction is with the skater who is overtaking.
A skater who has been, or is being, lapped may be instructed by the judges to move to the outside of the track to allow the oncoming skaters the right of way.
The judges signal to the skater with a yellow flag; the skater should remain on the track and continue the race.
Offenses A skater may not: deliberately impede another competitor with any part of the body;
slow down unnecessarily, so causing another competitor to slow down or collide; deliberately cross the track or in any way interfere with another competitor or with the result of the race.
Penalties Offenses may be penalized by disqualification, and a skater can be disqualified during a race.

A black flag is used to signal to the offender, who must leave the track immediately without impeding the other skaters.
A skater who is disqualified is not allowed to compete in the rerun.
RELAY RACES
Competitors Teams have two or four members, each of whom must take part. Only one competitor at a time from each team may skate in a race until relieved.
Substitutes may be allowed if a skater is injured during a race or contest.
If the substitution occurs during a heat or semi- or quarter-final, the substitute must remain in the team for the rest of the contest.
Relaying A skater may be replaced by another member

of the team at any time except during the last two laps.
The incoming team member is not in the race until he has touched, or is touched by, the skater who is being replaced.
The replaced skater must leave the track without impeding any of the other skaters.
A pistol signals the beginning of the last three laps, and a bell the beginning of the final lap.
Offenses Skaters may not impede, obstruct, or interfere with opponents, either on or off the track.
Offenses may be penalized by disqualification of the whole team.
Result The team of the first skater to reach the finishing line wins the race.

PURSUIT RACES
Competitors Each race is between two skaters.
Starting The skaters start opposite each other, each in the middle of the straight.
Duration Each race lasts a maximum of 10 laps.
Result The winner is the skater who overtakes the other one or who finishes in the faster time.
Heat winners qualify for the next round, in which the fastest qualifier is matched against the slowest qualifier, and the second fastest against the second slowest, and so on, until the winner is determined.

© DIAGRAM

Figure skating

There are three types of figure skating competition: single skating, pair skating, and ice dancing. Competitors perform compulsory movements and movements of their own choice. Marks are awarded for artistic impression and technical merit. Judges mark each competitor individually, and the winner is the skater or pair placed first by the majority of judges.

Rink The rink area for free skating and short programs should be rectangular. Maximum size: 60 × 30m. Minimum size: 56 × 26m. There must be a music reproduction system.
Music In both single and pair skating the music is selected by the competitors.

Officials There must be: a referee; a maximum of nine judges for both figure skating and ice dancing; two announcers; two secretaries; two timekeepers; and supplementary officials as necessary.

Duration In both single and pair skating, the short programs and the free skating sections have specified time limits.
For short programs the maximum time is two minutes. Skaters may finish in less time if they have attempted all the stipulated moves; no extra marks may be obtained for extending the program to the maximum time or repeating moves that have failed.
For free skating the maximum times are:
women, four minutes;
men, five minutes;
pairs, five minutes.
The skater must finish within 10 seconds before or after the specified time. The end of the time is signaled by a gong or whistle.
Sequence The compulsory figures or dances are skated first, followed by the short program and then the free skating or dancing.
There is a draw to decide the starting order in the compulsory section. The starting order in subsequent sections is decided by the competitors' performances in the previous section.

Restarts If a competitor is interfered with and is not at fault the referee may allow the program to be restarted. Such restarts occur after all the other competitors have performed. Any previous score is disregarded.

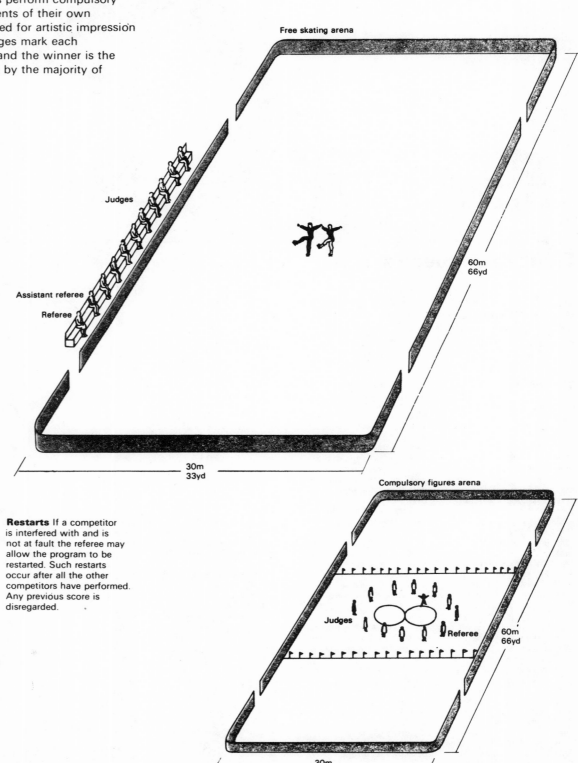

Free skating arena

Judges

Assistant referee

Referee

60m
66yd

30m
33yd

Compulsory figures arena

Judges

Referee

60m
66yd

30m
33yd

Dress must allow full freedom of movement. Costumes for ISU (International Skating Union) championships must be modest and dignified.
Skates usually have a single steel blade about 3mm wide. The blade is hollow-ground on the bottom to give two skating edges; figures are skated on the inside or the outside edge.

© DIAGRAM

ICE DANCING
Ice dancing consists of:
a) compulsory dances;
b) original set pattern dance;
c) free dancing.
The dance couple must consist of one woman and one man.
Compulsory dances
Competitors skate one of the following groups of dances:
1) Viennese waltz, kilian, quickstep;
2) Westminster waltz, paso doble, blues;
3) starlight waltz, rumba, Argentine tango.
Depending on the competition, the group is either drawn the previous evening or is specified when the competition is announced.

Original set pattern dance is treated as a fourth compulsory dance. Each couple chooses its own music, tempo, and composition, but the rhythm is announced annually by the ISU Ice Dance Committee.
The dance is to be composed of repetitive sequences consisting of either one half or one complete circuit of the ice surface. The choice of steps, connecting steps, turns, and rotations is free, provided the movements conform to ISU rules.
Free dancing The free dance consists of non-repetitive combinations of dance movements composed into a 4-minute program displaying the dancers'

personal ideas in concept and arrangement. Competitors choose their own music. All steps, turns, and changes of position are permitted, as are certain free skating movements appropriate to the rhythm, music, and character of the dance. Competitors are marked for their general knowledge and ability in dancing as well as for the originality and concept of their ideas.
SINGLE SKATING
Single skating consists of:
a) compulsory figures;
b) a short program that includes compulsory movements (this section is omitted from some competitions);
c) free skating.

The short program consists of seven prescribed free skating movements with connecting steps. It lasts for a maximum of two minutes. The connecting steps are also marked and should be kept to a minimum. Marks are deducted if unprescribed or additional elements are included.
PAIR SKATING consists of:
a) a short program that includes compulsory moves;
b) free skating.
The pair must consist of a man and a woman. They need not perform the same movements or always remain in contact with each other, but they must give a united, harmonious performance
Forbidden movements: swinging the lady while holding her hand or foot;

jumping toward the other partner; rotating with one partner gripping the other's leg, arm, or neck.
Lifting is permitted only with the hands; it is forbidden to hold the partner's legs. The partner may not be carried for more than three complete revolutions. The lifting arm must be fully extended. It is forbidden to turn the lifted partner in a horizontal position.
The short program consists of six compulsory moves with connecting steps. The connecting steps should be kept to a minimum; they are also marked. Marks are deducted if unprescribed or additional elements are included.

464

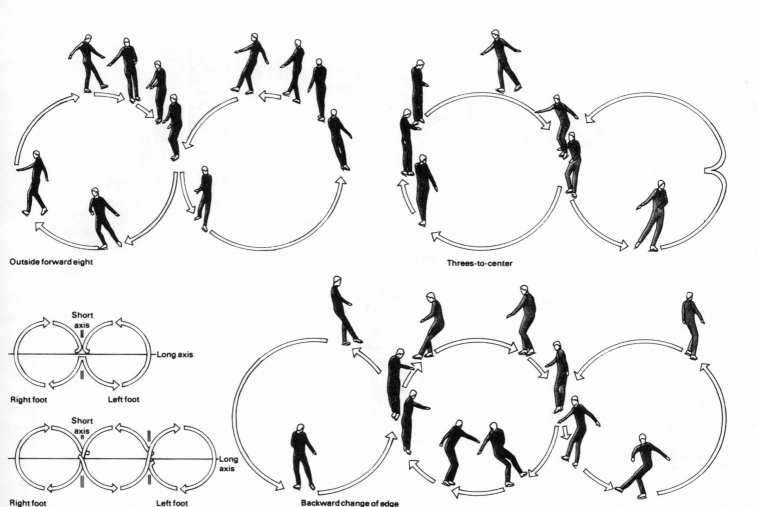

Outside forward eight

Threes-to-center

Short axis

Long axis

Right foot — Left foot

Short axis

Long axis

Right foot — Left foot

Backward change of edge

COMPULSORY FIGURES

Three compulsory figures are required in major championships. They are performed in order of increasing difficulty.
Every figure must be skated three times on each foot. There should be no pause between the repetitions. The execution of each figure should be flowing, graceful, and without effort.
Before the start of each compulsory figure the skater must indicate the long axis of that figure. The skater must not use the long axis of a previous figure, nor use any painted lines or marks on the ice as a tangent or axis, or to start or locate turns.
The skater must not start without the referee's permission.

At the beginning of each figure the skater must stand on the flat of his skates near the intersection of the figure's long and short axes. The skater must start from this position with a clean, single stroke from the edge (not point) of the skate. There must be no preliminary step, nor any unnecessary or exaggerated contortion of the body.
The change from one foot to the other must be made with a single stroke from the edge of the skate of the foot that is to become the free foot. There must be no pause. After a figure is finished the skater must change the tracing foot and continue in a straight line in the direction of the short axis. There should be no pause between the repetitions.

Carriage The head should be upright, relaxed, and held naturally;
the upper part of the body should be upright, but not stiff or bent forward or to the side at the hips;
the arms should be held gracefully;
the hands should be higher than the waist and the palms held easily, naturally, and parallel to the ice;
the fingers should be neither extended nor clenched;
the skating leg should be flexed and the knee slightly bent;
the free leg should be slightly bent at the knee, generally held over the tracing, with the free foot not too close to the skating foot;
the free foot should be carried slightly above the ice, the toe of the skate pointing down and out; exaggerated positions should be avoided.

Flow A lively and even flow should be maintained throughout the figure.
Motion The motion should be graceful and even, not stiff or with jerky, abrupt, flailing, or angular movements.
Speed A figure must be finished at a reasonable speed, or marks will be deducted.
Tracing The size of the figure must be approximately the same in its triple execution. Faults in the original tracing must be corrected in the succeeding tracing.
The circle is the basis of all compulsory figures. Each compulsory figure consists of two or three circles. These are tangent and traced continuously except for the brief interruption necessary for changing feet.

FREE SKATING

The skater selects movements from the officially approved list, with jumps, spins, steps, and other linking movements. This program should be executed, with a minimum of two-footed skating, in harmony with the music.
Spins Generally, spins must have a minimum of six rotations. If there is a change of foot or position during the spin, there must be a minimum of five rotations on each foot or in each basic position.

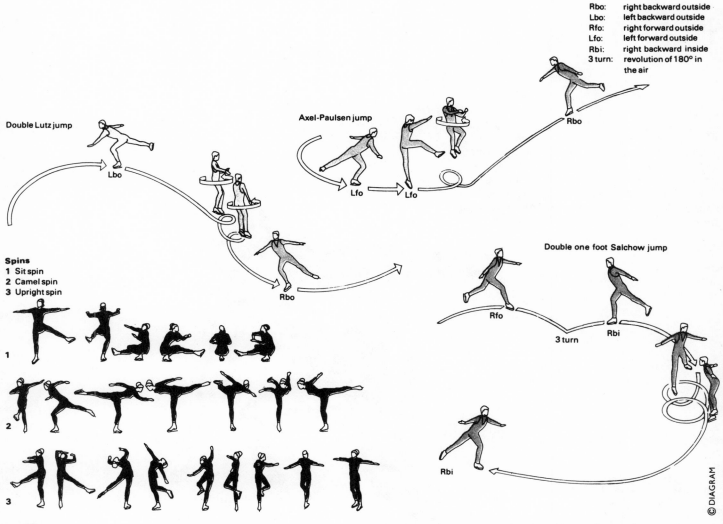

Double Lutz jump

Lbo

Axel-Paulsen jump

Lfo → Lfo

Rbo

Rbo: right backward outside
Lbo: left backward outside
Rfo: right forward outside
Lfo: left forward outside
Rbi: right backward inside
3 turn: revolution of 180° in the air

Double one foot Salchow jump

Rfo

3 turn

Rbi

Rbi

Spins
1 Sit spin
2 Camel spin
3 Upright spin

1

2

3

© DIAGRAM

SCORING

The scale of marks for each performance runs from one to six (to one decimal place).

Ice dancing The score from each judge is obtained as follows:
the marks for the compulsory group of dances are added;
the marks for the composition and presentation of the original set pattern dance are added;
the total marks for the compulsory group of dances and original set pattern dance are added together and divided by 2.5 to produce the total points for the compulsory dances;
the free dancing marks for technical merit and artistic impression are added to produce the total points for the free dancing;
the total points for free dancing are added to the total points for the compulsory dances to produce the points total for each judge.
In events without an original set pattern dance the points for the compulsory group of dances are added and divided by 1.5 to produce the total

points for the compulsory dancing.
This is then added to the total points for free dancing to produce the points total for each judge.

Single skating The score from each judge is obtained as follows:
the points for the compulsory figures are added together and divided by 1.5;
the short program marks for technical merit and artistic impression are added and the sum divided by 2;
the short program and compulsory figures totals are added together;
the free skating points for technical merit and artistic impression are added together;
the total points for free skating are added to the combined total for the short program and the compulsory figures.
In single skating events without a short program the mark for each compulsory figure is multiplied by an appropriate factor of value.
The results are added together and divided by the appropriate dividing factor, which is obtained by adding the factors of value of each

figure skated and dividing by 2.
This produces the total for the compulsory figures, which is then added to the free skating points to produce the points total for each judge.

Pair skating The score from each judge is obtained as follows:
the program marks for technical merit and artistic impression are added and the sum divided by 3;
the free skating marks for technical merit and artistic impression are added together;
the total points for the short program and free skating sections are added together to produce the points total for each judge.
In pair events that do not include a short program, the free skating marks for technical merit and artistic impression are added to produce the points total for each judge.

Compulsory figures

Each judge gives a mark for each figure.
The deduction of points depends on the degree or frequency of an error. Generally, an accumulation or combination of several different errors in a figure is penalized more heavily than a single serious error alone.
Taken into consideration are: the skater's start, carriage, and speed; the shape and symmetry of the figure; and the cleanness of the edges and turns.

Free skating Each judge awards two marks for each program: one for technical merit and the other for artistic impression.
The judges simultaneously display the marks they have awarded, using black numbers for whole marks and red numbers for decimals.

RESULTS

At the end of each part of the competition each judge places the competitors according to the total points he has awarded.
The competitor or pair placed first by the absolute majority of judges is the winner; the other places are similarly decided.
If two or more competitors or pairs have obtained a majority for the same place, the higher-placed will be the one who has been awarded that place by the greater number of judges.
If such majorities are equal, the lowest total of place numbers of those judges forming the majority decides between them.
Separate awards may be made for single free skating.

Skiing

Skiing sports are divided into three basic groups:
Alpine, Nordic, and biathlon. Alpine skiing
includes downhill, slalom, and giant slalom races,
and the Alpine combined event. Nordic skiing
includes cross-country, ski jumping, and the
Nordic combined. Biathlon combines cross-
country skiing with rifle shooting. All these skiing
sports are included in the Winter Olympics.

Skis are made of various
materials, though fiberglass
and plastic have largely
replaced wood and metal.
Extra grip is obtained from
metal edges along the running
surface.
The length and weight of the
skis vary with the competition,
and the size and preference
of the skier.

Downhill skis are heavier,
stiffer, and longer than those
for other racing events.
Slalom skis are shorter and
narrower, with the edges
welded to the skis to prevent
them from being torn off.
Giant slalom skis have
more flexibility and camber
than downhill skis and their
width is between that of
downhill and slalom skis.

Ski-jumping skis are
heavier, wider, and longer
than the others.
Cross-country skis are
narrow, light, and have a
simple binding to allow the
heels to move up and down.

Sticks (poles) are used for
balance, to help in climbing,
and to give impetus at starts
and turns.
They are made of steel or
aluminum tubing.
Handles are usually plastic,
and there is an adjustable
strap.
The basket, about 8cm from
the end, prevents the stick

from sinking too deep into
the snow.
The length of sticks used
varies with the skier's size and
preference; the top usually
reaches between the waist
and armpit when the arm is
hanging normally and the tip
of the stick is on the ground.

Officials Skiing competitions require a large number of officials.
Each event is supervised by a committee. The duties of officials and their assistants include setting and maintaining the course, starting, gate-keeping (in Alpine events), supervising the finish, and timing.
Many events require officials, who are not competitors, to make the track by skiing on the course before the competition begins.
There is a jury to decide protests, disputes, and other problems.

© DIAGRAM

Boots must fit to give maximum control over the ski edges and support for the ankles.
Racing boots are stiffer and fit higher than cross-country boots, which are lighter and lower-fitting for extra comfort.
Bindings hold the boots firmly to the skis. They also release the skier from the skis in case of a fall.

Waxing Racers wax the under surface of their skis to increase their speed. The type and amount of wax used varies according to temperature, snow conditions, etc. Waxing is particularly important on cross-country skis.

Dress must be warm, waterproof, and tight-fitting (to reduce wind resistance). Goggles may be used as protection from glare, wind, and snow spray, and to improve visibility in some conditions.
Downhill racers must wear crash helmets.

Penalties Competitors may be disqualified for not complying with regulations. Offenses include:
receiving unauthorized assistance;
not following the proper course (eg missing out a gate in racing events);
not giving way to an overtaking skier at the first demand;
finishing without at least one ski.

Alpine skiing

Alpine skiing includes three types of race: downhill, slalom, and giant slalom. There are also combined events comprising several races, either downhill, slalom, or both. There are races for men, women, and teams. General rules apply to all Alpine events.

Courses The snow must be as smooth and compact as possible.
Snow banks, straw, nets, etc should be used for protection against hazards.
Smaller obstacles should be removed from the course.
There must be direct communication between the start and finish.

Competitors The jury divides the skiers into groups according to previous performance.
Each group may have a maximum of 15 skiers. No nation may have more than four skiers in the first two groups.
Generally the group with the best competitors begins first and the others follow in sequence.
The starting order in each group is decided by drawing lots.

Giant slalom

Slalom

1 Men's
2 Women's

Downhill

Timing Electric timing apparatus is used for measurements to a hundredth of a second. Supplementary stopwatches are also used.
The starting time is recorded when the skier's lower legs cross the starting line.
With electric timing, the finishing time is recorded when any part of the skier's body or equipment crosses the finishing line; with hand timing the finishing time is when the skier's first foot crosses the line.

Re-runs A skier may appeal for a re-run because of:
obstruction;
objects on the course;
a missing gate;
a timing failure;
any other circumstances beyond his control that

interfered with his performance.
The re-run may be made at a full interval or half an interval after all the other competitors. The time for the re-run is the one recorded, even if it is longer than the competitor's original time.
A skier may be disqualified if he makes an unjustified appeal.

Team races Unless special conditions apply, a team consists of four skiers, and the times of the best three skiers in each race are averaged and used to calculate the combined result.
Points for each race are calculated from official tables, with the winning team receiving 0 points. If two teams have the same average, the team placing is determined

by the individual placing of the best skier.
The combined result is obtained by adding the points scored in the different races. If teams tie, the final result is obtained by their placing in the downhill race.

Start The starting area is reserved for competitors and officials.
The starting gate consists of two posts 75cm apart, and no more than 50cm high.
Competitors must be able to stand relaxed on the starting line, yet quickly reach full speed after starting. All outside help is forbidden.
The skier's poles must be stuck in the snow in front of the starting line. Only the poles may be used to start.
Skiers are warned 10 seconds before the start of the race,

and in races other than the slalom the last 5 seconds are counted out by the starter before he gives the command to start. (Alternatively, an automatic starting signal may be used.)
A competitor who, without just cause, is not ready to start at the appointed time will be disqualified.
A competitor who starts more than 3 seconds early in a race with fixed starting intervals will be disqualified for a false start.

Finish The approach to the finish must be adapted to the terrain, and the finishing area must be clearly visible as the competitors approach.
The finishing area must be wide and there must be a gently sloped outrun with smoothly packed snow. The area behind the finishing line must be completely fenced in.
The finishing line is marked by two poles connected by a banner. The width at the finish is determined by the terrain, snow conditions, and racers' speed. It is usually at least 6m.

Downhill racing

Skiers in downhill events race down the course as quickly as possible. Control gates are used to direct competitors over the course and to reduce the average speed. The winner is the skier who legally completes the course in the fastest time.

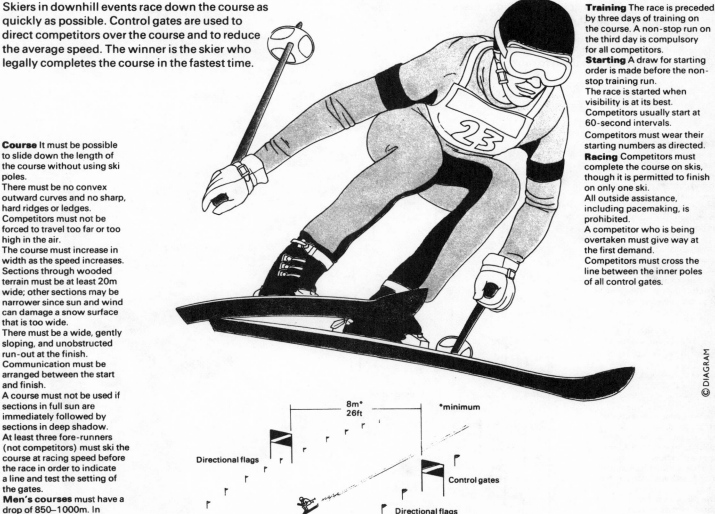

Directional flags

Control gates

Directional flags

8m*
26ft

*minimum

Course It must be possible to slide down the length of the course without using ski poles.
There must be no convex outward curves and no sharp, hard ridges or ledges.
Competitors must not be forced to travel too far or too high in the air.
The course must increase in width as the speed increases. Sections through wooded terrain must be at least 20m wide; other sections may be narrower since sun and wind can damage a snow surface that is too wide.
There must be a wide, gently sloping, and unobstructed run-out at the finish.
Communication must be arranged between the start and finish.
A course must not be used if sections in full sun are immediately followed by sections in deep shadow.
At least three fore-runners (not competitors) must ski the course at racing speed before the race in order to indicate a line and test the setting of the gates.
Men's courses must have a drop of 850–1000m. In Olympic and world ski championships, the best time for the course must not be less than two minutes.
Women's courses must have a drop of 400–700m. In Olympic and world ski championships, the best time for the course must not be less than 100 seconds.
If possible, women's downhill courses should be separate from the men's.

Control gates are used to direct competitors over the course, keep them away from dangerous areas, and to reduce the average speed for the run.
Gates consist of two flags; each flag is a rectangular piece of cloth between two vertical poles. The poles must be splinterproof and solid. Gates should be at least 8m

wide and placed, if possible, at right angles to the racing line. The lower edge of the flag must be at least 1m above the snow.
With the exception of the start and finish, gates are numbered consecutively down the course.

Men's courses are marked by red control gates. Women's courses are marked by alternating red and blue gates.
Direction flags are set on each side of the course: red flags down the left side and green flags down the right.

Training The race is preceded by three days of training on the course. A non-stop run on the third day is compulsory for all competitors.
Starting A draw for starting order is made before the non-stop training run.
The race is started when visibility is at its best. Competitors usually start at 60-second intervals.
Competitors must wear their starting numbers as directed.
Racing Competitors must complete the course on skis, though it is permitted to finish on only one ski.
All outside assistance, including pacemaking, is prohibited.
A competitor who is being overtaken must give way at the first demand.
Competitors must cross the line between the inner poles of all control gates.

Results Each competitor's time is announced unofficially until it is verified that the course was completed in a proper manner.
The official results are produced from the times of all racers who are not disqualified.
The winner is the competitor who legally completes the course in the fastest time.

© DIAGRAM

Alpine combined

The Alpine combined event comprises three races: downhill, slalom, and giant slalom. Points are awarded for each race according to official tables. These points are added together to give the final classification.

Sequence The downhill race usually precedes the slalom races.
The starting order for the downhill race is decided by a group draw.
The starting order for the slalom is determined by the result of the downhill race. The first five to finish in the downhill start the slalom in

reverse order (ie the fifth goes first, fourth goes second, etc). The remaining competitors start in the order in which they finished in the downhill. (A draw is used to settle starting order in cases of equality.)

Slalom

Competitors in the slalom follow twisting courses defined by pairs of flags (known as gates). A competition is decided by two runs down different courses. The winner is the competitor with the fastest aggregate time for the two runs.

Courses should test a wide variety of ski techniques. Traverses across the slope are interspersed with runs down it, and courses must include turns that allow maximum speed, precision, and neat execution. The snow must be as hard as possible.
In world and Olympic championships at least a quarter of each course must be on slopes exceeding a gradient of 30°.
Vertical drop World and Olympic championships: men 180–220m; women 130–180m.
Other international races: men 140–200m; women 120–160m.

Gates Slalom gates consist of two solid, uniform poles, which must be 3–4cm in diameter and extend 1.8m above the snow.
The gates must be alternately blue or red, with flags of the same color.
The distance between any two gates must be at least 0.75m, and not more than 15m.
Each gate must be between 4m and 5m wide.
In a hairpin gate the distance between the two verticals must be 0.75m.
The course must contain open and vertical gates, and two or three vertical combinations (consisting of between three and five gates) and at least four hairpin combinations.
For men's courses there are between 55 and 75 gates; for women's courses between 40 and 60 gates.
Except for the starting and finishing gates, the gates are numbered down the course, with the numbers on the outside of the poles.
Gates must not be set in monotonous combinations; nor must they spoil the fluency of a run by forcing sudden braking.

Difficult sequences of gates should not be set at the beginning or end of a course. The last gates should be fast, to enable a racer to finish at good speed.
The last gate should not be too near the finishing line (to avoid danger to officials), and should direct racers toward the middle of the finishing line.

Competitors There must be no more than 100 racers. The race committee may reduce the number for the second run, provided competitors have been told beforehand.
Courses may not be used simultaneously by two groups of competitors.

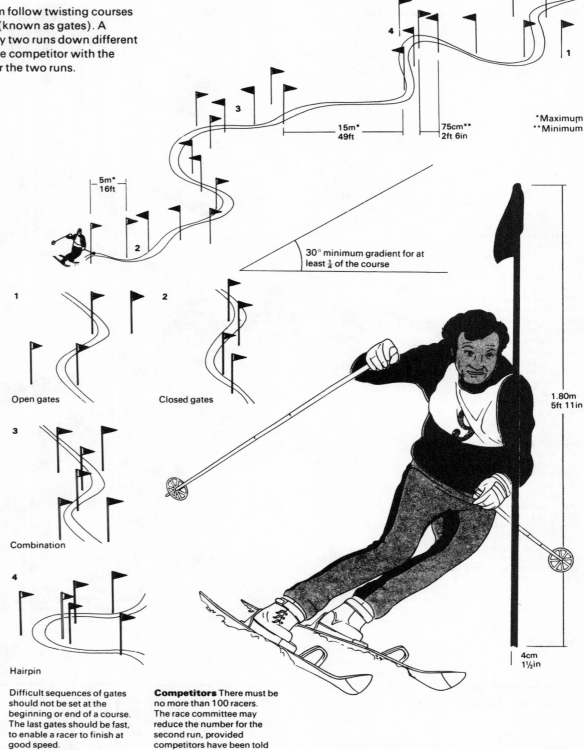

*Maximum
**Minimum

15m*
49ft

75cm**
2ft 6in

5m*
16ft

30° minimum gradient for at least ¼ of the course

1 Open gates

2 Closed gates

3 Combination

4 Hairpin

1.80m
5ft 11in

4cm
1½in

Starting Competitors start irregularly, by official decision, and may begin before the previous racer has finished.
Racers are divided into groups. In the first round they start according to their starting numbers.
In the second round the starting sequence is reversed. A competitor who is not at the start at the appropriate time may be disqualified.
Each competitor must start at the starting signal.

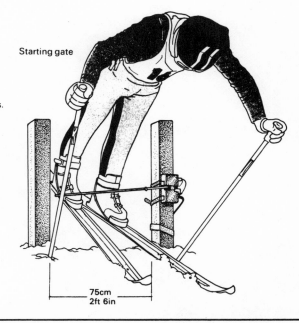

Starting gate

75cm
2ft 6in

Racing The course must be completed on skis, but a competitor may finish on one ski.
Racers must pass through all gates.
They must wear their starting numbers.
They may not receive any form of assistance.
They must cross the finish line with both feet.

Result The winner is the competitor with the fastest aggregate time for both runs.

Giant slalom

The giant slalom is longer than the slalom, the gates are farther apart, and competitors choose their own line between gates. A men's event consists of two runs, preferably on different courses; a women's event is usually only one run.

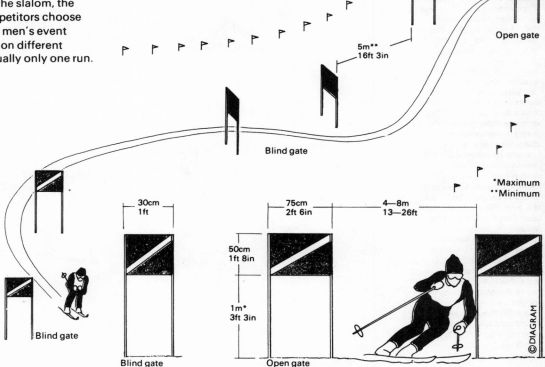

Courses are prepared as for downhill races, except at controls and turning sections, where they are prepared as for slalom races. Courses should be at least 30m wide, preferably on hilly and undulating terrain. The full width of the hill should be used whenever possible.
Vertical drop Men 250–500m; women 250–450m.
(Some competitions are allowed where the minimum vertical drop is not possible.)

Open gate

5m**
16ft 3in

Blind gate

*Maximum
**Minimum

30cm
1ft

75cm
2ft 6in

4—8m
13—26ft

50cm
1ft 8in

1m*
3ft 3in

Blind gate

Blind gate

Open gate

Gates Ordinary slalom poles are used, and there should be four poles at each gate. Minimum flag sizes are shown for blind and open gates. The flags should be set at right angles to the racing line, and gates must be 4–8m wide. Gates are alternately red and blue, and blue flags must be distinctly marked (preferably with a diagonal white stripe).

There must be at least 30 gates, excluding the start and finish. They should be set down the vertical line of the slope, at least 5m apart, and clearly distinguishable at high speed. The average vertical drop between gates should be at least 8m.
Figures are less important than in slalom races, and most of the gates should be

single. There should be a variety of long, medium, and small turns.
Direction flags may be used in bad visibility: red on the left of the course and green on the right.

Start Competitors start at 60-second intervals.
The starting order is reversed for the second run.

Result An event with two runs is won by the competitor with the fastest aggregate time. An event comprising only one run is won by the fastest competitor.

Ski jumping

Ski jumping requires strength, grace, and courage. Competitors make two jumps from a specially constructed hill, and points are awarded for style and technique as well as for the distance achieved.

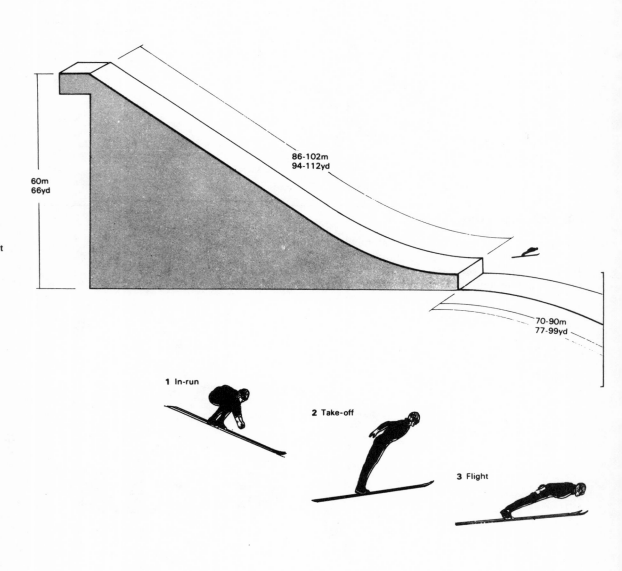

The jumping hill is constructed according to officially approved specifications.
Before training and competitions the hill must be smooth and hard from the in-run to the out-run, and must be tested to confirm its safety.
Before the start of competitions, trial jumps are performed by non-competitors; these help determine the starting place and the length and inclination of the take-off. Conditions must be consistent for all competitors.
The norm point (**P**) marks the ski-jumpers' expected landing point, extending to the table point (**TP**). The critical point (**K**) marks the maximum safe landing distance. These points vary according to the dimensions of the hill.
In some competitions two hills are used and the difference between their norm points must be at least 15m.
In some international competitions the norm point may not exceed 90m.
On hills with a norm point of over 80m, instruments for measuring the in-run speed and wind conditions must be used.
Point **P** is marked on the hill by a board, and on the snow by a blue line about 2m long on each side of the landing slope;
point **TP** is similarly marked by a board and green lines; and point **K** by a board and red lines.

Officials In international competitions five jumping judges must be appointed, each of whom makes an independent assessment of the jumps.

Jumping Competitors are divided into four groups. Each competitor has two jumps; a jump in the trial round is optional.
Competitors in the same class must begin from the same starting point.

The in-run (1) The ski-jumper adopts a relaxed crouched position adapted to the in-run. Ski poles or other aids for increasing speed are forbidden.

The take-off (2) must be a powerful action (varying according to the speed and profile of the hill), and made with boldness and precision. The knees must be straightened and the body stretched in a fast, rhythmic, and aggressive movement.

During the flight (3) the skis should be kept almost horizontal until just before landing. The skis should be parallel and in the same plane. The body should lean well forward and be as straight as possible at the hips. The legs and the upper part of the body should be taut, and the feet together. Arm movements must be controlled.

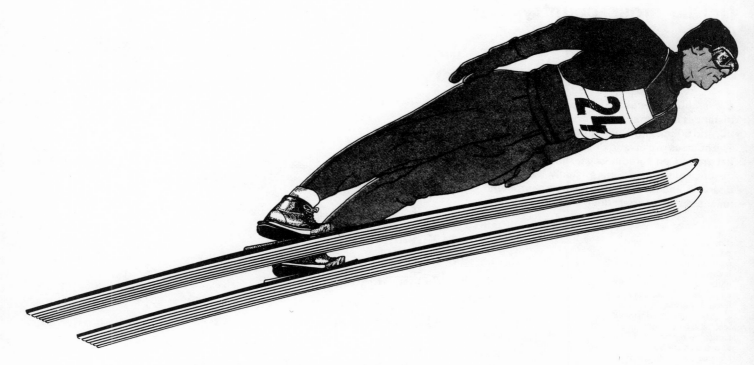

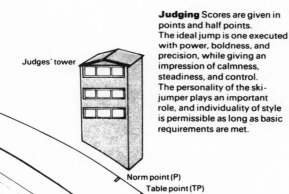

Judges' tower

Norm point (P)

Table point (TP)

Critical point (K)

Out-run
80-100m
88-110yd

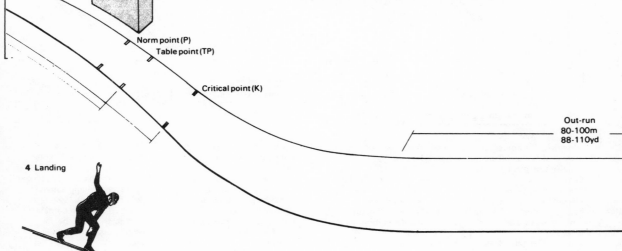

4 Landing

Judging Scores are given in points and half points.
The ideal jump is one executed with power, boldness, and precision, while giving an impression of calmness, steadiness, and control.
The personality of the ski-jumper plays an important role, and individuality of style is permissible as long as basic requirements are met.

The general impression of the entire jump determines the award of style points.
Judging begins at the moment of take-off. Any faults made at take-off are not penalized, however, as they will in any case influence the flight and the distance achieved.
Faults are less heavily penalized if they are

immediately rectified.
A standing jump is one in which the skier travels from the landing to the out-run in full balance. Any fall in the out-run is irrelevant. The standing jump scores between 6 and 20 points.
Falls A fall on the in-run loses 20 points; between 0 and 12 points are deducted for any other falls.

If a competitor touches the snow or his skis with both hands to maintain balance before reaching the out-run, this counts as a fall.
If a competitor has no control over the cause of the fall, he may be allowed to repeat the jump, or the jump may be declared a standing jump.

The landing (4) must be made with flexible but controlled movements and should not be too low. The ski-jumper should not prepare prematurely for the landing. Skis must be together (not more than a ski's width apart), with one foot in front of the other. Knees and hips are bent into the *telemark* position to counter the force of the

landing. The arms are spread for balance.
The ski-jumper then straightens up and continues to the out-run in a normal downhill position, holding himself as upright as the gradient and condition of the surface allow.

Results Distances are marked out before the competition, and boards are placed at 1m intervals on the sides of the landing slope.

Distances jumped are measured to the nearest ½m. They are taken from between where the feet land.
Each jump receives a total point score for style, and a total point score for distance.
The style score is reached by eliminating the highest and lowest of the judges' scores and adding the remaining three scores.

The distance score is calculated according to an official table, varying with the norm point of the hill.
The competitor with the highest total of points from his two jumps is the winner.

© DIAGRAM

Nordic cross-country

Cross-country races are held over a variety of distances and terrain. Men's races cover 10, 15, 30, and 50km, and women's races 5 and 10km. The courses run up and down hills as well as on flat ground, and gradients vary according to the distance of the race. Skiers usually start at intervals, and the winner is the competitor who finishes in the shortest time.

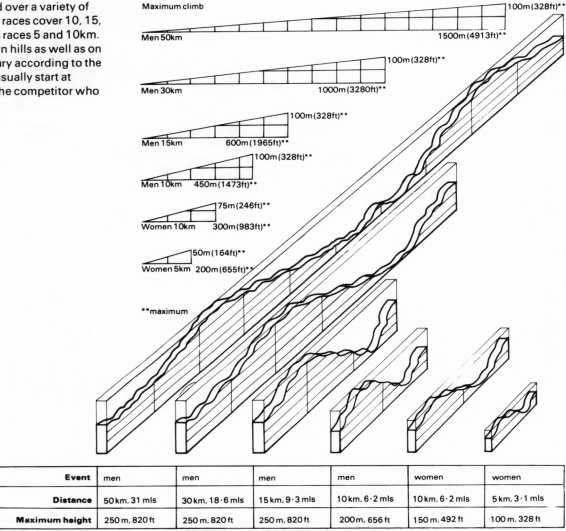

Maximum climb
Men 50km — 1500m (4913ft)** — 100m (328ft)**
Men 30km — 1000m (3280ft)** — 100m (328ft)**
Men 15km — 600m (1965ft)** — 100m (328ft)**
Men 10km — 450m (1473ft)** — 100m (328ft)**
Women 10km — 300m (983ft)** — 75m (246ft)**
Women 5km — 200m (655ft)** — 50m (164ft)**

**maximum

The course should ideally be one third flat, one third uphill, and one third downhill. It should be laid out as naturally and with as much variety as possible, preferably through woodland.
Courses should be designed to test the skier's technical, tactical, and physical abilities. Short-distance and relay courses are usually the most arduous. The degree of difficulty should relate to the level of the competition.
The most strenuous climbs should not occur within the first 2 or 3km, nor should there be long downhill runs in the final stretches.
The rhythm of the course should not be deliberately or frequently broken by sudden changes of direction or steep climbs.
Downhill sections must not be dangerous and changes of direction should not occur at the end of a run.
Conditions throughout the race must be consistent for all competitors.

Course measurements
Length
Men: 10, 15, 30, 50km
Women: 5, 10km
Height In world championships the maximum highest point for a cross-country course is 1650m.
The maximum differences in height between the highest and lowest parts of a course are:
5km course (women): 100m
10km course (women): 150m
10km course (men): 200m
15km+ courses (men): 250m
The maximum climb (the difference in height of any one climb, without an interruption of at least 200m) must not exceed:
5km course (women): 50m
10km course (women): 75m
Men's courses: 100m
The maximum total climb must not exceed:
5km course (women): 200m
10km course (women): 300m
10km course (men): 450m
15km course (men): 600m
30km course (men): 1000m
50km course (men): 1500m

Event	men	men	men	men	women	women
Distance	50km, 31 mls	30km, 18·6 mls	15km, 9·3 mls	10km, 6·2 mls	10km, 6·2 mls	5km, 3·1 mls
Maximum height	250m, 820ft	250m, 820ft	250m, 820ft	200m, 656ft	150m, 492ft	100m, 328ft

Marking The course is marked after every 5km, and at every 1km along the last 5km.
The direction of the race is marked by boards, arrows, flags, and ribbons. Each race is indicated by a different color:
Women: 5km blue, 10km violet, 5km relay red/blue.
Men: 15km red, 30km yellow, 50km orange, 10km relay green/yellow.
Starting Starts may be single or double, at intervals of 30 seconds. Group and mass starts are only permitted by special authorization.
Electric timing with an audible starting signal may be used. If hand timing is used, the starter warns the competitor 10 seconds before the beginning

of the race, and counts out the last 5 seconds.
The competitor must start with both feet behind the starting line, but with the poles in front of it.
Early starts If hand timing is used, the competitor is recalled. If electric starting is used, the competitor is allowed 3 seconds before his appointed starting time; alternatively, he is recalled to start outside the electric starting gate.
Late starts Competitors must not interfere with the start of other competitors.
Racing Competitors must follow the marked course and pass through all the controls. Only the skier's own propulsion may be used, and pacemakers are not allowed.

Both poles may be exchanged during the race, but only one ski; changes must be made without assistance.
Skis must be marked immediately before the start in order to prevent unauthorized changing of skis during the race. The course must be completed on at least one marked ski. Skis may be waxed by the competitor during the race.
When a competitor is overtaken he must always give way at the first request, even if the course has two tracks.
Any accidents, or any skiers who have retired from the race, must be reported at the next control or at the finish.

Finishing The competitor's finishing time is taken when his first foot crosses the line between the finishing posts or, with electric timing, when contact is broken.
The finish referee records the order in which the competitors complete the course.
Results Competitors are placed according to the difference between their starting and finishing times. This is recorded to 0.01 second with electric timing and to 0.1 second with hand timing.
If two or more competitors have the same time they are awarded the same placing, the competitor with the lower starting number being listed first.

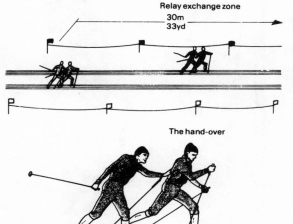

Competitors In world championships each country may enter four competitors, who are distributed separately into four groups. The team leader may decide on the distribution of his skiers. The groups start in reverse order, beginning with group four. In international competitions competitors are divided into three groups:
Group A: international competitors;
Group B: a maximum of 20 other competitors from the organizing country;
Group C: remaining competitors.
They start in the order B, A, C.

200m
220yd

100m
110yd

Reserves are only allowed to replace competitors after the draw in the event of illness or injury.
Competitors are permitted to train on and inspect the course prior to the race.
Timing Electric timing should be used whenever possible, together with hand timing as a check.
Competitors are timed along the course: once during a 10km course, twice during 15 and 30km courses, and at least three times during a 50km course.

Start and finish area The start and finish should be situated in the same area. This area should contain: loudspeakers and scoreboards; a temperature board, showing air and snow temperatures at intervals before and during the race;
rooms for medical treatment; general and official facilities. For a double start there must be two parallel tracks for at least 200m, and two parallel tracks at least 100m long at the finish.
Refreshment stations are provided at the start and finish, and along the course in races of more than 15km: two stations for races up to 30km in length, and four stations for races up to 50km.

Relay exchange zone
30m
33yd

The hand-over

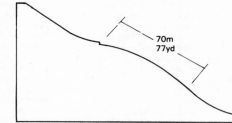

Relay races are organized according to the rules for cross-country skiing, with the following additions. Separate colors are used for the start numbers for each relay section. In world championships these are: first section, red; second, green; third, yellow; fourth, blue.
Skis are marked in the same colors as the relay sections.
Start There is a mass start, with competitors arranged in one or more arcs.
Skiers begin 2m apart, and each one has the same starting conditions.
The tracks must be parallel for the first 100m, and then converge into three separate tracks during the next 100m. There must be no sharp bends or corners in the first kilometer.
The relay exchange zone is a clearly marked area 30m long. The last 500m before the exchange zone must be at least double-tracked, and without sharp bends or corners.
The hand-over must take place within the relay exchange zone, when the racer touches his teammate. If the hand-over is illegal, the skiers may be recalled to perform a proper exchange.
Finish The last 500m must be at least double-tracked, and without sharp bends or corners.
A racer does not have to give way in the last 100m.
Teams consist of three or four racers. Each may run only one section.

Nordic combined

The Nordic combined competition consists of ski-jumping and cross-country skiing. Competitors take part in both events, and points are given for their performances. The winner is the competitor with the highest total of points from the two events.

70m
77yd

Duration The competitions take place on consecutive days. The ski-jumping normally precedes the cross-country.

Competitors There are separate draws for each event. Competitors are drawn in four groups. They perform in reverse order, with group 4 starting first.
Any specialist runners and jumpers taking part in a competition will be placed in separate groups.

The cross-country course is 15km in length. It must not include climbs, or excessively long flat sections. Technical difficulties must be less than for specialized cross-country events.
The total climb must be between 400 and 500m.
The course is indicated by green markers.

The jumping hill has a norm point of between 60 and 70m, and in world championships the norm must be 70m. Other installations and requirements are the same as for independent jumping competitions.
Results
Cross-country The time is measured in seconds and tenths of seconds, which are

then converted into points according to FIS tables.
Jumping Each competitor has three jumps. Each jump is awarded points for distance and style, and the lowest total is eliminated.
The final result is the total number of points from the cross-country and ski-jumping events.

Biathlon

Biathlon is a combined sport of skiing and shooting that was first included in the Winter Olympics in 1960. World championships are held every year. There are two broad types of competition: individual and relay.

The course must be laid out naturally and should vary as much as possible.
It should be set over undulating country within prescribed limits and differences in height.
It should be a true test of the competitors' strength, endurance, tactical knowledge, and ski technique.
The most strenuous part of the course should be around the halfway point.
Preparation All trees and stumps are cut down to ground level before the snow falls.
On the day of the race at least ten members of the tracking patrol ski over the course to ensure that weather conditions have not made it dangerous.
Marking The course is clearly marked with flags, and every fifth kilometer is indicated by boards at the side of the track.
Shooting ranges The start, shooting, and finish are generally at the same place.
The range is 150m, and the firing points should be even, firm, and clearly numbered.
Near the range is a test range so that competitors can have a trial shoot before the competition.
Shooting areas are marked off from spectators.
Organization Competitions are organized by the organizing committee, competition committee, jury, and officials.
The jury is responsible for arranging medical examinations, imposing penalties, and ensuring that competitions are carried out according to the rules.
Officials include the chief of the course, the chief of shooting, the chief of timekeeping and calculation, a doctor, and as many assistants as are necessary to man the butts and ensure adequate communication along the course.

Dress may be strengthened and protected on both elbows and on the right or left shoulder. Padded material may be used to alleviate the pressure of the sling used to carry the rifle.
Equipment A competitor may have only one pair of marked skis and one marked rifle.
If a ski or binding breaks one ski may be replaced, as may broken sticks and slings.
A spare weapon may be handed to the range officer for use if needed.
Weapons All non-automatic weapons with a caliber up to 8mm may be used, but magnifying optical sights are not allowed. The minimum trigger pressure is 1kg.
During the course there must be no round in the rifle.

Ammunition All ammunition, including reserves, must be carried by the competitors from the start.
Food and refreshments are provided for the competitors.
Procedure on the course
Competitors follow the flagged track, using no other means of propulsion than skis and sticks, and with no pacemaker.
Although competitors may wax their skis and repair equipment, no assistance is permitted beyond providing wax and handing over repair equipment.
If a competitor is overtaken, he must give way.
Competitors who observe any accident should report it at a control point.

Procedure at the firing range When he arrives at the firing point the competitor goes to the firing position allocated to him. There he loads his rifle with five rounds, which he fires in his own time, with his skis either on or off.
He fires five rounds from each of four firing points, and between the bouts of shooting there must be at least 3km of skiing.
The first and third shoots are in a prone position, when the rifle may be supported only by hands and held against shoulder and cheek, not propped on the ground.
The second and fourth shoots are in a standing position. Again, any support is forbidden, and the rifle must be held against shoulder and cheek, but not supported on the chest.
In both shooting positions the supporting arm may be supported by a sling as long as the rifle itself does not touch it behind the grip of the hand.
Penalties Serious offenses, such as taking short cuts, using means of propulsion other than skis and sticks, or changing the trigger pressure of the rifle, are penalized by disqualification.
Time penalties are issued for other offenses. For example, two minutes are added to the time of anyone who carries his rifle loaded around the course, and also for each shot not fired.

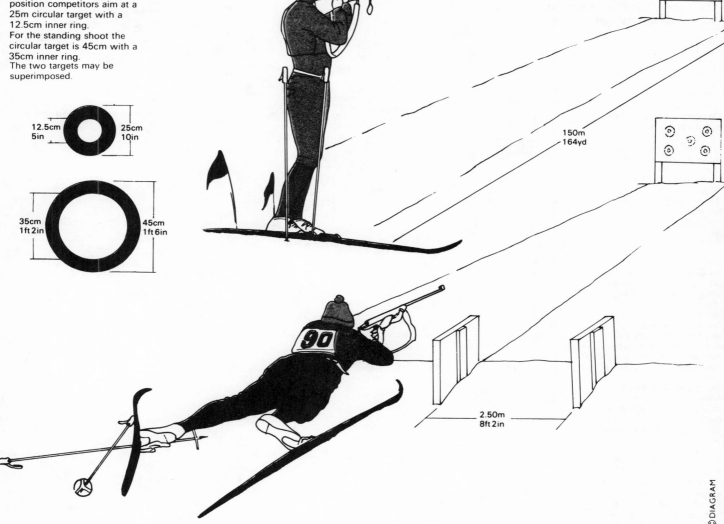

Targets For the prone position competitors aim at a 25m circular target with a 12.5cm inner ring.
For the standing shoot the circular target is 45cm with a 35cm inner ring.
The two targets may be superimposed.

12.5cm
5in

25cm
10in

35cm
1ft 2in

45cm
1ft 6in

150m
164yd

2.50m
8ft 2in

©DIAGRAM

Scoring The running time from start to finish (including the shooting) plus all penalty minutes equals the competitor's total time.
For hits in the inner ring there are no penalties. There is a one minute penalty for hits in the outer ring, and two minutes penalty for complete misses.

INDIVIDUAL EVENTS
20km Individual biathlon for seniors is skied over a 20km course, with four bouts of shooting at a range of 150m.
15km Individual biathlon for juniors is skied over a 15km course, with three bouts of shooting at a range of 150m.
10km Individual biathlon for seniors and juniors has prone shooting after approximately 2.5km and standing shooting after 7.5km.
The range is 150m and the targets are as for biathlon relay.
Penalty loops are 150m and relay penalty rules apply. Other rules are as for the 20km individual biathlon.

RELAY RACES
Relay races for seniors are skied over three or four times 7.5km, with two bouts of shooting. (In Olympic Games and world championships the relay race is four times 7.5km.)
Relay races for juniors are skied over three times 7.5km. (Those competitors who have passed their 21st birthday count as seniors from January 1 of the following year.)
Teams Relay events are for teams of three or four.
Skiing The handover takes place in the relay zone alongside the track, when the arriving competitor touches his starting teammate with his hand.

Shooting Each competitor shoots once lying and once standing, at 2.5km and 5km. Every competitor shoots eight rounds at five targets in each position.
If the competitor does not hit every target he must run a penalty course for each target not hit.
The penalty course is an oval loop 150m long, laid out on even ground near the shooting range.
Competitiors who incur penalties through missing targets or not having fired their eight rounds of ammunition are responsible for running the correct number of penalty circuits before the handover or crossing the finishing line.

JUNIOR RULES
Individual competitions
The running distance is 15km, with three bouts of shooting: prone, standing, prone.
There must be at least 3km skiing distance between shooting bouts, which can take place at one or several locations.
Relay races Rules are the same as for seniors, except that there may be only three persons in each team.
SMALLBORE BIATHLON
Individual competitions
are generally run under the same rules as full caliber competitions.
The range is 50m, the rifle caliber 5.6mm and the minimum trigger pressure 0.2kg.

Skibob racing

Competitors on skibobs attempt to cover a
marked course as rapidly as possible.
International events include downhill, giant
slalom, and special slalom races.

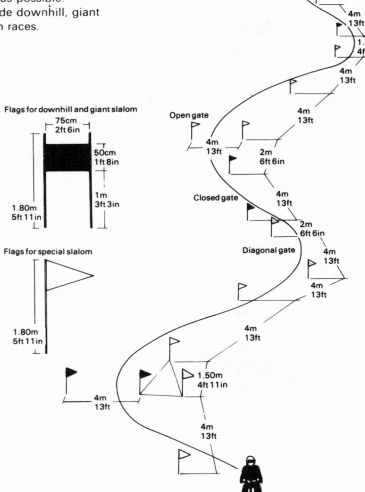

Section of special slalom course

Open gate

Closed gate

Diagonal gate

Flags for downhill and giant slalom

Flags for special slalom

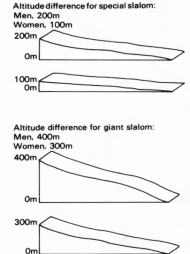

Altitude difference for special slalom:
Men, 200m
Women, 100m

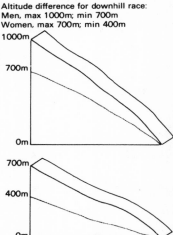

Altitude difference for giant slalom:
Men, 400m
Women, 300m

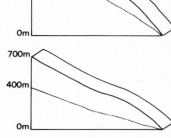

Altitude difference for downhill race:
Men, max 1000m; min 700m
Women, max 700m; min 400m

Competitions Downhill
and slalom events under the
surveillance of the FISB
(Fédération Internationale
de Skibob) are: world
championships, European
championships, other
international events.
Timing Electric timing
apparatus is used, with
additional hand timing in
case electric timing fails.
Electric timing is to
hundredths, and hand timing
to tenths, of seconds.
Result In single races, the
order of placing is based on
the time taken to cover the
course. If two competitors
record the same time, they
are placed together.
In combined events,
comprising more than one
race, points are scored for
each separate performance.

DOWNHILL RACES
Courses The altitude
difference between the
start and finish is normally
700-1000m for men's races,
and 400-700m for women's
races.
The length of all downhill
courses should be such that
the best competitor achieves
a time of about two minutes.
Downhill courses must be
completely ready and the
sticks placed at least one
day before the beginning of
the competition.
The terrain must be free of
stones, branches, roots, etc,
and any parts of the course
in wooded terrain must be at
least 20m wide.
There must be no
undulations, edges, ascending
or flat parts on the course,
and no narrow parts on fast
stretches. The finishing
stretch must be broad, long,
and softly moderate.
Any obstacle against which
a competitor might be thrown
must be covered with snow,
straw, or catch-nets.
There must be an obstacle-
free space at the outside of
curves to safeguard
competitors who leave the
course.

All gates must be arranged
to protect the competitors
against accidents, and the
last two gates before the
finish must be open.
Courses must be equipped
with easy means of transport
to the start.
Markings Red flags mark
the left side of the course
and green the right.
Gates consist of two
unbreakable vertical poles
with rectangular red flags.
Official training is an
integral part of the
competition and must last at
least one day.
The race cannot take place
if there have been no
perfect training conditions.
The course is closed to the
public during official
training.

Non-stop training Official
training must include a
non-stop training run down
the course.
Competitors must wear
starting numbers and begin
training within 15 minutes
of receiving the order to
start.
Competitors may make only
one run during non-stop
training and may not resume
a run interrupted by a fall or
for any other reason.
Official timing apparatus is
not in action, and there must
be no private timing.
Start Starting times are fixed
under the best conditions of
snow and visibility.
The starting area is under
cover, and a competitors'
shelter provided.

Competitors start the race at
60-second intervals. Ten
seconds before each
competitor starts, the starter
gives the command:
"attention." Five seconds
before the start, he counts
down from five to one before
giving the starting command:
"ab," "allez," or "go."
Competitors must be
allowed to look at the clock.
A competitor who is not
ready to start at his given
time will be disqualified
by the starter unless the
delay was caused by
circumstances over which he
had no control.
A competitor will be
disqualified if his steering
gear crosses the starting
line more than one second
before his official starting
time.

A competitor whose steering
gear crosses the starting line
more than one second after
his official starting time is
timed as if he had started one
second after his official
time.
The race A competitor is
liable to disqualification if he:
accepts outside help or
makes use of a pacemaker;
fails to clear the way when
requested by an overtaking
competitor;
fails to cross between the
gates;
takes a short cut;
fails to observe safety
regulations;
fails to cross the finishing
line on his skibob.
(A competitor is not
disqualified for losing his
foot skis.)

Skibob Competitors must use a single-track guidable skibob. It may be of any material—such as wood, metal, or plastic. Its total length must not exceed 2.30m when the front ski is followed in its trace by the rear ski.

Competitors must be amateurs. All entries for international events must be made through national associations.

Dress Competitors wear:
1 crash helmets (compulsory for races and official training);
2 ski boots;
3 foot skis (not exceeding 50cm in length);
4 starting number;
5 goggles (optional).

Officials for a skibob event are a race director, FISB judge, chief judge, start judge, finish judge, gate judges, course chief, course tracer, race secretary, starter and assistants, chief timekeeper and assistants, umpire, equipment officer, medical officers, chief and assistant stewards, press officers.

©DIAGRAM

GIANT SLALOM

Courses The altitude difference between the start and finish is 400m for men and 300m for women.
The course must be at least 20m broad, and of such a length that the best competitor achieves a time of about two minutes.
The course must have edges and slight undulations, but no ascending or flat stretches.

Gates There must be at least 31 gates, including those at the start and finish.
There must be at least 6m between successive gates, positioned so as to be easily recognizable even at high speed.

Gates consist of two unbreakable poles, with flags. Poles must be placed on a level, and at least 5m apart. Red-flagged gates alternate with blue-flagged gates; starting and finishing gates always have red flags.
All gates are numbered. The last two gates must be open.
Snow near the gates must be stamped or rolled to avoid deep furrows when skibobbers change direction or fall.

Training and inspection
Competitors train for at least one day with the course marked only by direction flags. The course is then closed for the whole day before the race.
The gates are put in position two hours before the start of the race, and competitors may familiarize themselves with the course by descending alongside the gates. They are forbidden to pass through the gates or practice direction changes alongside the course.

SPECIAL SLALOM

Courses The altitude difference between the start and finish is 200m for men and 100m for women.
The gradient must be fairly gentle, but sufficient to allow several clear changes of direction.
The snow must be stamped hard to avoid furrows during the competition.

Gates There must be 50 to 60 gates for men and 30 to 40 for women.
Gates consist of two unbreakable flagged poles, 3–4cm in diameter and with at least 1.80m above ground. Gates are in turn red, blue, and yellow, and the sticks as well as the flags are colored. All gates are numbered. The last two gates must be open.

Training and inspection
Training on the course takes place either in the morning or one day before the competition.
The gates must be in position at least 1½ hrs before the race, and competitors may familiarize themselves with the final course by ascending alongside it, either on foot or on skis. They must not go on the course itself.

Start Starting intervals for special slalom races may be different. Competitors must start after receiving the starting order.

Luge tobogganing

Competitors on luge toboggans make four runs down a purpose-built course. There are individual events for men and women, and a pairs event for men. Events are won by the competitors with the best aggregate times for the four runs. Speeds are similar to those achieved in bobsleigh events, though the courses are usually much more twisted and labyrinthine.

Course International courses are always artificial, with foundations of wood, cement, stone, or earth that become icy in winter conditions. They are iced mechanically when necessary.
Courses must be 1000–1500m in length, with a gradient of 9–10%. They should feature a left-hand bend, right-hand bend, hairpin, S bend, and labyrinth as well as straight sections. A starting ramp must be provided, and provision made for starting the shorter races. Control towers linked by telephone with the start and finish are compulsory, as are means for transporting toboggans, competitors, and officials to the starting line. Many courses are floodlit.
The race consists of four runs. The winner is decided on the basis of the lowest aggregate time for all four runs.

Labels on illustration: Start, Labyrinth, Hairpin bend, S-bend, Left-hand bend, Right-hand bend, Finish

Competitions The main competitions are the Olympic Games, world championships, European championships, and the European junior championships. Other international and national competitions are also held under the auspices of the FIL (Fédération Internationale de Luge de Course).
Events in major competitions are:
men's individual race;
women's individual race;
men's pairs race.
Women's and pairs' races are run over four-fifths of the men's individual course.
Competitors must be amateurs and members of a national association affiliated to the FIL.

Teams for the Olympics may have a maximum of four men and three women entered for the individual events, and two men's pairs. For other events teams may include twice these numbers.
Substitution is not permitted once a race is in progress. If a team member is injured during training, another team member may be nominated to take his place.
Officials The race director, starting and finishing officials, and timekeepers ensure the smooth running of races. Control is exercised by the jury (three persons drawn from national associations affiliated to the FIL), the chairman, technical delegates, and the FIL secretary.

Training Both systematic and non-stop training are compulsory.
Systematic training comprises a tour of the course under the guidance of the race director, training runs on a shortened start, and a thorough step by step study of the course's bends and curves.
Non-stop training ideally involves at least four runs for each competitor, including one run at night. Under adverse conditions every competitor must have made at least one run for the race to take place.
For Olympic races at least two training runs by each competitor must be timed and published.

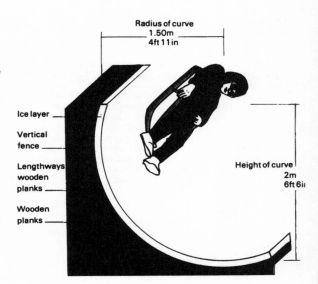

Labels on diagram: Radius of curve 1.50m 4ft 11in; Ice layer; Vertical fence; Lengthways wooden planks; Wooden planks; Height of curve 2m 6ft 6in

Toboggan May be of any type but must:
have room for one or two riders to sit safely;
have only one pair of runners;
not exceed 20kg if an individual toboggan or 22kg if a pairs toboggan (ballast may be used to bring it up to this weight, but must be firmly attached so that it cannot be jettisoned during a race);
not exceed the prescribed track dimensions;
be without braking or steering mechanisms of any kind.
The distance between the inside edges of the two runners may not exceed 45cm.
Once entered in a race competitors may alter, adapt, or exchange toboggans provided they do not breach any of these rules.
Toboggans are weighed and checked before each run.
Dress Crash helmets are compulsory for all training runs and races.
Further protective clothing, such as elbow and knee pads, are optional.

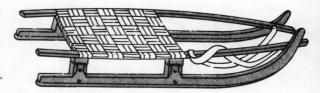

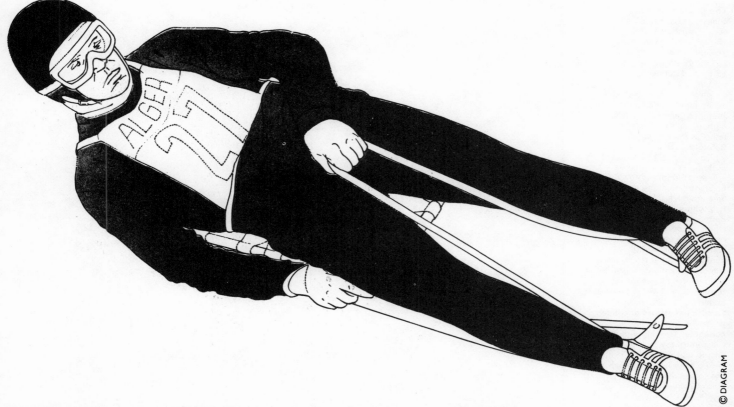

© DIAGRAM

The start A sitting start is compulsory for all events. Starting order is decided by lot, and varied over the four runs to ensure that conditions for all competitors are as equal as possible.
Only one toboggan may be on the course at a time, and the starter is notified by telephone from the finish when the course is clear.
The starter warns the next competitor as follows: "in 50 seconds; in 30 seconds; in 15 seconds." At 10 seconds before the start he gives the command: "Get ready, get set, go."

False start Whether the false start was due to a technical error or to an error by a competitor, a new start is compulsory.
Timing Electric timing apparatus, accurate to 1/100 of a second, is compulsory for Olympic and international races. At least two hand stopwatches are used as a check in case of a failure of the electronic apparatus. Competitors must repeat their runs after a timing failure.

Steering The competitor lies flat, with his body from the waist upward over the back of the toboggan.
He tends to control the toboggan on the straightways when plenty of speed has been gathered and does so with a movement of the body to deflect the airstream.
At bends the shoulders are used to push the toboggan into the right position and then the whole body and legs are used to pull the machine through and off the corners.

Offenses Competitors will be penalized for:
failing to wear a crash helmet;
warming toboggan runners before a race;
adding ballast to bring the toboggan over the allowed weight;
wearing weighted clothing (eg lead belts);
leaving the toboggan voluntarily during a race;
pushing, or allowing another person to push, the toboggan either at the start or during a race (except after a spill, when the toboggan may be pushed if it would otherwise be impossible to start moving again);

acting in a dangerous manner during training or a race;
training outside the approved hours;
failure to train;
infringing amateur status;
acting in a way deemed to be damaging to the sport or to the FIL.
Penalties vary from exclusion from a particular race to total disqualification, depending on the gravity of the offense.

Bobsleigh racing

Competitors on bobsleighs attempt to cover a specially built course as rapidly as possible. Teamwork keeps the bobsleigh from crashing into a solid wall of ice.

Start

Finish

The course To qualify for championship events, a course must be at least 1500m long and have a gradient between 8% and 15%. It must have at least 15 banked curves. On these corners, the walls are concave and may be as much as 6m high. The straight stretches must have walls high enough to keep the bobs on the course. Before the starting line, which is marked by a piece of timber, there is an area at least 15m long. After the finishing line, there is an area in which a bobsl halt without using brakes. Permanent courses have stone or concrete foundations on which wet snow and water freeze in wintry conditions. On some courses, electric equipment is used to keep critical places frozen. Runs with artificial icing must be at least 1200m long.

Control stations at critical points on the course are connected by telephone to the control tower. These ensure that the run is clear before each heat and keep the spectators informed, over a loudspeaker system, of a bobsleigh's progress.

Timing An automatic electric timing system is used that records in hundredths of a second on recording tape. The timing is also checked by two stopwatches.

Competitions Two-man and four-man bobsleigh events under the surveillance of the FIBT (Fédération Internationale de Bobsleigh et de Tobagganing): Winter Olympic Games, world championships, continental championships, some international and national events.

Results
Events usually consist of four runs. or heats, for each team. Two runs are made on two consecutive days, if weather conditions are suitable. The winner is the team with the lowest aggregate of times.

The team A two-man team consists of the captain, who steers, and the brakeman, who controls skids and stops the bob at the end of a race. The two middle men in a four-man team help push the bob at the start of a race and act as ballast. The transference of their weight is vital when cornering.

Training For world championships two-man teams train for a minimum of five days on the course, and four-man teams for four days. Teams entering other competitions train for a minimum of three days. Teams that have not had sufficient training may not be allowed to compete. A thorough knowledge of the course is essential for a fast, safe run.

The start The bobs are lined up in their running order, fixed by a draw, keeping the starting area clear.
A team not in position when its starting number is called is disqualified unless the delay is caused by circumstances over which it has no control.
The bobsleigh is set in motion either by a "flying start" or by a "standing start".
For both types of start, a team may push the bob as far as it likes, but must receive no help from anyone. If the permitted weights are not reached, ballast may be added to the bob.

Flying start The bob is placed up to 15m behind the starting line. The starter asks,

"are you ready?" The team captain answers, "yes." The starter then gives the command, "attention! go!" The team pushes the bob across the starting line, jumping on as it gains speed. Timing begins as soon as the front of the bob's runners crosses the starting line.

Standing start The bob is placed with the front of its runners on the starting line. The starter gives the same orders as for a flying start and the team pushes the bob, leaping on as it gains speed.

False start In the case of a false start, through no fault of the team, the team continues to the end of the course and begins again as soon as it returns to the start.

The race During a race, team members may get off the bobsleigh to push it or to change places.
If they have a spill or go off course, they may return and continue the race as long as all the team is on the bob when it crosses the finishing line.
If a team member is injured during a race, he may be replaced by a substitute at the discretion of the jury.
If the bob is damaged, it may be replaced by another of a similar type.

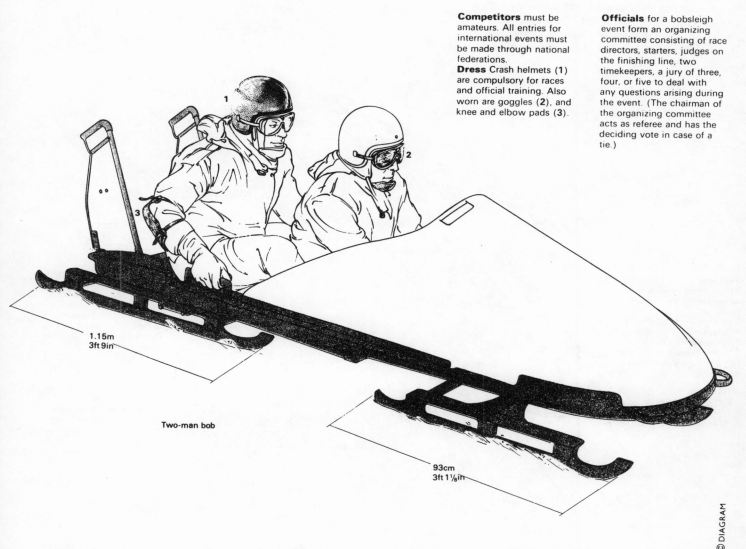

Competitors must be amateurs. All entries for international events must be made through national federations.
Dress Crash helmets (**1**) are compulsory for races and official training. Also worn are goggles (**2**), and knee and elbow pads (**3**).

Officials for a bobsleigh event form an organizing committee consisting of race directors, starters, judges on the finishing line, two timekeepers, a jury of three, four, or five to deal with any questions arising during the event. (The chairman of the organizing committee acts as referee and has the deciding vote in case of a tie.)

1.15m
3ft 9in

Two-man bob

93cm
3ft 1⅛in

© DIAGRAM

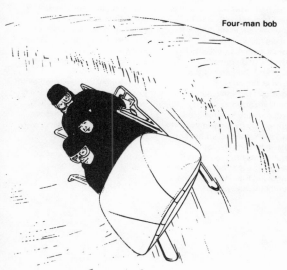

Four-man bob

Bobsleighs are constructed of steel and aluminum. They are fitted with streamlined cowls and handles on the sides for push starts. They are steered either by ropes leading to the front runners or by a steering wheel connected by cables to the front runners. The two front runners are attached to the front axle and steer the bob. The two rear runners are attached to the rear axle, which is fixed to the frame of the bob. Between the rear runners is a "harrow" type brake of hardened steel. The brake is used only in emergencies, as its serrated edge damages the surface of the run and can make it dangerous.

The maximum length of a four-man bob is 3.80m with a width of 0.67m. The combined weight of the bob and team must not exceed 630kg.
The maximum length of a two-man bob is 2.70m with a width of 0.67m. The maximum weight for the team and bob is 375kg.
If the permitted weights are not reached, ballast may be added to the bob.

Disqualification A team is liable to disqualification if any member:
does not wear a protective helmet during training and races;
wears spiked shoes when pushing a bobsleigh;
trains on a course outside authorized hours;
is considered to be physically or psychologically unfit to compete by the jury and by a doctor;
carries advertising on his clothes or bob;
carries ballast;
warms the runners of a bob before the start of a race;
uses any mechanical means to propel the bob;
accepts any outside help during a race;
refuses to abide by the decisions of the jury.

Pigeon racing

In pigeon racing all birds start from a single point, but each finishes in its own loft. The winning pigeon is the one that returns home in the fastest time, and this requires a complex timing system to ensure accurate results.

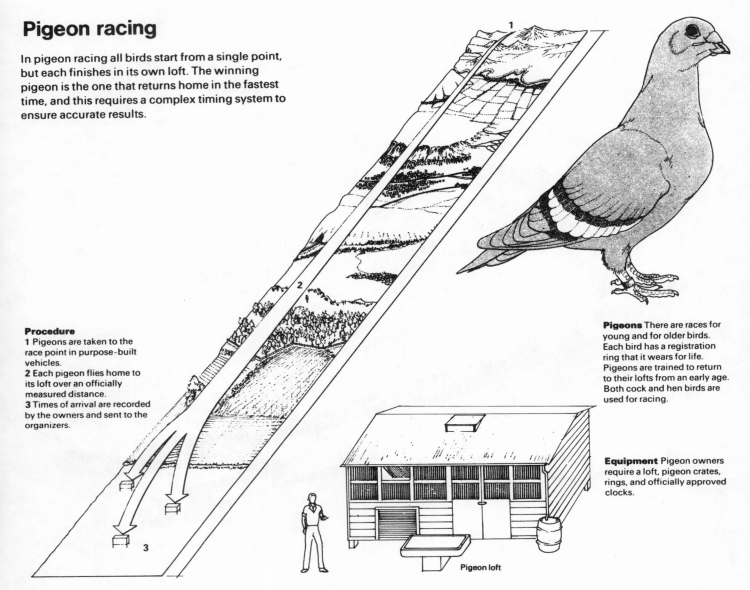

Pigeon loft

Procedure
1 Pigeons are taken to the race point in purpose-built vehicles.
2 Each pigeon flies home to its loft over an officially measured distance.
3 Times of arrival are recorded by the owners and sent to the organizers.

Pigeons There are races for young and for older birds. Each bird has a registration ring that it wears for life. Pigeons are trained to return to their lofts from an early age. Both cock and hen birds are used for racing.

Equipment Pigeon owners require a loft, pigeon crates, rings, and officially approved clocks.

Officials To organize and supervise pigeon racing many officials and assistants are required, including: race conveyors and assistant conveyors; liberators; marking officials; a clock committee.
Starting the race An owner submits his pigeons to the race marking committee. After the birds have been marked with racing rings they are kept in sealed enclosures until the race starts.
All the birds are conveyed together to the starting point from which they are liberated.

Distance Both young and older pigeons begin a season racing over about 60 miles. Later on, older birds will race over distances of up to 600 miles, but young pigeons are normally restricted to distances of up to 250 miles.
Timing For each race, officials place a rubber racing ring on one leg of each bird. The number on this ring and the bird's registration number are recorded. The racing ring also has an additional number on its inner side, which is secret.

The owners are officially informed of the liberation times of the birds. When a bird returns home its racing ring is removed and inserted into the clock, recording the time of arrival.
The clock is then returned to the race officials and checked against a master timer to calculate each pigeon's flying time.
Each owner's clock will have been submitted to the clock committee for 14 days before the race. The clocks are set by officials, and returned to their owners just before the race.

Returning home A pigeon is trained to return to its loft as quickly as possible and to enter the loft immediately it arrives home. The direction from which it approaches the loft will be dictated by the force and direction of the wind at the time.
To attract pigeons back to their loft, coopies (decoy birds) are sometimes used. These only fly around the loft and are trained to attract the racing birds to the loft landing board.
Stray birds that fail to return home are traced back to the owner by their rings.

Results The exact distance and flying time are divided by 60. Velocity, expressed in yards per minute, is then obtained by dividing distance by time.
The fastest pigeon wins the race.
Speeds may be combined over a season to calculate the best average speed.
Penalties Any bird that is raced without complying with the rules is disqualified.

Sled-dog racing

Sled-dog races are between harnessed dog teams, each controlled by a driver. Teams start at intervals, and the team with the shortest elapsed time wins. The number of dogs in a team varies with race distance and terrain. In world championships the minimum number of dogs is seven on the first day, and the course takes three days, with night rests.

Dress Starting-position numbers must be worn each day. All numbers must be returned at the end of each heat.

Equipment used is:
1 harness;
2 collar;
3 whip;
4 sled bag;
5 sled, with sufficient space to carry a dog;
6 sled brake;
7 sled brushbow;
8 snubline.
The sled bag, of canvas or similar material, is needed to carry any badly injured dog.

Harnessing All dogs except lead dogs must be harnessed with neck lines; lead dogs must also be harnessed, but may be run without neck lines.
No muzzles may be used, nor collars hooked as full choke collars.
The snubline is only to be used for hitching.

Competitors One driver ("musher") per team. Drivers often have a dog handler to assist them.
Officials Chief judge, judges, and course manager.

Procedure Teams must be in the holding area one hour before the first scheduled departure.
Each team, with its equipment, must be ready for inspection near the starting line ten minutes before its start time.
Any dog becoming unfit after departure must be carried on the sled.
Red markers indicate turns; green markers beyond an intersection or around a turn indicate a straight ahead.
Team and driver must run the full marked course, and all original dogs must return.

Start and finish Sleds start at intervals, usually every two minutes.
Timing is from when the sled's brushbow crosses the starting line until the first dog reaches the finishing line.
Starting order for the first day is drawn before the race. Starting order for succeeding days is determined by the elapsed time, the fastest team leaving first.

Racing rules A team coming within 20ft of the team ahead has right of way. The following team can require the team ahead to make way; or, if requested, to come to a full stop, but not when repassing or within a half mile of the start or finish lines.
Teams may not be assisted by pacing.
Outside assistance is only allowed in order to stop an unmanageable team; and then only by holding the sled unless race officials indicate otherwise.
Out of bounds If a team leaves the race trail, the driver must return to the point of deviation and continue from there.

Fouls Use of the whip other than for snapping is prohibited, except when dogs become unmanageable.
No interference with competing teams is allowed.
Drivers can be disqualified for: failing to attend the first day's drivers' meeting;
using any equipment not carried at the starting line; administering any forbidden drugs to the dogs or allowing anyone else to do so.
Cancellation In case of cancellation of the race after the first day, full prize money is still awarded.

© DIAGRAM

Greyhound racing

A greyhound race is between a usual maximum of eight, or in some places nine, greyhounds, over any distance between 230yd and 1200yd. The dogs are released from traps, and chase a motorized "hare" around the track. Prizes are awarded, and betting is a prominent feature. There is no international governing body, but the following rules and procedures apply fairly generally.

Registration All greyhounds racing on officially approved courses must be registered with the national governing body for the sport. They must also fulfill all race entry qualifications.

Identification Registered greyhounds have identity books or cards, giving: sufficient details of physical charàcteristics to distinguish that greyhound from all others; the name of its current trainer; details of innoculations; details of a bitch coming into season, whelping a litter, or being spayed; details of all trials, races, withdrawals, and disqualifications for fighting.

Age The age of a greyhound is reckoned from the first day of the month in which it was whelped. Greyhounds usually begin to race at either 12 or 15 months, depending on national rules.

Name A greyhound's name must be registered and be without advertising connotations. Any change of name must be registered and entered into the stud book.

Muzzles All greyhounds must wear approved safety muzzles when racing.

Racing jackets Each greyhound must race wearing an approved jacket, with the trap number shown on each side.

Jackets are colored according to trap number: the colors used vary from country to country.

Owners National rules vary, but in general: no owner may be under a minimum age; a greyhound must be registered and run in the true or approved assumed name of the *bona fide* owner; an owner may appoint and register an authorized agent to act for him; any change of ownership of a greyhound that is to race again must be notified and registered; all rules apply also to any part-owners or lessees.

Disqualification Any person may be disqualified for conspiring in any corrupt or fraudulent practice concerning greyhound racing — including the improper administering of drugs to greyhounds, offering or receiving bribes, willfully entering a disqualified greyhound for a race, making a false statement about a greyhound's documents or identity, or selling information about a greyhound with which he is connected.

Persons are also liable to disqualification for cruelty to a greyhound; and for acting in any official capacity or entering, owning, or having charge of a greyhound at any unauthorized course.

Race cards provide information on the racecourse, meeting, and officials, and give details of each race and each dog competing.

Categories of race These vary from country to country. Some countries have a grading system: greyhounds of the same grade compete, winners advance to the next grade, repeated losers fall a grade.

Other countries have a race system based on the greyhounds' training, with: open races, for greyhounds in the charge of any licensed trainer; races for greyhounds trained by trainers licensed at the racecourse concerned; kennel races, for greyhounds trained at courses with the same executive.

Other entry categories in the training-based system are: inter-racecourse races, between two or more teams representing different courses; private matches, between greyhounds with different owners and, usually, different trainers.

Special entry categories are: invitation races, for specified greyhounds; produce races, for members of a single litter. In many countries, any race may be declared: a sweepstake, with the entry fees or other payments by the owners being returned as prize money; a selling race, when one or more of the runners is to be offered for auction afterwards. Finally, any of the above may be held as: a normal race; a handicap race, with one greyhound having to run the full distance and others starting at the same time from traps that give them a number of yards' start; a hurdles race, over three or four sets of hurdles.

No-race is declared only if: there is a mechanical or other defect of the hare equipment or the starting traps; the hare is not kept within a reasonable distance from the leading greyhound; no greyhound completes the course within a reasonable time; there is any outside interference with the race.

Rerun A no-race may be rerun at the same meeting after a minimum time lapse. Whether a greyhound competes in a rerun is the option of the owner or, in his absence, his agent or trainer.

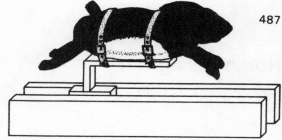

Hare The artificial hare is powered by electric motors and controlled by a licensed hare controller.

Starting traps

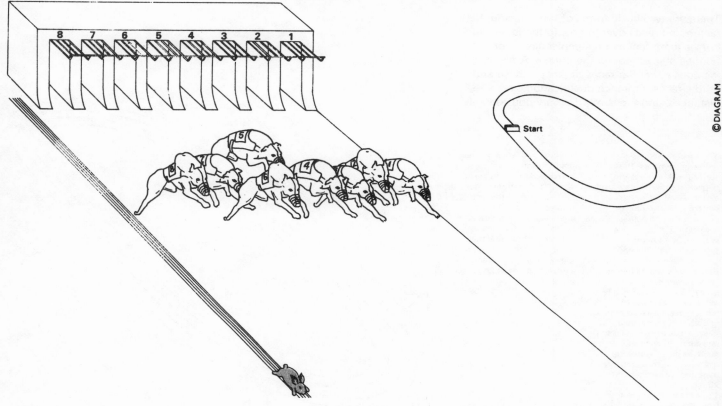

Start

©DIAGRAM

Racecourses Approved courses have:
a track with starting traps, a motorized artificial "hare," and a finish line with photo or ray-timing apparatus; an enclosed paddock with racing kennels; public enclosures; and, in some countries, a mechanical/electrical totalizator for betting.
Officials for an approved course are:
racing manager or secretary; stewards; judge(s); paddock steward(s); weighing clerk; starter; timekeeper; "hare" operator; security officer; veterinary surgeon; racecourse trainer. Officials' titles vary from country to country.
Traps Usually numbered from 1 to 8 (or 9), from the inside trap outward.
Each greyhound wears the number of the trap to which it is allocated and this number is given on the race card.

There may be reserves to take the place of any withdrawals. In non-handicap races, greyhounds are allocated by draw to traps from the inside outward, except that in some countries greyhounds classified as wide runners may be separately allocated to outside traps. In handicap races, the greyhound(s) running the full distance start(s) from the trap(s) nearest to the side of the track on which the hare passes the start. Runners benefiting from the handicap are placed in ascending order across the course from that side.
Paddock admission is limited to racecourse officials, holders of temporary appointments, stewards, licensed trainers and kennelhands in charge of any greyhound running at that meeting, owners of any greyhound running, and any person specifically authorized by the course authorities.

Kenneling procedure
This takes place before the first race of the meeting. Greyhounds are officially identified, and are weighed by a licensed official. Any greyhound varying more than a certain amount from its last running weight must be withdrawn.
After being inspected by the course veterinary surgeon, greyhounds are put in individual kennels and may be locked in at the request of their owners or trainers.
Paddock procedure Before a race, greyhounds about to run are taken from their kennels and reidentified. They are then fitted with the correct racing jackets and muzzles, and reexamined by the veterinary surgeon. After being paraded in front of the public enclosures, they are led to the starting traps and placed inside.
The start When all the greyhounds are in the traps, all persons other than the starter and his assistants must retire. The starter then gives the public signal for the hare to be started, and the traps are opened when the hare is approximately 12yd in front of them.

If a starting trap fails to open, the hare is stopped as quickly and safely as practicable—if possible, out of sight of the greyhounds. Failure of a greyhound to start after his trap opens is not in itself a reason for declaring "no-race."
Fighting Any greyhound that fights during a race is disqualified and its owner forfeits all rights in that race. There are procedures for reinstating disqualified greyhounds, but repeated fighting will result in permanent exclusion.
Out of bounds A greyhound that runs out of the defined course, whether it returns and crosses the finish line or not, is regarded as not completing the course.

Timing is by photo or ray-timing apparatus. Often the time for the first greyhound to finish is checked against a handheld stopwatch.
Timing is from when the starting trap's front reaches 45° to the perpendicular, until the winning greyhound's nose reaches the finish line. For handicap races, although the winner is still the first greyhound to reach the finish line, its race time is calculated by adding to its actual time a prescribed amount (0·60 of a second in some countries, 0·80 in others) for each yard of distance benefit received under the handicap.
Prizes A disqualified greyhound forfeits all rights in a race, and any prize already awarded must be returned. In case of a tie, prizes are, if possible, divided equally. Otherwise they are allocated by the mutual agreement of the owners; or, failing this, on the decision of the course authorities.

Horse racing

There are two basic forms of horse racing: flat racing and races over jumps. In the latter the horses jump fences (in steeplechases) or hurdles placed around the course. A meeting includes either flat races or steeplechase and hurdle races. Entrance qualifications, race distances, and types of prize vary considerably.

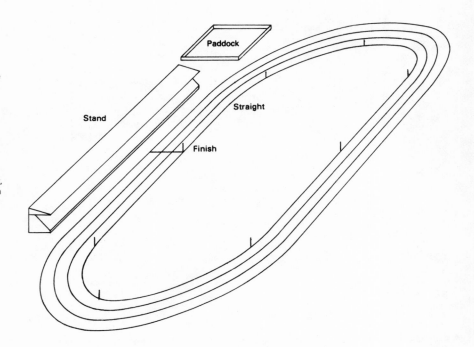

Paddock

Straight

Stand

Finish

The course Styles vary between countries. The surface may be grass, dirt, or packed snow; the layout a simple oval or a complex pattern with a number of possible starting points; the length 1 mile, 2½ miles, or more. Some courses provide for both flat and steeplechase/hurdle racing.

Steeplechases All fences except water jumps are at least 4½ft high. In the first two miles there are at least 12 fences, and at least six fences in each succeeding mile. In each mile there is at least one ditch, 6ft wide and 2ft deep, on the take-off side of a fence, and guarded by a bank and rail not more than 2ft high.
There is a water jump at least 12ft wide and 2ft deep,

guarded by a fence not more than 3ft high.
Hurdles All hurdles are at least 3½ft high from bottom bar to top bar. In the first 2 miles there are at least eight flights of hurdles, with another flight for each complete ¼ mile after that. As hurdles are made so that they are easily knocked over, a horse that hits a hurdle can usually keep going.

Fence

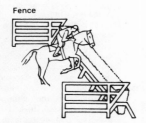

Water jump

Ditch

Hurdle

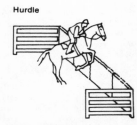

Officials who supervise meetings are known as stewards. Other officials include:
the racing secretary or "clerk of the course," in charge of the course and meeting arrangements;
the weighing officer or "clerk of the scales," who controls weighing out and weighing in;
the handicapper, who arranges the weights for handicap races;
the judge, who witnesses the finish and declares the result, after consulting photographs if necessary;
the camera patrol, who film crucial points of the race to help the stewards decide objections;
and the starter.

Types of race Races vary according to distance, type of horse entered, prize, and weighting system.
Race distances for flat races vary from ½–2¾ miles. Some countries (eg UK and Australia) concentrate on the longer races (1¼ miles and more), others (eg USA) on short races of 1 mile or less. Distances for steeplechases are 1½–4½ miles, and for hurdles 1½–3¼ miles.
Special categories include: novice races, for horses that have never raced before; maiden races, for horses that have never won;
auction plates, for horses bought in public auction as yearlings (weight allowances may be given in relation to purchase price);
selling races, in which the

winner is auctioned afterwards;
claiming races, in which horses may be claimed for purchase at a specified selling price.
(In countries in which claiming races are frequent, all horses in a race are listed for the same claiming price, and the system provides a way of grading horses, since the successful are moved up to higher price races.)
Weighting system
The normal load a horse carries (rider and equipment) can be altered by the addition of lead weights to give an overall "weight" to be carried. This allows four types of race:
open races, in which every horse carries the same weight;
weight for age races, in which

younger horses receive the benefit of a lighter weight;
condition (or allowance) races, in which a basic weight allowance for age and sex of horse is varied by added weight penalties for past successes (measured in prize money terms);
handicap races, in which the weights are adjusted to try to give horses an equal chance of winning.
In all steeplechase and hurdles, and some flat races, weight allowances are given to apprentices and jockeys with limited winning experience, providing that the prize money involved is below a certain amount.
Weighing-out Before a race all riders must be weighed. The trainer is responsible for his horse carrying the correct

weight, which includes hood and blinkers (if these have been declared for the horse), number cloth, martingale, breastplate, saddle, and clothing, as well as the jockey himself.
Lead weights may be added to the jockey's saddle to give the correct weight.
Crash helmet, whip, bridle, rings, plates, or anything worn on the horse's legs, are not included in the weight.
The start Before the race begins the horses are ridden in front of the stand. They must be at the starting post at the correct time. No preliminary jumps are allowed before a steeplechase or hurdle race.
The start is usually from starting stalls, but sometimes from a starting gate or by flag,

© DIAGRAM

Dress Jockeys wear:
1 crash helmet or "skull cap,"
which is compulsory;
2 shirt and trousers in the
owner's colors;
3 boots;
4 spurs;
5 Jockeys carry a whip.
The saddle is the rider's
responsibility, unless he is
an apprentice, when the
trainer is responsible.
It consists of:
6 saddle;
7 girth and surcingle;
8 stirrup irons;
9 leathers or webs;
and a number cloth.
If a rider is weighed out with
hood or blinkers, the horse
must wear them for the race.
Blinding hoods or any type of
shutter hood are forbidden.

Jockeys A jockey must be
licensed. He may operate
independently, unless he is
an apprentice, or he may be
retained by an owner.
A substitute jockey is allowed
either before or after the
weigh-out, providing there is
no unreasonable delay.

Horses The age of a horse is
taken from January 1 in the
year in which it was foaled.
Male horses are known as
colts to the age of five, and
horses thereafter; females as
fillies to five and mares
thereafter. A gelding is a
castrated colt or horse.

For flat races, a horse must
be a two year old before it can
race; for hurdles, a three year
old; and for steeplechasing,
a four year old.
In general, long races favor
older horses; young horses
dominate sprints.

Horse's age In flat racing
a race may be restricted
to a certain age group: two
year olds; three year olds,
or four year olds and older.
Horse's sex Some races are
for horses of one sex only:
fillies only; or colts and
geldings only.

with the horses started in a
straight line as far as possible.
In flat races the horses are
drawn for starting positions,
with number 1 on the inside.
An unruly horse may be
withdrawn by the starter.
No horse, when stalls are used,
may start from outside the
stalls or be held inside the
stalls.
A horse is considered to have
started once it has come
under starter's orders.
A false start may be
declared and the race
restarted if there is a fault in
the starting mechanism.
In steeplechase or hurdle
races, if the horses fail to
return after the recall signal,
the race is void. If only one
horse returns it is awarded
a walkover.

The race Each jockey must
try to give his horse the
chance to do as well as it can.
If a rider is dismounted, he
may remount; but the horse
must be remounted where
the rider fell. The rider may be
assisted in catching and
remounting the horse.
A horse will be disqualified
if it receives assistance from
anyone except its jockey in
jumping a fence or a hurdle
that it has refused.
If a horse misses a fence or
hurdle, or passes the wrong
side of a direction marker, it
must return and ride the
course correctly or be
disqualified.
A horse will also be
disqualified if its rider, by foul
riding, jeopardizes another
horse's chances.

A horse may be disqualified or
its placing altered:
if, in a steeplechase or hurdle
race, it crosses and interferes
with another horse at, or in
the home run from, the last
fence or hurdle;
if, in a flat race, it crosses
and interferes with another
horse in any part of the race.
Weighing-in After a race,
normally only the riders of the
first four horses are weighed
again.
If a jockey's weight exceeds
his weigh-out weight by more
than a permitted amount, it
is reported to the stewards, but
the horse is not disqualified.
If it falls below by more than
a permitted amount, the horse
is disqualified.
When the weigh-in reveals no
infringements, the stewards
confirm the result.

The finish The first horse
past the post wins, except in
the case of a disqualification.
If two or more horses finish
together, the judge's decision
is based on the order in which
their noses pass the post. In
this the judge is assisted by
the photo-finish camera.
Dead heat If two horses run a
dead heat for first place, each
is judged a winner and prize
money for the first two places
is divided equally between
them. This applies in dividing
all prizes, whatever the
number of horses involved.
If two horses run a dead heat
for second place and the first
horse is disqualified, these
horses become joint winners.
Walkover In a walkover a
horse need only be ridden
past the judge's box to be
declared the winner.

Prize The race may be:
a plate, with guaranteed prize
money;
a stakes or sweepstake, with
prize money made up from the
fees of entrants together with
"added money" paid by the
course;
a cup, with a prize that is
not in money form;
a private sweepstake, with no
"added money";
or a match, between the
horses of two different
owners on terms agreed by
them.

Harness horse racing

In harness racing horses are driven from a light, two-wheeled "sulky." Horses are trained to "trot" or "pace," and separate races are held for the two gaits. Horses race for purse money, and bets are placed by the public. (The rules given here are those of the United States Trotting Association. Similar rules apply in other countries.)

Colors Distinguishing colors are compulsory for drivers. Judges may bar from a race anyone they consider to be improperly dressed.

Protective helmets (1) with a hard shell and adequate padding must be worn by drivers. Chin straps must be used.

Whips (2) must not exceed 4ft 8in. Excessive use of the whip, and whipping under the arch of the sulky are prohibited. A crop is the only other permitted goading device.

The sulky (3) It is the responsibility of the owner and trainer to ensure that all sulkies used in the races have wheel discs of an approved type. The use of mudguards may be ordered by the presiding judge.

TROTTERS

Shoes (4) Trotters usually wear level shoes in front and swedge shoes behind. The swedge is a creased shoe providing traction when the horse's hind foot hits the ground. Shoes for trotters usually weigh 8oz each.

Toe weights Trotters often have toe weights (5) clipped to each hoof. Weighing 2–4oz, they are used to extend a horse's stride.

Trotting A high-stepping, diagonal gait. Right front and left hind legs are brought forward in unison, followed by left front and right hind legs.

Trotting

PACERS

Shoes (6) Pacers usually wear flat or half round shoes in front. Behind they usually wear a combination shoe, half round inside and half swedge outside. The half round portion is to reduce risk of injury, while the half swedge portion increases traction. Pacers' shoes weigh about 5oz each.

Hopples (or hobbles) (7) are leather straps encircling the front and hind legs on the same side to help the horse maintain its gait. If a horse wears hopples, it must wear them throughout a race. If a horse usually races hoppled, it needs the judges' approval to race free legged; if it usually races free legged, it needs approval to race hoppled. Any person attempting a fraud by removing or altering a horse's hopples, either before or during a race, is liable to be suspended or expelled.

The head pole (8) is a cue to keep the horse's head straight. Fastened alongside the head and neck, it must not protrude more than 10in beyond the horse's nose.

The gaiting strap (9) is fastened inside the shafts of the sulky to prevent the horse swinging the rear and traveling sideways on its gait.

Pacing A swaying, lateral gait. Right front and hind legs are swung forward in unison, followed by left front and hind legs.

© DIAGRAM

Pacing

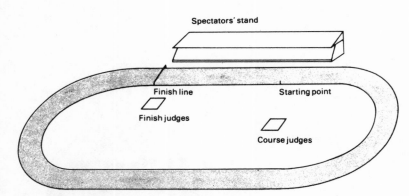

Spectators' stand

Finish line

Starting point

Finish judges

Course judges

The track is oval in shape. Lengths vary from ½–1 mile.
The starting point is marked on the inside rail. It must be at least 200ft from the first turn.
The wire (finish) is the real or imaginary line from the center of the judges' stand to a point immediately across and at right angles to the track.

A horse will only be placed if the driver is mounted in his sulky at the finish.
The winning horse is the one whose nose reaches the wire first. In a dead heat both horses count as winners. Where two horses tie in a summary, the winner of the longer dash or heat wins the trophy. If lengths are the same and horses tie in the summary and the time, both horses are the winners.
Timing Using an approved electric device or three official timers, times are taken from when the first horse leaves the starting point to when the winner's nose reaches the wire. Times must be publicly announced or posted, and are recorded in minutes, seconds, and fifths of seconds. In a dead heat the time is recorded for each winner.
Officials include: program director, presiding judge, paddock judge, starter, patrol judge, finish wire judge, timers, clerk of the course.
Length of races: as stated in the conditions for the meeting, and given in units of not less than $\frac{1}{16}$ of a mile.
Number of heats: as stated in the conditions for the meeting, usually one or three to a race.
There must be at least 40 minutes between the heats in a race.
A dash is a race decided by a single heat.

Paddock rules Except for paddock officials, the only persons authorized to enter the paddock are the owners, trainers, drivers, grooms, and caretakers of horses waiting to compete.
Horses must be in the paddock at least one hour before competing. Having entered the paddock, horses and the persons associated with them may only leave the paddock before the race for the purpose of warming up.

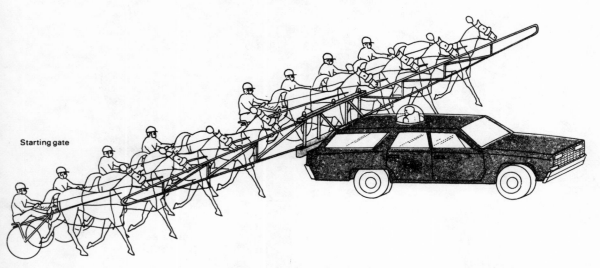

Starting gate

Post positions Post (or starting) positions are determined by lot for a dash or first heat. Post positions for subsequent heats, unless the published conditions state otherwise, are determined as follows: the winner of the previous heat takes the pole (or inside position) and the others are positioned according to their placings. Positions are settled by lot in the case of a dead heat.
Tiered starts A maximum of two tiers of horses, allowing 8ft per horse, is permitted to start in any race. Whenever a horse is withdrawn from a tier, horses on the outside move in to fill the vacant position.

Withdrawing a horse that has drawn or earned a position in the front tier does not affect the position of the horses in the second tier.
The starting gate must have arms perpendicular to the rail, and a screen or shield in front of the position for each horse.
The starter The horses are brought to the start by the starter, who controls them from the formation of the parade until he gives the word "go" at the starting point.

Starting procedure Horses are brought to the gate as near as possible ¼ mile before the starting point. The starting gate is then brought to the starting point with graduated speed: for the first ⅛ mile, not less than 11mph; for the next $\frac{1}{16}$ mile, not less than 16mph; from that point to the starting point, the speed is gradually increased until the starting point is reached. Only in the case of a recall may the speed be decreased in the course of a start. The starter gives the word "go" when the gate reaches the starting point.
Unless dismissed before the word "go," all horses that are not prevented by injury or accident must complete the course.

Recalls The starter may sound a recall only if:
a horse scores ahead of the gate;
there is interference;
a horse has broken equipment;
a horse falls before the word "go" is given;
a horse refuses to come to the gate before the gate reaches the pole ⅛ mile before the starting point.
No recall is possible after the word "go" has been given.
Recall signal A recall is sounded by the starter and signaled to the drivers by flashing lights. The starting gate proceeds out of the horses' path.

Starting violations
Drivers will be fined and/or suspended for:
delaying the start;
failing to obey the starter's instructions;
rushing ahead of the inside or outside wing of the starting gate;
coming to the starting gate out of position;
crossing over before reaching the starting point;
interfering with another driver during the start;
failing to come up into position.
Hearings are held before any penalty is imposed.

Age The age of the horses is reckoned from January 1 of the year of foaling, except for foals born in November and December, whose age is reckoned from January 1 of the succeeding year.

Race categories
Classified races are between selected horses, regardless of money won.
Conditioned races have specific entrance conditions, such as age, sex, or success over a given period.
Claiming races are those in which all starters may be purchased in conformity with the rules.
Handicap is a race in which performance, sex, or distance allowance is made. Post positions may be determined by claiming price.

Matinee is a race with no entrance fee, in which the premiums—if any—are other than for money.
Futurity is a race in which competing horses are nominated before being foaled.
Stake is a race for which entries close the year before the race and in which all nominating and starting fees are added to the purse.
Early closing races are those for which entries close at least six weeks before the race.
Late closing races are those for which entries close less than six weeks before the race.

Overnight events are those for which entries close not more than three days before the race (not including Sundays).
Coupled entry When a race includes two or more horses owned or trained by the same person, or trained by the same stable or management, they are normally coupled as an "entry." A wager on one of the horses counts as a wager on all horses in the entry.
In special events horses under separate ownerships but with the same trainer may be permitted to race as separate betting entries.

Money distribution
Dashes Unless the conditions state otherwise, the distribution is 45%, 25%, 15%, 10%, 5%.
Every heat a race As for a dash, with nothing set aside for the winner.
Two in three A horse must win two heats to win the race, and 10% is set aside for the race winner. The remainder is divided between the heats and distributed as if each heat were a dash. If the race is not decided after three heats, the heat winners or horses making a dead heat for first usually run in a fourth heat for the winner's 10%.

Placing system As for a two in three, a horse must win two heats to win the race. Other race placings are decided by a summary of heat placings. The summary is decided along the lines that a horse with a clear first place is higher than a horse with a tied first place or no place higher than second. Unless the conditions state otherwise, the money is divided 50%, 25%, 15%, and 10%.

Violations of driving rules No driver may:
change to the right or left if this would compel another horse to shorten its stride or be pulled out of its stride by its driver;
jostle, strike, hook wheels, or interfere in any way with another horse or driver;
endanger other drivers by crossing sharply in front of the field;
swerve in or out or pull up quickly;
crowd a horse or driver by "putting a wheel under him";
help another horse by causing confusion or interference among horses then trailing;
let any horse pass needlessly, or lay off normal pace to leave a hole that could easily

be kept closed;
in any way impede the progress of another horse or cause it to break from its gait;
change course after selecting a position in the home stretch, or by swerving or bearing in or out cause another horse to change its course or hold back;
drive in a reckless or careless manner;
shout loudly during a race, or use any goading device other than an ordinary whip or crop;
remove either foot from his stirrups from the word "go" until the race ends.
Breaking rules A horse that breaks from its gait must, where clearance exists, be taken to the outside and pulled back to gait.

It is a violation if a driver:
does not attempt to pull his horse to gait;
fails to take to the outside where clearance exists;
fails to lose ground by the break.
Drivers are then penalized as for a violation of a driving rule.
If there has been no violation, a horse is only set back if, at the finish, a contending horse on its gait is lapped on the breaking horse's hind quarter.
Complaints Any complaint by a driver must be made to the judges immediately the heat ends, unless he is prevented by accident or injury.

Action after violations
An offending horse may, for that heat or dash only, be set back in the placings behind any horse with which it interfered.
If an offense prevents another horse from finishing, the offending horse may be disqualified from receiving any winnings and its driver fined, suspended, or expelled.
In case of an offense by a horse coupled in an "entry," both horses may be set back if the judges consider that the finish was affected. Otherwise, horses in an "entry" are penalized separately.
Failing to finish Horses must contest every heat in a race. A horse failing to finish a heat will be ruled out, unless the failure was

caused by broken equipment or interference.
Inconsistent driving
Deliberately preventing a horse from winning, driving inconsistently, and racing to perpetrate or aid a fraud, are offenses punishable by fine, suspension, or expulsion. The judges may at any time substitute another driver.
Doping Blood, urine, and saliva tests may be used to determine the presence of forbidden drugs. Any person administering such drugs to a horse, or influencing or conspiring with another person to do so, will be fined and/or suspended, or expelled.

Impede by crossing sharply

Hook wheels

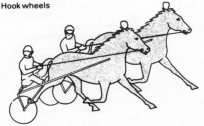

Impede by slowing down

Remove foot from stirrup

Strike an opponents horse

© DIAGRAM

Show jumping

A jumping competition is one in which the horse's jumping ability and the rider's skill are tested under various conditions over a course of obstacles. Certain defined errors are faulted, and, depending on the type of competition, the winner is the competitor with either the lowest number of faults, the fastest time, or the highest number of points.

A typical Grand Prix course:

1 brush and rails;
2 hog's back;
3 post and rails;
4 narrow stile
5 double-triple bar, planks and poles;
6 fancy gate;
7 treble-triple bar, parallel
8 white gate;
9 narrow stile;
10 water jump;
11 double-parallel poles,
12 oil drums and poles;
13 poles over a bank;
14 treble-triple bar, double oxer, post and rails;
15 stone wall;

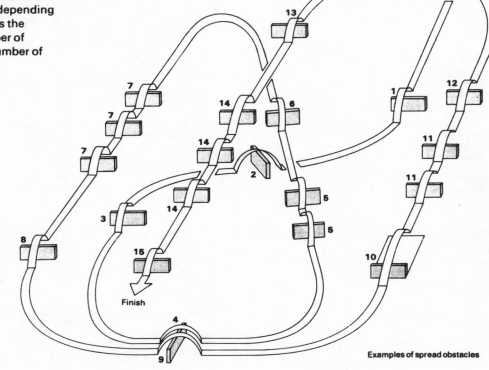

Examples of straight obstacles

Stone wall   Gate   Brush and rails

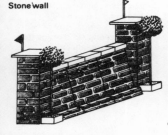

Examples of spread obstacles

Hog's back

Types of competition
Grand Prix
Nations' Cup
Puissance
Hunting
Six bars
Baton relay
Fault and out relay
Accumulator
Have a gamble stakes
Normal
Three-day event

Team competitions For CCI competitions an official team is composed of a maximum of a team captain, six riders, and 12 horses. Teams for the Olympic Games and Nations' Cup have four riders and four horses, of which only the best three scores are counted.
Individual competitions For CCIO and Olympic competitions riders may ride only one horse, and not more than three individuals may ride for any one nation. For other events competitors may enter three horses, but must declare at the beginning of the competition which one or two they intend to ride.

Officials include:
judges;
clerk of the course;
clerk of the scales;
timekeeper;
arena and collecting ring stewards.
Result Depending on the type of competition, the winner is the competitor or team with either the lowest number of faults, the fastest time with fewest faults, or the highest number of points.
The arena is enclosed, and while a horse is jumping all entrances and exits are shut. Once the competition has started, competitors are not allowed to enter the arena on foot, exercise their horses, or jump any of the fences, unless actually taking part.

The course From the starting line to the finishing line the maximum length of a course in meters is the number of obstacles in the course multiplied by sixty. The starting and finishing lines and all obstacles are marked with red flags on the right and white flags on the left.
Plan of the course A plan showing the general layout of the course is posted for the competitors' benefit. It shows:
the positions of the start and finishing lines;
the relative positions of obstacles, their type and numbers;
any compulsory passages or turning points;
the length of the course;

the track to be followed (a continuous line means that it must be followed precisely and a series of arrows indicates only the direction from which each obstacle is to be jumped);
the marking system to be used;
the time allowed and the time limit, if any;
the obstacles to be used in any jump-off, and the length of course and time allowed for the jump-off.

Horses must be: owned by a member of a national federation; registered with that federation; ridden by a person of the same nationality as the owner.

Riders must be at least 18 years of age (except for junior competitions) and possess an amateur license. A card of authorization from their national federation is compulsory for each show in a foreign country.

Dress Service dress may be worn at all competitions. For international events civilians are expected to wear hunting stock or white shirt, collar and tie, jacket, breeches, and black boots. For other events they should wear the uniform of a recognized riding club.

Saddlery There are no restrictions on saddles or bridles, but blinkers and hoods are forbidden. Only a running martingale is allowed. Whips exceeding 75cm or weighted at one end are also prohibited.

Triple bars

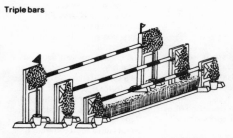

Double oxer

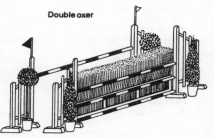

Parallel poles

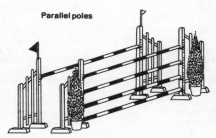

Obstacles are numbered consecutively in the order in which they are to be jumped. Multiple obstacles carry only one number, but each element has a different letter (for example 3A, 3B, 3C). As far as possible fences resemble natural hazards, but they are not absolutely fixed. Except in Puissance and Nations' Cup events obstacles never exceed 1.70m in height or 2m in width. The water jump never exceeds 5m width.

Types of obstacle:

A straight obstacle is one where the elements are placed vertically one above the other in the same plane, for example gates, walls, posts and rails, single rail.

Multiple obstacles are composed of two, three, or more fences, which have to be taken in successive jumps. The distance between any two parts is a minimum of 7m and a maximum of 12m. Banks, slopes, and ramps with or without fences are counted as multiple obstacles.

A spread fence is one that requires the horse to jump both height and width, for example triple bars, double-oxer, hog's back.

The water jump is a spread fence with a small guardrail or hedge on the take-off side (about 65cm high) and a ditch full of water between 4m and 5m in width. The limit of the jump is clearly marked on the landing side – at CCIs with a white strip of wood, at CCIOs and Olympic Games with a strip of white rubber approximately 5cm wide.

Fences for Nations' Cup competitions There are either 13 or 14 obstacles with heights varying between 1.30m and 1.60m. The course is normally about 800m and has to include at least one double or one treble obstacle, six fences not less than 1.40m high, two straight obstacles not less than 1.50m high, and a water jump with a minimum width of 4m. Spread obstacles may vary between 1.50 and 2.70m in width, with a height in proportion to their width.

Fences for puissance competitions There are between six and eight obstacles, of which straight fences must be at least 1.40m high. There may be a maximum of four jump-offs over a reduced number of fences, which may be raised and/or increased in width.

Olympic Games

Grand Prix (team) For round A the length of the course and the number and measurements of the obstacles are the same as for the individual event.

In round B only the best eight teams may participate. The jump-off is held over six obstacles 1.40–1.80m high; spread obstacles are increased to between 1.60 and 2.20m.

Grand Prix (individual) For round A the course does not exceed 1000m, with between 12 and 15 obstacles varying in height from 1.30 to 1.60m. Spread obstacles vary from 1.50–2.20m in width, and the water jump is at least 4.50m wide.

In round B the height of obstacles may be raised from 1.40 to 1.70m and the width increased to 2m, but there may not be more than 10 obstacles.

Knocking down an obstacle

Failure at the water jump

Procedure

Walking the course Before the start of the competition the rider is permitted to inspect the course and fences on foot.

The order of starting is decided by a draw. Competitors keep to the same order throughout each round of a competition.

Starting When his number is called, the competitor enters the arena already mounted. He does not cross the starting line until the judge gives the starting signal, normally a bell. The first round is not normally against the clock, but subsequent rounds may be. Once he has passed the starting line the competitor must jump the fences in the correct order and will be penalized for any errors, such as knocking over a fence, refusing a fence (in which case that fence must be taken again), or losing his way. If a horse knocks down a fence on a refusal, the rider must wait until it has been rebuilt before retaking it and continuing with the rest of the course. At the end of the course the rider must leave the arena still mounted and go straight to the weighing enclosure, where he will be weighed together with his saddlery.

Penalties

Obstacles knocked down
An obstacle is considered to be knocked down when any part of it is knocked down or dislodged, even if the falling part is arrested by another part of the obstacle. Touches and displacements are not counted, nor is an obstacle considered to be knocked down if it falls only

after the competitor has crossed the finishing line. Knocking down the top element is only penalized when an obstacle or part of an obstacle is composed of several elements in the same vertical plane.

When an obstacle has several elements not in the same vertical plane a competitor is penalized for only one mistake, irrespective of the number of separate elements knocked down.

Any element of a knocked-down obstacle that prevents a competitor from jumping another obstacle, or part of a multiple obstacle, must be removed before the competitor continues.

Falls A rider is considered to have fallen if he is separated from his horse, which has not fallen, in such a way that he has to remount or vault into the saddle.

A horse is considered to have fallen when its shoulder and quarters have touched the ground, or the obstacle and the ground.

Any fall is penalized wherever it takes place and whatever the cause. A competitor will be eliminated if he fails to continue the course from the point where the fall occurred or from any other point that does not reduce the length of the course.

When a horse or rider falls in knocking down or refusing an obstacle, or after any other disobedience, the penalties for both faults are added together.

A loose horse that falls, jumps an obstacle, goes to the

wrong side of a flag, or passes through the starting or finishing line is not penalized. A loose horse that leaves the arena is eliminated.

Disobedience Penalized as disobedience are:
a rectified deviation from the course;
a refusal, run-out, or resistance;
circling, except after a run-out or refusal;
crossing the track first taken between any two consecutive obstacles, except when specifically allowed by the course plan;
passing the obstacle and then approaching it sideways, zig-zagging, or turning sharply toward it.

Refusal It is a refusal if a horse stops in front of an obstacle to be jumped, whether or not the fence is knocked down or displaced. It is not a refusal if a horse stops at an obstacle without knocking it down or reining back, and then immediately makes a standing jump. It is a refusal if the stop is prolonged or if the horse steps back even a single pace, voluntarily or not, or if it takes more room to jump.

A competitor is eliminated if he knocks down an obstacle while stopping and then jumps the obstacle before it is re-erected.

If a horse slides through an obstacle the judge decides whether it is to count as a refusal or as an obstacle knocked down.

A competitor is eliminated after three refusals, or if he shows an obstacle to his horse after a refusal.

Running out A horse is considered to have run out if:
it is not fully under its rider's control and avoids an obstacle it should have jumped;
it jumps an obstacle outside the boundary flags.

The rider is eliminated if he fails to bring his horse back to jump the obstacle.

Resistance A horse is considered to offer resistance if at any time it fails to go forward.

A horse is eliminated if:
it resists its rider for 60 consecutive seconds;
it takes more than 60 seconds to jump an obstacle except in the case of a fall;
it fails to pass the starting line within 60 seconds of the signal to start.

Deviation A deviation from the course occurs when a competitor:
does not follow the plan of the course;
goes the wrong side of a flag;
jumps obstacles out of order;
jumps an obstacle outside the course, or misses the jump.

In order to correct a deviation, the competitor must return to the course at the point where the error was made.

If a deviation is rectified before the next obstacle is jumped, it is penalized as a disobedience. If a deviation is not so rectified, the penalty is elimination.

Competitors will be eliminated for receiving unauthorized assistance if any person in the arena draws their attention to a deviation in an attempt to prevent elimination.

Scoring There are three different tables for scoring show jumping. Most competitions are decided under table A.

Table A
First disobedience, 3 faults;
knocking down an obstacle or failure at the water jump, 4 faults;
second disobedience, 6 faults;
fall by horse or rider, 8 faults;
disobedience and knocking down an obstacle, 3 or 6 faults plus 6, 8, or 10 seconds;
third disobedience and other offenses stated in the rules, elimination;
exceeding the time allowed, $\frac{1}{4}$ fault for each second or part of a second.

Faults for disobedience are cumulative whether they are made at the same obstacle or not.

Faults are added together to give the competitor's score for the round(s).

The time taken by competitors may be used to decide cases of equality for first and other places, according to the conditions of the competition. In cases of equality of faults for first place, there may be one or more compulsory jumps-off, against the clock or not, according to the conditions of the competition.

Refusal at an obstacle   Fall by horse and rider

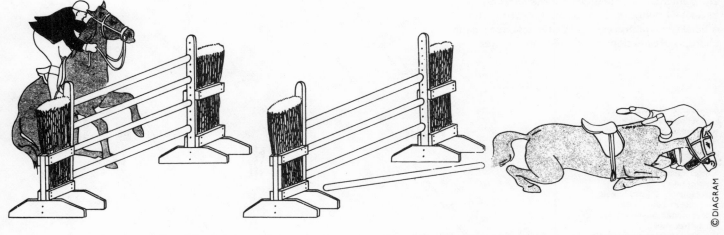

© DIAGRAM

Table B
Under this table jumping mistakes carry a penalty expressed in seconds. It may not be used if the length of the course is less than 700m.

Table C
This table is used for hunting competitions. Penalties are scored in seconds and added to the time of the round. The number of penalty seconds for each jumping mistake is calculated in relation to the length of the course and the number of times a horse is required to jump in the round.

Time and speed The timing of a round begins at the exact moment when the mounted rider passes the starting line, and ends when – still mounted – he crosses the finishing line.

Time allowed For international competitions the time allowed for each round is calculated from the length of the course and the following speed limits:
Normal: minimum 350m per minute;
Puissance: 1st round, 300m per minute; jump-off, no limit;
Hunting: minimum 350m per minute;
Six bars: no limit;
Nations' Cup: 400m per minute;
Olympic Games: 400m per minute.

The time limit is twice the time allowed in all competitions.

Recording time Time is recorded in seconds and tenths of seconds, and automatic timing devices are used in all international competitions.

Interrupted time The clock must be stopped when, for example, a rider knocks down a fence or his horse refuses to jump. It is not started again until the fence is rebuilt, at which point the rider is given the signal to recommence.

Time penalties are incurred as follows:
1) For knocking down an obstacle as a result of a disobedience:
6 seconds penalty for a single obstacle or the first part of a multiple obstacle;

8 seconds for the second part of a multiple obstacle;
10 seconds for the third or subsequent parts.
2) For knocking down part of a multiple obstacle and refusing or running out at the next part without knocking it down:
the clock is stopped as for a knock down resulting from a disobedience, and penalties of 8 or 10 seconds are imposed, depending on whether the disobedience was at the second, third, or subsequent parts.

Elimination Competitors are eliminated if they:
fail to enter the arena when called;
jump an obstacle in the arena before the starting signal, even if it is not in the course;
start before the signal, or fail to start within 60 seconds after it;
have three disobediences in a round, or show any obstacle to a horse after a refusal;
enter or leave the arena dismounted, except with the jury's permission;
have more than 60 seconds of resistance from their horse in any one round;
take more than 60 seconds to jump an obstacle (except in the case of a fall);
jump an obstacle without having corrected a deviation from the course;
jump an obstacle that is not in the course;
jump an obstacle in the wrong order;
pass the wrong side of a flag and fail to rectify the error;
exceed the time limit;
jump a knocked-down obstacle before it is rebuilt;

restart after an interruption before the signal has been given;
jump an optional obstacle in a jump-off either more than once or in the wrong direction;
fail to jump the whole obstacle after a refusal, run-out, or fall at any part of a multiple obstacle;
fail to jump out of a closed obstacle in the correct direction, or interfere with a closed obstacle;
fail to jump each part of a multiple obstacle separately;
fail to cross the finishing line mounted before leaving the arena, or their horses leave the arena before finishing the round;
accept a whip during a round, or any other unauthorized assistance at the jury's discretion;
fail to have the required minimum weight when weighing in at the end of each round;
enter the arena on foot after the start of the competition at the jury's discretion;
dismount before being given permission by the official in charge of weighing;
commit any other offense that the rules specifically state is penalized by elimination.

A jump-off takes place to decide the winner among competitors who are tied for first place after earlier rounds. Unless the rules state otherwise, the number of obstacles is reduced and individual fences may be raised or widened. For the first jump-off (except in Puissance or Nations' Cup) not less than half the original fences are retained, and for the second jump-off not less than six fences.
There are never more than two jumps-off unless the rules state otherwise. Either the first, or the first and second jumps-off may be against the clock. The jump-off may be decided by the number of faults plus the time taken to complete the round.
Special rules apply to Puissance jumps-off, in which the fences are made progressively higher until the winner is determined.
In the Nations' Cup the jump-off is timed and is over six obstacles. The winning team is decided by adding together jumping and time faults; if there are still teams with equal faults, the time taken is the decisive factor.

Dressage

Dressage competitions test the harmonious development of the horse's physique and ability, and demand a high degree of understanding between horse and rider. Competitors carry out official tests incorporating a variety of paces, halts, changes of direction, movements and figures.

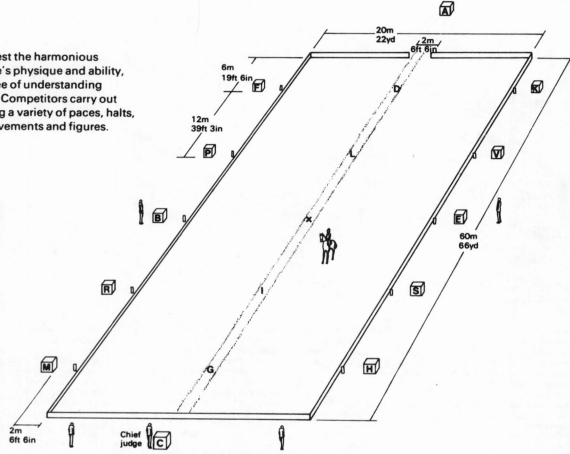

Arena International competitions must be in an arena measuring 60m by 20m. (An arena 40m by 20m may be used for less advanced tests.)
Arenas must be on perfectly flat ground.
There must be 20m between the arena and the public. Indoor arenas must be at least 2m from any wall.
The center line is a mown strip about ¾m wide. Center letters are marked with whitening or sawdust.
Outer markers have letters in black or white and are placed about 2m outside the arena. The entrance is marked by the letter A.

Officials International dressage events are judged by a jury of five members: three on one short side of the arena, and one on each of the long sides.

Tests The FEI (Fédération Equestre Internationale) issues the following tests for use at international level:
the Grand Prix (expert/ Olympic standard);
the Intermédiaire (advanced standard);
the Prix St Georges (medium standard).
the FEI also issues:
the Concours Complet (for use at three-day events);
the Free Style Test;
junior tests.

Horses must:
be currently registered with a national federation;
be owned by a member of that federation;
exceed 14.2 hands;
fulfill entry requirements for specific competitions (eg horses are excluded from Grand Prix competitions after competing in three Olympic Grand Prix).

Saddlery Compulsory are an English hunting-type of saddle and a double bridle. Prohibited are martingales and bearing, side or running reins of any kind, bandages, boots, and any form of blinkers.

Schooling No horse may take part in an official International Dressage Event (CDIO) if, in the town where the competition takes place, it has been schooled with anyone other than the competitor mounted in the three days prior to the first test or during the time of the entire event. (Training in hand may be undertaken by persons other than the competitor.)

Riders For all official events riders must:
be members of a national federation;
be at least 17 years of age for senior events;
be the same nationality as the horse's owner;
possess a card of authorization from their national federation for any show abroad;
possess an amateur license.

Dress Service dress may be worn. Civilians wear a black jacket and black riding trousers, or a dark coat and white breeches, also a top hat, hunting stock, and spurs.

Procedure At the judges' signal the competitor enters the arena at a collected canter, halts, and salutes.
The test is then carried out entirely from memory and all movements must follow in the order laid down in the test sheet.
If the test requires a movement to be carried out at a certain point in the arena, it is to be executed when the rider's body is over that point.
A change of pace at a marker should occur when the rider's body passes that marker.
A bell is rung whenever the competitor departs from the direction or pace given in the test sheet. The test must then be restarted from the point where the error occurred.
Timing apparatus is not stopped in such a case.
A fall by horse and/or rider does not result in elimination. The competitor is penalized by the time and by the effect of the fall on the execution of the movement and in the collective marks.
The test ends with a final salute, after which the competitor leaves the arena at point A.

Timing The time allowed is given on the test sheet. Timing is from the exact moment when the horse moves forward after the salute until the rider halts his horse and salutes after the test. Each second or part of a second over the time allowed is penalized by the loss of ½ point from each judge's score.

Penalties For every error, whether rectified or not, every omission, and every movement taken in the wrong order the competitor is penalized:
the first time by the loss of 2 points;
the second time by the loss of 4 points;
the third time by the loss of 8 points;
the fourth time by elimination, although he may continue the test to the end.

Marking Competitors receive two kinds of mark from each judge:
1) Movements and transitions are grouped into categories, which are given a mark from 0–10 by each judge. A mark of 0 means that a competitor performed nothing that was required.
2) Collective marks from 0–10 are awarded by each judge for the paces, impulsion, submission, and the rider's seat and use of aids.
(The collective marks and marks for certain movements can be given increased influence on the final result by using a coefficient fixed by the FEI.)

Test requirements Official tests include the following halts, paces, and movements.
The halt The horse should stand attentive, still and straight, with weight evenly distributed over all legs. The transition from any pace to the halt should be made progressively in a smooth, precise movement.
The half halt is intended to increase the attention and balance of the horse before the execution of several movements or transitions to lesser paces.
The walk is a marching pace, with the four legs following one another in well marked four time.
Walks are collected, medium, or extended according to the length of the stride.
There is also a free walk in which the horse is allowed complete freedom of the neck and head.
The trot is a two-time pace on alternate diagonals (near fore and off hind and vice versa) separated by a moment of suspension.
Steps should be free, active, and regular. The trot should always be entered without hesitation.
Recognized trots are collected, medium, and extended. (The collected trot is replaced by the working trot in tests below Grand Prix ride-off standard.)
The canter: a three-time pace. In the right canter the sequence is left hind leg, left diagonal (right hind and left fore leg), right fore leg, followed by a period of suspension with all four legs in the air.
Recognized canters are collected, medium, and extended. (The collected canter is replaced by the working canter in tests below Grand Prix ride-off standard.)
The counter (false) canter is a suppling movement on the circle. The horse remains bent to the leading leg.
Change of leg at the canter In a simple change of leg the horse is brought into a walk for one or two well-defined steps and then restarted into a canter with the other leg leading.
In a change of leg in the air the change is executed in close connection with the suspension that follows each counter stride.

Walk

Trot

Canter

©DIAGRAM

The collected paces The horse's quarters are lowered with all the muscles and joints acting as springs. This enables the horse to develop its impulsion in a forward and upward direction.
The rein back is a backward walk in which the legs are raised and set down simultaneously by diagonal pairs. The horse must be ready to halt or move forward without pausing at the rider's demands.
The submission A slight flexion of the jaw is a criterion of the horse's obedience and balance. Grinding the teeth and swishing the tail are signs of nervousness, tenseness, or resistance.
Transitions All changes of pace and speed should be quickly made but smooth. The same is true of transitions between passage and piaffer.

Changes of direction The horse should adjust the bend of its body to the curvature of the line followed, remaining supple and following the indications of the rider without any resistance or change of pace.
Counter-change of hand The rider changes direction by moving obliquely either to the quarter line, the center line, or the opposite long side of the arena.
The horse should be straight for an instant and then return on a line oblique to its line at the start of the movement. When the number of steps is prescribed, this must be strictly observed and the movement executed symmetrically.
Riding corners At collected paces, the horse must describe a quarter of a circle of approximately 3m radius. At other paces, the circle's radius should be approximately 6m.

The passage is a measured, very collected, very elevated, and very cadenced trot. Each diagonal pair of legs is raised and put to the ground alternately, gaining little ground and with an even cadence and a prolonged suspension.
In principle the height of the toe of the raised foreleg should be level with the middle of the cannon bone of the other foreleg. The toe of the raised hind leg should be slightly above the fetlock joint of the other hind leg.
The neck should be raised and gracefully arched with the poll at the highest point and the head close to the perpendicular.
Crossing the forelegs or swinging the forehand or the quarters from side to side are serious faults.

The piaffer is a movement resembling the very collected trot on the spot. The neck is raised, the poll supple, the head perpendicular, the mouth maintaining light contact on a taut rein. The alternate diagonals are raised with even, supple, cadenced, and graceful movement, the moment of suspension being prolonged.
In principle the height of the toe of the raised foreleg should be level with the middle of the cannon bone of the other foreleg. The toe of the raised hind leg just above the fetlock joint of the other hind leg.
The body of the horse should move up and down with a supple, harmonious movement without any swinging of either the forehand or the quarters from one side to the other.
Although executed strictly on the spot and with perfect balance, the piaffer must always be energetically executed.

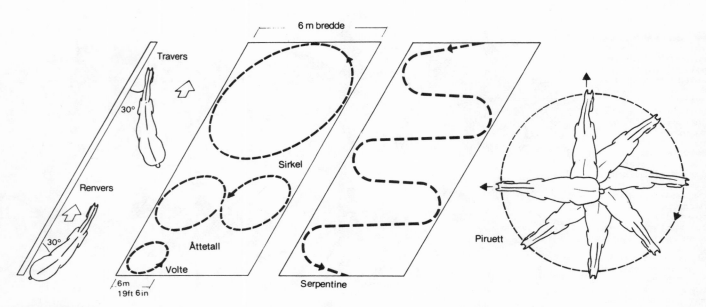

Lateral movements (work on two tracks) comprise the shoulder-in, the travers, the renvers, the on two tracks, the counter-change of hand, and the leg yielding. The aim is to bring balance and pace into harmony.

In all but the leg yielding, the horse is bent uniformly from poll to tail and moves with the forehand and quarters on two different tracks.

The distance between the tracks should not exceed one step.

The pace remains always regular, supple, and free. The forehand should always be slightly in advance of the quarters.

Shoulder-in The horse is slightly bent around the inside leg of the rider.

The outside shoulder is placed in front of the inside hind quarter. The inside legs pass and cross in front of the outside legs.

The horse looks away from the direction in which it is moving. The horse should not be at an angle of more than 30° to the direction in which it is moving.

Leg yielding resembles the shoulder-in, but the horse's body is quite straight except for a slight bend at the poll. The horse looks away from the direction in which it is moving.

Travers (head to wall) in which the horse moves along the wall with its head at an angle of not more than 30° to the wall. The horse is slightly bent around the inside leg of the rider and looks in the direction in which it is moving.

Renvers (tail to wall) is the inverse position of the travers, with the tail instead of the head to the wall. The horse looks in the direction in which it is moving.

On two tracks The horse's head, neck, and shoulders are always slightly in advance of the quarters.

The horse is bent slightly and looks in the direction in which it is moving.

The outside legs (on the side from which the horse is moving) pass and cross in front of the inside legs.

Counter-change of hand on two tracks (zig-zag). The judges concentrate on the changes of position of the horse, the movements of its legs, and the precision, suppleness and regularity of its movements.

Figures There are four figures: the volte, circle, serpentine, and figure of eight.

The volte is a circle of 6m diameter.

The circle has a stated diameter of 6m.

The serpentine The first loop is started by moving gradually away from the short side and the last loop is finished by moving gradually toward the opposite short side.

The figure of eight is executed following the same rules as for the serpentine inside a square with X as the center. The rider changes the bend of his horse at the center of the eight, making his horse straight an instant before changing direction.

The half-pirouette is a half-turn on the haunches. The forehand commences the half-turn, tracing a half-circle around the haunches, without pausing, at the moment the inside hind leg ceases its forward movement. The inside foot, while forming the pivot, should return to the same spot each time it leaves the ground.

The horse moves forward again, without a pause, upon completion of the half-turn.

The pirouette is a small circle on two tracks, with a radius equal to the length of the horse, the forehand moving around the haunches. The forelegs and the outside hind leg move around the inside hind foot, which forms the pivot.

The pace is not considered to be regular if the pivot foot is not raised and returned to the ground in the same way as the other hind foot.

The pivot foot should always return to the same spot.

Position of the rider All the movements should be obtained without apparent effort by the rider.

He should be well-balanced, with loins and hips supple, thighs and legs steady and well stretched downward.

The upper part of the body should be easy, free and erect, with the arms close to the body. Riding with both hands is compulsory.

Use of the voice is strictly forbidden and involves the deduction of at least two marks from what would otherwise have been scored for a movement.

Only women riding side-saddle are permitted to carry a whip.

Elimination Grounds for elimination are:
failure to obey judges' signals;
leaving the arena before completing the test;
a horse leaving the arena out of control;
a horse entering the arena when not actually competing;
a fourth error of course;
doping;
a horse going lame;
resistance (failing to enter the arena within 60 seconds of the starting bell, or refusing to continue the test for a period of 60 consecutive seconds).

Classification A competitor's marks from each judge are multiplied by coefficients where applicable. Penalty points for errors in the test and for exceeding the time allowed are next deducted from each judge's score. The judges' scores are then averaged to give the final score for each competitor. Team scores are obtained by adding the scores of the three team members.

In a competition with no ride-off, the winner is the competitor or team with the highest total; competitors with equal scores are given the same placing.

In a competition with a ride-off, the individual classification is determined by the marks obtained in the ride-off test; in case of equality after a ride-off the classification in the first test decides the classification.

In a competition with a ride-off, the points obtained in the ride-off do not affect the team classification; if two or more teams gain the same number of marks, the winning team is that whose worst competitor had the best result in the first test.

Ride-off test A ride-off test may be used to decide first place. (Compulsory for the Grand Prix at CDIOs and regional games. Special rules apply for Olympics.)

No more than 25% of the participants (to the nearest whole number above) may take part in the ride-off, and never more than 12 riders.

For the Grand Prix there is a special ride-off test. For the Intermédiaire and Prix St Georges, the initial test is repeated.

The order of starting is the same as for the initial test.

If a competitor withdraws or is eliminated during a ride-off, he is classified last of the competitors riding off. If several competitors withdraw or are eliminated, they are classified according to their points in the initial test.

Three-day event

The three-day event consists of three distinct equestrian competitions – dressage, endurance, and show jumping. They are held on three consecutive days, and each rider must ride the same horse throughout. The event is designed to test the harmonious development, speed, endurance, obedience, and jumping ability of the horse, and requires a perfect understanding between horse and rider.

Horses competing at international level must: exceed 14.2 hands; be at least 6 years old; be owned by a member of a national federation; be registered with that federation; be ridden by a person with the same nationality as the owner; be examined for fitness three times during the event.

Saddlery For the dressage, an English saddle and a snaffle or simple double bridle are compulsory. A dropped noseband is permitted, provided it is made of leather and used with a snaffle. Blinkers, bandages, martingales and bearing, and side or running reins are all prohibited.
For the endurance and jumping, the saddle is optional and a running martingale is allowed. Blinkers or hoods are not allowed.

Riders competing at international level must be in at least their 18th year and must possess an amateur license. They may take part only as nationals of their native countries, and as members of a national team. A card of authorization from their national federation is compulsory for each show in a foreign country.
A rider may ride only one horse in the team competition. A second horse may be ridden for the individual competition, but the team horse must be ridden first.

Dress Military dress, with a helmet or hard hat, is permitted for all stages of the event. For the dressage and jumping competitions, civilians are expected to wear hunting attire; for the endurance competition, they may wear either hunting attire, or a polo-necked sweater or shirt, white breeches, black boots, and black hunting cap or other hard hat.
Spurs are compulsory for the dressage competition.

Officials at three-day events are a president, judges, ground jury, appeal committee, technical delegates, a clerk of the course, veterinary officials, timekeepers, stewards, and jump judges.

International categories are:
CCI, or International Three-Day Event;
CCIO, or Official International Three-Day Event;
Olympic Three-Day Event.
All have the same three stages of competitions: dressage (day 1, and an extra day if required by the number of entries); endurance (day 2); show-jumping (day 3).
All have team and individual classifications.

Team competitions There are normally four members in a team, but only the marks of the best three are counted. A team of three may enter, but all three must complete the course. (CCI competitions are sometimes for teams of three, with only the marks of the best two members counted.)
In CCI competitions the number of teams entered by a nation is at the discretion of the organizers.
In CCIO and Olympic competitions, only one team per nation may enter.
There must be at least three teams for a competition to be valid.

Individual competitions All team members are automatically considered as individuals. (They compete only once, with their scores considered in both classifications.)
Additional individual competitors may also be entered, up to a maximum stated in the event rules.

Result The three competitions affect the final result in the ratio: dressage 3; endurance 12; jumping 1. Competitors can acquire penalty points in all competitions and bonus points in the steeplechase and cross-country.
The individual winner is the rider with least penalty or most bonus points.
The winning team is that with the lowest total penalty points or the most bonus points, after adding together the scores of the best three team members.

Order of starting is fixed by draw at the start of the event. It is the same for each competition. Team captains decide starting order within teams.

Examination of horses Horses are examined for fitness:
before the dressage competition;
after phase C and before the cross-country on day two;
before the jumping competition.
Judges must give reasons for elimination. There is no right of appeal.

Weight The minimum weight to be carried in the endurance and jumping competitions is 75kg. There is no weight restriction for the dressage test.
Competitors are weighed at the start of the endurance competition and before the jumping competition. If necessary, they may be weighed with all the equipment to be carried (bridle and whip excepted). Reweighing takes place after the endurance and jumping competitions, and riders must not dismount beforehand. The bridle may be included in these reweighings.

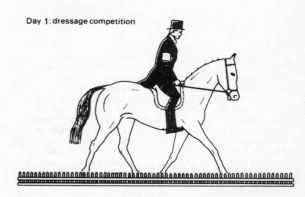

Day 1: dressage competition

Day 2: endurance competition

Day 3: jumping competition

DRESSAGE: DAY 1

The object is to test the harmonious development of the horse's physique and the degree of understanding between horse and rider.

Rules are generally as for other dressage competitions, with specific exceptions.

Type of test An officially approved (FEI) three-day event dressage test is used for CCIs and CCIOs. The degree of difficulty depends on the difficulty of the whole event.

Marking Each judge awards a competitor collective marks and 0–6 marks for each of the test's numbered movements.
Penalties for course error or for exceeding the time allowed are then deducted from each judge's sheet.
The judges' marks are next averaged, and the competitor's average mark converted into a penalty score by subtracting from the maximum marks obtainable.
Finally, the penalty score is multiplied by a factor calculated to give the dressage competition its correct importance relative to the whole event.
There is no casting vote or ride-off in the event of equality of marks.

ENDURANCE: DAY 2

The object is to prove the speed, endurance, and jumping ability of the fit, well-trained cross-country horse and to test the rider's knowledge of pace and riding across country.

Phases The endurance competition has four phases:
A) Roads and tracks
B) Steeplechase
C) Roads and tracks
D) Cross-country

Speeds and distances
Phases A and C: a total of 10–16km at 240m per minute for CCI; a total of 16–20km at 240m per minute for CCIO.
Phase B: 3000–3600m at 550–600m per minute (CCI); 3600 or 4200m at 600m per minute (CCIO).
Phase D: 5400–7200m at 400–450m per minute (CCI); 7200, 7650 or 8100m at 450m per minute (CCIO).

Course markings All courses are marked with yellow direction flags or signs, with the letter of the particular phase superimposed. Roads and tracks sections are marked at 1km intervals with numbered posts.
Red and white flags indicate compulsory sections, obstacles, compulsory changes of direction, and the start and finish of each phase. Riders must keep the red flags to their right and the white flags to their left.

Obstacles There are an average of three obstacles to every 1000m for phase B, and four to every 1000m for phase D.
Obstacles must be fixed. They must not exceed the prescribed dimensions, and only 50% of the obstacles may be of maximum height. Steeplechase obstacles are similar to those used on regulation steeplechase courses.
Cross-country obstacles should be imposing in shape and left as far as possible in their natural state. No obstacle may have a drop on its landing side greater than 2m from its highest point. Artificial obstacles must not demand an acrobatic feat of jumping for the horse nor give the rider an unpleasant or unfair surprise.
Obstacles are consecutively numbered. Each part of a multiple obstacle is numbered and judged independently. A single obstacle with several elements has a different letter for each element (eg 3A, 3B, 3C) and is judged as one fence.

The penalty zone is marked out with sawdust, chalk, or pegs. It extends 10m in front of, 20m beyond, and 10m to either side of each obstacle.

Start Competitors are normally started at intervals of less than 5 minutes for phase A. Starting times for other phases are based on the time allowed for the preceding phase. There is a compulsory halt of 10 minutes between phases C and D.
Phases A, B, and D must be started from a halt.

Pace Riders may choose their own pace. Phases A and D are normally ridden at the trot or slow canter; phases B and D at the gallop.

Dismounting Riders may walk beside their horses for phases A and C, provided they are mounted when passing the finishing post. In phases B and D they are penalized for dismounting (voluntarily or not) in the penalty zone; outside the penalty zone they are not penalized, provided they remount and continue from where they dismounted. Riders must not dismount until they have been weighed after phase D.

Timing The time allowed for each phase is the set distance divided by the set speed.
Timing is from the moment the horse's chest passes the starting post.
Time lost or gained in any one phase does not affect the time allowed for the next phase.
The time limit for phases A and C is one-fifth more than the time allowed. The time limit for phases B and D is double the time allowed.

Scoring Time penalties, time bonuses, and faults at obstacles are taken into account.

Time penalties For every second over the time allowed competitors lose:
for phases A and C, 1 penalty point;
for phase B, 0.8 of a penalty point;
for phase D, 0.4 of a penalty point.

Time bonuses Bonus points are awarded for completing phases B and D in less than the time allowed:
for phase B, 0.8 of a point for each second under the time allowed up to a maximum

speed of 90m per minute faster than the set speed; for phase D, 0.4 of a point for each second under the time allowed up to a maximum speed of 120m per minute faster than the set speed. There are no bonus points for completing phases A and C in less than the time allowed.

Faults at obstacles For a first refusal, 20 penalties; second refusal, 40 penalties; fall of horse/rider, 60 penalties. (Included as refusals are running out, circling, dismounting, and entering or leaving the penalty zone without jumping the obstacle.)

Elimination Grounds for elimination are:
arriving late at the start, or starting before the signal;
wilfully obstructing a competitor who is overtaking;
receiving assistance from a third party, except to catch a horse, adjust saddlery, or remount after a fall;
failing to obey red or white flags;
removing or altering flags;
any act of cruelty;
doping;
rapping a horse;
wearing spurs capable of wounding a horse, or excessively spurring an exhausted horse (less serious cases may be penalized by 60 points);
failing to carry the minimum weight, or dismounting before being weighed after phase D;
exceeding the time limit for any phase.

Penalty zone elimination The following faults cause elimination if they occur within the penalty zone:
third refusal at the same obstacle (phases B and D);
second fall of horse/rider in phase B;
third fall of horse/rider in phase D;
error of course not corrected;
missing an obstacle or flag;
retaking an obstacle already jumped;
jumping obstacles in the wrong order.

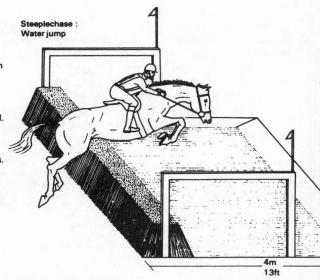

Steeplechase: Water jump

4m
13ft

Cross-country: Rails

Lane crossing

Fence

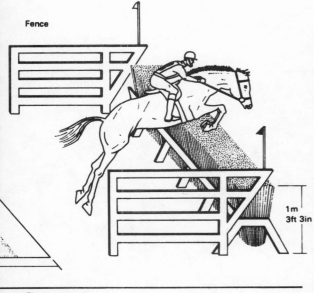

1m
3ft 3in

Elephant trap

CCI 1.80m
5ft 11in
CCIO 2m
6ft 6in

CCI	CCIO
2.80m	3m
9ft 2in	9ft 9in

JUMPING: DAY 3

Object The jumping competition is intended to test whether the horses can continue in service after the endurance competition.

The type of course depends on the difficulty of the whole event and on the intended influence of the jumping competition on the final result.

The track will be irregular and have changes of direction to test the horse's handiness. No acrobatic feat of jumping or turning will be required and no compulsory passage included.

Obstacles There will be 10 to 12 obstacles. All will be massive, imposing in shape and appearance, almost fixed, and set with wings or extensions. They will include a double resembling a road crossing, two fly fences (with both height and spread), and, where possible, a ditch or water jump.

No obstacle will be higher than 1.20m; at least a third will be this height.

Obstacles with spread only may not exceed 3m in spread for CCI, or 3.50m for CCIO competitions.

Fly fences will not exceed a spread of 1.80m (CCI) or 2m (CCIO) at the highest point, and 2.80m (CCI) or 3m (CCIO) at the base.

Speed and distance For CCI competitions the requirement is 700–800m at a speed of 350–400m per minute. For CCIO it is 750–900m at 400m per minute.

Penalties For:
a first disobedience, 10 penalties;
knocking down an obstacle or failure at the water jump, 10 penalties;
a second disobedience in the entire event, 20 penalties;
a third disobedience in the entire event, elimination;
a fall by horse and/or rider, 30 penalties;
jumping an obstacle in the wrong order, elimination;
an error of course not rectified, elimination;
exceeding the time allowed, ¼ mark for every second or part of a second;
exceeding the time limit (twice the time allowed), elimination.

Classification Penalties at obstacles are added to those for exceeding the time allowed.

Show jumping: Fancy gate

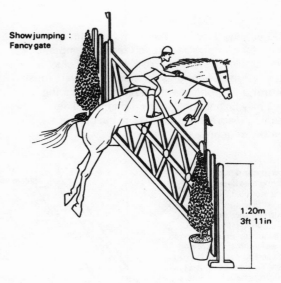

1.20m
3ft 11in

Wall and rails

Hog's back

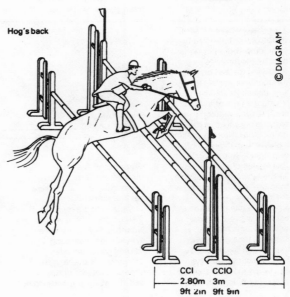

CCI	CCIO
2.80m	3m
9ft 2in	9ft 9in

© DIAGRAM

Polo

Polo is played by two teams of four players mounted on horseback. Each team attempts to score goals by striking a ball with its sticks between the opponents' goalposts. Players must control their ponies with the left hand, as the stick may be held only in the right hand. The winning team is the one to score the greater number of goals.

Diagram labels: 160yd / 146.40m · 30yd / 27.5m · 60yd / 55m · 300yd / 275m · Polo board · 11in / 28cm · 13ft / 3.96m · Ariss rail · 60yd line · 40yd mark · 30yd line · 40yd / 3.7m · 10ft / 3.05m · Goalpost · Safety zone · 8yd / 7.32m · 200yd / 183m

The ground comprises the playing area and a safety zone around it. No one other than officials and players' assistants may enter this zone during play.

The boards extend along either length of the playing area and are secured by iron pegs. They are designed to direct low balls back into play and are constructed in short sections, which may be easily replaced if damaged during a game.

The numbers 30, 40, and 60 are marked on the inside face of the boards at the appropriate lines on the ground. A mark is also made at the ends of an imaginary center line.

Where boards are not used, flags with the appropriate numbers are used to mark the ends of the lines, but they are fixed well beyond the sidelines to minimize the risk of collision.

Goalposts are of light construction, designed to break if collided with.

Officials The game is controlled by two mounted umpires, each generally responsible for one half of the field.

A referee stands off the field, and his decision is final in the event of any disagreement between the umpires.

Two goal judges stand behind each goal area and report to the umpires in cases of doubt or incidents near their goal. They signal with flags when a goal is scored. The beginning and end of each period is signaled by a bell rung by the timekeeper, who is also responsible for scorekeeping.

Team Each team consists of four players. Substitutes are only allowed to replace players who are ill or injured.

Scoring Goals are scored by striking the ball at any height between the opponents' goalposts or the imaginary vertical lines produced from them.

The right of way is one of polo's most important principles. Right of way is held by the player(s) following the ball on its exact line, or at the smallest angle to it, and taking it on the offside. It is a foul for another player to cross or pull up in the right of way, thereby making a player with the right of way check his pace.

Examples of right of way:
1) Player A hits the ball to X, follows its line, and assumes the right of way.
If player B can reach the ball at X without interfering with A's play, then B assumes the right of way and may strike the ball at B1. B must pull up if he can reach X only at the risk of fouling A. Provided he

keeps out of A's way throughout, B may then swerve and take a nearside backhander at B2.
2) Opposing players A and B share the right of way. No other player may enter it, even if he is meeting the ball on its exact line.
3) Player A is riding in the general direction of the ball, but at a slight angle to it.

He will have the right of way, provided he adjusts his course slightly in order to take the ball on his offside. After A has thus assumed the right of way, player B would not obstruct the right of way if he took the ball on his own offside at point X. If A fails to adjust his course, intending to take the ball on his nearside, he loses

the right of way by endangering B, who is approaching with the ball on his offside.
4) Player A hits the ball to X. Player B, riding to meet the ball on its exact line on his offside, is the player with the right of way. Player C, riding in at an angle, must not cross B's right of way. Player A may ride on and attempt to

take the ball on his offside, since this would not obstruct B's right of way.
5) Player A hits the ball to X and assumes the right of way. B rides for the ball, accompanied by A's partner C. It is a dangerous foul if C forces B across A's path, or causes him to pull up to avoid being sandwiched between A and C

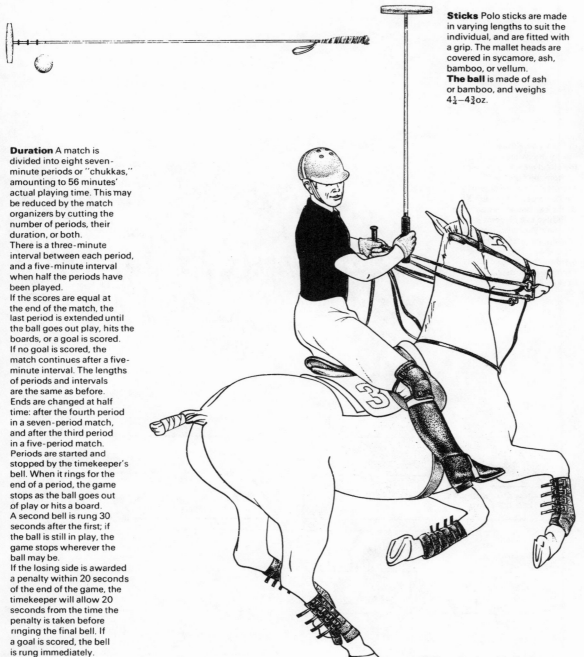

Sticks Polo sticks are made in varying lengths to suit the individual, and are fitted with a grip. The mallet heads are covered in sycamore, ash, bamboo, or vellum.
The ball is made of ash or bamboo, and weighs 4¼–4¾oz.

3¼in
8.3cm

Duration A match is divided into eight seven-minute periods or "chukkas," amounting to 56 minutes' actual playing time. This may be reduced by the match organizers by cutting the number of periods, their duration, or both.
There is a three-minute interval between each period, and a five-minute interval when half the periods have been played.
If the scores are equal at the end of the match, the last period is extended until the ball goes out play, hits the boards, or a goal is scored. If no goal is scored, the match continues after a five-minute interval. The lengths of periods and intervals are the same as before. Ends are changed at half time: after the fourth period in a seven-period match, and after the third period in a five-period match. Periods are started and stopped by the timekeeper's bell. When it rings for the end of a period, the game stops as the ball goes out of play or hits a board. A second bell is rung 30 seconds after the first; if the ball is still in play, the game stops wherever the ball may be.
If the losing side is awarded a penalty within 20 seconds of the end of the game, the timekeeper will allow 20 seconds from the time the penalty is taken before ringing the final bell. If a goal is scored, the bell is rung immediately.

Dress A polo helmet or cap with a chinstrap must be worn by all players. Polo boots and knee pads must be free of any buckles or studs that might damage another player's equipment. Sharp spurs are forbidden.
Distinguishing colors must be worn by both teams.
Ponies may be of any height. but must be calm in temperament. They must be able to see with both eyes, and blinkers or any form of noseband that restricts their vision are not allowed. Frost nails and screws on the shoes are forbidden, but a calkin (a small, spur-like projection) may be used on the hind shoes only. Rimmed shoes are permitted, but only if the rim is on the inside of the shoe. Bandages or boots must be worn on all four legs.

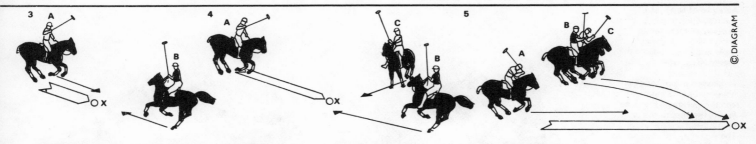

© DIAGRAM

6) A player does not gain the right of way merely by striking the ball, since another player might be following closer to the line of the ball.
7) If two players are following a ball hit by a third player, the player closer to the line of the ball has the right of way.

8) If two players are at equal angles from either side of the line of the ball, the player with the ball on his offside has the right of way.
9) Two players approaching the ball from exactly opposite directions should approach with the ball on their offsides. If a collision seems likely, the

player who actually gets the ball on his offside has the right of way.
10) If the line of the ball changes suddenly, by glancing off a player, for example, the right of way will almost inevitably change. The player who had the right of way may continue for a short distance along his original course without obstruction.

11) If a player misses a dead ball when trying to hit it back into play, the line of the ball for the purpose of defining the right of way is taken to be the same as the direction in which the player was then riding.

12) If the ball comes to a dead stop at any time, its line is considered to be the direction in which it was traveling before it stopped.

506

Starting play The opposing sides line up facing the umpire in the center of the ground, each team being on its own side of the half-way "T" mark.
The umpire bowls the ball underhand between the two ranks of players at a distance of not less than 5yd. The players must remain stationary until the ball has left the umpire's hand.
Ends are changed at half time and after every goal, unless the goal was awarded as a penalty for a dangerous or deliberate foul in an attempt to prevent a goal.
If a foul occurs after the first note of the bell in any but the last period, the game stops and the next period begins with the penalty for that foul being put into play as if there had been no interval.
If the ball hit the boards at the end of the previous period, it is treated as if it had gone over them.
Out of play The ball is out of play when:
a) it is hit over the boards or sidelines, the umpire bowls the ball in from the spot where it crossed the board or line, parallel to the back line (1);
b) it is hit over the back line by the attacking side, the defender hits the ball in from the point where it crossed the line, but not nearer than 4yd to the goalposts, boards, or sidelines (2);

c) it is hit over the back line by the defending side; the attackers take a penalty hit from the 60yd line opposite the point at which the ball crossed the line (3);
d) the ball becomes damaged or lodged in a player's clothing; the ball is bowled toward the nearer side of the ground at the point of the incident, but at least 20yd from the goalposts, boards, or sidelines (4)

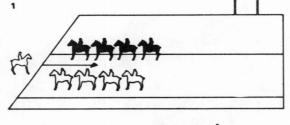
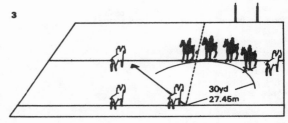
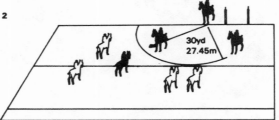
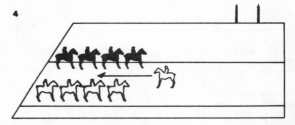

Misuse of the stick
It is forbidden to reach across or under an opponent's pony to strike the ball (1).
A player may not hit into the legs of an opponent's pony (2).
A player may only hook an opponent's stick if both he and the ball are on the same side of the opponent's pony, or in a direct line behind it. The stick may only be hooked when the opponent is about to strike, and not above shoulder height (3).
A player must not use his stick dangerously or hold it in such a way as to interfere with another player or pony.
If a player rides into the backhand stroke of an opponent in the right of way, he does so at his own risk, and without foul.

Penalty goals The umpire may award a penalty goal if he considers that a goal would have been scored but for a foul by the defending side. Ends are not changed after a penalty goal, and the umpire restarts the game by bowling the ball between the ranks of players 10yd from the offending team's goal.

Penalty hits The umpires decide on the gravity of an offense and award penalty hits at appropriate distances Where the hit results from the ball going out of play, the distances are fixed by the rules.
a) A free hit from a spot 30yd (or alternatively 40yd) from the offending team's back line, opposite the middle of the goal. The offending side must remain behind the back line until the ball has been hit, and may not stand behind the goal nor ride out between the goalposts where the hit is taken (5).

If the captain of the non-offending side wishes, the hit may be taken from the spot where the foul occurred, in which case no member of the other side may be nearer than 30yd to the ball. The players in the side taking the free hit must not be nearer the back line than the ball (6).
b) A free hit from a spot 60yd from the offending team's back line, opposite the middle of the goal. The offending team must be at least 30yd away from the ball; the players in the team taking the hit are free to.place themselves where they wish (7).

c) A free hit from the spot where the foul occurred(8). Positioning is as for (b), and the ball must be at least 4yd from the boards or sidelines. Free hits are also taken from the center spot, with positioning as for (b). Failure to carry out penalty hits correctly may result in: a penalty goal ; allowing the non-offending team members to position themselves where they wish ; retaking the hit unless a goal was scored or awarded.

If, having hit the ball over their opponents' back line, the attacking side does not allow the resulting free hit to be taken correctly, the hit is retaken from the 30yd line.
Unnecessary delay in taking a free hit may result in the umpire bowling the ball in from the same spot

5

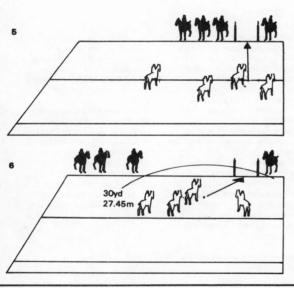

6

30yd
27.45m

7

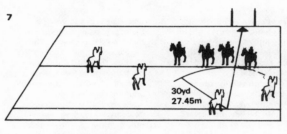

30yd
27.45m

8

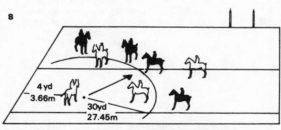

4 yd
3.66m

30yd
27.45m

"Riding off" or bumping between players riding in the same direction is permitted. Players must not:
bump at angles which may be dangerous to other players or their ponies;
strike with the head, hand, forearm, or elbow (although pushing with the upper arm is permitted);
attempt to seize another player, his equipment, or his pony;
zig-zag in front of another player when galloping, if doing so causes him to check his pace to avoid a fall;
ride across a pony's legs in an attempt to trip it;
ride at an opponent so as to intimidate him into pulling up or checking his stroke, even if no actual foul or crossing of the right of way took place.

3

©DIAGRAM

Accidents and loss of equipment The umpire stops the match if a player is injured or a pony goes lame. He will also stop the match if he considers that a pony's equipment is so damaged as to be a danger to other players and ponies.
If a player loses his helmet, the game will be stopped to allow him to recover it, but only when neither side will be favored by a stoppage. If a player falls from his pony without injury, the match will not be stopped. While dismounted, the player may not touch the ball or interfere with the game.

If a player is injured, 15 minutes are allowed for his recovery. If he is unable to continue after that interval, the game is restarted with a substitute player. Should the injury have been caused as a result of a foul by the opposing team, the injured player's captain may call on one of the opposition to retire, and the game will then continue with three players on either side.

27 <u>Sports on wheels</u>

Roller skating (speed)

There are speed roller skating events for men, women, and relay teams. Competitors race counterclockwise around an oval track. Procedures are similar to those for speed skating on ice.

Speed skates are light with a long, low wheelbase.

Starter

Timekeeper

22yd
20m

4.4yd
40m

Judges
Lapscorer

34ft 8in
10.50m

Track The width of the straight limits the number of skaters in a heat. Minimum widths are:
8ft for two skaters;
12ft for three skaters;
15ft for four skaters;
18ft for five skaters;
20ft for six skaters.
Races are always counter-clockwise around the track.

Officials At least three judges, a starter, timekeeper(s), a lap scorer, a recorder, two track stewards, and a competitors' steward.
Dress Competitors must wear numbers on their backs and left hips.
Start At the start of a race no part of a competitor's skates may be across the starting line; the tips of his skates may be on the line.
A competitor who deliberately starts before the starter's pistol or causes a false start is warned. For a third offense the skater is disqualified.

Overtaking The leading competitor has the right of way and may only be overtaken on the outside as long as he keeps to the inside of the track.
The responsibility for any obstruction or collision is with the overtaking skater unless the leading skater deliberately fouls.

Lapping A skater who has been, or is being, lapped may be ordered to give way. The judges will signal to him with a yellow flag, and the skater must then go to the outside of the track without impeding any other competitor.
A skater who has been lapped twice by the leading skater may be ordered off the track. The judges will signal with a blue flag, and the skater must then leave the track without impeding any other competitor.

Offenses A skater must not: deliberately cross the inside of the track with either skate; impede another competitor; touch another competitor with any part of his body; lose speed and so cause another competitor to slow down; improperly cross the track; conspire to produce an unfair result.
Penalties Offenses may be penalized by disqualification. A black flag is used to disqualify an offender during a race; the skater must immediately leave the track without impeding any other competitor.
A skater who is disqualified may not compete if a race is rerun.

Result The winner of an individual race is the first skater to reach the finishing line with one of his skates.
RELAY RACES Every team member must take part in a race.
One skater from each team skates until a teammate relieves him. Takeovers are by touch and are permitted at any point in the race except during the last two laps.
Substitutes are allowed in cases of injury or damage to a skate, but they must remain in the team for the rest of the competition.

Roller derby

Roller derby is a speed roller skating sport for teams of men and women. Competitors race around the track and gain points by lapping opponents. By contrast with conventional speed skating events, a good deal of body contact is permitted between competitors.

The track is oval, and usually 100-200ft around. The skating surface is usually hardwood coated with a thin veneer of plastic.
Teams Each team includes five men and five women.
Duration The men skate for a period of 12 minutes, and then the women skate for a similar length of time.

Procedure All the men skate together and then all the women. Competitors are not required to keep in lane. Tripping is prohibited, but pushing and jostling are both allowed.
Scoring Points are accumulated by lapping opponents.

Roller skating (artistic)

Skates for artistic events have a higher boot and larger wheels than the skates used for speed skating.

As in ice skating, there are international, national, and club championships in figure, pair, and dance skating. Figure events include compulsory figures and free skating, and dance events comprise compulsory dances and a program of free dancing.

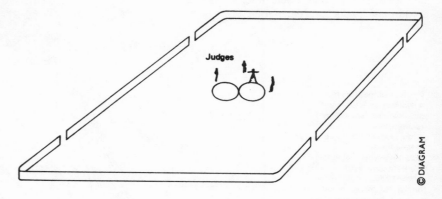

Judges

© DIAGRAM

Rink The skating surface is usually asphalt, asbestos, cement, or hardwood.

Dress Freedom of movement is a major requirement. Costumes are similar to those used for ice skating.

FIGURE SKATING

Events for single skaters comprise compulsory figures and free skating.

Compulsory figures for roller skating include circles, loops, rockers, counters, threes, and brackets.

All figures are performed on circles marked on the rink surface.

Each figure must be repeated three times consecutively. Skaters must start, at rest, from the point where the circles intersect.

Every stroke must be made with the four wheels, never with the toe-stop.

No impetus is allowed from the foot that is about to become the tracing foot.

Circles must be traced continuously except for a brief interruption to change the tracing foot.

Turns must be skated with a clean edge, without skids, scrapes, noise, or lifting of the wheels.

Execution The head should be upright, relaxed, and held naturally.

The body should be upright, but not stiff nor bent at the hips.

The arms should be held gracefully.

The hands should not be carried higher than the waist; the palms should be parallel to the floor and the fingers neither extended nor clenched.

The tracing leg should be flexible and slightly bent at the knee.

The free leg should also be slightly bent at the knee.

The free foot should not be too near the tracing foot and should be carried slightly above the rink surface with the toe pointing downward and outward.

All exaggerated positions should be avoided.

A consistent speed, rhythm, and even flow should be maintained; jerky, abrupt, and angular movements should be avoided.

Skaters may make only moderate use of their arms and free leg during the execution of compulsory figures.

Free skating Skaters perform unspecified movements to music of their own choice.

The length of program varies with the competition; competitors may finish up to 5 seconds before or after the time limit.

Falls A fall does not eliminate a skater from the competition.

A skater who falls through no fault of his own may be allowed to restart, possibly after an interval.

A skater who falls through his own fault will have his marks adjusted accordingly. He must continue from where he fell.

Scoring The scale of marks for each performance is from 1 to 6, with intermediate decimal places.

Compulsory figures Each judge gives a mark for each figure. Taken into consideration are:

good edge running, without flats or sub-curves;

superimposition;

clear turns made in the correct position;

maintenance of a consistent speed;

style, carriage, and movement;

the size of the figure.

Free skating Each judge awards two marks: one for the content of the program (difficulty and variety); the other for the manner of the performance.

Result A competition is won by the skater placed first by the majority of judges. Second and third places are similarly decided. Subsequent places are decided by the lowest totals of judges' placings.

PAIR SKATING

The two partners must give the impression of unison, though they do not have to perform all the same movements and may separate occasionally. They are always judged as a pair, never as individuals.

DANCE SKATING

Events comprise two, three, or four compulsory dances, followed by a program of free dancing to music of the competitors' own choice.

Compulsory dances One of the official groups of dances is chosen by the organizers before the competition begins.

Execution Basic head, body, and leg positions are the same as for figure skating.

Further requirements for dance skating are that competitors should:

raise and lower their bodies only by bending their tracing knees;

execute the dance with ease, avoiding all angular and stiff movements;

skate close together and execute all movements in unison;

keep footwork neat and make all steps accurately;

keep edges and turns smooth and clean;

pay careful attention to the time and rhythm of the music, coordinate all movements with the music, and express the music's character in the dancing.

Free dancing consists of a non-repetitive performance of novel movements, which can include variations of known dances or parts of dances, combined into a program with originality of design and arrangement.

All recognized movements are permissible, as are other movements appropriate to the rhythm, music, and character of the dance.

Unnecessary feats of strength or skating skill are counted against the dancers.

The separation of partners must not exceed the time needed to change positions.

Spins must not exceed 1½ revolutions.

Jumps and lifts where the man's hands are higher than waist level are not permitted. Toe-stops may be used in the interpretation of the music, but their use must be strictly limited.

Scoring Each compulsory dance is marked from 0 to 6, to one decimal point.

Two marks from 0 to 6 are awarded for the free dancing: the first for the contents of the program based on its harmonious composition, conformity with the music, variety, originality, beauty, and difficulty; the other for the manner of the performance based on the dancers' sureness, timing, rhythm, style, and carriage.

Result Marks for compulsory dances and for free dancing are given equal importance in the final result.

Cycle racing

Cycle racing is broadly divided into track and road racing. Both categories include a variety of different events at national and international level. Indoor events include special track races and stationary "races" on sets of rollers.

Dress Competitors must wear a jersey or undershirt with sleeves, and dark-colored racing shorts. Club members should wear club colors except in time trials.
A padded crash hat must be worn for track events.
Shoes should fit perfectly. Socks and gloves or mitts are optional, but are generally worn.

Machines For road racing any kind of cycle is allowed, provided it is propelled only by human force, has no streamlining, and does not exceed specified dimensions. For track racing free-wheel, gears, brakes, and wing-nuts are prohibited.
Tandems and multicycles must conform to general regulations.

Equipment For track racing, a cycle must consist only of frame, wheels, chainset, pedals with toeclips and straps, saddle, and handlebars. For road racing, a cycle must have brakes and, if ridden at night, lights and reflectors. For long rides a pump, a spare tube, and one or two feeding bottles mounted in a "cage" at the front are carried.

Competitors must be licensed by their clubs in accordance with national regulations.

Doping Any competitor found to be taking dope, ie any substance likely to affect his performance, is liable to disqualification.
A rider is barred from competing if he is taking drugs for medical reasons, but is not liable to disqualification.

Officials include a chief judge with one or more assistants, timekeepers, machine examiners, lap scorers, and starters if needed. A chief commissaire (steward) and at least one assistant commissaire are necessary at a road meeting.
Pacing marshals may be needed at a track meeting. At a roller event a gear examiner is needed.

Starts are at the drop of a flag, and may be made either standing or rolling.
Riders may be given a short untimed distance in which to settle down or clear a built-up area.

Finishes are determined by crossing a finishing line, at which point the riders are timed. On circuit races the riders may be timed for each circuit.

Dismounting A rider who has dismounted may complete the course carrying, dragging, or wheeling his machine, but must not receive assistance.

Refreshments Competitors may accept food and drink that are handed up to them.

Sanctions against offenders may include, in order of severity, a warning, a reprimand, a fine, relegation, disqualification, suspension, and withdrawal of licence. Amateurs may not be fined.

Claims and disputes over the results of races are settled at road meetings by the commissaires.
At track and roller meetings the chief judge acts as the chief official and deals with claims and disputes.

ROAD RACES

Road races must be held in conformity with the law of the country in which they are run, and with regard to local traffic regulations.
Pushing and hampering are banned, and riders must not help each other or accept assistance.
Glass containers, eg for drinks, are not allowed.

Stage races Competitors race over a number of stages. The best known is the Tour de France, in which competitors cover 3400km in 24 one-day stages.

Circuit races (criteriums) consist of several laps over a "ring" of roads. Lengths range from 1-80km.

Control points must be set up on long events.
Refreshments are generally provided at control points by the race organizers.

Pacing, in which one rider acts as pacemaker for another, is allowed only among members of the same team who are competing as such.

Illegal riding includes: pushing another rider in time trials or individual races (1); crossing in front of another rider to prevent him from moving on (2); fraudulent behavior such as attempting to take another's place.

1

2

1

2

Box (1) A tactic by which a rider rides just behind and to one side of another and thus prevents a third rider from overtaking without swinging right out.

Breakaway (2) Getting clear of the field.

Course des primes A race designed to give riders eliminated early from important events another chance of winning a prize.
Demi-fond A middle-distance motor-paced track event.
Domestique A team rider in road racing whose job is to help his leader win.
King of the mountains The title given to the winner of most points in hill climbs.
Lanterne rouge ("red lantern") A booby prize for the last man in a stage race.
Maillot jaune ("yellow jersey") Worn by the current leader in the Tour de France and some other major events.
Musette A sachel in which food and drink are handed up to a rider.

Omnium A track event comprised of races of several kinds.
Peloton The main bunch of riders in a road event.
Repêchage Another kind of "second-chance" race to allow additional riders to qualify for the next round of a progressive race.
Sag wagon The following vehicle in road events, used to pick up riders who have dropped out.
Stayer A track rider in a motor-paced race.

TRACK RACES
There are many different kinds of races held on tracks and on closed circuits (roads that are closed to the public). Tracks are usually hard-surfaced, but may be on grass.
Track markings include lines to mark handicap starts, finishing lines, and starting points for various standard distances.
The safety line is a line of distinctive color 1m from the inside edge of the track. No overtaking is allowed inside this line if the rider ahead is on or inside the line.
Sprints are races between two or three riders, over one or perhaps more laps of the track. Timing is over the last 200m only, the earlier part of the race being devoted to maneuvering for position.
Handicap races are over short distances, generally not more than 800m. At the start the riders are held upright and given a push-off.
Individual pursuit Two riders start on opposite sides of the track and race over the following distances: 3000m (women); 4000m (men's world championship); 5000m (professional). If one rider does not catch the other, the rider with the faster time wins.

Team pursuit is similar to an individual pursuit, but with two teams of four. Victory is decided on the times of the first three riders of each team.
Australian pursuit is a team pursuit with teams of up to eight riders. The race may be over a set number of laps or for a stated time.
Italian pursuit is between two or more teams of up to five riders. One rider from each team drops out at the end of each lap, and the finishing time of the last riders of each team decides the race.
Point-to-point A track event in which points are awarded for each lap or group of laps. The winner of the most points is the overall winner, even if he never finishes first.
Scratch races are events in which all competitors start together, but the term generally means long-distance races over such distances as 8km and 16km. Variants include: devil-take-the-hindmost, in which the last rider over the line in every lap is eliminated; and "unknown distance," in which riders do not know the total distance they have to ride until a bell sounds for the start of the last lap.
Madison racing is a form of team racing in which a pair of riders races, one on the track and one resting. The relays are effected by the outgoing rider pushing his partner.

Human pacing may be allowed in track events. Only one pacer may be on the track for each competitor, except during a changeover. Pacers must wear normal racing dress with crash helmets.
Men may pace women.
Motor pacing Track events of over 10km may be motor paced – with each rider preceded by a motorcyclist who sets the pace and affords some shelter from the wind. The pacer must be a licensed rider, and men may pace women.
Motorcycles used in motor pacing must be between 500cc and 1000cc.
Each machine must carry a roller 600mm wide and up to 35mm in diameter, supported on a frame projecting behind the rear wheels. The axis of the roller must be 350mm above the ground. The purpose of the roller is to prevent the following rider from getting too close to the pacer.
Motor cyclists acting as pacers may wear extra clothing to compensate for differences of physique, but may not wear loose padding. Loose or flapping garments that might give an unfair advantage as windbreaks for the stayer are not allowed.

1

2

Cyclo-cross (1) events take place in winter over open country. A course should include some woodland and fields, as well as paths and roads. It should not include hazards such as flights of steps. The maximum recommended distance is 24km. If a circuit is used, each lap should be at least 3km.
Hill climbs are for men only and generally do not exceed 5km. They may be much shorter, depending on the gradient of the hill.
Time trials Competitors set off at 1-minute intervals and race against the clock to cover a set distance in the least possible time. Each competitor is on his own, even in team events.
Distances for time trials are set by the organizers.
Short distances are up to 50km;
middle distances are up to 160km for men, 80km for women;
long distances are up to 160km and 12 hours for women, and 12 hours and 24 hours for men.

Roller races (2) These "stationary" races take place on sets of three rollers, two close together to support the rear wheel and the third spaced out to support the front wheel. The rollers are geared to dials that indicate the "distance" covered by the rider.
In general there can be up to four competitors. Each rider may be supported by an attendant. In some races the attendants leave go when the riders have "travelled" 200m. The end of an event is signaled by an audible signal, such as a pistol shot. A bell is rung for the last lap.
Gears for roller races are restricted to give all competitors a fair chance. Crank lengths are also controlled, and gears and cranks are inspected before each event.

© DIAGRAM

Motorcycle racing

There are many types of competition for motorcycles, with a wide variety of machines competing on various types of course. Road racing – on specially built circuits or sometimes on ordinary roads – has the largest following at international level. Races are held for several classes of motorcycle, and may be of any length.

The track should have a non-skid surface if possible. Yellow or white lines should be painted along the edges of the track if there is danger of the rider leaving the course. If the track passes under a bridge or between two walls it must be widened by at least 6ft.
Warning signs must be placed in advance of any dangerous points on the course.
The start line must be on a part of the track that is straight for at least 250yd and 33ft wide.

Dress Riders must wear protective leathers or an approved substitute. Clothing must form a complete covering, consisting of jacket, breeches, knee-length boots, and gloves. The boots must not have metal studs. In the past a rider's "leathers" were usually black, but recently colored leathers have become popular.
Helmets (1) must conform to strict safety standards and be in sound condition. The all-enveloping full-face style helmet is now the most popular. If an open-face type helmet is used, goggles or visors of a non-splintering material must be worn.
Classes The usual classes are for motorcycles with an engine capacity of:
50cc
125cc
250cc
350cc
500cc
750cc
Unlimited (751cc+)
Engines (2) Except for Production Motorcycle classes and US dirt track racing, there is no limit on engine design other than capacity limit.

Brakes (3) must be fitted, one on each wheel. They must be capable of controlling the machine independently.
Tires (4) must be fitted to a rim of at least 16in diameter. There are no restrictions on the type of tire, but it must conform to specifications of size published for each class of machine.
Number plates (5) must be fitted to both sides of the machine and on the front. They may be made of a rigid material or painted on the streamlining. In many countries different colors are used to indicate the various capacity classes.
Handlebars (6) must be not less than 20in in width. Stops must be fitted to ensure a minimum clearance of $1\frac{1}{4}$in between the handlebars and the tank to avoid trapping the rider's hand when on full lock. If streamlining is fitted, there must be at least 2in clearance between it and any part of the handlebar in whatever position.
Clutch and brake levers (7) must have an integral ball-end of at least $\frac{3}{8}$in diameter.

The seat (8) may not be any higher than $35\frac{1}{2}$in above the track surface when the machine is not loaded.
Footrests (9) must be fixed. Riders must keep their feet on the rests and will be excluded for not doing so.
A guard (10) must be fitted to prevent the drive chain or shaft being accidentally touched.
The exhaust pipe (11) must not project behind the machine or its bodywork. Exhaust gases must not foul the tire or brakes, or raise dust so as to inconvenience a following rider. Waste or surplus oil must not be discharged onto the track.
Fuel must be of a standard grade as supplied from normal commercial pumps.
Oil drain plugs must be tightly locked in position.
Streamlining is allowed subject to certain conditions. The front wheel, with the exception of the tire, must be clearly visible from both sides. Streamlining must not project forward of a line drawn vertically through the front wheel spindle, or to the rear of a similar line drawn through the rear spindle.

The rim of the wheel at the rear must be clearly visible to the rear of this line.
Normal mudguards are not considered to be streamlining, but neither they nor any part of the machine may project behind a line drawn vertically through the rearmost part of the rim of the rear wheel.
The rider, with the exception of his forearms, must be clearly visible from both sides and above.
Transparent material may not be used to avoid any of the rules governing streamlining.
Scrutineering Before the start of a race all machines will be carefully scrutineered to ensure that they conform to the required legal and safety standards.
A machine may be barred from racing if it is found to be defective during scrutineering.
The organizers may also ask for a machine to be stripped and scrutineered after a race.
Types of meeting
International meetings are held under the jurisdiction of the FIM (Fédération Internationale Motocycliste).

National, regional, and local organizations hold their own domestic meetings, governed by rules and class specifications that may differ slightly from those issued by the FIM.
Officials Stewards, up to five in number, are responsible for supervising a meeting. It is their duty to adjudicate any protests that might arise.
The clerk of the course is responsible for the actual meeting and organizes the events, and supervises the entries, starters, judges, timekeepers, and scrutineers.
Flag signals Riders must respond to all flag signals. Flags should measure 2ft 6in by 2ft.
Officially recognized flag signals are:
national flag, start;
checkered flag, finish;
black flag with rider's number, that rider to stop;
white flag, ambulance or other vehicle on the course;
yellow flag, danger;
green flag, course clear;
blue flag, rider behind;
blue flag waved, rider behind wishes to overtake;
red with vertical yellow stripes, oil on the course.

Sidecar combinations consist of a motorcycle and sidecar. The sidecar may be attached to either side.

Classes Sidecar racing events are usually divided into 500cc and 750cc classes.

Sidecar starts (1) In international sidecar racing events, starts are made with the engine running.

The wheels of the motorcycle must be at least 16in in diameter, measured over the outside of the tire.

The engine must not protrude beyond a longitudinal line drawn midway between the tracks formed by the rear wheel of the motorcycle and the sidecar wheel.

The sidecar wheel must be at least 10in in diameter. Wheels may be arranged to give two or three tracks. The overall width of the track must not be less than 2ft 6in, or more than 4ft, and only the rear motorcycle wheel may be driven.

Streamlining or coachwork is optional, but if fitted must have a ground clearance of at least 4in but not more than 1ft. The bodywork may not be more than 4ft above ground.

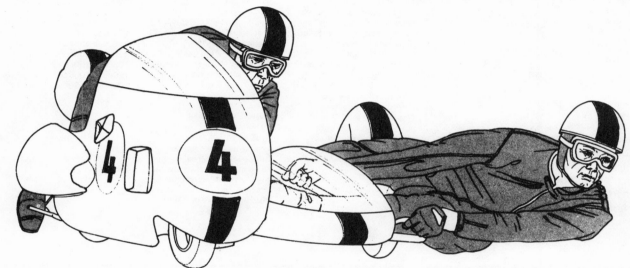

©DIAGRAM

Starters The maximum number of riders in a solo machine race is determined on the basis of one rider for every 40in of the course's width at its narrowest point, multiplied by one for every ⅝ mile of the course's length, or half that for sidecar races.

Starting positions may be arranged by means of a grid. Positions may be allocated by the organizers of the meeting according to the rider's known ability or, in the case of a final preceded by heats, according to the rider's total time for the respective heats. The position at the front of the grid on the inside of the track is given to the fastest rider. This is called pole position.

The start is signaled by the lowering of a flag.

Bump start (2) In races for solo machines the riders begin to push their machines when the flag drops and jump on as the engine fires.

Clutch start (3) The riders line up on the grid with their motors already running. Shortly before the flag drops, first gear is engaged and the machine is held on the clutch. As the flag drops, the clutch is released and the machine rapidly accelerated.

Le Mans start (4) The rider is required to run to his machine parked on the opposite side of the track, mount, and then kick-start his engine before accelerating away.

Rolling start (5) Riders are started while on the move. They line up together on the grid and then set off for a warm-up lap. As they pass the start line at the completion of the warm-up lap the flag is dropped and the race is under way.

A false start occurs when a rider moves forward from his position before the starting signal is given, even though, as in a grid start, he may not cross the actual start line. A 1-minute penalty is usually added to the offending rider's total time for the race.

Riding conduct The clerk of the course will immediately exclude any rider who is, in his opinion, guilty of riding in a foul, unfair, or dangerous manner.

The offending rider is shown the black flag and a black disc with his number; he must then leave the track as soon as possible.

The finish is signaled by the waving of the checkered flag as the leading rider completes his last lap. All riders are flagged off the track at the finish line, even though they may not have completed the required number of laps.

SPECIAL RULES

Among the classes with differing rules are the Formula 750 class, the Production Motorcycle class, and classes for scooters and mopeds.

Formula 750 class In order to qualify, a machine must be of a type that is in production and on sale to the general public. The engine capacity must be between 251cc and 750cc.

Production Motorcycle class

The rules of PR racing, as it has become known, vary from country to country, but generally machines should keep to standard, and skill and inexpensive maintenance are emphasized.

Scooters and mopeds may compete in class races of their own. Scooter dimensions must conform with the regulations.

The pedals of a moped must be capable of propelling the machine and starting the engine, but may be removed in certain road races.

Drag racing

Motorcycle drag racing is similar to drag car racing. Riders on specially prepared machines race in pairs over a straight 440yd track. A competition proceeds by a process of elimination – with the faster rider in each pair going into the next round.

Track The drag racing track, or "strip," is 440yd long and at least 50ft wide. There must be a braking area at least 800yd long at the end of the track.

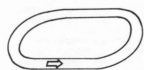

Burn-out (1) Competitors preheat and clean out their tires before the race.
Start The "Christmas tree" light system is used (as described under drag car racing).
Race procedure is generally the same as for drag car racing.

Classes There are two main divisions – street solo and competition solo. Both are further divided into six classes:
A (1301–2000cc)
B (1001–1300cc)
C (751–1000cc)
D (501–750cc)
E (351–500cc)
F (240–350cc)

Sprint

Sprints are races from point to point in a straight line on an approximately level, metaled surface. They are less than one mile in length, and are held between two or more competitors or individually against time. There are races for solo machines and for sidecar combinations.

Dress Protective clothing must be worn during practice and racing. It consists of jacket, breeches, knee-length boots, gloves, and an approved helmet.
Scrutineering All machines must be presented to the scrutineer before a meeting in order to ensure that they conform to regulations.
The start is made from a stationary position, with the engine running and the foremost part of the motorcycle 4in behind the start line.

Streamlining The only restriction on streamlining is that there must be a clearance of at least 2in between the streamlining and the extremities of the handlebars.
Throttle All machines must have a self-closing throttle.
Fuel There is usually no restriction on the type of fuel used.
Superchargers are permitted for sprint racing.
Brakes Solo machines require one brake operating independently on each wheel.
Tires may be of any type, but must have a cross-section not less than 2in.
Mudguards are optional.

Classes For solo machines the classes are:
up to 125cc;
125cc to 250cc;
250cc to 350cc;
350cc to 500cc;
500cc to 750cc;
750cc to 1000cc;
1000cc to 1300cc.

Speedway

Speedway racing is a highly specialized form of motorcycle sport. Riders on special speedway machines race around an ash or shale surfaced oval track. A special riding technique is needed as the machines have no brakes and riders are forced to broadside their machines through the bends at speeds of up to 70mph.

The track Speedway tracks are oval, usually with a lap length of 350yd. They are usually loosely surfaced with either ash or shale.

Races are usually over four laps. They are always ridden in a counterclockwise direction.

Speedway championships in order of priority are:
the individual speedway championship of the world;
the team speedway championship of the world;
the pairs speedway championship of the world;
approved international test matches;
national speedway championships;
any other approved international fixtures;
league fixtures;
any other speedway fixtures.
Championship meetings consist of 20 races, with four competitors in each race. Meetings are organized so that each competitor rides in five races and competes against each of the other competitors during the course of the meeting.

Scoring is 3 points for first place, 2 points for second, and 1 point for third.
Competitors Teams consist of four riders plus a reserve.
The start is made from a stationary position, with the engine running and the foremost part of the motorcycle right up to the starting tape or gate. A ballot is held beforehand to determine starting grid positions. Any rider who puts a wheel outside his grid before the start will be excluded.

Ice racing

Ice racing is similar to speedway. There are both individual and team events and the riders race around an ice track. Motorcycles have steel spurs attached to their rear wheels to grip the ice surface. Events are divided into heats, and points are awarded for the first three places in each heat.

The track is 300–400m in circumference. The minimum width for three drivers is 9m and for four drivers 12m. The maximum width on bends is 18m. The track must be surrounded by a snow safety wall at least 1.10m high.
Pits must be at least 40sq m in area and be equipped with heating.

Meetings International ice race meetings are normally open to 16 drivers and consists of 20 heats. There are individual and team competitions. Points are normally awarded to the first three riders in a heat.

Teams normally have seven or eight drivers. Each team is distinguished by its colors.
Starting positions are determined by ballot.

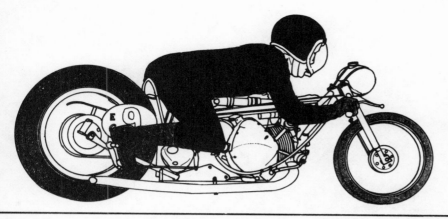

Street solo Normal road going bikes, but with any motorcycle-type engine and any modifications. The frame must be of the original type. Any gearbox may be fitted.

Competition solo The frame may be altered. Any engine or engines may be used. The engine can run on any fuel except hydrazine.

Sidecar combinations All the rules for solo machines apply to sidecar events. Other rules also apply.
Classes are usually:
up to 500cc;
500cc to 1300cc.

Wheels The three road wheels may be arranged to give either two or three tracks.
One of the wheels may be replaced by two wheels provided the distance between the vertical center lines does not exceed 8in.
Engine position is optional.
Passenger protection The passenger must always be protected from the road wheels and from the primary and final drive.
Ballast may be carried in addition to or in place of a passenger. If a passenger is replaced by ballast, it must weigh not less than 132lb and must be securely fixed.

©DIAGRAM

Machines Specialized motorcycles of not more than 500cc. They consist of little more than a simple frame, an engine (usually single-cylindered), two wheels, and a seat.
Brakes are prohibited.
Dress Team members wear distinguishing colors. Competitors in individual competitions wear numbers. Padded body protection is worn under the clothing.
1 approved helmet
2 goggles or visor
3 facemask
4 gloves
5 team uniform
6 steel-shod boots

Machines The referee will disqualify any motorcycle that he considers to be dangerous.
Brakes are prohibited as in speedway racing.
Rear tires have non-slipping steel spurs (**7**), which must not exceed 32mm in length.

Moto cross (scrambles)

Moto cross, or scrambles racing as it is also known, takes place on cross-country courses without prepared surfaces. Events are generally for solo motorcycles, although sidecar races are popular in Europe.

Dress Protective clothing must be of the approved type and consist of breeches, gloves, knee-length boots, and long-sleeved jersey. Helmets are compulsory and must be in a sound condition.

The course may be of any length and generally includes steep hills, extremely rough ground, and water hazards. Most courses are between one and three miles in length. Races can be held over a set distance, for example five laps, or a set time, for example 20 minutes.

The starting stretch must be long enough for safety.

The course should be clearly marked with flags and other indicators as to its width and direction of travel. It is forbidden to ride in the opposite direction to the race.

Starters The maximum number of riders in a race for solo machines is determined on the basis of one rider for every 3ft 3in of width of the course at the start line. Half that number is allowed for sidecar races.

The start is signaled by the lowering of a flag or by a signal light.

A speedway starting gate may also be used.

The start is made with the engines running.

A false start is signaled by an official stationed at least 200yd from the start line. This official will wave a red flag on a prearranged signal from the starter. The riders must stop at once and return to the start line.

Leaving the course If a rider leaves the course, he must return to it at the point at which he left it.

If a rider decides to retire, he must remove himself and his machine from the course as soon as possible.

Conduct Riders are prohibited from dangerous or unfair conduct in general, and from cutting across other riders in particular.

A rider who is about to be overtaken must not knowingly impede the progress of the overtaking rider.

The finish is signaled by the waving of the checkered flag as the first rider crosses the finish line.

Fuel must be of standard grade as supplied from normal commercial pumps.

Solo machines Events are usually for only three classes:
125cc, 250cc, and 500cc.

Handlebars (1) must be rounded or otherwise protected.

Clutch and brake levers (2) must have an integral ball-end at least ¾in in diameter.

The throttle (3) must be self-closing.

The engine (4) of any machine may be examined after the race to check conformity to class regulations.

The gearbox (5) is modified and strengthened.

A chain guard (6) must be fitted to the primary chain.

Exhaust (7) No exhaust pipe must project behind the machine.

Suspension (8) is modified to give extra strength.

Tires (9) Special knobby tires are used to improve traction. They may be of any type allowed in the regulations. Chains and non-skid devices are not permitted.

Mudguards (10) are compulsory.

Sidecars All the rules for solo machines apply to sidecar events. Other rules also apply.

The wheels of a scrambles combination must be at least 16in in diameter. They may be arranged to give two or three tracks. The distance between the tracks must be at least 32in.

The single sidecar wheel may be replaced by two wheels, provided that the distance between their tire centers does not exceed 8in at their closest point.

Passenger protection Adequate provision must be made to protect the passenger from the road wheels and from any other driven parts.

Trials

In trials riding the emphasis is on riding skill rather than speed. Trials are held in stages, partly on surfaced roads and partly on extremely rough ground. Competitors are started at intervals and the one who incurs fewest penalty points is the winner. There are events for solo machines and for sidecar combinations.

The course Trials are held partly on surfaced roads and partly on extremely rough ground.
The onus of following the marked course rests entirely with the rider.
A rider who leaves the course must rejoin it at the same point.
Penalties A rider is penalized if:
he dismounts;
he touches the ground with any part of his body;
he or his machine receives any outside assistance;
his machine ceases to move in a forward direction;
any part of his machine crosses an artificial boundary;
his machine travels outside any boundary marker;
he breaks or removes a tape or support.

Sidecar penalties are the same as for solo trials events, together with penalties incurred if the passenger touches the ground or receives outside assistance in maintaining his balance.
Trials machines are lightweight motorcycles designed to overcome the toughest terrain. They must comply with all the legal requirements for use on public roads.
Clutch and brake levers must have an integral ball-end of at least ¾in diameter.
Tires must be of a type approved by the governing body. It is forbidden to cut the treads or to fit chains or spikes.
Number plates must be fitted, one at the front, one at the rear.

Lights must be a permanent fitting and the use of torches or flashlights is forbidden.

Grasstrack racing

Grasstrack racing varies considerably from center to center. Some grasstrack meetings are simply speedways on grass, with riders broadsiding on speedway machines. Others have a variant of road racing, with machines that would not look out of place on a short road circuit.

©DIAGRAM

Courses Grass track courses are laid out in fields. They may be plain ovals or twisting "semi-road" tracks. The usual length is ½–1 mile.
Conduct The clerk of the course will exclude any rider who, in his opinion, is guilty of foul, unfair, or dangerous driving.
Fuel There are no restrictions on fuel types.
Machines vary with the type of track. Speedway machines are used on some tracks, "specials" suitable for short road races on others. There are events for solo machines and for sidecar combinations.
Throttle All machines must be fitted with a self-closing throttle.

Brakes Solo machines must have a brake on each wheel. Three-wheelers must be equipped with at least two brakes operating independently on different wheels.
Tires There are no restrictions on the type of tire, but chains and other non-skid devices are prohibited.

Chain guards Adequate chain guards must be fitted to protect the chain from fouling.

Sidecars must be rigidly fixed to the left-hand side of the motorcycle.
Passenger protection must be provided on three-wheelers from the rear wheel, the primary and final drive, and from the sidecar wheels.

Wheels may be arranged to give three tracks, each at least 16in in diameter measured over the outside of the tire. One of the wheels may be replaced by two wheels, provided that the distance between the vertical center lines of the two wheels does not exceed 8in.

Motor racing

Circuit racing

Cars are raced in many ways, but the best-known is circuit racing around specially prepared tracks. Single-seater racing cars, sports cars, production sedans, "stock" cars, and veterans all have their own circuit events. Races may run for a set number of laps or last for a specified time.

Circuits vary from banked speedways, lapped in under a minute, to 14-mile circuits with 30mph hairpin bends. All must comply with strict safety regulations, providing for marshals' posts, fire equipment, and safety barriers.
Officials of the appropriate governing body inspect circuits before awarding a racing license, and lay down the maximum number of cars allowed to start in a race.
Under FIA (Fédération Internationale de l'Automobile) regulations, tracks must be at least 30ft wide, with starting grid space of at least 2m by 8m for each car.

Vehicles All cars must:
have not more than four road wheels;
be of sound construction and mechanical condition;
have a full diameter steering wheel;
have a protective bulkhead between engine and driver's compartment;
have a complete floor;
have all doors and hinged and detachable parts securely fastened;
be fitted with sprung suspension between the wheels and the chassis.
Other requirements are listed under the various formulae.
Every car is checked before a race by official scrutineers to ensure that it complies with regulations.

Officials at a race meeting include: clerk of the course; secretary of the meeting; stewards; timekeepers; scrutineers and assistants; pit observers; road observers; flag marshals; finishing judges; handicappers; and starters.
Competitors must have a competition license.
Dress Drivers must wear:
an approved crash helmet, properly fastened;
goggles or visors (unless the car has a full-width windshield);
protective clothing covering arms, legs, and torso.
Practice Before a race, cars are tested on the circuit to make them as competitive as possible.
Each lap is officially timed to determine the cars' starting positions.

Starting All cars start together; their positions on the starting grid are determined by their performance in practice. The fastest are placed at the front, with the fastest car in pole position (the position in the front row that will give the driver most advantage going into the first corner).
The race is started when the starter lowers the flag.
Some races use a rolling start. A pace car leads the field, in their grid order, around one lap. It then drives off the circuit and the race begins. A car moving off before the flag incurs a time penalty.
Duration Circuit races last for a set number of laps or length of time (eg the Le Mans 24-hour race).
Formula One races (which are over a set number of laps) are arranged to give either 2 hours or 200 miles racing, whichever is the shorter.

Flags are used during races to give instructions to drivers. Internationally recognized signals include:
blue, motionless: another car following;
blue, waved: another car trying to overtake;
yellow: danger;
yellow with red stripes: slippery surface;
white: official non-racing vehicle on course;
red: stop race;
black: car indicated to stop.
The race Although drivers attempt to improve their race position, they are not allowed to drive dangerously and must reduce speed or stop if ordered to do so.
They may receive advice and mechanical assistance.
A car may be ordered to withdraw if it becomes unfit to race.
Result The winning car is the one that completes the distance first or is leading when the set racing time ends.

Single-seater racing

Helmets All motor racing competitors must wear helmets of an approved design.

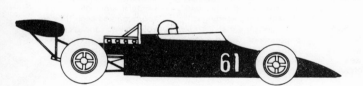

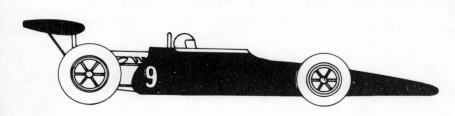

International Formula One
Up to 3000cc unsupercharged or 1500cc supercharged. These cars compete for the World Drivers' Championship and the World Constructors' Championship. Specifications govern bodywork and equipment. Tuning of the engine (other than supercharging) is unlimited. Maximum of 12 cylinders.

International Formula Two Up to 2000cc, with engines derived from production engines.

International Formula Three Up to 2000cc with engines derived from 4-cylinder production engines. All cars are fitted with an air restrictor over the induction system, limiting their power and speed.

Formula Ford Also known as Formula F, this uses production 1600GT Cortina engines, with only minimum modifications allowed (such as removing the air-cleaner and changing carburetor jets). Tires must be of standard road type, on 5½in wide wheels.

Formula 5000 Up to 5000cc. Engines must be of mass-production type with standard cylinder blocks and heads. Only engines with a single camshaft are eligible. Formerly known as Formula A in the USA.

Group 9 USAC Indianapolis type cars Up to 2999cc supercharged or 4490cc unsupercharged. Otherwise unrestricted.

Formula B A US formula for single-seater cars between 1100 and 1600cc, based on production engines. Similar to International Formula Two, but with tighter restrictions (eg no fuel injection). Raced in UK as Formula Atlantic.
Formula C US formula for 1100cc single-seaters.
Formula Sudam 1600, 1800 and 2000cc class, based on production cars with engines, chassis, and coachwork made or at least assembled in South America.
Formula Vee US and European formula similar to Formula Ford, but using Volkswagen 1300cc engines. No more than a specified amount of money may be spent on tuning.
Formula Super Vee As Vee, but using 1600cc Volkswagen engines that may be highly tuned.
Formula Libre This is an unrestricted formula. The organizers of the race establish their own classes and handicap certain cars if necessary.

© DIAGRAM

Sedan and sports car racing

In addition to single-seater formulae, circuit racing has many classes for sedan and sports cars.

FIA Group 5 Long distance open sports cars with two-seater bodywork. There is scope for all engine sizes, with cylinder capacity classes from below 500cc to over 5000cc. The World Sports Car Championship is for cars up to 3000cc. There is also a championship for 2000cc cars.

Sports cars Apart from the internationally regulated Group 5 for long distance cars, sports car racing is largely run on a national or even club basis, and recognized categories vary greatly from country to country. In general terms, there are opportunities for:
unmodified production cars;
modified production cars;
regulated hybrids built up from production engines and/or chassis;
cars built up from the kits and plans of small-scale manufacturers;
unregulated specials.
Cutting across these are engine-capacity categories, and races at local level often throw together a wide assortment of sports and even sedan cars racing together in classes based on engine size.

US sedan racing For American production sedan cars, with only limited modifications allowed. Cars are grouped into classes based on estimates of their capabilities.

US production car racing For production cars of mainly foreign origin, grouped into eight classes according to estimated potential performance. Group A, the highest, includes Corvette Stingray, Porsche 904, and Shelby Cobra 247.

Vintage racing Many countries have races held especially for vintage and thoroughbred cars. They are split up into various classes according to size and age.

Drag racing

The object of drag racing is to record the fastest time over a short straight track only 440yd long. Cars compete in pairs, and competitions are won by a series of elimination rounds against cars of the same category.

The track or "strip" must be 440yd long with a braking distance of a further half mile. The width of the track must be at least 50ft. There is a separate road along which cars return to the starting area.
Vehicles are of various classes, from mass-produced cars to highly specialized racing machines.
The most specialized cars have engines capable of producing up to 1500hp. Two engines may be permitted, but in US drag racing there is a restriction of 800cu in on engine capacity.
Some braking systems include special parachutes.
"Funny cars" are also raced: dragsters fitted with fiberglass replica sedan bodies.

Starting Cars compete in pairs.
They line up on the starting line and are started by the "Christmas tree" system.
In the center of the track is a pole with a vertical series of yellow, green, and red lights. These operate in sequence, starting from the top of the "tree." When the green light comes on, the cars can move off.
If a car moves before the green light, a red light comes on automatically and the car is disqualified.

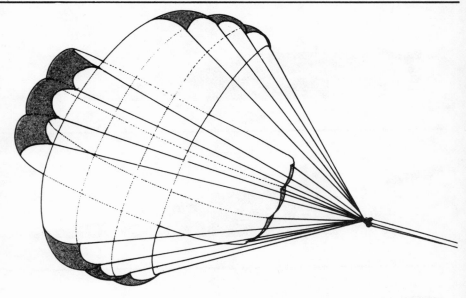

FIA Group 1 Series production four-seater touring cars, with only a minimum of modifications allowed.
"Blueprinting" the engine is permitted: the engine can be dismantled and reassembled to the manufacturers' exact specifications. There are various capacity classes.

FIA Group 2 Limited production four-seater touring cars, with more extensive modifications allowed.

FIA Group 3 Series production two-seater grand touring cars, with modifications governed as in Group 1.
FIA Group 4 Limited production two-seater grand touring cars, with modifications governed as in Group 2.

FIA Group 7 (Can-Am) For two-seater racing cars using commercial fuel and with full width bodies covering all mechanical parts. There are various capacity classes from under 850cc to over 5000cc.

The race If both cars start cleanly, it is a direct race to the finishing line.
If a car crosses into the opponent's lane, it is disqualified.
In every race cars are timed for both the elapsed time and terminal speed.
As each car starts, it breaks a timing light that is linked to another set of lights at the finish. As the car crosses the finishing line it breaks another light beam to record the elapsed time.
After it has crossed the finishing line the car passes through another light beam, connected to the finishing line, that records the car's terminal speed.

The elapsed time is the factor that decides the winner, though this may be modified by a time handicap system. It is possible for the losing car to record the faster terminal speed.

The result Time handicapping is not used in professional drag racing, but may be used in the amateur categories.
When handicapping does not apply, the first car to break the light beam at the finish wins. Otherwise the elapsed time is adjusted to include the time advantages given to the slower cars within the class.

Racers compete in a series of elimination races against cars in a similar category to produce the ultimate winners. There may also be awards for the fastest terminal speeds and the quickest times at a meeting.

© DIAGRAM

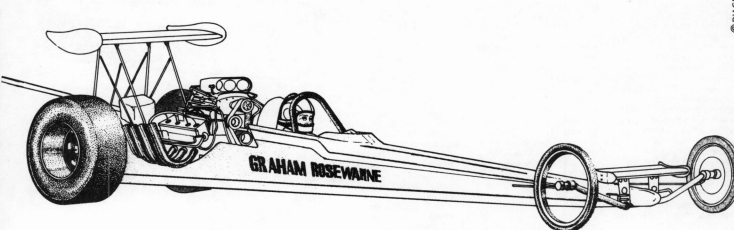

GRAHAM ROSEWARNE

Stock car racing

Stock car racing in the USA is for cars that in outside appearance are the stock production models available to the general public. They are, however, highly modified for racing and can achieve very high speeds. Stock car racing in the United Kingdom is much less streamlined – with stripped-down and modified cars racing and crashing on small oval tracks.

US STOCK CAR RACING
Track Usually an oval circuit with banks, but occasionally road race tracks are used.
Vehicles Of the several categories, the Grand National Championship division is the most famous. It has the following two classes:
Standard size cars Limited to cars with a minimum wheelbase of 119in, a maximum engine size of 430 cubic in (7 liters), and standard bodies complying with weight requirements.
Intermediate size cars Limited to cars with a wheelbase of 115-119in and a maximum engine capacity of 430 cubic in (7 liters).
Weight All GN cars must weigh at least 3800lb ready to race.

Races begin with a rolling start, and may be up to 600mi long.
UK STOCK CAR RACING
Competitions Cars begin in a massed start. Some contact between cars is allowed, but deliberate attempts to force other drivers off the track are forbidden.
Vehicles are divided into classes: senior, formula 2 stock cars, formula 2 superstox, and hot rods. Each class is governed by specific regulations. In some the shape of the car body has to be altered, the glass is removed and roll bars or cages have to be installed. Cars are numbered and brightly painted, with the color of the roof denoting the driver's status.

STADIUM RACING
Cars compete in groups around a loose-surfaced oval track ¼–½ mile long. There are various classes of car, from "banger" sedans to midget racers with 5 liter V-8 engines.

Rallying

Cars compete over a course divided into several stages. Penalty points are subtracted from a total number of points for each stage. The car with fewest penalty points wins the rally.

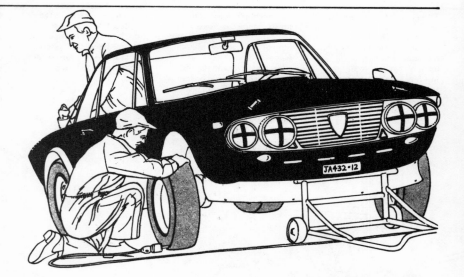

The route There may be one route, or several alternatives running from different starting points to a single destination. All routes are divided into stages, mostly over normal traffic routes. Each crew is given a route card with the exact distance between markers or changes of direction.
Competitors A driver and a navigator for each car.
Scoring Points are awarded for each stage completed, and penalty points are subtracted according to rally rules. Under international regulations, penalty points are subtracted for:
a) not reporting at a control (300 points);
b) not reporting at, or proving a visit to, a check (300 points);

c) not complying with the route card (150 points);
d) not obeying officials' instructions (150 points);
e) not being ready at a test, making a false start at a test, not completing a test or completing a test incorrectly (10 points plus the highest penalty incurred by any competitor in the class who completes the test correctly);
f) stopping in a non-stop section (150 points);
g) striking a marker or barrier (10 points);
h) every second taken to complete a test (1 point);
i) leaving a checkpoint before time (20 points);
j) arriving at a control after a specified time (10 points per minute);
k) breach of driving requirements (300 points);

l) covering a stage in less than ¾ of the specified time (300 points);
m) breach of lighting regulations (300 points);
n) excessive noise (300 points);
o) damage to the car (100 points).
A damaged or ineffective muffler system incurs exclusion.

Vehicles usually belong to sedan car racing groups 1–4. Special equipment is permitted. Most cars have a very accurate odometer.

HILLCLIMB

Competition In hillclimb competitions each car competes singly and makes two attempts to complete the course in the fastest time. Results are based on each car's better attempt. There is an overall winner as well as individual class winners.

Vehicles are organized in classes according to the number of entrants.
The course is on a hill, tarmac-surfaced, and at least 12ft wide. Lengths vary: in some countries ¾-1 mile is usual, in others the average is much longer.

SPRINTS
Sprint competitions are similar to hillclimbs, but the course is over a flat section of track. Events may be held on racing circuits or airfields.

SLALOM

Competition Slalom, or autotest, competitions are a test of maneuverability. Cars attempt the course singly. Each car starts with 0 points and receives 1 point for each second taken and 10 points for each marker touched. The winner is the driver with the fewest points at the finish.

Vehicles Many countries have three classes: production open, production closed, and specials. (Specials include such features as separate handbrakes for each rear wheel, or steering from front or back.)

The course is laid out with markers. It includes sections to be completed in reverse, and competitors are also required to back in and out of garages.

AUTOCROSS

Competition Cars compete against the clock over courses that do not include ordinary roads. Cars may race alone, or be started in pairs or threes. There are individual class winners and an overall competition winner.

Vehicles International regulations cover classes for production cars, buggies, and special cars. Nationally decided classes make further divisions according to engine capacity, engine position, and for cars with front- or rear-wheel drive.

The course is over grass or some other rough surface. Lengths are usually 500–800yd. The first corner must be at least 50yd from the start, and no straight may exceed 200yd. There is a 5-second penalty for touching a marker, and cars are automatically disqualified for crossing an imaginary line between any two markers.

RALLYCROSS

Competition Heats are usually between four to six cars and are held over three laps of the course. Winning times are recorded, and the event is won by the driver with the fastest time.

Vehicles Competitions are for sedan or production sports cars. Special custom-built cars are barred.
The course combines rough surfaces and tarmac, but does not include public roads.

HILL TRIALS

Competition Cars attempt to climb farthest up a steep hill. Measuring is to the point where the car fails to maintain unassisted motion. Cars are penalized for touching markers.

Vehicles There are three basic classes: production, specials, and 750.
Passengers Each car is allowed one passenger. Passengers may "bounce" the car to increase traction, but must keep their arms and legs within the car.
The course is marked out on a very steep, rough hill.

GRASSTRACK
All cars start together and race over an unsealed or grass course. The cars are put in classes by the organizers, but are usually sedans with tuned engines and special safety devices.

HIGH-SPEED TRIALS
Cars are timed over a rough circuit. They must either maintain a minimum speed of 50mph for a specified time or distance, or must cover a minimum distance in a specified time.

Karting

In karting, competitors race around one of three types of approved track: permanent, round-the-houses, or temporary. Karts are classified according to engine capacity.

Dress An approved style of crash helmet with goggles or visor must be worn; also a leather or heavy-duty polyvinyl chloride (PVC) suit and gloves.
All clothing must be securely fastened at the wrists and ankles. Boots and shoes that cover and protect the ankles are recommended.

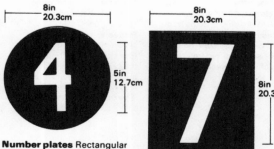

Eligibility to race
Chassis and engine Every kart must comply with national automobile club regulations and be in a sound mechanical condition.
It is the responsibility of competitors to keep their karts in eligible condition throughout the competition.
Scrutineering Competitors must make their karts available for inspection at any time required by the organizers.
The officially nominated driver is the only person eligible to drive a kart on the track during racing or practice.

Kart specifications
Chassis dimensions: wheelbase, track, and height must comply with official specifications.
1 Tires Pneumatic tires are obligatory, and are 9–17in in diameter.
2 The frame must be of sound construction.
3 Bumpers are compulsory at both front and rear.
4 Brakes are foot operated, either drum or disc type. Four-wheel brakes are compulsory for all gearbox karts.
5 Exhaust systems must comply with official regulations. Mufflers are compulsory.
6 The throttle must be foot operated.
7 The engine must be officially homologated (a standard production two-stroke engine). Supercharging is prohibited. 100cc engines may have only one cylinder; larger engines only two. Engines must have suppressors. There are price limits on engines for certain classes.
Drive Karts must be chain driven.
Weight Each kart class has a combined minimum weight for kart and driver.

50in** 1.27m

40in** 1.01m

Overall length 6ft 6in** 2m

**maximum

8in 20.3cm

5in 12.7cm

8in 20.3cm

8in 20.3cm

Number plates Rectangular plates must be fitted to the front, rear, and sides; circular plates only to the front and rear.
Restricted kart license holders must use black number plates with white numbers. International kart license holders use number plates according to class.

Types of event
Closed events, confined to members of the organizing club.
Restricted events, confined to the organizing club and up to 12 invited clubs.
National events, open to holders of a current international kart license.
International non-priority events, open to any holder of an appropriate competition license issued by a national automobile club that is a member of the FIA.
Entries are to be approved by competitors' own national automobile clubs.
International priority events are classified as such by the FIA, and are open to competitors under the same conditions as international non-priority events.

Classes Kart racing is divided into three classes:
Juniors for drivers aged 12 to 16, karts as Class 100 National, motors 100cc, no gearbox.
Class 1 is in two sections: Class 100 National and Class 100 International, motors 100cc.
Class 4 is in three sections: Class 210 Villiers, Class 250 International, and 125 International.
Cadet Motor Sport is a general category for schools, youth clubs, etc.

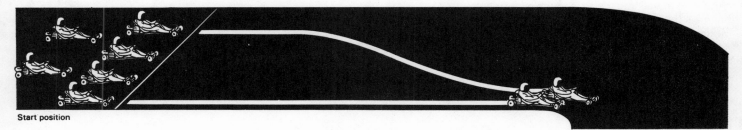

Start position

Administration Karting is organized by national automobile clubs that are members of the FIA.

Tracks National automobile club track licenses are issued to approved venues. Track regulations include the following:

tracks must have a minimum width of 20ft;

chicanes (where the track narrows) are not encouraged, but where essential must not exceed certain limits;

the track surface must be similar throughout;

track edges must be marked in an approved manner, and track markings must not constitute a hazard;

spectators must be protected by barriers and safety precautions.

There are three types of track:

Permanent, where shape can be determined at any time and all protective barriers are permanently in position;

Round-the-houses, tracks using public roads;

Temporary, other tracks.

Officials All officials should be present during practice and racing. Officials include:

kart steward;
club steward(s);
meeting secretary;
clerk of the course;
medical officer;
kart scrutineer;
chief timekeeper;
chief lapscorer and judge;
chief flag marshall;
starter;
chief course marshall with four or more assistants;
chief paddock marshall with two or more assistants;
general officials.

Signals are displayed to the drivers by flags or signal boards. Drivers are penalized for disobeying signals.

National flag A race with a rolling start begins at the moment the flag is raised. A standing start race begins the moment the flag is lowered.

Blue flag A stationary flag signals that another competitor is following close by. A waved flag signals that another competitor is trying to overtake.

White flag A service car is on the circuit.

Yellow flag A stationary flag signals danger and no overtaking. A waved flag signals serious danger and the need to be prepared to stop.

Yellow flag with red stripes Stationary, signals oil on the road ahead. Waved, signals that oil on the road is imminent.

Green flag Proceed, the hazard has been removed.

Red flag Complete and immediate stop for all karts.

Black and white warning board bearing a competitor's number indicates that the offending competitor will be flagged down if he repeats an offense.

Black flag with white number The driver of the kart with that number must report to the clerk of the course.

Black and white multi-checkered flag Finish.

Competitors The maximum number of starters is determined as follows:

Races under 500yd, 14 starters on tracks less than 25ft wide and 20 starters on wider tracks.

Races between 500–1000yd, 18 starters on tracks less than 25ft wide and 24 starters on wider tracks.

Races over 1000yd, 24 starters on tracks less than 25ft wide and 30 starters on wider tracks.

Practice Before racing a definite period is allowed for practicing. Drivers leave the paddock one at a time for the start; otherwise racing rules apply. Each driver must complete at least three laps' continuous running before racing.

Race procedure

Handicaps are based on an allowance of time or distance determined by either a timed performance in practice or a previous race, or by an assessment of performance by the organizers.

Handicaps are displayed on the official notice board not less than 15 minutes before the start of the race.

Starting positions are displayed before the race on the chief paddock marshall's board. The number 1 position is on the side of the track that is on the inside of the first corner. This position is taken by the competitor with the best preliminary performance.

Rolling start: for non-gearbox karts. Karts go round the course at a steady pace while awaiting the signal.

Standing start: for karts with a gearbox. Karts take up their position on the starting grid, with their engines running. Any driver unable to start raises his left hand and stays still.

Finish To be classed as finished, a kart must cross the finish line under its own propulsion not more than two minutes after the winner and having completed at least half of the race.

The first three finishers are weighed to check that they are not below the specified minimum weight limits for driver and kart combined.

Conduct Official instructions must be obeyed. These include: karts must be driven in an orderly manner;

all practicing and racing is in a clockwise direction, thus competitors must drive on the right and overtake on the left;

a driver who is forced to leave the track must rejoin it at the nearest practicable point to where he left it;

any driver leaving the track more than twice is excluded from the race;

refuelling during the race is forbidden.

Penalties In order of severity, the penalties that may be inflicted are: reprimand; fine or a time or point penalty; exclusion; suspension; disqualification.

Protests Any protests must be made in accordance with the general competition rules of the national governing body. A protest as to the validity of an entry must be made within two hours of the end of the official examination.

A protest against a handicap, the composition of a heat, etc must be made immediately upon notification.

A protest against a scrutineer must be made immediately.

A protest against any irregularity during a competition must be made within half an hour of the finish.

A protest against a result must be made within half an hour of announcement.

Appeals Any competitor may appeal against a decision affecting him. He must do so in writing to the stewards, enclosing the appropriate fee. Such an appeal must be made within one hour.

Gliding

In gliding, aircraft without engines are used. The gliders are towed into the air, and the pilots locate thermals (currents of warm air rising from the ground), using them to gain height before gliding downward to the next thermal. Competitors may be judged on altitude, distance, or speed.

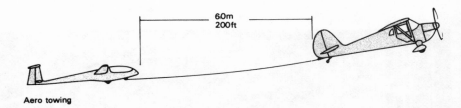

60m
200ft

Aero towing

Gliders Most gliders are monoplanes with long slender wings, able to make the best use of air currents. Gliders have a low sinking speed and can glide at very flat angles. Motor gliders, with an engine used only for take off, may be used.

Preparations for flight
There is a recommended cockpit check that must be made before take off.
Controls must be working freely and instruments must be checked and set as required.
Ballast may be used to make up the correct cockpit load.
The pilot and crew must be fastened in safety straps. The trim is set for take off, and the canopy locked shut. On motor gliders, additional checks should be made to ensure that there is sufficient fuel, that the propeller is free, and that people are clear of the take off path.

360m
1200ft

Auto launching

Bungey launching

Release point

Cumulus cloud

Prevailing wind

Aero tow take off

Thermal

Lake

Launching Gliders may be launched by aero towing, by car and winch, or by "bungey" launch.

Aero towing The glider is towed into the air by an airplane or "tug." The tug pilot is in command of both aircraft so as to avoid a collision. He is responsible for ensuring that the tow rope is suitable and that signals are fully understood, although the glider pilot chooses the moment to release the tow rope.
Once the glider pilot has released the tow rope, he should turn away so that it is fully clear to the tug pilot that the glider is free. The rope should not be released under tension, and it should fall only in the designated area of the airfield.

Auto and winch towing may be used on any flat ground, such as an airfield runway.
If there is any jerking or hesitation at the start of the launch, the car or winch driver must stop and await further signals before restarting. Should the glider pilot suspect power failure during the launch, he should release the rope at once while there is still room ahead to land.

Bungey launching is sometimes used to launch a glider from the top of a steep hill. A rubber rope is attached to the front of the glider and is pulled out into a "vee" shape by about six people on either side of the "vee." They walk or run as appropriate, stretching the rope until the glider leaves the ground.

Ground handling The glider should not be moved without crew on the windward wingtip and at either the tail or the nose. If the glider is moved into the wind, the nose must be held down and the tail up. If it is moved downwind, care must be taken to prevent the control surfaces from slamming. When the wind is strong, the airbrakes should be opened and the crew increased.
The crew runs with the glider to steady it until take off, and if the launch point slopes downhill, the crew can prevent the glider from overrunning by holding it back until the take off run starts.

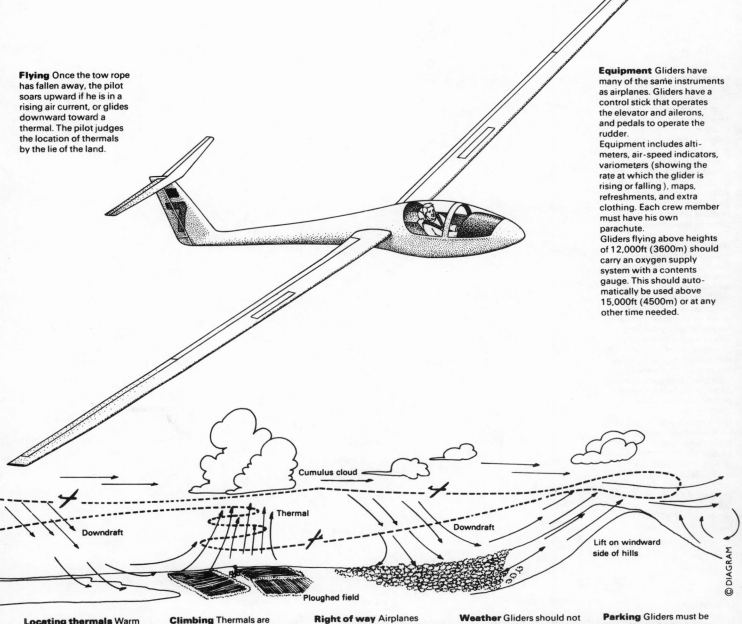

Flying Once the tow rope has fallen away, the pilot soars upward if he is in a rising air current, or glides downward toward a thermal. The pilot judges the location of thermals by the lie of the land.

Equipment Gliders have many of the same instruments as airplanes. Gliders have a control stick that operates the elevator and ailerons, and pedals to operate the rudder.

Equipment includes altimeters, air-speed indicators, variometers (showing the rate at which the glider is rising or falling), maps, refreshments, and extra clothing. Each crew member must have his own parachute.

Gliders flying above heights of 12,000ft (3600m) should carry an oxygen supply system with a contents gauge. This should automatically be used above 15,000ft (4500m) or at any other time needed.

Cumulus cloud

Thermal

Downdraft

Downdraft

Lift on windward side of hills

© DIAGRAM

Ploughed field

Locating thermals Warm air, and consequently updrafts, can be expected over open fields and over houses, particularly above cities. Upcurrents are indicated by cumulus clouds; a pilot who flies into a thunderstorm may be quickly carried up to 30,000ft (9000m). Geographical features such as ridges produce upward rising waves. Cold air, and consequently downdrafts, can be expected over woodland and lakes; down currents also flow over valleys.

Climbing Thermals are narrow, and the glider must turn in tight circles in order to stay within the effective area. A glider joining another in a thermal must circle in the direction established by the first glider.

A pilot should not change direction abruptly if there is another glider anywhere nearby, and he should ensure that he remains in full visibility of other pilots.

Right of way Airplanes must give way to aero tows and gliders, and gliders must give way to balloons; at all times it is each pilot's responsibility to avoid collision.

When two aircraft are converging at about the same height, the aircraft that has the other on its right must give way. If a headlong collision seems imminent, both aircraft must swing to the right.

When landing, the lower-flying aircraft has the right of way.

Air space is controlled by air traffic rules according to local conditions, to ensure safety both in the air and on the ground.

Weather Gliders should not be left out in winds of 20 knots (37kph) or more, as the risk of being blown over and damaged is high.

Lightning can strike down the winch wire, and car or tow launching should be suspended if a storm is imminent.

Low cloud may be hazardous to inexperienced pilots.

Launching should not take place in wet weather if the air temperature is below freezing, as ice on the wings can adversely affect efficiency and stalling speed.

Parking Gliders must be parked in such a way as to avoid being blown over or damaged in poor weather. If parked across wind, the windward wing should be weighted down, and the tail skid should be anchored on the side away from the wind. When unparking in strong wind, the pilot should be in the cockpit with crew at each wingtip, and the tail must be up before turning into the wind.

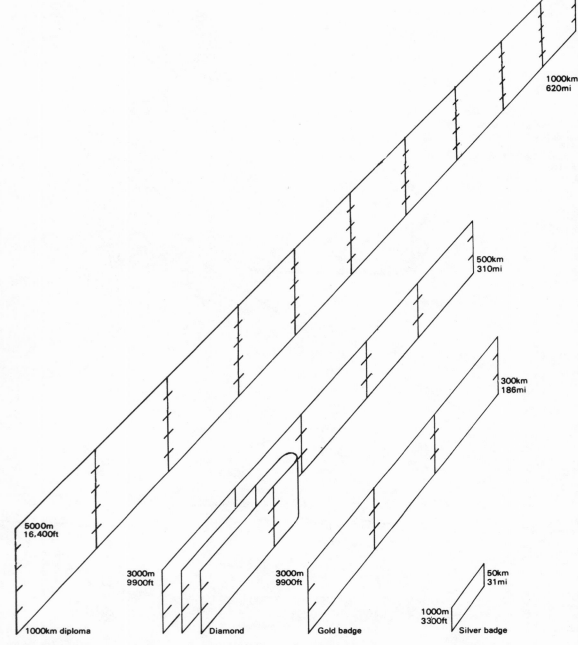

Competitions Many
countries hold an annual
competition, and world
gliding championships are
held every two or three years.
Competitions may be
judged on altitude, distance,
or speed.
There are three categories of
record: world, national, and
local; each category contains
single-seater, two-seater,
and women's classes.
Badges are awarded to solo
pilots for proficiency tests.
The simplest test requires the
pilot to know the basic air
rules, and to carry out three
solo flights of a circuit and a
turn in each direction, with
normal landings.
The Commission Inter-
nationale de Vol à Voile lays
down international standards
for the following badges:
Silver badge The requirements for this include a
duration flight of at least five
hours, a distance flight of at
least 50km (approximately
31mi), and a height gain of
1000m (approximately
3300ft).
Gold badge The requirements
for this include a distance
flight of at least 300km
(approximately 186mi) in a
straight line or around a
triangular course (which
need not necessarily be
completed provided that
300km is exceeded), and a
height gain of 3000m
(approximately 9900ft).

Diamonds These may be
added to gold or silver badges.
They are awarded for a
completed triangle or an
out-and-return flight of
300km; a distance flight of at
least 500km (approximately
310mi), and a height gain of
at least 3000m.
1000km diploma This is
awarded for a distance
soaring flight of 1000km
(approximately 620mi) or
more.

Evidence Proof that the
flights have achieved the
necessary standards is
supported by correctly
calibrated barographs
(showing the height
attained), and photographs
of the turn points taken
from the glider on distance
flights.

Signals It is essential that
signals between the person
in charge of the launching and
the winch or tow car driver
or tug pilot be clearly
understood.
Unless there is a radio or
telephone system in
operation, one of the
following three methods may
be used:
signaling with one bat;
signaling with two bats;
signaling with lights.

Airfield signals
A red and yellow striped
arrow pointing in a clockwise
direction indicates that a
right-hand circuit is in force.
A white double cross
indicates that glider flying is
in progress.
A white dumbell indicates
that aircraft and gliders are
confined to paved surfaces.
A dumbell with black bars
indicates that take offs and
landings must be made on
the runway, but taxying on
the grass is permitted.
A red L displayed on the
dumbell indicates that light
aircraft may fly from the
runway.
A large white L indicates that
a part of the airfield shall
only be used by light aircraft.

A white T indicates that take
offs and landings shall be
parallel to the shaft of the T
and toward the cross arm.
A white disc at the head of
the landing T indicates that
the direction of landings and
take offs may not be the
same.
A red panel with a yellow bar
indicates that the landing
area is in a poor condition.
A red panel with a yellow
cross indicates that the
airfield is unsafe and that
landing is prohibited.

Ballooning

Hot air balloons are maneuvered by regulating the temperature of the air within the envelope by means of a burner, thus causing the balloon to gain or lose height. Competitions may be based on flight duration, the highest altitude reached, or a particular journey over a given distance or region.

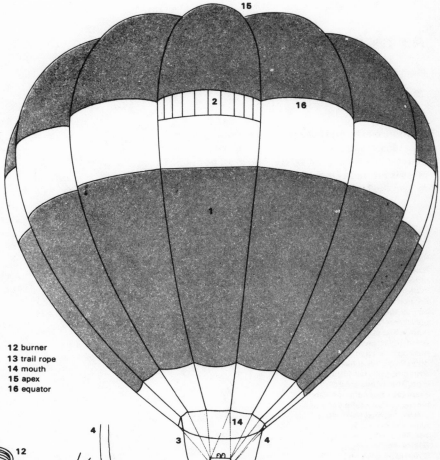

Balloons Hot air balloons vary in size between 20,000 and 140,000cu ft (566 and 3970cu m).

The envelope is made of light, high-tenacity nylon or polyester fabric, specially treated for impermeability and resistance to sunlight.
It has two controls:
the maneuvering or cooling vent, which can be opened in flight to release hot air and is operated by a line that closes the valve automatically; the ripping panel, a large section at the top of the envelope used on the ground to completely deflate the balloon.
The envelope is connected to the basket by stainless steel wires, which keep the fabric at a safe distance from the flame.

The basket is made of willow and rattan with interwoven stainless steel suspension wires.

The trailrope is 150–300ft (45–91m) long. It acts as a brake and stabilizer when landing.

Cylinders Gas is carried in lightweight cylinders strapped inside the basket. The cylinders are operated by an on-off valve. Only one cylinder is used at a time, although they are connected in series.

The burner is positioned above head level and is fed by liquid propane from six multiple jets.

Equipment may include: maps, altimeter, compass, electric variometer, ambient temperature thermometer, spare cylinders, refreshments, etc.
A vehicle and trailer are generally necessary for recovering the balloon.

Crew Balloons may carry a maximum crew of six, including a pilot. Other crew members may have special functions, such as navigation, instrument control, etc.

1 envelope
2 maneuvering or cooling vent
3 control
4 rip panel control
5 propane cylinder
6 altimeter, variometer, and compass
7 basket
8 suspension cables
9 load ring, plate, or frame
10 fire extinguisher
11 carrying handles
12 burner
13 trail rope
14 mouth
15 apex
16 equator

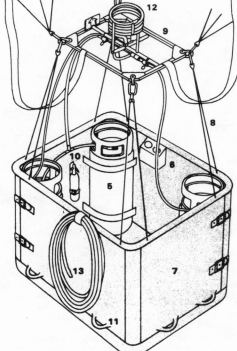

© DIAGRAM

Starting procedure The balloon is spread out with the basket on its side and the envelope down wind.
The neck of the balloon is flapped to trap some of the surrounding air, and is then held so that it forms a wide opening. The burner is ignited, successive bursts of flame warming the air inside the balloon and causing it to rise to a vertical position. The crew then enters the basket, and further heating lifts the balloon from the ground.

Maneuvering The balloon's movements are determined by the atmospheric conditions. Winds vary according to the altitude, and the balloon can only be steered by changing altitude by regulating the burner. More fuel is burned to gain height, less to lose it. The cooling vent may be used to cool the air more rapidly.
Balloons may fly at up to about 35,000ft (10,670m).

Landing A landing site must be in the direction of the wind, as the balloon cannot be steered to right or left. The approach is controlled by using the burner and cooling vent.
The trailing rope may be used to brake and stabilize the balloon, as landing should be achieved with as little vertical velocity as possible.

Wind direction

Burner low for level flight
Air cools, ascent slows
Air cools, descent begins
Air heated, continued ascent
Burner on, descent slows
Air heated for take-off
Dragging trail rope slows drift

Air racing

Formula air racing is designed to encourage low-cost racing and aircraft development while maintaining maximum safety. The most popular class is Formula One, but four other classes also race in the United States.

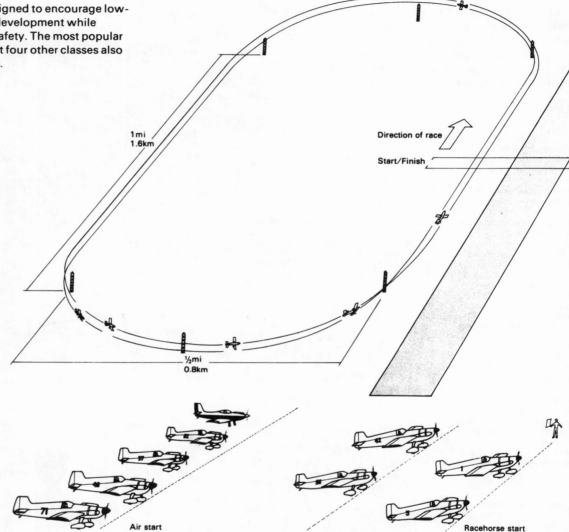

1mi
1.6km

½mi
0.8km

Direction of race

Start/Finish

Air start

Racehorse start

Racecourse The dimensions of the course are laid down in the rules for each class. For Formula One racing, the course should be as near as possible to 3mi (4.8km) in length. The course is six-sided, the corners being marked by six pylons about 30ft (9m) high. It has two straights, each 1mi (1.6km) long. The pylons are painted a conspicuous color, and are placed so that a pilot can see at least the next two pylons while flying around the course.

Officials

Stewards Each racing event is controlled by at least three stewards. They interpret and enforce the rules, and may fine competitors or ban pilots or aircraft for any infringements.

Other officials include the clerk of the course, the chief timekeeper, the chief starter, the chief judge, and members of the technical committee. This committee must include at least two pilots with racing experience. The committee inspects the aircraft and checks on the qualifications of the pilots.

Briefing The clerk of the course holds a briefing every day of the event on which practice, qualifying trials, or racing take place. All pilots must attend all briefings, or have a complete individual briefing before being allowed to compete.

Winning The winner of a race is the aircraft that crosses the finish line first, provided it has completed the required number of laps and has not incurred any penalties.

After crossing the finish line all aircraft must gain height and prepare to land.

Flags are used to signal to aircraft:
red and white flag, signals the start of a race or qualifying run;
white flag, signals the start of the last lap;
black and white checkered flag, signals the end of the race;
black flag, directs one or more aircraft to leave the course;
yellow flag, signifies an emergency.

Starts The number of aircraft starting is normally limited to seven or eight. There are two kinds of start: air starts and racehorse starts.

Air starts The competing aircraft take to the air individually and then take up formation on a pace aircraft. The pace aircraft dives across the starting line and then pulls away into the center of the course, releasing the racing aircraft.

If no pace aircraft is available, the competitors take up formation on the aircraft drawn nearest the number 1 pylon. Air starts are difficult to organize unless the aircraft are fitted with radios.

Racehorse starts The aircraft line up on the take off grid at one end of the runway, and are started by the drop of a flag. The order in which the aircraft line up is decided by their performance in the trials, the fastest qualifying aircraft having first choice, and so on.

The race begins when the starter lowers his flag, but the starting time is taken from the moment the first aircraft crosses the start line in flight after one preliminary "scatter" lap. Any aircraft that does not take off within 30 seconds of the first aircraft will be excluded.

Reserves The first alternate (reserve) aircraft should be ready for take off, as it will be eligible for the race if any of the qualifying aircraft fails to reach the start line.

Alternate pilots of an aircraft may race only in classes for which they are eligible. They must prove their eligibility in the same way as other pilots, but do not have to qualify the aircraft to be flown.

Handicap races Aircraft in handicap races are handicapped according to their estimated performance at full power.

Handicap races usually cater for stock production aircraft of widely varying performance. They are normally flown over a 100mi (160km) cross-country course.

Formula One racing airplanes have a length and a wingspan of approximately 16ft (5m). They must comply with the following rules:
Engine Any stock aero engine with a capacity of not more than 200 cu in (3277 cu cm).
Propeller must be fixed in pitch.
Airframe must weigh at least 500lb (approximately 230kg) when empty, with a wing area of at least 66sq ft (approximately 6sq m). It must have a fixed undercarriage and brakes.
Cockpit must comply with field of vision requirements.

Formula

Class		Power unit	Horsepower	Speed (mph)
1	Unlimited	Any piston engine	1500-3000	400+
2	Formula One	Any stock 200cu in engine	100	190-230+
3	T6 Harvard	Stock Wright	850	180-210
4	Sports biplane	Stock Lycoming	140	160-210
5	Formula V	Stock 1500cc Volkswagen	65	140-180

©DIAGRAM

Aircraft qualification To qualify for a race, aircraft must complete two laps of the course on the day before the race. The speed of the second lap is used to decide qualification.
Aircraft unable to qualify may be allowed to take part in heats if there are vacancies, but will rank behind qualified aircraft for finishing positions and prize money.

Pilot qualification Pilots must have flown at least 10 hours in their particular type of aircraft. They must have flown at least 500 hours as pilot in charge of an aircraft, or alternatively a minimum of 100 hours plus 10 hours in the particular type for every 100 hours short of 500 hours in charge.
They must have taken off and landed the type of aircraft at least five times during the 90 days before the race, and must have flown that type for two hours or any aircraft for 10 hours during the previous month.

Aircraft eligibility Aircraft must comply with their class specifications and must arrive at the course in time for inspection.
Class specifications prescribe design and structural standards for aircraft, the test program required before they are allowed to compete, and the modifications which are permissible on the engines.
All Formula Class racing aircraft are fully aerobatic.
Aircraft documents to be inspected before the race include:
entry form;
certificate of airworthiness or a permit to fly;
logbooks for engine and airframe; propeller maintenance record;
valid insurance certificate.

Aircraft equipment includes seat belts and shoulder harness, and may also include parachutes, protective helmets, fire-protective clothing, radio, and oxygen, according to the rules for the particular class.
Demonstrations Pilots must demonstrate their ability to take off safely in formation or fly in formation, and must fly five laps of the course (one at full power) before they may compete.
Pilots new to racing must fly 10 laps, including two at full power.

Safety No open containers of fuel are allowed in the pit area where the aircraft are prepared, and fire fighting equipment must be provided there. No smoking is allowed within 50ft (15m) of aircraft, and no alcohol is allowed in the pit area.
All aircraft must carry enough fuel for the race, plus one lap at full power and 20 minutes at cruising speed. They must keep a safe distance apart while racing.

Pylon turns Aircraft must fly outside the pylons when cornering. Flying inside (known as "cutting a pylon") may lead to penalties. Flying over the top of the pylon also constitutes a "cut."

Altitudes Aircraft must race at not less than 25ft (7.5m) above the ground, and not higher than 500ft (150m), unless a greater altitude is necessary for reasons of safety. In emergencies they must fly at not less than 300ft (90m).

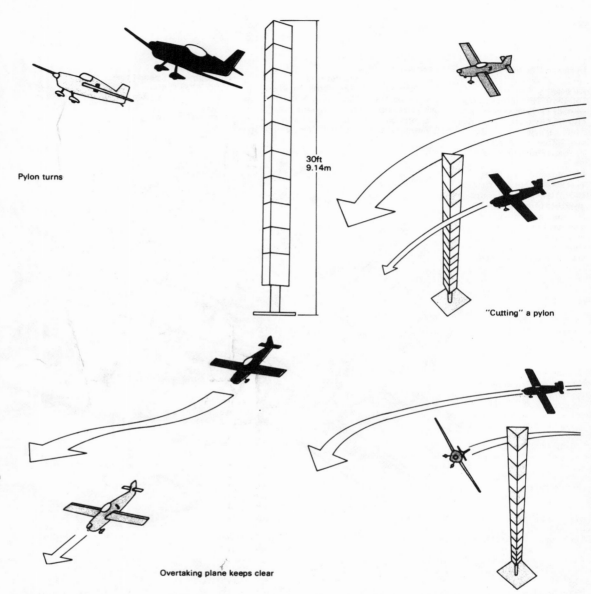

Pylon turns

30ft
9.14m

"Cutting" a pylon

Overtaking Aircraft must keep a safe distance apart during a race. The pilot of an overtaking aircraft is responsible for the safety of the maneuver, but the slower aircraft must keep to its course to avoid impeding the faster one. An aircraft must never overtake between another plane and a pylon, unless the slower aircraft is flying extremely wide.

Overtaking plane keeps clear

International civil aviation organization alphabet:

A Alpha
B Bravo
C Charlie
D Delta
E Echo
F Foxtrot
G Golf
H Hotel
I India
J Juliet
K Kilo
L Lima
M Mike
N November
O Oscar
P Papa
Q Quebec
R Romeo
S Sierra
T Tango
U Uniform
V Victor
W Whiskey
X X-ray
Y Yankee
Z Zulu

Emergencies An emergency is signaled by flying a yellow flag, and by radio from the air traffic control if radio is available in the aircraft. The lead aircraft must climb to at least 300ft (90m), giving way to any aircraft in difficulties, and other aircraft must follow suit. Aircraft must remain at the safety height until signaled by radio or by a red and white flag that the emergency is over.

Protests may be made as to the eligibility of an aircraft or its pilot, or the manner in which it is flown. Pilots, officials, or individuals entering aircraft may make protests, which must be in writing and handed in to the stewards within half an hour of the end of the race.

Penalties The stewards may exclude any aircraft or competitor for breaking the rules, or may fine them. The fines are deducted from prize money, and do not exceed the total prize money an offender has won.

Exclusion This penalty may be imposed for dangerous flying, unsafe condition of the aircraft or its pilot, unruly or unsportsmanlike behavior, or fraudulent description of an aircraft or its pilot.

Appeals An appeal may be made against any decision of the stewards. These appeals are made to the governing body of formula air racing in the country concerned.

Cancellation The stewards may cancel or postpone a race if they think the conditions are unsafe for spectators or contestants. If a race is stopped after the lead aircraft has completed half the course, the event is deemed to have been completed.

Weather A race is postponed or canceled if any of the following conditions prevail: visibility less than 1.8mi (3km); cloud lower than 330ft (100m); surface wind greater than 25 knots (46kph); excessive turbulence, cross winds, rain, or snow.

Aerobatics

Competitive aerobatics includes a large variety of maneuvers designed to test the skill of the pilots and the versatility of their aircraft. Pilots fly compulsory and free programs and are generally marked for each maneuver. The competitor with the highest score after the contest programs have been flown is the winner.

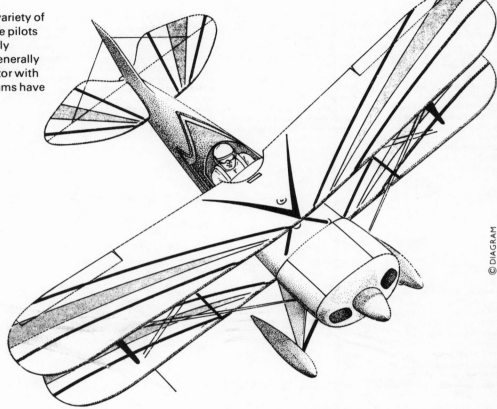

© DIAGRAM

Aircraft types Single-engined light aircraft are usually used. World championships and most international competitions are open to piston-engined aircraft only, which must be fully capable of performing the required maneuvers. They are usually 150–350hp and there is no division into classes.

All aircraft must have valid aerobatics certificates of air worthiness or the equivalent, as well as insurance certificates.

Replacements An aircraft may be replaced by another aircraft of the same type at any time during the contest, provided the change is officially recommended by the technical committee and approved by the jury. If an aircraft is damaged during flight, the flight may be repeated if the jury agrees.

Radio sets may not be used in international competitions. If a radio set is fitted in a competing aircraft, it will be sealed before flying begins.

Teams vary according to the rules of each competition. Solo entries are allowed if a national aero club is unable to send a team.

Competitors may be substituted within a specified time limit.

For world championships a team comprises at least three and not more than five pilots; there may be women's and men's teams. Other team members may include: chief delegate, team manager, judge and assistant, trainer, doctor, not more than three mechanics, interpreter.

Jury For world championships there is an international jury consisting of four members nominated by the international aerobatics commission of the FAI (Fédération Aéronautique Internationale) plus a chief judge, who has no vote.

The jury is responsible for ensuring that the championships are conducted in accordance with the regulations.

Judges For world championships and international competitions there is a board of judges consisting of a chief judge, a minimum of three and a maximum of nine international judges with their assistants, four positioning judges, and an administrative secretary. The positioning judges are placed at each corner of the performance zone. If electronic tracking equipment is used, they operate it and record its indications.

Other than at world championships, the board of judges may fulfill the role of the jury.

The technical commission is responsible for inspecting competing aircraft and certifying them airworthy. At world championships the committee comprises five engineers.

Briefing Daily briefings are held, which competitors, officials, judges, and jury members must attend.

Training flights Each competitor may make two training flights in order to familiarize himself with local conditions: one over and one away from the airfield where the championships are being held.

Each flight is limited to 20 minutes, except in international competitions, when a shorter period is normally allowed.

Weather conditions For world championships the cloud base must be at least 165ft (50m) above the maximum height at which competing aircraft will fly, and visibility must be at least 3mi (5km). If the conditions are worse than this or there are severe winds, the jury may halt flying.

If a majority of team managers agrees, the jury may decide to continue in slightly worse conditions than normally required, in order to complete the championships. If a competitor thinks that weather conditions are not sufficiently good, he can discontinue a flight and may, with the jury's agreement, repeat the flight later.

At other competitions, the minimum weather conditions required for contest flights may be determined by regional weather patterns.

Performance zone All competition flights must be performed within a zone of 1000m by 800m (approximately 1100yd by 880yd), which must be clearly marked.

Height In world championships and most international competitions, competitors must not fly lower than 100m or higher than 1000m (approximately 330ft and 3300ft).

Each competitor is allowed five minutes to reach operational height.

In other competitions, especially those that include less experienced pilots, the minimum height specified will often be between 300m and 500m (990ft and 1650ft).

534

World championship programs Pilots first fly three programs:
a known compulsory program;
an unknown compulsory program;
a free program of the competitor's choice.
The highest-placed third of the men competitors and the highest-placed half of the women competitors then compete in a fourth program, which is also free.
Each program has a draw to determine the competitors' starting order.
This curriculum changes periodically.

Program 1 The known compulsory program is composed of figures in both normal and inverted flight, performed continuously in the specified order.
There is a time limit of seven minutes.

Program 2 The unknown compulsory program consists of at least 15 figures chosen by the heads of delegations, and arranged by the jury with not more than five other delegation members.
Competitors are informed of details of the program at least 24 hours before they are due to fly, although they are not permitted to train for the program.
There is a time limit of seven minutes.

Program 3 The free program may consist of up to 30 figures, and must begin and end with level flight, either normal or inverted. There is a time limit of nine minutes.

Scoring For programs 1, 2, and 3 every judge rates the quality of each figure flown, and gives it a mark between 0 and 10. Judges take the precision and smoothness of the performance into account. The score for each figure is multiplied by a difficulty coefficient for that figure.
In program 4 each judge rates the total performance, taking into account the difficulty and versatility of the complete sequence, rather than marking individual figures.
The final score in each program for each competitor is found by eliminating the two highest and two lowest scores and averaging the remaining five judges' scores.

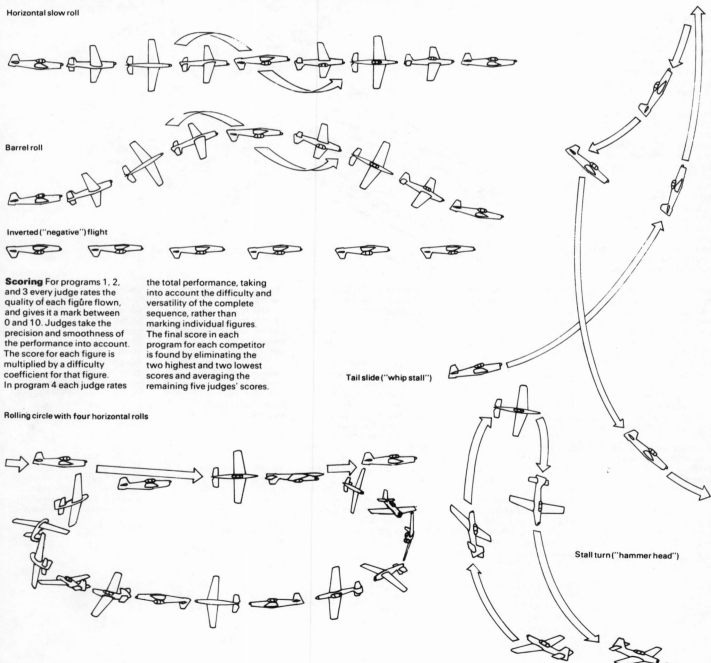

Horizontal slow roll

Barrel roll

Inverted ("negative") flight

Rolling circle with four horizontal rolls

Tail slide ("whip stall")

Stall turn ("hammer head")

Program 4 The final free program lasts for four minutes only, and any number of figures may be flown within that limit.
Other programs Many international competitions have a similar pattern to the world championships.

The second program may be free, with a reduced number of competitors going on to the third (unknown compulsory) program, and a still smaller number proceeding to the final free program. Some competitions consist of only two programs: possibly a known compulsory and a free program, each of between 8 and 15 figures.

Penalties Penalty points are incurred for various infringements.
Any figures flown after the time limit in the first three programs are not marked.
Any deviation by more than five seconds from the four minutes allowed for program 4 is penalized by 30 penalty points per second.

Penalties are incurred for flying too high or too low or outside the performance zone. Pilots are also penalized for interrupting the program to correct their course, or for circling to regain height.

Results vary according to the rules of each competition. In the world championships, the winners are the men and women pilots who do best in each of the four programs, and the overall champions are the man and woman to gain the highest total number of points in all four programs. There are also men and women team champions.

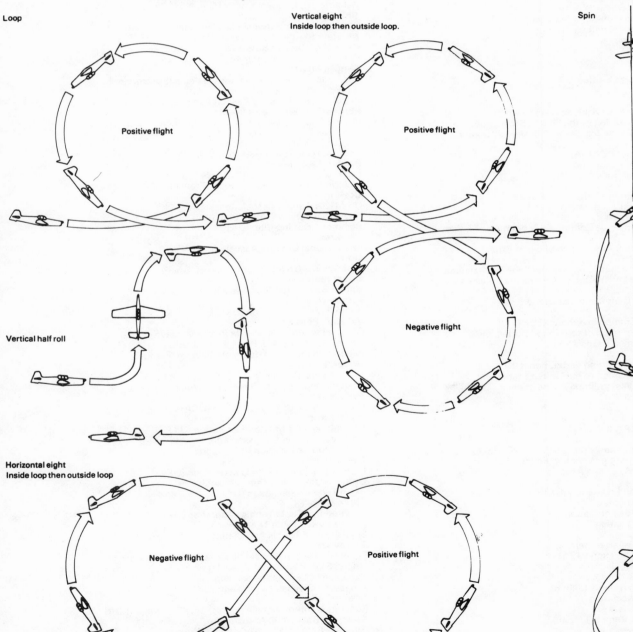

Loop

Positive flight

Vertical half roll

Horizontal eight
Inside loop then outside loop

Negative flight

Positive flight

Vertical eight
Inside loop then outside loop.

Positive flight

Negative flight

Spin

© DIAGRAM

Acknowledgments

The authors and publishers wish to extend their warmest thanks to the many sports associations, equipment manufacturers, and other organizations without whose kind and generous assistance this book could not have been compiled. Unfortunately, it is not possible to name them all individually, but special thanks are due to:

Organisationskomitee für die Spiele der XX Olympiade (Munich Olympics Committee)
The government tourist offices of France, Spain, and Switzerland
E Ayling & Sons Ltd, Racing Blade Specialists (Rowing)
R Bamber (Crossbow archery)
James Black (Aerobatics)
David Brown (Golf)
Nancy Clark (Speedball)
Keo Holdings (Surfing)
Leon Paul Equipment Co Ltd (Fencing)
Olympic yacht class organizations (Yachting)
Edwin Phelps, Racing Boatbuilder and Waterman to Queen Elizabeth II (Rowing)
Salter Bros Ltd (Rowing)
G Sambrooke Sturgess (Yachting)
Silva Compasses (London) Ltd (Orienteering)
Cyril A Sinfield (Athletics)
Peter Wells (Canoeing)
F Wilt (Athletics)

Governing sports bodies

Athletics
International Amateur Athletic Association (UK)
Amateur Athletic Union of the United States, Inc.
American Association for Health, Physical Education, and Recreation
Special Olympics, Inc. (USA)
Amateur Athletic Association (UK)
British Paraplegic Sports Society

Orienteering
Svenska Orienteringsförbundet (Sweden)
British Orienteering Federation

Modern pentathlon
Union Internationale de Pentathlon Moderne et Biathlon (Sweden)
Modern Pentathlon Association of Great Britain

Gymnastics
Fédération Internationale de Gymnastique (Switzerland)
National Association of College Gymnastic Coaches (USA)
British Amateur Gymnastic Association

Trampolining
Internationaler Trampolinverband (FDR)
Amateur Athletic Union of the United States, Inc
British Trampolining Association

Weightlifting
International Weightlifting Federation (UK)
Amateur Athletic Union of the United States, Inc
British Amateur Weightlifting Association

Boxing
Consejo Mundial de Boxéo (Mexico)
British Boxing Board of Control
Amateur Boxing Association (UK)

Wrestling
Fédération Internationale de Lutte Amateur (Switzerland)
United States Amateur Wrestling Foundation
British Amateur Wrestling Association

Judo
International Judo Federation (UK)
All Japan Judo Renmei
United States Judo Federation
British Judo Association

Karate
Zen Nihon Karatedo Renmei (Japan)
United Karate Federation (USA)
British Karate Association

Kendo
Zen Nihon Kendo Renmei (Japan)
British Kendo Association

Aikido
Zen Nihon Aikido Renmei (Japan)
British Aikido Association

Fencing
Fédération Internationale d'Escrime (France)
National Fencing Coaches Association of America
Amateur Fencing Association (UK)

Horseshoe pitching
National Horseshoe Pitchers Association of America

Darts
National Darts Association of Great Britain

Target and field archery
Fédération Internationale de Tir à l'Arc (UK)
National Field Archery Association of the United States, Inc
Grand National Archery Association (UK)
Field Archery Committee of Great Britain

Crossbow archery
Internationale Armbrust Union (Switzerland)
British Crossbow Archery Society
Eidgenössische Armbrust Schützen Verband (Switzerland)

Rifle and pistol shooting
Union Internationale de Tir (FDR)
National Rifle Association of America
Amateur Trapshooting Association (USA)
National Skeet Shooting Association (USA)
National Small-Bore Rifle Association (UK)
National Rifle Association (UK)
Clay Pigeon Shooting Association (UK)

Billiards and snooker
Union Mondiale Billiard (Belgium)
Billiard Congress of America
Billiards and Snooker Control Council (UK)

Skittles
Fédération Internationale des Quilleurs (Switzerland)
Amateur Skittles Association (UK)

Canadian fivepin bowling
Canadian Bowling Congress

Tenpin bowling
Fédération Internationale des Quilleurs (Switzerland)
American Bowling Congress
British Tenpin Bowling Association

Flat and crown green bowls
International Bowling Board (South Africa)
American Bowling Congress
English Bowling Association
Crown Green Bowling Association (UK)

Boules (boccie)
Federazione Internazionale Bocce (Italy)
Fédération Française de Boules (France)

Curling
US Men's Curling Association
Royal Caledonian Curling Club (UK)
Richmond Curling Club (UK)

Croquet
International Croquet Association (UK)

Golf
Professional Golfers Association of America

Court handball
United States Handball Association

Rugby fives
Rugby Fives Association (UK)

Jai alai (Pelota)
Federación Internacional de Pelota Vasca (Spain)
United States Jai Alai Players Association
Fédération Française de Pélote Basque (France)

Squash
International Squash Rackets Federation (UK)
United States Squash Rackets Association

Paddleball
National Paddleball Association (USA)

Badminton
International Badminton Federation (UK)
American Badminton Association
Badminton Association of England

Lawn tennis
International Lawn Tennis Federation (UK)
United States Lawn Tennis Association
Lawn Tennis Association (UK)

Table tennis
International Table Tennis Federation (UK)
United States Table Tennis Association
English Table Tennis Association

Volleyball
Fédération Internationale de Volleyball (France)
United States Volleyball Association
Canadian Volleyball Association
Amateur Volleyball Association (UK)

Basketball
Fédération Internationale de Basketball Amateur (FDR)
American Basketball Association
Amateur Basketball Association (UK)

Netball
International Federation of Women's Basketball and Netball Associations (New Zealand)
All-England Netball Association

Korfball
Fédération Internationale de Korfball (Netherlands)
British Korfball Association
Team handball
Internationale Handball Federation (Switzerland)
Canadian Team Handball Federation
British Handball Association
Speedball
AAHPER Speedball Committee (USA)
Gaelic football
Gaelic Athletic Association (Eire)
Australian football
Australian Football Council
American football
National Football League (USA)
Canadian football
Canadian Football League
Canadian Amateur Football Association
Rugby football
International Rugby Football Board (UK)
Eastern Rugby Union of America, Inc
Rugby Football Union (UK)
Rugby Football League (UK)
Soccer
Fédération Internationale de Football Association
(Switzerland)
United States Soccer Football Association, Inc
Football Association (UK)
Baseball
United States Baseball Federation, Inc
National Baseball Congress (USA)
Baseball Association (UK)
Softball
International Softball Federation (USA)
British Softball Federation
Rounders
National Rounders Association (UK)
Cricket
Test and County Cricket Board (UK)
Lacrosse
United States Inter-Collegiate Lacrosse Association
United States Women's Lacrosse Association
English Lacrosse Union
Roller hockey
American Roller Hockey Association
National Roller Hockey Association of Great Britain
Field hockey
International Hockey Rules Board (UK)
United States Field Hockey Association
All-England Women's Hockey Association
Hurling
Gaelic Athletic Association (Eire)
Shinty
Camanachd Association (UK)
Ice hockey
National Ice Hockey League (Canada)
British Ice Hockey Association
Bandy
Svenska Bandyförbundet (Sweden)
Swimming and diving
Fédération Internationale de Natation Amateur (Canada)
International Diving Association (UK)
Council for National Cooperation in Aquatics (USA)
Amateur Swimming Association (UK)
Amateur Swimming Union of Australia
Water polo
International Water Polo Association (USA)
United States Water Polo Association
Amateur Swimming Association (UK)
Surfing
Western Surfing Association (USA)
British Surfing Association
Water skiing
Union Mondiale de Ski Nautique (Switzerland)
American Water Ski Association
Canadian Water Ski Association
British Water Ski Federation
Rowing
Fédération Internationale des Sociétés d'Aviron
(Switzerland)
American Rowing Association
Amateur Rowing Association (UK)
Canoeing
Fédération Internationale de Canoë (Italy)
American Canoe Association
British Canoe Union
Yachting
International Yacht Racing Union (UK)
United States International Sailing Association
Royal Yachting Association (UK)
Royal Ocean Racing Club (UK)

Powerboat racing
Union Internationale Motonautique (Belgium)
Offshore Powerboat Club of Great Britain
Royal Yachting Association, Powerboat Section (UK)
Skating
International Skating Union (Switzerland)
Canadian Figure Skating Association
Canadian Amateur Speed Skating Association
National Skating Association of Great Britain
Skiing
Fédération Internationale de Ski (Switzerland)
United States Ski Association
National Ski Federation of Great Britain
Biathlon
Union Internationale de Pentathlon
Moderne et Biathlon (Sweden)
Ski Federation of Great Britain
Skibob racing
Fédération Internationale de Skibob (FDR)
United States Skibob Federation
Skibob Association of Great Britain
Bobsleigh and luge toboggan racing
Fédération Internationale de Luge de Course (Austria)
Fédération Internationale de Bobsleigh et de
Tobogganing (Italy)
Canadian Amateur Bobsleigh and Luge Association
British Bobsleigh Association
British Racing Toboggan Association
Pigeon racing
International Federation of American Homing Pigeon
Fanciers, Inc
Royal Pigeon Racing Association (UK)
Sled dog racing
International Sled Dog Racing Association (USA)
Lakes Region Sled Dog Club (USA)
Greyhound racing
American Greyhound Track Operators Association
National Greyhound Racing Club (UK)
Horse racing
Thoroughbred Racing Association of the United States
Jockeys Association of Great Britain
Racing Information Bureau and Jockey Club of Great
Britain
Harness horse racing
United States Trotting Association
Equestrianism
Fédération Equestre Internationale (Belgium)
Polo
United States Polo Association
Hurlingham Polo Association (UK)
Indian Polo Association
Roller skating
Fédération Internationale de Roller Skating (Spain)
United States Roller Skating Association
National Skating Association of Great Britain
Cycle racing
Union Cycliste Internationale (Switzerland)
American Cycling Union
North American Cycling Association (Canada)
British Cycling Federation
Motorcycle racing
Fédération Internationale Motocycliste (Switzerland)
American Motorcycling Association
Auto Cycling Union (UK)
Speedway Control Board (UK)
Motor racing
Fédération Internationale de l'Automobile (France)
United States Auto Club
Royal Automobile Club (UK)
International Rally Drivers Club (UK)
Drag and hot rod racing
National Hot Rod Association (USA)
British Drag Racing and Hot Rod Association
Karting
International Kart Federation (USA)
Royal Automobile Club (UK)
Gliding
Fédération Aéronautique Internationale (France)
Soaring Society of America (USA)
British Gliding Association
Ballooning
Fédération Aéronautique Internationale (France)
Balloon Federation of America
British Balloon and Airship Club
Air racing and aerobatics
Fédération Aéronautique Internationale (France)
United States Federal Aviation Administration
National Aeronautic Association (USA)
Formula One Air Racing Association (UK)
United Service and Royal Aero Club of the United
Kingdom

Games for Varying Numbers of Players

For any small group of two players or more (up to seven or eight)
Board games Game of goose 14, Alleyway 16, Snakes and ladders 16, Horseshoe 17, Many contemporary board games 18–19. **Tile games** Sap tim pun 63. **Target games** Marble games 66–68, Coin throwing games 70–71, Fivestones and jack 72–73, Jack-straws 75, Spellicans 74, Tiddlywinks games 76–77, Ball games 78–79, Darts games 301–303. **General card games** Napoleon 88, Purchase nap 88, Seven-card nap 88, Forty-five (even numbers only) 89, Spoil five 89, Auction pitch 96, Auction pitch with joker 96. **Dice games** Most dice games 118–133. **Gambling card games** Brag (seven-card and nine-card), Stop the bus 185, Card put-and-take 186, Lansquenet 188, Slippery Sam 188, Polish red dog 189, Hoggenheimer 190, Chinese fan-tan 191, Banker and broker 192, Monte bank (private) 192, Injun 194, Red dog 195, Six-spot red dog 196, Thirty-five 196, Yablon 198. **Word and picture games** Many games 200–211. **Games of chance** Spoof 212, Fan-tan 214, Dollar poker 214, Put-and-take top 215. **Children's card games** Snap 242, Slapjack 243, Beggar my neighbor 244, Crazy eights 249, Go boom 249, Card dominoes 249, Sequence 250, Knockout whist 251, Racing demon 252, Give away 253.

For any small group of three players or more (up to seven or eight)
General card games Loo (three-card and five-card) 88, Irish loo 88, Hearts games 94, Pope Joan 98, Michigan 100. **Gambling card games** Blackjack and variants 166–173, Poker games 174–183, Brag (three-card) 184, Horse race 187, Blücher 190, Thirty-one 196, Bango 198, Kentucky Derby 199. **Word and picture games** Most games 200–211. **Games of chance** Bingo 216, Lotto 216, Picture lotto 217, Roulette 218, Boule 221. **Children's party games** Most games 222–241. **Children's card games** Donkey 245, Pig 245, Pit 245, Happy families 246, Old maid 246, Authors 247, Black Peter 247, Le vieux garçon 247, I doubt it 248, Up and down cheat 248, Jig 249, Snip-snap-snorem 249, Play or pay 250, Linger longer 251.

Games that can be played by large groups of nine or more
Tile games Sebastopol 54, Tiddle-a-wink 54. **General card games** Oh hell 84. **Gambling card games** Blackjack 166, Poker games 174–183, Brag (three-card) 184, Polish red dog 189, Injun 194, Red dog 195, Six-spot red dog 196, Thirty-one 196. **Word and picture games** Most games 200–211. **Games of chance** Spoof, Dollar poker 214, Fan-tan 214, Put-and-take top 215, Bingo 216, Lotto 216, Picture lotto 217, Roulette 218, Boule 221. **Children's party games** Most games 222–241.

Games for a Specific Number of Players

For one player
Board games Halma solitaire 34, Solitaire board games 50. **Card games** Solitaire (Patience) card games 134–148. **Target games** Fivestones and jacks 72–75. **Children's games** Cup and ball 78.

For two players
Board games Ashta-kashte 12, Ludo 12, Pachisi 12, Contemporary board games 18, Backgammon and variants 24–25, Queen's guard 26, Ringo 26, Checkers (draughts) games 28–31, Lasca 32, Reversi 32, Conquest 33, Salta 33, Halma 34, Chinese checkers 35, Brax (for two players) 36, Chess 38, Shogi 42, Go (Wei-ch'i) 46, Go-moku 48, Hasami Shogi 48, Hex 49. **Tile games** Many domino games 52–57. **Target games** Conkers 69, Conquerors 69, Soldiers 69. **General card games** Euchre (two-handed) 86, Five hundred (two-handed), Ecarté 87, Hearts (two-handed) 94, All-fives 96, California Jack 96, Seven up 96, Casino 97, Draw casino 97, Royal casino 97, Spade casino 97, Bezique 101, Rubicon bezique 101, Piquet 104, Auction piquet 105, Imperial 105, Pinochle 106, Auction pinochle 106, Kalabriasz 107, Rummy 110, Gin rummy 110, Cribbage 112. **Double solitaire games** Russian bank 148, Spite and malice 148. **Small table games** Shove ha'penny 150, Shovelboard 151, Bagatelle 152, Burmese caroms 152. **Gambling card games** Fifteen 173. **Games of chance** Scissors, paper, stone 212, Spoof 212, Mora 213, Shoot 213. **Children's party games** Arm wrestling 233, Cock fighting 233, Stork fighting 233. **Children's card games** Persian pasha 243, War 243, Memory 244, Fish 247, Stealing bundles 248.

For three players
Board games Ashta-kashte 12, Ludo 12, Pachisi 12, Brax (for three players) 36. **Tile games** Blind Hughie 54, Block dominoes 54, Domino pool 54, Doubles 54, Draw dominoes 54, All fives 55, All threes 55, Bergen 55, Fives and threes 55, Matador 55, Picture dominoes 55, Mah jongg 58. **General card games** Preference 85, Euchre (three-handed) 86, Five hundred 86, Knaves 95, All fives 96, California Jack 96, Seven up 96, Casino 97, Calabrasella 100, Bezique (three-handed) 102, Auction pinochle 106, Skat 108, Cribbage (three-handed) 112, Austrian tarock 114, Tarocco 116. **Children's party games** Menagerie 242, Animal noises 243, War (for three players) 243.

For four players
Board games Ashta-kashte 12, Ludo 12, Pachisi 12, Brax (for four players) 36, Partnership block dominoes 54, Domino pool 54, Doubles 54, Draw dominoes 54, Fortress 54, Latin American match dominoes 54, All fives 55, All threes 55, Bergen 55, Fives and threes 55, Matador 55, Forty-two 56, Picture dominoes 57, Mah jongg 58, Mah jongg (American) 64. **General card games** Whist 82, Solo whist, 83, Boston 84, Vint 85, Euchre (four-handed) 86, Call-ace euchre 86, Railroad euchre 86, Five hundred (four-handed) 86, Auction forty-five 89, Contract Bridge 90, Auction bridge 93, Duplicate bridge 93, Grand 95, Polignac 95, California Jack 96, Seven up (four-handed) 96, Casino 97, Bezique (four-handed) 101, Auction pinochle 106, Partnership kalabriasz 107, Partnership gin rummy 110, Canasta 111, Cribbage (four-handed) 113. **Table games** Shove Ha'penny 150, Burmese caroms 152. **Children's card games** Menagerie 242, Animal noises 243, My ship sails 245, Stealing bundles 248, Rolling stone 251.

For five players
Tile games Blind Hughie 54, Sebastopol 54, Matador 55. **General card games** Call-ace euchre 86, Polignac 95. **Children's card games** My ship sails 245, Rolling stone 251.

For six players
General card games Call-ace euchre 86, Auction forty-five 89, Polignac 95, Partnership gin rummy 110. **Children's card games** My ship sails 245, Rolling stone 251.

Index of Games

Index of Sports